Jewish Literatures in Spanish and Portuguese

Jewish Literatures in Spanish and Portuguese

A Comprehensive Handbook

Edited by
Ruth Fine and Susanne Zepp

DE GRUYTER

ISBN (HARDCOVER) 978-3-11-053106-0
ISBN (PAPERBACK) 978-3-11-221558-6
e-ISBN (PDF) 978-3-11-056379-5
e-ISBN (EPUB) 978-3-11-056111-1

Library of Congress Control Number: 2022936930

Bibliographic information published by the Deutsche Nationalbibliothek
The Deutsche Nationalbibliothek lists this publication in the Deutsche Nationalbibliografie; detailed bibliographic data are available on the internet at http://dnb.dnb.de.

© 2025 Walter de Gruyter GmbH, Berlin/Boston
This volume is text- and page-identical with the hardback published in 2022.
Cover image: liuzishan/iStock/Getty Images Plus
Typesetting: Integra Software Services Pvt. Ltd.
Printing and binding: CPI books GmbH, Leck

www.degruyter.com

Contents

Ruth Fine and Susanne Zepp
Introduction —— 1

I Medieval Constellations

Rica Amrán
1   Jewish and *Converso* History in Medieval Spain: The Castilian Case —— 17

Yehoshua Granat
2   The Poetry of Sefarad: Secular and Liturgical Hebrew Verse in Medieval Iberia —— 39

Georg Bossong
3   The *kharadjāt* —— 55

Óscar Perea-Rodríguez
4   Jews and *Conversos* in Spanish *Cancioneros* and Portuguese *Cancioneiros* (c. 1350–1520) —— 81

II Early Modern Contexts

James Nelson Novoa and Carsten Wilke
5   1492–1700: Early Modern Iberian-Jewish Cultural History —— 157

Juan Diego Vila
6   *Converso* Spectres: The Lessons and Challenges of Spanish 'Golden Age' Prose —— 185

Joachim Küpper
7   From the Iberian Peninsula into the World: Leone Ebreo's *Dialoghi d'amore* and the 'Occidental' Concept of Love —— 221

Harm den Boer
8   The Literature of the Western Sephardim —— 251

Margalit Bejarano
9   Jews in the History and Culture of the Caribbean —— 297

III The Eighteenth and the Nineteenth Centuries

Tamir Karkason
10 The Iberian Diasporas in the Eighteenth and Nineteenth Centuries —— 319

Aliza Moreno-Goldschmidt
11 *Conversos* in Colonial Hispanic America —— 353

IV The Twentieth Century

Silvia Schenkolewski-Kroll
12 The Twentieth Century in Iberian and Latin American History —— 375

Daniela Flesler
13 Contemporary Jewish Literatures of Spain —— 417

Ilan Stavans
14 Mapping Twentieth Century Sephardic Literature —— 433

Saul Kirschbaum and Berta Waldmann
15 Jewish-Brazilian Literatures —— 447

Verena Dolle
16 Jewish-Mexican Literatures: Ashkenazic Tradition and Culture —— 475

Jacobo Sefamí
17 Sephardic Writing in Mexico —— 523

Saúl Sosnowski
18 Jewish Literatures from the Rio de la Plata Region (Twentieth Century) —— 547

V Contemporary Contexts

Leonardo Senkman
19 Historiography and Literary Essays on Latin American Jews in the New Millennium —— 581

Dieter Ingenschay
20 Contemporary Jewish Narrative in Twenty-first Century Latin America —— 603

Florinda F. Goldberg
21 Writing Cuban Belonging through Jewish Eyes —— 627

Index —— 645

Ruth Fine and Susanne Zepp
Introduction

Covering the time from the Middle Ages to the present, the compendium at hand is dedicated to the diversity of the Jewish chapters of world literature written in Spanish and Portuguese. Such a comprehensive survey of these areas of literary history – which took (and are taking) place in Europe, Latin America, and other parts of the world – has not been undertaken until now. The epistemic need for such a study lies in the fact that only this broad focus can reveal how diasporic Jewish literatures are closely related to literary history overall, yet simultaneously tied in with their own traditions. Moreover, their poetics were translated and adapted into an aesthetic praxis that has been formative and crucial for world literature.

This volume offers historical and socio-epistemological approaches together with questions of literary theory and literary history, thereby deepening our knowledge not only of the development of different traditions, but also of issues such as canonization, aspects of transmission, and the relevance of the respective texts today. The dialogue with the history of philological traditions and the scholarship of each respective period is intended to be of interest to specialists, scholars in training, and students alike.

The structure corresponds to the aforementioned objectives, tracing the diversity and development of the literatures in question as meticulously as possible. For this reason, the individual chapters have been arranged along a chronological axis which connects generic shifts and literary texts from different eras with a concurrent history of events. Within this chronological structure, you will find five sections corresponding to five historical periods: I. Medieval Constellations, II. Early Modern Contexts, III. The Eighteenth and the Nineteenth Centuries, IV. The twentieth Century, and V. Contemporary Contexts. Each section begins with a chapter that sets out the historical constellations pertaining to its respective place and time. These historical chapters place the epoch's foundational texts in their cultural and socio-historical contexts of emergence. Hence, with its historical accentuation and its simultaneous emphasis of textual analysis, the present handbook aims to draw attention to the significance of the respective texts in terms of literary history and within the context of their unique cultural settings. Of foremost interest in this regard are the respective aesthetic configurations, effectively represented in these texts by way of a nuanced interaction with a textual culture informed by sacred traditions.

One central thesis of this book is that amidst the diversity of Romance literatures, Jewish texts serve as particularly salient examples and also as important points of departure for a comparative or contrastive study. Several crucial aspects of the European and Latin American cultural multiplicity are represented in these texts, since hardly any other minority was forced to render problematic and to offer tentative answers to the question of 'identity' with such urgency, in such a nuanced manner, and over such an extended period of time – lasting even until today. Hence, as a history of transformations with regard to cultural belonging, Jewish history might provide heuristic categories for literary studies that advance research into other cultural belongings and their multiple correlations.

These processes of transformation have taken place in epochs in which essentialist thought was dominant. To highlight how strikingly Jewish literatures have managed, at least in part, to resist this essentializing dynamic we as editors have invited our contributors to consciously avoid terms that would imply these supposed essences. In the transition from the Middle Ages to the Early Modern period, for example, the belief in the existence of an essential difference between persons who were born to Christian parents and persons who had converted to Christianity emerged from the specific religious and socio-historical constellation of the Iberian Peninsula. This distinction was based on nothing less than biologistic reasoning, which did not see religious belonging as a choice. The related terms – such as 'Old Christians' and 'New Christians' – are placed in quotation marks throughout the entire handbook in order to draw attention to this specific historical semantics. The procedures of the Inquisition were also guided by biologistic reasoning. This includes the impactful and extremely questionable notion of *limpieza de sangre*. The literary texts of the time developed means of exposing the sheer preposterousness of such biologistic notions of identity. This is as true of the first picaresque novel in world literature, the anonymously published *Lazarillo de Tormes* (1554), as it is of the works of the author of *Don Quijote*. In his famous play *Retablo de las maravillas* (1615), Miguel de Cervantes satirized the identitarian-biologistic mindset of his times. It is to this critical tradition that our attention to concepts such as those mentioned above, but also to other essentialist terminologies, is indebted. This tradition teaches us that history is a continual process in which belonging is shared, shaped, and changed over time and place, and it teaches us how constructive it can be to let go of the notion of permanent, fixed 'identities'.

In terms of research, Romance studies have addressed Jewish traditions in phases of varying intensity. First, texts pertaining to the amalgamation of Hebrew with Romance languages were the ones to receive the most attention. This was followed by increased attention to the cultural effects of the encounters between Jewish, Christian, and Muslim cultures on the Iberian Peninsula. Likewise, significant analyses from the disciplines of historiography, cultural studies, the history of religion, and the history of philosophy have continuously contributed to the field; and yet, the former have a tendency to employ literary texts primarily as illustrative sources and not as objects of research in their own right.

In order to fill this scholarly gap, this handbook offers an integrative survey of Spanish- and Portuguese-language Jewish world literatures which addresses not only the coexistence of cultures, but also the dimensions and functions of a literary and linguistic space of negotiation in this context. This is implemented with a view to an integration of Jewish Literatures into literary history on the whole, thereby steering clear of isolationist approaches. European and Latin American literary history are characterized by various lines of tradition negotiating the encounters and coalescences of Christian, Jewish, and Muslim cultures. Precisely on account of their cultural diversity, the cultures of the Middle Ages and the Early Modern period were constituted in areas inseparable from, and profoundly interwoven with, a variety of religious traditions. As a result of the emancipation during the Enlightenment, Jewish perspectives were integrated into a dominantly Christian narrative. It is easily forgotten that Jewish and Muslim traditions were present in Europe's cultural history throughout the preceding centuries – the former, since the emergence of Christianity; the latter, since the rise of Islam. The Jewish chapters of European literature offer an ideal space for reflection on this cultural diversity, which the present book will address.

The Spanish- and Portuguese-language Jewish world literatures represent a complex configuration of three interwoven perspectives: Jewish self-understanding; external views on Jewish history in different scholarly disciplines; and a perspective pointing towards a potential universal significance of Jewish experience. The 21 chapters of this compendium aim to maintain a balance between national frameworks (such as Brazilian, Argentinian, or Mexican literary history) and transnational approaches. Accordingly, the handbook is more diversified at the transitions from the nineteenth to the twentieth and into the twenty-first century so as to be able to represent these epochs of complex changes as adequately as possible.

The epistemological questions of the volume at hand are inspired by the fundamental methodical parameters for the interpretation of Europe's Jewish history developed by the Simon Dubnow Institute in Leipzig under the aegis of Dan Diner and canonized in his *Encyclopedia of Jewish History and Culture*. In historiography and cultural studies, these factors have prompted a paradigm shift in the scholarly consideration of Jewish history. As a consequence of Dan Diner's *oeuvre*, Jewish history is no longer perceived and studied as a separate field; rather, the methodological integration of Jewish history into general history has become the central concern in, and scholarly standard of, any historical approach in this field. As a matter of principle, Jewish history – taken to be pluralistic, pertaining to Jews in complex intercultural frameworks – is studied in its transnational context. This approach counterbalances isolationist vantage points.

As for literary studies, the productive implementation of this critical methodological achievement is still in the making. This holds true for literary historiography proper as well as for those philological subdisciplines that are still stuck in the paradigm of 'national literature'. The acknowledgement of historical experience as a hermeneutic category downright contradicts an essentialist equalization of cultural background and mindset. Some endeavors to integrate various Jewish traditions of knowledge into a supposedly 'general' one have failed precisely as a result of the fact that, in struggling to resolve an alleged dissimilarity between them, such efforts inevitably concede and reproduce these very differences. Moreover, a productive permeability of disciplinary boundaries can only be achieved if the transnational, urban, mobile, and textual character of Jewish life-worlds receives comprehensive appreciation by specialists of historiography as well.

Erich Auerbach's 1946 *Mimesis: The Representation of Reality in Western Literature*, which has remained extremely relevant up to the present, offers a paradigmatic example of the interaction between established literary historiography and a perspective that transcends national frameworks. Auerbach confronts the cataclysms of modernity with a stance condensing historical experiences into a philological approach that transcends collectivist attributions. Auerbach's close readings and stylistic analyses – employed with a view to interpreting the representation of the 'real' in various literary forms – preserve Europe's cultural achievements as developed from pagan, Jewish, Christian, and secular traditions.

Auerbach's approach to literary history – which considers a text's structural composition while also including processes of reception into the analysis – was an inspiration for the volume at hand. This handbook may also serve as an impulse for further studies and endeavors with various other emphases, for instance in the fields of gender studies or the history of literary genres or epochs. The format – facilitating a synopsis in terms of both literary history and historiography proper while also relating to issues of theory and methodology – was designed to encourage students, scholars in training, and specialists to contemplate how the complex connections between experiences, cultural belonging, and texts in Spanish- and Portuguese-language literatures might be systematically integrated into future research, curricula, and teaching.

The first section of the volume, "Medieval Constellations", focuses on the rich and influential literary production of Jews in medieval Iberia as well as on the historical context in which it flourished. Four extensive chapters explore the main literary trends, the impact of the exposure to other cultures in the Peninsula (Christian and Muslim), and the developments that took place and influenced literary production from the initial period of Jewish settlement in Iberia to the massive waves of conversion.

In the opening chapter, Rica Amran offers a comprehensive diachronic account of Jewish history in medieval Iberia (with a special emphasis on Castile), stressing the differences between regions and periods. Representative examples of that diversity are found in the different social statuses of the Jews in small versus large communities or in the varying approaches of Christian theologians regarding the 'New Christians'. Moreover, Amran shows how the situation of the Jewish communities on the Peninsula before the events of 1391 was much better than the situation of the other European Jewish communities, though this changed radically after the period of widespread conversion. Amran's chapter convincingly displays the heterogeneity of this long period with the multiple paradoxes that operated within Jewish life in medieval Iberia, thus challenging monolithic and polarized approaches.

In the chapter "The poetry of Sefarad: Secular and liturgical Hebrew verse of medieval Iberia", Yehoshua Granat analyses the specificities and diversity of the medieval Iberian 'Golden Age' of Hebrew poetry in Al-Andalus, portraying not only its singularity in the context of the history of Hebrew verse but also the diversification undergone during its development. The chapter examines the singular traits of Iberian Hebrew poetry in medieval times, stressing the novelty of its metrical and formal design; the emergence of a new type of Hebrew secular verse in the Jewish courtly circles of al-Andalus; and the new developments in Hebrew liturgical poetry tradition (*Piyyut*) in medieval Iberia. As the author makes evident based on a close reading of selected texts, the medieval Hebrew poetry of Iberia (al-Andalus), under the unequivocal influence of Arabic poetry and poetics, offers outstanding artistic achievements that have rightly awarded it the denomination of the 'Golden Age' of Jewish literature. Although most of the secular poetry was forgotten during the following centuries until it was rediscovered by modern scholarship, liturgical Andalusian Hebrew poetry continues to be a central feature of the Sephardic liturgy and even of the liturgy of other Jewish communities.

In the context of the artistic creation of al-Andalus, Georg Bossong's chapter is devoted to the *kharadjat*: the final verses that appear at the end of Arabic and Hebrew strophic poems (*muwaššaḥāt*) written in Mozarabic, an early Ibero-Romance language. The *kharadjat* are the earliest known poems in that language, and one of its most important poets, Yehuda ha-Lewi, is rightly considered the first Spanish author known by name. Other Jewish authors of *kharadjat* are also among the greatest poets of Jewish al-Andalus. Bossong offers a rigorous and thorough overview of the main characteristics of *kharadjat*, of the fascinating history of their discovery, as well as of the controversial debate regarding their interpretation – between those who defend their Semitic origin (an approach also embraced by Bossong) and those who claim their origin lay in Castilian oral tradition. The chapter provides an innovative and significant perspective revealing the important Jewish component of the *kharadjat*, an aspect that is generally ignored by scholarship. Moreover, the *kharadjat* constitute a unique source of insight into a period in which the three monotheistic cultures interacted and influenced each other in medieval Spain. As Bossong states, in the world of al-Andalus, "Mixture and cross-fertilization reached peaks rarely found elsewhere in world literature".

Chapter 4, Óscar Perea Rodríguez's "Jews and *Conversos* in Spanish *Cancioneros* and in Portuguese *Cancioneiros*", concludes this first section by carrying the analysis of medieval Iberian Jewish literature into a later period, namely the mid-fourteenth century to the end of the fifteenth century. The chapter focuses on an important genre developed in those centuries: the *cancionero*, representative of the significant changes that affected the Iberian Jewish communities, i.e., the massive and forced conversions and the gradual weakening of Jewish life in the Peninsula. With his exhaustive analysis of these Castilian and Portuguese poem collections, Perea Rodríguez compellingly shows how they can be very useful sources for understanding the conflict-ridden evolution of Jews and conversos in Iberia in general and of their literature in particular. The chapter offers a diachronic examination of the genre from its initial manifestations to the age of the Catholic Monarchs and the expulsion, which is thematized in the Castilian *Cancionero general* and also in the Portuguese *Cancioneiro geral*. Based on a detailed presentation of the historical context of each period and a close reading of the texts, the author lucidly points out the contradictions that emerge. This reading shows the complex and diverse situation of Jews and conversos throughout the period in question, challenging essentialist and reductive readings that only consider the role of Jews and conversos as targets of mockery and disdain.

The second section of the volume, which is devoted to the Early Modern period, presents a myriad of approaches to the different cultural and literary manifestations of Jews and conversos within and outside the Peninsula after 1492. In Chapter 5, "1492–1700: Early Modern Iberian-Jewish Cultural History", James Nelson Novoa and Carsten Lorenz Wilke review the cultural, social and religious existences of Iberian conversos and their descendants between 1492 and 1700. The authors address some of the main problems faced by historians when trying to give an account of the lives and trajectories of this group, such as "the fluidity of religious identity, transcontinental migration, early modern tolerance and confessionalization". As in previous chapters, the authors try to focus on the diversity of the object of their study, avoiding preconceptions and generalizations. They recognize, for instance, the existence of converted Jews who accepted Christianity under duress and tried to preserve their faith and practices as well as others who found secure places in Europe and the 'New World' where they were able to maintain, either secretly or overtly, the Jewish religion. The authors' overview covers the development of converso life in Spain, Portugal, France, Italy, Amsterdam, and the New World – two centuries of social life and cultural production of the descendants of the medieval Iberian Jews. This early modern period was marked by trauma and estrangement, "but also assimilation, transformation and reinvention". The approach of the authors takes into account the many contradictions of the so-called "Nation" (*Naçao*) arising as a consequence of persecutions, expulsions, conversions, migrations, and a partial adaptation to the old-new religion, all leading to the singular hybridity and liminality that characterized the 'New Jews' and conversos of the Western Diaspora. The authors convincingly claim that this period of Western Sephardic life set a precedent for Jewish emancipation in the centuries to follow.

In Chapter 6, Juan Diego Vila rejects an essentialist approach in his examination of the corpus of converso literature, conceptualizing it through two perspectives: as an invisible marginality and as a manifestation of the concept of spectrality – a useful notion that facilitates the study of the writings of Spanish authors of Jewish origin in the 'Golden Age'. For Vila, the converso writers were protagonists of literary history, but silenced ones who challenged the canonical notions that prevailed in the history of Spanish literature. They represent the substance of a dynamics of exclusion carried out by the official literary discourse. Hence, his chapter serves as a critical overview of the controversial concept of converso literature in Early Modern Iberia. Vila focuses on two main examples – the works of Francisco Delicado and Mateo Alemán (*La lozana andaluza* and the *Guzmán de Alfarache*, respectively) – in an attempt to produce a general analytical concept of converso literature in which spectrality would be a central component. This being said, he challenges the notion of monolithic identities and points to the importance of defying cultural, ethnic and religious conceptual frontiers. He brings forth the point, often neglected in Spanish philology, that the texts of converso writers of Jewish origin represent a specific but multidimensional literary phenomenon, a multilayered and polyphonic textual constellation that constitutes an unavoidable keystone of Spanish literature.

Chapter 7, Joachim Küpper's "From the Iberian Peninsula into the World: Leone Ebreo's *Dialoghi d'amore* and the 'Occidental' Concept of Love", is dedicated to one of the most important and influential intellectuals of the period in question: Leone Ebreo. Küpper offers an exhaustive and innovative analysis of Ebreo's renowned *Dialoghi d'amore*, which was published after the author's death. The chapter focuses on the controversial question of the origin, significance, and influence of Ebreo's conception of love, posing crucial questions such as if this book is the first to introduce a notion, originating in the Jewish tradition, that combines the union of the souls with physical pleasures – a notion that would greatly influence European vernacular discourses on love from then on. Beginning with a short account of the life of the author, who belonged to one of the most renowned Iberian families, and a description of the book and its different editions, Küpper examines the evolution of the concept of love in the Western world, claiming that it cannot be explained as originating in Christianity, Islam or antiquity. His very innovative approach is that Iberian Jewish diasporic thought might have contributed significantly to the future development of the notion of love, minimizing the doctrinal and ethical constraints that characterized other literary paradigms. In this respect, *Dialoghi d'Amore* constitutes a most influential text in medieval and early modern Jewish diasporic thought about love, whose conceptual framework did not coincide with the dominant religious and philosophical traditions, rather presenting a combination of three substantial components: a non-sacred concept of language, a non-judgmental attitude towards sexuality, and an advancement of monogamy.

The following chapter by Harm den Boer, "The Literature of the Western Sephardim", offers a comprehensive study of the literature produced and read by the Sephardim of converso origin, discussing not only the main genres and their characteristics, but also the specificities that particularize this vast corpus and differentiate it from the Iberian as well as from the Jewish literature. This literature developed over the course of two centuries in different regions and contexts. Hence, one important claim is that there is no common denominator and that it is crucial to take into account its heterogeneity – not only of the corpus itself but also of its reception. Some 'New Jews' wanted to follow Orthodox Judaism as accurately as possible; others defied the rabbinical authorities and were keen to maintain their bonds with Iberian culture, especially in the realm of literary production; still others had an eclectic approach to religion and secular culture. The chapter commences by introducing the Western Sephardic Diaspora, its historical origin, its geography, and its social and religious constraints. Den Boer explains the place of the Bible in the writings of these authors as well as the centrality of the press in their literary enterprise. After these introductory remarks, the chapter discusses most of the genres cultivated by the Iberian Jews of the Western Diaspora, such as ethical and moral treatises, sermons and polemical literature, biblical commentaries, apologetic texts, but also the secular literature, including prose, poetry, and theater. One important conclusion of this exhaustive and illuminating study is that the use of the vernacular languages opened new paths and possibilities for Judaism that also benefitted the Iberian Catholic canon. Moreover, the author concludes by stating that literature was not only a means of entertainment for these 'New Jews', but also a way to recover and access the Iberian heritage they had left behind, both by readership and by creation. However, reading and writing interests went beyond Spanish and Portuguese literature, constituting a unique syncretic literary and intellectual phenomenon.

In Chapter 9, Margalit Bejarano offers a concise synopsis of the plural Jewish history and culture of the Caribbean, marked by a Sephardic historical experience whose contours were shaped by colonial history. In doing so, she not only provides a valuable overview of the early modern social and economic history of the Caribbean, but also elaborates the Iberian references in the language, culture, and literature of Caribbean Jewish history. The chapter is based on a thesis of the historian Yosef Kaplan, who has diagnosed a history of transformation in the Caribbean early modern period: Among the Dutch, English and French settlers of the Caribbean were Sephardic Jews, mostly conversos from Portugal, who had immigrated to Amsterdam, Hamburg, London, or Bayonne, where – according to Kaplan – they had turned from 'New Christians'to 'New Jews'. They considered themselves part of the *Nação*, the Spanish-Portuguese Jewish nation. The term "Nation" was not used in its modern sense but referred to a shared religious-cultural belonging. The chapter demonstrates how the numerous small communities of the *Nação* preserved both the Portuguese language and their Sephardic religious and cultural traditions. Thus, Bejarano portrays Caribbean Jewish history as a transnational diasporic history that connected Dutch, British, and French Jewry with the newly established Jewish communities in Latin America and North America.

The third section of the volume is devoted to the eighteenth and nineteenth centuries. It opens with Chapter 10, by Tamir Karkason: "The Iberian Diasporas in the Eighteenth and Nineteenth Centuries". This chapter offers an overview of the main trends in the Sephardic literature of the eighteenth and nineteenth centuries written in Ladino and in Hebrew, also considering the reception of this literature, i.e., the question of who its readers were and what interested them. As the author explains, in that period, most of the Sephardic literature was written in Ladino, and thus the Sephardic public, mostly unable to read Hebrew, could have access to it. Starting in the eighteenth century, we can witness an impressive flourishing of Ladino literature (both religious and secular) in the Ottoman Jewish communities, both in terms of quantity and in terms of quality, across a variety of literary genres. In the period discussed here, Ladino literature underwent a significant process of modernization and growth. Karkason illustrates this process by examining several texts, the *Me'am Lo'ez* being one of the major ones. Some of the genres that developed in the eighteenth and nineteenth centuries were unprecedented, while others corresponded to a previous tradition. There were also important historiographic works and an impressive amount of material published in the press. In the nineteenth century, the audience of Ladino readers grew vastly and enjoyed the secular genres without abandoning the Ladino translations of the Bible and the *Musar* literature. With this broad and instructive overview, Karkason persuasively demonstrates the vitality, openness, and diversity of Sephardic culture during the transition from the early modern to the modern period, as well as the centrality of Ladino as the main language of expression for the Eastern Iberian Diaspora.

Chapter 11, Aliza Moreno's "*Conversos* of Jewish Origin in Colonial Hispanic America", explains in historical terms the various circumstances that led to the arrival of the first 'New Christians' of Jewish origin to Hispanic America during the colonial era. The author presents an array of topics that illuminate the main characteristics of the subject matter: the role of the Inquisition in preserving information regarding the scope of the converso communities; some of the differences that can be pointed out with respect to the attitudes towards the conversos held in America as opposed to the Peninsula (i.e., the less crucial role played by 'purity of blood' in the 'New World'); the reasons for the conversos' arrival to the 'New World'; as well as their geographical distribution and the general characteristics of the group. As in all previous chapters, Moreno is well aware of the necessity of taking into account the diversity that characterized the history of the Jewish presence in Latin America; indeed, the varying times of arrival, the varying regions where the respective communities were established, and the varying historical circumstances all played a crucial role in generating this diversity. The author argues that there were three distinct migration processes which took place, respectively, in the colonial period, at the beginning of the republican period, and in the period starting at the end of the nineteenth century. There is no continuity between these waves of migration. Moreover, Moreno emphasizes that there are two important factors that the researcher should take into account when studying the subject: the motivation to travel to the 'New World' (whether economic and/or related to the search for a more equal social status) and the differences between the main centers in which the converso communities were established (Peru, Mexico, and Cartagena). Hence, this enlightening chapter demonstrates the need to approach the history of the conversos in Hispanic America with regard for the vast array of traits it presents.

In Chapter 12, Silvia Schenkolweski opens the section of this handbook dedicated to the twentieth century with an impressive survey of the history of the Jewish communities in Spain, Portugal, and Latin America (excluding the Caribbean). Throughout the chapter, the author draws our attention to the diverse historical conditions of Jewish migration movements. While there was hardly any Jewish presence on the Iberian Peninsula for centuries after 1492, in the twentieth century, this history changes for various reasons, which the author elaborates in detail. Schenkolweski's analysis of the Jewish history of Latin America in the twentieth century follows this standard of differentiation and precision. The chapter analyses how the respective political and social contexts in the individual countries of the continent shaped Jewish history. While the focus lies on the important communities of Argentina and Brazil, the chapter traces Jewish historical processes in seventeen countries. The compositional decision to comparatively discuss key events in the form of country overviews will allow readers to comprehend similarities and differences. In addition, the chapter provides a valuable contextualization within the larger scope of global historical events.

In Chapter 13, Daniela Flesler offers a comprehensive survey of the Jewish literary history of Spain in the twentieth century. Taking as its starting point a historical reflection on the Iberian constellation after the expulsion of 1492, the chapter provides detailed analyses of selected texts by Rafael Cansinos Assens (1882–1964), Solly Wolodarsky (1927–2014), and Esther Bendahan Cohen (b. 1964), tracing the return of Jewish storytelling and the representation of Jewish belonging. Simultaneously, the chapter develops the different thematic axes of Spanish Jewish literatures: While Rafael Cansinos Assens, who was born into a Catholic family in Seville, identified himself as a descendant of Iberian conversos and conceived of his writing as a continuation of early modern history, the chapter also presents the writing of Solly Wolodarsky, who came from an Ashkenazic Argentinian family and moved to Spain in 1969, as representative of the multifaceted field of Latin American-Jewish writing in Spain. With the *oeuvre* of Esther Bendahan Cohen, whose Sephardic family originates from Morocco, this dimension of Spanish-Jewish historical experience is also made accessible through literature. Flesler's chapter thus enables us to understand the great plurality of Spain's Jewish literatures.

In Chapter 14, Ilan Stavans explores the global landscapes of modern Sephardic literature. The layout of this chapter consciously transcends epochal and national boundaries and maps a literary field characterized by the multilingualism of its *oeuvres*, which were written in Ladino, Spanish, French, English, Arabic, and Hebrew. In this chapter, the term "Sephardic" refers to a literary tradition which had already established itself on the Iberian Peninsula long before 1492 and which continued to flourish in a variety of linguistic cultures after the expulsion. Thus, this chapter reveals the significance of migration for a transnational literary historiography, the methodological and theoretical implications of which are also highly relevant for current discussions of world literature. Language and historical experience replace traditional categories of a hitherto nationally organized literary historiography. The chapter's perspective therefore provides an opportunity to examine writers as diverse as Elias Canetti, Albert Cohen, Danilo Kis, Primo Levi, Angelina Muñiz-Huberman, and A. B. Yehoshua and to highlight the inscription of Sephardic experience in their writings.

Chapter 15, by Berta Waldman and Saul Kirschbaum, offers a concise overview of Brazilian-Jewish literatures. The focus is on texts from the nineteenth and especially the twentieth century. After a historical introduction, the chapter presents a large and thoroughly representative selection of authors and works in order to render the great diversity and range of Jewish writing in Brazil comprehensible. The chapter makes it evident that this corpus of literary texts is closely intertwined with Brazil's social and political history but can hardly be captured by the parameters of a national literary historiography. The individual historical experiences represented in the texts are too diverse to be described with traditional classifications. This does not mean that these texts do not have a share in the developments and tendencies of Brazilian literary history; on the contrary, many of them have initiated new trends. But the corpus presented by Waldman and Kirschbaum makes it clear that the specificity of these texts lies in the way they translate the historical experiences of migration, translingualism, and cultural diversity into literary techniques. From this perspective, the enormous potential of the diversity of Brazilian-Jewish literatures for reconceptualizing Brazilian literary history on the whole becomes evident. Indeed, the chapter suggests integrating questions of multilingualism and diverse belonging more strongly into the perception of Brazilian literatures.

In Chapter 16, Verena Dolle focuses on Ashkenazic-Mexican literature written in Spanish as an integral part of the history of the Jewish literary cultures of Mexico. The temporal focus is placed intentionally on texts produced since the 1970s whose techniques aimed quite explicitly to challenge paradigms of the national and notions of homogenization in Mexican literary history. These procedures addressed cultural, ethnic and gender diversity and multiplicity in a highly intentional manner. Verena Dolle's approach elaborates different stages of transformation in Ashkenazic-Mexican literatures. She demonstrates to what extent the procedures of the texts were primarily concerned with rendering diversity and plurality visible through language. The chapter elucidates the relevant narrative techniques with great clarity. Thus, the chapter is able to demonstrate how questions of Jewish belonging have been intertwined with feminist aims and how texts have emerged that sharply denounce and challenge patriarchal hierarchies. The fact that literary texts which explore themes of migration and multilingualism are also included here makes the breadth of the literary field examined in this chapter particularly transparent. Another focus of the analyses is the question of the representation of historical memory in Mexico's social and political constellations, which are at times also marked by offences against human rights and by extreme violence. The focus on female authors such as Margo Glantz, Sabina Berman, and Gloria Gervitz highlights the importance of Ashkenazic-Mexican writing for world literature.

In Chapter 17, Jacobo Sefamí examines the Sephardic literature of Mexico. In contrast to Ilan Stavans's chapter, this chapter focuses on a single country. Yet both chapters share the belief that the corpus of Sephardic writing is marked by a high degree of diversity, which is related to the representation of the experience of migration as well as to a profoundly anti-essentialist understanding of belonging. The chapter is thus also highly attentive to the religious-historical particularities of Sephardic liturgy, which has been made fruitful for the study of the linguistic representation of belonging. Thus, the chapter pays close attention to cultural transformations that have underpinned religious practices in Mexico and to the question of how the various texts have addressed issues of cultural memory. It explores these connections through four exemplary analyses: First, it examines a text by Angelina Muñiz that intertwines the life of Teresa de Jesús with contemporary events. In doing so, it shows that a differentiation of historical experiences does not automatically lead to a separating, isolating perspective, but rather allows diversity to be represented in language. The second exemplary reading examines the feminist aim of Rosa Nissán's writing. It demonstrates how the plural representation of Jewish historical experience is able to challenge essentialist social circumstances. The third exemplary study is dedicated to the writing of Myriam Moscona. The particular text examined focuses on the Bulgarian-Sephardic historical experience, the significance of this past for the challenges of the present, and the exploration of the Judeo-Spanish language as a mode of subverting the monolingualism of Spanish in Mexican literature. The last exemplary analysis is dedicated to the writing of Alejandro Tarrab, whose text 'literarizes' a family history and in so doing is able to address the role of historical memory in contemporary Mexico.

In Chapter 18, Saúl Sosnowski examines the Jewish literatures from the Río de la Plata region. The chapter offers a historical charting of the distinctive political, regional, and cultural constellations on both sides of the river. The focus of the chapter lies on texts that were written in the urban spaces of Buenos Aires and Montevideo. The chapter examines different generations of writers, each of which addresses Jewish historical experience in their texts in a different way. In addition to this chronological axis of analysis, which begins with the first authors of this canon (Gerchunoff, Tiempo, Grünberg, Eichelbaum), the chapter also includes a thematic axis that does not merely provide an overview, but rather a comparative panorama of this rich literary field, accentuated according to the authors' key issues. This includes texts by authors who reflect on the relations between Israel and the Diaspora (Rozitchner, Aguinis, Feierstein); subversive representations of official history (Bortnik, Rivera, Verbitsky, Viñas); texts by authors who focus on questions of belonging, integration, acculturation, assimilation and political militancy (Chejfec, Costantini, Dujovne Ortiz, Goloboff, Cozarinsky, Kohan, Orgambide, Rozenmacher); as well as texts marked by irony and humor (Blaisten, Shua, Steimberg, Szichman). An additional section is devoted to the rich lyrical tradition of the examined region (Futoransky, Gelman, Kamenszain, Pizarnik, Szpumberg and Toker).

Chapter 19 opens the final section of the handbook, which is devoted to contemporary literatures in Spanish and Portuguese. Authored by Leonardo Senkman, this chapter elucidates twenty-first-century Iberian and Latin American Jewish history on the basis of a rigorous and richly comprehensive research report. Thus, the author does not only introduce the most important historical processes of his subject matter, but also elaborates the current state of historiographical research. In doing so, he focuses on the epistemological issues that have taken center stage in historiographical works on the subject. Thus, Senkman also introduces three important research series that aim to unfold a plural approach to Iberian and Latin American Jewish history. He presents these transnational endeavors dedicated to the plurality of Jewish historical experience in a comprehensive manner, focusing on the complex negotiations between particular and collective history in the contexts he examines.

In Chapter 20, Dieter Ingenschay offers a comprehensive review of contemporary Jewish narrative in twenty-first-century Latin America. This chapter is characterized by its compositional point of departure in the diversity of representations of Jewish historical experience. Ingenschay interweaves this diversity with the history of the first two decades of the twenty-first century as well as with further considerations of a more theoretical and methodological nature. Thus, the corpus of contemporary Jewish narratives in Latin America is integrated into current debates on cultural theory while the theoretical potential of these literary contexts is highlighted. The fact that this is done on the basis of carefully chosen, exemplary analyses of individual texts makes the chapter extremely helpful. The criteria for choosing these literary texts are rendered transparent when the chapter organizes them according to key concepts such as linguistic reflection, the actualization of the historical novel and the generational novel, auto-fiction, and the criticism of religion.

The handbook concludes with Chapter 21, a case study by Florinda Goldberg on contemporary literary texts that focus on Jewish belonging in Cuba. At the start of her analysis, Goldberg evokes political and social contexts beginning in the 1960s, when many critical intellectuals left the country and made questions of heritage and belonging fruitful for their examinations of Cuban history. These reflections on Jewish belonging once again allude to the epistemic interest of this volume as formulated at the very beginning of this introduction: not to consider Jewish history and general history separately from each other and to demonstrate the relevance of these literary representations for general cultural-historical considerations. The texts chosen by Goldberg for her analysis originate from three authors who are presented as examples of these processes: Achy Obejas, Oscar Hijuelos, and Leonardo Padura.

This 21-chapter layout does not only highlight the diversity of Jewish literatures in the Spanish and Portuguese languages. The chapters themselves embody this diversity in their different compositional approaches as well as in their writing styles. Quite a few of our authors are in fact writers themselves, and some of them are part of the history they are presenting in this handbook. We have made a conscious decision not to minimize the resulting differences between the chapters in our editorial practice. This includes the texts whose Romance belonging is noticeable even in English translation. We do not consider this a flaw, but an invaluable resource for understanding history through language.

We would like to thank Samuel Walker, who edited a large part of the texts. He has shown great sensitivity in respecting the individual tone of each chapter while at the same time suggesting important linguistic revisions. Fray Hochstein also edited two chapters. We are deeply grateful for her dedication.

Sophie Meiners and Luise Mücker not only prepared the articles for typesetting according to the style sheet, but also carefully read each chapter and gave us valuable feedback. Without their careful, highly accurate and always constructive work, we would not have been able to complete this handbook. We thank them very much for this. A sincere thank you to Elena von Ohlen for her diligent proofreading. We also thank her and the entire team (Esra Akkaya, Lena Hein, Ofek Kehila, Sophie Meiners and Luise Mücker) for their determination and skill in producing an exemplary index for our handbook.

We are equally grateful to the De Gruyter team and especially to Ulrike Krauss, who has supported this project from the very beginning. The team comprising Christina Lembrecht, Katja Lehming, and Maxim Karagodin has been a continuous, trusted advisor on the part of the publishing house. For this we are deeply appreciative.

The Fundación Duques de Soria granted a research stay for one of the editors of this handbook at the 'Casa del Hispanista' in the *Convento de la Merced* in the Spanish city of Soria within the scope of the Observatorio Permanente del Hispanismo (OPH), which contributed significantly to the completion of the volume. We are most grateful for this.

We would also like to express our gratitude to our authors, who accepted our revisions and were always appreciative and very patient with us. Some of them completed their texts under difficult circumstances during the Covid-19 pandemic. They are role models in collegiality to whom we are deeply indebted.

Medieval Constellations

Rica Amrán

1 Jewish and *Converso* History in Medieval Spain: The Castilian Case

Abstract: This chapter offers a concise survey of medieval Jewish history on the Iberian Peninsula. The presentation is based on the insight that this history must not be presented in a one-dimensional way, but in its diversity and sometimes also in its contradictions. This is demonstrated through the regional and local differences in Iberian Jewish history to which this chapter draws attention.

Key Terms: Medieval Jewish History, history of the *conversos*, Iberian Peninsula, Castile

1 Beginnings

In all likelihood, the settlement of Jews in the Iberian Peninsula took place in antiquity, although the first archaeological and documental proof dates back only to the first century AD (Beinart 1962, 1–32). The arrival of Visigoths (González Salinero 2000) to Hispania did not provoke a major change in the relationship between minorities and the governing people. We can only observe a difference in this regard after Reccared's conversion in 587, which was undertaken with the intention of encouraging the religious unity of the kingdom and was predicated on the existence of a sole religion: Christianity. This, in turn, created a deterioration of the monarchy's relations with the Jewish minority as well as with other groups such as the Arians, whose religion had been practised by the Visigoths prior to the conversion to Christianity of the majority of their aristocracy.

If at the end the sixth century the situation had been tense, it became untenable after 612, when at the Thirteenth Council of Toledo it was decided to observe a more strict attitude towards the Jewish community. Among the Council's injunctions we could highlight the following:
1. All servants working for Jews were to be liberated.
2. Harsh punishments were to be meted out to those who continued to observe Jewish traditions.
3. Jews were excluded from important public positions in the kingdom.
4. Jews were forbidden from moving freely throughout the kingdom.
5. Commercial relationships between Jews and Christians were forbidden.
6. Jewish possessions came directly under the ownership of the Crown.

Fifty years later, the laws issued by the Seventeenth Council of Toledo were even more restrictive. This approach was justified with the claim that Jews had conspired to take over the Visigothic Kingdom with the help of their coreligionists from North Africa. At the Council, drastic measures were approved and the forced conversion of Jews was deemed the best solution. The result was that Jews became *de facto* enslaved. This could have resulted in the disappearance of the Jewish community from the Iberian Peninsula, but the Muslim arrival prevented it.[1]

1.1 Muslim Spain

Muslims founded an emirate in the central and southern regions of the Iberian Peninsula with the capital city of Cordova. Later on, the region became a caliphate. Nonetheless, the Muslim settlement of the Iberian Peninsula was difficult because of the conquerors' scarce knowledge of the geography, population, languages, etc. of the region. In their administration, they received the help of the Jewish community, some members of which acted directly as interpreters and statesmen. One of these was undoubtedly Hasday ibn Shaprut, who represents the model of the brilliant courtier: a doctor and a diplomat, he was knowledgeable of Greek and Latin in addition to Arabic and Hebrew. With the help of his secretary, Menahem ben Saruq, he brought from his trips all sorts of books and compiled an important library (Gonzalo Maeso 1972; Millás Vallicrosa 1953; Saenz Badillos 1991).

Interest in the Hebrew language on the Iberian Peninsula began to grow as early as the tenth century. This was due in part to the realization that this language was almost unknown outside Jerusalem, even among the Jewish population. Lexicographic research in the tenth century was therefore a difficult endeavor in al-Andalus. On the one hand, works on the Jewish language were guided by philological interest and the desire to explain the Bible, Jewish writings, faith and tradition. Yet at the same time, there developed a poetic production both religious and secular in nature, resulting in a period of great creativity. Menahem ben Saruq was born in Tortosa in 910 and established himself in Cordova at the same time that he began working as a secretary for Hasday ibn Shaprut's father, Isaac. He wrote festive and mourning poems on commission as well as others to be recited and sung in synagogues. Only after Isaac's death did he begin working with Hasday and composed letters and diplomatic treatises for him, such as those sent to Constantinople. We also know of an important linguistic study written around 958, the first Hebrew-Hebrew dictionary, known as *Mahveret*.

Menahem, according to his writings, believed in the unique character of Hebrew as a sacred language. He can thus be considered a pioneer of lexicographic and philological studies who opened new ground that would later be further explored by other

---

[1] The Muslim arrival was explained through the legend of Count Julian who, according to tradition, allowed Muslims to cross the Strait of Gibraltar and reach the Iberian Peninsula.

medieval scholars. His *Mahveret* quickly became well known in the Italian Peninsula, the Kingdom of France, and Central and Eastern Europe, and it attained great dissemination in regions where Arab was not even known. Nevertheless, this dictionary was frequently criticized, particularly by Dunas ben Labrat,[2] a poet and philologist who, like all great personalities in al-Andalus at that time, excelled in many fields of knowledge. Dunas bitterly opposed Menahem, for whom this dispute signaled the end of the support he had received from the ben Labrat family.[3]

Many relevant Jewish scholars were born in al-Andalus, such as Samuel ben Negrela,[4] poets such as Shlomo ibn Gabirol,[5] and later on Judah ha-Levi,[6] Moshé ibn Ezra[7] and Moshé ben Maimón, known as Maimónides, among many others. These names represent a mere fraction of the scholars who created a splendid period known as the Golden Age of Spanish Judaism (Millás Vallicrosa 1973).

1.2 The Christian North

In 778, the Carolingians rushed to the aid of the County of Barcelona, which had rebelled against the Emir of Cordova. They waited for a long time in front of the gates of Saragossa, since the Iberians did not trust them, before returning towards the Pyrenees. On a second incursion between 785 and 789, the inhabitants of Girona, Cerdaña and Urgel opened their city gates to them. In 801, a third expedition led by one of Charlemagne's sons, Louis, was successful in conquering Barcelona, which at the time marked the frontier with al-Andalus despite the Franks' intention of conquering the city of Tortosa. In 865, Charles the Bald separated Catalonia from Roussillon. When, in 985, the last caliph of Cordova decided to pillage the County of Barcelona, the Carolingians did not come to the County's aid. As a consequence, the region decided

---

2 We know that the Dunas Ben Labrat family originated in Bagdad and that Dunas's parents settled in North Africa between 920–925; this great scholar of Arabic and Hebrew letters was located in Cordova ca. 950.
3 Dunas rejects the philological and theological foundation of the *Mahveret* because some of its parts were contrary to rabbinic law. He also defended a comparison with Arabic in the philological study of Hebrew Scriptures, an idea firmly opposed by Menahem.
4 Samuel ben Negrala (996?–1056), also known as ha-Naguid (the prince) ,was born in Mérida and received his education in Cordova. He worked as personal secretary to the King of Granada and participated in several diplomatic missions on his behalf.
5 Shlomo ibn Gabirol (Málaga 1021–Valencia 1070) was one the most important Hispano-Jewish poets and a great philosopher. He is also known as Avicebrón.
6 Judah ha-Levi (Tudela de Navarra 1070–1141 Holy Land?) was a doctor and philosopher, particularly known for his poetic work *Zionids* (which revolves around the city of Jerusalem) and the *Kuzarí*.
7 Moshé ibn Ezra (Granada 1055/1060–1138) was a great poet, known for his compositions on the topic of exile (from al-Andalus to the Christian North).

to free itself from the Franks, becoming increasingly powerful and later on subduing the taifas (or little kingdoms) of Tolossa and Saragossa.

At the time, Catalonia was a poor region, overpopulated and governed by powerful landholders supported by a mass of enslaved people. This changed when a large group of peasants settled in the region and organized themselves with great success in rural communities (Assis 2006). In the Basque Country, Navarre (750–1035) expanded along both sides of the Pyrenees. During the reign of Sancho the Great (970–1035), its territory extended from Galicia to Catalonia. After Sancho's death, his four children divided the kingdom amongst themselves. Ferdinand (1035–1065) received Castile, while Ramiro attained the title of King of Aragon and annexed the neighboring counties, thus giving birth to the County of Aragon. The matrimonial union between Ramon Berenguer IV, Count of Barcelona, and the Aragonese Petronila resulted in the birth of Alfonso II (1162–1196), who inherited the kingdom and adopted Santiago as its capital city and Barcelona as its main economic center.

Castile in turn became a county led by Fernán González towards the end of the tenth century, remaining dependent on the Kingdom of León. In 1037, Ferdinand I of Castile and León conquered the Duero and Taxus rivers. Nevertheless, after his death in 1065, the kingdom went through a period of upheavals between 1072 and 1109 (Menéndez Pidal 1950; Martín 1988).

1.3 Navarre

The Jewish communities of Navarre had a large population during the Middle Ages. The cities with the largest Jewish populations were Tudela, Pamplona and Estella. In 1277, there was an assault on the Jewish community of this region, which was known as the *navarrería*. The attack on the Jewish community of Pamplona was particularly drastic. In 1328, following the death of the French king, the Jewish community of Estella was attacked. Such attacks became common and the affairs of the community became dependent upon foreign factors outside the kingdom and beyond the Iberian Peninsula. In general, we could say that the community lived relatively peacefully during the reigns of Charles II[8] and Charles III.[9]

---

[8] Charles II of Navarre (10/10/1332–01/31/1387), also known as Charles of Évreux or Charles the Bad – *le Mauvais*-, was Count of Évreux and reigned during 1349–1387.
[9] Charles III of Navarre (June 22 1361–September 8 1425), known as the Noble, was King of Navarre, Count of Évreux and Duke of Nemours. He was the son and successor of Charles the Bad and Joan of Valois and reigned during the years 1387–1425.

1.4 Castile

The destruction of the Caliphate of Cordova and the emergence of the taifa kingdoms, brought about by immigrant waves coming from North Africa – first the Almoravids (1086–1146) and later on the Almohads (1146–1232) – compelled Jews to move to the Christian North. There, the kingdoms had started to be organized but they lacked administrative experience, which Jews themselves, or at least their dominant class, had already become familiar with in al-Andalus.

Alfonso VI of Castile initiated a totally new policy with regard to Jews, as he was conscious of the need to reorganize the newly reconquered territories. To this end, he created very favorable conditions for the settlement of Jews in the territories of the Castilian Crown. In 1076, the *Fuero* of Nájera became the symbol of such changes. For instance, the assassination of a Jew was punished with the payment of 250 *sueldos*; in case the assassin was not found, the closest village to where the homicide had taken place was to be condemned to the payment of this fine or *caloña*. Alfonso VII issued the *Fuero* of Escalona in 1189, which permitted Jews direct access to markets, with the same rights as Christians, the possibility of having Christian or Jewish judges in mixed court cases, the right to swear on the Torah instead of on the Bible, etc. (Amran 1989).

The situation of Jews in the northern Iberian Peninsula was thus very different from that of Jews living in the rest of the European territories (Martín 1988, 603–622), and remained so until the thirteenth century, when new problems arose. During the reign of Alfonso X, the opposition between the nobility and the king, which had begun a few years earlier, reached its peak during the last years of the king's reign, when his son, the future Sancho IV, led the aristocratic party. The opposition between the nobility and the monarchy continued into the first years of the fourteenth century, when Alfonso XI ascended the throne as a child and was able to dominate the aristocracy for the next 50 years. But things changed again after his death, as Pedro I was opposed by his half-brother Enrique of Trastámara, one of the illegitimate sons of Alfonso XI and Leonor de Guzmán, who became the leader of the aristocratic party during the civil war that split Castile in two and resulted in the ascension of the illegitimate candidate as king in 1368.

With regard to the Jewish community, several issues became relevant starting at the end of the thirteenth century. First, many of the privileges previously obtained were abolished, including the participation of Jewish judges in mixes cases and the right to eat together with Christians, to hold public office, to work as doctors, etc. These privileges had been already taken away from the Jewish community under Visigoth rule, as well as throughout the rest of Europe. Ecclesiastical legislation also became threatening to the community, in particular the resolutions of the Council of Vienne (1311–1312) together with those of the Synod of Zamora that followed suit in 1313. Although neither set of resolutions was ever enforced, they became precedents for later legislations enacted at the beginning of the fifteenth century (Amran 1990).

All of the factors briefly touched upon here created a conflictive situation by the end of the fourteenth century, when the propaganda utilized by the Trastámara faction finally took hold in the population. To this must be added that there was a period of bad harvests, strong weather changes, famine and political instability as a result of the civil war. It was undoubtedly all of these forces that resulted in the persecutions of 1391 (Valdeón Baruque 2002).

1.5 Aragon

As in Castile, the monarchs of Aragon utilized the services of the Jewish minority to help them manage the administrative structures of the kingdom. For this reason, in 1239, James I (1213–1276) extended his royal protection to the Jews settling in Mallorca, Catalonia, and Valencia. Perpignan (Valdeón Baruque 1968, 1983) continued its association with the Crown of Aragon. This provoked the envy of many subjects and the enmity of the nobility, kept at a distance by Aragonese monarchs at this time as they were attempting to revindicate their rights.

James II (1291–1327) began a century-long policy of maintaining the privileges of the Jewish community while at the same time opening the kingdom's borders to the Jews exiled from France during the years 1306 and 1329. In 1333, his heir Alfonso V (1327–1336) issued a law that imposed supplemental taxes on the economic transactions of Jews. During Pedro IV's reign (1338–1387), the "Jewish element" was very active in the conquest of Mallorca.

The *aljamas* grew and became organized politically, administratively and judicially after the model of their Christian counterparts. Nonetheless, pressure from the Church deepened the differences between Christians and Jews. This was also the case outside of Aragon. In 1320, a movement known as *pastorellos* started in France, composed of large popular masses that pillaged all Jewish quarters on their pilgrimage to the Holy Places and that increased the disaffection already felt towards Jews. Some of these masses crossed the border and attacked the *aljama* of Monteclús, although a disaster was prevented thanks to the intervention of James II.

Another decisive factor was the bubonic plague that arrived on the Iberian Peninsula in 1348 and affected both Christians and Jews. As in other places, a rumor took hold that the disease had been caused by Jews who wanted to get rid of their fellow citizens.[10] Facing this danger, the Jewish communities tried to organize an institution composed of the *aljamas* of Aragon, Catalonia, Valencia, and Mallorca in 1354, but to no avail. In 1377, the Jewish population of Huesca was accused of the desecration of the Host. The plague of 1348 that provoked the persecution of Jews in the Kingdom of Aragon and, later on, in the whole Iberian Peninsula had serious consequences for

---

[10] The *aljama* of Jaca escaped from the plague but nonetheless suffered persecutions.

the Crown, particularly around the region of Saragossa. There, a large number of Jews died. At the same time, the nobility revolted. Similar developments could be observed in Barcelona and in the north of Catalonia.

In Mallorca, everything tended to be delayed. In around 1374, Jews were accused of worsening the situation of misery and famine because their loans suffocated the population. Despite this, the revolts here cannot be compared to those of 1391 and they did not endanger the existence of the Spanish Jewish community.

Another relevant fact was the accusation of Host desecration leveled against the Jews from the *aljama* of Barcelona in 1367, which ended with the execution of three Jews. As in Castile, the lower elements of society made Jews responsible for everything that went wrong.

2 Jewish Society in Medieval Christian Spain

The medieval Jewish community throughout Spain can be defined as a microsociety that, in many ways, paralleled Christian society. After the destruction of the Second Temple of Jerusalem, Jews brought their own institutions with them throughout the diaspora, both influencing and receiving the influence of the regions where they settled. In general, they organized themselves in small groups known as communities or *cahal*. The legal institution that encompassed one or more communities was called *aljama*.[11]

Spanish Jewish society was divided along the same lines as Christian society. There were three distinct groups: *mayores*, the upper class consisting of the economically powerful; *medianos*, the middle clas consisting of small traders, shoemakers, etc.; and *menudos*, the lower class consisting of widows, orphans, and the poor (Beinart 1968–1969, 221–225).[12]

In each Jewish community within the kingdoms of Castile-León, Navarre and Aragon, public life was governed by the most powerful families, the *mayores* who had land and possessions in the city and its surroundings. Some examples are, in Toledo, the families Abulafia, ibn Ezra, Alkafar, ibn Shoshan, and ibn Zadoq; in Barcelona, the families Abrevalia and Berfet; in Tarragona, the family Portel, etc. – all of whom appear time and again in the documents of the time. We could term them *court Jews*.

The social situation of Jewish communities in the peninsula was not the same in every place and at all times. Political changes affected them directly, a situation

---

11 The term *aljama* comes from the Arabic *al-jama'a*. It encompases many meanings, including assembly, council, and even armies composed of Moorish or Jewish soldiers. Later on, it took on the meaning of enclosed quarters where ethnic or religious minorities lived, as well as their property. Related terms are *aliama* and *alcama*.
12 In this particular point, we find a clear difference from Christian society.

which, for the most part, did not change after the *Reconquista*. Several attempts were made to compile a unified Christian legal code (e.g., *Siete Partidas* or the *Ordinance of Alcalá* of 1348), but Christian kingdoms were ruled alternatively by Visigoth, Roman or canonical law. On the other hand, the *aljama* legislation was unified and based on Jewish law (*halajá*).

Local characteristics gave each community its distinctive character. We can identify three distinct types based on the size of the respective community. a) The oldest and simplest type consisting in small groups in which every member takes part in community activities. According to Shlomo ibn Adret, "ni siquiera la mayoría tenía derecho a actuar en nombre de la comunidad" (nor even the majority had the right to act in the name of the community).[13] b) Small communities that had a tradition of managing their communal affairs in common and had trust in their community leaders. c) Larger communities with with an elective government such as in Barcelona, Toledo, Saragossa, etc.

The ruling body was known under a variety of names. Its functions also varied depending on the community. Community officers in Navarre-Aragon were called *mukadamim* (*advanced*), while in Castile they were called *neemanim* or *berurim* (faithful or enlightening), or also *mukdamim*. In turn, this group received the assistance of the *yoatzim* (advisors), who were the elders or notable people of the community and who were called "consejo de los diez, de los veinte o de los treinta, dependiendo del número que lo compusieran"[14] (council of the 10, 20 or 30, depending on how many people composed them). The *mukdamim* were the equivalent of Christian secretaries. The *berurim* were deputies that constituted an administrative group acting as magistrates, tax collectors, etc. (Suárez Fernàndez 1980, 103–104). The number of *berurim* or *mukdamim* varied in each community (10 in Toledo, 4 in Saragossa and Lérida, etc.).

Both the *berurim* and the councils had a responsibility towards the community. When there were important matters to discuss, the whole community was gathered in general assemblies with the intention of providing endorsement of their own opinions.

The main duties of the *berurim*, *mukdamim* and the council were the collection of taxes, the administration of justice within the *aljama*, the maintenance of synagogues, the organization of public education and of subsidies for the *Ezrá* (the community welfare system), and other such tasks.

---

13 Ben Adret, *Sheelot ve-teshuvot*, II, n.394. Shlomo ben Adret (Barcelona 1235–Barcelona 1310), also known as Rashba, was the most famous scholar of Jewish Law in the thirteenth and at the beginning of the fourteenth century. He was born in Barcelona in around 1235 and died in around 1310. He was a disciple of Nahmanides, the great Talmud scholar from Girona.
14 Beinart believes that towards the end of the thirteenth century, a council of 30 was formed that represented the three social classes, although the most prominent role in this council was represented by the so-called *court Jews* (Beinart 1968–1969, 229).

In order to accomplish all this, the community government was essential, and it took decisions only after they were approved by a majority vote (Ben Adret V n.126).[15] (There was no direct popular vote, which did not exist in Christian Spain either.) Nevertheless, this communal governance had its limitations. If it did not follow Jewish law or did not act according to legal norms and the principle of equality, it could be invalidated by a rabbinical authority (Ben Adret VII n.108). On some occasions, a rabbi took part in the assemblies in order to avoid illegal decisions. Once a motion was approved, it was valid as a municipal decree or *tacanot*. Once adopted by the *cahal*, final decisions were registered in the *pinkás* or *community registry*. On the Sabbath, after the rituals were performed, they were read out loud. Occasionally, there were complaints, but usually the decisions were approved by the whole congregation (the *cahal* gave its approval by uttering the word *amen*).

The violation of some of the measures adopted by the communal administration was punished with fines, corporal punishment or the *herem* and the *nidui*. Exclusion from the community was also a powerful weapon for the government of the *aljama*, and some monarchs tried to make use of it for their own interest, although they were not successful due to the fact that rabbinical authorities annulled all *herem* decreed by non-rabbinical authorities.

2.1 The Tax Problem: The Jewish *pecho*

For the Iberian monarchs, taxes were an important instrument of fiscal administration.[16]

There was no uniform method for the collection of taxes on Jews. They were required as a sum total from the *aljama*, which in turn was in charge of collecting them.

The Jewish population in northern Christian Spain was obliged to pay regular taxes, and they had to finance reparations of fortified cities and castles, supply horses for the army, and even contribute a special tax during war time.

Occasionally, the government resorted to loans from particular individuals. *Aljamas* became conscious of the danger to their subsistence involved in these loans, and decided accordingly to consider them as a tax, making in turn each individual contribute proportionally to their means to the payment of the amount demanded by the king (Ben Adret, *Sheelot ve-teshuvot*, III n.427).

The tax commission kept a registry that included all members of the community. If a foreigner resided in a city for over a year, he was included in the registry, and note was taken when an individual acquired wealth. The forms of payment varied from

---

15 According to Ben Adret, "La mayoría en cada ciudad era para el individuo lo que el Sanhedrín para todo Israel" ("the majority in each city was for the individual what the Sanhedrin was for the whole of Israel").*Sheelot ve-teshuvot*, V, n.126.
16 Haim Beinart considers that the collection of taxes was a crucial element in intercommunal relations (Beinart 1968–1969, 226).

community to community, allowing for the possibility of payment by installment. High dignitaries usually sought an agreement with the treasury and were, through special privileges, exempt from contributing to the tax on the *aljamas* (Suárez Fernández 1980). Thus, they harmed the community, as the wealthiest individuals avoided sharing in the payment of the fixed tax amount which then had to be paid by the middle and lower classes.

2.2 The Administration of Justice

The *aljama* had its own legal jurisdiction, and Jewish legislation differed from that of the Christian community. The Jewish court (*bet-din*, *bedimus*, *albedin*, a deformation of the word *bet-din*) was the oldest institution among the communities of the diaspora (Baer 1950, 5–7). Law was administered according to the law written in the *Torá* and the *Talmud*, with a rabbi acting as an appeals judge. Medieval judges were usually not official rabbis but rather educated men elected to the position of *dayán* (judge).[17] This was an honorary position which received no salary, gifts, or any monetary allotment for judicial expenses. The king confirmed the election of the judges as a way of making their appointment official.

The *bet din* made use of the available prisons to incarcerate the accused. In addition to detention in jail, they could resort to corporal punishment. The death sentence was rarely decreed and only when the defendants were determined to be *malsines*, that is spies or conspirators who could jeopardize the security of the *aljama*.

The *aljama* was very zealous of preserving its right to appeal directly to the king, for that allowed it to defend itself from abuses and arbitrariness (Suárez Fernández 1980, 107–108). *Aljamas* began to lose these rights at the end of the thirteenth and the beginning of the fourteenth century.

3 From 1391 to 1492: The "converso issue"

The fourteenth century is generally regarded as the end of the period of amicable relations previously established between the Castilian monarchs and the Jews settled in their territories (Baer 1981, 12–16; Suárez Fernández 1980, 35–38). This turning point coincided with a more general shift in social structures and in particular with a growing opposition between the nobility and the monarchy, which was fuelled by the former's attempts to preserve its rights and privileges. This was also accompanied by a grave social, political and economic crisis as a result of the spreading of the plague

---

17 In Castile, it was not necessary to be an ordained rabbi in order to be able to teach and act as a judge. (Beinart 1968–1969, 229).

in the Iberian Peninsula (which claimed the life of Alfonso XI), frequent droughts, and the periods during the fifteenth century when successive kings came to power while still very young.

In Castile, this situation was used by certain preachers to disseminate a clearly anti-Jewish message. That was the case of the archdeacon of Écija, Ferrán Martínez, in 1378, who was opposed by his superior cardinal Barroso and even by King Juan I. When King Enrique II ascended the throne while still a minor, Ferrán was able to take advantage of the Crown's social and economic instability to blame the Jews for the situation in Castile. As a consequence, a series of pogroms took place, first in Seville and later on throughout Andalusia, then in Valencia, Barcelona, and other locations. Numerous *aljamas* were attacked, material goods were pillaged, and many Jews were assassinated. During this time, a large number of Jews migrated to North Africa and an even larger number converted to Christianity (Amran 2001).

Prior to 1391, Jews who converted to Christianity did so as private individuals after being convinced of the truth of their new faith and upon receiving baptism. In 1391, the situation was rather different. Although some Jews continued to convert out of genuine conviction, many converted out of fear and in the belief that they could revert to their old religion once the danger subsided. In this they made a serious mistake, for once they converted to Christianity, the ecclesiastical institutions had the obligation to indoctrinate them (Meyerson 2004). From an economic and social standpoint, it should be noted that these new Christians, having taken steps towards conversion, now had opportunities open to them that had not existed for them before: they could apply for positions in the kingdom's administration and in the ecclesiastical hierarchy. Yet, as it was impossible for society to absorb all of them, social and economic competition began to be felt at the end of the fourteenth century.

The explosion of anti-converso sentiment in 1449 had Pedro Sarmiento as its main protagonist. Despite being disguised as religiously motivated, it had clear socio-economic incentives. The revolts provoked an opposition between new and old Christians. Pedro Sarmiento wrote the first *statute of purity of blood* according to which *judeo-conversos* and their descendants were prevented from participating in the city's administration. Although this *sentencia-estatuto* (sentence-statute) was never enacted and Pedro Sarmiento and his accomplices were severely punished, it was used as a model for future statutes of purity of blood, which the most prestigious institutions in the kingdom began to apply in the second half of the fifteenth century.

While the attacks of 1391 targeted Jews, the animosity of 1449 (Benito Ruano 1957, 2001; Amran 2002, 35–57) focused on new Christians. Although the entire fifteenth century is characterized by an opposition to the *judeo-conversos*, the Jewish minority, which had seen its numbers and privileges reduced, was also caught up in this opposition between new and old Christians. The Jews not only reminded the new Christians of their origins, but were also accused by the old Christians of trying to guide the former back to their old faith. It should also be noted that, in many cases, only part of a given family had converted, so that contact among conversos and Jews was frequent during festivities and ceremonies. Around this time, the accusation of being *bad Christians* and of a lack of faith in Jesus Christ was leveled against the conversos. It was regarded as necessary to suspect them all until they had proven their fidelity.

Alonso de Espina, the confessor of King Enrique IV and the author of *Fortalitium fidei* (1459), denounced the danger that conversos represented for Christianity. He proposed their expulsion. Espina catalogued 25 converso transgressions, which were later utilized as a guide by the Inquisition. They were divided as follows: a) The practice of Jewish ceremonies (observation of the Sabbath, circumcision, celebration of holidays, sending oil to synagogues, funerary rites, Jewish education, praying in Hebrew or the recitation of Jewish prayers in Spanish translation, etc.); b) Transgressions against the new faith (calumnies addressed to Jesus Christ and the Virgin Mary, performing work on Christian holidays, eating lamb on Passover, avoiding making the sign of the cross or celebrating baptism rites, etc.); c) Consanguinity in married couples, contact with non-Christian relatives, etc.

In 1461, Antonio de Oropesa made clear that part of the converso issue derived from the fact that there was no superior authority in charge of judging accusations against conversos, and concluded that if those who were in fact guilty were punished, the common people would cease to direct violence towards the entire group. Enrique IV seemed convinced, and asked Oropesa to organize an Episcopal Inquisition in the name of the king. He received papal approval on 15 March 1462. Nevertheless, due to the situation in Castile and Enrique's instability, the Inquisition was not established (Nirenberg 2002).

The Holy Office was finally established by petition of the Catholic Monarchs in 1478, when Pope Sixtus IV authorized it, although it only began to function in 1480.

The *Crónica de los Reyes Católicos* by Fernando del Pulgar mentions the 'converso heresy' in the following terms:

> Este año [1480] continuándose la inquisición comenzada en el Reyno contra los cristianos que habian seydo de linaje de judíos, é tornaban á judaizar, se fallaron en la ciudad de Toledo algunos homes é mugeres que escondidamente facian ritos judáicos. (Amran 2014, 95–97)

> This year [1480], as the inquisition begun in the Kingdom against the Christians who had been of Jewish lineage and were returning to Judaism continued, some men and women were found in the city of Toledo who were secretly performing Jewish rites.

And the *Crónica de los Reyes Católicos* by André Bernáldez indicates:

> La herética pravedad mosáica reinó gran tiempo escondida y andando por los rincones, no osando manifestar, y fue disimulada y dado lugar que pro mengua de los Prelados, é Arzobispo e Obispos de España que nunca la acusaron, ni denunciaron á los Reyes, ni á los Papas segun debían, y eran obligados [. . .], é quedaron los que se bautizaron cristianos y llamároslos conversos [. . .]. (Pulgar 432; Bernáldez 599–587)

> The heretical Mosaic depravity reigned for a long time hidden and concealing itself in the margins, not daring to manifest itself, and was disguised and able to take place to the detriment

of the Prelates, Archbishops and Bishops of Spain who never accused it, nor denounced it to the Kings, nor to the Popes as they should have done, and were obliged to do [. . .], and those who were baptised Christians and called converts remained [. . .].

3.1 Thinkers before the Sentence-Statute of 1449

This category includes a series of authors whose writings and preaching evinced a more divisive mentality that took shape little by little. Three facts that marked the passage from the fourteenth to the fifteenth century are to be highlighted with regard to this climate of growing animosity towards the conversos: the death of Enrique III of Castile in 1406; the ensuing regency of Catherine of Lancaster and Ferdinand I; and the appearance in the political-religious arena of the figure of friar Vincent Ferrer, an influential personality in the aforementioned change of mentality. In the *Crónica de Juan II*, we can read a description of Ferrer's arrival at the Castilian court:

> Fray Vicente, de edad de setenta años, [. . .] el qual así en Aragón como en Castilla con sus sanctas predicaciones convirtió a nuestras Sancta Fe muchos Judíos é Moros, é hizo muy grandes bienes [. . .] así se ordenó, se mandó é se puso en obra en las mas ciudades é villa destos Reynos [. . .].
> (Amran 1996, 146)

> Friar Vincent, at the age of seventy years, [. . .] who with his holy preaching converted many Jews and Moors to our Holy Faith both in Aragon and in Castile, and did great good [. . .] thus it was ordered, commanded and put into practice in most cities and towns of these kingdoms [. . .].

Friar Vincent, at first moved by mercy when he became aware of the events of 1391, preached in a different manner than Ferrand Martínez, that is without the desire to inflame the populace. According to him, no physical violence should be exerted in order to attain conversion:

> Contemplando maduramente los tristes cuanto desastrosas consecuencias,que en las multiplicadas esferas de la vida produjeron en esta Península Ibérica –exceptuando sólo el rincón de Navarra, por las causas oportunamente expuestas- los sangrientos sucesos de 1391; reconociendo, como hemos procurado hacerlo, el vario modo, con que la actividad de los pueblos cristianos, al obrar sobre la grey judía, ya movidas de la antigua y creciente malquerencia, ya jexcitados cual nunca por el celo proselitismo [. . .].
> (Amran 1996, 186)

> With a sober contemplation of the sad and disastrous consequences in the many spheres of life that the bloody events of 1391 produced in this Iberian Peninsula -excepting only the corner of Navarre, for the reasons duly explained-; we have to recognise, as we have tried to do, the various ways in which the activity of the Christians, when acting against the Jewish community, was either moved by their ancient and growing malice, or more excited than ever by the zeal of proselytism [. . .].

Nevertheless, there was a change in his attitude in the years 1411–1412 regarding the aggressiveness of his sermons. This was motivated by his desire to offer salvation to the Jewish community, for which he counted on the help of converso Pablo de Santa María (Cátedra). His proselytizing endeavors focused on the conversion of minorities, the integration of new Christians into the mainstream of society, and the exclusion of the unfaithful. He exerted a great deal of coercion in his sermons by obliging the entire population of a village to listen to them, including the minorities. His points of view were similar to those of previous preachers and he utilized the figure of the Antichrist as well as other apocalyptic imagery and content.

The *Laws of Valladolid of 1412* were a consequence of the situation created in these first years of the fifteenth century and were directly inspired by Vicent Ferrer, with the support of Catherine of Lancaster as well as of the friar's friend from youth Pope Benedict XIII. (The Pope was also responsible for the Bull of January 2, 1412, which was written along the same line as the Valladolid laws). In summary, these laws established that Jews must live in separate neighborhoods; that they could not be pharmacists, doctors or surgeons; that they could not trade in staple foods (flour, oil, lard, etc.); that they could not eat or drink with Christians; and that they could not be landlords or stewards. In addition, *aljamas* were forbidden from establishing their own taxes and tributes and Jews were obliged to wear a circular symbol known as a *rodela*. . . . In short, these laws aimed to make the daily functioning of the community as a whole as difficult as possible.

Vicente Ferrer (Vendrell 1953, 87–104) developed a friendship with Pope Benedict XIII's doctor, Yehoshua ha-Lorqui, and played an important role in his conversion (after which he would adopt the Christian name of Jerónimo de Santa Fe). These were relevant factors in the Disputation of Tortosa that began on 7 February 1413 and where the converso played a prominent role. The different messianic visions of the two religions occupied a prominent role among the points discussed in the disputation. The Christian participents relied on the Talmud to prove the superiority of the Christian faith: Jesus Christ was the awaited one.[18] Jerónimo wrote an opuscule composed of twenty-four chapters, to which the Jewish scholars had to respond. According to him, the conversion of Jews (the so-called "lost sheep of the flock") to Christianity would result in the spiritual victory of the Pope. He also described a higher (celestial) and a lower (earthly) Jerusalem.

In the Disputation of Tortosa, there were two points made on the figure of the Messiah which were to be paramount in their later influence on several messianic conceptualizations:

1. The nature of Jesus Christ: Christians considered him to be both God and man. For Jews, the Messiah was an upright man, a prophet that did not have any divine characteristics.
2. The function of the Messiah was, according to Christians, to redeem souls from hell. Jews expected the corporal and spiritual resurrection of the individual.

---

18 With regard to the figure of the Messiah, Judaism made three important predictions worth mentioning: the end of the political servitude of Israel; resurrection (corporeal as well as spiritual); acceptance of Jewish law by all the other nations.

The Talmud (which had already been discussed in Europe by Nicholas Donin under Pope Gregory IX) became the main topic of discussion after the disputation ended. This occurred at around the same time as the Council of Constance (November of 1414).

The conclusions of the Disputation of Tortosa (including those on the Talmud) were published in May–July 1415 and were not very different from those of the Laws of Valladolid of 1412 (Jiménez Soler 1950, 361–414). They called for the condemnation of the Talmud *in totum*[19] and the drastic separation of Jews in separate neighborhoods.[20]

As a consequence of Vincent Ferrer's preaching and the conclusions of Tortosa, some *aljamas* in Aragon were destroyed by impassioned followers of the preacher. Daroca was a special case, as all types of abuses were committed there. Judaism in Aragon, which was already debilitated after the events of 1391, almost became extinct in the first years of the fifteenth century until 1416. The situation only improved after the deposition of Benedict XIII and the death of Ferdinand I of Aragon. Both events resulted in the loss of influence of Vicente Ferrer and the partial recovery of Aragonese *aljamas*.

Three Jewish authors should be highlighted whose opinions were published in three books as a reaction to the Disputation, which the Jewish population was obliged to attend. R. Yosef Albo, a very active rabbi, wrote his *Book of Principles* (*Séfer ha-Iccarim*), in which he explains the articles of the Jewish faith. He discourses on the meaning of divine revelation and redemption as applied to conversos, in particular those who were forced to convert or who felt undecided, in an attempt to save them from desperation with the hope of receiving God's grace. He claims that all pains have been endured as a demonstration of the greatness of the Jewish faith.

Shem Tob ben Shem Tob was the author of the *Book of Beliefs*. In it, he summarizes his opinions as well as those of his contemporaries. He argues that philosophical rationalism is responsible for the current state of affairs, as it has brought about the destruction of *aljamas* as well as apostasy. He believes that the philosophically-inclined thinkers reject divine providence as well as the concepts of divine reward and punishment. He is convinced that these philosophical ideas are responsible for the physical destruction of Spanish Judaism. According to him, conversion has been but one more mistake in a long list of errors.

Finally, in his *Moral Epistle* (*Iggeret musar*), Salomón Alami reminds us of the events of 1391 and the Laws of Valladolid of 1412, both in Castile and Aragon. His advice is to leave Sepharad. According to him, the trials of his people can be attributed to the wealthy Jews (in particular the landlords) and their unethical lifestyle.

---

19 This also happened in the Kingdom of Aragon between 1413 and 1414.
20 Some of these measures had also been adopted back in 1413 and 1414. Regarding the great number of conversos (see Netanyahu 1994).

3.2 Thinker Coetaneous with the Sentence-Statute

Fernán Díaz de Toledo (Amran 2001, 56–66)

He was one of the most important officials in Juan II's court. Born in Alcalá de Henares, he probably converted in 1391, and he died in 1457. He was an expert on civil and canonical law and served as secretary to the king until 1420. After that date, he became *Relator* (that is, personal secretary to the king). He wrote an *Instrucción* addressed to the Bishop of Cuenca, Lope de Barrientos (Getino 146–159), on the topic of the sentence-statute. The beginning of this document is as follows:

> Lo que habeys de decir al Obispo mi Señor es esto. Que te véoslas manos, y me encomiendo a su merced, no sólo por mi, mas por toda esta pobre corrida Nación de Linaje de nuestro Señor Jesu Christo, según la carne, el qual es sobre todas las cosas, Dios bendito [. . .].
>
> (Díaz de Toledo, 343)

> What you have to say to the Bishop my Lord is this. That I see your hands, and I commend myself to his mercy, not only for myself, but for all this poor nation of the lineage of our Lord Jesus Christ, according to the flesh, who is above all things, blessed God [. . .].

Fernán Díaz de Toledo harshly objects to establishing any distinction between old and new Christians. He believes that the latter will end up leaving for "tierras de moros" (Moorish lands) as a result of people like those responsible for the Toledo revolt. Their new faith cannot defend them from their enemies:

> Según que cada día lo facen: mas aun los que son venidos y de ellos descienden, están escandalizados, diciendo que acertaron muy mal en venir a la fee; pues son mas perseguidos, que los Judios . . . que en todo Toledo de estos dies no hay duda, que a estos pase por voluntad de irse a tierra de Moros, o a otros Reynos a tornar Judios [. . .].
>
> (Díaz de Toledo, 343–344)

> They do it every day, but even those who descend from them are scandalised, saying that they were wrong to come to the faith; for they are more persecuted than the Jews. . . such that in all of Toledo there is currently no doubt that they are willing to go to the land of the Moors, or to other kingdoms in order to convert to Judaism [. . .].

He goes on to explain the opinion of the Toledo rebels about conversos:

> [. . .] el qual ha sembrado Zizaña en aquella Ciudad, diciendo, que los convertidos a la Fee, y los que vienen de ellos, no deben haber oficios, ni honras, ni Dignidades, ni aun deben ser recibidos por testigos entre los Fieles, fundándose por una razón, que dice la Ley de el fuero de el Juzgo de testigos, que dice que es canonizado, y fecho Decreto de ello [. . .].
>
> (Díaz de Toledo, 344)

> [. . .] who has stirred up much discord in that city, saying that those converted to the Faith, and those who convert from it, should not have offices, nor honours, nor titles, nor should they even be received as witnesses among the Faithful, based on the reason that the Law of the jurisdiction of the Court of Witnesses says that it is canonised, and a Decree has been issued about it [. . .].

Fernán Díaz de Toledo believes this constitutes blasphemy, for baptism transforms Jews into new men. Consequently, the Toledo rebels must be treated as heretics:

> Ya que el Santo Bautismo y la eficacia de él, el qual face el bautizado nuevo hombre y lo laba y lo quita de todo reato y culpa, y pecado [. . .]. (Díaz de Toledo, 345)

> Because Holy Baptism and the power of it, by which it makes the baptised person a new human being and washes away and takes away from him all guilt and sin [. . .].

He also referes to the origins of Jesus Christ and the Virgin Mary:

> Y yo no see como se aplicará a guardar lo que pertenece a nuestra Santa Fee el nuevamente convertido, mayormente de é Pueblo Israelítico, nin de los que vinieron de ellos, nin como honraron las fiestas de Nuestro Señor, que es nuestra cabeza y vino de aquel linaje a la carne, nin de quanto a la Virgen Gloriosa Nuestra Señora, María, su madre, nin de los otros Apóstoles, Santos y Martyres, que fueron de este mesmo linaje [. . .]. (Díaz de Toledo, 348–349)

> And I do not see how the new converts, especially those coming to our Holy Faith from Judaism, nor those who descended from them, will observe what corresponds to our Holy Faith, nor how they honour the feasts of Our Lord, who is our Lord and came from that lineage to the flesh, nor how they honour the Glorious Virgin Our Lady, Mary, his mother, nor the other Apostles, Saints and Martyrs, who were of the same lineage [. . .].

Fernán Díaz de Toledo argues that if conversos sin, they should be duly punished, but the upright believers must not pay for the new Christians who do not behave righteously:

> [. . .] que si algun Christiano nuevo hoy, que mal use; que es razon, e justicia, que siendo amonestado [. . .], y yo seré el primero que traeré la leña, en que lo quemen, y daré el fuego [. . .]. (Díaz de Toledo, 341)

> [. . .] if any New Christian should act improperly today; there is reason and justice for them to be reprimanded [. . .], and I will be the first to gather the firewood to burn them, and I will light the fire [. . .].

Juan de Torquemada (Amran 2001, 66–72; Tratado)

He was the uncle of Inquisitor Tomás de Torquemada and wrote in Latin his *Tractatus contra medianitas eismaelitas advesarios et detractores fidelium qui de populo iraelitico originem traxerum*.

Juan de Totquemada adopted a more theological approach than Díaz de Toledo and, to some extent, his work complements that of the *Relator*. First, he explains the title of his work: the enemies of Israel, according to the Bible, were the descendants of Esau as well as the Ishmaelites. Both represent those who hate Israel, i.e. Christians. Then, Torquemada moves on to analyze those who revolted against the conversos, who, according to his interpretation, ultimately acted against the king and the Church of Toledo. In order to justify their actions, they falsified the facts and accused conversos of heresy. The main purpose of it all was to remove new Christians from their positions and dignities.[21] The second chapter refutes the sanctions against the conversos, who were considered bad Christians until the fourth generation.

Torquemada does not accept social or economic discrimination among the Christian faithful or any distinction between old and new Christians (*Tratado*, 216). He believes this only results in damage to the Christian religion. He concludes that the measures adopted in Toledo were against the law; the premises were false and therefore the conclusion was unsound.[22] According to him, the only solution would be the annulment of the sentence-statute and the condemnation of the rebels (Amran 2001, 66–72).

Alonso de Cartagena (Amran 2001, 72–74)

He was the son of Pablo de Santa María. He was a theologian, historian, and the most important spokesperson for the conversos between 1435–1455. He was born in 1385 and converted in 1391. He studied at the University of Salamanca and specialized in philosophy, theology and law. He received his doctorate in 1406 and was appointed as a member of the Royal Council and as a papal nuncio in Castile. Around 1434 he was appointed Bishop of Burgos.

Alonso de Cartagena's *Defensorium unitates cristianos*, divided into three sections, begins by expressing St Augustin's ideas. After summarizing Biblical history, Cartagena arrives at Jesus Christ and explains the relation between old and new Israel by emphasizing the predestination, by divine grace, of Jesus's birth from Jewish lineage (Alfonso, 191). He does not distinguish between Old and New Testament, arguing that he who could read and understand the former could also comprehend the latter. He concludes by rejecting the sentence-statute after analyzing the contemporary converso society. He qualifies conversos in general as good Christians and indicates that their rejection was due in particular to economic and social reasons.

---

[21] "Quinto describitur processus antedictus impius, tupote impietatis et malignitatis consilio conceptus et formatos, cum dicitur super populum tuum malignaverunt consilium, deliberantes conversos adfidem Christi, de genere Israelitico sive Iudaeorum descendentes, nos esse admittendos danda, ad publica oficia, ad honores mundanas sive eclesiásticos . . ." (*Tratado*, 129–139).

[22] "Ex superioribus iam facile est ostendere quam domnatissima sit conclusio illa principalis quam praefeti impii Modiantae et Ismaelitae in suo processu iniquo et scandaloso, quem adversus noviter conversos de populo Isrelitico fecerunt, ex fundamentis sus eliciunt . . ." (*Tratado*, 191).

4 Isabel, Queen of Castile (1474–1504)

We cannot conclude this review of the history of Iberian Jews without mentioning Queen Isabella. There are several topics which have been systematically analyzed in studies of the period of the Catholic Monarchs. First, we should refer to the policy developed by the monarchs in matters pertaining to the so-called "unity of Spain", which they conceived of as a nation (Castro 1982 [1954], 197–198; Gil Pujol 2004, 39–93; Gifford 1934, 149–161; Ladero Quesada 1998, 95–129; Maravall 1954; Mitre Fernández 1982, 136–148; Sainz Rodríguez 1986, 171–210; Suárez Fernández 2000, 15–42; Suárez Fernández 1999, 123–161; Vallvé Bermejo 2002, 79–94). We must remember (as is well known) that "Spain" as a nation was at that time only a myth, a vague concept that had no historical basis.

Consequently, the concept of "unity" did not have any practicality, for Castile, Aragon, Valencia, Catalonia, and Mallorca continued to preserve their own jurisdictions. Moreover, when Granada and America were added to the possessions of the Catholic Monarchs, Castile had to respond to a new challenge: how to integrate them into the Kingdom.

The second essential topic pertaining to Isabella and Fernando's reign was the pacification of their territory. It started with Galicia, continued with the Castilian plateau and ended with complex Andalusia, where the rivalries between the Medina Sidonia and Ponce de León families had provoked a *de facto* civil war (Amran 2012, 17–36). The Santa Hermandad (Holy Brotherhood) (Ladero Quesada 2005), which existed prior to the Isabeline period, also played a crucial role and obtained large prerogatives in the composition of its squads as well as special jurisdiction over roads. By 1486, peace had been achieved. During the Catholic Monarchs' reign, much work was done on monetary reforms and charters, perpetual ownership rights, public debt, the military orders' pensions, etc.

On the other hand, the converso problem (Alcalá 2011) had become increasingly cumbersome since the end of the fourteenth century, and the monarchs attempted to control it by establishing the New Inquisition between 1478–1480 (Netanyahu 1999). Conversos became a social challenge for old Christians who competed with them and a real political enigma with regard to the support that they could offer the Catholic Monarchs (in fact, many converso families had supported Enrique IV against Isabella during the civil wars). As part of the royal programme of pacification of the kingdom, we can say that there was an interest in having them under control.

Regarding the fate of the remaining religious minorities, the expulsion of Jews from the kingdoms of Castile and Aragon in 1492, which had been preceded by the smaller (and often minimized) expulsion from Andalusia in 1483, should also be mentioned. Other relevant events include the royal policy regarding the Kingdom of Granada after the war (1482–1492) as well as the Muslim revolt of 1501 that resulted in the abolishment of the Capitulations of Granada of 1492 and the forced conversion of Muslims. Those who refused to convert were expelled from the kingdom on 12 February 1502. The expulsion of the *morisco* minority had thus began.

5 Conclusion

This chapter has offered an overview of the history of the Jewish and converso communities in the Iberian Peninsula, with particular emphasis on the Kingdom of Castile. We have attempted to explain the main points of conflict faced by these minorities. Nevertheless, we have also highlighted the moments in which Jews enjoyed a situation that was very different from Jewish historical experience in other European regions (France, England, the Holy Roman Empire).

As a result of their particular situation in the Iberian Peninsula, these Jews developed a different way of life and a different way of thinking. As the five peninsular kingdoms progressively took shape in a manner that resembled what was happening elsewhere in Europe, the situation of the Jewish minority in the Iberian Peninsula became more and more similar to that of its French, English, and German counterparts.

Bibliography

Works Cited

Sources

Crónica de los Reyes Católicos de Fernando del Pulgar. Ed. Cayetano Rosell, nº70, 1953, 432.
Crónica de los Reyes Católicos de Andrés Bernáldez. Ed. Cayetano Rosell, nº 70, 1953, 599–587.
Torquemada, Juan de. *Tractatus contra Medianitas e ismaelitas. Defensa de los judíos.* Ed. N. López Martínez and V. Proaño Gel. Burgos: Diócesis de Burgos, 1952.

Books and Articles

Alcalá, Angel. *Los judeoconversos en la cultura y sociedad españolas.* Madrid: Trotta, 2011.
Alonso Getino, Luis G. *Vida y obras de Fray Lope de Barrientos.* Salamanca: Anales Salmantinos, 1927.
Amrán, Rica. "La situación de los judíos en el reino de Castilla durante el periodo medieval." *Centenario del Código Civil Español* 3 (1989): 253–265
Amrán, Rica. "El sínodo de Zamora de 1313." *Instituto de Estudios Zamoranos Florián Ocampo*-CSIC 3 (1990): 411–415.
Amrán, Rica. "Las leyes de Valladolid de 1412." *Textures* 2 (1996): 181–192.
Amrán, Rica. *De judíos a judeo-conversos, reflexiones sobre el ser converso.* Paris: Université de Picardie-Indigo, 2001.
Amrán, Rica. "De Pedro Sarmiento a Martínez Siliceo: la génesis de los estatutos de limpieza de sangre." *Autour de l'Inqusition.* Ed. Rica Amrán. París: Université de Picardie-Indigo, 2002. 35–57.
Amrán, Rica. "La imagen de judíos y conversos en la *Historia de los hechos de Rodrigo Ponce de León*, primer marqués de Cádiz." *e-Humanista, Journal of Iberian Studies, Homenaje a Elena Romero* 20 (2012): 17–36.

Amrán, Rica. *Judíos y conversos en las crónicas de los Reyes de Castilla*. Madrid: Universidad Rey Juan Carlos-Dykinson, 2014.
Assis, Yom Tov. *Ensayos sobre cábala y misticismos judíos*. Buenos Aires: Marcial Pons, 2006.
Assis, Yom Tov. *The Golden age of Aragonese Jewry*. Oxford: Littman Library of Jewish Civilisation, 2008.
Baer, Isaac. "Ha-Yesodotve ha-atjalot shel irgun ha-kehilot ha-yehudiot ve-yemei ve-nai." *Zion* 15 (1950): 5–7.
Baer, Isaac. *Historia de los judíos en la España cristiana* (trad. de José Luis Lacave). Madrid: Altalena, 1981.
Beinart, Haim. "¿Cuándo llegaron los judíos a España?" *Estudios* 3 (1962): 1–32.
Beinart, Haim. "Hispano-jewish society." *Cahiers de Histoire Mondiale* 12 (1968–1969): 220–238.
Benito Ruano, Eloy. "D. Pedro Sarmiento, repostero mayor de don Juan II de Castilla." *Hispania* 27 (1957): 484–490.
Benito Ruano, Eloy. *Los orígenes del problema converso*. Madrid: Real Academia de la Historia, 2001.
Castro, Américo. *La realidad histórica de España*. México: Editorial Porrúa, 1982 [1954].
Cátedra, Pedro M. *Sermón, sociedad y literatura en la Edad Media. San Vicente Ferrer en Castilla (1411–1412)*. Salamanca: Junta de Castilla y León, 1994.
Cavallero, Constanza. *Los enemigos del fin del mundo. Judíos, herejes y demonios en el Fortalitium Fidei de Alonso de Espina (Castilla, siglo XV)*. Buenos Aires: Miño y Dávila, 2016.
Cohen, Jeremy. *Essential Papers on Judaism and Christianity in Conflict: From Late Antiquity to Reformation*. New York: New York Press University, 1991.
Gil Pujol, Xavier. "Un rey, una fe, muchas naciones. Patria y nación en la España de los siglos XVI-XVII." *La monarquía de las naciones. Patria, nación y naturaleza en la Monarquía de España*. Eds. Álvarez-Ossorio Alvariño, Antonio, and Bernardo José García García. Madrid, Fundación Carlos de Amberes, 2004. 39–93.
Gifford, David. "The development of a National Theme in Medieval Castilian Literature." *Hispanic Review* 3 (1935):149–161.
González Salinero, Raúl. *Las conversions forzosas de los judíos en el reino visigodo*. Roma: CSIC (Escuela Española de Historia y Arqueología en Roma), 2000.
Gonzalo Maeso, David. *El legado del judaísmo español*. Buenos Aires: Editora Nacional, 1972.
Jiménez Soler, Andrés. "Los judíos españoles a finales del siglo XIV y principios del siglo XV." *Universidad* 27 (1950): 361–414.
Ladero Quesada, Miguel Ángel. *La hermandad de Castilla. Cuentas y memoriales, 1480–1498*. Madrid: Real Academia de la Historia, 2005.
Ladero Quesada, Miguel Ángel. "Reinos y señoríos medievales (siglos XI a XIV)." *España. Reflexiones sobre el ser de España*. Madrid, Real Academia de la Historia, 1998. 95–129.
Leroy, Beatrice. *La Navarre au Moyen Age*. Paris: Albin Michel, 1984.
Maravall, José Antonio. *El concepto de España en la Edad Media*. Madrid: Instituto de Estudios Politécnicos, 1954.
Martín, José Luis. *La península en la Edad Media*. Barcelona: Teide, 1988.
Menéndez Pidal, Ramón. *El imperio hispánico y los cinco reinos*. Madrid: Instituto de Estudios políticos, 1950.
Meyerson, Mark D. "Samuel of Granada and the Dominican Inquisitor: Jewish Magic and Jewish Heresy in Post-1391 Valencia." *Friars and Jews in the Middle Ages and Reinassance*. Ed. Steven J. McMichael. Leiden, Brill, 2004. 161–189.
Millás Vallicrosa, José María. *Poesía hebraica postbíblica*. Barcelona: José Jané editor, 1953.
Millás Vallicrosa, José María. *Literatura hebraicoespañola*. Buenos Aires: Labor, 1973.
Mitre Fernández, Emilio. *Historiografía y mentalidades históricas en la Europa medieval*. Madrid: Universidad Complutense, 1982.

Monsalvo Antón, José María. *Teoría y evolución de un conflicto social: el antisemitismo en la corona de Castilla en la Baja Edad Media*. Madrid: Siglo XXI de España Editores, 1985.
Muñoz y Soliva, Trifón. *Noticias de los limos Sres obispos de Cuenca*. Cuenca: 1860.
Netanyahu, Benzion. *Los marranos españoles según las fuentes hebreas de la época (siglos XIV–XVI)*. Valladolid: Junta de Castilla y León, 1994.
Netanyahu, Benzion. *Los orígenes de la Inquisición española*. Barcelona: Crítica, 1999.
Nirenberg, David. "Mass Conversion and Genealogical Mentalities: Jews and Christians in Fifteenth-Century Spain". *Past and Present* 174 (2002): 3–41.
Sáenz Badillos, Ángel. *Literatura hebrea en la España medieval*. Madrid: Fundación Amigos de Sefarad-UNED, 1991.
Sainz Rodríguez, Pedro. *Visión de España*. Madrid: Fundación de Cánovas de Castilla, 1986.
Suárez Fernández, Luis. *Judíos españoles en la Edad Media*. Madrid: Ariel, 1980.
Suárez Fernández, Luis. *Nación, patria, estado. En una perspectiva histórica cristian*. Madrid: Unión Editorial, 1999.
Suárez Fernández, Luis. "Hispania: los fundamentos de la nación española." *España como nación*. Real Academia Española. Barcelona: Planeta, 2000. 15–43.
Valdeón Baruque, Julio. *Los judíos de Castilla y la revolución Trastámara*. Valladolid: CSIC, 1968.
Valdeón Baruque, Julio. *Los conflictos sociales en el reino de Castilla en los siglos XIV y XV*. Madrid: Siglo XXI editores, 1983.
Valdeón Baruque, Julio. *Pedro I el Cruel y Enrique de Trastámara*. Madrid: Santillana, 2002.
Vallvé Bermejo, Joaquín. "El tiempo de los moros." *Tópicos y realidades de la Edad Media*. Vol. 2. Ed. Eloy Benito Ruano. Madrid: Real Academia de la Historia, 2002. 79–104.
Vendrell, Francisco. "La actividad proselitista de San Vicente Ferrer durante el reinado de Fernando I de Aragón." *Sefarad* 13 (1953): 87–104.

Further Reading

Hernández Franco, Juan. *Sangre limpia sangre española. El debate de los estatutos de limpieza de sangre*. Madrid: Cátedra, 2011.
Kozodoy, Maud. *The Secret Faith of Maestre Honoratus. Profayt Duran and Jewish Identity in Late Medieval Iberia*. Philadelphia: University of Pensyvannia, 2015.
Menéndez Pelayo, Marcelino. *Historia de los heterodoxos españoles*. Madrid: Consejo Superior de Investigaciones Científicas, 1992.
Suárez Fernández, Luis. *Claves históricas para el reinado de Isabel y Fernando*. Madrid: Real Academia de la Historia, 1998.
Vallvé Bermejo, Joaquín. *Al-andalus, sociedad e instituciones*. Madrid: Real Academia de la Historia, 2000.

Yehoshua Granat
2 The Poetry of Sefarad: Secular and Liturgical Hebrew Verse in Medieval Iberia

Abstract: This chapter discusses the legacy of the Golden Age of Hebrew poetry that took place in medieval Iberia during the Andalusi period. It characterizes the unique qualities that differentiate this epoch from other periods in the history of Hebrew verse and examines the the emergence of a new brand of Hebrew secular verse in Jewish Andalusi courtly circles as well as transformative developments in the ancient tradition of Hebrew liturgical poetry (*Piyyut*) written by Jewish Andalusi poets of the time. The discussion is based on close readings of selected representative passages.

Key Terms: Hebrew poetry, Al-Andalus, Sefarad, Secular poetry, Piyyut (Hebrew liturgical verse), Scripture in poetry

1 Introduction

Hebrew verse has a vast and multifaceted history. Its earliest known examples are the most archaic poems that appear in the Hebrew Bible and are thought to have been written hundreds of years before the Common Era. In the post-biblical period Hebrew poetry continued to flourish and develop in a variety of schools and cultural centres around the Mediterranean Basin (and beyond), from late antiquity, throughout the Middle Ages, until modern times. Within this *longue durée* of literary creativity, the Hebrew poetry of medieval Iberia, and particularly that of *c*. 950–1150 Al-Andalus (Muslim Spain), highly influenced by Arabic poetry and poetics, is widely regarded as the superlative artistic achievement of an outstanding Golden Age. Samuel Ha-Nagid (993–1056), Solomon Ibn Gabirol (*c*.1022–1055), Moses Ibn Ezra (*c*.1022–1135) and Judah ha-Levi (*c*.1075–1141) are considered the four greatest luminaries of that celebrated age. The lives and oeuvres of these poets (alongside their contemporaries, predecessors and successors) have been the subject of ongoing scholarly work since the beginning of academic Jewish studies in the *Wissenschaft des Judentums* school of the nineteenth century. Rather than summarizing this massive and still evolving body of scholarship, the present essay seeks to sketch out, in broad lines, some focal con-

---

Acknowledgement: This research was supported by the ISRAEL SCIENCE FOUNDATION (grant No. 1907/20)

https://doi.org/10.1515/9783110563795-003

tours of this Golden Age of medieval Iberian Hebrew verse, bringing examples from selected passages of note.[1]

The first section of the essay concerns the conception of a distinctly Iberian school of Hebrew verse during the early Middle Ages, and of its creators as poets of "Sefarad." The second section focuses on the development of a novel kind of secular Hebrew poetry in Al-Andalus. Emerging within the socio-cultural context of Jewish courtly society in Spain, the hallmark of this corpus is a radically innovative and influential system of versification. The third and final section is dedicated to distinctively Iberian developments in the ancient tradition of Hebrew liturgical poetry (*Piyyut*).

2 "Song Dwells among the Men of Sefarad": Reception, Reputation, and Self-Regard

Abraham Ibn Ezra (1092–1167), the renowned medieval Jewish polymath – biblical exegete, poet, grammarian, mathematician, astrologer, and more – left his native Iberia around 1140 and began to wander around Italy, Provence, Northern France, and England. His journeys played a crucial role in "disseminating the poetics of the Spanish school in Western Europe" (Carmi 1981, 109).[2] It was probably at some point during this period that Ibn Ezra took part in an exchange of poems with Jacob Ben Meir Tam (widely known as Rabbenu Tam), a central authority on Talmudic literature and Jewish law (halakha), and the leading figure of twelfth century French Jewry (Reiner 2021). Rabbenu Tam had a keen interest in poetry. His poetic oeuvre is comprised of about 40 texts written in Hebrew and Aramaic, mainly *piyyutim* (liturgical poems) and didactic pieces, most of which are designed according to Andalusi verse forms. It is possible that it was in reaction to one of these pieces that Abraham Ibn Ezra wrote the following couplet (Meiseles 2012, 140):[3]

וּמִי הֵבִיא לְצָרְפָתִי בְּבֵית שִׁיר / וְעָבַר זָר מְקוֹם קֹדֶשׁ וְרָמַס
וְלוּ שִׁיר יַעֲקֹב יִמְתַּק כְּמוֹ מָן / אֲנִי שֶׁמֶשׁ וְחַם שִׁמְשִׁי וְנָמַס

Who allowed a Frenchman into the abode of song, / letting a stranger tread a holy place?
Be Jacob's song as sweet as manna, / I am the sun, whose heat makes manna melt!

This is a sharp-witted expression of a Hispano-centric view of (Hebrew) poetry ('song', שִׁיר), perceived as cultural capital in the exclusive domain of Iberian Jewry, of which

---

1 All Hebrew citations below are accompanied by English translations, based (with my revisions) on the translations mentioned in the references (in some cases, when no previous translation was known to me, the translation is my own and reference is made to the Hebrew text).
2 Cf. Schirmann 1997, 21–31.
3 Cf. Weinberger 1997, 6; Schirmann 1997, 29.

the wandering Ibn Ezra was considered to be a prominent representative (Freudenthal 2013, 35–65). That a foreigner (זָר), a non-Iberian (a Frenchman, in this case) would dare to compose Hebrew poetry (in the distinctly Andalusi fashion, presumably), is presented here as a presumptuous act of appropriation, doomed to failure. Moreover, this attempt is even regarded as an act of blasphemy, comparable to the forbidden entrance of a 'stranger' into 'a place of holiness [מְקוֹם קֹדֶשׁ]': a reference to the areas within the Jerusalem temple into which only priests and Levites were allowed. Ibn Ezra's metaphorical analogy between the composition of Hebrew verse à la Sefarad and the ancient, consecrated temple cult is certainly daring, yet not atypical. From its very beginnings, Hebrew Andalusi courtly verse did not shy away from employing even the most cherished elements of the sacred sphere as hyperboles, including in metapoetic contexts. A close precedent of Ibn Ezra's (mis)use of these holiest possible terms can be found in Ibn Gabirol's rebuke of a certain anonymous poet who tried to imitate one of his works. Invoking the biblical commandment not to go up the steps to the altar, lest one's "nakedness" be uncovered (Exod 20:26), the poet warns his anonymous imitator not to "go up the altar of song [בְּמִזְבַּח שִׁיר] by steps; / for as soon as you start your ascent – your most private parts are exposed" (Cole 2007, 85). This metapoetic employment of temple cult imagery is a remarkable reflection of the high regard in which the art of Hebrew verse was held in the Jewish culture of Al-Andalus, and Ibn Ezra's use of this trope in his epigram to Rabbenu Tam marks Hebrew verse as a particularly precious Hispanic territory, a core element of what Ross Brann describes as "Andalusi and Sefardi exceptionalism," or even "Andalusi and Sefardi singularity." "Andalusi Jews," writes Brann, were "[. . .] uniquely endowed with a flair for producing aesthetically marvelous and elegant Hebrew poetry" (Brann 2021, 8–9; 63). The epigram's second verse reveals that while "Jacob's [i.e., Rabbenu Tam's] song," may actually have sweetness to it, it is of only a rather superficial sort, because, when exposed to the sun, i.e., to Ibn Ezra himself, an authentic envoy of Sefarad, that superficially sweet song melts away, like the biblical manna (Exod 16:21).[4]

Rabbenu Tam reacted to the challenge of Ibn Ezra's epigram with a pronouncedly humble acceptance of the latter's superiority. In a short response poem, designed according to the same metrical scheme of the original epigram (with an additional rhyme at the first hemistich), the great French scholar declares that he is but "Abraham's slave" (Gen 24:34), bowing down in front of him.[5] To that gallant gesture Ibn Ezra responded with yet another epigram, designed according to the same metrical and rhyme scheme, but in a completely different vein from his earlier one:

---

[4] The poet's comparison of himself to the sun also occurs in Ibn Gabirol's verse; cf. Scheindlin 2016, 4–5.
[5] Meiseles 2012, 141: 'אֲנִי עֶבֶד לְאַבְרָהָם לְמִקְנָה / וְאֶקּוֹדָה וְאֶשְׁתַּחֲוֶה לְאַפָּיו' (Cf. Weinberger 1997, 6). However, there may arguably be a certain amount of ambiguity here; Elizabeth Hollender recently suggested that "Rabbenu Tam's deference to the mastery of Ibn Ezra is ironic, particularly given that he raised the technical stakes in his answer by adding a complicated rhyme scheme that Ibn Ezra then had to incorporate in his response" (Hollender 2020, 105, n. 39).

הֲנָכוֹן אֵל אַבִּיר עַם אֵל וְרוֹעָם / לְהַשְׁפִּיל רֹאשׁ בְּמִכְתָּב אֶל בְּזוּי עָם
וְחָלִילָה לְמַלְאַךְ הָאֱלֹהִים / אֲשֶׁר יִקּוֹד וְיִשְׁתַּחֲוֶה לְבִלְעָם

> Is it proper for a great shepherd of God's people / to abase himself in writing to one, despised of the people?

> Far be it for an angel of God, / to bend the knee and bow and prostate himself before Balaam!

"A celebrated leader of the God's people," as Rabbenu Tam is designated here, must certainly not abase himself by writing such a humble response to Ibn Ezra, who refers to himself as "despised of the people" (Ps 22:7). The meek self-appellation stands in sharp contrast to the poet's previous self-glorifying statement. At the same time, it does recall Ibn Ezra's well known acerbic poems of complaint on the discomforts of "vagabondage" (Freudentahl 2013, 59) that he suffered during his journeys. Ironically, it was in fact Ibn Ezra, rather than his celebrated correspondent, who was an actual 'stranger': an émigré from his native Al-Andalus, which had been brutally invaded by the Almohades not long after his departure. In hinting at these circumstances, the poet strikes an ironic note, in retrospect, with regard to the patronizing pride of his first epigram. This tone is further strengthened in the next verse, when Ibn Ezra refers to himself as Balaam; an image quite remote from the metaphor of the poet as a holy priest serving in the Temple of Song. Balaam, a gentile prophet (Num 22–24), is one of the most ambivalent figures in the Hebrew Bible and in post-biblical Jewish literature. Commanded by the Moabite king Balak to come and curse Israel, he ultimately, as a result of divine revelation, blesses them instead. Although the rabbis called him Evil Balaam, he was still regarded as no lesser a prophet than Moses. Indeed, one can detect here an implicit parody of a popular topos in secular Hebrew Andalusi poetry, in which the praiseworthy poet is compared to an illustrious biblical figure. Such a comparison was made by the young Judah Ha-Levi in a panegyric dedicated to the senior poet of his generation, Moses Ibn Ezra (Brener 1997, 13–14):

> Are not you most truly named after [Moses,] the faithful messenger? / For with both of you comes our freedom from bondage.
> Sweeten therefore our bitter cry, / and turn Marah and the sea into our most fragrant wine
> With song [בְּשִׁיר] that will suck honey from the rock / on the day that our tongues cleave unto our palates.
> From your West, make the dew of our clouds descend / like manna, and send quails for our spirit
> These, my rhymes, say: 'Let us go / and bow down before our king, our messiah'

It is noteworthy that ha-Levi's analogy between the biblical Moses, God's messenger and unparalleled prophet, and the Hebrew Andalusi poet Moses Ibn Ezra, is based purely on the latter's mastery of the art of verse: the sacred narrative of Israel's Exodus from Egypt and their miraculous sojourn in the desert becomes an allegory for the wonders that the magnificent poetry of the Andalusi master engenders in the minds of its readers.

Abraham Ibn Ezra's choice to compare himself to Balaam can be interpreted as an apologetic gesture towards Rabbenu Tam, which also betrays his sense of outsiderness, of being 'an Andalusi in France.' It can also be perceived as a telling reflection of his "post-classical" position during the "twilight of a Golden Age" (Weinberger 1997).[6] Despite the above, Ibn Ezra's sense of self regard as an Andalusi poet remained unshaken, as reflected in the self-appellation that ends his mnemonic poem on the rules of the Jewish calendar (probably composed in Italy): "By Abraham, the son of Meir: a Spaniard, master of poetry (סְפָרַדִּי אֲבִי שִׁירוֹת)" (Rosin 1891, 166). At any rate, the correspondence in verse between Ibn Ezra and Rabbenu Tam amply illustrates the impact of Andalusi poetry and its poetics on contemporaneous Jewish literati of Christian Europe, particularly in France (Hollender 2020). It is against that background that the advantage of 'authentic' Iberians over Franks in writing Hebrew poetry became somewhat of a literary topos, one that can also be found in the oeuvres of Judah Al-Ḥarizi (1165–1225) and Todros Abulafia (1247–after 1295).[7]

The *Book of Taḥkemoni* by Judah Al-Ḥarizi asserts a highly articulate Hispanocentric attitude to Hebrew poetry of his time, although it is mostly directed eastwards rather than northwards. Al-Ḥarizi, who travelled extensively throughout the Near East, "extols the Andalusi Hebrew literary tradition as the exclusive, transcendent paradigm for the production of elegant Jewish culture in Hebrew" (Brann 2021, 169). Through an elaborate discussion on the intrinsic Iberian inclination for poetry and the history of Hebrew verse in Al-Andalus, Al-Ḥarizi establishes the claim that "Song dwells among the men of Sefarad [וַיְהִי הַשִּׁיר בְּתוֹךְ אַנְשֵׁי סְפָרַד מַחֲנֶה]" (Yahalom and Katsumata 2010, 212; cf. Segal 2001, 177). His account of the history of Hebrew verse in the Iberian Peninsula heaps hyperbolic praise on the heads of the great Hebrew poets of Al-Andalus, especially Ibn Gabirol and ha-Levi, the latter of whom and his contemporaries he describes as divinely inspired prophet-poets: "age of the wondrous poets / known as the company of prophets [וְהוּא דוֹר הַמְשׁוֹרְרִים הַנִּפְלָאִים / הַקְּרוּאִים חֶבֶל נְבִיאִים]" (Yahalom and Katsumata 2010, 215; cf. Segal 2001, 179). In contrast, Al-Ḥarizi's own generation is humbly described as being minor epigones, unsuccessfully attempting to imitate their soaring predecessors. His harshest criticism, however, is reserved for the Hebrew poets he encountered in the East, who tried to follow the Andalusi masters in what he perceives to be an utterly incompetent manner. In particular, his fury is directed against a certain poet of Egyptian origin who resided in Damascus and unabashedly dared to compare his verse to that of Ibn Gabirol: "if only the late master could return to life and duly punish that arrogant imposteur!" (Yahalom and Katsumata 2010, 227; cf. Segal 2001, 185). Thus, as the above makes clear, the Golden Age of Andalusi Hebrew verse had a profound impact on the various centres of medieval Hebrew verse.

---

6 Cf. Schirmann 1997, 39–40.
7 Cf. Yahalom and Katsumata 2010, 219; Yellin 1932–1936, 2: 72–73.

3 "Enter the Garden of My Poems": An Emergent Universe of Hebrew Secular Verse

What makes a typical Hebrew poem of the Andalusi Golden Age distinct from earlier Hebrew verse, is its metrical and formal design. In particular, it was Dunash ben Labrat's invention of a new system of Hebrew versification that, in a sense, was the catalyst that ignited this seminal period of Hebrew poetry. "The adaptation of Arabic quantitate meters, based on distinctions between the lengths of vowels, endowed Hebrew for the first time with a precise (if not entirely organic) criteria for measuring the pace and weave of the line, which in turn intensified the focus on the language itself and on its lyric properties" (Cole 2007, 10).[8] The highly successful reception of this versification system facilitated the adoption of core elements from Classical Arabic poetry, far beyond the prosodical level, in terms of verse forms (the monorhymed polythematic *qaṣīda* and monothematic *qiṭ'a* as well as the strophic *muwashaḥ*), genres, themes, rhetorical devices, and so forth (Schippers 1994; Tobi 2004). A new type of Hebrew poetry thus began to evolve as a result of the direct and multi-dimensional influence of the Arabic model. This is especially remarkable given that the Jewish poets cultivated a pure form of biblical Hebrew as their poetic language of choice (here too they were inspired by an Arab ideal, this time the *faṣaḥa*, meaning eloquent poetic idiom).

Dunash's own perception of his prosodic innovation is expressed in a notable passage from his poem "Know, my heart, wisdom" (דעה לבי חכמה) (Decter 2018, 177; Mirsky 1992, 148):

וְהוֹדָה הַיּוֹצֵר / לְבָבוֹת, הַנּוֹצֵר / נְפָשׁוֹת, הַבּוֹצֵר / לְרוּחוֹת כַּבִּירִים
בְּשִׁירִים נִשְׁקָלִים, / חֲדָשִׁים, נִסְגָּלִים, / בְּמִבְטָא נִגְבָּלִים, / זְקוּקִים, נֶחְקָרִים –
וְשִׂים שִׁיר לִתְהִלָּה / לְהַשַּׂר רֹאשׁ כַּלָּה / אֲשֶׁר כָּלִיל כִּלָּה / גְּדוּדֵי הַזָּרִים
פְּאֵר וְהוֹד חָבַשׁ / וְיֶשַׁע אֵל לָבַשׁ [. . .]

> Thank the Creator of hearts, the Protector of souls, who reins in mighty winds,
> With metered, new, distinguished poems, measured in expression, refined, well-conceived,
> And set a song of praise for the prince, the *rosh kallah*, who utterly ruined foreign troops.
> He put on wonder and glory and wore God's victory [. . .]

Addressing himself, Dunash is here declaring what he sees his mission as a poet to be. Firstly, he is obliged to thank God and praise him – the traditional task of creators of liturgical poetry (*Piyyut*) for centuries. But his means to achieve that traditional end are decidedly modern. A sequence of no less than six consecutive adjectives accentuates Dunash's dedication to composing *metered* poems, accurately crafted in a novel

---

8 Alongside the more famous quantitive metre, designed as homological to the quantitive metre of Arabic poetry, there was another type of purely syllabic metre that was used mainly in liturgical poetry (*Piyyut*). It has been suggested that this alternative prosody was influenced by popular oral chants in the Romance vernacular (Fleischer 2010, 1: 103–112).

manner. He then focuses on a different end, distinct from the former, namely his commitment to "set a song of praise [or: glory] for the prince [לְהַשָּׂר / וְשִׂים שִׁיר לִתְהִלָּה]." The phrase used here is biblical in origin, and relates to the worship of God: "[...] song of praise and thanksgiving unto God [וְשִׁיר תְּהִלָּה וְהֹדוֹת לֵאלֹהִים]" (Neh. 12:46). As it is used in Dunash's poem, the object of poetic praise has shifted from the divine to the human sphere. This shift epitomizes the essence of the panegyric, the poetic genre that most directly reflects the socio-cultural setting of courtly Hebrew poetry. "Know, my heart, wisdom" is indeed an early example of a Hebrew Andalusi panegyric, dedicated to Dunash's patron, the famous Cordoban courtier, Ḥasdai (or: Ḥisdai) Ibn Shaprut: a leading figure at the court of the Caliph 'Abd al-Rahman III and head of Andalusi Jewry (Beinart 1992, 15–16). The main part of this full length *qaṣīda* highlights Ḥasdai's illustrious achievements in some detail. Lauded as a leader and protector of the Andalusi Jewish community, Hasdai's fame has reached across the Jewish world, as indicated by the title *Rosh Kallah*, conferred upon him by the Babylonian Geonic authorities in Iraq (Brann 2021, 211, n. 72). Moreover, Dunash stresses Ḥasdai's position as an eminent political figure of international renown, well beyond the confines of the Jewish community: "Every king trembles, and descends from his throne, and dispatches tributes to him in Sefarad [מְשִׁיבִים אֶשְׁכָּרִים / וְאֵלָיו לִסְפָרַד] / [...] Across East and West his renown is grand and great, Christendom and Islamdom seek his unstinting counsel [בְּחַסְדּוֹ נִדְבָּרִים / וּבֵית עֵשָׂו וְעֲרָב]" (Brann 2021, 61–62). Subsequently, alongside customary praises of Ḥasdai's benevolence towards the poor and the students of Torah, Dunash notes his support "for the composers of poems [לְעוֹרְכֵי הַשִּׁירִים]": a direct reflection of the courtly setting in which this very poem was composed. In retrospect, Dunash's brief mention of God's glorification in the poem's moralistic introduction may well be regarded as a rather apologetic statement of a continued commitment to the traditional role of poet-cantor (*paytan*), alongside his prestigious role as court poet.

Not all of the Hebrew Andalusi poets were necessarily court poets. Samuel Ha-Nagid, for example, was a political and military leader active in the kingdom of Granada who had a court of his own; and there is no evidence that either Moses Ibn Ezra or Judah Ha-Levi ever served as poets in a particular court (though they did dedicate lengthy panegyrics to various contemporary courtiers and dignitaries). Nevertheless, the courtly setting was a formative one in the emergence of the new type of secular Hebrew poetry in Al-Andalus. The status of poets in courtly circles was remarkably high, despite their utter dependency on the support of courtiers. Due to his command of the highly valued art of verse, the poet was an eminent, sought-after figure, rather than a mere courtly servant. This conception of the poet is epitomized in a famous short poem by Ibn Gabirol, which opens with the following resounding statetment (Scheindlin 2016, 6–7):

אֲנִי הַשָּׂר – וְהַשִּׁיר לִי לְעָבֶד

I am the prince, and the poem is my slave

It is the poet who leads the court musicians, like the concert master's violin, or rather oud (אֲנִי כִנּוֹר לְכָל שָׁרִים וְנוֹגְנִים). Moreover, it is he who, through his poems, creates "crowns for the kings and turbans for the heads of courtiers (לַמְּלָכִים / וּמִגְבָּעוֹת בְּרָאשֵׁי הַסְּגָנִים וְשִׁירֵי כַּעֲטָרָה" The profound confidence of a poet in the sovereign power of his own poems, hardly imaginable in a traditional rabbinic society, stems from the secularity of this new type of Hebrew verse, as manifested in the following line, attributed to Dunash (Cole 2007, 24):

וְגַן עֶדְנָךְ יְהוּ סִפְרֵי קְדוֹשִׁים / וּפַרְדֵּסָךְ יְהוּ סִפְרֵי עֲרָבִים

Let the sacred books be your Eden, / and the books of the Arabs your orchard

"The sacred books" (or: books of the holy) meaning scripture as well as probably also rabbinic canonical literature, are likened to the Garden of Eden (where, according to rabbinic doctrine, the pious will receive their just reward for their good deeds, including the study of holy writings). However, in the second hemistich of this programmatic verse another realm is defined: separate from the sacred one, yet perfectly legitimate. The "books of the Arabs" are likened to an orchard: a secular site dedicated to the joys of universal learning and aesthetic pleasure. Significantly, the orchard and Edenic garden imagery echo the typical setting in which courtly verse was usually publically performed, namely the *majlis*. This convivial gathering in a secluded palace garden was dedicated to wine drinking as well as to poetry, music, and dance, and was "the primary forum for the pursuit of sensuous pleasures in the Islamic world throughout the medieval period" (Brookshow 2003, 199). Andalusi courtly verse, in Arabic as well as in Hebrew, abounds with descriptions of these enchanted spaces. In the introductory poem in Moses Ibn Ezra's *dīwān* (a collection of a poet's works), the garden is transformed into a metapoetic metaphor. The poet addresses any person who is "sick at heart and cries out in bitterness [כָּל אִישׁ דְּוֵה לֵבָב וּמַר צֹרֵחַ]" and offers them consolation in the sweet scent of the garden of his poems (Goldstein 1971, 105):

בֹּאָה לְגַן שִׁירַי וְתִמְצָא לָךְ צֳרִי / עָצְבָּךְ וְשָׁם תָּגִיל כְּרֹן פֹּצֵחַ

Enter the garden of my poems, and find balm / for your sorrow, there you will rejoice and sing

It should be noted that whereas the biblical Psalmist finds his consolation and joy in God's Torah and commandments (Ps 119:47, 50), here it is the poet's own creations that ease the troubled soul.

The artistic freedom of Hebrew Andalusi courtly verse is impressively revealed in its secularized use of sacred imagery. This phenomenon already occurs in the work of the very first known Hebrew poet from medieval Iberia: Menaḥem ben Saruq, a pioneering Hebrew lexicographer, who was Dunash's predecessor as poet at Hasdai's court. Menaḥem's panegyrics are composed in a rather traditional manner, with no quantitate meter à la Dunash. Nonetheless, an unmistakable, full-fledged courtly mentality is on display in the hyperbolic praises of their addressees, which include secularized images drawn from descriptions of the Tabernacle in the Wilderness. In one such instance, the poet compares Ḥasdai to "the engraved plate / on Aaron's forehead [אֲשֶׁר / כְּצִיץ הַמִּפְתָּח / עַל מֵצַח אַהֲרֹן]" (Schirmann 1959, 1: 9). This is a reference to a passage in Exodus that describes how Aaron the High Priest wore a gold plate on his forehead on which was engraved the tetragrammaton, the letters of God's name (Exod 28:36). The very association of this supremely sacred object with a flesh and blood political leader, as distinguished as he may be, is striking. In another panegyric by Menaḥem, two dignitaries who arrived at Ḥasdai's court were likened to the high priest's ephod and breast place (Exod 28:4), as well as to the two cherubim that guarded the Ark of the Covenant (Exod 25:13) (Fleischer 2010, 1: 206). Such imagery was employed by Golden Age poets in a variety of thematic contexts. For example, Ibn Gabirol compared the skirts of a beautiful female court singer (*qayna*) – a figure well known in Muslim Andalusi courts (Reynolds 2017) as well as in Hebrew Andalusi courtly poetry (Granat 2013) – which were hung with bells and golden pomegranates, to the "robes of priests [אֲשֶׁר יָדְמוּ מְעִילֵי אַהֲרֹנִים]" (Scheindlin 2016, 158–159), following Exod 28:34. The image of the cherubim, mentioned above, also occurs quite often in poems of praise and friendship composed by Judah Ha-Levi (Berner 2005, 107; Granat 2018, 678–679), who was also bold enough to state, in a short epigram, that the well-groomed sideburns of a certain young man were so exquisite that they deserved to be engraved on the ephod of the high priest (Granat 2020, 545). One of the more remarakable examples of the use of these themes in a secular framework is the conclusion of a hedonistic *muwashaḥ* composed by Moses Ibn Ezra (Scheindlin 1986, 90–91; Carmi 1981, 325). The poem, phrased entirely in the imperative, calls on the reader to make the most of life's sensual pleasures. Addressed to an unnamed gentleman, the poem beckons him to take part in the joys of wine, music, and dance in the court garden, which is adorned with soothing water canals and the chirping of birds (וּשְׁתֵה עֲלֵי יֶבֶל נֵבֶל עָסִיס / יַיִן, לְקוֹל נֵבֶל עִם תּוֹר וְסִיס) – a compact scene of convivial *majlis*. Yet, it is in fact sexual enjoyment that is the subject of the text, as is clear from the introductory couplet: "Caress the lovely woman's breasts by night / and kiss the beauty's lips by morning light! (דַּדֵּי יְפַת תֹּאַר לְלֵיל חֲבֹק / וּשְׂפַת יְפַת מַרְאֶה יוֹמָם נָשֹׁק)." The final stanza elaborates on this by directing the addressee to take his "rightful portion [חָקְךָ]"of the world's delights. Just as the priests, "the heads of the righteous people ('רָאשֵׁי עַם צִדְקְךָ')," were entitled to partake in consuming the breast and leg of the Ram of Consecration (Exod 26:27–28), so is he, although in a rather different sense:

> אַל תֵּחֱשֶׁה לִמְצֹץ שָׂפָה וְרֹק
> עַד תֶּאֱחֹז חָקְךָ – חָזֶה וְשׁוֹק

> To suck the juice of lips do not be shy
> Until you take what's rightly yours: the breast and thigh!

As pointed out by Raymond Scheindlin: "[w]hat is shocking about these lines in not so much the explicit reference to sexuality as the almost midrashic association of sexual pleasure with the Ram of Consecration [...] Moses Ibn Ezra [...] has transformed the biblical account of the consecration of priests into a secular phantasy of induction into a radically different elite [...] the courtier class, the privileged devotees of beauty, of which Ibn Ezra was a most articulate member" (Scheindlin 1986, 95).

Such secularized transformations of sacred images should essentially be regarded as manifestations of a far-reaching artistic liberty. In their "vibrant, living poetry, what we call secular" (Menocal 2002, 109), the poets of the Hebrew Andalusi Golden Age felt remarkably free to explore the broad spectrum of the human condition (cf. Fleischer 2010, 3: 1491–1541) and chose not to shy away from religiously taboo areas, such as the sensuous and erotic.[9] In a similar way, though on an opposite note, they also gave uninhibited expression to the inconsolable pain of losing one's loved ones, as in Samuel Ha-Nagid's poignant cycle of laments over the death his brother Isaac. Indeed, extending beyond the boundaries of conventional genres, Hebrew verse provided these authors with a means to express their life experiences from the most personal and intimate of perspectives, as reflected in masterpieces such as the war poems of Samuel Ha-Nagid, Ibn Gabirol's poems of sickness and loneliness, the poems of exile by Moses Ibn Ezra or Ha-Levi's poems of his famous journey to the Land of Israel as an elderly man. Hebrew verse as art for its own sake enjoyed unparalleled prestige in the circles of poets and connoisseurs of poetry that thrived during the Andalusi Golden Age. It is no wonder, then, that Moses Ibn Ezra, the great classicist master of that era, was also the author of the first full-fledged treatise on the literary theory of Hebrew verse (Halkin 1975).

4 "My Heart Beheld You": Transformations in Piyyut

Piyyut, Hebrew liturgical poetry, evolved in the Near East during Late Antiquity. Beginning as an offshoot of that earlier literary tradition, the medieval Iberian school of *Piyyut* also transformed it, to a large extent, turning it into an integral element of Jewish Andalusi civilization, with close affinities to contemporaneous secular poetry and religious thought.

The prosody of early *Piyyut* was structured according to a free rhythm with a regular number of major stresses in each line, and, from around the sixth century onwards, on strophic rhymes, alternating from one stanza to the other. Though not abandoning these archaic patterns altogether, the Andalusi school of *Piyyut* gradually showed a preference for a more "modern" prosody of monorhymed poems in quantitate metre or *muwashaḥ*-like strophic poems (where some of the rhymes alternate but the end rhymes of each stanza recur throughout the whole piece), in quantitate metre or syllabic metre. Beyond these prosodic and formal features, perhaps the most signif-

---

[9] Though not without moments of ambivalence and retrospective compunction (Brann 1991); on the complexity of Ha-Levi's later poetic oeuvre in that regard, cf. Granat 2020.

icant shift was that the Hebrew poets of Sefarad regarded liturgical poetry not merely as "versified prayers," but, first and foremost, as literary works of art, no less expressive and exquisitely crafted than their secular poems, as is clear from the various metapoetic statements that appear in their *piyyutim* (Granat 2021, 258–268). Despite the essential distinction, in terms of performance settings and socio-cultural contexts, between the poetry of the synagogue and courtly secular verse, the influence of the latter on the former rises to the fore in certain thematic contexts. Most pertinent in that regard are allegorical, often quasi-dramatized, accounts of God's love for the people of Israel, in which the latter are depicted as a feminine figure. In numerous instances, the imagery in Andalusi *Piyyut* bears a striking resemblance to the sensuous language of erotic secular verse. In a poem by Ibn Gabirol, for example, the allegorical feminine figure of Israel beseeches God, "reclined upon golden couches in my palace [שׁוֹכֵב עֲלֵי מִטּוֹת זָהָב בְּאַרְמוֹנִי] [. . .] a handsome stag [צְבִי נֶחְמָד]," to turn to her, "the graceful gazelle [לְיַעֲלַת חֵן]." In return, she promises Him delectable delights from her precious stores: "the juice of my pomegranates, and my cinnamon, and my myrrh [עָסִיס וְרִמּוֹנִי, מוֹרִי וְקִנְּמוֹנִי]" (Carmi 1981, 314; Scheindlin 1991, 100–101).

In terms of subject matter, whereas early *Piyyut* relied extensively on rabbinic sources, Andalusi *Piyyut* became increasingly indebted to Greco-Arabic science, philosophy, and theology, typically through the mediation of contemporaneous strains of Jewish philosophy that aimed to achieve a synthesis between 'universal' conceptions – shared, to a large extent, by Muslim, Christian, and Jewish thinkers alike – and particular elements of Judaism. Of much importance in that field was *Al-Hidāya ilā farā'iḍ al-qulūb* (The Book of Direction to the Duties of the Heart) by the eleventh-century pietist (and *paytan*) Baḥya ibn Paqūda of Saragossa. As manifested in the very title of that influential treatise, itself profoundly influenced by Islamic Sufism, the emphasis is on individual consciousness, as emblemized by one's heart, and particularly on a sensitivity and awareness to God's presence in the universe, as well as within one's own spirit. Baḥya's book has been described as "the well from which the Spanish [i.e. Hebrew Andalusi] poets drew the ideas on which their philosophical and ethical poems were based" (Mirsky 1992, 171). The focus on the individual and the internalization of religious experience are indeed key features of Andalusi *Piyyut*. They are particularly conspicuous in the genre of introductory *piyyutim* (*reshuyot*) that were recited at the beginning of the morning service (Scheindlin 1991, 144–148). Several such pieces are so deeply personal that they are read as purely intimate soliloquies of the poet, expressing his search for the presence of God.

In one of his *reshuyot*, Ibn Gabirol specifies three 'witnesses' who keep the memory of God constantly present in front of him: the earth and the sky, which show God's greatness in creation and "the musings of my mind, when I look inside [הֶגְיֵג לִבִּי – בְּהַבִּיטִי בְּקִרְבִּי]" (Scheindlin 1991, 188–189). Immersed in a meditative state of introspection, the poet senses the divine presence within his own self, and the poem ends with a call to his own soul to constantly bless the Lord, thus implicitly giving a cue to each member of the congregation to join the communal service. At times, Ibn Gabirol casts serious epistemological doubts on the ability of any human being to approach God, since his body is made out of mere dust (וְאֵיךְ אוּכַל וּבֶעָפָר יְסוֹדִי), and only his heart and tongue are within his reach (מְאוּמָה אֵין לְבַד לִבִּי וְסוֹדִי / וְזוּלָתִי שְׂפָתַי אֵין בְּיָדִי). Nevertheless, so intense is the poet's passion for singing God's praises, that it overpowers this poignant self-doubt (cf. Zangwil 1923, 75).

The divine origin of the human soul is a recurrent theme in this devotional poetry, sometimes expressed by a direct address to the soul, as in the following words of a *tokheḥa* (devotional poem of self-admonition) by Baḥya ibn Paquda (Mansoor 2004, 448):

נַפְשִׁי מִתְּנוּמָתֵךְ עוּרִי / וְלִפְנֵי יוֹצְרֵךְ שִׁיר דַּבֵּרִי [. . .] / כִּי מִמְּקוֹר בִּינָה קֹרַצְתְּ / וּמִמַּעְיַן חָכְמָה לֻקַּחַתְּ / וּמִמְּקוֹם / מֵאֵת יְיָ מִן הַשָּׁמַיִם קָדוֹשׁ הוּבֵאת / וּמֵעִיר גִּבּוֹרִים הוּצֵאת

> My soul, rise from your slumber, / utter a song before you Creator [. . .] For you were formed from the font of knowledge, / taken from wisdom's well / brought from a holy place / and led forth from a heroes' city / from the Lord who is in heaven

Based on this concept, God himself is sometimes described as actually present inside the human psyche itself: "among my thoughts," as Isaac Ibn Ghiath (1038–1089) puts it, while claiming that the human soul is attached to God's heavenly throne, even though it is situated in the lowly earthly body (Scheindlin 1991, 194–195):

חֲקַרְתִּיךָ וְהִנֵּה בֵּין זְמָמַי / בְּעֵין לֵב אֶמְצָאָה אוֹתְךָ וְאֶרְאֶה
קְשׁוּרַת כִּסְאֲךָ נֶפֶשׁ נְפַחְתָּהּ / וְאִם שָׁכְנָה בְגוּף נִדְכֶּה וְנִכְאֶה

> I sought You out and found you among my thoughts, / in my heart's eye I find You and behold You
> The soul You breathed is attached to Your throne, / though residing in a battered, aching clod

The wonder of God's containment within the human mind is sharply accentuated by Ibn Gabirol as he juxtaposes it to God's ascendance over the whole world (Cole 2007, 97):

מְרוֹמוֹת לֹא יְכִילוּךָ לְשִׁבְתָּךְ – / וְאוּלָם יֵשׁ מְקוֹמְךָ תּוֹךְ סְעִפִּי

> The high heavens can't contain you / and yet you have a place within my thoughts

Ibn Gabirol's *Keter Malkhut* ('A Crown of Kingship'), widely considered "the greatest Hebrew religious poem of the Middle Ages, and indeed one of the major works of Hebrew literature since the completion of the Old Testament" (Lewis 2003, 1), is a large scale *baqqasha* (poetic personal prayer of supplication), in rhymed prose, that "combines sublime praise for God with philosophical contemplation and penitential themes" (Tannenbaum 2002, 58). In canto 29 of this monumental composition, the human soul is depicted, in elaborate detail, as a fiery substance, emanating from God's glory. Fashioned "from the flames of the fire of [divine] Intelligence [מִלַּהֲבוֹת אֵשׁ הַשֵּׂכֶל חֲצוּבָה]," God sends it to the body, as its guardian, "and it is a fire within it, and yet it does not consume it [וְהִיא כָּאֵשׁ בְּתוֹכוֹ וְלֹא תִשְׂרְפֵהוּ]" – much like the burning bush revealed to Moses (Exod 3:2). As throughout the whole composition, the canto ends with a re-contextualized biblical verse (Lewis 2003, 86–87).

> From the fire of the Soul the body was created and brought from nothingness to being
> 'Because the Lord descended upon it in fire' (Exod 19:18)
>
> כִּי מֵאֵשׁ הַנְּשָׁמָה נִבְרָא הַגּוּף וְיָצָא מֵאַיִן לַיֵּשׁ
> מִפְּנֵי אֲשֶׁר יָרַד עָלָיו יְיָ בָּאֵשׁ

The original context of this image is taken from Exodus 19:18, in which God reveals himself to the People of Israel at Mount Sinai, gives them the Torah and inaugurates Israel's covenant with God. The dramatic words describing this most defining moment of Israel's sacred history, are here transformed into an account of the making of an individual human being through the association of the fire of the divinely emanated soul with the material body. Indeed, ha-Levi, in one of his *reshuyot*, depicts a personal Sinai-like vision of God, revealed to the awakening poet (Scheindlin 1991, 164–165).

> My heart beheld You and was sure of You / As if it, itself, stood at Mt. Sinai
> I sought you in my visions, Your glory passed / through me, descending on my clouds
>
> וְלִבִּי רָאֲךָ וַיַּאֲמֵן בָּךְ / כְּאִלּוּ מָעֳמָד הָיָה בְּסִינַי
> דְּרַשְׁתִּיךָ בְּחֶזְיוֹנַי וְעָבַר / כְּבוֹדְךָ בִּי וְיָרַד בַּעֲנָנַי

Remarkably, this Sinai-like epiphany is envisioned as occurring within the self, between God and the human soul: "Halevi equates the individual's inward vision of God with the collective experience of revelation *par excellence*" (Tannenbaum 2002, 191).

These and similar poetic expressions of radically internalized religious experience are among the most original and profound literary achievements of Andalusi Piyyut. The spiritually introverted tone of these devotional lyrics is very different from the thriving, sometimes libertine, *joie de vivre* of much of the secular poetry of the time. But despite that striking difference, there is a common ground of vigorous poetic creativity, through which even the most sacred words of scripture were transformed by the poet into a means of expressing himself in well-crafted verse.

The *Sitz im Leben* of Jewish Andalusi courtly culture lasted for only a few generations, but the legacy of the Golden Age of Andalusi Hebrew verse that it created had a significant and long lasting impact on Jewish culture in the Iberian Peninsula and beyond. While most of the secular poetry written during this period fell into oblivion over the centuries, until it was re-discovered and published by modern scholars, liturgical Hebrew poetry by the great poets of Sefarad continued (and still continues) to be recited, sung, and appreciated in the synagogues of the Sephardi diaspora, as well as in those of other Jewish communities who have embraced it. Though necessarily far from covering the full range of such a complex and genuinely inspiring literary heritage, it is hoped that the bird's-eye view presented here has shed some light on a number of the most distinctive and defining dimensions of this wondrous age of Hebrew poetry in medieval Iberia.

Bibliography

Works Cited

Beinart, Haim. "The Jews in Castile." *Moreshet Sepharad, the Sephardi Legacy*. Ed. Haim Beinart. Jerusalem: The Magnes Press, The Hebrew University of Jerusalem, 1992. 1: 11–43.

Brann, Ross. *The compunctious poet: cultural ambiguity and Hebrew poetry in Muslim Spain*. Baltimore; London: Johns Hopkins University Press, 1991.

Brann, Ross. *Iberian Moorings: Al-Andalus, Sefarad, and the Tropes of Exceptionalism*. Philadelphia: University of Pennsylvania Press, 2021.

Brener, Ann. *Judah Halevi and his circle of Hebrew poets in Granada*. Leiden/Boston: Brill/Styx, 2005.

Brookshaw, Dominic P. "Palaces, Pavilions and Pleasure-gardens: the context and setting of the medieval majlis." *Middle Eastern Literatures* 6.2 (2003): 199–223.

Carmi, T. *The Penguin book of Hebrew verse*. London: Penguin, 1981.

Cole, Peter. *The Dream of the Poem: Hebrew Poetry from Muslim and Christian Spain 950–1492*. Princeton, N.J.: Princeton University Press, 2007.

Decter, Jonathan P. *Dominion Built of Praise: Panegyric and Legitimacy Among Jews in the Medieval Mediterranean*. Philadelphia: University of Pennsylvania Press, 2018.

Fleischer, Ezra. *Hebrew Poetry in Spain and Communities under Its Influence*. Jerusalem: Institute for Study of Jewish Communities in the East: Yad Yitshak Ben-Tsevi, 2010. 3 Vols. [Hebrew].

Freudenthal, Gad. "Abraham Ibn Ezra and Judah Ibn Tibbon as Cultural Intermediaries." *Exchange and Transmission across Cultural Boundaries*. Eds. Haggai Ben-Shammai, Shaul Shaked and Sarah Stroumsa. Jerusalem: Israel Academy of Sciences and Humanities, 2013. 52–81.

Goldstein, David. *The Jewish poets of Spain: 900–1250*. Harmondsworth: Penguin, 1971.

Granat, Yehoshua. "'Unto the voice of the girl's songs'": on singing women in the Hebrew poetry of medieval Spain." *Textures: Culture, Literature, Folklore, for Galit Hasan-Rokem*. Eds. Avigdoor Shin'an and Hagar Salmon. *Jerusalem Studies in Jewish Folklore* 28 (2013): 153–168.

Granat, Yehoshua. "To Alexandria, with the sound of bell and pomegranate: Yehuda Halevi's arrival at Alexandria in light of a newly identified poem by Aaron Ibn Al-ʿAmmānī." *Tarbiẕ* 85.4 (2018): 657–681 [Hebrew].

Granat, Yehoshua. "The mixed blessings of the western wind: Ambiguous longings in Halevi's Alexandrian poems of welcome and farewell." *Israel in Egypt: The land of Egypt as concept and reality for the Jews in Antiquity and the early medieval period*. Eds. Alison Salvesen et al. Leiden/Boston: Brill, 2020. 531–565.

Granat, Yehoshua. *Psalms recalled: Scriptural Psalms in the liturgical poetry of Yoseph Ibn Abitur*. Jerusalem: The Ben-Zvi Institute for the study of Jewish communities in the East, 2021 [Hebrew].

Halkin, Abraham S. *Kitab al-Muḥāḍara wal-Mudhākara* by Mosheh ben Yaʿaḳov Ibn ʿEzra. Jerusalem: Meḳitse Nirdamim, 1975.

Hollender, Elisabeth. "Sefarad in Tzarfat: Sefardi and Sefardi-Style Piyyutim in MS Bernkastel-Kues 313." *'His Pen and Ink are a Powerful Mirror': Andalusi, Judaeo-Arabic, and Other Near Eastern Studies in Honor of Ross Brann*. Eds. Adam Bursi et al. Leiden/Boston: Brill, 2020. 94–117.

Lewis, Bernard, tr. *The kingly crown (Keter malkhut)* by Solomon ibn Gabirol. Notre Dame, Ind.: University of Notre Dame Press, 2003.

Mansoor, Menahem, ed. *The book of direction to the duties of the heart* by Baḥya ben Joseph ibn Paḳuda. Oxford/Portland, OR: The Littman Library of Jewish Civilization, 2004.

Meiseles, Isaa, ed. *Shirat Rabbeinu Tam: the poems of Rabbi Jacob ben Rabbi Meir*. Jerusalem: Yitsḥak Maizlish, 2012 [Hebrew].

Menocal, Maria Rosa. *The ornament of the world: how Muslims, Jews, and Christians created a culture of tolerance in medieval Spain*. Boston/London: Little, Brown and Company 2002.

Mirsky, Aharon. "Hebrew Literary Creation." *Moreshet Sepharad, the Sephardi Legacy*. Ed. Haim Beinart. Jerusalem: The Magnes Press, The Hebrew University, 1992. 1: 147–187.

Reiner, Avraham (Rami). *Rabbenu Tam: interpretation, Halakhah, controversy*. Ramat Gan: Bar-Ilan University Press, 2021 [Hebrew].

Reynolds, Dwight F. "The Qiyan of al-Andalus." *Concubines and Courtesans: Women and Slavery in Islamic History*. Eds. Matthew S. Gordon and Kathryn A. Hain. New York: Oxford University Press, 2017. 100–123.

Rosin, David. *Reime und Gedichte des Abraham Ibn Esra*. Breslau: S. Schottlaender, 1891.

Scheindlin, Raymond. *Wine, women, & death: medieval Hebrew poems on the good life*. Philadelphia: Jewish Publication Society, 1986.

Scheindlin, Raymond. *The Gazelle: medieval Hebrew poems on God, Israel, and the soul*. Philadelphia: Jewish Publication Society, 1991.

Scheindlin, Raymond. *Vulture in a cage, poems by Solomon Ibn Gabirol*. Brooklyn, NY: Archipelago Books, 2016.

Schippers, Arie. *Spanish Hebrew poetry and the Arabic literary tradition: Arabic themes in Hebrew Andalusian poetry*. Leiden: Brill, 1994.

Schirmann, Jefim. *Hebrew Poetry in Spain and Provence*. Jerusalem: Bialik Institute, 1959. 4 Vols. [Hebrew].

Schirmann, Jefim. *The History of Hebrew poetry in Christian Spain and Southern France*. Edited, supplemented and annotated by Ezra Fleischer. Jerusalem: The Magnes Press, The Hebrew University and Ben-Zvi Institute. 1997 [Hebrew].

Segal, David Simha, ed., tr. *The book of Taḥkemoni: Jewish tales from medieval Spain* by Judah Al-Ḥarizi. London/Portland, OR: The Littman Library of Jewish Civilization, 2001.

Tanenbaum, Adena. *The contemplative soul: Hebrew poetry and philosophical theory in medieval Spain*. Leiden: Brill, 2002.

Tobi, Joseph. *Proximity and distance: medieval Hebrew and Arabic poetry*. Tr. Murray Rosovsky. Leiden: Brill, 2004.

Weinberger, Leon J. *Twilight of a golden age: selected poems of Abraham Ibn Ezra*. Tuscaloosa/London: University of Alabama Press, 1997.

Yahalom, Joseph, and Naoya Katsumata, eds. *Taḥkemoni, or Tales of Heman the Ezraḥite* by Judah Alharizi. Jerusalem: Ben-Zvi Institute, 2010 [Hebrew].

Yellin, David, ed. *Gan ha-meshalim yeha-ḥidot* by Todros Abulafia. Jerusalem, 1932–1936. 3 Vols.

Zangwill, Israel. *Selected religious poems of Solomon Ibn Gabirol*. Philadelphia: Jewish Publication Society of America, 1923.

Further Reading

Jayyusi, Salma Khadra, and Manuela Marín, eds. *The legacy of Muslim Spain*. Leiden: Brill, 1992.

Sáenz-Badillos, Ángel. *A history of the Hebrew language*. Tr. J. F Elwolde. Cambridge: Cambridge University Press, 1993.

Sáenz-Badillos, Ángel, and Judit Targarona Borrás. *Diccionario de autores judíos: (Sefarad, siglos X–XV)*. Córdoba: El Almendro, 1988.

Schirmann, Jefim. *The History of Hebrew poetry in Muslim Spain*. Edited, supplemented and annotated by Ezra Fleischer. Jerusalem: The Magnes Press, The Hebrew University and Ben-Zvi Institute, 1995 [Hebrew].
Rosen, Tova, and Eli Yassif. "The study of Hebrew literature of the Middle Ages: major trends and goals." *The Oxford Handbook of Jewish Studies*. Ed. Martin Goodman. Oxford: Oxford University Press, 2002. 241–294.

Georg Bossong
3 The *kharadjāt*

Abstract: The *kharadjāt* (Arabic plural of *khardja*) are the final verses in Mozarabic, an early Ibero-Romance language, which are found at the end of Arabic and Hebrew strophic poems, the so-called "girdle poems" (*muwaššaḥāt*). These verses are the earliest known poems in Ibero-Romance. Historically they extend from the middle of the eleventh century up to the reign of Alfonso X of Castile in the second half of the thirteenth century.

These poems shed a new light on the multicultural world of al-Andalus. They offer a precious testimony of this world where the three monotheistic religions mingled in a complex whole of mutual influences. The Jewish element played a crucial role in this process. The *kharadjāt* first came to light in Hebrew strophic poetry.

Judah ha-Levi is especially noteworthy in this context. He was not only the great classic of post-biblical Hebrew poetry, he was also the most fertile author of Romance *kharadjāt* and can rightly be considered as the "first Spanish poet known by name". His poems convey specifically Jewish meanings of messianic hopes, expressed in the form of apparently naive love poems. Their jewishness manifests itself in their constant reference to the intertext of the Hebrew Bible.

Key Terms: al-Andalus, Arabic and Hebrew poetry, Ibero-Romance language, Judah ha-Levi

1 The *kharadjāt* in the Context of Arabic Poetry

The golden age of postbiblical Hebrew literature unfolded in Spain, or more precisely in al-Andalus, the geographical and historical domain where the three monotheistic religions came together and influenced each other. Spain is the home of the great classical figures of postbiblical Hebrew poetry. The revival of Hebrew as a literary language spread from Spain.

It would have been unthinkable without the fertile cultural environment of Islamic Spain. The ancient language of the Bible, which had disappeared from everyday communication for ages, woke up to a new life. The language shook off the dust of centuries and rejuvenated again. It opened itself to the world and stepped out of the restricted domain of religion where it had been confined for so long. In Spain, it became possible to compose poetry on secular subjects, to sing on love and friendship, on the delights of wine and the beauty of nature. This great change did not come about all by itself. It resulted from external influences. The decisive factor was Arabic. In Islamic Spain, Arabic was evidently the dominating language, not only politically but also culturally. For Arabs and the peoples who had adopted the Arabic language, poetry was considered the pinnacle of culture. Among all arts poetry enjoyed the highest esteem. This veneration for Arabic poetry spread throughout the Muslim world, and so it also reached al-Andalus, the recently conquered Islamic domain on the Iberian Peninsula. Córdoba and other cities of al-Andalus became important centres for the cultivation of Arabic poetry, capable to rival Bagdad and the Orient.

The roots of Arabic poetry reach deeply into prehistoric times. Its origins are to be found in pre-Islamic Arabia with its tribal traditions. The classical models of this poetry, such as the famous seven *muʻallaqāt*, stem from bedouin times and had the Arabian desert as their setting. In later times, urban societies developed and the setting of poetry changed. It was in this later, urbanised form that Arabic poetry was practised in al-Andalus.

The complex history of Arabic poetry in the Muslim world and in the Iberian Peninsula cannot be traced here not even in its broad outline. Suffice it to say that Arabic poetry was an omnipresent and much admired model in Muslim Spain, for all religious communities, i.e. not only for Muslims, but also for Christians and Jews. Classical Arabic poetry was based on two structural principles: quantity, and monorhyme. The fundamental rhythm resulted from regular sequences of long and short syllables, as in Sanskrit, Persian, Greek, and Latin. And the all-pervading form of the *qaṣīda* has monorhyme as its most conspicuous structural feature. Monorhyme means two things: end-rhyme, and absence of any strophic structure. The same rhyme goes from the beginning of the poem to its end. A *qaṣīda* can contain more than a hundred verses, all bound together by one and the same rhyme. This is made possible by the linguistic structures of Arabic, an important point which cannot, however, be discussed here in detail. The principle of the monorhyme has far-reaching consequences for the internal structure of the poem as a whole, not only with respect to form, but also with respect to content. Due to the lack of strophic articulation, the structure of the whole poem is looser than in stanzaic poetry, it is less tightly bound together. It is possible to break out individual verses or passages of a few verses from a classical Arabic poem without problems; a *qaṣīda* is not necessarily composed as a unit. From the perspective of European sensibilities, a *qaṣīda* is to be understood as a structure consisting of individual parts that can be picked out and enjoyed in their own right and that are relatively autonomous in themselves. Such a poem is like a string of pearls that can be seen as a whole, but if you pick out the pearls, each fragment, indeed each individual pearl, still has its own value and beauty. Accordingly, the anthologies that fill entire libraries in Arabic literature are characterised by the fact that individual verses, considered as beautiful, have been extracted from longer poems that fit a certain theme. There are anthologies with a chapter about the beauty of nature in spring, about the scent of blossoms and about the stream flowing through a garden, and individual verses or short fragments are picked out for these individual themes, which are then strung together without taking the original context into account. This fits in with the overall loose, not tightly structured way of composing the whole poem.

In this context, the poets of al-Andalus introduced a revolutionary innovation: the *muwaššaḥa*, which may be translated as the "girdle poem". The *muwaššaḥa* is opposed to the *qaṣīda* in every respect, it is a kind of "anti-program" in structure and content. A *muwaššaḥa* is a tight composition from beginning to end; it is not possible to remove individual components without destroying the whole structure. The stanzaic form leads to a firmer joining, to a more coherent manner of composition, which gives the girdle poetry its peculiar character. The *muwaššaḥa* is indeed a revolutionary innovation in the framework of Arabic poetry, even though some of its components originated in Arabic poetry outside Spain, in the Orient. The essential points on the formal level are the strophic structure, and the refrain; the monorhyme schema gives way to more complex and variegated rhyme structures, where rhymes change from strophe to strophe, with identical returning rhymes ("refrains") at the end of each stanza. It is precisely through the overarching bond of the refrain that the individual verse becomes more integrated into a larger whole. The whole poem has a tightly composed form, it is directed towards a goal, it terminates in a punch line at the end; one cannot simply break out individual parts of it. This punch line, which might be a single or several lines, at the end of the poem, is the famous *khardja*, which will be discussed more in detail in the following pages. The term *muwaššaḥa* is a derivation from the noun *wišāḥ* "girdle" or "sash". A *wišāḥ* is a piece of decoration, a sash embroidered with pearls or gems. Literally the word *muwaššaḥa* means "girdled" or "belted", i.e. bound together by the returning rhyme at the end of every stanza. Linguistically the word is a passive participles of the 2nd stem, which here functions as a causative; its exact meaning is "provided with a girdle". In Hebrew the term has been translated by a simple attributive connection: *šir 'ezor* "girdle poem", which corresponds exactly to the German term "Gürtelgedicht". A poet who specializes in the composition of *muwaššaḥāt* is called *waššāḥ*, plural *waššāḥūn*, a form dedicated to professions, like *khabbāz* "baker" from *khubz* "bread". While most Arabic poets of al-Andalus wrote mainly traditional *qaṣīdāt*, an important minority of them were professional *waššāḥūn*. Let us now have closer look at the *khardja*.

A *khardja* is the final verse, or group of verses, of a *muwaššaḥa*, with a final repetition of the refrain at the end of the strophic composition. The word *khardja* is derived from the root √*kh-r-dj* which simply means "go out". Thus, originally it means nothing else but "exit", a word of everyday usage. In the various European languages, the term is transcribed in different forms, in English most often as <kharja>. In Spanish, the form <jarcha> has largely prevailed; in scholarly literature, one also finds <jarŷa>, with the attempt to somehow render the voiced sound /dj/ in today's Spanish orthography. The Spanish Arabist Corriente writes <xarja>. Whatever the transcription, phonetically these forms always represent the same word; written in the International Phonetic Alphabet it is [xardʒa]. The plural of the word in Arabic has the regular form *kharadjāt*. In his more recent publications, Corriente consistently uses this Arabic plural; his argument is that the plural of such an Arabism should not be formed according to the rules of the borrowing language, but of the donor language, just as in French the plural of the German musical term *le lied* is not *les lieds*, but *les lieder*. This argument is undoubtedly justified. Nevertheless, the majority of authors who have written on this subject prefer a European plural of the type <kharjas/ jarchas>. I find Corriente's argument convincing and will use the Arabic plural forms in the present publication

We can resume: the *khardja* contains the final repetition of the refrain. It takes on the rhyme which had been repeated all over the *muwaššaḥa*. But the *khardja* still has another outstanding feature: in the majority of cases, its language is different from the rest of the poem. Most of the times it is written not in classical standard Arabic, but in the spoken dialect (which is normally not used in written form). This bilingual usage is an immediate consequence of the diglossic situation reigning all over the Arabic world, since the beginnings up to the present day. For formal purposes the classical language is used, which is based on the language of the Qur'ān and of pre-Islamic poetry and which has remained unchanged ever since. This classical language differs substantially from the spoken vernaculars, which have evolved into numerous different varieties and which prevail in everyday oral communication. In al-Andalus, the local andalusí dialect was used in the majority of the *kharadjāt*. Arabic diglossia manifests itself in *muwaššaḥ* poetry by the fact that the *khardja* is mostly written in a form of vulgar Arabic, in contrast to the main body of the text. Often we also find a mixture of classical and colloquial forms; sometimes it is not easy to determine whether a text is intended to be classical or vulgar Arabic, there are intermediate forms, cases of doubt, and of deliberate ambiguities.

The *khardja* is embedded in a poetic genre, the *muwaššaḥa*, which differs from the classical Arabic *qaṣīda* by its stanzaic form and the resulting influences on its structure. In general the *khardja* is set off from this frame by its language, be it colloquial Arabic, be it a completely different language. In the context of al-Andalus, this completely different language was the Romance vernacular. In the multilingual, multicultural and multireligious society of Islamic Spain, varieties of Romance and Semitic languages mingled in a complex manner. On the base of the communicative pyramid we find a fundamental bilingualism with Romance and Arabic vernaculars side by side. Between colloquial and formal Arabic a situation of diglossia can be observed, i.e. a functional separation of a "high variety" and a "low variety". In the Romance domain, the place of the high variety was occupied initially by Latin. It took centuries for Latin to be replaced by the later written standard forms of Romance which evolved from the low varieties, in particular Old Spanish, Old Portuguese, and Old Catalan.

2 The Importance of the *kharadjāt* for Philological Research

The Romance and the Arabic vernaculars were common to all religious communities. There are many testimonies which show that Muslims – and even a Muslim king, namely al-Muʿtamid of Seville – had some knowledge of the Romance vernacular. And Arabic in all its varieties was widespread not only among Muslims but also among Christians and Jews. The only languages which were clearly confined to their respective religious spheres were Latin for the Christians and Hebrew for the Jews. At the top of the communicative pyramid the linguistic frontiers were sharply traced, whereas at its bottom the dominating picture is multilingualism and language mixture, irrespective of the religious borderlines. This situation is reflected in the *kharadjāt*, which thus offer a unique insight into the real life of communication and language mixing in al-Andalus. In this context, the term *khardja* takes still another, hidden sense. These final verses in a different language "go out/go beyond" the canons of the classical language, they imply a conscious transgression of the traditional rules of grammar and style. The *khardja* transcends the classical framework into which it is embedded. It recurs to popular, even vulgar forms of expression, which constitute a strong contrast to the classical language of the rest of the *muwaššaḥa*.

What role does the Romance element play in all this? All in all approximately 600 *muwaššaḥāt* have been preserved. Most of them have *kharadjāt* in colloquial Arabic. About one tenth of them, a bit more than sixty overall, contain *kharadjāt* written in an early Romance dialect, Mozarabic, the Vulgar Romance spoken at that time in the south and east of the Iberian Peninsula. This Romance dialect bundle appears here for the first time on the surface of the written tradition. One thing is particularly noteworthy: the writing of poetry in a form of Hispanic Romance, and thus writing poetry in a southern Romance language in general, starts in this context, in the context of the Arabic and Hebrew strophic poetry of al-Andalus. The oldest poems composed in a form of Spanish are found in this literature, in stanzaic poems of the *muwaššaḥa* type in Arabic or Hebrew. And they are transmitted in Hebrew and Arabic script. Below, we will come back to this topic.

According to certain traditions, the invention of this poetic form is attributed to a certain Muqaddam Qabrī, a blind poet from the small town of Cabra in central Andalusia, about 80 km south of Córdoba. He is said to have lived in the first half of the tenth century, that is, in the time of the highest deployment of Muslim dominance, when under ʿAbd al-Raḥmān III the Emirate was proclaimed a caliphate, and Hispanic Islam was on the peak of its political power and cultural splendour. In fact, we know nothing precise about this Muqaddam, we do not even know with certainty whether he existed at all, or whether this figure is a projection, a mere legend. However, one detail is thought-provoking, namely the geographical location of this town. Cabra is situated only 10 km from Lucena, and it is a well-known and well-attested fact that

Lucena was a dominantly Jewish town in that period. There was an important Jewish college, and in later times the names of important scholars and poets from Lucena have survived. It remains to be seen whether this is a mere coincidence, but it is at least conceivable that in the whole process of the emergence of *muwaššaḥa* poetry from its very outset the Jewish-Hebrew element played an important role, indeed that it crucially contributed to the birth of this form. What is really important is the mixture of the three elements that interpenetrate and mutually fertilise each other, namely the Arabic, the Romance and, from the very beginning, the Hebrew element. It is no coincidence that the birthplace of the *muwaššaḥa* lies precisely in this zone strongly marked by Jewish presence. It is also noteworthy that the oldest datable poems of this type were not written in Arabic but in Hebrew.

The blossoming time of poetry in this strophic form begins a bit later, around the middle of the eleventh century. In the first half of the eleventh century the textual tradition begins, and from the second half of this century on these poems appear in significant number. The actual heyday of this style of poetry is situated between the time of the *Reinos de los Taifas* and the time of the Almoravids up to the Almohads, essentially between 1050 and 1150. There was, however, a later after-bloom which extends to the reign of Alfonso X of Castile, in the second half of the thirteenth century. It has been a matter of dispute whether or not the *kharadjāt* are of popular origin: do they reflect an oral tradition of individual verses and short songs which flew from mouth to mouth, or are they the product of a conscious effort of a class of authors with literary education? Are these poems ultimately of anonymous, illiterate origin, or were they born in circles of sophisticate *literati* who handled language with virtuosity? The complex play of quotations and intertextual allusions which can be observed in some *kharadjāt* and their *muwaššaḥāt* point to an artistic, learned origin of these texts. On the other hand, many *kharadjāt* show a popular character, they sound as if they had been taken from an oral, anonymous culture, which must have flourished in the environment of these circle of poets. Frequently anonymous popular songs were copied and integrated into the formal and artificial context of the *muwaššaḥāt*, and it is precisely from this contrast that many compositions draw their enchantment. In my opinion, there are *kharadjāt* of both popular and of learned origin side by side. Every transmitted text must be analysed and interpreted individually, in order to reach convincing conclusions.

We now come to the discovery of the *kharadjāt* and its historical implications. The discovery of the *kharadjāt* was a scientific revolution, an event of enormous significance in different domains. First of all, this is valid for historical comparative linguistics. This discovery opened a window on a hitherto unknown Romance language, namely Mozarabic. The corpus of the *kharadjāt* proved to be the most extensive documentation of this extinct Romance language, which has its own characteristics and its own rules. It belongs clearly to the Ibero-Romance family, but it cannot be simply classified as a variety of Spanish, let alone of Portuguese, Catalan, or any other of the varieties present on the Iberian Peninsula. It shows remarkable archaic features in phonetics (such as *nohte*, an intermediate form on the way from Latin *nocte* to Spanish *noche*) and morphology (such as the conservation of final 3d person *-d* in the conjugation of verbs), as well as special developments in the lexicon, not just because of Arabic loans (which are of course numerous), but because of genuine Romance particularities. As an example we may quote the standard word for the concept "to speak", which is *hablar/falar* in Spanish/Portuguese, *parlar* in Catalan/French/Italian, but in Mozarabic it is *garrire*, from a classical Latin verb meaning "to gossip". Without any doubt Mozarabic had a distinctive physiognomy of its own, which assigns it an unmistakable place in Romance. It comes as no surprise that it has been classified as a Romance language of its own right in the standard reference work *Lexikon der romanistischen Linguistik*, alongside the other Ibero-Romance varieties. Before the discovery of the *kharadjāt* this was a completely hidden domain in historical comparative linguistics.

Apart from this, the discovery of the kharadjāt was important for the historical study of language contacts in a multilingual setting. Al-Andalus, the place where the three monotheistic religions lived together, was also a place of highly variegated contacts between languages. It is unique in the history of Europe insofar as here Romance and Semitic languages were in close interaction for centuries. Multilingualism and language mixing took a special shape on the soil of the Iberian Peninsula. There are traces of language-mixing and code-switching also in other literary works, especially in the poetry of Ibn Quzmān from Córdoba, written in the spoken Arabic dialect of his time, but the testimony of the *kharadjāt* is more variegated and far more extended. Here we can observe code-switching and contact phenomena between Romance and Arabic varieties in great number, and of different types. These poems are extremely precious documents of language contact phenomena, which must have been a general feature in daily life.

Societal multilingualism leads to language mixing. As was already stated, loans from Arabic are numerous. In the *kharadjāt* their proportion is variable, it ranges from nearly zero to almost 100%, which means that there are *kharadjāt* almost purely in Romance and also kharadjāt almost entirely in Arabic. This picture resembles what can be found in languages of the Islamic world which have undergone profound influence from Arabic and which also show a great array of Arabic loans. In languages like Persian, Turkish and Urdu the proportion of Arabic loans also can oscillate between almost zero to almost 100%. The testimony of the *kharadjāt* shows what Spanish could have become if the influence of Arabic would have lasted permanently, if the Reconquista had failed. Spanish would probably look more or less like the aforementioned Islamic languages today.

Apart from these consequences in the field of linguistics, the most conspicuous impact which the discovery of the *kharadjāt* had on any domain, was the study of medieval literature. The specialists of medieval poetry in various European countries discovered, to their utmost astonishment, that there existed a popular lyrical tradition which had simply passed unnoticed. This astonishment can be aptly resumed in the famous exclamation by Dámaso Alonso *¡Un siglo más para la poesía española!* "one more century for Spanish poetry". The possibility of oriental influences on European poetry, which had been a rather theoretical question, all of a sudden became very real, in the light of these little poems with their imageries and poetic language so similar to what was known from the *troubadours, trouvères* and *Minnesänger*. The debates on these questions, which touched metrics, contents, and the social relationship between men and women, were intense and heated. Of particular relevance was the problem whether the *kharadjāt*, with their popular, even folkloristic air, represented a popular poetry which up to then had remained unnoticed because it was oral. Were the *kharadjāt*, once they had come to light in written form after their discovery in Arabic and Hebrew texts, the reflexion of a pre-existing oral tradition, or were they the creation of the poets? It is impossible here to resume these extended and passionate discussions. Let us repeat here simply that a part of these poems reflects an oral tradition, while others are clearly the product of individual artistic creation.

3 The Chronology of Research on the *kharadjāt*

The following brief historical outline of the chronology of the discovery of the *kharadjāt* will be substantiating the claim that this discovery opened new horizons in many domains. I propose to call the history of the study of the Romance *kharadjāt* "khardjatology", a neologism that can be easily used in current Western European languages. This history can be divided into five phases, five periods, which are quite clearly separated from each other: prehistory, discovery, consolidation, challenge, new horizons. Let us start with prehistory.

It was in Hebrew, not in Arabic stanzaic poems, where the presence of Romance end verses was established for the first time – without, however, endeavouring to interpret them in detail. The *muwashshaḥāt* of Judah ha-Levi, who must be regarded as the most important *khardja* poet of all, was initially the sole focus of interest. The work of Judah ha-Levi was discovered in the 1830s, in the context of the emerging "Science of Judaism" (*Wissenschaft des Judentums*) in Central Europe and in Italy. One Jewish scholar who has distinguished himself in this context was the famous Rabbi Samuel David Luzzatto (1800–1886), by whom the first modern edition of songs of Judah ha-Levi was published in 1840, later followed by others. These editions of Luzzato contained mainly religious poems, liturgical pieces and songs of Zion, which have always been highly appreciated by the Jewish communities and have also become an important symbol of Judaism, an expression of the hope of returning to the Promised Land. We might say with some justification but also with all due caution, that Judah ha-Levi was in a certain sense a forerunner of Zionism. Especially in the second half of the nineteenth century, when the Zionist idea gradually began to spread in European Jewry, his Zion poems fell on fertile ground. They were discovered, edited and translated into European languages, especially into German, and in this way Judah ha-Levi was constantly present in the consciousness of the Jews. All the great figures of the "Science of Judaism" took part in this endeavour, such as Michael Sachs, Moritz Steinschneider, Abraham Geiger and others. Then in the twentieth century the great Jewish theologian, philosopher and Bible translator Franz Rosenzweig (1886–1929) presented his famous translation and interpretation of "92 hymns and poems of Jehuda Halevi" (1926). Of course, none of these authors was interested in the Romance end verses which appeared in some of his secular poems, but at least they were known to exist.

The first one to draw attention to the fact that there are indeed Romance verses to be found here which cannot be interpreted as Hebrew was Marcelino Menéndez Pelayo, the famous Spanish polygraph, in his inaugural speech to the Historical Academy in Madrid in 1898. He was an important forerunner, the first to realise that Judah ha-Levi was the first Spanish poet known by name, the first to reflect on the Romance character of these poems, and the first to try to decipher them.

The critical and up to now the most complete edition of the works of Judah ha-Levi was begun at the turn of the century. The editor was Haim Brody, who spent decades editing and commenting the poet's divan, both sacred and secular poems. This monumental edition was published in fascicles between 1894 and 1930 in Berlin. Brody was a first-rate Hebraist, but he did not actually make a serious effort to interpret the *kharadjāt*. He only made scattered remarks in his comments of the type "this is Romance, this is Spanish", without wanting or being able to propose a translation of his own; this was not his intention, and he would not have been able to do so. But in any case, since his publication of the divan of Judah ha-Levi it was established in the general philological discussion that a certain number of these *kharadjāt* were of Romance origin. Their existence was mentioned by the historian Yitzhak Baer in the 1930s in Germany and by the Hebraist José María Millás Vallicrosa in the 1940s in Spain. However, no one has really made a serious effort to scrutinize them. The fact that, in addition to the poems in Hebrew, there were also Romance poems transmitted in Arabic compositions, was completely unknown.

This situation changed in 1948, which can be called the actual beginning of the exploration of *kharadjāt*. At that time, Samuel Miklos Stern, a Jewish orientalist of Hungarian origin who was formed at the Hebrew University of Jerusalem and was teaching in Oxford, published an essay on Romance *kharadjāt* in Hebrew stanzaic poems in the journal *Al-Andalus*. Here again, the starting point were the Hebrew, not the Arabic songs, whose role was still unknown. This date (1948) marks the beginning of the first period of serious research. Stern was a first-rate philologist, both in the field of Oriental (Hebrew and Arabic) studies, as well as in the field of Spanish, and he was the first to attempt a large-scale interpretation of the *kharadjāt*, transmitted in Hebrew poems. Although not all of them had come to his attention, he was aware of the majority of the poems. He read and studied them in the manuscripts, and he presented a critical edition, which, however, does not meet today's standards. For the first time he also suggested serious interpretations within the framework of Romance. At this historical moment, his publication literally hit like a bomb, it was a bang that aroused extended scholarly discussions throughout Europe, starting in Spain, but then also in other European countries where philologists were interested in medieval poetry, especially in Italy and Germany. *Khardjatology* in the true sense of the word began in 1948, with the first relevant publication by Samuel Stern.

This phase can be called the "phase of discoveries". After the first examples of Judah ha-Levi, new texts were brought to light in rapid succession, first in Hebrew and then very soon also in Arabic poems, whose mere existence had been completely unknown until then. After Stern's ground-breaking publications new discoveries followed in rapid succession. Soon the Arabic filiation of this poetry was detected, and theoretical treatises by Arabic poetologists came to light, especially the poetological treatise *Dār al-ṭirāz*, literally "weaving site, textile factory", written by the Egyptian Ibn Sanā al-Mulk (1155–1211). The first and most important European researcher who has distinguished himself in this field was Emilio García Gómez (1905–1995), the head of the school of Spanish Arabists and leading representative of Spanish Arabic studies for more than a generation. García Gómez was the first to study *kharadjāt* transmitted in Arabic strophic poems. He published the first texts in the journal edited by him, *Al-Andalus*, in 1952. The publications of Stern and of García Gómez are based on the primary texts, they tried to arrive at critical editions, reconstructions and translations based on the original manuscripts. Their proposals formed the basis of extended and sometimes heated discussions, often led by authors who had no direct relationship with these texts, people who had no direct access to the original manuscripts and were often unable to classify them correctly due to a lack of knowledge of the Semitic languages and their writing systems. A fierce discussion broke out over the question of whether the *kharadjāt* represent a popular Hispanic poetry, an orally transmitted poetry, or whether they are artistic creations that can be explained as developments from oriental traditions.

These debates have been conducted with acrimony, deep trenches have opened up.

Among the representatives of the Hispanic thesis we find García Gómez himself, but also Ramón Menéndez Pidal (1869–1969), as well as, for example, Aurelio Roncaglia (1917–2001) in Italy or Theodor Frings (1886–1968) in Germany. The orientalists outside Spain held completely different views; they emphasised the oriental roots of these poems. Gustave Grunebaum (1909–1972), Wilhelm Hoenerbach (1911–1991) or Évariste Lévi-Provençal (1894–1956) belonged to this camp, among others. The 1950s were dominated by this great debate: is it folk poetry or art poetry? Moreover, there was an intense debate on another question: what does all this have to do with the poetry of the *troubadours*, with Occitan poetry in Southern France, which formed the first heyday of European poetry and about whose oriental origins there had always been much speculation. Ultimately, the German *Minnesang* was also supposed to derive from it. All these questions were intensively discussed in the 50s.

In the first phase we have on the one hand the discussion of these general historical connexions, on the other hand more and more new texts came to light. When the relevant manuscript collections were combed through carefully, new Romance poems were discovered and interpreted, sometimes quite uninhibitedly and with a lot of imagination. The danger was that the difficulties of the texts were passed over relatively quickly, and that the first interpretations were generally accepted. They soon became popular and rapidly found their way even into the general anthologies of Spanish poetry. Many authors have contributed to these interpretations, even persons who never had looked into the original manuscripts and whose knowledge of Semitic languages and writing systems was at best superficial. This phase of discoveries was followed by a phase of certainties, or better, pseudo-certainties, a phase of consolidation. The intensive research activity of the 1950s gave way to stocktaking. Various publications tried to compile all that had been published on the *kharadjāt* up to that point, and several attempts were made at a synthesis. Three authors in particular must be considered here: Heger, García Gómez, and Sola-Solé.

The first to be mentioned is Klaus Heger in Heidelberg (1927–1993), who at that time was still a *Romanist* and had not yet landed in the realm of general linguistics. In 1960, he published a supplement to the *Zeitschrift für Romanische Philologie* which contains a comprehensive survey of the entire research up to his time. The title of this volume in German *Die bisher veröffentlichten Kharjas und ihre Deutungen* reflects aptly its content; it is still an indispensable reference work, because the extensive discussion of the 1950s is clearly resumed and systematically summarised in this volume. Since some of these earlier publications had been published in obscure places and are difficult to access, Heger's publication has remained useful up to this day. In general, he abstains from giving his own interpretation and simply presents an account of the various attempts that had been presented until then.

A few years later, Emilio García Gómez presented a complete edition of the *kharadjāt* transmitted in Arabic poems, an edition which for the first time contains not only the Romance final verses, but also the complete texts of the related *muwaššaḥāt*. This work was first published in Madrid in 1965 under the title *Las khardjas de la serie árabe en su marco*. García Gómez brings the texts in Latin transcription; they are accompanied by translations into Spanish in the style of the author, namely in Spanish verses in exact rhythmic reproduction. This edition, too, is still indispensable today, even though it was heavily attacked in the following period for its often debatable interpretations. It should be used with caution.

The third summarizing work is by José María Sola-Solé (1924–2003), who has presented the first really complete collection of all the Arabic and Hebrew surviving *kharadjāt* including the corresponding *muwaššaḥāt*. The work was published in 1973 in Barcelona under the title *Corpus de poesía mozárabe*. However, he does not provide the texts of the *muwaššaḥāt* in the original, but only in a literal translation into Spanish prose. Moreover, he also presented independent new interpretations for most of the *kharadjāt*, some of which are very interesting and worthy of attention, while others are questionable. The presentation of all *muwaššaḥāt* in a Western language is without doubt a pioneering and highly deserving achievement, but today one must read it with a critical distance. These texts are difficult and complex, and in many cases the translations which Sola-Solé has provided are inadequate from today's point of view, sometimes simply wrong. With regard to the interpretation of *kharadjāt*, it must be noted that the author wants to give the impression that he has personally inspected all the original manuscripts. However, it is easy to show that he has not done so, but has copied essentially from Stern and García Gómez – including errors and oversights! But as a summary, as a truly comprehensive compilation, this book is still of great value.

The third phase, which can be defined by "new questions and new challenges", begins with a time lag of about fifteen years. After the aforementioned publications of the second phase it had become quiet around the *kharadjāt* research for a while. Most people thought that everything was clear, everything had been compiled and investigated. But then English scholarship stirred up the debate again. Two names have to be mentioned: Richard Hitchcock (Exeter) and Alan Jones (Oxford). From Hitchcock came some critical essays and also a useful bibliography, but not an independent edition; he helped to revive the debate. Alan Jones, a distinguished Arabist, is credited with several ground-breaking editions that have become fundamental. This third phase is marked by a fundamental critique of everything that had been published up to that point, the earlier certainties are radically questioned. Alan Jones went back to the Arabic manuscripts and produced a meticulous palaeographic edition where the original texts are photographically reproduced. This work was published in Oxford in 1988 under the title *Romance Kharjas in Andalusian Arabic muwashshaḥ poetry. A palaeographical analysis*. It shows the original texts in photographic reproductions which provide us with a clear picture of how difficult the edition is, how uncertain many of the interpretations previously considered safe are in the end, and how manifold the problems are that still need to be resolved. Alan Jones fundamentally questions most of the interpretations presented by the Spaniards, with García Gómez in the forefront, but also Sola-Solé. The situation can be described in the following pointed and somewhat polemical way: García Gómez has built a beautiful house, but in the Light of Jones' edition perhaps it is only a castle in the air. Or expressed with another metaphor, perhaps it is partly built on sand and has no solid foundation, while Alan Jones' edition is more reminiscent of a heap of rubble, of debris from a construction site. It is certainly all well and good to question everything, but often the author did not even dare to formulate anything positive at all, and some of the texts he published consist almost entirely of question marks. How ever one may judge this, the work of Alan Jones represents a necessary step, as a new phase in the long process of discovery, exploration and interpretation of the *kharadjāt*. In later editions he also critically edited the two main Arabic manuscripts where Romance *kharadjāt* are preserved. He insisted, in contrast to the romanistic literature on the topic, on the undeniable fact that the Romance *kharadjāt* are only a small part of a much larger whole and that the great majority of the *muwaššaḥāt* contain a *khardja* in vulgar or even in classical Arabic, and that the romance *kharadjāt* represent less than 1/10 of the totality of known *kharadjāt*. If one really wants to understand the romance *kharadjāt*, one first has to start with taking a closer look on the *kharadjāt* in vulgar Arabic, because the Romance poems only become fully understandable against the background of the Arabic ones in their phraseology and metaphorics. Alan Jones, as an Arabist, has been particularly insistent on such aspects.

Several scientific congresses took place afterwards, and there were fierce polemics about the question of metrics, which cannot be discussed in detail here because it risks becoming too technical. A large part of this polemic took place on the pages of the American journal *La Corónica*, specialized in problems of Old Spanish literature. The leaders of their respective camps were James T. Monroe from Berkeley and Alan Jones from Oxford; Federico Corriente from Zaragoza played a mediating role. At this point I can only give a brief summary.

The controversy over metrics began in the 1980s and continued well into the 1990s. This metric debate was conducted in part with polemical verve, even with passionate zeal. The controversy was now sparked by the question of metric forms: are these metric forms of Romance origin, that is, can it be said that not only the *kharadjāt*, but also their frame, the *muwashshaḥāt* in general, reflect a metric system that is ultimately based on orally transmitted Romance folk songs? Or do we have to assume that the metrics used here had oriental roots and were formed on the base of varying Arabic patterns? This dispute has been fiercely fought over the years, even with bitter and personal polemics between the individual opponents. Not only the reconstruction of García Gómez's text has been questioned, but also the whole system, the basic concept behind it, because García Gómez sees the *kharadjāt* as a reflection of popular Spanish poetry. He has partly bent the texts in such a way that they fit in with this idea, and he has also made numerous emendations in the texts which are not supported by palaeographic findings, but which are water on his mills and which are intended to prove that the metric schemes are to be interpreted in his way and not otherwise. García Gómez was violently attacked, sometimes in an unjust, personally denigrating manner, by the English researchers; and he defended himself just as violently and personally. In recent years, there still have been publications on the subject, but the polemic has become softer in the meantime and the opponents of yesteryear have partly reconciled.

I personally tend towards accepting the basic thesis of Federico Corriente (1940–2020), the leading representative of Spanish Arabic Studies in the last decades. He coined a felicitous term for the metric system of the *muwaššaḥāt* in al-Andalus: *'arūḍ modificado*, i.e. a modified classical Arabic metric system (*'arūḍ* means the schema of the 16 canonical metres, based on quantity). It can be shown in detail how classical metrics are modified and varied in a specific way, and how in the end something new is created from this. Such a new metrical system must not be attributed to Romance influence, but can be explained as an internal development of the Arabic metres. However, I would not be fundamentally opposed to the idea that certain features of Hispanic folk poetry might have played a role in the development of these metric forms out of the classical patterns of Arabic. Given the intensity of the linguistic contacts between the Romance and Arabic world, this does not seem a completely erroneous assumption. However, quantity remains the basic principle. I think that on the formal side meticulous in-depth studies of the texts will reveal new insights. Metrics will play a still more central role than in the past. The complex interplay of quantity and accent, once understood, will help to solve some long-standing riddles in the interpretation of the texts. The rhythm which can be detected in these poems can sometimes offer clues for the correct analysis of the text. It is a subtle combination of quantity and stress which determines the metrical structure. This structure is pluridimensional, it should not be reduced to a misleading simplicity. This methodological refinement will provide new perspectives which permit to improve our interpretation, in this text corpus. I have tried this approach for several *kharadjāt* with their *muwaššaḥāt*, with fascinating and quite novel results (see Bossong 2010, 99–162).

With regard to content, new and promising perspectives can be found in the domain of intertextuality. For a long time, these poems have been interpreted with too little attention to their context. Intertextual relations with other texts have in most cases not even been analysed for the *muwaššaḥa* in which they are embedded. The clues for understanding the *khardja* which can be found in its own *muwaššaḥa* have frequently been overlooked, because all the interest of scholars was concentrated on these little final verses. So, it is not surprising that other, more distant contexts have escaped the attention they merit. This observation is valid for the context of strophic poetry in general, be it in Arabic or in Hebrew, and for the context of the Hebrew Bible in particular, which is omnipresent in the Hebrew literature (while in the Arabic Islamic world there is nothing comparable with respect to the Qur'ān). It can be shown that this method will help to deepen our understanding of these texts in all their complexity. More details on this approach (with concrete examples) will be given below.

4 Example a: One *khardja* in Two Different *muwaššaḥāt*

In the following pages a few examples will be presented and interpreted. The reader should be aware, however, that in this publication technical details can only very sparsely be given. In the first example, one and the same *khardja* is used in two different *muwaššaḥāt*. Such a constellation is of particular interest, from a linguistic as well as from a literary point of view. The same Romance *khardja* appears in an Arabic and a Hebrew composition. The two authors are exact contemporaries, and they are the two most important writers of strophic poetry in the Arabic and in the Hebrew context respectively.

The Arabic author is Ibn Baqī, with his full name Abū Bakr Yaḥyà b. Aḥmad ibn Baqī al-Qurṭubī/ al-Ṭulayṭulī. He was born around 1080, maybe in Córdoba, maybe in Toledo, and died in Guádix near Granada in 1150.

The Hebrew author is Judah ha-Levi, the great classical figure of post-biblical literature, the famous "prince of Hebrew poetry" (ca. 1070, Tudela – ca. 1145, near Jerusalem). He was the most prolific of all *muwaššaḥa* writers in general, of both the Hebrew and the Arabic tradition. He has left no less than 12 Romance and 16 Arabic *kharadjāt* (and moreover 46 *kharadjāt* in Hebrew). It is remarkable that this poet of first magnitude in the history of Hebrew literature has also rightly been qualified as "the first Spanish poet known by name" (*el primer poeta castellano de nombre conocido*, Marcelino Menéndez Pelayo 1894, see Bossong 2010, 187–280).

It is a remarkable fact that both authors have made use of the same Romance *khardja*, apparently of anonymous popular origin, inserting it into their highly sophisticated strophic compositions in classical Arabic and in Hebrew respectively. For the research on the *kharadjāt* this is indeed a unique stroke of luck. Let us have a closer look on this text in its respective contexts. I give the text as I interpret it; it goes without saying that many details of such an interpretation are a matter of dispute, but this cannot be deepened here.

> *benid la paska (e) yo aun šin ele*
> *kom penad meu koračon por ele*
>
> "Easter is coming, and I am still without him.
> How my heart is suffering for him!"

One first point concerns the philological analysis. The double manuscript tradition is immensely helpful for deciphering the text. The Romance *kharadjāt* are transmitted in the Semitic writing systems which are notorious for their difficulties, especially when one considers that the copyist did not understand a single word of what he was writing; he used the Arabic or the Hebrew script for a language unknown to him. So, the problems in deciphering these texts are in many cases unsurmountable. But as soon as we dispose of a version in two different Semitic scripts, the difficulties are reduced or they disappear, since Arabic and Hebrew have problems of their own respectively, and may serve to elucidate each other. In the Arabic version, the first words of the khardja read like this:

> *nbḏ lyšqh*

This is simply incomprehensible gibberish if one tries to read it in Arabic. But in the light of the Hebrew manuscripts, everything falls in place. The poem of Judah ha-Levi has come down to us in three Dīwān collections conserved in later copies (Oxford 1971,

Oxford 1970, and Schocken 37). Moreover, there exists a Geniza fragment (Cambridge T.-S. H 15:46) which must be almost contemporary to the original composition by Judah ha-Levi. The poem of Ibn Baqī is transmitted in the famous manuscript Colin, which was paleographically reproduced and analysed in Jones 1988 (101–105). It is a well-known fact, even among those who do not master the Arabic language, that in the Arabic script diacritical points are of utmost importance. One point more at left, one point less at right completely changes the meaning of a passage. So, by the interchange of one diacritical point it becomes clear that *nbḏ* has to be read *bnḏ*; this is not meaningful in Arabic either, but its meaning is crystal clear in Romance: *beniḏ* "he comes". In Hebrew this reading is obvious and needs no emendation; the Hebrew script also has its problems, but other than Arabic. So in the light of Hebrew, the emendation in the Arabic text *nbḏ* → *bnḏ* can be established beyond any reasonable doubt. Unfortunately, such constellations are rather rare, and more often than not deciphering resembles guesswork with many uncertainties.

The emendation from *lyšqh* to *lbšqh* follows the same pattern. The letter <b> has just one diacritical point underneath, whereas <y> has two points in the same position. In the light of the Hebrew text it is evident that the nonsensical word *lyšqh* must be read as *lbšqh*. There is still an interesting point with respect to the initial words of the *khardja*. The ancient Hebrew manuscript from the Geniza reproduces in Hebrew letters the spelling of Arabic, where the sound /p/ does not exist and must be represented by means of the letter <b>: *lbšqh*. In contrast, the three later diwans have the correct Romance form, with its initial voiceless <p>: *lpšqa*. It seems that in the twelfth/thirteenth-century Arabic-speaking domain the Arabic graphic conventions influenced the Hebrew spelling when reproducing the Romance word. Hebrew is spelled as if it were Arabic which lacks <p>, whereas in the later copies from the sixteenth century, these Arabic resonances have completely disappeared and the voiceless consonant <p> could be freely used. It is remarkable that the Hebrew copyists must have been aware that the Romance word "Passover" had to do with their own *pesaḥ*, with its initial /p/; for how else would they have passed from an ancient *baška* to *paška*? It must also be noted that the Schocken manuscript (conserved in the Schocken Institute in Jerusalem) bears the indication ʿ*adjamī* "foreign, in a foreign (= non-Semitic) language" for the *khardja*. There was clearly a consciousness that this was a Romance text, and the Romance form of the word "Passover" was not totally incomprehensible to a Hebrew scribe.

It can be assumed that the Arabic *muwaššaḥa* by Ibn Baqī is older than the Hebrew one by Judah ha-Levi. It comes as a typical love song, with the usual topics of the genre in the literary tradition of al-Andalus. In the first stanza, the morning wind (*rīḥ al-ṣabā*) is evoked: it comes from the home of the beloved and lets flow the poet's tears in "humility"; it strikes the body of the poet with "emaciation", passionate love tortures him and causes pain to his "liver" (typically a seat of emotions in Arabic), the wind revives past sorrows. The second stanza is a complaint that the beloved has gone away, although the poet stands firm in faithful love. In the third stanza, the wind becomes the main protagonist again; the poet asks him to return to the home of the beloved and to bring him the greetings of the poet, kissing him in all humility. Stanza four accumulates other conventional images of Arabic love poetry; the curly locks of the beloved form the centre of a semantic field. Their curliness is compared with two letters of the Arabic alphabet which are equally curled with their rounded forms, namely *dāl* (د) and *nūn* (ن). Such comparisons are very much to the taste of the Arab poets; the modern reader just has to take a look at the form of the letters and the meaning becomes immediately visible. The curls are then compared with a curled stick and with a plait. At last, they are compared with a poisonous snake which defends its territory. This may seem quite unusual to a modern Western reader, but is absolutely common in Arabic. The fifth stanza brings the transition to the *khardja*, with the corresponding change of the perspective. While in the textual body of the *muwaššaḥa* love feelings are formulated from the perspective of the – male – lover, the *khardja* is put in the girl's mouth. All of a sudden, the roles are reversed: love is formulated from the perspective of the – female – beloved. In our poem the transition between these two perspectives takes its classical form: "Many girls are tortured by loving passion and its pains, they suffer from separation and distance, then they start singing" [follows the *khardja*].

All in all, Ibn Baqī's poem is a prototypical instance of a *muwaššaḥa* with its *khardja*. It contains the traditional imagery of the genre. The whole poem turns around two semantic poles: the morning wind, and the black curls. The wind bridges the distance between the lover and the beloved, it stirs up remembrance and carries the greetings to his home. The curls are simply beautiful and are compared to various objects with similar rounded forms. This metaphorical world gives place, in the *khardja*, to the plain and straightforward language of the girl which expresses her pain due to the absence of the beloved. The song of the girl stands in clear contrast to the sophisticated style of the preceding four and a half stanzas. Nothing more ingenuous than these words: "Easter is approaching, and I am still alone! My heart is suffering so much!" No metaphors, no rhetoric, plain and unpretentious language – and not Classical Arabic, but the spoken Romance vernacular! Such a contrast, stylistic as well as linguistic, forms the very essence of this stanzaic poetry, invented and developed in al-Andalus. This poem of Ibn Baqī unites all properties of the genre in an ideal combination. It is conventional, and it is prototypical.

The poem of Judah ha-Levi is of a different calibre. Undoubtedly, it has the same formal properties as Ibn Baqī's composition, the same metre, rhyme structure and refrain. The *khardja* is arguably identical in the Hebrew and the Arabic text. There remain zones of doubtful interpretation, but on the whole it is the same text in both versions. As we have seen earlier, the text written in Hebrew characters sheds light on the reading of the text written in Arabic script, and vice versa. While errors and difficulties are different, the underlying text is recognizably the same.

Judah ha-Levi lived in Granada for a while where he frequented Moshe ibn Ezra's circle of friends. This was a time when Hebrew poetry reached a peak. Moshe ibn

Ezra and his younger friend Judah ha-Levi were the outstanding figures of Hebrew letters, and they lived together in an atmosphere of friendly competition, where they spurred each other on to the highest performance. It was a golden age. Judah ha-Levi's poem bears witness to the atmosphere which reigned in this circle, whose members were not only poets of the highest rank, but also personal friends who lived closely together. The topic of this poem is grave, namely death. Of Moshe ibn Ezra's three brothers, the youngest, called Yehuda like the poet, died young, around the year 1090. Judah ha-Levi devoted his elegy to this sad event. The poem is directed to Moshe ibn Ezra. He is addressed in the title: "Peace (šalom) to the man whose joys are in exile and whose comforters have forsaken him". In the first strophe, Judah ha-Levi expresses his compassion with the brothers who are left alone by the loss of Yehuda; in the second stanza Moshe is addressed directly. This goes on in the third stanza; the dead brother appears in the mirror of dream, the surviving friends and relatives remember him, but he is no longer there, they are left alone with their despair; they lift their eyes to the height of God, but without response. Strophe four continues in the same vein: the beneficial rain which the dead brother had poured now has ceased; his illuminating lights are not shining any more. The fifth stanza contains the transition towards the *khardja*: The dead brother's song is "a spark in my heart", it resembles the song of the girl whose heart is stirred up because she expects in vain the beloved who does not come and does not keep his appointment. Easter does not bring union, but only separation forever.

When writing his *muwaššaḥa* Judah ha-Levi took Ibn Baqī's poem as a model. It stands to reason to assume that Yehuda took up a poem which circulated in his surroundings and adapted it to the personal circumstances we have seen, namely the death of his namesake. The poem of Ibn Baqī is a representative of a popular genre, whereas Yehuda's composition is individual and specific. It is a personal work, written in a specific situation. He followed the pattern of Ibn Baqī in metre, strophic structure and rhyme schemes, but the result is personal and unique. We find in Yehuda's text intertextual relations to the Arabic literary scene of his day but also, as is to be expected, to the Hebrew Bible. Hebrew cannot be imagined without a relation to the biblical intertext. Every phrase, every expression, sometimes almost every word reflects biblical usage. There are also references to the contemporary Arabic poetry, but the Hebrew Bible is predominant. In this poem, biblical quotations are less frequent than in other texts. Nevertheless, they are an integral part of the whole composition. With one exception all references come from the prophets: Isaiah, Jeremiah, and Daniel; one quotation is from the book of Psalms. Mostly the references to the Bible are allusive, they come in the form of rare verb forms which give a hint to a passage of the Bible. The semantic associations that come with these allusions are negative. Given the tragic and elegiac tone of the whole poem, the evocation of the prophets is generally in a gloomy mode. For instance, in the second stanza we find "the day when they [the horses] were swifter than the eagle". A similar formulation can be found in Jeremiah 4,13. The whole chapter in Jeremiah deals with the strong wind that comes up to destroy Jerusalem and its people; consequently, the wind is seen here as a force of destruction. This is in clear contrast with the "morning wind" in Ibn Baqī's *muwaššaḥa* where it is seen as a positive force capable to unite the lovers in spite of their separation.

Another example is the verbal root *ḥll* "pierce, wound" which occurs in Isaiah 14,10 ("you are also wounded like we") and in our poem in the first stanza ("the walls of my heart are wounded like theirs"). The grief over the death of the friend echoes the prophetic lament over the fall of the king. Resuming we might say that Ibn Baqī's song shows little adornment and is highly conventional, but in all its ingenuity it has a grace of its own. It is "popular" in the best sense of the word. Very likely it stems from a kind of orally transmitted folk song from which the wording of the *khardja* have seemingly been taken. It is the lament of a girl waiting in vain for her lover which missed the appointment and leaves her alone in spring, in the midst of the time of love, at Easter. All this sounds very authentic, and the effect is heightened by the use of the colloquial Romance language which contrasts with the Classical Arabic in the rest of the poem.

Contrary to that configuration, Judah ha-Levi's composition is a sophisticated work of art. Some verses are difficult to interpret, the whole poem is somewhat "artificial", in the best sense of the word. It contains many allusions and intertextual references, and it has emotional depth. The Hebrew poet has integrated the popular Spanish love song into a rigorously built composition which gives expression to the most universally felt tragic emotion: the omnipresence of death. In this way, the Romance verses of the *khardja* gain an unexpected profundity. The missed encounter between the lovers at Easter is transformed into a metaphor for man's mortality.

5 Example b: Two Different Versions of the Same *khardja*

In the preceding section we have presented the case of one *khardja* which appears in two *muwaššaḥāt*, one in Arabic, the other one in Hebrew, both written by the most important and most prolific *waššāḥūn*, namely Ibn Baqī and Judah ha-Levi. Apart from this constellation, other configurations can be observed. In the following pages, one example will be presented and shortly analysed; a more thorough analysis and interpretation can be found in Bossong 2010 (74–88).

In this case, one *khardja* appears in combination with two different Hebrew *muwaššaḥāt*. What makes this case even more interesting are the differences found between the two versions. The *khardja* is "the same", but not identical. The difference is not just between two versions, such as can frequently be found in texts transmitted in manuscript tradition. There are in fact two consciously differentiated versions. One text was written by the famous classic Yehuda ha-Lewi, the other one is the work of Ṭodros Abū l-ʿĀfiya (1247–1298), who lived almost two centuries later in the Castilian kingdom of Alfonso X el Sabio. Evidently, the later text is a copy of the older one, with specific alterations in form and content. The text from the classic period of Yehuda ha-Lewi is quoted and creatively developed further. Here are the two versions, in the form I have reconstructed (textual problems are not very difficult in this case):

Yehuda ha-Lewi

    bai-še meu qoračon de mib
        yā rabb ši še me tornarad
    tan mal me duoled lil-ḥabīb
        enfermo yed kuand šanarad
"my heart is departing from me,
    oh Lord, will it ever return to me?
It pains so badly for the beloved.
    He [the beloved] is sick, when will he recover?"

Ṭodros Abū l-ʿĀfiya

    bai-še meu qorason de mib
        yā rabbī ši še tornarad
    tan mal mi doler al-gharīb
        enfermo ed kuan šanarad
"my heart is departing from me
    oh my Lord, will it ever return?
So bad [is] my extraordinary pain.
    It [the heart] is sick, when will it recover?"

This is obviously the same text, but with a different perspective. In both versions the words are put into the mouth of the loving girl, but in the older one the girl worries about the health of the beloved, whereas in the more recent version the girl is concerned about her own heart and its health. Yehuda's version is original insofar as the real illness of the lover's friend is at stake, a constellation which is rare, or even non existent in Andalusian love songs. Ṭodros' version is more conventional, since worrying about one's own heart is quite common in lyrical poetry. For Ṭodros, Yehuda's text must have sounded old fashioned. It abounds in archaic linguistic features. For example, the object pronoun *mib* (from Vulgar Latin *mibi*, formed by analogy with *tibi*), instead of the current form *mihi* → *mi*. This pronominal form is current in the *kharadjāt* of the eleventh and twelfth centuries, but absent in later texts. Interestingly, this is an archaism which the Mozarabic of the *kharadjāt* shares with Sardinian, a particularly archaic Romance variety which often goes together with Mozarabic and contrasts with the rest of the Romance languages. It is remarkable that this archaic pronominal form rhymes with two different arabisms in the two versions of the text, namely *ḥabīb*, the omnipresent word for the "beloved", and *gharīb* "strange, surprising, extraordinary".

The same observation is valid for the verbal ending -*d* of the third person singular, from Latin -*t*; this form is also conserved as an archaism in Mozarabic and Sardinian but eliminated in the rest of the Romania. This verbal ending occurs in the rhyme position where it cannot be changed or eliminated. In contrast, in the interior of the verse Ṭodros replaces the archaic verbal form *duoled* by another form of this verb, the infinitive *doler*, which is neutral with respect to diachronic change. On the other hand he maintains the old form of the copula *(y)ed* which is not only archaic but also dialectal, being attested in Aragonese, the presumed mother tongue of Yehuda ha-Lewi, born in Tudela. The truncated form *kuan(d)* instead of *kuando* is also current in these poems, and can also be explained by the influence of Aragonese. In contrast, the archaic and/or dialectal form *qoračon* has been modernized and castellanised, being replaced by *qorason*.

Shortly summarizing, we observe that these two versions of one and the same text are separated by the diachronic evolution of Spanish during the time gap between 1090 and 1280. The more recent author has partially taken over the old forms, thus providing his verses a deliberately archaic flavour, and partially he modernised the text. He plays with the intertext of his great predecessor, integrating it into a completely different historical setting. Ṭodros Abū l-ʿĀfiya represents the sunset of a great tradition. His poetry is even more intricate and sophisticated than in the classical times of Yehuda ha-Lewi and his contemporaries. It is integrated into an extremely complex web of intertextual relations, which comprises not only the (classical and contemporary) Arabic love poetry and the language of the Hebrew Bible, but also the recent internal traditions of Hebrew poetry in al-Andalus.

6 The Significance of the Jewish Influence on the *kharadjāt*

Without any doubt, the strophic poetry of al-Andalus is the product of the coexistence of the three monotheistic religions and their respective cultural settings found in medieval Spain. Mixture and cross-fertilization reached peaks rarely found elsewhere in world literature. Nevertheless, when it comes to analyse the *kharadjāt* and their context, one element has perhaps not been stressed sufficiently. It is their Jewishness. Strophic poetry in general results primarily from the encounter of Arabic literary art and Hispanic popular traditions. But Hebrew and Jewishness plays a particularly significant, and even a decisive role in this context. In the following pages, this claim will be substantiated.

First, as we have seen in the chapter on the history of *khardjatology*, these texts were discovered for the first time in a Jewish context. Romance final verses in Hebrew poetry were known long time before they were found in Arabic poetry. This is due to the fact that the traditions of medieval Hebrew poetry had survived in the Jewish communities of Central Europe, especially in the synagogal services. Medieval poems continued to be recited in worship contexts, although their meaning was apparently erotic. The Jewish communities were accustomed to the religious interpretation of the biblical *Song of Songs*, and so they had no problem with love songs sung or recited in religious services. On the Muslim side, no such traditions existed, therefore the *muwaššaḥāt* with their respective *kharadjāt* disappeared even from popular memory. They were rediscovered from scratch in the twentieth century, by European researchers, not by their own communities. We can say that the existence of Romance *kharadjāt* in Hebrew poems was indispensable for the discovery of such *kharadjāt* in Arabic compositions. The priority in discovery corresponds to priority in scientific analysis. Before the exploration of Arabic, the *kharadjāt* in the Hebrew poems had already been scrutinized, albeit tentatively. Attempts at deciphering these enigmatic and fascinating texts began in this context.

The origin of the strophic poetry should be looked for in Southern Andalusia, in the region where the presumed inventor of these poetic form comes from. As we have seen earlier, the legendary inventor Muqaddam originates from Cabra, which is only a few kilometres from Lucena, an important centre of Jewish culture in the Middle Ages. It can be assumed that the Jewish community played a significant, perhaps decisive role in the invention and the development of strophic poetry.

The following point is of crucial importance. The Arabic composers of strophic poetry are all of minor rank, they are typical *poetae minores*. This assessment is valid even for the two most prolific authors, Ibn Baqī and al-Aʿmà al-Tuṭīlī. There is a short bilingual *khardja* by the king al-Muʿtamid of Seville, who was a remarkable poet. But none of the great names of Arabic poetry in al-Andalus appears on the list of the *waššāḥūn*, they all limited their work to the composition of classical *qaṣīdāt*. We have no *muwaššaḥāt*, let alone Romance *kharadjāt*, from Arabic poets of the first magnitude, such as Ibn Zaydūn, Ibn ʿAbdūn, Ibn Khafādja, or Ibn Zaqqāq. The picture is completely different when we compare it with the situation of Hebrew. The most important composer of Romance *kharadjāt*, Yehuda ha-Lewi, is at the same time the great classical author of postbiblical Hebrew poetry, he is the "prince of poets" of the revived Hebrew language, which had regained its shine as a medium of a refined literature in al-Andalus. It has rightly been claimed that Yehuda ha-Lewi was the "first Castilian poet of known name", and it was exactly this author who ranks in first place among the Hebrew poets of post-biblical times. The second most important author of Romance *kharadjāt* was Moshe ibn Ezra, who also belongs to the great classics of post-biblical Hebrew literature. We have mentioned Ṭodros Abū l-ʿĀfiya who lived about two centuries later and must also be classified as a Hebrew poet of the first rank. Resuming we can say that the Hebrew *waššāḥūn* occupy an important place in the Jewish literature of al-Andalus, whereas the role of the Arabic *waššāḥūn* in the Muslim literature of al-Andalus is much more limited.

Among all the *musaššaḥāt* which have come down to us, the Hebrew ones are the oldest, clearly older than the Arabic ones. The oldest text which can be dated with certainty is the work of a certain Yosef Ibn Caprel al-Kātib, secretary and court poet in Granada. It has been written between 1038 and 1041. This *khardja* is transmitted in a unique copy, probably from the time of its composition, conserved today as one of the treasures of the Bodleian Library in Oxford (Heb. Ms. e.100, f° 40 r°/v°, see Bossong 2010, 192 for details). It reads as follows:

tanto amare tanto amare	*ḥabībi tanto amare*
enfermieron uolyoš nidoš	*ya duolen tan male*
"to love so much,	my beloved, to love so much,
[my] clear eyes have become sick,	they are hurting so badly"

This venerable text is not only the first attested *khardja*, it is also the oldest attested poetic composition in any Ibero-Romance language (note that the only Arabic element is the omnipresent *ḥabīb* "beloved", the rest is pure Romance). Ibero-Romance poetry makes its first appearance in a Hebrew poem. We will later see that the Jewishness of this text goes far beyond the linguistic form and has to do with its content. In all likelihood this short poem is of popular origin. It seems that the poet has taken it from an oral tradition circulating in his environment and that he has embedded it in the formal context of his Hebrew *muwaššaḥa*. It is clear, then, that the date given above (ca. 1040) refers to the composition of the girdle poem as a whole, but not to the composition of the *khardja*, which is older and must be classified as anonymous. In contrast, there exists a poem by Yehuda ha-Lewi which can also be dated precisely because it makes allusion to an historical event. This text can be categorized as the oldest Ibero-Romance poem with a known author. According to the interpretations and reconstructions which I have proposed (Bossong 2010, 248–258) the text reads as follows:

deš do mio Sidielyo bénid	*tan bona al-bišāra*
kom rayo de šole éšid	*en wād al-ḥidjāra*
"from where does my Sidiello come?	what good tidings!
like a sunbeam he is rising	in Guadalajara"

The text refers to the visit of Yosef ibn Ferruziel, called "el Sidiello", in Guadalajara. He was an important personality in the Jewish community, influential in the court of the Castilian king. His visit to Guadalajara aroused messianic hopes. This visit took place between 1091 and 1095, and this must also be the date of the poem. It is evident that this poem is not of popular origin, it was composed by its author for a specific occasion. It is a personal creation of the poet, and this origin can also be detected when we analyse the text more in detail. The poem contains complicated allusions and sophisticated word-plays which are far away from the simple tone of Yosef ibn Caprel's composition. It is not a folk-song but a refined piece of art.

Let us resume for the present discussion that the very first samples of Romance *kharadjāt* – and so the very oldest lyrical productions in Ibero-Romance – have originated in a markedly Jewish cultural context. This observation is valid for dating the texts, but it is also valid for the interpretation of their content. The *muwaššaḥāt* where the *kharadjāt* are inserted follow the rules of the literary genre: at first sight they are love-songs, with numerous allusions to Classical and contemporary Arabic love poetry. But in these Hebrew texts, allusions to the Hebrew Bible abound, they are replete with quotations from the holy scriptures. There are two layers of intertextual relations, Arabic and Hebrew. This duality differentiates these texts from the contemporary Arabic girdle poems, where the relation to the holy scriptures is simply lacking: Arabic authors never quote the Qur'ān, whereas the Hebrew ones permanently use the Bible, with an astonishing degree of liberty.

In the poem of Yosef ibn Caprel, the apparent simplicity of the love topic is deceptive, it conceals a second, deeper layer of meaning. The love sorrow of the girl, longing for her absent lover, stands for the eternal suffering of the people of Israel longing for salvation by the promised redeemer. In Yosef's poem this deeper layer is not directly expressed, but it is obvious for any reader/hearer accustomed to the messianic reading of the biblical *Song of Songs*. In Yehuda's poem this messianic reading is explicitly formulated, since El Sidiello, the person to whom the poem is addressed, incorporates in his person the messianic hopes of the Jewish community of Castile.

Yehuda's poem is full of subtleties, as can be expected from one of the greatest poets of Israel. I just mention a complex word play, typical for a cultural environment where Arabic, Hebrew and Romance merged into one complex whole. The two rhyme words of the *khardja* are combined in an ingenious way. *Bišāra* "good tidings" is an Arabic word with a cognate in Hebrew, namely *beśora* (which occurs a few lines earlier in the text of the *muwaššaḥa*), and a cognate in Spanish, where *albricias* is a loan from Arabic. With one word which belongs to the three languages, the poet expresses his wish that the "good tidings" of the arrival of the redeemer may reconcile the three monotheistic religions. *Guadalajara* is a Castilian place name of Arabic origin, its meaning in Arabic is "river of stones" (*wād al-ḥidjāra*). This is put in relation with the biblical story of the young David who takes stones from a rivulet (*naḥal ha-avanim* "river of stones", see 1 Sam 17:40) and kills with them the overwhelming giant Goliath. Yehuda expresses his hope that El Sidiello might overcome the powerful enemies of Israel and establish a reign of peace for the persecuted and tribulated people.

We can draw the general conclusion that Hebrew girdle poems with Romance *kharadjāt* are often more profound than their Arabic counterparts. They convey messages which go beyond trivial love poetry. In form and content these gems of early Hispanic poetry are authentic works of art. Their Jewishness manifests itself in a dense web of intertextual relations and in the presence of deeper layers of meaning, beyond superficial literality.

Bibliography

Works Cited

Alonso, Dámaso. "Un siglo más para la poesía española." *ABC* 29.4 (1950) [repr. in *De los siglos oscuros al de Oro*. Madrid: Gredos 1958, 29–34].

Bossong, Georg. *Das Wunder von al-Andalus. Die schönsten Gedichte aus dem Maurischen Spanien. Aus dem Arabischen und Hebräischen ins Deutsche übertragen und erläutert.* München: Beck 2005, ²2018.

Bossong, Georg. *Das Maurische Spanien. Geschichte und Kultur.* München: Beck 2007, ⁴2020.

Bossong, Georg. *Die Sepharden. Geschichte und Kultur der spanischen Juden.* München: Beck 2008, ³2021.

Bossong, Georg. *Poesía en convivencia. Estudios sobre la lírica árabe, hebrea y romance en la España de las tres religiones.* Gijón: Ediciones Trea, 2010.

Corriente, Federico. "Nueva propuesta de lectura de las *xarajāt* con texto romance de la serie hebrea." *Revista de Filología Española* 74 (1994): 283–289.

Corriente, Federico, and Ángel Sáenz Badillos, eds. *Poesía estrófica.* Madrid: Universidad Complutense, 1991.

García Gómez, Emilio: *Las jarchas romances de la serie árabe en su marco. Edición en caracteres latinos, versión española en calco rítmico y estudio de 43 moaxajas andaluzas.* Madrid: Sociedad de Estudios y Publicaciones, 1965. Barcelona: Seix Barral, ²1975.

Heger, Klaus. *Die bisher veröffentlichten ḫarǧa-s und ihre Deutungen.* Tübingen: Niemeyer, 1960.

Hitchcock, Richard. *The Kharjas. A Critical Bibliography.* London: Grant & Cutler, 1977.

Jones, Alan and Richard Hitchcock, eds. *Studies on the Muwaššaḥ and the Kharja.* Oxford: Faculty of Oriental Studies, 1991.

Jones, Alan. *Romance kharjas in Andalusian Arabic muwaššaḥ poetry: a paleographical analysis.* London: Ithaca Press, 1988.

Luzzatto, Samuel David. *Bĕtulat bat Yĕhuda lĕquṭey shirim mi-dîwân r. Yĕhuda ha-Lewi* [Virgo filia Jehudae sive Excerpta ex inedito celeberrimi Jehudae Levitae divano]. Prag: M. I. Landau, 1840.

Luzzatto, Samuel David. *Dîwân. Yĕhuda ha-Lewi.* Lyck: M'kize Nirdanim, 1864.

Menéndez Pelayo, Marcelino. "De las influencias semíticas en la literatura española." *Edición nacional de las obras completas de Menéndez Pelayo*, VI, I. Madrid: CSIC, 1941 [1894]:191–217.

Millás Vallicrosa, José María. "Sobre los más antiguos versos en lengua castellana." *Sefarad* 6 (1946): 362–371.

Millás Vallicrosa, José María. *Yĕhudá ha-Leví como poeta y apologista.* Madrid: CSIC, 1947.

Millás Vallicrosa, José María. *La poesía hebraica postbíblica.* Barcelona: Janés, 1953.

Rosenzweig, Franz. *Jehuda Halevi. Zweiundneunzig Hymnen und Gedichte.* Berlin: Lambert Schneider, 1926.

Sola-Solé, José María. *Corpus de poesía mozárabe (las ḫarǧa-s andalusíes).* Barcelona: Hispam, 1973.

Stern, Samuel Miklos. *Les chansons mozarabes. Les vers finaux (kharjas) en espagnol, dans les muwashshahs arabes et hébreux.* Palermo: Manfredi, 1953 [repr. Oxford: Bruno Cassirer, 1964].

Stern, Samuel Miklos. *Hispano-Arabic strophic poetry.* Studies by Samuel Miklos Stern, selected and edited by L. P. Harvey. Oxford: Clarendon Press, 1974.

Zwartjes, Otto. *Love songs from al-Andalus. History, structure and meaning of the kharja.* Leiden: Brill, 1997.

Further Reading

Brann, Ross. *The compunctious poet. Cultural ambiguity and Hebrew poetry in Muslim Spain.* Baltimore: The Johns Hopkins University Press, 1991.
Brody, Ḥayyim. *Diwan Yĕhuda ben Shĕmu'el ha-Lewi.* 4 Vols. Berlin, 1894–1930 [Reprint A. M. Habermann. Gregg International Publishers, 1971].
Emery, Ed, ed. *Muwashshah: proceedings of the Conference on Arabic and Hebrew Strophic Poetry and its Romance Parallels, School of Oriental and African Studies (SOAS), London, 8–10 October 2004.* London: RN Books, 2006.
Heijkoop, Henk, and Otto Zwartjes. *muwaššaḥ, zajal, kharja. Bibliography of strophic poetry and music from al-Andalus and their influence in East and West.* Leiden: Brill, 2004.
Sáenz-Badillos, Ángel, and Judit Targarona Borrás. *Yehuda ha-Levi. Poemas.* Madrid: Alfaguara, 1994.
Schippers, Arie. *Spanish Hebrew poetry and the Arabic literary tradition. Arabic themes in Hebrew Andalusian poetry.* Leiden: Brill, 1994.
Shirman, Ḥayyim. *Ha-shira ha-'ivrit bi-Sĕfarad u-vĕ-Provence* [Hebrew poetry in Spain and Provence]. 2 Vols. Yĕrushalayim: Mosad Bialik & Tel Aviv: Dvir, 1954–1956.
Yellin, David. *Shirey 'ozer lĕ-Ṭodros ben Yĕhuda Abû l-'Âfiya* [girdle poems]. Yĕrushalayim: Weiss, 1935.

Óscar Perea-Rodríguez

4 Jews and *Conversos* in Spanish *Cancioneros* and Portuguese *Cancioneiros* (c. 1350–1520)

Abstract: This chapter presents the significance of both Spanish *cancioneros* and Portuguese *cancioneiros* for the scholarly examination of medieval Jewish history and literature on the Iberian Peninsula. Through a close integration of historiographical and literary analysis, all major *cancioneros* are examined and contextualized based on exemplary interpretations. The chapter is divided into six parts. The first part explains the importance of the historical context of warfare in the development of late medieval Iberian cultures. The second part presents *Cancionero de Baena* and *Cancionero de Palacio* as the two initial stepping stones of the new poetic style and their connection with the problems endured by both Jews and *conversos*. The third part explains the evolution that occurred during the reign of Enrique IV (1454–1474), while the fourth part is focused on the reign of the Catholic Monarchs (1474–1504) and on how the Castilian *cancioneros* can serve as proof of the issues endured by Jewish and converso populations during those uncertain times. The fifth part analyzes the influence of the expulsion of the Jews and of the Inquisition by examining the paramount example of Castilian poetry, the *Cancionero general* (1511), by Hernando del Castillo. Finally, the sixth part is centered on the expulsion of the Jews from Portugal, showing how this is reflected in the *Cancioneiro geral* (1516), by Garcia de Resende.

Key Terms: Cancioneros, Conversos, medieval Iberian history, Jewish cultural history

1 Introduction

In his pioneering work on the subject, Cantera Burgos pointed out that the *Cancionero de Baena* (Dutton PN1) was a veritable document of the coexistence of the three religions on the medieval Iberian Peninsula ("la entremezclada convivencia de gentes de las tres religiones entonces existentes en España" 1967, 80). This assessment was clearly in tune with Américo Castro's heterodox definition of medieval Iberian 'convivencia' (1954, 222–226), a concept that has been severely questioned over the last

---

Note: I shall use throughout this paper Brian Dutton's ID system to identify both poems and songbooks, according to the method designed by Tato García and Perea Rodríguez (2011, 93–94). I shall also use the PhiloBiblon system – manid and texid – to identify both manuscripts/printed books and texts mentioned here (see Faulhaber et al.). I am in debt to Charles Faulhaber, who read in depth a preliminary version of this paper, providing me with his valuable insight and clever suggestions, albeit any mistake this paper may contain is my responsibility only.

https://doi.org/10.1515/9783110563795-005

decades (Nirenberg 2006, 8–12; Soifer Irish 2009, 19–22; discussion in Szpiech 2013, Novikoff 2005, and Abate 2019). For our purposes, this historiographical dispute will be consciously avoided, since it seems to be irrelevant to our primary goal: attempting to assess if, in analyzing the evolution of Iberian Jews and conversos, *cancioneros* can be used as a legitimate historical source, witnessing either to that idyllic *convivencia* or to its constant deterioration.

Twenty years after Scholberg's significant contribution to the topic in 1971 (302–360), Arbós Ayuso once again encouraged researchers to examine Iberian *cancioneros* more closely as a cultural territory worthy of a more profound academic analysis (Arbós Ayuso 1982, 36). In her opinion, scholars would be able to find significant traces of Iberian Jews and their descendants, either those who remained faithful to their religion or those who – by force or voluntarily – converted to Christianity (Arbós Ayuso 1987, 139).

Let us recall that Menéndez y Pelayo, despite his ill-tempered analysis of the medieval Iberian *cancioneros* – focusing on such factors as their lack of poetic appeal ("hechizo poético de muchos de sus versos", Menéndez y Pelayo 1890, 2: 169) – did acknowledge that they had at least one outstanding ingredient: they informed their readers in a very explicit way of the life and customs of their time ("la actualidad histórica de que están llenos, la continua alusión a sucesos políticos del momento y las revelaciones, a veces muy explícitas y francas, que suelen contener sobre la vida y costumbres", Menéndez y Pelayo 1890, 2: 169). More recently, the value of *cancioneros* as a useful source for social history has been noted, so long as we "avoid from the outset the danger of regarding them as mere collections of texts or a fortuitous gathering of preexisting works" (Garcia 1998, 48). Thus, in order to understand the cultural sphere of Iberian *cancioneros* adequately, it seems necessary first to define the limit and scope not only of the literary genre to be analyzed, but also of its societal and historical significance.

I shall continue to use the Spanish word *cancionero* – or the Portuguese *cancioneiro* – instead of its putative English equivalent, 'songbook'. It is true that both terms can be used to refer to a book, whether written by hand or printed, that contains songs (Dutton and Roncero López 2004, 19) – that is, "the vehicle and the object of literature" (Garcia 1998, 51) – but the connotations of the Romance terms are much richer. In addition, we must understand 'songs' in the sense of 'lyrics', because most *cancioneros* were composed to be sung with musical accompaniment, in spite of the fact that the majority of extant *cancioneros* lack musical notation. At the end of the fourteenth century, the presence of that nuance caused one specific verse form, the *canción*, to become a literary genre for all practical purposes (Gómez-Bravo 2000, 161). *Canciones* therefore began to be ubiquitous, especially in the realm of love poetry (Whetnall 1989, 202–203; Dutton and Roncero López 2004, 77–80), while verse forms that had been dominant before, such as the *dezir* and *cantiga*, gradually fell away (Beltran 1988, 78–79).

Despite certain irregularities in its scholarly use (Severin 1994, 98–99), in medieval and early modern Iberian cultures the concept of *cancionero* connoted far more than just the physical object in which lyrics were either copied by hand or printed (Gálvez 2012, 11). It was also the name for a cultural phenomenon whose significance was repeatedly diminished during most of the twentieth century in favor of more popular – in both senses of the term – forms, such as the ballad or the epic (Gerli 1994, 26–27). This academic rejection was due in part to the immense prestige of Menéndez Pidal, who devoted his research precisely to these two genres, as well as to the fact that the overwhelming success of the Italianate poetry of the sixteenth century makes *cancionero* poetry appear to be a mere collection of enigmas, with its enormous bulk, its subtle conventions, its intricate topoi, and its stylized vocabulary (Perea Rodríguez 2012a, 290), containing plenty of "monotony and repetitiveness" (Garcia 1998, 53). Yet all these peculiarities are precisely what render *cancioneros* valuable historical sources for the study of medieval and early modern Iberian Jews and conversos. There are good grounds for an affirmative answer to the question of whether or not literature and history can complement each other to provide insights into the turmoil of this historical period ("si la literatura y la historia pueden complementarse o no para ofrecer una visión conjunta de ese turbado período español", Alcalá Galve 2011, 266).

The Iberian turmoil alluded to requires a brief explanation. One of its main causes was the stagnation of feudalism as a social and economic system in Western Europe (Dobb 1963, 50–51), and the consequences of which were severe in both the central and peripheral lands of the Iberian Peninsula (Valdeón Baruque 2001, 15–17). The scourge of war ravaged the five kingdoms of Portugal, Castile, León, Navarre, and Aragon by involving all of them, to a greater or lesser extent, in the Hundred Years' War (Mitre Fernández 2009, 17–20). As early as 1356, Castile and Aragon fought in the so-called *Guerra de los dos Pedros*, i.e., Pedro IV of Aragon against Pedro I of Castile (Lafuente Gómez 2014, 18–22). Immediately afterward, the Castilian Civil War began, with its decisive turning point at the Battle of Montiel in 1369 (Valdeón Baruque 2001, 32–37), when Pedro I was first defeated and later assassinated by his half-brother, Enrique de Trastámara, who succeeded him as the new king of Castile and Leon. Finally, the entire complexity of Iberian power relations exploded into a war between Castile and Portugal between 1383 and 1385 (De La Torre Gómez 2016, 18–21). This latter conflict was initiated by a controversial political maneuver of Juan I, Enrique II's son and heir, who wanted to marry Beatriz of Portugal, heiress of the Portuguese crown, in order to achieve political hegemony over the western half of the Iberian Peninsula (Olivera Serrano 2005, 82–83). The outcome of this war is of capital importance to understanding the cultural evolution of the Iberian *cancioneros* (Dutton 1990–1991, 7: I-V), as we shall see later.

In addition, the Iberian political landscape cannot be completely understood without bearing in mind that, from 1391 onward, an anti-Jewish component was added to the witches' brew (Wolff 1971, 7–9). Starting with the early conflicts in 1354 that eventually would spark the Castilian Civil War, the future King Enrique II made extensive use of anti-Judaism in his discourse, surely in order to increase popular support for his cause (Valdeón 2001, 80–83; Kaplan 2002, 18). His son and heir, Juan I, was considered a devout monarch, as his nickname 'the Pious' demonstrates (Olivera Serrano 2018, 282). However, nothing seems to have changed for the better for Jews during his rule; Shlomo ibn Verga mentioned in his *Shevet Yehudah* that in the times of Juan I, hard regulations were enforced against the Castilian Jews ("se multiplicaron sin cesar las calamidades [. . .], quitándoles sus modos de vida y decretando contra ellos duras normativas", Verga 1991, 213). The king's unexpected death in 1390 gave rise to profound disorder in the Kingdom of Castile, fueled by the Archdeacon of Écija, Ferrán Martínez, whose "inflammatory anti-Jewish sermons" motivated the mobs who "plundered and burned the Jewish community of Seville" (Aronson-Friedman and Kaplan 2012, 2). Unfortunately, the 1391 riots, inspired by the preaching of St. Vincent Ferrer, were but the deplorable crystallization of more than twenty years of anti-Jewish policies in the Iberian kingdoms (Castro 1982, 18–19). This event, referred to as the 'gran viraje' (Valdeón Baruque 1994, 32), decimated *juderías* all over the Iberian lands; it was the turning point that forever changed Iberian society with regard to the societal balance of a population living together with a variety of religious backgrounds (Mitre Fernández 1994, 23–38; Smail 2001, 113–117).

The year 1391 also marked the beginning of the so-called 'converso problem', one of the phenomena regarding the Iberian Peninsula that is most difficult to analyze, and one of the most uncomfortable for modern scholars (Benito Ruano 2001, 199–200). Recently baptized Jews began to feel that their sincerity in leaving behind their former creed was unlikely to be accepted at face value by their new coreligionists (Valdeón Baruque 1994, 29–30). Mass conversions or the conversions of public figures did not suffice to eliminate social rejection, for the so-called 'New Christians' were often perceived as concealed liars who continued to practice Judaism in the shelter of their homes (Domínguez Ortiz 1971, 17–25).

Since "only the Old Christian was [*seen as*] of pure Catholic ancestry" (Melammed 2004, 19), as soon as the anti-Jewish riots ceased, it was more than evident that the word converso began to be applied solely to the crypto-Jews, despite its polyvalent nature (Márquez Villanueva 2006a, 95–96). The not-so-subtle difference between *anussim* – those forced to become Christian – and *mesummad* – those who converted voluntarily – was basically disregarded (Gutwirth 1993, 102–104), despite the fact that the distinction was widespread in medieval Iberia, as shown in the *Libro del Alborayque*, which distinguishes between "christiano por fuerça [. . .] o christiano por voluntad" (Carpenter 2005, 68). The duality in converso identities, as shown here, lay behind the emergence of a certain type of anti-converso and pro-converso literature (Beinart 1992, 366; Jonin 1997, 124–126), while its impact could also be perceived in Castilian Spanish through several changes registered in the denominations of the whole social group (Bajo Pérez 2015, 73–96).

These facts and events were decisive in showing the Iberian kingdoms to be a society "deeply conscious of its divisions along the lines of ethnic and religious origins" (Netanyahu 1997, 43) and therefore susceptible to historical analysis in most literary works composed in Castile during the fifteenth century (Edwards 1992,

207–209). Nevertheless, scholarship has wavered on interpreting these reflections within the "amanerada poesía de los cancioneros" (Solá-Solé and Rose 1976, 371), as shown by bitter scholarly complaints that "little has been done to take full measure of the connection between *cancioneros* and Jews and conversos" (Rodríguez-Puértolas 1998, 187). Attempting to resolve this question, I shall analyze in chronological order all the events relevant to the issue, relating them to the cultural evolution of the Iberian *cancioneros*. The primary goal will be to point out how these poetry collections offer valuable insight into the historical trajectory of Iberian Jews and conversos (Baer 1966, 2: 300–302), providing qualitative knowledge of its societal, economic, and cultural significances.

2 Cultural Implications of the Fourteenth-Century Iberian Conflicts

It was only after Brian Dutton published the seven volumes of *El Cancionero castellano del siglo XV* in 1991 that scholars finally possessed the long-needed "research tool to undertake a global study of *cancionero* production in particular and also to reassess our perception of fifteenth-century literary life in general" (Garcia 1998, 48). In the seventh and last volume, Dutton referred to "En un tiempo cogí flores" as a sort of *Homo antecessor* for *cancionero* poetry (Dutton 1990–1991, 7: VII–VIII), composed by Alfonso XI himself for his mistress, Leonor de Guzmán. It is the only poem written in Castilian that was conserved in the Portuguese *cancioneiros* (Deyermond 1982, 200). This is the first step in a major cultural change, since both Castile and Portugal "fueron sede de una riquísima producción que se expresaba, como todas las escuelas trovadorescas de Europa, en una lengua convencional, con base, en este caso, en el gallego-portugués" (Beltran 1985, 259). But "En un tiempo cogí flores" is quite different from the classic Galician-Portuguese model, and through its verses it is crystal clear how lyric poetry began to abandon the Galician-Portuguese language in order to develop into a courtly Castilian poetry ("la poesía lírica empieza a abandonar el gallego-portugués para convertirse en una lírica cortesana y castellana", Dutton 1990–1991, 7: VIII).

This evolution, noticeable in the arrival in Castile of new rhyming patterns and schemes (Gómez Redondo 2017, 397), also had a decisive historical background deeply influenced by conflict. Alfonso XI and Leonor de Guzmán begot a large and illegitimate progeny: the Trastámara lineage, known as such because the oldest surviving son and head of the family, the future Enrique II, had already been appointed Count of Trastámara in 1345 (González Crespo 1988, 295). As mentioned before, the Trastámara family and its supporters incorporated anti-Jewish elements into their official discourse early on (Suárez Fernández 1991, 174–175), thus fostering a breeding ground for what is perhaps the very first conspiracy theory in Iberian history. Attempting to manipulate all sorts of collective emotions (Soyer 2019, 32–33), the intrigue turned Enrique II into the only legitimate son – and, therefore, heir – of Alfonso XI. In its earlier versions, the narrative depicted Pedro I as an illegitimate offspring, fathered by a Portuguese relative of his mother, Queen María de Portugal, who apparently bedded her during one of Alfonso XI's frequent absences from the royal bedchamber (De Los Ríos 1900, 58–65). Popular gossip later elaborated an even more nightmarish account, according to which Pedro I was actually born to a Jewish couple before being kidnapped by his alleged mother (Gimeno Casalduero 1972, 93–94). Queen María was said to have switched this Jewish baby boy with her recently born daughter, whose birth was kept secret, for she was given as compensation to the Jewish couple (Montes Romero-Camacho 2016, 127). The queen's sinister aim was to make it possible for this abducted child to inherit the Castilian throne, overriding the rights of Enrique de Trastámara (Estow 1995, XX). This is the reason behind the nickname *emperogilados* which was contemptuously received by the Petristas, the supporters of Pedro I (Perea Rodríguez 2009, 111), for they had followed a 'false king' referred to in some Castilian ballads as 'Pero Gil' (Castro 1970, 58), an illegitimate Jewish-born man who did not deserve the throne (Rodríguez-Puértolas 1998, 188). Today, it is absolutely evident that this was nothing more than one of the many apocalyptical prophecies that depicted Pedro I as the worst possible monarch (Beceiro Pita 2018, 323–324), but it has been recently considered to be a foundational link in the chain of the Spanish black legend (Kalinina 2018, 12–13).

More important for our purposes is the fact that this blatant lie had the chance to succeed because of Pedro I's generally lenient attitude toward the Jews (Valdeón Baruque 2004, 68). It has been argued that the king's appreciation was due to the extreme need the coffers of the monarchy had for the copious revenue generated by the special taxation paid by this minority, both the *servicio y medio servicio* (Ladero Quesada 1995a, 170–171) and the *cabeça del pecho de los judíos* (Ladero Quesada 1973, 219–221). But it seems quite likely that the perception of the last Castilian king of the Castilian House of Burgundy as a ruler who favored the Jews was based on the fact that he sought advice from counsellors of different religious backgrounds. Pedro I was keen to put into practice the poet Sem Tob de Carrión's advice on *la rosa et el espino* (Girón Negrón 2005, 251–259; Real Ramos 1996, 531–532), especially the metaphor "non val el açor menos por nasçer de mal nido / nin los enxemplos buenos por los dezir judío" ("the hawk is not worth less if born in a poor nest / nor are good proverbs bad if spoken by a Jew", *Proverbios morales* 64). It was therefore easy for his enemies to elaborate a negative perception of Pedro I, because intellectuals of both Muslim and Hebrew creeds often advised him, such as Lisān al-dīn Ibn al-Jaṭīb, officially a servant of Muhammad V, King of Granada (Marquer 2011, 1–3; Garcia 2010, 28–30), with whom the Castilian monarch maintained frequent epistolary contact (Garcia 1999, 28–37). Furthermore, we should not forget the notable presence in the royal administrative services of a few highly ranked Jewish officials, such as the royal scribe named Yahuda (Molina Molina and De Lara Fernández 1977, 13) and Abraham ibn Zarzar, the king's personal physician (Méndez Bejarano 1993, 102). Above all of them rises the figure of Samuel ha-Levi Abulafia, the king's *tesorero mayor*, who was not only a loyal adviser (Montes Romero-Camacho 2017, 103), but was also instrumental in the construction of the Sinagoga del Tránsito in Toledo (Gerber 2012, 44–47). However, his unblemished record of royal service was not shield enough to protect him from a spurious accusation forged by his enemies at the court, which finally condemned him to a terrible death in 1360 (Perea Rodríguez 2017a, 119–120).

The most interesting personality in this respect is the previously mentioned Sem Tob de Carrión (Márquez Villanueva 2006c, 29–30), the transliterated Spanish name of Šem Ṭov ben Ishaq ibn Arduṭiel – or perhaps Torrutiel (Roth 2007, 719). His literary production in Hebrew was overshadowed by his *Proverbios morales* (PhiloBiblon BETA texid 1434), a poem written "no solo con seriedad, sino con esperanza" (Díaz-Mas 2001, 32) and dedicated to Pedro I, the king in whom the Castilian Jews deposited their deepest trust to solve their problems of coexistence (Alcalá Galve 2011, 59). This mutually beneficial alliance between the Jews and the Crown (Castaño González 1995, 184) marked the conventional place of all Jewish communities, which "traditionally relied on royal patronage" (Boase 1978, 79), a vital alliance that in the fifteenth century would be retaken by the conversos (Perea Rodríguez 2007b, 170–171).

The stanzas in which Sem Tob praised the king displayed a variant of the old style of *cuaderna vía*, "clerecía rabínica" (Díaz-Mas 1993, 329), redolent of the gnomic themes typical of the poetry composed by the Spanish Jews (Díaz-Mas 2001, 46–47). Sem Tob is also an ephemeral testament to the cultural integration of Iberian Jews via "a Hebreo-Hispanic synthesis that was never to be" (Scheindlin 1997, 34). The *Proverbios morales* can consequently be considered a lyric epitaph: it rapidly turned from a petition for help in favor of the Jewish communities (Alcalá Galve 2011, 58–59) into the farewell address of a type of Castilian poetry that simply disappeared (Castro 1970, 98). Later, the irruption of a brand-new poetic fashion was fueled, in political terms, by circumstances quite unfavorable to the Jews, especially after the (in)famous speech of Enrique II in 1366, in which he accused Pedro I of bringing down the catholic faith because he was supposedly enriching Jews and 'Moors' ("acreçentando e enrriqueçiendo los moros e los judíos e enseñoreándolos e abaxando la fe cathólica de nuestro señor Ihesuchristo", quoted by Valdeón Baruque 1968, 39). It is easy to understand why the contemporary Jewish writer Samuel Çarça depicted Enrique II's soldiers as "evil men" and "foreigners" (Gutwirth 2000a, 164–165), in a sad prelude to the changes in religious policies that the Castilian monarchy was about to implement in the aftermath of the civil war.

Pedro I's defeat at Montiel was not only the culminating act of a coup d'état carried out by his brother, but also the beginning of an unprecedented hostile climate against the Jews, for the recently crowned Enrique II did nothing to prevent the atrocious attacks on the Castilian Jewries ("alentó, aprovechándolos, los anárquicos impulsos de la plebe: la pasividad del Trastámara ante el saqueo de las juderías fue la más rotunda de sus justificaciones", Gimeno Casalduero 1972, 92). Intimidating acts were already visible during the war in cities under siege, such as Cuenca and Miranda de Ebro (Montes Romero-Camacho 2016, 120), and even in battles, such as Nájera in 1367 (Rodríguez-Puértolas 1998, 188). When ideas reflecting those acts were incorporated into discourse emanating from the Crown (Soifer Irish 2016, 221–257), the political conception of the Castilian monarchy began to move away from the previously alleged coexistence of a tri-religious Iberia (Roth 2002, 9–10). In part as a result of his attitude toward the Jews, but also because history is written by the victors, the sidelined monarch was deliberately written out of most *cancionero* poetry, a clear operation of *damnatio memoriae* (Perea Rodríguez 2017a, 122–124) only partially counterweighted by foreign sources on the Castilian Civil War (Foronda 2010, 203–214). In fact, Pedro I's veiled appearances in *cancionero* poetry as a shadowy ghost became an essential feature of this genre in terms of political propaganda, as I have argued elsewhere (Perea Rodríguez 2017a; 2017b).

Dutton also pointed out another armed conflict as a key element in the shaping of the Iberian *cancioneros*: the war between Castile and Portugal that culminated in the resounding defeat of Juan I of Castile at Aljubarrota, the famous battle between the armies of Castile and Portugal in 1385 (Olivera Serrano 2005, 81–95). Thus, near the town and monastery of Alcobaça, Juan I of Trastámara was forced to give up his dream of uniting the two Iberian kingdoms under one crown (Olivera Serrano 2018, 293–299). The ensuing enmity between Castile and Portugal had dire consequences in cultural terms: their mutual disdain was especially detrimental to the poetry style that had been hegemonic, i.e., the "lírica tardía galleguizante al estilo de Macías" (Dutton 1990–91, 7: VII). After Aljubarrota, Galician poetry was the most obvious cultural victim in this hostile environment, for it practically vanished.

This Iberian cultural divorce affected virtually all interactions between the Crown and its literary agents, the troubadours, fomenting a complete revolution in the literary patterns of Iberian poetry (Boase 1978, 36–38). For these reasons, I have frequently advocated for considering 'poetry in the age of the Trastámaras' to be synonymous with what is often called *cancionero* poetry (Perea Rodríguez 2009, 255–256). It is no coincidence that the years 1350–1520, established by Dutton as the period of domination of *cancionero* poetry, match almost perfectly the time span of Trastámara rule in the Crowns of Castile and Aragon. During those years, the poetical harvest of Castilian poetry was the largest in the entire European continent during the Middle Ages (Dutton and Roncero López 2004, 5; Perea Rodríguez 2017a, 117–118). As Gómez-Bravo underscores, the confluence of both cultural and political factors "made poetry a widespread social phenomenon that went beyond a court elite" (2013, 33). The dynasty victorious in the civil war quickly realized poetry's enormous potential as a vehicle for apologetic and favorable messages (Nieto Soria 1988, 188); as the poet Gómez Manrique would say a few years later, ideas delivered in verse "se asientan mejor y duran más en la memoria que las prosas" (Manrique 2003, 214). Thus, the Trastamaran monarchs gladly fostered the creation, composition, and propagation of all kinds of texts provided that the messages delivered always justified, if only implicitly, their 'unfair seizure' of the Castilian throne.

Obviously, Portugal is the great exception to this maxim, and not only because it was never ruled by a Trastámara. Before the period of constant warfare of the second half of the fourteenth century, the zenith of Portuguese poetry had already passed with the death of King Dinis in 1325, the last important poet in Galician Portuguese (Dutton and Roncero López 2004, 10–15). The earliest extant Portuguese *cancioneiro* (Cohen 1987, 14–19), the *Cancioneiro da Ajuda*, was compiled in the late thirteenth century (Sharrer 2004, 42–44), while both the *Colocci-Brancuti* and *Vaticana* were copied in Italy in the sixteenth century from an earlier model (Tavani 1969, 77–179). However, the movement was moribund by the middle of the fourteenth century (Gonçalves 2016, 131), implying that there is almost a two-hundred-year gap between the thirteenth and, possibly, fourteenth-century *cancioneiro* manuscripts mentioned above and the next link in the Portuguese lyric chain: the *Cancioneiro geral*, compiled by Garcia de Resende and printed in 1516. As Deyermond explains, this fact "suggests that the Galician-Portuguese tradition of court lyric did not long survive Dinis's death in 1325" (Deyermond 1982, 198).

Despite what has been said before, there are a few traces of *cancioneiros* that perhaps did exist in the late fourteenth century, but no copy has survived. The most significant evidence in this regard is the *Livro de cantigas*, which Dom Pedro, Count of Barcelós, compiled around 1350 to be sent to Alfonso XI of Castile, Dom Dinis's grandson (Dutton and Roncero López 2004, 14–15). It has been argued that its content was, at least partially, integrated into the *compilação de reis e magnates* within the *Cancioneiro da Ajuda* (Marcenaro 2016, 586–587). A similar assessment could be made regarding the "gran volumen de cantigas, serranas y decires" (Gómez Moreno 1990, 60), described by Íñigo López de Mendoza, marquis of Santillana, as belonging to his grandmother, Doña Mencía de Cisneros (Deyermond 1982, 201–202), in whose library he said he read it during his childhood. Today, the *Cancionero de Baena* is the only link connecting the earlier Portuguese *cancioneiros* and the Castilian *cancioneros* of the fifteenth century, especially some of the compositions more in tune with the former trovadoresque tradition, such as those of Macías and Alfonso Álvarez de Villasandino (Lapesa 1953–1954, 52–58; Vallín 2003, 80–82). Thus, even though some scholars consider that the presence of some Galician poets in *Baena* contradicts – or at least diminishes – the alleged decadence of Galician-Portuguese poetry (Ventura 2006, 819–821), it is evident that the Castilian hegemony had begun by that time because "the Portuguese court had ceased to be a centre for poetry, and there was an awareness that Castile was taking over this role" (Deyermond 1982, 207).

3 The *Cancionero de Baena* and the *Cancionero de Palacio*: Two Sides of the Same Courtly Coin

Let us begin by establishing a basic premise: in literary terms, we are about to deal with a "form of transitional school in genre and technique as well as in language" (Deyermond 1982, 204). This is what defines *poesía de cancionero* during the period when Juan Alfonso de Baena shaped his collection, the very first anthology of medieval poetry written in Castilian Spanish (Dutton and Roncero López 2004, 1). There is one relevant factor that increases the archaic aura of the *Cancionero de Baena* (Dutton PN1): its compiler was guided by a peculiar criterion in the selection of its poems, preferring those more historical and philosophical to those based on pure courtly love topics (Beltran 2001a, 21–22). As a result, *Cancionero de Baena* can be read as a sort of poetic chronicle of the troubled years from 1380 to 1430 (Menéndez y Pelayo 1890, 2: 211), a remarkable appraisal if we consider that Juan II's reign was defined as such a unique blend of wars, celebrations, tournaments, and revolts, whose final result was a sort of Renaissance characterized by the simultaneous influences of Italian, classical, and troubadoresque literatures ("ce règne étrange, plein de guerres, de fêtes, de révoltes, de tournois, cette véritable renaissance où l'initiation simultanée aux oeuvres des anciens, des troubadours, des italiens", Puymaigre 1873, 1: 20). The aforementioned premise also reinforces the idea that a good many of the poems it contains are quite arid if considered without their historical background; they can only be fully understood through the prism of History ("si se leen sin sus connotaciones históricas, resultan áridos y vacíos; si se los encarna en su tiempo, cobran el colorido de la Historia", Blanco González 1972, 48).

The *Cancionero de Baena* thus offers an almost journalistic slant on contemporary events, a counterweight to what may be found in more traditional historiographical sources such as chronicles and official documents (Perea Rodríguez 2009, 256–257). That is why it is so appealing as a primary source for calibrating the interaction of Jews and conversos in the cultural history of the Iberian Peninsula. Since the secular Hebrew poetry of the period has been considered "epigonic and decadent" (Scheindlin 1997, 25), our focus here shall center on the poetry written mostly in Castilian Spanish, attempting to locate the presence of Jews and "conversos along the path of acculturation" (Glick 1997, 60).

The first thing to consider is that Juan Alfonso de Baena, compiler of the florilegium and occasional poet himself, was frequently alluded to as a converso (Cantera Burgos 1967, 81–82; Roth 2002, 165–166; 2007, 151–152). Many of the poetic attacks he received underscore aspects of typical converso idiosyncrasies and experiences, including his position as a scribe in the royal court (Márquez Villanueva 1965, 318) and his appreciation of typical Hebrew meals, such as *adafina* – the classic Jewish stew – and eggplants (Pomeroy 2010, 71–72). But we should recall that the Spanish word for eggplant is 'berenjena', and that the adjective 'berenjenero' was often taken as a synonym for converso (Gil 2009, 131; Macías 2010, 241). This joke largely surpassed its medieval boundaries, for it is even found in *Don Quijote* (D'Agostino 2011, 328); furthermore, 'berenjena' makes for an irresistible rhyme with 'Baena', a cheap shot among the burlesque blows that Juan Alfonso's rivals aimed against him in the many poetic dialogues in which he participated (Chas Aguión 2001, 42–50; Caíño Carballo 2018, 18–21). It is true that these 'social satires', mostly inherited from the Galician-Portuguese tradition of the *cantigas de escárnio e maldizer* (Scholberg 1971, 256), might entail a certain element of artistic license, meaning that they are not necessarily trustworthy (Scholberg 1971, 257). Nevertheless, Baena's Jewish origins are quite credible: he never rejected such accusations from other poets (Chas Aguión 2018, 127–140) such as Ferrán Manuel de Lando (Scholberg 1971, 306; Dutton and Roncero López 2004, 70–71); and he himself cast the same aspersions on other royal scribes, such as Álvar Ruiz de Toro (Chas Aguión 2014, 848–850). In addition, the little we know of Baena's life also points in the same direction (Márquez Villanueva 2006f, 184–185); he lived, for instance, in the parish of San Salvador in Córdoba (Nieto Cumplido 1979, 198–199), a well-known Jewish and converso neighborhood (Nieto Cumplido 1982, 41–42).

Whether Baena was a converso or not, his compilation indeed offers valuable insights concerning the complex coexistence of different religious groups in medieval Iberia, as shown by poems referencing "christianos, moros e judíos" (Cantera Burgos 1967, 80–83). Let us recall that "from 1400 to 1449 there is little evidence of serious popular agitation" (Mackay 1972, 58). Though it is perhaps exaggerated to define the first half of the fifteenth century as "el apogeo del marranismo" (Alcalá Galvé 2011, 82), there is no doubt that a certain benevolence obtained toward the Jews in Castile, especially in royal environments (Rubio García 1973, 151), an assessment based on the common-sense principle that a precarious coexistence was absolutely preferable to watching *juderías* be assaulted (Ruiz Gómez 1994, 141).

For these reasons, Juan II has generally been considered a protector of the Castilian minorities (Solá-Solé and Rose 1976, 372). He sought the advice of members of the Jewish communities, such as Abraham Bienveniste (Valdeón Baruque 1995, 75), and his court was such that, in Rodrigo Sánchez de Arévalo's *Suma de la Política*, it could be depicted as what a biblical Jewish monarchy might have looked like (Edwards 1992, 211–215). But the best evidence of this benevolent royal connection with the Jews is the fact that the king's own education was entrusted to Pablo de Santa María (c. 1350–1435), born Solomon Ha-Levi, chief rabbi of the city (Boase 1978, 93), who was named bishop of Burgos after his "spectacular conversion" to Christianity in 1390 and subsequent study of theology at the University of Paris (Rodríguez Puértolas 1998, 188). Considered one of the most important Iberian Humanists of the fifteenth century (Seidenspinner-Núñez 2000, 242–243), he wrote important works in both Latin and Spanish that had the effect of helping to create a sympathetic social environment for all conversos. First, his *Scrutinium Scripturarum* (c. 1434) provided theoretical support for contemporary conversions (Yisraeli 2018, 162–163), while at the same time incorporating traditions from Hebrew polemicists like Joshua Halorki and Shlomo Levi

(Glatzer 1995, 62–66). Secondly, and more importantly for our purpose, there is Santa María's *Siete edades del mundo* (Dutton ID 4279), a history of the world from its creation in *octavas reales*, the successor to the *cuaderna vía* for serious narrative poetry. This work represents a sort of historiographical *cancionero* which includes most of the literary ingredients we are analyzing here (Conde 1999, 29–30), while serving additionally as a vehicle for Jewish traditions (Gutwirth 2000a, 175; Szpiech 2010, 98–99).

The *Cancionero de Baena* provides a useful perspective from which to assay the "partial re-establishment of the position of the Jews and conversos in government and society which had been severely shaken by the pogrom of 1391" (MacKay 1972, 60). At the same time, it offers written testimony of the "process of acculturation that led eventually to the conversion of much of the Jewish upper classes to Christianity" (Scheindlin 1997, 37). Both of these elements are present in a poem by Pero Ferruz (Cantera Burgos 1967, 106–109), an old-fashioned love troubadour indebted to the Provençal school (Dutton and Roncero López 2004, 23–24), whose service as a tax collector in Toledo during the last quarter of the fourteenth century has served to identify him as converso (Perea Rodríguez 2009, 87–90). Ferruz daringly composed a burlesque starring the Jewish congregation of the synagogue at Alcalá de Henares (ID 1433, PN1-302 f. 105v: "Con tristeza e con enojos"). It seems they became a bit noisy during the early-morning Barechu and Shem'a Yisrael devotions at Shacharit (Perea Rodríguez 2013b, 27–29), for these "raucous Jewish prayers" (Lourie 1977, 138) apparently impeded anyone in the vicinity from getting a good night's sleep (Beinart 1992, 360):

[I] Con tristeza e con enojos
que tengo de mi fortuna,
non pueden dormir mis ojos
de veinte noches la una;
mas desque Alcalá llegué,
luego dormí e folgué
como los niños en cuna.

[II] Entre las signogos amas
estó bien aposentado,
do me dan muy buenas camas
e plazer e gasajado;
mas, quando viene el alva,
un rabí de una grant barva
óigolo al mi diestro lado.

[III] Mucho enantes que todos
viene un grant judío tuerto
que, en medio d'aquessos lodos,
el diablo lo oviesse muerto,
que con sus grandes bramidos
ya querrían mis oídos
estar allende del puerto.

[IV] Rabí Yehudá el terçero,
do posa Tello, mi fijo,
los puntos de su garguero
más menudos son que mijo;
e tengo que los baladros
de todos tres ayuntados
derribarién un cortijo.

(Baena 1993, 535)

It is possible that these verses were related to the uncertainties experienced by the Iberian Jewish communities concerning the accurate recitation of the Shem'a (Roth 2018, 30–33). In any case, Ferruz puts a satirical response in the mouths of the Rabbis (ID 1434, PN1-303, f. 105v-106r: "Los rabíes nos juntamos"). This farcical reply is a play on a well-known medieval literary topos: *Fortuna variabilis* (Gutwirth 2005, 155–156):

[I] Los rabíes nos juntamos,
don Pero Ferruz, a responder,
e la respuesta que damos
queredlo bien entender.
E dezimos que es provado
que non dura en un estado
la riqueza nin menester.

[III] El pueblo e los hazanes,
que nos aquí ayuntamos
con todos nuestros afanes,
en el Dio siempre esperamos
con muy buena devoçión,
que nos lleve a remissión
por que seguro bivamos.

[II] Pues alegrad vuestra cara
e partid de vos tristeza,
a vuestra lengua juglara
non le dedes tal pobreza,
e aun creed en Adonay,
qu'Él vos sanará de ¡ay!
e vos dará grant riqueza.

[IV] Venimos de madrugada
ayuntados en grant tropel
a fazer la matinada
al Dio santo de Israel
en tal son, como vos vedes,
que jamás non oiredes
ruiseñores en vergel.

(Baena 1993, 536)

Another instance of poetry that is humorous while also reflecting the respect fostered by the Castilian royal milieu toward Jews and conversos is that of Fray Diego de Valencia de Don Juan. This eminent doctor of theology has an interesting biography, characterized by his service to both the Crown and the Church in Castile and abroad (Perea Rodríguez 2009, 176–182). In one of his most distinguished poems (ID1637, PN1-511 f. 165v-166r: "Loarvos querría en arte de trobas"), the cultivated Fray Diego praised a certain "Simuel Dios-Ayuda", a Jew living in Astorga, where he converted to Christianity and took the name of Garci Álvarez de León (Cantera Burgos 1967, 101–103; Beinart 1992, 359):

[I] Loarvos querría en arte de trobas,
señor Don Simuel, por vuestra nobleza
e non con infinta por sotileza
por que vos me dedes reales nin doblas,
sinon solamente por las vuestras obras
que son çimentadas en grant cortesía,
e contra natura de la judería
en todos los fechos levados soçobras.

[II] Bien vos nonbró Semuel Dios-Ayuda
paresçe que fue grant maestre talán,
pues todos los pobres de vos siempre han
merçed e consuelo e muy grant ayuda,
ca vuestra palabra jamás non se muda,
aquel que dezides yo te daré algo
estas son señales de omne fidalgo:
dezir e fazer las cosas sin dubda.

(Baena 1993, 355)

As we can see, the poem contains a sly allusion to the Jew as moneylender in v. 4, "por que vos me dedes reales nin doblas", if only to imply that the concept does not apply to Don Simuel after his conversion. Nevertheless, in another poem (ID1627, PN1-501 f. 162v: "Johan de España muy grant saña"), the very same friar of "encyclopedic knowledge" (Bahler and Gyékényesi Gatto 1992 171) shows himself to be no longer benevolent, for he attacks Juan de España, a converso in the city of León. Juan de España is often referred to as Juan el Viejo (Amador de los Ríos 1865, VI: 309–311), a well-known author of a controversial treatise against the Jewish creed entitled *Memorial de los misterios de Christo* (Santonja Hernández 2009, 186). Here, Fray Diego does not hesitate to display in all its alleged crudity the Jewish origin of his opponent:

[I] Johan de España, muy grant saña
fue aquesta de Adonay,
pues la aljama se derrama
por culpa de Barçelay.

[III] E los sabios del Talmud,
a que llaman cedaquín
dize que non ha salud
el que no tiene beçím;
antes tienen por roín
el que non trae milán
quien non puede bahelá
non le cumple matanay.

[II] Todos fuemos espantados
maestros, rabíes, cohenín,
ca les fueron sus pecados
d'este sofar ahením,
pues non tenié baçín
quiso infinta fazer;
hora finque por manzel
pues tan mal pertrecho tray.

(Baena 1993, 343)

This poem, with its adaptation of a good number of words from Hebrew to Castilian Spanish, demonstrates Fray Diego's mastery of the lexicon of the Talmud (Solá-Solé and Rose 1976, 377). This fact, along with similar intellectual ingenuities, has caused him to be suspected of being a converso, although there is no consensus on this suspicion (Cantera Burgos 1967, 97–103; Girón-Negrón 2002, 252–254). Nevertheless, his poems unquestionably highlight an important cultural phenomenon, since they offer literary proof of how culturally intimate social relations were between the inhabitants of the tri-religious Castile ("las íntimas relaciones que existían entre cristianos y judíos o conversos del judaísmo", Cantera Burgos 1967, 97). Furthermore, they bear witness to the previously mentioned attitude of *laissez faire* in Juan II's courtly circles, especially with respect to understanding the complex spiritual concepts of Christianity. Despite doubts of the sincerity of those who were forced to convert after 1391 (Orfali 1994, 121–123; Melammed 2004, 16), it seems evident that, at least in the royal court, good will was extended to the acculturation of neophytes to their 'new' spiritual coordinates (Perea Rodríguez 2009, 181). Nevertheless, most of these lyrical debates over religion occurred while legal circumstances were making daily life more difficult for Jews (Rodríguez Puértolas 1998, 189; Valdeón Baruque 2001, 147–148), not only because of the restrictive laws approved in 1412 (Baer 1966, 2, 439–441; Melammed 2004, 17; Bodian 2007, 10–11), but also because it was during this period that the Dominican preacher Vicente Ferrer "became an apologist for forced conversion" (Daileader 2016, 117) with his anti-Judaic sermons (Cátedra 1997, 23).

Precisely for this reason, the dialogues compiled by Baena in his *Cancionero* must be considered as evidence for the existence of a courtly counterweight to the increasing social pressure against Jews and conversos. At the court, a path seems to have been cleared for poetic instruction to all new coreligionists, reinforcing the propaedeutic sense of "el importante papel que en la corte de Juan II tienen los pasatiempos y, entre ellos, las disputas poéticas" (Chas Aguión 2001, 77). One must also note the experience Baena, as a royal scribe, had in copying the works of another supporter of the same *propaideia*, Ramon Llull (Nieto Cumplido 1979, 218; Díaz Marcilla 2015,

626–627), which might have inspired his selection of debates for a courtly environment that fostered social integration of conversos.

This essentially benevolent behavior toward 'New Christians' was based on the fact that, since "conversions were essentially forced", most conversos were "poorly educated in Christian doctrine" (Aronson-Friedman and Kaplan 2012, 3). The strategy seemed to be effective, given the "surprisingly rapid assimilation of early generations of conversos into Christian society" (Seidenspinner-Núñez 2000, 241). The success achieved at court occurred thanks to a concept that once defined many Jewish lives (Baer 1966, 2: 508; Gutwirth 2007, 6–15): "cameral servitude" (Abulafia 2000, 714), that is, the special status acquired by some Jews because of their delicate services rendered in favor of the monarchy (Roth 2019, 159). It is evident that the very same status was inherited by many conversos in the Trastamaran milieu of the early fifteenth century (Márquez Villanueva 2006f, 180–181), as in the cases of Davihuelo, the converso jester of Juan II (Cantera Burgos 1967, 94–95; Perea Rodríguez 2009, 264), and García Álvarez de Alarcón, a prominent participant in philosophical and theological debates (Perea Rodríguez 2009, 166–167). This scribe, born in Madrid, was not only an occasional poet, but he also exercised a certain amount of influence on the rabbis at the Tortosa Council of 1412 (Fraker 1966, 58–60; Beinart 1992, 347–348). This event, albeit considered a pinnacle of Jewish intellectual life during the fifteenth century (Sáenz-Badillos 2005, 264–267), also marked the beginning of the profound decline of Mosaic Law in the Iberian Peninsula (Baer 1966, 2: 443–501).

Nevertheless, while it is sometimes a very thin line that separates comedic teasing from anti-Jewish rants, let us remember that many 'Old Christian' poets composed their verses with what can only be considered Jewish nuances (Cantera Burgos 1967, 109–111). To point out just one example of such a mixture of these two apparently opposed realities, let us get back to Fray Diego de Valencia. This great master of theology, Hebrew, and other difficult subjects, nevertheless composed erotic love poetry (Taylor 2007, 238–240; Proia 2012, 116–124), such as his best-known *En un vergel deleitoso* (ID 1631, PN1-505 fol. 164r), considered among "las más desvergonzadas [poesías] del *Cancionero de Baena*" (Cantera Burgos 1967, 104). Completely imbued, however, with the pedagogical and intellectual climate encouraged at the royal court, Fray Diego took part in a serious debate on the nature of the Trinity (Hames 2009, 201). It has been argued that some contributors to the explanation of this Catholic dogma were conversos (Castro 1982, 543), on the grounds of the influence of certain texts on this subject written by Islamic converts, such as the *Tahlīth al-waḥdāniyyab* (*La trinidad de la unidad*) (Monferrer-Sala and Mantas-España 2018, 22–23). Others, however, have denied this (Asensio 1992, 95–96), or have at least expressed concerns regarding the assumption that such work on the Trinity, with "indication of a high degree of enclosure", could only be composed by a converso (Glick 1997, 67).

Returning to Fray Diego, it is no surprise that he dealt seriously with the complexity of the Trinity, one of Catholicism's most difficult dogmas (Dutton and Roncero López 2004, 30–31), as seen in his poem "Virgen Santa muy pura" (ID

1629, PN1-503 f.163v). What sets him apart is his ability to do so by means of a joke in the comic dialogue between himself and Nicolás de Valencia (ID 1610, PN1-485 ff. 158v-159r: "Maestro señor pues sodes perfeto"). Here, Fray Diego astonishes us with his talents in composing a perilous burlesque, bordering on blasphemy, of the dogma of the Immaculate Conception:

[I] Señor, nos avemos que muger casada
que tenga marido, maguera cuitado,
que biva con él muy desconsolada,
si quier' tomar a otro, que faze pecado;
e yo sobre esto tengo maginado
que non faz' pecado nin comete error,
pues que lo fizo Dios, Nuestro Señor,
al Santo Joseph, que era desposado.

(Baena 1993, 330)

After reading these verses, it is evident that only a strong sentiment of mutual trust among the Castilian monarchy, the 'Old Christians', and both Jews and conversos could have created a culture in which compositions like this could be composed and recited. Let us recall here that a ballad on a similar theme, the *Relación de los zelos de San Joseph de hombre*, was severely prosecuted by the Spanish Inquisition on the Canary Islands during the supposedly "enlightened" period of the eighteenth century (Trapero 2018, 116–121). This shows how Fray Diego and Nicolás de Valencia could perform their burlesque debate in a much more tolerant climate under the auspices of Juan II (Perea Rodríguez 2013a, 36–39).

The debate between these two cultivated monks is not an isolated case of Castilian troubadours skilled in theological controversy: Alfonso Álvarez de Villasandino, the great *joculator* of his era (Márquez Villanueva 2006f, 176), must also be included. He was not only the poet who perhaps provided the initial impetus for the compilation of the *Cancionero de Baena* (Garcia 1998, 50–52), but also a master of the poetic techniques of the old-fashioned Galician-Portuguese school (Dutton and Roncero López 2004, 26–27). Among his well-documented literary relationships with conversos (Cantera Burgos 1967, 88–89), the three poems featuring a certain Alfonso Fernández Samuel stand out (Márquez Villanueva 2006f, 178–179). In addition to describing the latter as "the most amusing crazy man the world ever saw" (Calvo Pérez 1998, 231), Villasandino's burlesque is key to understanding the type of jokes endured by those who converted to Christianity as adults because of social pressure (Mota 2012, 194; Beinart 1992, 358–359).

In the first poem of this series (ID 1280, PN1-140 f. 45r: "Pues no tengo qué fazer"), Villasandino offers an account of the converso's life that shows how those who renounced their ancestors' faith became "a target for ridicule" (Mota 2012, 194–195). From spiritual aspects to physiognomy, the idea seems to be quite clear: once Jewish, always Jewish (Valdeón Baruque 2000, 28–32):

[I] Pues no tengo qué fazer
ora con los contadores,
contar quiero tus dolores,
Alfonso, a quien bel ver.
Todos deven bien creer
que, quanto en aquesta hedat,
non naçió tal mesumad
nin creo que ha de nasçer.

[II] Ya passan de los sesenta
años malos que nasçiste
que cada día corriste
grant fortuna con tormenta,
resçibiendo çiertamente
de palos y bofetadas;
si padesçen tus quixadas,
tu nariz lo representa.

(Baena 1993, 164)

The final poem of this series is designated as Fernández Samuel's last will and testament (ID 1282, PN1-142 ff. 45v-46r: "Amigos quantos ovistes"). It is a frequently misunderstood burlesque (Alcalá Galve 2011, 250), in which Villasandino makes fun of his friend by portraying him as dead and buried with the sacred elements of all three religions of the book: a cross, a copy of the Qur'an, and a copy of the Torah. The poet displays a surprisingly sophisticated use of Jewish religious vocabulary, which has led some scholars to wonder if perhaps we are dealing with the typical case of a converso attempting to eliminate suspicions against him by mocking others (Cantera Burgos 1967, 88–97).

Other poets who were certainly not conversos also participated in these anti-Jewish writings, whose topoi most likely came from the wide arsenal of motifs and patterns of popular literature (Glaser 1954, 40–41; Pedrosa 2007, 33). Such is the case of the Castilian magnate Pero González de Mendoza, the grandfather of the marquis of Santillana, who proudly proclaims the social gulf between his illustrious ancestors and the Jewish ancestors of the conversos by accusing the latter of smelling bad, a pejorative identifier that persisted over the years despite its evident falsehood (Gómez-Bravo 2018a, 15–16). But, in the very same *Cancionero de Baena*, we can also see that a high-ranking member of converso society, the royal physician Moshe ben Abraham Zarzar (Fraker 1966, 9–34; Roth 2007, 747), could join – under equal conditions and without any sort of harassment – the poetic debates of 1405 on the occasion of the birth of Juan II (Perea Rodríguez 2009, 174). His finely polished piece of *cancionero* poetry completely fulfills the typical requirements of this intricate style (ID 0503, PN1-230 f. 74v: "Una estrella es nasçida"). Furthermore, it clearly gives the lie to the tragic and false legend of Enrique III having been poisoned by his physician (Baer 1966, 2: 537), popularized from 1458 on by Alonso de Espina in his *Fortalitium Fidei* (Beinart 1992, 362–364; Caro García 2009, 98–102).

In the process of analyzing the *Cancionero de Baena* as a source for the cultural history of Iberian Jews and conversos, we must constantly bear in mind that contradictions of this kind were habitual (Menéndez y Pelayo 1890, 2: 178–179). They lie at the origin of confused statements based on an excessively straightforward reading of poems found in Baena's compilation, extrapolating from an anachronistic perspective without taking into account the sociological factors of fifteenth-century Castile (Nirenberg 2009, 167–168). This sort of anachronism is reflected in the general tone of negative amusement characterizing Fraker's approach to the Iberian *cancioneros*

(1966, 28–32) and maintained even in more recent analysis of the subject (Gerli 1994, 24–25). It is also evident in the qualification of jokes and burlesques against conversos as "sangrientos y despiadados" (Cantera Burgos 1967, 89). They are quite the opposite, for they show that many conversos were absolutely engaged in all aspects of daily life at the court.

This latter point must be elaborated. The *Cancionero de Baena* only shows us an elite of conversos, and therefore "it would be unwise to lump together all these men in our minds without making proper distinctions" (Fraker 1966, 30). The mass conversions after 1391 seem to have affected the higher-ranking members of Castilian society very little, whether they were Jews or conversos (Domínguez Ortiz 1991, 10–11), who perhaps only converted in search of a more secure social position, as in the case of Pablo de Santa María. Conversos undeniably included mostly "minor businessmen, merchants, and artisans, the makers and sellers of small goods" (Gitlitz 1996, 74). But even considering the impossibility of imagining Iberian conversos as a "homogeneous group [. . .] structured fundamentally around binary oppositions" (Gerli 2007, 3), they were much more visible and engaged than they would be after the establishment of the Inquisition in Castile in 1480, when no one could be explicitly accused of having a Jewish origin without facing terrible consequences (Scholberg 1971, 345–347). Furthermore, let us not forget that under Juan II, both Jews and conversos – especially those of higher rank – joined together in the court milieu with 'Old Christians', at least during that ephemeral period of benevolence toward minorities reflected in the poetic debates of *Cancionero de Baena* (Beltran 2002, 257).

Two exceptions to this general statement occurred during the last few years of Juan II's reign: both the rebellion against the conversos at Toledo and the ensuing enactment of the *Sentencia-Estatuto* by Pero Sarmiento radically changed the cultural climate (Netanyahu 1995, 547–548; Márquez Villanueva 2006d, 45–49), as will be explained later. While the lack of instruction from the Catholic Church toward the 'New Christians' was perhaps the most evident barrier to the social integration of conversos (Rábade Obradó 1999, 377–389; Pastore 2010, 71–84), the *Cancionero de Baena* remains an invaluable testament to how the royal court of Castile partially remedied that same problem for some high-status conversos. Since contemporary poets in Hebrew "failed to find a form of their own for the new message" (Scheindlin 1997, 29), Baena's compilation shows a notable level of nuance coming, one way or another, from the cultural interaction between Jews and Christians.

Together with the *Cancionero de Baena*, the *Cancionero de Palacio* (Dutton SA7) is the most representative poetry collection of the first half of the fifteenth century (Tato García 2012, 301). Leaving aside the problem of the date of its compilation – from 1437 to 1442 (Dutton 1979, 446) – and the problematic conditions of its material (re)production (Beltran 2005, 30–31), in literary terms we find there an extensive and prolific panoply of love songs, corresponding to the moment of creative fulfillment of *cancionero* poetry (Alvar and Gómez Moreno 1988, 99–100). The collection is also proof of the categorical success of those "discreteos de la erótica cortesana" (Beltran 1988, 45), consciously rejected by Baena in favor of his personal preference for political, astrological, theological, and philosophical themes (Boase 1978, 93). Comparing the two compilations, *Palacio* shows how the more complex poetic performances, especially dialogues and debates, were gradually abandoned in the first half of the fifteenth century (Chas Aguión 2010, 154), a disheartening fact if we consider that most of them were thought to stimulate creativity among antagonists (Nirenberg 2006, 413–414).

The *Cancionero de Palacio* offers a different perspective on the poetry of the Trastamaran court. This compilation was put together within a cultural space in which arts, literature, and creativity thrived (Boase 1978, 69–73), as evidenced by the importance of the manuscript's pictorial ornamentations (Gerli 2018, 132). In addition, the poets here should be included in one political faction (Orella y Unzúe 1976, 469–471): that of Pedro, Juan, and Enrique, the Infantes de Aragón, the sons of King Fernando I of Aragon and therefore the cousins of Juan II, with extensive possessions in Castile (Beltran 2001b, 75–79; Tato García 2003, 496). The feud between them and Juan II's favorite, Álvaro de Luna, was the focus of Castilian political intrigue until Don Álvaro's execution in 1453 (Valdeón Baruque 2001, 126–144), and its influence even extended into poetry collections like this one.

There is no mention in *Palacio* of Jews, not even with burlesque nuances. The presence of conversos, on the other hand, deserves to be regarded from a different perspective than what has been defined as the courtly dynamics of social integration (Perea Rodríguez 2013a, 23), for a new cultural element was added to those physical spaces at the court in which conversos used to socialize ("espacios de sociabilidad conversa", Muñoz Solla 2017, 77). Thus, when *Palacio* was being compiled – toward the end of the third decade of the fifteenth century – social circumstances were favorable for both Jews and conversos (Baer 1966, 2: 529). This freed converso authors from the constraints of their 'split identities' (Yovel 2009, 23–25); absent such constraint, they could concentrate on the composition of clever examples of passionate love poetry through the sublimation of the theme to its highest level, as this occurred at the end of the Provençal era (Lewis 1992, 21–22).

In the *Cancionero de Baena*, not many poets participated in this kind of poetry, with the exception of the siblings Diego and Gonzalo Martínez de Medina (Perea Rodríguez 2009, 246–249), whose converso background is irrefutable (Montes Romero-Camacho 2014, 345). Yet their verses show no traces of the stereotypical converso features mentioned above (Chas Aguión and Díaz Prieto 2018, 78). However, if love poetry was merely incidental in *Baena*, most of the poets in *Palacio* practiced it assiduously, to the exclusion of other themes. It is remarkable that two of the most active participants in the political life of the period, Constable Álvaro de Luna and King Juan II, appear in the *Cancionero de Palacio* only as genteel courtiers, playing witty word games in a "social ritual of court life" (Garcia 1998, 53), with no reference to the contemporary political turmoil that surely affected them (Boase 1978, 91–92).

Interspersed among those of many other members of the high nobility and the urban aristocracy, the converso voices in the *Cancionero de Palacio* are completely imbued with the literary fashion of love poetry. This is true, for instance, of García de Medina, a scribe and notary public associated with the literary court of Íñigo López de Mendoza, Marquis of Santillana (Perea Rodríguez 2013a, 43), who himself had a profound knowledge of Jewish topoi, as displayed by the use of the Ezekiel prophecies in his own poetry (Girón Negrón 2000, 165–168). In addition, Santillana was a steadfast patron of converso authors, especially in his birthplace, Carrión de los Condes, which contained a remarkable medieval *judería* (Gómez Moreno 2001, 84–86). García de Medina has only four poems in *Palacio*, but they are all inscribed within this privileged cultural environment and show the poet's affinity for the old Galician-Portuguese style (Álvarez Pellitero 1993, 181).

Juan Agraz is another converso poet clearly identified as such (Márquez Villanueva 2006f, 189), although not for his poems in the *Cancionero de Palacio*. He had already been noted as a converso in a poem by Juan Alfonso de Baena in defense of another obscure character, Juan Marmolejo (ID 6767 11CG-1026, f. 232v-233v: "Poderoso dominable"). Since that eliminate, Agraz became one of the 'usual suspects' in the anti-Jewish debates of the *cancioneros* (Scholberg 1971, 282; Perea Rodríguez 2015, 162–168). Despite this, his poem in *Palacio* shows no signs of that identification:

[I] En casa del Rey d'Espanya
do victoria Dios otorga,
a su muy noble conpanya
por el conde de Mayorga.

[II] Yo, el conde sin ventura,
vos saludo en Ihesu Cristo.
Ya sabedes que me visto
túnica de tierra pura
do jamás seré enbuelto;
a esi mundo non buelto
ninguno puede ser suelto
de que viene a tal clausura.

(Álvarez Pellitero 1993, 132–133)

Two more of the *Palacio* poets have been frequently identified as conversos. The first is Pedro de Santa Fe, whose *cancionero* is often considered the nucleus of the *Cancionero de Palacio* (Tato García 1999, 132–147). He shares a surname with the polemicist Jerónimo de Santa Fe, or Joshua Halorki in Hebrew (Beinart 1992, 347), who was one of the participants in the controversial Tortosa dispute of 1412 (Rodríguez Puértolas 1998, 189) and the author of *Hebraeo Mastix*, among many other anti-Jewish writings (Alba and Sáinz de la Maza 2011, 261–263). However, it seems unlikely that these two, despite the common surname, had any family connection (Tato García 2004, 18), a statement that can likewise be applied to the various poets surnamed 'Montoro', whose relationship with Antón Montoro 'el Ropero' have been generally discredited (Tato García 1998, 181–182).

The second poet is Juan de Torres, whose biography (Salvador Miguel 1977, 231–232; Mosquera Novoa 2016, 3–7) is especially marked by his role as Prince Enrique's agent during the 1449 uprising in Toledo (Vendrell 1945, 55). A personal relationship with Álvaro de Luna may be conjectured as well, precisely because of his participation in the *Cancionero de Palacio* (Haywood 2009, 48; Mosquera Novoa 2018, 237–238), a fact that reflects the remarkable protection Don Álvaro afforded to both Jews and conversos (Castro 1970, 79; Roth 2002, 89).

The problem in considering Santa Fe, Torres, and many others as converso poets lies in the fact that the topics they deal with are far away from those that have been perceived as typical of the "peculiaridad literaria de los conversos" (Asensio 1992, 89). Some scholars have misunderstood Castro's theoretical frame (Surtz 1995, 547), deriving from it a one-dimensional literary style valid for all converso authors: the writer burdened by a storm-tossed soul, constantly caught between the Scylla of his Jewish origins and the Charybdis of his status as a 'New Christian', who willy-nilly projects this vital tension in every one of his works. As obvious as it seems, it is important to emphasize that there is no "integral and univocal identity for the conversos" (Benito 2012, 45), nor is there only one converso way of writing ("una forma conversa de escribir", Round 1995, 557). The complexity of converso identity cannot be reduced to a monotone cliché in which they all are "portrayed as constantly threatened, marginalized and living under a specter of shame or abjection" (Gerli 2007, 3).

These considerations make *Palacio* an essential *cancionero* for the problem of converso identity, for it shows a model diametrically opposed to that of poets suffering from a tormented spirituality: it shows them completely integrated into a society in which their intellectual efforts would become crucial for the transformation of Humanism into the indispensable pillar of fifteenth-century Castilian culture (Kaplan 1996, 64–65). This supposed normality was surely behind the enormous success achieved by the converso poet *par excellence*: Juan de Mena. The great Cordovan troubadour not only had Jewish ancestors (Rohland de Langbehn 1998, 210–211; Roth 2002, 176–177), but was also protected, tellingly, by Álvaro de Luna during his years as chronicler and Latin secretary to Juan II (Tate 1986, 664–667; Roth 2007, 524–528). Despite this, many scholars have categorically rejected his converso origin (Salvador Miguel 1977, 148; Asensio 1967, 344–352; 1992, 90–96), arguing against it on a variety of cultural grounds (see discussion in Perea Rodríguez 2015, 161–162). The problem here is that Mena does not fit into either of the two habitual converso molds (Scholberg 1971, 235): he never stooped to parody as Antón de Montoro did, nor was he a misanthropic bel esprit, like Juan Álvarez Gato. There are no traces in his works of anything but an ordinary desire to achieve social status derived from the success of his works. For a converso, however, such a goal was only possible under the social shelter provided by a strong monarchy. That is precisely the purpose of Mena's masterpiece: the *Laberinto de fortuna*, o *Las Trescientas* (ID 0092, NH5-1 fols. 1r-42v: "Al muy prepotente don Juan el segundo"), the supreme example of how the elite group of conversos wanted the Trastamaran crown to be as strong as possible (Bermejo Cabrero 1973, 158). Only by achieving that goal were they able to circumvent the two antagonistic cultural types reserved for conversos, the witty joker and the troubled-soul writer, inaugurating instead a third one: the builder of a well-polished Castilian early Humanism, characterized by the maximum sublimation of love poetry in the royal milieu.

4 *Cancioneros* under the Reign of Enrique IV: A Hidden Reality Beneath the Cliché

Since Castilian *cancioneros* by far outweigh the lyric production of the rest of the Iberian Peninsula, I shall focus on them. However, this Castile-centered narrative does not imply the complete omission of compilations produced in the other Iberian kingdoms and, indeed, outside of Iberia. I shall omit only one category: medieval poetry on Jews and conversos written in Catalan. This literary tradition has been satisfactorily analyzed, from nuptial Jewish songs, *cants de noces* (Riera i Sans 1974, 8–10), to Hispano-Jewish liturgical chants (Díaz Esteban 1976, 167–171). We also know a good deal about the Valencian satirical *cançoner* (Martínez Romero 2010, 16–18), which includes quite a few witty but unmerciful burlesques against conversos. These were so cruel that St. Vicent Ferrer himself, in one of his most famous sermons (III 70, 20–32), condemned 'Old Christians' who dared to mock those "que·ls dien *retallat*" (Ysern i Lagarda 2003, 92). Spatial limitations compel me to omit this fascinating subject, which includes topics as interesting as the fact that *retallat*, one of the Catalan terms for conversos, is an uncouth and pejorative reference to circumcision.

The *Cancioneros* of this era shared a key continuity with the earlier ones: they still reflect a literature seriously influenced by the court, the hegemonic space for the flourishing of cultural activities and performances (Perea Rodríguez 2007c, 289–290). This is perfectly exemplified by the *Cancionero de Estúñiga* (Dutton MN54). Produced in Italy between 1442 and 1460 (Salvador Miguel 1977, 30–32), it contains an interesting blend of Aragonese and Castilian elements, uniting the works of a few poets born and raised in Aragon with those of a greater number of Castilian knights who had sided with the Infantes de Aragón in the earlier civil conflict (Valdeón Baruque 2001, 133–134). After being defeated by Álvaro de Luna and his supporters in the battle of Olmedo (1445), those knights fled to the service of the Infantes' brother, King Alfonso V the Magnanimous (Boase 1978, 94–100), whose Neapolitan court "ayudó y favoreció los poetas todos y hombres de letras que, en sus tiempos, por toda Italia y Sicilia se hallavan" (Marineo Siculo 2003, 87).

Leaving aside Juan de Mena, other poets included in the *Cancionero de Estúñiga* have been considered to be conversos, such as Pedro del Castillo, who was appointed by the Cartagena lineage as confidant between the family and the king of Castile (Salvador Miguel 1977, 77–78). Another one, indubitably a converso, is the well-known *mosén* Diego de Valera (Márquez Villanueva 2006e, 140) – son of Hernán Alfonso Chirino, the converso physician of King Juan II – whose poems here deal exclusively with love, particularly unrequited love, as befits the years he spent in Italy (Alvar 1998, 9). Perhaps the most important converso in *Estúñiga*, however, is Alfonso de la Torre, whose *Visión deleytable* is considered both a masterpiece of medieval thought, in line with the encyclopedic tradition of his era (Farcasiu 1992, 79), and a "shining testimony of semi-clandestine teaching of philosophy carried out in the shadows of the *aljamas*" (Márquez Villanueva 2000, 18). The problem is that none of the controversial ideas treated in the *Visión deleytable*, such as the references to unbelief (Girón Negrón 2009, 90–93), can be found in his *Estúñiga* poems. This is identical to the case of Fernando de la Torre, often identified as converso (Castro 1982, 87; Roth 2002, 102–103), but whose best-known poem is a perfect example of medieval courtly entertainment (Salvador Miguel 1987, 471–496). His *Juego de naipes* (ID 0594, MN54-96 f. 117r-124r: "Magnificencia y virtud") is based on an ingenious literary love conceit (Marino 2006, 212), following the fashion of the Neapolitan court (Beltran 2011, 412).

Another *cancionero* compiled outside of Castilian territory and closely related to the Navarre-Aragonese archetype of textual transmission (Beltran 2005, 44–45) is the *Cancionero de Herberay* (Dutton LB2), named for its owner, Nicolas Herberay des Essarts (†1552), a renowned French translator of Spanish literary works during the reign of François I (Boase 1978, 100–101). This *cancionero* captures the literary court of John I, King of Navarra, and the Queen regnant, his daughter Leonor ("cour litteraire de Juan, roi de Navarre, et de Leonor [sa fille], comtesse de Foix, regente", Aubrun 1951, XXXI), as well as the two wives of Juan I, Infante of Aragon (later Juan II of Aragon), Blanche of Navarre and Juana Enríquez. Between 1450 and1462, these three women and the first Trastámara to be crowned king of Navarre, together with his later disinherited heir, Prince Carlos of Viana, constituted the magnificent five of that courtly milieu ("las cinco figuras fundamentales en aquella corte", Conde Solares 2009, 8).

In *Herberay*, the only writer who is clearly converso is Juan Poeta (Roth 2007, 734), or Juan de Valladolid (Rubio González 1983–1984, 101–112), recognizable as such by his participation in polemic debates (Kaplan 2002, 40–57; Márquez Villanueva 2006f, 191–192). Even though he would eventually become the general model for the fierce mockery of crypto-Jewish poets (Perea Rodríguez 2015, 159–160), the only two of his poems included in *Herberay* (Aubrun 1951, 88) reflect his life in Naples, Mantua, and Milan (Menéndez Pidal 1991 [1924], 413–420) and therefore have little to do with his spiritual and social condition. The fact that *Herberay* shares quite a few poems with the *Cancionero de Palacio* is also representative of the cultural dominance of Castilian *cancionero* poetry throughout the Iberian Peninsula (Tato García 2003, 503–504). Indeed, in its pages we observe a victorious parade of lyrics glorifying love above all other subjects: "poemas de autores de casi todas las cortes ibéricas" seasoned by an "evidente prurito humanista, italianizante, y de defensa y elogio de las mujeres" (Conde Solares 2009, 1).

It is time now to return to Castile and to point out that those *cancioneros* produced during the reign of Enrique IV (1454–1474) have barely been studied. Only recently has some focus been turned to the in-depth exploration of the relevant manuscripts and the study of the most significant poets of that reign. For instance, the 14 poems and other texts of the *Cancionero de Salvá* (Dutton PN13), written by the practically unknown troubadour Gómez de Rojas, have remained in obscurity until very recently (Tomassetti 2018a, 172–175). This neglect is more difficult to understand given the fact that the poetic production of this era offsets the habitual – albeit mistaken – perception of this reign as a chaotic period in the history of Iberia

(Phillips 1978, 15–16). The *cancioneros enriqueños* show just the opposite: the remarkable reputation of Enrique IV, at least during the first decade of his reign (Suárez Fernández 2001, 132–148). There is, however, something more interesting for our general purpose: the fact that Enrique IV's prestige was popularized in poems composed by a group of poets in which conversos stood out: Diego de León, Pablo de Santa María, Pero Guillén de Segovia, and Ferrando Filipo de Escobar (Perea Rodríguez 2005, 41–58).

The present survey of these collections must begin with the *Cancionero de San Román* (Dutton MH1), compiled around 1454 (Deyermond 1982, 199) and once considered to be a second *Cancionero de Baena* (Dutton 1979, 448). These two share a rich textual tradition because they emerge from similar milieus (Proia 2018, 195–200), despite quite different poetical tastes (Weiss 1990, 45). Thus, the first poem in *San Román* is a significant sign of how the willingness to foster religious acculturation of neophytes at court had already disappeared. It is a curious *imitatio* of the very well-known *Coplas de la Gala* (ID 0141, MH1-254 ff. 372v-373r: "Non teniendo que perder"), composed by Suero de Ribera. This successful Castilian poet spent several years, from 1446 onward (Periñán 1968, 20–138), at the court of Alfonso V of Aragon (Salvador Miguel 1977, 185–188). Ribera's *Coplas de la Gala* is a refined literary text, embroidered with irony, that describes an ideal prototype of life for the gallant courtier (Scholberg 1971, 292). These are immediately followed in *San Román* by another poem (ID 0517, MH1-255 f. 373r-374v: "Contra la regla galana"), habitually attributed to Ribera as well (Scholberg 1971, 348–349; Kaplan 2012, 24–25), although it seems much more likely to be an anonymous parody of his *Coplas de la Gala* (Chas Aguión 2009, 143–144). In fact, this satirical *contrafactum* is a fiery tirade against those in the Trastamaran milieu who acted as fine courtiers despite converso origins, practices, and physiognomy:

[I] Contra la regla galana
que fize por dar dotrina,
qualquier persona malina
- que de contiendas ha gana -
replicó por arte vana,
pensando que me olvidé
otro estilo que yo sé
de gente bien cortesana.

[II] El galán, crespo e travado,
ha de ser - segunt apruevo -,
grant sabidor de renuevo,
mançebo çircunçidado
e con maliçias osado;
presumir que nunca peca,
con azeite - e non manteca -
sienpre comer adobado.

[III] El galán convién que tenga
la nariz luenga e bermeja,
la pluma tras el oreja,
arte de que se mantenga;
non curar de grant arenga
por fazer de su provecho,
al través e al derecho,
de qualquier parte que venga.

[IV] Sepan por qüalquier vía
el galán, día e noche,
diestro sin ningunt reproche
en todas mercadorías;
e, con grant sabidoría,
non dar nada sin misterio,
e ser, con gran vitoperio,
debdo de Santa María.

[V] El que fuere tal galán
del solar de la sinoga
fará muy alta la boga
sin levar menos afán;
bien creo se fallarán
algunos tales agora;
si los tienpos así van
a serviçio de la Tora,
si el fecho non se mejora.

(Perea Rodríguez 2011a, 188–189)

Here, as in the contemporary satirical *Carta-privilegio que Juan II dio a un fijodalgo* (Carpenter 2012, 297–298; González Rolán and Saquero Suárez-Somonte 2012, XCIII), the Iberian *cancioneros* exhibit for the first time the archetypical and wounding accusations based on aspects of "judaísmo sociológico" (Represa Rodríguez 1987, 34), such as being circumcised, operating moneylenders, following *kashrut*, having a different physiognomy, reciting the Torah and attending synagogue, being related to powerful converso families, and many more (Glaser 1954, 50–51; Beinart 1992, 357). This latter indictment constitutes the most polemic aspect of the converso reputation: the alleged power achieved during the reigns of Juan II and Enrique IV (Márquez Villanueva 1965, 318–319). Consequently, this poem should be considered a milestone in the process by which "poetry ceased to be, for converso and Old Christian alike, a place in which hermeneutic good faith could be proven" (Nirenberg 2006, 423).

Another significant example of how the Iberian *cancioneros* reflected the social and political changes that occurred after the 1449 Toledo revolt stems from Juan de Dueñas. His poetry can be found in three *cancioneros*, *Palacio*, *Estúñiga*, and *San Román*; but in the first two he appears as a young troubadour, interested solely in showing how skilled he was in the art of courtly love. These poems were probably composed before he sided with the Infantes de Aragón, for which he was exiled to Italy and incarcerated there at least until 1439, when he returned to the Iberian Peninsula (Marino 1985, 140–151). In the later *San Román*, on the other hand, the anonymous compiler selected more political poems, including those of Diego de Valera as well as Dueñas (Tomassetti 2018b, 79–80; Tato García 2010, 224), who proved to be a master of the controversial topos of the "sexualized Jewish woman" (Aizenberg 1984, 187) by praising a "Fermosa gentil judía" in one of his poems (ID 0476, MH-1 211, f. 352v). Dueñas was also the author of what can be seen as the very first real attack, based on social conflict, against conversos in the medieval Iberian literatures (ID 0457, MH1-191, ff. 346r-346v: "Alto rey más poderoso"):

[VI] Que ya tal es la costunbre
de tu reino, señor rey,
pues que peresçe la ley
y faz eclisi la lunbre,
y los valles que solía,

[VII] Esto digo porque veo
muchos viles prosperar
y otros que, sin errar,
biven sienpre con deseo;
y quando los tales prosperan,

si más creçe esta porfía,	los buenos se desesperan
luego querrán a la cunbre.	y aun a Dios pareçe feo.
[VIII] Y por esto, señor fuerte,	[IX] Antes, señor, devés dar
no devrías consentir	muy grand parte de tus algos
a los tales reçebir	a muchos pobre fidalgos
merçed ni bienes en suerte,	que en tu reino veo andar;
¡quánto más a los conversos,	que, señor, devés creer
de los buenos más adversos	que, al tienpo del menester,
que la vida de la muerte!	estos te án de aprovechar.

(Perea Rodríguez 2011a, 186–187)

This poem, as critics have noted, shows the opposition of some members of the Castilian aristocracy to Álvaro de Luna's policies in favor of the conversos (Vendrell 1958, 109–110; Kaplan 2002, 19–20). Dueñas urges Juan II to reject the converso bureaucrats at the royal chancery ("los burócratas conversos de la cancillería real", Scholberg 1971, 349), rewarding nobility instead, for only they were trustworthy ("los pobres hidalgos, únicas personas en quienes cabía sustentar su confianza", Salvador Miguel 1977, 80). Moreover, the poem clearly shows the profound "resentment of the social advancement and financial prosperity enjoyed by some conversos, and the perception that conversos, as agents of the monarchy, were responsible for economic crises" (Aronson-Friedman and Kaplan 2012, 3–4). Since this poem and others written by Dueñas were composed after the future Enrique IV entered Toledo in 1449 (Perea Rodríguez 2011a, 187–188), it seems acceptable to consider them as proof in verse of the events that occurred then when conversos had already "started to irritate the proletarian masses" (Márquez Villanueva 1965, 318) and the social turmoil was utilized by Álvaro de Luna's political opponents to root out any sort of social tolerance from the royal milieu.

The Toledo rebellion and its aftermath have been suitably treated in the historiographical literature (Benito Ruano 2001, 41–140; Amran 2012, 196–201), and most of its consequences relating to the cultures of the Iberian Peninsula have also been examined, including those affecting the *cancioneros* (Nirenberg 2006, 422–426; Kaplan 2012, 25–32). Yet some aspects remain to be clarified, for they are ensnared in the habitual negative depiction of both Enrique IV and his reign.

There is no doubt that the 1449 *Sentencia-Estatuto* of Pero Sarmiento, emanating from the uprising against Juan II, marked an early precedent for the place which the concept of 'blood purity' would occupy in the following centuries (Yovel 2009, 74; Hernández Franco 2011, 25–27; Kaplan 2012, 34–35). Because of a regrettable conjunction of political and economic factors (Kaplan 2012, 26–27), the *Sentencia-Estatuto* gave rise to one particularly unfortunate consequence: the normalization of anti-Jewish propaganda in political discourse, used as it was during the civil war (Suárez Fernández 2001, 86; González Rolán and Saquero Suárez-Somonte 2012, XXIV–XXV). The popular wrath crystallized against Álvaro de Luna because of the support he provided to both Jews and conversos (Netanyahu 1995, 237–238). In the *Crónica del Halconero*, he is made responsible for the good health and greater wealth of "infieles e herejes, e han judaizado e judaizan, e han guardado e guardan los más de ellos los ritos e ceremonias de los judíos" (Carrillo de Huete 2006, 523). The general setback caused by Luna's economic policies greatly affected daily life in Toledo, as popular discontent reached the "genealogical turn" (Nirenberg 2009, 250) that caused further social restrictions on the conversos (Vidal Doval 2013, 232–233). However, it is difficult to accept that this development was due to what today we would call racial discrimination (Kaplan 2012, 26), despite recent arguments to that effect (Nirenberg 2009, 260–261).

All of these factors greatly benefited the prince of Asturias, as is noticeable in the letter in which the rebels urged Juan II to "llamar al illustrísimo príncipe don Enrique, vuestro fijo primogénito" (Carrillo de Huete 2006, 526). Enrique's triumph in 1449 was therefore resounding, for he cleverly succeeded in arbitrating the confused quarrel between his father and the Toledo rebels (Perea Rodríguez 2011a, 190–193). Nevertheless, the perceptive young prince has not received historiographical credit for this. On the contrary, his actions have often been labeled as treason toward his father (Benito Ruano 1961, 13–31), as a ludicrous attempt to reward one of the king's favorites (Suárez Fernández 2001, 98–99), or even as mere personal ambition (Pastore 2010, 40; González Rolán and Saquero Suárez-Somonte 2012, LXXXII–LXXXIII). The habitual bias against Enrique IV is the only barrier preventing the acknowledgment of his actions as the masterful political maneuver they were, because he did square the circle: working in favor of the conversos while at the same time playing the role of 'Old Christian' standard-bearer (Perea Rodríguez 2011a, 190–191).

This latter assertion is proven by Enrique's presence in the *Cancionero de Vindel* (Dutton NH2), a collection of courtly amusements with a clear preponderancy of love poetry that demonstrates continuity between the court of Juan II and that of his son (Ramírez de Arellano y Lynch 1976, 36). However, *Vindel* also includes several disturbing anti-Jewish lampoons. The first, addressed to the king, is ascribed to an unknown poet known only as Furtado (ID 2388, NH2-79, 253–259: "Noble rey cuya potencia"), who mocks Mosén Lope, a jester or 'albardán', at the court of Alfonso el Magnánimo. Furtado did not mince words in disparaging Jewish customs, alleged physiognomy, and the circumcision of Mosén Lope, thus creating a hurtful literary template used time and again against converso jesters (Márquez Villanueva 2006f, 165):

[IV] ¿Veislo bien allá do'stá?
¡Si supiéssedes quién es!
Del linage de Judá,
sobrino de Banzabá,
del tribo de Manazés;
y maguer grave vos sea
de creher, mas bien es visto
que lo suyos en Judea
poblaron a Galilea,
¡parientes de Jesucristo!

[V] Y maguer que sin sentido
sus abuelos lo mataron,
vive bien arrepentido
por el tiempo qu'á perdido,
do crestianos l'enganyaron.
[............................]
Mas pochos día van atrás
qu'en secreto non adora
los *sus* cantos de la Tora,
con los libros de Humás.

[VI] Los ojos, puestos en trote,
la cara, suzia, humada,
las caxadas son d'escote,
la verga, sin capirote
la gracia, toda prestada.
Bien catada la figura,
segund vistes, he sus modos
de la fea catadura
que le puso la Natura,
non, por cierto, de los godos.

[VII] Respondiome el mensagero,
fatigado del viaje:
«Pues assí queréis, yo quiero
del presente cavallero
recontaros su linage:
desciende de Benjamín,
segund su cara designa;
son sus vicios, a la fin,
comer bien de un amín,
descorxar un'adefina.

(Ramírez de Arellano y Lynch 1976, 126–127)

More importantly, as other scholars have previously noted, *Vindel* shows us the future Enrique IV completely involved in this climate of converso mockery. In a poem attributed to him (ID 2354, NH-22, 113: "Mala pasqua vos do [sic] Dios"), the Prince of Asturias seems to take delight in deriding Juan Poeta for his circumcision (Perea Rodríguez 2007b, 157):

[I] ¡Mala pasqüa vos *dé* Dios
con vuestra lengua prolixa!
Pues havés vestido vos,
¿por qué no vestís la pixa?

(Ramírez de Arellano y Lynch 1976, 55)

This latter poem is essential to understanding the consolidation of Enrique IV's political path: he was playing the card of mocking conversos at court, while defending them outside of the palace walls. Furthermore, this point provides us with a useful bridge in attempting to explain how the depiction of the Toledo rebellion has been manipulated to portray Enrique IV's reign as a disaster in general (Alcalá Galve 2011, 249), but especially for both Jews and conversos (Mackay 1972, 57; Netanyahu 2000, 552–553). In fact, nothing could be farther from the truth than this sclerotic exaggeration, whose constant repetition has turned it into a historiographical cliché (Whinnom 1973, 22). Impartial data has never supported Enrique IV's "catastrophic political reputation [. . .] which has largely resulted from the rewriting of history by chroniclers under the regime of Fernando and Isabel" (Edwards 1992, 221). Quite the opposite was true, at least during the first ten years of Enrique's reign. Like Pedro I, Enrique IV had a number of Jewish counselors, such as Abraham Seneor, rabbi Jacob ibn Núñez, rabbi Simuel (Perea Rodríguez 2007b, 155–156), and especially Yosef ben Semtob, who was sent as ambassador to Portugal with full responsibility for arranging the king's own marriage to princess Joana (Baer 1966, 2: 508). In addition, his government was in large part dependent on the mutually beneficial alliance with conversos (Seidenspinner-Núñez 2000, 247), which accounts for the fact that poems in praise of the king were composed mostly by them.

The future king gladly accepted the support of his own mentor, the converso Alonso de Cartagena, who attacked Sarmiento's libelous *Sentencia-Estatuto* (Fernández Gallardo 2002, 76; Netanyahu 2000, 557–558), drawing on his profound knowledge of the theological aspects of the controversy (Rosenstock 2012, 118–119). Cartagena's was the most important voice in the literary outburst that followed the Toledo conflict (Giordano 2018, 227), and he was surely the architect of the argument that focused on the unity of all Christians, regardless of their origins, as a cornerstone of the defense of the conversos (Benito Ruano 2001, 26–28; Kaplan 2002, 20–27; Pastore 2010, 43–74). Among the many texts produced on this topic (Kaplan 2012, 31–32; González Rolán and Saquero Suárez-Somonte 2012, XXXV–XXXVII), Fray Alonso de Oropesa's *Lumen ad revelationem gentium* stands out (Castro 1970, 90–95; Kriegel 1997, 13–14). It advocates a rational response on behalf of those falsely accused of being 'crypto-Jews' by their envious neighbors (Ropero Berzosa 2018, 491–495). In addition, the *Instrucción del Relator*, by the converso Fernando Díaz de Toledo – royal notary, chief administrator of the Royal Council, and ally of Álvaro de Luna – holds a privileged position in this apologetic literature written in defense of 'New Christians' (González Rolán and Saquero Suárez-Somonte 2012, CVIII–CXII). Nor should we forget that Alonso de Cartagena's theological arguments may even have inspired the fine arts, as has been recently argued regarding Jan Van Eyck and his notable *Fuente de la Gracia* (Parada López de Corselas and Folgado García 2017, 18–19).

A significant step in the relation between the future Enrique IV and the conversos was taken when Juan II regained Toledo in 1451, because this entailed partial acceptance of some of the rebel claims (Benito Ruano 2001, 29), especially the controversial decision to deprive conversos of their offices in the city council (Valdeón Baruque 1995, 79). Four years later, Enrique IV, now king, reversed that decision in sympathy with the numerous conversos who had held such essential administrative positions in urban political environments (Márquez Villanueva 2006e, 144–145). Furthermore, the king wished to be crowned as 'emperor of the three religions' (Perea Rodríguez 2007b, 144–146), distancing himself from his father's policies that treated all conversos as 'crypto-Jews' (Netanyahu 1995, 716).

The *Cancionero del Conde de Haro* (Dutton GB1) is the most representative poetry collection of Enrique IV's reign. Although compiled in Castile, it shares some literary peculiarities with *Estúñiga* and the other Spanish *cancioneros* inspired by Italian cultural trends, such as the *Cancionero de Roma* (Dutton RC1) and the *Cancionero de Venecia* (Dutton VM1). The manuscript takes its name from Pedro Fernández de Velasco, first Count of Haro (Perea Rodríguez 2014, 108), known as 'el buen conde de Haro' and famous today as the owner of an impressive example of a noble library (Perea Rodríguez 2007a, 80–81). However, this *cancionero* was only completed by his son, the homonymous Pedro Fernández de Velasco, 2nd Count since 1470, and first member of the Fernández de Velasco family to be appointed Constable of Castile three years later (Franco Silva 2006, 13–79). These two members of Spain's highest nobility cooperated with Jews and conversos in the creation of cultural splendor

(Perea Rodríguez 2007a, 93–96), a wonder witnessed and described by an unexpected guest: Leo of Rozmital, a Bohemian pilgrim who visited Castile in 1466 (Boase 1978, 107–110). He describes how Jews, Muslims, and Christians lived together in harmony at the court of the 1st Count of Haro, because the latter allowed "each one to his own belief" (Rozmitála a Blatné 1957, 78). Furthermore, Rozmital underscored that the Count "is said to be a Christian, but no one knows what his belief is" (Rozmitála a Blatné 1957, 78).

The way in which people of different creeds lived together, which so greatly surprised Rozmital, is reflected in the *Cancionero del Conde de Haro*. Christian religious poetry is represented by Fernán Pérez de Guzmán, the Marquis of Santillana, Juan de Dueñas, and Gómez Manrique (Zinato 2001, 217). Yet the moral and religious tone of this *cancionero* allowed not only for political praise of Enrique IV – such as that by Escobar mentioned below – but also for popular ballads and *romances* more inclined to wisdom than to love (Dumanoir 2004, 80–83). Some converso authors can also be found, especially the great Juan de Mena, together with the relatively unknown Diego del Castillo (Perea Rodríguez 2007a, 56–61) and the enigmatic Juan Agraz. The latter was often attacked as a 'crypto-Jew' by other poets (Yovel 1998, 4–6), especially by Juan Marmolejo (Tosar López 2015, 1159), but all that we know of his life is that he was raised in Albacete and participated in the cultural circle of the second Count of Niebla, Enrique de Guzmán (Márquez Villanueva 1982, 400–401). However, since this *cancionero* is yet to be published, further information it may contain in relation to conversos remains to be analyzed in detail.

Another poetry collection worthy of attention is the *Cancionero de Martínez de Burgos* (Dutton MN33), compiled around 1464 in Burgos, the so-called *caput Castellae*, by Juan and Fernán Martínez de Burgos (Perea Rodríguez 2011a, 192–193). The latter are suspected of being conversos on the basis of allusions to the 'Old Law' and to 'David the Psalmist' in the prologue (Severin 1976, 14–16). In addition, the cancionero includes a composition entitled *Proverbios en rimo del sabio Salamón, Rey de Israel* (ID3663, MN33-12 fols. 92r-93v: "Amigos si queredes oír una razón"), in which aspects of Jewish cultural history are clearly traceable (Moreno Hernández 2008, 35–37). A comparable assessment can be made of the *Cancionero de Otte Brahe*, held by the Royal Library of Denmark and unknown to Dutton (Ortiz Hernández 2007, 48–49), but surely compiled during the reign of Enrique IV. As in the case of the *Cancionero del Conde de Haro*, Fernán Pérez de Guzmán and Juan de Mena are the authors of 23 of its 28 poems (Díez Garretas 2009, 384), but further analysis of the text is needed in order to assess the evidence of its possible converso sensibility.

A common trait of the *cancioneros enriqueños* is the perception that conversos lacked "a unified social reality, but [were] rather a group of heterogeneous, protean human beings whose practices, beliefs and circumstances could vary significantly" (Gerli 2007, 4). During the first decade of Enrique IV's reign, conversos enjoyed social stability and some, such as Fernando Felipe de Escobar, Pedro de León, and the anonymous continuator of Santa María's *Siete Edades del Mundo*, composed highly propagandistic poems to extol the king's virtues (Perea Rodríguez 2007b, 145–158). The most representative case is that of Pedro de León – Fray Luis de León's ancestor – who, employing messianism as a rhetorical tool, dared to prophesy that Enrique IV was the chosen one who would conquer Jerusalem (Perea Rodríguez 2005, 51–71). It is no coincidence that these poems were composed shortly after the fall of Constantinople to the Ottoman Turks, when continental Europe was shaken by rumors of growing efforts allegedly made by 'crypto-Jews' to 'Judaize' it (Lawee 2012, 353–354; Beinart 1992, 368). As a consequence of this environment, Castile was agitated around 1464 owing to Abraham ibn Ezra's calculations concerning the coming of the Messiah (Gutwirth 1995, 204; Carrete Parrondo 2000, 484–485), which served as the background for a diverse panoply of converso writings (Meyuhas Ginio 1989, 221).

These facts are important in order to underscore that converso poets in Castile did not first begin to use messianism to praise Queen Isabel and King Fernando (Kaplan 2002, 27); on the contrary, they had already used it in abundance in other panegyrics written between 1460 and 1475 (Castro 1970, 21–30; Alcoberro 2018, 78). In addition, the use of messianism as a literary device ran parallel to the emergence of another crucial propagandistic resource: Castilian neo-gothicism (Seidenspinner-Núñez 2000, 242–244). As one might expect, Alonso de Cartagena, in both his *Anacephaleosis* and his *Defensorium*, took responsibility for establishing this key notion in contemporary political ideology: the continuity of the Crown of Castile between the Visigoths and the Trastámaras (Kaplan 2002, 58–63). This concept rapidly became the backbone of Trastamaran propaganda (Villa Prieto 2010, 130–133), thus allowing converso "historiología a lo divino" (Tate 1970, 227) to become a specific feature of Castilian literature long before the advent of the Catholic Monarchs (Nieto Soria 1993, 245–246). But this fact notwithstanding, Isabel and Fernando eventually benefited more from messianism by associating it with both the Columbus enterprise (Milhou 1983, 338–340) and the conquest of Granada, the two messianic cornerstones of the modern Spanish state (Cepeda Adán 1956, 122–123).

Returning to Enrique IV, the period of relative calm for religious minorities under his reign turned into a disaster starting in 1464, when the king of Castile began to pile one political miscalculation on top of another (Valdeón Baruque 2001, 197–202). A significant factor in this crisis was the lack of harmony between the king and the select group of the intelligentsia, or *letrados*, the vast majority of whom were conversos (Seidenspinner-Núñez 2000, 242). If Enrique IV's superb management of the Toledo rebellion in 1449 was decisive in securing their support at the beginning of his reign (Márquez Villanueva 2006e, 145), the constant quarrels against minorities helped to usher in the subsequent turmoil, as Mosén Diego de Valera deplored in one of his epistles (Rodríguez Puértolas 2001, 93–96). The king's political mistakes triggered his inexorable fall into the hands of his unforgiving enemies, especially those nobles who had suffered under a Castilian monarchy, willing to reward 'new men' handsomely in the form of lands and titles (Miller 1972, 151–152). In a desperate attempt to reconcile with the aggrieved, Enrique IV again played the 'Old Christian' political card, as he had in 1449, this time abandoning completely his pro-converso policies. This had an immediate consequence: the eruption of vicious anti-Jewish riots, especially between 1462 and 1474 (Perea Rodríguez 2007b, 159–162).

Leaving aside the well-known events of 1465 which diminished the powers of the king – both the *Farsa de Ávila* and the *Sentencia Arbitral de Medina del Campo* (Valdeón Baruque 2001, 203–204) – an episode at court in 1466 symbolized better than anything the abyss that had grown between the king and his former converso allies: the attack on Pedro Arias, or Pedrarias, Dávila. He was the son of Diego Arias Dávila, a royal clerk of stainless character and one of Enrique IV's principal converso right-hand men (Rábade Obradó 1993, 132–137), especially as *contador mayor* (Palencia 1973, I: 39–40; I: 64–65) – an assessment that is abundantly attested in his Inquisition record (Carrete Parrondo 1986, 19–20). Diego's shrewd control of the levers of economic power is demonstrated by the fact that even Gómez Manrique, the well-known 'Old Christian' poet, praised him with a *cancioneril* composition (ID 0094, MN6b-44 fols. 229v–233v: "De los más el más perfecto"), acclaimed as a masterpiece of both philosophical thinking and satire (Atlee 2007, 173–174). When Diego passed away in 1466, his son inherited his bureaucratic posts and his enviable position at the royal court; but a certain enmity with Juan Pacheco (the powerful Marquis of Villena) developed into a political struggle with an unfortunate end (Palencia 1973, 1: 189). Stunned by Villena's constant accusations against Pedrarias, Enrique IV summoned the latter to the royal fortress of El Pardo in a friendly manner, but this was just an excuse to incarcerate him (Enríquez del Castillo 1994, 264–265). When Pedrarias realized the plot and, sword in hand, attempted to defend his life, the royal soldiers injured him badly ("con esta herida vivió Pedrarias asaz tiempo, pero jamás pudo ser curado hasta que murió della", Torres Fontes 1946, 285).

The *Pedrarias affair* was indeed a "symbol of Spanish Otherness" (Yovel 1998, 10), especially of its fragility (Perea Rodríguez 2007b, 164–166). Even Enríquez del Castillo, the most supportive chronicler of Enrique IV, emphasized the deplorable role played by the king on that occassion: "¡Ó, qué mal enxenplo de rrey! ¡Qué desonesta hazaña de prínçipe! [...] ¡El que devía de anparar su hechura real, mandalla prender e dar lugar a su muerte!" (Enríquez del Castillo 1994, 265). Like Pedrarias, in 1466 conversos felt betrayed by the same king they had constantly supported, by the same monarchy whose authoritarian principles they had upheld (Nieto Soria 1993, 247). The event ultimately led to a pervasive sense of the decline of "royal protection", which "would eventually be sacrificed" (Kaplan 2002, 25), a perception accurately portrayed by an author who mastered the literary art of satire (Scholberg 1971, 242–244): Juan Álvarez Gato. The life of the Madrid-born poet has been minutely dissected by Márquez Villanueva, who focused particularly on the failed attempts of Álvarez Gato's family to hide their converso origin (1960, 42–65). In his *cancionero* (Dutton MH2), which is probably autograph (Gómez Bravo 2011, 232), Álvarez Gato alludes to the 'Pedrarias incident' and to the king's role in it:

Pareçió muy mal, porque era muy notorio que le fue gran servidor. Y por esta causa, [*Álvarez Gato*] hizo las coplas siguientes en nombre d'un moço que se despide de su amo; y algunos cavalleros, por esta razón, se despidieron del rey.   (Álvarez Gato 1928, 96)

The allegory is transparent. Álvarez Gato, in the voice of a royal page, takes leave of his master, the king, and states that one by one the rest of the conversos will abandon him as well (ID 3114, MH2-48, fols. 40r-41r: "No me culpes en que parto"):

[I] No me culpes en que parto
de tu parte,
que tu obra me desparte
si m'aparto;
que los que me dieren culpa
en que partí,
yo daré razón de mí:
que tu culpa me desculpa.

[II] Que cosa pareçe fuerte
de seguir
quien remunera servir
dando muerte.
Írset*e* án todos los buenos
a lo suyo,
qu'eres bravo con el tuyo
y manso con los ajenos.

[III] Plázete de dar castigos
sin porqué;
no te terná nadie fe
de tus amigos;
y essos que contigo están,
çierto só
c'uno a uno se t'irán
descontentos, como yo.

[IV] Lo que siembras, hallarás,
no lo dudes;
yo te ruego que t'escudes,
si podrás,
qu'en la mano está el granizo,
pues te plaze
deshazer a quien te haze
por hazer quien te deshizo.

[V] Ya durarte no podría
sin mudança,
que muriose el esperança
que tenía;
que con obras de presente
c'as obrado,
ni tienes a Dios ganado
ni menos la buena gente.

[VI] Pues eres desconoçido
lastimero,
¡quédate con lo servido,
no lo quiero!
Pues el cabo da espirençia
que veré,
si me quieres dar liçençia;
si no, ¡yo la tomaré!

(Álvarez Gato 1928, 96–97)

This brooding poem, with its typical *cancionero* word play, matches a good handful of Álvarez Gato's meditations on the miseries of the world, which had turned him into an outstanding example of the troubled converso paradigm in literature (Kaplan 2002, 66–71). In light of the poets with whom he exchanged poetry, especially Hernán Mexía (Scholberg 1971, 244–245), he has a well-earned reputation as a reliable witness to the moment in which conversos, who constituted "an *intelligentsia* of sorts [. . .] anticipated the situation of conflict between intellectuals and the State which defines our own modern times" (Márquez Villanueva 2000, 18). Expressive of the feelings of resentment arising from the thwarted opportunities for conversos provided during Enrique IV's reign (Perea Rodríguez 2015, 155–156), Álvarez Gato's pessimistic writings inaugurated "la tradición sombría [. . .] de conversos desesperados, sin cómodo asiento en este mundo" (Castro 1982, 534–535), as seen in his memorable quotation, "la amarga muerte que de contino llovizna" (Márquez Villanueva 1960, 391). Without question, Álvarez Gato is the leading exemplar of the vital negativity that is a key feature for understanding a specific model of converso poetry produced in Castile during the Middle Ages and early Renaissance (Scholberg 1971, 245).

An identical sense of disaffection is noticeable in the writings of other contemporary conversos, such as Fernando de Pulgar, the *Bachiller* Alonso Palma (Márquez Villanueva 1976, 150), and the protonotary Juan de Lucena (Pastore 2010, 86–94), perhaps the leader in demonstrating just how profound the 'New Christian' resentment against 'Old Christians' was (Gilman 1979, 96; Contreras 1995, 470–472; Alcalá Galve 2011, 233–245). Enrique IV's descent was rapidly turning into a torpedo headed for the monarchy's ship of state (Miller 1972, 190–192); it was especially damaging to the conversos participating in the government of Castilian cities (Márquez Villanueva 2006e, 148). From this point on, poetry was just another weapon in the war between the king and the fractious nobility – a weapon, however, that was especially favorable to the king's own sister, the future Queen Isabel I (Weissberger 2004, 71–73).

In the period from 1464 to 1474, *cancionero* poetry was completely "weaponized" (Dutton and Roncero López 2004, 39–40), thus feeding into the historiographical perception of the "degenerate reign of Henry IV" (Gilman 1979, 94) and conveying his years of rule as "políticamente desastrosos" (Scholberg 1971, 242). The most prominent example must be the *Coplas de Mingo Revulgo* (ID 2024, MN67: "Mingo Revulgo, Mingo"), in which criticism of the king is wrapped in a pastoral allegory (Paolini 2015, 18–21). The poem has been attributed to Rodrigo – sometimes abbreviated as Ruy – Sánchez Cota (Scholberg 1971, 251), who owes his fame in part to having been mentioned as the 'antiguo autor' of the first act of *La Celestina* (Cantalapiedra Erostarbe 2017, 109). He was indeed a well-known converso writer who not only withstood various attacks from the caustic pen of El Ropero (Cota 1961, 10–11; Cantera Burgos 1970, 132–141), but was also the author of a notable piece of Jewish self-satire (Beinart 1992, 360–361), the *Epitalamio burlesco* (ID 2804, MN15-23 ff. 14r-16r: "Per Gonçález, Per Gonçález"). This poem, which can be read in the *Pequeño cancionero del marqués de la Romana* (Dutton MN15), was composed to mock the wedding of the poet's own sister, María Ortiz Cota (Cantera Burgos 1970, 8–9), to the already mentioned Pedrarias Dávila, the converso betrayed by Enrique IV and wounded by Castilian soldiers in 1466. Rodrigo was the son of Alonso Cota, a Toledan tax farmer (Cantera Burgos 1970, 21–44), whose family suffered the brutal consequences of the riots of 1449: their house was burned to the ground (Roth 2007, 179–181; Perea Rodríguez 2015, 149–150). Despite serving as living proof of the increasing hostility toward conversos in Toledo (Kaplan 2002, 93; Gerli 1994, 25–26), Cota's *Diálogo entre el Amor y un viejo* (ID 6103, 11CG-125 fols. 72v-75v: "Cerrada estava mi puerta") displays a refined troubadour interested in the courtly conventions of love poetry, which traditionally has been perceived as an obstacle to acceptance of his authorship of *Mingo Revulgo* (Perea Rodríguez 2015, 149–150).

In spite of recent arguments in favor of Rodrigo Cota (Cáseda Teresa 2019, 194–196), nowadays, it is generally accepted that the authorship of *Mingo Revulgo* should be attributed to Fray Íñigo de Mendoza (Mendoza 1968, IX–XII), a well-known converso author with powerful influence at court (Márquez Villanueva 2006f, 198–201; Perea Rodríguez 2015, 157). His criticism of Jews is often based primarily on theological disagreements (Alcalá Galve 2011, 280). He was also responsible for shaping another supreme example of criticism, the *Coplas de Vita Christi* (ID 0269, SA5-2, fol. 158v: "Aclara sol divinal"). These two crucial works, *Mingo Revulgo* and the *Coplas de Vita Christi*, were written to attack Enrique IV and to benefit the future Isabel I, who handsomely rewarded Fray Íñigo by appointing him as her private confessor (Rodríguez Puértolas 1989, 23–25).

Together with *Mingo Revulgo*, the zenith, or perhaps nadir, of slander and malice in the Castilian *cancioneros* is marked by the *Coplas del Provincial* (ID 4119, SM3-1, fols. 1r-23v: "El Provincial es llegado"), framed as a report from the head of a religious order, the *Provincial*, after his visit to one of its monasteries. This *cancionero* is based on exactly the kinds of vices actually indulged in by monks. Its verses are diametrically opposed to the metaphors in *Mingo Revulgo* (Scholberg 1971, 251–253) and well beyond the outermost limits of the gnomic and spiritual nuances of *Vita Christi* (Mendoza 1968, XIV–XV). *Provincial* was most likely composed by a group of people (Menéndez y Pelayo 1890, 2: 298; Rodríguez Moñino 1949, 459; Scholberg 1971, 336), although some scholars have denied this possibility (López Álvarez and Torrecilla del Olmo 1981, 240–241). In addition, a few particular names have been noted as possible authors, including Juan Hurtado de Mendoza, son of the Marquis de Santillana (Rodríguez Puértolas 2001, 97), and Juan Herrera de Toro, whose name appears in one of the main manuscript witnesses of the poem (Dutton SM3). Concerning its content, defamation was the primary tactic followed by the "maldizientes que hizieron las coplas del Provençial" (ID 3120, MH2-58, fol. 48v: "Unas coplas vi c'an hecho"; Álvarez Gato 1928, 107). Configured as a catalogue of injurious remarks against the "friars" of the convent, i.e., those members of the Castilian nobility who supported the king, the *Coplas del Provincial* emphasized – truthfully or not – the personal vices of these aristocrats, branding the men as "sodomita, cornudo, judío, incestuoso" and the women as "adúltera o ramera" (Menéndez y Pelayo 1890, 2: 289). Not surprisingly, finger-pointing at Jewish or converso ancestries and practices – again, truthfully or not – occurs often in these stanzas (Chicharro Chamorro 2003, 12–13):

[XXII] A ti, fraile bujarrón,
Álvaro Pérez Orozco:
en la nariz te conozco
ser de los de Faraón.

[XXIII] Y es tan grande que me asombra,
y a los diablos del infierno,

[XLII] A ti, fray Diego Arias, puto,
que eres y fuiste judío:
contigo no me disputo,
que tienes gran señorío.

[XLIII] Águila, castillo y cruz,
dime, ¿de dónde te viene?,

que hace en el verano sombra	pues que tu pija capuz
y rabos hace en invierno [. . .]	nunca lo tuvo ni tiene.

[XXX] Juan de Zúñiga es venido:
aqueste fraile perverso,
jugador y del partido
que no quiere ser converso.

[XLIV] "El águila es de San Juan,
el castillo, el de Emaús,
y en cruz pusiste a Jesús
siendo yo allí capitán."

[XXI] Pues merece ser de grados,
frailes, dadle la corona,
que es gran músico de dados,
gran ladrón de su persona [. . .]

[XLV] García, ¿está acá tu padre?
"¿A quién preguntáis por él?"
A ti, que dice tu madre
que eres hijo de Rusel.

(Rodríguez Puértolas 1989, 241–245)

What we have here is a thoroughgoing example of weaponized poetry (Rodríguez Puértolas 1989, 23), which clearly enlightens us as to why the partisans of the king were attacked as 'crypto-Jews': his enemies were looking to damage him in the eyes of his 'Old Christian' subjects, "because it served as a means of forging public opinion and demonstrating the harm Jews and Conversos were causing the state" (Beinart 1992, 368). For this reason, the significance of the *Coplas del Provincial* has often been called into question, and it has been considered as nothing more than pure invective with no literary merit. Nevertheless, this overstated judgment owes too much to Menéndez y Pelayo's analysis, based as it is on a concept of decorum that is perhaps *démodé* (Scholberg 1971, 285–287). A better edition is needed, especially with detailed biographical notes on those accused of being 'New Christians'. As one of the most important testaments to the social breakdown in Castile between 'Old Christians' and conversos at the end of Enrique IV's reign, the accusations it contains, albeit lurid – even obscene – deserve a more in-depth analysis.

Two final important details should be mentioned regarding the *cancioneros* of this era. Firstly, there is the ephemeral existence of another royal court parallel to Enrique IV's: that of his half-brother Alfonso el Inocente, who was raised to the throne in 1465 by rebellious members of the Castilian aristocracy (Valdeón Baruque 2001, 202–208). Until his death in obscure circumstances three years later (Morales Muñiz 1988, 251), noblemen and counsellors of the *rey intruso* Alfonso XII are documented as patrons of a large number of poems written with the clear aim of propagandizing his cause (Perea Rodríguez 2001, 35–36). The second detail is the suspected existence of several additional cultural circles around high-ranking members of the Castilian nobility, such as Beltran de la Cueva, Duke of Alburquerque (Perea Rodríguez 2006, 681–682), García Álvarez de Toledo, Duke of Alba (Pérez Priego 1999, 141), and Alonso Carrillo, Archbishop of Toledo (Gil Ortega 2015, 141–145). Few traces of these literary circles have been found, probably because of the loss of written sources during the turmoil of the last years of Enrique IV's reign. However, where there is written evidence, the remarkable role played by converso poets in those aristocratic milieus has been proved. The foremost example is Pero Guillén de Segovia, the converso accountant in service to Archbishop Carrillo, in whose court he played a prominent role alongside many other "letrados e cavalleros e ombres de fación" (Pulgar 2007, 179). Guillén de Segovia's *cancionero* (Dutton MN12 and SA10), transmitted fragmentarily via diverse copies from the fifteenth to the eighteenth century (Guillén de Segovia 1989, 18–20), reflects the common cultural pattern of the peculiar relationship between the Crown and the conversos at court during the reign of Enrique IV.

5 The Reign of the Catholic Monarchs: From Initial Hope to Final Despair

Before Isabel I was proclaimed queen in December 1474, the kingdom was ravaged by anti-Jewish riots (Perea Rodríguez 2011a, 201), especially in places with substantial converso populations, such as Carmona (1462), Toledo (1467), and both Jaén and Cordova (1473). It was probably after the riots when Antón de Montoro wrote one of the masterpieces of the Iberian *cancionero* (ID 1933 MP2-81, fols. 114v-115r: "O, Ropero, amargo, triste"), which has been highlighted as the most vivid testimony of the converso literary mentality in the Iberian Peninsula during the fifteenth century (Orfali 1994, 118):

[I] ¡O, Ropero, amargo, triste,
que no sientes tu dolor!
¡Setenta años que naciste
y en todos siempre dixiste
"*inviolata permansiste*";
y nunca juré al Criador!

[III] Los hinojos encorvados
y con muy gran devoción
en los días señalados,
con gran devoción contados
y rezados
los nudos de la Pasión,
adorando a Dios y Hombre
por muy alto Señor mío,
por do mi culpa se escombre…
¡no pude perder el nombre
de viejo puto y judío!

[II] Hice el Credo y adorar
ollas de tocino grueso,
torreznos a medio asar,
oír misas y rezar,
santiguar y persinar,
y nunca pude matar
este rastro de confeso.

(Rodríguez Puértolas 1989, 36–37)

El Ropero's bitter lament is devastating: no matter how hard he and other conversos attempt to prove that they are faithful Catholics, they are never capable of eliminating *el recelo* (Benito Ruano 2001, 17) or *este rastro de confeso*, i.e., the signs of their conversion (Perea Rodríguez 2015, 144–146). Montoro's ingenuity had no equal among the Iberian *cancioneros* because of his very unique, clever, ironic, and politically incorrect sense of humor (Roncero López 1996, 568–569; Márquez Villanueva 2006f, 186–189). In addition, he had a long life, and his literary activity runs almost throughout the entire fifteenth century (Perea Rodríguez 2011a, 202–203). It is therefore impossible to explore his poetry in depth here; suffice it to say that every single feature of the relationship between the *rastro de confeso* and *cancionero* poetry can undoubtedly be traced back to his astonishingly eloquent works (Beinart 1992, 361; Gerli 1994–95, 266).

The early years of Isabel and Fernando were marked by a civil war masquerading as a Portuguese invasion. The rights to the Castilian throne were claimed by Princess Juana, Enrique IV's daughter, although she was called *la Beltraneja* because of the libelous rumor that Beltran de la Cueva, duke of Alburquerque, was her real father (Suárez Fernández 2001, 124). Juana was defended by Afonso V of Avís, the Portuguese monarch, who was her maternal uncle and eventually her husband after May 1475 (Azcona 1998, 37–39). From 1475 to 1479, Afonso and Juana led a Portuguese army as well as an entire faction of the Castilian nobility that was interested, not so much in defending Juana, but rather in defeating Isabel and Fernando at all costs (Valdeón Baruque 2001, 211–217). The conflict caused a serious hiatus in the production of *cancionero* poetry, for poets and their patrons had more momentous issues to claim their attention. This gap is symbolized better than anything else by a sad milestone: the death of Jorge Manrique, the universally acclaimed Castilian poet, which occurred in the spring of 1479 during a brief and accidental skirmish in the context of this civil war (Lomax 1972, 61–62).

A year later, the Cortes Generales were held in Toledo, not only to reorganize the finances of the realm (Suárez Fernández 1989, 373–374), but also to introduce such measures as the *apartamiento*, that is, a ban on the living together of members of different religions (Ruiz Gómez 2005, 247–248). At the same time, the social condemnation of conversos increased (Domínguez Ortiz 1991, 151–152), a fact that Pulgar denounced in his chronicle, blaming those who cannot "sofrir que algunos que juzgáis no ser de linaje tengan honras y oficios de gobernación", together with those who disliked "ver riquezas en homes que, según vuestro pensamiento, no las merecen, en especial aquellos que nuevamente las ganaron" (Pulgar 2008, I: 347).

Despite the proverbial benevolence toward conversos that emanated from the Castilian monarchy, the Catholic Monarchs were greeted with mistrust. 'New Christians' surely began to experience even more their "disoriented converso mentality" (Edwards 1992, 207), especially those who, albeit gladly accepting of their new creed, received nothing but humiliating hostility and offensive incomprehension from 'Old Christians', who were always more inclined to perceive them all as *judaizantes* (Contreras 1995, 457–458). In this regard, it is crucial to underscore how the alleged interest of Queen Isabel I in providing "a public campaign of religious education" (Rubin 1991, 186) was a complete sham: no documented traces of a long-term plan along these lines have been found (Resines 1997, 67–70; Rábade Obradó 1999, 380–387). This catechetical failure, the origin of Américo Castro's notion of *vivir desviviéndose* – that is, the 'unliving' of conversos in the Spanish Golden Age (Castro 1982, 287) – could not be palliated by the personal initiatives undertaken by perhaps the only two peacemakers who enjoyed any real power: Fray Hernando de Talavera, confessor to Queen Isabel and later Archbishop of Granada, and the Gran Cardenal, Pedro González de Mendoza, Archbishop of Toledo (Ladero Quesada 1995b, 126–128). This abandonment of the conversos will be of primary importance in analyzing the poetry collections of the age of the Catholic Monarchs.

Moreover, a new perspective must be added to the literary and historical analysis of this period: the impact of the printing press. The first printers crossed the Pyrenees around 1472 (Odriozola 1982, 110), the *Trobes en lahors de la Verge Maria* (Dutton 74*LV) being the first collection of poems printed in the Iberian lands, sometime between 1474 and 1478 (Odriozola 1982, 111). Aside from four compositions in Castilian Spanish, the *Trobes* were written in Catalan and Valencian (Dutton 1990–1991, 6: 1–2). It was Antonio de Centenera, who set up shop in Zamora, who was responsible in 1482 for the first two printed *cancioneros* in Castilian Spanish (Odriozola 1982, 148): Fray Íñigo de Mendoza's *Coplas de Vita Christi* (Dutton 82IM) and Gómez Manrique's *Regimiento de príncipes* (Dutton 82˚GM). The proliferation of copies made possible an enormous expansion of the reading public, but since much of the funding for the early printing presses came from the upper bourgeoisie and the nobility, there was not a large market for social criticism (Infantes de Miguel 1989, 86). Isabel and Fernando, as a matter of conscious policy, promoted panegyrical verse in print, recognizing the substantial benefits it conferred in the form of social stability, but more importantly the propagandistic value of printing political messages. Indeed, it was precisely this latter fact that eventually moved them to seek to control the printing industry, ultimately leading to the imposition of censorship (Perea Rodríguez 2011a, 204–206). But this does not diminish the importance of the many extant manuscript *cancioneros*.

The *Cancionero de Gallardo* (Dutton MN17) is located just at the junction of the reigns of Enrique IV and the Catholic Monarchs. This manuscript, copied around 1550 (Azáceta 1962, 77–78), includes several compositions related to Jewish or converso topics mentioned above, such as Sem Tob's *Proverbios morales* and an incomplete version of *Coplas del Provincial* (Scholberg 1971, 296–300). *Gallardo* therefore resembles the *Cancionero de Juan Fernández de Híjar* (Dutton MN6), a splendid collection of doctrinal verses – some in favor of Enrique IV, such as those of the above-mentioned Escobar – along with a second part more connected to the Aragonese royal court (Azáceta 1956, 1: XL–XLII). The most engaging converso traces in *Híjar* are the satirical blows against Juan Poeta made by both Antón de Montoro and the count of Paredes (Scholberg 1971, 259–261), proving that these attacks and counterattacks on hybrid identities were already conventional in Iberian poetry (Kaplan 2002, 40–57). Comparable to these two *cancioneros* is yet another one that lies at the temporal frontier of two reigns: the *Cancionero de Egerton* (Dutton LB3), in which Gómez Manrique's eulogy of Diego Arias Dávila and the poetical debates between Montoro and his opponents stand out.

The *Cancionero de Oñate-Castañeda* (Dutton HH1), completed around 1485, is yet another of these mixed compilations which include works composed between 1440 and 1475 (Garcia 2017, 76–80). The prominence of Fernán Pérez de Guzmán, the first author included, is no surprise; but the most notable author here is Pedro de Escavias, whose poems, situated at the end of the manuscript, indicate his probable role as compiler of this *cancionero* (Garcia 1998, 54–56). A significant number of well-known authors, such as Fray Íñigo, Guillén de Segovia, Álvarez Gato, and the ubiquitous Montoro, add another layer of what has often been considered to be converso cultural identity to *Oñate-Castañeda*, along with two more poets whose converso roots have been largely discussed. The first is Diego de Burgos, scribe and secretary to the Mendoza family (Perea Rodríguez 2012a, 304; Perea Rodríguez 2015, 150–151) and the author of the *Triunfo del Marqués de Santillana* (ID 1710, 11CG-87 fols. 52r-63v: "Tornado era Febo a ver el tesoro"). The latter is a prodigious elegy of more than 1800 stanzas of *arte mayor* written in 1458 in memory of the just deceased Santillana, through which Diego de Burgos revealed himself to be a master of Iberian Humanism (Perea Rodríguez 2012a, 305–315). The second poet is the versatile Diego de San Pedro, whose proximity to the archetypical converso style has often been taken to indicate his origin (Márquez Villanueva 1966; Kaplan 2002, 106–129; Fontes 2005, 150–158; Roth 2007, 714–718), but this thesis has not been universally accepted as valid (see discussion in Perea Rodríguez 2015, 161). There are, however, striking similarities between some paragraphs of San Pedro's *Cárcel de amor* and Álvarez Gato's poem against Enrique IV in the context of the above-mentioned Pedrarias affair (Márquez Villanueva 1976, 148–150).

In the 1480s, Fernando and Isabel's consolidation of power was accompanied by the progressive conversion of both manuscript and printed *cancioneros* into propagandistic tools. This can be seen, at first subtly, in brief verse encomia such as those in the beginning and ending stanzas of the *Libro de los pensamientos variables* (Dutton MN59), a short treaty in prose dwelling on the importance of loyalty in an advisor (López Estrada 1988, 278–279). Its author might have been Pedro de Gracia Dei, a successful genealogist, chronicler, and poet who has sometimes been qualified as a converso (Perea Rodríguez 2002, 28–30). However, once the great aims of conquering Granada and expelling the Jews had been achieved in the first three months of 1492, the literary scene changed radically: the global political triumph of the Catholic Monarchs turned most Castilian and Aragonese *cancioneros* into nothing more than panegyrics (Perea Rodríguez 2011a, 204–205).

Handwritten *cancioneros* from 1492 to the death of Fernando in 1516 were composed *ad maiorem gloriam monarchiae*, as seen in the vast amount of poetry written in praise of both Isabel I of Castile (Perea Rodríguez 2007d, 1359–1377) and Fernando II of Aragon (Perea Rodríguez 2018, 250–257). Focusing on the Catholic Queen, the poems dedicated to her contained such embellished praise that some critics have argued for the existence of a personal cult (Lida de Malkiel 1946, 123–124), deeply influenced not only by the love poetry paradigm of her era, but also by the cult of the Virgin Mary (Jones 1962, 55–64; Dutton and Roncero López 2004, 42–43). From a more political perspective, the *Cancionero de Pero Marcuello* (Dutton CH1) is the best example of an exaggerated tribute acclaiming the Catholic Monarchs for the capture of Granada (Marcuello 1987, 8–9). But *Marcuello* is not a solitary milestone; Juan Barba's *Consolatoria de Castilla* (Dutton SA13) must also be included, for it is a perfect historiographical account in verse publicizing the Christian hegemony established after 1492 (Cátedra 1989, 17). The final addition to this group is the personal poetry collection – as yet unpublished – of the aforementioned Gracia Dei (Dutton NH2), in which the pattern of political propaganda in favor of Fernando and Isabel reached its apogee, as I have recently argued (Perea Rodríguez 2017b, 163–167).

In the *cancioneros* of this period, the second prominent theme was religion (Rodríguez-Moñino 1968, 37), sometimes mixed with wisdom literature (Perea Rodríguez 2015, 167–169). This blend, together with the fact that some of these poets, although aware of their origins, rejected their converso identity in order to demonstrate their Christian *bona fides*, makes it difficult to find any traces of Jewish religiosity. Fray Ambrosio Montesino is a representative case, because he excelled as a composer of religious poetry (Montesino 1987, 18–21) despite the fact that his father had been severely prosecuted by the Inquisition (Parada y Luca de Tena 2002, 19–23). In addition, the Aragonese Andrés de Li identified himself as a converso but rejected his heritage (Delbrugge 2012, 155–156). Nevertheless, his *Thesoro de la Pasión* was the first of many treatments of this supreme topic of the Christian faith among converso poets in Castile and Aragon (Gutwirth 2000b, 504–505; Delbrugge 2011, 50–57) as well as in Portugal (Afonso 2001, 39–41). Other remarkable treatments of this topic include Lucas Fernández's *Auto de la Pasión* (Valero Moreno 2003, 178–79) and the famed *Coplas de la Pasión con la Resurrección* (Dutton 90*CR), written by Diego Román (Román 1990, 15–18), identified as the same 'Comendador Román' of Toledo (Márquez Villanueva 2006f, 194–195) who was the butt of attacks by Antón Montoro found in several *cancioneros* (Lope 1990, 264–267; Perea Rodríguez 2015, 159).

The converso 'star' of Iberian poetry in the age of the Catholic Monarchs is, without doubt, Juan del Encina (Roth 2007, 201–203; Perea Rodríguez 2015, 161–162). Musician, poet, and literary theorist, his works are a compendium of Italian influences in Iberian poetry (Beltran 2014, 20–21) mixed with his own literary talent. Encina's lyrical approach reveals a pattern already seen in the *Cancionero de Palacio*: that of the conversos who sublimated their religious concerns into love poetry. This was, indeed, an extremely successful genre (Severin 2004, 40–42), as shown by the popularity of both the *Cancionero de Ramón de Llavia* (Dutton 86*RL) and the *Cancionero de Pedro Manuel de Urrea* (Dutton 16UC). In addition, Encina as a playwright is acknowledged as "el padre del teatro español" (Pérez Priego 1999, 140), with all that the early Renaissance lay theater implied regarding the defense of 'New Christians' (Castro 1961, 38–42). Ultimately, Encina is considered the first converso author more imbued in the vernacular Castilian literary tradition even than the 'Old Christian' authors, a feature also shared with the anonymous composer of a Judeo-Spanish version of the *Danza de la Muerte* (Hamilton 2012, 165).

This survey would not be complete without adding two more lyrical panegyrics related in one way or another to the Catholic Monarchs. First, there is Gracia Dei's *Crianza y virtuosa dotrina* (Dutton *89GD), printed around 1489 and dedicated to Princess Isabel, the Catholic Queen's eldest daughter (Perea Rodríguez 2002, 28–29). Secondly, there is *Panegírico a la Reina doña Isabel* (Dutton 09GP), printed in 1509 and considered the best literary example of Isabelline propaganda. Its author, Diego Guillén de Ávila, was the son of the converso Pero Guillén de Segovia (Magaña 2017, 677–684). Guillén de Ávila's Dantesque reverie, in which the virtues of Queen Isabel are unconditionally exalted (Magaña 2018, 149), represents in cultural terms the highest degree of cooperation between the group of conversos connected to the royal court and the Catholic Monarchs' political project (Perea Rodríguez 2007d, 1367–1368).

5 Conversos, Inquisition, and *Obras de burlas* in the *Cancionero general* (1511)

There is little point in focusing on the well-known hardships endured by the Jews after the infamous *Provisiones* of March 31, 1492 (Cohen 2002, 716), which left them with two options: conversion to Christianity or exile. Since approximately half of the Jewish population decided to leave (Ladero Quesada 1995a, 172), the immediate effect on Iberian *cancioneros* was the complete erasure of any Jewish-related topics. Only prominent members of the Castilian nobility, such as Diego López de Haro, the well-known ambassador and governor of Galicia (Perea Rodríguez 2007a, 174), could make use of Jewish historical and biblical characters in verse. His notable *Aviso para Cuerdos* (ID 4181, MH4-1 fols. 22r-52v: "Yo a cuerdos hablo y toco") reflects exemplarily the cautious approach taken by any poet willing to deal with topics related to Judaism during the late fifteenth and the early sixteenth centuries (Dutton 1990–1991: I, 579).

At some point around 1480, Castilian conversos must have felt as they had twenty years before: betrayed by the Crown's religious policies (Baer 1966, 2: 245–246). This feeling surely turned into deep concern once they realized the scope of the institution specifically designed to investigate the minutest actions of their daily lives: the Spanish Inquisition (Beinart 1992, 371–378). After the foundational papal bull of 1478 and the appointment of the first inquisitors two years later, the prosecution of alleged 'crypto-Jews' became "brutal, cruel, and harsh beyond justification" (Netanyahu 1997, 184). Today, this assessment is universally accepted, although a few scholars, in accord with what was written by fifteenth-century chroniclers (Valdeón Baruque 1995, 79), still try to blame the conversos themselves for this harshness (Ropero Berzosa 2018, 495). After the Inquisition began a "sucesión de procesos resonantes"

(Cavallero 2018, 95), conversos quickly realized that they had been betrayed yet again (Jiménez Monteserín 1980, 54). The key issue was that the Inquisitors did not maintain the lenient attitude that had been promised when judging "cosas livianas", i.e., small irregularities of faith or daily customs 'committed' by the 'New Christians' during the early stages of their conversions (Muñoz Solla 2017, 79–80). The failure of both the monarchy and the Inquisition to keep this promise in regard to the converso's "interim society" (Beinart 1992, 348) nipped in the bud any hope conversos might have entertained. Such severity was clearly manifested in the cruel prosecution of Andalusian 'crypto-Jews' between 1481 and 1483 (Baer 1966, 2: 330–332). A famous text written in those years, the *Católica Impugnación* of Fray Hernando de Talavera, is often considered to be the valedictory of the thwarted efforts made in defense of conversos: "el testamento espiritual de la España que no fue" (Avalle-Arce 1965, 386).

The institution of the Spanish Inquisition was paralleled by the increasingly restrictive control of printed books (Perea Rodríguez 2011a, 204–205). This practice had certainly not been unknown in the Iberian Peninsula, but it used to lie in the hands of the Catholic Church and was related to texts flagged as heretical for theological reasons, as when bishop Lope de Barrientos ordered that certain books by Enrique de Villena be burned in 1434 because of suspicion of witchcraft (Gascón Vera 1979, 318–319). Eventually, the monarchy achieved complete control of licensing the printing press in 1502 (Márquez 1980, 18–19), when a Pragmatic Sanction was issued to legalize what had been customary since 1480, the year in which the very first norms on the matter were established (Moll 1979, 51–52).

Let us examine more closely the only poem preserved to date which was intended to show clear opposition to the government of Isabel and Fernando. This composition, dated around 1489, is usually referred to as *Coplas del tabefe* (ID 0206, MN17-20, fols. 35r-36r: "Abre, abre las orejas"). When the rumors of its dissemination in Jerez de la Frontera reached their ears, Isabel and Fernando reacted immediately by applying the death penalty to two of its authors, while the third, Hernando de Vera, alderman of the city council, was prosecuted mercilessly (Perea Rodríguez 2011a, 205–208). Another witness to this hardline policy on censorship is an interesting document sent to the Burgos city council in 1492. Apparently, the Catholic Monarchs had been informed that, after the approval of an Inquisition court for Burgos, some of its citizens "fazen coplas e disen cantares" (Asenjo González 1999, 474–475), that is, began to compose verse and sing songs containing controversial accusations. The dismayed monarchs, envisioning Burgos wracked by insulting slurs, with its inhabitants making up verses probably accusing each another – truly or falsely – of being 'crypto-Jews', commanded the local authorities to punish both the composition and the singing of such chants (Perea Rodríguez 2011a, 209). One surviving echo of those *coplas e cantares* from Burgos might have been the musical refrain "Ea, judíos, a enfardelar, / que mandan los Reyes que paséis la mar", which the composer Juan de Anchieta took as the motif for a famous mass (Salinas 1958, 312). Although no copy of the latter is preserved, information about it was transmitted by *De Musica Libri*

Septem, a treatise on musicology written by Francisco de Salinas (Alcalá Galve 2011, 279), who, born in Burgos in 1513 (García Casar 1995, 21), might have heard some of the popular verses composed at that time as a child.

Within this context of censorship and intolerance, there was only one genre in the *cancioneros* of this period that allowed for the presence of Jews and conversos: burlesque compositions. The most outstanding poetry collection assembled during the reign of the Catholic Monarchs is the *Cancionero general* (Dutton 11CG), compiled by Hernando del Castillo and printed in 1511 (Rodríguez-Moñino 1968, 39), with eight more editions between 1514 and 1573. In addition to verses by converso poets already mentioned above – Álvarez Gato, Diego de Burgos, Ruy Cota, Fray Íñigo de Mendoza, Guillén de Segovia, Mena, Montoro, San Pedro, etc. – Castillo also included works by lesser-known converso poets, including a few anonymous pieces (Perea Rodríguez 2015, 162–163). In accordance with the importance of the topic, Castillo placed a series of religious poems at the beginning of the compilation (Darbord 1965, 283–285), some of them composed by those obscure converso poets. Mosén Juan Tallante is one of them, a converso from Murcia who enjoyed good connections with both the local and royal authorities (Perea Rodríguez 2015, 142–143). Ginés de Cañizares was another converso who lived in Valencia (McPheeters 380–384; Pérez Bosch 2009, 216–217) but had been "nascido y criado en las entrañas del Alcaná de Toledo", as Joan de Timoneda noted (Perea Rodríguez 2015, 148). Both Tallante and Cañizares shared the religious fervor of some 'New Christians' (Castro 1982, 200), for they wrote several of the most passionate and devout verses of the Iberian *cancionero*.

A different set of converso authors consists of those whose writings followed a pattern already described with regard to the *Cancionero de Palacio*: the sophisticated cultivation of love poetry stereotypes (Whinnom 1981, 39). Pedro de Cartagena is the outstanding example. A member of two prominent converso families, the Cartagenas and the Francos (Cantera Burgos 1968, 3–9; Avalle-Arce 1974, 287; Avalle-Arce 1981, 71–72), he is often considered to be the most refined love poet of this era (Perea Rodríguez 2015, 151), as witnessed by his famous Petrarchan composition (ID 0889, 11CG-140, fol. 84r: "La fuerça del fuego que alumbra, que ciega"). Other converso writers who specialized in love poetry include Antonio Franco, Cartagena's brother, who took his mother's surname (Macpherson 1998, 47; Perea Rodríguez 2015, 153); he is the author of a short 'invención' (ID 0921, 11CG-487 fol. 140r: "De la vida que perdí"). Also to be included in this list is Francisco Hernández Coronel, descendant of the notable Abraham Seneor, who took the surname of Coronel after performing a spectacular and theatrical conversion to Christianity in 1492 (Ladero Quesada 2003, 13–14; Perea Rodríguez 2015, 153–155). Francisco was the brother of Luis and Antonio Núñez Coronel, principal figures in the Cardinal Cisneros's Humanist circle in Alcalá de Henares (Perea Rodríguez 2010a, 616–617). His contribution to the *Cancionero general* is a spectacular gloss on the very same Petrarchan composition written by Cartagena, in which he outstripped the most common patterns of *cancionero* love poetry (ID 6739, 11CG-958 fols. 213v-214v: "Con tristes congoxas ni muero ni bivo"). His other known work is a contentious memorial in which he claimed compensation from the Crown for damages suffered by his father's business during troubled financial times in the past (Perea Rodríguez 2013b, 67–69). The last author of this group is Per Álvarez de Ayllón, another expert in courtly love poetry (Perea Rodríguez 2015, 158–159), who also enjoys a reputation similar to Encina's with respect to early modern Iberian drama (Avalle-Arce 1974, 340–352).

The majority of the converso poets and themes in the *Cancionero general* are found in its last section, the 'Obras de burlas' (Rodríguez-Moñino 1968, 47). This parade of burlesques is absent in the manuscript *Cancionero de Rennert* (Dutton LB1), dated around 1510 (Dutton 1990–1991, 1: 131) and in other respects practically identical to Castillo's collection. A smaller selection, however, does appear in the *Cancionero llamado guirlanda esmaltada de galanes* (Dutton 13*FC), which is basically an illegal and partial copy of *Cancionero general*, perhaps the first act of piracy in the history of Iberian printing. Most of the following assessments regarding conversos in *Cancionero general* can be applied to *Guirlanda esmaltada* as well as to all subsequent reprints of the *Cancionero general* in the sixteenth century which contain the burlesque section – those from the years 1514, 1517, 1520, 1535, 1540, and 1557, but not 1573. The *Cancionero de obras de burlas* (Dutton 19OB) should also be included in this latter group, for it is a separate printing of the burlesque section of Castillo's compilation that rapidly acquired a success of its own due to its erotic, not to say scabrous content (Cortijo Ocaña and Rubio Árquez 2015, IX–X).

Let us state at the outset that not all lampoons in the 'Obras de burlas' are related to conversos. When they are, however, they normally offer the most typical clichés and stereotypes, especially dietary habits such as the refusal to eat pork, the fastest way to allege that a converso was a 'hidden Jew' (Glaser 1954, 51–53). For this reason, converso burlesques in this section are among the oldest poems of the entire compilation (Perea Rodríguez 2012b, 326–327). This is logical, given the fact that if any protagonist of a converso joke had still been alive, the Inquisition would have immediately begun procedures against him, as the Holy Office was especially keen to prosecute conversos of the first generation, called *confesos antiguos* or *confesos de los viejos* (Muñoz Solla 2017, 81). This striking chronological divergence between the *Cancionero general*'s printing date of 1511 and the composition date of most of these lampoons of conversos can be explained by other reasons as well (Perea Rodríguez 2012b, 340–341). The first one is that a certain loosening of censorship occurred in Castile at the end of the fifteenth century, following the well-known chain of unfortunate deaths that gravely affected the Crown, which Bernáldez baptized as 'los tres cuchillos de dolor' of the Catholic Queen (Bernáldez 1962, 380). Thus, Prince Juan de Trastámara; Isabel of Castile, Princess and Queen of Portugal; and Prince Miguel – only a two-year-old baby boy – all passed away between 1497 and 1500 (Ladero Quesada 2005, 444–450). The ensuing political turmoil affected the Crown's control of the printing industry, especially after the death of Queen Isabel in 1504. In the following years, literary censorship was not as strict as it had been, a development which was essential to the preservation of real gems of poetry (Perea Rodríguez 2015, 169) such as Antón de Montoro's famous burlesque (ID 1928, 11CG-1010, fol. 230r: "Uno de los verdaderos"), in which he boldly and clearly explained the converso dilemma from his personal experience of going to the butcher shop and being unable to purchase anything but pork:

[1] Uno de los verdaderos,
del señor rey fuerte muro:
han dado los carniceros
causa de me hazer perjuro.
No hallando, ¡por mis duelos!,
con qué mi hambre matar,
hanme hecho quebrantar
la jura de mis ahuelos.

(Montoro 1990, 205)

This poem is the foundation of what Castro baptized the "sentido histórico-literario del jamón y del tocino" (1966, 14); furthermore, this expression has achieved fame as an antecedent of the 'duelos y quebrantos' used by Cervantes to describe Don Quixote's dietary habits (Castro 1966, 24–25; Wardropper 1980, 414–415). In short, the section of 'obras de burlas' is full of poems like this one, in which conversos are mocked as crypto-Jews, stressing the whole panoply of classic stereotypes: circumcision, dietary restrictions, supposedly 'long noses' and a 'peculiar physiognomy'. For this reason, to consider the analysis of poems linked to Castro's conceptual theory of "morada vital" as a "unicorn or snark" (Round 1995, 558) is false. Even though the search for a single converso mentality has been severely questioned (Roth 2002, 158), it is true that a certain 'Jewish touch' is indeed to be found in *cancioneros* (Aronson-Friedman and Kaplan 2012, 9), sometimes hidden in the form of simple rhetorical devices (Lope 1997, 112–114). The situation of being "at once wholly inside and wholly outside the society" (Gilman 1972, 137) surely did exist, as the 'Obras de burlas' conspicuously show.

On the other hand, sometimes the *Cancionero general* evinces traces of what Gutwirth termed "Hispano-Jewish Humour" (1990, 225). One remarkable example of this is Montoro's poem dedicated to the Corregidor of Córdoba (ID 0180, 11CG-986, fol. 226v: "Juan de Mena me lo dio"), an early appearance of the "non-conformist converso activist" that would achieve success in the following centuries (Ingram 2018, 5). Here, the author accuses the Corregidor of being a thief who has stolen a knife given to him by none other than Juan de Mena. Ropero alludes menacingly to his ancestry by suggesting that the Corregidor could suffer the same fate as Jesus Christ: being killed by Jews. This is blasphemy, only possible in a social and historical context long distant from the first decade of the sixteenth century, when Castillo put together his compilation:

[1] Juan de Mena me lo dio;
vos, señor, me lo tomastes:
¡en mis sayos pierda yo
si en ello algo ganastes!,
porqu'el linaje qu'es visto
de fuerças y de valor
que pudo con Ihesuchristo...
¡podrá con corregidor!.

(Montoro 1990, 252)

In addition to the *Cancionero general*, many other little-known collections contain converso burlesques. For instance, the British Library manuscript Egerton 482 (Lourie 1977, 130), not registered by Dutton, includes a lampoon accusing Jews and conversos of cowardice during a bullfight (Infantes de Miguel and Conde 2007, 90–101). Other early sixteenth-century *cancionero* manuscripts followed this pattern, such as the *Credo glosado contra los judíos* written by the unknown Juan de Carvajal (Perea Rodríguez 2011b, 290–292). In addition, the productive field of the printing press remains to be explored in depth for converso materials, especially *pliegos sueltos*, broadsheets or chapbooks. Worth noting is the *Pleito del Perro de Alba* (Sánchez Pérez 2010, 532–533), already in print in 1524 (Martín 2014, 300), a poem that repeatedly mocks the alleged 'cowardice' of Jews and conversos (Beinart 1992, 366–368), including a layer that might also be found in anti-Jewish popular dances of the Spanish sixteenth century (De Bunes Ibarra 2002, 794–797).

Let us highlight the fact that nontraditional literary sources, such as archival documents, can contain poems composed by conversos, as explained by Gutwirth (2011, 645–649). The most noteworthy example is that of Maestre Pedro de la Cabra, an Aragonese physician who wrote half a dozen typical *cancioneril* couplets found in a document in the Archivo de Protocolos Notariales of Saragossa (Marín Padilla 1998, 5–6). Poems like this are astonishing, for they show that the contact between Hebrew and Spanish poetry, well documented in earlier periods (Doron 2000, 227–228), must have continued at a similar scale during the fifteenth century. One key case is a poem contained in the proceedings of an Inquisitorial trial, a fundamental source for contemporary converso prayers (Fernández García 1995, 491–492). Its author was a certain Diego de Segura (Perea Rodríguez 2011a, 214), whose *Coplas por a.b.c.* have been preserved in the Inquisitorial confession of his brother, Pedro de Segura. The latter, a merchant born in Córdoba who lived in Valencia, confessed that his brother Diego composed some verses around 1480 that Pedro had learned by heart, a common practice among Jews and conversos to help them preserve their culture (Alcalá Galve 2011, 58). This composition, memorized by Pedro and copied down verbatim by the Inquisition's scribe, reflects with great clarity Diego's "longing for everything, large and small, that was sacred to the Jewish people" (Beinart 1992, 378):

[I] Adonay es el tu nombre,
segunt nos fue declarado,
en quien deve todo hombre
adorar muy inclinado;
y por más purificado,
en su nombre loaré,
y en ti sólo adoraré,
y librarme ás de peccado.

[II] Bendito es aquel varón
qu'en ti tiene su sperança,
que feziste al Rey Faraón
padecer tal tribulança,
y debaxo de su lança
sacaste los dotze tribus
libres y sanos y bivos,
y mostrásteles vengança.

[III] Cerca de la mar llegaron
de Faraón muy aflegidos,
y a Muisén se reclamaron
dando bozes y gemidos,
que se veían perdidos,
y Muisén los respondió:
"¡Esperat en vuestro Dio
y seredes acorridos!"

[IV] Del cielo fue decendido
una voz así disiente:
"Muisén: con tu vara erguida
por la mar fendiendo,
y venírseles ha a mientes
por dó pasen tus parientes,
y luego s'irá abriendo
de cómo yo los defiendo."

(Perea Rodríguez 2011a, 215–216)

7 Portugal and Iberian conversos: Resende's *Cancioneiro geral* (1516)

It is well known that many Castilian and Aragonese Jews decided to flee to Portugal in 1492 (Edwards 1995, 122), just as had happened after the crisis of 1391 (Afonso 2001, 28), a fact that converted the border between the two kingdoms into a hotbed of social tensions (Huerga Criado 1994, 16–17). Unfortunately, the *Ordenações Manuelinas*, issued in December 1496 by King Manuel I, *O Venturoso*, gave them less than a year to face the same choice they had faced in 1492: conversion to Christianity or the road into exile (Soyer 2014, 182–184). After 1497, Jews could no longer live in Portugal (Tavares 1987, 71–82); those who remained there as conversos endured the same conditions as in the rest of the Iberian Peninsula, "carrying with them the general stigma of being false Christians" (Tavares 1997, 96). Episodes like the Lisbon attacks of the spring of 1506 were the enraged crystallization of this social unrest (Pulido Serrano 2017, 306), forcing King Manuel to issue a decree for the protection of the endangered lives of his converso subjects (Rivkin 1995, 409–410). Despite such difficulties, the preservation of Jewish-influenced customs in Portuguese culture lasted throughout most of the sixteenth century, as witnessed in many documents from the Inquisitorial archives (Tavares 1994, 266–267).

The Trastamaran Isabel of Aragon and Castile, who was briefly Queen of Portugal between 1496 and 1498, has often been blamed as the chief instigator of the *Ordenações Manuelinas*. Advocates of this view exploit the rumor that the Catholic Monarchs' eldest daughter asked for the expulsion of the Jews as "a condition for the marriage of King Manuel of Portugal" (Beinart 2002, 43). Although this story is widespread, it is controversial in the eyes of current historiography (Alvar Ezquerra 2002, 132; 166 n. 27). In the eyes of Jews forced to abandon Portugal, however, Isabel was held to be responsible for the expulsion, as seen in her depiction in popular literature. For instance, in the Sephardic ballad "Éramos tres hermanitas / hijas del rey don Londrino" (Armistead 2000, 267–268), one of the king's daughters, acting as a first-person narrator, closely resembles Queen Isabel deciding the lamentable fate of her Jewish subjects. This widespread fabrication was later taken up by Humanists such as Diogo Pires (Soyer 2014, 179), popularizing this myth even more broadly.

The publication in 1516 of the *Cancioneiro geral* (Dutton 16RE) put an end to the gap of almost two centuries in the documentation of Portuguese poetry since the death of Don Dinís in 1325 (Fernandes 2010, 48). Its compiler, Garcia de Resende, was an authentic Lusitanian *alter ego* of Hernando del Castillo (Osório 2005, 295). Careful examination of Resende's compilation has suggested to some scholars the existence of a few other *cancioneiros*, such as one that is hypothetically attributed to the "abade que chaman Frei Martinho" (Fernandes 2018, 335). The courtly dimension in Resende's compilation is key to understanding the high level of cultural achievement at the court of João II between the years 1481 and 1495 (Morán Cabanas 2018, 363), even though Dias points out that some verses also show "momentos tenebrosos da corte do Príncipe Perfeito" (Resende 1990, 5: 359).

Regarding our main purpose here, let us begin by saying that before 1516, the only signs of Jews and conversos in the earlier Portuguese *cancioneiros* are two well-wrought *cantigas d'amor* composed by a certain Vidal from the town of Elvas (Barbieri 2005, 356). In them he adopts traditional Western techniques (Alvar 2001, 64), such as the *descriptio puellae* (Frateschi-Vieira 2018, 358–359) in praise of a Jewish woman. The lack of information on Vidal de Elvas, and on medieval Portuguese poetry in general, makes the *Cancioneiro Geral* all the more relevant, not only as a product of past traditions but also as a stepping stone toward the Portuguese poetry of the Renaissance, in which topics concerning Jews and conversos would be utilized by authors as successful as Gil Vicente (Girón Negrón 2011, 245).

One dimension in which both the Castillo and Resende compilations coincide is the fact that most of the poems in which Jews and conversos appear are concentrated in burlesque sections, such as the *Cousas de folgar e gentilezas* (Resende 1990, 5: 359–375), which can be considered a sort of modernization of the former *Cantigas de escárnio e maldizer* (Fernandes 2010, 49). It contains frequent attacks against Jews (Rodríguez Fernández 2000, 603), perhaps inspired by works such as André Dias's *Laudário*, composed around 1435 under the inspiration of the common Iberian climate of Dominican anti-Jewish hostility (Martins 1951, 14).

However, conversos and other minorities can also be found elsewhere in the *Cancioneiro Geral* (Rodríguez Fernández 2000, 610–621). For instance, in the *cantiga d'amor* (ID 7151, 16RE-1030 fol. 198v: "Em que me visseis viver"), the poet Aires Teles takes the well-known topic of the beautiful Jewish woman, but applies it instead to a *judeoconversa*, whose status is conveyed by a rubric stating that the lady "tinha duas leis":

> [I] Em que me visseis viver
> em outra lei atequi,
> senhora, como vos vi,
> conheci
> que na vossa hei-de morrer.
>
> [II] Pois que nam quero viver
> na lei que tive atequi,
> consenti,
> senhora, que desd'aqui
> na vossa possa morrer.
>
> [III] E pois que ja tenho a fee,
> senhora, dai vós a graça,
> qu'as obras forçado lh'ee
> qu'em vosso nome as faca.

(Resende 1990, 4: 126)

It seems fair to say that the *judeoconversa* inherited in Iberian literature a role comparable to that played by the Jewish woman, who was sexually objectified by Christian poets. This had already been evident in the era of Alfonso X el Sabio (Mirrer 1996, 33), being even more conspicuous in connection with another topos: that of "os judeus casamenteiros", Jewish matchmakers (Márquez Villanueva 2006b, 259).

The presence of conversos in Resende's *Cancioneiro geral* is dominated by jokes and accusations similar to those already seen in the Castilian *cancioneros* (Barbieri 2005, 360–361), such as the reference to the *ares maus*, or 'evil winds', to refer to Jewish habits (Rodríguez Fernández 2000, 605). There is, however, a substantial poem in which the different conditions of religious conversion in Castile and Portugal serve as the background of a sort of nationalist brawl (Faingold 1991, 34–35). It was written as a response to a "rifam" from some "castelhanos à porta do paço em Castela, andando laa o Duque dom Diogo" (ID 4943 16RE-82, fol. 67v: "Portugueses mantengaos Dios"):

> [I] Portugueses, mantengaos Dios
> y vos guarde de las manos
> de los crudos castelhanos.
> Qual prazeraa más a vos:
> ¿chofres, o bofes, o levianos?

(Resende 1990, 2: 47)

The Portuguese response, written by Fernam da Silveira, alludes to the roles played in the battle of Aljubarrota (1385) by the victorious Portuguese army and the defeated Castilian one (Barbieri 2005, 361–362), but adds insult to injury by equating Castilians with crypto-Jews, or more specifically, with "putos marranos" (ID 5460, 16RE-283, fol. 68r: "Castelhanos mantengaos Dios"):

> [I] Castelhanos, mantengaos Dios
> y guarde de tal afruenta
> qual fue la d'Aljubarrota,

> onde meus e teus avoos
> ali chofres nos a vos,
> nos como lindos galanos,
> vos como putos marranos
> fuyendo delante nos,
> nos vos valiendo las manos.
>
> (Resende 1990, 2: 47–48)

Line 7 immediately reminds one of Montoro's bitter lament of "viejo puto y judío". It is even more surprising if we consider that, sometime after the Portuguese Silveira claimed that all Castilians were 'marranos', in Golden Age Spanish literature the shoe was on the other foot, as 'Portuguese' was rendered a synonym of 'crypto-Jew'. This phenomenon emerges at approximately the same time that the pejorative 'marrano' was being taken as a synonym for 'Spanish' in Italy and other European countries (Díaz Esteban 2008, 594). It should be remembered that the Portuguese and the Castilians, as well as the other inhabitants of the Iberian Peninsula, were perceived by other Europeans as virtually identical, sharing the same undesirable burden of cultural influences somehow related to the Jews (Castaño González 2015, 194–195).

8 Conclusion

I hope to have made clear in the above how *cancioneros* and *cancioneiros* can be profitable sources for attempting to calibrate the complex and difficult evolution of Jews and conversos in the Iberian literatures. Their journey through Iberian history is impeccably reflected in these poetry collections, from their obscurity in the Galician and Portuguese *cancioneiros* at the turn of the fifteenth century to their surprising visibility in *Baena* and *Palacio* and the problems they endured during the age of *cancioneros enriqueños*. They reached the end of the road during the age of the Catholic Monarchs through sinister neglect and the forced transformation of an entire social and spiritual group into bait for the cruel parodies compiled in the Castilian *Cancionero general*, a sad fact also reflected in the Portuguese *Cancioneiro geral*. Since a significant number of these poems related to polemics against Jews and conversos still remains unpublished, it would be desirable to gather a complete corpus with all of the relevant compositions. This would allow us to gain a better understanding of the cultural role they played, either as prominent poets or as unexpected characters. Once this corpus is published, it will be possible to analyze more thoroughly the essential importance of Jews and conversos in Iberian poetry, especially of those members of the converso community "that, armed with the courage of its ancestral faith and the memory of Jewish past, stood alone against an entire establishment that sought unsuccessfully to destroy it" (Beinart 1992, 382).

Bibliography

Works Cited

Abate, Mark T. "Ever Since Castro: Thomas F. Flick, Medieval Spain, and *Convivencia*." *Convivencia and Medieval Spain. Essays in Honor of Thomas F. Glick*. Ed. Mark T. Abate. New York: Palgrave Macmillan, 2019. 1–61.

Abulafia, David. "The servitude of Jews and Muslims in the Medieval Mediterranean: Origins and Diffusion." *Mélanges de l'Ecole Française de Rome. Moyen Âge* 112.2 (2000): 687–714.

Afonso, Luís. "The Cultural Construction of the Jews in late medieval Portugal: contributions to a reevaluation." *Mitteilungen der Carl Justi-Vereinigung* 13 (2001): 22–46.

Aizenberg, Edna. "*Una judía muy fermosa*: The Jewes as Sex Object in Medieval Spanish Literature and Lore." *La Corónica* 12.2 (1984): 187–194.

Alba, Amparo, and Carlos Sáinz de la Maza. "La tradición judía como arma antijudía: los relatos rabínicos de Jerónimo de Santa Fe." *Violence et identité religieuse dans l'Espagne du Xve au XVII siècles*. Coord. Rica Amran. Paris/Amiens: Indigo et Côte-Femmes – Université de Picardie Jules Verne, 2011. 257–287.

Alcalá Galve, Ángel. *Los judeoconversos en la cultura y sociedad españolas*. Madrid: Trotta, 2011.

Alcoberro, Agustí. "La exaltación mesiánica de los Reyes Católicos y la expulsión de los judíos de los reinos hispánicos." *Revista de la Inquisición, Tolerancia y Derechos Humanos* 22 (2018): 77–90.

Alvar, Carlos. "La poesía de Mosén Diego de Valera (tradición textual y aproximación cronológica)." *Filologia romanza e cultura medievale. Studi in onore di Elio Melli*. Eds. Andrea Fassò et al. Alessandria: Edizioni Dell'Orso, 1998. 1: 1–13.

Alvar, Carlos. "Apostillas cancioneriles: de Vidal de Elvas a Álvarez de Villasandino." *Canzonieri iberici*. Eds. Patrizia Botta, Carmen Parrilla García and José Ignacio Pérez Pascual. Noia-Padova/A Coruña: Toxosoutos, 2001. 1: 59–75.

Alvar, Carlos, and Ángel Gómez Moreno. *La poesía lírica medieval*. Madrid: Taurus, 1988.

Alvar Ezquerra, Manuel. *Isabel la Católica. Una reina vencedora, una mujer derrotada*. Madrid: Temas de Hoy, 2002.

Álvarez Gato, Juan. *Obras completas*. Ed. Jenaro Artiles Rodríguez. Madrid: Los Clásicos Olvidados, 1928.

Álvarez Pellitero, Ana María (ed.) *Cancionero de Palacio*. Valladolid: Junta de Castilla y León – Consejería de Cultura y Turismo, 1993.

Amador de los Ríos, José. *Historia crítica de la literatura española*. Madrid: Imprenta José Fernández Cancela, 1865, 7 Vols.

Amran, Rica. "De 1449 a 1467: el problema converso y la construcción de la monarquía bajo los Reyes Católicos." *Identidades confesionales y construcciones nacionales en Europa (ss. XV-XIX)*. Dirs. José Ignacio Ruiz Rodríguez and Igor Sosa Mayor. Alcalá de Henares: Servicio de Publicaciones de la Universidad de Alcalá, 2012. 195–214.

Arbós Ayuso, Cristina. "Los cancioneros castellanos del siglo XV como fuente para la historia de los judíos españoles." *Proceedings of the Eighth World Congress of Jewish Studies*. Jerusalem: World Union of Jewish Studies, 1982. 35–42.

Arbós Ayuso, Cristina. "Judíos y conversos: un tema tópico en la poesía medieval." *Encuentros en Sefarad. Actas del Congreso Internacional «Los judíos en la Historia de España»*. Ciudad Real: Instituto de Estudios Manchegos, 1987. 137–152.

Armistead, Samuel G. "The memory of tri-religious Spain in the sephardic *romancero*." *Encuentros & Desencuentros. Spanish-Jewish Cultural Interaction Throughout History*." Eds. Carlos Carrete

Parrondo, Marcelo Dascal, Francisco Márquez Villanueva and Ángel Sáenz-Badillos. Tel Aviv: University Publishing Projects, 2000. 265–286.
Aronson-Friedman, Amy, and Gregory B. Kaplan. "Editors' Introduction." *Marginal Voices: Studies in Converso Literature of Medieval and Golden Age Spain*. Eds. Amy Aronson-Friedman and Gregory B. Kaplan. Leiden/Boston: Brill, 2012. 1–17.
Asenjo González, María. "Conflicto y propaganda: apéndice documental." *Orígenes de la monarquía hispánica: propaganda y legitimación* (ca. *1400–1520)*. Dir. José Manuel Nieto Soria. Madrid: Dykinson, 1999. 458–487.
Asensio, Eugenio. "La peculiaridad literaria de los conversos." *Anuario de Estudios Medievales* 4 (1967): 327–351.
Asensio, Eugenio. *La España imaginada de Américo Castro*. Barcelona: El Albir, 1992.
Atlee, Carl W. "A Reassessment of the Satirical Nature of Gómez Manrique's *Coplas para Diego Arias de Ávila*." *La Corónica* 35.2 (2007): 173–207.
Aubrun, Charles V. *Le chansonnier espagnol d'Herberay des Essarts (XVe siècle)*. Bordeaux: Féret et Fils, 1951.
Avalle-Arce, Juan Bautista. "Reseña de Fray Hernando de Talavera, *Católica impugnación*. Estudio preliminar de Francisco Márquez Villanueva, edición y notas de Francisco Martín Hernández. Barcelona, Juan Flors, 1961." *Romance Philology* 29 (1965): 384–391.
Avalle-Arce, Juan Bautista. *Temas hispánicos medievales*. Madrid: Gredos, 1974.
Avalle-Arce, Juan Bautista. "Más sobre Pedro de Cartagena, converso y poeta del *Cancionero general*." *Modern Language Studies* 11 (1981): 70–82.
Azáceta, José María, ed. *Cancionero de Juan Fernández de Íxar*. Madrid: CSIC, 1956, 2 Vols.
Azáceta, José María, ed. *Cancionero de Gallardo*. Madrid: CSIC, 1962.
Azcona, Tarsicio de. *Juana de Castilla, mal llamada La Beltraneja: 1462–1530*. Madrid: Fundación Universitaria Española, 1998.
Bahler, Ingrid, and Katherine Gyékényesi Gatto. *Of Kings and Poets: Cancionero Poetry of the Trastámara Courts*. New York: Peter Lang, 1992.
Baena, Juan Alfonso de. *Cancionero de Juan Alfonso de Baena*. Ed. Brian Dutton and Joaquín González Cuenca. Madrid: Visor Libros, 1993.
Baer, Yizthak. *A History of the Jews in Christian Spain*. Philadelphia: Jewish Publication Society of America, 1966, 2 Vols.
Bajo Pérez, Elena. *Vocabulario y fe. Los grupos étnico-religiosos de la Edad Media y la primera modernidad*. Mantova: Universitas Studiorum S.r.l., Casa Editrice, 2015.
Barbieri, Mario. "Hacia un estudio del tema judío y converso en el *Cancioneiro Geral* de Garcia de Resende." *Actes del X Congrés Internacional de l'Associació Hispànica de Literatura Medieval*. Coords. Josep Lluís Martos Sánchez et al. Alacant: Institut Interuniversitaru de Filologia Valenciana, 2005. 1: 355–363.
Beceiro Pita, Isabel. "La incidencia de la religiosidad en el enaltecimiento de las monarquías hispánicas de fines del medievo." *La espiritualidad y la configuración de los reinos ibéricos (siglos XII–XV)*. Dir. Isabel Beceiro Pita. Madrid: Dykinson, 2018, 321–363.
Beinart, Haim. "The great conversion and the *Converso* problem." *Moreshet Sepharad. The Sephardi Legacy*. Ed. Haim Beinart. Jerusalem: The Magnes Press, The Hebrew University, 1992. 1: 346–382.
Beinart, Haim. *The Expulsion of the Jews from Spain*. Oxford/Portland: The Littman Library of Jewish Civilization, 2002.
Beltran, Vicenç. "La *cantiga* de Alfonso XI y la ruptura poética del siglo XIV." *El Crotalón. Anuario de Filología Española* 2 (1985): 259–263.
Beltran, Vicenç. *La canción de amor en el Otoño de la Edad Media*. Barcelona: PPU, 1988.

Beltran, Vicenç. "*La poesía es un arma cargada de futuro*: Poética y política en el *Cancionero de Baena*". *Juan Alfonso de Baena y su* Cancionero. *Actas del I Congreso Internacional sobre el "Cancionero de Baena"*. Eds. Jesús L. Serrano Reyes and Juan Fernández Jiménez. Baena: Ayuntamiento de Baena, Diputación de Córdoba, 2001a. 15–52.

Beltran, Vicenç. "El *Testamento* de Alfonso Enríquez." *Convergences médiévales: épopée, lyrique, roman: mélanges offerts à Madeleine Tyssens*. Eds. Nadine Henrard et al. Louvain-La-Neuve: De Boeck, 2001b. 63–76.

Beltran, Vicenç. *Poesía española 2. Edad Media: Lírica y Cancioneros*. Barcelona: Crítica, 2002.

Beltran, Vicenç. "Tipología y génesis de los cancioneros: la reordenación de los contenidos." *Los cancioneros españoles: materiales y métodos*. Eds. Manuel Moreno and Dorothy S. Severin. London: Queen Mary & Westfield University, 2005. 9–58.

Beltran, Vicenç. "Morfología del cancionero. Los cancioneros castellanos." *La Tradizione della lirica romanza del Medioevo Romanzo. Problemi di Filologia Formale. Atti del Convegno Internazionale*. Ed. Lino Leonardi. Firenze: Edizioni del Galluzzo per la Fondazione Ezio Franceschini, 2011. 409–437.

Beltran, Vicenç. "Poesía musical antigua y cultura humanística: Juan del Encina entre Castilla e Italia." *'Vir bonus dicendi peritus': Studies in honor of Charles B. Faulhaber*. Eds. Antonio Cortijo Ocaña, Ana M. Gómez-Bravo and María Morrás. New York: Hispanic Seminary of Medieval Studies, 2014. 17–62.

Benito, Ana. "Inquisition and the Creation of the Other." *Marginal Voices: Studies in Converso Literature of Medieval and Golden Age Spain*. Eds. Amy Aronson-Friedman and Gregory B. Kaplan. Leiden/Boston: Brill, 2012. 43–67.

Benito Ruano, Eloy. *Toledo en el siglo XV. Vida política*. Madrid: CSIC, 1961.

Benito Ruano, Eloy. *Los orígenes del problema converso*. Madrid: Real Academia de la Historia, 2001.

Bermejo Cabrero, José Luis. "Ideales políticos de Juan de Mena." *Revista de Estudios Políticos* 188 (1973): 153–175.

Bernáldez, Andrés. *Memorias del reinado de los Reyes Católicos*. Eds. Juan de Mata Carriazo and Manuel Gómez-Moreno. Madrid: Real Academia de la Historia, 1962.

Blanco González, Bernardo. "Realismo y alegoría en el *Cancionero de Juan Alfonso de Baena*." *Cuadernos de Filología* 6 (1972): 29–75.

Boase, Roger. *The Troubadour Revival: A Study of Social Change and Traditionalism in Late Medieval Spain*. Boston/London: Routledge and Kegan Paul, 1978.

Bodian, Miriam. *Dying in the Law of Moses. Crypto-Jewish Martyrdom in the Iberian World*. Bloomington: Indiana University Press, 2007.

Caíño Carballo, Ana. *La poesía dialogada de Juan Alfonso de Baena: edición y estudio*. Madrid: Fundación Universitaria Española, 2018.

Calvo Pérez, Juan José. *La poesía de Alfonso Álvarez de Villasandino*. Burgos: Institución «Fernán González», 1998.

Cantalapiedra Erostarbe, Fernando. "Minerva's Dog and Other Problematic Points in *Celestina*'s Text." *A Companio to Celestina*. Ed. Enrique Fernández. Leiden/Boston: Brill, 2017. 108–123.

Cantera Burgos, Francisco. "El *Cancionero de Baena*: judíos y conversos en él." *Sefarad* 27.1 (1967): 71–111.

Cantera Burgos, Francisco. "El poeta Cartagena y sus ascendientes los Franco". *Sefarad* 28.1 (1968): 3–39.

Cantera Burgos, Francisco. *El poeta Rodrigo Cota y su familia de judíos conversos*. Madrid: Universidad de Madrid, 1970.

Caro García, Juan. *El Fortalitium Fidei: ¿un manual para conversos?* Ph. Dissertation University of Sevilla, 2009.

Carpenter, Dwayne E., ed. *Libro del Alborayque*. Mérida: Editora Regional de Extremadura, 2005, 2 Vols.

Carpenter, Dwayne E. "Polémicos privilegios: dos versiones de la primera sátira conocida en contra de los conversos." *Sefarad* 72.2 (2012): 295–324.

Carrete Parrondo, Carlos. *Fontes Iudaeroum Regni Castellae III. Proceso inquisitorial contra los Arias Dávila segovianos: un enfrentamiento social entre judíos y conversos*. Salamanca/Granada: Ediciones de la Universidad Pontificia de Salamanca/Universidad de Granada, 1986.

Carrete Parrondo, Carlos. "Mesianismo entre los judeoconversos castellanos." *Encuentros & Desencuentros. Spanish-Jewish Cultural Interaction Throughout History*. Eds. Carlos Carrete Parrondo et al. Tel Aviv: University Publishing Projects, 2000. 481–490.

Carrillo de Huete, Pedro. *Crónica del halconero de Juan II de Castilla*. Ed. Juan de Mata Carriazo y Arroquia. Estudio preliminar Rafael Beltrán Llavador. Granada: Universidad, 2006.

Cáseda Teresa, Jesús Fernando. "En torno a Rodrigo Cota y la autoría de las *Coplas del provincial*." *Sefarad* 79.1 (2019): 163–197.

Castaño González, Javier. "Las aljamas judías de Castilla a mediados del siglo XV: la *Carta Real* de 1450." *En la España Medieval* 18 (1995): 181–203.

Castaño González, Javier. "Men of the Nations of Portugal and Spain in Ferrara: The Socio-Economic Iberian Background." *Conversos, marrani e nuove comunità ebraiche in età moderna. Atti del convegno internacionale di studi*. Ed. Myriam Silvera. Firenze: Giuntina, 2015. 191–202.

Castillo, Hernando del. *Cancionero general recopilado por Hernando del Castillo (Valencia, 1511)*. Facsimile edition, with prologue and notes by Antonio Rodríguez-Moñino. Madrid: Real Academia Española, 1958.

Castillo, Hernando del. *Cancionero general*. Ed. Joaquín González Cuenca. Madrid: Castalia, 2004, 5 Vols.

Castro, Américo. *The Structure of Spanish History*. Tr. Edmund King. Princeton: University Press, 1954.

Castro, Américo. *De la edad conflictiva*. Madrid: Taurus, 1961.

Castro, Américo. *Cervantes y los casticismos españoles*. Madrid: Alfaguara, 1966.

Castro, Américo. *Aspectos del vivir hispánico*. Madrid: Alianza, 1970.

Castro, Américo. *La realidad histórica de España*. México: Porrúa, 1982.

Cátedra, Pedro M. *La historiografía en verso en la época de los Reyes Católicos. Juan Barba y su Consolatoria de Castilla*. Salamanca: Ediciones Universidad de Salamanca, 1989.

Cátedra, Pedro M. "Fray Vicente Ferrer y la predicación antijudaica en la campaña castellana (1411–1412)." *"Qu'un sang impur. . ." Les Conversos et le pouvoir en Espagne à la fin du moyen âge*. Coord. Jeanne Battesti Pelegrin. Aix-en-Provence: Publications de l'Université de Provence, 1997. 19–46.

Cavallero, Constanza. "Inquisición, decisión real y expulsión de minorías. El tribunal de la fe ante el destierro masivo de judíos y moriscos (1492, 1609, 1614)." *Revista de la Inquisición, Intolerancia y Derechos Humanos* 22 (2018): 91–114.

Cepeda Adán, José. *En torno al concepto de Estado en los Reyes Católicos*. Madrid: CSIC, 1956.

Chas Aguión, Antonio. *Juan Alfonso de Baena y los diálogos poéticos de su cancionero*. Baena: Ayuntamiento de Baena, 2001.

Chas Aguión, Antonio. "De ceremoniales, galanteo y técnica poética: los manuales de gentileza en la poesía de cancionero." *De la lettre à l'esprit. Hommage à Michel Garcia*. Ed. Carlos Heusch. París: Éditions Le Manuscrit, 2009. 139–163.

Chas Aguión, Antonio. "Concordancias y discordancias temporales en los intercambios poéticos de cancionero: el tiempo de creación y el tiempo de ejecución." *La concordance des temps. Moyen Âge et Époque moderne*. Ed. Gilles Luquet. París: Presses Sorbonne Nouvelle, 2010. 153–174.

Chas Aguión, Antonio. "Juan García de Vinuesa y Álvar Ruiz de Toro, poetas del *Cancionero de Baena*." *Bulletin of Hispanic Studies* 91.8 (2014): 843–854.

Chas Aguión, Antonio. "Avatares de una azarosa transmisión textual: poesía y poetas en la sección nuclear de Juan Alfonso de Baena en PN1." *Poesía, poéticas y cultura literaria*. Eds. Andrea Zinato and Paola Bellomi. Como/Pavía: Ibis, 2018. 125–145.

Chas Aguión, Antonio, and Paula Díaz Prieto. "Diego y Gonzalo Martínez de Medina. Escollos biográficos." *Escritura y reescrituras en el entorno literario del* Cancionero de Baena. Ed. Antonio Chas Aguión. Berlín: Peter Lang, 2018. 75–92.

Chicharro Chamorro, Dámaso. *Las* Coplas del Provincial *en su entorno social*. Jaén: Real Sociedad Económica de Amigos del País de Jaén, 2003.

Cohen, Mario Eduardo. "Las Provisiones de expulsión de 1492: vigencia en el espacio y en el tiempo." *Judaísmo hispano: Estudios en memoria de José Luis Lacave Riaño*. Ed. Elena Romero. Madrid: CSIC, 2002. 2: 715–726.

Cohen, Rip. *Thirty-Two Cantigas d'amigo of Dom Dinis: Typology of a Portuguese Renunciation*. Madison: Hispanic Seminary of Medieval Studies, 1987.

Conde, Juan Carlos. *La creación de un discurso historiográfico en el Cuatrocientos castellano:* Las siete edades del mundo *de Pablo de Santa María. Estudio y edición*. Salamanca: Ediciones Universidad de Salamanca, 1999.

Conde Solares, Carlos. *El Cancionero de Herberay y la corte literaria del Reino de Navarra*. Newcastle upon Tyne: Arts and Social Sciences Academic Press, 2009.

Contreras, Jaime. "Judíos, judaizantes y conversos en la peninsula ibérica en los tiempos d ela expulsión." *Judíos. Sefarditas. Conversos. La expulsión de 1492 y sus consecuencias*. Ed. Ángel Alcalá Galve. Valladolid: Ámbito, 1995. 457–477

Cortijo Ocaña, Antonio, and Marcial Rubio Árquez, ed. Las 'Obras de burlas' del Cancionero general *de Hernando del Castillo*. Santa Barbara: University of California Publications of eHumanista, 2015.

Cota, Rodrigo. *Diálogo entre el amor y un viejo*. Firenze: Felice Le Monnier Editore, 1961.

D'Agostino, Alfonso. "*Cide Hamete Berenjena*, apostilla sanchina." *Anales Cervantinos* 43 (2011): 327–329.

Daileader, Philip. *Saint Vicent Ferrer. His World and Life. Religion and Society in Late Medieval Europe*. New York: Palgrave Macmillan, 2016.

Darbord, Michel. *Le poésie religieuse espagnole des Rois Catholiques a Philippe II*. Paris: Centre de Recherches de l'Institut d'Études Hispaniques, 1965.

De Bunes Ibarra, Miguel Ángel. "Una danza contra judíos de finales del siglo XVI." *Judaísmo hispano: Estudios en memoria de José Luis Lacave Riaño*. Ed. Elena Romero. Madrid: CSIC, 2002. 2: 791–797.

De La Torre Gómez, Hipólito. *Fronteras. Estudios de historia de Portugal y de las relaciones peninsulares*. Madrid: Editorial Universitaria Ramón Areces, 2016.

De los Ríos, Ángel. "Cómo y por qué se llamó a don Pedro el Cruel Pero Gil." *Boletín de la Real Academia de la Historia* 36 (1900): 58–65.

Delbrugge, Laura. *A Scholarly Edition of Andrés de Li's* Thesoro de la Passion *(1494)*. Leiden: Brill, 2011.

Delbrugge, Laura. "Pragmatism, Patience and the Passion: The *Converso* Element in the *Summa de paciencia* (1493) and the *Thesoro de la passión* (1494)." *Marginal Voices: Studies in Converso Literature of Medieval and Golden Age Spain*. Eds. Amy Aronson-Friedman and Gregory B. Kaplan. Leiden/Boston: Brill, 2012. 141–160.

Deyermond, Alan. "Baena, Santillana, Resende and the Silent Century of Portuguese Court Poetry." *Bulletin of Hispanic Studies* 59 (1982): 198–210.

Díaz Esteban, Fernando. "Un fragmento de poesía litúrgica hispanohebrea en Barcelona." *Anuario de Filología* 2 (1976): 155–172.

Díaz Esteban, Fernando. "Literatura de los sefardíes occidentales." *Sefardíes: Literatura y lengua de una nación dispersa*. Coords. Iacob M. Hassán and Ricardo Izquierdo Benito. Cuenca: Ediciones de la Universidad de Castilla, La Mancha, 2008. 593–610.

Díaz Marcilla, Francisco José. "La influencia de Ramón Llull en el entorno del *Cancionero de Juan Alfonso de Baena*." *Antonianum* 90 (2015): 623–654.

Díaz-Mas, Paloma. "Un género casi perdido de la poesía castellana medieval: la clerecía rabínica." *Boletín de la Real Academia Española* 73.259 (1993): 329–346.

Díaz-Mas, Paloma. "Poesía medieval judía." *Judíos en la literatura española*. Coords. Iacob M. Hassán and Ricardo Izquierdo Benito. Cuenca: Ediciones de la Universidad de Castilla-La Mancha, 2001. 29–56.

Díez Garretas, María Jesús. "El *Cancionero de Juan Fernández de Híjar* (MN6) y *Diversi Rime en Spannol*, manuscrito GL. KGL. Samling, 435.20 de la Biblioteca Real de Copenhague (CR)." *Medievalismo en Extremadura: estudios sobre literatura y cultura hispánicas de la Edad Media*. Eds. Jesús Cañas Murillo et al. Cáceres: Universidad de Extremadura, 2009. 381–392.

Dobb, Maurice. *Studies in the Development of Capitalism*. New York: International Publishers, 1963.

Domínguez Ortiz, Antonio. *Los judeoconversos en España y América*. Madrid: Istmo, 1971.

Domínguez Ortiz, Antonio. *La clase social de los conversos en la Edad Moderna*. Granada: Universidad, 1991.

Doron, Aviva. "New Trends in the Conception of Hebrew Poetry in Thirteenth and Fourteenth-Century Spain in Relation to Spanish Literature." *Encuentros & Desencuentros. Spanish-Jewish Cultural Interaction Throughout History*. Eds. Carlos Carrete Parrondo et al. Tel Aviv: University Publishing Projects, 2000. 213–239.

Dumanoir, Virginie. "Textos poéticos romanceriles del siglo XV dentro de la *variatio* cancioneril." *Actas del XIV Congreso de la Asociación Internacional de Hispanistas*. Coords. Isaías Lerner et al. Newark: Juan de la Cuesta, 2004. 1: 75–84.

Dutton, Brian. "Spanish Fifteenth-Century *Cancioneros*: A General Survey to 1465." *Kentucky Renaissance Quarterly* 26.4 (1979): 445–460.

Dutton, Brian. *El Cancionero castellano del siglo XV (c. 1360–1520)*. Salamanca: Universidad de Salamanca, 1990–1991, 7 Vols.

Dutton, Brian, and Victoriano Roncero López. *La poesía cancioneril del siglo XV. Antología y estudio*. Madrid/Frankfurt: Iberoamericana-Vervuert, 2004.

Edwards, John. "*Conversos*, Judaism, and the Language of the Monarchy in Fifteenth Century Castile." *Circa 1492: Proceedings of the Jerusalem Colloquium: Litterae Judaeroum in Terra Hispanica*. Ed. Isaac Benabu. Jerusalem: The Hebrew University of Jerusalem and Misgav Yerushalayin, 1992. 207–223.

Edwards, John. "Portugal and the Expulsion of the Jews From Spain." *Medievo Hispano. Estudios* in memoriam *del Prof. Derek W. Lomax*. Madrid: Sociedad Española de Estudios Medievales, 1995. 121–139.

Enríquez del Castillo, Diego. *Crónica de Enrique IV*. Ed. Aureliano Sánchez Martín. Valladolid: Universidad de Valladolid, 1994.

Estow, Clara. *Pedro the Cruel of Castile, 1350–1369*. Leiden: Brill, 1995.

Faingold, Reuven. "Judíos y conversos en el teatro portugués pre-vicentino. La *Farsa do Alfaiate* en el *Cancioneiro Geral* de García de Resende." *Sefarad. Revista de Estudios Hebraicos y Sefardíes* 51.1 (1991): 23–50.

Faulhaber, Charles B., Ángel Gómez Moreno, Antonio Cortijo Ocaña and Óscar Perea Rodríguez (ed.) *PhiloBiblon – Bibliography of Old Spanish Texts (BETA: Bibliografía Española de Textos Antiguos)*.
<http://bancroft.berkeley.edu/philobiblon/beta_en.html> (23 March 2019).

Farcasiu, Simina. "Social Purpose and Scholastic Method: The *Visión delectable* of Alfonso de La Torre." *Circa 1492: Proceedings of the Jerusalem Colloquium: Litterae Judaeroum in Terra Hispanica*. Ed. Isaac Benabu. Jerusalem: The Hebrew University of Jerusalem and Misgav Yerushalayin, 1992. 79–97.

Fernandes, Geraldo Augusto. "Da necessidade – e do prazer – em se estudar o *Cancioneiro Geral* de Garcia de Resende." *Alétheia: Revista de estudos sobre Antigüidade e Medievo* 1.1 (2010): 48–60.

Fernandes, Geraldo Augusto. "Uma possível arte poética no *Cancioneiro Geral* de Garcia de Resende (1516)." *Poesía, poéticas y cultura literaria*. Eds. Andrea Zinato and Paola Bellomi. Como/Pavía: Ibis Edizioni, 2018. 331–344.

Fernández Gallardo, Luis. *Alonso de Cartagena (1385–1456). Una biografía política en la Castilla del siglo XV*. Valladolid: Junta de Castilla y León, 2002.

Fernández García, María de los Ángeles. "Criterios inquisitoriales para detectar al marrano: los criptojudíos en Andalucía en los siglos XVI y XVII." *Judíos. Sefarditas. Conversos. La expulsión de 1492 y sus consecuencias*. Ed. Ángel Alcalá Galve. Valladolid: Ámbito, 1995. 478–502.

Fontes, Manuel Da Costa. "Writing Under Persecution: *Cárcel de amor* and the Situation of Conversos." *'Entra mayo y sale abril': Medieval Spanish Literary and Folklore Studies in Memory of Harriet Goldberg*. Eds. Manuel da Costa Fontes and Joseph T. Snow. Newark: Juan de la Cuesta, 2005. 143–160.

Foronda, François. "La guerra civil castellana vista desde Europa: ¿una cuestión de memoria histórica?" *Memoria e Historia. Utilización política en la Corona de Castilla al final de la Edad Media*. Eds. Jon Andoni Fernández de Larrea and José Ramón Díaz de Durana. Madrid: Sílex, 2010. 201–219.

Fraker, Charles F. *Studies on the "Cancionero de Baena"*. Chapel Hill: University of North Carolina Press, 1966.

Franco Silva, Alfonso. *Entre los reinados de Enrique IV y Carlos V. Los Condestables del linaje Velasco (1461–1559)*. Jaén: Universidad de Jaén, 2006.

Frateschi-Vieira, Yara. "Uma inclusão problemática nos cancioneiros galego-portugueses: o inusitado retrato feminino nas cantigas de Vidal, Judeu d'Elvas." *Poesía, poéticas y cultura literaria*. Eds. Andrea Zinato and Paola Bellomi. Como/Pavía: Ibis, 2018. 345–359.

Gálvez, Marisa. *Songbook. How Lyrics Became Poetry in Medieval Europe*. Chicago: University Press Books, 2012.

Garcia, Michel. "In Praise of *Cancionero*: Considerations on the Social Meaning of the Castilian *Cancioneros*." *Poetry at Court in Trastamaran Spain. From the «Cancionero de Baena» to the «Cancionero general»*. Eds. E. Michael Gerli and Julian Weiss. Tempe: Arizona State University, 1998. 47–56.

Garcia, Michel. "Cartas del moro Benalhatib al rey don Pedro." *Atala. Revue d'études médiévales romanes* 10 (1999): 20–37.

Garcia, Michel. "Noticias del presente. Memoria del futuro. Escribir la historia en Castilla en 1400 y más adelante." *Memoria e Historia. Utilización política en la Corona de Castilla al final de la Edad Media*. Eds. Jon Andoni Fernández de Larrea and José Ramón Díaz de Durana. Madrid: Sílex, 2010. 15–41.

Garcia, Michel. "Nuevas consideraciones sobre el *Cancionero de Oñate*." *De lágrymas fasiendo tinta... Memorias, identidades y territorios cancioneriles*. Ed. Virginie Dumanoir. Madrid: Casa de Velázquez, 2017. 71–94.

García Casar, María Fuencisla. "Las comunidades judías de la Corona de Castilla al tiempo de la expulsión: densidad geográfica, población." *Judíos. Sefarditas. Conversos. La expulsión de 1492 y sus consecuencias*. Ed. Ángel Alcalá Galve. Valladolid: Ámbito, 1995. 21–31.

Gascón Vera, Elena. "La quema de los libros de don Enrique de Villena: una maniobra política y antisemítica." *Bulletin of Hispanic Studies* 56.4 (1979): 317–324.

Gerber, Jane. "The World of Samuel Halevi: Testimony from El Transito Synagogue of Toledo." *The Jew in Medieval Iberia, 1100–1500*. Ed. Jonathan Ray. Boston: Academic Studies Press, 2012. 33–59.

Gerli, E. Michael. *Poesía cancioneril castellana*. Madrid: Akal, 1994.

Gerli, E. Michael. "Antón de Montoro and the Wages of Eloquence: Poverty, Patronage, and Poetry in Fifteenth-Century Castile." *Romance Philology* 48 (1994–1995): 265–277.

Gerli, E. Michael. "The *Converso* Condition: New Approaches to an Old Question." *Medieval Iberia. Changing Societies and Cultures in Contact and Transition*. Eds. Ivy A. Corfis and Ray Harris-Northall. Woodbridge: Boydell & Brewer, 2007. 3–15.

Gerli, E. Michael. "Sight, Sound, Scent, and Sense: Reading the *Cancionero de Palacio*." *Beyond Sight. Engaging the Senses in Iberian Literatures and Cultures, 1200–1750*. Eds. Ryan D. Giles and Steven Wagschal. Toronto/Buffalo/London: University of Toronto Press, 2018. 123–140.

Gil, Juan. "*Berenjeneros*: The Aubergine Eaters." *The Conversos and Moriscos in Late Medieval Spain and Beyond. Volume One. Departures and Change*. Ed. Kevin Ingram. Leiden/Boston: Brill, 2009. 121–142.

Gil Ortega, Carmen. "Alfonso Carrillo de Acuña, un arzobispo proconverso en la Castilla del siglo XV." *eHumanista / Conversos* 3 (2015): 138–155.

Gilman, Stephen. *The Spain of Fernando de Rojas: The Intellectual and Social Landscape of "La Celestina"*. Princeton: University Press, 1972.

Gilman, Stephen. "A Generation of «conversos»." *Romance Philology* 33.1 (1979): 87–101.

Gimeno Casalduero, Joaquín. *La imagen del monarca en la Castilla del siglo XIV*. Madrid: Revista de Occidente, 1972.

Giordano, Maria Laura. "The *Virus* in the Language: Alonso de Cartagena's Deconstruction of the «Limpieza de Sangre» in *Defensorium Unitatis Christianae* (1450)." *Medieval Encounters* 24.1–3 (2018): 226–251.

Girón Negrón, Luis M. "Huellas hebraicas en la poesía del Marqués de Santillana." *Encuentros & Desencuentros. Spanish-Jewish Cultural Interaction Throughout History*. Eds. Carlos Carrete Parrondo et al. Tel Aviv: University Publishing Projects, 2000. 161–211.

Girón Negrón, Luis M. "*La rosa y el espino* de Santob de Carrión: breve nota sobre un motivo filosófico." *Dejar hablar a los textos. Homenaje a Francisco Márquez Villanueva*. Ed. Pedro M. Piñero Ramírez. Sevilla: Universidad de Sevilla, 2005. 1: 251–259.

Girón Negrón, Luis M. "«If There Were God»: The Problem of Unbelief in the *Visión Deleytable*." *The Conversos and Moriscos in Late Medieval Spain and Beyond: Departures and Change*. Ed. Kevin Ingram. Leiden/Boston: Brill, 2009. 83–96.

Girón Negrón, Luis M. "«Juro al Deu aí somos nós»: Some Notes on Gil Vicente's Jews and the Spanish and Portuguese *cancione[i]ros*." *La Corónica* 40.1 (2011): 243–293.

Gitlitz, David M. *Secrecy and Deceit: The Religion of the Crypto-Jews*. Philadelphia: Jewish Publication Society, 1996.

Glaser, Edward. "Referencias antisemitas en la literatura peninsular de la Edad de Oro." *Nueva Revista de Filología Hispánica* 8.1 (1954): 39–62.

Glatzer, Michael. "Crisis de fe judía en España a fines del siglo XIV y principios del siglo XV." *Judíos. Sefarditas. Conversos. La expulsión de 1492 y sus consecuencias*. Ed. Ángel Alcalá Galve. Valladolid: Ámbito, 1995. 55–68.

Glick, Thomas F. "On Converso and Marrano Ethnicity." *Crisis and Creativity in the Sephardic World, 1391–1648*. Ed. Benjamin R. Gampel. New York: Columbia University Press, 1997. 59–76.

Gómez-Bravo, Ana María. "*Decir canciones*: The Question of Genre in Fifteenth-Century Castilian *Cancionero* Poetry." *Medieval Lyric. Genres in Historical Context*. Ed. William D. Paden. Chicago: University of Illinois Press, 2000. 158–187.

Gómez-Bravo, Ana María. *Textual Agency. Writing Culture and Social Networks in Fifteenth-Century Spain*. Toronto: University Press, 2013.

Gómez-Bravo, Ana María. "El judaísmo como enfermedad en el discurso médico y literario del siglo XV." *eHumanista. Journal of Iberian Studies* 39 (2018a): 12–24.

Gómez Moreno, Ángel. *El prohemio e carta del marqués de Santillana y la teoría literaria del s. XV*. Barcelona: PPU, 1990.

Gómez Moreno, Ángel. "Judíos y conversos en la prosa castellana medieval (con un excurso sobre el círculo cultural del marqués de Santillana)." *Judíos en la Literatura Española*. Eds. Iacob M. Hassán and Ricardo Izquierdo Benito. Cuenca: Ediciones de la Universidad de Castilla-La Mancha, 2001. 57–86.

Gómez Redondo, Fernando. "La «vieja métrica» medieval: principios y fundamentos." *Revista de Filología Española* 97.2 (2017): 389–404.

Gonçalves, Elsa. *De Roma ata Lixboa. Estudos sobre os cancioneiros galego-portugueses*. Eds. João Dionísio et al. A Coruña: Real Academia Galega, 2016.

González Crespo, Esther. "El afianzamiento económico y social de los hijos de doña Leonor de Guzmán." *Anuario de Estudios Medievales* 18 (1988): 289–303.

González Rolán, Tomás, and Saquero Suárez-Somonte, Pilar. *De la* Sentencia-Estatuto *de Pero Sarmiento a la* Instrucción *del Relator*. Madrid: Aben Ezra Ediciones, 2012.

Guillén de Segovia, Pero. *Obra Poética*. Ed. Carlos Moreno Hernández. Madrid: Fundación Universitaria Española, 1989.

Gutwirth, Eleazar. "Conversions to Christianity in Late Medieval Spain: An Alternative Explanation." *Shlomo Simonsohn Jubilee Volume: Studies on the History of Jews in the Middle Ages and Renaissance Period*. Eds. Daniel Carpi et al. Tel Aviv: Tel Aviv University, 1993. 97–121.

Gutwirth, Eleazar. "Reacciones ante la expulsión: del siglo XV al XVII." *Judíos. Sefarditas. Conversos. La expulsión de 1492 y sus consecuencias*. Ed. Ángel Alcalá Galve. Valladolid: Ámbito, 1995. 195–217.

Gutwirth, Eleazar. "History and Intertextuality in Late Medieval Spain." *Christians, Muslims, and Jews in Medieval and Early Modern Spain*. Eds. Mark D. Meyerson and Edward D. English. Notre Dame: University of Notre Dame Press, 2000a. 161–178.

Gutwirth, Eleazar. "Lucas Fernández y Pierre Menard: el *Auto de la Pasión*." *Encuentros & Desencuentros. Spanish-Jewish Cultural Interaction Throughout History*. Eds. Carlos Carrete Parrondo et al. Tel Aviv: University Publishing Projects, 2000b. 503–517.

Gutwirth, Eleazar. "La ciudad y el diálogo: acerca de Pero Ferruz y los Rabíes de Alcalá." *Del pasado judío en los reinos medievales hispánicos: afinidad y distanciamiento. XIII Curso de cultura hispanojudía y sefardí de la Universidad de Castilla–La Mancha*. Coords. Ricardo Izquierdo Benito and Yolanda Moreno Koch. Cuenca: Ediciones de la Universidad de Castilla-La Mancha, 2005. 147–168.

Gutwirth, Eleazar. "Jews and Courts: An Introduction." *Jewish History* 21.1 (2007): 1–13.

Hames, Harvey. "It Takes Three to Tango: Ramon Llull, Solomon ibn Adret and Alfonso de Valladolid Debate the Trinity." *Medieval Encounters* 15.2–4 (2009): 199–224.

Hamilton, Michelle. "Text and Context: A Judeo-Spanish Version of the *Danza de la muerte*." *Marginal Voices: Studies in Converso Literature of Medieval and Golden Age Spain*. Eds. Amy Aronson-Friedman and Gregory B. Kaplan. Leiden/Boston: Brill, 2012. 161–182.

Haywood, Louise M. (2009): "Juan de Torres in the context of the *Cancionero de Palacio* (SA7)." *Bulletin of Hispanic Studies* 86.1 (2009): 46–54.

Hernández Franco, Juan. *Sangre limpia, sangre española. El debate de los estatutos de limpieza (siglos XV–XVII)*. Madrid: Cátedra, 2011.

Huerga Criado, Pilar. *En la raya de Portugal. Solidaridad y tensiones en la comunidad judeoconversa*. Salamanca: Ediciones de la Universidad, 1994.

Infantes de Miguel, Víctor. "Edición, literatura y realeza: apuntes sobre los pliegos poéticos incunables." *Literatura hispánica, Reyes Católicos y descubrimiento. Actas del congreso internacional sobre literatura hispánica en la época de los Reyes Católicos y el descubrimiento*. Ed. Manuel Criado del Val. Barcelona: PPU, 1989. 85–98.

Infantes de Miguel, Víctor, and Juan Carlos Conde. "*Antes de partir*. Un poema taurino antijudaico en el Toledo medieval (¿1489?)." *De cancioneros manuscritos y poesía impresa. Estudios bibliográficos y literarios sobre lírica castellana del siglo XV*. Madrid: Arco Libros, 2007. 87–104.

Ingram, Kevin. *Converso Non-Conformism in Early Modern Spain. Bad Blood and Faith from Alonso de Cartagena to Diego Velázquez*. New York: Palgrave Macmillan, 2018.

Jiménez Monteserín, Miguel. *Introducción a la Inquisición española*. Madrid: Editora Nacional, 1980.

Jones, Royston Oscar. "Isabel la Católica y el amor cortés." *Revista de Literatura* 21 (1962): 55–64.

Jonin, Michel. "Le *converso* ou «l'effacement de l'altérité»: sur une représentation littéraire de judéo-convers." *"Qu'un sang impur. . ." Les Conversos et le pouvoir en Espagne à la fin du moyen âge. Actes du 2ème colloque d'Aix-en-Provence, 18-19-20 novembre 1994*. Coord. Jeanne Battesti Pelegrin. Aix-en-Provence: Publications de l'Université de Provence, 1997. 123–37.

Kalinina, Elena. "Leyendas negras como un instrumento político y legal en la época de la Baja Edad Media y el principio de la época Moderna. El ejemplo de Pedro el Cruel (1350–1369) y Felipe II (1556–1598)." *Estudios de Historia de España* 20.1 (2018): 1–27.

Kaplan, Gregory B. "Toward the Establishment of a Christian Identity: The Conversos and Early Castilian Humanism". *La Corónica* 25.1 (1996): 53–68.

Kaplan, Gregory B. *The Evolution of* Converso *Literature. The Writings of the Converted Jews of Medieval Spain*. Gainesville: University Press of Florida, 2002.

Kaplan, Gregory B. "The Inception of *Limpieza de Sangre* (Purity of Blood) and its Impact in Medieval and Golden Age Spain." *Marginal Voices. Studies in Converso Literature of Medieval and Golden Age Spain*. Eds. Amy Aronson-Friedman and Gregoy B. Kaplan. Leiden/Boston: Brill, 2012. 19–42.

Kriegel, Maurice. "Alonso de Oropesa devant la question des conversos: une stratégie d'intégration hiéronymite?" *"Qu'un sang impur. . ." Les Conversos et le pouvoir en Espagne à la fin du moyen âge. Actes du 2ème colloque d'Aix-en-Provence, 18-19-20 novembre 1994*. Coord. Jeanne Battesti Pelegrin. Aix-en-Provence: Publications de l'Université de Provence, 1997. 9–18.

Ladero Quesada, Miguel Ángel. *La Hacienda real de Castilla en el siglo XV*. La Laguna: Universidad, 1973.

Ladero Quesada, Miguel Ángel. "El número de judíos en la España de 1492: los que se fueron." *Judíos. Sefarditas. Conversos. La expulsión de 1492 y sus consecuencias*. Ed. Ángel Alcalá Galve. Valladolid: Ámbito, 1995a. 170–180.

Ladero Quesada, Miguel Ángel. "Marco histórico: Iglesia, sociedad y educación." *Historia de la acción educadora de la Iglesia en España*. Coord. Bernabé Bartolomé Martínez. Madrid: Biblioteca de Autores Cristianos, 1995b. 1: 105–131.

Ladero Quesada, Miguel Ángel. "Coronel, 1492: De la aristocracia judía a la nobleza cristiana en la España de los Reyes Católicos." *Boletín de la Real Academia de la Historia* 100.1 (2003): 11–24.

Ladero Quesada, Miguel Ángel. *La España de los Reyes Católicos*. Madrid: Alianza, 2005.

Lafuente Gómez, Mario. *Un reino en armas. La guerra de los Dos Pedros en Aragón (1356–1366)*. Zaragoza: Institución «Fernando el Católico», 2014.

Lapesa, Rafael. "La lengua de la poesía lírica desde Macías hasta Villasandino." *Romance Philology* 7 (1953–1954): 51–59.

Lawee, Eric. "Sephardic Intellectuals: Challenges and Creativity (1391–1492)." *The Jew in Medieval Iberia, 1100–1500*. Ed. Jonathan Ray. Boston: Academic Studies Press, 2012. 352–394.

Lewis, Clive S. *The Allegory of Love. A Study in Medieval Tradition*. Oxford: University Press, 1992.

Lida de Malkiel, María Rosa. "La hipérbole sagrada en la poesía castellana del siglo XV." *Revista de Filología Hispánica* 8 (1946): 121–130.

Lomax, Derek W. "¿Cuándo murió don Jorge Manrique?" *Revista de Filología Española* 55 (1972): 61–62.

Lope, Monique de. "Sur un débat poétique entre Antón de Montoro et le commandeur Román." *Écrire a la fin du Moyen Age. Le pouvoir et l'écriture en Espagne et en Italie 1450–1530. Colloque International France-Espagne-Italie (Aix-en-Provence, 20-22 octobre 1988)*. Aix-en-Provence: Université, 1990. 253–267.

Lope, Monique de. "Les métaphores de l'identité *conversa* dans la poésie espanole du XVe siècles." *"Qu'un sang impur. . ." Les Conversos et le pouvoir en Espagne à la fin du moyen âge*. Coord. Jeanne Battesti Pelegrin. Aix-en-Provence: Publications de l'Université de Provence, 1997. 109–122.

López Álvarez, Celestino, and Francisco Torrecilla del Olmo. "El autor, sus pretensions y otros aspectos de las *Coplas del Provincial*." *Bulletin hispanique* 83.3–4 (1981): 237–262.

López Estrada, Francisco. "Anuncios renacentistas en el *Libro de los pensamientos variables*." *Homenaje a Eugenio Asensio*. Madrid: Gredos, 1988. 277–289.

Lourie, Elena. "A Fifteenth-Century Satire on Jewish Bullfighters." *Proceedings of the World Congress of Jewish Studies* 4 (1977): 129–139.

Macías, Uriel. "Ojos de berenjena: las mil y una recetas." *La mesa puesta: leyes, costumbres y recetas judías*. Coords. Uriel Macías and Ricardo Izquierdo Benito. Cuenca: Ediciones de la Universidad de Castilla, La Mancha, 2010. 241–269.

MacKay, Angus. "Popular Movements and Pogroms in Fifteenth-Century Castile." *Past and Present* 55 (1972): 33–67.

Macpherson, Ian. *The 'invenciones y letras' of the 'Cancionero general'*. London: Department of Hispanic Studies – Queen Mary University, 1998.

Magaña, Leticia. "*A nuestra gran Reina allí figuremos*: herramientas de propaganda política isabelina en el *Panegírico a la Reina Doña Isabel* (1509) de Diego Guillén de Ávila." *En Doiro antr'O Porto e Gaia. Estudos de Literatura Medieval Ibérica*. Ed. José Carlos Ribeiro Miranda. Porto: Estrategias Criativas, 2017. 675–686.

Magaña, Leticia. "Problemas de transmisión textual en el *Panegírico a la Reina Doña Isabel* (1509) de Diego Guillén de Ávila." *Poesía, poéticas y cultura literaria*. Eds. Andrea Zinato and Paola Bellomi. Como/Pavía: Ibis Edizioni, 2018. 147–160.

Manrique, Gómez. *Cancionero*. Ed. Francisco Vidal Gómez. Madrid: Cátedra, 2003.

Marcenaro, Simone. "Il presunto *Livro das cantigas* di don Pedro de Portugal, Conde de Barcelos." *Cantares de amigos. Estudos en homenaxe a Mercedes Brea*. Eds. Esther Corral Díaz et al. Santiago de Compostela: Universidade, 2016. 579–587.

Marcuello, Pedro. *Cancionero*. Ed. José Manuel Blecua. Zaragoza: Institución «Fernando el Católico», 1987.

Marín Padilla, Encarnación. *Maestre Pedro de la Cabra: médico converso aragonés del siglo XV, autor de unas coplas de arte menor*. Zaragoza: Edición de la Autora, 1998.

Marineo Siculo, Lucio. *Crónica d'Aragón*. Ed. Óscar Perea Rodríguez. *La historiografía humanista en los albores del siglo XVI: la* Crónica d'Aragón *de Lucio Marineo Sículo, traducida al castellano por el bachiller Juan de Molina (Valencia, Joan Jofré, 1524)*. Santa Barbara: UCSB-Publications of eHumanista, 2003.

Marino, Nancy F. "Un exilio político en el siglo XV. El caso del poeta Juan de Dueñas." *Cuadernos Hispanoamericanos* 416 (1985): 139–151.

Marino, Nancy F. "Fernando de la Torre's *Juego de naipes*, a Game of Love." *La Corónica* 35.1 (2006): 209–247.

Marquer, Julie. "La figura de Ibn al-Jaṭīb como consejero de Pedro I de Castilla: entre ficción y realidad." *e-Spania. Revue interdisciplinaire d'études hispaniques médiévales* 12 (2011): http://journals.openedition.org/e-spania/20900

Márquez Villanueva, Francisco. *Investigaciones sobre Juan Álvarez Gato: Contribución al conocimiento de la literatura castellana del siglo XV*. Madrid: Anejos del Boletín de la Real Academia Española, 1960.

Márquez Villanueva, Francisco. "The Converso Problem: An Assessment." *Studies in Honour of Américo Castro's 80th Year*. Ed. Marcel P. Hornik. Oxford: Lincombe Lodge, 1965. 317–333.
Márquez Villanueva, Francisco. "*Cárcel de amor*, novela política." *Revista de Occidente* 14 (1966): 185–200.
Márquez Villanueva, Francisco. "Historia cultural e historia literaria: el caso de la *Cárcel de amor*." *The Analysis of Hispanic Texts: Current Trends in Methodology*. Eds. Lisa E. Davis and Isabel Tarán. Jamaica, NY: Bilingual Press-Editorial Bilingüe, 1976. 144–157.
Márquez Villanueva, Francisco. "Jewish «Fools» of the Spanish Fifteenth Century." *Hispanic Review* 50.4 (1982): 385–409.
Márquez Villanueva, Francisco. "Hispano-Jewish Cultural Interactions: A Conceptual Framework." *Encuentros & Desencuentros. Spanish-Jewish Cultural Interaction Throughout History*. Eds. Carlos Carrete Parrondo et al. Tel Aviv: University Publishing Projects, 2000. 13–25.
Márquez Villanueva, Francisco. "Sobre el concepto de judaizante." *De la España judeoconversa. Doce estudios*. Barcelona: Bellaterra, 2006a. 95–114.
Márquez Villanueva, Francisco. "«Os judeus casamenteiros» de Gil Vicente." *De la España judeoconversa. Doce estudios*. In Francisco Márquez Villanueva. Barcelona: Bellaterra, 2006b. 257–263.
Márquez Villanueva, Francisco. "Presencia judía en la literatura española: releyendo a Américo Castro." *De la España judeoconversa. Doce estudios*. In Francisco Márquez Villanueva. Barcelona: Bellaterra, 2006c. 23–41.
Márquez Villanueva, Francisco. "El problema de los conversos: cuatro puntos cardinales." *De la España judeoconversa. Doce estudios*. In Francisco Márquez Villanueva. Barcelona: Bellaterra, 2006d. 43–74.
Márquez Villanueva, Francisco. "Conversos y cargos concejiles en el siglo XV." *De la España judeoconversa. Doce estudios*. In Francisco Márquez Villanueva. Barcelona: Bellaterra, 2006e. 137–174.
Márquez Villanueva, Francisco. "«Locos» judíos en la España del siglo XV." *De la España judeoconversa. Doce estudios*. In Francisco Márquez Villanueva. Barcelona: Bellaterra, 2006f. 175–201.
Martín, Adrienne L. "Antisemitismo canino en las *Coplas del perro de Alba*." *Creneida: Anuario de Literaturas Hispánicas* 2 (2014): 298–315.
Martínez Romero, Tomàs. *La literatura profana i antiga i el Cançoner satírich valencià*. Barcelona: Publicacions de l'Abadia de Montserrat, 2010.
Martins, Mário. *Laudes e Cantigas Espirituais de Mestre André Dias († c. 1437)*. Roriz: Mosteiro de Singeverga, 1951.
Melammed, Renee Levine. *A Question of Identity: Iberian Conversos in Historical Perspective*. Oxford: University Press, 2004.
Meyuhas Ginio, Alisa. "Las aspiraciones mesiánicas de los conversos en la Castilla de mediados del siglo XV." *El Olivo* 29–30 (1989): 217–233.
Méndez Bejarano, Mario. *Historia de la judería de Sevilla*. Sevilla: Castillejo, 1993.
Mendoza, Fray Íñigo de. *Cancionero*. Ed. Julio Rodríguez Puértolas. Madrid: Espasa-Calpe, 1968.
Menéndez Pidal, Ramón. *Poesía juglaresca y juglares. Orígenes de las litera-turas románicas*. Prol. by Rafael Lapesa, Madrid: Espasa-Calpe, 1991 [1924].
Menéndez y Pelayo, Marcelino. *Antología de poetas líricos castellanos*. Madrid: Librería de la Viuda de Hernando, 1890–1916, 14 Vols.
Milhou, Alain. *Colón y su mentalidad mesiánica en el ambiente franciscanista español*. Valladolid: Publicaciones de la Casa, Museo Colón, 1983.
Miller, Townsend. *Henry IV of Castile, 1425–1474*. Philadelphia/New York: J. B. Lippincott Company, 1972.

Mitre Fernández, Emilio. *Los judíos de Castilla en tiempos de Enrique III. El pogrom de 1391.* Valladolid: Ediciones de la Universidad de Valladolid, 1994.

Mitre Fernández, Emilio. "La Guerra de los Cien Años. Primer conflicto global del espacio europeo." *Clío & Crimen* 6 (2009): 15–35.

Mirrer, Louise. "The Beautiful Jewess: Marisaltos in Alfonso X's *Cantiga* 107." *Women, Jews and Muslims in the Texts of Reconquest Spain.* Ann Arbor: University of Michigan Press, 1996. 31–44.

Molina Molina, Ángel Luis, and Francisco de Lara Fernández. "Los judíos en el reinado de Pedro I: Murcia." *Miscelánea Medieval Murciana* 3 (1977): 11–40.

Moll, Jaime. "Problemas bibliográficos del libro del Siglo de Oro." *Boletín de la Real Academia Española* 59 (1979): 49–107.

Monferrer-Sala, Juan Pedro, and Pedro Mantas España. *De Toledo a Córdoba. Tahlīth al-waḥdāniyyab ('La Trinidad de la Unidad'). Fragmentos teológicos de un judeoconverso arabizado.* Madrid/Porto: Editorial Sindéresis, 2018.

Montes Romero-Camacho, Isabel. "El converso sevillano Nicolás Martínez de Medina (o de Sevilla), contador mayor de Castilla. Apuntes para una biografía." *Espacio, Tiempo y Forma. Serie III, Historia Medieval* 27 (2014): 343–379.

Montes Romero-Camacho, Isabel. "El mito del filojudaísmo de Pedro I. Leyenda y realidad." *El rey don Pedro I y su tiempo (1350–1369).* Ed. Manuel García Fernández. Sevilla: Editorial Universidad de Sevilla, 2016. 117–135.

Montes Romero-Camacho, Isabel. "Relaciones de poder entre los judíos y los conversos sevillanos al final de la Edad Media." *Judíos y conversos. Relaciones de poder en Galicia y en los reinos hispánicos.* Eds. Eduardo Pardo de Guevara y Valdés and María Gloria de Antonio Rubio. Santiago de Compostela: CSIC-Instituto de Estudios Gallegos «Padre Sarmiento», 2017. 95–138.

Montoro, Antón de. *Cancionero. Poesía completa.* Ed. Marithelma Costa. Cleveland: Cleveland State University, 1990.

Montesino, Ambrosio. *Cancionero.* Ed. Julio Rodríguez Puértolas. Cuenca: Diputación Provincial, 1987.

Morales Muñiz, Dolores Carmen. *Alfonso de Ávila, rey de Castilla.* Ávila: Institución «Gran Duque de Alba», 1988.

Morán Cabanas, María Isabel. "A figuração do poder real no *Cancioneiro Geral*: o caso de D. João II." *Poesía, poéticas y cultura literaria.* Eds. Andrea Zinato and Paola Bellomi. Como/Pavía: Ibis, 2018. 362–374.

Mosquera Novoa, Lucía. *La poesía de Juan de Torres.* Alessandria: Edizioni dell'Orso, 2016.

Mosquera Novoa, Lucía. "El cuerdo y el loco: un intercambio poético entre Álvaro de Luna y Juan de Torres." *Poesía, poéticas y cultura literaria.* Eds. Andrea Zinato and Paola Bellomi. Como/Pavía: Ibis, 2018. 235–247.

Mota, Carlos. "«Plázeme de tus Enojos». Alfonso Álvarez de Villasandino against Alfonso Ferrandes Semuel." *New Horizons in Sephardic Studies.* Dirs. Yedida K. Stillman and George K. Zucker. New York: SUNY Press, 2012. 185–201.

Muñoz Solla, Ricardo. "Solidaridad y conflictividad judeoconversas en el tribunal inquisitorial de Cuenca-Sigüenza (1491–1550)." *Judíos y conversos. Relaciones de poder en Galicia y en los reinos hispánicos.* Eds. Eduardo Pardo de Guevara y Valdés and María Gloria de Antonio Rubio. Santiago de Compostela: CSIC-Instituto de Estudios Gallegos «Padre Sarmiento», 2017. 73–94.

Netanyahu, Benzion. *The Originis of the Inquisition in Fifteenth Century Spain.* New York: Random House, 1995.

Netanyahu, Benzion. *Toward The Inquisition. Essays on Jewish and Converso History in Late Medieval Spain.* Ithaca/London: Cornell University Press, 1997.

Netanyahu, Benzion. "The Old-New Controversy About Spanish Marranism." *Encuentros & Desencuentros. Spanish-Jewish Cultural Interaction Throughout History*. Eds. Carlos Carrete Parrondo et al. Tel Aviv: University Publishing Projects, 2000. 545–578.

Nieto Cumplido, Manuel. "Aportación histórica al *Cancionero de Baena*." *Historia. Instituciones. Documentos* 6 (1979): 197–218.

Nieto Cumplido, Manuel. "Juan Alfonso de Baena y su Cancionero: nueva aportación histórica." *Boletín de la Real Academia de Ciencias, Bellas Artes y Nobles Artes de Córdoba* 52 (1982): 35–57.

Nieto Soria, José Manuel. "Apología y propaganda de la realeza en los cancioneros castellanos del siglo XV. Diseño literario de un modelo político." *En la España medieval* 11 (1988): 185–221.

Nieto Soria, José Manuel. "Las concepciones monárquicas de los intelectuales conversos en la Castilla del siglo XV." *Espacio, Tiempo y Forma, Serie III, Historia Medieval* 6 (1993): 229–48.

Nirenberg, David. "Figures of Thought and Figures of Flesh: 'Jews' and 'Judaism' in Late-Medieval Spanish Poetry and Politics." *Speculum* 81.2 (2006): 398–426.

Nirenberg, David. "Was there Race before Modernity? The Example of "Jewish" Blood in Late Medieval Spain." *The Origins of Racism in the West*. Eds. Miriam Eliav-Feldon et al. Cambridge: University Press, 2009. 232–264.

Novikoff, Alex. "Between Tolerance and Intolerance in Medieval Spain: An Historiographic Enigma." *Medieval Encounters* 11.1 (2005): 7–36.

Odriozola, Antonio. "La imprenta en Castilla en el siglo XV." *Historia de la imprenta hispana*. Ed. Carlos Romero de Lecea. Madrid: Editora Nacional, 1982. 91–219.

Olivera Serrano, César. *Beatriz de Portugal. La pugna dinástica Avís-Trastámara*. Santiago de Compostela: Instituto de Estudios Gallegos Padre Sarmiento-CSIC, 2005.

Olivera Serrano, César. "Juego divino y reparación regia: Juan I de Castilla y Beatriz de Portugal." *La espiritualidad y la configuración de los reinos ibéricos (siglos XII–XV)*. Dir. Isabel Beceiro Pita. Madrid: Dykinson, 2018. 281–320.

Orella y Unzúe, José Luis de. *Partidos políticos en el primer renacimiento (1300–1450)*. Madrid: Fundación Universitaria Española-Seminario Suárez, 1976.

Orfali, Moisés. "El judeoconverso hispano: historia de una mentalidad." *Xudeus e Conversos na Historia. I.- Mentalidades e Cultura*. Ed. Carlos Barros. Santiago de Compostela: Editorial de la Historia, 1994. 117–134.

Ortiz Hernández, Juan Pablo. *Poética doctrinal: la edición del* Cancionero de Otte Brahe. Ph.Diss. Dir. Kenneth Brown. Calgary: The University of Calgary, 2007.

Osório, Jorge A. "Do Cancioneiro «ordenado e emendado» por Garcia de Resende." *Litera. Revista da Faculdade de Letras, Línguas e Literaturas – Universidade do Porto* 22 (2005): 291–335.

Palencia, Alonso de. *Crónica de Enrique IV*. Ed. Antonio Paz y Melia. Madrid: Atlas, 1973–1975, 3 Vols.

Paolini, Devid, ed. *Las coplas de Mingo Revulgo*. Salamanca: Ediciones de la Universidad, 2015.

Parada López de Corselas, Manuel, and Jesús R. Folgado García. "Jan Van Eyck, Alonso de Cartagena y la *Fuente de Gracia*." *Boletín del Museo del Prado* 53 (2017): 16–31.

Parada y Luca de Tena, Manuel. *Fray Ambrosio Montesino, poeta renacentista y predicador de los Reyes Católicos. Apuntes genealógicos sobre una familia conversa de Huete*. Madrid: Real Academia Matritense de Heráldica y Genealogía, 2002.

Pastore, Stefania. *Una herejía española. Conversos, alumbrados e Inquisición (1449–1559)*. Madrid: Marcial Pons, 2010.

Pedrosa, José Manuel. "El antisemitismo en la cultura popular española." *El antisemitismo en España*. Coords. Gonzalo Álvarez Chillida and Ricardo Izquierdo Benito. Cuenca: Ediciones de la Universidad de Castilla-La Mancha, 2007. 31–56.

Perea Rodríguez, Óscar. "La corte literaria de Alfonso «el Inocente» (1465–1468) según las *Coplas a una partida* de Guevara, poeta del *Cancionero general*." *Medievalismo. Boletín de la Sociedad Española de Estudios Medievales* 11 (2001): 33–58.

Perea Rodríguez, Óscar. "La utopía política en la literatura castellana del siglo XV: el *Libro de los Pensamientos Variables* (BNM, ms. 6642)." *eHumanista. Journal of Iberian Studies* 2 (2002): 23–62.

Perea Rodríguez, Óscar. "Enrique IV de Castilla en la poesía de cancionero: algún *afán* ignorado entre las mil *congoxas* conocidas." *Cancionero general* 3 (2005): 33–71.

Perea Rodríguez, Óscar. "Una posible corte literaria del siglo XV: la de Beltrán de la Cueva, Duque de Alburquerque." *Convivio: estudios sobre la poesía de cancionero*. Eds. Vicenç Beltran and Juan Paredes Núñez. Granada: Universidad de Granada, 2006. 633–684.

Perea Rodríguez, Óscar. *Estudio biográfico sobre los poetas del «Cancionero general»*. Madrid: CSIC, 2007a.

Perea Rodríguez, Óscar. "Enrique IV de Castilla y los conversos. Testimonios poéticos de una evolución histórica." *Revista de Poética Medieval* 19 (2007b): 131–175.

Perea Rodríguez, Óscar. "El entorno cortesano de la Castilla Trastámara como escenario de lucha de poder. Rastros y reflejos en los cancioneros castellanos del siglo XV." *Res Publica. Revista de Historia de las Ideas Políticas* 18 (2007c): 289–306.

Perea Rodríguez, Óscar. "«Alta Reina esclareçida»: un cancionero ficticio para Isabel la Católica." *Isabel la Católica y su época. Actas del Congreso Internacional*. Eds. Luis Ribot, Julio Valdeón and Elena Maza. Valladolid: Instituto Universitario de Historia Simancas, 2007d. 2: 1355–1383.

Perea Rodríguez, Óscar. *La época del "Cancionero de Baena". Los Trastámara y sus poetas*. Baena: Ayuntamiento de Baena, 2009.

Perea Rodríguez, Óscar. "Francisco Hernández Coronel, poeta converso del *Cancionero general*." *Homenaje a Eloy Benito Ruano*. Coord. Juan Francisco Jiménez Alcázar. Madrid: Sociedad Española de Estudios Medievales, 2010a. 607–622.

Perea Rodríguez, Óscar. "*Quebrantar la jura de mis abuelos*: los conversos en los cancioneros castellanos del tardío medievo (1454–1504)." *La Corónica* 40.1 (2011a): 183–225.

Perea Rodríguez, Óscar. "Lírica anticonversa de los siglos XV y XVI: el *Credo glosado contra los judíos*, de Juan de Carvajal." *Violence et identité religieuse dans l'Espagne du Xve au XVII siècles*. Coord. Rica Amran. Paris/Amiens: Indigo et Côte-Femmes – Université de Picardie Jules Verne, 2011b. 307–325.

Perea Rodríguez, Óscar. "*Night Moves*: Nocturnality within Religious and Humanist Poetry in Hernando del Castillo's *Cancionero general*." *eHumanista. Journal of Iberian Studies* 22 (2012a): 289–329.

Perea Rodríguez, Óscar. "Sobre la datación cronológica de las 'Obra de burlas' del *Cancionero general*." *Estudios sobre el* Cancionero general *(Valencia, 1511): poesía, manuscrito e imprenta*. Coords. Marta Haro Cortés, Rafael Beltrán Llavador, José Luis Canet Vallés and Héctor H. Gassó. Valencia: Universitat de Valencia, 2012b. 1: 325–347.

Perea Rodríguez, Óscar. "*Quebrantar la jura de mis abuelos*: los conversos en los primeros cancioneros castellanos medievales (1396–1454)." *Lo converso: orden imaginario y realidad en la cultura española (siglos XIV-XVII)*. Eds. Ruth Fine et al. Madrid/Frankfurt am Main: Iberoamericana-Vervuert, 2013a. 19–54.

Perea Rodríguez, Óscar. "La peligrosa fidelidad de los conversos a la monarquía hispánica: el memorial de agravios de Francisco Hernández Coronel al Rey Católico (1515)." *Les minorités face au problème de la fidélité dans l'Espagne des XVe-XVIIe siècles*. Coord. Rica Amran. Paris: Indigo-Université de Picardie Jules Verne, 2013b. 61–79.

Perea Rodríguez, Óscar. "Mencía de Mendoza, condesa de Haro." *Damas de la Casa de Mendoza. Historias, leyendas y olvidos*. Ed. Esther Alegre Carvajal. Madrid: Ediciones Polifemo, 2014. 95–130.

Perea Rodríguez, Óscar. "«*Este rastro de confeso*»: *Converso* Poets and Topics in Medieval and Early Modern Spanish *Cancioneros*." *Las 'Obras de burlas' del* Cancionero general *de Hernando del Castillo*. Eds. Antonio Cortijo Ocaña and Marcial Rubio Árquez. Santa Barbara: University of California-Publications of *eHumanista*, 2015. 125–172.

Perea Rodríguez, Óscar. "Pedro I y la propaganda antipetrista en la génesis y el éxito de la poesía cancioneril castellana, I." *La Corónica* 45.2 (2017a): 109–132.

Perea Rodríguez, Óscar. "Pedro I y la propaganda antipetrista en la génesis y el éxito de la poesía cancioneril castellana, II." *La Corónica* 46.1 (2017b): 151–181.

Perea Rodríguez, Óscar. "La anónima elegía a la muerte del Rey Católico (Dutton 18*EF): poesía funeral en memoria de un monarca postergado." *Poesía, poéticas y cultura literaria*. Eds. Andrea Zinato and Paola Bellomi. Como/Pavía: Ibis Edizioni, 2018. 249–275.

Pérez Bosch, Estela. *Los valencianos en el* Cancionero general: *estudio de sus poesías*. Valencia: Publicacions de la Universitat, 2009.

Pérez Priego, Miguel Ángel. "Juan del Encina y el teatro de su tiempo." *Humanismo y literatura en tiempos de Juan del Encina*. Ed. Javier Guijarro Ceballos. Salamanca: Ediciones de la Universidad, 1999. 139–146.

Periñán, Blanca. "Las poesías de Suero de Ribera. Estudio y edición crítica anotada de los textos." *Miscellanea di Studi Ispanici* 16 (1968): 5–138.

Phillips, William D. *Enrique IV and the Crisis of Fifteenth-Century Castile, 1425–1480*. Cambridge, Mass: The Medieval Academy of America, 1978.

Pomeroy, Hilary. "Yantar e identidad religiosa." *La mesa puesta: leyes, costumbres y recetas judías*. Coords. Uriel Macías and Ricardo Izquierdo Benito. Cuenca: Ediciones de la Universidad de Castilla, La Mancha, 2010. 69–88.

Proia, Isabella. "Hacia una edición de las poesías de fray Diego de Valencia de León: unas notas exegéticas al decir «En un vergel deleitoso»." *Rumbos del hispanismo en el umbral del Cincuentenario de la AIH. II: Medieval*. Eds. Aviva Garribba and Patrizzia Botta. Roma: Bagatto, 2012. 116–125.

Proia, Isabella. "Morfología de las tradiciones textuales en el *Cancionero de San Román* (MH1)." *Poesía, poéticas y cultura literaria*. Eds. Andrea Zinato and Paola Bellomi. Como/Pavía: Ibis, 2018. 181–200.

Pulgar, Fernando de. *Claros varones de Castilla*. Ed. Miguel Ángel Pérez Priego. Madrid: Cátedra, 2007.

Pulgar, Fernando de. *Crónica de los Reyes Católicos*. Ed. Juan de Mata Carriazo y Arroquia. Prol. Gonzalo Pontón. Madrid: Marcial Pons, 2008 [ed. facsímil de Madrid: Espasa-Calpe, 1943], 2 Vols.

Pulido Serrano, Juan Ignacio. "La masacre de 1506 en Lisboa. Versiones críticas del obispo Jerónimo Osorio, el padre Mariana y fray Benito Feijoo." *Carolvs. Homenaje a Friedrich Edelmayer*. Ed. Francisco Toro Serrano. Alcalá la Real: Ayuntamiento, 2017. 305–310.

Rábade Obradó, María Pilar. *Una elite de poder en la corte de los Reyes Católicos: Los judeoconversos*. Madrid: Sigilo, 1993.

Rábade Obradó, María Pilar. "La instrucción cristiana de los conversos en la Castilla del siglo XV." *En la España Medieval* 22 (1999): 369–393.

Ramírez de Arellano y Lynch, Rafael W. *La poesía cortesana del siglo XV y el* Cancionero de Vindel. *Contribución al estudio de la temprana lírica española*. Barcelona: Vosgos, 1976.

Real Ramos, César. "Nacer en el espino (los *Proverbios morales* de Santob y la paremiología castellana en el siglo XIV)." *Nunca fue pena mayor. Estudios de literatura española en homenaje a Brian Dutton*. Eds. Victoriano Roncero López and Ana Menéndez Collera. Cuenca: Ediciones de la Universidad de Castilla, La Mancha, 1996. 531–542.

Represa Rodríguez, Armando. "Una carta de esponsales y otras prescripciones sobre el matrimonio entre judíos y conversos castellanos." *Encuentros en Sefarad. Actas del Congreso Internacional*

"Los judíos en la Historia de España". Coords. Francisco Ruiz Gómez and Manuel Espadas Burgos. Ciudad Real: Instituto de Estudios Manchegos, 1987. 33–40.

Resende, Garcia de. *Cancioneiro Geral*. Ed. Aida Fernanda Días. Lisboa: Imprensa Nacional – Casa da Moeda, 1990, 6 Vols.

Resines, Luis. *La catequesis en España. Historia y textos*. Madrid: Biblioteca de Autores Cristianos, 1997.

Riera i Sans, Jaume. *Cants de noces dels jueus catalans*. Barcelona: Curial, 1974.

Rivkin, Ellis. "Los cristianonuevos portugueses y la formación del mundo moderno." *Judíos. Sefarditas. Conversos. La expulsión de 1492 y sus consecuencias*. Ed. Ángel Alcalá. Valladolid: Ámbito, 1995. 408–419.

Rohland de Langbehn, Régula. "Power and Justice in *Cancionero* Verse." *Poetry at Court in Trastámaran Spain: from the* Cancionero de Baena *to the* Cancionero general. Eds. Michael E. Gerli and Julian Weiss. Tempe: Arizona State University, 1998. 199–219.

Rodríguez Fernández, José Luis. "Minorías religiosas e étnicas no *Cancioneiro Geral* de Garcia de Resende." *Professor Basilio Losada: ensinar a pensar con liberdade e risco*. Eds. Isabel de Riquer et al. Barcelona: Publicacions de la Universitat de Barcelona, 2000. 603–623.

Rodríguez Puértolas, Julio. *Poesía crítica y satírica del siglo XV*. Madrid: Castalia, 1989.

Rodríguez Puértolas, Julio. "Jews and Conversos in Fifteenth-Century Castilian Cancioneros: Texts and Contexts." *Poetry at Court in Trastamaran Spain. From the «Cancionero de Baena» to the «Cancionero general»*. Eds. E. Michael Gerli and Julian Weiss. Tempe: Arizona State University, 1998. 187–197.

Rodríguez Puértolas, Julio. "La poesía de la Baja Edad Media." *Judíos en la literatura española*. Coords. Iacob M. Hassán and Ricardo Izquierdo Benito. Cuenca: Ediciones de la Universidad de Castilla, La Mancha, 2001. 87–109.

Rodríguez-Moñino, Antonio. *Poesía y cancioneros (siglo XVI)*. Madrid: Real Academia Española, 1968.

Román, Comendador. *Coplas de la Pasión con la Resurrección*. Ed. Giussepe Mazzocchi. Firenze: La Nuova Italia, 1990.

Roncero López, Victoriano. "Algunos temas de la poesía humorística de Montoro." *Nunca fue pena mayor. Estudios de literatura española en homenaje a Brian Dutton*. Eds. Victoriano Roncero López and Ana Menéndez Collera. Cuenca: Ediciones de la Universidad de Castilla, La Mancha, 1996. 567–580.

Ropero Berzosa, Alfonso. "Judeoconversos y espiritualidad heterodoxa en tiempos de Carlos V." *Cuadernos de Historia Moderna* 43.2 (2018): 485–504.

Roth, Norman. *Conversos, Inquisition, and the Expulsion of the Jews from Spain*. Madison: The University of Wisconsin Press, 2002.

Roth, Norman. *Dictionary of Iberian Jewish and Converso Authors*. Madrid-Salamanca: Aben Ezra Ediciones, Universidad Pontificia de Salamanca, 2007.

Roth, Norman. "Some Customs of Jews in Medieval Spain." *From Catalonia to the Caribbean: The Sephardic Orbit from Medieval to Modern Times. Essays in Honor of Jane S. Gerber*. Eds. Federica Francesconi et al. Leiden: Brill, 2018. 27–42.

Roth, Norman. "Dar «uma voz» aos judeus: representação na Espanha." *Dimensões* 42 (2019): 151–164.

Rosenstock, Bruce. "Against the Pagans: Alonso de Cartagena, Francisco de Vitoria, and *Converso* Political Theology." *Marginal Voices: Studies in Converso Literature of Medieval and Golden Age Spain*. Eds. Amy Aronson-Friedman and Gregory B. Kaplan. Leiden/Boston: Brill, 2012. 117–139.

Round, Nicholas G. "La «peculiaridad literaria» de los conversos, ¿unicornio o «snark»." *Judíos. Sefarditas. Conversos. La expulsión de 1492 y sus consecuencias*. Ed. Ángel Alcalá. Valladolid: Ámbito, 1995. 557–576.

Rozmitála a Blatné, Jaroslav Lev. *The Travels of Leo of Rozmital through Germany, Flanders, England, France, Spain, Portugal and Italy, (1465–1467)*. Ed. Malcolm Letts. Cambridge: Hakluyt Society, 1957.

Rubin, Nancy. *Isabella of Castile: The First Renaissance Queen*. New York: St. Martin's, 1991.
Rubio Árquez, Marcial. "Hacia una edición crítica del *Cancionero de obras de burlas provocantes a risa* (Dutton, 190B)." *Poesía, poéticas y cultura literaria*. Eds. Andrea Zinato and Paola Bellomi. Como/Pavía: Ibis, 2018. 213–222.
Rubio García, Luis. *Estudios sobre la Edad Media española*. Murcia: Universidad de Murcia, 1973.
Rubio González, Lorenzo. "Juan de Valladolid: Un poeta de juglaría en el siglo XV." *Castilla. Estudios de Literatura. Boletín del Departamento de Literatura Española de la Universidad de Valladolid* 6–7 (1983–1984): 101–112.
Ruiz Gómez, Francisco. "Juderías y aljamas en el mundo rural de la Castilla medieval." *Xudeus e Conversos na Historia. II. – Sociedade e Inquisición*. Ed. Carlos Barros. Santiago de Compostela: Editorial de la Historia, 1994. 111–152.
Ruiz Gómez, Francisco. "La convivencia en el marco vecinal: el régimen apartado de las juderías castellanas en el siglo XV." *Del pasado judío en los reinos medievales hispánicos: afinidad y distanciamiento. XIII Curso de cultura hispanojudía y sefardí de la Universidad de Castilla–La Mancha*. Coords. Ricardo Izquierdo Benito and Yolanda Moreno Koch. Cuenca, Universidad de Castilla–La Mancha, 2005. 247–288.
Sáenz-Badillos, Ángel. "Intelectuales judíos y conversos en el siglo XV." *Dejar hablar a los textos. Homenaje a Francisco Márquez Villanueva*. Coord. Pedro Manuel Piñero Ramírez. Sevilla: Universidad de Sevilla, 2005. 1: 261–280.
Salinas, Franciscus. *De Musica. Faksimile-Nachdruck herausgegeben von Macario Santiago Kastner*. Kassel: Bärenreiter, 1958.
Salvador Miguel, Nicasio. *La poesía cancioneril. El 'Cancionero de Estúñiga'*. Madrid: Alhambra, 1977.
Salvador Miguel, Nicasio, ed. *Cancionero de Estúñiga*. Madrid: Alhambra, 1987.
Sánchez Pérez, María. "Un libelo antijudío en la literatura popular impresa del siglo XVI." *Revista de Literatura* 72 (2010): 531–553.
Santonja Hernández, Pedro. "Sobre judíos y judeoconversos en la Baja Edad Media. Textos de controversia." *Helmántica. Revista de filología clásica y hebrea* 60 (2009): 177–203.
Sharrer, Harvey L. "Estado actual de los estudios sobre el *Cancioneiro da Ajuda*." *O Cancioneiro da Ajuda cen anos despois. Actas do Congreso realizado pola Dirección Xeral de Promoción Cultural en Santiago de Compostela e na Illa de San Simón os días 25–28 de maio de 2004*. Santiago de Compostela: Xunta de Gallicia, 2004. 41–54.
Scholberg, Kenneth R. *Sátira e invectiva en la España medieval*. Madrid: Gredos, 1971.
Seidenspinner-Núñez, Dayle. "Conversions and Subversion: *Converso* Texts in Fifteenth-Century Spain." *Christians, Muslims, and Jews in Medieval and Early Modern Spain*. Eds. Mark D. Meyerson and Edward D. English. Notre Dame: University of Notre Dame Press, 2000. 241–261.
Severin, Dorothy S. *The "Cancionero de Martínez de Burgos": A Description of its Contents, with an Edition of the Prose and Poetry of Juan Martínez de Burgos*. Exteter: Exeter Hispanic Texts, 1976.
Severin, Dorothy S. "«Cancionero», un género mal nombrado." *Cultura Neolatina* 54 (1994): 95–105.
Severin, Dorothy S. *Del manuscrito a la imprenta en la época de Isabel la Católica*. Kassel: Reichenberger, 2004.
Smail, Daniel Lord. "Hatred as a Social Institution in Late-Medieval Society." *Speculum* 76.1 (2001): 90–126.
Soifer Irish, Maya. "Beyond *Convivencia*: Critical Reflections on the Historiography of Interfaith Relations in Christian Spain." *Journal of Medieval Iberian Studies* 1.1 (2009): 19–35.
Soifer Irish, Maya. *Jews and Christians in Medieval Castile. Tradition, Coexistence, and Change*. Washington D.C.: The Catholic University of America Press, 2016.
Solá-Solé, Josep M. & Rose, Stanley E. "Judíos y conversos en la poesía cortesana del siglo XV: el estilo políglota de Fray Diego de Valencia." *Hispanic Review* 44.4 (1976): 371–385.

Soyer, François. *The Persecution of the Jews and Muslims of Portugal. King Manuel I and the End of Religious Tolerance (1496–7)*. Boston/Leiden: Brill, 2014.

Soyer, François. *Antisemitic Conspiracy Theories in the Early Modern Iberian World. Narratives of Fear and Hatred*. Boston/Leiden: Brill, 2019.

Suárez Fernández, Luis. *Los Reyes Católicos. La conquista del trono*. Madrid: Rialp, 1989.

Suárez Fernández, Luis. *La expulsión de los judíos de España*. Madrid: Mapfre, 1991.

Suárez Fernández, Luis. *Enrique IV de Castilla: la difamación como arma política*. Barcelona: Ariel, 2001.

Surtz, Ronald E. "Características principales de la literatura escrita por judeoconversos: algunos problemas de definición." *Judíos. Sefarditas. Conversos. La expulsión de 1492 y sus consecuencias*. Ed. Ángel Alcalá. Valladolid: Ámbito, 1995. 547–556.

Szpiech, Ryan. "Scrutinizing History: Polemic and Exegesis in Pablo de Santa María's *Siete edades del mundo*." *Medieval Encounters* 16.1 (2010): 96–142.

Szpiech, Ryan. "The Convivencia Wars: Decoding Historiography's Polemic with Philology." *In A Sea of Languages: Rethinking the Arabic Role in Medieval Literary History*. Eds. Susan Akbari and Karla Mallette. Toronto: University Press, 2013. 135–161.

Tate, Robert Brian. *Ensayos sobre la historiografía peninsular del siglo XV*. Madrid: Gredos, 1970.

Tate, Robert Brian "El cronista real castellano durante el siglo XV." *Homenaje a Pedro Sáinz Rodríguez*. Madrid: Fundación Universitaria Española, 1986. 3: 659–668.

Tato García, Cleofé. "Poetas cancioneriles de apellido «Montoro»." *Revista de Literatura Medieval* 10 (1998): 169–184.

Tato García, Cleofé. *Vida y obra de Pedro de Santa Fe*. A Coruña: Toxosoutos, 1999.

Tato García, Cleofé. "El *Cancionero de Palacio* (SA7): Ms. 2653 de la Biblioteca Universitaria de Salamanca (II)." *Cancioneros en Baena. Actas del II Congreso Internacional* Cancionero de Baena, In Memoriam *Manuel Alvar*. Ed. Jesús L. Serrano Reyes. Baena: Ayuntamiento de Baena, 2003. 1: 495–523.

Tato García, Cleofé. *La poesía de Pedro de Santa Fe*. Baena: Delegación de Cultura, 2004.

Tato García, Cleofé. "Un acercamiento al problema de las atribuciones en el *Cancionero de Palacio* (SA7)." *Convivio. Cancioneros peninsulares*. Eds. Vicenç Beltrán and Juan Paredes. Granada: Universidad de Granada, 2010. 215–233.

Tato García, Cleofé. "Prolegómenos a la edición del Cancionero de Palacio (SA7)." *El texto medieval: de la edición a la interpretación*. Eds. Pilar Lorenzo Gradín and Simone Marcenaro. Santiago de Compostela: Universidad, 2012. 299–318.

Tato García, Cleofé, and Óscar Perea Rodríguez. "De Castillo a Dutton: cinco siglos de cancioneros." *La Corónica* 40.1 (2011): 89–102.

Tavani, Giuseppe. *Poesia del duecento nella penisola iberica: problemi della lirica galego-portoghese*. Rome: Ateneo, 1969.

Tavares, Antonio Augusto. "Aspectos da cultura dos cristãos novos em Portugal na primera metade do século XVI." *Xudeus e Conversos na Historia. I. – Mentalidades e Cultura*. Ed. Carlos Barros. Santiago de Compostela: Editorial de la Historia, 1994. 265–274.

Tavares, María José Pimenta Ferro. *Judaismo e Inquisição. Estudos*. Lisboa: Editorial Presença, 1987.

Tavares, María José Pimenta Ferro. "Expulsion or Integration? The Portuguese Jewish Problem." *Crisis and Creativity in the Sephardic World, 1391–1648*. Ed. Benjamin R. Gampel. New York: Columbia University Press, 1997. 95–103.

Taylor, Barry. "The Lady Is (in) the Garden: Fray Pedro (*sic*) de Valencia, «En un vergel deleitoso» (*Baena* 505)." *From the* Cancioneiro da Vaticana *to the* Cancionero General: *Studies in Honour of Jane Whetnall*. Eds. Alan Deyermond and Barry Taylor. London: Department of Hispanic Studies Queen Mary, University of London, 2007. 235–244.

Tomassetti, Isabella. "Historia, política y cortesía: Diego de Valera y el *Cancionero de San Román* (MH1)." *Studi Romanzi* 11 (2015): 53–74.

Tomassetti, Isabella. "En el entorno del *Cancionero de Salvá* (PN13): Gómez de Rojas y su poesía." *eHumanista. Journal of Iberian Studies* 40 (2018a): 171–194.
Tomassetti, Isabella. "«*Do serví más sin error / resçebí pena y desgrado*»: la poesía de Diego de Valera entre ideología cortés y denuncia política." Eds. Andrea Zinato and Paola Bellomi. *Poesía, poéticas y cultura literaria*. Como/Pavía: Ibis, 2018b. 75–92.
Torres Fontes, Juan. *Estudio sobre la "Crónica de Enrique IV" del Dr. Galíndez de Carvajal*. Murcia: CSIC-Instituto Jerónimo de Zurita, Seminario de Historia de la Universidad de Murcia, Sucs. de Nogués, 1946.
Tosar López, Javier. "Juan Marmolejo y Juan Agraz: proyecto de edición y estudio de su poesía." *Estudios de literatura medieval en la Península Ibérica*. Coord. Carlos Alvar. San Millán de la Cogolla: Cilengua, 2015. 1157–1166.
Trapero, Maximiano. *La Inquisición española contra el Romancero. Proceso inquisitorial sobre dieciocho romances que circulaban en Canarias en el siglo XVIII*. México: Frente de Afirmación Hispanista A.C., 2018.
Valdeón Baruque, Julio. *Los judíos de Castilla y la revolución Trastámara*. Valladolid: Universidad, 1968.
Valdeón Baruque, Julio. "Sociedad y antijudaísmo en la Castilla del siglo XIV." *Xudeus e Conversos na Historia. II. – Sociedade e Inquisición*. Ed. Carlos Barros. Santiago de Compostela: Editorial de la Historia, 1994. 27–46.
Valdeón Baruque, Julio. "Motivaciones socio-económicas de las fricciones entre viejocristianos, judíos y conversos." *Judíos. Sefarditas. Conversos. La expulsión de 1492 y sus consecuencias*. Ed. Ángel Alcalá Galve.Valladolid: Ámbito, 1995. 69–88.
Valdeón Baruque, Julio. *El chivo expiatorio. Judíos, revueltas y vida cotidiana en la Edad Media*. Valladolid: Ámbito, 2000.
Valdeón Baruque, Julio. *Los Trastámaras. El triunfo de una dinastía bastarda*. Madrid: Temas de Hoy, 2001.
Valdeón Baruque, Julio. *Judíos y conversos en la Castilla medieval*. Valladolid: Ámbito, 2004.
Valero Moreno, Juan Miguel. "La pasión según Lucas Fernández." *La Corónica* 31.2 (2003): 177–216.
Vallín, Gema. "Villasandino y la lírica gallego-portuguesa." *Cancioneros en Baena. Actas del II Congreso Internacional* Cancionero de Baena, In Memoriam *Manuel Alvar*. Ed. Jesús L. Serrano Reyes. Baena: Ayuntamiento de Baena, 2003. 2: 79–85.
Vendrell, Francisca. *El Cancionero de Palacio. Manuscrito nº 594*. Barcelona: CSIC, 1945.
Ventura, Joaquim. "Poetas en gallego en el *Cancionero de Baena*: contra el tópico de la decadencia." *Convivio. Estudios sobre la poesía de cancionero*. Eds. Vicenç Beltran and Juan Paredes. Granada: Universidad, 2006. 813–821.
Verga, Selomoh ibn. *La vara de Yehudah (Sefer Sebet Yehuda)*. Ed. and tr. María José Cano. Barcelona: Riopiedras, 1991.
Vidal Doval, Rosa. "«Nos soli sumus christiani»: *Conversos* in the Texts of the Toledo Rebellion of 1449." *Medieval Hispanic Studies in Memory of Alan Deyermond*. Eds. Andrew M. Beresford et al. London: Tamesis, 2013. 215–236.
Villa Prieto, Josué. "La ideología goticista en los prehumanistas castellanos: Alonso de Cartagena y Rodrigo Sánchez de Arévalo. Sus consideraciones sobre la unidad hispano-visigoda y el reino astur-leonés." *Territorio, Sociedad y Poder. Revista de Estudios Medievales* 5 (2010): 123–145.
Wardropper, Bruce. "«Duelos y quebrantos», Once Again." *Romance Notes* 20 (1980): 413–416.
Weiss, Julian. *The Poet's Art: Literary Theory in Castile, c. 1400–60*. Oxford: Society for the Study of Medieval Language and Literature, 1990.
Weissberger, Barbara F. *Isabel Rules. Constructing Queenship, Wielding Power*. Minneapolis: University of Minnesota Press, 2004.
Whetnall, Jane. "Songs and *Canciones* in the *Cancionero general*." *The Age of the Catholic Monarchs, 1474–1516. Literary Studies in Memory of Keith Whinnon*. Eds. Aland Deyermond and Ian Macpherson. Liverpool: University Press, 1989. 197–207.

Whinnom, Keith. "Introducción." Diego de San Pedro, *Obras completas*. Madrid: Castalia, 1973, 3 Vols. 1: 3–26.
Whinnom, Keith. *La poesía amatoria de la época de los Reyes Católicos*. Durham: University of Durham, 1981.
Wolff, Philippe. "The 1391 Pogrom in Spain. Social Crisis or Not?" *Past & Present* 50.1 (1971): 4–18.
Yisraeli, Yosi. "From Christian Polemic to a Jewish-Converso Dialogue. Jewish Skepticism and Rabbinic-Christian Traditions in the *Scrutinium Scripturarum*." *Medieval Encounters* 24.1–3 (2018): 160–196.
Yovel, Yirmiyahu. "Converso Dualities in the First Generation: The *Cancioneros*." *Jewish Social Studies* 4.3 (1998): 1–28.
Yovel, Yirmiyahu. *The Other Within. The* Marranos: *Split Identity and Emerging Modernity*. Princeton: University Press, 2009.
Ysern i Lagarda, Josep-Antoni. "Sant Vicent Ferrer: Predicació i societat." *Revista de Filología Románica* 20 (2003): 73–102.
Zinato, Andrea. "*Auctoritates* y poesía: el *Cancionero de Fernán Pérez de Guzmán*." Eds. Patrizia Botta et al. *Canzonieri iberici*. Noia: Toxosoutos, 2001. 2: 215–230.

Further Reading

Corfis, Ivy A. "Conquest and Conversion in the Hispanic Chivalric Romance: The Case of *Reinaldos de Montalván*." *Medieval Iberia. Changing Societies and Cultures in Contact and Transition*. Ed. Ivy A. Corfis and Ray Harris-Northall. Woodbridge: Boydell & Brewer, 2007. 3–15. 70–84.
Girón Negrón, Luis M. "«Muerte, cates / que non cates»: el «discor» 510 de Fray Diego de Valencia en el *Cancionero de Baena*." *Revista de Filología Española* 82.3–4 (2002): 249–272.
Gómez-Bravo, Ana María. "Ser social y poética material en la obra de Antón de Montoro, mediano converso." *Hispanic Review* 78.2 (2010): 145–167.
Gómez-Bravo, Ana María. "Vida en fragmentos: el *libro* de Juan Álvarez Gato y la memoria autobiográfica". *Romance Quarterly* 58.3 (2011): 231–248.
Gómez-Bravo, Ana María. "Material Poetry and the Compiler's Textual Self: Compilation and Textual Agency in Hernando Del Castillo and Garcia de Resende." *Calíope: Journal of the Society for Renaissance and Baroque Hispanic Poetry* 23.2 (2018b): 21–43
Lacave Riaño, José Luis. *Juderías y sinagogas españolas*. Madrid: Mapfre, 1992.
Macpheeters, David W. "The XVth Century Converso poet Ginés de Cañizares." *Symposium* 6 (1952): 380–384.
Márquez, Antonio. *Literatura e Inquisición en España (1478–1834)*. Madrid: Taurus, 1980.
Nieto Cumplido, Manuel. "La revuelta contra los conversos de Córdoba en 1473." *Homenaje a Antón de Montoro en el V centenario de su muerte*. Montoro: Imprenta San Pablo, 1977. 31–49.
Nirenberg, David. *Communities of Violence: Persecution of Minorities in the Middle Ages*. Princeton: University Press, 1996.
Perea Rodríguez, Óscar. "Juan Álvarez Gato en la villa y corte literaria del Madrid tardomedieval." *La villa y la tierra de Madrid en los albores de la capitalidad (siglos XIV–XVI)*. Coord. Eduardo Jiménez. Madrid: Al-Mudayna, 2010b. 49–77.
Puymagre, Théodore Joseph Boudet, Count of. *La cour littéraire de Juan II, roi de Castille*. Paris: Librairie A. Franck, 1873, 2 Vols.
Rodríguez-Moñino, Antonio. "El cancionero manuscrito de Pedro del Pozo (1547)." *Boletín de la Real Academia Española* 29 (1949): 453–509.

Rosenstock, Bruce. *New Men, Conversos, Christian Theology and Society in Fifteenth-Century Castile*. London: Queen Mary U of London – Department of Hispanic Studies, 2002.

Salvador Miguel, Nicasio. "Cisneros en Granada y la quema de libros islámicos." *La Biblia políglota complutense en su contexto*. Coord. Alfredo Alvar Ezquerra. Alcalá de Henares: Universidad, 2017. 154–184.

Scheidlin, Raymond P. "Secular Hebrew Poetry in Fifteenth-Century Spain." *Crisis and Creativity in the Sephardic World, 1391–1648*. Ed. Benjamin R. Gampel. New York: Columbia University Press, 1997. 25–37.

Toribio Fernández, José Alberto. "Antón de Montoro en el *Cancionero de burlas* (sic) *provocantes a risa*." *Homenaje a Antón de Montoro en el V centenario de su muerte*. Montoro: Imprenta San Pablo, 1977. 17–28.

Valverde Madrid, José. "En el centenario de Antón de Montoro." *Homenaje a Antón de Montoro en el V centenario de su muerte*. Montoro: Imprenta San Pablo, 1977. 5–13.

Wertheimer, Elaine. "Converso «Voices» in Fifteenth-And-Sixteenth-Century Spanish Literature." *The Conversos and Moriscos in Late Medieval Spain and Beyond. Volume One. Departures and Change*. Ed. Kevin Ingram. Leiden/Boston: Brill, 2009. 97–119.

Whitenack, Judith A. "Conversion to Christianity in the Spanish Romance of Chivalry, 1490–1524." *Journal of Hispanic Philology* 13 (1988–89): 13–39.

II Early Modern Contexts

James Nelson Novoa and Carsten Wilke

5 1492–1700: Early Modern Iberian-Jewish Cultural History

Abstract: This chapter presents a general picture of the cultural, social and religious life of Iberian Judeo-converts and their Jewish descendants between 1497 and 1700. It aims to provide a glimpse of some of the many problems involved in describing their lives and paths such as the fluidity of religious identity, transcontinental migration, early modern tolerance and confessionalisation. While some of those who accepted Christianity under duress continued steadfast in that faith, many others, after careful negotiations, managed to secure places in Europe and even the New World in which forms of Jewish belief and practice were able to flourish either in secret or overtly. Basing itself on the most up-to-date bibliography this chapter gives a general overview of the situation of New Christians in Portugal and Spain, as well as the Western Sephardic diaspora in the Mediterranean, Northern Europe, and the Americas in a constantly changing political and social landscape during the early modern period.

Key Terms: Iberia, Sephardim, *Conversos*, New Christians, Diaspora

1 Introduction

Ever since Greek-speaking Jews arrived on Iberian soil in the first century CE, the Jewish immersion into Ibero-Romance vernacular speech and literature impresses with its intensity and permanence. In medieval Christian Spain, while Jewish literary expression was mainly in Hebrew and Aramaic, "most of the Hispanic elements employed on an everyday basis by the average medieval Sephardi may have differed little, if at all, from the popular forms used by their average Christian neighbors" (Bunis 1992, 403). Jewish speech was mainly recognizable on the level of the lexicon through the presence of Hebraisms. After 1492, the Jewish exiles in North Africa and the Balkans continued using Spanish among themselves. Linguistic isolation, the original blend of peninsular dialects, as well as borrowings from Hebrew and local languages shaped a separate Jewish Castilian. Called "Judeo-Spanish," "Ladino," or "Judezmo," this language will not be the object of the present chapter, nor the manifold history of its speakers and writers. We will only deal with the sociocultural conditions of those Jews who, converted to Christianity, stayed in the Peninsula or emigrated at a later date. The spoken and literary languages of these conversos soon became indistinguishable from those of their Iberian environment, though the way of using standard Spanish and Portuguese would often be affected by their social and migratory history, as well as by their cultural singularity, on which this chapter will focus.

A vulgar insult of unknown origin, *marranos* (pigs), which for good reason is rare in written sources, became the label by which Jewish romantic historiography has named persons that were Christian by church affiliation, but Jewish by racial origin, inner conviction, secret practice, or social exclusion. However, one should not uncritically assume these four features to overlap in a society that discriminated against persons of Jewish origin irrespective of their religious persuasion. Scholarship thus distinguishes between a social category of conversos, that is, Spanish Catholics of Jewish ancestry, and a fraction of "crypto-Jews" among them. In Inquisitorial parlance, the latter were classified as *judaizantes* (Judaizers). In Portugal, converts were generally known as *cristãos-novos* (New Christians). Rabbinic Hebrew applies the technical term *anusim* (forced ones) to all Jews who were made Christians or Muslims against their will. Finally, none of all these terms should be applied to persons of converso stock who either joined the Sephardic exiles outside the Peninsula or founded Jewish communities by themselves.

Fraught with discontinuity, the history of the conversos and their Jewish descendents in the early modern world can be synthesized in quite different ways. The nineteenth-century historian Meyer Kayserling first distinguished an ethnic group of "Portuguese Jews" among the Sephardim (Kayserling 1971)[1]. Cecil Roth focused on the historical experience of forced conversion that shaped the "marrano diaspora" (Roth 1974). Jonathan Israel conceived the Sephardi and converso diasporas as an economic network (Israel 2002); and Yosef Kaplan inserted the "Western Sephardim" or "New Jews" into a narrative of (early) modernization (Kaplan 1994; 2000).[2]

All these aspects need to be taken into consideration jointly, and the use of a modern European standard language is a major distinctive criterion. Even after "returning" from clandestine to normative Judaism, the descendants of the conversos used Iberian literary genres and social practices, such as devotional printing, occasional verse, or even theater performance. Writers within the Portuguese Jewish communities transferred forms of expression that were proper of Iberian Christianity —such as the pastoral novel, plays and epic poetry— to non-Christian religious content within a non-Iberian setting, a hybrid creative activity that considerably enlarges the boundaries of the Hispanic literatures.

The history of the "Portuguese nation" thus presents a certain continuity, but it crosses moments of profound historical transformation in religious, socioeconomic, and cultural sense that should not be downplayed. It is also dispersed in an almost global geographical space and integrated local cultural environments as different as Iberian Catholic urbanity, indigenous Andean villages, Moroccan ghettos, or the City of London. With their peculiar symbiosis of Hispanicity and Jewishness, the Sephardim

---

[1] With a framework of Portuguese-Jewish ethnicity, see also Azevedo (1989), Wilke (2009).
[2] For modernization narratives focusing on intellectual history, see also Faur (1992); Yovel (2009); Boccara (2014).

should not be reduced to this inner duality; they were the inhabitants of a kind of third mental space, in which Iberian heritage melted into a global culture. Steeped in modern Iberian languages and forms of cultural expression, they were denizens of a mythical Sepharad, an imagined place of origin however distant in time and space from it.

2 Conversos in Early Modern Iberia

2.1 Spain

Below the tomb of King Fernando III of Castile, which his son Alfonso X the Wise had built in Seville in 1279, four epitaphs in Spanish, Latin, Arabic, and Hebrew celebrate the memory of the deceased (Nickson 2015). Spain, which was a self-conscious haven of religious and cultural pluralism back then, became an exclusively Catholic domain in less than two-and-half centuries, its rulers receiving in 1494 the papal title of "Catholic Monarchs" in recognition of their zeal to complete the country's unity in the sphere of the sacred.

Explaining this shift from religious, legal, and cultural diversity to an obsession with purity has always been a challenge for Spanish historiography, and Spanish-Jewish historiography in particular (Méchoulan 1978). A simplistic periodization places the decisive turnabout in the year 1492, the moment of the conquest of Moorish Granada, the expulsion of the Jews, the birth of the Hispano-American empire, and a peak in the activity of the newly-founded Inquisition (Bennassar 1991). However, the repression and survival of tri-religious Spain should rather be seen as a long-term feature of the country's medieval and early modern history, which presents itself as a meandering itinerary with moments of violently enforced inclusion and exclusion, but also peaceful coexistence, assimilation and clandestine resistance of minorities.

Though not tolerating any non-Catholics officially, early modern Spain counted with two numerous communities of forced converts and their descendants. With all caution, one may estimate for the early sixteenth century at least 500,000 Moriscos and 250,000 conversos (Ladero Quesada 2016, 217). While the former lived in closely knitted agricultural communities, where they could pass on religious ritual and literature in Aljamiado (Spanish in Arabic characters), the latter mostly engaged in urban crafts and trades with less of a cultural resilience and social cohesion. After generations of assimilation and mixed marriages, being a converso was a result of social stigma rather than ancestral tradition. Yet it is to some extent legitimate to speak of a "History of the Jews in Modern and Contemporary Spain" as Julio Caro Baroja (1995) did in his three-volume classic, or at least of a Jewish history in that period. The history of Spanish Judeoconverts passes through three distinctive stages, roughly corresponding with the fifteenth, sixteenth, and seventeenth centuries.

In the fifteenth century, at least from the forced conversions of 1391 to the foundation of the Inquisition in 1478, converts succeeded in entering the patriciate and clergy of many Spanish cities. Their minority background was made invisible through name change, the repression of Hebrew books and schooling as well as mandatory participation in Catholic public practice, but the memory of Jewish ways was still strong inside the families and, what is more, kept alive by occasional contacts with professing Jews still living in Spain. The sheer numeric strength of the conversos favored locally the emergence of compact crypto-communities, such as the one of Ciudad Real, where Judaic ritual practices were still followed in private quite extensively (Beinart 1981). During its first and extremely cruel phase between 1480 and 1495, the Inquisition thoroughly destroyed these urban centers of converso life. In Extremadura, a prophetic and messianic movement flared up in reaction to this cataclysm. Many conversos fled to Portugal. But most of them undertook the tenacious efforts of social integration and mobility in spite of the dishonor that was attached to their lineage.

The sixteenth-century converso experience was dominated by these integration conflicts. While Jewish secret practice was eradicated in most places, family memories lived on in a transformed and erratic shape. The stigma of Inquisitorial persecution was upheld by the institution of the *inhabilidad*, denounced by *sanbenitos* displayed in the parish churches. The profusion of "purity of blood" regulations, a genre of private law that excluded conversos from many ecclesiastical, civil, and military corporations, had a less systemic impact and could be circumvented by bribes and protection. Six generations after mass baptism, the group of Judeoconverts was set apart by social prejudice rather than by religious culture or ideological deviance. Américo Castro ([1948]) claimed that men and women of converso lineage, members of educated urban classes who were uprooted from Judaism yet also marginalized by Christian society, developed skeptical and nonconformist worldviews that lay behind the more profound and dissident literary works of Spanish early modernity. Authors of converso background powered the Erasmian movement and its quest for inclusive norms such as piety, virtue, or prudence, as opposed to particular ones such as dogma, custom, and rank. Some of them ironically formulated an anti-code of honor, embodied in the passionate lovers of the *Celestina* or the anti-heroes of the picaresque novel. For some historians, the converso factor explains why, at the height of Spain's military and economic expansion, worldviews of mystical transcendence or this-worldly disillusion (*desengaño*) could invade elite literature.

The description of the conversos as a "social class" (Domínguez Ortiz 1955)[3] or as a "caste" is deemed far too rigid in recent literature, which has identified converso identity negatively by its liminal, slippery, and heterogenous character, yet has claimed it as a ferment of modernity (Fine 2013; Ingram 2018). The analysis of converso history in terms of competing social elites unduly diminishes the survival of a secret religiosity of

---

[3] See also Contreras (1992).

Jewish inspiration. Remote townlets offered a refuge to remnants of the fifteenth-century crypto-Jewish movement. In the Mancha region, a raid of 1588 unearthed a big family network, in which the secret transmission of Jewish practices by the women (Melammed 1999) and the oblique reading of Catholic devotional texts by some literate male leaders nourished a religious revival (Révah 2003, 167–174). The last refuges of Spanish crypto-Judaism were the region of Ciudad Rodrigo in Extremadura (Huerga Criado 1994) and the singular community of the "Chuetas" on the island of Majorca, target of an Inquisitorial mass arrest as late as 1677.

During the seventeenth century, Spain became the main destination for "New Christian" immigrants from Portugal, many of them refugees of the Inquisition. The expansion of their dynamic merchant networks after the peninsular union of 1580 opened, as Fernand Braudel famously put it, a "century of the Portuguese" in Atlantic commerce. Unlike the sedentary Castilian conversos, the "Portuguese" were extremely mobile within a far-flung diaspora mainly built on solidarities of local and family origin, as well as Jewish and Portuguese symbolic identities. These families, which were often of humble origins from the border regions of Beira and Trás-os-Montes, started as peddlers in Galicia and Extremadura, continued as export traders on the New Castile wool fairs, and ended up as merchant-bankers in Madrid running a commerce and contraband network with Portuguese Jewish communities in Italy, France, and the Netherlands. From 1627, they entered into banking schemes with the crown, became active in the administration of army supplies, monopolies and taxes. The appearance of these "Portuguese" provoked the Spanish Inquisition to a new intensity of anti-Jewish persecution, which peaked around 1655 and evidenced the vulnerability even of the economic elite (López Belinchón 2001).

The ten thousand or more Portuguese New Christians who were scattered throughout early modern Spain did not only share specific fears. Their family structures and memories, their cross-border business ventures, and their Luso-Spanish bilingualism blended their members into the imagined ethnic network that they called the *nação*. Identification with this community did not necessarily imply an actual practice of crypto-Judaic ritual, which was, in any case, reduced to little more than Sabbath rest, abstention from pork, and certain fast days. Women were frequently the transmitters of religious family tradition, while the male intellectual elite, physicians trained in Salamanca and Alcalá or amateur poets and writers protected by the magnates, represented a secular culture fully immersed in the aesthetic and scientific curiosities of the age. Jewish knowledge was obtained obliquely, from Christian sources (Yerushalmi 1998), except for the small-format prayer books that were smuggled in from Amsterdam. Yet the Portuguese fully participated in Spanish cultural consumption patterns; they attended theaters, bullfights, and church sermons, read Catholic devotional literature, imperial histories, and poetry. The social frameworks of literary production included *academias*, contests among amateur poets, and *tertulias*, learned gatherings of intellectuals for the display of eloquence and wit. New Christians occasionally formed separate circles, which may have become a forum for crypto-Jewish and free-thinking ideas (Yerushalmi 1971; Muchnik 2014).

Defended by the crown during the long reigns of Philip IV and Charles II, the "Portuguese" merchant network and financial elite continued thriving at least until the 1680s, despite the attacks by the Inquisition against many of its members (Sanz Ayán 1988, 163–168, 232–234, 286–290, 336–376). Economic instability, migration to Jewish communities abroad, assimilation into the Old Christian Spanish majority, and a massive country-wide sweep by the Holy Office in the 1720s put a temporary end to Jewish presence on Spanish soil (Alpert 2001).

2.2 Portugal

Throughout the Middle Ages Jews had lived in Portugal in decidedly more peaceable conditions than their co-religionists in the neighbouring kingdoms of Castile and Aragon, knowing neither major pogroms nor forced mass conversions (Tavares 1992). They enjoyed a considerable degree of legal autonomy and could be found in all levels of society, from the lowly to those higher up in finance, banking, international commerce and public office. The introduction of the Inquisition to Spain in 1478 saw the arrival of some conversos of which a number apparently openly embraced Judaism in Portugal (Soyer 2007a, 84–138). The expulsion of 1492 brought most of the exiled Spanish Jews into Portugal as they were accepted by João II upon the payment of a fee with the understanding that the bulk of them would stay for less than a year and make their way abroad (Soyer 2007a, 84–138; Tavares 2010).

On December 5, 1496 João II's successor, Manuel I (1495–1521), made public his decree forcing Portugal's Jews to leave the kingdom giving them until October of the following year to part or embrace Christianity. The playing out of the terms of Manuel's expulsion decree changed over the course of the first half of 1497. Sometime after Easter of 1497, the children of Portugal's Jews were forcibly taken from their parents, baptized, and handed over to Christian foster parents. In May 1497 Manuel made out an edict to those who freely accepted the Christian faith, promising to return their children and to grant them a twenty-year amnesty during which there would be no inquiry undertaken regarding their religious practices. When thousands of Jews nonetheless assembled to embark in Lisbon during late summer, King Manuel prevented them from leaving the country and had them forcibly converted to Christianity (Soyer 2007a, 138–181).

The full religious integration of the newly minted Christians was an overriding concern of the monarchy. Resentment grew alongside suspicions regarding their true orthodoxy. In the few years following the general conversion, examples of violence became frequent, the most serious of which was the pillaging and slaughter in Lisbon's New Christian quarter in 1506 (Yerushalmi 2015; Soyer 2007b). While the privileges Manuel I offered to the conversos were again renewed on April 1512 for another sixteen years, thus extending the period of grace until 1534, at the same time he began to pursue the creation of a Spanish-style tribunal of the Inquisition to deal with the religious deviance of the conversos (Marcocci 2011). It was his successor and son João III who was to fulfill his father's desire for the establishment of a tribunal of the Inquisition in Portugal. The institution was to last until 1821 (Marcocci and Paiva 2013). It was officially granted by papal sanction in 1531 though it did not actually begin to function until 1536 in part, at least, thanks to the work of an important New Christian lobby in Rome that did what they could to put obstacles in the path of João III's designs.[4]

The effective preservation and extention of Jewish belief and practice among Portugal's conversos had been a topic of much debate in historiography. The lines are generally drawn between the position of I. S. Révah, who held that a the Inquisition was founded to repress the peculiar "marrano" religiosity that largely persisted among the converts, and the view of Antonio José Saraiva, who held that the converts of 1497 assimilated quickly, shedding all real vestige of Jewish belief and practice; however, since they formed most of Portugal's commercial bourgeoisie, they were persecuted by the traditional social elites.[5] According to Saraiva, the Inquisition reinforced preconceptions about the New Christian's inherent Jewishness and thus became a "factory of Jews." From 1558 onwards, in addition, an increasing number of blood statutes barred New Christians from the ecclesiastical, military and administrative spheres and the distinction itself was only to be abolished in 1773 (Olival 2004; Rêgo 2011). The social stigma that was the result of these exclusionary measures enhanced the menace of the tribunal for the lives and livelihood of the New Christians who, counting still about 60,000 persons in 1542, fled Portugal in a steady trickle during the three centuries after the forced conversion (Saraiva 2001, 16).

There are, however, clear instances that some converts chose to embrace some form of syncretic adherence to Judaism. At the same time many lived their lives, at least apparently, as Catholics, some even making it a point of publicly flaunting a Catholic identity.[6] Yet the custom addressing all the New Christians as an ethnic group apart, a *nação hebrea*, was not only owed to the memory of their Jewish origins. Both the proyected image which was superimposed on them and their response to menace contributed to crystalizing their group identity. The category of the *nação* was at once social and political, as a part of the kingdom's economic and fiscal organization, and imaginary. Belonging to a nation meant a certain possibility of organization and structure, a way of manifesting itself in the world. It is difficult to pinpoint when the term itself was used for the first time, but already by 1525, it was as much attributed to them as internalized by them in Portugal and abroad. It encompassed all those

---

[4] For the foundational years of the Portuguese Inquisition the classic work remains Herculano (1968). A recent book which sheds crucial light on this period is Marcocci (2004).
[5] The documents of this controversy, which took place in 1969–1971, were translated in Saraiva (2001, 234–341).
[6] The wide spectrum of possible religious identity options available to New Christians is taken up in Graizbord (2008).

who had Jewish ancestry in Portugal, bringing them together with a common narrative and past regardless of their outward religious adhesion. Undoubtedly, their common plight as descendants of Portuguese Jewry independently of their religious professions was the impetus for solidarity networks; and the communal organization that the New Christians undertook in their struggle against the activities of the Inquisition further contributed to galvanizing them behind a common ethos.

In this regard some form of organization on the part of New Christians in Portugal and abroad was the precondition for their repeated temporary successes in reverting the functioning of the tribunal of the Inquisition. They obtained, most notably, prohibitions of the confiscation of the property of the accused in 1536, 1546–1547, 1558, 1577 and 1649, an important general pardon in 1605 (López-Salazar Codes 2010; Stuczynski 2007), an edict of grace in 1627 and a suspension of the tribunal itself from 1674 to 1681 (Lloyd 2016). It was this shared menace and the response to it, be it flight or resistance in Portugal, which contributed to crystalizing the idea of belonging to a common nation irrespective of religious expression.

The specificity of the Portuguese context in the sixteenth and seventeenth centuries would impact the sociability and cultural expression of the New Christians in and outside Portugal and the subsequent constitution of the diaspora. By the first half of the sixteenth century, important segments of the Portuguese population were bilingual, especially those who had privileged access to schooling, with both Spanish and Portuguese as working languages. Most of Portugal's important authors in the period used both languages, since Spanish had a literary prestige which surpassed that of Portuguese both outside and in the Iberian Peninsula. This only increased during the Iberian Union of 1580–1640 under the Habsburg crown during which knowledge of both languages was essential for many members of the populace (Buescu 2004; Vasquez Cuesta 1989). As will be seen, this bilingualism is evident both among New Christians and the Jewish communities of Portuguese origin which flourished in the second half of the sixteenth and the seventeen century. Many of these communities lived in a state of diglossia, regularly availing themselves of both languages for para-liturgical uses, cultural expression and the production of community documents.

3 The New Christian Diaspora

The Portuguese Inquisition was the powerful push-factor in the emigration of New Christians; but the pull-factors that turned the refugees into a successful merchant network were economic rather than religious. Refugees increasingly chose the trade hubs of the North Sea region, though these, unlike the Mediterranean cities, did not admit any public practice of Judaism at the time. The Portuguese New Christians obtained their settlement charters as a nominally Catholic merchant corporation, the so-called "Portuguese Nation," alongside the Flemish, Dutch, Hanseatic, English, and Italian "nations".[7]

By a fatidic coincidence, Portugal's Jews were forced to become Christians shortly before the India trade made Lisbon overnight into Europe's most global port city. Since 1501, the royal "Casa da Índia" monopolized the spice imports, its European outlet being the consulate (*feitoria*) in Antwerp. The Lisbon-based converted Jews immediately competed on this route with the most powerful Italian and German trade networks of the time. The Antwerp municipality gave in 1511 a favorable charter to the "Portuguese Nation," whose leading firm, the brothers Franciso and Diogo Mendes, obtained around 1525 a privileged access to the Casa da Índia and thereby a dominance over the route (Almeida 1993; Magalhães 1998). Their networks extended further to England and the Mediterranean, and when several of their associates had joined Ottoman Jewries, the imperial authorities submitted the Mendes family in 1532 to a series of trials for heresy and treason. The prosecution occasioned in 1545 the flight of the Mendes heiresses to Italy and Constantinople. Emperor Charles V responded in 1549 with the expulsion of many New Christians from Antwerp, and Portugal closed its *feitoria* (Leone Leoni 2005). Antwerp's Portuguese colony, however, continued to thrive thanks to religious conformism, Spanish royal concessions, and the exploitation of new commodities, most importantly, the sugar of Brazil. The small but affluent "Portuguese Nation" on the Scheldt was involved in the cultural life during Antwerp's Golden Age, which included an elite taste in Spanish letters and the Humanist and Protestant enthusiasm for Biblical literature. The colony counted almost one hundred families at the eve of the Dutch Rebellion, which would lead to an ephemeral Calvinist rule in Antwerp. During that time, in 1581–1585, the municipality took the bold measure of opening the city to Jewish settlement. Inquisition reports show religious gatherings among the Portuguese, animated by Jews from the Mediterranean (Prins 1927; Pohl 1978).

After the Spanish recapture of Antwerp in 1585, much of the Iberian trade relocated to competing commercial hubs that offered greater economic and religious freedom. After the turn of the seventeenth century, several Dutch, German, and Danish ports allowed the establishment of public Jewish communities. We will discuss this new diaspora separately and continue focusing on those European regions where the "Portuguese Nation" had to remain in a grey zone between a merchant corporation and a religious community.

New Christians tried to gain a foothold in London but were expelled twice, first in 1542 and again in 1594, when the execution of the Queen's physician Rodrigo Lopes, accused of conspiracy with Spain, stirred up an anti-Jewish mood that also resounds in Shakespeare's *Merchant of Venice*. António Fernandes Carvajal, who arrived in 1635, headed again a small nucleus that would evolve into a Jewish community. At

---

7 The classic study of these corporations remains Goris (1925).

that time, Portuguese merchants ran the war finances of the Spanish crown and could place their agents safely among the elite of Brussels and Antwerp.

Already during the Mendes crisis, Antwerp's New Christians had looked upon France as a refuge. In 1550, they could obtain a charter from King Henry II, which invited "the merchants and other Portuguese that are called New Christians" on advantageous conditions. A further letter of 1574 assured those in Bordeaux against inquiries about their private religious practice. It is known that two major sceptic thinkers of the time, Michel de Montaigne of Bordeaux and Francisco Sánchez at the University of Toulouse, had Iberian converso background. The Portuguese colonies, however, gained momentum only after the division of the Netherlands made France into a neutral sanctuary for Iberian trade: while the Dutch navy blockade of the Scheldt was compensated by the overland route from Rouen, Spanish embargoes forced the Dutch to unload in Bordeaux or in the Basque ports near the border. Apart from acting as intermediaries in these transactions, Portuguese merchants also shipped French fabrics from Normandy and Brittany to the Iberian empire. Counting about two thousand members during the first half of the seventeenth century, the "Portuguese Nation" based in the French ports was an essential link in the Atlantic trade system between Seville and Amsterdam (Israel 2002, 245–268). It built up a religious culture of its own, equidistant to Iberian Catholicism, the Jewish diaspora, and the local environment (Nahon 1992; Wilke 2019). Intense relations with Dutch and Italian Jews inspired a semi-clandestine religious life in the Southwestern corner of the country, while in the big cities of Bordeaux, Nantes, and Rouen, various other alliances were possible. The Portuguese community here fell apart into a crypto-Jewish majority and a Catholic minority that pursued a militant integration strategy. Conflicts between both camps reached their high point in 1633, when the Spanish Inquisition recruited the Catholic New Christians in Rouen for its cause, provoking mutual accusations in front of the French courts and mass arrests from both parties. Richelieu's intervention and a huge bribe protected the crypto-Jews of Rouen against their Spanish and local enemies (Révah 1961).

While the Rouen settlement declined after the mid-century and had disappeared by the 1680s, the most populous center of the "Portuguese nation" emerged in Saint-Esprit, a suburb of Bayonne, under the protection of the local governors, the dukes of Gramont (Zink 1994). A triangle of rural communities, specialized in the crossborder trade, settled in Peyrehorade, La Bastide-Clairence and near the Gramont castle in Bidache. These communities served as end points of adventurous contraband trips of their male members into Spain, where they worked in trade and finance, especially tax adminstration. While living under such amphibic conditions, the Portuguese under Gramont protection obtained garantees of tacit toleration in 1656 and passed to a fairly orthodox Jewish practice, undergoing circumcision, adopting Hebrew names, keeping separate cemeteries, a synagogue, and a rabbi, while their living conditions still entailed nominal Catholicism, at least for life cycle events (Graizbord 2004; Wilke 2015).

For generations, switching between two religious registers was part of everyday life and basis of professional activities for the Portuguese in France. Their cultural life reflected this adaptive culture. While Spanish and Portuguese were spoken in the families and in commercial life until the eve of the French Revolution, most members were fluent in French, and those in the Southwest often spoke Basque as well. The crypto-Jewish communities of France hosted improvised literary circles of which important fragments and indirect testimony remain. The poets João Pinto Delgado and Antonio Enríquez Gómez, who printed their works in Rouen and Bordeaux, apparently found a part of their audience in this local environment. It is possible to point to contacts with French intellectuals and even relations of protection by local authorities.

With the influx of Inquisition refugees in the early eighteenth century, the community of Bayonne grew to some 3,500 members, while that of Bordeaux prospered with the French colonial expansion (Nahon 2003). Here, the double life lasted until 1723, when Jewish practice was finally recognized, but the same step took until 1756 in the Southern Netherlands and until 1777 on the entire French territory including Paris. The French Sephardim remained marked by their long experience of religious flexibility, manifest in instances of free-thought and close social relations with non-Jews. The two Sephardi communities of France were the first European Jews who, in 1790, obtained the equality of political rights.

4 The Western Sephardim

4.1 The Mediterranean

The Iberian Jewish and the New Christian diaspora was thoroughly interconnected in the Mediterranean. The expulsion of 1492 saw the flight of many Spanish Jews to the Maghreb where they integrated into existing Jewish communities or formed new ones. After the 1496 expulsion a number of Portuguese Jews managed to make it there as well (Tavim 1997). After the mass conversion there were regular instances of Portuguese New Christians joining these communities, a process often fraught with difficulties (Huerga Criado 2003). The ultimate destination for many was the Ottoman Empire where long established Greek-speaking (Romaniote) Jewish communities thrived and prospered. Islamic law placed them, alongside Christians, in a position of inferiority but in incomparably better conditions than in most other European localities. It was natural that Constantinople and Salonica should become a place of refuge (Hacker 1992; Tavim 2013).

Throughout the sixteenth century Portuguese merchants managed to establish safe havens in the Italian peninsula where they could have the right to reside, a recognition of the importance of their mercantile networks. The invitations were rendered public, though only after years of delicate planning with local authorities. The various Italian states also had to contend with the Roman Inquisition created in 1542. At the outset generally the invitations granted them the right to live in the respective states with the agreement that they would live as Christians. Conversion or reversion to Judaism was only possible later in the second half of the century.

In 1534 Ercole II (1534–1559) allowed *hebrei hispani* to settle in the Duchy of Ferrara. This term meant Spanish and Portuguese conversos who wanted to embrace Judaism and were accorded the same privileges as those Jews from Spain who arrived in 1492 (Leone Leoni 1993, 143–147). Four years later the Duke made out an invitation to Spanish and Portuguese *marrani* specifically seeking them out in the commercial hub of Antwerp (Leone Leoni 1993, 143; Segre 1996). Ferrara was to be, for a short time, a veritable cultural centre for the Western Sephardic diaspora. Thanks to the press managed by Abraham Usque and Yom Tov Atias, conversos who had embraced Judaism, Ferrara became, between 1552 and 1555, a bastion of Iberian and properly speaking Iberian Jewish culture in the Italian peninsula. The press printed important liturgical works in Spanish for the use of Spanish and mostly Portuguese New Christians who wished to embrace normative Judaism but did not have a command of Hebrew alongside literary works which, however, betray some form of converso connection. The intended readership was, of course, not limited to the duchy but rather catered to the growing, predominantly Portuguese diaspora. That this central Italian locality should become such a hub of return to Judaism was certainly singular and, indeed, short lived (Andrade 2006). In 1597 the Duchy passed to the Papal States and a ghetto was created there in 1627.

Similar invitations that followed in other Italian cities searched to preclude apostasy. In the Papal States, the port city of Ancona in 1547 attracted Portuguese merchants active in mercantile networks linked to the Adriatic, the Balkans and the Ottoman Empire, but their charter was soon withdrawn by the zealous Pope Paul IV and twenty-five of its members were executed in 1556 as apostates (Cooperman 1998). Meanwhile in 1549, Duke Cosimo de' Medici of Tuscany had granted Spanish and Portuguese New Christians the right to reside in Pisa, considering them on a par with other Tuscan residents and guaranteeing them freedom from inquisitorial prying (Frattarelli Fischer 2008, 15–68). Tellingly, news of the privileges was made out through an undated letter in Spanish directed to "persons of the nation in Rome" who were almost exclusively Portuguese, testimony to the kind of diglossia which the *nação* operated under (Novoa 2005). The arrival of important New Christian lawyers, doctors and merchants to Pisa in the following years would be at the basis of one of the most important communities of the Mediterranean.

In almost all of these cases the invitees were conversos who appeared as successful professing Portuguese Catholics. In exchange, they were granted the freedom to live without inquisitorial prying and to practice their professions. Financially savvy rulers understood the benefit they could derive from the growing New Christian mercantile networks that, by the middle of the sixteenth century, spanned from the Levant to the Atlantic world. The reliable availability of expensive goods and the policies of steady investment in trade helped create an era of unprecedented prosperity of many members of the Portuguese New Christian diaspora in the seventeenth century (Israel 2002).

One of the most innovative and dynamic contexts for Sephardic life in the sixteenth and seventeenth centuries was the Ottoman Empire, which must always be considered alongside developments in the Italian peninsula and the Eastern Mediterranean. Throughout those centuries new communities sprang up especially in localities like Istanbul, Salonica and Smyrna, often taking the place names of the purported origins of their members, some communities fused and others disappeared. The conversos who became Jews and joined their ranks contributed to cultural life and leadership. Some, such as the Portuguese Dona Beatriz de Luna/Dona Gracia Nasi and her nephew João Micas/Joseph Nasi (1524–1579) were known for their wealth, international connections and attained an almost mythical status even in life. Both reached the Sublime Porte after stays in Antwerp and Venice and contributed to fostering a sense of community once there (Roth 2003).

Others brought European culture and learning to the Levant. They either came with an academic formation undertaken in Iberia in the case of conversos who became Jews in the Ottoman Empire or were the descendants of exiles who maintained a continuity and identification with the place of origin of their families. It was in Salonica that the Portuguese physician João Rodrigues de Castelo Branco, better known as Amatus Lusitanus (1511–1568), finally openly embraced Judaism and completed his best-known work, the *Curationum Medicinalium Centuriae Septem*, after an itinerary which followed the path of many fellow conversos in the sixteenth century.

Under the guise of Ottoman subjects, Iberian Jews were able to settle in Venice as go-betweens, intermediaries between the *Serenissima* and its natural enemy, yet also main trading partner. The Iberian origins of many of them conditioned the literary production which was evinced in the Venetian presses.

Iberian 'New Jews'[8] were finally able to openly settle in Venice in 1589 thanks to the intervention of a Portuguese former converso, Daniel Rodriga. A merchant, he convinced Venetian authorities that the *Ponentini* ("Westerners," as they came to be known in distinction from the Ottoman Sephardim) would be useful to the Republic of Venice due to their presence in the trading hub of Spalato. In this way Venice could gain the upper hand in trade with the Ottoman Empire over its rival, the Republic of Ragusa, where Iberian Jews had a longstanding presence since the expulsion (Ligorio 2018). This new category was not without controversy from Rome, as it meant the tacit acceptance of apostasy, essentially allowing baptized Catholics to renounce their religious faith and espouse Judaism. In 1589 Rodriga managed to obtain an official charter establishing the *Ponentini* as former Christians turned Jews in the *Serenissima*.

---

8 For the term New Jews and its problematics see Kaplan (1996).

Years later, in 1633 they even had their own space within the city in the form of the *Ghetto Novissimo*; and in the seventeenth century, the city of the lagoon could boast five synagogues, two of which were related to the Iberian Jewish presence there, the Levantine and Spanish *schole*. One important *ponentino* denizen was the Portuguese Emanuel Aboab (1555–1629) who penned parts of his *Nomología o discursos legales* in the city where he served as hakham to the Iberian Jewish community for several years. The rich archival documentation in Spanish and Portuguese held in the state archive of Venice is testimony to the vibrancy of Sephardic cultural life there, with the constant arrival of new members from Iberia and the diaspora (Arnold 2006).

The Grand Duchy of Tuscany followed a similar pattern with the creation of the Iberian Jewish communities of Pisa and Livorno. From the 1570s onwards, Portuguese Jews in Pisa were regularly called *ebrei levantini*; and many had indeed arrived there after a spate in the Ottoman Empire (Toaff 1990). They coexisted with an important New Christian community which was for the large part Portuguese and lived, at least publicly, as Christians. Among them were prominent doctors and well-respected men such as Damião Dias, Estevão de Castro and Rodrigo da Fonseca, all professors of medicine at the University of Pisa, the last two being the authors of many books. Others were active in international commerce with the Levant, the Maghreb and even the Americas making them especially sought after by the Medici authorities, intent on turning the Grand Duchy of Tuscany into an important state.

The water shed decision of Grand Duke Ferdinando de' Medici (1587–1609) to make out the 1591–1593 the *Livornine* edicts allowed New Christians, predominantly Portuguese, to live as Jews in Pisa and Livorno, even if they had previously lived as Catholics. It would establish the port city of Livorno as a major Iberian cultural hub in the early modern period (Trivellato 2009). The use of Spanish and Portuguese was maintained until the nineteenth century with alternation between the two. In the middle of the seventeenth century at least two devotional texts, translations from Hebrew, were printed in the port city in Spanish for a readership of New Jews. Later on, from the eighteenth and well into the nineteenth century Livorno would be known as a major hub for printing works in Hebrew, destined to Sephardic communities in the Maghreb, North Europe and even the Americas (Bregoli 2014).

While the Viceroyalty of Naples, under the Hispanic monarchy had effectively expelled Jews from the south of Italy there for two centuries at least there were instances in which the presence of Judaizing conversos was brought to the attention of religious and civil authorities. These were Iberians who had settled in the south of Italy and formed important communities with prominent individuals linked to international commerce and the life of the court in Naples (Huerga Criado 2012; Mazur 2013). In this context an author worthy of note is the Portuguese converso doctor Miguel de Silveira (1580–1644?) who, after years in the literary circles of Madrid during which he was object of Inquisitorial investigations on account of suspected crypto Judaism, settled in Naples where he published the epic poem *El Macabeo* in 1638.

4.2 Northern Europe

When the emigration of Portuguese New-Christians reached Protestant cities, political authorities were still reluctant to admit the public practice of either Catholicism or Judaism. At the same time, they were committed to liberty of conscience and eager to attract the trade routes for Iberian commodities. Branching out on the North Sea shores, Portuguese merchants had to shed Catholicism and engage in the complicated "return" to Judaism in an environment where there was neither an existent Jewish community nor any interest to establish an Italian-style Jewry with ghettos, distinctive clothing, and Talmudic autonomous jurisdiction. The Portuguese Nation had to invent a newly defined Jewish culture and social profile, negotiated not only with its Protestant environment but also with its Catholic-educated members. After having been New Christians, the migrants did not simply return to an ancestral faith but became, as it were, New Jews (Kaplan 1996).

In Amsterdam, the first Portuguese merchant families, Veiga and Pimentel, appear in notarial documents in 1595, coming from Antwerp. In Hamburg, there were already seven families at the time, among them the famous physician Rodrigo de Castro. Within the Hanseatic League, Hamburg showed the greatest openness towards immigrants; and the city needed the Sephardim to develop its considerable trade relationships with the Iberian world (Kellenbenz 1958; Poettering 2019). Yet even here, the open practice of Judaism was seen as an offense to Christianity, and due to the pressure of the Lutheran clergy and commercial competitors, the charter given to the "Portuguese Nation" in 1612 admitted only wealthy merchants, whom it treated as foreign residents, prohibiting most crafts and trades, real estate ownership, and especially the possession of synagogues and cemeteries.

The Portuguese of Hamburg could thus practice Judaism, but had to hold their prayer assemblies discretely in residential buildings. The three congregations were unified into a single one, "Bet Israel" in 1652. It had 1,200 members at the time, governed by a community board (*Mahamad*) and a chief rabbinate. An intellectual and literary life developed around doctors such as Benjamin Mussafia, rabbis such as David Cohen de Lara, and poets such as Moseh de Gideon Abudiente, who in 1666 also became a propagandist of the messianic pretender Sabbatai Zvi. Jews in Hamburg were part of the social elite, displaying status symbols such as carriages and servants from Africa, but their life included an experience of marginalization by the law, polemical campaigns of the Lutheran clergy, organized proselytism, and occasional molestations by the mob (Studemund-Halévy 1994–1997).

The Jews of Hamburg buried their dead on a cemetery that they had acquired in 1611 in the neighboring city of Altona, on Danish territory, and many of them lived between two political frameworks. The King of Denmark tried in 1619 to invite Jewish merchants by granting them many of the rights that Hamburg denied, but the Portuguese colony that formed in Glückstadt could in no way compete with its big neighbor. Only when Hamburg submitted its Jews to increased fiscal pressure at the end of the seventeenth century, part of the Portuguese community moved indeed to the Danish side and set up a new community in Altona in 1703.

Even in Amsterdam, which would stand out as a beacon of religious liberty, the Portuguese immigrants lived initially as crypto-Catholics or members of the Reformed Church, the sole cult that was publicly admitted at that time. In 1603, James Lopes da Costa brought a Jew from the Ashkenazi community of Emden to conduct clandestine services. In contrast to the famous foundation legend stating that the city authorities discovered these hidden Jews and willingly admitted them in their midst, official acceptance was the result of long negotiations, in which the famous jurist Hugo Grotius intervened. As neither side had an interest in formalizing a distinctive Jewish statute, the Jewish community was included in the liberty of conscience on the condition that their leadership, the *mahamad*, committed to repress any offensive tendencies among the members. This agreement, signed in 1616, allowed the community to build up its internal life free from state control, since it was the *mahamad* who upheld a far-reaching control of public and private morals, a strict censorship of Jewish printing, and a repression of religious deviance as well as potentially unsettling controversies with Christians.

The confrontation between the *mahamad* and free-thinking rebels – most famously exemplified by Spinoza's excommunication – is the most visible manifestation of a constitutive tension within the Sephardic community of Amsterdam, which pitted a strong and sometimes repressive oligarchy against a widely acculturated membership (Albiac 1987; Yovel 1989; Kaplan 1992; Révah 1995). The former New Christians had been accustomed to treat Judaism as a family tradition in a rather flexible manner; most of them even continued trading under false Christian identities with family members in Portugal, Spain and France. The Portuguese Jews of Amsterdam thus represent, in Yosef Kaplan's words, an "alternative path to modernity": they were immersed in the classical, Iberian, and local cultures of their environment, but their form of modern Jewishness, quite unlike the individualized choices of the emancipation age, took pride in ethnic cohesion and collective confessional self-affirmation (Kaplan 2000; Swetschinski 2000). Emerging from an amorphous crypto-religion, the founders invested an impressive amount of ambition and resources into the design of formalized institutions. Synagogue prayer had been organized by three separate congregations, which all merged into a unitary community in 1639, named "Talmud Torah" (Study of the Law) after the Sephardi sister community of Venice. The Jews of Amsterdam acquired cemetery plots in 1602 and in 1614, where splendidly sculpted marble slabs defied the traditional ban on images. Since 1608, they hired rabbis from Italian and Ottoman Sephardi communities. They ran a central boys' school from 1616, where teaching followed the systematic pedagogy of the age; and they started training their own rabbis from 1637 at the academy "Ets Haim", which built up what is now the oldest Jewish institutional library in the world. Authors and printers published since 1610 hundreds of books in Iberian languages and provided European Jewry from 1627 with Hebrew imprints. The community built in 1675 a monumental synagogue that rivalled with baroque churches while being based on contemporary scholarly reconstructions of the Temple of Jerusalem.

With its visual culture and the solemnity of its public acts, Amsterdam Jews perfected the political aesthetics of Jewish communal life with the intent of becoming a player in multiconfessional Dutch society, whereas their symbolical culture extolling honor and lineage manifestly took its inspiration from the Iberian tradition (Kaplan 2001). While the poet Daniel Levi de Barrios compared the "Jewish popular government" to the Dutch estates, this imaginary republic was meant to cover the Western Sephardic diaspora in its entirety. The institution that best exemplifies the translocal spirit of lineage that animated the *nação* is Dotar, a lottery society founded in 1615 in order to endow poor brides "of this Portuguese Nation, and the Castilian, among residents from St. Jean-de-Luz to Danzig, including France and the Netherlands, England and Germany" (Bodian 1997, 48).

Though the vitality of Iberian languages over two centuries is remarkable, the Sephardi communities should not be seen as linguistic enclaves. Their members were mostly polyglot and needed to master local languages in their everyday life. Spinoza, whose family had immigrated from Antwerp and Nantes, was surrounded by Dutch and French communication from his childhood; he studied Hebrew and literary Spanish at the community school. Like other young Jews who reflected on an academic career, he took private lessons in Latin, which would open the European scholarly world to him. Yet he famously confessed that he felt fully at ease only in his native language, by which he obviously meant Portuguese.[9]

The literary expression of the Amsterdam Sephardim was Jewish in content and Iberian in form, not leaving out any baroque genre, not even Quevedo-inspired satire, Jesuit-style sermons or allegorical theater. Religious books, such as those written by Rabbi Menasseh ben Israel, were meant to impress fellow Talmudists, but they also provided Jewish instruction to Jews who had received all their literary culture outside the fold. Amsterdam imprints were also destined to encourage the silent audience of clandestine readers in the New Christian diaspora, and finally they searched to spread favorable ideas about Judaism among Christian theologians and Hebraists (Rauschenbach 2019). Subjects of internal communication circulated in manuscripts, which contained family history and occasional verse, sometimes kabbalah and other esoteric lore, poetic celebrations of Inquisition victims, and often elaborate polemical treatises against the Christian religion, which were too bold to be printed. By their learned rhetoric and calligraphy, these manuscripts demonstrate a wish to vindicate a conceptual and symbolical identity within a multi-confessional environment.

The Amsterdam Jews, whose economic mainstay was the Iberian trade, often entertained close relations with their countries of origin and sometimes even travelled there under false Catholic identities. Only when the Dutch West India Company developed

---

9 Spinoza, letter XIX to William van Blijenbergh, dated January 5, 1665 (Van Vloten and Land 1914, 69).

an anti-Spanish policy of colonial expansion, alternative commercial strategies opened within the Dutch empire overseas. Among the Jewish settlers and promotors of Dutch Brazil, these perspectives could evoke messianic expectations, and Menasseh ben Israel explicitly claimed in a 1650 pamphlet that the global dispersion of the Jews prepared the imminent messianic age. This belief became a strong unifying ferment between Jews and Puritan groups when Menasseh ben Israel undertook a major propagandistic initiative to open England for Jewish settlement, appealing at the same time to the economic benefits that Jewish trade would have for English commercial expansion. Though Ben Israel was able to gain Oliver Cromwell for his plan, the Parliament's opposition to a formal admission only allowed in 1656 a tacit toleration of prayer meetings in particular houses (Schorsch 1978). When the Anglo-Jewish community established in 1664 a formal community framework under the congregational name "Saar Hasamaim" and gained a more formal charter of protection, its merely unofficial readmission protected it from legal discriminations that persisted elsewhere, even in Amsterdam (Kerner 2018).

In the late seventeenth century, the three thousand Portuguese Jews of Amsterdam were at the center of a well-connected community network that embraced the big Sephardic communities of Hamburg, London, Bordeaux, and Livorno, smaller colonies in places such as Rotterdam, The Hague, Dublin, and Copenhagen, but most importantly, a first cluster of Jewish communities on the American coast. Gaining a foothold overseas allowed the Sephardim to integrate the Dutch, English, and French colonial economies and to withdraw progressively from the Iberian trade route, which had initially been the key of their prosperity in foreign lands.

5 The Diaspora Overseas

5.1 North America

A unifying element between the confessional frontlines of a divided Europe, the Sephardi diaspora also reached far beyond the Christian world. While a large group of Iberian Jewish emigrants had found refuge in the Ottoman Empire and in Sharifian Morocco, smaller segments of the diaspora left Europe in order to act as commercial intermediaries with local populations. This is the case of the New Christians who in the sixteenth century reached the fortresses of Portuguese India, mostly Goa and Cochim, and who, in the last named place, mingled with the Malabar Jews in the nearby Hindu city of Mattancherry (Tavim 2003). In the early seventeenth century, Sephardic arms traders from the Netherlands settled under the protection of African kings in present-day Senegal (Mark and da Silva Horta 2013). The major overseas destination, however, was the New World.

America was all but a safe haven in the beginnings of colonization. A Spanish royal edict of 1501 barred the passage to the Indies to all persons of Jewish or Muslim ancestry; and those who succeeded in evading this prohibition faced the same religious persecution as in the mother country. One of Cortés's conquistadors, Hernando Alonso, was accused of crypto-Judaism and publicly executed in 1528, barely seven years after the fall of Tenochtitlán (Uchmany 2001, 191). From 1570, tribunals of the Inquisition were set up in Lima, Mexico City, and Cartagena de Indias (Greenleaf 1969; Chuchiak 2012).

Judeo-converts nonetheless reached the Spanish-American colonies. Some circumvented controls through document fraud or bribery, others pretended to be crew members or personal attendants of Old Christian settlers. Already in the sixteenth century, conversos of Spanish origin were established in the viceroyalty, their Jewish identity being often no more than a vague genealogical rumor (Rubinstein and Dabbah Mustri 2002). Portuguese-born New Christians, who showed a greater degree of cohesion, joined them after the union of the crowns. They frequently evaded the Seville bureaucracy by a detour via the Cape Verde islands, where they embarked on slave ships chartered by their compatriots. The most famous exemption that Philip II granted to a group of them was part of a plan to occupy and develop New Spain's northern borderlands. In 1579, Luis de Carvajal the Elder from northern Portugal was made governor and captain-general of Nuevo León and received the privilege to settle a hundred families of his choice upon this huge territory. In the course of a ruthlessly successful colonizing enterprise, Carvajal was denounced to the Inquisition and died in prison in 1590. While he seems to have been a sincere Catholic, his settler communities kept crypto-Judaic customs; and his nephew, Luis de Carvajal the Younger, was the head of a secret community in the mining town of Pachuca. When he was arrested by the Inquisition, he chose to die impenitent at the stake in 1596. His spiritual autobiography and other manuscript writings, kept as evidence by the Inquisition, constitute the first extant Jewish writings of the American continent (Toro 1944; Perelis 2016).

A new immigration wave of New Christians, nearly all of them merchants of Portuguese birth, arrived in the 1620s. This group ran a vast network of trade services, which soon encompassed New Spain from the urban centers of Mexico and Puebla to the most distant mining towns and along the trade route that linked Acapulco to China and the Philippines. Their activity lasted for a quarter century only, until a large-scale persecution by the Inquisition crushed the entire crypto-Jewish community, 150–250 persons (Alberro 2001, 181), in the years of 1642–1649. Culminating in three huge autodafés and some twenty capital executions in Mexico City, the persecution was a sequel to similar major razzias in South America.

Since the trial records are extant and have been repeatedly studied, the defendants of New Spain are probably the best known historical nucleus of secret Judaism (Liebman 1970; Hordes 1980; Wachtel 2001, 103–247). The immigrants appear in a peculiar colonial situation. In New Spain, white Iberian settlers formed a small elite among the larger indigenous, black, and mixed populations, and they recruited each other readily into positions of command in the administration and the church. As a part of the racial "upper crust," the Portuguese rather had to fear the revenge of slaves, servants, and neighbors, who knew how vulnerable their masters were to denunciations (Alberro 1996, 420).[10] However, the Inquisition also persecuted some individuals of mulatto and indigenous background who had been admitted into the secret of the Judaizers, and a community of mestizo Jews in Pachuca claims this heritage still today.

5.2 South America and the Caribbean

The "discovery" of Brazil in 1500 by Pedro Álvares de Cabral provided a new territory for members of the *nação* to settle in. Rather than a colony along the model of Hispanic America the early colonization of Brazil was organized along the lines of hereditary captaincies which were leased out. Historians of this period point out that New Christians arrived in Brazil from the outset of colonial expansion there, with many working in the exploitation of the commodity which gave the name to the country, brazil wood, and in sugar plantations (Mello 1996; Novinsky 1972; Salvador 1976; Salvador 1978).

An independent tribunal of the Inquisition was never created in Brazil as it had been in Portuguese India in 1560. Instead, the tribunal of Lisbon oversaw doctrinal purity by sending regular inquisitorial visitations. The first such visitation, conducted in 1591–1593, alerted authorities as to the significant presence of Judaizers in the north east of Brazil, with clear instances of well-entrenched Judaizing practices among them (Mello 1991). This first visitation brought the attention of religious authorities to a number of prominent promoters of the *marrano* heresy in Brazil, among them the man who would go down in history as the first Brazilian author, Bento Teixeira (1561 – ca. 1600), a teacher of Latin originally from Porto who was accused of having partially translated the Bible in addition to indoctrinating people into the Jewish faith. Sent to Lisbon where he stood trial, it was in prison where, apparently, he penned his epic poem, the *Prospopeia*, in which he celebrated the exploits of the family of the governor of the captaincy of Pernambuco, Jorge d'Albuquerque Coelho (1539–1602), perhaps with a view of returning there. The poem was published posthumously a year after his death in 1601. A second visitation in 1618–1620 was sent to Salvador de Bahia, a third in 1627–1628 to the southern captaincies and later, in 1763–1769 to Grão-Pará (Pereira 2011).

Brazil and the La Plata region were the destinations of a busy contraband route that developed in the course of the Peruvian silver boom. South America quickly became a sought-after destination for peninsular conversos desirous of either living

---

10 For an extensive study on race relations see Schorsch (2009).

a life as Christians without the harassment dealt to them in Spain or as crypto Jews, which was deemed to be more possible in the vast expanse of the American continent.

The tribunals of the Inquisition of Lima and Cartagena de Indias, respectively created in 1570 and 1610, at outset were more concerned with the arrival of Protestants, the beliefs of slaves or problems of moral turpitude. Very soon however, they were alerted to the reality of Judaizing New Christians who maintained some form of attachment to Jewish belief and practice. Especially important was the role of New Christian women in the transmission of this often syncretic form of Judaism. They were often accused of being the primary culprits in having passed on the tradition to their offspring, keeping alive practices through the preservation of ritual and religious observation. The rich holdings of these tribunals, albeit a partial source, indicate the resilience of Jewish belief among descendants of Iberian Jews in the New World (Escobar Quevedo 2008).

A disproportionate amount of those who were interrogated were Portuguese. Some were able to reach the Spanish possessions in South America from Europe; others had originally settled in Brazil and went on to seek fortune in Spanish America, especially in the silver mines of Potosí. Many of the most affluent were *asentistas* in the slave trade. The decade of the 1630s was to see numerous trials of members of the "Portuguese Nation." One such Judaizer was the prominent physician Francisco Maldonado de Silva (1592–1639), a descendant of Portuguese New Christians who lived in Santiago de Chile. Calling himself "Eli Nazareno," he was a noted crypto Jewish leader and in his 1639 trial by the tribunal of Lima in which he was condemned to death, it became known that he had maintained correspondence in Latin with Jews from Rome, receiving instruction and advice on matters of normative Jewish faith and practice (Böhm 1984). One of the most prominent sets of trials condemned the great merchant Manuel Bautista Pérez[11] and some of the most important Portuguese converso merchants based in Lima in the so-called "Great Complicity" (*gran complicidad*) between 1637 and 1639 of being secret Jews (Moreno Cebrían and Sullón Barreto 2014). As the century progressed, the many trials available are testimony to instances of Jewish life which lived out among members of the *nação* in Spanish America.

The crackdown on the crypto-Jewish trade system of Spanish America was in part motivated by fear that these men might become a fifth column in a Dutch or Portuguese invasion. A turning-point was indeed the conquest of Pernambuco by the Dutch West India Company in 1630. During a quarter century Judaism was able to be openly practiced in northeastern Brazil. The congregation "Zur Israel," the first synagogue in the Americas, was founded in 1636 in Recife under the leadership of the Portuguese-born Dutch-trained rabbi Isaac Aboab da Fonseca (1605–1693). One source attests that the number of Jews in Dutch Brazil was as large as 1,450, half of the white settler population. Their life as an integral part of the colonial elite, the

---

[11] On this Peruvian network, see Studnicki-Gizbert (2007).

economy and the military, with significantly less religious constraints than in Europe, shaped a new Jewish self-assurance and had an important impact on Portuguese Brazil (Feitler 2003). The short-lived experience of openly lived normative Judaism ended in 1654 with the Portuguese reconquest of the territory (Vainfas 2010).

The large number of Jews that was expelled from Brazil found havens in the Caribbean possessions that North European powers had started to wrest from the Spanish Empire. As planters and traders, Sephardic Jews occupied a peculiar social position between the Protestant elite and the enslaved black majority in these sugar economies. Daniel Levi de Barrios presented Anglo-Jewry in 1688 as a global map stretching from the Caribbean via Europe to India:

> *Ya, en seis ciudades anglas, se publica*
> *luz de seis juntas de Israel sagrada:*
> *tres en Nieves, London, Iamaica,*
> *quarta y quinta en dos partes de Barbada,*
> *sexta en Madras Patân se verifica.* (Barrios 1688, 55–56)

("The light of six Israelite communities already shines forth in six English cities: three in Nieves, London, and Jamaica, the fourth and fifth in two places of Barbados; the sixth can be found in Madras-Patan.")

The Dutch Sephardim had meanwhile entered the plantation economy in Suriname, South America, and the trade of Curaçao, which became a hub of commerce and contraband with the Spanish Empire. Finally, the year of the loss of Brazil, twenty-two Jewish refugees from Pernambuco arrived in New Amsterdam, the future New York, where they were the founders of what would become in 1706 the congregation "Sheerit Israel" and, two centuries later, the world's biggest Jewish community.

6 Conclusion

We have overviewed, if only in an inevitably partial manner, two centuries of the social life and cultural production among the descendants of the medieval Iberian Jews, be they conversos who remained in Spain and Portugal or emigrants who left to inhabit New Christian hubs or fully fledged Iberian Jewish communities. Transnational and cross-religious, this imaginary "Nation" progressively shifted its center of gravity from Toledo and Lisbon to Amsterdam and Livorno. At the same time, the undoubtedly largest share among the descendents of the late medieval converts integrated into their Spanish and Portuguese surroundings, which were lastingly transformed by this process. According to a 1932 historian, the Jewish revival among the "marranos" teaches "that protracted martyrdom, unexampled in history, proved powerless to vanquish the indomitable Jewish spirit" (Roth 1974, 374). From a different angle, the very same history could also be presented as "a spectacular case of attempted assimilation"

(Netanyahu 1972, 205). In Iberian Jewish history, the early modern period is a time of profound trauma and rupture, but also of quiet assimilation, transformation and reinvention. Part of its inner contradictions are due to the fact that in the concept of the "Nation," normative definitions of religion were replaced by an ethnic identification and ancestral fidelity (Wachtel 2001, 28–29) and that, moreover, the religiocide of 1497, religious hybridity, persecution, and migration had made Luso-Jewishness into something constitutively "marginal, atypical, and liminal" (Stuczynski and Feitler 2018, 15).

Massive persecution, but also the search for economic opportunities and religious freedom prompted the turn to dispersion, migration and settlement in new places. Resettlement was achieved through communal organization, political negotiation and social compromise with the new surroundings, but also through cultural adaptation. In exile, the "New Jews" adopted new patterns of sociability while being united in the attachment to their rich Iberian Jewish heritage. As a symbol of this cultural and linguistic heritage, Sefarad transformed into a kind of imagined community or mental space, which the more distant it became in a geographical sense, the more it was turned into a continuous creation of memory, collective and individual.

Iberian Jewish literary creation, which embraced the literary genres, styles and forms of multiple traditions, was a place for exchange, intertwining and negotiation between the literary trends of the Iberian Peninsula and the social and religious exigencies that its authors had to contend with. These early and decisive centuries of Sephardic life set a precedent to Jewish emancipation in the centuries to follow, not only because of the Portuguese Jews successful socio-economic integration, but also by a peculiar cultural expression that molded Judaism in the languages and forms that were shared with early modern contemporaries.

Bibliography

Works Cited

Alberro, Solange. *Inquisición y sociedad en México, 1571–1700*. Mexico City: FCE, 1996.
Alberro, Solange. "Crypto-Jews and the Mexican Holy Office in the Seventeenth Century." *The Jews and the Expansion of Europe to the West, 1450 to 1800*. Eds. Paolo Bernardini and Norman Fiering. New York: Berghahn Books, 2001. 172–185.
Albiac, Gabriel. *La sinagoga vacía: un estudio de las fuentes marranas del espinosismo*. Madrid: Hiperión, 1987.
Almeida, A. A. Marques de. *Capitais e capitalistas no comércio da especiaria: o eixo Lisboa-Antuérpia (1501–1549)*. Lisbon: Cosmos, 1993.
Alpert, Michael. *Crypto-Judaism and the Spanish Inquisition*. New York: Palgrave, 2001.
Andrade, António Manuel Lopes. "Os senhores do desterro de Portugal: Judeus portugueses em Veneza e Ferrara a meados do século XVI." *Veredas* (2006): 65–108.
Arnold, Rafael. *Spracharkaden: Die Sprache der sephardischen Juden in Italien im 16. und 17. Jahrhundert*. Heidelberg: Winter, 2006.

Azevedo, J. Lúcio de. *História dos cristãos-novos portugueses*. Lisboa: Clássica, ³1989.
Barrios, Daniel Levi de. *Historia de la Gran Bretaña*. Amsterdam, 1688.
Beinart, Haim. *Conversos on Trial: The Inquisition in Ciudad Real*. Jerusalem: Magnes Press, 1981.
Bennassar, Bartolomé, and Lucile Bennassar. *1492: Un monde nouveau?* Paris: Perrin, 1991.
Birnbaum, Marianna. *The Long Journey of Gracia Mendes*. Budapest: CEU Press, 2003.
Boccara, Elia, *L'invenzione marrana: Ricostruzione dell'anima in un'alba di modernità*. Florence: Giuntina, 2014.
Bodian, Miriam. *Hebrews of the Portuguese Nation: Conversos and Community in Early Modern Amsterdam*. Bloomington: Indiana University Press, 1997.
Bregoli, Francesca. *Mediterranean Enlightenment: Livornese Jews, Tuscan Culture, and Eighteenth-Century Reform*. Stanford: Stanford University Press, 2014.
Buescu, Ana Isabel. "Aspectos do bilinguismo português-castelhano na época moderna." *Hispania* 61.1, no. 216 (2004): 13–38.
Bunis, David M. "The Language of the Sephardim: A Historical Overview." *Moreshet Sepharad: The Sephardi Legacy*. Vol. 2. Ed. Haim Beinart. Jerusalem: Magnes Press, 1992. 399–422.
Böhm, Günter. *Historia de los judíos en Chile*. Vol. 1. Santiago de Chile: Editorial Andrés Bello, 1984.
Caro Baroja, Julio. *Historia de los judíos en la España moderna y contemporánea*. Madrid: Istmo, ³1995.
Castro, Américo. *España en su historia: Cristianos, moros y judíos*. Buenos Aires: Losada, [1948].
Chuchiak, John F. IV. *The Inquisition in New Spain, 1536–1820: A Documentary History*. Baltimore: John Hopkins University Press, 2012.
Contreras, Jaime. *Sotos contra Riquelmes: Regidores, inquisidores y criptojudíos*. Madrid: Anaya & M. Muchnik, 1992.
Cooperman, Bernard Dov. "Portuguese *conversos* in Ancona: Jewish Political Activity in Early Modern Italy." *In Iberia and Beyond. Hispanic Jews Between Cultures*. Ed. Bernard Dov Cooperman. Newark: University of Delaware Press, 1998. 297–352.
Domínguez Ortiz, Antonio. *La clase social de los conversos en Castilla en la edad moderna*. Granada: Universidad de Granada, 1955.
Escobar Quevedo, Ricardo. *Inquisición y judaizantes en América española (siglos XVI-XVII)*. Bogotá: Editorial Universidad del Rosario, 2008.
Faur, José. *In the Shadow of History: Jews and Conversos at the Dawn of Modernity*. Albany: SUNY Press, 1992.
Feitler, Bruno. *Inquisition, juifs et nouveaux-chrétiens au Brésil: Le Nordeste, XVIIe et XVIIIe siècles*. Louvain: Leuven University Press, 2003.
Fine, Ruth. "La literatura de conversos después de 1492: Autores y obras en busca de un discurso crítico." *Lo converso: Orden imaginario y realidad en la cultura española (siglos XIV–XVII)*. Ed. Ruth Fine et al. Madrid: Iberoamericana Vervuert, 2013. 499–526.
Frattarelli Fischer, Lucia. *Vivere fuori dal Ghetto: Ebrei a Pisa e Livorno (secoli XVI–XVIII)*. Torino: Silvio Zamorani Editore, 2008.
Goris, Jan Albert. *Etude sur les colonies marchandes méridionales (Portugais, Espagnols, Italiens) à Anvers de 1488 à 1567: Contribution à l'histoire des débuts du capitalisme moderne*. Louvain: Librairie Universitaire, 1925.
Graizbord, David L. *Souls in Dispute: Converso Identities in Iberia and the Jewish Diaspora, 1580–1700*. Philadelphia: University of Pennsylvania Press, 2004.
Graizbord, David. "Religion and Ethnicity among 'Men of the Nation': Towards a Realistic Interpretation." *Jewish Social Studies: History, Culture, Society* 15.1 (2008): 32–65.
Greenleaf, Richard E. *The Mexican Inquisition of the Sixteenth Century*. Albuquerque: University of New Mexico Press, 1969.
Hacker, Joseph. "The Sephardim in the Ottoman Empire in the Sixteenth Century." *Moreshet Sefarad: The Sephardic Heritage*. Vol. 2. Ed. Haim Beinart. Jerusalem: Magnes Press, 1992. 109–133.

Herculano, Alexandre. *History of the Origin and Establishment of the Inquisition in Portugal*. Tr. John C. Branner. New York: Ktav, 1968.

Hordes, Stanley. *The Crypto-Jewish Community of New Spain, 1620–1649: A Collective Biography*. New Orleans, Louisana: PhD Tulane University, 1980.

Huerga Criado, Pilar. *En la raya de Portugal: Solidaridad y tensiones en la comunidad judeoconversa*. Salamanca: Ediciones Universidad de Salamanca, 1994.

Huerga Criado, Pilar. "El marranismo ibérico y las comunidades sefardíes." *Entre Islam y Occidente. Los judíos magrebíes en la Edad Moderna*. Ed. Mercedes García-Arenal. Madrid: Casa de Velázquez, 2003. 49–68.

Huerga Criado, Pilar. "Cristianos nuevos de origen ibérico en el Reino de Nápoles en el siglo XVII." *Sefarad* 72 (2012): 351–387.

Ingram, Kevin. *Converso Non-Conformism in Early Modern Spain: Bad Blood and Faith from Alonso de Cartagena to Diego Velázquez*. Cham, Switzerland: Palgrave Macmillan, 2018.

Israel, Jonathan I. *Diasporas within a Diaspora: Jews, Crypto-Jews and the World Maritime Empires, 1540–1740*. Leiden: Brill, 2002.

Kaplan, Yosef. "The Intellectual Ferment in the Spanish-Portuguese Community of Seventeenth Century Amsterdam." *The Sephardi Legacy*. Vol. 2. Ed. Haim Beinart. Jerusalem: Magnes, 1992. 288–314.

Kaplan, Yosef. *Ha-pezurah ha-sefaradit ha-maaravit* [*The Western Sephardi Diaspora*, in Hebrew]. Jerusalem: Ministry of Defence, 1994.

Kaplan, Yosef. *Judíos nuevos en Amsterdam: Estudios sobre la historia social e intelectual del judaismo sefardí en el siglo XVII*. Barcelona: Gedisa, 1996.

Kaplan, Yosef. *An Alternative Path to Modernity: The Sephardi Diaspora in Western Europe*. Leiden: Brill, 2000.

Kaplan, Yosef. "'Gente Politica': The Portuguese Jews of Amsterdam vis-à-vis Dutch Society." *Dutch Jews As Perceived by Themselves and by Others*. Eds. Chaya Brasz and Yosef Kaplan. Leiden: Brill, 2001. 21–40.

Kayserling, Meyer. *História dos judeus em Portugal*. Trs. Gabriele Borchardt Corrêa da Silva and Anita Novinsky. São Paulo: Livr. Pioneira, 1971.

Kellenbenz, Hermann. *Sephardim an der Unteren Elbe: ihre wirtschaftliche und politische Bedeutung vom Ende des 16. bis zum Beginn des 18. Jahrhunderts*. Wiesbaden: Franz Steiner, 1958.

Kerner, Alex. *Lost in Translation, Found in Transliteration: Books, Censorship, and the Evolution of the Spanish and Portuguese Jews' Congregation of London as a Linguistic Community, 1663–1810*. Leiden: Brill, 2018.

Ladero Quesada, Miguel Ángel. *Judíos y conversos de Castilla en el siglo XV*. Madrid: Dykinson, 2016.

Leone Leoni, Aron di. "Documents inédits sur la 'Nation Portugaise' de Ferrare." *Revue des études juives* 152.2 (1993): 137–176.

Leone Leoni, Aron di. *The Hebrew Portuguese Nations in Antwerp and London at the time of Charles V and Henry VIII*. Jersey City: Ktav, 2005.

Liebman, Seymour B. *The Jews in New Spain: Faith, Flame, and the Inquisition*. Coral Gables FL: University of Miami Press, 1970.

Ligorio, Benedetto. "Una nuova *élite* mercantile in Adriatico orientale: Le esportazioni dei sefarditi ragusei verso la *Serenissima*." *Revue des études sud-est européenes* 56 (2018): 123–136.

Lloyd, Ana Paula. "Manuel de Gama de Pádua's Political Networks: Service, Subversion and the Disruption of the Portuguese Inquisition." *Journal of Levantine Studies* 6 (2016): 251–275.

López Belinchón, Bernardo. *Honra, libertad y hacienda: Hombres de negocios y judíos sefardíes*. Alcalá de Henares: Universidad de Alcalá, 2001.

López-Salazar Codes, Ana Isabel. *Inquisición portuguesa y Monarquía Hispánica en tiempos del perdón general de 1605*. Lisboa: Colibri-CIDEUS/UE, 2010.

Magalhães, Joaquim Romero. *Portugueses no mundo do século XVI: espaços e produtos*. Lisbon: CNCDP, 1998.

Marcocci Giuseppe. *I custodi dell'ortodossia: Inquisizione e chiesa nel Portogallo del Cinquecento*. Roma: Edizioni di Storia e Letteratura, 2004.

Marcocci, Giuseppe. "A fundação da Inquisição em Portugal: um novo olhar." Lusitania Sacra 23 (2011): 17–40.

Marcocci, Giuseppe, and José Pedro Paiva. *História da Inquisição portuguesa 1536–1821*. Lisboa: A Esfera dos Livros, 2013.

Mark, Peter, and José da Silva Horta. *The Forgotten Diaspora: Jewish Communities in West Africa and the Making of the Atlantic World*. Cambridge, UK: Cambridge University Press, 2013.

Mazur, Peter. *The New Christians of Spanish Naples 1528–1671: A Fragile Élite*. London: Palgrave Macmillan, 2013.

Méchoulan, Henry. *Le Sang de l'Autre ou l'honneur de Dieu: Indiens, juifs et morisques au Siècle d'Or*. Paris: Fayard, 1978.

Melammed, Renée Levine. *Heretics or Daughters of Israel? The Crypto-Jewish Women of Castile*. New York: Oxford University Press, 1999.

Mello, José Antônio Gonsalves de. "Um tribunal da inquisição em Olinda, Pernambuco (1594–1595)." *Revista da Universidade de Coimbra* 36 (1991): 369–374.

Mello, José Antônio Gonsalves de. *Gente da nação*. Recife: Editora Massangana, 1996.

Moreno Cebrían, Alfredo, and Gleydi Sullón Barreto. "Somos cristianos no judíos: Portugueses en la 'gran complicidad' y el auto de fe limeño de 1639." *Boletín del Instituto Riva-Agüero* 37 (2014): 1–29.

Muchnik, Natalia. *De paroles et de gestes: Constructions marranes en terre d'Inquisition*. Paris: EHESS, 2014.

Nahon, Gérard. "Le modèle français du marranisme: Perspectives nouvelles." *Inquisição: Ensaios sobre mentalidade, heresias, e arte*. Eds. Anita Novinsky and Maria Luiza Tucci Carneiro. Rio de Janeiro: Edusp, 1992, 227–265.

Nahon, Gérard. *Juifs et judaïsme à Bordeaux*. Bordeaux: Mollat, 2003.

Netanyahu, Benzion. *The Marranos of Spain from the Late 14th to the Early 16th Century, According to Contemporary Hebrew Sources*. New York: American Academy for Jewish Research, 1972.

Nickson, Tom. "Remembering Fernando: Multilingualism in Medieval Iberia." *Viewing Inscriptions in the Late Antique and Medieval World*. Ed. Antony Eastmond. Cambridge, UK: Cambridge University Press, 2015. 170–186.

Novinsky, Anita. *Cristão novos na Bahia*. São Paulo: Editora da Universidade de São Paulo, 1972.

Novoa, James W. Nelson. "Tre lettere di Pedro de Salamanca, documenti per la storia dell'insediamento dei nuovi cristiani in Toscana nel Cinquecento." *Bollettino storico pisano* 74 (2005): 357–367.

Olival, Fernanda. "Rigor e interesses: os estatutos de limpeza de sangue em Portugal." *Cadernos de Estudos Sefarditas* 4 (2004): 151–182.

Pereira, Ana Margarida Santos. "Terceira visitação do Santo Ofício às partes do Brasil: Capitanias do Sul, 1627–1628." *Politeia: História e Sociedade, Vitória da Conquista* 11.1 (2011): 35–60.

Perelis, Ronnie. *Narratives from the Sephardic Atlantic: Blood and Faith*. Bloomington: Indiana University Press, 2016.

Poettering, Jorun. *Migrating Merchants: Trade, Nation, and Religion in Seventeenth-Century Hamburg and Portugal*. Berlin: De Gruyter, 2019.

Pohl, Hans. *Die Portugiesen in Antwerpen, 1567–1648: zur Geschichte einer Minderheit*. Wiesbaden: Steiner, 1978.

Prins, Izak. *De vestiging van de marranen in Noord-Nederland in de zestiende eeuw*. Amsterdam: Hertzberger, 1927.

Rauschenbach, Sina. *Judaism for Christians: Menasseh ben Israel (1604–1657)*. Lanham: Lexington Books, 2019.

Rêgo, João Vaz Monteiro de Figueirôa. *A honra alheia por um fio: Os estatutos de limpeza de sangue no espaço de expresão ibérica (sécs. XVI–XVII)*. Lisboa: Fundação Calouste Gulbenkian, 2011.
Révah, I. S. "Autobiographie d'un Marrane: Edition partielle d'un manuscrit de João (Moseh) Pinto Delgado." *Revue des études juives* 119 (1961): 41–130.
Révah, I. S. *Des Marranes à Spinoza*. Paris: Vrin, 1995.
Révah, I. S. *Antonio Enríquez Gómez, un écrivain marrane*. Paris: Chandeigne, 2003.
Roth, Cecil. *The House of Nasi: The Duke of Naxos*. New York: Greenword Press, 1948.
Roth, Cecil. *A History of the Marranos*. New York: Schocken Books, ⁴1974.
Rubinstein, Becky and, Herlinda Dabbah Mustri. *Autores judeoconversos en la Ciudad de México*. Mexico City: Gobierno del Distrito Federal, 2002.
Salvador, José Gonçalves. *Os cristãos novos. Povoamento e conquista do solo brasileiro (1530–1680)*. São Paulo: Livraria Pioneira Editora, Editora da Universidade de São Paulo, 1976.
Salvador, José Goncalves. *Os cristãos novos e o comércio no Atlântico meridional*. São Paulo: Livraria Pioneira Editora, Editora da Universidade de São Paulo, 1978.
Sanz Ayán, Carmen. *Los banqueros de Carlos II*. ORT: Universidad de Valladolid, 1988.
Saraiva, António José. *The Marrano Factory. The Portuguese Inquisition and its New Christians 1536–1765*. Translated, revised and augmented by Herman Prins Salomon and I.S.D. Sassoon. Leiden: Brill, 2001.
Schorsch, Ismar. "From Messianism to Realpolitik: Menasseh ben Israel and the Readmission of the Jews to England." *Proceedings of the American Academy for Jewish Research* 45 (1978): 187–208.
Schorsch, Jonathan. *Swimming the Christian Atlantic: Judeoconversos, Afroiberians and Amerindians in the Seventeenth Century*. Leiden: Brill, 2009, 2 Vols.
Segre, Renata. "La formazione di una comunità marrana: i portoghesi a Ferrara." *Storia d'Italia. Annali XI/1: Gli ebrei in Italia. Ed*. Corrado Vivanti. Torino: Einaudi, 1996. 779–841.
Soyer, François. *The Persecution of the Jews and Muslims of Portugal: King Manuel I and the End of Religious Tolerance (1496–7)*. Leiden: Brill, 2007 (=2007a).
Soyer, François. "The Massacre of the New Christians of Lisbon in 1506: a New Eyewitness Account." *Cadernos de Estudos Sefarditas* 7 (2007): 221–243 (=2007b).
Stuczynski, Claude B. "New Christian Political Leadership in Times of Crisis: the Pardon Negotiations of 1605." *Bar –Ilan Studies in History. V: Leadership in Times of Crisis*. Ed. Moises Orfali. Ramat Gan: Bar-Ilan University Press, 2007. 45–70.
Stuczynski Claude B., and Bruno Feitler. "A Portuguese-Jewish Exception? A Historiographical Introduction." *Portuguese Jews, New Christians, and "New Jews:" A Tribute to Roberto Bachmann*. Eds. Claude B. Stuczynski and Bruno Feitler. Leiden: Brill, 2018. 1–28.
Studemund-Halévy, Michael. *Die Sefarden in Hamburg: Zur Geschichte einer Minderheit*. Hamburg, 1994–1997, 2 Vols.
Studnicki-Gizbert, Daviken. *A Nation upon the Ocean Sea. Portugal's Atlantic Diaspora and the Crisis of the Spanish Empire, 1492–1640*. New York: Oxford University Press, 2007.
Swetschinski, Daniel M. *Reluctant Cosmopolitans: The Portuguese Jews of Seventeenth-Century Amsterdam*. Oxford: Littman Library, 2000.
Tavares, Maria José Pimenta Ferro. *Los judíos en Portugal*. Madrid: Editorial Mapfre, 1992.
Tavares, Maria José Pimenta Ferro. "The Castilian Jews in Portugal: An Approach to their History." *Hispania Judaica Bulletin* 7 (2010): 175–192.
Tavim, José Alberto Rodrigues da Silva. *Os Judeus na expansão portuguesa em Marocos durante o século XVI: origens e actividades duma comunidade*. Braga: Edições APPACDM, 1997.
Tavim, José Alberto Rodrigues da Silva. *Judeus e cristãos-novos de Cochim. História e memória (1500–1662)*. Braga: Edições APPACDM, 2003.
Tavim, José Alberto Rodrigues da Silva. "Sephardic Intermediaries in the Ottoman Empire." *Oriente Moderno* 93 (2013): 454–476.

Toaff, Renzo. *La nazione ebrea a Livorno e a Pisa 1591–1700*. Firenze: Leo S. Olschki editore, 1990.
Toro, Alfonso. *La familia Carvajal: Estudio histórico sobre los judíos y la Inquisición de la Nueva España en el siglo XVI*. Mexico City: Patria, 1944, 2 Vols.
Trivellato, Francesca. *The Familiarity of Strangers: The Sephardic Diaspora, Livorno, and Cross-Cultural Trade in the Early Modern Period*. New Haven: Yale University Press, 2009.
Uchmany, Eva Alexandra. "The Participation of New Christians and Crypto-Jews in the Conquest, Colonization, and Trade of Spanish America, 1521–1660." *The Jews and the Expansion of Europe to the West, 1450 to 1800*. Eds. Paolo Bernardini and Norman Fiering. New York: Berghahn Books, 2001. 186–202.
Vainfas, Rolando. *Jerusalem colonial: Judeus portugueses no Brasil holandês*. Rio de Janeiro: Civilização brasileira, 2010.
Vasquez Cuesta, Pilar. *A língua e cultura portuguesas no tempo dos Filipes*. Lisboa: Publicações Europa-América, 1989.
Van Vloten, Johannes, and Jan Pieter Nicolaas Land, eds. *Benedicti de spinoza opera quotquot reperta sunt*. Vol 3. The Hague: Martinus Nijhoff, 1914.
Wachtel, Nathan. *La Foi du souvenir: Labyrinthes marranes*. Paris: Seuil, 2001.
Wilke, Carsten L. *História dos judeus portugueses*. Lisboa: Edições 70, 2009.
Wilke, Carsten L. "Contraband for the Catholic King: Jews of the French Pyrenees in the Tobacco Trade and Spanish State Finance." *Purchasing Power: The Economics of Modern Jewish History*. Eds. Rebecca Kobrin and Adam Teller. Philadelphia: University of Pennsylvania Press, 2015. 46–70.
Wilke, Carsten L. "Semi-Clandestine Judaism in Early Modern France: European Horizons and Local Varieties of a Domestic Devotion." *Religious Changes and Cultural Transformations in the Early Modern Western Sephardic Communities*. Ed. Yosef Kaplan. Leiden: Brill, 2019. 113–136.
Yerushalmi, Yosef Hayim. *From Spanish Court to Italian Ghetto: Isaac Cardoso: A Study in Seventeenth-Century Marranism and Jewish Apologetics*. New York: Columbia University Press, 1971.
Yerushalmi, Yosef Hayim. "Connaissance du judaïsme et préparation spirituelle chez les marranes revenus au judaïsme au cours du XVIIe siècle." *Sefardica*. Tr. Cyril Aslanoff. Paris: Chandeigne, 1998. 235–254.
Yerushalmi, Yosef Hayim. *The Lisbon Massacre of 1506 and the Royal Image in the Shebet Yehudah*. Cincinnati: Hebrew Union College Press, ²2015.
Yovel, Yirmiahu. *Spinoza and other Heretics*. Princeton: Princeton University Press, 1989, 2 Vols.
Yovel, Yirmiyahu. *The Other Within: The Marranos, Split Identity and Emerging Modernity*. Princeton: Princeton University Press, 2009.
Zink, Anne. "Une niche juridique: L'installation des Juifs à Saint-Esprit-lès-Bayonne au XVIIe siècle." *Annales – Histoire, Sciences Sociales* 49.3 (1994): 639–670.

Further Reading

Barnett, Richard David, and Walter M. Schwab, eds. *The Western Sephardim: The History of Some of the Communities Formed in Europe, the Mediterranean, and the New World After the Expulsion of 1492*. Grendon: Gibraltar Books, 1989.
Beinart, Haim, ed. *The Sephardi Legacy*. Jerusalem: Magnes Press, 1992, 2 Vols.
Bethencourt, Francisco. *The New Christians of Jewish Origin, 1497–1773*. Forthcoming.
Melammed, Renée Levine. *A Question of Identity: Iberian Conversos in Historical Perspective*. Oxford: Oxford University Press, 2004.
Meyuḥas Ginio, Alisa. *Between Sepharad and Jerusalem: History, Identity and Memory of the Sephardim*. Leiden: Brill, 2014.

Juan Diego Vila

6 *Converso* Spectres: The Lessons and Challenges of Spanish 'Golden Age' Prose

Abstract: The present study starts from the critical tensions that organize the recognition of *converso culture* in the seemingly homogenous context of the Spanish sixteenth and seventeenth centuries. For this, the canonizing devices of the literary and the production of invisible marginalities are attended to, and the outstanding works of Francisco Delicado and Mateo Alemán are chosen for an exemplary close-reading. We postulate that Spectrality organizes the cultural field under study and that the recognition of the converso constellation could be resolved both in minimal forms such as insults or jokes and in the consolidation of hostile stereotypes typical of anti-Jewish writing. These two options, in the imaginary constellation of literature, ask of each critic a special reading commitment to articulate and interpret the spectral dynamics of such figurations.

Key Terms: Converso Literature; Hispanic Canon; Spectrality Principle; Dissent Readings; Spanish Golden Age Prose

1 Thinking Converso Literature in the Twenty-First Century

The status of converso literature is an issue that is far from being resolved, even among the most renowned specialists. Is converso literature an exclusive subgroup of "Spanish literature"? When this constellation is proposed, is it understood that the defining thing is the works or are the inquiries addressed to some form of biographism? In strictly literary terms, what would be the substantial and defining aspect of a "Converso literature"?

These and similar questions divide the opinions of specialists to the point that, in the latent virulence of the confrontations, it is possible to recognize the weight of conditioning factors that precede and influence the debate. Sometimes, this has to do with the conceptualization of the literary in general; many other times, it is due to the value granted to the particularism of the Jew or the converted Jew in a certain culture.

The conflicting views on so-called "Converso literature" are a product of their time, a variable it would be a huge mistake to ignore. What is important in this regard is to be aware of the evolution of the intellectual field of literary criticism and, in light of what has been done already, to adjust and put into new perspectives those theoretical critical legacies that today can still be considered valid or to be facilitators of new contemporary approaches.

Controversial themes like those in question call for an ethical procedure by the researcher, since the prerogative of being in tune with the legitimate ways of reading in our time only belongs to us and to those who share our time. And, if we talk about predecessors, it seems only honest to admit that their readings have served as guiding beacons of the current times.

I want to start my reading with an epistemic contextualization, since those who strive for the recognition of a specificity of converso literature always do so in the larger context of some national literature whose existence and defining characteristics are considered indisputable. Usually, the existence of something called "Spanish literature of the sixteenth and seventeenth centuries" or, "Spanish literature of the Renaissance and Baroque" or, with even more grandeur, "Golden Age Spanish literature", is accepted, without major controversy. Even the most prominent Hispanists, past or present, accept this combination of territory, language and time to define a type of literature. Nobody would call these categorical criteria into question. But the same is not the case if, on the contrary, it is postulated that, within that bigger set of "Spanish literature", it is possible to read a minor subset called "Converso literature" or that this, in turn, would put into question the existence and assumed parameters of the bigger set.

To insist on this fact is, in our opinion, not a minor gesture; it allows us to make visible the extent to which the tension existing between both levels depends less on the supposed 'shortcomings' attributed to the conversos – like the angry voices of the detractors of the moment would want us to believe, but, on the contrary, on the need to silence any dissent that might question the basic operation of "national literature": its natural territorial essentiality.

So, we can accept, without further detours, that something called Spanish literature exists and that its difference conforms, naturally, to the very debatable geographical boundaries of the nation known to its current scholars. The converso, on the other hand, cannot conform to such standards of predictability, ergo, it must be discredited. In such a way, then, that – for the sake of the necessary scientific predictability of the literary discipline – any entity that repels the resulting descriptive naturalization is neutralized and rendered invisible.

But what, since the nineteenth century, was presented as a logical fact, perfectly verifiable when it came to prescribing what was proper to a certain national literature and to introducing it into Western and European literary historiographies, has ended up being the subject, in the most contemporary of perspectives, of an unavoidable debate.

The literary is no longer seen as an deterministic inevitability, the magical frontiers of the Spanish nation and the supposedly univocal spirit of its people, but rather is read as a process of a historically, socially and politically determined human construction, to the point that, not without reason, this is the path along which many recent theorists question the alleged neutrality of the term "Contemporary Spanish Literature". Does it exist? Is it recognizable? How does literature in Catalan, Galician or Basque figure into this idea? Is it logical to continue thinking, when it comes to literature, that autonomous communities do not exist?

The agenda of scholars of twenty-first-century Spanish-language literary production does not ignore the fact that the current conflictive relationship between literature and nation is the result of the theoretical recognition of the prevailing critical evolution, from the Enlightenment to the present day, of veiled imperialist and ethnocentric practices. Nor is it a minor fact that the existing discomfort with 'the Spanish' as a neutral and objective category can be explained, broadly speaking, by the recognition that such a notion is subsidiary to reading practices that have brought into play very varied strategies of minoritization, neutralization and invisibilization of what is perceived as subaltern. In Topuzián's words:

> Today, the study of any national literature, without anticipating the total neglect or overcoming of the paradigm of the historiography of national literatures (. . .) has to make increasingly room for translations, foreign literatures, exiled and migrant writers, multilingualism, cosmopolitism and universal, world, global or transnational literature, i.e., to a set of issues that before were apparently restricted only to the well-defined environment of comparative literatures."
> (Topuzián 2017, 51. My translation)

The reason for the previous digressions goes far beyond the imaginary illusion that this is a diagnosis only valid for our times. Given that, if we look back, we can see how this inappropriate set of phenomena was already present a long time ago and had been the object of expurgation or silencing in the unrefined histories of literature that, since the late nineteenth century, continue to fertilize, surprisingly, pedagogy and research in the field of study itself.

Today we accept that the generalized perception of the Hispanic was the result of successive tensions among literary forms from other national confines – beginning in the Renaissance with Italy and concluding in the eighteenth century with France. It also assesses the guiding principles, tinged with exoticism, with which Spain was built in Europe (Fuchs, 2011). However, it should not be ignored that the censorious disposition of the diverse is not a novelty of the first modernity, nor that the confessional and cultural variables of the past – the Spain of the three religions – deserve, in the historiographic project, a respectful and egalitarian treatment.

The usual literary histories do not integrate, when thinking about what is specific to Spain, writing in Arabic or Hebrew, even knowing the scientific, philosophical or poetic transcendence of the culture in *al-Andalus*, and neither do they value the so-called "Silver Century" of Jewish literature in Spain (Fine, 2006). Nor is there a perspective integrating the mass of translations, because even when they evoke the existence of the school of translators in Toledo, they do not value the circulation of the resulting writings and the dialogues enabled by them because what is proper to Spain should not attend to what is pointed out as foreign. A similar attitude also legitimizes the devaluation of all exiled authors whose works, mostly in Spanish, end up purging an exile from the canon that, in countless cases, mirrors the previous trauma experienced by the author. Since the expulsion of the Jews from the Iberian Peninsula in 1492, the establishment of the Confessionalization processes throughout Europe and the subsequent eradication of the *Moriscos* in the seventeenth century, the Spanish empire encouraged countless collective diasporas and individual exiles, but literary historiography prefers to forget these circumstances since the capacity for guilty oblivion is inversely proportional to the possibility of imagining, only in aesthetic terms, a matrix devoid of any political or ideological taint.

From all of which it follows that we should not ignore the context of the current epistemic crisis that the fusion of the national with literature is going through, since it will be crucial for repositioning, in a new light, the controversy over the much-questioned converso literature. For, in fact, the only thing that differentiates both possible constellations – the current one of plurilingualism and plurinationalities in the twenty-first century and the past one of confessional confrontations in the sixteenth and seventeenth centuries – is not settled by the transcendence of the productions nor by the aesthetic dimension ascribable to one or several sides but rather, by the communicational positioning of the opposing poles. Of course, if anything has historically defined the polemics on converso literature, it is that its defenders constantly have found themselves in reactive positions in the face of ubiquitous contextual denials that, like the well-known example of Américo Castro, insisted time and again on supposed 'problematic' aspects of converso literature. For, in the end, the critical collective interested in the converso literature was always required to certify the full legitimacy of the critical-analytical categories it implemented. It is a totalitarian yearning that, in truth, the same actors who censured the 'heretical' position could never have satisfied. Indeed, if the rejoinder generated by the reproached critics in their attack on the converso had not been concerned with generating defenses of their perspective, but with questioning the presumed natural objectivity from which an alternate imaginary constellation was attacked, the evolution of this polemic would have been very different.

And to this must be added, a strategy of discrediting that we could call a 'normalization device'. Certainly, in more than one case, the expected conformity or agreement to some thesis has been withheld, inasmuch as the problematic of the converso literature should be uniformly endorsed in a set of analogous cases, similar dispositions, practices or experiences, strictly related works. While in my opinion, the great challenge of the converso constellation is to enter subtly into situations without guiding precedents, into works and feelings that are not necessarily constant and uniform. All of which, in short, should lead us to admit, without half-measures, that in the categorical difficulties or crises of our times there is a clear and excellent opportunity to redefine, rewrite and reconfigure the possibilities of a converso constellation in the literary, historical, philosophical and cultural axes of times and spaces in which its existence was contested.

2 Epistemic Limits of Previous Perspectives and New Critical Paths for Converso Constellations

What is evident is that, beyond the real obstacles and the expectation that the "literature of converts" would end up confined as a passing fad in the memory of the elders in our academy – a feeling very similar to the one that continues to arouse the emergence of feminist and gender studies in various places – our starting point is quite different. Not only because an endless number of forgotten and marginalized texts of the Hispanic converso past have been published in reliable studies but also because of a congress held in Jerusalem that brought together specialists of various interests who were able to offer brilliant statements of the question in their respective fields of work together with specific proposals on possible future channels of research in the field.

It seems to me unavoidable to consider two of the proposals collected there because they clarify, in a superb way, what could be a way forward with this controversy. The first approach I am referring to was that of Augustin Redondo, a specialist of indisputable trajectory and breadth of criteria who, precisely, came to point out the unfeasibility of reiterating presumed certainties that subsequent critical research had managed to challenge or limit. The second, more hopeful, was the responsibility of Ruth Fine, one of the convening professors and hostess of the conference, who, based on the very careful textual tours on converso works and authors she had made in her professional career, came to propose an alternative horizon in terms of which converso literature was restructured, far from the expeditious assurances, as a horizon of works, interpretations and avenues of analysis still pending investigation.

For Fine the great pending task is not so much the sighting of exegetical protocols lacking in rigor but a pedagogy and progressive forming of new habits, perspectives and strategies of signification that will redefine and produce new types of researchers. After all, the narrow-mindedness of the past contributed to the invisibility of the multiple levels of heterogeneity that define the corpus of converso literature. It is not a minor fact that her proposal goes beyond an endless number of standardizations and reductionisms that the apparently positive label of converso literature concealed. Wouldn't it be more appropriate to start by admitting that we are dealing with chronologically variable 'literatures', changeable according to the confines of emergence, changeable, in short, according to whether or not they inscribe their artistic praxis in one, several or no socially shared genre.

The biographical variable, when analyzing authors and their works, is usually a source of many misunderstandings. In the first place, because a large number of their critical points remain veiled from our understanding, a phenomenon that can be explained by the policies of social control of the "converted" subjects, marked by persecution and the practices of shame to be assumed by the individuals thus labeled. And, secondly, because any clarification external to the author does not illuminate, with the necessary clarity, the inner experience in the face of a generic and disqualifying label. As Fine argues, what kind of "convert" does the critic think of? Does one analyze an apostate by conviction, a coerced Judeo-convert, someone who perceives himself as a new Christian, but is labeled a *Marrano* or "crypto-Jew"?

This potential for mutually exclusive horizons that are also mutable, fluctuating and potentially hybrid, as the individual transits his difference throughout his existence, strongly discourages any interpretation that insists, somewhat naively, on monovalent senses, authorial positions and desired effects. The converso phenomenon, to a great extent, needs readers and scholars who are fond of constellations of meanings whose exact determination, in many cases, may be subject to reevaluations, changes of weighting and blind spots where the devised architecture could seem on the verge of collapse.

The convert, by definition, is on the run. It is this disposition to drift –essentially imaginary but also physical – which makes it inexcusable, in any historically respectful perspective of the phenomenon, to take into account the so-called "Converso geography", all marked by conflicts and social tensions, but of different kinds. Could the consequences of the decree of expulsion of the Jews in 1492 be put on an equal footing with, for example, the *auto de fe* carried out in 1632 on the occasion of the scandal caused by the *Cristo de la Paciencia*?

To all of which can be added the variable of language with, specifically, the horizon of the first readers. We agree with Fine that it is imperative to accept that even if there is in this group of authors some who could have expressed themselves in Hebrew, the most important thing is still the acceptance that the basal language – mother tongue for many of them – is Spanish. This is a material fact which anchors artistic production to the Hispanic intellectual field of each era, even when it is possible to read dialogues with the Mosaic cultural legacy, its wit and writings accessible to a few.

The latter variable greatly conditions the profile that each critic institutes to define the horizon of potential first readers of these works. Indeed, certain critical sectors make firm bets on the exhumation of a set of potential converso readers, with which these works and their circulation would constitute, to a certain extent, a resistant and counter-hegemonic cultural production. Regardless of how comforting the postulation of readers in tune with the suggested dissidences may be, it lacks the critical reality of reliable testimonies of such decoding skills. The converso writer may express his life situation or give indications of certain differences or experiences of segregation suffered, but there is no certain evidence of a reading work in accordance with the marks, winks, or subtle refractions that would transform communication into a key discourse between individuals with similar competencies. A phenomenon for which more than one critic of all converso literature wielded the flimsy excuse that the work had not been included in certain inquisitorial indexes of banned works or that, for instance, the necessary expurgations or censorship had not taken place. The fact that this had not happened was an indisputable verdict of the dissident decoding competencies that were sought to be outlined when thinking about the audience of a certain work. A strategy that is debatable, to be sure, but within the reach of many.

Restrictively linking the existence of the converso literature to the highly improbable exhumation of a group of readers who are also conversos is an argumentative path beset by failure. Because it contributes, as Fine argues, in a very debatable way, to the thesis of watertight cultural compartments without dialogues.

It is typical of any majority position that, by manifesting itself through some means of writing, the expression of one's own hierarchies of values becomes recognizable, legible and interpretable for the general public. For the converso author, on the other hand, writing becomes a dangerous fatality. He cannot express himself and his experience freely for fear of persecution.

And from this should follow – in my opinion – the acceptance that one of the most singular marks of converso literature ends up being the acceptance that, perhaps very particularly, it is written for an audience deaf to the most personal differences; the bitter certainty that the intimate writing is, most probably, condemned to dwell confined, without suitable readers to release it. A phenomenon by which the flourishing of a converso literature would not depend so much on irrefutable documentary certifications but, on the contrary, on critical interventions and reading operations at the level of works and authors historically oppressed in their differences.

For that reason, Fine values the perspective of Gilman (1972) in a very different way, who, by postulating the notion of a "Converso situation", managed to transcend the determinisms of previous works and critics. Because the "Converso situation" depends on "the awareness of the difference, in relation to a society that designates and particularizes new Christians in a negative way" (Fine 2013, 513). And it is from this perspective that the whole subject turns into a valid ethical inquiry because it is within the reach of anyone to recognize "the call of the one who has not been heard, the silenced" (Fine 2013, 513), and thus make recognizable the one "whose right to name the shame of his identity has been denied" (Fine 2013, 514). From this vantage point then, and thanks to the contributions of Hartman (1995) and Levine Melammed (2004), according to Fine converso literature would be a very particular type of traumatic writing marked by the imperative of memory, individual and collective, that defined the converted Other.

But the contributions of this reading are not exhausted here since, if up until now it had been patiently deconstructing the idea of a rigid and scientifically regulated and recognizable field, it will contribute in its conclusions, under the protection of a typology bequeathed by Angel Alcalá, the possibility of considering a number of variables of the converso literature as subversive.

3 The "Spectrality Principle" in Converso Literature

Following these two distinguished professors, I propose, and I believe that this would be especially useful as far as the imaginative prose of the sixteenth and seventeenth centuries in Spain is concerned, a sort of constructive principle, achievable by means of diverse rhetorical strategies, which would allow the critical recognition of writings in which the converso problematic manifests itself.

That is to say, I'm suggesting that the reading work of any critic interested in a converso literature should attend to what could be called the "Principle of Spectrality". This is a hypothesis in which I decisively distance myself from any biographical speculation or historicist bias, since I am interested in highlighting not the identity of the creators but, rather, the imaginary construct governed only by verbal sophistication.

Every spectre – Derrida's (1998) thesis and analysis is exemplary and profoundly illustrative – is an entity that reigns in the territory that demarcates life and death. It is a figure of that which cries out for the overcoming of binarisms of the existent, insofar as it concentrates, willingly, existence and non-existence at the same time. Its emergence, or haunting of the reader or listener, rejects any dynamic that pursues identification, for the spectre reveals himself as much against what was, as against what would no longer be. For this very reason, I postulate that converso literature manifests itself in spectral forms and procedures, such as seemingly incidental mockeries, ominous silences or very brief mentions of the Jewish and converso cultural legacy. These function, in the texts under analysis, as marks that destabilize the natural dynamics of the representation of what is reputed to be valuable for existing. They are spectres that haunt, in the narrative normality, the triumph of the same. They are vestiges of a civilization that refuses to perceive itself as concluded and proscribed beyond the rule of law. They are marks, sometimes simple traces, that update, under an unsuspected and unprecedented return, what once flourished.

I chose the "Principle of Spectrality" because Derrida's notion of "Specter" evokes the status of subjugation that would define the feasibility of these readings – regarding what we want to recognize as real in an exclusive way –in that it talks about the existing tension between two orders that want to be exclusive: the land of the living and the land from which those who should be perceived as non-existent or justly dead return shamelessly. Because it turns specific, in the confrontational imbalance, the reduction of the real in front of a surplus or a very minor part that rebels in its difference and anomie, any spectre is, in sum, an epistemic scandal; the founding abjection of its status neither disables nor hinders its aided contextual spell. So, the spectres, in a political perspective, attentive to the strategies of domination and community restraint, do not need to be real to be invested of unlimited power.

This allows me to suggest, consequently, that the task of reading any converso literature must attend to a set of variables that enable the tracing of Spectrality indexes in the works under analysis. For a systemic proposal – such as the one we also seek to offer here – cannot ignore the fact that, in the imaginary architecture devised for the works, the converso or dissident can be read according to the variables of geographical and temporal distribution of the story, according to whether or not the expectation of a figurative blurring of the converso culture is respected or, on the contrary, a frank overwriting based on hostile stereotypes, and, fundamentally, to the extent that the occurrence of thematic indications of the writing adjust – or not – to the ways of figuration of the subjugated other: its silencing, its insult, its mockery.

Indeed, the variable of imaginary geographies alerts us to the inexcusable difference that would exist between the outline of Jewish and converted figures in Spain or beyond the magical borders of the empire which outlawed the existence of Jewish communities in its interior and coerced those believers who did not agree to follow the path of territorial expulsion to become "Christians".

From this fact follows, also, the forced attention to the converso temporalities. Of course, the expulsion effectively ordered in 1492 explains the impossibility of finding a work of fiction that points out the existence of Jewish characters in Spain in post-1492 settings, but it also says, after the implementation of the protocols of *limpieza de sangre*, that the possible recognition of a "new Christian" in the pages of a book is never exempt from a tacit and expeditious devaluation. Since the handicap of being a "New Christian", in juridical and cultural terms, prevents him from becoming the main character of the story altogether.

The "Principle of Spectrality" determines, through the two variables of space and time, the scope and limits that are plausibly suitable for the representation of a Jewish or converso protagonist or secondary character recognizable as such in fiction. And it has an impact, as a limiting factor, on the degree of operability and symbolic weight within the story that will be recognized by the culture of origin.

Prototypical expressions of Jewish speech in Spain or the recovery of the Mosaic culture, particularly food or practices internalized in everyday life by religious observance, will be legible indications, in an unstable axis that will be stretched between veiled suggestion or hostile censorship, to outline what some troubled character in the street or some other hostile character seeks to manifest. And it is evident, in this sense, that in terms of Spectrality, the cultural must be analyzed in its particular combination with the personal.

There are few cases in which the cultural difference is in tune with everything that readers already know about a character, basically because, for this to happen, it is necessary to think of novel settings outside Spain or prior to 1492. With the same criteria, it is necessary to pay attention to how, in many cases, what many protagonists or secondary figures are silent about ends up being suggested to the specialized critics and to the readers as a whole, by merely differentiating clues of foreign horizons that contrast with dominant norms.

For example, let us think of all the signs that, throughout history, have articulated the so-called Semitic palate and the Jewish dietary laws. It is important to emphasize how the limitations of critics, prone to read the Mozarabic legacy of the past victors and reluctant to recognize records of the banned memory of the Jewish people, end up acting as enhancers of the Jewish and converso cultural spectrality.

It is well known that, in the cultural historical perspective, the Spaniards tended to reappropriate and forget the Mozarabic singularity in a process of rewriting what would be recognizable as the Andalusian difference of Spain, while, by this appropriation, they made even more invisible the specificity of Jewish dialogue with Muslim culture on the peninsula.

However, there is a clear exception to this tendency. If the author needs, due to his ideological position, to stretch the differences to unimaginable extremes, it is very likely that the minimal signs of divergent cultural aspect will end up manifesting themselves in an endless string of evidence, whose only purpose is to carve out a stereotype that he seeks to attack. A position that, evidently, is that of Quevedo in his *Buscón*. In this drift, what ends up prevailing is the idea that culture defines the subject, is part of his or her conviction, and smooths out any sifting or punctual analysis that one may wish to elaborate, critically, on his or her personality. Because what is at stake here is the assumption that what constitutes and makes individuals communicate is their very "race".

If Spectrality becomes visible in fictional characters and in the culture of origin that authors confer upon them, it usually occurs in writings that insistently recover the interaction with an "other", an "other" that speaks to them and defines them. For, except in the case of perspectives that condemn differences or in pamphlet literature, the centrality of the action does not fall, equanimously, on those who are different but, on the contrary, on those who are in contrast "honest and without fault", i.e. probably the majority of the New Christians whose ancestors converted several generations before.

And here, in short, a very evident communicational economy prevails. In the first place, when the dialogue deals with the recognizable confessional difference, it is notorious how the lines of the tainted *Marranos*, crypto-Jews or, simply, shameful 'New Christians', bet on pretense or on simple and pervasive silence. Secondly, when the other recognizes the Jew or the convert, the display of the subsequent insults takes precedence – neatly inventoried by many critics who would never have recognized a converso literature – or it leads to mockery and jokes that always have them as the laughable subjects of the anecdote. An expressive restriction that fits, in terms of Spectrality, with the entity that the speaking subject is willing to recognize as the one that is different: they are minor, anecdotal, insignificant, like that brief clause in which the dominant textual normality decides to inscribe the spectral evocation of difference.

To better illustrate my point and show how the Concept of Spectrality may be applied here, I will in the following discuss four prominent works of literary fiction in general terms, before focusing on two of them for a close reading: *La Lozana andaluza* by Francisco Delicado, *Guzmán de Alfarache* by Mateo Alemán, *Don Quixote* by Miguel de Cervantes Saavedra and *El Buscón* by Francisco de Quevedo.

4 Beacons of Hispanic Prose of the Sixteenth and Seventeenth Centuries

These works of literary fiction were chosen because, in chronological terms, they cover a temporal term sufficiently illustrative of nuances and variations that will allow us to understand, in all its scope, the constructive principle of Spectrality to guide our analysis.

La lozana andaluza, dated 1528 in the only edition that has been preserved and set, primarily, in Rome prior to its sacking on 6 May, 1527, via which Charles V settled his conflict with the so-called "League of Cognac" in his favor, which serves as the extra textual reference, for the "generations of the expulsion" or the ones immediately after that.

The relatively close dating of the works of Alemán and Cervantes – both with two parts, 1599–1604 for the Sevillian, 1605–1615 for the Alcalaíno – make them play, in our analysis, drastically different roles when it comes to community references. Not only because they are almost a century older than Delicado's text, but also because, historiographically, the daily life of the "New Christians" at the end of the sixteenth century and the beginning of the seventeenth century has very different particularities.

The case of the *Buscón*, originally thought of as a collective work, exposed to incessant rewritings in literary encounters of various tenors where the adventures of Pablos is a source of mockery and constant laughter from the audience and mirrors, in its journey to the later printed edition, the changes in social attitudes, particularly on the part of Spain's noble elites, in face of the monarchy's easing of the hostile laws towards the descendants of Jews, a phenomenon that would culminate in the so-called "reflux of the Portuguese" to Madrid and other urban centers.

In terms of Spectrality, the four novels articulate perfectly coherent chronotopic variations. In *La Lozana* and *El Guzmán* the adventures of the protagonists unfold between Spain and Italy – foreignness that would allow for the possibility of Jewish characters in the narrative framework –, but while Delicado's text makes Aldonza's exile a one-way trip, in Mateo Alemán's story there is a return and this, of course, has a particular impact on the plot and the type of representation conferred to the conversos in the text. Cervantes and Quevedo, on the other hand, narrate the adventures of the protagonists in an exact and perfect domestic closure, since in the case of the author of *Don Quixote* what is beyond the peninsular only counts when retrospective accounts of secondary creatures are given.

It is important to note, in this preliminary diagnosis of the corpus, the type of privileged approach that the weight of a possible Jewish or converso cultural legacy has received, in the usual literary criticism and histories, since, *lato sensu*, this perspective tends to naturalize standards of latent anti-Semitism. In the case of *La lozana andaluza*, little is at stake, in ideological terms, when accepting a writing potentially permeable to cultural differences. For the vast majority, *La lozana* is the great dialogical work and it does not feel forced to read into it the removed memory of an expelling Spain. In the cases of *Guzmán* and *Quixote*, however, there is a tendency to prefer the critical speculation according to which the converso differences are not enough to name and prescribe the narrative logic of the two most prominent texts of the period.

While lastly, and contrary to the discomfort evident in many eminent Quevedoists, the *Buscón* tends to be placed in the stereotypical space of anti-converso fiction. Quevedo – we continue to hear these defenses today – was not anti-Semitic; his disagreements, in any case, are strictly confessional. And so it is not surprising that no attempt is usually made to investigate the functioning of this text in a critical constellation that works in favor of the legibility of a converso literature.

These disagreements, however, are far from being obstacles that discourage our reading, since we understand, that they meet the criteria referred to above that allow for the application of the principle of Spectrality.

It is not insignificant, either, that literary historiography warns us, with respect to the biography of the authors, of the richness of four well-differentiated experiences. Quevedo, undoubtedly, as the most acclaimed incarnation of the most orthodox Catholicism of his time and his lineage – as he himself and his memoirists reinforce – is free of any taint. Mateo Alemán, on the other hand, is the "New Christian" par excellence. His Jewish ancestors were well known in his time – for this reason he was called, sarcastically, "of *poca sangre*" – and his scholars have been able to confirm this condition. These facts should be recovered since, given the impossibility of hiding or blurring in the confusion of presumed communitarian similarities, the Sevillian author redoubled his efforts to pamper the greatest religious orthodoxy, a typical gesture of the conversos who feel compelled to remember again and again that they have renounced that past that haunts them.

Of Cervantes, on the other hand, there is no precise documentary evidence. Many non-Spanish critics want to read in his progenitors' occupations and in the incessant family moves a veiled sign of a past to be hidden. But what is striking here, due to the memorialist agenda of the Spaniards, is that any possible speculation of a converso condition continues to be maniacally forbidden. Cervantes, of course, is a privileged synecdoche to refer to Spain, but not just any kind, one that is solely related to the Castilian imaginary and the *reconquista batalladora*.

This perspective, in the case of Delicado, is speculatively inverted. Many believe that his family was Jewish and, probably, that they were part of the first generations of New Christians – this also is a hypothesis – but nobody reveals the author's confessional profile and neither does it seem to matter much to them that a different cultural tradition was certified for his character. Delicado, after all, had preferred to emigrate from Spain to Italy.

Of the four works mentioned I have chosen *La Lozana andaluza* and *Guzmán de Alfarache* for an exemplary close-reading to demonstrate their characteristics with regard to the proposed principle of spectrality and their positioning within the constellation of converso literature.

5 The Exiles of *La Lozana andaluza*

La Lozana andaluza is one of Delicado's least debated works when considering its possible inclusion in some converso constellation, though in recent decades, annotators and editors of the text have progressively begun to question many of the basic aspects that would allow such affiliation. I believe that a first and necessary step in the reconsideration of the text as converso literature is, in this case, a closer look at the logical, rhetorical or editorial traps with which, voluntarily or involuntarily, academic approval has been prevented, in order to inscribe it into the symbolic-discursive constellation of the converso universe. An important aspect to consider here is how paratextual devises are used to guide the reading. Since most of these texts are mainly accessible in editions mediated, fixed, annotated and prefaced for the big publishing houses. Here, of course, we are not attacking the unequivocal advantage of being able to work with reliable versions. The problem is that, in many cases, the apparently marginal territories of prologue and notes can hardly be considered "neutral". It is through them that the editor usually has the advantage of conditioning and hierarchizing different readings of the text.

While a principle of generality and legitimization of the basics to be considered in the reading of the respective text is what organizes the prologue, particularisms, debates and points that are not settled in the critical debate usually become footnotes. The processes of canonizing certain works, based on the "Hispanic" category, make everything invisible that, like the converso matter, could be perceived as an unstable variable. One of the clearest examples of this phenomenon can be found in the way in which the universe of Jewish and converso culture of the Diaspora is presented and problematized in the editions of Francisco Delicado's *La Lozana andaluza*. None of the three editions most widely used by scholars – the one by Bruno Damiani in Castalia in 1969, the one by Claude Allaigre in Cátedra in 1994 and the most recent one by Jacques Joset and Folke Gernert in Galaxia Gutemberg in 2007 – clearly prioritizes the converso component. This becomes more notorious as the strategies of prologues and respective notes are opposed to what their precedents and the remaining specialists were able to interpret or demonstrate over the last forty years. Of the multiple flanks that Delicado's text offers for a possible converso understanding, I will only refer to two: the author's debatable condition as a descendant of Jews and the culinary recipe book of Mamotreto II.

If the work should be included into the converso worldview by exclusive merit of Delicado's biography, Damiani rushes to clarify that "we must recognize the possibility mentioned by Vilanova that he belonged to a family of converted Jews" and adds, immediately, that the "hypothesis" is sustained in some textual data according to which we should understand that the exile was "a voluntary migration, maybe motivated by the fear of some complaint regarding his Judaic ancestry" (Damiani 1969, 11). He cannot, like the vast majority, draw a reliable biographical profile in the absence of documentary evidence, but that does not prevent him from confirming that his departure was not forced and that "perhaps" the only certainty was the "fear of some accusation" founded in the – now probable – "Jewish" family background (ibid.).

It is also striking that being or not being of Judaic ancestry only matters, eventually for some, when thinking of Delicado and not for all the Spanish authors who are considered models or relatively close generic precedents, to understand the dimension of such a two-faced work.[1]

Allaigre's prologue does not consider it necessary at all to introduce a biographical portrait, a gesture that Joset and Gernert's version undoes, but, of course, with new nuances. For, although they express that "whatever his family religious condition, the important presence of the Converso culture is undeniable" (Joset and Gernert, xxxi), such an assertion, for other reasons, doesn't seem to matter much in what follows. For although the circle of possible family affiliations for Delicado and his family is limited, since they could have been, all of them or only our author, both Jews and conversos[2] – with the varied sincerities that we could attach to this adjective – what counts is the critical preference for turning textual data on which previous opinions are based into cultural testimony of an age that relegates the uncertain particularisms of the author to a place where they cannot be settled.[3]

---

[1] One of the criticisms that the "celestinesco" genre usually received was the instability or notorious genre fluctuation of the works; all of them read as hybrids of the rhetorical arts and poetic molds and unhappy marriages of prose and theater. It is worthwhile to corroborate, with a detailed analysis, the point to which this "textual segregation" for stylistic and formal "impurity" is not subsidiary to a previous marginalization: the classlessness of their authors, most of the time typified capriciously as "minor" for being obvious carriers of the stigma of religious conversion.

[2] Let us remember how Joset and Gernert outline this changing spectre: "Usually the speculation is that Delicado was son of Jewish parents, forced to leave Spain due to the massive expulsion of their coreligionist in 1492, according to the suggestion of Bubnova (1987:59). But, once again, it was not proved if our author was a Jew or a Convert, even though, backing his Judaism, Costa Fontes (1993 and 1994) refers to the presence of the traditional Jewish diatribe against the Trinity in the *Lozana*. A more theological argument is held by Mac Kay (1985a:175–178), who considers that the *Lozana* is a continuation of the dispute of Fernando del Pulgar against the practices of the Inquisition in defense of the converted young women. Other critics, like Molho (1950:80), Márquez Villanueva (1973a:93) or Mac Kay himself and Semerau (1989:446) found the Hebrew linage of the author on the names used in the novel. Finally, some critics, like Stoll (1995:31–33), suppose that Delicado, or the main character of his novel, are undoubtedly converts, emphasizing how the *Lozana* describes the stages of a typically Sephardi exile (see Allaigre, 1994)" (Joset and Gernert 2007, xxx–xxxi. My translation).

[3] From these initial passages of Joset and Gernert I am interested in pointing out two aspects. First, how the focus of stable categories – being Hebrew, Jew or converso – in the summary of the perspectives and positioning of the specialists clouds the religious category's complexity in the context of

6 *Converso* Spectres: The Lessons and Challenges of Spanish 'Golden Age' Prose — 199

This takes place to such an extent that, on an equal footing with this register, there is the memory of the mentioned "latent anti-Semitism in the description of the Judeo-Converso world" (Joset and Gernert 2007, xxxi). This is a hypothesis for which only the necessarily contrary identity of the author is recovered – as if minorities did not reproduce the stigma with which they are usually stigmatized, or even transform into a sign of positive belonging the very thing with which the other describes them.[4]

The text seems to have something of Jewish, Converso, Hebrew[5] or Sephardi in it, but it is not explained why none of it can justify or support a coherent reading. And a perhaps unintentional reductionism is once again evident when speculating on the random condition of a text without an audience that characterized the work. This point is very well documented, but the underlying problem[6] is, in our opinion,

---

community intolerance. Let us remember, from a strictly historical angle, how many subjects were persecuted for alleged and suspected religious insincerities in the process of adoption of a new creed due to the longing or the need for integration in the social structure. And how, categorically, the hypothesis that the phenomenon of conversion sets up is invalidated in itself: the fact of having been, in two different moments of their life, faithful to different spiritualties. Can a convert, in fact, close his own past in a satisfactory way? Why, when converted personalities are represented, only the destination faith is important in conversion? What is complex and problematic is not, indeed, just that there are no trustworthy documents and that everything is solved by inferences and critical deductions based on the reading of the work, but rather that Delicado, in his family context and his world, could be crossed and subjected by these various and unsteady spiritual oscillations.

4 Let us remember, in this order of ideas, the assertions of Pierre Bourdieu (1985) when he typified the discursive practices of the minority groups, clarifying up to which point the assumption of the value standards and the perceptive protocols of reality can be oriented, in countless examples, by devices of adaptation to the prevailing common sense. These practices would imply, to a certain extent, an incantation of what one does not want to be real with respect to oneself. There are countless examples, both in the past and today, in which women can emphatically state that they do not feel represented by the positions of feminists, or the cases of homosexuals who clamor for a return to the coherence of the heterosexist universe. That a Converso or *Judaizante* would find themselves trapped before any circumstance of public elocution that would limit a positive or defensive preaching of his own identity should not cause astonishment. Nor, indeed, that, for the sake of an effective blurring of their own belonging, in a conscious or unconscious way, they replicate and seem to share the discriminatory judgments about their own collective. To which we should add, if this were not convincing, the supreme fictional example left to us by Cervantes when he created the character of Ricote, in his *Quixote* of 1615, marked by the expatriation of 1609 and, at the same time, a staunch defender of the expulsion decree.

5 It is worth noting how this categorization implies an ambiguity that is not always properly clarified. Can it be affirmed that, in Spain, in the thirteenth to seventeenth centuries, there are or were "Hebrews"? To what extent is this homologation of the notion of "Jew" with that of "Hebrew" not useful in terms of the prevailing verbal and physical violence? It is well known today that the symbolic coordinate exalts the variable "Hebrew" by referring to the Old Testament coordinate prefiguring the Christian New Testament – the so-called *veritas hebraica* – insofar as, unequivocally, any mention of a Jew connotes the deicidal people. A good and well-documented approach to the phenomenon can be read in Fine 2008, 411–418.

6 To support this hypothesis, and in the absence of specific documentation on the publishing history of the *Lozana* in Venice, Joset and Gernert draw an understandable, though not necessarily decisive,

that it proves that the non-inclusion of the text in any inquisitorial index –particularly in those that banned the edition and circulation of volumes "Hebrew or in any written language, containing Jewish ceremonies" – would explain, without further ado, the thesis that, quite possibly, it lacked readers. It goes without saying, in this regard, that not everything inventoried by the indexes was well catalogued and that many other texts are also known whose "inappropriateness" did not cause their prohibition.

This point is very well documented but the underlying problem is that it takes for granted that the lack of inclusion of the text in any index of the Inquisition —very particularly in those that prevented the publishing and circulation of volumes in "Hebrew or in any language written that contain Judaic ceremonies" — would explain, per se, the thesis that very possibly it has lacked readers.

The question about the audience, allegedly phantasmagorical and almost non-existent, does not seem to be incidental,[7] the identification of two notorious flanks of potential inquisitorial condemnation – the obvious eroticism and the notorious Semitism – may well be the basis, in a different way but with analogous validity, of

---

analogy with a text by Alvise Cinzio published in 1526: *Della origine delli volgari proverbii*. According to the editors "the book raised fierce and vehement protests on the part of the Venetian Franciscans, the target of Cinzio's scorn in his paremiological compilation" and the dispute would have been settled with the general establishment of editorial controls and the authorization given to the order to destroy all the anathematized copies. It is evident that the fact that this happened is not enough to certify that a similar attitude was adopted with a text in another language and, by virtue of this, presumably destined to a type of reader with different competences from the local Italian. It should be noted, moreover, that if Cinzio's work is fiercely against the Franciscans, Delicado does not focus his anti-ecclesiastical attacks against any order in particular and his satires or degraded refractions of the religious figure represented could well have gone unnoticed under the protection of epochal aesthetics in which the vices of the religious moved to laughter but not necessarily to scandal since such "faults" were not assumed as legitimate condemnations of this or that current of spirituality.

7 It goes without saying, that even if it is true that the editors' statement about the reception of the work – "In spite of the enormous efforts, it has not been possible to find a reader of that extensive period who openly or obliquely affirms having read the *Lozana*" – this does not lead us to conclude that, necessarily, it lacked readers and that its impact was null and void. In the first place, because the value of these testimonies, at least at the dawn of the sixteenth century, could not be conclusive, since if we relate the number of copies of the different printings with this type of news produced by the readers, we will notice that in many cases, not only in the *Lozana*, the percentage of "proofs of reading" compared to the number of copies in circulation is far from being a simple correspondence. In most cases it is much lower or even non-existent. Secondly, because it is difficult to accept as objective the alternative of "obliquely having read" the text, since it is enough to consult the specialized bibliography of the period to corroborate that these links are indeed recognized. That Joset and Gernert typify them as non-existent because they do not share them is admissible, but their reading need not be the only possible one. In fact, if we focus on the interaction of Miguel de Cervantes with the work of Francisco Delicado, there are two well-known works that question this path: Vilanova (1952, 5) and Bubnova (1990).

a hypothesis about clandestine and circumscribed consumption among those who, clearly, were libertines or conversos or Jews or all of the above.

The prologue opts for a speculation in which the law of hostility triumphs and denies outright the possibility that, outside their homeland, the migrant communities had articulated forms of resistance based on their condition as minorities.

Not everything that the editor or the critics ignore is nonexistent. But it is evident how all these uncertainties are oriented, in a gesture that minimizes reading discomfort, towards a significance that transforms the religious belonging or cultural interaction of a collective in exile into irrelevant data. For even if it should be accepted that Delicado's was perhaps a forced exile, it would seem evident that the "Hispanic" readmission must be conceived from the hypothetical position of a *vox clamans in deserto*.

It is a singular detail that these critics do not notice how the conflicting or blind spots of the preliminary studies lose all accordance with the notes prepared for the prologue text. For the matrix of many of the notes is the concretization of an insignificant diaspora. What is mentioned there as converso or *Judaico* will not be put in relation to what happens in the following magisterial statement unless, clearly, the principle of non-reiteration of what has already been illuminated must take precedence. Thus, in practice, the reader interested in the systematic nature of the Mosaic material in the work must reread it from its margins and, in addition, have a good memory.

And this, undoubtedly, is what two of our editors do when annotating Mamotreto II of Delicado's text. Since, in Damiani's case, nothing is mentioned about the very evident Semitic matrix of the recipe book wielded by the protagonist before her aunt. And although his ignorance could be objected to, he cannot be reproached for his incongruity. Our two other versions, on the other hand, admit the centrality of the converso experience to declare the complexities of the text but accompany their remarks with paradoxical gestures.

In the case of Allaigre's very meticulous version we focus on his footnote 6 in which he openly expresses that: "Preparing *hormigos* with oil was for Jews or Conversos" and that this is an "important feature of *Lozana* that I have not discussed in the Introduction but that I studied in Allaigre 80, 181–200" (Alleigre 1980, 178).

The ambiguity – and the tacit hierarchization of the object that follows from this sentence – is quite striking. Whoever seeks clarity and coherence on the subject matter discussed should abandon Delicado's text and refer to another work whose access to the reader can be considered neither immediate nor simple.[8]

Joset and Gernert, on the other hand, subject the entire passage of the cookbook to a thorough analysis in which one can see consistency with some of the details

---

8 Besides the "*hormigos* with oil", Allaigre links the Jewish or converso palate to eggplant dishes – "they were considered typical of Jews" – and the so-called "cazuela mojí", which "also can be interpreted as the insistence on the already mentioned Converso characteristic" (Allaigre 1980, 178).

stated in the respective prologue.[9] But it should not be overlooked that the *Galaxia Gutemberg* collection admits a third section in which notes for specialists are developed and that there, on the contrary, the certainty obtained in this matter is subjected to a polemical sifting by virtue of which what was considered as converso is reappropriated for another cultural domain that is intended to be exclusive and allogenic: the *Morisco* world.

Specialists on Delicado are not unaware that, based on a masterful article by Monique Joly (1989) on Aldonza's recipe book, it follows that many of the delicacies of the Andalusian woman could be decoded as unequivocal signs of the Moorish influence in the south of Spain.[10] And in her reading, the evidence of texts contemporaneous or relatively close to Delicado's work, and also the testimony of such diets still existing in northern African countries, are united.

The point here, however, is that the references to some of the conclusions of the French Hispanist are organized according to a possible but not conclusive or proven principle, which would be the thesis that in any culture it is possible to postulate isolated and uncommunicated worlds. The recipe book in its totality could be typical of the Moors and it would also be admissible, even, that there were examples whose finding in the Jewish and converso palate was improbable or not documented, but from this it does not necessarily follow, for every critical reader, that it should be retained as logical and unique corollary that Aldonza initiates her trip to Rome for a probable Moorish condition. The current studies on the multiple coexisting cultures in the Spanish "Golden Age" – not only those that are thought and categorized according to religious belongings – invalidate any reading based on hypotheses of clear categories and watertight communities. This criterion allows us to point out how, in short, the pruritus of controversy and debate that animates this third section of the most recent edition contributes, to the invisibility of data and indications that can also be justly linked to converso culture.

This world, according to this brief overview of three editions, seems condemned to suffer a semiological limbo: either it does not exist and nothing is mentioned about it; or it exists, but its discourse is postponed for a better occasion; or, if it is provisionally admitted to exist, this existence is relativized through a counter position

---

9 In Mamotreto II, n. 11, Joset and Gernert held: "A whole class of 'oatmeals' (*hormigos, talvinas, zahínas*) from the Arabic or Jewish cooking, as well as the 'turnips withour bacon'" (p.15) ("Se agrupa toda clase de 'gachas' (*hormigos, talvinas, zahínas*) de la cocina árabe o judía, así como los 'nabos sin tocino'").

10 In extra note 15.5 of the Joset and Gernert's edition, the words of J. del Val are recovered. In a previous edition (1967) he, when referring to the cookbook of the main character, had insisted on the affinity this Andalusian confectionery has ("con las golosinas que nos aportaron los árabes" [with the candy the Arabs provided us with]). In that note also, they insist on the hypothesis by Monique Joly: "in the text there are abundant lexical marks that seem to indicate that, at least in this first stage of the *Retrato* Delicado put certain effort in presenting Aldonza as a possible descendant of *Moriscos*" (Joset and Gernert 2007, 379).

that works the unthinkable wonder of secrecy. In such a way the flourishing of a new critical territory, ignored until then, finds its best configuration.[11]

6 The *Guzmán* and the Existential Ordeal of "Knowing His Blood"

The *Guzmán de Alfarache* is the text used to construct, in its link with the *Lazarillo de Tormes*, the picaresque genre. And it is important to remember that, by virtue of Mateo Alemán's public status as a "New Christian", two critical corollaries have been developed that have influenced, with varying degrees of success, the evolution of the critical field in general and of the novel in particular. The first of these is the one that establishes that every author of picaresque books is a converso – a phenomenon already studied in the previous pages. The second, on the contrary, is the one that centers the confessional problem of the protagonist's conversion. The dispute about it affected, in the first place, the lawfulness of such an author – a public converso – preaching about the right confessional virtue to an anonymous public that could be made up of "Old Christians".

But it also impacted the general readings that were postulated to settle the meaning of the text. Was *Guzmán* a champion of Tridentine Catholicism – as many argued – or, on the contrary, should he be recognized as a simple impostor? Was his conversion sincere or not, and what should follow from it?

The whole of *Guzmán* tenses up towards the final scene of his conversion to a strong Catholicism. But in the entire novel there are only four scenes in which the universe of the converso – from Jew or Muslim to Christian – is summoned. Much has already been written about the axes of meaning that are stretched between the fate of the protagonist and that of the exemplary *morisco* lovers Ozmin and Daraja, the first of the four occurrences, and I also set aside, in order to focus my reading, a fourth allusion in which the mockery is articulated, very briefly, with respect to a "New Christian". What I am interested in highlighting, in the two remaining sequences, is how, in accordance with the postulation of converso Spectrality, the possibility

---

11 The general effect of a reading focused on the proposed passages would suggest certain discomfort with which, *prima facie*, could be understood as a relatively clear evidence of a different culture as point of departure and background of the imaginary coordinate of Delicado. It would not be mistaken even to wander if the notes are not the final stitch of a process of *damnatio memoriae* that the editor must carry out so that the work manages to enter the domain of the authorized Spanish. Is it necessary to remind up to which point the Hispanic culture dealt with and better understood the Moor cultural memory than the Jewish one? Is it risky to sustain that the different elocutive strategies used in the annotations thought for the foreign cookbook of Aldonza have the oxymoronic purpose of calling the attention for words or practices that, immediately after, are going to be confined to the irresoluble or the irrelevant for that edition?

of reading this signifying constellation is articulated by virtue of the emergence of minimal forms: an insult and a mockery. Minimal forms at the discursive level that break, evocatively, the preeminence of the narrative voice by integrating others who insult and mock the presumed converso. The first of these two is stated narratively when the protagonist has already expressed the longing to "know his blood". This leads Guzmán on a long Italian adventure that begins in the third book of the First Part with his arrival in Genoa and culminates in the last chapter of the second book of the Second Part with his flight to Spain, from the same city, with the goods he has stolen from his relatives.

Guzmán's arrival in Genoa calls into question the inclusive logic of the supposedly beneficial conversions through the problematic acceptance of a relative, who appears "hecho un espantajo de higuera" ("a figtree scarecrow") and who aspires, clearly, to become "de los Godos" ("of a noble origin") against the background of a family branch in better economic conditions (Alemán 1992, Part I, Book 3, 378).

In a grotesque interlude that could well be read as the inversion of the public scandal that surrounded the condemned prisoners of the Inquisition with its proclamations and spectacular executions, Guzmán invades the community space of the "nobility of that city" announcing, to whoever would listen, that because of "who he was" his repulsive presence was justified by the phantasmatic affiliation of his dead father with one of the distinguished Genoese families (Alemán 1992, Part I, Book 3, 378). The narrator does not spare us the precise effect of such an unexpected presence. The whole community was "so angry that they hated him to death". And he also feels obliged to justify, to a certain extent, the elemental and primary passion of the citizens by comparing it to the feelings that the readers themselves would have if, like the Genoese, they were exposed to such an unpleasant ordeal: to identify with the poor, the different, the despicable.

Guzmán evokes, without half-measures, the cultural effect of the reunion between two worlds, and thus he specifies

> A persona no pregunté que no me socorriese con una puñada o bofetón. El que menos mal me hizo fue, escupiéndome a la cara, decirme '¡Bellaco, marrano! ¿Sois vos ginovés? ¡Hijo seréis de alguna gran mala mujer, que bien se os echa de ver!' Y como si mi padre fuera hijo de la tierra o si hubiera de doscientos años atrás fallecido, no hallé rastro de amigo ni pariente suyo.
> (Alemán 1992, Part I, Book 3, 378–379)[12]

An insulting speech, with no clear origin of its production, other than being the least offensive of an endless number of anonymous verbal abuse and physical attacks, would explain the violent reactions to which he was exposed in his search and

---

[12] "I didn't ask anyone who wouldn't help me with a punch or a slap. The one who did me the least harm was, spitting in my face, saying to me, 'You swine! Are you from Genoa? You must be the son of some great bad woman, for you are well missed!' And as if my father were a son of the earth or had died two hundred years ago, I found no trace of a friend or relative of his." (My Translation)

arouses, as if between the lines and perhaps without being aware of it, an evident tension within the two parental figures of his project of affiliation. Guzman searches for a father who seems to have vanished "two hundred years ago" and may be rejected by all that of his mother, "gran mala mujer" (a very bad woman), is certified in him. If we leave aside what could seem an evident parody of the fate of the Jew Jesus before the Sanhedrin, mistreated and spat on in the face when he is captured, we can see that the reflection that Guzmán adds to the polemic and affronting phrase is far from the naivety or supposed spontaneity that the memorial project of his life pretends to make us believe. Since what first stands out is how, in the face of the segregation of his own mother as unworthy, he officiates – by implicit means – the revelation of a similarity that the interlocutor pretends does not exist. Guzmán denies – through the "as if" – both that his father does not have his ancestors in Genoa, and that it is impossible to find a "friend" or "relative of his". The narrator does not invalidate the verbal insult but, on the contrary, the effect pursued by the insult: to reduce all the ignominy and shame that his person should arouse to a single and exclusive link, his mother. And it is central that we emphasize that the defense that the son seeks, through all the impossibilities that he preaches of the father, supposes the tacit affirmation that, for him, the same arguments should be valid.

The converso drama – as revealed by the clear disgrace of being typified as a "Bellaco marrano" – is structured as distressing and unstable balance between the daily evidence – what the offenders read in the body of the son who searches for his relatives – and the longing for a perfect erasure of his figure, in such a way that his non-existence can be certified. In the centre, however, we find the basic doubt of the drama of inclusion: "Are you Genoese?"

The *Guzmán* leaves no doubt; the so-called religious conflict is a civic-political conflict. It is about the conditions of citizenship, whether it should be granted to those who are different, and the requirements for their admission and integration, involving equal opportunities. The ultimate and basal rejection is not being called a "marrano" but rather not being able to be a citizen.

This device of segregation is neither novel nor typical of Genoa, since it is impossible not to detect, in the anonymous accusation, the multiple and numerous testimonies of Jews and conversos afflicted, for existing in a non-place, for lacking, beyond the typical geographical hardships and typical of the diaspora, the symbolic space to exist. But I do believe that the choice of Genoa, as the capital city that liberates the discrimination veiled until then in the story, is not the result of the author's random imagination.

Alemán's Genoa is twinned with the historical Genoa in the structural dilemma of accepting or rejecting the Jews expelled from Spain, or their descendants, and I do not think it is random, either, that the reason for this trip, in the text of the galley-slave writer, appears as a return to the father's past, since this Italian "dream" seems to liberate, as a brilliant veiled allegory, the fate of the Spanish Jews in the various Italian regions.

In fact, everything seems to begin with the offensive observation that leads to the rejection of Guzmán wrapped in "rags and patches" like a "fig tree scarecrow", just as, according to historians, the overcrowded ships of exiles arrived at the Genoese port (Alemán 1992, Part I, Book 3, 378). And this analogy seems to be confirmed by the fact that the resolution on the acceptance or rejection of 'the different' is played out on the same constructive principle, with regards to the real event, and in fiction: the disruption of families.

For if the *Guzmán* narrates how the protagonist's son is expelled from the apparent paternal city, researchers on the Jewish presence in Genoa will remind us of the tragic fact of what happened to the first boats of exiles: after having authorized the resupply for a few days in a meager confinement of the port, the Genoese took possession of the offspring of the exiles and forced the parents to follow an uncertain course on the high seas, perhaps because, in a gesture that transcends the biologization of culture, they considered that the offspring of Jews could be 'recovered' with the 'right' upbringing. Genoa, however, was a repeated and habitual destination in successive migrations, and the history of the Jewish presence in the port city seems to be an example of what will occur, with less intermittency and alternations, in the rest of the Italian city-states.

From Genoa to the papal confines in Rome, Guzmán follows an itinerary in which, suggestively, his face as a wandering beggar is emphasized. It is also symptomatic that all his resting points in the Italian peninsula are precisely those that were unstable for exiles – in the continuous swing of public and political opinion towards the Jews. The experiences of the son in Italy, according to what we believe to be a great allegorical key declared by the insult of "Bellaco, marrano!", may well symbolize, from another level of memory and discourse, the untold story of the expelled families, a story that Spain did not want to hear but which is its responsibility, since it embodies the future which was aborted by the expulsion.

For this reason, then, it is highly striking that the insult and mockery against the Jews acts as a symbolic customs duty in the return to Spain. Guzmán, in the second passage I will analyze has already arrived in Zaragoza, has returned extremely rich, because of the goods stolen from his relatives in Genoa and, as if it were a logical consequence of the possession of a capital different from that which he least legitimately had when he left, he is once again afraid. Fear of ceasing to be, for being stolen, fear that, in the end, the money will disclose his identity.[13]

---

[13] This loss of identity that the *pícaro* fears is nothing else than the unveiling of his essence since, as the reader remembers, the fortune is not his own and in the potential plundering of what he managed to steal from his relatives, the capacity to deny his converso ancestry is at stake. In fact, the whole deliberate deception of Don Beltrán can be read as a masterful rewriting of the sequence of the chests of sand in the *Cantar del Mío Cid* and in this return to Spain, the citizenship card that certifies his long-established Hispanicity, he wants to pretend, would be explained in the ability to keep what, once, the *campeador* stole from the moneylenders Vidas and Raquel. Only a good Spaniard – as is

The notion of limits and territorial specificity are not, at any point, variables to be ignored. And here, it is worth emphasizing how the joke that we will analyze occupies the center of a whole chapter that, apparently, would be crossed by a series of displacements, inversions of causalities and logical breaks whose primary function would seem to be to blur, behind a false disposition to narrative accumulation, the vertebral axes of what the joke, as the argumentative and allegorical core of the passage, would be pointing out in another level of meaning.

The humorous interlude that Guzmán evokes is intertwined, somewhat chaotically, with two isotopies whose consistency and instances of reoccurrence throughout the chapter seem to be, voluntarily, hidden from the reader's consideration because what is recalled should be placed, within the story, as a simple self-sufficient sequence in itself and without further corollaries.

The first isotopy is clearly the territory of legality insofar as it can be thought of as a natural fact or as a cultural convention. And it is evident how the masking of this constructive principle in *Guzmán* is achieved through the annihilation of such disjunction in function of a double negation of alternative paths. The beginning of the chapter starts with the reminder that

> Cuando con algún fin quiere acreditar alguno su mentira, para traer a su propósito testigos, busca una fuente, lago, piedra, metal, árbol o yerba con quien la prueba, y luego alega que lo dicen los naturales. Desta manera se les han levantado millares de testimonios. Él es el que miente y cárgaselo a ellos.[14]   (Alemán 1992, Part II, Book 3, 353)

This same narrative section opposes, however, the disavowal of natural knowledge, the irrationality of the human being in community. For the "Arancel de Necedades" [Tariff of Necessities], as legislation regulating the *pícaro*'s passage through Zaragoza and, perhaps, his entry into Spain, is said to be enunciated by "la Razón, absoluto señor" ["Reason, the absolute lord"] that knows nothing superior to it (Alemán 1992, Part II, Book 3, 333). This counterpoint between the false wisdom of naturalism and the very evident blindness of a triumphant rationalism has a clear link with another thematization that, to a certain extent, could well be interpreted as a concrete case to be settled between the ridiculed positions and is the one so well studied by the ever-present Monique Joly (1985): the juridical problem of the second marriages of widows.

The alarm that – with unusual moralizing – the protagonist claims to warn of the liberal customs of the widows of Zaragoza is based on the contraposition

---

suggested between the lines – knows how to enjoy what was stolen from the Jews. And Guzmán, although he does not expressly admit it, understands the challenge perfectly, hence his fear.

14 "When for some purpose someone wants to prove his lie, to bring witnesses to his purpose, he looks for a fountain, lake, stone, metal, tree or grass with whom he can prove it, and then he alleges that the natives say so. In this way thousands of testimonies have been raised. He is the one who lies and attributes it to them." (My translation)

of two legalities: the juridical one – different from territory to territory – and the theological-moral one of universal claim. Both, in their asynchrony and dystopia, make a counterpoint – not always evident – of the diverse effects of civil legislation and religious norms, and produce a result, somewhat unforeseen and rarely exposed when analyzing the *Guzmán*: the possibility that the subjects are diverse because they are told by different legalities, thus relativizing, not the persons, but the subjective frameworks in which they are trapped.

In contrast to an alarmed *pícaro* who, because he finds himself rich, has already forgotten what would seem to be proper to those of his condition, Alemán ironically opposes, as Joly pointed out, an innkeeper with quasi-philosophical overtones. A detail that, for the stereotypes of the representation in use, would only be viable in aesthetics akin to a surrealism that does not yet exist. And this counts because, rhetorically, the anecdotal motif of the liberal widows is what authorizes the focus on the themes of money and honor to become plausible as logical corollaries. The widows could be exposed to embezzlement of their symbolic capital because of the danger of seeing their capital endangered. And this is indeed relevant because the reader's attention is shifted to the causes of what could be a reprehensible conduct – according to the different communities – while, in an inverse gesture, consideration of the results of such dangerous relationships within a community is omitted: infamous births.[15]

This undeveloped and substantive theme in the case of the protagonist acts as a key phantasmatic, since the *galeote*'s autobiography, which pretends to be an integral confession, silences the interdict that, with respect to his person, is ridiculed as a magical entry clause that authorizes his return to Spain. And this, in our opinion, is reinforced by two very precise contextual aspects. The fact that – in the *cazurra* dimension – the jocular "Arancel" is said to be useful for "todos los nacidos y que adelante sucedieren" and, secondly, because the joke that his memory evokes acquires, from this vantage point, all its significant dimension.

The reader will know – once he has read the "Arancel" – that the cheerful disposition, the uncontrollable laughter, and the prior demand for payment as a customs fee, has a mocking explanation: that Guzmán has blown his nose and contemplated his secretions as if they were "pearls" (Alemán 1992, Part II, Book 3, 339). But what is interesting here is that the extortive tone of the payment, without the traveler understanding it, is what releases the device of infamous control in *Guzmán*.[16]

---

15 Note how both stay in Spain – the one that is specified from the birth of Guzmán until his Italian exodus and the one that is taken up again with the return analyzed here until his exile in the overseas confines of galleys – and are "figured" from the meditation of the undesirable births: the promiscuous mother who deceives the father and the widows who expose themselves to get pregnant. See, moreover, how the absence of offspring for the supposed widows illuminates the anguishing alternative and eventual certainty that for him to be and exist in Spain it would be logical – unreal as it may sound – "not to have been born".

16 Another evident irony – although concealed by the course of the action – is the one that follows

6 Converso Spectres: The Lessons and Challenges of Spanish 'Golden Age' Prose — 209

The *pícaro* clearly feels uncovered in some sense, as if one of the multiple deceptions that underpinned the plausibility of his false identity had collapsed. All of which justifies, for the sake of his readers, that in order to explain this uncomfortable sensation he appeals to the remembrance of an analogy that contains the already announced joke. A playful passage that says, without intending to, what really distresses him:

> Cuando esto me decía, estaba yo de lo pasado y con lo presente tan confuso, que se me pudiera decir lo que a cierta señora hijadalgo notoria que, habiendo casado con un cristiano nuevo, por ser muy rico y ella pobre, viéndose preñada y afligida como primeriza, hablando con otra señora, su amiga, le dijo 'En verdad que me hallo tal, que no sé lo que me diga; en mi vida me vide tan judía' Entonces la otra señora con quien hablaba le respondió: 'No se maraville Vuestra Merced, que trae el judío metido en el cuerpo.'[17]   (Alemán 1992, Part II, Book 3, 342)

The joke is reconstructed, mentally, in the uncomfortable territory of potential punishment.[18] Everything happens delayed, in the confines of uncertainty which consolidates when the "laughter and uproar of the guest", prolonged for no apparent reason, makes him fear "that I would drop dead there" if the truth of his offence was not revealed to him and if this, after all, was not one of those that – as is presupposed – could be settled with a fine, like the one that has been demanded of him (Alemán 1992, Part II, Book 3, 342).

Guzmán knows he is at fault but doesn't know why exactly. And here it is important to realize that this imperfect certainty recovers, according to the internal logic of the joke, the deep awareness that, regardless of what his mind thinks as a potential explanation, it will be the contextual Other who, in all certainty, has within his reach an incontrovertible reason for the mockery.

That Other, whose overflowing laughter is the effect, sign and exercise of a power that Guzmán does not have. An Other who, as the joke denounces, has the ability to redefine the diverse horizons of possible positioning of the individual, for the benefit of cruel evidence that was pretended to be postponed and postponed forever. An

---

from the confrontation of what really happens in the misunderstanding and the equivalences that follow: Guzmán fears to be recognized either as a thief, or as an effeminate, or, in the end, as a simple descendant of conversos. The innkeeper, in turn, clarifies what he knows, that they are simple snot, impure excretions of his organism, shameful matter that should not be "revered" or contemplated by the producer himself.

17 "When he told me this, I was so confused about the past and with the present that I could say to myself what a certain notorious lady, who, having married a New Christian, because he was very rich and she was poor, seeing herself pregnant and afflicted as a first-time bride, talking to another lady, her friend, said to him, 'Truly I find myself such that I do not know what you say to me; in my life I have never seen myself so Jewish': 'Do not marvel, Your Mercy, that you have the Jew in your body'." (My translation).

18 Although our readings do not coincide substantially, the approach proposed by Glaser (1954) could prove useful.

Other who – even with the face of a friend or cordial interlocutor – can remind him that "he has the Jew in his body".

The anti-Semitic joke is organized as a clear equivocation or lexical entendre. For if "señora hijodalgo" uses "Jewess" as a culturalized meaning of *medrosa* or *insegura* – an axis in which the naturalization of the oppressive forge of a secular stereotype, in which fear of the other was consolidated as a distinctive variable of their personality, and not as a primary result of the community interaction between Christians and Jews – the friend, in turn, forces her to recognize that, being married to a 'New Christian', biological reason rules.

This tension between the legality of culture and the legality of nature – which had already been developed in the discursive context of the chapter – reaches an unthinkable limit here. For what the joke teaches through the playful staging – in the process of subjection of the different – is how the cultural, the supposed perception of values or distinctive signs in the different, in this case the fear of other Jews, ends up biologizing itself because if the 'New Christian' is perceived as an insincere Christian, as a crypto-Jew, it is necessary that the mother gives birth to a Jew, a *medroso*, which reveals, on another narrative level, that Guzmán is afraid.

The discursive restraint that the mockery releases also demonstrates how the symbolic domination of the other is not always resolved by force but, on the contrary, and in a large number of cases, by an almost involuntary and uncontrollable recall of the immemorial contexts of acculturation of the minority. No one tells Guzmán that he is inferior and, as such, oppressible, because the text will demonstrate that everything is resolved in a grotesque joke, in a wild horizon of the world upside down, about snot. But this does not count because the memory of the *pícaro-galeote*-writer has the ability to recall innumerable occasions in which others, similar to him, were reproached and mocked about their differences.

Guzmán, before the laughter of the Other, voluntarily submits to the idea that what is laughable in him would be nothing other than the possibility of being considered 'just another Jew', a wide scope dynamic in which one's own perception and categorization of what is real have yielded to the affronting standpoint of the other. For that, and nothing else, is the drama of those who know they have been called by that which the dominant culture defines as an insult. The *pícaro* knows he is affected by minoritizing speech and images. And it is logical that, in such a context, the game of mirroring between concrete situation and joke concentrates on all the points that, in his own existence, are perceived as a source of community scorn. Guzmán is already rich, like the 'New Christian' of the story, and as fortunate in business as his father, also a 'New Christian', could have been. And his birth, needless to insist, could only be explained as the self-interested and objectionable union of two parents who only got together because the Levantine was "very rich and she was poor".

This foregrounds the determinism of the stereotype – through the potential equalization in the macula of the male figures – as well as the forbidden vision of that which can only be said, due to its seriousness, from the point of view of mockery.

6 Converso Spectres: The Lessons and Challenges of Spanish 'Golden Age' Prose — 211

That which, nefariously, would have occurred in a womb, a womb inhabited by a monster or, as the mockery says, by a Jew who got in where he shouldn't have. Because Guzmán, wherever he is, knows he was conceived where evil cohabited. Is he the Jewish monster or is he different? Is he just one, or is there a double? What is it that the mother gave birth to?

The intended comicality of the joke is also articulated in two evident translations. The first one implies the disarticulation between the enunciative and discursive context within the evocation, and the second one officiates the reconfiguration of the communicative horizons between the two women. Guzmán presents the case speaking of a *señora hijodalgo* and her 'New Christian' spouse, but the repetition of the dialogue between the women makes it clear, that it is all a question of Jews. For the Jew, his affective-familial ties and his descendants, should not be referred to as 'New Christians' but, on the contrary, as the blood, with all rigor, commands.

The joke lies within the fact that the *señora hijodalgo* supposes that her objectionable relationship with a "new Christian" does not have consequences. She believes that the horizon of shared beliefs with her friends keeps her safe of having become another member of the group of the damned. And she does not realize that the economic strengthening she pursued with the liaison, far from exalting her, has weakened her even more.

If she, as the story refers, profaned the economy of the descendant of Jews, he, without her noticing it, has entered her body. She wanted to obtain financial security but she unwittingly sacrificed the sanctuary of her identity. She can continue to think that Jews are the others and everyone will continue to make fun of her because she, from then on, is one of them. The joke operates with the illusory deregulation of certain social categories that the reader of the *Guzmán* should consider as unchangeable in order to understand the semantic game and the laughter. For the pretended neutrality of the linguistic similarities is undone by the biological evidence that puts the evaluations in their right place. This also emphasizes, in a serious dimension, the phobic attitude of the 'Old Christians' evident in the phantom of the invasion. Because the joke preaches that money is what would have authorized the 'New Christians' to break the magical boundary that should keep the Christian communities separated from the Jewish or converso ones and because it is repeated, in the imaginary coordinate, like the marvelous intrusion of her uterus, or, in the political version, as a kingdom fornicated by the Semitic monster.

The Jew, according to the joke, hides in and lives at the expense of the notorious unscrupulous female matrix that only knew how to be cautious with the reproduction of money. A denunciation that, clearly, becomes enunciable insofar as it transfers the responsibility of the 'Old Christians' to a simple woman, since the *señora hijodalgo* encourages the annihilation of Spain.

It does not escape me, at this point, that the virulence of the anti-Semitic evocation – in the mental course of the protagonist – is enhanced markedly when the reader realizes that these enunciations come from the mouth of a converso author in whose environment the persecutions had not ceased and that his inclusion, in the course of the story, is strategically placed, as a border joke between the "pure" here of Spain and the foreign degradation from which the *pícaro* comes. How, one is tempted to ask, could Alemán have echoed such a discourse? Is it a testament to the weak position of the 'New Christians' of his time, a naive concession to the supposed camaraderie generated by the mockery? Does it preach, in a way, that conversos should be readmitted in exchange for taxes? What, in short, is Alemán's scriptural position on conversos?

7 Converso Spectres: Tentative Lessons, Challenges to Assume

Historically, the literature of conversos fought its battles on two opposing fronts. On the one hand, there was a certain tendency to focus on the collective encompassed by the definition. Increasing, analysis after analysis, the list of authors whose ancestors had been Jews or conversos was for many the touchstone that would legitimize the respective critical interests. However, to a certain extent, the first gesture of affiliating individuals to the same confessional group shifted the focus of esthetic problems to pseudo-historiographic territories, where everything seemed to be reduced to the task of certifying belonging.

It would be evident that one of the great merits of these initial approaches did not reside, mainly, in the 'scientific' achievements of their theses but, on the contrary, in the breaking of a wall of silence with which, in the academy, a difference destined to subsist mute and without discourse, was confined. Insisting on the significance of a social category that, at least hypothetically, was destined not to produce difference – for a converso should have been and should have been perceived as a Christian, without the addition of 'New' or 'Old' – is what enabled a discourse and, by extension, a wide critical field of inquiry.

This took place to the point that, in retrospect, it can be seen how the battle between critics over the fair or exaggerated ascription of an author to one or another confessional position served to postpone, strategically, the detailed consideration of the facts that, in each studied section, the researcher of converso literature had analyzed, systematized and interpreted. For the denial of the label applied to the author hindered the legibility of a difference in multiple dimensions and ways in which it was articulated in a social plexus that was desired to be non-signifying. As if the recognition of the existence of conversos had been in practice a mere nominal difference with no impact on the subjectivities achieved.

The recovery of a constellation called converso literature, regardless of the partial or broader failures that could have been enunciated as the critical polemics awakened by this or that author, implied the habituation to a protocol of disruptive enunciability within a canonical tradition that, by its own vertigo, had been adapting to monological normalization. In such a way that, consequently, it should always be kept in mind how the progressive installation of precedents – in the mutant contexts of critical production – liberated the value, incidence and centrality of the subjection of the converso other in one's own culture.

Indeed, as soon as certain confessional certainties began to be validated and the basic ideological corollaries, determined by such membership, ceased to be questioned, the critical collective began to focus, more wearily, on what the diverse productions of these authors could reveal and refine about their condition and their unavoidable context of production. Little by little, the critical path of the converso literature was integrating not only the elusive and diverse representation of the respective difference – in singular works or grouped by authorship, genre and period – but also the unavoidable counterpoints of other authors and, of course, other represented objects.

Indeed, if anything distinguishes the reading practices of many scholars interested in the converso literatures, it is that they are not afraid to break the tyranny of categorical compartments in order to pursue their inquiries. A progressive acceptance that a pure "essence" of the converso would not reveal itself no matter how many efforts were made was the natural corollary of a logical confinement that developed in the critical cultural field of the first decades. Would it have been possible to prescribe, abstractly, the "essence" of the converso – in historical, cultural, aesthetic terms – when, precisely, the hybrid status of such subjects had been established?

What would be the outcome of such enterprises when – as we have seen – it was always enough to point out that this or that variable that was thought to be converso – a trade, a culinary dish, a practice, a place of residence or a simple profession – was not exclusive to the collective, in order to invalidate the analysis? The corollary of common sense, in the face of these onslaughts or retorts to potential advances, always aspired to dwell unscathed. There may have been conversos, but none of their characteristics is predictable; the 'New Christians' may have dwelled together with the 'Old Christians', but it is impertinent to assume that any achievement or something of their collective worldview or individual sensitivity can be thought of as an autonomous or privileged legacy to Iberian culture.

For all these reasons, then, it is important to value how, in the last few decades, an alternative path of inquiry has been fostered, one that prioritizes the potentiality of the hybrid, the richness of the changeable and the ever-present challenge of instability. For all this, in epistemic terms, honors the basic assertion that all change – as voluntary or forced conversions were – implied an ontological scandal. Thus, indeed, current studies of converso literature have renounced the illusion of purity and the need to validate their achievements and advances with exclusive criteria that contribute to the aseptic distinctions of hermetic communities.

And this also explains why those who work in converso literature tend to enrich their research with contributions from specialists of other subjugated minorities of the period – *Moriscos*, Protestants – with protocols of analysis implemented by readers of transnational phenomena – diasporic literatures, of exile, trans-territorial, of Hispanic expression in non-Hispanic contexts. Moreover, in tune with these perspectives, a diverse revision of the processes of representation of the 'Old Christians' themselves and of other collectives in the discursive productions of the 'New Christians' should be considered.

For by accepting that the way in which the figuration of the 'New Christian' is approached is unstable, not always precise, dogmatic or univocal, we allow for the possibility of similarly uncertain drifts in the readings that were produced of the dominant collective. This tension between collective and individual, between culture and figuration of its constituents, opens the period to the most critical point of any enterprise interested in the converso literature: the authorial positioning.

Certainly, I am aware that sooner or later one will be confronted with the final question of authorial intentionality, the dilemma surrounding the degree of awareness of certain authors in the face of aesthetic problems and the implications of certain rhetorical decisions in their works, the question that unfolds, like a sea of uncertainty, around the achievements of such tasks in the reception of the first readers and, obviously, in posterity. Is converso literature an exploration of the diverse modes of decoding a dissent whose expression was pursued, or, in the end, is it a hypothetical and conjectural construct generated by academic agendas of later centuries? Although it may be frustrating to face the possibility that there is no single answer or that, from another point of view, the exclusivity of a single possible meaning cannot be certified, I believe that this initial tension must be inverted in order to honor, in a new light, what could be a different approach in face of this apparent limitation. And this would be achieved, in my opinion, if we could demystify the culturally generated expectations about the value and meaning of an answer. For in literature, and in so many other fields of culture, what is really challenging are not the answers but the questions that the critic may ask himself and, above all, the search process they undertake for the elucidation – albeit partial, provisional, subject to revision – of the dilemma that guided their work.

Converso literature must be addressed, in my opinion, as a paradigm of inclusive analysis, potentially in dialogue with the similar but also with the alien and even hostile, as a project of critical work that illuminates our knowledge of the past but also honors, ethically, the urgent dilemmas of modernity in terms of segregation, persecution and harassment of minorities of all kinds, as a legacy of synchronicity, through artistic consumption, of divergent times and spaces.

For if we accept that we do not all read in the same way, nor in a similar way after some time or after several re-readings of the same text or of others, it should be simpler to admit that the disposition to the assault of multiple, elusive senses, of random and changing refraction, rather than detracting from the enterprise, honors it and liberates it in all its potential. This is the minimum tribute that, after many centuries of oblivion and marginalization, such geniuses and their respective texts deserve.

Converso literature also establishes a reading policy, since the critic embarks, as a substitute, on a converso position when thinking about the production and consumption of that particular work. I believe that, if the analysis does not empathize with the position of the author or of the potential first readers, it will inevitably miss many particularisms.

In this sense, then, to think of a cartography of the converso in the Spanish prose of the sixteenth and seventeenth centuries implies the initial acceptance of a set of crucial limitations. Spain, at that time, canonized in historiographic and literary perspectives as the moment in which state monologism triumphed – one single faith, one single 'race', one single valuable genre – looked, *a priori*, like a potential wasteland: There were no longer any Jews in Spain – unless we were to overestimate the inquisitorial obsession with the so-called *Judaizantes* or crypto-Jews – and the status of the conversos, under the label of 'New Christians', was potentially emerging as a path of progressive and incessant critical dissatisfaction. For if there were – as was well attested in the individual or collective baptismal certificates of so many relatively voluntary or decidedly forced rites –, it becomes inevitable to accept that no converso would agree to his inscription, or that of his family, in a category that worked as a constant reminder of the alleged impurity according to which his community segregation would be legitimate.

How to read that which, in theory, would have no mark or significant trace in the culture of a period? How to interpret and understand the processes of artistic representation in which the profiled figures would invoke references already untraceable in the compositional medium itself or, also, subjects whose public verification would seem impossible and could only be understood as the result of an obsessive mystification in their regard? Why and to what extent are the evocations of "New Christians" reliable, whose only condition of phenomenal possibility is to be realized as an example of a generic collective that repels and aborts all singular individuation? What is it that determines that between reality and literary series all conceivable links and ways of articulation appear aborted, discontinuous, torn?

The journey through the authors of the period I chose for my reading proposal seeks to dwell in the astonishment of the survival of the allogenic in writings in which purification and extermination testify to its failure. It attends, without preconceptions, to the design of worlds dreamed by the pen in which a certain order of cohabitation or co-presence unfolds. It integrates, with the caution that the subject deserves, the apparent oblivion or figurative dissolution of some collective.

For in the "golden" literature of the sixteenth and seventeenth centuries, what is characteristic to the Jew and the converso – in their infinite and various nuances – would seem to be their 'being and not-being' in the texts, to be an image that the critic glimpses at times, whose presence resists the reader's expectations – and that sometimes triumphs, while in other contexts, it seems to stand, threatening, before the eyes of the author. From which follows, in my opinion, the spectral status of its representation.

In the spectre, moreover, time collapses. For if the withdrawal of temporality from life determines that what is already dead cannot access the future, the opposite is true of the spectres. They are vestiges, traces, fleeting refractions of a past that reach the present and threaten the future; they are signs of a resistance that opposes its dissolution and, fundamentally, oblivion. Insofar as the emergence of the spectral in every culture openly founds a politics of memory. The spectre activates, in the face of critics and readers as a whole, the figure of an impossible mourning.

The spectre seeks to activate the reminder and the value of that which was considered dead since, coming from the past, he actualizes the latency of something unfinished, he releases the memory of what could have come to our present but was not successful and establishes, irreverently, the relevance for the living of a voice and a discourse that, as proper of the dead, is typical of the defeated, the loser, the segregated from the respective cultural reality.

Any critical enterprise interested in the recovery of a converso literature is therefore enriched by the integration of discursive productions that, like Quevedo's *Buscón*, display their anti-Semitism openly. Given that between this hostile position and its counterpart – in various positions that testify to the diverse entity of the Jew and the converso in the respective form – the only traceable difference ends up being the way in which they receive, negotiate and welcome in their own artistic praxis the inhabitation of the spectral. On the reading commitment of each critic depends the ethical listening of that world which resists – courageous even in defeat – repulsion, oblivion, annihilation.

Bibliography

Works Cited

Allaigre, Claude. *Sémantique et littérature: le "Retrato de la Loçana andaluza."* Échirolles: Imprimérie du Neron, 1980.
Allaigre, Claude. "Introducción." Francisco Delicado. *La lozana andaluza*. Madrid: Cátedra, 1994.
Batallion, Marcel. "Introduction." *La vida del Lazarillo de Tormes/La vie de Lazarillo de Tormes*. Paris: Aubier/Flammarion, 1968.
Bourdieu, Pierre. *¿Qué significa hablar?*. Madrid: Akal, 1985.
Braudel, Fernand. *El Mediterráneo y el mundo mediterráneo en la época de Felipe II*. México: Fondo de Cultura Económica, 1987.
Bubnova, Tatiana. *Francisco Delicado puesto en diálogo: las claves bajtinianas de 'La lozana andaluza'*. México: Universidad Autónoma de México, 1987.
Bubnova, Tatiana. "Cervantes y Delicado." *Nueva Revista de Filología Hispánica* 38.2 (1990): 567–590.
Butler, Judith. *Mecanismos psíquicos del Poder. Teorías de la sujeción*. Madrid: Editorial Cátedra, Universidad de Valencia, Instituto de la Mujer, 1997.

Cabo Aseguinolaza, Fernando. *El concepto de género y la literatura picaresca*. Santiago de Compostela: Universidad de Santiago de Compostela, 1992.

Castro, Américo. *La realidad histórica de España*. México: Porrúa, 1954.

Castro, Américo. *Hacia Cervantes*. Madrid: Taurus, 1957.

Cavillac, Michel. "El Buscón y los 'Guzmanes': el personaje de Alonso Ramplón." *"Guzmán de Alfarache" y la novela moderna*. Madrid: Casa de Velázquez, 2010. 219–231.

Cervantes Saavedra, Miguel de. *El ingenioso hidalgo don Quijote de la Mancha*. Prólogo de Marcos A. Morínigo. Edición de Celina Sabor de Cortazar e Isaías Lerner. Buenos Aires: Editorial Huemul, 1983.

Costa Fontes, Manuel da. "Anti-Trinitarism and the Virgin Birth in La lozana andaluza." *Hispania* LXXXVI (1993): 197–203.

Costa Fontes, Manuel da. "The Holy Trinity in La lozana andaluza." *Hispanic Review* LXII (1994): 249–266.

Cros, Edmond. *Ideología y genética textual. El caso del 'Buscón'*. Madrid: Planeta-Cupsa, 1980.

Deleuze, Gilles, and Félix Guattari. *Kafka, por una literatura menor*. México: Ediciones Era, 1978.

Delicado, Francisco. *Retrato de La lozana andaluza*. Edición J. del Val. Madrid: Taurus, 1967.

Delicado, Francisco. *La lozana andaluza*. Edición, prólogo y notas de Bruno Damiani. Madrid: Clásicos Castalia, 1969.

Delicado, Francisco. *Lozana, die Andalusierin*. Traducción A. Semereau, notas de Angus Mac Kay. Nördlingen: Greno, 1989.

Delicado, Francisco. *La lozana andaluza*. Edición, prólogo y notas de Claude Allaigre. Madrid: Cátedra, 1994.

Delicado, Francisco. *La lozana andaluza*. Edición, prólogo y notas de Jacques Joset y Folke Gernert. Madrid: Galaxia Gutenberg, 2007.

Derrida, Jacques. *Espectros de Marx. El estado de la deuda, el trabajo del duelo y la nueva internacional*. Madrid: Editorial Trotta, 1998.

Dunn, Peter N. "El individuo y la sociedad en La vida del Buscón." *Bulletin Hispanique* LII (1950): 375–396.

Eribon, Didier. *Reflexiones sobre la cuestión gay*. Barcelona: Editorial Anagrama, 1999.

Fine, Ruth. "El Antiguo Testamento y el Quijote: un caso de sincretismo escriturario." *El 'Quijote' en Buenos Aires. Lecturas cervantinas en el cuarto centenario*. Eds. Alicia Parodi, Julia D'Onofrio and Juan Diego Vila. Buenos Aires: Eudeba, Asociación de Cervantistas, Instituto de Filología y Literaturas Hispánicas "Dr. Amado Alonso", 2006. 65–82.

Fine, Ruth. "Lo hebreo, lo judío y lo converso en la obra de Cervantes: diferenciación o sincretismo." *Languages and Literatures of Sepharadic and Oriental Jews*. Ed. David M. Bunis. Jerusalem: Misgav Yerushalaim and the Bialik Institute, 2008. 411–418.

Fine, Ruth. "La literatura de conversos después de 1492: autores y obras en busca de un discurso crítico." *Lo converso: Orden imaginario y realidad en la cultura española (Siglos XIII–XVIII)*. Eds. Ruth Fine, Michèle Guillemont and Juan Diego Vila. Madrid/Frankfurt: Iberoamericana/Vervuert, 2013. 499–526.

Fuchs, Barbara. *Una nación exótica. Maurofilia y construcción de España en la temprana Edad Moderna*. Madrid: Ediciones Polifemo, 2011.

Gilman, Stephen. "The death of Lazarillo de Tormes." *Publications of the Modern Languages Association* LXXXI (1966): 149–166.

Gilman, Stephen. *The Spain of Fernando de Rojas*. Princeton: Princeton University Press, 1972.

Glaser, Edgard. "Two anti-semitic Word plays in the Guzmán de Alfarache." *Modern Language Notes* 69 (1954): 343–348.

Hartman, Geoffrey. "On Traumatic Knowledge and Literary Studies." *New Literary History* 26.3 (1995): 537–563.

Ife, Barry. *Lectura y ficción en el Siglo de Oro. Las razones de la picaresca*. Barcelona: Crítica, 1992.
Johnson, Carroll. "El Buscón: D. Pablos, D. Diego y D. Francisco." *Revista Hispanófila* LI (1974): 1–26.
Joly, Monique. *La bourle et son interpretation. Espagne XVIè/XVIIè Siècles*. Lille: Atelier National de Réproduction des Thèses, 1986.
Joly, Monique. "Du remariage des veuves: à propos d'un épisode du Guzmán." *Amours légitimes – Amours illégitimes en Espagne (XVIè–XVIIè Siècles)*. Ed. Augustin Redondo. Paris: Publications de la Sorbonne, 1985. 327–339.
Levine Melammed, René. *A question of identity: Iberian Conversos in Historical Perspective*. Oxford: Oxford University Press, 2004.
López Baralt, Luce. "La estética del cuerpo entre los moriscos del Siglo XVI, o de cómo la minoría perseguida pierde su rostro." *Le corps dans la société espagnole des XVIè et XVIIè siécles*. Ed. Augustin Redondo. Paris: Publications de la Sorbonne, 1990. 335–348.
Mac Kay, Angus. "The Hispanic Converso-predicament." *Transactions of the Royal Historical Society* XXXV (1985): 159–179.
Márquez Villanueva, Francisco. "El mundo converso de La lozana andaluza." *Archivo Hispalense* LVI (1973): 87–97.
May, Terence. "Good and Evil in the Buscón: A Survey." *Modern Language Review* XLV (1950): 319–335.
May, Terence. "A Narrative Conceit in La Vida del Buscón." *Modern Language Review* LXIC (1968): 327–333.
Molho, Michael. *Usos y costumbres de los sefardíes de Salónica*. Madrid: Instituto Arias Montano, 1950.
Molho, Maurice. "Cinco lecciones sobre el Buscón." *Semántica y Poética. Góngora, Quevedo*. Barcelona: Editorial Crítica, 1977.
Molho, Maurice. "El pícaro de nuevo." *Modern Language Notes* 100.2 (1985): 199–222.
Nagy, Edward. "El anhelo de Guzmán de Alfarache de 'conocer su sangre': una posibilidad interpretativa." *Kentucky Romance Quarterly* 16 (1970): 75–95.
Parker, Alexander. "The Psychology of the Picaro in El Buscón." *Modern Language Review* XLII (1947): 58–69.
Parker, Alexander. *Los pícaros en la literatura. La novela picaresca en España y Europa (1599–1753)*. Madrid: Gredos, 1975.
Parodi, Alicia. "San Pablo, raptos, caídas, aguijones y agujas en la representación del Quijote de 1615." *Siglo de Oro español en España y América*. Ed. María Celia Salgado. Neuquén: Editorial de la Universidad Nacional del Comahue, 2006. 195–202.
Redondo, Augustin. "Del personaje de don Diego a una nueva interpretación del Buscón." *Actas del V Congreso de la Asociación Internacional de Hispanistas*. Burdeos: Universidad de Burdeos, 1977. Vol. 2: 699–711.
Redondo, Augustin. *Otra manera de leer el 'Quijote'*. Madrid: Editorial Castalia, 1998.
Redondo, Augustin. "Los goces laicos del carnaval." *Revista Ñ*. 21 May 2005.
Redondo, Augustin. *Revisitando las culturas del Siglo de Oro. Mentalidades, tradiciones culturales, creaciones paraliterarias y literarias*. Salamanca: Ediciones Universidad de Salamanca, 2007.
Redondo, Augustin. "Revisitando el concepto de literatura de conversos. El caso del Lazarillo, progenitor de los libros de pícaros." *Lo converso: Orden imaginario y realidad en la cultura española (Siglos XIII–XVIII)*. Eds. Ruth Fine, Michèle Guillemont and Juan Diego Vila. Madrid/Frankfurt: Iberoamericana/Vervuert, 2013. 241–265.
Rico, Francisco. *La novela picaresca y el punto de vista*. Barcelona: Seix Barral, 1982.
Ruta, Caterina. "Aspectos iconológicos del Quijote." *Nueva Revista de Filología Hispánica* XXXVIII.2 (1990): 875–886.

Stoll, André. "Sepharads Widerstand. Zur poetischen Produktivität derl jüdischen Kultur Spaniens nach dem Verteribungsedikt." *Sepharden, Morisken, Indianeirinnen und ihresgleichen: die andere Seite der hispanischen Kulturen*. Bielefield: Aisthesis Verlag, 1995.
Tarelli, Francesco. "El Dómine Cabra del Buscón. Lectura de las claves simbólicas." *Nueva Revista de Filología Hispánica* XLVI.1 (1998): 47–66.
Topuzián, Marcelo, ed. *Tras la nación. Conjeturas y controversias sobre las literaturas nacionales y mundiales*. Buenos Aires: Eudeba, 2017.
Vila, Juan Diego. "Aunque claramente sepa que yo soy hijo de un azacán: sueños, verdades calladas y linaje en el delirio caballeresco de don Quijote." *Releyendo el Quijote, cuatrocientos años después*. Ed. Augustin Redondo. Paris: Presses de ls Sorbonne Nouvelle, Centro de Estudios Cervantinos, 2005 c. 51–64.
Vila, Juan Diego. "La faz implícita: la construcción del caballero en el Quijote de 1615." *Peregrinar hacia la dama. El erotismo como programa narrativo del Quijote*. Kassel: Edition Reichenberger, 2008. 44–66.
Vilanova, Antonio. "Cervantes y La lozana andaluza." *Ínsula* 77 (1952).

Further Reading

Amran, Rica. *Judíos y conversos en el reino de Castilla. Propaganda y mensajes políticos, sociales y religiosos (Siglos XIV–XVI)*. Valladolid: Junta de Castilla y León, Consejería de Cultura y Turismo, 2009.
Rodríguez de la Flor, Fernando. *Era Melancólica. Figuras del imaginario barroco*. Barcelona: José J. de Olañeta, Edicions UIB, colección Medio Maravedí, 2007.
Redondo, Augustin, ed. *Les problèmes de l'exclusion en Espagne (XVIè–XVIIè sièles)*. Paris: Publications de la Sorbonne, 1983.
Roth, Cecil. *Histoire des marranes*. Paris: Editions Liana Levi, 1990.
Vivar, Francisco. *Quevedo y su España imaginada*. Madrid: Visor Libros, 2002.
Wachtel, Nathan. *La lógica de las hogueras*. Buenos Aires: Fondo de Cultura Económica de Argentina S.A., 2014.

Joachim Küpper
7 From the Iberian Peninsula into the World: Leone Ebreo's *Dialoghi d'amore* and the 'Occidental' Concept of Love

Abstract: This chapter provides a thorough examination of Leone Ebreo's *Dialoghi d'amore* – maybe conceived in Ladino, but first printed in Italian – while presenting some hypotheses regarding the significance of Abrabanel's ideas on love for a long-standing controversy: what are the origins of the conceptualization of love current in 'Occidental' literature from the Middle Ages onward? Given the date of production, it is evident that Abrabanel's text may not be considered as a 'site of emergence' (M. Foucault) of certain components of such a concept, but rather as the first textual manifestation extant of an attitude towards the syndrome of a union of the souls and physical pleasures that is peculiar to the Jewish tradition, and that might have inspired European vernacular discourses on love from the "Dark Ages" onward.

Key Terms: Leone Ebreo, conceptualization of love, Romantic love, medieval Christian literature, Arabic literature

1 Judah ben Isaac Abrabanel (Leone Ebreo): An Early Modern Jewish Intellectual

Leone Ebreo's *Dialoghi d'amore* are one of those works, whose titles are familiar to everyone working in the broader field, but which are hardly ever studied except by specialists. This first section will therefore provide some relevant information about the author.

Judah ben Isaac Abrabanel, later known as "Leone Ebreo", was born in Lisbon around 1460. He died in Naples, Italy, sometime after 1521.[1] He came from one of the most illustrious families of the early modern European Jewry. His father, his grandfather and his great-grandfather had held important positions as advisors at the Castilian and at the Portuguese courts and were learned people. Judah was instructed by his father in all matters concerning the Jewish tradition, including philosophy (Maimonides). Since he was educated in a period before the watershed date of 1492, it is

---

[1] The exact dates are not available. As to the following overview, see Hiram Peri's and Avraham Melamed's entry in the *Encyclopaedia Judaica* ("Abrabanel, Judah."), as well as Aaron Hughes's entry "Judah Abrabanel" in the online *Stanford Encyclopedia of Philosophy*; see also Pflaum, Heinz [i. e.: Hiram Peri]. *Die Idee der Liebe*.

probable that he learned much about the Islamic tradition as well; and it need not be mentioned that he was familiar with the religious and general culture which was dominant in the countries where he lived. As an adolescent, Judah started studying medicine; he is listed in the register of Lisbon physicians from 1483. In that same year, however, he and his family had to leave Portugal. It cannot be determined to what extent there was an anti-Judaic background to this event. In any case, there seems to have been a political context. Judah's father, Isaac, was accused of having taken part in the high treason for which the Duke of Braganza, Ferdinand II, was executed. Isaac Abrabanel, too, was sentenced to death, but managed to flee with his family. – After their flight, the family first settled down in Spain and succeeded in regaining a relevant position. Judah became the private physician of the *Reyes católicos*. His father supported Queen Isabel in raising funds for the siege of Granada and for Columbus's expedition. In 1492, however, the Abrabanel family rejected the attempts of Isabel and Ferdinand at persuading them to receive baptism. They belonged to those Iberian Jews who preferred losing their social position and their belongings to abandoning their traditions. One may thus assume that Judah Abrabanel had a clear awareness both of the similarities and the differences between the religion of his fathers and the creed that was the basis of social and intellectual life in the countries where he spent his life. – The family moved to the Apennine Peninsula. It was at this time that Judah became known under the name of "Leone" (the Lion).[2] In Naples, where the family first settled down, Judah was welcomed by King Ferdinand I, and after a short while he was given the same position he had held at the Spanish court. But when the French King invaded the city in 1495, violence against the Jews got out of hand during the ensuing turmoil; the Abrabanel family fled to the territories of the Republic of Genoa. There, too, the situation became dangerous in 1501; they returned to Naples, where the ideological climate had become less fierce in the meantime. Although Spain regained the control of the city in 1504, Judah Abrabanel was able to reassume an outstanding position; he became the private physician of the Spanish Viceroy. But in 1510, the Spanish implemented the decrees concerning Jews unwilling to convert, which had been established on the Iberian Peninsula some 20 years before, in the Vice-Kingdom of Naples also. Judah Abrabanel fled to Venice, then returned to Naples once again; and it seems that it was his eminent skill as a physician which earned him, in the year 1520, a personal privilege by the Emperor Charles V exempting him from the special taxes non-Christians had to pay in medieval and early modern Europe.

As already mentioned, Abrabanel was trained as a medical doctor. From a modern perspective, it may seem astonishing that a physician became known as a writer of philosophical treatises. During the age in question, such a constellation was less striking than in later times. It is rooted in the structure of medieval universities. In many schools, the disciplines of the liberal arts curriculum belong-

---

[2] The name alludes to the comparison between the biblical Judah and a young lion (*Genesis* 49:9).

ing to the *quadrivium* were mainly taught by professors of medicine. There is not any exact information about whether or not Abrabanel attended university.[3] Be that as it may, the combination of medicine and philosophy in a learned person was not as exceptional as it appears from a present-day perspective. Maimonides or Rabelais would be further prominent examples.

2 The *Dialoghi d'amore*: A Masterpiece of Renaissance Discourse

The text that has earned its author a place in the Western canon, the *Dialoghi d'amore*, was not published until after his death.[4] In addition to the dialogues composed in Italian, the incunable (Rome 1535) comprises five poems in Hebrew. It is an unresolved controversy amongst specialists whether the printed text is the original or whether the manuscript it was based on was in Ladino; that is, Spanish written in Hebrew characters, and interspersed with Hebrew words and expressions. The second print edition (Venice 1541) bears on its frontispiece the words "[. . .] per Leone medico, di natione hebreo, et dipoi fatto Christiano"/"by Leon, medical doctor, Jew by birth, then converted to Christianity". This description is repeated on the title page of the third edition (1545). However, there are no documents that substantiate the claim that Leone ever converted to Christianity.[5] It is sensible to attribute the alleged conversion to the pre-Counter-Reformation ideological climate that prevailed in the years of the text's publication. Even in a relatively tolerant country like Italy, it would hardly have been possible to print a text whose author's name explicitly referred to another religion without saying that he had finally embraced Christianity.

The text was either not completed, or part of the manuscript was lost. Three of the four dialogues announced at the beginning have been passed down to the present. The last dialogue would have dealt with the effects of love – so far, it has not been discovered.

---

[3] During that period, studies at a medical school were not the only way to become a physician; being trained on the job by an experienced practitioner – as had typically been the case in ancient times – was an accepted alternative method.

[4] For details regarding the complicated history of the text's redaction and publication, see Novoa (2009, 45–66).

[5] The extent to which Abrabanel was committed to his cultural roots becomes evident in one of the poems contained in the first print of the *Dialoghi*, in which he laments the loss of his son. The child had been kidnapped by the Spanish – or, according to other sources, by the Portuguese – King in order to exert pressure upon the father in the matter of conversion. In other sources one may read that Judah Abrabanel himself sent his son to Portugal in order to prevent a kidnapping that was imminent in Spain; in any case, he resisted the pressure and thus accepted that the child was raised in Portugal as a Christian and was not permitted to see his family ever again.

The *Dialoghi* were a widespread text in early modern Europe. There are no less than twelve contemporaneous editions in Italian,[6] three translations into Spanish[7] and two into French; there is one early Latin translation, and a Hebrew translation was written by Joseph Baruch of Urbino. Writers like Baruch Spinoza, Giordano Bruno, Robert Burton and Baldassare Castiglione referred to Abrabanel's text, or to specific arguments found therein. Ronsard and Montaigne criticized the work. In Portugal, the *Dialoghi* were listed on the *Index librorum prohibitorum* from 1581 onwards, in Spain from 1590 onwards. In 1593, they appeared on the Roman *Index*, which was binding for the entire Catholic world. Yet this did not prevent the concept of love as developed in the dialogues from pervading the whole corpus of European literature – narrative, lyric, and dramatic – in the second half of the sixteenth and in the seventeenth century.

The dialogues announced in the title are set in a period situated after Columbus's and Magellan's expeditions,[8] at an unspecified location, on three or four days over a time span of two or three weeks. There are two interlocutors – one male, the other female – regarding whose identity there are no other clues than the fact that both are familiar with the erudite culture of the European fifteenth and sixteenth centuries. Numerous references to "our own Rabbi Moses", that is, Maimonides (Ebreo 2009, 157), as well as other similar expressions suggest that they are meant to be of Jewish belonging. They bear the names "Filone" and "Sofia". Their relation is to be seen as simultaneously literal and allegorical. On the literal level, they represent a human couple: Filone tries to conquer Sofia. On the allegorical level, their relationship embodies the text's main thesis: Sofia, wisdom – that is, the highest level of insight the human intellect can attain in life – is in need of permanent instruction and guidance by love; united, they would then be "Filo-Sofia", philosophy.

Although the *Dialoghi* are the first text of the genre in which a female and a male interlocutor exchange their arguments on an equal level,[9] feminist criticism does not seem to have included them in its canon so far. In fact, Sofia is equal to Filone in terms of intellectual skills, but it is Filone who holds the role of the magister. He expounds theses; she responds by raising critical questions and asking for further clarification; he answers the questions. The ratio of textual segments articulated by Sofia to portions of the text articulated by Filone thus turns out to be about 1:8.

---

[6] The last one was published in 1607.
[7] One of these was written by the famous chronicle author Garcilaso de la Vega, el Inca.
[8] Quotes from the original and translations into English are taken from the following editions: *Dialoghi d'Amore*. Ed. Delfina Giovannozzi. Bari: Laterza, 2008; *Dialogues of Love*. Trs. Cosmos Damian Bacich and Rossella Pescatori. Toronto: University of Toronto Press, 2009; in rare cases, where the translation is particularly infelicitous, I have made minor emendations.
[9] There is, of course, the (fictitious) exchange of letters between Abaelard and Héloïse; but an exchange of letters is, as far as genre is concerned, different from a (fictitious) oral dialogue.

As for the genre, dialogues were nothing novel in the premodern period. Throughout the Middle Ages, such texts mainly revolved around the question of which religion is the "true" one. Ibn Gabirol, one of Abrabanel's main intellectual references, had made an important contribution to this variant (*Fons vitae*, first half of the eleventh century). Roughly three hundred years later, Petrarch had revivified the classical pagan tradition; that is, the form of dialogue that ends without a definitive solution as to the problem of whose positions are right and whose are wrong.[10] From Petrarch's *Secretum* (1347–1353) onward, there is an uninterrupted genre history in early modern times, culminating in well-known texts such as Castiglione's *Cortegiano* (written 1508–1516, first printed in 1528) or Bembo's *Asolani* (first printed in 1505, revised version 1530).

At first sight, the content of the *Dialoghi* also seems conventional. The text's primary source is Plato's *Symposium* and its thesis that love is the driving force behind all human endeavors: beginning at the baser level of love for beautiful bodies, *eros* may lead to an ascent to the highest regions of transcendental knowledge, to the realm of the pure Ideas. In addition, the exposition of almost every argument contains an implicit reference to Aristotle, to the catalogue of virtues and vices as given in the *Nicomachean Ethics*, to the concept of the good life (*eudaimonia*) and to Aristotle's position that a reasonably conceived middle way (*mesotes*) is the guideline to follow in all problems posed by the practical existence of human beings. One may also encounter references to standard questions of medieval scholasticism, for instance to the controversy concerning *intellectus agens*.[11] The author is well informed about the teachings of the Stoics and the Epicureans. He knows Greek mythology in great detail, and is versed in all other questions one may expect in a text written by a highly cultured European from the age in question. His immediate sources from the post-classical tradition are Ibn Gabirol's already mentioned *Fons vitae*, the first important text transmitting the teachings of Neo-Platonism, as well as Ficino's translations of Plato and Plotinus with their harmonizing drive.[12] Abrabanel's attitude towards religion, including his own, seems to be influenced by Maimonides's treatise *Dux neutrum/The Guide for the Perplexed* (written around the year 1200), which nowadays is considered a sort of anticipation of the Enlightenment's stance on faith.

The pivotal question to be discussed will thus be the following: Is there any relevance of the *Dialoghi*, which would render them more than just another example

---

10 – a variant which Augustine had condemned in *Contra academicos* (III) as a vehicle for relativism to make its way into the domain of the "veritas una et eadem semper" (*De libero arbitrio* II, 12, 33).

11 The controversy revolved around the question of whether human reason is capable of accessing abstract levels of knowledge by itself, or whether it needs to be illuminated by a higher, trans-personal intelligence – and whether this illumination may or may not be identified with what Christian theology calls grace.

12 Yet – as I should like to say parenthetically, in order to avoid misunderstanding – Ficino does not integrate Judaism, but only the Christian tradition into the one broad body of universal knowledge that also comprises the writings of the pagan philosophers.

of the many documents exhibiting the fusion of Neo-Platonism and Neo-Aristotelianism that is so typical of the intellectual discourse of the Renaissance? The thematic accents that can be extrapolated from the titles of these dialogues do not seem very promising in this respect. The first dialogue focuses on what love is – considered from a human perspective ("D'amore e desiderio"/"On Love and Desire"). Dialogue two is entitled "De la comunità d'amore" ("On the Universality of Love"), while dialogue three deals with the "Origin of Love" ("De l'origine d'amore"). The latter two are chiefly concerned with theoretical speculations on the structure of the cosmos, as well as with the manifold fables humans tell about the gods, which are supposed to reveal this structure. All these items are standard topics of Renaissance discourse.

In essence, the text's second and third sections ("De la comunità d'amore"; "De l'origine dell'amore") are a scholastic treatise, presented as a dialogue, which expounds the Neo-Platonic assumption that the cosmos is governed by the principle of love. Accordingly, Filone gives prominence to the idea that the goal of love is not possession, but the pleasure of the lover in his union with the idea of the beautiful and the good, embodied in the beloved. The individual steps of the argument are derived from the (Neo-)Aristotelian categorization of the physical and the practical (man-made) world. In addition to this miscellany, the Stoic concept of a correspondence between the macrocosm on the one hand, and man as microcosm on the other, happens to be at play – that is, typical features of the Renaissance worldview, which one would label, since Foucault's *The Order of Things*, as "analogical discourse".

Finally, what Filone conveys to Sofia – and via Sofia to the readers of the text – is a complete compendium of the contemporaneous standard ontology, based on Plato and Plotinus, and detailed by categories derived from Aristotelian logic. In this sense, the text is typical of the genre. It demonstrates the author's perfect mastery of a given field of learning; at the same time, it is apt to serve as a device for readers to acquire the corresponding body of knowledge. In certain cases, Renaissance dialogues may have had a tendency to open up questions, and to leave them unresolved. They thus may be a textual realization of what has become known as the 'plurality' of the Renaissance – as opposed to the Middle Age's supposedly monolithic worldview. Yet such conceptualizations should not lead one to neglect the continuities between the two epochs and their textual sedimentations. In its origin, the Renaissance dialogue is a written transposition of the dialogical mode of instruction between master and student as it was common practice in European universities from the Middle Ages onward. Its modernity mainly consists in its being conceived in the vernacular rather than in Latin. Consequently, it addresses a broader public and thus serves as a powerful instrument of the divulgation of higher knowledge in an age without a generally accessible education system. By way of the printed book, knowledge was able to leave the secluded circles of the universities and spread into society at large. One may even hypothesize that Abrabanel wrote his text particularly for Jewish readers – who were in almost all cases denied access to universities, unless they were ready to convert to Christianity. Above all else, the *Dialogues* are a masterpiece of Renaissance pedagogy.

3 The Conceptualization of Love in Abrabanel

Yet there are passages in the text that exceed the limits of contemporary 'normal' discourse.[13] My argument will foreground one such strand that is remarkable in terms of conceptual innovation. Starting from the points presented by Abrabanel, I will present a (speculative) contribution to a question which regards the broader era: what are the *conceptual* roots of the phenomenon we call 'literature' in the West? The corresponding implications of Abrabanel's dialogues, namely, their first section, are certainly not to be understood as 'original' in the literal acceptation of the term. The *Dialoghi* may rather be the first written documentation of arguments predating the production of this specific text.

It is at the end of the third dialogue, that the term "union" puts an end to all Platonic spiritualization pervading the text's previous sections. Once again, Filone thematizes his unfulfilled physical desire, and Sofia reacts in a most coquettish way (which only further kindles the flames): if she is not prepared to reciprocate, this demonstrates that she is an imperfect object of love; and since love is the search for what is perfect – as Filone has expounded repeatedly – he should not love her. Moreover, since love, according to Filone, originates in divine wisdom, and as all Sofia's wisdom has been imparted to her by him, he should love God, or himself, rather than her. The (rhetorical) controversy is not brought to a definitive resolution, as there is still one major point left, namely, the question of the effects of human love. Since Filone had promised to resolve this question as well, he consents to the deferral; but not without reminding Sofia that he expects her to fulfil her obligations towards him if he agrees to the "pagamento di resto d'obligo" (Ebreo 2008, 367), the "payment of the rest of my debt" (Ebreo 2009, 359). The text as it has been handed down thus closes with an open ending – whatever the reasons for this may be, the work's suggestiveness is certainly heightened by this feature, which Abrabanel, if he crafted this effect voluntarily, may have derived from a reading of Petrarch's *Secretum*.

To recall the configuration at the basis of this strand of the *Dialoghi*, which is apparent right from the start: the relation between Filone and Sofia, understood as figures in the literal sense, is one of courtship. Filone loves Sofia. He tries to persuade her to reciprocate and to surrender to his wishes for carnal union. Sofia does not reject him unconditionally. She seems to harbor sympathies, perhaps even authentic feelings for Filone. Yet when it comes to the question of whether or not the carnal pleasures constitute an integral part of "true love"/"vero amore", she has many questions. The reason behind her reserved attitude seems not to be prudishness or lack of love. Rather, this attitude is implicitly based on the fact that, in those days, the woman,

---

[13] The term is meant in the sense of Thomas S. Kuhn's concept of "normal science" (Kuhn 1962). – My basic hypothesis concerning the unconventional stance Abrabanel takes with respect to questions currently discussed in main-stream Renaissance discourse also applies to his attitude towards biblical hermeneutics (see Küpper 2021).

and not the man, had to bear the possible consequences – such as parenthood – if an affair did not lead to a legal marriage.[14] Accordingly, Sofia reacts to Filone's impetuous demands as articulated right from the beginning not by putting an abrupt end to the situation, but by initiating a discussion on the question of what love is. The first dialogue's central part is governed by Sofia's intention to create a situation, which yields the opportunity for her to convince Filone that her resistance is based on reasonable argument; whereas Filone hopes that he will be able to persuade Sofia that his position is right – namely, that physical union is a necessary, logical part of true love.

The points exchanged by the interlocutors shall not be presented in detail. They consist of topical references to Aristotle's *Nicomachean Ethics* and Plato's conception of *eros*. The main point made by Sofia is that the longing for carnal pleasures comes to an end, according to Aristotle, as soon as the initial need is satisfied. One may anticipate the line of Filone's argument by which he tries to convince her that this will not occur: what he feels for her is not mere physical desire. For him, the beauty of her body is a symptom of the beauty of her soul. So far, this is a standard Platonic argument: the beauty of material objects, including human bodies, triggers in their beholder the desire to experience a more refined beauty free of the corruptibility of the material world – finally, the beauty of the Ideas and the Divine. Love, in the sense of longing for physical beauty, receives a legitimization as a first step within a hierarchy of sensory and mental operations, the final aim of which is cognizance in its purest form. At the end of such a classical Platonic 'ascension' stands the perfect harmony of two de-sexualized souls assisting each other in the attempt to view the Ideas – a process which, more or less, also corresponds to contemporaneous Neo-Platonic theories of love as may be found in Ficino's *De amore* or in Bembo's *Asolani*.

Even so, Abrabanel has *his* dialogue finish with an outright denial of the Platonic conception. There is no attempt at modulating the transition 'backward' from spiritual to physical love; the change is abrupt.[15] After hours of highly sophisticated philosophical dialogue, Filone relapses into an even more unveiled articulation of his demands for sex than at the beginning. What takes place is an outburst of physical desire. He laments his "pena per il mancamento de l'unione: la quale né ragione né volontà né prudenzia possono limitare, né resisterli" (Ebreo 2008, 55), his "suffering" caused by "the incompleteness of the union [. . .], [a suffering] which neither reason nor will nor prudence can limit or resist" (Ebreo 2009, 69). This graphic articulation of erotic desire is preceded by a carefully constructed argument within the framework of Aristotelian and Neo-Platonic theory: true love does not, as Filone concedes, consist in a longing for corporeal union. It is primarily a desire for a union of two souls who feel attracted

---

14 – which in that age was considered a legal affair according to the logic of social status and riches, but not a matter of 'true love'.

15 The abrupt character of this shift translates into form what is articulated at the level of content: all concepts aiming at blurring the distinction between *eros* and *agape* (Platonism, Neo-Platonism, mysticism of any variant) are illusionary constructs neglecting the reality of the *physis*.

to each other on the basis of similarity. This union can be achieved indeed, since the two instances involved are merely spiritual. Yet as the two souls inevitably belong to different bodies, the spiritual union provokes the desire for physical union as well, in order to make it perfect. Corporeally, the lovers will always remain two distinct units. Hence, the desire for accomplishing a total union can never be fulfilled. Yet as the souls of "true" lovers *are* already united, the desire for perfecting the union by realizing it on the corporeal level will always persist. Consequently, physical desire between such lovers will never turn into disinterest provoked by satisfaction,[16] but will be enduring (Ebreo 2008, 50–55; Ebreo 2009, 65–69). – By making use of classical Aristotelian as well as Platonic concepts, Filone succeeds in theoretically substantiating his erotic desire, and is able to counter Sofia's objection that her physical surrender will be the first step towards ending his love.

The argument brought forward by Filone consists in an astute exploitation of the discursive margins opened up by the hybridization of Platonism and Aristotelianism – which, as such, was typical of that age. On Filone's part, there is no problematizing of the premise that the (Platonic) union of the souls is the overall aim to be attained by love amongst humans. Yet Filone then refers to Aristotle's basic objection to his teacher's idealism: when it comes to (living) human beings, the intellect (the rational soul) is inevitably linked to a body, whose needs cannot be ignored. Moreover, if perfection consists in the harmony of the diverse – a (Neo-)Platonic concept once again – the unity of souls indeed calls for the unification of the corresponding bodies, in order to make the harmony perfect.

4 The Origins of the 'Occidental' Concept of Love – An Unresolved Question

The ideas I will link to Abrabanel's theory of love are hypothetical, the argumentation will be symptomatic. I shall extrapolate positions that are not documented from explicitly articulated textual material. Such an approach might appear hazardous. Indeed, it is uncommon in the humanities; and even more so in philology, where textual evidence is mandatory, if one wants to substantiate a claim. If I allow myself to suggest some conceptual lines according to the path just outlined, I do so for three different reasons. Firstly, it is highly improbable that there will ever be a reliable textual basis as would enable an irrefutable answer to the question I will discuss. Secondly, the prevailing, more or less speculative replies to the issue I am referring to seem problematic. Finally, said question is central for the conceptualization of Occidental literature as a whole.

---

16 – or even into disgust after having had too much of it, as is typically the case with equally desirable material goods like wine or food.

The unresolved problem I am referring to is that of the origins of the Occidental concept of love, which is typically characterized by the term 'romantic love'. It is older than the age of Romanticism, and still alive today. Although we hardly ever act according to it, it regulates the thoughts and feelings of Westerners concerning love and sexuality. Since the beginnings of general literacy in the nineteenth century, and the inception of visual mass culture in the twentieth century, it has penetrated all strata of society. It has thus become trivialized, but is more widely spread than ever before in its long history; and it seems that it is gaining ever more popularity in non-Western cultural communities as well (India, China).

The basic features of this concept are exclusiveness (there is only one "true love" in a life); an extremely high intensity (finding the one true love is the most important thing in life); a consequential disregard for all opposing circumstances (social conventions, material interests, moral imperatives); the striving after a union of the souls (whatever that may be; in our times this feature typically translates as a 'deep mutual understanding'); and the experience of an everlasting physical attraction, albeit in a somewhat 'clean' sense.[17] – The beginnings of this concept are to be found in medieval love lyrics, in the poetry of the troubadours, and in courtly romance. With the Petrarchan *Canzoniere* (1327–1369), it becomes the common patrimony of the West. It is subsequently divulged by poetry, by dramatic texts, and later on by novels and motion pictures. Yet where does this conception of love derive from?

Our (not completely uninformed) clichés convey that the Occident has been erected on two pillars: classical pagan culture and Christianity. It is probably not necessary to detail the extent to which the current conception of love is opposed to the basic beliefs of the religion dominant in the West. From a Christian standpoint, the function of love between the sexes is procreation. Corporeal pleasures deriving from physical love are sinful, since they divert from the only right aim in life, the love of God. To a certain extent, the two other monotheistic traditions share this view. Especially in case love and desire focus on one specific object, there is the looming menace of idolatry. Within Christianity however, this position is amplified in a way that is unfamiliar to both Judaism and Islam. On the basis of its own premises, Christian theology is forced to demonize physical desire. If Jesus was indeed resurrected physically, and through his own power, he cannot have been a prophet only – one must assume that he was, or rather is, (a) God.[18] Such an unheard-of act, God's self-sacrifice in order to redeem the world, only makes sense if one assumes that it is consistently impossible for humans

---

17 Romantic love does not allow for all the 'unorthodox' practises (sexual fetishism, sadism, masochism, etc.) popularized in our age by the adult film industry.

18 The logical chain, which may already be found in the Pauline epistles, was initially considered so uncommon and bold that it took approximately three centuries of fierce discussions – and, ultimately, the personal intervention of Constantine, the one who promoted the new religion to an exclusive position in his empire – to enforce this dogma. It was only at the Nicene Council (325 CE) that Arianism – the belief that Jesus was not more than an exceptional human – was definitively anathematized.

to redeem themselves. Christianity's central dogma requires casting all humans as sinners. The first explicit articulation of this new anthropology[19] is to be found in Paul's *Letter to the Romans*. Yet not all humans are murderers or thieves. There might even be some who never lie. The emerging Christian theology thus had to look for a behavioral pattern that would allow it to reasonably postulate that all human beings – without any exception[20] – are marred by sin. The solution devised by Paul was elaborated by Augustine.[21] Sexuality – conceived as the revolt of the body against the control exerted by reason, that is, the component of humans that establishes their likeness to God ("similitudo") – is by no means the gravest sin. Yet its ubiquity, its presence even while humans are sleeping, testifies to the assumption that all humans are sinners, hence in need of redemption. – To put it in a more concise way: the discourse on love in Occidental literature does not derive from a Christian background, it is, rather, conceptually situated in a clear-cut opposition to this background.

One might object that, the doctrinal obstacles notwithstanding, there is a broad strand of literary texts dealing with something close to what was later called 'romantic love' as early as the eleventh century. Still, it would be an anachronism to assume that the thematization of love was as unproblematic during that age as it has become in posterior times; and it would be an even greater misconception to believe that the privilege literary discourses gained in modernity proper – namely, to articulate what is not tolerated in pragmatic discourses – applies to the period in question.[22] In literary texts from the High Middle Ages onward, one does encounter the thematization of erotic love, including its praise as supreme bliss.[23] Yet in reaction, there is the consistent

---

19 The difference with regard to classical (pagan) moral philosophy lies in the latter's – never problematized – assumption that the mind of an educated man is able to restrain the bodily drives by means of its own insight.
20 In fact, there are (extremely restricted) exceptions. Jesus is free of sin; according to traditional, that is, Catholic theology; this applies also to the *theotokos*, Mary, who is consequently taken to have been conceived in an 'immaculate' way.
21 See *Romans*, *1 Corinthians*, and *De civitate Dei* (esp. XIV).
22 As to the endeavors made by Renaissance poets and theoreticians to bring about the first elements of what would become, more than four centuries later, the concept of literary autonomy, see my "Zu einigen Aspekten der Dichtungstheorie in der Frührenaissance." (2006).
23 Michel Foucault's ingenious idea to conceptualize the West's obsession with sex as a consequence of Christianity's attempts to systematically repress sexuality (*La volonté de savoir*. 1976 = vol. I of *Histoire de la sexualité*) may, indeed, yield a convincing explanation for the fact that 'talking about sex' is common in modern Occidental everyday culture to an extent which is assessed as shocking by people from cultural backgrounds that are, in principle, much more welcoming towards erotic practices than the West (India, China, Japan, etc.). With regard to literary texts, there are certain problems concerning periodization. Auricular confession as a systematic practice – by which Western people 'learned', according to Foucault, to thematize those parts of their daily lives whose verbalization is prohibited in other cultures by a strict taboo – set in, step by step, after the year 1215 only. The highly illuminating textual evidence produced by Foucault, the detailed catalogues of possible sexual transgressions figuring in the manuals which helped priests to conduct the weekly interviews with believers, date

tendency to neutralize this concept by converting it into mysticism. The evolution of the figure of Beatrice – from Dante's *stil novo*-like poems in the *Vita Nova*, where she is presented as an object of desire, but also already as a possible guide to spiritual salvation, to her total conversion into a mediator of divine revelation in the *Commedia* – is representative of the fate of the concept of love-as-passion under the reign of Christian orthodoxy. One could trace a comparable line of evolution with regard to Arthurian romance. Even Petrarch made concessions to such a conceptualization, resulting in a 'sublation' of earthly into spiritual love.[24]

At least until the middle of the nineteenth century,[25] Occidental literary history thus manifests an axiological paradox. On the one hand, there is the continuous, explicit articulation of erotic desire and even actual sexual practices in literary texts of all genres; on the other, there are the symptoms of attempts to repress these tendencies. At times, this was done by means of censorship, that is, by taking measures with a view to restricting the circulation of the texts in question. At other times, it was done by indicating to poets and writers how to manage the problem within the limits of the acceptable, namely via an 'absorption' of erotic love by mystic or Platonic concepts. These attempts notwithstanding, the thematization of what is hardly acceptable from the dominant religion's standpoint has become, by the latest from the middle of the fourteenth century onward, the centerpiece of all of Occidental literary texts – which raises the question of how to explain the emergence and persistent re-emergence of the corresponding discursive configuration.[26]

---

from the period of the Counter-Reformation; that is, from an age during which Catholicism's attention to questions of sexual practices had increased dramatically, for reasons which derived from the internal dissent between the traditional and the Reformed Churches regarding sexuality and grace.

24 – which I tend to consider impregnated with superficiality laid bare, and thus as an ingenious device to convey the contrary: the speaker's voluntary or involuntary persistence in erotic love (see my article quoted in n. 50).

25 Behavioral norms have changed dramatically since the cultural revolution of 1968 – so much so that it is frequently forgotten what Western culture's recent past looked like in this respect. Need I remind readers that Flaubert had to stand trial for having written *Madame Bovary* (1857)? It is undecidable whether the reason for his acquittal is to be sought in the support he is said to have had on the part of the Imperial court, or in the barrister's ruse to give the portrait of Emma's desires for romantic love a moralizing touch by hinting at the fact that it led to a premature death. One could adduce a plethora of famous literary texts in order to demonstrate that well into the second part of the nineteenth century, physical love, if not under wedlock, was considered a highly problematic issue in Christian cultures (*La dame aux camélias* (1848); *Effi Briest* (1896); *Anna Karenina* (1877), etc.). Yet, as I should like to say in anticipation of the further course of my argument, its thematization and its appealing presentation was a (literary) fact, in contrast to the situation in other cultural communities.

26 Once again, I emphasize that I am dealing with concepts and their discursification – not with 'drives' in a naturalistic sense. The difference will become fully transparent in the following paragraphs, where I will briefly discuss the phenomenon's discursification within other cultural communities, whose members are, on the level of (sexual) drives, of course no different from Westerners.

Might the second 'pillar' mentioned above – that is, the textual corpus from pagan antiquity – be considered a possible source for the concept of romantic love as presented in Occidental literary texts from the High Middle Ages onward? The Greeks and Romans of the classical age did not have anything that might compare to the dogma of original sin. Within their various religious and ethical systems, they did not need such a concept. All texts and material artifacts such as amphoras, frescoes and friezes that remain extant seem to demonstrate that they enjoyed the pleasures of the body in quite an uninhibited way.

The classical conception of love differs, however, dramatically from 'romantic love' as detailed above.[27] I shall limit my cursory remarks to a prominent example for which I would claim a representative status. The written tradition of love lyrics begins with Sappho. There is only one poem that has been preserved in its entirety (fragment 1 in the edition by Lobel/Page). It consists of a poeticized imploration, addressed to *Athanat' Aphrodita*, immortal Aphrodite, the goddess of love, by the lyrical I who refers to herself as "Sappho". The poetess, as can be inferred from her imploration, has fallen in love,[28] but there is no reciprocation – so far, this is quite a conventional setting; love poems are always and in all cultures primarily texts about unfulfilled love;[29] if there is fulfilment, there is not much reason for sublimation by means of poeticization. Sappho asks the goddess to come to her assistance on her chariot drawn by holy birds; and then one may read words that mark a basic cultural difference, which all those who try to refute Erich Auerbach's theses on the intellectual history of the West[30] will not be able to annihilate. The poetess says (addressing the

---

27 As I state on various occasions, all conceptual delimitations I am dealing with are, of course, to a certain extent constructs (which, the way I see it, should nonetheless have a sound *fundamentum in re*). In the very early phase of (documented) Western love lyric – Iberian, Occitan or Provençal – there are indeed vestiges of the classical conceptualization of love, but vestiges that disappear rapidly in the course of the genre's further evolution. As I shall stress in the course of the argument presented here, it seems to be the reception of Platonism – and its 'fusion' with explicit monotheism – that is responsible for the evaporation of the classical conceptualization of love as essentially promiscuous, and for the emergence of the concept of the one and only object of love. Basic Platonic concepts were well-known in the West, (well) before the period of systematic translations of the original works.
28 It is irrelevant for the problem at stake that the beloved seems to be a female person.
29 This would be my basic objection to the much-quoted position of Denis de Rougemont (*L'amour et l'Occident*, 1939). De Rougemont starts his argument by referring to the narrative of Tristan and Iseult, which does end with the death of both lovers. He connects this motif to the (preceding) troubadour lyrics, which are mainly about unfulfilled love, but where death caused by love typically does not occur, for most evident reasons – within lyrical poetry, in most cases bound to a first-person discourse, there would be no one able to present a fatal outcome.
30 With this possibly somewhat cryptic remark, I resume a longstanding controversy, documented in a plethora of my publications, with my esteemed colleagues from Classics departments worldwide. The latter scholars share, with almost no exception, the attitude of regarding the West as being in direct continuation of the classical pagan age. As to Auerbach's objection to such conceptualizing, see *Mimesis: The Representation of Reality in Western Literature* (2013).

goddess): "You [Aphrodite], O blessed one[,] [...] ask the reason for my troubles and why *again* I invoke you." Aphrodite then replies (this is the wish of the poetess; or rather, what she asks for[31]): "Whom am I *this time* persuading to take you back into her heart? Who *now* has wronged you, Sappho?" (vv. 13–20).[32] – With the occurrence of the adverb δηὖτε ("again") three times within a passage of no more than four lines, the poem foregrounds the presentation of the situation as one that is not unique, but rather a repetition of preceding and analogous situations. The text's scheme of reference – ritual discourse, whose basic structure is repetition – perfectly matches the situation stylized in the poem. – To put it in abstract terms: in pagan antiquity,[33] there is no discursive link[34] between passionate love and exclusiveness. The pattern first to be found in Sappho is omnipresent in archaic Greek poetry. It is echoed by the love lyrics of Roman pagan antiquity and its frivolities,[35] and it governs the theorizations on the part of philosophers. Love is a variant of *philia* (friendship) in a very broad sense. There are many love objects of different profile in a person's life. Above all, love is just one component amongst others, when it comes to the question of what happiness (*eudaimonia*) consists in.[36]

---

[31] This important nuance is astonishingly neglected in much of the scholarly literature. It is of primary importance insofar as it lays bare that the entire situation depicted in the poem is not to be understood as a literary transposition of a 'real' encounter, but rather as a stylization of the way in which the lyrical I conceives of what the essence of (her) love is; in short: the poem presents a conceptualization of love.

[32] σὺ δ', ὦ μάκαιρα, / μειδιαίσαισ' ἀθανάτωι προσώπωι / ἤρε' ὄττι δηὖτε πέπονθα κὤττι / δηὖτε κάλημμι / κὤττι μοι μάλιστα θέλω γένεσθαι / μαινόλαι θύμωι τίνα δηὖτε πείθω/ μαισ' ἄγην ἐς σὰν φιλότατα; τίς σ', ὦ / [Ψά]πφ', ἀδικήει [...]; as to my reading, see also Mace (1993).

[33] The article by Mace quoted in the preceding note shows that the link between the adverb δηὖτε and the depiction of erotic desire may be observed in further poems by Sappho, in poems by Alcman, Ibycus, and above all by Anacreon. David A. Campbell describes the adverb as "almost a catchword of Greek love poetry" (Campbell 1983, 9).

[34] I am not referring to facts and practices. I am talking about normative modelling structures.

[35] The love elegy as represented by poems of Tibullus, Propertius, Catullus and Ovid is considered to be one of the rare original creations of Latin/Roman literature. It does differ from the tradition established by Sappho. Without going into the details, it should be evident that it is hardly conceivable to consider it to be the basis of the Occidental concept of romantic love. The occasional presence of the motif of *foedus aeternum* notwithstanding, the discrepancies with regard to medieval and post-medieval Western love lyrics are enormous. The reference scheme of the Roman love elegy is not tragedy, but comedy. The (male) lover is, at least in tendency, a ridiculous person, while the (female) beloved typically has further lovers, or is outright venal. The relationship is frequently arranged by panderers. There is jealousy, infidelity, the constant presence of rivals, and even the motif of venereal disease. Succinctly put: although the tone differs from Greek archaic lyric, the underlying concept of promiscuity as the 'regular' pattern of the relation between the sexes is preserved.

[36] Conceptualizations of any phenomena are always and by necessity constructs. It would be nonsensical to postulate that there are absolutely no continuities between 'classical' and 'Occidental' love. It is a matter of dominant features. – Scholars who contest the above views typically adduce two counterexamples: the story of Phaedra, and the Androgyne myth as expounded in Plato's *Symposium*.

Without being too audacious, one may hypothesize that the feature of exclusiveness to be observed in the majority of post-classical love lyrics results from the blending of a spiritualization of physical love – as developed in Plato's *Symposium* – with explicit monotheism.[37] If what is to be seen in the beloved more intensely than in any other life form is no longer the multitude of the Ideas, but the one and only God as the site of supreme truth and beauty, it follows, logically speaking, that this privileged person should be as unique as the one to whom she is to direct the beholder's vision. Under monotheistic conditions, the legitimization of physical love by way of a spiritualizing maneuver tends to reproduce the uniqueness of the relation between God and believer in the relation between beloved and lover. – If considered as a partial structure, such a conceptualization – which distinguishes the Western modelling of love from the Greek and Roman patterns – is in itself unrestrictedly acceptable from a Christian perspective. This configuration may indeed be found in one such concept, which is even typically

---

It is true that Phaedra passionately loves Hippolytus. Yet in Euripides, this love is caused by a spell cast on Phaedra by Aphrodite – who happens to be furious, because Hippolytus has rejected her, or rather the idea of carnal love as such. Phaedra, in particular her love, is an instrument devised by the goddess in order to bring about Hippolytus' downfall. In Seneca, the mythical horizon, though still present, begins to recede, a line then to be continued by Racine: Hippolytus is not just some good-looking young man. He is the son of Theseus, Phaedra's husband. When Phaedra beholds Hippolytus, she sees, as she explicitly says, in his face and his body the face and the body of Theseus, whom she loved when he and she were young. Yet the young Theseus first favoured Phaedra's sister Ariadne; and it was only after having forsaken her – and having engaged in several further adventures – that he proposed to Phaedra. When the action of the dramatic texts I am referring to takes place, Theseus is no longer young – and neither is Phaedra. Is it reasonable to assume that there are no traces of a concept like romantic love in pagan antiquity, with the exception of one example, namely Phaedra? Or should one not rather assume that the Phaedra myth is either a story of the terrible revenge gods take on humans rejecting the *nomoi* established by them (Hippolytus); or the tragedy of a human being who is no longer young and who tries to repress by all means the realization that youth, physical attractiveness and splendor are gone forever (Phaedra)? – Regarding the Androgyne myth – which has been interpreted in the reception of Plato's writings since the Renaissance as a story that stylizes exclusiveness as the most important feature of true love – I should like to point out one particular element, which is linked to the (original) contextualization and its implications on the level of meaning. It is Aristophanes, the author of comedies, who narrates the story of the first human beings, who have some kind of spherical/globular bodies, with two heads, four hands and four feet. Apollo divides these bodies into two parts at Zeus's command, which is issued out of anger over the pride and arrogance of the Androgynes. Aristophanes has difficulties to control his hiccups when he starts delivering his speech – which means he ate and drank too much; and he laughs before he begins to speak. In other words: the fable is not to be taken seriously, but provides a comic or ludic aetiology for what is an uncontested fact of (as I should say) the sentimental life of all human beings. Under the pretext of looking for the one 'half' who would be our only and ideal partner, we constantly keep looking. The farcical story as narrated in Plato does not stylize a concept of exclusive love – hardly imaginable for Plato and his age; it gives a somewhat grotesque explanation for what love is, and legitimately so, from a classical pagan standpoint: a very promiscuous matter.

37 – under which label I also comprise 'pagan' variants of explicit monotheism, such as Neo-Platonism and its concept of *to hen*.

and specifically Christian: namely in the idea of marriage as an indissoluble bond, which echoes, as we may read in Paul, the bond between Christ and the Church (*Ephesians* V, 33). What is missing – in order to complete this partial structure, and produce the concept of romantic love – is precisely the one ingredient unacceptable from a Christian perspective: the element of legitimate erotic desire.

5 The Contribution of Jewish Thought to the Emergence of Romantic Love – An Alternative to the Assumption of an 'Arabic Connection'

The configuration devised in Abrabanel's text adds this missing element of intense physical desire and its fulfilment to the spiritualizing, monotheistically inspired concept. What enabled the author to present this feature as legitimate is all too evident to require being detailed: in Judaism, there is no dogma of God's self-sacrifice; consequently, there is no need to assume that all humans are sinners by necessity. Accordingly, there is no need to identify a symptom of this common sinfulness, and thus no reason to reprimand sexuality. There are, of course, conventional taboos; traditional Judaism is not a domain of uninhibited hedonism. Still, there is no generalized incrimination of physical pleasure as something to be avoided, or submitted to rigorous discipline.

Abrabanel certainly did not 'invent' – by way of writing his text – the concept of romantic love. Such an assumption would be nonsensical, since the concept had already existed for several centuries, when the author conceived his text.[38] Put in Foucauldian terms, I suggest considering the *Dialoghi* (the actual *énonciation*) as a manifestation of an *énoncé* – that is, as the encoding of a discursive pattern which predates the actual text.[39] My suggestion is to discuss the hypothesis that Occidental love literature – and what would remain of literature if we were to eliminate all the works dealing with love? – owes its origins neither to the dominant religion, nor to the classical heritage, but to a fusion of the spiritualizing tendencies of Platonism, the 'monistic' tendencies of monotheism, and a third conceptual component which is

---

[38] The period in which Abrabanel's text was produced is characterized by a much more liberal attitude towards the thematization of physical pleasures in literary texts than previous, and certain subsequent, periods. One may think of the 'Renaissance' of the pastoral, beginning with Sannazaro's *Arcadia* (1504). One might also think of the renewed reception of the love lyrics by Roman poets on the part of the French *Pléiade* poets. To put it succinctly: the contextual conditions were favorable to a divulgation of ideas which, as such, might have existed previously, but could hardly have been explicitly articulated outside of Abrabanel's own community during those times.

[39] For Foucault's elucidating differentiation of *énonciation* and *énoncé*, see *L'archéologie du savoir*. Paris: Gallimard, 1969, esp. 98–138.

free from Christianity's reprimanding of bodily pleasures, as well as from the Platonic and Neo-Platonic debasement of all beauty affected by materiality.

I have avoided labeling this third component 'Judaism', for the simple reason that I should first like to make some remarks on the competing alternative that has had its propagators starting with Jean-Charles-Léonard Simonde de Sismondi,[40] who is followed in the twentieth century by Ramón Menéndez Pidal (1938), and, in more recent times, by scholars such as María Rosa Menocal.[41] There is a widespread thesis that the emergence of literary texts praising physical love in the Christian Occident is due to Islamic influences.

The origins of this assumption are to be found in the age of Romanticism and its obsession with detecting 'roots'. In accordance with the biblical tradition – which regained some influence after the end of the Enlightenment – but also in reaction to the findings initiated by Napoleon's expedition to Egypt, these roots were identified as being 'oriental'. In Romantic literature, there are innumerable accounts of real or fictional oriental journeys, driven by the nostalgia to find what had been lost in the process of rationalization and the concomitant 'disenchantment' of the world. Romantic writers conceived of the Orient as consisting of three components: the Holy Land of biblical times; the Egypt of the pharaonic age; and, finally, the contemporary Orient characterized by a religion, Islam, which appeared to many enlightened Europeans to be quite as archaic as the cult of ancient Israel and the mysteries of classical Egypt. Since the latter two existed only in the form of ruins and remains, fantasies regarding 'life' were projected upon the contemporaneous Muslim Orient. As may be extrapolated from the texts, but as is also evident from famous paintings of that age, oriental life became, as it were, emblematized by the concept of the 'harem' and was thus associated with the (male) fantasy of a place of unrestricted carnal pleasures.

---

40 *De la littérature du Midi de L'Europe* (1813). – For a detailed account of the history of research, going back to the first stages of the 'Arabic' theory in early modern times, see Menocal, María Rosa. *The Arabic Role in Medieval Literary History: A Forgotten Heritage*. Philadelphia, PA: University of Pennsylvania Press, 1987. 79–88.

41 *The Arabic Role in Medieval Literary History*. – It might serve as indirect evidence of the fragile textual basis on which Menocal establishes her argument that she has frequent recourse to quite anecdotal material when it comes to the question of how the Muslim cultural influence might have spread into territories where there was no actual Muslim presence. In addition to some rather hazardous speculations concerning the private life of Eleanor of Aquitaine, Menocal presents the first entrance of the tradition of Arabic love poetry into the region north of the Pyrenees as follows (see 27–30): In the year 1064, 1,000 Muslim girls allegedly became enslaved by Guillaume de Montreuil, who took them to his castle in the Provence. In exile, these girls, moved by nostalgia, continued what they had done at home, that is, they permanently sang songs according to the Arabic tradition of love poetry. These songs pleased the 'Christian' noblemen and -women to the extent that they immediately started emulating them. – With regard to non-Hispanists amongst my readers, I should like to add that I am quoting only the most important titles from a fund of articles and books that has acquired enormous dimensions over the years. Still, the point is not even one of quantity. Rather, it is a matter of the establishment of the 'Arabic connection' thesis as a sort of *doxa* which hardly anyone thinks of problematizing.

It was already Gérard de Nerval – by conceiving the first *Voyage en Orient* (1851) deeply impregnated with irony – who laid bare these speculations as being in diametrical opposition to what could actually be observed in the Muslim world: interaction between the sexes is restricted to marriage. The latter is a social duty aiming at procreation. Any verbalization of physical desire is subject to a strict taboo.[42]

Nerval remained an isolated figure, however. For reasons of its appeal to more or less conscious desires, the cliché of the 'sensuous Orient' continued to have resonance; and it was adopted by modern literary studies – a discipline that owes its emergence to the same intellectual configuration as Orientalism, namely Romanticism:[43] Love – in the sense of the term as it may be extrapolated from the Western literary patrimony – was assumed to have its 'roots' in the Islamic textual tradition. In our times, the corresponding claim comes with all the attractions conferred upon it by the imperatives of political correctness. It praises the 'subaltern' of the modern world – who were and continue to be 'shamelessly oppressed' by the ruling powers – as the ones who have been producing the 'really valuable' things all along.[44]

The thesis is not implausible in itself. Within Islam, there is no narrative of God's self-sacrifice, hence no assumption of general sinfulness and no systematic reprimanding of sexual pleasures.[45] The problem to be discussed consists in the fact that the potentialities opened up by the general configuration are made use of by the actual textual production in a way which matches the phenomena observable in medieval Western love literature obliquely at best – if at all.

Within the new religious context, establishing its discursive control from the early seventh century onward, certain literary traditions dating from pre-Islamic times and

---

[42] Regarding this point, see Küpper (2017b).

[43] See Gumbrecht (1986/7). See also my more extensive elaboration on the point in *The Cultural Net: Early Modern Drama as a Paradigm*. (Küpper 2018a), Part III.

[44] The politicized background of her 'reconstruction' of medieval literary history is frankly articulated by Menocal (1987, 6–16, and passim). The argumentation is remarkable indeed: because the traditional view of a 'homogeneous' Western culture, based on the classical heritage and the Christian tradition, is problematic (a point with respect to which I agree), any alternative view is to be credited with truth, even without further proof. – There is an additional factor which may explain the largely unquestioned adoption of the above thesis by almost all Western medievalists: there is no denying that the medieval Latin West is indebted to the 'Arabic connection' as regards the transmission of the textual basis of its standard philosophy, the works of Aristotle. In addition to the Stagirite's writings, a considerable textual corpus thematizing more scientific issues (medicine, astrology, mathematics) migrated from the Arabic territories first to Spain (and partly to Italy), and then to places like Paris, Oxford and Cambridge – becoming a relevant component of epistemic knowledge without the reception of which the present-day Occident would most probably not look the way it does. – One may find a quite adequate description of the scenario in Menocal, who takes the evidence of influence in the field of learning as applying also to literary texts – for which, by contrast, there is hardly any such evidence (1987, 54–61 and 137–154).

[45] Of course, there are various taboos established by the patriarchal tradition. As already stated, this feature applies to traditional Judaism, as well. It does not constitute a differential trait.

originating from a Bedouin background, which gave expression to erotic love, were at first preserved,[46] and even continued for a limited time, producing the 'new' genre of *gazal*. In the beginning, the dominant strand of this genre thematizes a conceptualization of love which may be paralleled to what is familiar from the love poetry by the great Roman authors. The accent is on sensuality. There is no idealizing of exclusiveness. The concept of a 'spiritual union' between two lovers, understood as human beings, is not to be found. Yet, as early as in the ninth century, the erotic elements recede, and give way to a formulaic solidification – frequently accompanied by a religiously oriented ambiguity.[47] It is not very astonishing to see that this evolution produced, as its counterpart, texts whose main characteristic is sexual explicitness to the point of obscenity.[48]

In the more serious Arabic lyrics[49] of Islamic times, the eroticism tends to be more and more absorbed by religious mysticism.[50] On the level of motif, this move

---

[46] There seems to be a consensus amongst Arabists that pre-Islamic Arabic poetry did not produce any poems which treated love as their central topic. References to erotic elements are contained within poems whose general tenor is either epideictic or lampooning. Carnal love, practiced with whomsoever, is presented as one of many pleasures the male person concerned is said to have experienced (or is said to have never had the chance to experience). Poems making love the center of attention seem to emerge only in Islamic times.

[47] As almost all publications by professional Arabists, Susanne Enderwitz's *Liebe als Beruf: Al-Abbas Ibn Al-Ahnaf und das Gazal*. Beirut and Stuttgart: Steiner, 1995, does not refrain from incidentally presenting the Arabic poetry of the time as an inspiration for 'Western' love literature from the eleventh century onward. Even so, Enderwitz consistently relativizes her corresponding assessments, and, in the final analysis, leaves the question unresolved. The general characterization of Arabic poetry from the seventh and eighth centuries as given in the book is useful, to a certain extent.

[48] This 'carnivalesque' strand, sometimes apostrophized as 'higazic' gazal or as 'kufic' gazal, is represented e.g. by the works of Abu Nuwas (eighth century); see Bauer (1998). – Bauer, who is an Arabist, shares his discipline's high esteem for Arabic love poetry; but he also stresses in a most transparent, even polemical way that the widespread equalizations of Arabic and Western love poetry from the Middle Ages are misguided (see in particular 68–73).

[49] Arabists make use of the term 'udritic' gazal for this form of love poetry.

[50] There is religious mysticism also in the Christian West, in particular bridal mysticism, which is based on the parallel established by Paul between husband and wife on the one hand, and Christ and the Church on the other (*Ephesians* V, esp. 32). Moreover, there is Marianism, which does not exist in the Islamic tradition, at least not in a way that would be worth mentioning. From the last poem of Petrarch's *Canzoniere*, the "canzone alla Vergine", one may gather how close to each other the rhetorical and stylistic patterns of (Western) love lyric and Marianic mysticism are (see my "Palinodie und Polysemie in der Mariencanzone." (Küpper 2002); as to the general question of the close links, on the level of images and rhetoricization, between the concept of *passio* in a Christian understanding on the one hand and in a secular acceptation on the other, see Auerbach (1941)). In other words: it is possible to hypothesize that secular love lyric is an 'illegitimate' derivative of religious poetry. If one follows this line of argument, there is no need for the construct of an Islamic, or any other exogenous inspiration. Starting as early as in the first century CE, there is a rich tradition of mystical literature within Christianity, which always includes the blurring of the boundaries between *agape* and *eros*. – I would like to briefly explain why I am less inclined to consider this hypothesis than the one detailed

frequently translates as a link between passionate love (*'ishq*) and the physical death of both lovers, combined with vaguely circumscribed ideas of being united 'in death'; or, occasionally, in the world beyond, 'in Allah'.[51]

The background of this 'sublative' tendency – which might at first seem to be parallel to the abovementioned constellation within Western frameworks – is doctrinal, but in a way that differs from the Christian scenario. Not only does Arabic poetry[52] make use of the language of the *Quran*, seen as a linguistic code; it also imitates its mode of articulation, which is characterized by the absence of a comprehensive narrative continuity.[53] The holy text of the Muslim religion consists in large part of sections of a limited number of lines constituting sense units of their own. To an extent that is much

---

above: the eroticism of mystical literature, as shocking as it may be at times, is in any case a 'veiled' eroticism. There is never any – explicit – thematization of physical desire. As modern readers, we have a tendency to immediately decode an angel's spear of fire 'transverberating' a female body as a phallic symbol and to thus read the scene as an erotic fantasy of the mystic (in this case: of Teresa of Ávila). Yet if one indulges in such an approach, there is no need to discuss how to explain the emergence of eroticism in literary texts at all, since such is their (hidden) essence anyway, according to Freud at least (see "The Relation of the Poet to Day-Dreaming." 1998, 300–304). This being said, the question concerning the actual texts remains unresolved: how come there is, from a certain period onward, an – explicit – thematization of topics which were acceptable only in a (very) hidden way within the 'autochthonous' (meaning: Christian) discursive tradition? – With a primary focus on Bernard of Clairvaux, Étienne Gilson has demonstrated in an exemplary fashion why it is problematic to conceive of the Occidental discourse on love present in literary texts from the troubadours onward as being influenced by the mystical tradition: the discursive differences are all too important. Early Western love lyric, especially the seminal Occitan or Provençal corpus, is concise and transparent, while mystic discourse is allusive and opaque (Gilson 1934).

51 See Gruendler 2015.

52 There is a problem of terminology involved here that needs to be addressed. Whenever the term 'poetry' is made use of in manuals of Arabic literary texts, or in scholarly publications on these texts, it has to be understood as an opposite term to 'prose', the criterion being versification. References to the 'huge tradition of Arabic poetry' to be found on almost every page of the specialized scholarly literature are to be decoded as apostrophizing to an overwhelming extent texts which would rather be labeled 'pragmatic' from a Western perspective (encyclopedic texts; scientific texts; panegyric texts; letters; petitions, etc.). Such a (merely) rhetorical definition of poetry is at odds with the concept that seems to first emerge in Aristotle's *Poetics* and has become so familiar within intra-Western discussions that we do not even realize anymore to what extent it is specific. The Stagirite gives expression to the view that versification is not a sufficient criterion for what he calls *poiesis* in his tract (which may best be translated as 'literature'); the natural philosopher Empedocles may not be called a poet, even if he presented the results of his 'research' in verse (Ch. 1, 1447b 15–23). – If one endeavors to scrutinize what is signified by the ubiquitous term of 'the huge tradition of Arabic poetry' according to the two criteria, 1) literary (vs. pragmatic) and, 2) thematic focus on erotic love (vs. various other foci), one would perhaps be astonished to see on how narrow a textual basis the widely accepted assumption of an Arabic origin of Western love lyric rests.

53 The enormous impact of the *Quran* on Arabic literature in Islamic times becomes evident, once again, if one takes into consideration that pre-Islamic Arabic literature does contain important descriptive elements.

greater than in 'Western' texts – with the exception of the mystical tradition – the mode of articulation thus tends to be allusive and suggestive. This profile is corroborated by the high frequency of metaphorical expressions, which are laid bare by breaches of context. These two mutually reinforcing features account for the extremely broad interpretability of the *Quran*.

Secular texts written in imitation of this mode of articulation share the latter characteristic. Their semantic profile is characterized by ambiguity and instability in a way that transcends the phenomena we are referring to when applying said categories to 'Western' literary texts. Whether the "cup" one reads of in most of Hafez's poems[54] contains wine; or whether the substance the speaker is keen to drink from it is sensual pleasure; or whether it is divine knowledge; whether the "beloved" apostrophized in many poems is a human being, the sun, the soul (that is, the speaker's own), or the intellect in a Neo-Platonic understanding of the term;[55] whether "kissing" and "embracing" is meant physically or as a metaphor for spiritual union – this remains consistently undecidable.[56]

This feature is supported by an element that stands in direct contradiction to one of the main characteristics of 'romantic love' as expounded above: in almost all cases the beloved is not portrayed with any individuality. The situations depicted in the poems remain abstract. They are not about meeting one specific woman in one specific place on one specific day,[57] but about an encounter with someone – human or super-human – whose beauty triggers in the beholder or lover an impetus in the literal sense, the direction of which remains without specification. It may be that the ultimate goal is physical union with the one who conveys the beauty of the cosmos to the beholder. Yet it may just as well be that the goal is union with the source from which all earthly beauty originates or emanates. The ambiguities resulting from such

---

54 Hafez wrote his poems mainly in Farsi, with some interspersed formulations in Arabic; but his poetry was systematically modeled on the classical Arabic gazal. Accordingly, what I am arguing above also holds true for the poems by Abu Nuwas (eighth century).

55 Neo-Platonism had made its way into Iranian intellectual and poetic discourse starting in the sixth century, after Emperor Justinian had deprived the academy – where 'pagan' philosophy was taught – of its financial basis. The texts were well known in translation from the eighth century onward.

56 Such undecidability with regard to elements which could possibly be read as referring to (earthly) love may even have been implemented by the authors, in order to favor a reading along mystical patterns, hence to protect the texts from attacks by religious officials. Regardless of this externally conditioned factor, it is extremely difficult to render mystical texts of any provenience in translation – particularly because their referential dimension is multifaceted, vague or allusive to the point that the 'exact meaning' must always remain opaque. This said, a mere glance at the many translations of Hafez's works (or of parts of them) may suffice to gain an impression of the poems' mode of articulation, and to appreciate the enormous distance that separates them from Western-style love poetry (see e.g. the most recent English translation by H. Wilberforce Clarke, London: Octagon Press, 1974; or the well-known nineteenth-century German translation by Friedrich Rückert [reprint Zürich: Manesse, 1988]).

57 As a striking instance, I am referring to the famous sonnet of *innamoramento* from Petrarch's *Songbook* (*Canz*. III).

structures generate a sort of 'love' poetry that is situated in discursive proximity to philosophical or even religious and theological reflection. The reasons for this situation – meaning, that the possibilities, which seem in principle to be granted by the general doctrinal configuration regarding physical pleasures, are not seized upon – remain to be discussed.

There is one (quantitatively less significant) sub-corpus that eludes the above characterization: the *muwashshahas* from the Iberian Peninsula – dating from the eleventh and twelfth centuries[58] – are indeed about a kind of love that may be understood as physical. Yet there is nothing to be found in them that could be compared to the fusion of eroticism and spiritualization characteristic of 'romantic love'.[59] The expressly carnal implications, most frequently articulated in an informal, popular tenor and pronounced by a figure distinct from the lyrical speaker,[60] are concentrated in the last section of these poems, the *kharjas*. In contrast to the first and longer part – conceived in many cases in classical Arabic – these are hybrid texts. They consist of Arabic, Romance and Hebrew words and characters. It may be that the cultural hybridity, to which their wording refers, is the condition of their existence.[61]

This assumption is all the more plausible in that the Islamic world outside of Spain did not produce something that comes close to a love literature as it is understood in

---

58 – which are taken by many Hispanists of the second half of the twentieth century, amongst others by Menocal, as irrefutable evidence for the postulate of an 'Arabic connection'. – It needs to be emphasized that the generic term is applied to poems written in the non-Iberian Muslim world also. It supports my speculations as developed above that these latter *muwashshahas* do not display the physical explicitness that characterizes the final parts of the Iberian *muwashshahas*. Another detail to be mentioned (silenced in almost all cases by the propagators of what I am calling the 'Arabic connection' thesis) is the fact that many of the Iberian *muwashshahas* are not only written in Hebrew characters to a large extent, but can also reliably be attributed to authors of Jewish belonging. For an extensive analysis of the corpus, mainly from the perspective of linguistics, while also taking into consideration problems of content, see Georg Bossong's contribution to this handbook ("The *kharadjat*", esp. section 6).

59 The scholar who, in 1948, first published these poems – which had been forgotten for a long period – Samuel Miklos Stern, most honestly resisted the temptation to give his discovery more importance than it actually has. According to him, a comparison between these texts and early Provençal poetry evinces that the assumption of the latter as having been "influenced" by the former is hardly tenable Stern (1948)). See also Stern (1974).

60 In most cases, the wording and the style suggest that the author of the poem intends to invite readers to conceive these final lines as being spoken from the perspective of a young (female) person of humble origin.

61 In this respect, it is quite telling that the variant of this new form, which emerged on the Iberian peninsula, was rejected in all other parts of the Arabic-speaking world (Menocal 1987, 95); Menocal (1987, 91–113) refers to the linguistic hybridity as the (only) reason for the rejection. I would suggest that there might have also been a rejection of the concepts articulated in these texts. – I do not wish to contradict Menocal's praise of the Iberian *muwashshahas*. There is no denying that the texts are interesting in many respects. Yet vindicating them as the (ever-lacking) piece of evidence for the proof of the 'Arabist' theory is somewhat bold.

the West. Profane literature[62] in general is a marginal phenomenon within traditional Islamic contexts. The reasons for this condition are systemic.[63] In contrast to the Hebrew and the Christian *Scriptures*, the divine words to be read in the *Quran* are not conceived as having been mediated by humans, by prophets or evangelists; but as directly articulated, orally or scripturally, or as dictated by Allah. In consequence, the language of the *Quran* is seen as sacred. Ultimately, the problem here discussed is contingent upon the fact that it was this variant of the pre-existing Arabic language that became the basis of its standardization: written standard Arabic is defined as being the language contained in the *Quran*. After the end of the very early period – that is, from the *umma*'s consolidation onward – profaning a code that is the language of the holy text by using it to write about frivolous things is considered more and more a problematic thing, if not – at least amongst devout Muslims – a punishable crime.

Given the taboo concerning classical Arabic – emerging during the process of the canonization of those texts which came to be comprised under the title of "*Quran*" – the section of the discursive field[64] we call literature is related in the traditional Muslim world[65] to the further sections (philosophy; theology; pragmatic discourses of various kinds) in a way that differs from what we spontaneously assume to be the case when we are talking about 'Western' phenomena.[66] It may thus not be fortuitous that the tendencies towards a mystical 'sublation' of love-as-passion, while becoming

---

62 Let me stress once again what I said in n. 52 concerning terminology. In addition, I should like to highlight that my above assessment is relative (of course). The formulation of the "marginality of the phenomenon we call literature in the West" is meant to denote the situation of the pre-modern Islamic world in comparison to the contemporaneous Latin West.

63 – which may also account for the fact that such marginality is still perceptible in the present-day Arab world.

64 As to M. Foucault's concept 'champ discursif', see *L'archéologie du savoir*, 44–101.

65 It need not be mentioned that there are literary texts (as we understand the term) in the Arabic world from the period of the Western penetration into these regions onward. Yet even into the twentieth century, such texts remain a controversial item. At times, they are tolerated to a certain extent; at others, they are ostracized by *fatwahs* issued against writers who took advantage of the privilege of literary discourse in the modern, Occidental sense – meaning: to hold views, to insinuate positions considered unorthodox within the societal framework in which the texts originate.

66 There are some literary texts that reoccur in the publications by all those advocating the thesis in question. One of the centerpieces is a famous poem by the Persian poet Nezami (the ascription is not uncontested) known by the title "Layla-wa-Majnun" (ca. 1192), which deals, indeed, with a lover driven mad by his unsatisfied desire. Yet it ends with the premature death of the female person, and with the lover's demise as soon as he realizes that the object of his desire is no longer alive. It must be added that there is no physical consummation that takes place prior to the death of the protagonists. It is only from a modern perspective that one can conceive a reading that abstracts the narrated story from its moralizing background. Rather than being a thematization of 'tragic love', the poem stylizes a warning about the dangers that accompany erotic desire. Its basic pattern may be considered paradigmatic for the stylization of love (in the sense of personally focused desire) in the (serious) Arabic literature of Islamic times.

more and more recessive in the 'West', constantly gain in importance in the course of pre-nineteenth century Arabic literary history.

It is an aspect of minor importance that the most famous *gazals* – poems said to be erotic, but in the manner characterized above – by Hafez, Rumi, and Saadi (all of Persian origin, writing mainly in Farsi) date from the thirteenth and the fourteenth centuries; which is to say: they are posterior by at least 200 years to the emergence of Western-style love lyrics. Another point that needs being mentioned: as to content, classical Arabic poetry – whose formal and rhetorical sophistication shall remain uncontested – happens to consist mainly of texts in the epideictic mode; that is, of panegyrics, and, to a smaller extent, of their opposite: (drastic) satirical lampooning with the latter section comprising a graphic thematization of sexual facts and practices.[67]

I would like to add that my view of the entire discursive scenario takes into consideration the theoretical discussions of a concept of passionate love, *amor hereos*, ascribed to Avicenna (*Canon medicinae*) – which also turns out, if one takes a closer look at the sources, to be a hybrid phenomenon combining Greek, Jewish, Roman, Christian, and Arabic features.[68]

I wish to supplement this section of my argument by saying that Arabic poetry does not need to be proclaimed the 'source' of Western love poetry in order to be highly valued, both conceptually and aesthetically. As is frequently the case, the somewhat forced 'revaluation' of various non-Western cultural phenomena as being 'equal' to Western phenomena might ultimately be nothing more than an (unconscious) expression of condescension.[69]

---

67 Without being an expert in the field, I would suggest interpreting this – at first sight astonishing – co-presence of mystical and obscene texts along the lines developed by Bakhtin with regard to medieval Western literature: a highly coercive discursive system produces, as it were, its "carnivalesque" inversion, if only with a view to enabling, from time to time, a channeling of the frustrations resulting from the rigidity characterizing the official discourse. – Apart from the language of the *Quran*, there have always been the various vernaculars of oral communication in the Arabic world; but until the nineteenth century, they did not produce something that comes close to what we understand as literary texts – which is not dissimilar from the Occidental situation. On a systematic basis, popular manners of speaking made their way into Western literary discourse also only during that period. As in the Latin West, there are incidental hybridizations of standard and popular parlances in a limited number of Arabic texts as early as in premodern times. Yet these tendencies cannot be compared to literary paradigms like 'realism' and 'naturalism' emerging only in the nineteenth century, and extant in both cultures.
68 See Küpper (2018b). In said article, I address a point I am neglecting in this paper: *amor hereos* is, for various reasons, to be considered as a conceptualization of erotic desire that stands in contrast to important features of romantic love.
69 For an extended discussion of this problem and the intricate questions linked to it, see Küpper (2018a, 232–291).

6 The *Dialoghi d'amore*: A Document of Jewish Diasporic Cosmopolitanism

In conclusion, I would like to highlight the main point of my argument once again: if Western literature's concept of love can hardly be explained as originating in Christianity, or in pagan Antiquity – and if there are some critical points to be raised when it comes to ascribing it to the influence of an Islamic literary tradition – one might hypothesize that Jewish diasporic thought may have made an essential contribution to it; or – taking the Iberian scenario into consideration – one might assume that the Jewish tradition may have helped diminish the textual effects of the abovementioned doctrinal pressures which increasingly deprived 'serious' Arabic poetry of the actual possibility to articulate what, in principle, it could have expressed, as far as the ethical level is concerned.

Conceptually, such a view would be consistent; this point does not require a detailed explanation. The reserved attitude of monotheistic systems vis-à-vis the 'adoration' of human beings is inflected, within Judaism, by the necessity to enhance procreation – the latter feature being a consequence of its characteristic as a 'tribal' monotheism.[70] For reasons differing from a Christian framework, Judaism thus contains a strong valuation of monogamy[71] which is absent, as demonstrated above, from that (restricted) part of Islamic poetry that indulges in the thematization of the pleasures of the body.

As to a philological substantiation of the suggested hypothesis, there is the problem of a lack of broader textual evidence concerning the period in question.[72]

---

[70] The one characteristic precludes the 'mixing' with tribes, who pray to other deities; the other precludes proselytizing. In order to survive, traditional (that is, non-secular) Judaism must guarantee a continuously high level of reproduction. There is no other way to preserve the existence of Yahweh's chosen people than to multiply – precisely – within the tribe's limits.

[71] In my statement above, I am referring to the consolidated phase of the Jewish faith, and not to the age of the patriarchs. As to the biblical text, the turning point might be marked by the valuation of King Solomon's attitude regarding the point in question. – One might argue that polygamy is conducive to an even higher level of reproduction than strict monogamy. In terms of long-term sustainability, however, the latter structure has two important advantages, especially in the case of tribes consisting of a limited number of individuals. Long-term nuclear families dedicate much more attention to raising their offspring than informally organized clans. The second advantage of strict monogamy is the prevention of frictions amongst the male members of the tribe, which are in particular a consequence of 'closeness' – that is, of social relations typical of smaller communities without a multilayered hierarchy separating the favored males from the multitude of those disfavored by polygamous structures.

[72] Starting in the period of emancipation in Europe, a broadly documented Jewish literary and artistic production emerges; and there are, of course, literary texts from the period before the destruction of the Temple. No one would contest that the *Song of Songs* is an important source of inspiration for the Western discourse on love – which is a point apt to further substantiate my speculations; and which I do not address here, because it is so evident.

In this respect, the situation of diasporic Judaism needs to be taken into consideration. The biographical circumstances of Judah Abrabanel, which I did not expound without reason at the beginning of this paper, are paradigmatic for people of Jewish origin; and not only in the century under consideration here, but during the entire period from the destruction of the Temple up to the age of the European Enlightenment. What distinguishes Abrabanel from other protagonists of Jewish origin is his belonging to the small intellectual elite of his age. In addition, he wrote in a period when print technology enabled a preservation of many texts which previously would have sooner or later fallen prey to the innumerable pogroms taking place periodically in medieval Europe.[73]

Be that as it may. The *Dialoghi d'Amore* constitute a piece of textual evidence of a kind which hardly exists in the case of the 'Muslim hypothesis': in medieval and early modern Jewish diasporic thought,[74] there were configurations of concepts that may help explain the emergence of a type of literary text in the West, whose conceptual framework was not in congruence with the dominant religious and philosophical traditions.

I might add one remark that is perhaps quite banal. Medieval love literature is not a Peninsular phenomenon only. It emerged all over Western and Southern Europe. The Muslim influence, however, was limited to the Iberian Peninsula.[75] Jewish diasporic

---

[73] – by which I mean texts that were not considered to be important enough to preserve the manuscripts under any circumstances: that is, literary texts, in contrast to ritually relevant ones.

[74] As I have stressed on various occasions, Abrabanel's philosophical thoughts are for the most part unoriginal – which is, in the age concerned, not a marker of inferior quality. Within my speculative frame of reasoning, I allow myself to extend this feature to his utterances concerning physical love. I consider them to be not of his own 'invention', but rather representative of the corresponding discursification within his community. The reason I believe this speculation to be tenable is the fact that there is indeed plenty of textual evidence in the Jewish tradition for an 'affirmative' attitude towards the sensual pleasures – as far as 'normal' practices are concerned. As is well known, Judaism reprimands all practices *contra naturam*. Yet the background of these strictures is a different one than within Christianity. As is evidenced by rules such as the obligation to marry the widow of a brother even if the male partner is already married to another woman, the logic of Jewish sexual hygiene is maximum reproduction – which, in turn, is conditioned by Judaism's status as a tribal monotheism. Within Christianity, reproduction, while necessary, is not a vital problem, since there is another means of preserving and even enlarging the impact of the 'right' belief – namely by proselytizing. For this reason, Christianity was able to systematically reprimand sexuality, although it had to tolerate it within certain limits, of course. The tolerance concerns the fulfillment of the divine mandate to multiply, while the reprimanding regards any sort of pleasure linked to it. What is accepted is the minimum necessary for procreation and for the catharsis of sexually relevant body fluids (a point that explains in part why Christian moral theology has always been more indulgent with regard to male than to female sexual desire). Sexual pleasure, and all practices that might incite it, are a sin from the traditional Christian standpoint, Catholic no less than Protestant.

[75] – and to parts of Sicily, but in this case for a rather short period only. It is one of the close to innumerable argumentative twists to be found in the book of Menocal (1987, 115–135) that the author – while providing a detailed account of the corpus of *scuola siciliana* poems conceived in the Arabic language – does not mention that, although the linguistic code at Frederick II's court was, to some

life, in contrast, was to be found everywhere, in France, in Italy, in Spain, in England and in the territories of German language. Yet the main point I would like to stress is the following: the condition for the emergence of a phenomenon like serious 'love literature'[76] is a configuration comprising three components: a desacralized concept of language; a non-reprimanding attitude towards the pleasures of sexuality; and a basis for rejecting promiscuity.[77] Within classical pagan, Christian and Muslim cultures one encounters – in varying configurations – one or two of these prerequisites; within Jewish diasporic culture all of them are given.

There will never be definitive answers to the questions raised in this chapter. The era I am dealing with here – namely the incubation period of discursive phenomena that do not reach the level of textuality until the eleventh century[78] – was for a long time called the "Dark Ages". In the present, it has become fashionable to incriminate this label as a superficial cliché. It is reasonable indeed to assume that there was a significant production of cultural artifacts during the period in question.[79] Yet it is also a fact that, as far as texts – literary ones in particular – are concerned, there is not, from the time of the Roman Empire's collapse (476 CE) to the instauration of the Empire by Charlemagne (800 CE), sufficient written testimony extant, which would allow for the establishment of theses that could be considered 'reconstructions' in terms of discourse archaeology.

Still, we are able to ponder the different possibilities of how to hypothetically explain what we are unable to reconstruct. This assessment comprises the critical discussion of the implications of current hypotheses; and it intends to continue reflection upon the possibility of new and more convincing ones. Doing (cultural, intellectual) history is a variant of hermeneutics – and there is never an end to interpretation.

---

extent, Arabic, the ideological parameters were not Muslim. Not least for that reason, the poems in question have little in common, in terms of their conceptual substratum, with the mystically informed texts of classical Arabic love poetry.

76 I insist on the epithet 'serious'; a carnivalesque thematization of love can well do without the third prerequisite mentioned.

77 It is only this latter criterion that opens up the perspective for the idea of 'spiritual' union, so essential for Western conceptions of love.

78 My argument is thus based on a framing of the period under scrutiny as differs from the majority of the research conducted so far: I do not hold that William of Aquitaine was a sort of *creator ex nihilo* of what was to become the 'standard' Western concept of erotic love. I rather suggest assuming that there was – quite as in the case of medieval epic – a long-lasting oral prehistory of the texts that have been passed down, a period in which the diverse components out of which 'Western love' is composed might have interacted and then become fused into a comprehensive concept.

79 We may leave it open whether or not these artifacts would be able to compete in terms of quantity and quality with the artifacts from previous or subsequent periods.

Bibliography

Works Cited

Primary Sources

Ebreo, Leone. *Dialoghi d'Amore*. Ed. Delfina Giovannozzi. Bari: Laterza, 2008.
Ebreo, Leone. *Dialogues of Love*. Trs. Cosmos Damian Bacich and Rossella Pescatori. Toronto: University of Toronto Press, 2009.

Secondary Literature

Aristotle. *Poetics*. Ed. and tr. Stephen Halliwell. Cambridge, MA: Harvard University Press, 1995.
Auerbach, Erich. "Passio als Leidenschaft." *PMLA* 56 (1941): 1179–1196.
Auerbach, Erich. *Mimesis: The Representation of Reality in Western Literature*. Tr. Willard R. Trask. Princeton, NJ: Princeton University Press, 2013.
Bauer, Thomas. *Liebe und Liebesdichtung in der arabischen Welt des 9. und 10. Jahrhunderts: Eine literatur- und mentalitätsgeschichtliche Studie des arabischen Gazal*. Wiesbaden: Harrassowitz, 1998.
Diner, Dan. *Versiegelte Zeit: Über den Stillstand in der islamischen Welt*. Berlin: Propyläen, 2005.
Enderwitz, Susanne. *Liebe als Beruf: Al-Abbas Ibn Al-Ahnaf und das Gazal*. Beirut and Stuttgart: Steiner, 1995.
Foucault, Michel. *L'archéologie du savoir*. Paris: Gallimard, 1969.
Foucault, Michel. *La volonté de savoir*. Paris: Gallimard, 1976.
Freud, Sigmund. "The Relation of the Poet to Day-Dreaming." *Art and Interpretation: An Anthology of Readings in Aesthetics and the Philosophy of Art*. Ed. Eric Dayton. Peterborough: Broadview Press, 1998. 300–304.
Gilson, Étienne: *La théologie mystique de Saint Bernard*. Paris: Vrin, 1934.
Gruendler, Beatrice. "'That You Be Brought Near'. Union beyond the Grave in the Arabic Literary Tradition." *Love after Death: Concepts of Posthumous Love in Medieval and Early Modern Europe*. Eds. Bernhard Jussen and Ramie Targoff. Berlin, Munich and Boston, MA: De Gruyter, 2015. 71–95.
Gubbini, Gaia. "L'haleine de l'esprit: Traces olfactives d'oc et d'oïl." *Les cinq sens au Moyen âge*. Ed. Éric Palazzo. Paris: Les Éditions du Cerf, 2016. 745–758.
Gumbrecht, Hans Ulrich. "*Un souffle d'Allemagne ayant passé*: Friedrich Diez, Gaston Paris, and the Genesis of National Philologies." *Romance Philology* 40 (1986/7): 1–37.
Ḥāfiẓ. *The Dīvān*. Tr. Henry Wilberforce Clarke. London: Octagon Press, 1974.
Ḥāfiẓ. *Ghaselen*. Tr. Friedrich Rückert. Zürich: Manesse, 1988.
Hegel, Georg Wilhelm Friedrich. *Aesthetics: Lectures on Fine Arts*. Tr. Thomas M. Knox. 2 Vols. Oxford: Clarendon Press, 1975.
Hughes, Aaron. "Judah Abrabanel." *The Stanford Encyclopedia of Philosophy*. https://plato.stanford.edu/entries/abrabanel/. Winter 2016 Edition. (5 February 2018).
Kuhn, Thomas S. *The Structure of Scientific Revolutions*. Chicago, Il: U. of Chicago Press, 1962
Küpper, Joachim. "Zum romantischen Mythos der Subjektivität. Lamartines *Invocation* und Nervals *El Desdichado*." *Zeitschrift für französische Sprache und Literatur* 98 (1988): 137–165.

Küpper, Joachim. *Petrarca: Das Schweigen der Veritas und die Worte des Dichters*. Berlin and New York, NY: De Gruyter, 2002.
Küpper, Joachim. "The Traditional Cosmos and the New World." *MLN* 118 (2003): 363–392.
Küpper, Joachim. "Zu einigen Aspekten der Dichtungstheorie in der Frührenaissance." *Renaissance – Episteme und Agon*. Eds. Andreas Kablitz and Gerhard Regn. Heidelberg: Winter, 2006. 47–71.
Küpper, Joachim. "Philology and Theology in Petrarch." *MLN* 122 (2007): 133–147.
Küpper, Joachim. *Discursive Renovatio in Lope de Vega and Calderón: Studies on Spanish Baroque Drama: With an Excursus on the Evolution of Discourse in the Middle Ages, the Renaissance, and Mannerism*. Berlin and Boston, MA: De Gruyter, 2017 (=2017a).
Küpper, Joachim. "Sentimental Revivals: Gérard de Nervals's *Voyage en Orient*." *Spectral Sea: Mediterranean Palimpsests in European Culture*. Eds. Stephen Nichols, Joachim Küpper and Andreas Kablitz. New York, NY and Bern: Lang, 2017. 157–202 (=2017b).
Küpper, Joachim. *The Cultural Net: Early Modern Drama as a Paradigm*. Berlin and Boston, MA: De Gruyter, 2018 (=2018a).
Küpper, Joachim. "The Secret Life of Classical and Arabic Medical Texts in Petrarch's *Canzoniere*." *Petrarch and Boccaccio: The Unity of Knowledge in the Pre-Modern World*. Ed. Igor Candido. Boston, MA and Berlin: De Gruyter, 2018. 91–128 (=2018b).
Küpper, Joachim. "Leone Ebreo's Dialoghi d'amore: Elliptical Revelation?" Modern Language Notes 136 (2021): 1134–1153.
L-Suli, Abu Bakr Muhammad Ibn Yahya. *The Life and Times of Abu Tammam*. Ed. and Tr. Beatrice Gruendler. New York, NY and London: New York University Press, 2015.
Mace, Sarah T. "Amour, Encore! The Development of δηὖτε in Archaic Lyric." *Greek, Roman and Byzantine Studies* 34 (1993): 335–364.
Menocal, María Rosa. *The Arabic Role in Medieval Literary History: A Forgotten Heritage*. Philadelphia, PA: University of Pennsylvania Press, 1987.
Novoa, James W. Nelson. "Appunti sulla genesi redazionale dei *Dialoghi d'amore* di Leone Ebreo alla luce della critica testuale attuale e la tradizione manoscritta del suo terzo dialogo." *Quaderni d'italianistica* 30 (2009): 45–66.
Peri, Hiram, and Melamed, Avraham. "Abrabanel, Judah." *Encyclopaedia Judaica*. Eds. Michael Berenbaum and Fred Skolnik. Detroit, MI: Macmillan Reference USA, 2007.
Pflaum, Heinz. *Die Idee der Liebe: Leone Ebreo: Zwei Abhandlungen zur Geschichte der Philosophie in der Renaissance*. Tübingen: Mohr, 1926.
Pidal, Ramón Menéndez. "Poesía árabe y poesía europea." *Bulletin hispanique* 40 (1938): 337–423.
Rougemont, Denis de. *L'amour et l'Occident*. Paris: Plon, 1939.
Simonde de Sismondi, Jean-Charles Léonard. *De la littérature du Midi de L'Europe*. Paris: Treuttel et Würtz, 1813, 4 Vols.
Snell, Bruno. *The Discovery of the Mind: The Greek Origins of European Thought*. Tr. Thomas G. Rosenmeyer. Cambridge, MA: Harvard University Press, 1953.
Stern, Samuel Miklos. "Les vers finaux en espagnol dans les muwaššahs hispano-hébraïques: Une contribution à l'histoire du muwaššah et à l'étude du vieux dialecte espagnol 'mozarabe'." *Al-Andalus* 13 (1948): 299–343.
Stern, Samuel Miklos. "Literary Connections between the Islamic World and Western Europe in the Early Middle Ages: Did they Exist?" *Hispano-Arabic Strophic Poetry: Studies by Samuel Miklos Stern*. Ed. Leonard P. Harvey. Oxford: Clarendon Press, 1974. 204–230.

Further Reading

Astell, Ann W. *The Song of Songs in the Middle Ages*. Ithaca, NY: Cornell University Press, 1995.
Foucault, Michel. "The Order of Discourse." *Untying the Text: A Post-Structuralist Reader*. Ed. Robert Young. Tr. Ian McLeod. London: Routledge, 1981. 48–78.
Kierkegaard, Søren. *Stages in Life's Way*. Tr. Walter Lowrie. Princeton: Princeton University Press, 1940.
Lévi-Strauss, Claude. *Structural Anthopolgy*. Tr. Monique Layton. London: Allen Lane, 1968/1977, 2 Vols.
Matter, E. Anne. *The Song of My Beloved: The Song of Songs in Medieval Christianity*. Phildelphia, PA: University of Pennsylvania Press, 2011.

Harm den Boer
8 The Literature of the Western Sephardim

Abstract: This chapter deals with the vernacular literature written, produced, and – to a lesser degree – consumed by Sephardim of *converso* origin from the sixteenth until the end of the eighteenth century. Given the geographical dispersion, the large chronological span and the frequently blurred religious identity of the so called 'New Christian' Diaspora – of which a part remained Christian, another embraced formal Judaism and still another escaped confessional affiliations or traveled between them – the literature studied here does not belong to an easily definable group of producers or readers, nor is this literature itself clearly distinguishable from other literatures.

Key Terms: Early Modern diasporic literature, Judaism in Spanish and Portuguese, religious and secular dimensions of Western Sephardim, Iberian literature, Sephardic belonging

1 Defining Western Sephardic Literature

This chapter treats Spanish and Portuguese émigrés of converso descent belonging to Jewish communities in the so-called Western Sephardic Diaspora (Venice, Livorno, Amsterdam, Hamburg, Bayonne, Bordeaux, London, as well as settlements in the New World such as Pernambuco, the Antilles, Surinam, New York). The authors reviewed here were Jewish, but for some part of their lives they could have been observant Christians, whether still living in the realms of Spain and Portugal or living outside the Peninsula without officially joining a Jewish community. Examples of such authors include João Pinto Delgado (ca. 1585–1653), who was born in Portugal, lived for several years in France without formally belonging to Judaism, and finally joined the Sephardic community of Amsterdam, where he was known as Moses Delgado. This author wrote and published works in France and in the Netherlands: those published in France reflected an identification with Hebrew biblical heroes but no explicit religious affiliation, whereas those written and printed in Amsterdam were overtly and apologetically Jewish. Miguel de Barrios (1635–1701), the best-known author among the Western Sephardim, was born a Christian in Montilla, Andalusia. Around 1658, he fled Spain, travelling through Italy and the New World before establishing himself in the Netherlands, where he soon joined the Sephardic community of Amsterdam. While the first work of this author was published in the Spanish Netherlands – present-day Belgium –, Barrios had previously finalized it in Amsterdam. Before that, he had probably written a part of his poetry and plays while still living in Spain. Barrios addressed himself at times to an Iberian Catholic or general audience, at times to a Jewish readership from Amsterdam. In his case, it is perhaps more important to examine the difference between his various publications than to pin a religious identity on the author depending on where he lived. It is remarkable that even Sephardic authors born and raised as Jews could address themselves to non-Jewish readers. Indeed, one of the features of Western Sephardic Literature and culture in general is precisely its secular dimension.[1]

Even the element 'Western' in the formulation 'Western Sephardic Literature' escapes easy definitions; I do not refer here to the geographical distribution of former conversos in the early modern world, but rather to their converso origin. In Western Sephardic literature, we occasionally come across authors who were traditional Sephardim, resident in Northern Africa or the Ottoman Empire, rather than former conversos. Their texts belong to the literature of the Western Sephardim insofar as they addressed themselves to ex-converso readers in the vernacular language and in the Latin alphabet.[2]

With regards to language, although the principal literary languages of the Western Sephardim were Spanish and Portuguese, they also expressed themselves in Hebrew, Latin, French or other languages. Generally, the choice of one of these alternative languages targeted a distinct readership and corresponded to a distinct necessity: Hebrew was the language for rabbis and students and was used for exchanges with the Jewish world; Latin was the language for communication with learned circles in Europe; local languages were either used for interaction with the surrounding society or were embraced by the Sephardim in substitution of their native languages, generally decades after their migration, when the ties with the Hispanic world had loosened.[3] In some cases, the use of a language other than Spanish and Portuguese could represent an overlap, as seen in some – albeit very few – bilingual liturgical texts in Spanish and Hebrew or in multilingual publications commemorating important festivities. However, more often than not, such publications of the same text in various languages reflected the different readerships addressed in them. In spite of the multiplicity of languages, the choice of Spanish or Portuguese was relatively clear-cut. Portuguese was the spoken language of the majority of the Western Sephardim and the current language in their religious congregations, as can be seen from their records (Kerkhof 2003; Kerner 2019, 86; Arnold 2006). As a *literary* language,

---

[1] In his Ph.D. thesis, Swetschinski (1979) had already pointed out the secular dimension of Sephardic literature in relation to the Portuguese Jewish merchant elite; see his later publication (Swetschinski 2000, 297–302), also Den Boer (1994, 69–70, 73–75).

[2] The general feature of Eastern Jewish Sephardim is their use of the Hebrew alphabet and their specific language, *Judeoespañol*. Some traditional Sephardic poetry among Western Sephardim can be explained by the migration of Eastern Sephardim from Northern Africa or the Balkans to the Netherlands, see Levie Bernfeld (2018).

[3] Speaking for the whole Western Sephardic Diaspora, Portuguese and Spanish were replaced by the local languages from the second half of the eighteenth century onwards. The Emancipation of the Jews in each country – whether or not propelled by the French Revolution – was the definitive moment in this process.

Portuguese competed with Spanish among the former conversos. The choice of one or the other language is elucidated in the discussion of the different literary genres below. Regarding Spanish, it is necessary to make some remarks on its use in Western Sephardic literature. Contrary to the Spanish used by the Eastern Sephardim, which evolved into distinct variations of the language, known as Judeo-Spanish[4] (referring to the language spoken in the Ottoman Empire) and Haketía (referring to the Spanish spoken in Northern Africa, i.e., present-day Morocco) – which both were written in Hebrew characters – the Spanish of the Western Sephardim was largely the language with which the conversos were raised in Spain and its territories.[5] This Spanish, and even more so the Portuguese spoken and written by the Western Sephardim, incorporated Hebrew words and expressions related to Jewish worship and communal life ("meldar", "esnoga", "mahamad", "kahal kados", etc.); however, the use of such words or expressions was limited (Kerkhof 2003; Arnold 2006). The most important factor affecting the Spanish of the Western Sephardim was the interference from Portuguese as the native language of either the writer or the community to which he belonged. In many Spanish works of the Western Sephardim, we find traces of Portuguese syntax – notably the *infinitivo pessoal* – as well as Portuguese lexical variations; spelling patterns also reveal the difficulties faced by the speakers where Portuguese and Spanish phonology "clash", particularly with regard to the sibilants (Kerkhof 2003; Arnold 2006).

2 Western Sephardic Literature in Iberian and Jewish Studies

Until now, I have taken the notion of 'literature' for granted. It is, however, important to examine the textual genres practiced in the Sephardic converso diaspora, not only in relation to Hispanic (that is Spanish and Portuguese) literature, but also with regard to Jewish or Hebrew literature. As will be shown, the vernacular literature of the Western Sephardim originated from a religious need: to provide former conversos with texts that helped them reconnect with traditional Judaism. Such texts included the Bible, the works used for liturgical purposes, and a series of treatises, ranging from practical instructions on the observance of Judaism to works of an ethical or philosophical character. Given the primary importance of all these doctrinal texts, even if they belong to genres that are nowadays not considered "literature", they nevertheless constitute the fundament of Western Sephardic culture. Moreover, from a Jewish

---

[4] I mention the term used by a majority of scholars nowadays; names such as "Judezmo" and "Ladino" are also used, however (Bunis 2016).
[5] When their native language was Portuguese, they would acquire knowledge of Spanish by reading or they were instructed by Spanish, sometimes Christian, instructors.

perspective, they can be called "literary", because Jewish – that is, Hebrew – literature always had a strong intertextual relation with the Bible and rabbinic writing, at least in the premodern era. From an Iberian perspective, many of the texts discussed here are frequently considered secondary to or derivative of the canonical literature of the so-called Golden Age,[6] which is principally constituted by poetry, drama and prose fiction. Modern Spanish and Portuguese readers are somewhat disappointed by the literary creations of the Western Sephardim, which were produced on the periphery and were only of marginal influence upon the Iberian – that is, Spanish and Portuguese – literary canon. Poets like Miguel (Daniel Levi) de Barrios or David Abenatar Melo, if studied at all, are inevitably compared against the standard set by the many great poets of the Spanish and Portuguese seventeenth century; from such a perspective, qualifications as "secondary" or "epigonic" have been frequent.

Because of its use in religious, philosophical and political discourse, early modern non-fictional prose has not enjoyed much appreciation in literary studies. Perhaps only the humanistic dialogue enjoys a better reputation. The intellectually challenging and even entertaining dialogues of Western Sephardic polemical literature, as can be found in the *Danielillo* (Caplan 1868; Orfali 1997) and the *Marrakesh Dialogues* (Wilke 2014), are nevertheless hardly known among literary scholars of the Iberian world. Only Samuel Usque's *Consolação às tribulações de Israel* (*Consolation for the tribulations of Israel*, 1553) has made it into the Iberian – that is, Portuguese – literary canon. What has been said of the dialogue applies all the more to the religious and philosophical treatise, as the genre itself is only studied by a handful of specialists of Iberian literature. Consequently, the speculative or polemical texts of the Western Sephardic Diaspora are rarely read as literary texts. Even the Portuguese and Spanish sermons delivered in synagogues all over the Diaspora and occasionally written down or printed, some of them veritable showcases of literary devices, have not received the attention they deserve.[7]

Conversely, from the perspective of Jewish literature or Jewish Studies, the vernacular literature of the Western Sephardim has also been rather neglected. Although many works and authors have received some attention – not least thanks to the efforts of Meyer Kayserling (1868, 1890) –, this has been more often than not indirect, that is, by way of secondary sources rather than close readings. Perhaps the Spanish and Portuguese works written by the Western Sephardim have been considered more as transitory works than as contributions to Judaism in their own right. For many scholars of Jewish Studies, Spanish and Portuguese remain foreign languages. It is only through the work of a small number of eminent pioneering scholars that we are better informed about Western Sephardic literature's contribution to Judaism and Jewish

---

[6] The Spanish and also the Portuguese literature produced in the sixteenth and seventeenth centuries.

[7] For an overview of the sermons among the Sephardim of Amsterdam, written down and printed in Spanish and Portuguese, see Den Boer 1996, 213–268.

history (Roth 1974 [1932]; Yerushalmi 1971, 1989; Kaplan 1989; Salomon 1982, 1988). The situation is changing, however, and recent studies in the field have been accompanied by an excellent knowledge of Spanish, Portuguese and the Iberian cultural background.[8]

3 Western Sephardic Literature and the Role of Printing

Literature in the sense of the printing of texts was of fundamental importance to the establishment of new Jewish communities in the Western Sephardic Diaspora. The activities of the press founded by Abraham Usque and Yomtob Athias in Ferrara provide the best example of this fact. Under the protection of the Dukes of Este, Iberian conversos founded a Jewish community in that city in the second half of the sixteenth century and provided the new members with translations of the Jewish Bible and liturgy in Spanish. The *Biblia en lengua española traduzida palabra por palabra de la verdad hebraica por muy excelentes letrados* (1553) represented a monumental effort to render the Jewish biblical canon into a translation that inserted humanist philological criticism into traditional techniques of literal translation as practiced in Jewish Iberia during the Middle Ages. The so-called "Ferrara Bible" was intended for the Jewish re-education of a converso readership no longer familiar with Hebrew – but was also sold to Christian readers interested in the *hebraica veritas* (Hassán and Berenguer-Amador 1994; Lazar 1996). Thus, the Usque press set a standard for future ex-converso communities, serving the needs of former Marranos and, whenever desired or possible, also attending to the curiosity of the non-Jewish reader. The press founded by Usque and Athias produced editions of the Psalms and the prayer books in small formats that served the needs of conversos reverting to Judaism who could participate in worship by following Hebrew services at the synagogue with the help of a very literal Spanish translation; of course, these books would serve them privately as well.

In 1553, the Jewish Ferrara press also published a work in Portuguese, the *Consolação às tribulações de Israel* (*Consolation for the tribulations of Israel*) by Samuel Usque. Employing the Renaissance genre of the dialogue as well as a pastoral style, Usque portrays allegorical shepherds who lament the fate of the people of Israel and try to make sense of the recent catastrophes in Iberia: the pogroms and murders of 1391, the growing intolerance leading to the expulsion from Spain, the

---

[8] Examples: Bodian (1997), Swetschinski (2000), Rauschenbach (2012), Perelis (2016), Dweck (2019), Fischer (2020). The many studies by Yosef Kaplan, Michael Studemund-Halévy and Carsten Wilke should also be mentioned.

mass conversion in Portugal and the relentless persecution by the Inquisition. The intense melancholy of the dialogues, its poetical Portuguese language and the way the author offers comfort to his readers by reminding them of God's promise to his chosen people make the work a classic of both Jewish and Portuguese literature (Yerushalmi 2014, 53–81; Wilke 2014, 128–135).

The same press published two titles addressed to a broader, also non-Jewish audience: a work of prose fiction in Portuguese, *Menina e moça* (*Maiden and Modest*, 1554), by Bernardim Ribeiro, as well as the Spanish treatise *Visión deleitable de todas las ciencias* (*Delectable vision of all sciences, 1554*), a new edition of a popular encyclopedic work on the sciences, couched in allegorical language and leading up to the ultimate knowledge – the intellectual knowledge of God. Written by the fifteenth-century converso Alfonso de la Torre, the *Visión deleitable* draws a large part of its content from Maimonides' *Guide of the perplexed*, in addition to other, Christian sources (Giron-Negrón 2001); it had circulated in many manuscripts and editions in Spain, but became popular among diasporic Jewish readers, as two later versions by Francisco de Cáceres (Amsterdam 1623 and 1663) demonstrate (Den Boer 2010).

The vernacular printing by Usque and Athias in Ferrara in many ways serves as a model and, in fact, set the standard for printing afterwards and elsewhere in the Western Sephardic Diaspora: between the second half of the sixteenth century and the beginning of the nineteenth century, works in the vernacular were steadily produced for the benefit of the conversos who returned to formal Judaism in the communities of Western Europe. Although the Bible, liturgical works and Jewish learning would dominate, printing presses evolved and came to embrace many genres and readers. Of course, the production, the type and the scope of works published in the different centers of the Western Sephardic Diaspora at different times varied according to local conditions and particularities. Before examining this literature more closely, also taking into account the circulation of handwritten texts, a brief overview of the geographic distribution of printing presses will be presented.

In Italy, Venice became the center of Sephardic book production after the brief but intense printing activity of the former conversos in Ferrara. As it was a city with an important Jewish ghetto, also situated at the crossroads between West and East, between Western and Eastern Sephardim, Sephardic works were printed there in both Hebrew and Roman scripts (Arnold 2006, 93, 347–351). Already in 1552, around the same time as the start of the activities in Ferrara, prayer books were being printed there in bilingual editions (Hebrew and Spanish). In 1568, an early Spanish translation of Leone Ebreo's *Dialoghi d'amore* was written by the Sephardic Jew Guedellah Yachia and dedicated to King Philip II of Spain, whom the author provided with the epithet "Católico defensor de la fe"; in an added section, the *Diálogos de Amor* were accompanied by a short treatise on the *Opinions of the ancient philosophers on the Soul*, by Doctor Aron Afia (Nelson Novoa 2005). These Sephardim, descendants of the Jews who had been expelled from Spain in 1492, apparently felt confident enough to publish works in a city where Spanish literature was printed, sometimes with overt heterodox content (*La Celestina*, the *Diálogo de Mercurio y Carón* by the Reformist Alfonso de Valdés, several editions of a Spanish translation of the New Testament). In the seventeenth century, works specifically addressed to former conversos were printed in Venice. In 1609, an abridged Spanish version of Yosef Caro's Halakhic work *Sulhan Arukh*, by Moses Altares, appeared with the title *Libro del mantenimiento del alma* (*Book of the soul's maintenance*); it was based upon a previous version in Hebrew characters.[9] In 1627, rabbi Isaac Athias published his work on the 613 commandments printed (*Tesoro de preceptos*) with Gioanne Caleoni, and rabbi Moses de Toledo (seventeenth century), an itinerant Sephardic scholar from Jerusalem, had a huge moral work called *The Trumpet* (*La trompeta*) published in Venice in 1643; finally, the work of David Mugnon, *Tratado de la oración y meditación y conocimiento propio del Dio* (*A treatise on Prayers and Meditation and the Knowledge of God*) was published at the press of Imberti in 1654, a Christian printer family who also printed Jewish works in Hebrew and Italian.

Other Italian cities with Sephardic communities, such as Pisa, Livorno or Florence, occasionally had editions printed as well; however, they never reached the level of output of Ferrara and Venice. Altogether, Sephardic printing in Italy was either a short-lived affair or played a minor role in the Western Sephardic Diaspora, where only Amsterdam rose to the position of a Jewish printing center, both in Hebrew and in Spanish and Portuguese.

Like Italy, France was one of the initial safe havens for 'New Christian' refugees and from the sixteenth century on, Jewish communities arose, notably in Rouen, Bayonne and Bordeaux (Novoa and Wilke 2022), but Jewish worship was officially recognized only in the eighteenth century. Jewish printing in vernacular languages was therefore a precarious affair in France during the sixteenth and seventeenth centuries. Laurence Maury printed works by the conversos Antonio Enríquez Gómez, João Pinto Delgado and Manuel Fernandes Villareal; however, none of these include explicitly Jewish content. Two treatises by rabbis of Bayonne, Abraham Vaez and Isaac da Costa, were printed in France without mention of place or printer; a voluminous paraphrase of the Bible by rabbi Isaac da Costa, *Conjeturas sagradas sobre los Profetas Primeros* (*Sacred Conjectures on the First Prophets* 1722), was issued with the false imprint of Leiden, but certain typographical lapsus indicate that it was really printed in France.

Northern Germany and England offered occasional examples of Jewish vernacular printing. In Germany, the restrictions on Jewish life in Hamburg – due to the role of the Lutheran clergy – meant that many works related to the Sephardic community were printed in Amsterdam, or were printed with false addresses. Of the approximately fifteen works printed in Hamburg during the seventeenth and eighteenth centuries,

---

9 *Mesa de el alma*, a Ladino translation in Hebrew characters by Meir ben Semuel ben Benveniste, printed in Thessaloniki in 1568 (Schwarzwald 2017, above all 290–292).

only five titles bear the city's name on their title pages: a Hebrew grammar by Abudiente, two liturgical works printed in 1662, a treatise on penitence by Maimonides likewise printed in 1662, and a non-Jewish collection of poems and songs printed as late as 1764.

In England, Jews were admitted from 1655 on due to the efforts of Menasseh ben Israel, although it was not until 1664 that they established a formal congregation under the name of Sha'ar Hashamayim. Vernacular printing in Spanish and Portuguese only started from the eighteenth century onwards and included sermons, liturgy and some major works by Daniel Israel López Laguna, haham David Nieto and Jacob de Castro Sarmento, totaling some 40 works (Roth 1960).

It was the Netherlands where Sephardic printing far outperformed the publishing activities of the other communities of converso origin. The Sephardic community had found in the city of Amsterdam conditions for printing that were not easily found elsewhere, and it soon knew how to benefit from the opportunities offered by the Dutch printing press thanks to its place on the crossroads of trade routes, its excellent infrastructure and not least a freedom of expression not enjoyed in other parts of Europe. The first Spanish and Portuguese works printed in the Netherlands had been produced in Dordrecht in 1584 – probably still addressed to colonies of 'New Christian' merchants secretly practicing Judaism in Antwerp. Around 1604, works related to the first Jewish communities of Amsterdam started to come off the presses, still concealing the printer's address and identity – a fact that reflects the initial insecurity of the new Jewish communities with regard to their status. Some ten years later, works produced by and for the Sephardim were printed with explicit mention of Amsterdam and the printer's full name on their title page (Offenberg 1991; Den Boer 2006a, 2006b; Den Boer 2018a, 2018b). In 1627, Menasseh ben Israel became the first Jewish printer, to be followed by a whole range of Jewish printers who published both in Hebrew and in the Iberian vernacular languages: Immanuel Benveniste, David de Castro Tartas, Jacob de Cordoba, Selomoh Querido, Solomon Proops and several others ... A total of more than 750 works in Spanish and Portuguese were printed in Amsterdam between 1600 and 1800 (Den Boer 2003).[10] This number is all the more impressive if counted together with the literature produced in manuscript, of which some 400 copies are presently extant. Manuscript culture was an important feature of early modern literary and cultural circulation, coexisting with printed texts; in the case of Western Sephardic literature, many works that are only extant in manuscript were part of a clandestine or semi-clandestine polemical literature directed against Christianity; such works were expressly forbidden for publication by the Sephardic congregations in Europe, as they endangered relations with the surrounding majority society.

---

10 If we exclude the works of the poet Daniel Levi (Miguel) de Barrios, which often consisted of single leaves or previously used leaves with some new inserts, the total is approximately 500 editions, still an impressive amount. For a Bibliography of Spanish and Portuguese Printing in the Northern Netherlands, see Den Boer 2003.

4 Educating former conversos: Religious Instruction in Spanish and Portuguese

The Spanish and Portuguese literature of the Western Sephardim arose out of the need to provide 'New Christians' who were returning to formal Judaism with texts. As the former conversos no longer had sufficient command of Hebrew, their reintegration into Judaism required instruction in their own language, and it was through the printing press that they were served. Ferrara turned out to be the place where, around the second half of the sixteenth century, such a press could be founded. The so-called "Ferrara Bible" and prayer books formed the basis of many re-editions during the seventeenth and eighteenth centuries in Amsterdam.[11] The text of the subsequent Spanish Bible and liturgical editions underwent only minor changes until 1671, when Jacob Judah Leon published a revision of the Psalm translation to which he added a paraphrase, and 1740, when rabbi David Nieto of London presented a revised text of the Mahzor (the *Orden de Ros Hasanah y Kipur*), followed by a revised edition of the daily prayers in 1771 (Kerner 2018, 71).

From the start of vernacular printing for the Western Sephardim, other genres of Jewish works were also printed: instructions on the commandments, moral and ethical treatises, and a whole range of texts that constituted a veritable canon of Judaism made available in Spanish and Portuguese. Translations, original works written by rabbis resident in the Sephardic communities, treatises composed by ex-conversos drawing from both Iberian Catholic sources and newly acquired Jewish knowledge, poetical compositions, drama, etc. – very soon, Sephardic literature comprised many genres and directions. These will be briefly discussed below, divided into the categories of prose, poetry and theatre. Born out of necessity and initially still focused on the newly established communities of conversos who had returned to Judaism, the vernacular presses occasionally addressed a non-Jewish public as well: economic opportunities for printers, the personal ambitions of writers, the social aspirations of a merchant elite, or the interaction of Jewish scholars with a Christian environment all contributed to the creation of a diversified literary production that reflects the multifaceted religious and social identity of the Western Sephardic Diaspora.

5 Reading and Censorship

Before we turn to the several genres of literature produced in the Western Sephardic Diaspora, two further introductory remarks must be made. Firstly, among the

---

[11] I have counted eight editions of prayer books printed in Venice between 1550 and 1623 (Den Boer 2015).

regulations of the established congregations of the Western Sephardic Diaspora, provisions were made for the control of the circulation of texts. The governing boards defined sanctions against those members who published or circulated works against other religions (read: Christianity) or which were in conflict with religious orthodoxy, Books were printed with the approval of the rabbis and authorities of the congregations but were issued from within the community; thus, this censorship was effective only insofar as authors and members of the community would subject themselves to the rules (Swetschinski 2000, 19–20, 243–249; Den Boer 1996, 79–103; see also Kaplan 2000, 143–154; Kerner 2018).

Finally, Sephardic culture consisted of far more than just the production of its own texts: members of the Sephardic communities also brought books with them or had access to all kinds of reading depending on their economic status, their interests, and the availability of books in their environment. Important studies have been made on reading habits among the Western Sephardim; they show that Iberian literature was not only an important remnant of the cultural past but was actively acquired and read even after many years of living outside of Spain and Portugal. Italy, the Spanish Low Countries and the bookstores of Amsterdam provided easy access to Iberian literature: historical, literary, political and religious. However, reading interests often went quite beyond Spanish and Portuguese literature, constituting, as one scholar has defined it, a veritable "patchwork culture" (Swetschinski 2000, 286–310, Kaplan 2002; Studemund-Halevy 2003).

6 Prose: Introductory Remarks

Although not the most literary of all genres from a present-day perspective, non-fictional prose certainly prevailed in the written vernacular production of the Western Sephardim. Hundreds of titles, in print and in manuscript, are extant in libraries all over the world. In addition to the all-encompassing variety known as the "Treatise" – the most traditional of forms,[12] – Jewish contents received new impulses through the adoption of early modern discursive forms, such as the humanistic dialogue and the sermon, which combined the Jewish practice of the *derush* with the elaborate eloquence of baroque discourse.[13] Historiography was also present in Samuel Usque's *Consolação às tribulações de Israel* (1553), and in *La vara de Juda* (Judah's scepter,

---

[12] Although the treatise in its most traditional form is an argumentative discourse without contradiction, treatises can include dialogical parts, aphorisms, or stories, thereby incorporating other genres.
[13] In his edition of the Spanish "Diálogos de Marrakesh" (2014, 3–29), Carsten Wilke discusses the importance of Jewish contents transmitted through new literary models: "The scholastic *quaestio*, the dogmatic treatise, the Humanist dialogue, the Reformation catechism, the versified hagiography and martyrology of the Counter-Reformation, the Baroque sermon, the political pamphlet, the convert's spiritual autobiography, the freethinkers' obscene pasquinada, and many others" (2014, 5).

1640 and 1744) the Spanish translation of Solomon ibn Verga's *Shevet Yehudah*; also, in many works by Daniel Levi (Miguel) de Barrios and in a whole range of texts on secular themes such as military victories, weddings and visits by princes and sovereigns, all reflecting the diplomatic endeavors and social aspirations of a Sephardic merchant elite (Schwetschinski 2000, 301–302; Den Boer and Israel 1991). The foremost specialist in highly contrived, panegyrical prose discourses was Joseph Penso de la Vega, an author emblematic of Western Sephardic culture itself (Pancorbo 2019). It is impossible to deal here with this prose output in any depth. Only the principal directions and most influential genres will be discussed, starting with the reception of the Bible and the "vernacular library of Jewish learning" among the former conversos.

7 The Role of the Bible

The Spanish Bible (1553), translated by Abraham Usque and others, was an extraordinary achievement in many respects. Among the major challenges were, of course, the financing of such an enterprise and the permission to have the Bible printed in the Christian environment of the Duchy of Ferrara. Above all, however, it was the process of preparing the translation itself that represented the greatest difficulty. The technique used to translate the Bible was based upon traditional literal renderings that the conversos had inherited from Jewish Spain, but the translation was also a new endeavor that required the consultation of Jewish sources, such as the Targum and rabbinical commentaries by Rashi, Ibn Ezra, Kimhi and others, as well as the Latin interlineal translation of Santes Pagnino. The Ferrara translation was realized by a team of scholars, versed in Hebrew and Latin, who sought to maintain the principle of literal translation while at the same time producing a Spanish in accordance with new Renaissance ideals – an almost impossible enterprise, as Usque himself admitted in the prologue. The anachronistic words of old translations and a syntax that intended to preserve the character of the Hebrew original – in other words, the word-for-word principle referred to as 'Ladino' – clashed with the ideal of "polished language" and irritated many future readers, becoming a true obstacle to understanding the sacred text. Later editions of the entire Jewish Bible or of parts of it often reflect the ambiguous relation of the former converso readers to this Spanish Jewish Bible, admired for the spell of its arcane diction, which conferred a sacred quality, and/or abhorred for its obscure and outdated language. The subsequent editions of the Bible produced in Amsterdam during the seventeenth and eighteenth centuries thus progressively introduced adjustments, without, however, fundamentally changing the original Ferrara translation (Den Boer 1994).

It is often stated that the Ferrara Bible was meant to reintegrate former conversos into formal Judaism, as it permitted them to participate in worship while they still lacked knowledge of Hebrew and of the liturgical practice. However, exactly how the

Bible was used in the Western Sephardic Diaspora and how the Scripture was regarded in a time when its nature as a revealed text began to be challenged by philological and historiographic examinations has only recently come to the attention of scholarship. The existence of a vernacular Bible available in print was a novelty in the early modern Jewish world, and its consequences deserve careful consideration. On the one hand, it can be argued that the Spanish translation served the traditional purpose of the Bible in Jewish worship. Thus, many editions were made of the Pentateuch and Prophets for liturgical use (Humasim and Haphtarot); together with the continuous editions of the Spanish translation of the prayer books, these books served the former converso worshipper in the synagogue and at home, just as in the rest of the Jewish world. The practical purpose of such texts is apparent, for instance, in the case of the first edition of the *Humas o cinco libros de la Ley divina*, printed together with the *Libro de las Aphtaroth*, by Menasseh ben Israel in 1628. The rabbi of Amsterdam had organized the text from the Spanish Ferrara Bible into a convenient octavo format that the worshipper could carry with him; he arranged the Parashiot (the weekly pericope readings) so that the user could easily find them, marked the corresponding readings of the Haphtarot, added numbers in the margin to show where the Hazan or cantor would call for the reading of the Torah, and included tables in the book, providing both an overview of the order of the readings and a synthesis of the chapters of the Pentateuch. In subsequent editions, more tables and practical indications followed. All of these served the purpose of enabling worshippers to participate in services despite their lack of familiarity with the Hebrew spoken and read therein. Exactly who these worshippers were, or how long they relied on liturgy in translation before using the Hebrew text – if at all – is not known. A series of questions therefore remains: Did only newcomers use the vernacular editions? Was a female readership targeted? Do the continuously printed editions indicate an influx of newcomers into the community? Or do they perhaps show that even Sephardim born in the communities still preferred to use translations?

However pragmatic and traditionally Jewish the use of the vernacular Bible may have been, the fact that editions of the entire Bible circulated in the Western Sephardic world and that they became available in a convenient format[14] also allowed for the emergence of a new dimension of reading the Bible, namely as a text that could be meditated upon individually, at home, either following traditional usage or guided by personal interests.[15] The implications of this individual exploration of the Sacred

---

14 The *Biblia en lengua española* of Ferrara and the subsequent editions in Amsterdam of 1611, 1630 and 1646(?) were all in folio; the Spanish Bible printed by Athias in 1661 was in octavo and printed in the same format in 1726. The last Spanish Bible was printed together with the Hebrew text in folio in Amsterdam in 1762 (Den Boer 1994).

15 Upon studying the role of the vernacular Bible within the Sephardic community, Kromhout and Zwiep (2017, 153) conclude that among the Sephardim, the Bible was still not regarded as an autonomous text but was "never eclipsed by its rabbinic amplifications" as in Ashkenazi Judaism. Fisher

Text, as well as the modernity of this phenomenon, have recently come under careful scrutiny (Fisher 2020).

In addition to the vernacular Bible and liturgy, other works were also provided in order to integrate former conversos into Judaism, in such an amount and of such a quality that they form an impressive library of Jewish knowledge in the Spanish and Portuguese languages (Yerushalmi 1980). Between 1553, the year of publication of Samuel Usque's *Consolation for the tribulations of Israel*, and 1750, almost 150 works of prose were printed: ethical or moral treatises, paraphrases and studies of the Bible, sermons and discourses, special prayers, historiography, etc. Although such works often contain a remark that they were addressed to "those of our Nation" or to those who "did not know the Holy Language", such is their variety that it is difficult to reconstruct a standard reader for them, as the following example will show.

8 Explaining the Commandments in Spanish and Portuguese

Works such as the *Declaração das 613 encomendanças de nossa Sancta Ley* (*Declaration of the 613 Commandments of our Sacred Law*, 1627) by Abraham Farrar and rabbi Saul Levi Mortera; *Tesoro de preceptos* (Treasure of commandments) by Isaac Athias; *Compendio de Dinim* (1687) by David Pardo; *Tesouro dos Dinim* (Treasure of dinim/commandments, 1645–1647) by Menasseh ben Israel; and *Libro de mantenimiento del alma* (Book on the Soul's Care) by Moses Altares are all on Jewish Law, but differ considerably. Whereas *Mantenimiento del alma*, *Tesouro dos Dinim* and *Compendio de Dinim* provide practical instructions on how the commandments are to be observed in daily practice – with differences in length, structure, moral digressions, and language – the *Tesoro de preceptos* and *Declaração das 613 encomendanças* list all the commandments, providing the biblical text with a commentary and with rabbinic opinions; they therefore establish the rationale behind the commandments.

Now, whereas all these books served the purpose of providing former converso readers with insight into the commandments and their observance, some had a practical and didactic orientation, while others satisfied newcomers in their curiosity regarding the backgrounds and the tradition of the (rabbinic) practice of Judaism.

What this single example shows is that the vernacular library of Judaism produced by the Western Sephardim over two centuries cannot be seen as a homogeneous library produced for the purposes of re-education. Producers, readers and the individual communities all had their interests and priorities regarding Jewish texts in

---

(2020) offers detailed insight into the primary role of the Bible in the Sephardic curricula, where rabbinic commentaries were only studied by advanced students.

the vernacular. Early treatises published in the first half of the seventeenth century reflected an urge to integrate and to discipline the newcomers, insisting on the importance of *teshuvah* or repentance among those who returned to Judaism. This tendency was embedded in a narrative that regarded the Inquisition as a divine punishment for the conversos' abandonment of the God of Israel, which appealed to a sense of guilt among conversos for not having left Portugal or Spain earlier on account of their attachment to a life of material ease.[16] Such texts gained a new urgency in the 1660s under the spell of the pseudomessiah Sabbatai Zvi.

Many works produced in the initial years of the Western Sephardic communities also reflect the difficulty felt by some newcomers in accepting normative Judaism and rabbinic authority. Uriel da Costa notoriously challenged the latter in his *Propostas* sent to the Sephardic community of Venice in 1613 and later, when all rabbis ruled against him, managed to publish an extended version of his theses as *Exame das tradições fariseas* (*Examination of Pharisaic Traditions*, ed. Salomon 1993) in Amsterdam in 1624. It is exceptional that a copy of this work has survived, given the scandal it provoked and the immediate efforts made to confiscate copies and even to burn them all; since 1993, the modern reader can now access the text of this precursor of Spinoza.

Immediately prior to the publication of the *Exame*, the physician Samuel da Silva had fiercely attacked Da Costa's theses, debunking them on the basis of the only valid source of truth: the divinely guided authority of Oral Law. The question of the place of rabbinical authority or Oral Law in Judaism would remain an urgent issue among the Sephardim's religious establishment, as is apparent in several works: Imanuel Aboab of Venice countered attacks such as those by Da Costa with his *Nomología o discursos legales* (*Science of the Law or legal discourses*; 1627). Menasseh alluded to the challenge to Oral Law in his *Resurrección de los muertos* (*Resurrection of the Dead*, 1636). Even before the Da Costa case, a certain Isaac de Castro (a Portuguese Jew from Hamburg) had already published a booklet in Amsterdam on the same matter: *Sobre a ubrigação dos sábios* (*On the obligation of the Rabbis*, 1612).

It was a personality such as the merchant Abraham Pereira (Tomás Rodríguez Pereira), who left Madrid to live openly as a Jew in Amsterdam, who came to embody the model behavior that was required of the conversos. He made great efforts to adapt to normative Judaism, regretting that he was too old to learn Hebrew; instead, he devoted large sums of money to works of piety, founding a Yeshivah in the Holy Land. He was the author of two works in Spanish: *La certeza del camino* (Amsterdam 1666) and *Espejo de la vanidad del mundo* (1671) reflect a guilty conscience with regard to his

---

16 The treatise on repentance by Maimonides was translated twice, first by Samuel da Silva, *Libro de la tesubá*, Amsterdam 1612; then by haham David Cohen de Lara, rabbi of Hamburg, *Tratado de penitencia*, Leiden 1660. Similar works include: the translation of Gerondi's *Sendero de vidas* by Joseph Salom Gallego (a Sephardic Jew from Thessaloniki) and the *Enseña a pecadores* by Isaiah Horowitz, published in Amsterdam in 1666 with a penitential poem "Viduy penitential" composed in Hebrew and translated into Spanish by Solomon de Oliveira.

converso past as well as his full submission to Jewish Law and rabbinic authority. For these works of pious devotion, Pereira employed an arsenal of Catholic Iberian texts, which he 'Judaized' for their new purpose (Méchoulan ed. Pereyra 1987). In their reliance on Iberian Catholic sources for the construction of a Jewish identity, Pereira and the writer Barrios have been regarded as the Marrano "split souls" par excellence.

However, quite different, not necessarily tormented paths to Judaism were also possible, even those that departed from the mainstream narrative of repentance and submission. In Venice, a merchant called David Mugnon published a treatise on prayer, meditation and the knowledge of God (*Tratado de la oración, meditación y conocimiento del Dio*, 1654) that reflects a personal path to Judaism, centered on an intense meditation on the Psalms and containing a strong mystical component inspired by both Spanish devotional literature and Kabbalah. This work also displays a striking indifference towards the scrupulous practice of the Jewish Commandments. Mugnon, as much an autodidact as Pereira, had fashioned a very personal practice of Judaism.[17]

9 Different Readerships

To further illustrate the argument that Jewish learning or texts could function very differently among different former conversos, we can turn to a common source in the works of Abraham Pereira and David Mugnon: the *Tratado del temor divino* (*On the Fear of God*) by Eliahu de Vidas,[18] printed in Amsterdam in 1633. Whereas Pereira uses the text to instill the awe and fear of God in his readers, in an effort to induce them to repent and correct their ways, Mugnon sees the awe of God as a path to self-knowledge, leading to prayer and meditation and thereby to an encounter with the divinity.

In sum, the argument made here is that in spite of the repeated references to the readers of "our nation" who no longer know Hebrew, or who need instruction in the Spanish and Portuguese works of Jewish learning, there is no standard converso reader to whom these formulations allude. Consider, for instance, the works of Menasseh ben Israel. It is true that in his *Tesouro dos dinim* (*Treasure of commandments*, 1645–1647, reprint 1710), he specifically targeted the former converso with a daily exercise,[19] even addressing himself to the women of his Portuguese nation;[20]

---

[17] A critical edition and study of this work is underway by Den Boer and Wilke.
[18] The work is a partial translation of *Reshit Hokhma* by Eliyahu de Vidas (sixteenth century), based on the Zohar.
[19] "Thereby I have given you, reader, an excellent daily exercise, use it to your good to fulfill your obligation".
[20] *Tesouro dos dinim*, "To the most noble and virtuous women of his Portuguese Nation" (Portuguese); the author presents the last part of his work dedicated not only to the commandments regarding the house, but also including a treatise on the married woman with many moral instructions (Menasseh Ben Israel, dedication, 3–4).

but in *Conciliador*, after a long assessment of the content of the work and of all the Jewish and gentile authorities he consulted, the rabbi asserted that "this writing is in my poor native speech, because I [. . .] hope to be of use to the men of my Spanish nation [. . .] most of whom do not know Hebrew"; to which he then added: "I hope that soon it will be spread in other languages".[21] To which reader was rabbi Menasseh really addressing himself, and if it was those of his nation, why does he call them "Spanish" here, and why does he write in Spanish anyway?[22] Why did he dedicate a volume of the Pentateuch and the Prophets, the proper book for Jewish Bible reading, to a Christian friend? Why were so many of his works issued in Spanish and Latin versions? Of course, the rabbi had in mind a diversified audience and the commonplace of serving the needs of the men of his nation was first and foremost a justification of the usefulness of the time he spent writing.

The former conversos, the 'New Jews' of the Sephardic Diaspora, had a wealth of texts at their disposal, for instruction, piety, curiosity and – why not? – entertainment. However, in addition to the Bible and the prayer books, some works enjoyed particularly popularity. Sephardic libraries typically contained some works on the Commandments and on Oral Law, such as those previously mentioned, and some classics turn up frequently: the *Duties of the hearts* by Bahya ibn Paquda, available in a Spanish (1610) and a Portuguese (1671) translation,[23] the *Delectable vision* by Alonso de la Torre and *Cuzary* by Judah ha-Levi. The work by Bahya met the needs of the Jewish reader looking for a personal involvement with Judaism; the *Vision deleitable* was read as a spiritual journey; and *Cuzary* was attractive both as an encyclopedia of Judaism and as a dialogue between the religions in which Judaism excelled. *Cuzary's* translator, rabbi Jacob Abendana (1630–1685), had extensive contacts with Christian Hebraists and dedicated the work to the British merchant-diplomat Sir William Davidson. Abendana thus represents another case of the Sephardic author with an eye for the gentile environment in addition to Menasseh ben Israel, Jacob Judah Leon Templo and others.

Against the background of the intense anti-Jewish literature to which conversos had been exposed, it was only to be expected that the Jews of converso origin would look for works in which their religion was defended or acknowledged for its qualities (Feitler 2015). Thus, the apologetic *Excelencias de los hebreos* (Excellencies of the Hebrews, 1679), by Isaac (Fernando) Cardoso, would become another standard item on the Western Sephardim's bookshelves. Cardoso presented a counter-discourse to the praises of the (Catholic) Spanish nation and its anti-Jewish discourse. Cardoso's learned rebuke was cherished by many former converso readers.

---

21 *Conciliador* (1632, 7).
22 In the second volume, the author addressed the criticism that his first volume, discussed above, "was more for learned than for common readers". See Rauschenbach (2012, 69).
23 See Den Boer (2018c) for the special adjustments in the Portuguese translation by Samuel Abas, ordered by rabbi Moses Raphael d'Aguilar.

10 Manuscript Literature and Religious Controversy

A great part of the manuscript literature produced in the Western Sephardic Diaspora dealt specifically with polemics, defending Judaism and attacking Christian readings of the Old Testament. The impressive corpus of over three hundred polemical manuscripts in Spanish and Portuguese that are extant today reflects how important this genre was among former conversos – and among Christian readers interested in this Jewish literature that was now available in vernacular language. This literature did not so much contribute great novelties to the vast arsenal of anti-Christian arguments and biblical exegesis as it presented this arsenal in highly effective literary forms inherited from Christian Renaissance culture, such as the scholastic *quaestio*, the treatise or humanistic dialogue and even poetry. Texts by Orobio de Castro, Saul Levi Mortera, Eliyahu Montalto, Isaac Troki or Isaac Naar circulated in many copies, some of them in beautiful calligraphic codices that included illustrations. These belong to a literature that circulated semi-clandestinely, as printed distribution was explicitly forbidden in the Sephardic communities; understandably, given the particularly incisive character of many texts. Some texts and authors have received scholarly attention in recent decades,[24] with Abraham Gómez Silveira (1656–1741) as one of the most interesting figures in this genre due to the enormous volume of his polemical oeuvre, its extremely playful nature and the author's extensive Christian and Jewish reading (Brown and Den Boer 2000; Den Boer 2019). Language and literary devices, used in all variations but with an unmistakably Iberian character, played an important role in Sephardic polemical literature and further enhanced its attractiveness. Authors such as Barrios or Estevão Dias (Wilke 2014), as well as scholars and rabbis such as Isaac Orobio (Wilke 2018) and David Nieto, all exploited literary and rhetorical devices. The Spanish and Portuguese polemical literature was written from the sixteenth until the eighteenth century in different places and different contexts within the Western Sephardic Diaspora: sometimes, the arguments and dialogues reflected confessional tensions within the 'New Christian' *nação* (Wilke 2012); on other occasions, an exposure to Christian proselytism against which the rabbis wanted to protect the former conversos; and in many cases, the calligraphed copies in beautiful bindings of the early eighteenth century[25] seem to reflect a cherished *lieu de memoire* of religious and cultural identity. A general assessment of the Sephardic literature of controversy, with an overview of its production, extant copies and new critical editions is long due.

---

[24] On Orobio: Kaplan 1989, Wilke 2018; on Mortera: Salomon 1988, Fisher 2020, 167–23; the *Marrakesh Dialogues*, Wilke 2014; the "Danielillo", Orfali 1997; see also Mulsow 2002.
[25] That is to say, years after the time in which a real polemic had taken place.

11 Preaching to former conversos: Sermons as a Genre

Another important genre of the religious prose written in the Western Sephardic Diaspora that is extant in a considerable corpus is the sermon literature in Spanish and Portuguese, both in printed and manuscript form, totaling over two hundred homilies. Impressive as this number may be, it represents only a small portion of the sermons that were actually delivered in the communities of the Western Sephardim. Only counting the weekly sermons of the Portuguese Jewish congregation of Amsterdam from 1639 until 1800, we arrive at over 8,000 sermons,[26] which could be multiplied by a minimum of three or four when we take all the Sephardic congregations in Europe and the New World (Curaçao, for instance) into account.

Sermons were meant for oral delivery and would have been written down only in summarized form by the rabbis or their disciples. The extant sermons of Saul Levi Mortera are all in Hebrew, whereas he delivered them in Portuguese, probably only the sermons that were deemed of importance would have been recorded.

For the former conversos, the sermon was perhaps the only part of the Jewish service that was familiar to them, as it was very similar to the preaching they were accustomed to in Iberian Catholic services. This could well explain why sermons occupied a strategical position in religious instruction (Den Boer 1996, 214–215; Fisher 2020, 76–80).

In the carefully arranged printed sermons, many of the characteristics of the act of speaking must have gone lost. On the other hand, many of the sermons still show evident signs of orality, such as repetitions, exclamations and theatricality.

The sermons delivered in the Western Sephardic Diaspora, also known as "daras", dealt with a central issue, quite like contemporary Christian sermons. The sermon started with an initial biblical verse (Hebrew: *nose*) taken from the weekly Torah reading, followed by a quotation from rabbinic literature (the *ma'amar*). Then a central subject would be discussed. The sermons that appeared in print from the second half of the seventeenth century onwards had some additional features that reflect training in and conscious employment of classical oratory among the preachers. Particularly, the use of tropes and rhetorical devices made them very similar to the baroque Iberian, or more generally to the Jesuit sermon. Indeed, Sephardim read Catholic sermons, admiring in particular António Vieira's eloquence and "ingenious discourse".[27]

---

[26] Menasseh wrote that he composed 450 sermons over a period of twenty-five years, none of which have survived. Saul Levi Mortera is supposed to have delivered about 1,450 sermons; over 500 survive in manuscript, in Hebrew.

[27] It was the Portuguese critic António José Saraiva who coined Vieira's baroque style as "discours ingénieux" (1971).

As for the subjects of these sermons, present issues within the congregations were generally not addressed directly – when they were, then only by visiting rabbis or in moments of crisis. Preachers would pick a topic that corresponded to the weekly reading of the Torah – e.g., why Simhat Torah should be a day of joy –, but frequently they spoke about virtues and vices in a general way, avoiding criticism against members of the congregation. Quite to the contrary, preachers dressed their moral exhortations in a flattering robe, adopting a humble position and praising their "noble" and proud audience.

The rhetoric of the sermon was carefully planned. Rabbi Moses Raphael de Aguilar wrote a treatise on rhetoric and logic for his pupils in Amsterdam, in which he pointed out the three sorts of discourses: judicial, demonstrative and deliberative; he further commented on the structure of exordium, narration, confirmation and peroration along classical lines. In many of the sermons delivered by Western Sephardic preachers, trained in Amsterdam or other communities, we find a strict application of these rhetorical principles, already present in titles such as "Sermão moral e gratulatório" – where "moral" indicated the treatment of virtues and vices with an exhortation at the end of the sermon and "gratulatory" referred to the expression of gratitude required by the liturgical date or the circumstances. The argumentative content of the sermons – regarding, for example, the duty of the generous to be silent and that of the recipient to voice his gratitude – often displayed a strict application of logic, evident in the syllogisms used by the preachers. As for style, the Western Sephardim adopted the Ciceronian model, with long phrases and multiple forms of repetition, to which they added surprising comparisons or metaphors. Sermons remained understandable, however, and never reached the conceptual or rhetorical density of António Vieira or Hortensio Paravicino, the Iberian preachers that often appear as models.

Why were sermons printed or preserved in careful handwriting? Important events for the community were often commemorated in sermons. Rabbi Isaac Aboab de Fonseca and rabbi Jacob Abendana wrote sermons that were included in *Elogios a la felice memoria*, a volume of poetry dedicated to Abraham Núñez Bernal and Isaac Almeida Bernal, who died as martyrs in autos-da-fé in Spain in 1655. A function similar to that of preserving the collective memory of martyrdom was served by sermons celebrating the deliverance of conversos who had escaped inquisitorial persecution: Samuel Mendes de Solla, born in Lisbon and himself a 'New Christian' who had fled Portugal, celebrated the arrival of his mother and family in one such sermon; Gabay Isidro and Samuel da Silva Miranda also presented a narrative of Exodus, with Miranda delivering his homily precisely on the sabbath of Pesach.

The inauguration of the new Portuguese Jewish synagogue in Amsterdam in 1675 was commemorated in homilies that were published in an elegantly bound book together with engravings by the Dutch artist Romein de Hooghe. Its printer, David de Castro Tartas, addressed himself to imaginary visitors to whom he presented the marvels of the building's construction and the eloquent discourses pronounced by seven eminent orators of Talmud Torah (the Sephardic congregation of Amsterdam). Funeral sermons were printed at the death of leading rabbis – in Amsterdam and in London – or of other leading personalities, commissioned by their families. Sermons were held on the birth, wedding or death of the Prince or King in the communities of Amsterdam, Curaçao and London. One particular sermon of this kind merits attention as occasion and discourse were particularly bound together: the sermon pronounced by rabbi Samuel Mendes de Solla after the Prince of Orange had imposed a peace upon the quarreling Sephardic community of Curaçao in 1750. In the sermon *Triunfo da união*, Solla used all his skills to mask his own role in the bitter conflicts, reaching out to the opposing party in a gesture of conciliation.

One particular reason for the printing of sermons found in the Sephardic community of Amsterdam was the debut of a young preacher who had finished his studies at Ets Haim, the community's religious school. Accompanied by dedications, official approbations and praises, these works were not only a souvenir for the preacher himself but also heightened the status of Ets Haim as an institution capable of producing trained scholars who could compete with Christian theologians. In some way, these sermons were a counterpart to the academic dissertations published around the same time in Christian society.

12 Secular Eloquence: The Panegyric Genre

The baroque oratory present in the sermons was also employed in discourses written in the wake of historical or social events that were important to the Sephardic merchant elite. Writers such as Miguel de Barrios, Manuel de Leão and, above all, Joseph Penso de Vega wrote elaborate discourses celebrating military victories, royal visits or other events that demonstrated the involvement of the Sephardim in the political and social happenings of their time. Leão and Penso would typically leave the question of religious confession outside of their texts, whereas Barrios wrote a miscellaneous work on the history of the Sephardic community of Amsterdam and its institutions, *Triunfo del gobierno popular* (1684), as well as several prose texts addressed to other congregations and personalities. However, he had also written political discourses and treatises dedicated to Spanish, Portuguese and other European kings, princes and nobles; in most of these flattering, pompously erudite and increasingly contrived writings, he had carefully avoided any confession of his religion. Towards the end of his life, he increasingly introduced Jewish references, Kabbalistic speculations and messianic expectations into works dedicated to Christian sovereigns – claiming an importance as writer or prophet he felt had been denied to him.

Fiction was scarce in the Western Sephardic Diaspora. In the context of their involvement with literary academies, some authors, such as Gómez Silveira and

Penso de la Vega, wrote playful texts using Lucianesque dream-fiction, in which prose and verse alternated. Penso published three novellas in *Rumbos peligrosos* that follow the conventions of the Iberian baroque or "courtly" novel, full of a contrived, witty language, but other authors did not follow suit, and Penso himself dedicated himself mainly to all forms of highly contrived oratory. He had written funeral discourses on the death of his mother and father, in which he displayed the entirety of his Jewish learning, albeit without claiming a religious role: to his congregation, he spoke as a lay preacher. Penso also published a series of *Discursos académicos* (1685), which treated the frivolous topics discussed in the Sephardic literary academies with all the skills and excesses of baroque discourse, as well as *Ideas posibles* (*Possible fictions*, 1692), in which he translated imaginary discourses that Italian Jesuit authors had composed and added some imaginary discourses of his own, including what Joseph would have said to Potiphar's wife in order to resist her advances. But Penso is best known for his *Confusión de confusiones*, his dialogues between a merchant, a philosopher and a broker on the workings of the stock exchange. This work, a classic in the field of economics, has enjoyed a steady increase in studies: on the impact of stock trading and crisis among the Sephardim, including Penso himself, as well as on the hyper-baroque style and the wealth of sources the author used, many of them from Italian writers (Nider 2019; Pancorbo 2019, 144–162). It is remarkable and yet highly illustrative of Western Sephardic culture that an author such as Penso, who was born a Jew in the Sephardic world, would still present such a worldly outlook on life.

13 Poetry: Introduction

Spanish and Portuguese poetry was widely cultivated throughout the Western Sephardic Diaspora from the sixteenth century until well into the eighteenth century, comprising thousands of compositions. The precise number will remain difficult to establish as long as dispersed handwritten sources have not been fully explored. Although Spanish and Portuguese – the vernacular languages of the Sephardim – prevailed for over two centuries, poetry was also written in other languages: Latin among the first converso émigrés and in scholarly circles; Hebrew among rabbis and their students. As for the languages of the host countries, the particular cultural environment in Italy and the relative proximity of Italian dialects to Iberian Romance languages account for the fact that the Sephardim of certain communities, such as those of Venice, Livorno and Pisa, started to use the local language relatively soon. However, in most of the Western Sephardic Diaspora, the local language only became current when the Sephardim ceased to be in active exchange with the Iberian world or when they received civil rights.

14 The Choice of Spanish and Portuguese

Even though most Iberian 'New Jews' were of Portuguese origin and spoke Portuguese, the vast majority of their poetry was written in Castilian. This choice is not surprising, as in Portugal itself Castilian had risen to a language of prestige during the sixteenth and seventeenth centuries, adopted by many Portuguese poets.[28] Moreover, as a substantial portion of the poetry written by Western Sephardim was not religious or confessional in nature, and thereby not exclusively addressed to Jewish readers, the adoption of Spanish guaranteed a larger international audience than Portuguese. In religious poetry, on the other hand, a reason for choosing Castilian over Portuguese was the use of the Spanish Bible translation printed in Ferrara in 1553, with successive editions printed in Amsterdam between 1611 and 1762 (Den Boer 2008).

15 The Lyrical Voice and the Role of the Bible

Although poetry certainly occupied a prominent place within the Spanish and Portuguese literature of the Sephardim, the modern reader might be disappointed by the general absence of a lyrical or confessional tone. Although discrimination, persecution and exile belonged to a shared converso experience, the poetic expression of melancholy, lament or indignation is only found in a minor part of Sephardic poetry, which was perhaps more preoccupied with a reassertion of Jewish identity than with the memory of individual suffering. A profoundly exilic voice, as is present in Samuel Usque's *Consolação às tribulações de Israel* (1553; Usque 2014) or in Neo-Latin verse by the converso exile Diogo Pires (1517–1599; Tucker 1992), is not found in the same intensity and on the same level among the later conversos who returned to Judaism and wrote in Spanish and Portuguese. Among those converso poets who were still living as (formal) Christians and under the influence of the Inquisition, whatever suffering could be directly related to their condition as a persecuted minority had to be expressed in a veiled manner, as in the case of some poems in the autobiographical mode by Antonio Enríquez Gómez (1600–1663), printed in his *Academias de las musas* (1642; Pedraza Jiménez 2015).[29] Significantly, his only composition containing an overt confession of Judaism, the *romance* "Al felicísimo tránsito de Juda el Creyente, llamado don Lope de Vera y Alarcón", transferred the experience of religious martyrdom to an 'Old Christian' hero.[30]

---

28 See the references given by Novoa and Wilke in this volume.
29 Particularly, the part "Elegías y epístolas: el contenido autobiográfico", 97–105.
30 The poem only circulated in manuscript form, because of its polemical content. The poem is also known under its faulty title "Romance al divín mártir Juda Creyente", from the manuscript copy at the Bodleian. For a modern edition, see Brown 2007, especially 160–183.

It was above all in biblical poetry that converso and former converso Sephardic poets found a way to channel their individual experiences into a meaningful framework, reconnecting with the history of the Hebrew people. Epic poetry, the most prestigious literary genre of its time, proved to be particularly popular in this regard. Between 1604 and 1656, five long poems authored by Jewish or converso poets were published in Diaspora: *La Machabea* by one "Estrella Lusitano" (Lyon, but really The Netherlands, 1604), *David* by Jacobo Uziel (Venice 1624), *Poema de la reina Ester* by João Pinto Delgado (Rouen 1627), *El Macabeo* by Miguel Silveira (Napels 1638) and *Sansón nazareno* by Antonio Enríquez Gómez (Rouen 1656).[31] All of these compositions reflected the ambition to revive classical epic poetry through the stories of the biblical heroes. Although their authors refrained from dealing with actual questions of confession and did not present an overt conflict with Christianity, against the Iberian backdrop of continuous vilification of Jews and Judaism, praising the deeds and virtues of Hebrew heroes in defiance of their oppressors was a significant statement in itself (see also Díaz Esteban 1994). In these biblical poems, the traditional Christological readings of Old Testament heroes were left out; in the case of Pinto Delgado, this omission was supplemented by a subtle polemical stance (Zepp 2014, 117–160). A Catholic Iberian reader would regard these works, if at all available, as Old Testament narratives with an exemplary function, like those of the biblical heroes in the hugely popular editions of the *Flos Sanctorum Vida de los Santos* by Alonso de Villegas;[32] the converso reader, on the other hand, would feel encouraged by the identification with a Hebrew past of heroism and sacrifice (Den Boer 2011).

In the openly Jewish context of the Sephardic former converso congregations, biblical poetry was present in a variety of ways. Two former conversos with a personal history of inquisitorial persecution found a way of dealing with their past through rhymed translations of the Psalms, the biblical text that played such a significant role in shaping early modern devotion. David Abenatar Melo (Fernão Áclvares Melo) published his *CL Salmos de David* in Hamburg in 1626 (Den Boer 1997); a century later, Daniel Israel López Laguna offered a translation of the Psalms in different metrical forms, with the title *Espejo fiel de vidas*, printed in London in 1720 (Fine 2009). Although both realized their poetical versions with considerable artistic freedom, they felt a special allegiance to the literal Spanish translation of the Ferrara Bible: Melo went out of his way to declare that he had not diverged in any way from the "divine text of the Ferrara *ladino* [translation]", whereas Laguna conceded that if a reader missed elegance in his verses, this was because he wanted to follow the literal meaning of this Spanish bible translation, always "bound to truth" (Den Boer 2008,

---

[31] Miguel Silveira and Antonio Enríquez Gómez were conversos who had left Spain; Jacob Uziel was a descendant of the expelled Jews of Spain, not a former converso; "Estrella Lusitano" and Pinto Delgado were conversos who had embraced Judaism in the Netherlands. See Den Boer (2011).
[32] This work, precisely because it celebrated biblical heroes before the advent of Christ, was very popular among conversos (Kaplan 2018, 22).

337–338). And thus, between their reencounter with Judaism, symbolized by the Spanish truth of the Ferrara Bible, and their need to find meaning through the most personal of all biblical texts, these authors inserted some remarkable expressions of their own sufferings. Melo famously did this in his version of Psalm 30 (Den Boer 2008, 337) and in Psalm 123, where he lent a particular Iberian and autobiographical voice to David's words, lamenting that his soul was "oppressed and afflicted by the scorn, contempt, laughter and play of evil men, who live their live calmly. And they take us to be burnt in harsh fire!"[33]

16 The Poet Daniel Levi de Barrios

Daniel Levi de Barrios (1635–1701), the best known and most prolific of the poets of the Western Sephardic Diaspora, also turned to the Psalms in some of his finest poetry. In *Días penitenciales* (Penitential Days), a collection of religious poems related to the period of introspection and contrition leading up to Yom Kippur and the Jewish New Year, he included a rhymed translation of Psalm 51, together with other poems that echo the Psalms but are derived from Hebrew compositions belonging to the liturgy of Yom Kippur and Rosh Hashanah, which was already available in translated editions in the Western Sephardic Diaspora.[34] The author had included some of these penitential poems in earlier publications addressed to a general Iberian and therefore also Christian audience. In the collection printed in 1685, he presented one of these poems with an unequivocal confession of converso guilt that must have resounded among the readers of Christian past in the Sephardic Diaspora: "I confess that I have idolized / and stained myself in filthy water".[35] Such expressions of regret for the Christian past were, however, rare among the voluminous oeuvre of the Andalusian poet and in the literature of the former conversos in general.

Barrios, raised with the poetical traditions of the Spanish baroque, was a professed admirer of Góngora and other prominent Spanish poets. Consequently, many of his compositions were highly contrived, full of mythological references, rhetorical

---

33 De escarnio está oprimida
de malos que se ven en su sosiego,
con desprecio afligida
con risa, mofa y juego
nos llevan a quemar en duro. (den Boer 1997, 777)
34 The poem "Acto primero de contrición" is a free translation of the Viduy by Rabbenu Nissim, which was extant in Spanish translation in the various editions of the *Mahzor de Roshasanah y Kipur*, printed in Ferrara in 1552 and reprinted many times in Amsterdam during the seventeenth century. See Scholberg (1962, 162–168, 345–346).
35 "Confiesso que idolatré / que me manché en la agua inmunda", in *Dias penitenciales*, Amsterdam, 1685. The text was first edited by Scholberg (1962, 168–175).

devices and wit. His most ambitious poem, *Imperio de Dios en la armonía del mundo* (1674, ²1700), which was never completed due to a lack of financial resources, belongs to a genre of speculative philosophical/religious poetry that had its admirers in the poet's time. In its complete version, it was to comprise ten sections that reflected the ten choirs of universal harmony. Apart from describing the Creation, including the celestial, terrestrial and aquatic world, it would also contain the "Trumpet of Man with the voice of his creation, empire and fall", and it would end with a "Mirror of God's justice and mercy" (Den Boer 1996, 288–289). Only the first section on the Creation, in versions of 125 and 127 stanzas, have come down to us. Barrios also wrote an extensive poem on Free Will in which he presented thirteen "objections" to the concept, together with thirteen poetical answers. Skillfully, he managed to phrase the question in such a way that both Iberian Catholic readers and his own Jewish readers could admire the doctrinal content of his poem – which he probably had taken from Menasseh ben Israel's *Conciliador* (Scholberg 1962, 90). Perhaps emboldened by the praises he received from Spanish readers, the poet even forayed into religious discussions with members of his Sephardic community, notably with the physician and philosopher Isaac Orobio de Castro. Given his lack of any form of rabbinical training, this was a task for which he was ill-prepared. Consequently, he was harshly criticized or even censored more than once (Kaplan 1989, 230–232). Among his fellow Jewish readers, his religious poetry never attained the level of recognition he enjoyed among Iberian Christians, something he often bemoaned. The poet became further estranged from his community by taking upon himself the role of visionary and prophet, influenced by the messianic pretender Sabbatai Zvi. Particularly in his later work, he concocted esoteric interpretations of historic events that were full of Kabbalistic derivations, both of Hebrew and of Spanish, seemingly convinced of the imminent coming of the messianic age. Although hardly readable, such compositions are a fascinating testimony to the poet's baroque creativity and to his conflicted Marrano mind (Den Boer 1999).

In some areas, however, Barrios was quite successful: he was a gifted author of humoristic verse, using wit and learning to his advantage in satirical poetry and in parodies of mythological stories, so-called "fábulas burlescas". In his early years in Amsterdam, he had still written and published mythological and amorous poetry addressed to the general Iberian reader, even occasionally traveling to the Spanish court in Brussels. His collections *Flor de Apolo* (1665) and *Coro de las musas* (1672) had met with harsh criticism from the rabbis of Amsterdam, who censored Barrios because of his treatment of mythological deities, his flattery of Spanish kings and nobles and his "lascivious verse", not at all befitting a Jew (Den Boer 1995, 85–89). Some years before, the poet Jacob, alias Manuel, de Pina had also caused a scandal with the publication of his satirical and erotic verses (Den Boer 1995, 84–86, 116). As for Barrios, the censorship did not prevent the poet from having his works printed by Flemish printers or from having an Amsterdam printer use the false imprint of "Brussels" or "Antwerp" (Den Boer 1995, 54). Due to his chronic poverty, but also in the social context of the Western Sephardic elite's contacts with several European courts, Barrios continued to address himself to Christian patrons until the end of his life. He also used his skills as a witty poet with an acute eye for detail in works dedicated to Jewish subjects and personalities of the Western Sephardic Diaspora. One example is his "Alabança jocosa de la Ley divina", a praise of the Law of Moses written in a combination of jocular and serious verse, which extracts maximal effect from the traditional comparison between the Torah and a bride (Scholberg 1962, 86–87). In a similar style of easy verses displaying spontaneous wit, he composed hundreds of occasional poems on every noteworthy event within his community of Amsterdam and other congregations of the Western Sephardic Diaspora, flattering his patrons and lending a quasi-aristocratic prestige to their social and religious lives. Together with his chronicles in prose and verse of the institutions of Talmud Torah – the best known collection is *Triunfo del gobierno popular* (1684) – and other Sephardic communities in Europe, many of these occasional pieces are still consulted for the valuable biographical and historical details provided by the poet, however embellished his presentation of them was (Pieterse 1968).

What can be observed in the work of Daniel Levi de Barrios can be extended to much of the poetry written in the former converso Diaspora: many of the compositions produced by a considerable number of poets and "poetasters" constitute valuable testimonies to the social life of the Western Sephardim rather than lasting creations of poetical force. Many of these poets are only known for a small number of verses, written on the occasion of a book being printed a wedding or a funeral. Sometimes, poems were written within the framework of socialization, in the worldly "academias" or socio-artistic gatherings that coexisted with religious life throughout the Western Sephardic Diaspora. Here, representatives of the merchant class, physicians, Jewish scholars and poets would meet to attend and participate in entertaining or learned literary discussions, often enriched by musical and even theatrical performances (Kaplan 1989, 286–302).[36] Such *academias* or salons were fundamentally different from the formal Yeshivot and from the societies organized for religious study among adult former conversos (Fisher 2020, 64–65). They belonged to the secular dimension of Sephardic life and could – occasionally or regularly – welcome non-Jewish attendees. A good indication of the social role and activities of the former conversos is provided by the poems in praise of important political events, such as the victories against the Turks at Vienna (1683) and Buda (1686), the Glorious Revolution under King Stadholder William III (1688–1689), or the journey of the Queen-to-be Maria Anna of Neuburg from Germany to Portugal with a stopover in the Netherlands (1687). All of these events were accompanied by the involvement of an elite of Sephardic merchants, known for their diplomatic efforts and financial services to European courts. Poets such as Barrios, Duarte/Moses Lopes Rosa or Manuel de Leão lent artistic prestige to their patron's activities and did not confront their readers with matters of religion (Swetschinski 2000, 298–299; Den Boer 1991).

---

36 For the Italian context, the "Academia de los Sitibundos" in Livorno, see Pancorbo 2019, 44–51.

17 Poetry and Jewish Life in the Western Sephardic Diaspora

As for Jewish life, even poetry written to commemorate Jewish martyrs who died in autos-da-fé in the Iberian world originated in a social context. A printed volume dedicated to Abraham Núñez Bernal and Isaac de Almeida Bernal, both burned alive (in Córdoba and Santiago de Compostela) in 1655 for refusing to recant their Judaism, contained two sermons and some fifty poems written by twenty or more members of the communities of Amsterdam and Hamburg. Some of the compositions are variations on the same motto, and many of them display similar patterns, indicating a special gathering where these poems were recited (Den Boer 1995, 137–138). A collection of poetry dedicated to the martyrdom of Isaac de Castro Tartás contained poems in different metrical forms written by Moses Pinto Delgado, Jonas Abravanel, Jacob de Pina and other poets (Roth 1962). Such volumes kept the memory of the martyrs alive and established them as models not only for their religion but also for the "nobility" or "honor" of their lineage: a very Iberian sense of Jewish identification (Bodian 1997, 81–82).

Behind the public sphere of Sephardic social life and of poetry in print, there also existed a considerable manuscript circulation. As mentioned above, a great part of these handwritten texts, many of them of considerable length, contain religious controversy, i.e., arguments against Christianity that were bound to remain unpublished lest they expose the Western Sephardic communities to harsh criticism or persecution in the Christian societies they lived in. Poetry also played its part in this literature – compositions in honor of Jewish martyrs burned in autos-da-fé were of course instrumental in strengthening the faith of the conversos who had returned to formal Judaism in the communities of the Western Sephardic Diaspora. Poetry also functioned as a mnemotechnical device or artistic synthesis of polemical arguments, as is evident in a poem by one Moses Belmonte that is often titled "Arguments against the gentiles" and appears in many of the copies of the treatises of Saul Levi Mortera, Montalto or Orobio de Castro (edited in Brown and Den Boer 2000, 182–184).

18 Apologist and Jester: The Poetry of Abraham Gómez Silveira

A very particular position in this polemical literature is occupied by Abraham Gómez Silveira (1656–1741), who authored an extensive oeuvre extant only in manuscript, with the exception of a collection of seven sermons and a short humoristic discourse spoken within the context of a literary academy of Portuguese Jews living in Antwerp (Brown and Den Boer 2000; Den Boer 2019). The many volumes he left us constitute a polemical work that originated as a refutation of the proselytizing efforts of the French Huguenot preacher Isaac Jacquelot, who had addressed his *Dissertations sur le Messie* (1699) to the Jews. Silveira's reply soon developed into a multivolume polemical work, including a substantial portion of poetry, his favorite forms being "coplas", stanzas of four eight-syllable verses (also called *redondillas*). Insofar as they serve to sustain arguments through verse, and on account of their frequent aphorisms, they remind the Iberian reader of the *Proverbios* of the medieval Spanish Jew Sem Tob, although Silveira would have been unaware of the latter. Despite their dialectical qualities, these *coplas* adopt the tone of common-sense wisdom, and they are full of very Spanish expressions, including *refranes* of popular tradition. More often than not, the *coplas* also contain wit and laughter, not only directed at the (Christian) opponent, but also as an instrument of fideistic skepticism, as a mark of human folly. The work of this long-lived scholar and writer has been receiving a steady increase in attention, as the exploration of his voluminous handwritten works reveals one of the most singular writers of the whole Western Sephardic Diaspora: a voracious reader of whatever theological, philosophical and literary texts he could find, with an uncontrollable need to insert Spanish expressions and wordplays into his writing. Some humoristic or irreverent poems have come to light that can now also be attributed to Silveira, one on the life of the pseudomessiah Sabbatai Zvi and another on Jesus Christ and the Magdalene, in which Jesus appears as a *pícaro* (both in Brown and Den Boer 2000), as well as a nonsensical poem on the Grand Turk and the virtues of chocolate, with a diatribe against the Inquisition (González Quiroz 2015).

Due to recent efforts by scholars, the manuscript poetry written and produced in the Western Sephardic Diaspora has been rescued from the libraries and collections where it lay dormant. Frequently, this poetry is found in miscellaneous collections. Some are remnants of a literature that was no doubt recited in *tertulias*, academies or other gatherings but did not make it into print: in the early modern era, many texts still circulated in manuscripts – if at all. The poetical activity of David del Valle Saldaña (Brown and Den Boer 1997), only partially extant, may be mentioned by way of example. In one work, we read that it was recited at the *Sociedad Amigable* in the house of the Pinto family in Amsterdam, again indicating a literary or cultural salon where Spanish and Portuguese were cherished – although by then they had received the company of French culture. Some of Saldaña's works were perhaps too occasional to be printed – and at least one of them, a collection of erotic, not to say pornographic verse, would surely not have been meant to be published at all. Although Amsterdam was as ever the center of Western Sephardic cultural production, also for manuscripts, there are testimonies of activities in other communities as well. The Braidense library of Milan contains a collection of Spanish poetry, both non-Jewish and Jewish, that might have circulated in Italy (Brown 1998, 63–64); in Hamburg, one Bento Guilhelmo Rahmeijer had a chapbook of poetry and prose in Spanish, Portuguese and French with some compositions that appear to reflect literary gatherings in the early seventeenth century in the Hanseatic city (Brown 2018).

Anti-Christian polemical literature, including poetry, was widespread throughout the entire Western Sephardic Diaspora.

19 Chapbooks in Exile

Personal collections of poetry, and of literature in general, offer insight into the taste of former converso individuals, and frequently also reflect the practice of literature in more intimate circles, such as that of the family. In miscellaneous collections, we often find well-known Spanish and Portuguese poetry that was read aloud or sung – sometimes with an indication of Dutch, French or English melodies. In several chapbooks, a variety of Spanish and Portuguese poems by known authors such as Lope, Góngora or Quevedo coexisted with compositions by converso or Jewish former converso poets, such as Enríquez Gómez, Barrios or Pina. These testimonies reflect the ongoing attachment that former conversos felt to Iberian culture, although we should be aware of some very particular readings of Christian religious subjects. Thus, in a seventeenth-century miscellaneous manuscript belonging to the Sephardic community of Amsterdam, the well-known and playful "Quintillas al Nacimiento" (stanzas at the Nativity) by Gerónimo Cáncer were reproduced with extensive anti-Christian glosses (Brown and Den Boer 2000, 278–280).

Another manuscript volume of poetical miscellanea that provides us with insight into how Iberian culture might have been enjoyed in an intimate setting stems from Amsterdam and was written in the early eighteenth century. It contains some short comical plays that were taken from Spanish collections of *Entremeses,* together with a short Jewish play, "Entremés de Parho" (Farse of Pharaoh), in which Moses manages to free his people from the oppression of Pharaoh. The latter includes some comical elements, such as the character of the *gracioso*. The collection also features a large poem – totaling no less than 90 stanzas – titled "Exhortation of sinners and comfort for the afflicted", which retells the story of Genesis in simple, often moralizing verses, no doubt meant to be sung. The very same poem appears embellished with illustrations in a late eighteenth-century manuscript written down by Solomon Saruco in The Hague; here the poem was called "Sacred poetry to demonstrate the greatness of the Ruler" (Poesías sacras para manifestar la grandeza del Soberano) and had over 1000 Stanzas.[37] Undoubtedly, such an extensive poem, preserved in a beautiful binding, with its double attachment to Judaism and to the Spanish language, was still meaningful to a Sephardic family in the Netherlands almost two hundred years after the first Iberian immigrants arrived there.

---

[37] A manuscript with this title, copied by "Selomoh Saruco" in 1748, is extant at Ets Haim/Livraria Montezinos of the Portuguese Jewish Community in Amsterdam, ms. EH 48 D 30. Saruco was a tutor at the house of the wealthy Lopes Suasso family in The Hague (Lieberman 2011, 158), and it is very probable that he would have written this manuscript for his patrons.

It is precisely in such collections and private chapbooks that other insights into the private lives of the converso immigrants are to be discovered. In some of them, we encounter Portuguese poems that are very different from the polished baroque compositions written and recited in refined circles. Such is the case of a poetic dialogue between two Portuguese Jewish women in Amsterdam, Sara and Rica, who complain of the boredom of their existence and the life of luxury they left behind in their home country: "in my land, sister, in the house of my father there was much comfort; there I did not have to stick my hand in cold water and lived a gentle life" . . . (Den Boer 2001, 198–199). However fictitious, such conversations in plain and lively Portuguese reflect real emotions felt by persons and families that still felt estranged in their new environment and could not help but look back at the lives they had left behind – in spite of religious persecution. Another very plain but moving poem is found in the middle of the aforementioned volume comprising Spanish plays and a large biblical play, also in Spanish. In the Portuguese "Lamentations on Death", we do not find a moralizing composition on mortality and the virtuous life, but instead a scene almost taken from real life. Here the voice of a young woman expresses her terrible anguish at the idea of death and decay. She confesses that if she accidentally pricks her finger when sewing, she already gets anxious, thinking of the worms in her grave . . . When she visits her friends' house and wants to have fun, she is stricken with melancholy and cannot but think of her mortality. Then she bursts out in an emotional cry:

O mein arche o mein lifie!	Oh my heart (Dutch: *hartje*), o my love (Dutch: *liefje*)!
Que vos hão de amortalhar!	You will be wrapped in a shroud!
E depois para enterar	and afterwards, to be buried,
levarvos hão no *esquiphe*!	you will be taken in a boat (Dutch: *schipje*)![38]

Her Portuguese mixed with exclamations in Dutch, the language heard in everyday life, this anonymous fictive character visualizes being taken by boat to be buried: an unequivocal reference to the burial place of Amsterdam's Sephardic Jews at Ouderkerk.

20 Theatre in the Diaspora: The Popularity of the *comedia*

The establishment of Jewish communities of Iberian conversos in Europe between the second half of the sixteenth century and the first half of the seventeenth century coincided with the emergence of theatre in Spain. The presence of public theatres in the major cities together with the formula of the *comedia* introduced by Lope de Vega attended to the needs of a heterogeneous urban audience and decisively contributed to the enormous popularity of drama in the Iberian Peninsula. It could only be

---

38 Manuscript Cod. Hisp. 30 at the State and University Library of Hamburg, Germany, ff. 30r-31v.

expected that the conversos who left Spain and Portugal would take their fondness for drama with them on their way to the different regions of Europe where they settled.

The attendance of theatrical performances by the emigrated conversos – whether living as Christians or as Jews – is well documented. In sixteenth- and seventeenth-century Italy, there already existed a Spanish culture, and the linguistic barrier was low for the Iberian newcomers. Many sources testify to the attendance of theatre and spectacles by conversos and Iberian Jews in Italy. In Livorno, the Sephardim were known for their fondness for attending dramas and comedies in Italian and Spanish, and they were also active in producing and financing plays (Bregoli 2014, 233). The community's authorities intervened in 1665 following unspecified "scandals" that allegedly occurred in a theatre, prohibiting men, women and children from attending spectacles. This decision was, however, not upheld for long (Toaff 1990, 314, quoted by Pancorbo 2019, 51).

As for 'New Christians' and Jewish conversos living in France, the situation must have been similar.[39] In Northern Europe, where the local languages would have been an obstacle, the Sephardim still enjoyed going to the theatre, where they could attend Spanish *comedias* in translation. Soon, *aficionados* of theatre among the Sephardim of Amsterdam organized staged performances themselves. The wealthy Isaac de Pinto celebrated his wedding in 1648 with a staging of *La vida es sueño*, the famous play by Calderón, probably with actors from the Spanish court at Brussels; the event took place at Pinto's residence in Rotterdam, with many guests who came over from Amsterdam (Salomon 1975, 41). The Sephardim of that city founded their own companies and rented warehouses to perform *comedias*, apparently with such success that they caught the eye of the municipal authorities, who objected to such performances, wary that they might affect the revenues of the city theatre. We do not know which plays were actually performed. It is reasonable to presume that the big hits of Golden Age Spanish drama were also performed in these Sephardic theatres; this is suggested by two collections of *comedias* that were printed in Amsterdam by a Sephardic printer in 1697 and 1704, precisely around the time the above-mentioned companies were active. These collections contained works by Calderón, Matos Fragoso, Moreto, Rojas, Vélez Guevara, Solís and Zárate – all popular authors in the second half of the seventeenth century. Small adjustments in the printed texts indicate that these works reflected the taste of the Sephardic immigrants and would have been performed: all too explicit references to Christianity were left out and substituted by more neutral formulations.[40] The Amsterdam Sephardim continued their theatrical activities well into the eighteenth century. In 1726, a further collection of *comedias* was published, this time of famous biblical plays by Lope, Calderón and the converso playwright

---

[39] Wilke mentions how the converso author Antonio Enríquez Gómez attended French theatre (1994, 302–303); see also the article by Novoa and Wilke in this volume.
[40] For instance, exclamations to the Virgin Mary or to Jesus Christ have been substituted by more neutral formulations like "Dios" or "Dios Bendito" (Den Boer 1995, 150).

Antonio Enríquez Gómez. The Sephardic printer or publisher dedicated it to Manuel Jiménez, son of the prominent Manuel de Belmonte.[41] Although the Sephardic community of Amsterdam had grown progressively more familiar with Dutch and its elite increasingly read and expressed itself in French, such was the taste for Iberian theatre that in 1758, a play by Voltaire was translated into Spanish and printed for the Sephardim Moses Gavilán and Abraham Morales. They dedicated it to the director of the "Colegio de la comedia española", expressing their hope that the company could continue its activities.[42]

21 Sephardic Playwrights and Jewish Drama

Theatre was also written by the former conversos, including works with a Jewish setting. Already around 1558, Solomon Usque wrote a Purim drama about Esther that was performed several times in the ghetto of Venice. Usque was thus the author of one of the earliest Jewish plays. In 1559, it was performed for the first time for a group of Venetian nobles, and it was staged again in 1592. Leon Modena came to know of it and created his own version of the play, not being a great admirer of Usque's verses and style (Adelman and Ravid in Modena 2020, 235).

A further – again, indirect – testimony to the fact that plays were written by Italian Sephardim stems from the documentation of a trial by the Italian Inquisition following an accusation of blasphemy in a play that was staged during Carnival in Pisa. The accused were young Portuguese men, both Catholic and Jewish, who had staged an *entremés*, a comical interlude by a Spanish author. However, together with the text of the confiscated *entremés*, there were some leaves of another short play, titled "About the doctor and his servants", by an anonymous author who appears to have been Jewish.[43] Finally, two short plays by a certain Raphael Montes or "Nieto de Montes" are extant in manuscript. They were written to celebrate the visits of the Grand Duke Ferdinando II and Vittoria della Rovere to the cities of Livorno and Pisa, where Jews participated in the festivities. In both of these works, full of baroque flattery and meant for the public sphere, there is of course no Jewish content (Félix-Álvarez 1994).

Invariably, we are best informed about Amsterdam with regard to theatrical practices and plays. Here, the earliest work we know of is a Portuguese allegorical play

---

[41] *Comedias nuevas de los mas célebres autores y realzados ingenios de España*. Amsterdam: 1726 (Den Boer 1995, 151).
[42] "Dedicatoria al señor don Enrique Gomes Soares, director del Colegio de la Comedia Española", signed by Gavilán and Morales in Amsterdam on 12 January 1758. *Bruto*. Amsterdam: G. and J. De Broen, 1758, ff. *2r-v (Den Boer 1995, 151–152).
[43] "Un dotor i lo que izieron sus criados" On this work, see Bellomi 2019, 459; and Nider 2012, who first studied its fragmentary text.

performed in the synagogue, the *Diálogo dos montes* (Dialogue of the Mountains), the result of a collaboration between Rehuel Jessurun (Paulo de Pina) and rabbi Saul Levi Mortera. According to several manuscript copies that have been preserved, the play was performed in 1624. More than one hundred years later, it was printed as an "interesting and very old" ("antiquíssima") piece, a kind of *lieu de mémoire* of the early years of the Portuguese Jewish congregation in Amsterdam. Its publisher revealed that it was also a tribute to the president of the present *mahamad*, who was a descendant of Rehuel Jessurun.

It is of course remarkable that a play, however religious in content, would have been created and performed in the center of one of the first congregations of the Amsterdam Sephardim, taking into account the traditional Jewish objections against theatre and spectacles. In communal regulations drawn up a few years later, the joint authorities of the three Sephardic congregations of Amsterdam forbade further use of the synagogue for all types of spectacles related to festivities, annoyed by all the installations and alterations of the sacred space and order (Swetschinski 2000, 286; for the regulation Pieterse 1968, 155). However, a general stance on theatre itself was not formulated.

The performance of a drama such as the *Diálogo dos montes* in a synagogue of the Western Sephardic Diaspora would probably remain an exception. The content of the work, a dispute between the seven mountains of Palestine regarding which one deserves the most honor in the eyes of God, stems from a Midrashic tradition. The winner of the competition was, predictably, Mount Sinai; the play was performed on Shavuot, commemorating the giving of the Torah on Sinai.

The dramatic content of the play is limited; it is rather a staged dialogue in the framework of Iberian religious one-act plays, the *autos*, but without action and without a real conflict. The disputation between the mountains, each represented by an actor (a member of the community), was an amicable one, basically consisting in recited sermons in which each mountain's preeminence was backed by scriptural and rabbinic quotations – this was the part written by rabbi Saul Levi Mortera. The more entertaining element was the appearance of a group of musicians between the parts of the play; their songs gave voice to the feelings of restoration, gratitude and hope of the reborn community of Jews (Polack, ed. 1975, xxi–xv).

Thirty years after the performance of the *Diálogo*, a further play appeared in an entirely different context. Jacob (Manuel) de Pina published a volume of humorous and satirical poems titled *Chanzas del ingenio y dislates de la musa* (*Plays of wit and follies of the Muse*), including a parodical comedy titled *La mayor hazaña de Carlos VI* (*The greatest achievement of Charles VI*), an obvious reference to a comedy with the same title about Emperor Charles V by the Spanish dramatist Jiménez de Enciso (Mata Induráin 2018). The authorities of Talmud Torah were scandalized by the obscene content of the work and did not hesitate to prohibit it, threatening its author with excommunication. Pina had a powerful patron, however, and no doubt through the intervention of Moises Curiel, alias Jerónimo Nunes da Costa, the work was permitted again – only to be prohibited afterwards. The comedy itself was quite daring, portraying Charles VI (obviously referring to Charles V) of Habsburg as a foolish, bawdy Emperor surrounded by ridiculous noblemen, fulfilling his ultimate wish of retirement in Yuste, in a convent of nuns. If performed at all, this comedy would have been enjoyed privately, outside of the sphere of the Sephardic congregation. Its author did not have the vocation of a transgressor, however: he also wrote serious poetry, such as poems in honor of converso martyrs burnt in *autos-da-fe* and a Portuguese poem on the death of rabbi Saul Levi Mortera, published in 1660, only a few years after his *Chanzas* (Den Boer 1995, 116, 329–333).

22 Secular and Jewish Drama by Daniel Levi de Barrios

The most prominent among the poets of the Western Sephardic Diaspora, Daniel Levi de Barrios, cultivated all literary genres; he also dedicated himself to writing plays. He had included three *comedias* of the cloak and dagger genre in *Flor de Apolo* (1665), his first published work, still intended for a general Iberian audience. It is possible that he had written the plays in Spain, before arriving in Amsterdam. They are not different from the common cloak and dagger plays of young noblemen and women entangled in amorous pretensions. One of them, *The Spaniard from Oran* (*El español de Orán*), is set against the backdrop of rivalling Spaniards and Moors in Oran, but without religious implications.[44] The dramatic qualities of the three plays were sufficient for several re-editions in Spain during the eighteenth century. We do not, however, have information regarding any performance of any of these three plays in Barrios's time – neither in Amsterdam nor in the Spanish Low Countries, which he still visited at the time the three plays were published. In *Coro de las musas* (1672), Barrios included some minor dramatical pieces to celebrate events at the court of Brussels, and according to Barrios's own inscriptions these short plays were performed there. Even after refraining from the visits he had made to the Spanish Low Countries, the poet would continue to address works to Spanish and Portuguese patrons, and this also applies to his dramatical production. In 1690, he published *Nubes no ofenden al sol* (*Clouds do not offend the Sun*), an allegorical play celebrating the royal wedding of Charles II of Spain to Maria Anna of Neuburg. The no less than fourteen mythological characters in the play represented such a variety of entities as Germany, Spain, Great Britain, Amsterdam, the Sacred Prophecy, "Common Accidents" and prominent kings and personalities, including King Louis XIV of France, William III of Orange, and Don Manuel de Belmonte. The latter, one of the wealthiest members of the Amsterdam Sephardic congregation, exercised several diplomatic functions in European courts: he was resident

---

44 Barrios's brother Juan had gone to Oran and served in the army there (Scholberg 1962, 6–7).

of the Spanish King and Count Palatine of the Holy Empire. Representing the political constellation of the anti-French or anti-Turkish Holy League, the work was both a contrived flattery directed at the royal wedding and a reflection of Barrios's political-messianic expectations. It is hard to imagine the work being performed.[45]

In 1665, Barrios had published a Jewish work, addressed to his Jewish audience: *Contra la verdad no hay fuerza* (*No force can stop the truth*), an allegorical play celebrating the martyrdom of three conversos who were burned at the stake in autos-da-fé staged in Cordoba. The work is modelled after Calderón de la Barca's *Los encantos de la culpa* and has been characterized as a Jewish "auto sacramental", although "comedia alegórica" fits better, because the "sacramental" element of the Catholic *autos* is difficult to transfer to a Jewish work, nor was there any intent by the author to explain theological concepts. Like the Ulysses of Calderon's *Los encantos de la culpa*, the main character of *Contra la verdad*, "Will" (Albedrío), is besieged by enemies who try to seduce him. In the case of Barrios's play, these are Appetite and Error, led by Lie. Only when Will is convinced by Understanding and assisted by Truth and Zeal can he free himself from the grip of Lie and return to the Law of Moses. The protagonist then follows the example given by the steadfastness of the three honored martyrs. After performing an act of contrition, professing his offenses, Will joins the martyrs and is burnt at the stake. In a final battle, Virtue and Zeal prove that God rewards the righteous. Given the exalted atmosphere obtaining around the time the play was published due to the excitement stirred up by the pseudomessiah Sabbatai Zvi, it is conceivable that Barrios's play was actually performed in his community – although most certainly not in the synagogue. *Contra la verdad no hay fuerza* contains quite elaborate stage directions, although this fact alone is no guarantee of an actual staging. Barrios also wrote some minor works he called "autos" that were short allegorical plays in praise of certain institutions of the Sephardic community of Amsterdam; these plays with few characters and minimal stage requirements could well have been staged in these societies (Lieberman 1996).

23 Iberian Allegorical Drama in Hebrew: Joseph Penso

That theatre was indeed appreciated within the sphere of the Sephardic community is further attested by a play written in Hebrew by Joseph Penso (1650–1693), who later styled himself "De la Vega", when he was only seventeen years old. Alternatively known as *Pardes soshanim* and *Asire Hatikvah* (*Prisoners of Hope*), it was published

---

[45] The author had dedicated the preceding introductory "loa" to Manuel Francisco de Lira, hoping that the latter would pass it on to the King, probably without much success. Lira had occupied a military role in the Spanish Netherlands and Barrios had known him; by 1690, Lira resided in Madrid, where he housed visiting ambassadors.

in 1673 and applauded by a whole range of personalities of the Amsterdam Sephardic congregation, including the rabbis Isaac Aboab da Fonseca, Moses Raphael de Aguilar, Abraham Cohen Pimentel and Solomon de Oliveira. Poets like Barrios and Pina also contributed to the praises, the latter with puns on his not understanding it because of its language... *Prisoners of Hope* is a short allegorical play in three acts, called an "auto moral", encouraging the youth to abandon their lives of worldly pleasures and return to the service of God and his Law, with a plot very similar to Barrios's *Contra la verdad no hay fuerza*. Here, it is a King (representing Will), besieged by the Devil and his helpers Appetite, Woman and Pleasure, who is led back to God and religious observance by Reason, Truth, Providence and an Angel. There is no information available regarding an actual performance of the play; however, we do know that it was printed a century later in Livorno (1770), where Penso had stayed for a period of about ten years (between 1670 and 1683), during which he was actively engaged in the congregation and contributed to literary life through the foundation of a literary academy, the "Academia de los Sitibundos" (Academy of the Thirsty).

24 The Enduring Popularity of Iberian Drama in the Western Sephardic Diaspora

In addition to the elaborate dramas in Baroque style written by authors with a literary vocation, there also existed drama on a more modest level, written in a plain but entertaining style. The pieces that have come down to us in print and in manuscript were possibly conceived to be performed in a small circle or to be read aloud. In 1699, two short plays were published in Spanish and Portuguese. The Spanish play on the Esther story was accompanied by riddles and rhymes and was conceived to be enjoyed during Purim, as the title page reveals. The *Comedia de Amán y Mardoqueo* was presented by its editor, the printer Isaac Cohen de Lara, as the adaption of an originally one-act play, written by an author from Hamburg, to the formula of the three act *comedia* – whether Lara took this work from a Yiddish Purimspiel or from a Sephardic author is not known (Praag 1940, 14). The work is somewhat clumsy, with its Spanish exhibiting interferences from Portuguese and faulty versification (in *quintillas*), but it is entertaining and has a joyous popular character. The Portuguese play *Jahacob e Essau* was printed some months later; again, it was presented as the adaptation of the work of a previous "famous author". The story of rivalry between Jacob and Esau was also a popular subject for Purim performances and in the Portuguese version, use was apparently made of Jewish legends regarding the famous story, with elements not present in the biblical narration (Praag 1940, 97, 101). Although again popular in tone, the work is typical for the culture of the former conversos in that it brings together elements of Jewish tradition and Iberian dramatical and poetical forms. Particularly striking in this regard is the appearance of Silvio and Montano in the service of Laban: these shepherds, in the best pastoral tradition of the eclogue, remind one of the pastoral shepherds in Tirso de Molina's biblical play *La venganza de Tamar*.

A further example of a short play that would have been read or performed among the Sephardim in a Jewish context can be found in an Amsterdam manuscript dated around 1700. Presented as a "Book of *entremeses* (interludes) and other curiosities", it contains four well-known Spanish short comical plays, preceded by another short play in Spanish with a biblical subject, the "Entremes of Pharaoh". This work by an anonymous Jewish author is rudimentary in language and form – with a quite arbitrary spelling, as if written by a scribe with no formal education. It centers around the imminent exodus of the people of Israel conducted by Moses. The principal characters are Moses, Israel and Pharaoh, and again there is the Iberian element, represented by the *gracioso* "Filo". The play is in verse, as was common in Iberian theatre, and as it is only 295 verses long, it could have been performed as an "entremés" or interlude, perhaps between the acts of a larger play (Brown 2018).

Within the genre of the (probable) Purim play, one example by Isaac de Matatia Aboab is the most elaborate. The merchant Aboab (Amsterdam 1632–1707) is known for a great number of works he commissioned in writing, reflecting his broad interest and above all his moral and religious preoccupations. Among his works is a *comedia* on the life of Joseph in three parts, *El perseguido dichoso* (translated as "Harassed but Happy"), in fact consisting of two *comedias* and a one-act epilogue. The work appears to have been authored by Aboab himself and is written in Spanish, with interferences from Aboab's native Portuguese. More elaborate than the above-mentioned Purim plays insofar as it displays a variety of metrical forms and reminiscences of Spain's classical writers, such as Garcilaso de la Vega, Góngora and Carvajal, the play nevertheless contains considerable formal shortcomings. Its structure is particularly unbalanced, with a supposed division into three parts that in fact total, at best, two and a half. Moreover, the first two parts are themselves divided into three acts of a very unusual extension: in each part, acts one and two are extremely short, whereas the third act is extraordinarily long. *El perseguido dichoso* also exhibits defects in rhyme and meter (McGaha 1998, 230). Altogether, the *comedia*-in-parts is again the product of an amateur rather than a skilled writer, but its plot is well-developed and the playwright knew how to exploit the dramatical contents of the biblical story of the exemplary steadfastness of Joseph, making good use of the techniques of the *comedia*, particularly the effects of disguise and recognition. Thus, Joseph's identity remains hidden from his brothers for a long time and is only revealed after a series of tests; Joseph himself is tested by his future wife Aseneth, who is wearing a veil, etc. Particularly entertaining is the instant power of attraction the young Joseph has over women, causing an authentic battle between multiple female rivals. The carnivalesque element is further provided by Pharaoh's majordomo, who functions as the *gracioso* in the second part of the play, "silly, vulgar, always drunk" (Györegy 2018, 78).

In the middle of the eighteenth century, Spanish theatre was still well and alive, as attested by the publication of a Spanish translation of Voltaire's *Brut* that contains references to a company of the Spanish Theatre among the Amsterdam Sephardim. It is interesting to note that the publishers of the translation, Gavilán and Morales, are also mentioned by one of the Sephardic poets of eighteenth-century Amsterdam, the Spanish-born physician David del Valle Saldaña (1699/1700–1755). In addition to his erotic and occasional poetry, employed at weddings and other events within the community or dedicated to the House of Orange, this author left us five short pieces of theatre, comprising both "Loas" and "Coloquios" that would have been used as interludes during theatrical performances – Saldaña even mentioned the titles of some of the *comedias* to which they belonged (Brown 1997, 38–39). One "Loa" was on the birth of the "Hereditary Prince of Orange" William V; another "Loa" and a "Coloquio" (Dialogue) were on the peace recently achieved with France; and an interesting further "Loa", again paired with a "Coloquio", thematized the "Triumph of Peace and Cure of the Comedy". In the latter, the allegorical characters Public, Comedy and Worry were thankful to Peace, hoping that it would re-establish the practice of the Spanish Theater of the Amsterdam Sephardim! In all these short plays by Saldaña, the characters "Gavilán" and "Morales" functioned as the *graciosos*, i.e., the comical types: no doubt played by the aforementioned Abraham and David themselves (Brown 1997). All in all, these pieces by David del Valle Saldaña offer precious insight into the activities of a Theater Company in Amsterdam:[46] At a time when the Sephardim of the Netherlands were ever more familiar with Dutch and French culture, some *aficionados* still made great efforts to uphold their love of Spanish and of the performance of Iberian *comedias*.

Theatre, it can thus be concluded, was prominently present in the life of the Western Sephardim. As soon as they had the opportunity, the Iberian newcomers visited theatres in the lands where they established their communities. These former conversos eagerly read what was being produced in Spain, and they staged Spanish *comedias* or shorter plays in their own theaters, occasionally meeting with resistance from the rabbis and other zealous community members. But even among rabbis, there were lovers of the dramatical genre as well, or some who recognized its edifying and community-building function – think of Mortera. The plays that are now preserved in text represent only a small part of the theatrical practices of the Western Sephardim, and whilst they can hardly measure up to the brilliant drama produced by Spain's great playwrights, they demonstrate the vitality of Iberian life and, again, an enthusiasm for the production of Jewish drama that is hard to overestimate.

---

46 Kenneth Brown offers a full edition of all these pieces in his work on the poetry of David del Valle Saldaña (1997, 247–322).

25 Conclusion

In its wealth of texts and genres, the literature produced by the Sephardim of converso origin is difficult to assess in terms of established paradigms, as fragments or extensions of "Jewish", "Spanish" or "Portuguese" literatures. As this literature was produced over the course of two centuries in what is globally called the Western Sephardic Diaspora but refers to different places and different contexts, one important conclusion seems to me that there is no common denominator for the whole. Rather, authors and their preoccupations were as varied as the conversos themselves: Some, traumatized by their past, wanted to conform as quickly as possible to traditional Judaism, relying heavily on Spanish Bible translations, prayer books and devotional works to readjust themselves. Others challenged rabbinic authority and preserved their Iberian lifestyle in the realm of literature. Still others would be simultaneously observant Jews and "reluctant cosmopolitans". The Spanish and Portuguese literature produced in the Diaspora offered options for everyone. Particularly considering the vast output of Jewish literature in the vernacular, ranging from the Bible translations initiated in Ferrara to the numerous ethical and moral treatises, sermons and polemical literature, it is evident that definitions such as "re-education for ex-conversos" or "marrano literature" are too reductive. Not only on the part of the readers, but also on that of the authors and producers (printers, editors), a wide range of interests, backgrounds and motivations can be observed. Spanish editions of the Pentateuch and the Prophets prepared the 'New Jewish' reader to attend services at the synagogue, reflecting traditional Jewish practice, but the several Spanish editions of the entire Bible, of biblical commentaries and of the Psalms allowed for many other uses of the Bible as well, whether traditional, personal or critical. The treatises in Spanish and Portuguese included practical, detailed or learned instructions on the commandments and rabbinical law, but also personal explorations of Judaism; their authors were trained rabbis or devout merchants; finally, their readers, often addressed as if they were one collective – those of the Nation who no longer knew Hebrew (or Judaism) – could be returning conversos, Sephardim born and raised in the new communities, or even interested Christian readers. The Spanish and Portuguese apologetical and polemical texts similarly included many different readers, both uninstructed and highly educated, and the discussions and questions they treated pertained not only to differences between Jews and Christians, but also reflected differing directions and hesitations within the 'New Christian' or converso Diaspora itself.

A second conclusion regards the role of literature in the Western Sephardic Diaspora. The use of the vernacular opened up a new dimension for Judaism, widening readership and creating bookshelves of Spanish and Portuguese literature on which the Iberian Catholic canon was expanded with Jewish texts in those languages. Jewish-Christian polemics acquired new dynamics through the adoption of Iberian literary genres such as the humanistic dialogue or the baroque ingenious discourse. It is clear, then, that among the Sephardim, literature was not only a form of entertainment – important in itself for social cohesion – but reached further and deeper. Language and literary expression occupied a central place in the Western Sephardic Diaspora and were present in every genre of their literature, both secular and religious. Perhaps only by experiencing the arcane spell of the Spanish literal Bible translation, the moving laments of the shepherds of Samuel Usque's *Consolation*, the contrived poetry of Miguel de Barrios, the baroque exuberance of Penso de la Vega, the popular Castilian wisdom of Gómez Silveira's polemical poetry, or the fictive conversations of anonymous Portuguese women enclosed in their Amsterdam houses. . . can we really grasp the contribution made by the literature of the Western Sephardim.

Bibliography

Works Cited

Aboab, Imanuel. *Nomología, o, Discursos legales*. Ed. Moisés Orfali. Acta Salmanticensia. Biblioteca de pensamiento y sociedad. Salamanca: Universidad de Salamanca, 2007.

Bellomi, Paola. "El fénix sefardí. Sobre la existencia de un teatro judeo-ibérico en Italia (Proyecto E.S.THE.R.)." *Sefarad* 79.2 (2019): 447–467.

Bregoli, Francesca. "Mediterranean Enlightenment: Livornese Jews, Tuscan Culture, and Eighteenth-Century Reform." *Stanford Studies in Jewish History and Culture*. Stanford, CA: Stanford Univ. Press, 2014.

Brown, Kenneth. "El Parnaso sefardí y sus cancioneros, siglos 17–18." *Actas del XII Congreso de la Asociación Internacional de Hispanistas, 21–26 de agosto de 1995, Birmingham*. Eds. Aengus M. Ward et al. Birmingham: University of Birmingham. Department of Hispanic Studies, 1998. 60–69.

Brown, Kenneth. *De la cárcel inquisitorial a la sinagoga de Amsterdam: (edición y estudio del 'Romance a Lope de Vera' de Antonio Enríquez Gómez)*. Colección Creación literaria. Clásicos. Toledo: Consejería de Cultura de Castilla-La Mancha, 2007.

Brown, Kenneth. "Four New 18th-Century Sephardic Literary Texts in the Hamburg University Library." *Caminos de leche y miel: Jubilee Volume in Honor of Michael Studemund-Halévy*. Eds. Harm den Boer, Anna Lena Menny, Carsten Wilke, David M. Bunis, Ivana Vučina Simović and Corinna Deppner. Barcelona: Tirocinio, 2018. 246–287. 2 Vols.

Brown, Kenneth, and Harm Den Boer. *El barroco sefardí : Abraham Gómez Silveira, Arévalo, prov. de Avila, Castilla 1656 – Amsterdam 1741 : estudio preliminar, obras líricas, vejámenes en prosa y verso y documentación personal*. Kassel: Reichenberger, 2000.

Bunis, David M. "Handbook of Jewish Languages." *Judezmo (Ladino)*. Eds. Lily Kahn and Aaron D. Rubin. Leiden/Boston: Brill, 2016. 365–450.

Caplan, Abraham Cohen. *Danielillo o Respuestas a los Cristianos, escrito en Amsterdam por I.M. en el año de 1738*. Bruselas: B.G. van Gelder, 1868.

Da Costa, Uriel. *Examination of Pharisaic traditions = Exame das tradições phariseas: facsimile of the unique copy in the Royal Library of Copenhagen*. Ed. Herman Prins Salomon. Leiden: Brill, 1993.

Den Boer, Harm. "La Biblia de Ferrara y otras traducciones españolas de la Biblia entre los sefardíes de Europa occidental." *Introducción a la Biblia de Ferrara. Actas del Simposio Internacional sobre la Biblia de Ferrara, Sevilla, 25–28 de noviembre de 1991*. Eds. Iacob M. Hassán and Ángel Berenguer-Amador. Sevilla: Sociedad Estatal Quinto Centenario, 1994. 251–96.

Den Boer, Harm. *La literatura sefardí de Amsterdam*. Alcalá de Henares: Instituto Internacional de Estudios Sefardíes y Andalusíes, Universidad de Alcalá, 1995.

Den Boer, Harm. "El mito del milenio sefardí." *Mitos : actas del VII Congreso Internacional de la Asociación Española de Semiótica, 4–9 noviembre 1996*. Eds. Alberto Navarro González, Juan Carlos Pueo Domínguez, Alfredo Saldaña Sagredo and Túa Blesa. *Asociación Española Semiótica de Blesa*. Zaragoza: Universidad de Zaragoza, 1999. 696–702.

Den Boer, Harm. "Exile in Sephardic Literature of Amsterdam." *Studia Rosenthaliana* 35.2 (2001): 187–99.

Den Boer, Harm. *Spanish and Portuguese Printing in the Northern Netherlands 1584–1825. Descriptive Bibliography*. Leiden: IDC, 2003.

Den Boer, Harm. "Isaac de Castro, Albert Boumeester and Early Sephardi Printing in Amsterdam." *Omnia in Eo: Studies on Jewish Books and Libraries in Honour of Adri Offenberg Celebrating the 125th Anniversary of the Bibliotheca Rosenthaliana in Amsterdam*. Ed. Irene Zwiep. Louvain: Peeters, 2006a. 228–246.

Den Boer, Harm. *Sephardic Editions, 1550–1820: Spanish and Portuguese Books Written and/or Published by Sephardic Jews of Early Modern Europe*. Leiden: Brill, 2006b.

Den Boer, Harm. "La Biblia entre los judíos sefardíes de Amsterdam y otras colonias en Europa occidental." *La Biblia en la literatura española. II. Siglo de Oro* 2. Eds. Rosa Navarro Durán and Gregorio del Olmo Lete. Madrid: Trotta 2008. 315–349.

Den Boer, Harm. "The Visión Deleitable under the Scrutiny of the Spanish Inquisition: New Insights on Converso Literature." *European Judaism* 43.2 (2010): 2–17.

Den Boer, Harm. "Hacia un canon de la poesía religiosa judeo-conversa." *Calíope* 17.1 (2011): 19–42.

Den Boer, Harm. "The Ferrara Bible and the Amsterdam Jews." Conversos, *marrani e nuove comunità ebraiche in età moderna: atti del convegno internazionale di studi organizzato dal Museo nazionale dell'ebraismo italiano e della Shoah: 28–29 aprile 2014, Sala della musica, Chiostro di S. Paolo, Ferrara*. Vol. 2. Eds. Myriam Silvera. Atti della *Fondazione Museo nazionale dell'ebraismo italiano e della Shoah*. Firenze: Giuntina, 2015. 119–129.

Den Boer, Harm. "Isaac Orobio de Castro as a Writer: The Importance of Literary Style in the 'Divine Warnings against the Vain Idolatry of the Gentiles'." *Isaac Orobio: The Jewish Argument with Dogma and Doubt*. Ed. Carsten Lorenz Wilke. Berlin: De Gruyter, 2018a. 77–91.

Den Boer, Harm. "La Machabea and the First Portuguese of the Northern Netherlands." *Portuguese Jews, New Christians, and 'New Jews' A Tribute to Roberto Bachmann*. The Iberian Religious World 4. Leiden/Boston: Brill, 2018b. 303–333.

Den Boer, H. "Samuel Abas and his Portuguese translation of Bahya's 'Duties of the Hearts': A particular form of censorship and cultural transfer" *Caminos de leche y miel: Jubilee Volume in Honor of Michael Studemund-Halévy*. Eds. Harm den Boer, Anna Lena Menny, Carsten Wilke, David M. Bunis, Ivana Vučina Simović and Corinna Deppner. Barcelona: Tirocinio, 2018c. 142–184.

Den Boer, Harm, and Jonathan I. Israel. "William III in the Eyes of Amsterdam Sephardi Writers: The Reactions of Miguel de Barrios, José Penso Vega and Manuel de León." *The Anglo-Dutch Moment: Essays on the Glorious Revolution and Its World Impact*. Ed. Jonathan I. Israel. Cambridge: Cambridge University Press, 1991. 439–461.

Díaz Esteban, Fernando. "La poesía épica de Miguel de Silveira." *Los judaizantes en Europa y la literatura castellana del siglo de Oro*. Ed. Fernando Díaz Esteban. Madrid: Letrúmero, 1994. 103–129.

Dweck, Yaacob. *Dissident Rabbi: The Life of Jacob Sasportas*. Princeton University Press 2019.

Enríquez Gómez, Antonio. *Academias morales de las Musas*. Eds. Milagros Rodríguez Caceres, Felipe B. Pedraza Jiménez, and Rafael Carrasco. Ediciones críticas 16. Cuenca: Universidad de Castilla-La Mancha, 2015.

Feitler, Bruno. *The Imaginary Synagogue: Anti-Jewish Literature in the Portuguese Early-Modern World (16th–18th Centuries)*. Boston: Brill, 2015.

Fine, Ruth. "The Psalms of David by Daniel Israel López Laguna, a Wandering Marrano." *The Conversos and Moriscos in Late Medieval Spain and Beyond*. Ed. Kevin Ingram. Leiden/Boston: Brill, 2009. 45–62.

Fisher, Benjamin E. *Amsterdam's People of the Book Jewish Society and the Turn to Scripture in the Seventeenth Century*. Cincinnati, OH: Hebrew Union College Press, 2020.

González Quiroz, Mabel. *Relación Verdadera del Gran Sermón: edición y estudios: chocolate e inquisición en un manuscrito satírico sefardí*. Ed. Mabel González Quiroz. Literatura de los siglos de oro de España y América 14. Barcelona: Paso de Barca, 2015.

Hassán, Iacob M., and Ángel Berenguer-Amador, eds. *Introducción a la Biblia de Ferrara: actas del simposio internacional sobre la Biblia de Ferrara: Sevilla, 25–28 de noviembre de 1991*. Sevilla: Sociedad Estatal Quinto Centenario, 1994.

Jessurun, Rehuel. *Diálogo dos montes*. Ed. Philip Polack. Colección Támesis Serie B, Textos. London: Tamesis Books, 1975.

Kaplan, Yosef. *From Christianity to Judaism the Story of Isaac Orobio De Castro*. The Littman Library of Jewish Civilization. Oxford: Oxford Univ. Press, 1989.

Kaplan, Yosef. *An Alternative Path to Modernity: The Sephardi Diaspora in Western Europe*. Leiden: Brill, 2000.

Kaplan, Yosef. "El perfil cultural de tres rabinos sefardíes a través de sus bibliotecas." *Familia, religión y negocio. El sefardismo en las relaciones entre el mundo ibérico y los Países Bajos en la Edad Moderna*. Ed. Jaime Contreras, Bernardo García García, and Ignacio Pulido Serrano. Fundación Carlos de Amberes; Ministerio de Asuntos Exteriores. 2002. 269–286.

Kaplan, Yosef. "*From Christianity to Judaism* Revisited: Some Critical Remarks More than Thirty Years after Its Publication." *Isaac Orobio: The Jewish Argument with Dogma and Doubt*. Ed. Carsten Wilke. Studies and Texts in Scepticism 2. Boston, MA: De Gruyter, 2018. 15–29.

Kayserling, Meyer. *Sephardim. Romanische Poesien der Juden in Spanien: ein Beitrag zur Literatur und Geschichte der Spanisch-Portugiesischen Juden*. Leipzig: Mendelssohn, 1859.

Kayserling, Meyer. *Biblioteca española-portugueza-judaica: dictionnaire bibliographique des auteurs juifs, de leurs ouvrages espagnols et portugais et des oeuvres sur et contre les juifs et le judaïsme : avec un aperçu sur la littérature des juifs espagnols et une collection des proverbes espagnols*. Strasbourg: Trubner, 1890.

Kerkhof, Maxim. P.A.M. *Over het Portugees en het Spaans van de Sefardische joden in Amsterdam in de 17e, 18e en 19e eeuw*. Maastricht: Shaker, 2003.

Kerner, Alex. *Lost in Translation, Found in Transliteration: Books, Censorship, and the Evolution of the Spanish and Portuguese Jews' Congregation of London as a Linguistic Community, 1663–1810*. Leiden: Brill, 2018.

Kromhout, David, and Irene E. Zwiep. "God's Word Confirmed. Authority, Truth, and the Text of the Early Modern Jewish Bible." *Scriptural Authority and Biblical Criticism in the Dutch Golden Age: God's Word Questioned*. Eds. Dirk van Miert, Henk J. M. Nellen, Piet Steenbakkers, Jetze Touber, and Rijksuniversiteit te Utrecht. Oxford, UK: Oxford University Press, 2017. 133–154.

Lazar, Moshé. *Biblia de Ferrara*. Biblioteca Castro. Madrid: Ed. de la Fundación José Antonio de Castro, 1996.

Levie Bernfeld, Tirtsah. "Confrontation between East and West Balkan Sephardim in Early Modern Amsterdam." *Caminos de leche y miel: Jubilee Volume in Honor of Michael Studemund-Halévy*. Eds. Harm den Boer, Anna Lena Menny, Carsten Wilke, David M. Bunis, Ivana Vučina Simović and Corinna Deppner. Barcelona: Tirocinio, 2018. 328–362. 2 Vols.

Lieberman, Julia Rebollo. *El teatro alegórico de Miguel (Daniel Leví) de Barrios*. Newark: Juan de la Cuesta, 1996.

Lieberman, Julia Rebollo. *Sephardi Family Life in the Early Modern Diaspora*. HBI Series on Jewish Women. Ed. Julia Rebollo Lieberman. Waltham, Hanover: Brandeis University Press, University Press of New England, 2011.

Mata Induráin, Carlos. "De Lisboa a los Países Bajos: Manuel (Jacob) de Pina, poeta y dramaturgo sefardí, y su cancionero de burlas Chanzas del ingenio y dislates de la musa (1656)." *La poésie d'exil en Europe aux XVIe et XVIIe siécles = La poesía del exilio en Europa en los siglos XVI y XVII = Writing poetry in exile in early modern Europe*. Eds. Rafaèle Audoubert, Aurélie Griffin, and Morgane Kappès-Le Moing. New York: Instituto de Estudios Auriseculares (IDEA), 2018.

Modena, Leon. *The Autobiography of a Seventeenth-Century Venetian Rabbi: Leon Modena's Life of Judah*. Eds. Mark R. Cohen, Theodore K. Rabb, Howard E. Adelman, and Natalie Zemon Davis. Princeton: Princeton University Press, 2020.

Mulsow, Martin. *Moderne Aus Dem Untergrund Radikale Frühaufklärung in Deutschland 1680–1720*. Hamburg: Meiner, 2002.

Nider, Valentina. "El *Entremés de un dotor y lo que iziero[n] sus criados*, inédito, en los papeles de la Inquisición de Pisa: ¿un scenario?" *Por tal variedad tiene belleza. Omaggio a Maria Grazia Profeti*. Eds. Antonella Gallo and Katerina Vaiopoulous. Firenze: Alinea, 2012. 323–336.

Nider, Valentina. "'Confusión de confusiones' de José Penso de la Vega (1688) y la 'Tabla de Cebes' a través de Agostino Mascardi (con una mirada a los 'Pensieri' de Alessandro Tassoni)." *Festina lente. Augusta empresa correr a espacio: studia in honorem Sagrario López Poza*. A Coruña: Servizo de Publicacións, 2019. 207–227.

Offenberg, Adri K. "Spanish and Portuguese Sephardi Books Published in the Northern Netherlands before Menasseh Ben Israel (1584–1627)." *Dutch Jewish History: Proceedings of the Symposium on the History of the Jews in the Netherlands*. Tel Aviv: Tel-Aviv University, 1991. 77–96.

Orfali, Moisés. "Il 'Danielillo' da Livorno, testo e contesto." *Zakhor; rivista di storia degli ebrei d'Italia* 1 (1997): 207–220.

Pancorbo, Fernando José. *José Penso de Vega: la creación de un perfil cultural y literario entre Ámsterdam y Livorno*. Storia dell'ebraismo in Italia. Studi e testi, XXXI. Florence: Leo S. Olschki, 2019.

Pedraza Jiménez, Felipe. "'La variedad, sal del entendimiento': Antonio Enríquez Gómez y las Academias morales de las Musas." *Academias morales de las Musas*. Eds. Milagros Rodríguez Caceres, Felipe B. Pedraza Jiménez, and Rafael Carrasco. Ediciones críticas 16. Cuenca: Universidad de Castilla-La Mancha, 2015. 97–105.

Pereyra, Abraham de. *Hispanidad y judaismo en tiempos de Espinoza : estudio y edición anotada de la 'Certeza del camino' por De Abraham Pereyra, Amsterdam 1666*. Ed. Henry Méchoulan. Salamanca: Ediciones Universidad de Salamanca, 1987.

Pieterse, Wilhelmina Chr. *Daniel Levi de Barrios als geschiedschrijver van de Portugees-Israelietische gemeente te Amsterdam in zijn Triumpho del govierno popular*. Amsterdam: Scheltema & Holkema, 1968.

Pinto Delgado, João. *The Poem of Queen Esther*. Tr. David R. Slavitt. New York: Oxford University Press, 1999.

Praag, J. A. van. "Dos comedias sefarditas." *Neophilologus* 25.1 (1940): 93–101.

Rauschenbach, Sina. *Judentum für Christen: Vermittlung und Selbstbehauptung Menasseh ben Israels in den gelehrten Debatten des 17. Jahrhunderts*. Berlin/Boston: De Gruyter, 2012.

Roth, Cecil. *A History of the Marranos*. New York: Sepher-Hermon Press ^{5}1974 [1932].

Roth, Cecil. "The Marrano Typography in England." *The Library* 5–XV.2 (1960): 118–128.

Roth, Cecil. "An Elegy of Joao Pinto Delgado on Isaac de Castro Tartas." *Revue Des Etudes Juives* 121 (1962): 355–366.

Salomon, Herman Prins. "The De Pinto Manuscript: A 17th-Century Marrano Family History." *Studia Rosenthaliana* 9.1 (1975): 1–62.

Salomon, Herman Prins, ed. Saul Levi Mortera: *Tratado da verdade da lei de Moisés: escrito pelo seu próprio punho em Português*. UC Biblioteca Geral 1, 1988.

Saraiva, António José. *Le discours ingénieux*. Lisbon: Ramos, 1971.

Scholberg, Kenneth R. *La poesía religiosa de Miguel de Barrios*. Ohio State University Press, 1962.

Schwarzwald, Rodrigue, O. "Thessaloniki 1568 and Venice 1713: Language Differences in Two Ladino Books." *Actas del XVIII Congreso de Estudios Sefardies*. Eds. Elena Romero Castelló, Hilary Pomeroy and Shmuel Refael Vivante. Madrid: CSIC, 2017. 289–306.

Studemund-Halévy, Michael. "Codices Gentium. Semuel de Isaac Abas, coleccionista de libros hamburgués." *Familia, religión y negocio. El sefardismo en las relaciones entre el mundo ibérico y los Países Bajos en la Edad Moderna*. Eds. Jaime Contreras Contreras, Bernardo José García García, and Juan Ignacio Pulido Serrano. Madrid: Fundación Carlos de Amberes, 2003. 287–319.

Swetschinski, Daniel. *The Portuguese Jewish Merchants of Seventeenth-Century Amsterdam: A Social Profile*. Ann Arbor: University Microfilms International, 1982.

Swetschinski, Daniel. *Reluctant Cosmopolitans: The Portuguese Jews of Seventeenth-Century Amsterdam*. London: The Littman Library of Jewish Civilization, 2000.

Toaff, Renzo. *La nazione ebrea a Livorno e a Pisa (1591–1700)*. Storia dell'ebraismo in Italia. Studi e testi, IX. Florence: L.S. Olschki, 1990.

Tucker, G. Hugo. "Didactus Pyrrhus Lusitanus (1517–1599), Poet of Exile." *Humalova Humanistica Lovaniensia* 41 (1992): 175–198.

Usque, Samuel. *Consolation aux tribulations d'Israël (1553)*. Eds. Carsten Lorenz Wilke and Yosef Hayim Yerushalmi. Trs. Lúcia Liba Mucznik, Anne-Marie Quint, and Nicole Siganos. Péninsule. Paris: Chandeigne, 2014.

Valle Saldaña, David. *El afrodiseo y otras obras jocosas y festivas*. Eds. Kenneth Brown and Harm Den Boer. Mérida: Editora Regional de Extremadura, 1997.

Wilke, Carsten Lorenz. "Conversion ou retour? La métamorphose du nouveau chrétien en juif portugais dans l'imaginaire sépharade du XVIIe siècle." *Mémoires juives d'Espagne et du Portugal*. Ed. Esther Benbassa. Paris: Publisud, 1996. 53–67.

Wilke, Carsten Lorenz. "Midrashim from Bordeaux: A Theological Controversy inside the Portuguese Jewish Diaspora at the Time of Spinoza's Excommunication." *European Journal of Jewish Studies* 6.2 (2012): 202–247.

Wilke, Carsten Lorenz. *The Marrakesh Dialogues: A Gospel Critique and Jewish Apology from the Spanish Renaissance*. Studies in Jewish History and Culture, Vol. 45. Leiden/Boston: Brill, 2014.

Wilke, Carsten Lorenz. "Torah Alone: Protestantism as Model and Target of Sephardi Religious Polemics in the Early Modern Netherlands." *Polemical Encounters: Christians, Jews, and Muslims in Iberia and Beyond*. Eds. Mercedes García-Arenal and Gerard Albert Wiegers. University Park: The Pennsylvania State University Press, 2018. 357–376.

Yerushalmi, Yosef Hayim. *From Spanish Court to Italian Ghetto: Isaac Cardoso: A Study in Seventeenth-Century Marranism and Jewish Apologetics*. New York: Columbia University Press, 1971.

Yerushalmi, Yosef Hayim. *The Re-Education of Marranos in the Seventeenth Century*. Cincinnati: Judaic Studies Program University of Cincinnati, 1980.

Yerushalmi, Yosef Hayim. "Un classique juif en langue portugaise. Consolation aux tribulations d'Israël de Samuel Usque." *Consolation aux tribulations d'Israël (1553)*. Ed. Carsten Lorenz Wilke. Tr. Lúcia Liba Mucznik, Anne-Marie Quint, and Nicole Siganos. Péninsule. Paris: Chandeigne, 2014.

Zepp, Susanne. *An Early Self: Jewish Belonging in Romance Literature, 1499–1627*. Stanford Studies in Jewish History and Culture. Stanford: Stanford University Press, 2014.

Further Reading

Besso, Henry V. *Dramatic Literature of the Sephardic Jews of Amsterdam in the XVIIth and XVIIIth Centuries*. New York: Hispanic Institute in the U.S., Sección de Estudios Sefardiés, 1947.
Den Boer, Harm. "El teatro entre los sefardíes de Amsterdam a finales del siglo XVII." *Diálogos Hispánicos* 8.3 (1988): 679–690.
Den Boer, Harm. "Francisco de Caceres, litterator en koopman in talen te Amsterdam." *Een gulden kleinood. Liber amicorum aangeboden aan de heer D. Goudsmit ter gelegenheid van zijn afscheid als bibliothecaris van 'Ets Haim/Libraria Montezinos' van de Portugees-Israëlietische Gemeente te Amsterdam*. Eds. Harm Den Boer, Jeanne Brombacher, and Peter Cohen. Apeldoorn: Garant, 1990. 55–70.
Den Boer, Harm. "La representación de la comedia española en Holanda." *Cuadernos de Historia Moderna* 23 (1999): 113–127.
Den Boer, Harm, and Monserrat Gómez García. "Los Salmos de David (Abenatar Melo)." *Die Sefarden in Hamburg: zur Geschichte einer Minderheit*. Ed. Michael Studemund-Halévy. Hamburg: Buske, 1997. 753–780.
Fine, Ruth. "De la liturgia al relato testimonial: los 'Psalmos de David' de Daniel Israel López Laguna." *Calíope: journal of the Society for Renaissance and Baroque Hispanic Society* 17.1 (2011): 177–198.
Girón-Negrón, Luis M. *Alfonso de La Torre's 'Visión Deleytabl' Philosophical Rationalism and the Religious Imagination in 15th Century Spain*. Medieval Iberian Peninsula Vol. 14. Leiden: Brill, 2001.
Hernando Álvarez, Julio-Félix. "Teatro hispanojudío en Toscana durante el siglo XVII." *Los judaizantes en Europa y la literatura castellana del siglo de Oro*. Ed. Fernando Díaz Esteban. Madrid: Letrúmero, 1994. 193–214.
Leoni, Aron di Leone, and Grazia Secchieri. *La nazione ebraica spagnola e portoghese di Ferrara (1492–1559) : i suoi rapporti col governo ducale e la popolazione locale ed i suoi legami con le nazioni portoghesi di Ancona, Pesaro e Venezia*. Storia dell'ebraismo in Italia. Firenze: L.S. Olschki, 2011.
Méchoulan, Henry. "La Sepmaine au secours de l'orthodoxie juive à Amsterdam au début du XVIIe siècle." *Du Bartas, 1590–1990 actes du colloque international d'Auch-Le Bartas-Pau (6–8 avril 1990)*. Ed. James Dauphiné. Mont-de-Marsan: Editions InterUniversitaires, 1992. 427–445.
Peiró, Angeles Navarro. "El 'Conciliador' de Menasseh ben Israel." *Los judaizantes en Europa y la literatura castellana del siglo de Oro*. Ed. Fernando Díaz Esteban. Madrid: Letrúmero, 1994. 313–319.
Roth, Cecil. *Magna Bibliotheca Anglo-Judaica; a Bibliographical Guide to Anglo-Jewish History*. London: Jewish historical Society of England, 1937.

Margalit Bejarano
9 Jews in the History and Culture of the Caribbean

Abstract: This chapter examines the rich diversity of Sephardic Caribbean Jewish history and culture. Following a comprehensive overview of the colonial history of the Caribbean, it analyzes the legal framework of Jewish settlements. It provides a survey of the economic history of the Caribbean, the particularities of religious and community life, including the particular circumstances of enslavement, and an analysis of the Iberian impact on the language, culture, liturgical works and literature of Caribbean Jewish history.

Key Terms: Sephardic Caribbean, economic history, colonial history, Jewish settlements, Spanish-Portuguese Jewish nation

1 Introduction

At the turn of the seventeenth century, France, England and the Dutch Provinces conquered the small Caribbean islands that were considered by Spain to be *islas inútiles* (useless islands), challenging the Spanish monopoly that was stipulated in the Treaty of Tordesillas.[1] In the new colonies that they founded on the islands and along the Wild Coast (today the Guianas), agricultural staples were cultivated for the benefit of their metropoles, converting the sugar plantations into a new Eldorado.

Among the Dutch, English and French settlers there were Sephardic Jews, most of them *conversos* from Portugal who had migrated to Amsterdam, Hamburg, London or Bayonne, where they had been transformed – according to the historian Yosef Kaplan – from 'New Christians' into 'New Jews' (Kaplan 2003). They considered themselves to be part of the *naçao*, the Spanish-Portuguese Jewish nation. The term "nation" was not used in its modern sense, but signified their belonging to the same ethnic group. This comprised conversos who had genuinely adopted Catholicism, crypto-Jews, 'New Christians' who had returned to living openly as Jews, and descendants of Jews who had been expelled from Spain and lived in Europe or under Ottoman rule (Arbell 2002, 10–12; Studemund-Halévy 2016, 7–8). Kinship was often stronger than religious differences.

These Sephardim established small communities throughout the Caribbean, where they continued to speak Portuguese and preserved their religious traditions and their social patterns. They created networks – strengthened by endogamy –

---

[1] The Treaty of Tordesillas (1494) divided the newly discovered lands – and those to be discovered – between Spain and Portugal.

based upon family relations, economic interests and a common cultural background (Loker 1991, 20). The *naçao* was actually a transnational diaspora with unique characteristics that linked Dutch, British and French Jewry with the newly founded Jewish communities in the Americas. Ironically, the Jews who had been expelled from Spain, and whose presence in its colonies was forbidden, carried their Iberian culture to the Caribbean territories that Spain had lost. This chapter will trace the history and culture of the Sephardim in the Caribbean in the seventeenth and eighteenth centuries, giving special attention to their Iberian legacy.

2 The Historical Background: The Caribbean

Due to the special circumstances in the colonies and the interest of the respective governments in strengthening their white populations, the Sephardic Jews who settled in the Caribbean were able to obtain privileges that were denied them in Europe. England, France and the Dutch Provinces started to establish permanent settlements in the Guianas and on the small Caribbean islands at the beginning of the seventeenth century. Small colonies on the Virgin Islands were later established by Denmark. With the foundation of the Dutch West India Company (WIC) in 1621, Dutch merchants became the most successful in the Caribbean (Goslinga 1971, 34–38). They traded illegally with the Spanish colonies and supplied technical knowledge that promoted the growth and processing of sugar cane among the French and British settlers, particularly after the loss of their own colony in Northern Brazil.[2] The introduction of the sugar industry converted the early settlements that had been based on small-scale farming into plantation societies for the benefit of the metropoles (Knight 1978, 36–40; Dunn 1973, 16–20; Klein 1986, 50–51). The cultivation of sugar cane could be highly profitable and attracted adventurers who wished to enrich themselves. It was, however, a risky endeavor, as it depended on credit for the purchase of enslaved people and machinery and was subject to the fluctuations of the price of sugar on the world market. In a region that suffered from hurricanes, earthquakes, volcanic eruptions and tropical diseases, prosperity was challenged by insecurity. On the other hand, the region's natural beauty, its eternal summer, the comfortable lifestyle it offered and the hope of prosperity were very tempting.

The Caribbean colonies became essential sources of profit for the European powers that imposed a monopoly on the trade within their respective domain. Thus,

---

[2] The Dutch conquered Pernambuco in 1930 and established a prosperous colony based on the cultivation of sugar cane. In 1954, Portugal defeated Holland in Brazil, and the Jews were forced to flee from the Portuguese colony. Some returned to Amsterdam; others settled in the Caribbean, and many of the Dutch settlers – including some Jews – relocated to the Caribbean. A group of 23 Jews that reached New Amsterdam became the first Jewish settlers in the United States.

the Navigation Act of 1651 allowed the British colonies to use only English boats and to trade exclusively with Britain and its domains. This economic system was typical to the period of mercantilism; the Caribbean colonies were characterized by monocultures of sugar cane and the production of other tropical staples, such as coffee and cotton, that combined agriculture with industry. They were forced to be dependent on their respective mother countries, to which they exported their products and from which they imported their consumer goods (Dunn 1973, 25; Hurwitz and Hurwitz 1971, 38).

The colonizing process was carried out by private companies such as the WIC and the *Compagnie des Îles d'Amérique*, which were granted public functions to control not only the economy, but also the local politics in the colonies (Knight 1978, 41–43). The WIC granted private patents to patroons, who in turn recruited colonists and were responsible for their settlement (Goslinga 1971, 101–104). The majority of the population, however, was "recruited" in Africa through brutal coercion and was brought to the Caribbean by the colonizing companies that dominated the transatlantic slave trade. The historian Franklin Knight defined the Caribbean colonies as *exploitation colonies*: "The typical exploitation colony was one in which a minority population of Europeans usually but not always dominated and managed a majority of non-Europeans to produce some export commodity primarily for the European market" (Knight 1978, 56–58; Dunn 1973, 44–45).[3]

Enslaved persons were considered to be 'portable property' and were treated with cruelty by their masters.[4] Nevertheless, white men tended to grant freedom to the children they had with enslaved women, thus creating the basis of the free population of color. Caribbean society was structured as a pyramid divided horizontally into three 'castes': white people, free people of color and enslaved people. Within each 'caste', there were differences of origin, class, occupation and legal status. White people, who comprised the small upper triangle, were divided between two distinct classes. The upper class included nobles, owners of large plantations – many of them not actually present in the colonies – as well as rich merchants and professionals. The lower class were small-scale merchants, artisans, teachers, peasants, etc. (Knight 1978, 94–113; Hurwitz and Hurwitz 1971, 26, 60–62). The free people of color found themselves "between the heaven of the white man's superior position and the hell of degradation of the slave. . . in an eternal purgatory from which there was no purgation" (Hurwitz and Hurwitz 1971, 65). Their status was based primarily on the color of their skin. Enslaved people were divided between those born in Africa (*bozales*) and those born in the colonies (*criollos*), as well as according to their occupations (Klein 1986, 60–64; Cohen and Greene, 1972).

---

[3] Knight contrasts the exploitation colonies of the Caribbean with the *settler colonies* of North America.
[4] According to the Black Code (*The Code Noir*, 1685), Article XLIV: "We declare slaves to be charges, and as such enter into community property."

All white people, regardless of their economic and social conditions or their political affiliations, enjoyed a superior status with respect to the other two 'castes'. This privileged position was also the basis of the Jewish legal and social status in the colonies.

3 Settlement and Legal Framework

The 'New Christians' who migrated from Portugal following its unification with Spain (1580) found their first haven in Amsterdam, and from there they spread to other European cities.[5] The Dutch who rebelled against the Spanish crown were more interested in trade and profits than in religious unity and were therefore tolerant towards Catholics and Jews who contributed to their economy (Goslinga 1971, 23, 104; Faber 1998, 11–12). Many of the 'New Christians' were merchants and professionals, but Amsterdam also attracted indigent Jews who became a burden on the community's coffers. The leaders of Amsterdam's Sephardic community, who wished to assist their poor coreligionists but also to protect the image of their community, sponsored the settlement of the newly arrived Jews in the Dutch Caribbean colonies, subsidizing their maritime voyage and providing guidance, protection and spiritual leadership to their communities (Loker 1991, 20–22; Ben-Ur 2016, 30).

The two major Jewish communities in the Dutch Caribbean were established in Curaçao and Surinam. Following the loss of their colony in Brazil, the Dutch authorities, who recognized the potential contribution of the Jews to the sugar plantations and to international trade, tried to attract them to their Caribbean colonies. The WIC granted Jewish settlers *lettres patentes* that assured their economic protection and their religious freedom. Tolerance, however, had its limits: Jews were not allowed to trade on Sundays and were obligated to serve in the militias on the Sabbath and on Jewish holidays. Moreover, there were differences in the legal status of the Jews in each colony that stemmed from the local circumstances (Arbell 2002, 58–59, 125–131; Loker 1991, 22–24; Gerber 2014, 5–6).

Curaçao was conquered by the Dutch in 1634, and the first Jewish settlers arrived in the 1650s under the condition that they cultivate the land. The first group of permanent Jewish settlers, headed by Isaac Da Costa, arrived in 1659 and was settled in the *Joden Quartier* (Jewish Quarter). The authorities assisted the Jews in acquiring land, horses and enslaved people, but only a handful were successful as plantation owners. The semiarid soil and the lack of water made the island inadequate for agriculture, and the WIC transformed it into a 'depot' for enslaved people and a commercial center. Most of the Sephardic Jews became merchants and their knowledge of Spanish

---

5 In 1656, Oliver Cromwell revoked the edict of expulsion of the Jews from England (1290) and permitted their resettlement. London became home to the second-largest community of Sephardic-Portuguese Jews.

was a valuable asset for trade with the Spanish Main (Emmanuel and Emmanuel 1970, 40–48; Arbell 2002, 125–131). It has been estimated that in the middle of the eighteenth century, the Jews of Curaçao numbered between 1,300 and 1,500 persons – almost half of the white population (Emmanuel and Emmanuel 1970, 213, 226, 277).

Surinam was first occupied by England (1630), whose government was interested in encouraging the settlement of members of "the Hebrew Nation" and granted them exceptional liberties that included economic, religious and judicial freedom as well as permission to work on Sundays. When the Dutch conquered Surinam in 1667, they maintained these privileges. In addition to the freedom to practice their religion, Jews were allowed to own enslaved people and were exempt from military service in times of peace (Arbell 2002, 82–90). In Surinam, the center of Jewish life was the *Joden Savanne*, an autonomous region that was called "Jerusalem on the Riverside". Aviva Ben-Ur summarizes its special status:

> Jodensavanne is the fullest expression of the privileges granted to Jews in the Atlantic world. Jodensavanne represented territorial autonomy: the village and its immediate environs, which Jews referred to as "the savannah," belonged to the Jewish community. Homeowners in Jodensavanne owned only the houses they built, purchased or inherited. The plots of land they occupied were the collective patrimony of Suriname's Portuguese Jewish community. According to communal bylaws, houses could be sold only to Portuguese and Spanish Jews; the Ashkenazim (Jews of Germanic origin) were excluded. (Ben-Ur 2016, 40–41)

The Sephardim in Surinam established sugar plantations that carried biblical names, such as *Mahanaim, Beer Sheba, Hebron* and *Carmel*, reaching a maximum of 2,000 Jews and 115 plantations in the eighteenth century.[6]

In the British colonies, the Jewish population was not as concentrated as in the Dutch ones. The largest Jewish community was founded in Jamaica, which became the most successful plantation colony under the British. Its history dates back to the sixteenth century, when Jamaica was a neglected colony under Spanish rule. The Spaniards apparently preferred to ignore the presence of crypto-Jews from Portugal since they were useful for trade with other colonies. The crypto-Jews welcomed the British conquest in 1655, after which they increasingly settled in Port Royal – a commercial center dominated by buccaneers that was destroyed in an earthquake in 1692 (Dunn 1973, 35, 183). Gradually, control of Jamaica passed into the hands of the plantation owners who dominated the island's economy and politics. Jewish immigration, especially from England, continued throughout the enslavement period. Most of the Jews engaged in trade, but there were also several plantation owners. Jews were granted religious and economic freedom but were considered unequal to British citizens: they had to pay a special tax, called the "Jew's Tribute"; they could

---

[6] These figures are based on Arbell (2002, 91–92). According to Robert Cohen, the Sephardic population reached its peak in 1786 with 852 persons (Cohen 1991, 63–64).

own only a limited number of enslaved people; and they were not allowed to hold public office. In 1730, the Jews numbered 900 in a population of 7,148 white people. By the beginning of the nineteenth century, there were 2,000 Jews in Jamaica among a white population of about 15,000 people, who in turn constituted only 4.4% of the total population, 90% of which was enslaved (Hurwitz and Hurwitz 1971, 57; Gerber 2014, 6; Knight 1978, 238).

Jews from Brazil and Europe also immigrated to the French colonies, but in 1685, France decreed their expulsion. Although there are indications of their continued presence, they were not able to live openly as Jews, nor to establish communities (Loker 1991, 24–26).[7] Jews also settled in the Danish colonies, particularly St. Thomas. Here, their status was similar to that observed in the other Protestant colonies.

4 Transformation of the Legal Status and Relations with the Local Population

The status of the Jews was shaped not only by the laws decreed in the mother country or by the colonies' authorities but also by the attitude of the local Christian population. According to Zvi Loker: "Generally speaking the Jews in the British Islands enjoyed peaceful coexistence with the Protestant majority" and "[g]ood relations in particular developed between the Jewish settlers and the Dutch Reformed Church, headed by the local 'classis'" (Loker 1991, 32). Nevertheless, Jews suffered from discrimination and anti-Semitic attacks motivated by prejudices, religious zeal and economic competition (Faber 1998, 45, 60–61).

Jewish merchants who traded illegally with the Spanish colonies were exposed to special peril in case they were captured by Spanish privateers and handed over to the Inquisition. The successful contraband trade practices of the Jews with the Spanish Main aroused the envy of the local white bourgeoisie, who considered them to be "a distinct alien minority". The Jews had to negotiate the maintenance of their privileges with the local governments, such as the permission to work on Sundays or to be exempt from service in the militia on the Sabbath and on Jewish holidays. In Surinam, the Sephardic Jews obtained additional privileges such as exemption from forced public works and the permission to conduct their community's own judiciary system (Wilmot 2014, 261; Emmanuel and Emmanuel 1970, 82–84; Van Lier 1982, 20–22).

The social status of the Jews within the dominant 'caste' was inferior, especially in the British colonies. On the other hand, they alone developed economic ties with the free people of color and with the enslaved. The latter were allowed to trade only in the Sunday markets, and the Jews – who did not rest on that day – provided them with merchandise (Wilmot 2014, 364–365).

---

7 *The Code Noir*, Article Premier.

The inferior social status of the Jews was manifested in their exclusion from holding positions of civil servants. In the British colonies, Jews obtained full civil rights in 1831 – six months after the free population of color and two years before the abolition of slavery. In the Dutch colonies, the status of the Jewish faith became equal to that of other denominations in 1825, but at the same time, Jews lost the privileges that they had received from the WIC and the Dutch government (Emmanuel and Emmanuel 1970, 48, 335–337).

Legal equality in the Protestant Caribbean colonies was obtained during a period of economic decline. Jews from Curaçao, St. Thomas and other islands started to look for new opportunities in the United States and in the new independent republics of Latin America. The Caribbean Jews sided with the cause of the colonies fighting against the Spanish Empire, which had persecuted their ancestors and forbade their entry into its territories. The *Libertador* Simón Bolívar had close relations with the Jews of Curaçao, especially with Mordechay Ricardo, who had sheltered him in his home after his defeat in Porto Cabello. Bolívar, who was a Freemason, encouraged non-Catholics to settle in the republic of Gran Colombia (comprising Venezuela, Colombia, Ecuador and Panama), granting them religious freedom as long as they practiced in the privacy of their homes. In 1819, he signed a decree that gave "the members of the Hebrew Nation the right to establish themselves, with guarantees of religious liberty and political rights, given to other citizens" (Arbell 2002, 160, 301; Capriles Goldish 2009, 10, 99).

Several Sephardic communities were established in the port towns of Venezuela, Colombia and Panama. The first was the community of Coro (Venezuela) – 60 miles from Curaçao – where the liberal attitude of Bolívar was not shared by the Catholic population. The Jews prospered economically, but anti-Semitic eruptions in 1855, accompanied by cries of "mueran los judíos, viva su dinero" (death to the Jews, long live their money), forced many of them to return to Curaçao (Capriles Goldish 2009, 66–70; Arbell 2002, 302–304).[8] With time, however, the Sephardic Jews were integrated into the Catholic society in Colombia also, achieving social and political prominence.

5 Economic Transitions

The economy of the Caribbean colonies was based on plantations of sugar and other staples that were owned by European settlers who depended on the manpower of enslaved people from Africa. The first Sephardim who engaged in agriculture were refugees from the Dutch colony in Pernambuco who brought to the Caribbean their experiences and techniques from the sugar plantations of Brazil. They were joined by new settlers from Amsterdam, London and other European cities. For the Portuguese Jews, the plantation period lasted from the mid-seventeenth century to the

---

[8] On the history of the Jews of Coro, see Isidoro Aizenberg (1983).

mid-eighteenth century. During this period, they were involved in the development of innovations in the production of sugar and other staples as well as in the processing of chocolate and vanilla (Loker 1991, 47; Arbell 2002, 40–48).

The most prosperous agricultural center of the Sephardim was the Jewish village of *Joden Savanne* in Surinam, which, according to the historian Robert Cohen, was "the most privileged Jewish community in the world":

> Economically, they [the Surinamese Jews] were not only traders and merchants, but often also plantation owners and slave-owners. Demographically, they were [. . .] a sizeable proportion of the white population throughout the eighteenth century. (Cohen 1991, 1)

Dutch Jews also received concessions from the WIC to settle in Curaçao, where they established sugar and tobacco plantations in the *Joden Quartier* along the shore. Curaçao, which developed into a commercial center, challenged the Spanish monopoly with its contraband trade. Since agriculture could not adequately provide for their large families, most Jews preferred to engage in commerce and maritime activities, taking advantage of their knowledge of languages and their family and communal networks (Israel 2014, 32–37; Emmanuel and Emmanuel 1970, 62).

The most profitable business in the Caribbean was the slave trade, but it was monopolized by settlement companies such as the WIC and the Royal African Company. Thus, the participation of Jews in the slave trade was marginal. Furthermore, the British colonies imposed restrictions on the ownership of enslaved persons by Jews, and only a small number of them could make it as plantation owners. In Jamaica, most of the Sephardim traded with the Spanish colonies or were merchants in the Jamaican villages. They also acquired real estate in the towns and traded goods in the Sunday markets of the enslaved (Faber 1998, 32–37, 65–68, 82; Arbell 2002, 29, 75, 208, 251).

Most of the Sephardim engaged in maritime occupations, i.e., as merchants, ship owners, sailors or insurance agents. Their major commercial center was established in Curaçao, which served as a depot for the WIC. The Sephardim distributed the goods imported from Europe throughout the Caribbean colonies and the Spanish Main, benefitting from their knowledge of Spanish. They used small freighters, that exposed them to the risks of shipwreck. They were also menaced by Spain, that tried to protect its colonies from contraband, as well as by British privateers, that wished to dominate the contraband business (Israel 2014, 29–31; Emmanuel and Emmanuel 1970, 69–73, 142, 215–216). Thus, one of the functions of the Jewish communities was the redemption of captives who fell into the hands of pirates.

6 Religious and Communal Life

The Jews in the Caribbean established semi-autonomous communities according to the model of Amsterdam, whence they imported most of their spiritual leaders and whose bylaws they adapted to local conditions. They continued to use Portuguese and Spanish as their communal languages and turned to the Amsterdam leadership when they needed help. According to Hilit Surowitz-Israel, "all religious authority resided in the Amsterdam community and Curaçao functioned as its satellite" (Surowitz-Israel 2014, 111).

Curaçao was considered "the mother community of all the Caribbean islands", and it served as their model. Each year, the veteran rich families that formed its elite elected from among themselves the *ma'amad* – the executive committee of the congregation – which consisted of a *presidente*, a *parnas* (vice president) and a *gabay* (treasurer). The minutes of their sessions were written in Portuguese. The members of the *ma'amad* decreed regulations, nominated religious and lay officials and imposed the *imposta da naçao* (the community's tax) as well as the *finta* (poll tax). The *ma'amad* had absolute authority over the members of the community through its power to ban religious transgressors or persons who refused to fulfill their communal obligations as well as through the protection of the Dutch authorities and the communal leadership in Amsterdam (Surowitz-Israel 2014, 110–111; Loker 1991, 43; Nahon 2014, 68–73).

The Sephardic synagogues in the Caribbean followed the unique tradition of covering their floors with sand. The reason is explained by Mordechai Arbell:

> One idea is that clandestine *converso* synagogues in Portugal or in Dutch Brazil, where Portuguese conversos used to come to pray, had sand-covered floors so as to muffle the sound of the steps of those who came to pray. The Caribbean Jews explain the meaning of the sand by saying that as long as they are not back in Jerusalem, they are still trodding in the desert. (Arbell 2002, 19)

The first synagogue in Curaçao was constructed in 1674, and its first religious leader, *Haham* Yoshiahu Pardo, was sent from Amsterdam in the same year. He established the yeshiva *Etz Chaim*, which trained cantors and other religious officials. The *haham* (rabbi) was responsible for religious services and for the education of boys, and he headed the court of the community (Emmanuel and Emmanuel 1970, 55, 118).

One of the central functions of the Caribbean communities was to assist poor families, widows, orphans and other persons in need as well as to take care of the dying and to ensure the proper handling of the deceased. In Curaçao, there were 29 distinct Sephardic charities for purposes such as the secret assistance of respectable families that had become impoverished, the collection of dowries for poor brides, and the gathering of funds for the redemption of ransomed captives. The Caribbean Sephardic communities also had special funds that were dedicated to their coreligionists in the four holy cities of the Land of Israel (Jerusalem, Hebron, Safed and Tiberias). The attachment of the communities to their historical homeland was also manifested in the customs of placing sand from the Holy Land on the eyes of the deceased before burial and of mixing it with the sand that was spread on the synagogue floor (Emmanuel and Emmanuel 1970, 153–155; Arbell 2002, 23–26, 142).

Religious life was characterized by rivalries and conflicts between lay and religious leaders as well as between competing religious factions. In the mid-eighteenth century, the monopoly of *Mikve Israel* – the official community of Willemstad (Curaçao) – was threatened by the poor Jews of Ostrabanda, who established their own synagogue (Roitman 2014, 87–88). Another source of internal tensions was the presence of Ashkenazim from Eastern and Central Europe who had followed in the footsteps of the Sephardim and settled in the Caribbean. Iberian Jews preferred to maintain contact exclusively with other Sephardic communities and to preserve endogamy within their ethnic group. In Paramaribo (Surinam), German Jews established a separate synagogue and punished members who visited the Portuguese synagogue or took Portuguese spouses (Arbell 2002, 26; Van Lier 1982, 19–20; Goldish 2014, 317).

Jews shared the prejudices of Christian society towards the population of color. The shared offspring of Jews and people of color could join the community as members but were denied equal rights. In Barbados, the preamble to the Hebrew Vestry Act stated that "no person whose original extraction shall be proved to have been from a *Negro* shall be deemed or allowed to choose or be chosen a Vestry-man under this Act" (Watson 2014, 210–211). The regulations of the community of Surinam stipulated that "all Jewish 'mestizos', people of color, 'mestizas' (sic) and 'castices' who carry the name of, or are known to be descendants of the Portuguese/Spanish nation will be considered 'Congreganten'".[9] Their status, however, was different from that of the *yehidim* (full members) (Arbell 2002, 108–109). In 1759, the Jewish people of color of Surinam established a society named *Darchei Yesharim* (Ways of the Righteous), which was the only such community in the Caribbean.

The process of secularization that took place in the nineteenth century aroused conflicts between the liberals, who called for a reform of the religious services, and the conservatives, who opposed the innovation of rituals or other areas of religious life. The decline of rabbinical authority as well as personal rivalries aggravated the conflict between lay and religious leaders, and in the case of Curaçao, a schism ultimately resulted in the foundation of the "Dutch Jewish Reform Community" (Emmanuel and Emmanuel 1970, 371–380). Throughout the nineteenth century, most of the Caribbean communities (with the exception of Surinam) adhered to the Reform movement and adopted its doctrines and liturgy. In this process, which is beyond the scope of the present chapter, the Amsterdam community lost its role as a model and a source of inspiration for the Caribbean Sephardim, and its place was taken by the Reform congregations of the United States. The historian Mordechai Arbell regarded this process as one of the reasons for the assimilation that ultimately led to the "comfortable disappearance" of the Caribbean communities – with the exception of Panama. The Reform prayer books and the customs imported from the US disconnected the Caribbean Jews

---

9 "Mestizos" is a historical term for people of both European and indigenous ancestry; "castices" is a historical term for people of Portuguese origin living in the East Indies.

from their Spanish-Portuguese roots, and they became estranged from religious practice. At the same time, they maintained their ethnic identity and continued to view themselves as part of the Spanish-Portuguese Jewish nation (Arbell 1998, 25–28).

7 Language and Culture

As in religious and communal life, the source of inspiration for the culture of the Caribbean Sephardim was rooted in Amsterdam and other Sephardic European centers. According to Miriam Bodian, the acculturation of 'New Christians' who returned to Judaism was facilitated by their forced Catholicization in the Iberian Peninsula:

> They spoke European languages . . . and were in close touch with the currents of European intellectual and political life. For many ex-Conversos, Jewish loyalties, however powerful, were anchored not in rabbinic tradition but in ethnicity, ancestry, and hostility to the Church. [. . .T]he new diaspora that emerged in the Atlantic states did not reproduce the characteristics of traditional Jewish societies [. . . and] its adaptation to rabbinic life was distinctive, with, for example, greater emphasis on the Bible than was prevalent in other Jewish cultures and a high reliance on prayer books and Bibles in Spanish. (Bodian 201, 23)

The central element of the Iberian culture that was brought over to the Caribbean was language, and it remained the major component of Sephardic identity. Portuguese and Spanish were spoken in daily life within the family and in economic interactions and they formed the basis of community life. Knowledge of Hebrew was limited to religious services, whereas the synagogue's further functions were conducted in Portuguese. In addition, some prayers were recited in Portuguese or in Spanish, such as the "bendigamos" recited after meals (Eckkrammer 2016, 277–285; Emmanuel 2016, 319).

The use of Iberian languages by the Caribbean Sephardim is reflected in the names, in the wills and in the tombstones of the Sephardic communities. According to Sephardic custom, the firstborn son or daughter was named after the paternal grandfather or grandmother and the second after the maternal grandparents, even if they were still alive. The names were mostly taken from the Bible. The surnames were of Hebrew or Arabic origin, of Hispano-Portuguese origin, or were a combination of both (e.g. Cohen-Henriquez or Levy-Maduro) (Arbell 2002, 135–136; Ben-Ur 2016, 171–176; Eckkramer 2016, 283–285).

Wills were important legal documents for the Jewish merchants who risked their lives on journeys on the high seas, and they became an important source of information for historians. Most of the early wills from the British as well as from the Dutch colonies were written in Spanish or in Portuguese. In addition, Jews of color in Surinam used Portuguese – together with Dutch – when writing their wills (Loker 1997, 23–34; Faber 2014, 285–286; Ben-Ur 2014, 179). The tombstones of the seventeenth and eighteenth centuries were written mostly in Hebrew, Portuguese or

Spanish. Gradually, however, the local languages took precedence, testifying to the tendencies of secularization and assimilation which began in the nineteenth century. The tombstones also reflect several other aspects of the history and culture of the Caribbean Jews that found expression in the composition of epitaphs, in the iconography and in the ornamentation. These also contribute to the study of economic and demographic transitions and of the impact of the local environment on the Sephardic Jews (Studemund-Halévy 2016, 429–436).

In his study of the epigraphs and iconography of the gravestones of Bridgetown (Barbados), Michael Studemund-Halévy points out the persistence of ties with Amsterdam even in the final resting places of the Sephardic Jews. Wealthy merchants would prepare their gravestones during their lifetime, importing Carrara marble which was carved with Hebrew inscriptions in Amsterdam or other European cities (Studemund-Halévy 2016, 439–440). The influence of Iberian culture was manifested in the engravings of human figures and other elements of iconography and ornamentation. Studemund-Halévy refers to the images of skulls, skeletons and crossbones as instances of *memento mori* that reflect Christian influence, while Rachel Frankel suggests that this imagery was related to the Vision of the Valley of Dry Bones of the prophet Ezekiel (Chapter 37), symbolizing national revivification (Studemund-Halévy 2016, 447–448; Frankel 2014, 137).

In her analysis of tombstone inscriptions in Suriname and Jamaica, Frankel observes:

> The use of Portuguese indicates the cultural, if not sacred, status that the language retained among the Sephardi Jews in Suriname [...]. The prevalence of Hebrew and Portuguese or Hebrew and Spanish epitaphs on the inventoried gravestones of Cassipora Creek, Jodensavanne, Hunt's Bay, and Paramaribo's old Sephardi cemeteries suggests that mourners sought to affirm Jewish tradition as well as their Iberian heritage. (Frankel 2014, 135–136)

Frankel notes the difference between the Dutch cemeteries in Surinam on the one hand, where "[t]he absence of trilingual epitaphs – Hebrew, Portuguese (or Spanish), and Dutch [. . .] – suggests that Jodensavanne's Jews preferred and hoped to perpetuate their cultural isolation", and Hunt's Bay Cemetery in Kingston on the other hand, where "trilingualism suggests that the Jamaican Jewish community was in the process of absorbing new cultural traits and perhaps anticipating future generations of English speaking progeny" (Frankel 2014, 136–137).

In addition to the official languages of their metropoles, the Caribbean populations developed their own Creole languages. Papiamento, spoken in the ABC colonies (Aruba, Bonaire and Curaçao), was created by a mixture of European and African languages, and was used for communication between the Protestant Dutch, Sephardic Jews, free people of color and enslaved people. Some researchers claim that Papiamento was influenced by the languages spoken by Sephardic Jews. Asunción Lloret Florenciano and Susann Fischer argue that "the influence of the Sefardic Jews (be it Spanish, Portuguese or Judeo-Spanish) on Papiamento was only marginal [. . .] [but that] the Sefardim together with the slaves were the first to use Papiamento for daily life, and thus to support its use on Curaçao as a *Lingua Franca*" (Lloret Florenciano and Fischer 2016, 234). Sephardic women did not speak Dutch, and they used Papiamento in their interactions with the enslaved. "The black nannies became mediators between the black and the white populations" (Lloret Florenciano and Fischer 2016, 245–247; Eckkrammer 2016, 280–282).

The Creole language that developed in Surinam was Sranan Tongo, an English-based language mixed with the African languages of the enslaved as well as Dutch and Portuguese. Among themselves, the Sephardic Jews of Surinam spoke the "Portuguese Jewish language", but in their daily communication with the rest of the population, they used Sranan Tongo (Ben-Ur 2014, 176–177; Eckkrammer 2016, 286).

In the nineteenth century, Sephardic communities gradually abandoned the use of Portuguese in their communal activities. The emergence of the Latin American republics and the immigration of Caribbean Jews to the port cities of South America strengthened the use of Spanish as the language of the Sephardic Jews. At the same time, English became a predominant language in the communities' ties with the Reform movement of the United States. Curaçao – the mother of the Caribbean communities – switched from Portuguese to Dutch when it came to writing the community's minutes (Ben-Ur 2014, 179; Eckkrammer 2016, 288–289, 311–313).

8 Liturgical and Literary Works

Hebrew served as the sacred language for religious practices, with liturgical and rabbinical books imported from Amsterdam and London. A handful of religious works were composed in the Caribbean even though there were no local Hebrew publishers. Zvi Loker presents three examples:

1. A *Benedictions for Circumcisions* composed by the *hazan* (cantor) Moses López in 1794, which was "The only known Hebrew Prayer Book printed for the exclusive use of a Caribbean territory" (Barbados).
2. A prayer book composed by *hazan* David Hisquiau Louzada in Surinam, apparently after a revolt of Maroons in the 1760s, seeking the Almighty's "protection from black slaves who revolted and escaped, attacking the plantations from time to time, plundering and even killing".
3. *Azharot* (Warnings): liturgical poems enumerating the 613 Commandments, composed by Rabbi Gabbay Izidro, who served as a spiritual leader in Surinam and Barbados. Loker concludes that "The composition of *Azharot* presupposes a sound knowledge of both the Hebrew language and metrics. Its use in the Caribbean sugar colonies of the New World shows a relatively high degree of Judaic culture" (Loker 1991, 45, 82–83; Loker and Cohen 1982, 75–77).

The Caribbean plantation societies of the seventeenth and eighteenth centuries were not a fertile environment for intellectual life, and only a small number of Sephardic Jews were involved in literary production – generally under the influence of their previous experience in Europe. The poet Daniel López Laguna was born in Portugal to converso parents who settled in Southern France. While studying at the university in Spain, he was imprisoned by the Inquisition but was able to flee to Jamaica, where he openly returned to Judaism. He worked for 23 years on his masterpiece *Espejo fiel de vidas que contiene los Psalmos de David en verso* (The true mirror of life, that contains the Psalms of David in rhyme) (Perelis 2014, 322–324; Arbell 2002, 255–256). In his essay on López Laguna, Ronnie Perelis presents his work as an exceptional case of a converso who wrote about his previous experience as a crypto-Jew. In the introductory paratexts of the Psalms, López Laguna himself claims:

> To the Muses I was inclined / From the time of my Youth / My adolescence in France / Sacred schooling I was given. / In Spain I mastered the Arts / Eyes opening to virtue / I escaped the Inquisition. / Today in Jamaica in Song / The Psalms give to my harp. / The Desires, first born in my prison cell / I have now fulfilled. (Perelis 2014, 324)[10]

Jamaica, in López Laguna's words, was the place where he was able to give expression to his experience in the prison cell of the Inquisition. But although he had lived there for several years, he does not refer to Jamaica in his poems.

Another converso who used his literary talent in the service of religion was Samuel Mendes de Sola, who was sent from Amsterdam to serve as the second *haham* of the *Mikve Israel* congregation of Curaçao.[11] Samuel Mendes de Sola was born in Lisbon. His father and other relatives had been persecuted by the Inquisition, but the family succeeded in escaping to Amsterdam, where Samuel completed his rabbinical studies. Harm den Boer has analyzed his sermons, which reflect Mendes de Sola's exceptional eloquence as well as his vast knowledge of both rabbinical studies and classical sources. Mendes de Sola published works in Portuguese, Spanish and Hebrew, both in Amsterdam and in Curaçao. He defended the use of classical profane sources in his religious writings, saying that: "do mesmo lugar donde bebe a aranha o veneno que mata, chupa a abelha o mel que deleita" (from the same place where the spider drinks the poison that kills, the bee sucks the honey that delights) (den Boer 2016, 343).

David de Isaac Cohen Nassy (1747–1806), who lived in Surinam, wrote its history and was part of its intellectual elite, represents an entirely different case. Over the course of his turbulent economic life, he worked as a notary, plantation owner, community leader and medical doctor. Cohen Nassy served as secretary and *parnas* of the Jewish community in the Jodensavanne congregation *Beracha Ve-Shalom* and

---

[10] A different translation of Laguna's verses appears in Arbell (2002, 256).
[11] Samuel Mendes de Sola was involved in a conflict that split the Curaçaoan community in the middle of the eighteenth century (see Surowitz-Israel 2014, 112–115).

played an active role in reforming its statutes. He was also involved in the leadership of the Jewish community of Paramaribo and promoted Jewish educational programs (Bijlsma 1982, 65–73). Cohen Nassy himself had a broad education and was greatly inspired by the French Enlightenment. He was the author of the *Essai historique sur la colonie de Surinam* (Historical Essay on the Colony of Surinam), published in 1788, which also includes the history of the Jews of Surinam. He was one of the founders of *Docendo Docemur* (We are taught by teaching), a literary society established in Paramaribo by Sephardic Jews for the common study of history, literature and philosophy.

Referring to the books as a major source of inspiration for Surinamese culture, Robert Cohen prepared an inventory of the books in Cohen Nassy's library, which was later completed by Gérard Nahon. More than 80% of the books were in French, 12% in Spanish, 3.5% in Dutch, and only a small number in Portuguese and Hebrew respectively. This distribution demonstrates both the centrality of the French Enlightenment and the scarcity of Hebrew documents when it comes to the sources that shaped Cohen Nassy's thought (Cohen 1991, 181–239; Nahon 2016, 366). Robert Cohen analyzed the works and activities of David Cohen Nassy in the context of a literary and scientific awakening among the intellectual elite of Surinam which took place during the second half of the eighteenth century. This process coincided with the decline of the plantation economy and the emergence of urban life, which caused the integration of the Surinamese Jews into the cultural life of Paramaribo (Cohen 1991, 94–123).

During the nineteenth and twentieth centuries, the creativity of Caribbean Jews lost its religious content, blended into the general cultural environment and reflected the broader processes of integration and secularization (Capriles Goldish 2009, 89, 115, 237–240).[12]

9 The Decline of Sephardic Life in the Caribbean

The decline of Sephardic life in the Caribbean originated in the political, economic and social transitions of the region. During the American War of Independence, the British colonies were forbidden to trade with the Thirteen Colonies and were thus disconnected from their sources of supply as well as from their export markets. The Dutch colonies were hit hard by the conquest of Holland by the French revolutionaries and the restrictions on trade imposed by the "patriots" who founded the Batavian Republic. During the British occupation of Curaçao (1800–1803, 1807–1816), the authorities confiscated ships and merchandise and imposed heavy taxes (Hurwitz and Hurwitz 1971, 46; Emmanuel and Emmanuel 1970, 283–290). In addition to the

---

[12] For a list of Jewish authors in Curaçao in the nineteenth century, see Emmanuel and Emmanuel 1970, 444–456.

European wars, the population of the Caribbean suffered from a series of hurricanes, epidemics and drought as well as from economic crises.

The cultivation of sugar beet in Europe, motivated by the destruction of the French colony of Saint-Domingue and the foundation of the Republic of Haiti, caused a decline in the price of sugar on the international market. The British authorities were not interested in maintaining their monopoly on the West Indies and shifted their focus to East Asia and other regions (Hurwitz and Hurwitz 1971, 50–55). With the abolition of slavery by the British Parliament (1833), and later by France (1848) and Holland (1863), the white population lost its legal privileged status. In Jamaica, the free people of color were granted legal equality in 1830, and, consequently, Jews were granted full emancipation but lost much of the communal autonomy that had protected their status. The decline of the Sephardic communities was manifested in two parallel demographic processes: emigration and assimilation.

Emigration was caused by the economic and political transitions that diminished the socio-economic status of the Jewish population. Curaçaoan Jews emigrated to St. Thomas, which was an area of free trade under Danish rule. Prosperity, however, was temporary, and many of the Jews of St. Thomas and Curaçao continued their wanderings, settling in the Dominican Republic, Panama, Costa Rica or the United States. Since many of the immigrants were single men, the balance between men and women was shaken, leaving a surplus of unmarried women in the communities of origin. In the countries of destination, the Jewish population was often too small to offer a Jewish marriage market. This, along with declining religiosity, increased the number of weddings between Jewish men and Catholic women, and later also between Jewish women and Catholic men.[13]

The paradigmatic case of emigration is that of the community of Curaçao, which from the "mother of the Jewish communities in the Caribbean" became the source of a new diaspora, dispersed throughout the circum-Caribbean countries, that continued to preserve business and family networks and to maintain the Curaçaoan Sephardic identity. The ex-Curaçaoan Sephardim integrated into the economic elite of their new countries and in many cases gradually assimilated to the Catholic population. In his study of the Jewish history of the Dominican Republic, Enrique Ucko has used the term "fusion", arguing that there was a voluntary assimilation of the Sephardic Jews – most of whom came from Curaçao – and the Dominican population. Although they adopted the Catholic faith, the descendants of the Sephardim remained proud of their Jewish ancestry and preserved the memories and customs of their Judaism (Ucko 1994, 51–73).

In her book *Once Jews: Stories of Caribbean Sephardim*, Josette Capriles Goldish analyzes the history of the transnational Caribbean Sephardic diaspora of the nineteenth and twentieth centuries, focusing on family networks in four centers: Curaçao, Coro (Venezuela), the Danish colony of St. Thomas and Barranquilla

---

13 On the impact of migration on the situation of Jewish women, see Capriles Goldish 2009, 241–254.

(Colombia). She compares the different patterns of assimilation against the backdrop of varying local contexts and attitudes towards the Jews as well as internal factors such as the existence of Jewish institutions and education. Her conclusion is that despite assimilation, family relationships persisted, and that even after four or five generations, Jews and Catholics with common ancestors consider themselves "cousins" and are proud of their Jewish-Sephardic ancestry and its values such as morality, liberalism and education (Capriles Goldish 2009, 257–264).

10 Conclusion

The Caribbean islands – with the exception of Cuba, Hispaniola and Puerto Rico – remained outside the sphere of influence of the Spanish Empire, but Iberian culture was brought to the colonies by the Spanish-Portuguese Jews, who were part of the transnational diaspora of the Western Sephardim. Coming from Amsterdam, London or other European centers of 'New Christians' who had returned to Judaism, they represented an Iberian culture that was further developed in the context of Protestant colonies during the era of the plantation economy.

In the hierarchical system of the plantation societies, Jews occupied a privileged position that was denied them in Europe by virtue of belonging to the white upper 'caste'. They differed, however, from the Christian elite in their religion, social status, cultural legacy, and often in their economic occupations. Their special role in the development of the colonies' economies derived from their domination of languages, their previous economic experiences and their commercial networks that extended between Europe and the Americas.

The networks of Spanish-Portuguese Jews were instrumental in the construction of a common identity among small communities dispersed throughout colonies that belonged to different European countries. Religious uniformity was acquired through the acceptance of the spiritual authority of Amsterdam. There were close relations between the different communities, in part because of many marriages between relatives that strengthened these networks. The Portuguese and Spanish languages were a central element in the identity formation of the Sephardim. In addition to their use as colloquial languages that facilitated the interaction between the dispersed communities, they were incorporated into the prayer books, thus being consecrated as part of the religious legacy of the Caribbean Sephardim.

The eighteenth century was the golden age of the Caribbean Sephardim. Their eventual decline was triggered by economic crises and constant migrations as well as by the diminution of religion caused by secularism and assimilation. Their sense of belonging, like that of their ancestors who were expelled from Spain, transcended religious and national divisions, and they preserved with pride their Jewish-Spanish-Portuguese heritage.

Bibliography

Works Cited

Aizenberg, Isidoro. *La comunidad judía de Coro, 1824–1900: una historia*. Caracas: Biblioteca de Autores y Temas Falconianos, 1983.

Arbell, Mordechai. *Comfortable Disappearance: Lessons from the Caribbean Jewish Experience*. Jerusalem: Institute of the World Jewish Congress, 1998.

Arbell, Mordechai. *The Jewish Nation of the Caribbean; The Spanish-Portuguese Jewish Settlements in the Caribbean and the Guianas*. Jerusalem: Gefen, 2002.

Ben-Ur, Aviva. "The Cultural Heritage of Eurafrican Sephardi Jews in Suriname." *The Jews in the Caribbean*. Ed. Jane Gerber. Oxford/Portland, OR: The Littman Library of Jewish Civilization, 2014. 169–193.

Ben Ur, Aviva. "Jerusalem on the Riverside: Jewish Political Autonomy in the Caribbean." *A Sefardic Pepper-Pot in the Caribbean. History, Language, Literature, and Art*. Ed. Michael Studemund-Halévy. Barcelona: Tirocinio, 2016. 30–54.

Bijlsma, Roelof. "David de Is. C. Nassy, Author of Essai historique sur Surinam." *The Jewish Nation in Surinam: Historical Essays*. Ed. Robert Cohen. Amsterdam: S. Emmering, 1982. 65–73.

Bodian, Miriam. "The Formation of the Portuguese Jewish Diaspora." *The Jews in the Caribbean*. Ed. Jane S. Gerber. Oxford/Portland, OR: The Littman Library of Jewish civilization, 2014. 17–27.

Capriles Goldish, Josette. *Once Jews: Stories of Caribbean Sephardim*. Princeton: Markens Weiner Publishers, 2009.

The Code Noir [The Black Code]. Édit du Roi, Touchant la Police des Isles de l'Amérique Française. Paris, 1687. 28–58. http://chnm.gmu.edu/revolution/d/335/ (16 September 2019).

Cohen, David, and Jack Greene. *Neither Slave Nor Free – The Freedmen of African Descent in the Slave Societies of the New World*. Baltimore/London: The Johns Hopkins University Press, 1972.

Cohen, Robert. *Jews in Another Environment: Surinam in the Second Half of the Eighteenth Century*. Leiden/New York/Copenhagen/Köln: Brill, 1991.

den Boer, Harm. "Perfil literario de Samuel Mendes de Sola." *A Sefardic Pepper-Pot in the Caribbean. History, Language, Literature, and Art*. Ed. Michael Studemund-Halévy. Barcelona: Tirocinio, 2016. 327–361.

Dunn, Richard S. *Sugar and Slaves: The Rise of the Planter Class in the British West Indies, 1624–1713*. London: Jonathan Cape, 1973.

Eckkrammer, Eva-Martha. "Communicative Practices in a multilingual society: A diachronic case study on the Sefardi community of Curaçao." *A Sefardic Pepper-Pot in the Caribbean. History, Language, Literature, and Art*. Ed. Michael Studemund-Halévy. Barcelona: Tirocinio, 2016. 272–316.

Emmanuel, Isaac S. "El portugués en la sinagoga Mikvé Isael de Curaçao." *A Sefardic Pepper-Pot in the Caribbean. History, Language, Literature, and Art*. Ed. Michael Studemund-Halévy. Barcelona: Tirocinio, 2016. 317–323.

Emmanuel, Issac S. and Suzanne A. *History of the Jews of the Netherlands Antilles*. Cincinnati: American Jewish Archives, 1970, 2 Vols.

Faber, Eli. *Jews, Slaves and the Slave Trade*. New York/London: New York University Press, 1998.

Faber, Eli. "The Borders of Early American Jewish History." *The Jews in the Caribbean*. Ed. Jane S. Gerber. Oxford/Portland, OR: The Littman Library of Jewish civilization, 2014. 281–288.

Frankel, Rachel. "Testimonial Terrain: The cemeteries of New World Sephardim." *The Jews in the Caribbean*. Ed. Jane S. Gerber. Oxford/Portland, OR: The Littman Library of Jewish civilization, 2014. 131–142.

Gerber, Jane. 2014. "Introduction." *The Jews in the Caribbean*. Ed. Jane Gerber. Oxford/Portland, OR: The Littman Library of Jewish Civilization, 2014. 1–14.
Goldish, Matt. "The Strange Adventures of Benjamin Franks, an Ashkenazi Pioneer in the Americas." *The Jews in the Caribbean*. Ed. Jane S. Gerber. Oxford/Portland, OR: The Littman Library of Jewish civilization, 2014. 311–318.
Goslinga, Cornelis Ch. *The Dutch in the Caribbean and the Wild Coast 1580–1680*. Gainesville: University of Florida Press, 1971.
Hurwitz, Samuel J., and Edith F. Hurwitz. *Jamaica: A Historical Portrait*. New York: Praeger, 1971.
Israel, Jonathan. "To Live and to Trade: The Status of Sephardi Mercantile Communities in the Atlantic World during the Seventeenth and Eighteenth Centuries." *The Jews in the Caribbean*. Ed. Jane S. Gerber. Oxford/Portland, OR: The Littman Library of Jewish Civilization, 2014. 29–43.
Kaplan, Yosef. *Minozrim Chadashim Lihudim Chadashim* [From New Christians to New Jews]. Jerusalem: The Zalman Shazar Center for Jewish History, 2003.
Klein, Herbert S. *African Slavery in Latin America and the Caribbean*. Oxford/New York: Oxford University Press, 1986.
Knight, Franklin W. *The Caribbean – The Genesis of a Fragmented Nationalism*. Oxford/New York: Oxford University Press, 1978.
Lloret Florenciano, Asunción, and Susann Fischer. "Papiamentulo as a Sefardic Koiné in the Caribbean." *A Sefardic Pepper-Pot in the Caribbean. History, Language, Literature, and Art*. Ed. Michael Studemund-Halévy. Barcelona: Tirocinio, 2016. 233–271.
Loker, Z., and Robert Cohen. "An eighteenth-Century Prayer of the Jews of Surinam." *The Jewish Nation in Surinam: Historical Essays*. Ed. Robert Cohen. Amsterdam: S. Emmering, 1982. 75–86.
Loker, Zvi. *Jews in the Caribbean: Evidence on the History of the Jews in the Caribbean Zone in Colonial Times*. Jerusalem: Misgav Yerushalayim, 1991.
Loker, Zvi. "Caribbean Jewish Wills – A Historical Source." *Judaica Latinoamericana*. Vol. III. Jerusalem, Magnes Press, 1997. 23–33.
Nahon, Gérard. "Amsterdam and the Portuguese Naçao of the Caribbean in the Eighteenth Century." *The Jews in the Caribbean*. Ed. Jane S. Gerber. Oxford/Portland, OR: The Littman Library of Jewish civilization, 2014. 67–83.
Nahon, Gérard. "Nefusot Yehuda (Bayonne) et beraha ve-Shalom (Surinam): Livres et lecture au XVIIIème siècle." *A Sefardic Pepper-Pot in the Caribbean*. Ed. Michael Studemund-Halévy. Barcelona: Tirocinio, 2016. 362–428.
Perelis, Ronnie. "Daniel Israel López Laguna's 'Espjeo fiel de vidas' and the Ghosts of Marrano Autobiography." *The Jews in the Caribbean*. Ed. Jane S. Gerber. Oxford/Portland, OR: The Littman Library of Jewish civilization, 2014. 319–328.
Roitman, Jessica. "A Flock of Wolves Instead of Sheep: The Dutch WIC, Conflict Resolution and the Jewish Community of Curaçao in the eighteenth century." *The Jews in the Caribbean*. Ed. Jane S. Gerber. Oxford/Portland, OR: The Littman Library of Jewish civilization, 2014. 85–105.
Studemund-Halévy, Michael. "More than Images: Sefardi Sepulchral Iconography in the Jewish Cemetery in Bridgetown, Barbados." *A Sefardic Pepper-Pot in the Caribbean. History, Language, Literature, and Art*. Ed. Michael Studemund-Halévy. Barcelona: Tirocinio, 2016. 429–488.
Surowitz-Israel, Hilit. "Religious Authority: A Perspective from the Americas." *The Jews in the Caribbean*. Ed. Jane S. Gerber. Oxford/Portland, OR: The Littman Library of Jewish civilization, 2014. 107–118.
Ucko, Enrique. "La fusión de los sefardíes con los dominicanos." *Presencia judía en Santo Domingo*. Ed. Alfonso Lockward. Santo Domingo: Taller, 1994. 51–73.
Van Lier, R.A.J. "The Jewish Community in Surinam: A Historical Survey." *The Jewish Nation in Surinam: Historical Essays*. Ed. Robert Cohen. Amsterdam: S. Emmering, 1982. 19–27.

Watson, Karl. "Shifting identities: Religion, Race and Creolization among the Sephardi Jews of Barbados, 1654–1900." *The Jews in the Caribbean*. Ed. Jane S. Gerber. Oxford/Portland, OR: The Littman Library of Jewish civilization, 2014. 195–222.
Wilmot, Swithin. "Jewish Politicians in Post Slavery Jamaica: Electoral Politics in the Parish of St. Dorothy, 1849–1860." *The Jews in the Caribbean*. Ed. Jane S. Gerber. Oxford/Portland, OR: The Littman Library of Jewish Civilization, 2014. 261–278.

Further Reading

Cooper, Sara-Louise. "'Des fils invisibles nous relient': Comparative Memory in Caribbean Life-Writing". *Francosphères* 5 (1), 2016, 5, 25–38.
Ledent, Bénédicte. "Caribbean Writers and the Jewish Diaspora: A Shared Experience of Otherness." *The Cross-Cultural Legacy: Critical and Creative Writings in Memory of Hena Maes-Jelinek*. Ed. Gordon Collier, Geoffrey V. Davis, Marc Delrez. Leiden, Brill Academic Publishers; 2016. 201–218.

III The Eighteenth and the Nineteenth Centuries

Tamir Karkason
10 The Iberian Diasporas in the Eighteenth and Nineteenth Centuries

Abstract: This chapter presents the key trends in the Sephardic literature of the eighteenth and nineteenth centuries – primarily written in Ladino (Judeo-Spanish), but also in Hebrew – from a panoramic perspective, while also offering a profile of the intended audience of this literature. Not all genres of Sephardic literary creativity can be included in my discussion, particularly when it comes to the nineteenth century, when the scope of the Ladino corpus expanded significantly. Rather, this chapter attempts to identify the most prominent genres of this literature in terms of both quantity and quality.

In the eighteenth and, even more so, in the nineteenth centuries, the bulk of Sephardic literature was written in the local Ladino vernacular rather than in the high-status language Hebrew. Therefore, Ladino literature was accessible to broad Sephardic audiences who were not literate in Hebrew. Starting in the eighteenth century, Ladino literature began to appeal to a broader audience than ever before, both through the expansion of the use of the vernacular and through the diversification of literary genres along with the strengthening of their popularizing tendencies.

Key Terms: Ottoman Jewish History, Rabbinic literature, *belles-lettres*, *Haskalah* (Jewish enlightenment), Westernization

1 Introduction

Over the course of the two centuries following the expulsion of the Jews from Spain (1492), the vast majority of the Sephardic literary corpus was composed in Hebrew, the liturgical lingua franca of the Jewish world. These works were intended primarily for members of the rabbinical elite and to a lesser extent for other literate Jews. In the nineteenth century, however, this situation changed, and a growing proportion of Sephardic literature was published in Ladino (Judeo-Spanish), the vernacular of the Sephardim in the Ottoman Empire (Bunis 2011; Bunis 2016, 365–377). A pivotal work in the context of this transformation was the rabbinical anthology *Me'am Lo'ez* (1730–1777), which for the first time addressed Jewish men from beyond the ranks

---

Note: Funding Details: This project has received funding from the European Research Council (ERC) under the European Union's Horizon 2020 research and innovation programme (grant agreement No 801861). I also thank the The Salti Institute for Ladino Studies at Bar-Ilan University, headed by Prof. Shmuel Refael, for the generous support of this study.

of the rabbinical elite, including those from other classes, while also indirectly addressing women.

In the nineteenth century, alongside processes of Ottoman modernization and reform, this popularization of Ladino literature continued, and a growing number of works were written for men from outside the rabbinical elite as well as for women. Throughout the eighteenth century, Sephardic literature had included only a small number of works that were not based primarily on Jewish sources. This trend also changed in the nineteenth century, as Sephardic literature – particularly those works written in Ladino – adopted genres that had previously been virtually absent, such as *belles-lettres* and theater, or genres that appeared for the first time on a large scale in the context of the European enlightenment and the *Haskalah* (Jewish enlightenment), such as non-fictional works, historiography, and ethnography.

2 The Eighteenth Century

Jews living in the major cities of the Ottoman Empire in the eighteenth and nineteenth centuries, in the provinces of Western Anatolia and the Southern Balkans, were mostly descendants of immigrants who came to the Empire from Iberia ("Sephardim"). Soon after their expulsion from the Iberian Peninsula, they had settled in the Ottoman Empire, possibly encouraged by Sultan Bayezid II (Ray 2013, 11–75). With varying degrees of autonomy, the Ottoman sphere enabled the Jewish communities to preserve their unique Sephardic cultural heritage, including the Judeo-Spanish vernacular they spoke in their old homeland, Ladino (Hacker 1992; Ben-Naeh 2008).

Scholars have long debated the precise number of Jews expelled from Spain in 1492, but a figure of around 80,000 seems reasonable (Ray 2013, 39). The majority of the exiles and their descendants settled in the Ottoman Empire, forming the Eastern Sephardi Diaspora. Starting in the seventeenth century, a Western Sephardi Diaspora also developed, comprised mainly of the descendants of *Anusim* (i.e., *conversos*, forced converts to Christianity) whose ancestors also moved from the Iberian Peninsula to the Ottoman Empire following the expulsion, but later migrated to Western Europe and returned to Judaism after several generations of detachment from Jewish religious tradition. These migrants established new Jewish communities in Amsterdam, Hamburg, London, Livorno, and other Western European cities (Israel 1985; Kaplan 1994; Kaplan 2000; Israel 2009). These communities included prosperous merchants who established an elaborate network of commerce in the ports of the Mediterranean and in the New World, constituting the Western Sephardi Diaspora. This group reached its peak in the seventeenth century, but probably never numbered more than 10,000 people (Kaplan 1994, 50).

Starting in the seventeenth century and particularly in the eighteenth century, some of these people, mainly from Italy, migrated to Ottoman port cities such as

Aleppo, Izmir, Salonica, and Tunis, where they maintained flourishing business ventures. These families, who came to be known as "Francos," spoke various European languages, including Portuguese and Italian, and in the nineteenth century also French. According to agreements signed with the Ottoman Empire, the "Francos" were considered foreign citizens. This distinguished them from the local Jewish community, exempted them from taxes, and served as a catalyst for internal conflicts in the communities in which they lived (Rozen 1992; Trivellato 2009).[1] The "Francos" are associated with the processes of modernization in Ottoman Jewry, particularly in the second half of the nineteenth century; they also influenced the corpus of Ladino literature.

Beginning in the fifteenth century, the Ottoman Empire launched a series of major conquests in Europe, reaching the gates of Vienna in 1683. By the late seventeenth century, the Ottomans no longer presented a real threat to Central Europe and the expansion of the empire effectively halted. During the Tulip Period (1718–1730), the Ottomans focused their efforts on the internal strengthening of the empire. During and after this period, reforms were introduced in the army, and for the first time a Muslim printing house (1729) and university (1734) were established in Istanbul. In 1774, however, the Ottomans were defeated by the Russians and lost additional territory.[2]

Like other non-Muslims in the empire, such as Orthodox Christians and Armenians, Ottoman Jews were organized in separate communities that enjoyed some degree of autonomy in internal jurisdiction, tax collection, the election of their leadership, and the management of their internal affairs.[3] Most Ottoman Jewish men engaged in commerce and peddling, crafts, or work in the community institutions. The members of the prosperous elite were involved in such areas as tax collection and the provision of supplies to the authorities. Some of them served as senior financial agents (the two types of agent were known as a *bazargan* and a *sarraf*) in the service of governors and sultans, representing what Yaron Ben-Naeh (2018) referred to as "Ottoman-Jewish courtiers."[4]

The crisis of Sabbatianism[5] seriously undermined the social and cultural stability of Ottoman Jewry from the 1650s on, leading to growing ignorance of the meaning of the Jewish commandments and customs among Ottoman Jewish communities.

---

[1] Aron Rodrigue has suggested that, at least in Salonica, local Jews gradually assimilated with the "Francos," thereby acquiring foreign citizenship (Rodrigue 2014, 446).
[2] For a detailed description of the Ottoman Empire in the eighteenth century, see: Quataert (2000, 37–53).
[3] In the mid-nineteenth century, the Ottoman Empire recognized these organizations as *millet* communities, and their heads – including the chief rabbi (*hahambaşı*) – were recognized as the official representatives of the *millet* communities.
[4] For a synthetic review of Ottoman Jewry from the expulsion generation through the eighteenth century, see: Benbassa and Rodrigue (2000, 1-64). See also Ayalon 2017.
[5] Sabbatianism was a messianic movement that emerged in the mid-seventeenth century around the character of Shabbetai Şevi (1626–1676), a Jew born in Izmir who declared himself to be the Messiah. The movement spread with astonishing speed around the Jewish world (Scholem 2016).

The new trends in Ladino literature in the eighteenth century were in part a direct response to this crisis.

2.1 Rabbinical Literature in Hebrew

From as early as the sixteenth and seventeenth centuries, we find evidence of the existence of a large group of rabbinical scholars in Jewish communities across the empire, and particularly in Istanbul and Salonica, who aspired to secure rabbinical positions. Members of this group indeed went on to serve as rabbis of various communities within Ottoman Jewry (Ben-Naeh 2008, 292–304). Some of these scholars found positions in *yeshivot* – institutions intended to facilitate studies using the traditional *chevruta* (study pair) method for adults who had acquired a certain status and received a salary in return for their studies. In addition, individual young men who intended to adhere to this study track were also admitted to these institutions. As Ben-Naeh has explained, the rabbinical elite had a pyramidal structure:

> Those who lacked exceptional intellectual faculties, ties with influential people, distinguished lineages, or wealth had to make do with rabbinical posts in medium and small communities in the outlying provinces. If they insisted on remaining in a big city, they could barely make a living by teaching in congregational or private *yeshivot*, or by tutoring pupils'. (Ben-Naeh 2008, 296)

All the works published during the first 250 years following the expulsion from Spain were written by members of the rabbinical elite, and the vast majority appeared in Hebrew – the elevated "holy tongue" dedicated to liturgical and religious works, and only rarely employed for treatises on other subjects. The publication of works written in the Ladino vernacular was relatively rare, though a short flurry of such publications can be found in the third quarter of the sixteenth century, mainly as part of the effort to make rabbinical literature accessible to *Anusim* returning to the fold of Judaism (Borovaya 2017).

Rabbinical literature in Ladino flourished from the 1730s on, when it began to address broader audiences than in the past. Rabbinical literature in Hebrew was also published in the eighteenth and nineteenth centuries, but its relative weight within the total corpus of Sephardic literature in the Ottoman Empire gradually fell, mirroring the rise of Ladino writings and new literary genres. The scholars of the eighteenth and nineteenth centuries in the Balkans and Anatolia devoted their Hebrew-language treatises mainly to the same subjects that had been examined by their predecessors in the sixteenth and seventeenth centuries: religious edicts, exegesis (of the Bible, the Mishna, the Tosefta, Midrashim, Maimonides, etc.), and sermons. The scope of Kabbalistic and *Musar* literature also expanded (Borenstein-Makovetsky 2001; see also Borenstein-Makovetsky 1997). Leah Borenstein-Makovetsky has examined some 500 rabbinical works printed in Hebrew in Anatolia and the Balkans between 1750 and 1900.[6] Of these, approximately 210 were published in Izmir (around one-third of which were works by the eminent religious arbiter R. Haim Palachi, 1788–1868), approximately 80 in Salonica, and around 60 in Istanbul. The remaining works were published in Edirne, Bursa, Rhodes, and other cities (Borenstein-Makovetsky 2001, 127). The intended audience of these works was almost always the rabbinical elite, but from the eighteenth century onward, they were also aimed at other literate, affluent Jews, known as *ba'alei ha-batim* (Borenstein-Makovetsky 2001, 145; see also Ben-Naeh 2015a, 286–287).

2.2 Rabbinical Literature in Ladino

In the Sephardic communities of the Ottoman Empire, a large proportion of boys attended the *Talmud Torah* from the age of five. The teachers inculcated their students with the ability to read Hebrew and to understand the prayers and the Bible, and also provided a basis in the *Halakhah*. The lessons were conducted in the Ladino vernacular, and the teaching method was based on Ladino translations of the Bible and the accompanying explanations, as well as on learning the material by rote. The students began by learning the letters of the Hebrew alphabet, went on to study vocalization and its diacritical symbols, and then studied prayers and the Bible with the help of Rashi's commentary (Ben-Naeh 2008, 253–254). Among women, who were excluded from the traditional educational frameworks, literacy was virtually unknown until the last quarter of the nineteenth century, with very rare exceptions (Karkason 2018, 73–77). Even among men, the literacy rate was only partial: contrary to the popular perception, literacy was never shared by the entire Jewish male population. Many boys from poor families did not attend a *Talmud Torah*, or were forced to end their studies after three or four years in order to help provide for their family. Therefore, "despite the effort of the congregation, there were children who did not study at all and upon reaching maturity could not even write their names" (Ben-Naeh 2008, 254). Some other boys ended their studies around the age of 12 or 13, while an even smaller proportion continued on to the *yeshiva* frameworks and gained a broader literacy in Hebrew. The level of Hebrew knowledge among those who did not continue to *yeshiva* after the *Talmud Torah* was generally quite limited, and was almost non-existent among men from poorer backgrounds and women in general.

The lack of knowledge of Hebrew and the distancing from Castilian Spanish in the Jewish public sphere were probably the main reasons for the wave of original publications and translations into contemporary Ladino. The eighteenth century was

---

[6] Dozens of works have survived in manuscript form, but it is clear that many treatises, both manuscripts and printed works, were lost and are not in our possession (Borenstein-Makovetsky 2001, 127–128).

a revolutionary one for the Sephardic literature of the Ottoman Empire, as the center of gravity shifted from Hebrew to the Ladino vernacular, which had previously been confined mainly to speech and oral culture. This transition was manifested in four main genres during this century: Biblical exegesis, and particularly the exegetical anthology *Me'am Lo'ez* (1730–1777); the new, more accessible Ladino translations of the Bible published by Abraham Assa (1710 – ca. 1780); *Musar* literature translated into Ladino; and the poetic form known as *coplas*, whose roots are older, but which emerged as a literary genre in the eighteenth century.

These genres reflected the emergence of a relatively broad audience literate in the local vernacular – one that for the first time extended beyond the confines of the narrow rabbinical elite and the *ba'alei ha-batim* and also addressed men from lower social classes as well as women. These phenomena strengthened in the nineteenth century, as the scope of Ladino literature widened considerably and new genres were introduced, expanding the boundaries of the Sephardic bookshelf.

2.3 *Me'am Lo'ez*

The rabbinical anthology *Me'am Lo'ez*, and particularly its classic volumes on the Pentateuch, is the flagship of Ladino literature. *Me'am Lo'ez* includes a Ladino commentary on the Bible, written in an accessible register designed to appeal to a relatively wide audience. The anthology was initiated by R. Jacob Huli (1689–1732), who was born in Jerusalem but lived and worked in Istanbul. Huli "sought to compose a popular collection in Ladino of the Jewish religious literature over the generations, from the Mishna through to the literature of his own time, to be edited according to the order of the verses in the 24 Books of the Bible" (Landau 1981, 35). The works of Huli and his successors focus mainly on the Midrash, Halakhah, and Aggadah, though they also touch on the Kabbalah, *Musar*, sermonizing, and other fields (Landau 1981, 36).

All the volumes of *Me'am Lo'ez* including commentary on the Torah were published in the Ottoman capital, Istanbul. Huli himself wrote and published a commentary on Genesis (1730), and he also wrote half the commentary on Exodus, up to the Torah portion *Terumah*. This latter work was published shortly after his death (1733). His work was continued by R. Yitzhak Magriso, who wrote and published the second half of Huli's commentary on Exodus (1745–1746) as well as commentaries on Leviticus (1753) and Numbers (1764). R. Yitzhak Arguete wrote and published a commentary on Deuteronomy in two volumes (1772, 1777) (Romeu Ferré 2000, 9–46). In the latter half of the nineteenth century, additional commentaries in the *Me'am Lo'ez* format were published in Salonica, Izmir, Jerusalem, and Istanbul, covering some of the Early Prophets (Joshua), the Latter Prophets (Isaiah), and the Ketuvim or Writings (Esther,

Ruth, Ecclesiastes, and the Song of Songs) (Romeu Ferré 2000, 10; Meyuhas Ginio 2015, 359–360).[7]

Jacob Huli, who was born during the tail end of the Sabbatean crisis, was concerned about the prevailing ignorance among the Jewish public regarding the meanings of the commandments and customs. This ignorance led many to violate Halakhic laws, as Huli noted in his introduction to the Genesis volume of *Me'am Lo'ez*: "As for the precepts of Judaism, nobody is able to read a ruling from the *Shulhan Arukh*[8] because people do not know Hebrew, and thus nobody knows the rulings one is obliged to follow" (Huli 2014, 29–30). In the eighteenth century, Huli and his successors sought to fill the lacunas in popular knowledge, restore a widespread familiarity with the canonical texts, above all the Bible, and make Judaism more appealing to the general population. Alisa Meyuhas Ginio suggests that Huli and his successors sought to bridge "the cultural gap that existed between the Hebrew-writing rabbinical élite on the one hand and the rank and file Judeo-Spanish speaking and Ladino-reading on the other." Accordingly, they "needed a new modern type of language, closer to the everyday language yet at the same time including many Hebrew words and expressions" (Meyuhas Ginio 2010, 118–119).

Huli and his successors authored their works with the intention that they be read aloud in the synagogue or at home, and there is extensive evidence that this was indeed the case. Therefore, their impact extended beyond literate audiences to include Jewish men and, even more so, Jewish women who had never learned to read and write; for the first time, women were able to follow the public reading of the Torah (Quintana 2006, 175–176; Meyuhas Ginio 2010, 120–122). This trend continued over the following decades.

Huli's desire to influence his readers and to provide them with an entry point into familiarization with Judaism led him to produce a relatively free interpretation of the Talmudic story, which was suited to his readers' level of understanding and to their expectations; he adjusted "the sources to his society and his era" (Landau 1981, 36). Huli modified the Talmudic stories he quoted and translated: He did not hesitate to add positive epithets to characters who were referred to in neutral terms in the Talmud; he enhanced the supernatural component in the Aggadot he presented; he added stories from the oral tradition to Talmudic tales; etc. (Landau 1981, 42–45). Accordingly, some of the stories were reinterpreted and became "almost a new tale with a different meaning" (Landau 1981, 45).

---

[7] For reasons that have not yet been sufficiently clarified in the research, but that probably relate both to literary quality and to the changes in the target population, the volumes of *Me'am Lo'ez* examining the Prophets and Ketuvim did not acquire the same canonical status as the volumes from the eighteenth century.
[8] The *Shulhan Arukh* (literally: "Set Table") is the most widely consulted of the various legal codes in Judaism. This book was authored in Safed by Joseph Karo (1488–1575) in 1563 and published in Venice in 1565.

Me'am Lo'ez introduced enormous changes into Ladino literature from the eighteenth century onward. Its impact on the creation of an audience for Ladino literature, including its readers, men and women, as well as those who heard it read aloud, was immeasurable.

2.4 Eighteenth-Century Translations of the Bible

In addition to *Me'am Lo'ez*, the eighteenth century also saw significant growth in the field of Ladino translations of the Bible. Such translations, written in the Latin alphabet (Ferrara 1553) as well as in Rashi script (Istanbul 1547; Salonica 1565–1585), had appeared as early as the mid-sixteenth century (Cohen D. 2011, 204; Cohen D. 2019, 200–208). However, by the eighteenth century, these texts were inaccessible to the vast majority of the emerging audience, as their language had become outmoded with the passage of time. The main figure in the generation of *Me'am Lo'ez* who led the process of change in this respect was Abraham Assa of Istanbul, about whose life very little is known. Assa's most lasting legacy is his Ladino translation of the Bible, beginning with the Pentateuch (1739) and followed by the Prophets (1743), the Five Scrolls (1744), and the remaining Ketuvim (1745).

In his introduction to the book of Prophets, Assa explains the educational ideology that lay behind his work. He quotes earlier Sephardic figures who explained that "what sustains the Jews in this exile is their ceaseless reading of the Bible," and expresses his own view "that the reason for the expulsion from Spain was that people did not read the written Law [the Bible and Talmud]." While during the period from the Muslim rule in Spain to his own day, there had been "more than five thousand [Sephardic] rabbis of universal fame, the masses did not read the Bible," argues Assa (quoted in Lehmann 2005a, 34). Assa sought to fill the vacuum caused by what he regarded as the painful deterioration of the generations. Thus, in contrast to the hyper-literal approach of the sixteenth-century translators, he preferred more accessible language and adopted a more liberal approach in rendering the Hebrew biblical text into the Ladino vernacular of the day (Lehmann 2010).[9]

2.5 Ladino Translations of *Musar* Literature

Alongside the biblical translations and commentaries, the middle of the eighteenth century also saw the emergence of *Musar* (literally "ethics") literature in Ladino. The works, published by members of the rabbinical elite, included both translations from Hebrew and original treatises. The objective of *Musar* literature, which had its

---

9 Assa's translations of the Bible, like other aspects of his extensive work, deserve further research.

origins in the Middle Ages, was to encourage the strengthening of faith and the correction of moral conduct. The authors of *Musar* works sought to present their readers with an ideal human role model, so that, as Lehmann suggests, this genre constitutes "a literary system that represents the symbolic universe of rabbinic tradition." Lehmann explains that "Musar literature is a prime instrument in the construction of a meaningful set of cultural references for its readers, who are invited to see and understand the world through the prism of musar's worldview" (Lehmann 2005a, 5).

Like the authors we discussed in the context of the other genres, the writers and translators of *Musar* literature also sought to expand the audience for Ladino literature and enhance the accessibility of Ladino books. All these fields together combined to create a "Judeo-Spanish print culture" (Lehmann 2005a, 43) that paralleled the consolidation of print cultures among Muslims, Orthodox Christians, and Armenians across the Ottoman Empire (Ben-Naeh 2001, 75).

Elena Romero (1992, 107–140) enumerated 29 *Musar* works published in Ladino in the eighteenth and nineteenth centuries, of which we will touch on just two here. The first is Elijah ha-Kohen's *Shevet Musar*, which was printed in Hebrew in Istanbul (1712) and translated into Ladino by Abraham Assa (Istanbul 1748, 1766; Salonica 1800; Izmir 1860, 1889). The second is the work *Pele Yo'ets*, written by Eliezer ben rabbi Isaac Papo and printed in Hebrew at Istanbul (1824). This work was translated into Ladino by Eliezer's son, Judah Papo (Vienna 1870–1872; Salonica 1899–1900).

Lehmann has coined the term "the vernacular rabbis" to refer to these authors and translators, along with others such as Isaac Bechor Amarchi, Isaac Farhi, Abraham Palachi, Ben-Tsion Roditi and Isaac Badhab (Lehmann 2005a, 44). Most of these figures belonged to the second rank of Ottoman Jewish rabbinical leaders, and their Ladino translations and writings offered them a chance to enhance their status within the religious world in particular, and Ottoman Jewish society in general, as cultural agents appealing to broad audiences. These rabbis "had in mind a clear image of an intended reading public, and their texts must thus be understood as representation of what *they* as an elite believed appropriate for the non-learned public to whom their writings were addressed" (Lehmann 2005a, 60). In works such as *Pele Yo'ets*, this led them to translate moral themes into vivid stories (Lehmann 2005a, 52–61). In this respect, the *Musar* literature continued the trend established by *Me'am Lo'ez*.

This literature also addressed women as an explicit (albeit indirect) target audience.[10] In the work *Shevet Musar*, for instance, Elijah ha-Kohen tells the male reader that "what he hears, he should tell his wife and people of his household when he returns home in the evening" (quoted in Lehmann 2005a, 68). Lehmann (2005a, 68) also quotes a call in the *Pele Yo'ets*, that was published one century after the *Ma'am Loez*, for literate women to disseminate their religious knowledge to their

---

10 It is also worth mentioning a Ladino prayerbook written specifically for Jewish women in Salonica in the sixteenth century (Schwarzwald 2012).

friends: "How good is it if [...] each group appoints a women who can read and they spend the hour with [study]. An advantage is that they will look for ways to teach their daughters [to read]." Such indirect references to women planted the seeds of the emergence of women readers in Ottoman Jewry, a phenomenon that can first be found in the latter quarter of the nineteenth century.

As Lehmann has demonstrated, *Musar* literature played a central role in the establishment of a Ladino print culture that appealed to a wider circle of readers than in the past, including both men and women readers. Moreover, starting in the second half of the eighteenth century, modern literature in Ladino, and particularly *belles-lettres* and non-fiction works of various types, sought "to educate and entertain." In so doing, Lehman observes, "they were following the model that had been evolving since the early eighteenth century" (Lehmann 2005a, 206).

2.6 *Coplas*

The poetic form known as *coplas* first began to appear in print in the eighteenth century. *Coplas* are rhyming verses with a clear plot and an emphasis on narrative that were accompanied by original or borrowed tunes. The genre has its roots in the pre-expulsion literary tradition, and Hispanic culture in general is familiar with the model of narrative poems intended to be presented orally (Pedrosa 1995). The Sephardic *coplas* also have roots in Hebrew poetry, for example in the *Piyyutim*. The printing of *coplas* and the emergence of this genre in the eighteenth century formed part of the didactic trend discussed above, "which sought to draw the masses closer to Jewish scholastic engagement and a renewed familiarity with the Jewish way of life" (Refael 2004, 19). In the eighteenth century, *coplas* mainly presented versions of the traditional texts – the Pentateuch, the Five Scrolls, Aggadah and Midrash, and Halakhah. Many of the *coplas* were devoted to the Jewish festivals, including songs for Hanukkah and Tu BiShvat, Purim songs (including facetious *kinnot* ["dirges"]), genuine dirges for Tisha B'Av and the other fast days, etc. (Refael 2004, 33–34, 38–39).

Activities in this field continued in the nineteenth century and thereafter, but the genre acquired a different and more modern character. Most of the *coplas* were now "songs in which Jewish society sought [...] to perpetuate its history, document its heroes, and comforts its pains and crises through lyrical means" (Refael 2004, 13). Particularly in Salonica, *coplas* were also devoted to the forces and ravages of nature (such as hail, famine, and fires), to poverty, and to current events (the Ottoman constitution, the drafting of Jews into the Ottoman army, etc.) (Refael 2004, 39, 189–225). The scope of activity in this genre expanded considerably during the nineteenth century: in Salonica, for example, 79 printed editions of *coplas* were published in the nineteenth century, compared to just 11 in the previous century (Refael 2004, 38).

Refael also notes that *coplas* printed in Salonica account for over half the total number of printed works in this genre (134 titles), compared to 16 percent in Istanbul and six percent in Izmir. Moreover, the *coplas* published in Salonica cover the full range of themes addressed by this genre, whereas the scope elsewhere was more partial (Refael 2004, 37–41). Refael suggests that the importance of this city in the field of *coplas* can be attributed to "a local ideological foundation for nurturing Jewish thought that flourished in Salonica" (Refael 2004, 41).[11]

2.7 La Guerta de Oro

The borders of the Ladino library expanded significantly in the eighteenth century alongside the expansion of the audience for literature in this language. In this context, it is worth devoting special attention to a work that anticipated trends that would strengthen considerably in the following century. This work is *La Guerta de Oro* (The Garden of Gold, Livorno 1778), arguably the first "secular" book in Ladino.[12] This 128-page work represents an eighteenth-century example of the trends of "Westernization" that would come to characterize a large part of the Ladino corpus over the following century, particularly in its second half. Its author, David Attias, was a Jewish native of Sarajevo (then within the boundaries of the Ottoman Empire) who migrated to the port city of Livorno in 1769. This city formed part of the independent Duchy of Tuscany and was an important commercial and economic center (Bregoli 2014), which its population included many merchants from the Western Sephardic Diaspora.

La Guerta de Oro included, among other fields of content, an introduction to the Italian language, including a simple phrasebook; a presentation of the Greek alphabet; a short essay on physiognomy, the contemporary theory that a person's appearance, and particularly their facial features, could provide significant insight into their character and capabilities; a type of abridged commercial guide concerning the "rational" ways to appeal to a potential business partner; and a letter from a young Ottoman Jew living in Europe, perhaps modeled on Attias himself, to his mother in the Ottoman East. Lehmann has identified in this letter some proverbs of Jean de la Fontaine (d. 1695) and citations from Jacques Savary's *Le parfait négociant* (1675), a classic text of mercantilism (Lehmann 2005b, 51, 59–60, 62–63). These themes had not hitherto appeared in Ladino literature, thus testifying to its flexible and open character even at this relatively early stage and anticipating future developments. Attias himself was aware of the pioneering nature of his endeavor, explaining that:

---

[11] This issue deserves further study, including a comparative geographical analysis of the areas where the various literary genres in Ladino were published.
[12] Angel Berenguer Amador (2016) recently published this work in Latin transliteration, accompanied by a linguistic study.

> All [other] nations publish many kinds of books, but, among us, there is nobody who publishes any kind of book in our Levantine [!] Spanish language [Ladino] – neither history, ancient or modern, nor books on geography or other sciences, and not even a book dealing in commerce that is the dearest thing to us Jews.
>
> (quoted in Lehmann 2005b, 52)

As this comment shows, as someone living in the *tsafon* (the North – a Hebrew term Attias preferred to *ma'arav* – the West), the author explicitly addressed a Jewish audience in the *mizrah* – the East, his own Ottoman homeland. Attias wrote for his fellow Jews in Anatolia and the Balkans in "our Levantine Spanish language." Although he had lived in distant Livorno and been profoundly exposed to Western culture over the course of the decade preceding the publication of the book, he considered himself a member of the Eastern Sephardic Diaspora, a Ladino speaker, and someone who felt a kinship with the Jews of Anatolia and the Balkans. This is reflected in his use of terms such as "among us" and "our" in the above quote.

According to Lehmann, Attias espoused a worldview that sanctified the "ideal of a merchant community guided by the values of commercial pragmatism." This worldview did not shy away from criticizing the prevalent greed among merchants; it also advocated the acquisition of Western European knowledge, including foreign languages, so that Jewish merchants could communicate properly with the non-Jewish world. Attias adhered to a rational and enlightened approach and believed in human autonomy – values he contrasted with the contemporary character of Ottoman Jewry and which formed the basis for his call for comprehensive change (Lehmann 2005b, 57).

In the latter quarter of the eighteenth century, a work such as *La Guerta de Oro* could only have been composed outside the boundaries of the Ottoman Empire, in a Western European commercial center. While a native of the Ottoman Empire, it should also be emphasized that Attias was born in Sarajevo, which is twice as far from Istanbul as it is from Vienna. His orientation antedated by at least six decades the emergence of significant patterns of "Westernization" in the Ottoman Empire itself, which occurred during the Reform era. It thus turns out that the trend towards "Translation and Westernization" in Ladino, to use the title of one of the articles by Olga Borovaya (2001) examining Ladino *belles-lettres* in the late nineteenth century, was not invented in this century. In the context described above, *La Guerta de Oro* anticipated many of the dramatic transformations that would come later (see also Borovaya 2017, 233–238).

3 The *Long Nineteenth Century*

The "Long Nineteenth Century," beginning with Napoleon's invasion of Egypt (1798) and ending with the First World War (1914–1918), presented the Ottoman Empire with a wide range of domestic and external pressures. Donald Quataert noted that this century saw the emergence of a largely new phenomenon "in that many of the territorial losses resulted from revolts and rebellions on the part of Ottoman subjects against their suzerain or sovereign" (Quataert 2000, 55).

During this period, the Ottoman rulers were forced to confront national revolts in the Balkans as well as the growing presence of the Western powers inside the Empire. In order to cope with this double challenge, the Ottoman state sought "to eliminate intermediating groups – guilds and tribes, Janissaries and religious communities – and bring all Ottoman subjects directly under its authority" (Quataert 2000, 64). To this end, a series of constitutional and administrative reforms were introduced, known as the Tanzimat (literally "reorganizations," 1839–1876).

The main instruments of reform were two orders issued in 1839 and 1856, the latter of which declared the state's obligation to ensure equality between all subjects, including equal access to public schools and to civil service positions. This order abolished the poll tax (*jizya*) that had hitherto been imposed on non-Muslim subjects in accordance with Islamic religious law. Both before and during the Tanzimat period, the empire experienced significant processes of administrative and technological modernization. The provinces of the empire were restructured (1864) and a law was enacted introducing compulsory education (1869). Postal (1834) and telegraph (1856) services were established, and from the 1830s on the number of newspapers in Turkish and other languages expanded. Relations with Western Europe also intensified, allowing for the more rapid dissemination of Western ideas, knowledge, and lifestyles. The affinity to the West was particularly apparent in the main urban centers and among the non-Muslims that tended to concentrate in these areas, including the Jews (Lewis 2002, 74–128; Hanioğlu 2008, 72–108).

This increasing Western orientation was also reflected in changes in Jewish education. Some Jews chose to send their children to the modern schools established by the state, or even to institutions run by European missionaries. Starting in 1854, modern schools were also launched within the Jewish community, with a curriculum that included secular studies, European languages, and Turkish. The *Alliance israélite universelle* ("the Alliance") was established in France in 1860 with the goal of promoting "regeneration" (*régénération*) in Jewish communities in Eastern Europe and the Mediterranean basin, whose leaders were regarded as "traditional." In order to establish a "rational" and "progressive" society with a pro-French orientation, the founders of the Alliance were convinced that the members of these communities had to be transformed into "useful" citizens. The main tool for this purpose was school, which was expected to correct the "defective" past of those who entered its gates. From 1865, the Alliance opened dozens of schools in the Ottoman Empire, and starting in the latter years of the century the graduates of these institutions formed the core of the local Jewish bourgeoisie (Rodrigue, 1990; Rodrigue 1993).

The processes of modernization in the empire continued, and indeed intensified, during the subsequent Hamidian period (1876–1908), under the rule of Sultan Abdul Hamid II (1842–1918). During this period, the empire advanced both a pan-Islamist agenda and the ideology of "Ottomanism," which emphasized equality among all male subjects of the empire, in part with the goal of ensuring the loyalty of Christian citizens in the Balkans and in Eastern Anatolia (Quataert 2000, 67–68). The means of communication in the empire continued to expand and diversify despite the imposition of strict censorship on the media (Yosmaoğlu 2003, 15–30).

The Hamidian regime faced opposition, particularly from the Young Turks, who from the 1880s on sought to establish a centralized and parliamentary system that would unify the disparate groups across the empire. The Young Turks staged a military coup in July 1908, seizing power in the empire and announcing elections to the Ottoman parliament. During the early years following the revolution, the new rulers relaxed the regulations on publishing and the press in the center of the empire and in the provinces. The fifteen years that followed the coup of the Young Turks were a period of great instability in the Ottoman Empire – firstly due to the Balkan Wars (1912–1913), in which the empire lost almost all its remaining footholds in Europe, and later during the First World War (1914–1918), which effectively eliminated the empire and led to the establishment of a Turkish republic in Anatolia and in a small part of Eastern Thrace (1923) (Zürcher 2004, 93–175).

3.1 "Westernizers" and "Enlighteners" (*Maskilim*)

Throughout the nineteenth century, a wide range of rabbinical literature continued to be published, with an increasing emphasis on the popularizing trends that had emerged over the course of the previous century. However, beginning in the middle of the nineteenth century, the dominant tone in Ladino literature was set by the "Westernizers." This circle advocated the partial adoption of Western culture ("Westernization"), manifested particularly in lifestyle, mentality, and material culture.[13] While the trend toward Westernization had its roots in earlier periods, and had also apparent in *La Guerta de Oro*, this process accelerated in the mid-nineteenth century, and even more so following the establishment of the network of Alliance schools across the empire.

Beginning in the last quarter of the eighteenth century, the classic model of Western self-understanding advocated the legal emancipation, acculturation, and integration of Jews in local society. As Yaron Tsur has shown, in the Islamic countries, which were colonial or semi-colonial societies, an "imperialist mutation" of this pattern of identity developed during the second half of the nineteenth century. This "mutation" sought to ensure legal emancipation within the Muslim majority society, but at the same time acculturation and integration in the cultural and economic networks of one of the Western powers, usually France (Tsur 2010, 49). The Westernizers'

---

[13] The use of the term "Westernizers" is not intended to negate the self-agency of those to whom it is applied or who used it themselves. For a critique of the use of the paradigm of "Westernization" in Ottoman modernity studies, see Rubin (2009, 123–124, 132).

desire to integrate into Western culture was not necessarily the product of colonial "oppression," but often reflected an internal and autonomous dynamic based in the strong desire of Jews in the Islamic countries to better their socio-economic status in a world of increasingly rapid changes.

Unlike the Jewish Westernizers in the Arab Middle East and North Africa, who abandoned their Judeo-Arabic vernacular and adopted French (Tsur 2010, 48–49), most of the Ottoman Jewish Westernizers in Anatolia and the Balkans continued to work mainly in their Ladino vernacular, at least until the end of the nineteenth century (Abrevaya Stein 2004, 58–59). I would argue that there were two main reasons for this. The first is that the Ottoman Jews were subjects in a semi-colonial system, rather than a colonial one – a factor that limited the penetration of French. The other is that the status and prestige of Ladino among Anatolian and Balkan Jews were stronger than that of Judeo-Arabic among the Jews of the Arab Middle East, because Ladino had, since the eighteenth century, undergone a process of cultural and linguistic unification that was not seen in the communities that spoke Judeo-Arabic dialects (Karkason 2018, 48).[14] The main genres employed by the Westernizers in the nineteenth century were the Ladino press, *belles-lettres*, and theater, and their activities also exerted a crucial influence on the development of non-fiction literature.

In addition to the Westernizers, a distinct circle of around hunderd *maskilim* (Jewish enlighteners) also emerged in the Ottoman Empire beginning in the 1830s (Karkason 2018). The *Haskalah* (Jewish enlightenment) movement appeared in Berlin in the second half of the eighteenth century. According to Shmuel Feiner's definitions, the *maskilim* joined together:

> [. . .] in a unique Jewish enterprise of modernity and have considered themselves to be responsible for an unprecedented historic move [. . .] – the rehabilitation of traditional society in light of the values of enlightenment, the distribution of broad general knowledge of the world of nature and the human being, the education of the young generations for their integration in life as productive citizens that have access to European society and culture [. . .]. And mostly, mental preparation for moving [. . .] from the "old world" to the modern age.
> (Feiner 2010, 38–39; See also Feiner 2001)

The Berlin *Haskalah*, which peaked during the last three decades of the eighteenth century, first spread across the German-speaking lands, including Austria. During the first quarter of the nineteenth century, the centers of the *Haskalah* shifted to Galicia (on the periphery of the Austro-Hungarian Empire), the Russian Empire, and Italy. The earliest extant documentation of the Ottoman *Haskalah* and its products is from the year 1850, but we can date the phenomenon to a decade or more before that, around the beginning of the Tanzimat (Karkason 2018, 20, 102–105). The Ottoman

---

14 Tsur has discussed this process of cultural unification in Ladino at length, arguing that it centered around *Me'am Lo'ez*, and has noted the unique nature of this phenomenon among the Jews of the Islamic countries (Tsur 2016, 50–54).

maskilim maintained an affinity with the trends of the European *Haskalah* and sought to use these to cope with processes of modernization in their unique Ottoman Jewish context (Karkason 2018, 53–55).¹⁵

The *Maskilim* participated in various processes of modernization, authoring books and articles on various non-rabbinical subjects (foreign languages, science, historiography, ethnography, etc.) and engaging in intensive journalistic activities. They published mainly in Hebrew, the lingua franca of the *Haskalah*, as well as in their mother tongue, Ladino. The three most prominent Ottoman *maskilim* were Judah Nehama of Salonica (1825–1899); Barukh Mitrani (1847–1919), who wandered around Europe and Asia; and Abraham Danon (1857–1925), who was active in Edirne, Istanbul, and Paris. The *Maskilim* established modern schools that taught foreign languages and Hebrew grammar and literature and founded associations whose buildings housed "secular" libraries. They also arranged classes in Jewish studies and provided training for youths from poor backgrounds enabling them to work in crafts or agriculture (Benbassa and Rodrigue 2000, 106–109; Cohen J. and Abrevaya Stein 2010; Karkason 2018).

It is important to stress that the three main groups within the Ottoman Jewish intelligentsia – the Westernizers, the rabbinic elite, and the *maskilim* – existed across a spectrum and were not mutually exclusive (Karkason 2018, 51–53).

3.2 The Ladino Press

The first Jewish newspaper in the world was the *Gazeta de Amsterdam*, which was founded in Amsterdam in 1678 and intended for the members of the Western Sephardic Diaspora (Schnitzer 1987; Sánchez Vasco 2017). This newspaper was written in Castilian Spanish, using the Latin alphabet. The Eastern Sephardic Diaspora would have to wait many years for the first newspaper to appear in Ladino, using the Rashi Hebrew script. The first Ladino newspaper was *Sha'are Mizrah/Las Puertas de Oriente*, which appeared in Izmir in 1845–1846 and was edited by Rafael Uziel (1816–1881). Moshe David Gaon (1965) and Dov Cohen (2021, 601–655) have found that 300 Ladino newspapers were subsequently published, mainly in the major urban centers of Istanbul, Izmir, and Salonica.¹⁶

Sha'are Mizrah was one of the first newspapers in any language to appear in the Ottoman Empire, just five years after the first private Turkish newspaper was founded in the Ottoman capital, Istanbul (Saba Wolfe 2015, 427–428; see also Şişmanoğlu

---

15 See also the classification by Cohen J. and Abrevaya Stein (2010) concerning the "Sephardic scholarly worlds," which served as the conceptual foundation for my exploration of the *maskilim* and for other studies (see, for example, Noy 2017).
16 An Annotated Bibliography of about 4,000 items in Ladino from the years 1490–1960 was published in Hebrew (Cohen D., 2021).

Şimşek 2010, 109–110). Uziel's newspaper was biweekly, though it was published erratically and with various interruptions, apparently ceasing to appear after 16 issues. The main themes covered in the newspaper would continue to occupy the Ladino press over the following decades. These included foreign news, news from the Jewish world, and reports on the Ottoman Empire and its Jews, as well as items of municipal and local interest, reports on the markets, and exchange rates. These were accompanied by factual articles from the fields of history, geography, philosophy, science, etc. (Bunis 1993, 8–33; Saba Wolfe 2015).

Over the course of the three decades following the appearance of *Sha'are Mizrah*, additional Ladino newspapers and journals were established, including *Or Israel* (Istanbul 1853–1854), *El Lunar* (Salonica 1864–1865), and *Journal Israelit* (Istanbul, 1860–1871). These journals published similar content to that of *Sha'are Mizrah*, and also began to publish literary works in installments. During the same period, the Scottish missionary service began to publish the Ladino newspaper *El Manadero* (Istanbul, 1854–1855). This journal formed part of the sub-genre of missionary literature in Ladino,[17] whose goal was to encourage Ottoman Jews to convert to Christianity – an objective that enjoyed little success (Borovaya 2012, 37–43).

Mirroring the trend in the Turkish press of the time (Meral 2013, 138–139), the 1870s saw the publication of the first Ladino journals intended for the general population. Three popular journals, one in each of the metropolises, were particularly prominent: *La Buena Esperansa* (Izmir 1871–1917), edited by Aaron de Yosef Hazan (1849–1931); *La Epoka* (Salonica 1875–1911), edited by the Halevy Ashkenazi family; and *El Tiempo* (Istanbul 1872–1930), whose editor was David Fresco (1853–1933), the most eminent Ladino journalist of all times. Other important journals published in Istanbul included *El Nasyonal* (1873–1878) and its successor *El Telegrafo* (1878–1931). The popular Ladino newspapers were printed in many hundreds of copies, and in the twentieth century in thousands (for instance, see Naar 2016, 15). Each copy was shared by several readers and the content also reached those with a low level of literacy and, indirectly, even the illiterate, for whom the newspaper was read aloud.[18] In addition to the small number of journals that continued to be published over periods of many years, many others appeared and disappeared rapidly, most of them surviving no longer than a year or two. According to my research, the average lifespan of the 44 Ladino newspapers published in Istanbul was approximately seven years, though this figure is skewed significantly upward by a small number of publications that were published over a long period.

---

[17] The preliminary state of research into missionary literature in Ladino makes it difficult to present a more detailed summary here. Dov Cohen has identified 70 books published in Ladino after 1829 by Christian missionary groups. These include full or partial translations of the New Testament as well as polemical works challenging Jewish beliefs (Cohen D. 2011, 161, 169–170; Cohen D. 2021, 671–679).
[18] On the popular journals in Ladino, see: Abrevaya Stein (2004, 55–76); Borovaya (2012, 43–47).

Beginning in the 1860s, Ladino newspapers were published throughout the Ottoman Balkans and even in Vienna, where there was a well-established and prosperous Sephardic community (Stechauner 2019, 49–55), as well as in nearby Pressburg (today Bratislava, the capital of the Slovak Republic). In the 1870s, Ladino newspapers also began to appear in Palestine – a phenomenon that expanded in the early twentieth century. New journalistic genres emerged in the last quarter of the nineteenth century, such as literary and scientific journals that promoted Westernization in the spirit of the Alliance and journals that were directly associated with the *Haskalah* movement (examples of these trends will be given below).

The relative freedom of the press introduced following the Young Turk Revolution of 1908 led to a softening of the Ottoman censorship system and greater leeway than in the past. This encouraged an unprecedented surge in the press, including the publication of journals in numerous languages across the empire, including Ladino. This development was also facilitated by the maturation of the first and second generations of graduates of the Alliance schools, which dramatically expanded the readership of the Ladino press. In 1908–1910, a total of 34 new journals were established in Salonica, Izmir, Istanbul, and nearby Edirne, though most of these publications only survived for a brief period. The lighter censorship also facilitated the emergence of satirical journalism that used humor to criticize the political situation, the economic and cultural elites, and social disparities. This genre employed prose, poetry, and short vignettes of daily life. The most important journal of this type was *El Jugeton* (Istanbul 1908–1931), edited by Elia Rafael Carmona (Magid 2010, 130–132).

After the Young Turk Revolution, the Ladino press became the arena for a debate and struggle between "assimilators," Zionists, and Socialists; Alliance graduates were prominent among all three groups.[19] In the following decades, the Ladino press continued to provide a platform for the struggle between these and other groups (Bunis 1999). Ladino journals also appeared among the migrant communities in the United States, Latin America, Israel, and elsewhere. In the 1960s and 1970s, Ladino ceased to serve as a living language transmitted to the next generation, and accordingly the Ladino press ceased to exist as a sustainable phenomenon.

3.3 Belles-lettres

The Ladino *belles-lettres* genre developed alongside the emergence of popular journalism. From the 1870s on, Ladino journals published numerous short stories and novels, most of which were translated either from Western European languages (mainly French) or from Hebrew. Several hundred Ladino works of this type were published over the following seventy years.

---

19 On this phenomenon in the Salonican press, see Naar (2016, 22–24).

The serialized novel emerged as a genre in France in the 1830s, followed rapidly by other countries (Borovaya 2012, 149–150), including the Ottoman Empire and its Turkish press (Meral 2013, 139, 146). When it arrived to the Ladino-speaking Ottomans, "this new genre, referred to as *romanso*, soon earned a leading position in the Sephardi literary market" (Borovaya 2012, 140). In most cases, the translators/adaptors of the *romansos* abridged the original works and simplified their messages in keeping with their perception of the audience (Borovaya 2012, 166–192). Novels extending over hundreds of pages were converted into booklets of just 16–32 pages. In many cases, the stories were printed in the journals in a format that allowed the reader to detach them from the surrounding material and combine them into a single work. In other cases, the stories appeared as separate publications.

The main target audience for these works were readers who had attended the modern schools established in the Ottoman Empire from the 1850s on, and particularly the *Alliance* schools. The emergence of this genre in the 1870s and its rapid development at the turn of the century mirrored the expansion of these educational institutions across the empire, enabling the formation of circles of "new readers" – both men and women. Prior to the emergence of these schools, very few Ottoman Jewish women were literate, and they became an indirect audience for Ladino literature during the eighteenth century. The later spread of girls' education, primarily through the Alliance network, turned women into an intended audience of the *romanso* genre, which was also innovative in Sephardic literature in terms of the appearance of the first women literary protagonists (Borovaya 2012, 151).

Borovaya (2012, 150–155) has divided the Ladino novels into two categories: love stories and adventure stories. Eva Illouz (1997) highlighted romantic love as a leitmotiv in popular stories, metaphors, products, and theories and explained that individuals interpret their experiences in this field through common symbols and meanings. Romantic love was a familiar emotion in Ottoman culture; it is also documented in some Hebrew sources and more extensively in popular Ladino literature. Until the late nineteenth century, however, it was not usually a factor in choosing a life partner, and falling in love was not a prerequisite for marriage. Marriage continued to be defined as the product of social suitability and sociopolitical and economic expediency, rather than as a manifestation of romantic love (Ben-Naeh 2015b, 62–68; Ben-Naeh 2017, 30). Therefore, "since western love stories had no counterparts in the domestic canon, the Sephardi literati who created the love story as a subgenre of Ladino *belles-lettres* fully relied on the [Western] European model" (Borovaya 2012, 150). Well-known love stories that were translated into Ladino include Alexandre Dumas fils's *La Dame aux camélias*, Antoine François Prévost's *Manon Lescaut*, and Jacques-Henri Bernardin de Saint-Pierre's *Paul et Virginie*.[20]

---

[20] Some of these love stories were also translated into Turkish during this period (Meral 2013, 146–148).

In contrast to the *romansos*, the presence of the travelogue genre in all Jewish literatures since the Middle Ages and the popularity of some of these works, such as *Sefer Eldad Ha-Dani* (The Book of Eldad the Danite), facilitated the absorption of adventure stories. This genre includes translations of Jonathan Swift's *Gulliver's Travels*, Alfred Assolant's *Aventures merveilleuses maquis authentiques du capitaine Corcoran*, and Jules Verne's *Les Enfants du capitaine Grant*.

Borovaya has shown that "only a small number of Ladino novels published as chapbooks indicate on the title page both names: the author of the foreign source and the rewriter." Usually we find only the name of the foreign author, only the name of the rewriter, or no names at all (Borovaya 2012, 156). When the name of the Ladino translator or adaptor is provided, a wide range of terms are used to describe their function, such as *trezladado* (translated), *imitado* (imitated), *adaptado* (adapted) and *rezumido* (summarized) (Borovaya 2012, 157; Cohen D. 2011, 127). In previous centuries, the identity of the author of a work had usually been clear, and in most cases, this was a Sephardic rabbinical figure, of lesser or greater importance; now, the act of rewriting blurred the question of authorship in Sephardic literature.

To illustrate the adapted and abridged character of most of the *romanso* works in comparison to their originals, I will rely here on Borovaya's conclusions regarding the translation prepared by Alexander Benghiat (1863–1924) of the French novel *Paul et Virginie*. The Ladino version, entitled *Pablo y Virginia*, was published as a separate booklet in Jerusalem in 1912, at the printing house of Shlomo Israel Cherezli (1878–1938). Borovaya explains:

> The attractive aspect of the novel was the sad love story, whereas the long monologues of the old man [the narrator] could not interest most Sephardic readers and were deleted. The rewriter also deleted all philosophical discourses and descriptions of nature. They did not advance the plot and were alien to Ladino belles-lettres anyway. Consequently, the readers received a 21-page long moving story about the love of two young people, separated by implacable circumstances, which caused their tragic death. (Borovaya 2002, 271)

Thus, a French novel extending over more than 300 pages was transformed into a short story of about 20 pages, in a process whereby the adaptor decided what parts the readers should be made familiar with. The same was true of many other works in this genre. The sphere of *belles-lettres* led to considerable transformations in Ladino literature, as readers – men and women – were exposed to new themes drawn from Western literature. These themes influenced and were influenced by the culture and lifestyle of the growing audience for this literature.

The press and *belles-lettres* formed the focus of the reading culture of Ottoman Jews from the 1870s on. Other genres were also represented, however, some of which we shall mention now.

3.4 Theater

The genre of modern theater in Ladino was extensively investigated by Elena Romero (1979) in her monumental three-volume study on the subject, as well as more recently by Olga Borovaya (2012, 193–238). Jews participated in the Ottoman theatrical industry, both in Puppet Theater (*orta oyunu*) and Shadow Theater (*karagöz*), and also staged performances in their own communities, particularly in bathhouses and cafés. Three Ladino plays from the sixteenth century are known to us (Cohen D. 2011, 153–154), but a modern theater only began to emerge in the Ottoman Empire in the 1860s. The popularity of this genre increased from the 1890s on and reached its peak during the first three decades of the twentieth century. As in the case of the short story, Ladino theater drew on Western – and particularly French – culture. Almost all the plays staged in Anatolia and the Balkans were translated versions of works by Molière, Victor Hugo, Fyodor Dostoevsky, Shakespeare, George Bernard Shaw, and others (Romero 1979; Romero 2009, 157).[21] In the twentieth century, a handful of original plays were staged, such as David Elnecave's *Los Macabeos* (Istanbul 1921) (Romero 2009, 158).

As in the case of short stories, the plays presented in Anatolia and the Balkans were also adapted in various ways. For example, David Yosef Hasid, who adapted Molière's *L'Avare* (*The Miser*) into Ladino (Salonica 1884), titled his play *Han Benyamin*, probably in "honor" of an actual Salonican Jew renowned for his greed and miserly character. The names of other characters in the Ladino play were also converted into Hispanic variants – Enrico, Matilde, Sinyor Eduardo, etc. Borovaya has demonstrated that the Ladino versions tended to be "more exciting and touching" than the originals, in an attempt to appeal to local tastes. By way of example, the question "You are my sister?" in the original is translated into Ladino as "Oh God! You are my sister!?" (Borovaya 2012, 228–232). Thus, the theatrical adaptations were very similar to those in the genre of *belles-lettres*.

3.5 Non-Fictional Works

The number of non-fictional works published in Ladino before the nineteenth century was relatively small. The first medical treatises in Ladino appeared in the mid-sixteenth century (Cohen Starkman 2017, 48, 78–86, 115–121) and were associated with the medical literature written in Hebrew by Sephardic Jews in the Ottoman Empire (Buskila 2021). Ḥoshev Maḥshavot, a Ladino arithmetic textbook, was published in Istanbul in 1737, and Ladino legal texts also appeared during the eighteenth century (Yerushalmi 1971; Cohen D. 2011, 151–154). In the second half of the nineteenth

---

[21] It is worth noting that in many cases, the Ladino versions of English-language works were based on their French translations.

century, the genre of non-fictional works expanded significantly, accompanying the process of modernization and the Ottoman reforms. Dozens of works were published in the empire on a wide range of subjects: geography, history and biography, ethnography, science, education, economics, law (including collections of Ottoman laws), etc. (Cohen D. 2011, 155–164; Cohen D. 2021, 439–589). These included speeches and polemical articles, dictionaries, and egodocuments.

The growth of non-fiction genres is associated with the appearance of scientific journals in Ladino during the second half of the nineteenth century. Of these, we may mention *El Lunar* (Salonica 1864–1865), edited by the *maskil* Judah Nehama (Karkason 2018, 210–211, 298, 303), as well as three literary and scientific journals edited by David Fresco in Istanbul: *El Sol* (1878–1880), *El Amigo de la Familia* (1881–1886), and *El Instruktor* (1888).[22] Thus, for example, in *El Lunar*, Nehama published translated and adapted versions of articles that had appeared shortly before in the Hebrew journal *Hamagid*, which was published in Lyck in Eastern Prussia between 1856 and 1903. The versions published in *El Lunar* were significantly shorter than the Hebrew originals and were adapted for the local audience. They included, by way of example, a detailed article about the ten lost tribes; an excerpt from an article about the story of Chang and Eng Bunker, who were the original "Siamese twins;" and a short piece about the medical demerits of tobacco (Karkason 2018, 210–211).

Non-fiction literature in Ladino has yet to be studied in depth and deserves further attention. In the following, I will discuss in slightly more detail one sub-genre of this field: Ottoman Jewish historiography from the second half of the nineteenth century.

3.6 Historiography

"Native" historical writing by Sephardim about the Ottoman Empire is known to us from as early as the sixteenth century (Usque 1965; Yerushalmi 1996, 53–75; Ben-Naeh 2015a). However, the Ottoman *maskilim* were the first to compose modern historiography about Ottoman Jewish communities, drawing on the methods of the *Wissenschaft des Judentums*. Judah Nehama wrote historical treatises about the Jews of Salonica as early as the 1860s, but more dramatic change in this field came in the 1880s with the work of Abraham Danon and his colleagues in Edirne.

Aware that Ottoman Jews had not properly documented their history and that valuable material had been lost forever, the maskilic society *Dorshei ha-Haskalah* in Edirne (1879–1889), headed by Danon, sought to establish a historical journal in Hebrew and Ladino called *Yosef Da'at/El Progreso*. The journal would include articles "about the history of the Jewish diaspora in Turkey, and all that happens to our people living under the gracious rule of the Ottoman sultans" (Danon A. 2014, 393).

---

22 For further details, see: Abrevaya Stein (2000); Abrevaya Stein (2004, 123–149).

In 1888–1889, a total of 21 issues of the journal appeared. The Hebrew section was devoted to original sources that had hitherto remained unknown or unresearched. These sources were held in Danon's collection or were sent to him from other personal archives after he encouraged his readers to do so in the introduction to the first edition:

> In the vineyard of our Oriental histories, precious treasures are hidden: we do not know much of the habits and traditions of the various communities, nor the relations with the venerated government and with the other nations living under its protection [. . .]. Let our wise men rise up, let each one search in his own place or town of residence for the memories of his brothers and neighbors. Let them call to the hidden manuscripts: come out! And to our ancient Turkish histories: reveal yourselves!
> (Danon A. 2014, 393)

The Hebrew section of *Yosef Da'at* was intended mainly for *maskilim* and exponents of the *Wissenschaft des Judentums* around the Jewish world, the vast majority of whom were Ashkenazim. Most of the Hebrew section consisted of original articles. By contrast, the Ladino section of the journal was devoted mainly to material that had been translated, adapted, or summarized from historical studies on Ottoman Jewry. It was intended for Ladino-speaking Ottoman Jews who were interested in history – the members of *Dorshei ha-Haskalah* themselves as well as others in the Ladino-speaking domain who were interested in acquiring knowledge. Danon and the editorial board chose to make available to the Ladino-speaking readers sections from Heinrich Graetz's (1817–1891) *Geschichte der Juden* ("History of the Jews," 1853–1876), which was originally written in German; these sections constituted the vast majority of the Ladino section of *Yosef Da'at*. In keeping with the declared goals of *Yosef Da'at*, Danon translated or adapted solely those sections from Graetz that dealt with the history of Ottoman Jewry in the sixteenth and seventeenth centuries, focusing in particular on the story of Sabbatai Șevi and his movement (Karkason 2018, 236–237, 303–304).[23] Beginning in the 1880s, Danon's articles appeared in several prestigious journals of the *Wissenschaft des Judentums* in the various European languages (for example, he published eight articles in the Parisian *Revue des Études Juives* between 1896 and 1922). Danon's studies in this period focused on the folklore, ethnography, and historiography of the Sephardic Jews (Karkason 2018, 247).

I would argue that the activities of Judah Nehama and Abraham Danon, and particularly the journal *Yosef Da'at*, laid the foundations for the extensive historiographic studies by Sephardim in the twentieth century – a subject that is beyond the scope of our discussion here. The two most important historians of Ottoman Jewry during the first half of the twentieth century were "late *maskilim*" who continued on the path blazed by the Ottoman *Haskalah*. The first of these was Shlomo Abraham Rosanes

---

[23] Danon was also one of the first writers to discuss the phenomenon of the followers of Shabbetai Șevi ("*Dönme*") who lived in Salonica until the 1920s. He published a series of articles on this community in the period from 1897 to 1910, including the short book *Études sabbatiennes*, which was published in Paris in 1910 (Karkason 2016, 135–136). On the Dönme community, see Baer (2009).

(1862–1938), who was born in Rusçuk (today Ruse, Bulgaria) but worked mainly in Sofia, and who published a five-volume study in Hebrew on Ottoman Jewry: *Korot ha-Yehudim be-Turkiya ve-Artsot ha-Kedem* ("A History of the Jews in Turkey and in the Eastern Lands," Husiatyn, Sofia, and Jerusalem 1907–1945). The second was Abraham Galanté (1873–1961), who was born in Bodrum and was mainly active in Istanbul. Galanté published dozens of articles on Ottoman and Turkish Jewish history, most notably the nine-volume *Histoire des Juifs de Turquie* ("History of the Jews of Turkey"), published in French in Istanbul (1985). Moreover, the journal *Yosef Da'at* served as a prototype for later Hebrew journals that discussed the Jews of the Islamic countries – from Abraham Elmaleh's *Mizrah Uma'arav* (Jerusalem 1919–1932)[24] through Isaac Raphael Molho's *Otsar Yehudey Sepharad* (Jerusalem 1959–1970) and on to *Pe'amim*, which has been published in Jerusalem since 1979.

3.7 Women Writers

Until the nineteenth century, literacy in Hebrew and a knowledge of the fundamentals of Judaism were almost exclusively a male preserve. As Tova Cohen and Shmuel Feiner have shown (2006, 36), this led to "the exclusion of women from canonical Jewish culture in general and from the literature of the *Haskalah* in particular." However, as we have seen, from as early as the sixteenth century, and certainly from the eighteenth century on, Ladino literature addressed women as an indirect audience.

In the last quarter of the nineteenth century, following the expansion of education for Jewish girls in the Ottoman Empire (mainly, but not only, those from Westernized bourgeois families), women became a direct and principal audience for genres such as *belles-lettres* and the theater. As early as 1860, some *maskilim* advocated the advancement of education for girls in the Ottoman Empire – a phenomenon that was paralleled among diverse ethnic groups around the empire in the same period (Davis 1986, 45–60). In 1867, Barukh Mitrani, who was 20 at the time, published the following trenchant criticism in *ha-Magid*:

> [...] The state of education of the girls is very bad, because all the women and girls in our city [Edirne] are like the beasts in the forest, to the disgrace of humankind. [They] do not know how to write and read at all, and they have no wisdom! Oh! Our laziness caused this [...] and has caused for our women in our land[25] this state of ignorance and stupidity [...]!
>
> Oh! Why should the girls be less than the boys? Were they not created in the shape of God also? Do they not carry the name "human"? Why should they be ignorant like beasts in the forest? Therefore, I call upon you, the educated (*maskilei*) of my people in our land, I shout at you, please hurry to bring the salvation of education (*yesha ha-haskalah*) also to your daughters!

---

24 See the recent article by Campos (2017).
25 i.e., the Ottoman territories in Western Anatolia and the Southern Balkans.

Remove the shame of their ignorance from them and yourselves, and from your sons... Open their ears to ethics, religion and knowledge, have mercy on them and on their takers [husbands] and pave paths for education (*haskalah*) in their hearts [. . .]! (Banim 1867, 163)

As early as the 1870s, Roza Gabbay (ca. 1855–1941), a woman from a wealthy and well-connected Istanbul family, composed an essay on manners and customs (Gabbay 2014, 62–65). Other women writers are known, mainly from the late nineteenth century onward. We will mention just two here. Reina Cohen from Salonica wrote an autobiography that is currently being edited by Gila Hadar;[26] Reina Cohen also published the essays *Las muchachas modernas* (Salonica 1898) and *Por los modernos* (Salonica 1899), as well as a commentary in Ladino on the Book of Daniel (Salonica 1901) (Martin-Ortega 2013; Hadar 2015). The second was the playwright Laura Papo (Bohoreta) from Sarajevo (1891–1942), who had lived in Istanbul during her adolescence (1900–1908) (Papo 2012). It is reasonable to assume that further research will uncover additional enlightened women who produced non-fiction works along the lines of Esther Moyal (1873–1948), who was active in the contemporary *Nahda* Arab enlightenment movement (Levy 2012).

4 Conclusion

This chapter has offered a survey of Sephardic literature in the eighteenth and nineteenth centuries, primarily in Ladino, but also in Hebrew. It is undeniable that during the nineteenth century, and particularly in its second half, Ladino literature underwent significant processes of modernization, expansion, and diversification. However, it seems fair to note that Ladino literature in the eighteenth and nineteenth centuries was characterized as much by continuity as by innovation. This is demonstrated by the *Me'am Lo'ez* project, which began in the 1730s and continued well into the nineteenth century, as did the *Musar* literature translated into Ladino. The *coplas* genre began to flourish in the eighteenth century, growing and diversifying further in the following century while also undergoing a thematic change that led it to focus on developments and daily life in the Ottoman Jewish communities.

Most of the "new" genres of the nineteenth century also have roots in earlier periods. Thus, for example, while Ladino theater was an essentially new genre, Ottoman Jews had written plays since as early as the sixteenth century and participated in the Turkish theatrical world. The "Westernized" work *La Guerta de Oro*, published in Livorno in 1778, predated by several decades the modernizing trends in Ottoman Jewry. This work forms part of the genre of non-fiction works in Ladino,

---

[26] An exception from this autobiography will soon be published in an anthology edited by Julia Phillips Cohen (for now, see Cohen J. 2018).

which developed in the nineteenth century but had deep roots in the preceding century.

In all probability, the modernizing processes of the nineteenth century could not have put down roots among Ladino-speaking Jews to such a massive extent or gained such a broad audience were it not for the efforts by eighteenth century authors – beginning over one hundred years earlier – to appeal to new audiences. From the 1730s on, the circle of Ladino readers gradually grew, expanding step by step from the narrow rabbinical elite. At first, the "new readers" were mainly exposed to "religious" genres based clearly on the Jewish sources – most notably the monumental *Me'am Lo'ez*. For the first time, Ladino literature appealed to readers beyond the rabbinical elite, including those who were literate only in Ladino; it also appealed indirectly to illiterate Jews – both men and women – who listened to works such as *Me'am Lo'ez* as they were read out loud in the synagogue or at home. In the second half of the nineteenth century, the processes of modernization in the Ottoman Empire and in its Jewish communities, along with the spread of modern, broader education through the Alliance network and other educational institutions, vastly increased readership. In this period, the target audience was increasingly exposed to new and more "secular" genres, including the press, *belles-lettres*, and the theater. At the same time, they continued to be exposed to *Me'am Lo'ez* and the Ladino translations of the Bible, developing a Sephardic culture that embraced extensive and diverse fields of content.

This chapter, which has attempted to synthesize the existing research, thus creates a picture of Sephardic culture during a period of transition from the early modern to the modern period. This was a flexible and open culture that drew on diverse genres for both "religious" and "secular" needs, turning to increasingly broad audiences. Following these developments, and toward the end of the nineteenth century, Ladino became a popular written language for women and men in the Sephardic communities of Anatolia and the Balkans and in their diasporas around the world.

5 Epilogue

The establishment of the nation-states on the ruins of the Ottoman Empire dealt a deathblow to Ladino. The new states – firstly Serbia and Bulgaria, and later Greece (which assumed control of Salonica in 1912) and the Republic of Turkey – encouraged Jews within their borders to adopt the local national language at the expense of Ladino (Benbassa and Rodrigue 2000, 116–158). The Holocaust of the Jews of Greece and Macedonia eliminated several of the most important and dynamic of the Ladino-speaking communities, above all Salonica – *sivdad i madre de Israel*. Moreover, the Jews who emigrated from Turkey and the Balkans during the first half of the nineteenth century, particularly to the United States, Latin America, France, and Israel, abandoned Ladino relatively quickly in favor of the languages of their newly adopted countries (Refael 2020, 19–37), even if at first they sought to preserve it by various means, such as a local Ladino press (Ben-Ur 1998; Ben-Ur 2001; Satinger 2018).

These processes gradually rendered Ladino obsolete as a language of daily communication – first outside the home and later inside. Among Sephardim in the various nation states, Ladino had, by the 1960s or the 1970s at the latest, become a language confined to the private and domestic sphere, mainly among older generations, while it was almost completely excluded from the public domain. Its use was confined to such realms as the local synagogue, and its chain of transmission was cut so that it no longer serves as a mother tongue (Refael 2020, 83–100, 141–196). Ladino's future is bleak, but its splendid past continues to be worthy of research and study.

Bibliography

Works Cited

Abrevaya Stein, Sarah. "Creating a Taste for News: Historicizing Judeo-Spanish Periodicals of the Ottoman Empire." *Jewish History* 14.1 (2000): 9–28.
Abrevaya Stein, Sarah. *Making Jews Modern: The Yiddish and Ladino Press in the Russian and Ottoman Empires*. Bloomington: Indiana University Press, 2004.
Ayalon, Yaron. "Rethinking Rabbinical Leadership in Ottoman Jewish Communities." *Jewish Quarterly Review* 107.3 (2017): 323–353.
Baer, Marc David. *The Dönme: Jewish Converts, Muslim Revolutionaries, and Secular Turks*. Stanford: Stanford University Press, 2009.
Banim [Barukh Ben Yitzhak Mitrani]. "Masa Turkiya ha-Eiropit." *ha-Magid* 11.21 (1867): 163.
Ben-Naeh, Yaron. "Hebrew Printing Houses in the Ottoman Empire." *Jewish Journalism and Printing Houses in the Ottoman Empire and Modern Turkey*. Ed. Gad Nassi. Istanbul: Isis Press, 2001. 73–96.
Ben-Naeh, Yaron. *Jews in the Realm of the Sultans: Ottoman Jewry in the Seventeenth Century*. Tübingen: Mohr Siebeck, 2008.
Ben-Naeh, Yaron. "Hebrew Sources on the Death of Sultan Osman: A Chapter in Jewish Historiography under Islam." *Jerusalem Studies in Arabic and Islam* 42 (2015a): 283–363.
Ben-Naeh, Yaron. "Old Sentiments, New Times: Love as a Factor in Marital Connection among Ottoman Jews." *El Prezente* 8–9 (2015b): 61–83 [Hebrew].
Ben-Naeh, Yaron. "The Ottoman-Jewish Family: General Characteristics." *Open Journal of Social Sciences* 5 (2017): 25–45.
Ben-Naeh, Yaron. "Ottoman Jewish Courtiers: An Oriental Type of the Court Jew." *Jewish Culture and History* 19.1 (2018): 56–70.
Ben-Ur, Aviva. "The Ladino (Judeo-Spanish) Press in the United States, 1910–1948." *Multilingual America: Transnationalism, Ethnicity, and the Languages of American Literature*. Ed. Werner Sollors. New York: New York University Press, 1998. 64–77.
Ben-Ur, Aviva. "In Search of the American Ladino Press: A Bibliographical Survey, 1910–1948." *Studies in Bibliography and Booklore* 21 (2001): 11–52.
Berenguer Amador, Angel. *El libro sefardí "La güerta de oro" de David M. Atias (Liorna, 1778): edicion y estudio linguistico del verbo*. Zaragoza/Portico/Lausanne: Sociedad Suiza de Estudios Hispanicos. 2016.

Benbassa, Esther, and Aron Rodrigue. *Sephardi Jewry: A History of the Judeo-Spanish Community, 14th-20th Centuries*. Berkeley: University of California Press, 2000.

Borenstein-Makovetsky, Leah. "Rabbinic Scholarship: The Development of Halakhah in Turkey, Greece and the Balkans, 1750–1900." *Jewish Law Association Studies* 9 (1997): 9–18.

Borenstein-Makovetsky, Leah. "Halakhic and Rabbinic Literature in Turkey, Greece and the Balkans 1750–1900." *Pea'mim* 86–87 (2001): 124–174 [Hebrew].

Borovaia, Olga V. "Translation and Westernization: *Gulliver's Travels* in Ladino." *Jewish Social Studies* 7.2 (2001): 149–168.

Borovaia, Olga V. "The Role of Translation in Shaping the Ladino Novel at the Time of Westernization in the Ottoman Empire (A Case Study: *Hasan-Pasha* and *Pavlo y Virzhinia*)." *Jewish History* 16.3 (2002): 263–282.

Borovaya, Olga. *Modern Ladino Culture: Press, Belles Lettres, and Theater in the Late Ottoman Empire*. Bloomington and Indianapolis: Indiana University Press, 2012.

Borovaya, Olga. *The Beginnings of Ladino Literature: Moses Almosnino and His Readers*. Bloomington and Indianapolis: Indiana University Press, 2017.

Bregoli, Francesca. *Mediterranean Enlightenment: Livornese Jews, Tuscan Culture, and Eighteenth-Century Reform*. Stanford: Stanford University Press, 2014.

Bunis, David M. "The Earliest Judezmo Newspapers: Sociolinguistic Reflections." *Mediterranean Language Review* 6–7 (1993): 5–66.

Bunis, David M. "Judezmo: The Jewish Language of the Ottoman Sephardim." *European Judaism* 44.1 (2011): 22–35.

Bunis, David M. "Judezmo (Ladino)." *Handbook of Jewish Languages*. Eds. Lily Kahn and Aaron D. Rubin. Leiden/Boston: Brill, 2016. 365–450.

Bunis, David M., ed. *Voices from Jewish Salonika: Selections from the Judezmo Satirical Series "Tio Ezrá i su mujer Benuta" and "Tio Bohor i su mujer Djamila"*. Jerusalem and Thessaloniki: Misgav Yerushalayim, The National Authority for Ladino Culture, and Ets Ahaim Foundation of Thessaloniki, 1999 [English, Hebrew and Ladino].

Buskila, Tali. "The Beginning of Life in Ottoman Jewish Society: Fertility, Childbirth, and Childhood, in the Jewish Communities of the Pre-Modern Middle East." Doctoral Thesis, Hebrew University of Jerusalem, 2021 [Hebrew].

Campos, Michelle U. "*Mizrah Uma'arav* (East and West): A Sephardi Cultural and Political Project in Post-Ottoman Jerusalem." *Journal of Modern Jewish Studies* 16.2 (2017): 332–348.

Cohen, Dov. "The Ladino Bookshelf: Research and Mapping." Doctoral Thesis, Bar-Ilan University, Ramat Gan, 2011 [Hebrew].

Cohen, Dov. "Novedades bibliográficas en el estudio de las ediciones de biblias sefardíes (siglo xvi)." *Sefarad* 79.1 (2019): 199–224.

Cohen, Dov. *Thesaurus of e Ladino Book 1490–1960: An Annotated Bibliography*. Jerusalem: Ben-Zvi Institute, 2021 [Hebrew].

Cohen, Julia Phillips. *Becoming Ottomans: Sephardi Jews and Imperial Citizenship in the Modern Era*. Oxford/New York: Oxford University Press, 2014.

Cohen, Julia Phillips, and Sarah Abrevaya Stein. "Sephardic Scholarly Worlds: Toward a Novel Geography of Modern Jewish History." *The Jewish Quarterly Review* 100.3 (2010): 349–384.

Cohen, Julia Phillips and Sarah Abrevaya Stein, eds. *Sephardi Lives: A Documentary History, 1700–1950*. Stanford: Stanford University Press, 2014.

Cohen, Julia Phillips. *Notes from the 2018 Meyerhoff Lecture*. 31 October 2018. https://katz.sas.upenn.edu/resources/blog/notes-2018-meyerhoff-lecture. (13 September 2021).

Cohen, Tova, and Shmuel Feiner. *Voice of a Hebrew Maiden: Women's Writings of the 19th Century Haskalah Movement*. Tel Aviv: Hakibutz Hameuchad, 2006 [Hebrew].

Cohen Starkman, Mira. "A Generic and Thematic Study of Judeo-Spanish (Ladino) Medical Literature." Doctoral Thesis, Bar-Ilan University, Ramat Gan, 2017 [Hebrew].

Danon, Abraham. "The First Journal Devoted to the Sephardi Past Appears on Edirne (1888)." *Sephardi Lives: A Documentary History, 1700–1950*. Tr. Shir Alon. Eds. Julia Phillips Cohen and Sarah Abrevaya Stein. Stanford: Stanford University Press, 2014. 392–393.

Davis, Fanny. *The Ottoman Lady: A Social History from 1718 to 1918*. New York: Greenwood Press, 1986.

Feiner, Shmuel. "Towards a Historical Definition of the *Haskalah*." *New Perspectives on the Haskalah*. Eds. Shmuel Feiner and David Sorkin. London: Littman Library of Jewish Civilization, 2001. 184–219.

Feiner, Shmuel. *The Jewish Enlightenment in the 19th Century*. Jerusalem: Carmel, 2010 [Hebrew].

Gabbay, Rosa. "An Etiquette Handbook for Sephardi Women (1871)." *Sephardi Lives: A Documentary History, 1700–1950*. Tr. Michael Alpert. Eds. Julia Phillips Cohen and Sarah Abrevaya Stein. Stanford: Stanford University Press, 2014. 62–65.

Gaon, Moshe David. *A Bibliography of the Judeo-Spanish (Ladino) Press*. Jerusalem: Ben-Zvi Institute, 1965 [Hebrew].

Hacker, Joseph. "The Sephardim in the Ottoman Empire in the Sixteenth Century." *Moreshet Sepharad: the Sephardi Legacy, Vols. I–II*. Ed. Haim Beinart. Jerusalem: Magnes Press, 1992. 109–133.

Hadar, Gila. "Reina Cohen: Soferet u-mistikanit yehudiah mi-saloniki be-mifne ha-meah ha-19 ve-tehilat ha-meah ha-20." *El Prezente* 8–9 (2015): 149–166 [Hebrew].

Hanioğlu, M. Sukru. *A Brief History of the Late Ottoman Empire*. Princeton: Princeton University Press, 2008.

Huli, Ya'akov. "A Rabbi in Istanbul Interprets the Bible for Ladino Readers (1730)." *Sephardi Lives: A Documentary History, 1700–1950*. Tr. Olga Borovaya. Eds. Julia Phillips Cohen and Sarah Abrevaya Stein. Stanford: Stanford University Press, 2014. 28–31.

Illouz, Eve. *Consuming the Romantic Utopia: Love and the Cultural Contradictions of Capitalism*. Berkeley/Los Angeles/Oxford: University of California Press, 1997.

Israel, Jonathan I. *European Jewry in the Age of Mercantilism, 1550–1750*. Oxford: Clarendon Press, 1985.

Israel, Jonathan I. "Jews and Crypto-Jews in the Atlantic World Systems, 1500–1800." *Atlantic Diasporas: Jews, Conversos, and Crypto-Jews in the Age of Mercantilism, 1500–1800*. Eds. Richard L. Kagan and Philip D. Morgan. Baltimore: Johns Hopkins University Press, 2009. 3–17.

Karkason, Tamir. "Sabbateanism and the *Ma'aminim* in the Writings of Abraham Elmaleh." *El Prezente* 10 (2016): 123–142.

Karkason, Tamir. "The Ottoman-Jewish *Haskalah* (Enlightenment), 1839–1908: A Transformation in the Jewish Communities of Western Anatolia, the Southern Balkans and Jerusalem." Doctoral Thesis, The Hebrew University of Jerusalem, 2018 [Hebrew].

Kaplan, Yosef. *The Western Sephardi Diaspora*. Tel Aviv: Misrad ha-Bitahon, 1994 [Hebrew].

Kaplan, Yosef. *An Alternative Path to Modernity: The Sephardi Diaspora in Western Europe*. Leiden: Brill, 2000.

Lehmann, Matthias B. *Ladino Rabbinic Literature and Ottoman Sephardic Culture*. Bloomington: Indiana University Press, 2005a.

Lehmann, Matthias B. "A Livornese 'Port Jew' and the Sephardim of the Ottoman Empire." *Jewish Social Studies* 11.2 (2005b): 51–76.

Lehmann, Matthias B. "Assa, Abraham Ben Isaac." *Encyclopedia of Jews in the Islamic World*. Ed. Norman A. Stillman. First published online: 2010. https://referenceworks.brillonline.com/entries/encyclopedia-of-jews-in-the-islamic-world/assa-abraham-ben-isaac-SIM_0002460. (05 November 2018).

Landau, Luis. "The Transformation of the Talmudic Story in *'Me'am Lo'ez'*." *Pe'amim* 7 (1981): 35–49 [Hebrew].
Levy, Lital. "Partitioned Pasts: Arab Jewish Intellectuals and the Case of Esther Azhari Moyal (1873–1948)." *The Making of the Arab Intellectual (1880–1960): Empire, Public Sphere, and the Colonial Coordinates of Selfhood*. Ed. Dyala Hamzah. London: Routledge, 2012. 128–163.
Lewis, Bernard. *The Emergence of Modern Turkey*. New York: Oxford University Press, 2002.
Magid, Moshe. "Periodical Literature." *Jewish Communities in the East in the Nineteenth and Twentieth Centuries: Turkey*. Ed. Yaron Ben-Naeh. Jerusalem: Ben-Zvi Institute, 2009. 123–136 [Hebrew].
Martín Ortega, Elisa. "Las primeras escritoras sefardíes, entre tradición y modernidad: el caso de Reina Hakohén de Salónica." *Miscelánea de Estudios Árabes y Hebraicos* 62 (2013): 145–175.
Meral, Arzu. "A Survey of Translation Activity in the Ottoman Empire." *Osmanlı Araştırmaları/The Journal of Ottoman Studies* XLII (2013): 105–155.
Meyuhas Ginio, Alisa. "The History of the *'Me'am Lo'ez'*: A Ladino Commentary on the Bible." *European Judaism* 43.2 (2010): 117–125.
Meyuhas Ginio, Alisa. "Tsa'ar gidul banot u-vituyav bi-shnayim mi-sifrei ha-hadracha shel ha-yehudim ha-sephardaim: *Me'am Loez* (1730) u-*Pele Yo'ets* (1824; 1870)." *El Prezente* 8–9 (2015): 357–374 [Hebrew].
Naar, Devin E. *Jewish Salonica: Between the Ottoman Empire and Modern Greece*. Stanford: Stanford University Press, 2016.
Noy, Amos. *Experts or Witnesses: Jewish Intelligentsia from Jerusalem and the Levant in the Beginning of the 20th Century*. Tel Aviv: Resling, 2017 [Hebrew].
Papo, Eliezer. "Estado de la investigación y bibliografía anotada de la obra literaria de Laura Papo 'Bohoreta'." *Sefarad* 72.1 (2012): 123–144.
Pedrosa, Jose Manuel. "Coplas sefardíes y pliegos de cordel hispánicos." *Sefarad* 55.2 (1995): 335–357.
Quintana, Aldina, "The Structure of the Narrative in R. Jacob Culi's *Me'am Lo'ez*." *Pe'amim* 105–106 (2006): 151–179 [Hebrew].
Quataert, Donald. *The Ottoman Empire 1700–1922*. Cambridge: Cambridge University Press, 2000.
Ray, Jonathan. *After Expulsion: 1492 and the Making of Sephardic Jewry*. New York: New York University Press, 2013.
Refael, Shmuel. *"I Will Tell a Poem": A Study of Judeo-Spanish (Ladino) Coplas*. Jerusalem: Carmel, 2004 [Hebrew].
Refael, Shmuel. *Ladino Here and Now*. Tel Aviv: Tel Aviv University Press, 2020 [Hebrew].
Rodrigue, Aron. *French Jews, Turkish Jews: The Alliance Israélite Universelle and the Politics of Jewish Schooling in Turkey, 1860–1925*. Bloomington and Indianapolis: Indiana University Press, 1990.
Rodrigue, Aron. *Images of Sephardi and Eastern Jewries in Transition: The Teachers of the Alliance Israelite Universelle, 1860–1939*. Seattle: University of Washington Press, 1993.
Rodrigue, Aron. "The Beginnings of Westernization and Community Reform among Istanbul's Jewry, 1854–65." *The Jews of the Ottoman Empire*. Ed. Avigdor Levy. Princeton/Washington, DC: Darwin Press and The Institute of Turkish Studies, 1994. 439–456.
Rodrigue, Aron. "Salonica in Jewish Historiography." *Jewish History* 28.3–4 (2014): 439–447.
Romero, Elena. *El teatro de los sefardies orientales* (Volumes I–III). Madrid: Instituto "Arias Montano," 1979.
Romero, Elena. *La creación literaria en lengua sefardí*. Madrid: Editorial MAPFRE, 1992.
Romero, Elena. "Theatre." *Jewish Communities in the East in the Nineteenth and Twentieth Centuries: Turkey*. Ed. Yaron Ben-Naeh. Jerusalem: Ben-Zvi Institute, 2009. 155–162 [Hebrew].
Romeu Ferré, Pilar. *Las llaves del Meam loez. Edición crítica, concordada y analítica de los Índices del Meam loez de la Torá*. Barcelona: Tirocinio, 2000.

Rozen, Minna. "Strangers in a Strange Land: The Extraterritorial Status of Jews in Italy and the Ottoman Empire in the Sixteenth to the Eighteenth Centuries." *Ottoman and Turkish Jewry: Community and Leadership*. Ed. Aron Rodrigue. Bloomington: Indiana University Press, 1992. 123–166.

Rubin, Avi. "Ottoman Judicial Change in the Age of Modernity: A Reappraisal." *History Compass* 7.1 (2009): 119–140.

Saba Wolfe, Rachel. "Puertas de luz [sha'are or]: ha-iton *Sha'are Mizrah* (Izmir, 1845–1846) ka-kol ha-mevaser shel ha-haskalah ha-yehudit ha-sephardit." *El Prezente* 8–9 (2015): 421–469 [Hebrew].

Sánchez Vasco, Marta Isabel. "*Noticias principales y verdaderas* y *La Gazeta de Amsterdam*: Visión comparada de dos gacetas de Flandes y Holanda durante el siglo XVII Autores." *Libros de la Corte* 15 (2017): 54–69.

Satinger, Margalit. "The Judeo-Spanish (Ladino) Israeli Press (1948–1958): Between National and Ethno-Sephardic Contents." Doctoral Thesis, Bar-Ilan University, Ramat Gan, 2018 [Hebrew].

Scholem, Gershom. *Sabbatai Sevi: The Mystical Messiah, 1626–1676*. Intro. Yaacob Dweck. Tr. R. J. Zwi Werblowsky. Princeton: Princeton University Press, 2016.

Schnitzer, Shmuel. "The Gazette, First After All." *Kesher* 40 (1987): 3–10 [Hebrew].

Schwarzwald, Ora. *Sidur para mujeres en ladino, Salónica, siglo XVI*. Jerusalem: Ben-Zvi Institute, 2012 [Hebrew and Spanish].

Şişmanoğlu Şimşek, Şehnaz. "The Anatoli Newspaper and the Heyday of the Karamanli Press." *Cries and Whispers in Karamanlidika Books: Proceedings of the First International Conference on Karamanlidika Studies (Nicosia, 11–13 September 2008)*. Eds: Evangelia Balta and Mathias Kappler. Wiesbaden: Harrassowitz Verlag, 2010. 109–123.

Stechauner, Martin. "The Sephardic Jews of Vienna: A Jewish Minority Crossing Borders." Doctoral Thesis, University of Vienna, 2019.

Trivellato, Francesca. *The Familiarity of Strangers: The Sephardic Diaspora, Livorno, and Cross-Cultural Trade in the Early Modern Period*. New Haven: Yale University Press, 2009.

Tsur, Yaron. "Modern Identities of Jews in Muslim Lands – The Arab-Jewish Option." *Pea'mim* 125–127 (2010): 45–56 [Hebrew].

Tsur, Yaron. *Notables and other Jews in the Ottoman Middle East 1750–1830*. Jerusalem: The Bialik Institute Press, 2016 [Hebrew].

Usque, Samuel. *Consolation for the Tribulations of Israel (Consolação ás Tribulações de Israel)*. Tr. Martin A. Cohen. Philadelphia: Jewish Publication Society of America, 1965.

Yerushalmi, Yosef Hayim. "'Privilegos del Poderozo Rey Karlo' (1740): A Neapolitan Call for the Return of the Jews, and its Ladino Translation." *Studies in Jewish Bibliography, History and Literature, in Honor of I. Edward Kiev*. Ed. Charles Berlin. New York: Ktav, 1971. 517–541.

Yerushalmi, Yosef Hayim. *Zakhor: Jewish History and Jewish Memory*. Seattle: University of Washington Press, 1996.

Yosmaoğlu, Ipek. "Chasing the Printed Word: Press Censorship in the Ottoman Empire, 1876–1913." *Turkish Studies Association Journal* 27.1–2 (2003): 15–49.

Zürcher, Erik J. *Turkey: A Modern History*. London: I.B. Tauris, 3rd ed. 2004.

Further Reading

Abrevaya Stein, Sarah. *Family Papers: A Sephardic Journey through the Twentieth Century*. New York: Farrar, Straus and Giroux, 2019.

Alexander-Frizer, Tamar. *The Heart is a Mirror: The Sephardic Folktale*. Detroit: Wayne State University Press, 2008.

Alexander-Frizer, Tamar, and Eliezer Papo. "El enkanto de la majia – Sephardic Magic: History, Trends and Topics." *El Prezente* 5 (2011): 9–31.

Ben-Naeh, Yaron. "Moshko the Jew and his Gay Friends: Same-Sex Sexual Relations in Ottoman Jewish Society." *Journal of Early Modern History* 9.1–2 (2005): 79–108.

Ben-Naeh, Yaron, Dan Shapira and Aviezer Tutian. *Debar Šepatayim: An Ottoman Hebrew Chronicle from the Crimea (1683–1730). Written by Krymchak Rabbi David Lekhno*. Boston: Academic Studies Press, 2021.

Ben-Ur, Aviva. "Ladino in Print: Toward a Comprehensive Bibliography." *Aviva Jewish History* 16.3 (2002): 309–326.

Bunis, David M. "Modernization and the Language Question among Judezmo-Speaking Sephardim of the Ottoman Empire." *Sephardim and the Middle Eastern Jewries: History and Culture in the Modern Era*. Ed. Harvey Goldberg. Bloomington: Indiana University Press, 1996. 226–239.

Cohen, Julia Phillips. "Oriental by Design: Ottoman Jews, Imperial Style, and the Performance of Heritage." *American Historical Review* 119.2 (2014): 364–398.

Crews, Cynthia. *Extracts from the Meam Loez (Genesis) with a Translation and a Glossary*. Leeds: Proceedings of the Leeds Philosophical Literary Society, 1960.

Danon, Dina. *The Jews of Ottoman Izmir: A Modern History*. Stanford: Stanford University Press, 2020.

Diaz-Mas, Paloma. *Los sefardies: Historia, lengua, y cultura*. Barcelona: Riopiedras Edicione, 1986.

Ginio, Eyal. "Jews and European Subjects in Eighteenth-Century Salonica: The Ottoman Perspective." *Jewish History* 28.3–4 (2014): 289–312.

Goldish, Matt. *Jewish Questions: Responsa on Sephardic Life in the Early Modern Period*. Princeton: Princeton University Press, 2008.

Gruss, Susy. *Las novelas de Judá Haim Perahiá: Salónica 1886 – Xanthi 1970*. Barcelona: Tirocinio, 2020.

Hacker, Joseph. "The Sephardi Sermon in the Sixteenth Century – Between Literature and Historical Source." *Pe'amim* 26 (1986): 108–127 [Hebrew].

Hassán, Iacob M. "Visión panorámica de la literatura sefardí." *Hispania Judaica* 2 (1982): 25–44.

Held, Michal. *Let Me Tell You a Story/Ven te kontare: The Personal Narratives of Judeo-Spanish Speaking Storytelling Women, An Interdisciplinary Study*. Jerusalem: Ben-Zvi Institute, 2009 [Hebrew].

Held, Michal. "The People who Almost Forgot: Judeo-Spanish Online Communities as a Digital Home-Land." *El Prezente* 4 (2010): 83–101.

Held, Michal. "'Verso una nueva vida' (Towards a New Life): The Ultimate Voices of the Sephardic Community of Salonica." *Ladinar* 9 (2017): lix–lxxix.

Karkason, Tamir. "Between Two Poles: Barukh Mitrani between Moderate *Haskalah* and Jewish Nationalism." *Zutot* 18 (2021): 108–118.

Martín Ortega, Elisa. "Itzhak Benveniste and Reina Hakohén: Narrative and Essay for Sephardic Youth." *Sepharad as Imagined Community Language, History and Religion from the Early Modern Period to the 21st Century*. Ed. Mahir Saul and José Ignacio Hualde. New York: Peter Lang, 2017. 147–161.

Manrique, David M. *Dize la muerte: Estudio y edición de la copia cuatrocentista de la Danza de la Muerte aljamiada (Ms. Parma 2666)*. Barcelona: Tirocinio, 2019.

Mays, Devi. *Forging Ties, Forging Passports: Migration and the Modern Sephardi Diaspora*. Stanford: Stanford University Press, 2020.

Naar, Devin E. "Fashioning the 'Mother of Israel': The Ottoman Jewish Historical Narrative and the Image of Jewish Salonica." *Jewish History* 28.3–4 (2014): 337–372.

Naar, Devin E. "'Turkinos' Beyond the Empire: Ottoman Jews in America, 1893 to 1924." *Jewish Quarterly Review* 105.2 (2015): 174–205.

Papo, Eliezer. *And Thou Shalt Jest with Thy Son: Judeo-Spanish Parodies on the Passover Haggadah*. Vols. I–II. Jerusalem: Ben-Zvi Institute, 2012 [Hebrew].

Sánchez, Rosa, and Marie-Christine Bornes Varol, eds. *La presse judéo-espagnole: support et vecteur de la modernité*. Istanbul: Libra Kitapçılık ve Yayıncılık Ticaret, 2013.

Sciaky, Leon. *Farewell to Ottoman Salonica*. Istanbul: Isis Press, 2000.

Aliza Moreno-Goldschmidt

11 *Conversos* in Colonial Hispanic America

Abstract: This chapter analyzes the different historical circumstances that led to the arrival of the first 'New Christians' of Jewish origin to Hispanic America during the colonial era. We will also examine the main characteristics of this group as well as their impact within colonial society. As the documents of the Inquisition constitute the main source for the study of this phenomenon, we will carry out a general assessment of these documents and try to point out some of the peculiarities of the *converso* phenomenon in each of its geographical enclaves.

Key Terms: converso history, colonial history, Tribunals of the Inquisition

1 Beginnings

Anyone who wishes to inquire into the history of the Jewish presence in Latin America must understand that the arrival of these immigrants has taken place at various times, in various regions and under various historical circumstances. As we will show in the present chapter, we can generally speak of three independent phases of migration – during the colonial period, at the beginning of the Republican period and, lastly, a phase of modern migration beginning towards the end of the nineteenth century. These different waves have no direct connection to one another. For this reason, to state that the first traces of Jewish life documented in Iberoamerica date back to colonial times is just as correct as the claim that the Jewish communities currently existing in Latin America are the result of the migrations that began during the second half of the nineteenth century. The main topic that will occupy us in this chapter will be the colonial era, but towards the end, we will also take a brief look at the Jewish presence in Latin America in modern times.

2 The Colonial Period

Within the single year of 1492, two events took place that would prove to be decisive for the history of Spain: the expulsion of the Jews and the arrival of Columbus to the American continent, which began the period of Spanish conquest. This coincidence has given some reason to suppose that among the crew of Columbus's expeditions, there may have been some converts of Jewish origin.[1]

---

[1] Although it is generally not an accepted opinion among academics, there are some researchers who

Although it should be noted that, in legal terms, the 'New Christians' of Jewish origin were prohibited from participating in the campaigns of conquest as well as the colonization enterprise (Domínguez Ortiz 1988, 128–129), it is known that compliance with these regulations was not always exercised with the same rigor. Thus, it is feasible that individuals of Jewish origin may have reached the American continent as early as the time of the conquest. The difficulty in obtaining conclusive answers regarding the possible presence of conversos of Jewish origin in the campaigns of conquest and during the early colonial period lies in the lack of historical sources; since, according to the regulations, the presence of 'New Christians' was prohibited in the colonies, this kind of information was generally omitted from official documents.

By the second half of the sixteenth century, the first two Tribunals of the Inquisition were instituted in the Spanish colonies, one in Mexico City and the other in Lima, the respective capitals of the two Viceroyalties. The jurisdiction of the Inquisition of Lima encompassed the territories of what is now Panama, Colombia, Venezuela, Ecuador, Peru, Bolivia, Argentina, Uruguay and Paraguay. For its part, the district of the Inquisition of Mexico encompassed the territories of what is now Mexico, Guatemala, Nicaragua, Hispaniola, Cuba, Puerto Rico and Jamaica, forming a jurisdiction that was both continental and insular. It was a pretentious division, we could almost say, disconnected from reality. Although it is true that the jurisdiction of the Inquisition in Hispanic America was not absolute, since its authority did not include the evangelized native population – whose faith and religious practices continued to be under the responsibility of the religious orders – the immense territory that each of these courts had to govern constituted a serious obstacle. Moreover, it was totally at odds with the situation in the Peninsula, not only due to the lack of common sense in the distribution of territory but also concerning the standards that governed the inquisitorial courts. According to Escandell Bonet's calculation, the inquisitorial district of Peru included an approximate territory of three million square kilometers, while that of Mexico included about two million square kilometers (Escandell Bonet 1993, 53). It soon became clear that it would be impossible to carry out a truly efficient and comprehensive inquisitorial function with just two branches for the entire continent. Several years later, it was decided to institute a new court that could alleviate the difficult work of the other two. Three cities were taken into consideration: the city of Santa Fe de Bogotá, favored for being a city of the Royal Audience as well as the most important of the New Granada territory, the city of Santo Domingo, favored for its central port location and for the frequent arrival of fleets from the Peninsula, and finally, Cartagena de Indias, which would ultimately be chosen. The establishment of the Tribunal of the Inquisition in Cartagena de Indias had an immediate impact on the other two American courts, first and foremost in terms of the consequent geographic redistribution. The new

---

consider that Columbus himself could have been of Jewish origin. See for example: Wiesenthal 1973 and Madariaga 1940.

court became responsible for the jurisdiction of the regions today corresponding to Colombia, Venezuela, Panama, Hispaniola, Cuba, Puerto Rico and Nicaragua.

The establishment of the Inquisition on the American continent constitutes a fundamental turning point for the reconstruction of the presence of 'New Christians' of Jewish origin in the New World, thanks to the meticulous written records that this institution kept of the trials it carried out. The Inquisition, which prosecuted the various possible heresies against the Catholic religion, was also in charge of penalizing those individuals who were suspected of preserving Jewish beliefs and practices. Consequently, starting with the institution of the Inquisition in the American colonies and especially from the first half of the seventeenth century, we have a significant quantity of documents from which we can learn about different aspects of the ethno-social group of conversos who arrived in the Americas during the colonial period.

While it is uncontroversial that the quantity of sources provided by the Inquisition's archives is enough to support a historical inquiry, it is still pertinent to evaluate the quality and the nature of these documents in order to establish whether or not they constitute reliable sources, especially if we take into account that they are almost the only kind of written material from the colonial period in Hispanic America that may serve the modern historian to reconstruct the history of the 'New Christians' of Jewish origin.

The reliability of inquisitorial documents has been a subject under debate not only in the American context. Some scholars, such as Rivkin and Netanyahu, have dismissed any use of these sources as a matter of general principle.[2] According to this approach, the Inquisition was a manipulative organ which had different goals from those officially declared – not sincere religious concerns but, on the contrary, social and economic interests – and as a consequence produced documents which do not constitute reliable testimonies, but only reflect the manipulative means to obtain certain goals. Distrust of the Inquisition as an institution led these scholars to disregard all the different kinds of inquisitorial documents.

On the other hand, researchers who are of the opposite opinion and consider that the declared goals of the Inquisition do generally correspond to its true motivation trust inquisitorial documents as highly reliable sources, in this case also as a general principle. Among this group we can mention scholars such as Domínguez Ortiz (1991, 1993), Caro Baroja (1996a, 1996b), Révah (1959–1960), Beinart (1981, 1992) and Dedieu (1986).

In a way, both approaches may be regarded as problematic, both the *a priori* condemnation of the inquisitorial documents and the automatic acceptance of them – as in the case of Beinart, who simply assumes that "the Conversos' way of life was

---

[2] See some representative examples: Rivkin 1957–1958, 1980; Netanyahu 1995, 137. See also some additional negative approaches in: García Cárcel 2000, 103; Domínguez Ortiz 2000, 57–82.

recorded in the Inquisition trial" (Beinart 1992, 58) without presenting clear criteria for the critical reading of these sources.

In the context of this historiographical discussion, it is worth mentioning an interesting argument presented by Yerushalmi: The documents of the Inquisition are so complete and detailed to the point that they include the voices of witnesses who contradict the accusations as well as those of inquisitors who question the guilt of the defendants (Yerushalmi 1971, 24). Without contradicting the fact that the verdict of many trials could have been biased, the inquisitorial records, are far from being monophonic – not only at the quantitative level, insofar as they include the testimonies of several agents, but also at the qualitative level, insofar as these diverse voices sometimes also offer us different or even contradictory perspectives. These, in fact, are living voices captured in writing.

The thoroughness of the inquisitorial records allows us to add another argument for the reliability of said sources. In many cases, the testimonies contained in the inquisitorial documents include very specific and detailed descriptions that the inquisitors simply could not have invented or manufactured. Examples of this can be found, among other places, in the detailed testimonies on Jewish life in European communities outside the Iberian territory. The knowledge possessed by the inquisitors of the seventeenth century regarding Judaism was limited to the very 'warnings' that the Holy Office offered to its officials and that were publicly presented for the recognition of the crime at issue (García 1995). On the other hand, these officials, who for the most part never left the territories of the Spanish kingdom, never encountered any Jew who freely practiced their faith, much less Jewish public life in the various European communities. Even so, we can find in the inquisitorial records accurate descriptions of Jewish life in communities such as Venice, the Ottoman Empire, Amsterdam and others (Moreno-Goldschmidt 2016b).

Inquisitorial documents are worth being studied as relevant and valuable historical sources. There is no compelling reason to discredit these archives. However, it is no less important to note that we must take into consideration – not only as a theoretical reflection, but as the most basic methodological prerequisite – that the documents left behind by the Spanish Inquisition present us with serious challenges and thus must be read critically.

The critical reading of the inquisitorial sources for the study of the converso societies must take into consideration different aspects such as the type of inquisitorial document in question as well as the possible interests of the person whose testimony is recorded there (Moreno-Goldschmidt 2018, 46–58). In the context of our chapter, it is appropriate to emphasize an additional aspect: heretical practices were the *raison d'être* of the Holy Office and its function consisted in discovering, penalizing and correcting this type of behavior. This was the central engine of all inquisitorial activity. As for the defendants, it is highly probable that they tried to hide any information that may have implicated them or that they even 'confessed' to false facts in a desperate attempt to reach an end to the torture or to the trial itself. If someone raised false testimony to implicate another person, for the purposes of revenge or for any other reason, it is clear that this falsehood would be manifested in the parts of the testimony that spoke of supposed religious practices or beliefs. However, the inquisitorial documents recorded not only the alleged transgressions of the Catholic religion, but also many other aspects of the lives of these persons which, had it not been for the secret archives of the Holy Tribunal, would very possibly have been lost in eternal oblivion.

In their trials, the prisoners had to present their detailed genealogy and an account of their lives in which they told of their families, their occupations, their migrations, etc. In addition, throughout the various testimonies, both the defendants and the prosecution and defense witnesses provide detailed accounts of their family (or extramarital) relationships, their social lives, their businesses, their conflicts, their moments of leisure, and their worries. Not only do these aspects of the documents present us with a unique possibility to learn about the daily lives and social relations of a significant number of people, but this type of information can generally be considered highly reliable as it does not directly concern the persecutory goals of the Inquisition and there is no reason to suspect plagiarism or distortion. In fact, the information that must have been most insignificant in the eyes of the inquisitors is of the greatest value to the modern historian due to its nature and its reliability.[3]

Thus, in our effort to reconstruct the history of the 'New Christians' in the Americas, having as historical sources almost exclusively the inquisitorial documents, we should be aware that conclusions about the social, economic or even cultural realities of this group will be more reliable, while the reconstruction of their religious lives will be much more challenging.[4]

3 The Concept of *limpieza de sangre* [purity of blood] in the Colonial Context

Throughout the seventeenth century, in Peninsular Spain and in the Spanish American colonies, the existence of the Tribunals of the Inquisition as regulatory and executive bodies, responsible for crimes of faith as well as the presence of conversos within Hispanic society, were both historical realities. However, it is important to point out some essential differences between the Spanish institutions and the social realities in the distinct socio-geographical context of the Americas. For example, we have already mentioned the significant gap between the enormous areas of jurisdiction of

---

3 See two excellent books that exemplify this kind of study based on trial documents: Davis 1985; Ginzburg 1982.
4 It should be noted that despite what has been pointed out here, there are serious scholars who address the religious world of the 'New Christians'. Regarding the religious experience of the conversos in Hispanic America, see Nathan Wachtel's studies: Wachtel 2001, 149–171; Wachtel 2013 [2001].

each inquisitorial tribunal in the colonies in contrast to a greater number of tribunals for much smaller areas in the Peninsula. Evidently, this fact was not just a matter of numbers, but directly affected the ability of each tribunal to carry out the functions expected of it.

On a social rather than a bureaucratic level, there is another important difference between the reality in the Peninsula on the one hand and that of the colonies on the other – a difference that had a deep impact on the lives of 'New Christians' and that has not been sufficiently considered by several of the scholars who have studied the topic of 'New Christians' in the American context: the impact and even the very meaning of the concept of *limpieza de sangre* [purity of blood] within the complex ethnic and social panorama of colonial America.

When addressing the issue of *limpieza de sangre* within Spanish society in the early modern period, it is critical to understand that its effects took place on two different levels. The origin of the concept goes back to the legal sphere: *The Statutes of Purity of Blood* were a set of laws that prevented individuals of convert origin from accessing certain circles and certain public functions within Spanish society. These legal documents aroused intense debate within Spanish society, especially during the fifteenth and seventeenth centuries (Sicroff 1985). The statutes also affected the processes of migration to the colonies as well as some of the official Spanish institutions in America. However, it is of great importance to understand that although the concept itself refers to legal regulations, this concept was also present in the social sphere, being a stigma that was part of the Iberian idiosyncrasy in all strata of society. As effectively formulated by Yerushalmi, for conversos of Jewish origin,

> the statutes [were] as forceful a reminder of their Jewish extraction as the insults to which they were often subjected in daily life. For the term "New Christian" was both a social stigma and a legal category. (Yerushalmi 1971, 16)

The stigma surrounding the 'New Christians' in Spain was a general feeling, an inherent part of the social environment of the time, or as defined by Granjel, "in the Spanish society of the Modern World, 'purity' was equivalent to 'honor', presented as the greatest of all goods" (Granjel 1993).[5] In Spain and Portugal, the conception of an alleged 'purity of blood' became indeed a central and dominant aspect of the ideology and social mentality of the time, but it was an invisible social superiority, since the supposed ethnic, cultural and religious gaps were not distinguishable at first glance. In the Iberian society of the early modern period, the 'New Christian' was the object *par excellence* that symbolized 'otherness'. But this 'other' was constituted by people born in the Iberian Peninsula, who spoke the same language, who shared the same social and cultural experiences, who attended the same churches, who in many cases sincerely shared the same faith

---

5 See also: Contreras (1991, 132).

and who lived according to the same values and idiosyncrasies. In many aspects, it was de facto a completely imaginary 'otherness'.

In spite of the fact that both Spain and its colonies were ruled by the same crown, it would be a serious mistake to apply concepts from continental Spanish society to the American reality without reevaluating them;[6] this is indeed the case when it comes to the meaning and impact of the laws of the alleged 'purity of blood' in the new context. As far as 'New Christians' are concerned, the general conception of 'purity of blood' was not essentially transformed in the 'New World'. However, the ethno-cultural panorama that lay before the eyes of the conquerors and colonizers was entirely different from the European one. In this new reality, ethnic differences became the most basic and dominant aspect of life and social dynamics. The various ranges of skin color were transformed into the most important factor in determining social status. Caucasians, who constituted the vast majority in Europe, represented the dominant minority in the conquered lands, and as Céspedes del Castillo affirms,

> for the Castilian immigrants, their settlement in the Indies meant a generalized social ascent. (Céspedes del Castillo 1999, 69)

In the 'New World', 'otherness' was transformed into something that could be perceived by the senses. Europeans perceived differences on the surface, not only in color, but also in culture and idiosyncrasy. In front of them, they saw indigenous people that were weakening in body and spirit, with customs that had, from the perspective of the colonizers, to be evangelized. On the other hand, they saw the people of color who had been kidnapped from Africa (by Europeans or their ancestors) to supply the labor force in the colonial enterprise – people of color who were seen as objects, as slaves. The 'other' thus became the vast majority, with whom the colonizers shared their daily lives. In this new reality, the stigma of the 'otherness' of the 'New Christians' was unfailingly transformed. This does not mean that the heritage of 'New Christians' was no longer considered impure, but the differences that separated old and 'New Christians' in Europe, already difficult to distinguish, became blurred in America to the point that they were perhaps non-existent. They all had come from Europe, they had the same skin color, they shared the same mother tongue, they dressed in the same fashion, they lived in the same neighborhoods, they sat next to each other in churches, they entertained themselves by playing the same card games and drinking the same wine, and they had sailed to the 'New World' under similar circumstances. In Martínez's words:

---

[6] An example of the error to which this type of attitude can lead is what Martínez criticizes regarding the application of the European caste system to the understanding of the new social organization in colonial America (Martínez 2008, 3).

> The transfer of the Castilian discourse of *limpieza de sangre* to Spanish America did not mean, however, that it remained the same in the new context [. . .] in Spanish America, the notion of purity gradually came to be equated with Spanish ancestry, with "Spanishness," an idea that had little significance in the metropolitan context.
> (Martínez 2008, 2)

At this point, a distinction should be made between the Spanish 'New Christians' and those who came from Portugal. Undoubtedly, those who reaped the greatest benefit from this change of panorama were the Spanish 'New Christians' – regarding whom, precisely because of their integration into colonial society, we have almost no information. In fact, the number of Spaniards (without Portuguese origins) who were judged by the courts of the Inquisition in America on suspicion of having 'judaized' was very small. This fact does not mean that Spaniards from converted families did not come to America, but rather that these individuals had less difficulties to integrate into the Spanish society of the American colonies.

The attitude of colonial society towards the Portuguese in general and towards the 'New Christians' of Portuguese origin in particular (who constituted a high percentage of the former) was, however, different. On the one hand, they were also part of the ethnic elite as they were European colonizers. Furthermore, the attitude towards the Portuguese was more complex than in the case of other foreign merchants (French, English, etc.). They were not Spanish, and that in itself already made them an 'other', but the historical, cultural and political relationship (especially during the period between 1580 and 1640, when the Spanish and Portuguese crowns were united) was much closer and therefore their treatment was more familiar. One example of this attitude can be found in a quote from the governor of Cartagena de Indias, Pedro de Lodeña, from 1586:

> There are a huge number of foreigners and Portuguese here who have lived in this city for days and even years [. . .].
> (AGI 1586)

According to this assertion, there were two categories or levels of foreigners: the Portuguese on the one hand and the rest of the European foreigners on the other. In their position as foreigners, the Portuguese continued to arouse suspicion and the question of their 'purity of blood' became relevant. Even so, in these cases too, the whole picture must be taken into account. Let us not forget the great ethnic, cultural and social variety that constituted the colonial reality. Thus, despite the alleged 'dubious' ancestry of the Portuguese and the fact that they were foreigners rather than Spaniards, they still had much more in common with the Spanish population than with all the rest of the groups that constituted 'otherness' in the 'New World': indigenous people and people of color.

In this light, it is interesting to address the question of the conversos' motives for immigrating to the Hispanic colonies. According to some scholars, the main reason for the arrival of the Portuguese conversos was the fear of the European Inquisition and the hope of living a more peaceful life in a place far from Iberian soil (Garavaglia and Marchena Fernández 2005, 360; Liebman 1984, 31). Adding to this argument, Alberro makes the following point:

> [T]heir long experience at evading the curiosity and vigilance of the Christian population in general, the relative inability of the bulk of the population to recognize their heterodox practices, the weakness of institutional networks – especially the Inquisition's – and finally, the elite status that they shared with other Europeans gave them a good chance of surviving, as had been their hope when they embarked for America. (Alberro 2001, 182)

Alberro's description indeed reflects some aspects and peculiarities of the reality of the colonies, but were these *de facto* advantages indeed also *a priori* motivations? Let's remember that, at this historical point, Spanish and Portuguese 'New Christians' also had the opportunity to settle outside the Iberian domains, including several places where Judaism was not only not prohibited, but where new communities of the Western Sephardic diaspora were flourishing and where many former conversos created their own Jewish communities – places such as Amsterdam, Livorno, Hamburg, etc. In light of this, the idea that the 'New Christians' embarked to the Americas in order to avoid the inquisitorial persecutions appears insufficient.[7]

We can safely affirm that what attracted these conversos to the colonies was in general not different from what led other merchants – Spanish, Portuguese or of any other nationality – to embark to America: the great commercial opportunities in these territories precisely at a time when the mercantile system was booming and especially taking into account the extensive connections that existed between converso merchants residing in different enclaves of Europe, Africa and America.

Thus, we can conclude that there are two important facts that must be taken into consideration for a better understanding of the phenomenon of the conversos in Hispanic America: on the one hand, it is clear that the main motivation of their journey to the 'New World' were the economic opportunities. On the other hand, beyond their original reasons, the reality of the American colonies offered them several advantages in contrast to the reality of other enclaves where they could have resided. Unlike the 'New Christians' who remained in the Iberian Peninsula, conversos in the 'New World' came to enjoy a more equal social status, as described above. Furthermore, if we compare the situation of the conversos who wanted and were able to return openly to Judaism in the communities of the Western Sephardic Diaspora with the situation of the conversos who decided to migrate to the American colonies, we can affirm that the latter enjoyed certain advantages. Although they experienced a more radical geographical change, on a cultural level their new home was a familiar environment, in

---

[7] According to Novinsky, in some cases it was easier for the conversos to embark to the 'New World' rather than travel to other countries in Europe, in spite of the greater distance (Novinsky 1994, 515). But even if this is true, this fact can only explain some particular cases and not the phenomenon in general.

which the language, customs and values were similar to those known in Iberian societies (Hordes 2005, 45–46; Alberro 2001, 174).

4 Who Arrived in Colonial Hispanic America?

In spite of the fact that 'New Christians' came from different parts of Europe and settled in different cities and towns on the American continent, the documents from the three American Tribunals of the Inquisition demonstrate that many of them belonged to the same social-ethnic group. This allows us to formulate a general picture of the profile of the converso immigrants.

One of the most prominent characteristics of this group was their Portuguese origin. The great majority of the individuals accused of Judaizing by the American tribunals were either born in Portugal or had a Portuguese family connection. Of the people whom the Mexican Inquisition accused of Judaizing between 1589 and 1604, 73% were born in Portugal. 43% of the Spanish-born Mexicans accused of 'judaizing' from this period were from towns close to the border with Portugal, while the parents of many others were born in Portugal (Gitlitz 2019, 95). The data from the Peruvian Inquisition reveals the same tendency. As Schaposchnik affirms concerning the people sentenced in the context of the "Great Complicity" (1635–1639), the vast majority were born in Portugal, while a substantial minority were from Spain, most of whom had family connections to Portugal. Only one was born in the 'New World' (Schaposchnik 2015, 105–106). In Cartagena, 83.6% of the prisoners suspected of observing Jewish practices were born in Portugal and a large percentage of the rest, born in Spain, had family origins in Portugal (Moreno-Goldschmidt 2018, 96–97).

Since we are interested in understanding the general phenomenon of the 'New Christians' in the Americas rather than just the 'crypto-Jews', it is very important to mention what Kaplan has explained in various contexts:

> The Marranos in colonial America were part of a great diaspora that encompassed almost the entire world from the Ottoman Empire to Mexico, from North America to Goa, from the Iberian Peninsula to Peru. The feeling of belonging to a common ethnic group, the Nação, connected individuals and families who did not always share the same religion [. . .] However, relations between the Jews and the conversos were not always serene, and harmony did not always prevail among members of the respective groups. There is no lack of cases in which the difference in religion gave rise to tension, rivalry, and conflict. (Kaplan 2013, x–xi)

Most of the Portuguese immigrants in Spanish America were part of this *Nação* regardless of their beliefs or degree of identification with the Jewish legacy of their ancestors. In this sense, not just the numbers of prisoners of the Inquisition, but also the very presence of individuals of Portuguese origin may serve as an indication of the dimensions of the phenomenon and of the impact of this group during the colonial period. Thus, it will be relevant to mention the presence of Portuguese beyond the context of the Inquisition.

Of course, in areas where the Inquisition was active, this persecutory body put not all Portuguese inhabitants on trial. Thus, it is also important to understand their proportion among the general population. For example, in the mining centers of New Spain such as Pachuca or Zacatecas, the Portuguese population rates attained 15 percent; this was also the case in the port of Veracruz and in such big cities as Guadalajara and Mexico City (Israel 1990). As for Cartagena de Indias and according to the statistics presented by Vila Vilar, in the year 1630, there were around 1,500 residents; of these, 193 were foreigners, 154 of whom were Portuguese. In other words, the Portuguese constituted about 80% of the foreigners in the city. And perhaps most significantly, they made up 10% of the overall Caucasian population (Vila Vilar 1979, 4).[8]

A second general characteristic of this group was its deep involvement in commercial activities of various kinds, starting with small peddlers and including some of the most influential traders of the colonial capitals, who were involved in important international commercial networks, such as Manuel Bautista Perez in Lima (Wachtel 2013 [2001], 50–68; Silverblatt 2004, 47–53; Schaposchnik 2015, 59–60, 108–109; Mateus Ventura 2003, 400–404), the Gramajo family in Cartagena (Mateus Ventura 2003, 394–399)[9] and Simon Vaez in New Mexico (Uchmany 1983; Hordes 2005, 37–45, 55–57). Those networks were possible thanks to the wide-ranging connections among members of the *Nação* – both Jews and conversos – in different geographical locations including several cities in Europe, Africa and Hispanic America. In fact, these kinds of commercial links could be found all over Hispanic America. Referring to the Peruvian case, Mateus Ventura argues that family ties functioned as an effective mechanism for the preservation of family and regional belonging. The sense of belonging of a shared heritage, allied to religious complicities maintained in secrecy, completed the defining triangle of their commercial association criteria. The lasting contact and distribution of commercial interests between family members who remained in Portugal or Seville and those who were in Peru conferred on some families the status of a transatlantic structure (Mateus Ventura 2003, 393–394). These circumstances were also very common in other enclaves in the 'New World'. Ventura's analysis is largely correct, except for the assessment of the religious element, particularly with regards to the range attributed to it. While it is true that in many cases the fact of secret religious complicity under dangerous circumstances could have strengthened the trust and ties between certain merchants of the *Nação*, it is also true that this was not an exclusive characteristic. There are no documents that can corroborate the narrative that all members of the Portuguese nation preserved a 'crypto-Jewish-iden-

---

8 See also: Israel (2002, 29).
9 For more about the Gramajo family in Cartagena de Indias, see Moreno-Goldschmidt (2018, 144–145, 192–197).

tity'. Yet, the awareness of belonging to the same group with its distinct social and commercial relations was a general reality that included sincere Christians, committed 'crypto-Jews' and a wide range of situations in between. Perelis makes a similar assertion regarding the networks among the members of the *Nação* around the world:

> these secret Jewish communities were connected through a complex web of familial, economic, and cultural ties to a global network of fellow conversos and openly professing Jews living throughout Europe and the Americas. (Perelis 2016, 1)

In contrast to Ventura, Perelis points out the contact not just between the 'New Christians' in Hispanic America and other 'New Christians' in the Iberian Peninsula, but also with former conversos who openly returned to Judaism in Western Europe – the 'New Jews', as they are termed by Yosef Kaplan. However, Perelis uses a very problematic conceptual formulation: "secret Jewish communities". In some cases, these communities might have been secret, but they were neither *Jewish* nor *communities*. This probably is a matter of semantics, but it is important to clarify in order to avoid possible confusions. First of all, it should be stated clearly that not all conversos had a 'crypto-Jewish religious identity'. For those who indeed had a religious identity related to their ancestors, Iberian 'crypto-Judaism' during the colonial period was in no way equivalent to normative Judaism. This was not just a matter of being outside of the law and forced into secrecy, but there were deep differences, starting with the fact that the great majority of 'crypto-Jews' had no access to Jewish sources of learning and never experienced a comprehensive Jewish life. Even in cases of great devotion, the lack of knowledge and the absence of normative Jewish traditions and environments led to a new reality in which faith and practices played distinct roles, in contrast to conventional Jewish religion. This situation is described very well by Wachtel:

> Marrano religiosity, diverse and complex, cannot be reduced to these interactions. We know that it comprised a vast horizon of possibilities, and that the tension between Christianity and Judaism also resulted in polemics whose mutual neutralization could lead, if not necessarily to unbelief and skepticism, to a kind of religious relativism. (Wachtel 2013 [2001], 244)

Regarding the concept of "communities" used by Perelis, it is also imperative to make a clear distinction, especially considering that this term is commonly used to refer to the administrative and social structures of centers of Jewish life in different historical contexts. The Jewish communities of the world have nothing in common – neither in colonial times nor even today, neither in the context of the Sephardic diaspora nor in any other cultural context – with the cases of 'crypto-Jewish' individuals who came to maintain contact with one another. The 'crypto-Jewish' tradition was mainly kept in the intimacy of the home, and the cases in which some individuals knew about each other and communicated about it usually were spontaneous conversations or, in rare cases, sporadic meetings in which rituals were not always carried out but mainly information was exchanged, accompanied by a mutual declaration of faith. We cannot speak of any official structure or infrastructure, nor of a communal religious life. It would not even be correct to suppose that there was a single religious model, but on the contrary, each individual or family fulfilled their own rules. From no perspective would it be appropriate to refer to these individuals as a religious community.

But what is more important to clarify in this context is that Perelis's statement mistakenly excludes the Portuguese who had no connection with religious Judaism. There were several characteristics and aspects that made these individuals part of a group with a common consciousness of belonging (Gitlitz 2019, 98–102), with Jewish roots probably being one of these. However, identification or commitment to that religion was not necessarily a relevant reality for many of them, and still they were part of the *Nação*.

5 Peru, Mexico and Cartagena – Peculiarities of Each Center

As Wachtel has pointed out, "the history of Marranism on the American continent presents considerable differences by region and period" (Wachtel 2013 [2001], 248), so in spite of the common characteristics described above, it is interesting to examine some of the main peculiarities of the phenomenon in the different areas where the Inquisition had its tribunals in the American continent. Without pretending that the conversos only settled in Peru, Mexico or Cartagena, thanks to the documents produced by the Inquisition, we have much more information about their presence in these geographical areas. Among the differences that we will mention, we will address some social peculiarities as well as some differences regarding the inquisitorial activities of each tribunal.

First, we can consider numbers. Of course, there were no censuses that might provide us with exact data, nor can we accept the premise that the Inquisition arrested and prosecuted all the 'New Christians' on the continent. However, the comparison of the respective numbers of prisoners might help us to understand the dimensions of the phenomenon in each place. According to Hordes, in Mexico, about 250 trials were held of people who can be categorized as 'judaizing' 'New Christians' (Hordes 2005, 59). According to the data provided by Schaposchnik, in Peru during the „Great Complicity" – that is to say, by far the period of the greatest activity against 'New Christians' (1635–1639) – there were approximately 110 trials for the heresy of 'crypto-Judaism' (Schaposchnik 2015, 100). In Cartagena de Indias, throughout all the years of the Inquisition's activity, there were 87 cases of people prosecuted on suspicion of 'crypto-Judaism' (Álvarez Alonso 1999, 117), and during the most active period (between 1610–1660), there were 71 cases (Splendiani 1997, 121–128).

Based on this data, we could infer that the phenomenon was significantly more prominent in Mexico, followed by Peru and finally by Cartagena as the area with the lowest rate. However, to this data we must add other factors that may affect this conclusion to some extent. First, it should be noted that the Cartagena tribunal was instituted more than thirty years after the tribunals in Peru and Mexico, which could explain the lower number of 'crypto-Jews' prosecuted in Cartagena. Even so, it should also be noted that the time of greatest activity against 'New Christians' in all three courts only began in the 1630s (Schaposchnik 2015, 79, 82). Another fact to consider in this context is that while the main waves of persecution in Peru and Cartagena took place in the 1630s, in Mexico this happened almost ten years later, which could at least partially explain the higher number of conversos that arrived and settled in the area.

There is another fundamental difference between the Mexican case on the one hand and the cases of Peru and Cartagena on the other, which is possibly also due to the fact that the persecutions in Mexico occurred at a later time, facilitating a more solid establishment of social structures. In the vast majority of cases, those who first arrived in the 'New World' were single men or married men who had left their families behind. In fact, in many cases, the original intention of many of them was not to settle in the 'New World', but to make a fortune and return, or at least to settle and later bring over their families. In fact, in both Peru and Cartagena, almost all 'crypto-Jewish cases' prosecuted by the Inquisition were men. In contrast, the case of Mexico was different. Not only were there several women prosecuted by the said court, but the documents allow us to conclude that some of these women played central roles among the conversos.

It is also interesting to consider the contrast between what was happening in the 'Old' and the 'New Worlds' in terms of the role that women came to play within 'crypto-Jewish' groups. In the Iberian Peninsula, mainly because the only environment in which 'crypto-Jewish' culture could be manifested was not in public but in the private sphere (in most cases, the privacy of the home), women came to play a relatively active and central role (Levin Melammed 1999). In this sense, we can find a greater similarity to the Mexican case (Alberro 2001, 177), in which several families managed to settle and establish themselves in their new American home. On the contrary, the situation in Peru (Schaposchnik 2015, 105–106) and Cartagena was radically different, as it was very rare to find women involved in these affairs. Thus, despite the fact that the converso phenomenon was statistically less significant in Peru and New Granada, it developed there in a very peculiar and almost unique direction.

One final point to be mentioned in this context is the question of endogamy. It is well known that one of the tendencies among the converso groups in their different enclaves was the inclination to form endogamous families. This trend can be observed both in the case of Mexico (Uchmany 1983, 129–130) and, in lower numbers, in that of Peru. However, in New Granada, the men who got married or involved in stable concubinage did so with local or 'Old Christian' women. In fact, we know about these cases thanks to the defendants' arguments regarding the difficulty or impossibility of observing 'crypto-Judaism' due to their 'Old Christian' spouses (see, for example, Moreno-Goldschmidt 2018, 146–148, 201–202).

There is still another interesting difference between the respective activities of the American Tribunals of the Inquisition. The concept of "Great Complicity" is widely used in the study of the Inquisition in the Americas. Since colonial times, this has been the concept used to refer to the period of peak activity against alleged 'crypto-Jews'. These were waves of incrimination in which, after a chain of testimonies, a very large number of individuals were prosecuted on suspicion of 'crypto-Judaism'. Each of the American courts had its "Great Complicity" and, in fact, the long list of incriminations that were collected in these testimonies on many occasions also involved individuals who were in other geographical locations, both in the American continent and in Europe. In these cases, the agents of the Inquisition sent the testimonies to their colleagues in the various inquisitorial branches so that they could continue with the investigation in the areas under their jurisdiction. In fact, it should be observed that the "Great Complicity" in Cartagena began after a testimony that had arrived from Peru. The chain of testimonies in Peru started in 1634; in 1639, the great *auto-da-fé* took place in which the convicts of the Great Peruvian Complicity were sentenced. In the case of Cartagena, the chain of testimonies of the "Great Complicity" also took place in the second half of the 1630s. However, and in spite of the fact that some accusations were sent from the latter two tribunals to Mexico, the "Great Complicity" took place there only years later, between 1642 and 1649 (Uchmany 2001, 198; Uchmany 1983, 139).

Why did the peak of persecutions take place later in Mexico than in Peru and Cartagena, and in spite of the fact that the converso phenomenon was apparently more significant in Mexico?

Both Hordes and Uchmany identify political reasons for the intensification of the persecution of the Portuguese 'New Christians' in Mexico – particularly the separation of Spain and Portugal in 1640 and the dismissal of the Count-Duke of Olivares by King Felipe IV in 1643 (Hordes 2005, 50–55; Uchmany 1983, 132–134). This argument could be very persuasive, especially taking into consideration the chronological proximity of the said political changes to the dates of the persecutions in Mexico. However, a panoramic analysis allows us to understand that these could not have been the only reasons, because they do not explain why no particular waves of persecution against the Portuguese took place in Cartagena and Peru in the 1640s, nor do they explain why the accusations coming from the other "Great Complicities" of the 1630s did not lead to significant trials in Mexico.

Alberro, who like the other two scholars mentioned above also explains the persecutions of the 1640s in light of the aforementioned political events (Alberro 1988, 533–545), argues that the reason for the relatively low rate of persecutions during the 1630s in the Mexican context was the close relations between the Portuguese 'New Christians' and the inquisitors (Alberro 2001, 181). But in fact, it is not just from Mexico, but also from Cartagena that we have proofs of close ties of this kind

(Moreno-Goldschmidt 2016a), and yet these relationships did not prevent the chain of accusations and inquisitorial trials against conversos in the New Granadan context.

There is also the possibility that the reasons that led to different courses of action in the various courts did not have to do with large-scale policies but, on the contrary, with the inquisitorial agents in power. It is worth pointing out, for example, a particular figure: Juan de Mañozca was involved in the three American courts at different times, starting in Cartagena as an inquisitor and later presiding over the institution in Peru during the main wave of persecutions against the 'New Christians' that culminated in the *auto-da-fé* of 1639 (Silverblatt 2000). In the 1640s, when the great wave of persecution took place in Mexico, he was Mexico's bishop and archbishop, while his cousin Juan Sáenz de Mañozca was inquisitor (Uchmany 1983). This idea might provide an explanation, but it should be studied in greater depth before a conclusion can be reached.

It is almost impossible to trace the further history of the Portuguese 'New Christians' who lived in Spanish America during the colonial era to our own times. Some conversos possibly returned to Europe and subsequent generations of those who remained in America integrated into the local population. We cannot refer to a community that maintained a consciousness of belonging throughout the intervening centuries. In some specific cases, there are families who believe they are descended from these conversos (Hordes 2005, xvii), but it is not possible to speak of a Jewish continuity that reaches to the present time.

6 The First Jews on the American Continent and the Modern Jewish Communities

As we have already mentioned, Jewish presence was officially prohibited in all Spanish and Portuguese colonies. After the Dutch expeditions organized by the West India Company, the first Dutch colonies in the 'New World' emerged in the first half of the seventeenth century, and with them came the possibility of legal and official Jewish immigration to the American continent. Indeed, in Recife, the first Jewish community, *Tzur Israel*, was established, and after the reconquest of this city by the Portuguese forces, many of its members moved to Curaçao, where the *Mikve Israel* community was founded in 1659, building the first synagogue in American history (Emmanuel and Emmanuel 1970, 51–61). Most of these Jews came from Amsterdam and originally belonged to the same group of Portuguese 'New Christians' as those who were prosecuted by the Spanish Inquisition in Peru, Mexico and Cartagena, with the difference that, before arriving in America, they had officially adopted Judaism and formed part of a normative Jewish community. Moreover, once in the Dutch colonies in America, they continued to be allowed to openly live Jewish lives, in contrast to the Spanish and the Portuguese colonies (Emmanuel and Emmanuel 1970, 37–98).

With the very beginning of the Republican period in the first decades of the nineteenth century, apparently thanks to the support offered by the Jews of Curaçao to Simón Bolívar (Emmanuel and Emmanuel 1970, 295–301), the "Libertador" authorized entry and freedom of residence to all people without distinction of religion or origin. Once these policies were established, many Sephardic Jews migrated, mostly from the Dutch colonies, to the various territories under the rule of Bolívar, mainly in today's borders of Venezuela and Colombia, along the Caribbean coastline. In terms of Jewish practice, these small communities maintained connections with and functioned primarily under the guidance of the *Mikve Israel* community of Curaçao, which by then was well established and had a stronger tradition, but they did not build solid and independent community infrastructures and, for the most part, assimilated over the course of a few generations (Sourdis Najera 2001, 155–159).

Some waves of migration that are worth mentioning although they were not especially large began to take place in the first half of the nineteenth century. These were two independent processes, one beginning in Germany and England (Martínez Ruiz 2021; Avni 1992, 106–112) and the other in Morocco (Avni 1992, 102–106). However, the Jewish communities that exist today in all Latin American countries are in their vast majority the result of migration processes that began in the second half of the nineteenth century and whose peak took place in the first half of the twentieth century. These were mainly due to the respective economic and political crises both in Eastern Europe (Avni 1992, 157–192; Laikin Elikin 1998, 51–71), where the largest Jewish community of the time was located, and in the decaying Ottoman Empire (Bejarano 2012).

Bibliography

Works Cited

Alberro, Solange. *Inquisición Y Sociedad En México, 1571–1700*. Mexico City: FCE, 1988.
Alberro, Solange. "Crypto-Jews and the Mexican Holy Office in the Seventeenth Century." *The Jews and the Expansion of Europe to the West 1450–1800*. Eds. Paolo Bernardini and Norman Fiering. New York, Oxford: Berghahn Books, 2001. 172–185.
AGI, Santa Fe 37, R6, N69. Carta del gobernador Pedro de Lodeña fechada el 13 de agosto de 1586.
Álvarez Alonso, Fermina. *La Inquisición En Cartagena de Indias Durante El Siglo XVII*. Madrid: Fundacion Universitaria Espanola, 1999.
Avni, Haim. *Judíos En América*. Madrid: Editorial MAPFRE, 1992.
Beinart, Haim. *Conversos on Trial: The Inquisition in Ciudad Real (Hispania Judaica)*. Jerusalem: Hebrew University Magnes Press, 1981.
Beinart, Haim. "The Conversos in Spain and Portugal in the 16th to 18th Centuries." *Moreshet Sepharad. The Sephardi Legacy*. Vol. 2. Ed. Heim Beinart. Jerusalem: Hebrew University Magnes Press, 1992. 43–67.

Bejarano, Margalit. "The Sephardic Communities of Latin America." *Contemporary Sephardic Identity in the Americas*. Eds. Margalit Bejarano and Edna Aizenberg. New York: Syracuse University Press, 2012. 3–30.
Caro Baroja, Julio. *Inquisición, brujería y criptojudaísmo*. Barcelona: Galaxia Gutenberg, 1996a.
Caro Baroja, Julio. *Los judíos en la España moderna y contemporánea*. Madrid: Istmo, 1996b.
Céspedes del Castillo, Guillermo. "La organización del espacio físico y social." *Historia general de América Latina* 3.1 (1999): 57–74.
Contreras, Jaime. "Family and Patronage: The Judeo-Converso Minority in Spain." *Cultural Encounters: The Impact of the Inquisition in Spain and the New World*. Eds. Mary Elizabeth Perry and Anne J. Cruz. Berkeley: University of California Press, 1991. 127–145.
Davis, Natalie Zemon. *The Return of Martin Guerre*. Harmondsworth: Pinguin Books, 1985.
Dedieu, Jean Pierre. "The Archives of the Holy Office of Toledo as a Source for Historical Anthropology." *The Inquisition in Early Modern Europe*. Eds. Gustav Henningsen, John Tedeschi, and Charles Amiel. Dekalb: Northern Illinois University Press, 1986.
Domínguez Ortiz, Antonio. *Los judeoconversos en España y América*. Madrid: Istmo, 1988.
Domínguez Ortiz, Antonio. *La clase social de los conversos en Castilla en la Edad moderna*. Madrid: Csic, 1991.
Domínguez Ortiz. Antonio. *Los judeoconversos en la España moderna*. Madrid: Editorial Mapfre, 1993.
Domínguez Ortiz, Antonio. "Las presuntas 'razones' de la Inquisición". *Historia de la Inquisición en España y América* 3 (2000): 57–82.
Emmanuel, Isaac S., and Suzanne A. *History of the Jews of the Netherlands Antilles*. Vol. 1. Cincinnati: American Jewish Archives, 1970.
Escandell Bonet, Bartolomé. "Estructura geográfica del dispositivo inquisitorial americano." *Historia de la Inquisición en España y América*. Vol. 2. Madrid: Biblioteca de Autores Cristiano, 1993. 48–60.
Garavaglia, Juan Carlos, and Juan Marchena Fernández. *América Latina de los orígenes a la independencia*. Barcelona: Crítica, 2005.
García Cárcel, Ricardo. "Son creíbles las fuentes inquisitoriales." *L´Inquisizione romana: metodologia delle fonti e storia istituzionale*. Trieste: Edizioni Università di Trieste, 2000. 103–116.
Ginzburg, Carlo. *The Cheese and the Worms: The Cosmos of a Sixteenth-Century Miller*. Baltimore: Johns Hopkins University Press, 1982.
Gitlitz, David. *Living in Silverado – Secret Jews in the Silver Mining Towns of Colonial Mexico*. Albuquerque: University of New Mexico Press, 2019.
Granjel, Mercedes. "Judaísmo y pureza de sangre en la Universidad de Salamanca: la formación del médico en el siglo XVI." *Proyección histórica de España en sus tres culturas: Castilla y León, América y el Mediterráneo*. Ed. Eufemio Lorenzo Sanz. Valladolid: Junta de Castilla y León, Consejería de Cultura y Turismo, 1993. 295–302.
Hordes, Stanley M. *To the End of the Earth: A History of the Crypto-Jews of New Mexico*. New York: Columbia University Press, 2005.
Israel, Jonathan I. "The Portuguese in Seventeenth Century Mexico". *Empires and Entrepots: The Dutch, the Spanish Monarchy and the Jews, 1585–1713*. London: Hambledon Press, 1990.
Kaplan, Yosef. "Foreword." *The Faith of Remembrance*. Nathan Wachtel. Philadelphia: University of Pennsylvania Press, 2013. ix–xiv.
Laikin Elikin, Judith. *The Jews of Latin America*. New York: Holmes and Meier, 1998.
Levin Melammed, Renée. *Heretics or daughters of Israel?: the crypto-Jewish women of Castile*. New York: Oxford University Press, 1999.
Liebman, Seymour B. *Requiem por los olvidados – los judíos españoles en América 1493–1825*. Madrid: Altalena, 1984.

Madariaga, Salvador de. *Christopher Columbus: Being the Life of the Very Magnificent Lord Don Cristóbal Colón*. New York: Macmillan, 1940.

Martínez, María Elena. *Genealogical Fictions: Limpieza de Sangre, Religion, and Gender in Colonial Mexico*. Stanford: Stanford University Press, 2008.

Martínez Ruiz, Enrique. "Los asquenazíes del Caribe: redes transatlánticas de comercio y migración entre Frankfurt y Bogotá, a través del Imperio británico en el siglo xix." *Historia Crítica* 80 (2021): 57–79.

Mateus Ventura, Maria d. G. A. "Los judeoconversos portugueses en el Perú del siglo XVII – Redes de complicidad." *Familia, Religión y Negocio – Sefardismo en las relaciones entre el mundo ibérico y los Países Bajos en la Edad Moderna*. Eds. Jaime Contreras, Bernardo José García García, and Juan Ignacio Pulido Serrano. Madrid: Fundación Carlos de Amberes, 2003. 391–406.

Moreno-Goldschmidt, Aliza. "Portuguese New Christians among the Local Elites in Seventeenth-Century Cartagena de Indias." *Journal of Levantine Studies* 6.1–2 (2016a): 295–312.

Moreno-Goldschmidt, Aliza. "Integración religiosa y social de los conversos en las comunidades de la Diáspora Sefardí Occidental a la luz de fuentes Inquisitoriales." *Sefarad* 76.1 (2016b): 159–196.

Moreno-Goldschmidt, Aliza. *Conversos de origen judío en la Cartagena colonial – vida social, cultural y económica durante el siglo XVII*. Bogotá: Pontificia Universidad Javeriana, 2018.

Netanyahu, Benzion. "¿Motivos o pretextos? La razón de la Inquisición." *Judíos. Sefaraditas. Conversos – La expulsión de 1492 y sus consecuencias*. Ed. Ángel Alcalá Galve. Valladolid: Ambito, 1995.

Novinsky, Anita. "Consideraciones sobre los cripto-judíos hispano-portugueses: el caso de Brasil." *Judíos. Sefaraditas. Conversos – La expulsión de 1492 y sus consecuencias*. Ed. Ángel Alcalá Galve. Valladolid: Ambito, 1995. 513–522.

Perelis, Ronnie. *Narratives from the Sephardic Atlantic: Blood and Faith*. Indianapolis: Indiana University Press, 2016.

Révah, Israël Salvator. "Les Marranes." *Revue des Études Juives* I.CXVIII (1959–1960): 3–77.

Rivkin, Ellis. "The Utilization of Non-Jewish Sources for the Reconstruction of Jewish History." *Jewish Quarterly Review* Vol. XLVIII (1957–1958): 183–203.

Rivkin, Ellis. "How Jewish were the New Christians?" *Hispania judaica. Studies on the History, Language, and Literature of the Jews in the Hispanic World. I: History*. Eds. Joesp Maria Solà-Solé, Samuel G. Armistead, and Joseph H. Silverman. Barcelona: Puvill, 1980. 105–115.

Schaposchnik, Ana E. *The Lima Inquisition – The Plight of Crypto-Jews in Seventeenth Century Peru*. Madison: The University of Wisconsin Press, 2015.

Sicroff, Albert A. *Los estatutos de limpieza de sangre: controversias entre los siglos XV y XVII*. Madrid: Taurus, 1985.

Silverblatt, Irene. "New Christians and New World in Seventeenth-Century Peru." *Comparative Studies in Society and History* Vol. 42.3 (2000): 524–546.

Silverblatt, Irene. *Modern Inquisitions: Peru and the Colonial Origins of the Civilized World*. Durham: Duke University Press, 2004.

Sourdis Najera, Adelaida. *El registro oculto: los sefardíes del Caribe en la formación de la nación colombiana, 1813–1886*. Bogotá: Ministerio de Educación Nacional, 2001.

Splendiani, Anna María. "Cincuenta años de Inquisición en el Tribunal de Cartagena de Indias, 1610–1660." Vol. 4. Bogotá: Centro Editorial Javeriano, Instituto Colombiano de Cultura Hispánica, 1997. 121–128.

Uchmany, Eva Alexandra. "Simón Vaez Sevilla." *Michael: On the History of the Jews in the Diaspora* 8 (1983): 126–161.

Uchmany, Eva Alexandra. "The Participation of New Christians and Crypto-Jews in the Conquest, Colonization, and Trade of Spanish America, 1521–1660." *The Jews and the Expansion of Europe to the West 1450–1800*. Eds. Paolo Bernardini and Norman Fiering. Herndon: Berghahn Books, 2001. 186–202.

Vila Vilar, Enriqueta. "Extranjeros en Cartagena (1593–1630)." *Jahrbuch für Geschichte Lateinamerikas. Anuario de Historia de America Latina* 16 (1979): 147–184.
Wachtel, Nathan. "Marrano Religiosity in Hispanic America in the Seventeenth Century." *The Jews and the Expansion of Europe to the West 1450–1800*. Eds. Paolo Bernardini and Norman Fiering. Herndon: Berghahn Books, 2001. 149–171.
Wachtel, Nathan. *The Faith of Remembrance: Marrano Labyrinths*. Tr. Nikki Halpern. Philadelphia: University of Pennsylvania Press, 2013 [2001].
Wiesenthal, Simon. *Sails of Hope: The Secret Mission of Christopher Columbus*. New York: Macmillan, 1973.
Yerushalmi, Yosef Hayim. *From Spanish Court to Italian Ghetto*. Seattle and London: University of Washington Press, 1971.

Further Reading

Feros, Antonio. *Speaking of Spain: The Evolution of Race and Nation in the Hispanic World*. Cambridge: Harvard University Press, 2017.

IV **The Twentieth Century**

Silvia Schenkolewski-Kroll
12 The Twentieth Century in Iberian and Latin American History

Abstract: The chapter surveys twentieth century Jewish communities in Spain, Portugal, and Latin America (without the Caribbean). These countries absorbed Jewish immigrants under different circumstances: in Iberia Jews returned after centuries of expulsion; in Latin America the chapter traces how Jewish life was organized depending on political and social conditions in each country. 17 countries are surveyed; 14 of them in detail according to their importance on the basis of communal organization, with emphasis on the important communities of Argentina and Brazil, while 3 others were places of random Jewish settlement. The country surveys are preceded by a comparative discussion of issues common to the shaping of the communities, such as relations abroad, influence on immigration, and settlement policy. The conclusion from the comparative and differential analysis is that domestic policy in each country, coupled with worldwide factors such as the Holocaust and the establishment of Israel, contributed to the organizational patterns of the individual communities so as to meet their communal, cultural, and religious needs. In addition, they maintained trans-national ties that ensured their relationship with Israel.

Key Terms: Iberia, Latin America, Twentieth Century, Jewish Communities

1 Introduction

This chapter is structured according to the states that comprise the present-day geographical distribution of the countries surveyed. It will begin with Spain and Portugal, the two mother-countries of Latin America. A general introduction will be followed by the individual states themselves. The order is neither geographic nor alphabetical: at first it follows the level of importance of the Jewish community in each state, which explains why Argentina comes first, followed by Brazil, Chile, Uruguay, and Mexico. The order of countries with smaller Jewish communities is arbitrary, followed by those in which no organized community existed, due to the small number of Jews residing there.

The subjects discussed for each country depend to a great extent on published research dealing with them. In every case, the dominant issues are relations between government, the majority society, and the Jewish community; the threefold relationship between government, community, and the State of Israel; communal organization; diverse ideologies and political groupings; education; press; and culture. The headings intend to reflect the essence of what is discussed in each sub-section of the chapter.

Due to the importance of Argentina and Brazil, and the fact that they are dealt with at relatively greater length, additional sub-headings have been added.

This chapter addresses the twentieth century with its prolegomena and its consequences, if it is necessary, regarding the Jewish history in Iberia and Latin America (except for the Caribbean area that is addressed in another chapter). These two geopolitical areas have idiomatic common denominators (Spanish and Portuguese); having being Latin American countries the most important part of Spain and Portugal colonies, with all that means regarding social and cultural heritage. Regarding Jews, there is no doubt about the rich history in both kingdoms, since the Visigoth era, through the Muslim and Christian domains, until late fifteenth century, id est, the expulsion of the Jews from Spain (1492) and the forced conversion in Portugal four years later (1496). Given the coincidence of the above-mentioned facts with the discovery of the New World, both in the metropolis and the colonies, the presence of Jews and the practice of Judaism became illegal. Its observance and its punishment were implemented by the Inquisition of the two countries, both in Europe and in America. This situation continued up to the nineteenth century, when the final abolition of the Inquisition took place in Spain (1834) and in Portugal (1923), as well as the independence of all the colonies that brought about, in both cases, freedom of worship (Avni 1992, 19–55, 97–102).

From that moment on, the history of the Jewish presence in Iberia and its colonies in America splits in two. From the last decades of the nineteenth century, immigrants who legally live as Jews, who gather in some sort of communities and then in proper communities, started to arrive to both sides of the Atlantic Ocean. These are parallel, not related processes (Avni 1992, 157–198).

2 Spain: From Toleration to Legal Status

In Spain, the step that followed the abolition of the Inquisition was, in 1869, the abolition of the Decree of Expulsion, according to the liberal Constitution passed the same year. In practice, there was a Jewish immigration with isolated cases, especially from the North of Africa, who came to be a thousand people at the beginning of the twentieth century. The first synagogue opened its doors in 1917, and it worked under the name of "oratory", a fact that is not strange taking into account that the Constitution of the Restoration in 1876 prohibited the public worship of creeds that were not the Catholic creed. In 1924, under a constitutional monarchy regime, the descendants of the people expelled from Spain received the Spanish citizenship, something that benefited especially the Jews from the Balkans and had repercussions during the Second World War when, sheltering in this citizenship, 3,235 Jews could be saved. During the times of the Second Republic and until the start of the Civil War, Jewish refugees came from Germany (Avni 1982a, 172).

Spain under Franco's regime stayed officially neutral during the entire Second World War (even showing sympathy to the Nazi regime). Haim Avni, in his book *España, Franco y los Judíos* (1982), comes to the conclusion that the *Generalísimo* allowed the arrival of Jews into Spanish land, but he didn't have any interest in that the Jewish refugees settled in the country. That was the reason why he received them without discrimination when they were part of groups of refugees of other nationalities, but that was not the case when they were isolated Jews or Jewish groups. The policy was that Spain was a place of passage to other destinations. According to Avni, Franco could have done greater efforts to save Jews, including those with the Spanish citizenship. On the other hand, countries like United States and Great Britain could have pressed on the regimen, but they did not do it, neither aid organizations like JDC (Joint) could act in the best way, partly because of the lack of support from a well-organized local Jewish community. Only at the end of the war, when it came to the Hungarian Jews, the allied powers put pressure on Spain, and this country managed to save 4000 Jews granting them visas. In total, 11,535 Jews found shelter in Spain or through Spain (Avni 1982a, 173–193).

The end of the war did not bring about changes in the legal situation of Jews in Spain. They kept being, like the rest of the non-Catholics, people who could practice their worship only in private. Only in the 1960s and as a consequence of the bonds with the United States and an opening to the world fostered by the increasing tourism, there was a possibility of change. In 1968, on the occasion of the consecration of Madrid's synagogue, the 1492 edict of expulsion was abolished again, like in 1868, but not their legal situation. Only with the enactment of the new Constitution in 1978, the "ideological, religious and worship freedom of individuals and communities" was achieved (Avni 1982a, 195–209). According to this Constitution, in 1992, Agreements regulating the situation of non-Catholics, even the Jews, were reached. But the previous legal situation didn't prevent the growth of Jewish communities. Several thousands of Moroccan Jews arrived in the 1950s and 1960s, and in the 1970s they were joined by Jews coming especially from Argentina, seeking shelter from the persecutions of the Military Board (Avni 1982a, 199–200).

The community not only grew numerically but, from the 1950s and 1960s, community services started to be organized in Madrid, like a synagogue that, in 1968, laid publicly its cornerstone, adding to its functions the activities of a community center. Also in those years, an elementary school and the Macabi youth organization were founded. At the end of the 1970s, there were in Spain two well-organized communities in Madrid and in Barcelona, and there were also others of lesser importance in Seville, Malaga and Valencia. In 1965, the Sephardic Federation of Spain (Federación Sefaradí de España) was founded as the representative of the communities before the Spanish government and the Jewish World Congress. A maximum expression of the relationships between the government and the Jewish community of Spain was the visit of King Juan Carlos to the synagogue at Balmes street in 1992, on occasion of the 500th anniversary of the expulsion of the Jews from Spain (Rein and Weisz 2011,

174–175). Despite this, at late twentieth century, there still was a feeling of "otherness" regarding the Jew, or as Rein and Weisz express (2011, 173): "Without a doubt, the secular Christian anti-Semitism, reinforced by modern anti-Semitic movements in other European nations, keep influencing the image of the Jew in Spain".

3 Portugal: Return, Crypto-Jews, and Refugees

With regard to Portugal, as a consequence of the liberal revolution in 1820, the General Courts not only abolished the Inquisition, but also declared that all Jews, and not only the descendants of the expelled, could go back to Portugal. This statement materialized when at late nineteenth century an immigration of Jews from North Africa, especially from Morocco, began. In 1892, the Moroccan-Jewish community was officially recognized.

In 1923, an unusual event took place, and it put its seal to the Portuguese Judaism. Samuel Schwartz, a Polish Jew, a mine engineer, got in contact with crypto-Jews in the area of Tras os Montes. This discovery was the beginning of a process of rapprochement and return to Judaism by a community that preserved habits and traditions for centuries. At the same time, an officer from the Portuguese army, Arthur Carlos de Barros Basto, of crypto-Jewish origin, returned openly to Judaism and spread it among the people with his same origin. Barros Basto founded a synagogue in Oporto and another one in Braganza. The discovery of the crypto-Jews aroused special interest within the Sephardic communities of Europe, which tried to help that movement, for example, the "Marrano-Portuguese Committee". Until the first half of the 1930s, this return to Judaism had some success, but not enough to endure, due to the socio-cultural situation of the crypto-Jews and the lack of understanding about it by external elements who saw in the return a mission, without taking into account the actual situation of the objects of their cares (Milgram 1993a).

Portugal, like Spain, remained neutral during the Second World War, which allowed the refugees who escaped from the occupied Europe to have asylum in Portugal, staying in the place or being this country a route to another countries, for example, Cuba. Between July 1940 and December 1941, 8,346 Jews left Lisbon to trans-Atlantic destinations. It should be noted that, during this period, Portugal consuls issued visas and passports to Jewish refugees. At the end of the war, there was a total of 400 Jewish residents and 650 refugees (Wikipedia, 8.1.2020). Up to the end of the Salazar's regime, Jewish presence was tolerated despite some anti-Semitic expressions that were addressed to fight opponents and didn't coincide with the small number of Jews who lived in Portugal. The return to democracy in 1974, the 1976 Constitution and the 2001 Religious Freedom Law completed the legal aspect of the settlement of Jews in Portugal (Martins 2010, 151–153). In 1987, the then president of Portugal Mario Soares apologized to the Jewish communities of Portuguese origin for the responsibility of Portugal related to the Inquisition and the persecutions of Jews. By late twentieth century, there were four communities in Lisbon, Porto, Belmonte, and Madeira. It should be noted that Belmonte's community, officially recognized in 1989, whose members are descendants of crypto-Jews returned to Judaism. In 2003, a population of 5,000 Jews was estimated, mainly Sephardic Jews and descendants of crypto-Jews, and a thousand from Central Europe and refugees of the *Shoah* (Wikipedia, 8.1. 2020).

Both in Spain and in Portugal, they were small communities with a very important historical past, which, thanks to the evolution of thought and the changes in the policies of their governments, could consolidate a Jewish life after hundreds of years.

4 Latin America: International Relations, Emigration, and Settlement Policy Influence Stabilization of the Jewish Communities

The beginning of the twentieth century in Latin American found, regarding Jews, processes and facts that were the results of what happened the previous century. Like in Iberia, the abolition of Inquisition and the freedom of worship proclaimed in all the countries of the continent allowed the free admission of Jews, both to Euro-America (countries with a high percentage of European immigration) and to Indo-America (countries with a majority of original and mestizo population). This legal situation favored the rooting and institutionalization of individuals who came the previous century from Northern Africa, Western and Central Europe, and mainly the principle of the creation of community frameworks by the massive immigration coming from Eastern Europe since the last decades of nineteenth century, also from the Ottoman Empire and the Balkans. This occurred both in groups organized by a colonizing institution, Baron Hirsch's JCA, and by immigrants coming by their own means. These facts validate that the reticence of Jews to appear as such before a majority society that still maintained prejudices of Catholic tradition had mostly disappeared (Avni 1992, 157–170).

Internal and external elements that influenced the conformation of Jewish communities of Iberian America can be considered. The first ones include governmental policies and mutual influences in the majority society, and the second ones include the international events, existing also relationships between both of them. Argentina and Brazil were the main countries that developed an immigration policy (Avni 1992, 157–161, 163–164). The external elements most influential in the configuration of the Jewish communities in the territories of Latin America were, on one hand, the events in the international sphere, as the two World Wars, the closing of the immigration to United Stated and, without a comparison, the Nazi regime and its fatal consequences, the Holocaust. On the other hand, the reaction of the different governments to those facts and the internal policies dictated or not by their relations of the local Jewish community and the relations regarding the Jews and the Judaism in general. We should take into account that the creation of the State of Israel (1948) was a new (strong) parameter between the governments and the local communities. We could say that this was a change of status both at the collective level and at the particular one: the fact that the Jews had also a "homeland" as a support.

Since this is about the relationship between different countries, it is not possible to arrive to an absolute periodization, but roughly it can be defined that the international events were the common denominator that influenced in all of them, but, in each particular case, it is necessary to take into account domestic events and local influences. This premise is also valid regarding the anti-Semitism.

During the first half of the twentieth century, the immigration kept flowing to the countries that had a clear immigration policy like Euro-America (Argentina, Brazil, Chile and Uruguay), and also Mexico (Indo-America). Process that underwent a bigger boom in 1922 and 1924 with the closing of the free immigration to the United States (system of quotas), and suffered restrictions during the 1930s and the Second World War due to changes in the policy of the governments abovementioned. On the other hands, on the verge of the Second World War and during the war, countries like Bolivia, Ecuador and Peru allowed the arrival of Jewish refugees who founded new communities (Avni 1992, 274–275). After the creation of the State of Israel, the topic of the Jewish immigration ceased to be a problem in Latin America. The Jewish immigration had as the main goal Israel, including *olim* of Latin America. At the same time, a process of shifting from Iberian America, mainly to the United States, started at the second half of the twentieth century (Della Pergola 2011, 313–327).

All immigration is considered transnational and, in the case of the Jewish immigration, it can be defined as "trans-territorial", because the nationality, in the sense of "people" doesn't change, but the territories or the places of settlement change. Anyways, that immigration brought about a baggage of ideologies that were transplanted to the immigration country, on one hand, they maintained the bonds with the places of origin, and, on the other hand, they served as the basement of new organizations or influenced groups already institutionalized. In our case, both the Zionist movement as its enemies from the left, communists and Bundists, had great influence in those categories. An example of the relationships between the local Zionist movement, the majority society and the governmental spheres was consequence of the creation of the Latin American Department of the Jewish Agency in New York in 1943, with the intention of getting the support of those countries for the postwar policy of the WZO, the creation of a Jewish state, when it was necessary to find a solution for the Holocaust survivors. With that purpose, Committees in support of a Hebrew Palestine (Comités Pro-Palestina Hebrea) were formed in Latin American countries. These influenced on the recognition of a Jewish state. This was the task of local Zionist elements related to famous politicians and intellectuals from each country that organized and promoted the activities of the committees (Avni 1992, 294–296; Avni 1994, 366–368). Methodologically, this introductory survey will take into account shared themes and topics that justify a comparative study, while what distinct characteristics for each country will be discussed separately.

Argentina and Brazil, the two large focus of Jewish immigration had shared prolegomena in the colonizing project of Baron Maurice de Hirsch and its continuation by the JCA (Jewish Colonization Association). The Baron planned the massive immigration of Jews from Russia and their settlement in the North of Argentina, in lands apt to very large-scale colonization. The expert examination verified the impossibility of the project. Therefore, after the Baron's death (1896), JCA tried to consolidate the existing colonies and to found another ones at a pace according to the immigration current selected at the origin (Avni, 2018). In 1913, there were 13 colonies in Argentina (Avni 1982b, 145–165). In the Jewish colonies, the first agricultural cooperatives of Argentina were founded. By 1910, they got to five, and in the period between the two wars they covered all the colonies of the JCA, and the Jewish colonies founded independently. Their mission was to protect the interests of the settlers doing joint transactions to buy machinery and to sell the harvest, as well as representing the interests of the settlers before the colonizing institution. In 1928 the Agrarian Fraternity (Fraternidad Agraria) was founded; it was a second-degree cooperative that gathered all the Jewish cooperatives (Schenkolewski-Kroll, 2001). In that time, mid-1930s, the total amount of settlers in Argentina was 20,382 people settled in 2,833 agricultural unities, plus 13,000 paid workers – JCA owned by then 600,000 hectares. Another 1,120 settlers lived in colonies not related to JCA (Avni 1992, 166).

In Brazil, colonization was more modest. At the beginning of the twentieth century, following the colonizing policy of the state of Rio Grande do Sul, JCA bought land to establish colonies with a mixed agriculture system that required less land that the extensive crops of Argentina. So the Phillipson Colony was founded in 1903 and the Quatro Irmaos Colony in 1911. The latter had, in 1915, 232 families and a total amount of 1,678 personas. In the 1920s, only there were 72 families left, and in the first one, from de 122 family, only 17 remained in 1926 (Avni 1992, 166–167).

The severe JCA's regime regarding the settlers, bad harvests and other calamities provoked that many settlers abandoned the fields and others occupied their places. Some settled as independent farmers, but most of them went to the towns and cities. According to H. Avni, both in Argentina and in Brazil, JCA played an important role in the absorption of Jewish immigration in these countries (Avni 1992, 167).

Parallel to agricultural colonization, masses of immigrant arrived to Euro-America turning it into that. That was the case of Argentina, the South of Brazil, Uruguay and Chile. All of them had a marked immigration policy, but they did not change in the policy of ownership of land or industrialization. This brought about that immigrants had to work as share-croppers or paid laborers in the fields, or focusing in the cities they were engaged in commerce, art crafts or small industries. The independent Jewish immigration suffered the same hardships that the general immigration, with the additional problem of not having generally a country to return. The Jewish population in Argentine came to 115,600 people, on the eve of the First World War. In Brazil, at the end of this war, the number of Jewish immigrants is estimated between 5,000 and 7,000. During the war the total of Jews settled in Uruguay is estimated in 1,700; and in Chile, 500 (Avni 1992, 168–169).

Given the policy of manufactured products import, in the urban scene, the immigrant, in order to survive, only could innovate in the marketing of products and directing their business to the social layers that could not afford to buy merchandise in cash. Therefore, the system of sale in payments by peddlers was created with great success. The peddler supplied their merchandise to Jewish merchants already established, who supplied them with the first products. In Buenos Aires, these sellers in installments organized themselves in cooperatives. Another working possibility would have been to elaborate art crafts products, which was possible when in the middle of the First War the lack of imports influenced on the industrialization of these countries and, as a consequence, there was more employment and the economic well-being increased. The consequence of that situation was a process of deproletarization that was gradually changing the life, work and needs of the immigrants. For example, in the 1920s, there was already in Argentina a group of university professional Jews, who arrived to the country when they were children or were born already in Argentina. In general terms, this process continued later, and, for that reason, most Jews in Euro-America could be considered part of the middle class, devoted to commerce, industries and liberal professions (Avni 1992, 171–172). And some of them belonged to the ends of the scale: the high-middle class or the lower class. This model remains valid until the economic crisis of the end of the century. This crisis that affected communities like the ones in Brazil, Uruguay, Venezuela and specially Argentina was the result of changes in economic policies like the free imports and irruption of chains of supermarkets that ruined small business. The communities had to confront the "new poverty", founding new institutions or adapting the existing ones (Kliksberg 2001).

5 Argentina

5.1 Emigration, the Government, and Majority Society prior to and after the Establishment of the State of Israel

Argentine legislation at the end of the nineteenth century passed the Immigration Law, established the Civil Registry and secular education that prepared the terrain for the settlement of non-Catholic inhabitants. This occurred in an oligarchical republic thirsty of inhabitants but afraid of proletarian elements. In 1902, the Residency Law was passed; it allowed to expel from the country "undesirable" elements. Among them, there were Jews from the entire proletarian spectrum. In 1912, there was an electoral reform required specially by the Radical Party, which led to elections where all the social classes were represented. From the 1916 election to October 1930, date of the military revolution, a period considered the real Argentine democracy took place, all under the administration of the Radical Party. This did not prevent that in January 1919 the Tragic Week occurred, when a workers strike ended up in a confrontation against the police that led to a general strike strongly repressed by the police and the army. This repression policy revealed the fear the dominant class felt for a proletarian uprising like in Germany and Hungary. In this framework, a pogrom in the Buenos Aires Jewish neighborhoods triggered, organized and implemented by the Argentine Patriotic League, which devoted to "hunt the Russian" (the Jews), devastating clubs, libraries and Jewish properties, and arresting hundreds of Jews. All those disasters tried to be justified by the discovery of an alleged Bolshevik plot that intended to establish a Soviet government. The 1930 military revolution, the result of the 1929 crisis, the dissatisfaction with the Radical regime and the expectations of conservatives to go back to power, brought to the administration elements who sympathize with Fascism that stayed in power thanks to the electoral fraud that prevailed until early 1940s. In 1934, when due to the anti-Semitic policy of the Nazi regime the immigration permits were more necessary, they were diminished. The community activities were not restricted, except for the prohibition of using Yiddish in public acts. Despite the great influence of the Nazi propaganda and the abundance of anti-Semitic publications, no law was passed that explicitly discriminated against Jews. When the Peronist regime took power in the 1946 democratic elections, this ambivalence endured, on one hand, Perón tried to win the Jewish public who did not support him in the election and, on the other hand, he allowed that anti-Semitic elements acted freely. From the Jewish point of view, it was a hassle, but they did not hinder their activities like those of the Zionist movement (Avni 1992, 250–253; Schenkolewski-Kroll 1996, 19–31).

The relationships of the triangle formed by the Argentine government, the local community and Israel influenced in different ways in the configuration of Argentine Judaism.

Eichmann's abduction and condemnation (1961, 1963) brought about an explosion of anti-Semitism sustained on what the government defined as the usurpation of Argentine sovereignty. This led to a temporary increase of emigration to Israel. The Six-Day War that won enthusiasm of the local community and the sympathies of the Argentine public in general didn't bring substantial changes in the relationship with Israel (except for *Tnuat Aliá*). The consequence of the crisis of the Yom Kippur War was the beginning of change of perspective that led to a critical glance to Israeli politics. The military regime (1976–1982) produced mass arrests and missing people: among them, the number of Jews was much greater than their percentage within the population. The efforts to release them and offer them sanctuary in Israel by representatives of the Jewish Agency contrasted with the selling of weapons from Israel to Argentina. In all, between 300 and 400 people were saved (Avni 1995; Avni 2001; Senkman 1995; Barromi 1999). The fall of the military regime after the failed

Malvinas War brought about not only the restoration of democracy, but also radical changes in concepts: the acceptance of ethnic-cultural pluralism instead of the ideal of the melting pot so many times trumpeted as an integral part of "Argentinity" (Avni 1995, 377).

The last decade of the century treated here was characterized by facts unknown up to that moment due to their dimension: the economic crisis and the attacks against the Embassy of Israel (1992) and the AMIA building (1994). The deep economic crisis above mentioned led to the impoverishment of part of the Jewish middle class, in a process that was the reversal of the one that had featured the social climbing of the community. That led to the foundation of aid institutions like Tzdaká and the adoption of social measures by the communities. The attacks by foreign terrorist elements that found complicity in Argentina and left 27 dead at the Embassy and 85 at AMIA moved the collectivity and some members decided to emigrate. Given the circumstances and ideological-social changes, the destination of the emigration was not only Israel, but also United States, Canada, Mexico and Spain (Avni 1995, 373; Kliksberg 2000; Blaistein 2000; Escudé and Gurevich 2003).

5.2 Geographical Diffusion and Communal Organization

Of the four republics of the "south cone", Argentine had not only the most numerous Jewish community (it amounted to 282,000 in 1970), but it also was, at the beginning of the twentieth century the most organized. The Jews congregated mainly in some Buenos Aires neighborhoods, in the main inland cities and in surrounding areas of the Jewish colonization. In all of them, there were institutions that provided religious or charitable services. A census carried out by JCA in 1909 confirmed these facts and was the foundation for the configuration of a Jewish education network in the urban centers along with the ones at the colonies. In Buenos Aires the Argentine Republic's Israelite Congregation (Congregación Israelita de la República Argentina) was founded in 1868 by Jews from Western Europe; and the Latin Israelite Congregation (Congregación Israelita Latina, in 1891, by the Jews from Morocco. The Society of Burials of the Ashkenazi from Buenos Aires was founded in 1894. Its institutionalization according to a legislative decree enacted by the Argentine government regulating the activities of the mutual associations (1938), and the expansions of its functions established the AMIA (Israelite-Argentine Mutual Association, by its acronym in Spanish: Asociación Mutual Israelita Argentina) in 1941. Other institutions that had a crucial relevance in health and social aid were also created, like the Israelite Worker Union (Unión Obrera Israelita) in 1896. In 1900 the Ezrah Society (Sociedad Ezrah) that founded the Israelite Hospital (Hospital Israelita) was created. Completing the health sector, in 1916 the Argentine Israelite League against the Tuberculosis (Liga Israelita Argentina contra la Tuberculosis) was established. Social aid was concreted when ladies from the Israelite Congregation founded, in 1908, the Aid

Society of Israelite Ladies (Sociedad de Socorros de Damas Israelitas) who sustained an orphan asylum for girls. In 1915, a home for old-aged people was established, to which an orphan asylum for boys was annexed. Continuing the aid to refugees from the First World War, Soup Kitchens and the Israelite Philanthropic Association (Asociación Filantrópica Argentina) were opened. All these institutions were maintained by the installments and donations of thousands of members and adherents in the city of Buenos Aires and cities, towns and colonies in the interior of the country (Schenkolewski-Kroll 1996, 33–36).

In addition, in the interior of the country, there were organized communities that provided services to their members: first of all, traditional burials and religious services, but also education, social assistance, and culture. In 1934, there were in Argentina 800 settlements where Jews lived, whose configuration during the whole twentieth century showed that the majority were in the Great Buenos Aires area. For example, according to the 1960 census, almost 80% of the Jews lived there. Most of the remaining 20% lived in the littoral area (Avni 1972, 14–16).

Along with the institutions founded and sponsored by Jewish immigrants from Europe, the Sephardic immigration coming from the Ottoman Empire was additional to the Moroccan immigration above mentioned. The Sephardic Jews from Turkey organized several societies that were not connected between them and they just achieved a common organization in the 1940s with the foundation of the Israelite-Sephardic Community Association (Asociación Comunidad Israelita-Sefaradí). The Jews from Syria, Aleppians and Damascenes, more religious than other Jews, mainly the first ones, also configured their religious and educational institutions. Unless the Ashkenazi who, regardless their internal differences, sought the common denominator to join forces, the Sephardic sector prevailed in remaining faithful to the ancestral origin of each group. There were adherents to the Zionist movement, but they did not have the politization of the Ashkenazi sector. In 1972, the FESELA (Latin American Sephardic Federation, by its acronym in Spanish: Federación Sefaradí Latino-Americana) at the request of the Zionist World Organization, opening branches all over Latin America. Buenos Aires was one of the main points where it activated the CIDICSEF (Center of Research and Diffusion of the Sephardic Culture, by its acronym in Spanish: Centro de Investigación y Difusión de la Cultura Sefaradí), which published *Sefardica*. In a total of 187,000 Jews in 2003, in the relation of the 37,400 Sephardic Jews with the majority group, up to the second half of the twentieth century, the last period of the acculturation process, the use of Yiddish was also an obstacle. Only DAIA with the responsibilities it assumed managed, already in the 1930s, a permanent collaboration between both groups (Bejarano 1978; Bejarano 1996; Bejarano 2011).

All these organizations reflected the presence of an organized community that provided services to its members. Parallel and also since the 1870s, the Jewish immigration for human trafficking started, pimps who brought Jewish women and girls from impoverished regions of Eastern Europe to work in the brothels of Buenos Aires and the interior of the country. The fact that the majority society got mixed up or could get mixed up by the decent Jews and the *tmeim* (impure in Hebrew), called like that by the former, was one of the incentive to make an absolute division between them, and even to refuse them the right to a Judaic burial (Avni 1992, 182–183).

5.3 Political-Ideological Movements in Local Communities

Up to the First World War, the political-ideological currents of the Jews in Europe had been consolidated in the local Jewish community. The "Lovers of Zion" were the first ones that organized from 1897, the year of the First Zionist Congress. Then, the immigrants who arrived after the failed 1905 revolution in Russia followed and completed the Jewish political landscape. So we could find all the spectrum of Jewish workers parties in the area of Residency, Galizia and Poland: Poalei Zion (Workers of Zion), territorialists, Bundists, Russian-speaking socialists and different kinds of anarchists (from terrorists to unionists). All of them found an auspicious terrain within the mainly proletarian environment of the local community. The members of the different parties founded clubs and libraries. They organized Jewish labor unions. They made propaganda and tried to publish newspapers that mostly were ephemeral. The most successful were the Bundists, who along with Poalei Zion survived the second decade of last century. The Bundist organization Avangard maintained twelve consecutive years its newspaper *Der Avangard* (1908–1920). The differences between the identification with the Comintern or with the Socialist International marked a gap in the movement. Some of the members who adhered to the first one integrated the Jewish idiom section of the Argentine Communist Party founded in 1920. To that section also the members of the Poalei Zion incorporated after the 1921 schism when they abandoned the Zionist movement. Immigration between wars, especially from Poland, brought about changes in the activities of the Bund. Given the deproletarization process that underwent the Jewish community, Bund started to take care of cultural and educational activities that characterized it the following decades (Schenkolewski-Kroll 1996, 37–38).

The first two decades of the twentieth century, parallel to what was mentioned before, were the years of shaping of the local Zionist movement. Unlike the situation in Europe, where the Zionism tried to conquer firmly rooted communities, in Argentina the Zionist parties took the responsibility of organize them as such, besides concreting their specific goals. The abovementioned "Lovers of Zion" became in 1913 the Zionist Federation, which was recognized by the World Zionist Organization as a "territorial organization". It was the representative of this organization before the local Judaism and, in a certain way, before the official authorities (Schenkolewski-Kroll 1996, 39–49).

The local Poalei Zion, founded in 1906, had two goals in its action, on one hand, as we have seen, as part of the Jewish proletariat, on the other hand, as part of the Zionist movement. It acted almost exclusively in the City of Buenos Aires. Officially according to the WZO, it was considered *Sonderverband* or a special association. The collaboration between them referred specifically to the sale of the *shekel*, before the Zionist Congresses, and the campaigns in support of the National Funds. During the First War, it is worth mention the mass demonstrations due to the Balfour Declaration, which expressed the sympathies of the Jewish community for the Zionism (Schenkolewski-Kroll 1996, 39–49). A more concrete fact was the departure to Europe of 52 volunteers of the local worker Zionism to enroll in the ranks of the Hebrew Battalion (Senkman 1983).

From its first years, the local Zionism asked the central entity to send representatives to take care of propaganda, clarification and education. In 1919, it just achieved that a representative came to the campaigns, being the ideological aspect only a secondary product of the mission. Up until the beginning of the Second World War, that was the WZO policy regarding Argentine Zionism. Only when the European doors were closed, representatives started to arrive with ideological-educational purposes in the formal and non-formal field. This was intensified after the war and it became routine after the creation of the State of Israel (Schenkolewski 1988).

The Zionist Federation and Poalei Zion probably were the most important organizations of the Zionism in Argentina, but they are not the only ones. In 1926, WIZO was founded, named in Argentina OSFA (Organización Sionista Femenina Argentina), with great success and branches in almost every place with Jewish inhabitants. The Revisionist Party dated from 1930 and had separate activities because they separated from the WZO. From mid-1930s youth movements started to act and they were pioneers of the whole range of Zionist ideology. They peaked when they established training farms (*hajsharot*), in 1946 and with the ideological *aliyah* and the foundation of *kibbutzim* after the creation of the State of Israel (Schenkolewski-Kroll 1996, 49; Schenkolewski-Kroll 2005).

5.4 Ideological Movements, Centralized Organization, and Communal Control

As noted above, the Zionist movement considered one of its goals the community organization. The expansion of the domestic and imported anti-Semitism in the fourth decade gave place, in 1935, to the organization of the Delegation of Argentine Israelite Associations (Delegación de Asociaciones Israelitas Argentinas, DAIA), whose objective, up to now is fighting against anti-Semitism and the community representation before the government, the majority society, and also being the representative of Argentine Judaism before transnational Jewish instances. From the beginning, DAIA was the "umbrella institution" for all Jewish organizations in the country, without distinction of class, origin or character. It included all the range of society from Ashkenazi, Sephardic and Oriental Jews' origins. Only the anti-Zionist left forged a parallel organization. The Zionist parties and the institutions that adhered to it, despite being a minority, had a leading role in DAIA's organization and activities. DAIA participated in the foundation of the World Jewish Congress. It led the campaigns to aid the victims of the Second World War; in some opportunities along with Keren Hayesod, and mainly up to now, it kept denouncing every anti-Semitic event perpetrated in the country (Schenkolewski-Kroll 1991; Schenkolewski-Kroll 1996, 233–278).

The second institution to which the Zionist movement directed its efforts was the Burial Society (Sociedad de Entierros), which, in practice, played the role of community. Since the massacre of European Judaism, the Zionist movement felt it was the inheritor of the annihilated communities, and as such, it tried to emulate their intellectual and social values. The Burial Society was the most powerful institution in the community due to its economic solvency from the monopoly on the Ashkenazi burial, which allowed it to donate or invest its money at its discretion. For instances, in 1935, it created the AMIA's Education Commission (*Vaad Hajinuj*), which rendered its services and centralized all Jewish education in Buenos Aires and surrounding areas. With the creation of the State of Israel, after having declared officially being a community (1949) and having passed the electoral reform that allowed a proportional representative system to the result of elections, the Zionist parties had the predominance in AMIA for decades (Schenkolewski-Kroll 1993; Schenkolewski-Kroll 1996, 279–295).

The Communist Jews had a great boom in Argentina during the 1920s and 1930s, it could be said until the creation of the State of Israel. The Soviet Union program of establishing a Jewish settlement in its territory aroused a lot of enthusiasm among a public who found in that program a counter-answer to the Zionist movement. In 1924, Procor (by an acronym in Yiddish, Association for Promoting the Productivization of Declassed Jewish Masses in the Soviet Union) was founded. It backed Gezerd "Organization of Workers' Colonization" (Schenkolewski-Kroll 1990).

At the beginning it had two thousand adherents in Buenos Aires, without taking into account the 23 places in the hinterland, even in the colonies. This identification was not strange because it was a movement with similar objectives. Procor received representatives from the United States in 1929 and 1935, and twice sent delegations to the Jewish autonomous area of Birobidzhan. There was also intent of emigration and colonization of that territory by a group of Jews from Argentina and Uruguay (Schenkolewski-Kroll 2002).

Although, during the war, the Soviet Union was part of the allied powers, the communist Jews kept having a separatist stance regarding the aid to the victims of the war, because the aid backed by DAIA was linked to the collaboration with Zionist funds. Thus, the Organism of Direct Aid to the Jewish Victims of the War in Europe was founded and it sent its money through the Joint. The "conquer of AMIA" was another of the objectives of the communist Jews, being AMIA the most powerful institution in the community due to its economic solvency. The communist Jews took power only in 1946, and kept it partially up to 1948. All the efforts to change the traditionalist-national character of the institution were not successful. The emergence of the State of

Israel was welcomed by the communist Jews and the Soviet Union backed the young state. Following that traditional line marked from Moscow, the approved the trials of Moscow and Prague at beginning of the 1950s. These postures marginalized them in a community that had been conquered by the Zionist movement. The communist Jews endured emphasizing the educational and cultural activities. Among them, the ICUF (by is acronym in Yiddish, Federation of Cultural Jewish Entities of Argentina) theatre and the Domingo F. Sarmiento school (Schenkolewski-Kroll 1990; Schenkolewski-Kroll 1993; Schenkolewski-Kroll 2009; Schenkolewski-Kroll 2011; Senkman 2017).

5.5 Changing Beliefs: From Liberalism to Orthodox, Conservative, and Reform

Up to the 1960s, the Jewish population was in general liberal, not religious, infused of a national character. If it needed religious services, it received them from the orthodoxy. There were isolated cases the Israelite Congregation of the Argentine Republic (CIRA, by its acronym in Spanish: Congregación Israelita de la República Argentina) that practiced a conservative rite. In that decade, on one hand, the influence of Agudat Israel and Jabad increased. The first one managed to have more votes than Mizrahi in the AMIA's elections. The second one increased thanks to a policy of expansion by the Lubawitz rabbi. At the same time, representatives of the conservative and reformist currents arrived from the United States, and they influence massively on the community with the foundation of the Latin American Rabbinical Seminary (Seminario Rabínico Latinoamericano, 1962), which had a conservative nature, occupied and renewing the activity in abandoned temples. All these currents have the common denominator of the place of residency, without aspirations of *aliyah*. Despite that, the general character of the community kept being Zionist and backing Israel (Babis 2009; Schenkolewski-Kroll 2012; Bargman 2017; Goldman 2011).

5.6 Ideological Tendencies and Jewish Education

All these political-ideological currents described above put the accent on the education of the future generations, each one according to their conception of the world. This was noted mainly in the city of Buenos Aires and its surrounding area where most of the Jewish population lived. So, along with traditional *Talmud Torá* schools with a Zionist character and workers' schools, especially Bundist, communist and from Left Poalei Zion were created. This was the school overview when the abovementioned Education Commission was created (Zadoff 1994).

The school politization was less noticeable in the hinterland where, since the beginning JCA founded and maintained the schools in the colonies. When the JCA schools passed to the power of the State, the Jewish part, along with the complementary schools of the provinces passed to the system of the Religious Courses of the Argentine Republic, run by CIRA. All these schools were complementary to the official mandatory education that ruled in Argentina. As a consequence of the foundation of the Federation of Argentine Israelite Communities *Vaad Hakehilot* (Federación de Comunidades Israelitas Argentinas *Vaad Hakehilot*, 1952), two organisms merged in the Central Council of Education *Vaad Hajinuj Hamerkazí* (Consejo Central de Educación Vaad Hajinuj Hamerkazí). A main change in the network of Jewish schools was the result of reforms in the national school system, when in 1967 the complete day of education system was approved; the system did not allow the continuity of the double – a system who did not allow the existing continuity of the whole day education between the public school and the Jewish school. The only solution was the transformation of the Jewish school into a comprehensive school recognized by the government that also taught the official curricula. This model is the one that rules up to now. In the same way, the arrival of the new ideological currents abovementioned diminished the Zionist party influence on education; schools self-defined as keepers of the plurality, as well as the particular Jewish identity were created. Each one of them highlighted its particularity and the relations with a central organism were debilitated (Avni 1985).

5.7 Economic Life, Press, and Culture

The tendency to an economic rise that benefited the community, which from the 1930s established cooperatives of credit and banks, was reflected in a cultural boom both in Yiddish and Spanish. For example, in 1938, 31 periodical publications were published in Yiddish, among them three newspapers, and 27, in Spanish. The data varied and, by the end of the century, digital journalism was added (Avni 1972, 78, 84).

Both in the city of Buenos Aires and the provinces, libraries and cultural societies, which developed their activities in Yiddish and gradually passed to the Spanish language, were created. Among them, the one that considered its goal being a bridge between the Jewish and the Argentine cultures, using the national language, outstood. In 1926, the Argentine Hebraic Society (Sociedad Hebraica Argentina) was founded; for more than ninety years, it developed programs with courses and conferences on Jewish and general history and literature. It published books and philosophical and through journals, like *Davar*. Its library is place for scholars. At the same time, it developed social activities and sports. In the hinterland, Hebraica's activities were emulated founding similar institutions. Informal education, social activities and sports are developed in different environments and, since the 1960s, there is an umbrella organization, FACCMA Argentine Federation of Maccabean Community Centers (Federación Argentina de Centros Comunitarios Macabeos) (Avni 1972, 82–83; Schenkolewski-Kroll 2017a, 73–90; Schenkolewski-Kroll 2017b, 531–546).

6 Brazil

6.1 Stages prior to Communal Organization

As noted, Brazil has a common denominator with Argentina regarding the JCA colonization, but not in the case of its institutional level at the beginning of the twentieth century. There were Sephardic communities organized in the Amazon region and Rio de Janeiro, which were not apt for absorbing Jewish immigration to Eastern Europe. In the south, in Porto Alegre and other villages that surrounded the Jewish colonization, small communities were established. Similar nodes were formed in Curitiba, Salvador, Recife and Natal. Given the characteristics in Río de Janeiro and Sao Paulo, the most important communities were formed there. At the beginning of the century, the spreading across such a big country was related to the newspaper *A Columma*, which concentrated the efforts to defend the honor of the Jews, because the same scourge devoted to human trafficking that disturbed Jews in Buenos Aires existed in Río de Janeiro. This newspaper was not successful regarding its efforts to unite the three communities acting in Rio: the Sephardic community, the Center of Rio de Janeiro, founded in 1912 by francophone people, and the Yiddish speaking Beit Yaacov synagogue. But the newspaper did have positive results backing the Brazilian Committee of Aid to the Victims of the War, founded in 1916. The committee was headed by the leaders of the Zionist organization founded in Rio in 1913. The immigration after the war favored the growth of the communities, especially in Sao Paulo and Río de Janeiro (Avni 1992, 173–174; Milgram 1995).

JCA contributed to their consolidation by sending to Brazil Rabbi Isaías Raffalovich to organize the activities of the different institutions, trying to coordinate them. These efforts were not successful due to the intrinsic differences between the groups. The rabbi did manage, thanks to his official position, to establish good relationships in official spheres and to get the support of rich Jews who were away from the collectivity. In the second half of the 1920s religious, charitable and entertainment institutions emerged; they lasted in the following decades. From these years, there was an abundance of journals in Yiddish (Avni 1992, 182).

6.2 Ideological-Political Movements

The Zionist movement in Brazil had its prolegomena even during Herzl's life, among the Sephardic people from the north of Brazil. The writer of the newspaper *A Columma* already mentioned, backed the Zionist movement in his publication, but he saw in it especially an ideological, not a practical, current, which has to be supported economically. In 1908, the KKL central contacted a Jew from Sao Paulo, originally from Lithuania, to represent the KKL interests in that city and state. The report of the situation he sent to the Zionist central talk about some 200 Jews who do not have any kind of organization and lack community services, who live in the same conditions that the rest of the inhabitants, because there was a separation between the Church and the State and allows the greatest freedom of speech. This apparently optimal situation did not stimulate the identification with Zionism. Only the relatively massive arrival of the immigration from Eastern Europe, rooted in the Jewish tradition, managed to establish permanent Zionist institutions with the impulse given by the Balfour Declaration (Milgram 1995).

Leftist anti-Zionist Jews who arrived in Brazil during the 1920s had influence on the creation of the Brazilian Communist Party (PCB, by its acronym in Portuguese,1922). They were immigrants from Eastern Europe, mainly from Poland and Rumania. We should differentiate between a minority of activists devoted to the revolutionary cause, and the Jews who sympathized with the PCB but not were involved in the clandestine practice. According to Milgram, all of them conformed, within the community framework a subculture that was ruled in Yiddish. As in any Jewish migration process, they found rivals there from the old world like Zionists and capitalists. In 1928, the Brazilian Jewish left was institutionalized with the foundation of the Brazilian Society in support of Judaic Colonization in the Soviet Union BRAZCOR, by its acronym in Portuguese (Sociedade Brasileira Pro-Colonizacao Judaica nao Union Sovietica), which gathered communists and Bundists who backed the policy of productivization of Jewish masses in the Soviet Union. At the same time, given the policy of limitation of the *aliyah* to Eretz Israel of the British mandate, on one hand, and, on the other hand, the initiative of the Soviet Union to institute a federated socialist Jewish republic, the controversy between Zionists and communists reached a peak. In 1934, with the declaration of Birobidjan as an autonomous territory of that republic, the interest increased in the Jewish-communist circles, and delegations from both the United Stated and Argentina traveled there, and there was also an emigration from Argentina and Uruguay to Birobidjan. That was not the case in Brazil: in that country, the identification was limited to economic aid and rhetoric and journalistic propaganda. The newspaper *Der Unhoib* (The beginning) was the spokes media of the communist Jews grouped in the Workers Center Morris Vinchevsky. They had some success founding an elementary school named Arbeter Shule, and a proletarian kitchen named Arbeterkich. The 1935 government repression broke into the kitchen, arrested the people who were there, and some of them were expelled from the country. This coincided with the anti-communist policy of the government, especially noticeable when they were foreign Jews.

Milgram sums up the situation of the communist Jews in the concerned period as a marginal subculture with a universalist ideological orientation. This position did not have chances to thrive in a free enterprise society, without racial impositions and with perspective of fast social promotion. The state repression, the Zionist competition and the practical distancing from the proletarian spheres did not lead to the crystallization of an alternative community organization. Later on, and according to the same community processes in other countries, the creation of the State of Israel finally defined the place of the Brazilian communist Jews (Milgram 2001).

6.3 Changes in Religious Denominations and Their Influence on Education

Parallel to the left organizations mentioned before, during the 1920s and 1930s synagogues were founded in Sao Paulo and Río, many of them according to the origin of their members and the orthodox rite. In 1936, in Sao Paulo, the first liberal synagogue of Brazil was established. According to Marta Topel, with the socio-cultural ascent of the second generation, the perception of the Sao Paulo Judaism from the 1960s could be defined as liberal Judaism, on one hand, and secular Judaism, on the other hand, conforming an ethnic-cultural identity. This changed gradually from the 1980s with the presence of Jabad, the opening of new synagogues and the services added by this current that attracted an audience that went through a process of *hazará betshubá* with all the implications. Topel explains that situation as a consequence of the weakening of some identity models like the communities of origin, the Holocaust and the Zionism. The Brazilian Jewish population achieved a 100.000 people stability that was maintained from the 1980s through the end of the century (Topel 2011; Della Pergola 2011, 315).

Jewish education in Brazil was never centralist like in Argentina; it was characterized by its federal system that comprehended school spread all over the country. From the 1940s, the schools were organized according to the current Jewish-ideological lines, undergoing transformation according to the ideological and social changes in the communities. For instance, the process of *tshuvá* in Sao Paulo brought about a change in the character of educational institutions. Religious educators entered non-religious Jewish schools; new orthodox schools and traditional educational sites *yeshivot* and *kolelim* were created. This does not mean that there was just one general line in the country. The common denominator of all the currents is the preservation of Jewish identity, within an integration process in a multiracial and pluralist society like Brazil's. In the 1990s, 30 Jewish schools were functioning in Brazil; they comprehended half of the 20.000 school age children (Topel 2005).

6.4 Informal Education and Cultural Aspects

Informal Jewish education was represented in Brazil by the same Zionist youth movements, classical pioneers coming from Europe to Euro American countries. They achieved their peak with the creation of the State of Israel and during the following years there was an ideological *aliyah* that ended up with the establishment of Kibbutz Bror Jail and settlement in other existing *kibbutzim*. For both ideological and socio-economic reasons in Israel and Brazil, from the 1970s, they lost their vitality and only remains of them act among the youth and the children of the less favored social layers of the Jewish community, especially Hashomer Hatzair. At the same time, social and sport clubs were formed with the intent of attracting the Jewish youth and avoiding assimilation processes. This kind of institutions became community centers that render different types to services along the life cycle of the members (Chazan 2017).

The most famous example is the Brazilian Association A Hebraica (Associaçao Brasileira A Hebraica) in Sao Paulo, founded in 1953 with the objective of providing the Jewish families an adequate place for entertainment. Since its beginnings, it had a suitable property for sports and social life. In the 1960s and 1970s, it added, following the example of Hebraica Buenos Aires, cultural activities. It managed to have thousands of members becoming a community center that renders services reaffirming Jewish identity in the Brazilian mosaic. Since among their founders there were supporters and activists of the Zionist movement that was its orientation, without getting to a practical Zionism (Unpublished).

6.5 Anti-Semitism and Immigration Policy

Anti-Semitism in Brazil did not have a concrete expression until the fourth decade. With the foundation of the Brazilian Whole Action (1932), with a fascist and top to down orientation, anti-Semitic propaganda started to be published, like the Portuguese translation of the Protocols of the Elders of Zion, adapting them to what they considered the Brazilian reality, besides other 90 publications of the same character. This propaganda was very influential on the middle class, army officers and intellectuals. The president Getulio Vargas, elected in 1930, considered the Action an allied that served him to suffocate leftist uprisings in 1935 and 1937. In this year, they fabricated an alleged uprising, the "Cohen Plan", with a distinctly antisemitic stamp. The direct consequence was the declaration of martial law that brought about the abolition of the Constitution and the instauration of the Estado Novo. The decree (12.3.1937) banned the existence of all political parties and their symbols; even the Action, which tried to rebel without success. "The avenues of direct participation of the organized anti-Semitism in the state power had been cut off, but the ideological affinity with many of those in power remained" (Avni 1992, 253–256).

This situation brought about a policy of obstruction to the arrival of immigrants and refugees when it was most needed. The immigration from Germany quote, specified in the 1934 Constitution, would have allowed the entry of 308 Jews in condition to be farmers. JCA bought the land in Rezende and prepared in Germany families to be colonized. Despite everything, the government refused to give the permits because they were Jews. In other cases, out of the few authorizations the Brazilian diplomats could distribute – 1000 in total, between France, Belgium, and the Netherlands –

only 803 came to be effective. The common denominator was the antisemitic policy of some high ranked officials related to immigration. Despite this situation, an estimated 17,500 Jews entered Brazil during the Nazi era, most of them were claimed by their families, others had special permits got by individuals, and a third group obtained the permanent residence after having disembarked as tourists. In the postwar years up to the 1990s, anti-Semitism was encouraged, not at a large scale, by Nazi elements in the states of the south and by Arab immigrants. That is the reason why it is a Neo-Nazi and anti-Zionist anti-Semitism (Avni 1992, 269–272; Milgram 1993; Avni 2003, 22–25).

7 Chile: A Community Wavering between Local and World Events

As it happened in other countries of the continent, during the second half of the nineteenth century, isolated Jews from Western Europe arrived to Chile with commercial purposes. They got assimilated to the majority society without leaving Jewish heirs (Bohm 1988). The Jews who constituted the base of the community organization came from Eastern Europe and the Ottoman Empire. Part of them came directly and others through Argentina, where some were residents who sought in Chile new horizons, for instance, former JCA settlers. The same adaptation process suffered in other immigration countries occurred also in Chile, as well as the changes in a second generation that acquired liberal professions at the university and was integrated to the life of the country and also to the political parties and even managed to be members of the Legislative branch (Avni 1992, 169, 181; Nes El 1988).

The beginnings of an organized Jewish community in Chile date from 1906 when in Santiago a group of Ashkenazi gathered for the religious services of New Year, but only three years later, they established a religious or social society called the "Commercial Center of Charity" (Centro Comercial de Beneficiencia). The Sephardic people native from Monastir, only in 1916 established in Temuco, in the south of Chile, the "Macedonian Center" (Centro Macedónico). The little tolerant Catholic environment that prevailed in Chile is reflected in the omission of the term "Jewish" or "Israelite" in the name of these societies (Nes El 1988, 167; Avni 1992, 172–173). The Balfour Declaration and the international support obtained led the community activist to add the adjective "Israelite" to the names of their organizations. Chilean Jews convoked a Congress in September 1919, which has representatives of 13 organizations. In that opportunity, the Zionist Federation of Chile (Federación Sionista de Chile) was founded and then was declared the representative institution for the whole collectivity, a function that it maintained. This organization put down roots and kept organizing annual congresses. In 1930, seven organizations from the capital and five from other cities, with a total of 108 delegates, were represented. The union tendency was manifested when, in 1920, the Ashkenazi from the capital had gathered in the Israelite Circle (Círculo Israelita) and four youth organizations of Sephardic and Ashkenazi people were grouped in 1928 in the Israelite Youth Association (Avni 1992, 172–173, 177, 183; Nes El 1988, 169).

During the second half of the 1930s, Chile's Jewish population increased with the arrival of immigrants, mainly refugees of the Nazi regime. In 1935, there were complaints before Chile's president (Arturo Alessandri) because second-level officials placed obstacles to the entry of Jews. This attitude was replaced by a close collaboration between the Ministry of Foreign Relations and the Committee for the Protection of the Israelite Immigrant of Santiago; they reached an agreement that allowed the entry of 60 families each year. The big increase of applications led to up to 300 permits being issued the last months of 1938. Some criticism by the public opinion about the way the entry of immigrants was managed and the complaints about a "Jewish avalanche" led to the cancellation of all the agreements in force. In December 1939, the president ordered the creation of an Investigation Commission to analyze all the procedures regarding Jewish immigration. The disastrous consequence was the official closure of immigration. The estimates are that, during the whole Nazi era, between 10.000 and 12.000 refugees entered Chile (Bohm 1997, 216–222; Avni 1992, 272–273).

Chilean Judaism had communities outside the capital in Valparaíso, Viña del Mar, Temuco, and Concepción. All of them rendered religious and social services according to the circumstances. It can be said that there was an abandonment of the communities of the hinterland and a concentration in Santiago. In 1970, it is estimated that 90% of the Jews lived in the capital. In 1930, the Hebrew Institute for the elementary and secondary education was founded. The Israelite Public Hospital (Policlínico Público Israelita) dates from 1922, and the Israelite Stadium (Estadio Israelita) of a social and sport nature dates from 1948. Macabi is from the 1950s. The local collectivity adopted also organizational types typical of the country, like the creation of groups of volunteer firefighters. Thus the Israel Bomb of Santiago (Bomba Israel) was founded. The year above mentioned, there were 40 Jewish institutions affiliated to the Representative Committee of the Israelite Collectivity of Chile (Comité Representativo de la Colectividad Israelita de Chile). The main organizations were based in the common place of origin of their members. The Zionist Federation, which, in the past, represented the whole collectivity, grouped local representatives of the different political tendencies in force in Israel and it was very important both for its natural activity and for the controlling the recollection of contributions in support of the Zionist cause and the distribution of those funds between the local needs and the donations to Israel. The Representative Committee had a congruent policy of neutrality regarding the Chilean political environment at any level. This policy was put to a test during the 1970 presidential elections that took Allende to power, marking a milestone in the history of the Chilean Judaism. Despite Allende's repeated declarations that the Jewish collectivity was not going to suffer any harm during his administration, it is estimated that around 8000 Jews abandoned Chile: 3000 of them headed to Israel. In the 1990s, only half of the Jews registered at the beginning of the 1970s (from 30.000

to 15.000) were living in Chile. The fear of the implementation of a Marxist regime was the cause of this exodus. The direct consequence was processes of institutional fusion derived from the demographic reduction. In 1972, the *Kehilá Ashkenazí* and the Israelite Circle merged, creating the Kehilá Israelite Circle (Kehilá Círculo Israelita). A year before, the Israelite Stadium and Macabi had done the same. Another effect of the emigration was the crisis of spiritual direction due to the lack of rabbis. This situation was overcome with the arrival of the conservative rabbi Angel Kreiman, who was very popular within the community and outside it thanks to his ecumenical activities.

The military coup that brought down Allende in 1973 verified again the consequence of the Jewish collectivity regarding governments. Both the rabbi and the Representative Committee and the Jewish press congratulated the new government and wished it success in its enterprises. These wishes got concrete through a contribution of the collectivity to the campaign of national reconstruction (Sznajder 1993).

"During Allende's administration, the ethnic-religious worry, broadly expressed, had disguised the real socio-economic worry of the majority of the Chilean Jewish leadership. When Allende fell, Chile entered another kind of crisis, but in this one the socio-economic sector, to which the majority of the Jewish leaders in Chile belonged, did not feel threatened" (Sznejder 1993, 146). Anti-Semitism in Chile came from political circles influenced by Nazism and from the large number of Palestinians living in the country, around 300.000 (Avni 1992, 256; Eisenberg 1994, 42–43).

8 Uruguay: Ideological and Communal Division within a Liberal Majority Society

Contrary to what has been said regarding Chile, where the Catholic tradition influenced the covert way the Jewish community was organized at the beginning, Uruguay was a country that, already at early twentieth century, separated the Church from the State and where the liberal secular spirit prevailed. It is estimated that, in 1910, 150 Ashkenazi and Sephardic people lived in Uruguay. In 1909 and 1911, they organized respectively their community life. We have to take into account that the closed vicinity with a numerous and organized community like Buenos Aires' influenced the Montevideo's one, for example, the Argentine Jewish journalism circulated in Uruguay. In the same way that Argentine collectivity went through stages in its economic structure, the same process took place in Uruguay, only with some chronological delay (Avni 1992, 169; Raicher 2003, 3–35).

Despite the restrictive dispositions that ruled regarding immigration, between 1936–1944, 9,199 Jews entered Uruguay, enhancing the human flow of the community. This happened because the 1934–1938 dictatorship, despite being such, did not paralyze the criticism by liberal and leftist elements. During the constitutional regime that followed, and although Uruguay adhered to the anti-immigration policy of the Evian conference, in fact, Jewish refugees, especially from Germany and Austria, entered the country. This was the last great demographic contribution to the Uruguayan Judaism. According to Della Pergola, the number of Jews achieved a 32,000 people maximum in 1970, with a reduction of up to 23,000 in 1995, a tendency that continued through the twenty-first century, not only because of the *alya*, as will see below, but because of the emigration to the United States, other countries of the continent, Spain, and even Australia, partly as a result of the 1982 and 2002 economic crises (Raicher 2001, 63–77; Della Pergola 2011, 315; Shorer Kaplan 2018, 117–141).

Up to the years of that immigration noted above, during the 1930s there were already in Uruguay four communal institutions: the Israelite Community (Askenazi); Comunidad Israelita), the Sephardic Israelite Community (Comunidad Israelita Sefaradí), the Hungarian Israelite Society (Sociedad Israelita Húngara), and the Synagogue Community of Montevideo (Comunidad Sinagogal de Montevideo), which afterwards was denominated New Israelite Community (Nueva Comunidad Israelita) and grouped German speaking Jews. The four communities founded the Israelite Central Committee of Uruguay (Comité Central Israelita del Uruguay). There were also *landsmanschaften* and aid organizations for the Jewish immigrant like HIAS, which, from 1933, performed a significant action. There were also financial institutions that gathered members of different ideologies: the Israelite Bank, of the Jewish left, and the Israelite Commercial and Industrial Center (Centro Comercial e Industrial Israelita), of the Zionist community sector. This type of organizations suggests that in Uruguay all the ideological spectrum of the Zionist movement, and also communist and bundist were acting. In Uruguay, a community organizational unite was not achieved, unlike Argentina that had an "umbrella organization" like DAIA, and an institution at community level like AMIA that concentrated all the Ashkenazi sector (Raicher 2003, 70–99, 121–144).

The leftist non-Zionist sectors maintained their policy of loyalty to the Soviet Union, both at the time of the Molotov-Ribbentrop Pact and during the first year of the creation of the State of Israel, when the USSR backed Israel. Its change of position renewed the separatism between the two community sectors. The non-Zionist left continued its activities, but its influence declined. The removal of Jewish life in the USSR provoked criticism, but only a minority abandoned its ranks. For the following years, given their tendency to mix with sectors of the majority society with similar ideology, the Jewish valued were getting lost (Raicher 2003, 144–147, 232).

Formal and informal Jewish education is part of that ideological differentiation that prevailed in all the community environments, being less noticeable in formal education. Up to 1962, in Montevideo, only Jewish schools linked to different ideological currents in force in the community functioned. Unlike other communities like Mexico's, where public education were deprived, in Uruguay, it had a high level as in Argentina, therefore, the foundation of the Uruguayan-Hebrew Integral School (Escuela Integral Hebrea Uruguaya,) 1962 for the whole education cycle, was a challenge that was successful and gathered all the non-religious Zionist sectors. At the same time, the Yavneh school fulfilled the same mission in the religious Zionist sector (Raicher 2003, 212; Raicher 1973).

Informal education had, from the 1930s, all the range of pioneer youth movements brought from Europe. In the 1940s, the Zionist Youth Federation of Uruguay was founded, where seven youth movements were represented. At the same time, two institutions were formed, a Zionist non-party one devoted to sports named Macabi, and a second social named Hebarica. Both merged in the 1950s under the name of Hebraica-Macabi (Raicher 2003, 212).

The Zionist movement was very important by its actions and its practical results. Uruguay is the country with the greater percentage of *aliyah* to Israel from Latin America proportionally to the number of Jews. It was that during all the periods from the creation of the State of Israel: up to 1993, more than 9,000 Jews arrived to Israel. Also, in difficult times, like the Independence War, there were volunteered in Majal, and during the Six-Day War, the phenomenon was repeated. It is important the example of the Jativá Mordejai Anilevich, representative of the leftist Zionism, and the link between the Hashomer Hatzair movement and the MAPAM party, a contingent that left as volunteers to Israel in 1967 (Shorer Kaplan 2018; Ben Dror 2017).

Especially worthy of mention, given the liberal democratic character of the majority society and of the government regimes of the 1940s, the collaboration of the Zionist movement with political and intellectual figures who backed the policy of the World Zionist Organization, founding in Montevideo, like what happened in another Latin American countries, an Uruguayan Committee in support of a Hebrew Palestine (Comité Uruguayo Pro Palestina Hebrea). Uruguay had a practical implication in the United Nations resolution regarding the partition, because, along with Guatemala, its representative to the UNSCOP commission backed the project. It was also the first country of the continent that had diplomatic ties with Israel (Raicher 1993, 231–243).

9 Mexico: A Community unto Itself Imbued with Jewish Values

Mexico is an Indo-American country bordering on the United States, whose geographical position influenced the configuration of the Jewish community. The positivist regime in force in that country at the end of the nineteenth century promoted the European immigration, so some Jews from Western Europe, as well as from the United States, arrived. Given the fact that they were away from the tradition and the character of the regime and particularly the Catholic environment full of prejudices, prevented an organized community to make up. Only in 1904, Jews gathered for the big holidays, the same happened a year afterwards thanks to the aid of Bnei Brith representative from the United States. At the same time a group of immigrants from

Damascus and Aleppo, more traditionalist and with less economic resources the above mentioned, started to reunite. The visit of the rabbi from El Paso, Texas, influenced on the foundation of the Mount Sinai Charity Society (1923) of the Damascenes. The Aleppians gradually separated from the Damascenes founding eventually, in 1938, the Maguén David Community (Comunidad Maguén David). The Ashkenazi founded in 1922 the community called "Nidjei Isroel". Post-revolutionary policy of the vindication of the indigenous and mixed-race population, the limitation of the rights and the activities for foreigners could have restricted the establishment of a steady Jewish community. However, during the first decade after the war a community was consolidated due to the proximity of United States and the contribution of its Judaism (Avni 1992, 193–195).

The first restrictions on immigration to the United States (1922, 1924) started to increase the Jewish immigration to Mexico, which was received as part of the foreigners with capital and skills who would contribute to the country's development. In practice, poor Jewish immigrants from Eastern Europe, trying to get to the United States, ended up in Mexico. Given those circumstances, American Jews, not wanting to turn to illegal methods, helped with the settlement of the newly arrived in Mexico through Bnei Brith. The principles were similar to the already mentioned for Euro-America, especially the street trade. There was also in Mexico a process of economic status improvement. In 1930, the Jewish population had 16,000 people, most of them settled down in the capital (Avni 1992, 195–196).

The nature of an Indo-American society – nationalistic and partly xenophobic – forced particularly the Ashkenazi sector to develop an intense community life. Up to 1930, there were three religious institutions. In the social and youth area, in 1922, the Young Men's Hebrew Association was founded with an American influence. A cultural club of socialists and revolutionaries called I. L. Peretz Cultural Association (Asociación Cultural I. L. Peretz) was founded in 1922. In 1927, it split, giving birth to the Radical Worker Center (Centro Obrero Radical). Because of the atmosphere prevailing in the majority society, this kind of organizations only acted within the community. In 1925, the Zionist movement emerged solidly rooted among Ashkenazi and Sephardic people. This, the Kadima United Zionist Organization (Organización Sionista Unida Kadima) was established that year, gathering the general Zionists and whose main objective was to collect money for the National Funds. Like in other countries, there were internal rivalries between general Zionists and several political factions within Zionism. In 1935, the Poalei Zion was formally organized; it had made up years before the Pro-Worker Palestine League (Liga Pro Palestina Obrera), which campaigned in support of the KAPAI, the Fund of Land of Israel Workers (Caja de los Obreros de la Tierra de Israel). Given the circumstances prevailing in 1938, the differences between the different groups did not prevent the creation of the Central Jewish Committee of Mexico (Comité Central Judío de México), or the Israelite Sport Center (Centro Deportivo Israelita) in 1950. During the 1920s and 1930s, journalism in Yiddish and Spanish was developed. At the end of the period approximately ten synagogues were functioning, most of them Orthodox, belonging to Bet El Community Center (Centro Comunitario Bet El) from the conservative line (Avni 1992, 197; Gojman de Bakal 2009; Wikipedia 17.1.2020).

Since the beginning, each community founded a traditional educational institution like *Kutab* or *Talmud Torá* and also more modern schools like "Yiddishe Shul". At the end of 1941, the religious school Yavne and the Tarbut school, both comprehensive schools, were founded. The same process happened in the schools of the Mount Sinai (1941) and Sephardic Union (1943) communities. Jewish education in Mexico outstood for the gradual increase of the school population. Given the situation of public education in México, where the government did not have an enough number schools to satisfy the needs of the whole population, private schools – among them the Jewish institutions – were a solution. These schools had a higher level that the public ones, were recognized by the State, and had to comply with the regulations like the secular education, approved to stop the Catholic influence in this sector, but that also affected the teaching of Judaism. Jewish education in Mexico achieved the maximum number of students in the whole Latin America.

Also in Mexico, like in other countries of the continent, from the 1960s, the US Conservative movement took position in the community life. Likewise, in the 1970s, Orthodox currents, not specially Jabad, arrived to the country, so the *talmudei torá* and *yeshivot* multiplied. By the end of the twentieth century, the mentioned institutions acted in a community of 40,000 people, and they were joined by Orthodox institutions according to the "return to Judaism" currents. It could be said that the Mexican community, even though rooted in the country, given the socio-ethnographic circumstances, was a closed society with a 94 percent of Jewish school attendance and 3 percent of exogamous marriages (Avni, Bokser Liwerant and Fainstein 2011, 563–570).

Regarding the Mexican government policy related to Jewish immigration in the 1930s and 1940s, when the admission of Jewish refugees was more necessary, the Mexican government acted like other Latin American countries, Brazil and Argentina, limiting Jewish immigration that achieved in this case about 2,000 people. This policy was, partly, consequence of the antisemitic influence of the "golden shirts", influenced by the Nazi propaganda that spread through the country, mainly before Mexico sided with the allies in 1942 (Avni 1992, 257; Gojman de Backal 1988, 174–191).

In relation to Mexican policy regarding the creation of the State of Israel, (the positive case of Uruguay was discussed above), according to the hypothesis of Judit Liwerant, Mexico "found in the abstention a way that allowed it not to get involved or commit with distant geopolitical problems". Another explanation could be that it tried to show the United States its independence, when the latter was making efforts so that the Latin American backed the partition. A last argument is the influence of the Syrian-Lebanese community settled in Mexico (Bokser Liwerant 1993, 203–229).

In 1975, there was another "breakdown" in the triangle made up by the Mexican government, the Jewish community and Israel. Mexico voted in favor of the UN

Resolution 3379, which condemned Zionism as a form of racism and discrimination. This was the result of the third-world position of the Mexican government of that time. This vote provoked a reaction within the local Jewish community, and also the interference of transnational Jewish institutions: the one with more practical results was the intervention of the Jews from United States who declared a boycott to the tourism to Mexico. All the pressure against the government led to the recognition of a "mistake". In 1991, Mexico voted for the revocation of this resolution thanks to a policy change regarding United States, and in the domestic front, the admission of otherness and pluralism counteracted the anti-Zionist and antisemitic tendencies (Bokser Liwerant 1997, 319–349).

In two Indo-American republics, a Jewish community was formed as a consequence of immigration permits during the years of the Nazi regime before and during the Second World War. These countries were Ecuador and Bolivia that, up to that moment, only had a few dozens of Jewish inhabitants.

10 Ecuador: A Refuge for Jews during the Second World War

Ecuador achieved, in 1935, an agreement with a Jewish organization from Paris, in order to colonize several thousands of Jewish immigrants in almost half a million hectares the Ecuadorian government made available for the enterprise. The organization did not have the economic resources to invest in the necessary infrastructure for such a project and everything came to nothing. In fact, few immigrants arrived during 1936 and 1937. In 1938, there was an attempt to expel the Jewish refugees who did not comply with the commitment to engage in agriculture. This was annulled and, since then and during the war, the consulates of Ecuador in Germany and other European countries granted visas. In 1943, there were in Ecuador 2,200 Jews, most of them in Quito, but also in Cuenca, Ambato and the port of Guayaquil. By the end of the century, the country had a Jewish population of only 900 people belonging to a middle class that has economic security and is engaged in industry, commerce and services (Eisenberg 1994, 31; Avni 1993, 274–275; Della Pergola 2011, 315).

11 Bolivia: A Country of Transit during the Second World War

Bolivia opened its doors to immigration in 1938 as a policy for the development of the country; in fact, it was an opportunity for Jewish refugees when they needed it the most. Bolivian consuls issued the visas and hundreds of Jews arrived to the country.

The criticisms for the increase of prizes due to the arrival of European immigrants and for having sold for exorbitant sums visas that should have been issued for free, with the addition of the suicide of the president of the Republic, led to the close of immigration, but in the interim, between 9,000 and 10,000 Bolivian visas had been issued. Many of these refugees passed to neighboring countries, mainly Argentina. It is estimated that, in 1943, there was in Bolivia 5,150 people who formed communities in La Paz, Cochabamba, Santa Cruz, Potosí, Sucre and Oruro (Avni 1992, 275–276).

After the end of the war and with the creation of the State of Israel, part of these communities decreased the number of members or ended up disappearing like the case of Sucre. By the end of the twentieth century 700 Jews lived in Bolivia (Della Pergolla 2011, 315). The Israelite Circle of La Paz (Círculo Israelita de La Paz) is the organization that manages two synagogues and a school, functioning in parallel with WIZO and B'nai B'rith (Eisenberg 1994, 34–35).

12 Panamá: Encounter with the Diaspora and Return to the Sources

In 1876, the first Jews arrived to Panamá, they were Sephardic coming from Curazao, and founded the Kol Shearit Israel congregation, which exists until today. In the twentieth century, Jews from Syria, and also Ashkenazi from Europe and USA were incorporated. According to the social makeup of the country, where, due to a strong American influence, there is not a solid national awareness, each of the components of the ethnic mosaic maintains its cultural and work features. So, among the Jews, there are differences between the groups abovementioned. The descendants of the first Sephardic people engaged in the financial, banking and air transport sectors. The people with Syrian origin are engaged in commerce within the "Free Zone". The Ashkenazi, whose number is decreasing gradually for their emigration to USA, Israel and other countries, tend to get inserted in development and construction firms, as well as to engaged in liberal professions. In the 1970s, for political reasons, a last big group of emigrants from Syria arrived; it was very welcomed by their countrymen. From then on, the Jewish population increased, reaching more than 5,000 people by the end of the twentieth century. Orthodox religious tendencies, which spread across all the Latin American Judaism, had a very singular repercussion in Panama, thanks to the rabbi Sion Levy, who was for more than fifty years the spiritual chief of the majority group of Syrian and Sephardic Jews. Thanks to his charisma and the authority that emanated from his personality, he achieved that habits brought by tradition become rules of life for most of the community that became an orthodox community both in public and in private. On the other hand, the religious rules introduced in all the schools of the collectivity led secular Ashkenazi and old Sephardic Jews to found the Yitzhak Rabin school (Siebzehner 2017; Della Pergola 2011, 314).

13 Venezuela: From a Developing Community to Decline Due to Government Policy

The national census in Venezuela registered, in 1891, 247 Jewish residents, a number that was on the rise. In 1907, the Israelite Charity Society was founded; in 1919 it became the Israelite Society of Venezuela, gathering there all the Jews in the country. The emigration from Central and Eastern Europe grew since 1934. By then, Venezuela imposed restrictions to the Jewish immigration that were in force until after the 1950s. Despite that, in 1943, around 600 Jews from Germany entered the country, and they were joined by other hundreds after the Second World War. In 1950, the community reached 6,000 people. In 1958, more than a thousand came from Egypt, Lebanon and Syria. To these we should add an unknown number of immigrants from Latin American countries, rising the number to 20,000 by the 1980s, a number that was maintained until the 1990's. The community had all its institutions, outstanding among them the Herzl-Bialik elementary and high school, to which 90% of the Jewish children of Caracas attended. Hebraica was the community center. It should be noted also that the Ashkenazi community named Israelite Union of Caracas (Unión Israelita de Caracas), and Sephardic Israelite Association of Venezuela (Asociación Israelita de Venezuela) that along with the Zionist Federation, B'nai B'rith and the Union of Hebrew Women (Unión de Mujeres Hebreas) made up the umbrella organization named Confederation of Israelite Organizations of Venezuela (Confederación de Organizaciones Israelitas de Venezuela), founded in 1967. The big change happened in 1999 when the Chávez regime started bringing about an economic crisis, an antisemitic rhetoric marked by the support to Iran, Syria and Hamas that, along with the breakdown of diplomatic relations with Israel, incited the emigration of Jews. Most of them went to Miami, also to Israel and other Latin American countries. We should clarify that the emigration phenomenon was not only Jewish but part of a general process of the Venezuelan population. In 2009, there were 12,200 Jews in this country and that tendency was still in effect. The community decrease brought about the lack of solvency for the institutional support, a result of the impoverishment of the members, the reduction of the number of students at the community school and of members at Hebraica (Roniger 2011, 271–285; Eisenberg 1994, 27–28).

14 Peru: From the Periphery to the Capital; Decline Due to Government Policy

Like other countries as Chile and Argentina, in the second half of the nineteenth century some Jews coming from Western Europe arrived to Peru as representatives of foreign companies and professionals hired by the government. Up to de 1920s,

Peru tried to attract, without much success, European immigration, due to the lack of economic opportunities, political instability and poor health conditions. Then, the immigration was restricted to avoid the arrival of immigrants from other parts of the world. This policy was accentuated in 1936, and Peru closed its doors during the Second World War. Despite that, Jewish refugees kept arriving through a high payment for their visas. At the end of the we, 4,000 Jews lived in Peru, 1,200 in the hinterland, and the rest in Lima. It is estimated that 20% were of German origin, 20% Sephardic, and 60% from Eastern Europe (Trahtemberg 1989, 23–24).

Outlining the Jewish life in Peru during the twentieth century, we can say that the first one to arrive during the second decade were Sephardic coming from the Middle East and the North of Africa, who made contact with the remaining of the almost extinct community of German Jews. The third decade was characterized by the arrival of young people from Eastern Europe; many of them tried their luck in the hinterland. The 1930s were years of economic stabilization both in the capital and in the provinces, and of the institutional development of the three sectors: the Israelite Charity Society (Sociedad de Beneficiencia Israelita), 1870, of the German Jews, enhanced by the refugees' immigration; the Sephardic Israelite Charity Society (Sociedad de Beneficiencia Israelita Sefaradí, 1925); the Israelite Union of Peru (Unión Israelita de Perú, 1926) formed by the people from Eastern Europe (Trahtemberg, 24–26).

The 1940s and the 1950s were characterized by the community integration and unification of the services for the three congregations: cemetery, unified foreign representation through the Association of Israelite Societies of Peru (Asociación de Sociedades Israelitas de Perú). As part of the Zionist work, the Peruvian Committee in Support of a Hebrew Palestine (Comité Peruano Pro Palestina Hebrea) was founded in 1945. In 1946, the Jewish integrative school León Pinelo, the youth movements Betar and Hanoar Hatzioní were founded, as well as a series of Zionist institutions like the National Funds and WIZO. This development was, partly, the result of a migration process of the Jews in the provinces to Lima and the gradual disappearance of the communities in the hinterland. The causes of this process were the search of economic opportunities, a better education and the community socialization, mainly for the youth. These were the years of the first generation of Jews graduated from Peruvian universities (Trahtemberg 1989, 65–69).

The 1960s brought stability to the community and was the decade for the generational change. The community grew up to reach a maximum of 5,300 people. The Hebraic club, like similar institutions in the neighboring countries, became the social and sport center of the community. During the 1970s, a reverse process started. Due to the 1968 military coup that destabilized many people, the economic deterioration of the country, the first signs of an anti-Zionist and antisemitic journalism, the increase of crime and lack of safety influenced on the emigration from Peru. At the end of that decade, the collectivity had been reduced to a fifth. a process that would be accentuated in the 1980s and 1990s as a consequence of the worsening of this situation. Jews emigrated to Israel, the United States, Canada, and other countries of the continent (Eisenberg 1994, 33; Della Pergola 2011, 315). Along with these processes and as a consequence of the incorporation of the third generation into the Peruvian society, Jewish names can be found in the political and cultural spheres of the country (Trahtemberg 1989, 75).

15 Colombia: Emigration and Organization under the Shadow of Official and Popular Anti-Semitism

Colombia was not a country that developed an immigration policy. In the third decade of the twentieth century, thanks to a twenty-year peaceful period, European immigrants started to arrive from different countries, attracted by the opportunities of an almost unexploited country. This fact was not consented by a local oligarchy that was afraid of the competition of the new immigrants and that put pressure on the government to prevent a massive immigration. These were the conditions that waited for the Ashkenazi and Sephardic people who arrived at that time and afterwards until the 1940s; to these we should add the aggravating circumstance of being Jews, because this attitude was joined by an antisemitic aspect both in the people and the government. What happened in Europe, the Bolshevik revolution and the identification of the communist with the Jewish did not only influence on conservative elements, but also in some part of liberal oligarchy. Ashkenazi Jews suffered specially this situation, without knowledge of the language, they had to go through an adaptation period. 1930s events, the German National Socialist regime and its consequences did not open Colombia's doors to Jewish immigration, in many cases, not even for family reunions. The Foreign Affairs Minister issued in January 1939 a notice ordering "to put all the humanly possible obstacles to the visas for new passports to Jewish elements". These obstacles were applied despite the estimate of a total of 6,000 Jews in the country. Given the circumstances, the fraudulent purchase of visas was the only possibility to access Colombia. In practice, outside Bogota, communities were formed in Barranquilla, Cali and Medellin (Hernández 2011, 175–187; Leal Villamizar 2011, 221–240).

The typical door to door trading with sale in payments that characterized the Jewish immigration in its first steps in other countries of the continent, also thrived in Colombia and fulfilled a social function making available to the underprivileged classes merchandises that were exclusively for the middle and high classes. This commercial innovation prompted calls for a boycott and generated waves of anti-Semitism based on the alleged enrichment of the Jews in detriment of the Colombian people (Hernández 2011, 188–194).

Despite the hostile atmosphere, the Jews started to organize themselves and, in 1929, the Israelite Center of Bogotá (Centro Israelita de Bogotá) received its legal status. The center grouped the Ashkenazi sector. In 1935, the magazine *Nuestra*

Tribuna was founded, published both in Iddish and Spanish. *Nuestra Tribuna* was a publication that denounced anti-Semitism from an attitude that was connected with the Hebrew Federation, representative of the Zionism in the community. Up to 1945, the three Jewish community of the capital were already founded, and in 1938 the Montefiore Israelite Association (Asociación Israelita Montefiore) was added, founded by Jews of German origin, and also the Sephardic Hebrew Community of Bogota (Comunidad Hebrea Sefaradí de Bogotá, official recognition, 1945). Over time, the second generation, born and raised in Colombia, managed a greater collaboration between the three sectors. This materialized in a common cemetery, the foundation of the Hebrew Colombian School (Escuela Colombo Hebrea) in 1948, and a home for old-aged people (*Beit Avot*). In the 1960s, the Federation of Jewish Communities of Colombia (Federación de Comunidades Judías de Colombia) was created. Another important institution is the Office of Human Relations of the Jewish Community Foundation (Oficina de Relaciones Humanas de la Fundación de la Comunidad Judía) that is in charge of the relations with non-Jewish institutions and people on humanitarian, cultural and clarification topics (Tesone Milhem 2011, 245–264).

Given domestic circumstances that affected the country, the Jewish population decreased, being in 1995 5,000 people. This process continued until de twenty-first century (Della Pergola 2011, 315).

16 Paraguay: A Country Marked by Anti-Semitism that Opened Its Doors to Refugees

The Jewish community of Paraguay had, at early 1930s, around a thousand people of different origins: Ashkenazi from Eastern Europe and Sephardic Jews. During the 1920s a relatively large number of immigrants arrived from Poland. The ethnic differences and the lack of university studies, according to Seiferheld, hindered the integration of that first generation to the Paraguayan society, something that did happen with the second one. Already in 1913, the Society Latin Israelite Temple (Sociedad Templo Israelita Latino), of the Sephardic Jews, was founded, in 1916 the Israelite Alliance of Paraguay (Alianza Israelita de Paraguay), that followed the Ashkenazi rite, was formed, being the most important of all the institutions the Hebraic Union Society of Paraguay (Sociedad Unión Hebraica de Paraguay), dating from 1920. There was also a ladies' organization, another one of Polish residents and some attempts of a youth organization. Some Jews participated on the local communist left wing. Like in other countries of the continent, the refugees of the National Socialist regime formed their own institutions. In 1936, they founded what became the Israelite Union in Support of the Mutual Aid (Union Israelita Pro Socorros Mutuos). During the war, in 1943, the Hanoar Hatzioni was founded, among other institutions, and it published the magazine *Hebraica*.

Paraguay was a country where, up to 1937, there was free immigration, despite the existing anti-Semitic influences, mainly the German propaganda. That year a law was passed that restricted immigration, turning it selective, defining some features that, without explicitly naming them, were referred to Jewish immigrants. The Paraguayan Ministry of Foreign Affairs, in the memos to its consuls, ordered directly not granting visas to the Jews. In practice, many times, these orders were not carried out due to deals made still in Europe or other resources to avoid prohibitions. The estimates are than more than 5,000 passports and visas were issued by Paraguay, mainly for people from Germany and Austria (Seiferheld 1985a, 97–111, 165–177).

Many refugees went through Paraguay to bordering countries with stricter immigration policies, but with more possibilities to adapt, like Argentina, Brazil and Uruguay.

Despite the prevailing anti-Semitic atmosphere, only in 1941, there was a Jewish institutionalization against this tendency. That year the Israelite Circle (Círculo Israelita) was constituted: its objective was the propaganda for the Israelite collectivity and the fight against anti-Semitism. From this organization the Israelite Committee in Support of the Allies (Comité Israelita Pro Aliados) arose, which had relations with the Committee in Support of the Allies of Paraguay (Comité Pro Aliados de Paraguay). Even though Paraguay supported the allies from 1942, the Nazi influence and anti-Semitism kept being in force. In September 1944, the Latin American Committee of the Jewish Agency in Support of Palestine (Comité Latinoamericano de la Agencia Judía Pro Palestina), turned to the Paraguayan government asking for support to get a homeland for Jews. There is no news that in Paraguay a Committee in Support of a Hebrew Palestine (Comité Pro Palestina Hebrea) has been constituted as in other Latin American countries. Regarding the relations of this committee with the local Jewish community, it is worth mention its participation in the First Latin American Zionist Congress, held in Montevideo in March 1945. Allegedly it was the first time that the Jews from Paraguay were represented in a transnational Jewish forum. The purpose of Zionism renewed the distrust of the Paraguayan government regarding the Jewish community, which was catalogued as internationalist, without attachment to the new land (Seiferheld 1985b, 129–133, 214–249).

During the second half and until the end of the twentieth century, the abovementioned institutions kept acting, and to them it should be added the State of Israel Integrative School (Escuela Integral Estado de Israel), which concentrates 70% of the Jewish school population. The Israelite Representative Council of Paraguay (Consejo Representativo Israelita del Paraguay) was also founded regarding the people and government of the country (Shields, 8.1.2020).

17 Costa Rica: A Homogenous Community under the Zionist Banner

Costa Rica, one of the few countries in the continent (if not the only one) that enjoys a permanent democracy, had a *sui generis* relation regarding the Jews. Some isolated immigrants of Sephardic origin arrived to the country at the beginning of the twentieth century. Later on, in the early 1930s, Jewish immigrants arrived from Zelechow, Poland. They recommended each other and that is the reason why, in Costa Rica, there was almost uniformity of origin. Up to 1936, the arrival of 399 Polish Jews had been registered. These, like in other countries of the continent, at the beginning, were engaged in the door-to-door trade and selling in installments; this fact generated a negative reaction of the local merchants (Avni 2013, 227).

Like all the other countries of the continent, Costa Rica also participated, in July 1938, in the above-mentioned Evian Conference. As the rest of the participants, the only category of – immigrants considered acceptable was farmers. According to the proposal of Central American countries, including Costa Rica, the quota of refugees admitted in each of them should be proportional to their territory extension. Another condition was that the governments would not commit to cover the budget regarding the refugees (Avni 2013, 215–216).

Costa Rica was in excellent conditions to fulfill those requirements because, in 1937, thanks to the acquisition of the state of Tenorio for the Refugee Economic Corporation (REC), refugees could establish there as farmers. Despite the positive aspects, the plan failed. The legal purchase was carried out, but the estate could not be registered in the Public Registry. In order to make the situation legal, it was turned into a commercial company depending on the REC but not according to original purposes. This was the outcome of the opposition of the president of the country to the arrival of Jews to Costa Rica. According to the immigration laws in force, the president could make definite decisions in this aspect. This policy gravitated also in the admission of isolated Jewish refugees. On those decisions the prevailing antisemitic propaganda had an influence, based on the argument that the Polish Jews would become door to door salesmen and there would be a risk of "flooding" of the country by these immigrants. In fact, up to 1941, 556 "Polish" entered Costa Rica. In sum, the Costa Rica's aid to Jewish refugees during the Second World War was almost inexistent (Avni 2013).

Despite that situation, in 1943, as in other countries of the continent, the Committee in Support of Hebrew Palestine was constituted gathering Jews and gentiles that supported this demand. Thanks to that influence, the support of the Costa Rican government at the UN for the partition and the creation of the State of Israel was obtained.

At the end of the twentieth century, the Jewish community of Costa Rica had 2,500 people (Della Pergola 2011, 314). The beginnings of its organization dated from 1931 with the foundation of the Zionist Organization that, in 1948, was absorbed by the Zionist Israelite Center of Costa Rica (Centro Israelita Sionista de Costa Rica), founded in 1934, which carried out also the functions of *kehila*. Parallel and with a similar process, in 1945, the Women Organization was absorbed by the WIZO, created in 1940. Due to the Zionist character of the community, the dates for the fusions are not surprising, as well as the assertion of the authors of *The Jew in Costa Rica* about that the Zionist Israelite Center and WIZO were the institutional pillars of the community. To them we should add the United Zionist Youth and the Israel Student Organization. In the 1950s, we could add the Israelite Ladies that did charitable work in the lower classes of the majority society, a singular fact in the Jewish community fact. In the same decade, the Bene Berith Lodge and the youth movement Hanoar Hatzioni started to act. The community also has a comprehensive Hebrew-Spanish school with the name of Chaim Weizmann. Up to the end of the past century, the Zionist character and the permanent support to Israel hardly influenced on the *alyah* of the Costa Rican Judaism (Schifter Sikora et al. 1979; Eisenberg 1994, 21).

18 Guatemala: Traces of Communal Organization and Ties to Israel

Except for Panama and Costa Rica, treated above, the rest of the Central American countries does not have Jewish communities that numerically have the conditions to constitute a collectivity with all its attributes. Guatemala reached, during the 1970s, a total of 1,900 Jews, a number that decreased to 1,000 in the 1990s, due to the violence that ravaged the country during the previous decade. They were professionals, technicians and business people. The community have three synagogues and a Bene Berith Lodge. The relations of Guatemala with the State of Israel were excellent since the beginning. Being a Guatemalan delegate a member of UNSCOP, he voted in favor of the partition, and Guatemala was the first country of the Western hemisphere, after the United States, that recognized the creation of the State of Israel. Israel-Guatemala relations were characterized by the agro-technological help of Israel to this country (Eisenberg 1994, 14; Della Pergola 2011, 144).

19 Other Central American Countries

El Salvador reached, during the 1970s and 1980s, a maximum of 800 Jews, with a dramatic reduction to 100 in the 1990s, a situation from which it did not recover (Eisenberg 1994,18).

Honduras is not among the countries with a Jewish population (Della Pergola 2011, 144). In the 1990s, Eisenberg notes the presence of forty Jewish families. They belong to the higher class, with a high percentage of exogamous marriages. Due to their social positions and their cultural and intellectual level, some Jews occupied high positions in the Honduran administration (Eisenberg 1994, 16).

Nicaragua, too, is not listed among the countries with a Jewish population. According to the B'nai B'rith report, fifty resident families abandoned the country in 1979, as a consequence of the Sandinista regime that confiscated assets and properties. They started to return under the Violeta Chamorro's administration (Eisenberg 1994,19).

20 Conclusions

The establishment of Jewish communities in the Iberian Peninsula and Latin American, from the end of the nineteenth century and during the twentieth century, was the consequence of immigration to countries like Spain and Portugal that, in a distant past, had a Jewish population, and in Latin American, the Jews were established for the first time after the independence of the republics of this continent. We must take into account the Catholic background and the anti-Semitism that varied according to the circumstances of the different countries. Most of them put obstacles to the Jewish immigration when, in front of the Nazi danger, the Jews needed it the most. That is testified by the result of the Evian Convention. Given the circumstances of the Second World War and its consequences, the *Shoah*, there was a positive change in the government policies, a fact that was demonstrated by the support of the creation of the State of Israel.

In general terms, except for Argentina and Brazil where colonization projects were developed, in the rest of the countries, there was only an urban immigration that, at the beginning, was a population constituted by workers, artisans and door to door salesmen, who afterwards climbed to higher socio-economical strata. By the end of the period treated here, due to an economic crisis a "new poverty" emerged that affected Brazil, Venezuela and mainly Argentina.

The community organization varied according to the prevailing conditions in each place; and in all cases the religious, cultural and social needs of the community members were covered. The ideologies brought from the countries of origin influenced the organizational process and, at the same time, the immigrants maintained the transnational bond with analogous communities. In many cases, especially in numerous communities, the ideological currents (Zionism, communism, Bundism) influenced the formal and non-formal Jewish education, as well as the journalism and the culture. During the second half of the twentieth century, due to orthodox and conservative currents originally from the United States, there were changes in the religious-cultural profile of the communities.

In terms of demographics, the general trend indicates a reduction of the number of Jews due to emigration, low birth rate and assimilation.

Bibliography

Works Cited

Avni, Haim. *Judaism in Argentina. Social Position and Organizational Type*. Jerusalem: Hebrew University of Jerusalem, 1972. (Hebrew)

Avni, Haim. *España, Franco y los Judíos*. Madrid: Altalena, 1982a.

Avni, Haim. *The History of the Jewish Immigration to Argentina 1810–1950*. Jerusalem: Magnes Press,1982b.

Avni, Haim. *Emancipation and Jewish Education: A Century of Argentinian Jewry's Experience 1884–1984*. Jerusalem: The Zalman Shazar Center, 1985. (Hebrew)

Avni, Haim. "The Spanish-Speaking World and the Jews." *Terms of Survival. The Jewish World since 1945*. Ed. Robert S. Wistrich. London: Routledge, 1990. 358–382.

Avni, Haim. *Judíos en América. Cinco siglos de Historia*. Madrid: Mapfre, 1992.

Avni, Haim. "Jewish Leadership in Times of Crisis: Argentina during the Eichmann Affair (1960–1962)." *Studies in Contemporary Jewry* XI (1995):117–135.

Avni, Haim. "The Impact of the Six-Day War on a Zionist Community: The Case of Argentina." *The Six-Day War and World Jewry*. Eds. Eli Lederhendler et al. College Park: University of Maryland, 2001.137–166.

Avni, Haim. "Costa Rica and the Jews during the Holocaust." *Judaica Latinoamericana* VII. Ed. AMILAT. Jerusalem: Editorial Universitaria Magnes, Universidad Hebrea, 2013. 215–236.

Avni, Haim. *Argentina ¿Tierra Prometida? El Barón de Hirsch y su Proyecto de Colonización Judía*. Buenos Aires: UAI, Teseo, 2018.

Avni, Haim, Judit Bokser Liwerant and Daniel Fainstein. "Tres modelos de Innovación Educativa en México. Un Análisis a Tres Voces." *Pertenencia y Alteridad. Judíos en/de América Latina: Cuarenta Años de Cambios*. Eds. Haim Avni, Judit Bokser Liwerant et al. Madrid: Iberoamericana – Vervuert, 2011. 563–600.

Babis, Deby. "De Sinagoga Ortodoxa a Centro Comunitario Conservador, Cambios en la Comunidad Judía de Buenos Aires." *Judaica Latinoamericana* VII. Ed. AMILAT. Jerusalem: Editorial Universitaria Magnes, Universidad Hebrea, 2009. 53–78.

Bargman, Daniel. "Tipografías Judaicas y Redes Transnacionales: una Aproximación Antropológica a las Identidades y Religiosidades Judías en Buenos Aires." *Judaica Latinoamericana* VIII. Ed. AMILAT. Jerusalem: Editorial Universitaria Magnes, Universidad Hebrea, 2017. 215–240.

Barromi, Joel. "Argentina Veinte Años Después. Una Revisión de las Políticas de Israel Hacia los Judíos Argentinos Durante la Junta Militar (1976–1983)." *Encuentro y Alteridad. Vida y Cultura Judía en América Latina*. Eds. Judit Bokser Liwerant and Alicia Gojman de Backal. Mexico City: Fondo de Cultura Económica, 1999. 673–690.

Beit Hatfutsot. *Jewish Community of Santiago*. Dbs.front- READ Me.Mdat dev.B (5 March 2020).

Bejarano, Margalit. "Historia de la Comunidad Sefaradita de Buenos Aires 1930–1945." *Legado de los Judíos de España y Oriente*. Ed. Issachar Ben Ami. Jerusalem: Magnes Press, 1978. 161–170. (Hebrew)

Bejarano, Margalit. "L´Integration des Seppharades en Amerique Latine: Le Cas des Communautés de Buenos Aires et de la Havane." *Memoires Juives de Espagne e du Portugal*. Ed. Esther Benbassa. Paris: Publisud, 1996. 207–219.

Bejarano, Margalit. "Comunidad y Religiosidad: Cambios en la Identidad Colectiva de los Sefaradíes en América Latina." *Pertenencia y Alteridad. Judíos en/de América Latina: Cuarenta Años de Cambios*. Eds. Haim Avni, Judit Bokser Liwerant et al. Madrid: Iberoamericana – Vervuert, 2011. 603–620.

Ben-Dror, Graciela. "El Rol del Movimiento Sionista-Socialista Mordejai Anilevich en el Uruguay, 1964–1976." *Judaica Latinoamericana* VIII. Ed. AMILAT. Jerusalem: Editorial Universitaria Magnes, Universidad Hebrea, 2017. 185–213.

Blastein, Nora. "Alianza Solidaria: una Red de Protección Social Comunitaria en la Argentina." *La Lucha Contra la Pobreza en América Latina-Deterioro Social de las Clases Medias y Experiencias de la Comunidades Judías*. Ed. Bernardo Kliksberg. Buenos Aires: Fondo de Cultura Económica, 2000. 101–125.

Bohm, Gunter. "Vida Judía en Chile y en Perú Durante el Siglo XIX." *Judaica Latinoamericana*. Ed. AMILAT. Jerusalem: Editorial Universitaria Magnes, Universidad Hebrea, 1988. 32–40.

Bohm, Gunter. "'Judíos en Chile': un Informe Confidencial de la Embajada Alemana en Santiago, de Junio 1939." *Judaica Latinoamericana* III. Ed. AMILAT. Jerusalem: Editorial Universitaria Magnes, Universidad Hebrea, 1997. 207–226.

Bokser Liwerant, Judit. "El Movimiento Sionista, la Sociedad y el Gobierno de México frente a la Partición de Palestina." *Judaica Latinoamericana* II. Ed. AMILAT. Jerusalem: Editorial Universitaria Magnes, Universidad Hebrea, 1993. 203–229.

Bokser Liwerant, Judit. "Fuentes de Legitimación de la Presencia Judía en México: El Voto Positivo de México a la Ecuación Sionismo=Racismo y su impacto sobre la Comunidad Judía." *Judaica Latinoamericana* III. Ed. AMILAT. Jerusalem: Editorial Universitaria Magnes, Universidad Hebrea, 1997. 319–349.

Chazan, Meir. "The Creation of the Relations between Israel and Brazil from Pioneering Perspective: Between Diplomacy and Kibbutz." *Jews and Jewish Identity in Latin America: Historical, Cultural, and Literary Perspectives*. Eds. Magarlit Bejarano, Yaron Harel et al. Boston: Academic Studies Press, 2017. 208–231.

Della Pergola, Sergio. "¿Cuántos Somos Hoy? Investigación y Narrativa Sobre la Población Judía en América Latina." *Pertenencia y Alteridad. Judíos en/de América Latina: Cuarenta Años de Cambios*. Eds. Haim Avni, Judit Bokser Liwerant et al. Madrid: Iberoamericana – Vervuert, 2011. 305–340.

Eisenberg, Warren W. *The Quest for Pluralism: Jews in a Changing Latin America*. Ed. Bnai Brith Center for International, Governmental and Israel Affaires. Washington DC, 1994.

Escudé, Carlos, and Beatriz Gurevich. "Limits of Governability, Corruption and Transnational Terrorism: the Case of 1992 and 1994 Attacks in Buenos Aires." *Estudios Interdisciplinarios de America Latina y el Caribe* 14.2 (2003): 127–148.

Gojman de Backal, Alicia. "Minorías, Estado y Movimientos Nacionalistasde la Clase Media en México: Liga Antichina y Antijudía (Siglo XX)." *Judaica Latinoamericana*. Ed. AMILAT. Jerusalem: Editorial Universitaria Magnes, Universidad Hebrea, 1988. 174–191.

Gojman de Backal, Alicia. "Inmigración de Judíos Polacos a México en ek Siglo XX." *Judaica Latinoamericana* III. Ed. AMILAT. Jerusalem: Editorial Universitaria Magnes, Universidad Hebrea, 1997. 45–72.

Gojman de Backal, Alicia. "Los Judíos Estadounidenses en México. La Creación del Yugnt Geselshaft y su Revista *Nuestra Palabra*." *Judaica Latinoamericana* VI. Ed. AMILAT. Jerusalem: Editorial Universitaria Magnes, Universidad Hebrea, 2009. 123–141.

Goldman, Daniel. "El Movimiento Conservador en Latinoamérica y el Legado del Rabino Marshall Meyer." *Pertenencia y Alteridad. Judíos en/de América Latina: Cuarenta Años de Cambios*. Eds. Haim Avni, Judit Bokser Liwerant, et al. Madrid: Iberoamericana –Vervuert, 2011. 639–654.

Hernández, José Angel. "La emigración judía: ¿Colombia, país de asilo? Años 20, 30, 40." *Los Judíos en Colombia. Una Aproximación Histórica*. Eds. Adelaida Sourdis Nájer and Alfonso Velazco Rojas. Madrid: Casa Sefarad Israel, 2011. 175–194.

Jewish Virtual Library. *Chile Virtual Jewish History Tour*. dbs.front/READ Me.md at dev.B. (5 March 2020)

Kliksberg, Bernardo. *La Lucha Contra la Pobreza en América Latina-Deterioro Social de las Clases Medias y Experiencias de las Comunidades Judía*. Buenos Aires: Fondo de Cultura Económica, 2000.

Kliksberg, Bernardo. "Una Comunidad Judía en Peligro. Los inquietantes interrogantes del judaísmo argentino y latinoamericano." *Temas de Actualidad Social* 1. Buenos Aires: AMIA, 2001. 4–19.

Leal Villamizar, Lina María. "Colombia frente a la cuestión judía. 1935–1939." *Los Judíos en Colombia: Una Aproximación Histórica*. Eds. Adelaida Sourdis Nájer and Alfonso Velazco Rojas. Madrid: Casa Sefarad Israel, 2011. 221–240.

Martins, Jorge. *A República e os Judeos*. Lisboa: Vega, 2010.

Milgram, Avraham. "Rezende e outras Tentativas de Colonizacao Agricola a Refugiados Judeos no Brasil (1936–1939)." *Judaica Latinoamericana* II. Ed. AMILAT. Jerusalem: Editorial Universitaria Magnes, Universidad Hebrea, 1993. 57–68.

Milgram, Avraham. "El Intento de volver conversos de Portugal al Judaísmo en los años 1925–1931." *Gesher* 126 (1993): 90–99. (Hebrew).

Milgram, Avraham. "Precursors of Zionism in Brazil before the Turn of the 20th Century." *The Journal of Israeli History* 16.3 (1995): 257–266.

Milgram, Avraham. "O 'millieu' Judeo-Comunista do Rio Janeiro nos anos 30." *Judaica Latinoamericana* IV. Ed. AMILAT. Jerusalem: Editorial Universitaria Magnes, Universidad Hebrea, 2001. 213–234.

Nes El, Moshé. "Natalio Berman, Dirigente Sionista y Parlamentario Chileno." *Judaica Latinoamericana*. Ed. AMILAT. Jerusalem: Editorial Universitaria Magnes, Universidad Hebrea, 1988. 167–173.

Raicher, Rosa Perla. "La Educación Judía en Uruguay; Informe de Investigación No. 2", Tel Aviv: Instituto Horowitz, Universidad de Tel Aviv, 1973. (Hebrew)

Raicher, Rosa Perla. "El Comité Uruguayo Pro Palestina Hebrea (1944–1948). Su Acción y Cauces de Pensamiento." *Judaica Latinoamericana* II. Ed. AMILAT. Jerusalem: Editorial Universitaria Magnes, Universidad Hebrea, 1993. 231–243.

Raicher, Rosa Perla. "Los Judíos Refugiados del Nazismo, 1933–1941." *Judaica Latinoamericana* IV. Ed. AMILAT. Jerusalem: Editorial Universitaria Magnes, Universidad Hebrea, 2001. 63–77.

Raicher, Rosa Perla. *Uruguay, la comunidad israelita y el pueblo judío*. Montevideo: Ed. Universidad Hebrea de Jerusalén, Universidad de la República, 2003.

Rein, Raanan and Martina Weisz. "Fantasmas del pasado, desafíos del presente: nuevos y viejos "otros" en la España contemporánea." *El otro en la España contemporánea- Prácticas, discursos y representaciones*. Eds. Silvina Schammah Gesser and Raanan Rein. Sevilla: Tres Culturas, 2011. 161–186.

Roniger, Luis. "Globalización, Transnacionalización y las Comunidades Judías: El impacto del Chavismo en Venezuela." *Pertenencia y Alteridad. Judíos en/de América Latina: Cuarenta Años de Cambios*. Eds. Haim Avni, Judit Bokser Liwerant et al. Madrid: Iberoamericana – Vervuert, 2011. 271–302.

Schenkolewski, Silvia. "Cambios en la Relación de la Organización Sionista Mundial hacia la Comunidad Judía y el Movimiento Sionista en la Argentina, hasta 1948." *Judaica*

Latinoamericana. Ed. AMILAT. Jerusalem: Editorial Universitaria Magnes, Universidad Hebrea, 1988. 149–166.
Schenkolewski, Silvia. "Zionists Versus the Left in Argentina." *Zionism and Its Opponents*. Eds. Haim Avni and Gideon Shimoni. Jerusalem: Hassifriya Hazionit, 1990. 181–189. (Hebrew).
Schenkolewski-Kroll, Silvia. "The Influence of the Zionist Movement on the Organization of Argentinian Jewish Community-the Case of DAIA, 1933–1946." *Studies in Zionism* XIII (1991): 17–28.
Schenkolewski-Kroll, Silvia. "La Conquista de las Comunidades: El Movimiento Sionista y la Comunidad Ashkenazí de Buenos Aires (1935–1949)." *Judaica Latinoamericana* II. Ed. AMILAT. Jerusalem: Editorial Universitaria Magnes, Universidad Hebrea, 1993. 191–201.
Schenkolewski-Kroll, Silvia. *The Zionist Movement and the Zionist Parties in Argentina, 1935–1948*. Jerusalem: Magnes Press, 1996. (Hebrew)
Schenkolewski-Kroll, Silvia. "El Cooperativismo Agrícola Judío en la Argentina: su Función Socioeconómica y su Identidad Etnica, 1901–1948." *Judaica Latinoamericana* IV. Ed. AMILAT. Jerusalem: Editorial Universitaria Magnes, Universidad Hebrea, 2001. 209–219.
Schenkolewski-Kroll. "The Jewish Communists in Argentina and the Soviet Settlement of Jews on Land in the URSS." *Jews in Eastern Europe*. Ed. Mordechai Altschuler. The Institute of Contemporary Jewry. 3, 49, (2002): 79–98.
Schenkolewski-Kroll, Silvia. "Los Movimientos Juveniles: una Faceta Carente en la Historiografía Sionista de la Argentina." *Judaica Latinoamericana* V. Ed. AMILAT. Jerusalem: Editorial Universitaria Magnes, Universidad Hebrea, 2005. 47–61.
Schenkolewski-Kroll, Silvia. "Comunistas y no Sionistas en Argentina y la Ayuda a las Víctimas de la Segunda Guerra Mundia ldesde el Prisma del Joint." *Judaica Latinoamericana* VI. Ed. AMILAT. Jerusalem: Editorial Universitaria Magnes, Universidad Hebrea, 2009. 337–350.
Schenkolewski-Kroll, Silvia. "Ideology and Propaganda in the Collective Memory's Construction: Zionism and Communism in Argentina." *Rebels Against Zion: Studies on the Jewish Left Anti-Zionism*. Ed. August Grabski. Warsaw: Jewish Historical Institute Emanuel Ringelblum, 2011. 125–138.
Schenkolewski-Kroll, Silvia. "Religious Zionism in Argentina." *Studies in Religious Zionism: Developments and Change*s. Eds. Yehuda Friedlander and Dov Schwartz. Ramat Gan: Bar Ilan University Press, 2012. 451–472. (Hebrew)
Schenkolewski-Kroll, Silvia. "Informal Jewish Education: Argentina's Hebraica Society." *Jews and Jewish Identity in Latin America: Historical, Cultural, and Literary Perspectives*. Eds. Margarlit Bejarano, Yaron Harel et al. Boston: Academic Studies Press, 2017a. 73–90.
Schenkolewski-Kroll, Silvia. "Transnacionalismo y Educación Judía no Formal: el Caso de Macabi Buenos Aires." *Judaica Latinoamericana* VIII. Ed. AMILAT. Jerusalem: Editorial Universitaria Magnes, Universidad Hebrea, 2017b. 531–549.
Seiferheld, Alfredo M. *Nazismo y Fascismo en el Paraguay: Vísperas de la II Guerra Mundial, 1936–1939*. Asunción: Ed. Histórica, 1985a.
Seiferheld, Alfredo M. *Nazismo y Fascismo en el Paraguay: Los años de la guerra 1939–1945*. Asunción: Ed. Histórica, 1985b.
Senkman, Leonardo. "El Primer Grupo de Voluntarios Argentinos al Batallón Hebreo (1918) y el Album que en su Honor Editó M. Padalevsky." *Michael on the History of the Jews in the Diaspora* VIII. Eds. Daniel Carpi and Shlomo Simonsohn. Tel Aviv: Tel Aviv University Press, 1983. 30–42.
Senkman, Leonardo. "Israel y el Rescate de las Víctimas de la Represión: una Evaluación Preliminar." *El Legado del Autoritarismo. Derechos Humanos y Antisemitismo en la Argentina Contemporánea*. Eds. Leonardo Senkman and Mario Sznajder. Buenos Aires: Nuevohacer, 1995. 283–324.

Senkman, Leonardo. "Identidad Transnacional de Judeocomunistas Argentinos en los Albores del ICUF." *Judaica Latinoamericana* VIII. Ed. AMILAT. Jerusalem: Editorial Universitaria Magnes, Universidad Hebrea, 2017. 131–160.
Shields, Jacqueline. "Paraguay Virtual Jewish History Tour" (8 January 2020).
Shifter Sikora, Jacobo, Lowell Gudmunson and Mario Solera Castro. *El Judío en Costa Rica*. San José: Editorial Universidad a Distancia, 1979. 295–371.
Shorer Kaplan, Maya. "La Comunidad de Uruguay, Emigrantes y Emigrantes a Israel: Principales Tendencias y Características." *Ecos del Nuevo Ulpan* 103 (2015): 32–37. (Hebrew)
ShorerKaplan, Maya. "Patterns and Structure of Social Identifications: Uruguayan Jews Migrants to Israel and other Countries, 1948–2010." *Jewish Population and Identity – Concept and Reality in Honor of Sidney Goldstein*. Eds. Sergio Della Pergola and Uzi Rebhun. Cham, Switzerland: Springer, 2018. 117–141.
Siebzehner, Batia. "Autoridad y Religiosidad: Transformaciones en la Comunidad Judía de Panamá." *Judaica Latinoamericana* VIII. Ed. AMILAT. Jerusalem: Editorial Universitaria Magnes, Universidad Hebrea, 2017. 267–289.
Sznajder, Mario. "El Judaísmo Chileno y el Gobierno de la Unión Popular." *Judaica Latinoamericana* II. Ed. AMILAT. Jerusalem: Editorial Universitaria Magnes, Universidad Hebrea, 1993. 136–148.
Tesone Milhem, Vivianne. "Expansión de la comunidad judía de Bogotá." *Los Judíos en Colombia: Una Aproximación Histórica*. Eds. Adelaida Sourdis Nájer and Alfonso Velazco Rojas. Madrid: Casa Sefarad Israel, 2011. 245–264.
Topel, Marta F. "O Movimiento de Teshuváem Sao Paulo e o Esgotamento do Judaísmo Secular no Brasil: Algumas Reflexoes." *Judaica Latinoamericana* V. Ed. AMILAT. Jerusalem: Editorial Universitaria Magnes, Universidad Hebrea, 2005. 83–93.
Topel, Marta F. "Brooklyn y Jerusalén en los Trópicos: El Movimiento de Teshuvahen la Comunidad Judía Paulista." *Pertenencia y Alteridad. Judíos en/de América Latina: Cuarenta Años de Cambios*. Eds. Haim Avni, Judit Bokser Liwerant et al. Madrid: Iberoamericana – Vervuert, 2011. 621–637.
Trahtemberg, León. *Los Judíos de Lima y las Provincias del Perú*. Lima: author's edition, 1989.
Wikipedia, *History of the Jews in Portugal*, 8 January 2020.
Wikipedia, *History of the Jews in Mexico*, 17 January 2020.
Zadoff, Efraim. *Historia de la Educación Judía en Buenos Aires (1935–1957)*. Buenos Aires: Editorial Milá, 1994.

Further Reading

AMILAT (ed.), *Judaica Latinoamericana, Estudios Histórico-Sociales*, Jerusalén: Editorial Universitaria Magnes, (Vol. I) 1988, (Vol. II) 1993, (Vol. III) 1997, (Vol. IV) 2001.
AMILAT (ed.), *Judaica Latinoamericana, Estudios Históricos, Sociales y Literarios*, Jerusalén: Editorial Universitaria Magnes, (Vol. V) 2005, (Vol. VI) 2009, (Vol. VII) 2013, (Vol. VIII) 2017.
Avni, Haim. *Judíos en América. Cinco siglos de Historia*. Madrid: Mapfre, 1992.
Avni, Haim. *Argentina ¿Tierra Prometida? El Barón de Hirsch y su Proyecto de Colonización Judía*. Buenos Aires: UAI, Teseo, 2018.
Avni, Haim, Judit Bokser Liwerant et. al., eds. *Pertenencia y Alteridad. Judíos en/de América Latina: Cuarenta Años de Cambios*. Madrid: Iberoamericana – Vervuert, 2011.
Lisbona, José Antonio. *Retorno a Sefarad: La política de España hacia sus judíos en el siglo XX*. Barcelona: Riopiedras Ediciones, 1993.

Daniela Flesler
13 Contemporary Jewish Literatures of Spain

Abstract: This chapter examines contemporary Jewish literature in Spain focusing on three writers that are emblematic of the return of Jews and Judaism to Spain in the twentieth century. The writings of Rafael Cansinos Assens (1882–1964), Solly Wolodarsky (1927–2014) and Esther Bendahan Cohen (1964–) are analyzed as exemplary case studies of different emphases in contemporary Jewish literatures in Spain. The chapter explores the major role that Spain's Jewish history plays in the work of these three writers.

Key Terms: Rafael Cansinos Assens, Solly Wolodarsky, Esther Bendahan Cohen, Spanish Jewish writers, Jewish literature in Spain

1 Jewish Returns

This chapter focuses on three writers that are emblematic of the return of Jews and Judaism to Spain in the twentieth century and, thus, of Jewish literature written in contemporary Spain.[1] From their different religious backgrounds, nations of origin and historical moments in the long twentieth century, Rafael Cansinos Assens (1882–1964), Solly Wolodarsky (1927–2014) and Esther Bendahan Cohen (1964–) explore what it means to be Jewish in Spain in light of Spain's long and conflictive Jewish history, and the different modes of identification with that history and with Jewish identity. These writers, within their time, witnessed a set of historical milestones encapsulated in a double return to Spain, first of significant numbers of Jews and second of the open practice of Judaism. It is, therefore, not surprising to find these milestones thematized in these writers' fictional work. Their work contributes to Jewish-Spanish literature in a process similar to Dieter Ingenschay's definition of Jewish-Latin American literature in this volume: "an open corpus of literary works that contribute to the discussion, continuation and (re)shaping of the (self-)consciousness of the group of people who 'identify' as Jewish Latin Americans" (Ingenschay). Cansinos, Wolodarsky and Bendahan's writings and personal trajectories

---

[1] This chapter does not provide an exhaustive list of Jewish writers in contemporary Spain. For general reference, Jacobo Israel Garzón's annotated list "Autores judíos contemporáneos de la Península Ibérica" is extremely useful. Significant Jewish writers of the twentieth century not analyzed in this essay include Leopoldo Azancot (Seville 1935–Madrid 2015) and Marcos Ricardo Barnatán (Buenos Aires 1946–), who moved with his family to Madrid in the 1960s. See Beckwith (2006), for an analysis of Leopoldo Azancot's novel *Novia judía*.

encapsulate and become emblematic of the different layers of meaning and diversity present in their identification as "Jewish" in twentieth and twenty-first century Spain.

Rafael Cansinos Assens was born in a Spanish Catholic family in Seville but came to identify himself as a descendant of *conversos* and was regarded by his contemporaries as Jewish. His extensive Jewish-themed oeuvre explores the historical context that made his identity claim possible and reflects on his belonging in relation to Spain's Jewish history. He is an early representative of an important phenomenon in Spain today, that of (Catholic-raised) Spaniards who identify as having Jewish ancestry. Solly Wolodarsky was born in an Argentine Ashkenazi family in Buenos Aires and moved to Spain in 1969. Many other Argentine Jews (mostly Ashkenazi and non-religious) arrived in Spain in the 1970s and later in the 1990s. Wolodarsky was an important figure in the development of a public sphere for Jewish culture in Spain, and in the legitimation of the role of secular Ashkenazi Jews in it. Esther Bendahan Cohen, born in a Moroccan Sephardi family in Tetouan, emigrated as a child to Madrid in the early 1970s, at a time when important numbers of Moroccan Sephardi families did, transforming the composition of Spain's Jewish communities. Both in her institutional role in the *Centro Sefarad-Israel* and in her literary work, Bendahan carves a space for the presence of Jewish culture in general and Sephardi culture and identity in particular in contemporary Spain.[2]

The official return of Jews to Spain in the twentieth century was preceded by a return of the figure of the Jew in public discussions in the late eighteenth century and nineteenth centuries. At this time, a variety of arguments about the place of Jews in Spain's history brewed in political debates over the gradual decline of Spain as a world power. These discussions gained urgency as Spain's progressive loss of its overseas empire culminated in the humiliating 1898 defeat by the US in the Spanish American War. Jews were at the center of heated political debate on the issue of the abolition of the Inquisition, the role of Church and State, and freedom of conscience and individual rights. These were, at their core, debates about modernity itself and Spain's place in a modern world order (see Álvarez Chillida 2002, 100–101; Gold 2009, 102–103; Rozenberg 2010, 74–78; Ojeda-Mata 2006).

Spain's re-encounter with "real" Jews took place in Morocco at the time of the 1859–1860 Hispano-Moroccan War. When Spanish troops triumphantly entered the city of Tetouan on February 6, 1860, the Jews of Tetouan received the Spaniards as liberators. Many articles in the Spanish press commented on the surprise of Spaniards at encountering descendants of the Jews expelled from the Peninsula in 1492, who still spoke "Spanish" (González García 1991, 67–79, Rozenberg 2010, 43–45).[3] At

---

[2] The Center was created in 2007 as part of Spain's diplomatic efforts towards the Jewish world and Israel. It was added to pre-existing Centers or "Casas" dedicated to cultural relations and public diplomacy with different parts of the world: Casa América, Casa Asia, Casa Árabe, Casa África.

[3] A first-hand account of this reception appears in Pedro Antonio de Alarcón's *Diario de un testigo de la Guerra de Africa* [*Diary of a Witness of the War of Africa*]. The episode also appears in Benito

the same time, since the mid-nineteenth century, historians such as José Amador de los Ríos had begun to re-assess the role of Jewish culture in Spanish history (see Friedman 2011, 2014; Bush 2011; Shinan 2013). Their work influenced some of the most important political figures of the second half of the nineteenth century in Spain, such as Emilio Castelar (1832–1899), famous for his passionate defense of religious freedom during the preparation of the 1869 Constitution (Ojeda-Mata 2006, 59; Shinan 2016).[4]

The efforts at a rapprochement with Sephardi Jews coalesced in the early twentieth century around the figure of a close friend of Castelar, the senator Ángel Pulido y Fernández. He became the leader of 'philosephardism,' a movement that sought to expand Spain's influence in the Mediterranean and advance Spain's colonial ambitions on Morocco through the cultivation of links with Sephardi Jews.[5] The philosephardists' campaign brought the history of Sephardic Jews into the public sphere and produced concrete results. The 1915 appointment of the Jerusalem-born Jewish scholar Abraham Shalom Yahuda to a Chair for Hebrew Literature and the History of the Jews in Spain in the Middle Ages at the University of Madrid, the creation of *Casa Universal de los Sefardís* [Universal House of Sephardi Jews], an organization established in 1920 in Madrid to promote economic and cultural cooperation and, most importantly, the granting of Spanish nationality to a number of Sephardi Jews through a 1924 royal decree.[6]

Pérez Galdós' *Aitta Tettauen*. The Judeo-Spanish language has its origin in old Castilian, but it is a live language that has evolved in contact with and influenced by other languages (Hebrew, Arabic, Turkish, Italian, French), not an archaeological remnant of old Castilian, as it is often represented (Hassán 2006, 42). Rather than an expression of love for Spain, the use of the Judeo-Spanish language among Sephardi Jews was an affirmation of their own Jewish minoritary identity, a differentiating element that explains why many referred to the language as "judío" or "judesmo" (Hassán 2006, 45). See also Paloma Díaz-Mas (1992, 72–101, 198).

4 The Inquisition was abolished for good by order of the Regent Queen María Cristina in April 1834. The Jewish population of Spain in the second half of the nineteenth century was about 400 people, most of whom had emigrated from Gibraltar and North Africa. There were also some Ashkenazi financiers from prominent European families. The 1869 Constitution guaranteed freedom of religion and abrogated the remaining anti-Jewish legislation.

5 As he related it, he "discovered" the Sephardim during a cruise along the Danube in 1880 in which he became fascinated by three Sephardi businessmen who spoke to him in Judeo-Spanish. Returning to the Balkans in 1903, he met Enrique Bejarano, the Romanian director of a school in Bucharest and a great admirer of Spain, who informed him about the two million Sephardi Jews who lived around the world, spoke Judeo-Spanish and felt a close attachment to Spain. Back in Spain, Pulido began a campaign to promote ties with these communities, writing articles and giving speeches in the Senate. These were collected in his 1904 book *Los israelitas españoles y el idioma castellano* [*The Spanish Israelites and the Castilian Language*] (Díaz-Mas 1992, 153–155; Garzón 1992, xi–xxi; Rohr 2007, 15).

6 See Friedman and González for more on the fascinating figure of Yahuda, who held the first Jewish studies chairmanship created in the Western Hemisphere in a secular university in the modern era (Friedman 2019; González 2019). The 1924 decree was intended for Sephardim who had enjoyed the protection of Spain's diplomatic agents in the Ottoman Empire. Few people (between four and five thousand) were able to obtain nationality this way, either for lack of clear information or because the process was arduous and required documents that many did not have (Rohr 2007, 27; Avni 1982,

The far-reaching consequences of Pulido's writings and the philosephardi campaigns can still be felt in Spain today. Much of the rationale and language of the 2015 Law of Nationality for Sephardi Jews, which provides a path to citizenship to those who can prove descent from Jews expelled from Spain in 1492 is connected to these early twentieth century philosephardi views of Sephardi Jews.[7]

2 Rafael Cansinos Assens

Rafael Cansinos Assens was a privileged witness to the philosephardi efforts of Pulido, to the arrival of Yahuda in Madrid and the inauguration of the first synagogue in Madrid on February of 1917. Cansinos' "discovery" of his family's converso roots and the beginnings of his deep relationship with Judaism coincided with the beginning of the philosephardi campaigns. Through Pulido he met José Farache, a Gibraltar Jew living in Madrid, who probably told him about the Jewish origin of the last name "Cansino," present among members of Gibraltar's Jewish community (Garzón 2011, 9). As Garzón explains, many of Cansinos' contemporaries identified him as Jewish. In Pulido's *Españoles sin patria*, published in 1905, Pulido calls Cansinos "a renown Spanish journalist descendant of Israelites" (Garzón 2011, 10, 22). The accusation of being Jewish was the main reason why Cansinos was denied a journalist credential in 1940, upon the end of the Spanish Civil War, by the Francoist authorities, which meant he could not publish in Spain (Garzón 2011, 11). Borges, who considered himself a disciple of Cansinos, famously described this Jewish identification in the poem "Rafael Cansinos-Assens," written upon Cansinos' death in 1964 and included in *El otro, el mismo*: "Bebió como quien bebe un hondo vino / Los Psalmos y el Cantar de la Escritura / Y sintió que era suya esa dulzura / Y sintió que era suyo aquel destino" (Aizenberg 1980, 534–535; Garzón 2011, 13) [As with deep drinks of vintage, so did he drink/ the Psalms and the Song of Solomon, / He felt that such a sweetness was his own, / He felt that all this was his destiny].[8] In terms of his work, Esther Bartolomé Pons sees him as "uno de los más destacados representantes de la literatura judía en España" [one of the most prominent representatives of Jewish literature in Spain] (Bartolomé Pons 1983, 4). As Carmen de Urioste argues, Cansinos' profound interest in Judaism has to be seen in the historical context of the philosephardi campaigns taking place at the time. Cansinos was an active participant in these efforts. As explained by Allyson González, Cansi-

---

31–33; Ojeda-Mata 2006, 66). Notwithstanding its limitations, the decree was an important precedent for the modern rapprochement of Spain and the Jews. See Garzón, "El Doctor Pulido" for more on the far-reaching consequences of the philosephardi campaign.
7 For more on the philosephardi echoes in this Law, see Linhard 2014, Aragoneses 2016, McDonald 2019, Aliberti 2020. For Spain and the Jews under Franco, see Avni 1982, Rohr 2007, Linhard 2014.
8 Translation by John Hollander (Borges 1972, 197).

nos' own Jewish self-identification speaks of a time of profound change, of "complex desires for personal and national regeneration" (González 2019, 421–422).

Cansinos' explicitly "Jewish" ouevre is comprised of several books, in addition to numerous journalistic articles and poems: *El candelabro de los siete brazos* (1914), *Las bellezas del Talmud* (1920), *España y los judíos españoles. El retorno del éxodo* (1920), *Cuentos judíos contemporáneos* (1921), *El amor en el Cantar de los Cantares* (1930), *Los judíos en la literatura española* (1937). His novel *Las luminarias de Janucá* (1924), which narrates his own identification with Judaism through the figure of an alter ego, the poet Rafael Benasar, and his collection of short stories *Los judíos en Sefarad* (1950), which further explores some of the key themes and characters of *Luminarias* are especially pertinent for our purposes.

Las luminarias de Janucá was published by Editora Internacional in Madrid in 1924, re-published in Buenos Aires by Candelabro in 1961, and recently re-published in Spain again by the Rafael Cansinos Assens Archive (Fundación Arca) in 2011. This novel has been characterized as a historical document narrating the creation of the first Jewish community in Madrid at the time of World War I (Garzón 2011, 13); as a novel "de valor documental" [of documentary value] (de Urioste). It is characterized as such by Cansinos himself, when, for the re-edition of 1961, he calls his text a "monument:" "una obra que, aparte de su mérito literario, es un monumento que consagra un momento culminante y feliz en la historia de las relaciones, no siempre fraternales, entre españoles y sefardíes" [a work that, besides its literary merit, is a monument that consecrates a culminating and happy moment in the history of the not always friendly relationship between Spaniards and Sephardi Jews] (*Luminarias* 26). The novel, in effect, narrates Pulido's political efforts, the arrival in Spain of Yahuda, the lives of some of the Jewish inhabitants of Madrid at the time, and the opening of the first official synagogue in Madrid for the celebration of Hanukkah in December of 1916.

But, most potently, the text excavates Jewish identity at the beginning of the twentieth century in Spain. It explores the available ways of being Jewish in Spain at this time, with special attention to the profound and often anguished identity search that its protagonist, Rafael Benaser, undertakes and embraces. In parallel to the description of the philosephardi campaigns, the novel describes Rafael's acknowledgment of his "difference," and the discovery and subsequent embrace of his converso ancestry. Early in the novel, we read that "[s]iempre había parecido a Rafael Benaser que un misterio latía en lo recóndito de los anales familiares" [Rafael Benaser always thought that a mystery lay in the family's remote past] (*Luminarias* 29). The text comes back once and again to this idea: the protagonist has always felt different. Different from his classmates as a child, from his fellow countrymen as an adult (*Luminarias* 31, 36, 284). This difference was acutely perceived by the priests, he notes: "[n]o me sentían enteramente suyo" [they did not perceive me as entirely theirs] (*Luminarias* 95–96).

One day, browsing through old manuscripts, he finds the family name in reference to an Inquisitorial process. This moment of recognition and revelation provides the clue to understand his family history, his parents' struggles, the unshakable "old sorrow" that has accompanied his family for generations: "Y el joven, inclinado sobre aquellos papeles que conservaban como un lienzo sagrado huellas del dolor de su raza, sintió que las lágrimas fluían de sus ojos por aquel dolor antiguo, y que en su alma nacía una conciencia nueva de su vida y de su destino" [leaning over the papers that contained the traces of his people's suffering as a sacred canvas, the young man felt his tears fell for that old sorrow, and in his soul a new conscience about his life and his destiny was born] (*Luminarias* 34–35). Rafael explains that he cannot have absolute certainty but that he does not need it. Just the possibility that it might be true is enough to accept a lineage and a legacy that, he argues, he cannot refuse (*Luminarias* 44–46). In parallel to the acceptance of this inheritance, Rafael develops friendships with the few Jews who live in Madrid at this time. He observes how they live hiding their Jewish identity, and how they meet in secret (*Luminarias* 67). Their secrecy finds parallel in the secrecy of past conversos (*Luminarias* 49, *Los judíos* 47–57).

In her analysis of converso return narratives, Dalia Kandiyoti explains that returns are often marked by failure. But this impossibility does not prevent many social actors from "returning" and finding, or producing remnants of that past, and seeing themselves as remnants, even where other people might see nothing (Kandiyoti, *The Converso's Return* 6–7, 18). Rafael sees himself precisely this way, as a remnant, and so do his friends. Doctor Salomon (whose character in the book stands in for Yahuda) tells Rafael, "por todas partes, en España, me salen al encuentro los vestigios de la tradición de nuestra raza. Piedras antiguas, vestigios de templos y de juderías y *reliquias vivas*, como usted mismo, me acogen en este país" [everywhere, in Spain, I meet with vestiges of our people's tradition. Old stones, vestiges of temples and Jewish quarters, and *live remnants*, just like yourself, meet me in this country] (*Luminarias* 183, my emphasis). But Doctor Salomon is the exceptional witness who can see these vestiges.

Doctor Salomon's capacity to see these traces of the past and Rafael's willingness to remember, the obligation towards the past that he feels and acts upon, appear in stark contrast to the collective amnesia that Rafael observes in the people of Spain. He reflects upon the "olvido más afrentoso que un odio" [oblivion more shameful than hate] that exists towards Jews and Spain's Jewish history (*Luminarias* 67–68). In the short story "Amnesia ofensiva," included in the collection *Los judíos en Sefarad*, Cansinos' protagonist strives in vain to find concrete evidence of the Jewish past in Spanish cities. Yet, what distresses him the most is the fact that his interlocutors, those who inhabit streets, buildings, towns and landscapes where Jewish people once lived, have developed a selective blindness, a specific forgetfulness towards that past. Moreover, by forgetting the Jews who lived there, they absolved themselves of any responsibility for their absence (*Los judíos* 159–160). Cansinos Assens himself fell prey to a form of amnesia. His writings, admired by his contemporaries, remain all but forgotten in the current canon of Spanish literature. The partial rescue from oblivion of Cansinos' work occured in the context of a renewal of interest in "things Jewish" towards the end of the twentieth century in Spain, coinciding with the preparations for the Fifth Centenary of the 1492 Expulsion.⁹

3 Solly Wolodarsky

Since the mid 1980s, many cultural and political initiatives at the local, regional and national levels have engaged with the memory of Jewish Spain and attempted to officially reconnect Spain with the Jewish world. Since then, all things "Sepharad" have been widely marketed throughout Spain, from cultural festivals, museums, former synagogues and Jewish quarters, to historical novels, music and cookbooks. The symbolic "welcoming back" after 500 years of the commemorations of 1992 was accompanied by an increasing visibility in the publishing industry (see Flesler, Linhard and Pérez Melgosa 2011). Historical novels with Jewish topics related to Spain such as *El último judío* by Noah Gordon and *La judía de Toledo* by Lion Feuchtwanger have become bestsellers in Spain after their translation, as have many of those written by Spaniards, such as Toti Martínez de Lezea's *La calle de la judería* (1998), Lucía Graves' *La casa de la memoria* (1999), Ildefonso Falcones' *La catedral del mar* (2006), Martí Gironell's *El pont dels jueus* (2007), and Agustín Bernaldo Palatchi's *La alianza del converso* (Roca 2010). Other related important novels about Spain's Jewish history written by Spaniards are Carme Riera's *Dins el darrer blau* (Premio Nacional de Literatura, 1994), its sequel *Cap al cel obert* (2000), José Manuel Fajardo's trilogy *Carta del fin del mundo* (1996), *El converso* (1998), and *Mi nombre es Jamaica* (Premio Alberto Benveniste 2010). Many of these novels thematize the Holocaust, with or without connections to Spain: Maria Àngels Anglada's *El violí d'Auschwitz* (2003), Antonio Muñoz Molina's *Sefarad* (2001), Juana Salabert's *Velódromo de invierno* (Premio Biblioteca Breve 2001), Adolfo García Ortega's *El comprador de aniversarios* (2002), Chufo Lloréns' *La saga de los malditos* (2003), Clara Sánchez' *Lo que esconde tu nombre* (2010).¹⁰

---

9 Just like *Las luminarias de Janucá* was republished in 2011 after its first edition in 1924, *Los judíos en Sefarad* was re-published in Spain in 2008 (Hebraica Ediciones) also thanks to the efforts of the Cansinos Assens Foundation. Several of its short stories had been published in 1938–1939 in the journal *Judaica* in Argentina. The collection was published in Buenos Aires in 1950 by Editorial Israel, with a prologue by Cansinos' friend César Tiempo.
10 See Linhard (2014), Beckwith (2020) for analysis of several of these novels. Paloma Díaz-Mas has analyzed how in a number of these texts, often published with funding provided by local and regional cultural institutions, the Jewish plot is part and parcel of an effort to recognize the local or regional past (Díaz-Mas 2003, 170). See also Beckwith, "Transitions" for the intimate relationship between historical novels from the 1980s and 1990s and the Spanish cities they depict and promote. Hackl writes a very critical review of the "Sepharad industry," epitomized, in his view, by Muñoz Molina's text.

Solly Wolodarsky, born in Buenos Aires and having moved to Madrid in 1969, was one of the protagonists of this cluster of new initiatives that sought to make Jewish history and culture visible again in Spain. In 2004, he founded the radio program *Radio Sefarad*, a project of the Federation of Jewish Communities of Spain which he also directed for several years. He was also involved with one of the first cultural /touristic projects that sprang out of the creation of the *Red de juderías de España* (Network of Jewish Quarters of Spain) in 1995, that of the Jewish festival in the town of Hervás, in Cáceres, Extremadura.[11] Looking to revitalize the cultural life of the town and attract tourists, Juan Ramón Ferreira, Hervás' mayor and founding member of the *Red de juderías*, decided to stage one of Wolodarsky's plays. Behind the idea was Miguel Nieto, a well-known theatre director who specializes in popular performances by non-professional actors. Nieto suggested the play *Los conversos*, written by Wolodarsky in 1985. Although the play was highly experimental and had been intended for an audience that was knowledgeable about Jewish culture and history, the production, directed by Nieto and performed by non-professional actors from Hervás, was a big success. The play, performed over three consecutive summers, became the central event of and gave its name to the festival, still today called "Los conversos."[12]

Wolodarsky was also witness of the negotiations about Jewish identity that emerged as Sephardi and Ashkenazic Jews brought back Judaism to Spain in the later part of the twentieth century. Moroccan Jews began arriving in Spain in significant numbers after Morocco's independence in 1956, and, especially, following the Six Day War in 1967. These Moroccan immigrants rapidly became a numerical majority and organized the structures of today's official Jewish community in Spain based on the principles of Orthodox Judaism. A few years later, significant numbers of Argentine Jews emigrated to Spain as part of a larger group of political exiles escaping from the persecution of the military dictatorship established in Argentina in 1976. A second and larger wave of immigrants arrived following the 2001 Argentine economic crisis, looking for better economic and professional opportunities. Because of their different origins and paths of incorporation to Spanish society, these two groups, Sephardi Moroccans and mostly Ashkenazi Argentines, brought with them diverging visions about questions of religious observance, cultural norms and social integration (see Garzón 2014; Álvarez Chillida 2002; Rein and Weisz 2011).

Wolodarsky's most important work, *Los conversos*, can be read as a reflection on precisely these issues of contemporary import. It foregrounds Spain's Jewish history

---

11 The *Red de Juderías* was one of the tangible results of the 1992 commemorations. Funded by Spain's central government and the local councils of participating cities, the association promotes these cities' Jewish legacy through tourist routes and cultural activities. See Flesler and Pérez Melgosa (2008 and 2020) for an analysis of this initiative and its effects in towns and cities throughout Spain.
12 Several plays related to Jewish local history and legend (including antisemitic legends) have been staged in Hervás' festival after this first play. See Cohen (1999) and Flesler and Pérez Melgosa (2010 and 2020) for more on this festival.

as a way to articulate a reflection on contemporary questions of Jewish belonging. Samuel, the play's protagonist, is a secular Jewish Latin American tourist who visits Toledo in the late twentieth century. While contemplating the *Sinagoga del Tránsito*'s historic Main Prayer Room, Samuel reconsiders a question that haunts him: why should he, as an agnostic intellectual, continue identifying as a Jew? Immersed in his thoughts, Samuel dreams that he is in front of Daniel of Toledo, a fifteenth century rabbi who decided to go into exile in 1492 to preserve his faith. Daniel's brother Isaac is the third protagonist of the play. In contrast to Daniel, Isaac remained in Toledo and converted to Christianity. Samuel wants to hear directly from Daniel and Isaac about the reasons behind the decision each of them made when confronted with the choice of exile or conversion. He is confident that their answers will help him solve his personal dilemmas as a secular Jew.

As the brothers explain and justify their lives and choices to Samuel, their apparently opposite positions begin to show their interdependence. Daniel sees betrayal and cowardice in his brother's decision to convert and accuses Isaac of having betrayed his people only to keep the family's fortune. But we learn how, ironically, it was thanks to Isaac's "betrayal" that he was able to send money to Daniel so the rabbi could to complete his spiritual education and his pilgrimage to the promised land. The play also reveals the shadows of Isaac's moral pragmatism when we see him as an informer, exposing Judaizing-converts when the Inquisition directly threatens his family.

Isaac's testimony dismantles the binary logic that opposes a 'heroism' of those who maintained their Jewish faith, by going into exile or practicing Judaism in secret after converting, to the supposed 'treason' of the assimilated converso. As the play continues to unveil the complexity of the converso condition, it deploys the term "converso" beyond religion, into the realms of culture. Thus, when Rabbi Daniel accuses Isaac of having broken his covenant with God, allowing his children to marry Christians and erasing their lineage through the purchase of noble titles, Isaac exclaims, pointing to the audience: "-¡Ahí tienes a mis descendientes! ¿Cuántos con mi sangre encuentras hoy en las calles de toda España? Tienen una patria cierta, no ambulante. Poseen un linaje, una religión que no los diferencia . . . ¡Ahí están los frutos de mi sacrificio!" [-Behold my descendants! How many people with my blood do you find today in every street of Spain? They aren't nomads, but have a secure homeland, they are not exiles. They have a lineage, a religion that does not set them apart . . . There you have the fruits of my sacrifice!]. For Isaac, his conversion was the price he paid to assure his descendants' life. It also assured his brother's Judaism. His words attempt to conjure up the converso component in Spanish society, challenging and directly addressing the (Spanish) audience.

We can read this interpellation as an intervention in the discussions within Spain's newly formed Jewish communities, at a time when Moroccan and Argentine Jewish immigrants were debating appropriate modes of inserting themselves within a national community which was undergoing an accelerated process of modernization, democratization and secularization. When the play addresses the audience directly to point out Spain's ancestral converso legacy, converting, in the sense of surviving their own historical circumstances, including immigrating and adapting to a new environment, becomes not the exception but the common experience that Samuel, Daniel, Isaac and the audience share. Implicitly, this redefined "conversion" becomes the common ground that today's Spanish Jews share with the rest of the population in Spain. In the context of a country in which Judaism has been, and still is, a suspect identity associated with foreignness, *Los conversos* refashions Spain, with its Jewish legacy, as a legitimate home for each of these three groups.

In the year 2000, moved by the enthusiastic reception of his play in Hervás, Wolodarsky wrote a play specifically tailored for the town, with the action set in its streets and local historical references incorporated in the plot. Thus was born *La conversa de Hervás*, the central piece of the festival from 2000 to 2007. This play uses theatrical conventions of the cloak and dagger comedies from the Spanish Golden Age to tell the story of Manuel Alvarado, a prominent local converso. The play, a denunciation of Jewish scapegoating, emphasizes the inclusion of Don Manuel and his family in the cultural, social and religious life of the town, presenting them not as conversos who happen to live in Hervás but rather as people from Hervás who are conversos. Wolodarsky's novel *El judío de Hervás* (2007) further developed the character of Manuel Alvarado, cementing the relationship of Jewish and converso characters to a particular Spanish local space, something that he also explored in his other late works, *Maimónides, el Sefardí* (2005) and *Avapiés* (2009), about the Jewish connections of the iconic Madrid neighborhood Lavapiés.

4 Esther Bendahan Cohen

Like Wolodarsky, Esther Bendahan Cohen is both a writer and a key public figure in the panorama of Jewish culture and its dissemination in contemporary Spain. She has been the director of cultural programming at the *Centro Sefarad-Israel* since its inauguration in the year 2007, and as such, she has played a key role in Spain's official efforts to strengthen diplomatic links with Judaism, the Sephardi diaspora and Israel. Bendahan's writing captures with particular poignancy the difficulty of avoiding well-established clichés when speaking for and about Sephardi Jews in contemporary Spain. She is critical of the origin and use of the romantic myths of historic loyalty and love for an Iberian homeland and the Spanish language and the idealization of *convivencia* that emerge in Spanish public discourse when the name *Sepharad* is invoked.[13] Yet, she is also aware that these myths often provide the means through

---

[13] See Díaz-Mas (1992) and Iacob M. Hassán (2006) for the dispelling of many of the myths surrounding Sephardi Jews. The cliché of their centuries-old attachment to the homeland that rejected them has been pervasive because this understanding of the Sephardim has served Spanish interests and, at

which the experience of Sephardi Jews finds articulation within contemporary Spain. Her work explores this tension between the need to fully normalize the presence of Jews in general and the Sephardim in particular within contemporary Spanish society and the desire to dispel the many prejudices and misconceptions that still circulate about them.

The discourse of Sephardi Jews ancestral love for Spain has become the most expedient, and at times the only available rhetorical instrument to articulate a claim of legitimacy, belonging and authority for Spanish Jews. Within Spain, participating in the country's mythologies of medieval *convivencia* and of Sephardi Jews as zealous preservers of Spanish culture and language provides a social right to inhabit a shared space. These time-sanctioned myths still provide the available grammar through which it is possible to speak, and to be listened to, as Sephardim in Spain. Frequently, Bendahan's narratives inhabit these spaces and deploy their grammar. Yet, as critics like Campoy-Cubillo observe, Bendahan's fiction stays away from essentialist definitions of identity (Campoy-Cubillo 2012, 87). Her writing also embarks in critical explorations of these received notions, exposing their mythical nature in the form of narrative voices that interrogate characters' notions of genealogy, identity and national belonging.

Bendahan's first novel, *Soñar con Hispania* (2002), co-written with Israel-based Chilean Jewish writer Ester Benari, undertakes such examination through the relationship of its two protagonists, José de la Villa, a Spanish professor of medieval literature, and Sofía Corzo, a Jewish Israeli computer programmer. As they correspond through email, we find out that Sofía is a widow who maintains a genealogical website dedicated to the Sephardi Corzo family and José is researching the life-stories of two fifteenth century Jewish women from his hometown in Spain who had Sofía's same last name. Just like in Cansinos' and Wolodarsky's work, we find here a reflection on the connections between present and past, and how contemporary protagonists position themselves and claim a factual or affective genealogy with those Spanish Jews who either converted or went into exile in 1492. But the novel also bursts the romantic bubble imagined by José, when he assumes that Sofía is a descendant of one of the two sisters. Just as we cannot know what exactly happened to them in the fifteenth century, the novel ruptures the fallacy of the possibility of tracing a genealogical straight line from them to Sofía, as it reveals that Corzo is not her last name, but her deceased husband's.

Bendahan's 2006 novel *Déjalo, ya volveremos*, is the story of a Moroccan Sephardi family who leaves Tetouan for Madrid in the early 1970s. With clear autobiographical overtones, the novel is extremely aware of the way the average Spanish reader may

---

times, Sephardi interests as well. See Flesler and Pérez-Melgosa (2020) for more on the currency and deployment of myths about Sepharad and *convivencia* in Spain today. See Martin-Márquez (2008), Calderwood (2018), for *convivencia* in relation to Spain's Arab and Muslim heritage.

see Jews and Judaism.[14] It uses the perspective of a child narrator who tells us of her family's life in Tetouan, her arrival in Madrid and her progressive adjustment to her new home. In Madrid, she confronts the ignorance and prejudice of her school classmates towards Jews, and her difference from them. In a narrative arch that coincides with the Jewish festive cycle and Jewish holidays, the protagonist adapts to her surroundings in Spain, while finding her home in her Jewish practice. The novel gives a nod to the notion of Spain as a place of "return" for Sephardi Jews, as an ancestral home. The family, says the narrator, "eran españoles de siempre" [had always been Spaniards] (*Déjalo* 238). This nod, which undoubtedly sits well with the Spanish audience that would buy and read the novel, is, however, also tinged with feelings of ambivalence and nostalgia for other lands and paths taken and not taken in successive exiles and migrations.[15]

5 Conclusion

As Dalia Kandiyoti explains in reference to diasporic writing in her book *Migrant Sites*, the homeland is far from being an uncontested space and source of identification (*Migrant Sites* 37). Indeed, "the condition of multiple rediasporization that characterizes the trajectories of many communities may make the assumption of a single place of origin impossible or moot" (*Migrant Sites* 38). Kandiyoti uses the oxymoronic formulation "migrant sites" to characterize these dwelling places, a term that encompasses both the local and the translocal, the national and the transnational, fixity and mobility (*Migrant Sites* 39). Jewish literature in contemporary Spain explores Spanish Jewish identity as a condition belonging to these interstitial, in-between spaces of deep contact, not only in terms of geographical mobility but also, especially, of temporal movement. Spain's Jewish past has an overwhelming presence in contemporary Jewish writing in Spain. In his review of Cansinos Assens' *Luminarias*, Borges explained that the novel "es conmovedora en el teatro antiguo de tantas glorias y vejámenes" [is moving in the old theatre of so many glories and humiliations] (in Aizenberg 1980, 536). That is, what makes this novel so moving is precisely that place of enunciation from "the settings of the old tragedy," as Cansinos himself calls Spain in "Amnesia ofensiva." The fact of writing from this precise location, of striving to give voice to the experiences that emerge from it,

---

14 In 2016 Bendahan published the book *Tetuán*, recounting her memories of the city and her recent trips there. Even more explicitly than *Déjalo, ya volveremos*, this book emphasizes the identity ties between the Jewish community of the Moroccan Protectorate and Spain and the "Spanishness" of Bendahan's family.
15 In her article, "El mundo literario judío como paradigma del exilio ¿literatura judía?" Bendahan affirms that Jewish literature is intrinsically related to exile, both the real, personal exile of Jewish writers and the concept of exile as a constitutive part of Jewish identity (Bendahan 2014, 29–31).

becomes, in Cansinos, Wolodarsky and Bendahan's work, the main reason for the existence of their writing. And the existence of this new writing, in turn, carries with it the possibility of adding new significations to "the settings of the old tragedy."

Jewish literature written in contemporary Spain is characterized by the significance that many writers place in the rich and conflictive Jewish history of Spain. Although this literature is being written from a variety of perspectives and obeys the very different interests and circumstances of different writers, it shares a common interrogation about the place and belonging of Jews and Jewish culture to Spain. Written during the twentieth and twenty-first centuries, the creation and circulation of this writing coincides with the physical return of Jews to Spain, and it participates in the growing visibility of Judaism and Jewish culture in Spain's public sphere.

Bibliography

Works Cited

Aizenberg, Edna. "Cansinos-Assens y Borges: en busca del vínculo judaico." *Revista iberoamericana* 46.112–13 (1980): 533–544.

Álvarez Chillida, Gonzalo. *El antisemitismo en España: la imagen del judío, 1812–2002*. Madrid: Marcial Pons, 2002.

Aliberti, Davide. "Back to Sefarad? A Comparative Analysis of the 2015 Iberian Citizenship Laws for Sephardic Jews." *Transcultural Spaces and Identities in Iberian Studies*, edited by Mark Gant & Susana Rocha Relvas, Cambridge Scholars Publishing, 2020. 236–60.

Aragoneses, Alfons. "Convivencia and Filosefardismo in Spanish Nation-Building." *Max Planck Institute for European Legal History Research Paper Series* 5 (2016): 1–34.

Avni, Haim. *Spain, the Jews, and Franco*. Philadelphia: The Jewish Publication Society of America, 1982.

Bartolomé Pons, Esther. "Rafael Cansinos Assens: fracaso y gloria para el poeta de una hora tardía (o de cómo un judío milenario se convierte en maestro ultraísta)". *Ínsula* 444–445 (1983): 3–4.

Beckwith, Stacy N. "Between Eros and Dios: Leopoldo Azancot's *Novia judía*." *Religious Perspectives in Modern Muslim and Jewish Literatures*. Eds. Glenda Abramson and Hilary Kilpatrick. London and New York: Routledge, 2006. 299–310.

Beckwith, Stacy N. "With Sepharad as a Void: Recent Reckoning with the Holocaust in Spanish Fiction." *Spain, the Second World War, and the Holocaust: History and Representation*. Eds. Sara J. Brenneis and Gina Herrmann. Toronto: Toronto University Press, 2020. 536–551.

Beckwith, Stacy N. "Transitions Back to Sepharad in Spanish Historical Novels from 1985 through 2001." (unpublished manuscript).

Bendahan, Esther. *Déjalo, ya volveremos*. Barcelona: Seix Barral, 2006.

Bendahan, Esther. "El mundo literario judío como paradigma del exilio ¿literatura judía?" *El Judaísmo: Contribuciones y presencia en el mundo Contemporáneo*. Cuadernos de la Escuela Diplomática Número 51. Madrid: Escuela Diplomática España y Centro Sefarad Israel, 2014. 29–45.

Bendahan, Esther. *Una hora solamente, de la orilla del día*. Salamanca: Confluencias, 2016.

Bendahan, Esther. *Tetuán*. Antequera: Confluencias, 2016.

Bendahan, Esther, and Esther Benari. *Soñar con Hispania*. Santander: Tantín, 2002.

Borges, Jorge Luis. *Selected Poems 1923–1967*. Ed. Norman Thomas di Giovanni. London: The Penguin Press, 1972.

Bush, Andrew. "Amador de los Ríos and the beginnings of modern Jewish studies in Spain." *Revisiting Jewish Spain in the Modern Era*. Eds. Daniela Flesler, Tabea Linhard and Adrián Pérez Melgosa. Special Issue of the *Journal of Spanish Cultural Studies* 12.1 (2011): 13–33.

Calderwood, Eric. *Colonial al-Andalus. Spain and the Making of Modern Moroccan Culture*. Cambridge: Harvard University Press, 2018.

Campoy-Cubillo, Adolfo. *Memories of the Maghreb. Transnational Identities in Spanish Cultural Production*. New York: Palgrave, 2012.

Cansinos Assens, Rafael. *Las luminarias de Janucá. Un episodio de la historia de Israel en España*. Madrid: Arca Ediciones, [1924] 2011.

Cansinos Assens, Rafael. *Los judíos en Sefarad*. Ed. Jacobo Israel Garzón. Madrid: Hebraica Ediciones, [1950] 2006.

Cohen, Judith R. "Constructing a Spanish Jewish Festival: Music and the Appropriation of Tradition in Imagined Iberian Jewish Communities." *The World of Music* 41.3 (1999): 95–114.

Díaz-Mas, Paloma. *Sephardim: The Jews From Spain*. Chicago: University of Chicago Press, 1992.

Díaz-Mas, Paloma. "Judíos y conversos en la narrativa española de los años 80 y 90." *El legado de Sefarad. Los judíos sefardíes en la historia y la literatura de América Latina, España, Portugal y Alemania*. Ed. Norbert Rehrmann. Salamanca: Amarú, 2003. 167–180.

Flesler, Daniela, and Adrián Pérez Melgosa. "Marketing *Convivencia*: Contemporary Tourist Appropriations of Spain's Jewish Past." *Spain is (Still) Different: Tourism and Discourse in Spanish Cultural Identity*. Eds. Eugenia Afinoguénova and Jaume Martí-Olivella. Lanham, MD: Lexington Books, 2008. 63–84.

Flesler, Daniela, and Adrián Pérez Melgosa. "Hervás, *Convivencia*, and the Heritagization of Spain's Jewish Past." *Journal of Romance Studies* 10.2 (2010): 53–76.

Flesler, Daniela, Adrián Pérez Melgosa and Tabea Linhard. "Introduction: Revisiting Jewish Spain in the Modern Era." *Journal of Spanish Cultural Studies* Special Issue 12.1 (2011): 1–11.

Flesler, Daniela, and Adrián Pérez Melgosa. *The Memory Work of Jewish Spain*. Bloomington: Indiana University Press, 2020.

Friedman, Michal. "Jewish History as "Historia Patria": José Amador de los Ríos and the History of the Jews of Spain." *Jewish Social Studies* 18.1 (2011): 88–126.

Friedman, Michal. "Reconstructing 'Jewish Spain': The Politics and Institutionalization of Jewish History in Spain, 1845–1940." *Hamsa. Journal of Judaic and Islamic Studies* 1 (2014): 55–67.

Friedman, Michal. "Abraham Shalom Yahuda: A Jewish Orientalist among Sepharad, Zionisms, and the British Empire." *The Jewish Quarterly Review* 109.3 (2019): 435–451.

Garzón, Jacobo Israel. "El Doctor Pulido y los Sefardíes." In Pulido, Angel. *Los israelitas españoles y el idioma castellano*. Ed. Jacobo Israel Garzón. Madrid: Riopiedras, 1992. ix–xxiii.

Garzón, Jacobo Israel. "Autores judíos contemporáneos de la Península Ibérica." *Raíces. Revista judía de cultura* 14 (1993): 27–43.

Garzón, Jacobo Israel. "Rafael Cansinos Assens, el judaísmo y *Las luminarias de Janucá*." In Cansinos Assens, Rafael. *Las luminarias de Janucá. Un episodio de la historia de Israel en España*. Ed. Jacobo Israel Garzón. Madrid: Arca Ediciones, 2011. 9–24.

Garzón, Jacobo Israel. "El retorno a Sefarad y los Judíos de España." *El Judaísmo: Contribuciones y presencia en el mundo Contemporáneo*. Cuadernos de la Escuela Diplomática Número 51. Madrid: Escuela Diplomática España y Centro Sefarad Israel, 2014. 329–61.

Gold, Hazel. "Illustrated Histories: The National Subject and 'the Jew' in Nineteenth-Century Spanish Art." *Journal of Spanish Cultural Studies* 10.1 (2009): 89–109.

González, Allyson. "Abraham S. Yahuda (1877–1951) and the Politics of Modern Jewish Scholarship." *The Jewish Quarterly Review* 109.3 (2019): 406–433.

González García, Isidro. *El retorno de los judíos*. Madrid: Nerea, 1991.
Hackl, Erich. "El caso Sefarad: Industrias y errores del santo de su señora." *Lateral: Revista de Cultura* 6.78 (2001): 20–29.
Halevi-Wise, Yael, ed. *Sephardism: Spanish Jewish History and the Modern Literary Imagination*. Stanford: Stanford University Press, 2012.
Hassán, Iacob M. "Los sefardíes como tópico." *Raíces* 67 (2006): 41–47.
Kandiyoti, Dalia. *Migrant Sites: America, Place, and Diaspora*. Hanover and London: University Press of New England, 2009.
Kandiyoti, Dalia. *The Converso's Return. The Afterlives of Conversion in Contemporary Literature and Culture*. Stanford: Stanford University Press, 2020.
Linhard, Tabea. *Jewish Spain. A Mediterranean Memory*. Stanford: Stanford University Press, 2014.
Martin-Márquez, Susan. *Disorientations. Spanish Colonialism in Africa and the Performance of Identity*. New Haven and London: Yale University Press, 2008.
McDonald, Charles A. "Return to Sepharad: Citizenship, Conversion, and the Politics of Jewish Inclusion in Spain." PhD dissertation, New School for Social Research, 2019.
Ojeda-Mata, Maite. "Thinking about 'the Jew' in Modern Spain: Historiography, Nationalism and Antisemitism." *Jewish Culture and History* 8.2 (2006): 53–72.
Rein, Raanan, and Martina Weisz. "Ghosts of the Past, Challenges of the Present: New and Old "Others" in Contemporary Spain." *El Otro en la España Contemporánea. Prácticas, discursos y representaciones*. Eds. Silvina Schammah Gesser and Raanan Rein. Sevilla: Fundación Tres Culturas, 2011. 161–186.
Rohr, Isabelle. *The Spanish Right and the Jews, 1898–1945. Antisemitism and Opportunism*. Brighton, England: Sussex Academic Press, 2007.
Rozenberg, Danielle. *La España contemporánea y la cuestión judía. Retejiendo los hilos de la memoria y la historia*. Madrid: Casa Sefarad-Israel and Marcial Pons, 2010.
Shinan, Nitai. "Estudio preliminar." In Amador de los Ríos, José. *Los Judíos de España: Estudios históricos, políticos y literarios*. Ed. Nitai Shinan. Pamplona: Urgoiti, 2013.
Shinan, Nitai. "Emilio Castelar y los judíos: una reevaluación." *Miscelánea de estudios árabes y hebreos* 65 (2016): 101–118. http://www.meahhebreo.com/index.php/meahhebreo/article/view/891/1032
Urioste Azcorra, Carmen de. "El pensamiento judío de Rafael Cansinos-Assens." *Magazine Modernista* 14 (2010). http://magazinemodernista.com/2010/02/15/el-pensamiento-judio-de-rafael-cansinos-assens/.
Wolodarsky, Solly. *Los conversos: pieza teatral en dos partes*. Madrid: La Avispa, 1985.
Wolodarsky, Solly. *El rabí no cree en Dios*. Madrid: Fundamentos, 1997.
Wolodarsky, Solly. *La conversa de Hervás*. Madrid: La Avispa, 2000.
Wolodarsky, Solly. *Maimónides, el Sefardí*. Madrid: La Avispa, 2005.
Wolodarsky, Solly. *El judío de Hervás*. Madrid: Hebraica, 2007.
Wolodarsky, Solly. *Avapiés*. Madrid: Hebraica, 2009.

Further Reading

Aliberti, Davide. *Sefarad. Una comunidad imaginada (1924–2015)*. Madrid: Marcial Pons, 2018.
Álvarez Chillida, Gonzalo and Ricardo Izquierdo Benito, eds. *El antisemitismo en España*. Cuenca: Universidad de Castilla-La Mancha, 2007.
Avni, Haim. *España, Franco y los judíos*. Madrid: Altalena, 1982.

Benmayor, Rina and Dalia Kandiyoti, eds. *Reparative Citizenship in Spain and Portugal: Sephardi Jews, Reconciliation, and Return*. Berghahn Books, forthcoming.

Brenneis, Sara J. and Gina Herrmann, eds. *Spain, the Second World War, and the Holocaust: History and Representation*. Toronto: Toronto University Press, 2020.

Friedman, Michal Rose. "Unsettling the 'Jewish Question' from the Margins of Europe: Spanish Liberalism and Sepharad." In *Jews, Liberalism, Antisemitism: A Global History*. Abigail Green and Simon Levis Sullam, eds. London: Palgrave Macmillan, 2020. 185–208.

Garzón, Jacobo Israel. *Escrito en Sefarad. Aportación escrita de los judíos de España a la literatura, la erudición, la ciencia y la tecnología contemporáneas*. Madrid: Hebraica Ediciones, 2005.

Goode, Joshua. *Impurity of Blood. Defining Race in Spain, 1870–1930*. Baton Rouge: Louisiana State University Press, 2009.

Izquierdo Benito, Ricardo, Uriel Macías and Yolanda Moreno Koch, coord. *Los judíos en la España contemporánea, historia y visiones, 1898–1998*. Cuenca: Universidad Castilla-La Mancha, 2000.

Lisbona, José Antonio. *Retorno a Sefarad: la política de España hacia sus judíos en el siglo XX*. Barcelona: Riopiedras, 1993.

Manrique Escudero, Mónica. *Los judíos ante los cambios políticos en España en* 1868. Madrid: Hebraica Ediciones, 2016.

Marquina, Antonio & Ospina, Gloria. 1987. *España y los judíos en el siglo XX: la acción exterior*. Madrid: Espasa Calpe.

Martín Corrales, Eloy and Maite Ojeda Mata, eds., *Judíos entre Europa y el norte de África (siglos XV-XXI)*. Barcelona: Bellaterra, 2013.

McDonald, Charles A. 2021. "Rancor: Sephardi Jews, Spanish Citizenship, and the Politics of Sentiment." *Comparative Studies in Society and History* 63, no. 3, 722–751.

Ojeda Mata, Maite. 2013. *Modern Spain and the Sephardim: Legitimizing Identities*. Washington D.C.: Lexington Books.

Rother, Bernd. *Franco y el Holocausto*. Madrid: Marcial Pons, 2005.

Schammah Gesser, Silvina and Raanan Rein. *El Otro en la España Contemporánea. Prácticas, discursos y representaciones*. Sevilla: Fundación Tres Culturas, 2011.

Ilan Stavans
14 Mapping Twentieth Century Sephardic Literature

Abstract: This chapter explores the literary tradition that predated and resulted the Spanish expulsion in 1492, which continues to manifest itself in numerous diasporas and in multiple languages, from Ladino to Spanish, French, English, Arabic, and Hebrew. It discusses immigration as a defining factor of the tradition and looks at trends such as *Marranismo* and Crypto-Jewishness. It highlights influential writers like Elias Canetti, Albert Cohen, Danilo Kis, Primo Levi, Angelina Muñiz-Huberman, and A. B. Yehoshua.

Key Terms: Intellectual trends, Ladino, multilingualism, Sephardic diaspora, Spanish Expulsion

1 Introduction

> Travelling, one accepts everything;
> indignation stays at home.   – Elias Canetti, *The Voices of Marrakesh: A Record of a Visit* (1967)

Sephardic literature is an amphibious term used to refer to a series of narrative traditions: the one directly linking to *La Convivencia*, the period of coexistence in Spain of the three Abrahamic religions: Judaism, Christianity, and Islam; the dispersion that took place as a result of the Alhambra Edict of 1492, in which Jews were expelled from Spain and later on Portugal, taking them to other places in Europe like Italy and Netherlands, as well as northern Africa and the Balkan region; and the portion of the population in the Ottoman Empire (Syria, Lebanon, Turkey, and Greece, commonly known as Levant) that traced its roots to the Iberian Peninsula. This vast geographical spread sometimes generates confusion, in particular given that after the Destruction of the Second Temple in Jerusalem in 70 CE a portion of the dispersed population settled in the Mesopotamian region (Iran and Iraq) and elsewhere; this tradition, known as Mizrahi, isn't Sephardic per se.

The purpose of this encyclopedic guide to the topic is to delineate the parameters of Sephardic literature and to appreciate its vitality from the early days of the twentieth century to the present. The name *Sfarad* is used in the Hebrew Bible as a moniker of Spain. Given the plurality of experiences within Sephardic literature, a number of languages have been used as conduits of expression. The principal ones are Spanish, Portuguese, Ladino, Dutch, Italian, and French. The latter become the *lingua franca* of large segments of the Sephardic diasporas when, as part of the *Haskalah*, e.g., Jewish Enlightenment, the intellectual elite embraced it as a channel to modernize the infrastructure of a slew of Jewish communities within the Ottoman Empire. In terms of genres, the birth of Sephardic literature is directly linked to liturgy – and, more comprehensively, poetry – where it thrived. The Hebrew poets of medieval Spain remain an inspiration for contemporary Sephardic writers. Those origins were defined by the transactions of conversos, New Christians, and Crypto-Jews, whose plight also remains a topic of enormous interest. Another line of inquiry has been philosophy, which has mutated in Sephardic literature into autobiographical writing devoted to large metaphysical, conceptual, and linguistic topics. Nowadays, the tradition is represented by poetry and autobiography. Interestingly, unlike Ashkenazic literature, whose motor is fiction, stories and novels aren't as central, even though the earliest literary attempts in Sephardic literature were in those realms.

Thematically, readers are attracted to a series of tropes. First and forest is the idea travel, physically and existentially. Sephardic literature is represented as a quest, with a specific moment of departure and another of arrival. This pilgrimage has a micro and a macro level: the individual is conceived as part of a historical chain that connects with the expulsion of 1492. Discussion of reconvening in the lost homeland is also frequent. It features motifs like keys, a door, a mezuzah waiting to be kissed, and some on. Needless to say, Israel as present in the tradition; it doesn't compete with Spain as a site of reunification, though.

All this makes Sephardic literature tacitly messianic in its nature. Other motifs are the dichotomy between freedom and determination, with an undercurrent of fatalism is an overall attitude toward life; since to a large extent Kabbalah developed in the Sephardic world, Sephardic literature is understood to have mystical power; the dialogue between humans and the divine is seen as not only essential but unavoidable; cuisine, along with religious rituals, are featured as the glue keeping communities together; and the fragile line separating the private and public realms is an obsession; there is a constant dialogue with medieval and renaissance texts, such as the Hebrew poet Shmuel ha-Nagid and Judah ha-Levi and *converso* poets Daniel Leví de Barrios and João Pinto Delgado, and novels like *La Celestina*, *Lazarillo de Tormes*, the autobiography of Luis de Carvajal the Younger, and others; finally, since the tradition is structurally polyglot, translation, both as practice and as a topic of reflection, is an ongoing concern.

2 Aterritorality

At the core of Sephardic literature is an emphasis on the journey is tangible in an array of prominent Sephardic autobiographical meditations, including Primo Levi's *Survival in Auschwitz* (1954), also known by the title of *If This Is a Man*; Elias Canetti's three-volume *Memoirs* (1999), André Aciman's *Out of Egypt* (1994), Victor Perera's *The*

Cross and the Pear Tree (1996), Lucette Lagnado's *The Man in the White Sharkskin Suit* (2007), and a multi-volume by Angelina Muñiz-Huberman (2013–2016) look at the Sephardic past through the prism of family history. All written in English, they focus on the tightly-knit communities of Levant, and their diasporas across the Americas, especially the United States, as proof of survival dexterity. Similar autobiographical odysseys are present in French, Italian, German, and Israeli literatures, including the work of Levi, Canetti, and Muñiz-Huberman.

Until the end of the fifteenth century, Jews outside of the Middle East lived dispersed all over Europe. The various governments offered special dispensation for them to settle in specific areas. In Spain, those areas were called *juderías*, most of which were neighborhoods in larger urban areas such as Toledo, Gerona, and Córdoba. A large community developed in the Iberian Peninsula. Over time, the contact between the three Abrahamic religions – the other two are Christianity and Islam – gave place to what came to be known as *La Convivencia*, which, according to scholarly debates, goes from the Muslim Umayyad conquest of Hispania in the early eighth century until the expulsion.

Prior to 1492, the foundation behind this outlook was a cadre of experimental poets writing in Hebrew that favored a type of liturgical poem called *piyut*, meant for use in religious services. They include Shmuel ha-Nagid, who, aside from writing poetry, was a military figure, a Talmudic scholar, and a merchant of immense importance in Muslim Spain, and Shlomo ibn Gabirol, known in Latin as Avicebron. He was primarily known for his poetry, portions of which have been integrated into the Yom Kippur liturgy. Yet in European intellectual circles, his work *Fons Vitae*, written in Arabic (its title is *Yanbu' al-Hayat*), was well known, although his authorship was only acknowledged in the mid-nineteenth century. Moses ibn Ezra, who wrote substantially about rhetoric, especially the use of metaphor, differed with Maimonides and was arguably the most important philosopher and biblical commentator of Jewish Spain.

Perhaps the most resonant of the Jewish poets in medieval Spain was Judah ha-Levi, a physician, poet, and philosopher whose book *Kitab al-Ḥujjah wal-Dalil fi Nuṣr al-Din al-Dhalil* (completed in 1140), known in its Hebrew translation by Judah ibn Tibbon as *Sefer ha-Kuzari*, is built as a dialogue between a rabbi and the king of the Khazars. It is an essential philosophical disquisition on various aspects of Judaism, such as the names of the divine, how the universe was created *ex nihilo*, the value of the oral tradition, and so on. Along with Maimonides's *Guide for the Perplexed* (ca. 1190), ha-Levi's treatise is of fundamental importance in medieval Jewish theology. Likewise, his diverse poetic explorations are influential. He wrote love poems, elegies, riddles, travel verses, and laudatory poems about friendship, a number of which have been canonized in Jewish liturgy as Shabbat hymns. One of the most enchanting and a primer of the Sephardic outlook is "My Heart Is in the East." It displays, in full splendor, the forking paths of Sephardic identity:

> My heart is in the east, and I am in the far-away west.
> How can I savor food? How might it be sweet to me?
> How might I render my vows and bonds, while
> Zion is under the might of Edom and I am in Arab bondage?
> It would be good for me to leave behind all goods from Spain
> while I behold in my eyes the precious dust of the forsaken sanctuary. (Stavans 2021a, 46)

ha-Levi represents diaspora life for Jews as a forking path between their individual location, in his case, Spain, and Jerusalem, the site of King Solomon's destroyed temple, as the source for constant longing. In the context of aterritoriality, that dualism is a constant. Toward the end of his own life, having lived in various locations in Christian and Muslim Spain, he traveled to Egypt and from there set off for Jerusalem. He probably made it, although rumors have it that he died at sea. It is also said that he was killed by an Arab horseman.

Although premodern when judged by the parameters of the European Enlightenment, these cadres of Hebrew poets continue to exert enormous appeal among Jewish readers. Heinrich Heine, the German Romantic poet and among the first Jews to enter a national literary canon (even though, as in the case of Mendelssohn's descendants, Heine's family converted to Lutheranism when he was young), was infatuated with them to such an extent that he translated some of them into German. Emma Lazarus used Heine's versions as her source for her English versions.

The road to Spain as a unified nation exacerbated the tension among the three religions. The year 1492 is an *annus mirabilis* when everything fell apart. It marks the time in which *La Reconquista*, the drive to homogenize Spain under a Catholic faith, brought together King Ferdinand of Aragon and Queen Isabella of Castile, known as *los reyes católicos*, the Catholic Monarchs, meaning their partnership was based on an agreement established by the Catholic Church. Harassment against Jews and Muslims intensified. Other European nations had already expelled them from their midst: England in 1290, the Duchy of Austria in 1421, and Ravenna in 1491. Others would quickly follow suit: Portugal in 1496, Nuremberg in 1499, and several papal states in 1569. In other words, there was a continental rush to narrow the path minorities – especially Jews – had in emerging nationalistic projects.

The defining characteristic in pre-1492 Spain was the perfidious role that *El Santo Oficio*, the Spanish Inquisition, played in every aspect of life. As an institution, it pushed non-Catholics to either convert or leave. Those choosing conversion sometimes embraced it wholeheartedly. Others engaged in it only as a public act, keeping a hidden identity in the domestic realm, thus living a double life. As the question of *limpieza de sangre*, purity of blood, became a referendum in Spain on people's identity, a new class of people, known as conversos, meaning converts, spread all over the Spanish kingdom. The nomenclature includes important variations on the converso type: *cristiano nuevo*, New Christian; *marrano*, describing a converso in a derogatory sense; its Hebrew equivalent, *anusi*; and Crypto-Jew, a hidden Jew. Aside from the Alhambra Decree, as the Edict of Expulsion is known, other important events took place that year. In an effort to find a new maritime route to India, which was impeded by a Turkish blockade in the Mediterranean Sea, the Genoese admiral, whose ancestry has been suggested to have been partially Jewish, sailed from the Canary Islands to the Caribbean. With funds from Queen Isabella, Columbus set foot on the island eventually known as Hispaniola, now divided between Haiti and the Dominican Republic.

The end of *La Convivencia* dispersed Jews to a number of places: from the Netherlands to Italy, from the Balkans to Turkey and Northern Africa, or Jerusalem and its surroundings, and into the Western Hemisphere. Ladino, also known as *Judezmo* and *judeo-español*, was a language made of Spanish and Hebrew elements and until the late nineteenth century was written in Hebrew characters, though there was a flourishing Ladino publishing industry (using Hebrew characters) well into the twentieth century. Ladino was used to create poetry, lyrics, and storytelling. An emergent consciousness came to the fore, which might be called "the converso split," a dense web of transnational connections among *cristianos nuevos*, who possessed Jewish family roots but had abandoned them, yet felt united by the ostracism they were subjected to. They were rejected not only by the Spanish Inquisition and the old Christian majority of Spanish society, but also by Jews. Metaphorically, this group suddenly became the new Jews, a loosely defined people with strong cultural ties, who took it upon themselves to help each other, at times quietly and at other times overtly, against adversity.

Through conversion, those whose genealogy included Jewish elements often became devoted Catholics. This switch was projected into their work. They embedded secret messages in their work to alert readers about the double consciousness they inhabited. Poets like Santa Teresa de Jesús and Fray Luis de León, the latter the author of important exegetical works on the *Book of Psalms* and other biblical narratives, were to various degrees suspected of Judaizing. The same ought to be said of the anonymous author of *Lazarillo of Tormes* (1554), a novel considered the first in Europe in the picaresque genre. The acerbic critique it makes of the Catholic Church was possible only through some distancing from it, which is what conversos experienced in their daily life. The same goes for Fernando de Rojas, author of *La Celestina* (1499). The entire narrative is made of a series of dialogues that follow the tradition of courtly love. One of its protagonists is a hybrid between a healer and a matchmaker. If one takes a narrow view of Sephardic culture, all these authors should not be considered part of it. After all, they or their ancestors had abandoned the Jewish faith. Yet that duality, to be an outcast while retaining a certain sensibility connected to one's past, was a feature – religious, intellectual, and emotional – a number of them manifested.

The case of Baruch Spinoza, the Dutch philosopher responsible for the *Tractatus Theologico-Politicus* (1670), is pertinent. He himself rejected his Judaism; as punishment for his ideas, the Amsterdam community in which he lived proclaimed a *herem*, an excommunication. Nobody was allowed to relate to him. Still, his Jewishness defined his worldview. And that worldview, especially in the realms of ethics and government, was the cornerstone in the shaping of essential documents like the US Constitution, written during the Philadelphia Convention in 1787. Américo Castro, a prominent early twentieth century Spanish cultural historian, author of *The Structure of Spanish History* (1954), concluded that the New Christian mentality was shaped by a sense of pride, not shame, in secrecy. He even speculated, without any tangible evidence, I should add, that Miguel de Cervantes Saavedra, author of *Don Quixote of La Mancha* (1605–1615), might have had "Jewish blood". A few scholars read the first sentence of his novel – *"En un lugar de la Mancha de cuyo nombre no quiero acordarme, no ha mucho tiempo que vivía un hidalgo de los de lanza en astillero"*; in my English translation: "In a place of La Mancha of which name I do not care to remember, there lived, not long ago, a hidalgo who has a lance on the shelf" – as evidence of attempting to hide one's origins.

One of the most significant Sephardic writers, whose odyssey showcases the tortured nature of a double life forced by the Spanish Inquisition, is Luis de Carvajal the Younger. He arguably is the most famous martyr of the Spanish Inquisition in the Americas, which, although not as lethal as its counterpart in the Iberian Peninsula, nevertheless established a similar reign of terror. Carvajal's uncle, the Spanish-born, Crypto-Jewish governor of the northern Mexican state of Nuevo León, was aware that in New Spain, as Mexico was known in the sixteenth century, the Spanish Inquisition was more lenient. The uncle brought along his extended family, asking them to retain their secret Jewishness at home. Among them was Luis de Carvajal the Younger, who became known under his chosen name, Joseph Lumbroso, a.k.a. *El Iluminado*. He rediscovered his Jewish roots in his early twenties and became obsessed with them. Never having read the Hebrew Bible, he taught himself a few tenets he discovered in it. Soon, he became convinced he was a biblical prophet endowed with the task of bringing back to their old faith those members of the tribe who had distanced themselves from it.

As Carvajal began to proselytize among other Crypto-Jews in New Spain, the Spanish Inquisition tracked his activities. He, his mother, and his sister were eventually arrested and put in prison. They were interrogated by inquisitors who wanted to know every detail of their endeavor. To extract precise information, they were tortured. Inside the prison, Carvajal communicated surreptitiously with his relatives by sending them messages in *mamey* peels. The inquisitors intercepted these messages. The Carvajals repented, at least publicly. The story takes a surprising twist. Carvajal was released from prison, at which point he proselytized again. And he drafted an autobiographical narrative in which he described in detail – in the third person – all his activities, including his and a friend's decision to circumcise themselves on the bank of the Panuco River. That narrative is the first memoir by a Jew written in the New World. Not long after, Carvajal and his relatives were arrested again and burned at the stake, in the Plaza del Quemadero in downtown Mexico City, in the most important auto-da-fé ever to take place in the Americas. (Against the background of a lost manuscript, the graphic novel illustrated by Steve Sheinkin, *El Iluminado* [2012], recounts his ordeal.)

As Sephardim built new communities, their literature reflected the historical events affecting them. One example is Daniel Levi de Barrios, a.k.a. Miguel Barrios. Born in Spain and wanting to connect with his Jewish heritage yet understanding he needed to keep it secret, he escaped the Inquisition by traveling to Algeria, Italy, France, and then the West Indies. Levi de Barrios serves as a connection with the nascent Ottoman Empire under Suleiman the Magnificent. It was there that the movement known as *Sabbatanism*, in which Levi de Barrios participated, took shape. Its central figure was Shabbetai Zvi, the false messiah, a rabbi, and kabbalist from Smyrna, in the Ottoman Empire, whose claim to be the messiah persuaded thousands of followers. In the year 1666, just as his prophesy of a new age was to arrive, he was arrested in Constantinople by the grand vizier Ahmed Köprülü. While in prison, Zvi converted to Islam. His unexpected move shocked his followers. Some abandoned Judaism; others followed him in conversion, creating a subwing of the movement that, in its antinomianism, argued for sin as a road to salvation. (In 1967, Gershom Scholem wrote a lucid biography of Zvi and his movement.) The impact on Levi de Barrios was deep. As a convert, he looked at Zvi as a redeemer like Jesus Christ. But after the conversion to Islam, he became an antinomian, becoming persuaded that redemption was attainable through sin. He set out to write a treatise – now lost – on the divine presence in the modern world. Afterward, he kept his distance from all types of religion. In time, he became a successful poet as well as the author of *comedias* and history books. Whereas Carvajal was himself convinced of, and ultimately doomed by, his messianic powers, Levi de Barrios, getting his feet wet on Shabbetanism, emerged from the experience as an astute champion of enlightened ideas. This duality would define successive generations: some would fear doom while others would embrace hope.

3 A Bookshelf of Classics

In the eighteenth and nineteenth centuries, Sephardic writers included Benjamin Disraeli, who was baptized at an early age and displayed little interest in Judaism, and, on the opposite side, Grace Aguilar, a novelist, poet, and advocate for religious and education reform whose most important poems meditate on the biblical characters of Hagar and Ishmael. But unlike Yiddish literature, which I discuss in the following chapter, the Sephardim never fully developed a coherent modern literary tradition. Instead, there are figures here and there who acknowledge the Spanish heritage as impacting their oeuvre.

Among them is Greek-born Swiss novelist Albert Cohen, who worked for the International Labor Organization and wrote humorous, idiosyncratic novels, like *Belle du Seignior* (1988), full of idiosyncratic Ottoman characters. These two positions, rejection and embrace, are notable across the tradition. Arguably the most famous twentieth century Sephardic writer is Bulgarian novelist and cultural critic Elias Canetti, who grew up in Ladino but wrote in German. Quite prolific, he alternated between novels and book-long essays. His most famous novel is *Die Blendung* (1935), known in English translation as *Auto-da-Fé*, a phantasmagoric exploration of life under fascism. His two most important nonfiction books are *Masse und Macht* (1960), known as *Crowds and Power*, a probing study of the psychology of the masses under fascism; and *Der andere Prozess* (1969), titled *Kafka's Other Process* (1969) in English, in which he explored, in minute fashion, the sentimental life of the author of *The Metamorphosis* with his lover Felice Bauer. Canetti's style could oscillate from the lyrical to the phantasmagoric. This is clear in his multivolume autobiography, especially in *Die Gerettete Zunge* (1977), translated as *The Tongue Set Free*. The reader is able to sense a delicious mix of Ladino, German, and English, and the respective cultures they represent, in its pages.

Other Sephardic writers include Italian activist and member of Parliament Natalia Ginzburg; chemist and Holocaust survivor Primo Levi, also Italian; and Serbian short-story writer Danilo Kiš, who spent the last period of his life in France. Born in Palermo, Sicily, and prominent anti-fascist and for a while a member of Italy's Communist Party, Ginzburg's work focuses on the tension between the domestic and public spheres in Italian family life, especially among the intelligentsia during the Second World War portraits. Her novel *Family Lexicon* (1963) is a vivid, surgically-delivered, empathetic portrait, with an added focus on family language, that is anchored in the death of Leone Ginzburg, an influential anti-fascist journalist, editor, writer, and teacher, and Natalia Ginzburg's first husband. It chronicles the plight of Italian Jews under the regime of Benito Mussolini and the death of celebrated poet Cesare Pavese, whom she published while an editor in Turin at the publishing house Eunaudi. Ginzburg (née Natalia Levi) also published Primo Levi, Italo Calvino, and another Sephardic writer, Carlo Levi, author of *Christ Stopped at Eboli* (1945).

Influenced by Bruno Schulz, Jorge Luis Borges, and Vladimir Nabokov, his volumes of stories *A Tomb for Boris Davidovich* (1976), about betrayal and deception in the Soviet bloc, and *The Encyclopedia of the Dead* (1983), a postmodern meditation on tyranny, are lucid instances of this tradition. A. B. Yehoshua, the Israeli novelist, sought to understand the continuity between the expulsion in 1492 and a sprawling Sephardic family tree in his epic novel *Mr. Mani* (1989). Faulknerian in language as well as in structure, it tells the story of various generations in reverse chronological order, with the youngest descendant, an Israeli, starting the tale, and the last one, an Iberian, concluding it.

It is important to make a distinction between this tradition and its Mizrahi counterpart. The latter term describes Jews from Middle Eastern and North African descent. After the destruction of the Second Temple, as Jews were exiled in the Roman Empire, a very small number stayed in Jerusalem and the surrounding areas and persisted in their religious practices. The expulsion from Spain also brought Jews into North Africa and the Middle East, which means that a portion of Mizrahim have Sephardic blood. Occasionally in their work, Iraqi-born Israeli author Sami Michael and Tel Aviv-based Orly Castel-Bloom delve into the junction between the forking paths of Sepharad and Magreb.

An ethereal quality present in Mizrahi literature is personified – if such a verb might be used to describe such a ghost-like individual – in Monsieur Chouchani. While I confess to knowing almost nothing about him, not even his first name, let alone his date of birth, I feel the urge to include him in this survey. He was a rabbi, a Talmudist, and a conversationalist who deliberately left no trace, especially in published form. Two major Jewish thinkers of the twentieth century, Emmanuel Levinas and Elie Wiesel, about whom I will reflect in depth later, befriended him in Paris. Wiesel, upon finding out Monsieur Chouchani had died in 1968, procured a proper Jewish tomb and burial in Montevideo, Uruguay, where he passed away. He apparently had a prodigious mind and was able to recite entire sections of the Talmud. Yet he lived, by all accounts, an itinerant life and was often homeless. In countless ways, his existence is symbolic of the wandering ways of Mizrahi, and for that matter all, Jewish literature.

The most wide ranging of Sephardic authors is Angelina Muñiz-Huberman. A refugee of the Spanish Civil War, her family moved to France and subsequently to Mexico, where she went to school. Her household was Catholic. One day, Muñiz-Huberman saw her mother sweep the kitchen. She took the garbage she piled in the center not through the door, but through the window. When the daughter asked why, the mother responded that it was a custom she had learned as a girl. Eventually, Muñiz-Huberman figured out such behavior was frequent among Crypto-Jews. This led her to a voyage of discovery. She eventually became a scholar of Jewish mysticism, a poet, and a novelist whose oeuvre, such as *The Confidantes* (1997), deals with the legacy of secrecy among conversos. In her work, she returns to the medieval Hebrew poets – Hanagid, ibn Gabirl, Ezra, and ha-Levi – to find continuity. She empathizes with Iberian writers like Santa Teresa de Jesús and Fray Luis de León, and she connects with kabbalists and other mystics.

Muñiz-Huberman's oeuvre is in constant dialogue with medieval and renaissance literature. She is engaged in a dialogue with rebels like Sor Juana Inés de la Cruz but also with Kabbalistic texts like the *Zohar* (in fact, she edited a couple of anthologies of Jewish mysticism) and with narratives by New Christians like *La Celestina* and *Lazarillo de Tormes*. This conversation, present in other Sephardic writers too, establishes a bridge between the present and the past. One of those authors is the nineteenth-century U.S. poet Emma Lazarus. She translated into English the medieval Hebrew poets Shmuel Hanagid, ibn Gabirol, Ezra, and Judah ha-Levi. In Lazarus's' case, there is a caveat: she knew neither Hebrew nor Spanish. Her renditions re based on German poet's Heinrich Heine's translations.

Lazarus, of course, is famous for her poem "The New Colossus," arguably the most famous sonnet in the United States, inscribed in a plaque in the pedestal of the Statue of Liberty, welcomed immigrants sailing to America between 1892 and 1954. The famous last six lines read:

> "Keep, ancient lands, your storied pomp!" cries she
> With silent lips. "Give me your tired, your poor,
> Your huddled masses yearning to breathe free,
> The wretched refuse of your teeming shore.
> Send these, the homeless, tempest-tost to me,
> I lift my lamp beside the golden door!" (Lazarus 2005, 67)

These lines are a leitmotif announcing America's relationship with the rest of the world, its stance toward immigration, and its vision of the so-called American Dream, a magnet for a large numbers of poor Yiddish speakers from the Pale in the last third of the nineteenth century. Interestingly, before "The New Colossus," Lazarus wrote another sonnet, titled "1492," that feels strikingly similar in structure and content. The last four lines read:

> "Ho, all who weary, enter here!
> There falls each ancient barrier that the art
> Of race or creed or rank devised, to rear
> Grim bulwarked hatred between heart and heart!" (Lazarus 2005, 72)

In regards to Ladino, a number of twentieth century Sephardic authors have deliberately switched to it in order to reconnect with a lost part of their own experience. Or else, Ladino might be used as a motif to explore issues like immigration, as in the case of Mexican poet Myriam Moscona's *Tela de sevoya/Onioncolth* (2017). There are other examples in which an Ashkenazic writer, such as Argentine Juan Gelman, responsible for *Dibaxu* (1994), who created a concoction that is halfway between Spanish and Ladino.

Abraham Joshua Heschel, the Polish-born American philosopher and civil rights activist, who wrote a biography of Maimonides (1935), once published an essay suggesting that the Sephardic sensibility is precise, almost mathematical, and allergic to expressions of disquiet and nervousness and that it sees itself best reflected in liturgical chants. While these might be generalizations, Sephardic literature indeed oscillates toward certain motifs and moods. One is the motif of the lost key. It symbolizes an abandoned door that belongs to the past, although nobody remembers exactly where that door is located. The key invokes nostalgic moods and shares a feeling that the family is both the conduit for continuity to last and its saboteur. Along the way, the key showcases an urge for travel by a people with shifting diasporic addresses to find connections across borders to be able to replicate certain patterns of religious behavior.

4 The Reflective Eye

This last section is about scholarship on Sephardic literature. The outcome here is mixed. Although there has been somewhat of an outburst in the early decades of the twenty-first century, the field still remains largely unexplored. In part, it is the result of a global movement toward multiculturalism. Looking at Jewish culture beyond the confines of Ashkenaz has brought along a refreshing interest to alternative traditions. Likewise, the emergence of a more diverse Israeli culture represented by heterogeneous immigrant waves, from Turkey to Ethiopia, have pushed the country to pay closer attention to Sephardic voices.

Ironically, one of the early academic studies to focus on conversos was Cecil Roth's *A History of the Marranos* (1932). Américo Castro, a non-Jewish historian from Spain. His book *The Structure of Spanish History* (1954), produced after his country's civil war and to a large extent a response to it, was among the first to attempted a decentralize view against a monolithic understanding of Catholicism. It was followed by the work by scholars like Hayim Yosef Yerushalmi, who wrote lucidly on Spanish and Italian Jewish life in the renaissance and beyond, although not specifically about Sephardic literature. (His book *Zakhor* [1982], not centered on any specific Sephardic concern, is an extraordinary disquisition on Jewish memory and Jewish historiography.) Decades later, David M. Gitlitz's *Secrecy and Deceit: The Religion of the Crypto-Jews* (1996) delved deeper into the topic of a closeted identity at the core of Sephardic culture. Yirmiyahu Yovel's *The Other Within: The Marranos, Spilt Identity and Emerging Modernity* (2009) explores Sephardic life from a strictly economic perspective.

As suggested before, modern translations of Sephardic poets have proliferated in recent times. Among the best medieval poems in translation are in Peter Cole's *The Dream of the Poem: Hebrew Poetry from Muslin and Christian Spain, 950–1492* (2007). Ammiel Alcalay gathered a sample of Israeli writers, a number of them Sephardic, in *Keys to the Garden* (1996). My anthology *The Schocken Book of Modern Sephardic Literature* (2005) served as an invitation to look at the menu of international possibilities, showcasing the continuity of this literature from figures like Emma Lazarus to Victor Perera. Mair Saul and José Ignacio Hualde's *Sepharad as Imagined Community: Language, History, and Religion from the Early Modern Period to the 21st Century* (2017) appreciate the Sephardic journey from a linguistic viewpoint as do the chapters included in Joshua J. Miller and Anita Norich's *Languages of Modern Jewish Cultures: Comparative Perspectives* (2016). An important volume is David A. Wacks' *Double Diaspora in Sephardic Literature: Jewish Cultural Production Before and After 1492* (2015).

Book-length studies on the Sephardic side of figures like Primo Levi, Elias and Venza Canetti, and A. B. Yehoshua are unavailable. The same goes for comparative analysis of memoirs, Sephardic literature of the Shoah, and, although a handful of doctoral dissertations in Hebrew have been written, a full-fledge exploration of Sephardic literature in Israel remains an elusive idea. I might also take this opportunity to comment on Sephardic museums and special library collections. Again, the landscape in this regard is bleak. In countries like France, Holland, Denmark, Italy, and Greece there are Jewish museums which feature the local history of Jewish, including, obviously, Sephardic material. But none of them make a case for establishing a lineage in connection with Sephardic literature. Neither does Beit Hatfutzot in

Tel-Aviv, known as a museum that collects artifacts from all the Jewish diasporas. Likewise, there is no world organization such as YIVO Institute for Jewish Research in New York and the Yiddish Book Center in Amherst, Massachusetts, both of them dedicated to safeguarding Yiddish literature. My hope is that in the next few decades a gathering of individuals and institutions will orchestrate an effort to create such an address where Sephardic literature will be housed.

In my book *Jewish Literature: A Very Short Introduction*, I meditate on what makes modern Jewish literature "modern" (although it starts with the European Enlightenment, it might be traced back to 1492), "Jewish" (there is a specific Jewish sensibility that coheres across the various diasporas), and "literature" (the People of the Book have expanded their horizons).[1] Among my central arguments is that Jewish literature is aterritorial, e.g., it does not have an address; that is, it engages with Jewish as a civilization without being fixed in a national territory. In other words, no specific flag, anthem, currency, etc. Of course, all Jewish writers belong to specific countries: Franz Kafka was Czech, Isaac babel was Russian, and Bruno Schulz was Polish. What makes them Jewish, though, are their supranational qualities. It is in this context that Sephardic literature ought to be appraised: a transnational, multilingual tradition whose practitioners belong to specific national contexts yet they are connected by a Jewish sensibility as well as specific parameters that insert them in the bifurcating paths that define the Sephardic tradition.

Bibliography

Works Cited

Aciman, André. *Out of Egypt*. New York: Farrar, Straus, and Giroux, 1994.
Alcalay, Ammiel, ed. *Keys to the Garden: New Israeli Writing*. San Francisco, CA: City Lights, 1996.
Bassani, Giorgio. *The Garden of the Finzi-Continis*. Tr. William Weaver. New York: Harcourt Brace Jovanovich, 1977.
Canetti, Elias. *Auto-da-fé*. Tr. C. V. Wedgwood. New York: Farrar, Straus, and Giroux, 1984.
Canetti, Elias. *The Memoirs of Elias Canetti: The Tongue Set Free, The Torch in My Ear, The Play of the Eyes*. Tr. Joachim Neugroschel. New York: Farrar, Straus, and Giroux, 1999.
Canetti, Veza. Yellow Street: A Novel in Five Scenes. Tr. Ian Mitchell. New York: New Directions, 1991.
Canetti, Veza. *The Tortoises*. Tr. Ian Mitchell. New York: New Directions, 2001.
Cole, Peter, Tr. *The Dream of the Poem: Hebrew Poetry from Muslin and Christian Spain, 950–1492*. Princeton, NJ: Princeton University Press, 2007.
Derrida, Jacques. *Monolingualism of the Other*. Tr. Patrick Mensah. Stanford, CA: Stanford University Press, 1998.
Derrida, Jacques. *Of Grammatology*. Tr. Gayatri Chakravorty Spivak. Baltimore: Johns Hopkins University Press, 2016.

---

1 See Stavans 2021b. This guide is based on the first chapter.

Gelman, Juan. *Dibaxu*. Barcelona: Seix Barral, 1994.
Ginzburg, Natalia. *Family Lexicon*. Tr. Jenny McPhee. New York: New York Review of Books, 2017.
Lagnado, Lucette. *The Man in the White Sharkskin Suit: My Family's Exodus from Old Cairo to New York*. New York: Ecco, 2007.
Lagnado, Lucette. *The Arrogant Years: One Girl's Search for the Lost Youth, from Cairo to Brooklyn*. New York: Ecco, 2011.
Lazarus, Emma. *Selected Poems*. Ed. Esther Schor. New York: Library of America, 2005.
Levi, Primo. *Collected Works*. 3 vols. Tr. Ann Goldstein. New York: W. W. Norton, 2015.
Levinas, Emmanuel. *The Levinas Reader*. Ed. Seán Hand. Oxford: Blackwell, 1989.
Modiano, Patrick. *The Search Warrant*. Tr. Joanna Kilmartin. New York: Random House, 2000.
Modiano, Patrick. *In the Café of Lost Youth*. Tr. Chris Clarke. New York: New York Review Books, 2016.
Moscona, Myriam. *Tela de sevoya/Onioncloth*. Los Angeles: Les Figues Press, 2017.
Perera, Victor. *The Cross and the Pear Tree: A Sephardic Journey*. New York: Alfred A. Knopf, 1996.
Stavans, Ilan, ed. *The Schocken Book of Modern Sephardic Literature*. New York: Schocken Books, 2005.
Stavans, Ilan, ed. *Oy, Caramba! An Anthology of Jewish Stories from Latin America*. Albuquerque: University of New Mexico Press, 2016.
Stavans, Ilan. *Selected Translations: Poems 2000–2020*. Pittsburgh, PA: University of Pittsburgh Press, 2021a.

Further Reading

Asscher, Omri. *Reading Israel, Reading America: The Politics of Translation between Jews*. Stanford, CA: Stanford University Press, 2019.
Balbuena, Monique R. *Homeless Tongues: Poetry and Languages of the Sephardic Diaspora*. Stanford, CA: Stanford University Press, 2016.
Castro, Américo. *The Structure of Spanish History*. Tr. Edmund L. King. Princeton, NJ: Princeton University Press, 1954.
Gilman, Sander L. *Jewish Frontiers: Essays on Bodies, Histories, and Identities*. New York: Palgrave Macmillan, 2003.
Gitlitz, David M. *Secrecy and Deceit: The Religion of the Crypto-Jews*. Philadelphia: Jewish Publication Society of America, 1996.
Hoberman, Michael. *A Hundred Acres of America: The Geography of Jewish American Literary History*. New Brunswick, NJ: Rutgers University Press, 2019.
Kellman, Steven G. *The Translingual Imagination*. Lincoln: University of Nebraska Press, 2000.
Kellman, Steven G. *Nimble Tongues: Studies in Literary Translingualism*. West Lafayette, IN: Purdue University Press, 2020.
Kirsch, Adam. *The People and the Books: 18 Classics of Jewish Literature*. New York: W. W. Norton, 2016.
Levinas, Emmanuel. *Nine Talmudic Readings*. Tr. Annette Aronowicz. Bloomington: Indiana University Press, 1990.
Matt, Daniel, tr. and ed. *Zohar*. 12 Vols. Stanford, CA: Stanford University Press, 2018.
Mendelson-Maoz, Adia. *Multiculturalism in Israel: Literary Perspectives*. West Lafayette, IN: Purdue University Press, 2014.
Miccoli, Dario, ed. *Contemporary Sephardic and Mizrahi Literature: A Diaspora*. New York: Routledge, 2017.
Miller, Joshua J., and Anita Norich, eds. *Languages of Modern Jewish Cultures: Comparative Perspectives*. Ann Arbor: University of Michigan Press, 2016.
Roth, Cecil. *A History of the Marranos*. Philadelphia: Jewish Publication Society of America, 1932.

Saul, Mair, and José Ignacio Hualde, eds. *Sepharad as Imagined Community: Language, History, and Religion from the Early Modern Period to the 21st Century*. New York: Peter Lang, 2017.

Slucki, David, Avinoam Pratt and Gabriel N. Finder, eds. *Laughter After: Humor and the Holocaust*. Detroit, MI: Wayne State University Press, 2020.

Sokoloff, Naomi B., and Nancy E. Berg, eds. *What We Talk about When We Talk about Hebrew (and What It Means to Americans)*. Seattle: University of Washington Press, 2018

Stavans, Ilan. *The Inveterate Dreamer: Essays and Conversations on Jewish Culture*. Lincoln: University of Nebraska Press, 2001.

Stavans, Ilan. *Singer's Typewriter and Mine: Reflections on Jewish Culture*. Lincoln: University of Nebraska Press, 2012.

Stavans, Ilan. *The Return of Carvajal: A Mystery*. University Park: Pennsylvania State University Press, 2018a.

Stavans, Ilan. *On Self-Translation: Meditations on Language*. Albany: State University of New York Press, 2018.

Stavans, Ilan. *The Seventh Heaven: Travels though Jewish Latin America*. Pittsburgh, PA: University of Pittsburgh Press, 2019.

Stavans, Ilan. *Selected Translations: Poems 2000–2020*. Pittsburgh, PA: University of Pittsburgh Press, 2020.

Stavans, Ilan. *Jewish Literature: A Very Short Introduction*. New York and Oxford: Oxford University Press, 2021b.

Wacks, David A. *Double Diaspora in Sephardic Literature: Jewish Cultural Production Before and After 1492*. Bloomington, IN: Indiana University Press, 2015.

Yerushalmi, Hayim Yosef. *Zakhor: Jewish History and Jewish Memory*. Seattle: University of Washington Press, 1982.

Yovel, Yirmiyahu. *The Other Within: The Marranos, Spilt Identity and Emerging Modernity*. Princeton, NJ: Princeton University Press, 2009.

Saul Kirschbaum and Berta Waldmann

15 Jewish-Brazilian Literatures

Abstract: This chapter provides a survey of the Jewish literatures of Brazil. Jewish-Brazilian literature began to gain a profile of its own with the emergence of an organized Jewish community in Brazil with a modicum of freedom of expression. This happened, in turn, due to mass emigration from Europe, predominantly Eastern Europe, at the end of the nineteenth century and throughout the twentieth century. It should be noted that as early as 1957, on the occasion of Samuel Rawet's publication of *Contos do Imigrante* (Immigrant Tales), Jacó Guinsburg registered "the *de jure* emergence of immigration literature in our letters" (Guinsburg 1957). Often, the history of Brazil's Jewish literatures is dated back to the colonial era. The presence in colonial Brazil of 'Judaizing' 'New Christians' – that is, unwillingly converted Jews who secretly practiced Judaism to avoid conflicts with the Inquisition – is well known. Even if this minority did produce literary works, as in the case of the authors Bento Teixeira, Ambrósio Fernandes Brandão and Antônio José da Silva (known as "the Jew"), their texts, perhaps precisely in view of the climate of repression, do not, in our estimation, present distinctly Jewish qualities. These writings are therefore not the main focus of this chapter.

Key Terms: Brazilian Literature, Twentieth Century, Twenty-first Century, Immigration, Belonging.

1 Introduction

The panorama of Brazilian-Jewish literature encompasses all literary genres: prose, poetry, essays, and chronicles. In view of the controversy over the issue, we avoid entering into a discussion of what characterizes literature as "Jewish". Criteria such as theme, author's ethnicity and language of expression have been widely discussed, without leading to any consensus.[1] Nevertheless, one should recognize the echo of a dissonance between the texts listed ahead and the dominant Brazilian literature,[2]

---

[1] See, for instance, Wirth-Nesher (5754/1994).
[2] "When Kafka indicates that one of the goals of a minor literature is the "purification of the conflict that opposes father and son and the possibility of discussing that conflict," it isn't a question of an Oedipal phantasm but of a political program. "Even though something is often thought through calmly, one still does not reach the boundary where it connects up with similar things, one reaches the boundary soonest in politics, indeed, one even strives to see it before it is there, and often sees this limiting boundary everywhere ... What in great literature goes on down below, constituting a not indispensable cellar of the structure, here takes place in the full light of day, what is there a matter of

which varies from author to author; Samuel Rawet, in his commentary on the work of Clarice Lispector, perceives a particular relationship of the immigrant writer to both the Portuguese language and to the perception of Brazilian reality, distinct from that of the native writer – a relationship always mediated, necessitating, in a certain way, "interpretation".[3] This difference establishes a literary space that Deleuze and Guattari called "minor literature" (Deleuze and Guattari 1986 [1975]).

2 Jewish History in Colonial and Imperial Brazil

Throughout the period prior to Brazil's independence, Jewish life found no expression there, suppressed by the permanent threat of the Inquisition. As Regina Igel records: "During Portuguese rule, inquisitorial oppression stifled, in addition to religion, any other related cultural and artistic activities of the Jewish community in Portugal and Brazil. Consequently, for practical purposes, there was no Jewish literary expression in the entire territory dominated by the Portuguese. It took many decades after 1822, the date of Brazil's independence from Portuguese administrative power, before Jews from various nations entered the former Portuguese colony with their personal identity, free from subterfuge and confident in the freedom to practice their religion" (Igel 1997, 9).

Further on, regarding Jewish literature, the researcher clarifies that some works can be considered to have managed to cross the barrier: "In the colonial period, it is alleged, expressions of mosaic roots broke through the gag of the Inquisition and revealed themselves, in a covert way, through three literary works. In them, according to some critics, their authors were able to preserve a Jewish nature that was veiled, but still noticeable: Bento Teixeira, in the poem *Prosopopeia*, Ambrósio Fernandes Brandão, in the *Dialogues of the Great Things of Brazil*, and Antônio José da Silva, in the short story *Works of the Little Devil of Pierced Hand* (Igel 1997, 9). Even in the subsequent period – that is, during the period of the Empire (1822–1889) and the first decade of the Republic (1889–1900), there was no distinctly Jewish literary production, despite the arrival of Jews no longer subject to inquisitorial control. Regina Igel notes: "The expression of Jewish experiences and their cultural-religious complexity in Brazilian literature is of contemporary origin. As a literary phenomenon, it has been driven mainly by immigrants established here in the early twentieth century, by their descendants born in Brazil, and by refugee survivors of World War II" (Igel 1997, 28).

---

passing interest for a few, here absorbs everyone no less than as a matter of life and death." (Deleuze and Guattari 1986 [1975], 48)

3 Cf. Rawet's interview with Ronaldo Conde, "A Necessidade de Escrever Contos" (1971).

3 Jewish Immigration in the Twentieth Century

Jewish presence in Brazil becomes significant only in the twentieth century, with immigrants from Eastern Europe, notably Russia and Poland, fleeing pogroms and the very poor conditions of survival there. According to Jeffrey Lesser, between 1881 and 1900, a total of 1,000 Jews arrived – an average of 50 per year – while from 1901 to 1942, that number rose to 67,836 – an average of 1,615 per year – in a steeply ascending curve (Lesser 1995, 316). However, according to data from CONIB (Confederação Israelita do Brasil), this presence barely reached 0.06% of the country's total population.[4]

Groups of immigrants of the same geographical origin, with a common culture and traditions, tend to create institutions that enable the maintenance of bonds of solidarity and the preservation of their culture. Among these institutions, it is common to find clubs, theater groups, newspapers and magazines. This tendency towards cohesion, towards "talking to equals", is reinforced when there are problems in welcoming the minority, as occurred with the Jews in the first half of the twentieth century, between the manipulation of the *Estado Novo* dictatorship – which elected the Jews as scapegoat in their search for legitimation – and widespread anti-Semitism among the population driven by the preaching of the low clergy of the Catholic Church.

When some of the members of such a community dedicate themselves to producing literature, it is common for questions related to the immigration process to find relevant space among the topics addressed. This is what happened in Brazil. As Regina Igel reports: "Jewish themes entered Brazilian literature as a literary reaction to the typical problems of the first moments of Jewish immigration to Brazil, mainly from Europe. Appearing in the middle of the twentieth century and in Portuguese, it is a literature endowed with a specific, circumscribed identity, particular to the experiences of Jews in Brazilian territory" (Igel 1997, 1).

Jacó Guinsburg, reviewing the publication of *Contos do Imigrante*, by Samuel Rawet, in 1957, points out this phenomenon as follows: "The narratives gathered there carry the seal of a fiction writer who masters the current possibilities of the short story and uses them for a very original theme, at least in Brazilian literature. Indeed, this collection focuses, in some of its short stories, on aspects of Jewish immigration in Brazil and, in fact, marks the *de jure* emergence of this subject in our letters" (Guinsburg 1957). In Brazil, Guinsburg continues, tensions between immigrants and the hegemonic population opened up space for "a series of writers focused on the themes of discrimination, prejudice, anti-Semitism, resistance and the tendency to assimilation, conflicts of minds and generations, etc." (Guinsburg 1957).

---

4 Available at https://www.conib.org.br/historia/ (10 March 2022).

4 Authors and Works

In what follows, we present the main Brazilian writers of Jewish belonging, whether still active or already deceased. In our panorama, the authors' belonging and the use of Portuguese as their language of expression prevail as criteria. Thus, we include the work of Clarice Lispector despite the fact that Jewish themes are not evident in it. Notwithstanding the thorough research that underlies this work, omission of some authors is not impossible. In addition, given the disparities between research sources (from periodicals to recent publications in books), it is possible that some dates pertaining to the birth and death of authors and to the publication of works are not entirely accurate. The authors are presented in alphabetical order, by last name.

Lúcia Aizim was born in Ukraine in 1915 and died in 2006 in Rio de Janeiro (Brazil). A poet, her book of poems *Alma Pastora das Coisas* (Shepherdess Soul of Things) was published in 1974. What stands out in her poetry is its unique and personal rhythm as well as thematic figurations in which Judaism transpires as hybrid matter interspersed with tropical, Brazilian elements. This mixture, drawn in different dimensions, creates a singular poetics with different resonances, announcing the foreigner brought into the national body. It also reflects a contemplative attitude focused on the Jewish tradition, which nourishes itself, however, from daily life. Aizim also wrote *Folhas Soltas* (Loose Leaves), 1969; *Errância* (Wandering), 1978; *Exercício Efêmero* (Ephemeral Exercise), poetry, 1982; *Cantos e Baladas* (Songs and Ballads), 1985; *A Casa de Pássaros* (The House of Birds), short stories, 1992; and *Saga*, 1997.

Bernardo Ajzenberg was born in 1959 in São Paulo (Brazil). A writer, translator and journalist, his first work of fiction, the novel *Carreiras Cortadas* (Careers Cut Short), was published in 1989. Silvio Goldman, the narrator-protagonist of the novel *Variações Goldman* (Goldman Variations, 1998), is the son of a middle-class Jewish family from São Paulo, guided by bourgeois values, in which prestige, success, accommodation and discrimination make their mark. It is by the comic bias that one measures the distance between the narrator and the Jewish tradition, experienced by him and his family as an automatically fulfilled movement, as a compromise between the desire to get rid of an inheritance received and to perpetuate it, revealing a position of which he is no longer sure, for there is a teaching whose meaning has been lost. This is reminiscent of Kafka's literary universe, where messengers circulate but the messages do not reach their destination. Ajzenberg also wrote: *Goldstein & Camargo*, a novel, 1993; *Efeito Suspensório* (Suspensory Effect), 1993; *A Gaiola de Faraday* (Faraday's Cage), 2002; *Ilha Deserta* (Deserted Island), 2003; *Excursão à Caverna da Destruição* (Tour to the Cave of Destruction), 2005; *Homens com Mulheres* (Men with Women), 2005; *Olhos Secos* (Dry Eyes), 2009; *Pelé – Minha Vida em Imagens* (Pelé – My Life in Images), 2009; and *Gostar de Ostras* (To Love Oysters) 2017.

Moacir Aparecido Amâncio was born in Brazil in 1949. A journalist, essayist, poet and professor of literature, he is responsible for a wide range of poetic works. He premiered with the publication of *O Saco Plástico* (The Plastic Bag) in 1974, followed by *Do Objeto Útil* (Of The Useful Object) in 1992. In the latter work, the author encounters objects with his gaze, without aiming to reproduce the roundness of the world. On the contrary, he denies it in the name of a proper glance, supposedly in the movement of the eye that looks at the eye – or, as he says in his verses: "dentro deste olho / um outro olho espreita o branco" ("within this eye / another eye lurks the white"), eventually engendering in the poems a rhythm and an imaginary attentive to the representation of the real. In this book, although more discursive and less hermetic than those that would follow, lay the foundations of a poetic project taken as the axis of the production of the others.

One of Amâncio's poetic coordinates is the checking of the association of lyricism with the obligatory passage of the world by the subject and its conjugated expression, since his poetry is constructed through the emptying of feelings, memory and confidences, although there is a manifest desire to tell and make contact with the real. In this case, the mimesis is made by flashes, shards, capable of bringing into language a color, a light, a fruit, an animal, a body or parts of a body, outside the chain that governs the real, as if they were isolated parts.

On a second plane, the reference to a lyrical subject is emptied, so much that the pronoun "I" does not appear in any composition of the author, although it appears in the gaze that selects and composes, as in the poetic writing itself. It is a covert subject, giving way to objects, things, fruits, animals, and, on a more abstract plane, colors, sounds, rhythms – floating beings that need to be touched by the writing to anchor in the text, which can be a living room, a kitchen, a garden, or any other space. However, for the scene to occur, the object must enter the arc of the gaze; must be seen by an eye, and for this to take place, it is necessary for the object to be affected by the light, and thus the scene is composed, while avoiding at all costs any form of mirroring, of reflection, which would provoke paralysis of the movement: "un ojo, sí, pero / en sí no refleja" [an eye, yes, but / in itself it does not reflect] (Amâncio, *Colores Siguientes* 1999, 15). Thus, as soon as scene and text are inscribed, they are transfigured, a matter of fragile presence, which soon passes.

Being Jewish by choice and engaged in the study of the Hebrew language and the Jewish tradition, exile – a recurring theme in Jewish diasporic literature – is not part of his life experience, except in a broad sense, as a trace impressed on the condition of contemporary man. Nonetheless, the strangeness of and in language emerges as a place of exile in his poetry. In it is contained the biblical imperative of remembering (*zakhor*). The Hebrew language, one of the sources of production of this strangeness, marks the place where the sacred, the legacy of the dead and of the history of the Jewish people, has been filed since its first book and programmatically evoked in the others.

Os Mortos	The Dead
Doem, os falhos enigmas,	Hurt, the flawed puzzles,
Não no vago corpo deles,	Not in their vague body,
Doem em nós, alguns leitores,	[But] in us, some readers,
Os esquecidos da língua	The forgotten ones of the language
Onde se guardam escritos.	Where writings are kept.
Deveremos aprendê-la	We must apprehend it.
– alfabeto e reconquista –	– alphabet and reconquest –
para soletrar iguais	to spell equal
dimensões de solidão?	dimensions of solitude?

(Amâncio, *Do objeto útil* 1992, 38)

The traffic between languages stresses this place, destabilizes it permanently to maintain it, but as "earthquake matrix", which always has to be restored, reinvented. Thus, when sprouting in the white of the page, the poetic word creates a fleeting order. Image suspended in the abyss, it alludes to itself, strangely, but also evokes internally an ancient linguistic model, loaded with the mythical and mystical past that calls for transmission. The poem is the unstable place of transmission (*Makom-haMakon*). In this way, the snapshot contains the tradition; the unstable contains the past; the limited contains the infinite, the poem; each determined poem contains the indeterminate. For Moacir Amâncio, writing is to be on the very axis of ambiguity and to remain there, in exile, the focus of light attracted by the pull of secret waters, so it lurks in the shadows and weaves in secret.

Amâncio also published: *Estação dos Confundidos* (Season of the Confused), 1977; *Chame o Ladrão – Contos Policiais Brasileiros* (Call the Thief – Brazilian Police Tales), 1978; *O Riso do Dragão* (The Dragon's Laugh), 1981; *José J. Veiga – Literatura Comentada* (José J. Veiga – Commented Literature), 1982; *Súcia de Mafagafos* (Mafagafos's carousal), 1982; *Mariana e o Pavão Misterioso* (Mariana and the Mysterious Peacock), 1990; *Crônicas Escolhidas* (Selected Chronicles), 1991; *Figuras na Sala* (Figures in the Room), 1996; *Os Bons Samaritanos e Outros Filhos de Israel* (The Good Samaritans and Other Children of Israel), 1997; *O Olho do Canário* (The Eye of the Canary), 1997; *Colores Siguientes* (Next Colors), 1999; *Contar a Romã* (To Tell the Pomegranate), 2001; *Dois Palhaços e uma Alcachofra* (Two Clowns and an Artichoke), 2001; *O Talmud* (The Talmud), 1997; *Óbvio* (Obvious), 2004; *Ata*, 2007; *Yona e o Andrógino* (Yona and the Androgyne), 2010; and *Matula*, 2017.

He organized the collections *Cronistas do Estadão* (Chroniclers of Estadão), 1991, and *Ato de Presença: Hineni* (Act of Presence: Hineni), 2005.

Ben Abraham (pseudonym of Chaim Nekrycz) was born in Poland in 1924 and died in São Paulo (Brazil) in 2015. His work focuses on the sufferings of the victims of the Shoah. A writer and historian, he published: . . . *E o Mundo Silenciou* (. . . And the World Remained Silent), 1972; *Além do Infinito* (Beyond Infinity), 1973; *Holocausto – o Massacre de 6 Milhões* (Holocaust – the Massacre of 6 Million), 1976; *Izkor*, 1979; *O Trajeto* (The Path), 1982; *Desafio ao Destino* (Challenge to Destiny), 1984; *Segunda Guerra Mundial – Síntese* (World War II – Synopsis), 1985; *O Anjo da Morte: Dossiê*

Mengele (The Angel of Death: Mengele Dossier), 1985; *Yom HaShoah*, 1988; *Diário de um Repórter* (Diary of a Reporter), 1989; *De Varsóvia a Entebbe* (From Warsaw to Entebbe), 1992; *Mengele: a Verdade Veio à Tona* (Mengele: Truth Came to the Fore), 1994; *Memórias* (Memories), 1996; and *As Incríveis Travessuras de Ricardinho* (Ricardinho's Incredible Pranks, 1998.

Paulo Blank was born in Rio de Janeiro (Brazil) in 1949. A psychoanalyst and writer, he published *O Tal do Judeu* (The Jew) in 1989, *Cabala: o Mistério dos Casais* (Cabala: The Mystery of Couples) in 2005 and *Mensch: a Arte de Criar um Homem* (Mensch: The Art of Creating a Man) in 2016. The latter, as of now his most recent work, is a kind of *Bildungsroman* that presents the childhood of the narrator, who was brought up by his mother and grandmother, Polish immigrants who emigrated to Rio de Janeiro on the eve of World War II.

Roney Cytrynowicz was born in São Paulo (Brazil) in 1964. A historian, journalist and fiction writer, his first book of fiction, the collection of short stories *A Vida Secreta dos Relógios e Outras Histórias* (The Secret Life of the Clocks and Other Stories), was published in 1994. One of the axes of his fiction is the figure of his grandfather, who takes us back to Bom Retiro in São Paulo, a neighborhood with a large Jewish population that is now preferred by Koreans, a group belonging to a more recent immigrant movement. The narrator's grandfather, in the short story that gives the title to the collection, fixes clocks, an activity that alludes to the biblical injunction to repair the world – in Hebrew *tikkun olam*, a phrase that points to the need to return to perfection by obeying the precepts.

Cytrynowicz also published: *Memória da Barbárie* (Memory of Barbarism), 1990; *Guerra sem Guerra: a Mobilização e o Cotidiano em São Paulo durante a Segunda Guerra Mundial* (War without War: Mobilization and Daily Life in São Paulo during World War II), 2000; *A Congregação Israelita dos Pequenos* (The Israeli Congregation of the Little Ones), 2003; *Quando Vovó Perdeu a Memória* (When Grandmother Lost her Memory), 2006; *A Duna do Tesouro* (The Dune of the Treasure), 2009; and *Ciência e Arte: a Trajetória de Lilly Ebstein Lowenstein entre Berlim e São Paulo 1910–1960* (Science and Art: the Trajectory of Lilly Ebstein Lowenstein between Berlin and São Paulo 1910–1960), 2013.

Alberto Dines was born in 1932 in Rio de Janeiro and died in 2018 in the same city. A journalist, professor, biographer and writer, he published: *29 histórias curtas* (29 Short Stories), a collaboration, 1960; the volume of short stories *Posso?* (Can I?), 1972; *Morte no Paraíso, a Tragédia de Stefan Zweig* (Death in Paradise, the Tragedy of Stefan Zweig), 1981, with an expanded version published in 2004; *O Baú de Abravanel: uma Crônica de Sete Séculos até Sílvio Santos* (Abravanel's Trunk: a Chronicle of Seven Centuries until Sílvio Santos), 1990; *Vínculos do Fogo: Antonio José da Silva, o Judeu, e Outras Histórias da Inquisição em Portugal e no Brasil* (Bonds of Fire: Antonio José da Silva, the Jew, and Other Stories of the Inquisition in Portugal and Brazil), 1992; *Histórias do Poder: Militares, Igreja e Sociedade Civil* (Stories of Power: Military, Church and Civil Society), 2000; and *A Rede de Amigos de Stefan Zweig: sua Última*

Agenda 1940–1942 (The Network of Friends of Stefan Zweig: His Last Phonebook 1940–1942), 2014.

Sara Riwka Erlich was born in 1935 in Recife (Brazil). A psychiatrist, psychoanalyst and writer, she published: *Histórias que Precisavam ser Contadas* (Stories that Needed to be Told), a collection of short stories, 1963; *No Tempo das Acácias* (In the Time of Acacias), a collection of chronicles and short stories, 1978; *Transpoemas*, 2001; and *Outros Tempos I e II* (Other Times I and II), essays, 2003.

Boris Fausto was born in São Paulo (Brazil) in 1930. A lawyer, historian and political scientist, he published: *Crime e Cotidiano: a Criminalidade em São Paulo 1880–1924* (Crime and the Everyday: Criminality in São Paulo 1880–1924), 1984; *Negócios e Ócios* (Businesses and Idleness), 1997; *Fazer a América* (Making America), 1999; *Céu da Boca* (Palate), 2006; *Getúlio Vargas*, 2006; *O Crime do Restaurante Chinês: Carnaval, Futebol e Justiça na São Paulo dos Anos 30* (The Crime of the Chinese Restaurant: Carnival, Football and Justice in São Paulo in the 1930s), 2009; *Memórias de um Historiador de Domingo* (Memories of a Sunday Historian), 2010; and *O Brilho do Bronze: um Diário* (The Glitter of Brass: A Journal), 2014.

Janette Diamant Fishenfeld was born in 1931 in Niterói (Brazil) and died in Rio de Janeiro in 1993. A writer and biologist, she published the chronicles *Imagens no meu Espelho* (Pictures in my Mirror) in a monthly column in the magazine *Aonde Vamos?* in 1965. Her collection of tales *Os Dispersos* (The Scattered Ones) is from 1966.

Jacques Fux was born in 1977 in Belo Horizonte (Brazil). A mathematician and writer, his first work of fiction, *Antiterapias* (Antitherapies), was published in 2014. In *Meshugá – um Romance sobre a Loucura* (Meshugah – a Novel about Madness), published in 2016, the author plays with comic episodes of extravagant Jewish characters, accentuating their excess and its proximity to madness and breaking with the criteria of plot development usually associated with the novel genre. Madness, then, manifests itself as a way of escaping from the impossibility of assimilation. Fux also published *Literatura e Matemática: Jorge Luis Borges, George Perec e o Oulipo* (Literature and Mathematics: Jorge Luis Borges, George Perec and Oulipo), 2011, and *Brochadas: Confissões Sexuais de um Jovem Escritor* (Going Limp: Sexual Confessions of a Young Writer), 2015.

Alfredo Gartenberg was born in Vienna in 1897 and died in Rio de Janeiro (Brazil) in 1981. A journalist, theater critic and writer, he published the following works before moving to Brazil: *Per-versus*, a collection of satirical poems, 1920; *Mentiras da Vida* (Lies of Life), 1922; and *A Montanha de Vidro* (The Glass Mountain), 1932. While living in Brazil, he wrote the novel *O J vermelho* (The Red J) in 1976 and the biographical novel *Jacob Frank, o Messias da Sarjeta* (Jacob Frank, the Messiah of the Gutter) in 1980.

Zevi Ghivelder was born in Rio de Janeiro in 1934. A lawyer, journalist and writer, he published: *As Seis Pontas da Estrela* (The Six Points of the Star), a novel, 1969; *Sonetos Atentos* (Attentive sonnets), poetry, 1990; and *Missões em Israel, o Refém Emocional* (Missions in Israel, the Emotional Hostage), news reports, 1993.

Judith Grossmann was born in Rio de Janeiro in 1931, the daughter of immigrants from the Russian border with Romania, and died in 2015. A professor of literary theory and writer, she published: *Linhagem do Rocinante: 35 poemas* (Rocinante's Heritage: 35 Poems), 1958; *O Meio da Pedra* (The Middle of the Stone), short stories, 1970; *A Noite Estrelada: Estórias do Interim* (The Starry Night: Stories of the Interim), 1977; *Outros Trópicos* (Other Tropics), a novel, 1980; *Temas de Teoria da Literatura* (Themes of the Theory of Literature), 1982; *Cantos Delituosos* (Punishable Songs), a novel, 1985; *O Espaço Geográfico no Romance Brasileiro* (Geographical Space in the Brazilian Novel), 1993; *Meu Amigo Marcel Proust Romance* (My Friend Marcel Proust Novel), 1995; *Vária Navegação: Mostra de Poesia* (Varied Navigation: Poetry on Display), 1996; *Nascida no Brasil* (Born in Brazil), a novel, 1998; *Fausto Mefisto Romance* (Faust Mephisto Novel), 1999; *Pátria de Histórias: Contos Escolhidos de Judith Grossmann* (Homeland of Stories: Selected Short Stories by Judith Grossmann), 2000; and *Todos os Filhos da Ditadura* (All the Children of the Dictatorship), a novel, 2011.

Halina Grynberg was born in Poland in 1948. In her first book of fiction, *Mameloschn: Memória em Carne Viva* (Mameloschn: Memory in Living Flesh), published in 2004, the author configures the account of her life as a kind of *Bildungsroman*, punctuated by the *Shoah*. Belonging to the second generation after the catastrophe, Grynberg records the effort to move away from a history marked by the destruction and the trauma experienced by her as the inheritance of her parents. Nomadism and the condition of geographical exile make the family strive to carry with them the mother tongue – the *mameloschn* – the soil of affection, tradition and culture. Yiddish gains a new meaning after the Second World War, as it begins to register the debris and the ghost of the destruction of the Jews of Eastern Europe. Grynberg also published *Paulo Moura – um Solo Brasileiro* (Paulo Moura – a Brazilian Solo) in 2011.

Jacó Guinsburg was born in Bessarabia in 1921 and came to Brazil with his family at the age of three. He died in São Paulo in 2018. An editor, essayist, translator, and professor of theater and literature, Guinsburg was the first writer in Brazil to produce fiction about the *Shoah*. His short story "O Retrato" ("The Portrait") was published in 1949 in the magazine *O Reflexo* (number 8). The narrative focuses on the war as observed from Brazil, in a first-person account in which the character-narrator is the son of parents who emigrated from Romania. In four pages, the story marks the course of the war, enough time for the young narrator to move from his position of indifference with regard to his origin towards identification with it, as he suffers with his father the disasters of a world that, in the end, has been dismantled. Guinsburg also published *Aventuras de uma Língua Errante: Ensaios de Literatura e Teatro Ídiche* (Adventures of an Errant Language: Essays on Yiddish Literature and Theater) in 1996, *O que Aconteceu, Aconteceu* (What Happened, Happened) in 2000, and *O Noviço* (The Novice) in 2000.

Marcos Iolovitch, a writer, was born in Russia in 1907 and died in 1984 in Rio Grande do Sul (Brazil). His novel *Numa Clara Manhã de Abril* (On a Clear April Morning) was published in 1940 and his prose poems *Preces Profanas* (Profane Prayers) were published in 1949.

Paulo Jacob was born in Manaus (Brazil) in 1923, where he died in 2003. A judge and writer, by virtue of his profession he got to know thoroughly the interior of the state of Amazonas. Jacob published: *Muralha Verde* (Green Wall), 1964; *Andirá*, 1965; *Chuva Branca* (White Rain), 1968; *Dos Ditos Passados nos Acercados do Cassianã* (Of the Past Sayings in the vicinities of Cassianã), 1969; *Chãos de Maiconã* (Grounds of Maiconã), 1974; *Vila Rica das Queimadas*, 1976; *Estirão de Mundo* (Worldwide Spruce), 1979; *A Noite Cobria o Rio Caminhando* (Night Covered the River Walking), 1983; *O Gaiola Tirante Rumo do Rio da Borracha* (The Boat Cage Departing Towards the River of Rubber), 1987; *Dicionário da Língua Popular da Amazônia* (Dictionary of the Popular Language of the Amazon), 1985; *Um Pedaço de Lua Caía na Mata* (A Patch of Moonlight Fell on the Jungle), 1990 – this is the only publication with Jewish topics; *O Coração da Mata, dos Rios, dos Igarapés e dos Igapós Morrendo* (The Dying Heart of the Forest, of the Rivers, of the Streams and of the Igapos), 1991; *Amazonas, Remansos, Rebojos e Banzeiros* (Amazonas, Backwaters, Rebojos and Banzeiros), 1995; *Assim Contavam os Velhos Índios Ianomanes* (Thus Narrated the Old Ianomane Indians), 1995; and *Tempos Infinitos* (Infinite Times), 1999.

Noemi Jaffe was born in São Paulo in 1962. A writer, teacher and literary critic, her first work, the collection of poems *Todas as Coisas Pequenas* (All Small Things), was published in 2005. Jaffe also wrote: *Quando Nada Está Acontecendo* (When Nothing is Happening), 2011; *A Verdadeira História do Alfabeto* (The True History of the Alphabet) and *O que os Cegos Estão Sonhando* (What Blind People Are Dreaming), 2012; *Irisz: as Orquídeas* (Irisz: the Orchids), 2015; *O Livro dos Começos* (The Book of the Beginnings), 2016; and *Não Está Mais Aqui Quem Falou* (Never Mind), 2017.

Luis Sérgio Krausz was born in 1961 in São Paulo (Brazil). A professor of Jewish Literature, translator and fiction writer, his first novel, *Desterro: Memórias em Ruínas* (Banishment: Memories in Ruins), was published in 2011. His fictional work thematizes the difficulties of assimilation faced by Jewish immigrants and other issues related to exile and diaspora. The emphasis is on those who came from Central Europe, which lends originality to his work. His texts blend fictional elaboration with personal memories, creating an empathy with the reader through this identification. Krausz also published: *As Musas: Poesia e Divindade na Grécia Arcaica* (The Muses: Poetry and Divinity in Ancient Greece), 2007; *Rituais Crepusculares: Joseph Roth e a Nostalgia Austro-Judaica* (Crepuscular Rituals: Joseph Roth and Austrian-Jewish Nostalgia), 2008; *Passagens: Literatura Judaico-Alemã entre Gueto e Metrópole* (Passages: Jewish-German Literature Between Ghetto and Metropolis), 2012; *Deserto* (Desert), 2013; *Ruínas Recompostas: Judaísmo Centro-Europeu em Aharon Appelfeld* (Recomposed Ruins: Central European Judaism in Aharon Appelfeld), 2013; *Bazar Paraná* (Paraná Bazaar), 2015; *O Livro da Imitação e do Esquecimento* (The Book of Imitation and Forgetfulness), 2017; *Outro Lugar* (Another Place), 2017; and *Santuários Heterodoxos: Subjetividade e Heresia na Literatura Judaica da Europa Central* (Heterodox Sanctuaries: Subjectivity and Heresy in Central European Jewish Literature), 2017.

Bernardo Kucinski was born in 1937 in São Paulo. A journalist, political scientist and writer, his first work of fiction, the novel *K*, was published in 2012. The double reference to Kafka is not accidental: firstly, the presentation of the central character by the first letter of his name only and, secondly, the Kafkaesque universe faced by the protagonist within the labyrinths of the Brazilian military dictatorship (1964 to 1985) as he searches for his daughter, a political militant who has disappeared. As in the novels of the Jewish-Czech writer, the search is unfruitful – the labyrinth has no way out. Kucinski also published *Você Vai Voltar para Mim* (You Will Come Back to Me) in 2014, *Os Visitantes* (The Visitors) in 2016, and *Pretérito Imperfeito* (Imperfect Past Tense) in 2017.

Meir Kucinski was born in Poland in 1904 and died in São Paulo (Brazil) in 1976. He came to Brazil at the age of twenty-nine and came to play an important role in Jewish intellectual life, journalism and the teaching of Yiddish language and literature. His language of expression was Yiddish, and his narratives were translated into Portuguese. Refusing to erase the violence inherent in human relations, and particularly refusing to treat the Jews as a homogeneous block, Kucinski depicts the Jewish family in a state of conflict, intent on concealing and repressing an unwanted story. The book *Imigrantes, Mascates e Doutores* (Immigrants, Peddlers and Doctors), published in 2002, includes short stories originally published in Israel in 1963. Many of these narratives elaborate the problems faced by Jewish immigrants in their attempts to adapt to Brazilian conditions.

Trudi Landau was born in Germany in 1920 and died in Brazil in 2015. A writer, she published *Crônicas do Meu Tempo* (Chronicles of My Time) in 1981, *Vlado Herzog: o que Faltava Contar* (Vlado Herzog: What Was Still to be Told) in 1986, and *Carlinhos Querido* (Dearest Carlinhos) in 1992.

Esther Regina Largman was born in Salvador (Brazil) in 1934. A writer, teacher and historian, she wrote the novels *Jovens Polacas* (Polish Girls) in 1992, *Jan e Nassau: Trajetória de um Índio Cariri na Corte Holandesa* (Jan and Nassau: Trajectory of a Cariri Indian at the Dutch Court) in 1996 and *Tio Kuba nos Trópicos* (Uncle Kuba in the Tropics) in 1999. She also wrote *O Milionésimo Café de Augusta e Da janela* (Augusta's Millionth Coffee and From the Window) in 2003 and the non-fiction work *Judeus nos Trópicos* (Jews in the Tropics) in 2003.

Michel Laub was born in Porto Alegre (Brazil) in 1973. A lawyer, journalist and writer, his first book, the collection of short stories *Não Depois do que Aconteceu* (Not After What Happened), was published in 1998. His novel *Diário da Queda* (Diary of the Fall, 2011) departs from a traumatic event that gives meaning to the whole. It is this violent episode experienced by the narrator with a group of boys that will mark not only his adolescence, but also his adult life, characterized by a past of troubled relationships, including his own family history. It is the work of remembrance that brings to the fore the questions of the boy who becomes conscious, little by little, of the hatred that he and his fellow students at a Jewish school direct towards the only non-Jew in the schoolroom. The collective disdain for João (this is the name of the non-Jewish pupil), who is repeatedly humiliated and buried in the school's sandbox, reveals to the narrator the emptiness of his father's discourse on anti-Semitism.

The plot's construction is a daring one; in its ceaseless transit between delicate poles of human nature, it shows how the excluded can assume the role of the oppressor and, in a general way, how these roles are interchangeable. Along the way, the novel alludes to multiple resonances: to the absence of a protection network, which throws the characters into unimaginable situations; to the exploration of the "biographical space" that gives voice to experience; to different forms of annihilation; to unfathomable abysses of unsuspected humanity; to traumatic memory transformed into an object of inquiry; to oblivion; to the discussion of the ethical duty of remembering. Finally, the diversity of accounts of the past traces an intricate cartography that signals the paths of the fall and its recognition. To weave together so many threads, the novel gathers and intertwines three diaries, and the story arises out of the confrontation of three generations, represented by the grandfather, the father and the son/narrator. Written in the first person, it is not clear at first that the novel is a work of autofiction, since the author attributes to the protagonist/narrator some of his own (albeit shuffled) biographical information, which may lead the reader to think that it is an autobiography. The generational confrontation gives rise to a thematic segment focused on individual and collective memory. As the grandfather is an escapee from the Auschwitz concentration camp, the motto is that we (the Jews) cannot forget the mass murder committed by Nazi fascism. The grandfather escapes from the camp, travels to Brazil (Porto Alegre), marries a non-Jewish woman who converts to Judaism and never, at any time, refers to his experience as a prisoner and survivor. He ends up committing suicide, leaving behind sixteen volumes of written memories. His son, then at the age of fourteen, opens the door and finds his father killed by a bullet. As the grandfather never referred to his life at Auschwitz, the reader expects the volumes to reveal what was hidden. But they do not. Instead, they deal with how life should be and not how it is or was.

If the grandfather does not refer to his status as an immigrant or to his victimization by Nazism, the father does it for him, determining what cannot be forgotten: what a majority is capable of doing to a minority, according to a rigid scheme of perpetrator and victim. Ironically, he will suffer from Alzheimer's and will lose his memory, diminished by the degenerative disease, which metaphorizes the ethical injunction to remember. The narrator/son, on the other hand, recounts the remarkable experience of his life at the Jewish school, where a poor non-Jewish student, the son of a bus conductor, has been admitted, which will highlight another side of the story. Within this institution, the Jews are hegemonic, and João the non-Jew, a minority, is the laughingstock of his schoolmates. They bury him every day in the sandbox, making a mockery of him, until he turns thirteen, when his father decides to throw a party to reciprocate the invitations of his schoolmates, who used to invite him to their *bar mitzvah* celebrations. The party, the food, and the invited family members all bear the marks of poverty. João's schoolmates conspire to throw him upwards thirteen times, just as they used to do with the others, except that on the thirteenth throw they will let him fall to the ground.

The narrator wonders if he participated in this attack due to pressure from his schoolmates, whether he was active in the elaboration of the idea, whether it was the fault of others or rather his own: "I don't know if I did it simply because I was mirroring my classmates' behaviour, João being thrown into the air once, twice, with me supporting him right up until the thirteenth time and then, as he was going up, withdrawing my arms and taking a step back and seeing João hover in the air and then begin the fall, or was it the other way round: what if, deep down, because of that plot hatched in the previous days, because of something I might have said or an attitude I might have taken, even if only once and in the presence of only one other person, quite independently of the circumstances and any possible excuses, what if, deep down, they were also mirroring my behaviour?" (Laub 2011, 22). No one dampens the fall of João, which causes him to become paraplegic. This event causes the narrator to reassess his position in the world.

He rejects his father's discourse on anti-Semitism, for "even though so many had died in the concentration camps, it made no sense to be reminded of this every day" (Laub 2011, 48). As a result of the fall, the narrator is forced to move to a public school, where he approaches João. The two are in the same class. Now it is João, strengthened, who denounces the narrator to their new schoolmates and tells of his disloyalty and his participation in the incident. In a prose that oscillates between violence, lyricism and irony, with interludes of almost documentary neutrality in the description of smells, tastes, sounds, facts and feelings, the novel delineates the unusual journey of a man who needs to make a decisive choice to guide his life. In the last pages of the novel, the son of the narrator is born, who will have to cope with an ambiguous existential inheritance, at the same time fourth-generation victim and second-generation oppressor. Laub also published: *Música Anterior* (Previous Music), 2001; *Longe da Água* (Away from the Water), 2004: *O Segundo Tempo* (The Second Time), 2006; *O Gato Diz Adeus* (The Cat Says Goodbye), 2009; *A Maçã Envenenada* (The Poisoned Apple), 2013; and *O Tribunal da Quinta-feira* (The Court of Thursday), 2016.

Jaime Lerner was born in São Paulo (Brazil) in 1959. At the age of seven, he emigrated with his family to Israel, where he studied film and television. Later, he lived in London, where he obtained his master's degree in cinema in 1984. In 1985, he returned to Brazil, where he has lived ever since in Rio Grande do Sul. Lerner published: *Grupo de Risco* (Group of Risk), a novella, 1990; *Entre Quatro Paredes* (Between Four Walls), short stories, 1995; *O Vizinho – Parente por parte de Rua* (The Neighbor – Relative by Part of the Street), a work of children's literature, 2005; *O Fazedor da Utopia* (The Maker of Utopia), 2016; *Dois Amantes* (Two Lovers); and *A Origem* (The Origin), 2015.

Eliezer Levin was born in the agricultural colony Barão Hirsch (Rio Grande do Sul, Brazil) in 1930 and died in São Paulo. An engineer, entrepreneur, novelist, short story writer and chronicler, he is the author of several works that discuss the daily life of Jewish immigrants and their descendants in the neighborhood of Bom Retiro, São Paulo. His first work, the novel *Bom Retiro: o Bairro da Infância* (Bom Retiro: Childhood Neighborhood), was published in 1972. It describes the protagonist's effort to establish his Jewish identity.

Levin also published: *Herança Judaica* (Jewish Heritage), a work of political science, 1980; *Sessão Corrida: que me dizes, Avozinho?* (Rally Time: What Do You Have to Say, Grandpa?), 1982; *Crônicas do Meu Bairro* (Chronicles of My Neighborhood), 1987; *Nossas Outras Vidas* (Our Other Lives), chronicles, 1989; *Adeus, Iossl* (Good-bye, Iossl), a novel, 1994; and *Roberto Blanco, aliás Berl Schvartz* (Roberto Blanco, aka Berl Schvartz), 1997.

Tatiana Salem Levy was born in Lisbon in 1979, where her family was exiled during the Brazilian military dictatorship (1964 to 1985). They returned to Brazil shortly after Tatiana's birth. She currently lives between Rio de Janeiro and Lisbon, dedicating herself to journalism and literature. A translator and writer, her first work, the novel *A Chave da Casa* (The House in Smyrna), was published in 2007 in Brazil and Portugal, having merited several translations. In this novel, the author updates the drama experienced by Jewish immigrants expelled from Muslim countries, who remained in a kind of limbo, not knowing if they would be allowed to return later. As a result, they created the habit of preserving the keys to their houses, counting on the possibility of returning one day. In many cases, as in the novel, the keys were handed down from generation to generation, making exile an inheritance. Levy also published: *A Experiência do Fora: Blanchot, Foucault e Deleuze* (The Experience of the Outside: Blanchot, Foucault and Deleuze), 2003; *Dois Rios* (Two Rivers), a novel, 2011; *Curupira Pirapora*, a work of children's literature, 2012; *Tanto Mar* (So Much Sea), another work of children's literature, 2013; *Paraíso* (Paradise), 2014; and *O Mundo não vai Acabar* (The World will not End), 2017. In addition, she organized a collection of short stories by various writers, *Primos* (Cousins), in 2010.

Clarice Lispector was born in 1920, when her family traveled through Ukraine on its way to Brazil, where she arrived only two months old. She died in Brazil in 1977. She was married to the ambassador Gurgel Valente, which allowed her to live for several years in Europe during part of World War II. During this period, she volunteered daily at a hospital, where she assisted wounded Brazilian soldiers. Living in these conditions, she certainly became aware of the persecutions to which the Jews were subjected. However, this topic is not addressed in her work.

In 1944, still very young, Clarice completed her first novel, *Perto do Coração Selvagem* (Near to the Wild Heart). It is already perceptible in her debut work that what is at stake in her writing is not on the factual level of what "is" in space and time, but on the level of what is to be – eclipsing itself. It is this climate of principle-base, foundation, root, that endows her work with a vocation for the abyss, an atmosphere of genesis, a taste of archeology.[5]

---

5 See Pessanha (1989).

The work of Clarice Lispector is animated with this movement oriented towards the origin, which seeks to be the searching eye that opens the beginning – what is going to happen. This results in the non-intellectualism of most characters, a focus on rudimentary psychological life or on the "poor in spirit."

1961 is the year of publication of *A Maçã no Escuro* (The Apple in the Dark), a novel that proposes to build a man's life from the original loss of human form and language. Unleashed from any duties, from family life, and from the established order, which has been destroyed, it will be up to the protagonist to construct a new order. He will even give up word and thought in order to remake his life from ground zero. The world of language, however, is not easy to recreate. Slowly, the protagonist acknowledges that he has attempted an impossible adventure. He will be reabsorbed by the common language, mired in *cliché*, and his act will be called a crime. Thus, the trajectory of the protagonist imitates the shape of the apple, because it is a circular pilgrimage.

This movement of deconstruction is also found in *A Paixão Segundo G. H.* (The Passion According to G. H.), published in 1964. It is Lispector's first novel narrated in the first person. In it, the character named only by the initials G. H. submits to an unlearning of human things. While she inspects a room left empty by the dismissal of her maid, a cockroach emerges from the inside of the wardrobe. In a panic, G. H. crushes the insect and looks, fascinated and enraged, at her agonized victim, who also looks at her, unleashing a process in which G. H. is emptied of her personal life. Between the will to maintain her human individuality and the compulsion to follow a path that would lead her to the inhuman, G. H. struggles painfully until she yields to the attraction of that impersonal reality that integrates her into the exteriority of living matter. Thus, the role that the cockroach plays is to break down the system within which the narrator lived.

As with Martim from *A Maçã no Escuro* (The Apple in the Dark), G. H. returns to the system she had transgressed, but brings with her the dimension of her limits, the experience of suffering, necessary to achieve what in the novel is called "neutral." The "neutral" for Lispector is pure identity, in which the difference between subject and object is annulled, both of them intertwined in a reciprocal vision without transcendence.

Protagonism, in the texts of Clarice Lispector, has a close relationship with the word, with the fact of wanting to speak. Lispector's hero is one who leaves the world of created things, of creatures, and crosses over to the side of creation. Thus, the narrator of *Água viva* (Living Water) repeats insistently that she writes "for deeply wanting to speak." Perhaps it is here that we can identify a Jewish dimension in the author's work, for the idea of creation by the word is a distinctly Jewish concept. For example, in Genesis 1: 3, we read, "And God said, Let there be light; and there was light"; or, in 1: 6–7, "And God said, Let there be a firmament in the midst of the waters, and let it divide the waters from the waters. And God made the firmament; and divided the waters which *were* under the firmament from the waters which *were* above the firmament: and it was so." This creative power of the word is implied in the double meaning of the Hebrew term *davar*, at the same time "word" (of God) and "thing." This novel was published in 1973, and by 1979 it had already reached its tenth edition.

Clarice Lispector's last novel, *A Hora da Estrela* (The Hour of the Star), was published in 1977. The name Macabea, attributed to the protagonist, refers to the heroes of the biblical tradition (albeit outside the canon of the Hebrew Bible). However, the protagonist traverses an anti-heroic trajectory, characterized by poverty – both material and spiritual – and social marginalization. In this way, the novel must be understood in an ironic key. In search of some autonomy, the heroine looks for a fortune teller. Soon after a promising future has been predicted, she is killed by a car in the Rio de Janeiro's traffic and dies. In an interview, the author alludes directly to her Jewish origin, but makes such a turn in the construction of the sentence that she ends up amalgamating her Brazilian belonging with the initial statement: „I am Jewish, you know. [. . .] In short, I am Brazilian, and that's final, once and for all." (Coutinho 1980, 168).

Lispector also published: *O Lustre* (The Chandelier), 1946; *A Cidade Sitiada* (The Besieged City), 1949; *Alguns Contos* (Some Tales), 1952; *Feliz Aniversário* (Happy Birthday), 1960; *Laços de Família* (Family Ties), 1960; *A Legião Estrangeira* (The Foreign Legion), 1964; *O Mistério do Coelho Pensante* (The Mystery of the Thinking Rabbit), 1967; *A Mulher que Matou os Peixes* (The Woman Who Killed the Fishes), 1968; *Uma Aprendizagem ou O Livro dos Prazeres* (A Learning or The Book of Pleasures), 1969; *Felicidade Clandestina* (Clandestine Happiness), 1971; *Água Viva* (Living Water), 1973; *A Imitação da Rosa* (Imitation of the Rose), 1973; *A Via Crucis do Corpo* (The Via Crucis of the Body), 1974; *A Vida Íntima de Laura* (Laura's Intimate Life), 1974; *Onde Estivestes de Noite?* (Where Have You Been at Night?), 1974; *Um Sopro de Vida (Pulsações)* (A Breath of Life (Pulsations)), 1978; *Quase de Verdade* (Almost Real), 1978; *A Bela e a Fera* (Beauty and the Beast), 1979; *A Descoberta do Mundo* (The Discovery of the World), 1984; *Como Nasceram as Estrelas: Doze Lendas Brasileiras* (How the Stars Were Born: Twelve Brazilian Legends), 1987; *Aprendendo a Viver* (Learning to Live), 2004; and *Outros Escritos* (Other Writings), 2005.

Elisa Lispector was born in Ukraine in 1911 and died in Rio de Janeiro (Brazil) in 1989. A writer, her first novel, *Além da Fronteira* (Beyond the Border), was published in 1945. In her best-known work *No Exílio* (In Exile), from 1948, the author records the difficulties faced by the Jews who emigrated to Brazil – fleeing from the terrible conditions to which they had been subjected in Eastern Europe since before the Second World War – in their effort to adapt to the new environment, until the euphoric end marked by the creation of the State of Israel, which occurred in the same year as the publication of the work. She also published: *Ronda Solitária* (Lone Round), a novel, 1964; *Muro de Pedras* (Stone Wall), a novel, 1962; *O Dia Mais Longo de Thereza* (Thereza's Longest Day), a novel, 1965; *Sangue no Sol* (Blood in the Sun), short stories, 1970; *A Última Porta* (The Last Door), a novel, 1975; *Inventário* (Inventory), short stories, 1977; *Corpo a Corpo* (Hand-to-Hand), a romance, 1983; *O Tigre de Bengala* (The Bengal Tiger), short stories, 1985; and *Retratos Antigos – Esboços a Serem Ampliados* (Old Portraits – Sketches to be Enlarged), 2011.

Cíntia Moscovich was born in Porto Alegre (Brazil) in 1958. A journalist and writer, her first book, the collection of short stories *O Reino das Cebolas* (The Kingdom of Onions), was published in 1996. The author introduces Judaism as one of the structuring elements of her work. The family, intergenerational encounters and the transformations that are outlined create entanglements, oppositions, clashes, and struggles. In this context, "being Jewish" is a changing concept and many of the conflicts between parents and children are related to this transformation. The Jew in Brazil, immigration, changes of habit and language, mixed marriages, and the memory of ancestors are all topics that are treated by the author with sharpness and humor. The experience of the *Shoah* and its effects on the Jews of the second and third generations also enter into the stories of the writer. In the novel *Por Que Sou Gorda, Mamãe?* (Mother, Why Am I Fat?), published in 2006, the description ". . . counting forkfuls. As in a concentration camp" emphasizes the suffering of the overweight protagonist, who has to starve to lose weight (Moscovich 2006, 231). The doctor has recommended the reduction of her diet to three forkfuls per meal and a maximum of six forkfuls a day. In the narrative, food is available in excessive amounts and must be diminished by the compulsive protagonist, but it was scarce and almost nonexistent among the squalid inmates of the concentration camps. By means of comparison ("as in a concentration camp"), an analogy is constructed which designates two crossed and antagonistic realities, establishing the ironic tone of the text. This applies to the naming of things that seem out of place. The essential ambiguity of irony lies in accepting, at the same time, conflicting meanings that confuse the reader, who must take a shortcut to get there. It should be noted that the supply of food in excess can be understood as a diasporic Jewish family trait, and that the titular question is rightly addressed by the protagonist to her mother.

The quotation: "the father, like the commander of an extermination camp, took control of the cart (from the airport)", from the short story "O homem que voltou ao frio" ("The Man Who Returned to the Cold"), is one of several similar passages to be found in this narrative, which describes the stay of an unwanted Finn in Porto Alegre, construing him as the victim of a conjugal mismatch. Through recourse to the mention of Nazi concentration camps, the account evokes the misfortune of the presence of this young man, who has arrived in an untimely manner to stay and marry a young woman he met in Israel. Already upon his arrival, his death at the end of the narrative is foreshadowed. The Finn, a non-Jew, cannot convert to Judaism but wants to marry the Jewish girl from Porto Alegre. Belonging to the third generation after the Shoah, the movement of the writer is ambiguous, because she detaches herself from a history marked by the destruction and trauma experienced by her as an inheritance and, at the same time, employs it in the construction of figures of language, trampolines for the attainment of grace and irony, motivated by the contrast and disproportion between what was the collective slaughter of the Second World War and the more or less prosaic situations of the life of a relatively wealthy and bourgeois Jewish family in the city of Porto Alegre, Brazil. This treatment of the Shoah theme through the use of humor and irony is a transgressive mark of the author's writing. Moscovich also published: *Arquitetura do Arco-Íris* (Architecture of the Rainbow), short stories, 2004; *Duas Iguais: Manual de Amores e Equívocos Assemelhados* (Two Alike: Manual of Loves and Similar Misconceptions), a novella, 1998; *Anotações Durante o Incêndio* (Notes During a Fire), short stories, 2006; *Esta Coisa Brilhante que é a Chuva* (This Brilliant Thing that is Rain), short stories, 2012; and *Mais ou Menos Normal* (More or Less Normal), a child/young adult novel, 2014.

Joseph Nichthauser was born in Poland in 1928 and died in Belo Horizonte (Brazil) in 2010. A survivor of the *Shoah*, he published *Quero Viver... Memórias de um ex-Morto* (I Want to Live... Memoirs of a Former Dead Person) in 1976 and *A morte de um Carrasco* (Death of an Executioner) in 2003.

Rosa Palatnik was born in Poland in 1904 and died in Brazil in 1981. A writer of short stories, she contributed to Yiddish newspapers from São Paulo, Rio de Janeiro, Buenos Aires, New York and Tel Aviv. In Brazil, she published in Portuguese translation: *Kroshnik-Rio: dertseylungen* (Krusnik-Rio: tales), 1953; *Baym Geroysh fun Atlantik: dertseylungen* (Facing the Whirlwind of the Atlantic), 1957; *Dreytsn dertseylungen* (Thirteen Stories), 1961; *Geklibene dertseylungen* (Selected Stories), 1966; *Parokhet ha-ketifah: Mivhar sipurim* (Velvet Ark: Selected Short Stories), 1972; and *Dois dos Justos* (Two of the Just), short stories, 1975.

Maurício Eskenazi Pernidji was born in 1930 and died in 1994. He published the novel *A Última Polaca ou Sarah Pede: Por Favor, Não Tragam Flores à Minha Sepultura* (The Last Polish Girl or Sarah Asks: Please Do Not Bring Flowers to My Grave) in 1985 and, together with Joseph Eskenazi Pernidji, the historical novel *Homens e Mulheres na Guerra do Paraguai* (Men and Women in the War of Paraguay) in 2000.

Samuel Urys Rawet was born in 1929 in the Polish *shtetl* Klimontow. Due to the poor economic conditions to which Polish Jews were subjected after the reconstitution of Poland as an independent state, his father, like many other Polish Jews, emigrated to Brazil in 1932, seeking to gather resources to bring his family, which happened only in 1936, when Samuel was seven years old. He died in Brazil in 1984. Faced with the need to survive amid a hegemonic population that is not always welcoming, members of a minority often experience the need to demarcate the difference that separates them from the majority group or to strengthen an identity that allows them to live with the autochthonous population without totally losing this identity; or, instead, they experience the need to integrate themselves radically into this population, breaking with their original group by erasing differential marks. In other words, in all situations the foreigner is led to look at himself through the gaze of the other.

The strangeness linked to the consciousness of his Jewishness and the perception of the difference resulting from this condition helps to explain the fact that of the ten short stories comprising Rawet's first collection, *Contos do imigrante* (Immigrant Tales) – containing works written since 1951 and published in book form in 1956 – five feature a Jewish character in a crisis situation resulting from the difficulties of acceptance by the group in which he tries to integrate. As we shall see, in two of these short stories, "A prece" ("The Prayer") and "Gringuinho" ("Little Gringo"), the group whose acceptance the foreigner seeks is part of the hegemonic, non-Jewish population. In the other three stories, the conflict is established in the relationship between the protagonist and a group of Jews. In one of them, "O profeta" ("The Prophet"), the protagonist's family rejects him for his insistence on remaining faithful to the memory of the Shoah and to the habits of life in Europe; reciprocally, he criticizes and rejects his family for having opted for assimilation and diminished the importance of the barbarism to which the Jews, like himself, had been submitted in the Nazi period. In another tale, "Judith," the protagonist is rejected by her family for having married a non-Jew; and in "Réquiem para um solitário" ("Requiem for a loner)", the protagonist, a successful immigrant, is plagued by the guilt of having come to Brazil, abandoning his first family to Nazi extermination.

The short story "A prece" ("The prayer") is narrated without concern for chronology. The initial scene already marks the end of the plot: Ida is returning to her tenement after a day of exhausting work and is harassed by children who are residents of the same house. The narrative continues alternating, without warning, between events from different times. Thus, Rawet reflects the tumult of Ida's thoughts and the reader realizes that the protagonist's life has plummeted from tragedy to tragedy, from displacement to displacement. How is Ida seen by the tenants? By the children, as a very strange figure, an object of mockery that almost comes to physical aggression. Her speech is nearly incomprehensible, which exacerbates her estrangement and encourages her ridicule. The story reaches its climax on a Friday afternoon, when Ida, exhausted by work and the tropical sun, prepares, nevertheless, for her first Shabbat in the tenement. The scene, so familiar to Jewish families from Eastern Europe, is bizarre for non-Jewish eyes, mainly because of the candles, which evoke the possible presence of a deceased in the children's imagination. Called by the children, the adults share their bewilderment: they find Ida with her hands covering her eyes and a scarf on her head, reciting her prayer. Slowly, common sense returns to the tenants, when one of them calls them to reason: "– Vamos sair, minha gente. Nâo é nada! Isso é reza lá da terra deles" [–Let's leave, folks. It's nothing! This is praying from their land] (Rawet 1956, 35).

"Gringuinho," perhaps the author's best-constructed tale, included in the collection *Os cem melhores contos brasileiros do século* (The One Hundred Best Brazilian Short Stories of the Century), is another narrative in which the Jewish protagonist finds himself in the inescapable contingency of relating to a group of non-Jews. If the end of "The Prayer" is optimistic – after all, Ida has recognized her right to be different and is accepted as a tenant – the end of "Gringuinho" is less promising: unable to cope with the rejection of his schoolmates and feeling abandoned by his mother, the boy protagonist, in order not to succumb to melancholy, chooses to flee from external reality. He runs to fetch the onions ordered by his mother in an attempt to magically hasten time and stop being a child; he wants to be an adult as soon as possible – the only way, in his view, to stop being harassed.

At the time of the writing of *Immigrant Tales*, the Jewish population in Brazil experienced remarkable growth as a result of the arrival of refugees from the war in Europe. These different immigration conditions provoked estrangement not only from the hegemonic, non-Jewish population, but also from the Jewish communities established in Brazil for some time. Certainly, these early Rawetean protagonists are dated. There are no more "Idas" and "Little Gringos" in Brazil. Nowadays, being Jewish is an asset, associated with good expectations regarding entry into the qualified labor market, corporate networks and good social relations in general (Grün 1999). Nevertheless, Rawet made use of the difficult relationship between a Jewish protagonist and a group of non-Jews in later works also, such as the short stories "Natal sem Cristo" ("Christmas without Christ"), "Reinvenção de Lázaro" ("Reinvention of Lazarus"), "Lisboa à Noite" ("Lisbon at Night") and "O Casamento de Bluma Schwartz" ("The Wedding of Bluma Schwartz"), in addition to the novella *Abama*.

This allows him to look at himself, in his Jewish condition, through the eyes of the other, as in a game of mirrors. Rawet published: *Contos do Imigrante* (Immigrant Tales), 1956; *Diálogo* (Dialogue), 1963; *Abama*, 1964; *Os Sete Sonhos* (The Seven Dreams), 1967; *O Terreno de uma Polegada Quadrada* (The Land of One Square Inch), 1969; *Viagens de Ahasverus à Terra Alheia em Busca de um Passado que Não Existe Porque é Futuro e de um Futuro que Já Passou Porque Sonhado* (Voyages of Ahasverus to a Foreign Land In Search of a Past That Does Not Exist Because it is Future and of a Future That Has Already Passed Because It Was Dreamt), 1970; *Devaneios de um Solitário Aprendiz da Ironia* (Daydreams of a Lonely Apprentice of Irony), 1970; *Consciência e Valor* (Consciousness and Valor), 1970; *Homossexualismo, Sexualidade e Valor* (Homosexuality, Sexuality and Valor), 1970; *Alienação e Realidade* (Alienation and Reality), 1970; *Eu-Tu-Ele* (I-Thou-He), 1972; *Angústia e Conhecimento: Ética e Valor* (Anguish and Knowledge: Ethics and Valor), 1978; and *Que os Mortos Enterrem Seus Mortos* (Let the Dead Bury Their Dead), 1981. He also produced theatrical pieces, such as *Os Amantes* (The Lovers), 1957, and *Um Lance de Dados* (A Throw of Dices), unpublished, which alludes directly to the poem by Stéphane Mallarmé (1842–1898).

Samuel Reibscheid was born in São Paulo (Brazil) in 1937, the son of immigrant parents, and died in 2011. A doctor and writer, his first book, the collection of short stories *Breve Fantasia* (Brief Fantasy), was published in 1995. His work, captured by the eye as a kind of postmodern polaroid, does not fear excess. Excrement, mutilation, and death signal the disorder of irrationalism, negating any frames of reference from a world in progress. His fiction is based on a history that systematically victimizes minorities, highlighting the continuity of prejudice and intolerance. Reibscheid also published *Memorial de um Herege: Vida e Morte de Isaac ben Maimon* (A Heretic's Memorial: Life and Death of Isaac ben Maimon) in 2000 and *Exílio – as Histórias da Grande Peste* (Exile – The Stories of the Great Plague) in 2007.

Malka Lorber Rolnik was born in 1922 in Poland and died in Curitiba (Brazil) in 1987. A writer, she published *Os Abismos* (The Abysms) in 1990 and *Mundo Jovem* (Young World) in 2000.

Paulo Rosenbaum was born in São Paulo (Brazil) in 1959 and is a doctor, poet and novelist. His first work of fiction, the novel *A Verdade Lançada ao Solo* (The Truth Thrown to the Ground), was published in 2010. His approach to Judaism has a mystical bias. The novel *Céu Subterrâneo* (Underground Sky), published in 2016, is a metaphor that not only joins the high and the low, but also exposes what is below the visible surface of the ground. The intended object is not any common cave, but the Tomb of the Patriarchs that the biblical Abraham purchased for Sarah's grave (Gen. 23). Over time, Abraham, Isaac, Rebecca, Jacob and Leah would also be buried there. It is precisely this place, so dear to Jews and Arabs, that brings together an important part of the events of this novel. A scriptural reading is, however, not the only one possible, as the book may also be read in a postmodern key. The extension of time that the novel encompasses and the mystery to be unraveled create a postmodern climate in which man inhabits a world full of icons and signs that oppose everyday objects and demand the attribution of meaning. In this way, mysticism and postmodernity are related in a very particular way. Rosenbaum has also published a book of poems, *A Pele que Nos Divide* (The Skin that Divides Us), in 2017. and the novel *Navalhas Pendentes* (Dangling Razors), 2021.

Isaac Schachnik was born in Recife (Brazil) in 1918 and died in the same city in 2003. He published: *Judaísmo em Prosa e Verso (Pessach Bossa-Nova)* (Judaism in Prose and Verse (Pesach Bossa Nova)), a poem, 1986; *Página Um e Outras Páginas* (Page One and Other Pages), 1984; *Um Casaco de Peles* (A Fur Coat), short stories, 1994; and *Páginas Leonísticas* (Lionistic Pages), 2001.

Boris Schnaiderman was born in Ukraine in 1917 and died in São Paulo (Brazil) in 2016. A translator, teacher, and essayist, his first book of fiction, the novel *Guerra em Surdina* (Muted War), was published in 1964. Among the combatants who embarked for war on 2 July, 1944 was Sergeant Boris Schnaiderman, who did everything he could to be summoned. The struggle was for democracy, but it was the children of a country under dictatorship who went to combat. Written many years after the end of the war, the author works with the reminiscences deposited in his memory and fictionalizes them, rather than opting for the provision of testimony. Thus, he chooses to employ enunciative practices that allow him to transcend the scope of personal experience, because he is interested in the undiluted human aspects of the public scene. Schnaiderman also published: *A Poética de Maiakóvski* (The Poetics of Mayakovsky), 1971; *Projeções: Rússia, Brasil, Itália* (Projections: Russia, Brazil, Italy), 1977; *Leão Tolstói: Antiarte e Rebeldia* (Leo Tolstoy: Anti-Art and Rebellion), 1983; *Turbilhão e Semente: Ensaios Sobre Dostoiévski e Bakhtin* (Whirlwind and Seed: Essays on Dostoevsky and Bakhtin), undated; *Contos Reunidos* (Collected Tales), 1994; *Os Escombros e o Mito: a Cultura e o Fim da União Soviética* (The Debris and the Myth: Culture and the End of the Soviet Union), 1997; *Encontros* (Meetings), 2010; *Tradução: Ato Desmedido* (Translation: Excessive Act), 2011; and *Caderno Italiano* (Italian Notebook), 2015.

Luis Schwarcz was born in São Paulo (Brazil) in 1956. An editor and writer, he published: *Minha Vida de Goleiro* (My Life as a Goalkeeper), 1999; *Em Busca do Thesouro* *da juventude* (In Search of the Treasure of Youth), 2003; *Discurso Sobre o Capim: contos* (Speech on Common Grass: Tales), 2005; *Éloge de la Coïncidence* (Praise of Coincidence), 2005; and *Linguagem de Sinais* (Language of Signals), 2010.

A Brazilian born in Porto Alegre in 1937 and the son of immigrants from Eastern Europe, **Moacyr Scliar** brings to his literature the marks of this double identity. He died in Brazil in 2011. What makes him stand out in the context of Brazilian literature is his thematization of the phenomenon of Jewish immigration, particularly in Rio Grande do Sul. Scliar observed the Jewish community from within, with humor and irony, employing such instruments as parody and inversion.

In Scliar's works, combinations between the local and the foreign are updated in different ways: in hybrid figures such as the centaur in *O Centauro no Jardim* (The Centaur in the Garden) or the mermaid in *O Ciclo das Águas* (The Cycle of Waters); in a plot that is articulated in such a way as to bring out the cultural shock between immigrants and Brazilians or between the first generation of immigrants and that of their children who have already adapted to the country (*A Guerra no Bom Fim* [The War in Bom Fim]); in the construction of characters who live the conflict of having to choose between the tradition of their parents and the hegemonic culture (*Os Deuses de Raquel* [Rachel's Gods]); and in the use of certain formal matrices of Jewish culture (the parable, the intertextuality with the Bible and the Kabbalah), all three of them presented in another key.

In *A Guerra no Bom Fim* (The War in Bom Fim), the author's first novel, published in 1972, it is through a child's eyes that we see a parade of hostile non-Jewish characters: a Polish alcoholic, threatening to make mincemeat of the Jews; people of color, who are depicted as scary and aggressive except for Macumba, with whom the protagonist Nathan exchanges his plate of Jewish food for some rice and beans. As for the gentile woman, she embodies the instinct of evil that always passes through the body. She is lubricious, as in the case of the Madalena, whom Elias marries, taking her to Bom Fim (a Jewish neighborhood in Porto Alegre), to the disgrace of his family and the curiosity of the younger ones: "E daí, meus judeuzinhos? Querem me comer?" (So, my little Jews? Do you want to eat me?) (Scliar, *A Guerra no Bom Fim* 1972, 45). To this list of intimidating figures is added that of the German, associated with Nazism, who will, in fact, transpose the "final solution" from Germany and Poland to Porto Alegre by transforming, in a scene of cannibalism, an older Jew into barbecue on a carnival day. Living in the illusion of emancipation and enrichment, in indifference to the tradition of the ancestors, and lacking a Jewish education, the incomprehensiveness and at the same time the deepest aspiration of Scliar's (anti-)heroes seem to aim at conciliating a Jewish "spirit" with a *goyish* body, seeking to eliminate the difference at least on the plane of appearances. Thus, the cult of the *goyish* body in the case of the centaur Guedali begins with the selection of food that differs from the traditional Jewish diet. The beet soup, fish, and unleavened bread of Passover are tasty foods for the Jews, but not for Guedali, whose huge horse's belly and long intestines call for more adequate sustenance. To the great regret of his parents, Mayer Guinsburg also insists on eating pork, precisely in order to violate the Jewish dietary rules and to dream with the materiality of the *goyish* body. In Scliar's accounts, the bodies of the Jews undergo the most grotesque and distressing metamorphoses. It is in physical uniqueness and disease that Jews manifest their fragility. Rosa's toothed vagina (*A Guerra no Bom Fim*) and the equine part of Guedali (*O Centauro no Jardim*) are ways of pointing out the difficulty and even the impossibility of confronting the outside world, beyond stigmatizing the difference. Second generation Jewish immigrants in the writings of Scliar seek redemption in the conscious forgetting of their collective past, and the magical key that will change their situation is enrichment. This is their biggest project. To achieve it, it will be necessary for them to set their origins aside and to secularize the past by means of the homogenizing power of capitalism, which will force the Jews to move away from the strict sphere of their community and to begin to conduct themselves like the bourgeoisie. However, even if distanced from their roots, these characters cannot get rid of them. Scliar's characters can be defined as exiled from themselves. In this condition, they are led to situate the object of their integration outside of themselves, which leads them to an incessant movement. In this transit, there is a search and, at the same time, the certainty of a lack, which causes the characters to oscillate without finding their point of balance. If this exile from the self is what characterizes Scliar's Jewish characters, it is also one of the questions posed by contemporary literature in general, which points to emptiness as one of the defining traits of present-day man. There are two components that could be highlighted in Scliar's work: the expression of an ethnic identity and the manifestation of a national way of feeling and thinking. Scliar lies both outside of and within his group, adopting as a theme the condition of the one who is different, identifying with him but also writing in the hegemonic language, inserting, in his colloquial style, his critical view of reality and his depictions of its anti-heroes into the literature that has been developing in Brazil in recent decades. Living within the experience of cultural hybridization with which he deals in his writing, the mixture of two worldviews and two collective memories so far apart, Moacyr Scliar is the most fruitful representative of this particular encounter in contemporary Brazilian letters. Scliar also published: *O Carnaval dos Animais* (The Carnival of Animals), 1968; *A Guerra no Bom Fim* (The War in Bom Fim), 1972; *O Exército de um Homem Só* (The One-Man Army), 1973; *Os Deuses de Raquel* (The Gods of Rachel), 1975; *A Balada do Falso Messias* (The Ballad of the False Messiah), 1976; *O Ciclo das Águas* (The Cycle of the Waters), 1977; *Mês de Cães Danados* (Month of Damned Dogs), 1977; *Doutor Miragem* (Doctor Mirage), 1978; *Os Voluntários* (The Volunteers), 1979; *O Centauro no Jardim* (The Centaur in the Garden), 1980; *Cavalos e Obeliscos* (Horses and Obelisks), 1981; *Max e os Felinos* (Max and the Felines), 1981; *A Festa no Castelo* (Feast in the Castle), 1982; *A Estranha Nação de Rafael Mendes* (The Strange Nation of Rafael Mendes), 1983; *O Olho Enigmático* (The Enigmatic Eye), 1986; *O Tio que Flutuava* (The Uncle Who Floated), 1988; *Um País Chamado Infância* (A Country Called Childhood), 1989; *A Orelha de Van Gogh* (Van Gogh's Ear), 1989; *Cenas da Vida Minúscula* (Scenes of the Tiny Life), 1991;

No Caminho dos Sonhos (Dream Paths), 1992; *Sonhos Tropicais* (Tropical Dreams), 1992; *Um Sonho no Caroço do Abacate* (A Dream in the Avocado Seed), 1995; *Contos Reunidos* (Collected Tales), 1995; *Minha Mãe Não Dorme Enquanto Eu Não Chegar e Outras Crônicas* (My Mother Does Not Sleep Until I Arrive and Other Chronicles), 1996; *A Majestade do Xingu* (The Majesty of the Xingu), 1993; *Mulher que Escreveu a Bíblia* (The Woman who Wrote the Bible), 1999; *A Colina dos Suspiros* (The Hill of Sighs), 1999; *Os Leopardos de Kafka* (Kafka's Leopards), 2000; *O Mistério da Casa Verde* (The Mystery of the Green House), 2000; *Pra Você Eu Conto* (To You I Tell), 2000; *Ataque do Comando P. Q.* (Attack of the Commando P.Q.), 2001; *O Imaginário Cotidiano* (The Daily Imaginary), 2001; *Eden-Brasil*, 2002; *O Sertão Vai Virar Mar* (The Backwoods Will Turn into Sea), 2002; *O Irmão que Veio de Longe* (The Brother Who Came from Afar), 2002; *Na Noite do Ventre, o Diamante* (In the Night of the Womb, the Diamond), 2005; *O Olhar Médico: Crônicas de Medicina e Saúde* (The Medical Look: Chronicles of Medicine and Health), 2005; *Ciumento de Carteirinha* (Card-Carrying Jealousy), 2006; *Câmara na Mão, o Guarani no Coração* (Camera at Hand, Guarani at Heart), 2006; *Os Vendilhões do Templo* (The Moneychangers of the Temple), 2006; *Manual da Paixão Solitária* (Handbook of the Lone Passion), 2008; *Deu no Jornal* (Published in the Newspaper), 2008; *O Menino e o Bruxo* (The Boy and the Wizard), 2009; *Histórias que os Jornais Não Contam* (Stories that the Newspapers Do Not Tell), 2009; *Eu Vos Abraço, Milhões* (I Embrace You, Millions), 2010; and *Caminhos da Esperança (a Presença Judaica no Rio Grande do Sul)* (Paths of Hope [The Jewish Presence in Rio Grande do Sul]), undated.

Samuel Szwarc, a lawyer, journalist, public relations professional and writer, published *Contos Judaicos e Outros Nem Tanto* (Jewish Stories and Others Not So Much) in 1995.

Célia Igel Teitelbaum was born in 1945 and died in 2019 in São Paulo (Brazil). She published *Passagem-paisagem* (Passage-Landscape), poetry, in 1983 and *Nem lá, nem cá* (Neither there nor here), a novel, in 2012.

Adão Voloch was born in 1914 in the Filipson colony in Rio Grande do Sul and died in Rio de Janeiro (Brazil) in 1991. He published the novels: *O Colono Judeu-Açu: o Romance da Colônia Quatro Irmãos – Rio Grande do Sul* (The Judeu-Açu Settler: The Novel of Colônia Quatro Irmãos – Rio Grande do Sul), 1984; *Um Gaúcho a Pé* (Gaucho Afoot), 1987; *Os Horizontes do Sol* (The Horizons of the Sun), 1987; *Ben-Ami: Um Homem Louco Pinto* (Ben-Ami: A Mad Man I Paint), 1988; *Sob a Chuva Nasceu Nucleary* (Under the Rain Was Born Nucleary), 1989; and *Os Desgarrados de Nonoai* (The Torn of Nonoai), 1989.

Ronaldo Wrobel was born in Rio de Janeiro (Brazil) in 1968. A lawyer, chronicler, short story writer and novelist, his first work, the novel *Propósitos do Acaso* (Purposes of Chance), dates from 1998. His most publicized work, *Traduzindo Hannah* (Translating Hannah), was published in 2010. The novel takes place in the dictatorial government of Getúlio Vargas (1937–1945), who is obsessed with establishing strict vigilance over all acts of the population, including their correspondence, especially in foreign languages. For this purpose, it is necessary to call upon a Yiddish expert. The reading of the letters exchanged between the sisters Hannah and Guita leads the protagonist to immerse himself in the relations between the members of the Jewish community of Rio de Janeiro. Wrobel also published: *Raiz Quadrada e Outras Histórias (contos)* (Square Root and Other short Stories), 2001; *Nossas Festas Infanto-Juvenis* (Our Juvenile Parties), 2007; and *O Romance Inacabado de Sofia Stern* (Sofia Stern's Unfinished Novel), 2016.

Samy Wurman was born in 1971. An economist and auditor, he has published: *Sexo com Nexo* (Sex with Nexus), 1997; *Olhos de Céu* (Eyes of Heaven), a novel, 2001; *Numa Gota de Tempo uma Vida* (In a Drop of Time a Life), 2014; and *Heranças Malditas* (Cursed Inheritances), 2015.

Finally, we list authors for whom literature has not occupied the center of their interests, which does not detract from the quality of their works: **Frida Alexandr** (1906–1972), *Filipson*, chronicles, 1967; **Leôncio Basbaum** (1907–1969), *Uma Vida em Seis Tempos* (A Life in Six Times), memoirs, 1976; **Konrad Elkana Charmatz** (1910–1986), *Pesadelos* (Nightmares), memoirs, 1976; **Rosane Chonchol**, *O Rabino e o Psicanalista* (The Rabbi and the Psychoanalyst), short stories, 1986; **Rachelle Zweig Dolinger** (born 1938), *Mulheres de Valor: uma Memória de Mulheres que se Destacaram na Comunidade Judaica do Rio de Janeiro* (Women of Value: a Memoir of Women who Excelled in the Jewish Community of Rio de Janeiro), 2004; **Francisco Dzialovsky** (born 1952), *O Terceiro Testamento* (The Third Testament), short stories, 1987; *Devoração* (Devoured), novel, 2001; **Moisés Eizirik** (1919–?) *Aspectos da Vida Judaica no Rio Grande do Sul* (Aspects of Jewish Life in Rio Grande do Sul), chronicles, 1984; *Imigrantes Judeus* (Jewish Immigrants), chronicles, 1986; **Leão Pacifico Esaguy** (1918–2010), *Contos Amazonenses* (Amazonian Tales), 1981; *O Aleijadinho, um Romance na Amazonia* (Aleijadinho, a Novel in the Amazon), 1982; **Martha Pargendler Faermann** (ca. 1922–2014), *A Promessa Cumprida* (The Promise Fulfilled), memoirs, 1990; **Haim Grünspun** (born ca. 1927), *Anatomia de um Bairro: o Bexiga* (Anatomy of a Neighborhood: Bexiga), memoirs, 1979; *Meu Pai me Matou* (My Father Killed Me), memoirs, 1987; **Mary Hirschfeld**, *Seja Lá o que For* (Whatever It Is), 1988; **Abrahão Iovchelovitch**, *O Sacrifício do Médico* (The Physician's Sacrifice), a novel, 1958; *Ecos da Eternidade* (Echoes of Eternity), 1980; **Mathilde Maier** (ca. 1907–?), *Os Jardins de Minha Vida* (The Gardens of My Life), memoirs, 1981; **Samuel Malamud** (ca. 1908–ca. 2000) *Do Arquivo e da Memória* (From the Archives and From Memory), 1983; *Escalas no Tempo* (Stopovers in Time), memoirs, 1986; *Recordando a Praça Onze* (Recalling Praça Onze), memoirs, 1988; *A Segunda Guerra Mundial na Visão de um Judeu Brasileiro* (The Second World War in the Eyes of a Brazilian Jew), undated; *Contribuição à Memória da Comunidade Judaica Brasileira* (Contribution to the Memory of the Brazilian Jewish Community), a documentary, 1992; **Alberto Moghrabi** (born 1955), *Pequenos Contos de Enredo Indeterminado* (Small Tales of Undetermined Plot), chronicles, 2001; *Umas Histórias – crônicas* (Some Tales – Chronicles), 2003; *Tempo Passa Tempo* (Time Pastime), chronicles and novellas, 2007; **Eva Nicolaiewsky**, *Israelitas no Rio Grande do Sul* (Israelites in Rio Grande do Sul), memoirs, 1975; **Moysés Paciornik** (ca. 1914–ca. 2008), *Brincando de Contar Histórias* (Playing Storytelling), chronicles, 1973; **Anita D. Panek** (born 1930), *Carta aos Meus Netos: uma Autobiografia* (Letter to My Grandchildren: An Autobiography), 2000; **Olga Papadopol** (born 1925), *Rumo à Vida* (Towards Life), 1979; **I. Podhoretz**, *Memórias do Inferno* (Memories of Hell); **Sonia Rosenblatt**, *Lembranças Enevoadas* (Clouded Memories), memoirs, 1984; **Sultana Levy Rosenblatt**, *Uma grande mancha de sol* (A Great Spot of Sun), 1951; **Jacques Schweidson** (1904–1995), *Judeus de Bombacha e Chimarrão* (Jews of Bombacha and Chimarrão), memoirs, 1985; *Saga Judaica na Ilha do Desterro* (Jewish Saga on the Island of Desterro), memoirs, 1989; **Guilherme Soibelman**, *Memórias de Philipson* (Memories of Philipson), 1984; **Alexandr Storch** (1908–?), *Os Lobos* (The Wolves), autobiography, 1983; **Américo Vértes** (1910–?), *Entre Duas Evas* (Between Two Eves), 1969; **Samuel Wainer** (1910–1980), *Minha Razão de Viver, Memórias de um Repórter* (My Reason for Living, Memoirs of a Reporter), 1988; **Amália Zeitel** (1933–1992), *O Sétimo Dia* (The Seventh Day), theater, 1982; *Morangos com Chantilly e Outros Contos* (Strawberries with Cream and Other short Stories), 1992.

5 Trends and Perspectives

In the twentyfirst century, Brazilian Jews still perceive themselves as a minority, culturally different from the hegemonic population. But they no longer feel foreign or discriminated against in any way. They are no longer "undesirable",[6] "suspects", "agents of international Communism", or "controllers of world finance". Their integration into Brazilian society is complete. They fully participate in the country's social, economic, cultural and political life. Under these conditions, Jewish writers are no longer immigrant writers. Issues related to geographical and cultural relocation, to the past in Europe's *shtetlach* and ghettos, or to the early days in the host country cease to be dominant in literary production, surviving, in some cases, as nostalgia for living with grandparents or as memories of an outdated era.

In a process that is currently intensifying, active Jewish writers cease to be dedicated to specifically Jewish themes and instead reflect, like non-Jews, on universal issues, social relations, and the human condition. Perhaps it is no longer possible to speak of a "Jewish-Brazilian literature", as integration promotes a progressive dissipation of particularism.

---

[6] We use here the concept of "desirable" and "undesirable" immigrants as formulated by Jeffrey Lesser (2001, 20). In the author's analysis, the Jews were undesirable immigrants because they would not contribute to the "whitening" of the population, nor would they provide labor for farming.

Bibliography

Works Cited

Amâncio, Moacir. *Do objeto útil*. São Paulo: Editora Iluminuras, 1992.
Amâncio, Moacir. *Colores siguientes*. São Paulo: Musa Editora, 1999.
Confederação Israelita do Brasil. https://www.conib.org.br (10 March 2020).
Coutinho, Edilberto. "Uma mulher chamada Clarice Lispector." *Criaturas de Papel*. Rio de Janeiro/Brasília: Civilização Brasileira/INL, 1980. 165–170.
Deleuze, Gilles, and Félix Guattari. *Kafka: Toward a Minor Literature*. Tr. Dana Polan. Minneapolis, MN: University of Minnesota Press, 1986 [1975].
Falbel, Nachman. *Judeus no Brasil*: estudos e notas. São Paulo: Humanitas/Edusp, 2008.
Grün, Roberto. "Construindo um lugar ao sol: os judeus no Brasil." *Fazer a América*. Ed. Boris Fausto. São Paulo: Editora da Universidade de São Paulo, 1999. 353–381.
Guinsburg, Jacó. "Os Imigrantes de Samuel Rawet." *Paratodos* II. 30 (August 1957).
Igel, Regina. *Imigrantes judeus / Escritores brasileiros: o componente judaico na literatura brasileira*. São Paulo: Perspectiva: Associação Universitária de Cultura Judaica: Banco Safra, 1997.
Lesser, Jeffrey. *O Brasil e a questão judaica*: imigração, diplomacia e preconceito. Tr. Marisa Senematsu. Rio de Janeiro: Imago, 1995.
Lesser, Jeffrey. *A negociação da identidade nacional*: imigrantes, minorias e a luta pela etnicidade no Brasil. Tr. Patricia de Queiroz Carvalho Zimbres. São Paulo: Editora UNESP, 2001.
Moscovich, Cíntia. *Por que sou gorda, mamãe?* Rio de Janeiro/São Paulo: Record, 2006.
Nascimento, Lyslei. *Dicionário de Escritores Judeus Brasileiros*. http://www.letras.ufmg.br/padrao_cms/?web=nej&lang=1&page=839&menu=515&tipo=1. (10 March 2022).
Pessanha, José Américo. "Clarice Lispector: o itinerário da paixão." *Remate de Males* 9 (1989): 181–198.
Rawet, Samuel. *Contos do imigrante*. Rio de Janeiro: Editora J. Olympio 1956.
Rawet, Samuel, and Ronaldo Conde. "A Necessidade de Escrever Contos". Interview. *Correio da Manhã/Anexo*. Rio de Janeiro, 07 December 1971.
Wirth-Nesher, Hana. *What is Jewish literature?* Philadelphia, PA/Jerusalem: The Jewish Publication Society, 5754/1994.

Further Reading

Vieira, Nelson H. "Símbolos Judíos de Resistencia en la Literatura Brasileña." *Judaica latinoamericana: estudios histórico-sociales*. Ed. AMILAT. Jerusalem: Editorial Universitaria Magnes, Universidade Hebraica, 1988.
Vieira, Nelson H. *Jewish voices in Brazilian literature: a prophetic discourse of alterity*. Florida: University Press of Florida, 1995.
Vieira, Nelson H. "Hibridismo e alteridade: estratégias para repensar a história literária." *Cadernos do Centro de Pesquisas Literárias* 4.2 (1998): 7–15.
Vieira, Nelson H. "Displacement and Disregard: Brazilian-Jewish Writing and the Search for Narrative Identity." *Literary Cultures of Latin America: A Comparative History*. Eds. Mario J. Valdés and Djelal Kadir. Oxford: Oxford University Press, 2004.

Vieira, Nelson H. *Contemporary Jewish writing in Brazil: an anthology*. Lincoln/London: University of Nebraska Press, 2009.
Waldman, Berta. *Entre passos e rastros: presença judaica na literatura brasileira contemporânea*. São Paulo: Perspectiva/Fapesp/Associação Universitária de Cultura Judaica, 2003.

Verena Dolle
16 Jewish-Mexican Literatures: Ashkenazic Tradition and Culture

Abstract: The focus of this article is on the specificity of Ashkenazic-Mexican literature written in Spanish. It shows how it emerged in the 1970s, authored by second and third generation immigrants and how it focused on challenging the up to then homogenizing national discourse and featured commentaries on Jewish and global topics, claiming ethnic but also gender plurality. The article traces different phases of Ashkenazi-Mexican literature: in the 1970s and 1980s that part of Mexican society obtained literary visibility for the first time, often in fictional texts narrated in third-person singular. In the 1990s, this was followed by autobiographical explorations – mostly by female authors – of hybridity and hyphenated identity in the 1990s with particular emphasis on female empowerment and the challenging of patriarchal hierarchies. The article also deals with topics of migration to Mexico and (post-traumatic) memory as entangled history and the dynamics between remembering and oblivion. To put it in a nutshell: Ashkenazi-Mexican authors, such as Margo Glantz, Sabina Berman, and Gloria Gervitz, do no longer figure as representatives of a peripheral, marginal literature, but are in the center of a Mexican literature now conceived as one full of linguistic and literary cosmopolitism beyond national boundaries.

Key Terms: Ashkenazic-Mexican literature, immigration, cosmopolitanism, entangled history, crisis of *mexicanidad*, hybridity

1 Introduction: Ashkenazic Tradition and Culture in Mexico and Hegemonic Discourse

> True literary history now, in the twenty-first century, must aspire to a
> global perspective in spatial as well as temporal terms.   (Pettersson et al. 2006, IX)

In a concise article on Mexican narrative fiction of the twentieth century that forms part of a volume on Hispanic American literary history, J.C. González Boixò and J. Ordiz Vázquez very briefly touch on Jewish authors in a subchapter on a genre of female Mexican narrative from the last decades of the twentieth century (cf. Boixò and Ordiz Vázquez 2019, 210–213). According to the authors, the characteristic trait of this female narrative is the (mostly autobiographical) search for identity and orientation, which involves searching for cultural roots in a society deeply shaped by patriarchal and Christian structures. As works that represent explorations of Jewish culture in particular, González Boixò and Ordiz Vázquez refer to Esther Seligson's

La morada en el tiempo (1981) as well as Angelina Múñiz-Huberman's *Tierra adentro* (1977) and *De magia y prodigios* (1987) (cf. 2019, 211). Beyond mention of this partially autobiographical genre written mostly by women, no allusion to Jewish literature as a form of ethnic literature or to any other related genres is made, nor is any attention paid to the heterogeneous Jewish traditions and communities of Mexico.

Nevertheless, when dealing with Jewish Mexican – or Mexican Jewish – literature, one has to take into account the plurality and diversity covered under the term "Jewish", i.e., the manifold Jewish traditions present in Mexican culture to this day, as a means to counteract any homogenizing or "othering" attitudes (cf. Cánovas 2011, 62; Lockhart 2013b, 11). This multiplicity encompasses communities of Sephardic, North African, Ashkenazic, and Syrian origins – the latter being divided into a Halabi and a Shami community from Aleppo and Damascus respectively – in addition to the different languages originally spoken, including those in extinction (Ladino, Yiddish). In modern-day Mexico, there is a "caleidoscopio de culturas judías" (cf. Sefamí and Lehmann 2018, 9; Cánovas 2011, 62). These are shaped deeply not only by their countries of origin and even by the segregational tendencies of Jewish communities in Mexico – "Ashkenazíes, sefaradíes y judíos originarios de países árabes conformaron subcomunidades" (Kraus 2011, 64) – but also by ideological topics, as Zadoff (2001) has indicated with reference to the 1940s and 1950s.

This diversity has been pointed out as early as 1980, when the first anthology of Latin American Jewish literature in English was published in the US, giving visibility to this specific literary production from the southern part of the continent. In her introduction to the anthology, Roberta Kalechofsky highlights not only the differences between Jewish and non-Jewish groups, but also those between Jewish communities themselves, drawing on their heterogeneity (cf. Kalechofsky 1980, viii) and thus affirming the need:

> [...] to become acquainted. Judaism, religion, people, and history, is deep and broad and global, fragmented and unified, separated and whole. This century, this post-holocaust generation century, finds us, not weakened but, to our surprise, in the process of self-discovery, of where we have been and where we are everywhere: [...] and the process of self-discovery is the process of recovery, and of establishing a humane and humanly possible definition of 'universal' and 'particular'. (Kalechofsky 1980, vi–vii)

As a means to underscore the anthology's approach to Jewish Latin American literature and reveal the breadth of its spectrum, Kalechofsky provides a quote from Mexican Ashkenazic writer Esther Seligson, who sharply criticizes an overly homogenized and narrow definition of what can be classified as "Jewish":

> To speak of Judaism in such global terms as the "Jewish tradition", as belonging solely to the Ashkenazic or the Sephardic, is absurd. That which is Jewish does not rest on blood or race, nor does it rest on uniformity of origin, nor even less on rigidity of thought and action.
>
> (Seligson in: Kalechofsky 1980, 11)[1]

At the same time, she challenges any hegemonic claims within the diverse Jewish communities to being representative for all or hierarchically above the others: "Neither Ashkenazim nor Sephardim have the exclusive privilege of having preserved Judaism". Taking into account strategic reflections and calling for a peaceful co-existence, she asks: "Ought we then to continue to foment in our children an antagonism which is not only anachronistic but –considering the narrow dwelling-ground – effectively disperses our communal identity for others as well as for Jews themselves, with respect to our continuing desire to be a source of living waters?" (Seligson in: Kalechofsky 1980, 11).

With a focus on heterogeneity and the position of the Jewish groups with respect to the majority community, Florinda Goldberg and Saúl Sosnowski stress the importance of a "middle ground" (Goldberg 2011, 747) regarding the fundamental characteristics of Jewish existence, an existence in-between, i.e. between different communities and belongings.

Sosnowski places the focus "on the hyphen" (Sosnowski 1987, 23) as an element indicating both a connection to and a distinction from the majority, a usually non-Jewish community, and one's own respective diasporic existence: "marca de frontera y tercer participante del continuo juego dinámico entre los elementos que separa y une" (Goldberg 2011, 745–746).

For Latin America and Jewish Latin American writers in particular, I adhere to Lockhart's tentative definition, as quoted by Goldberg (2011, 745, n. 12):

> By writers whose works reflect a Jewish identity I mean to say that their writing *in large part* deals with the *so-called* Jewish concerns, which *include but are not limited* to the problematics of identity, assimilation, traditions, immigration, the Sephardic heritage of Latin America, Yiddishkeit, Judaism/Jewishness, self-hatred, anti-Semitism, the Holocaust, Zionism and Israel.

To this, I'd like to add Kalechofsky's characterization according to which the "writings in [the] anthology [. . .] represent the spectrum of Jewish thought and sensibility in Latin America, a blend of Judaism, Eastern Europe, a particular country, and the influences of Spanish and Indian cultures" (Kalechofsky 1980, viii–ix). Focusing on Mexico in particular, Sosnowski highlights that "Jewish Mexican literature as a whole [is] marked by the following topics: the country, the belonging to it, questions of identity" (Sosnowski 2004, 266–267).

While Jewish literature in vernacular languages became visible in Argentina and Brazil relatively early in the twentieth century (cf. Chapter 18 of this volume), this was

---

[1] The text is taken from her 1978 editorial in the Mexican Jewish review *Aquí estamos* and translated by Roberta Kalechofsky. (Punctuation has been corrected without further comment.)

not the case in Mexico. This was due to a highly particular official hegemonic discourse on national collective identity, which influenced literary expression until the 1960s, as many scholars have pointed out (cf., to name just a few, Igler 2008, 99–100; Cánovas 2011, 62; Lockhart 2013b, 11; Caufield 2015, 1). This identity, formed after the Party of the Institutionalized Revolution (PRI) began to constitute a strict one-party system in the 1920s, was 'the homogenizing ideal of *mestizaje*' (miscegenation or mixture between Spanish and Indian ethnicities), a concept that essentially excludes all other groups.[2] According to scholars, this concept of identity thwarted expressions of difference, diversity and plurality over a considerable span of time in the twentieth century. Heterogeneity in literature and civil life first started to appear in the 1960s, due to an obvious crisis regarding this discourse and the PRI itself. Simultaneously, broader Western movements of liberalism, anti-authoritarianism, pacifism, and feminism questioned traditional beliefs, and the 1968 movement in particular had strong repercussions in Mexico. Students protested against the State and stood up for their cause (cf. Lomnitz-Adler 2018). In 1968, expressions of heterogeneity and protests which attempted to establish a (more) pluralistic society came to a violent end: First, the independent UNAM Campus was occupied by soldiers on 19 September and, several weeks later, the unarmed students' protests on the Plaza de Tlatelolco in Mexico City ended with ca. 300 protestors shot dead by the Mexican army on 2 October (with an until now unclear, only estimated number of victims, long silenced by official discourse and researched by engaged intellectuals such as Poniatowska, *La noche de Tlatelolco*, 1971). The massacre was a traumatic experience for many citizens, resulting in many breaking ties with the associated national identity and the idea of "mexicanidad" (cf. Igler 2008, 99–100; Caufield 2015, 4). Ever-growing groups within civil society began questioning the PRI's hegemonic discourse and its claim to represent all Mexicans. In turn, they started expressing their differences and plurality with respect to ethnicity, political opinion, religion, and gender.[3] Below, Esther Seligson captures this spirit in a retrospective commentary on her journalistic works of the 1970s:

> Entonces, la sensación de libertad intelectual y física no era ficticia, y la literatura, el arte y las ideas políticas se intercambiaban con *un sentido cosmopolita y universalista que excluía todo morbo por la 'identidad nacional'*. La pintura joven, el teatro universitario y la creación literaria rompieron estructuras anquilosadas [...], y no sólo como un eco de lo que ocurría en el mundo, sino como una reacción natural de continuidad debida a la apertura de los espíritus hacia su entorno. Tampoco es coincidencia que esa ruptura en el terreno cultural haya incidido en la conciencia política para reclamar igual derecho a la libre creatividad y al cambio (reclamo abruptamente silenciado a partir del 2 de octubre de 1968).
> (Seligson 1988, 11–12, italics mine, V.D.)

---

[2] Judith Laikin Elkin put it in a nutshell: "The centrality of race to the concept of Mexicanidad and the impossibility of Jews being included in la raza raise impassable barriers for Mexican Jews" (Laikin Elkin 1987, 314; quoted in Cypess 2010, 1).
[3] Caufield (cf. 2015, 7) takes up Bokser Liwerant's notion of "plural identities" (Bokser 2008).

The 1970s were deeply influenced by the Tlatelolco massacre. For Seligson, these years represent a period of awakening, liberty, change, and an opening towards the world and universal issues. National issues, ossified structures and national identity were no longer central fixtures, whereas the 1980s were characterized by a feeling of "una falta de osadía intelectual y creativa, de derrumbe y carencia de alternativas políticas" (Seligson 1988, 12). Bokser Liwerant refers to the entangled effects of globalization and multiculturalism as a legitimation of diversity, whereby space was created for the Other who was different in terms of ethnicity, politics, religion or gender. This included public expressions of the "particular judío" (Bokser 2011, 295).

In her retrospective gaze, Seligson highlights the extent to which the dominant Mexican literary discourse and public perception were shaped by works on the topics of *mestizo* national identity. These were written above all by white (criollo) men, with female writers a scarcity. Some highly influential essays are *El perfil del hombre* by Alfonso Reyes, 1936, and *El laberinto de la soledad* by Octavio Paz, 1950 (cf. Schmidt-Welle 2004, 776). Up until the 1970s, other major topics in Mexican literature were the achievements (and failures) of the Revolution. Such topics gave rise to a highly prolific novelistic subgenre (the "novela de la Revolución" with different phases from Mariano Azuela, *Los de abajo*, 1919, to Juan Rulfo, *Pedro Páramo*, 1955, and Carlos Fuentes, *La muerte de Artemio Cruz*, 1962) and to works that dealt with economic growth in the 1940s and 1950s, i.e., the "milagro mexicano", and the building of modern Mexican society (cf. Carlos Fuentes, *La región más transparente*, 1958). This all took place in the realm of *mestizaje*, resulting in other ethnic groups of immigrants not being considered, as Ashkenazic writer Sefchovich still points out in 2008. In the 1960s, Carlos Fuentes and Octavio Paz received global (i.e., Western) attention for their contributions to Mexican literature.

Carlos Fuentes – together with Peruvian writer Mario Vargas Llosa, Columbian writer Gabriel García Márquez, Cuban writer Alejo Carpentier, and Argentine-French writer Julio Cortázar – became part of the new "boom" generation in Latin American literature, a term standing for the tremendous commercial success, lasting until the 1980s, that put Latin America on the literary map of Europeans and North Americans. At the expense of plurality and heterogeneity, Latin American literature was labelled and exoticized as a literature representing above all "magic realism" rather than a realistic worldview. It was not until the beginnings of the post-boom phase in the 1980s that this attitude was called into question for being too narrow. The Western expectation that Latin American authors should write only on topics of magical realism was increasingly challenged from within, as we see in the 1996 Mexican literary manifesto *Crack*. At the same time, many more female writers were coming to the fore, some of whom were or have been extremely successfully (e.g., Chile's Isabel Allende, the bestselling Latin American female author ever, and the Mexican writers Carmen Boullosa and Laura Esquivel), vehemently challenging the passive role ascribed to women over a long period of time in *machista* patriarchal Latin American societies. There were many Jewish writers among them as well.[4]

Before moving on to Ashkenazic literary production in Mexico, we need a short definition of what is understood by both Jewish and Ashkenazic literature. According to Frakes's article in the *Encyclopaedia Judaica*, Jewish literature can be defined as:

> (1) works written by Jews on Jewish themes in any language; (2) works of a literary character written by Jews in Hebrew or Yiddish or other recognized languages, whatever the theme; (3) literary works written by writers who were essentially Jewish writers, whatever the theme and whatever the language. (Frakes 2007, 84)

For reasons of limitation, I will only focus on works corresponding to the first definition given by Frakes, i.e., "works written by Jews on Jewish themes in any language", and will furthermore specify the language as Spanish (with one exception) and Mexico as the territory where the writers of Ashkenazic origin are located or have ties. I will focus solely on works that highlight the presence of Ashkenazic tradition and culture in Mexico. I will not cover any works written in Yiddish by first generation immigrants (cf. Rubinstein 1997; Waldman 2001; Astro 2003; Cimet 2013 on Kahan, J. Glantz, and I. Berliner; cf. 526 in this Handbook), but rather give attention to works written in Spanish by second and third generation immigrants, which appeal to a broader public. It must be noted that writing in Spanish is an obvious sign of (linguistic) adaptation to Mexico and signals a generational decline in the use of Yiddish. Lockhart highlights the challenging role of Jewish-Mexican literature as a:

> writing that speaks to the specificity of the diverse Jewish cultural, ethnic, and religious experiences not as separate from but as part of Mexican reality and all the sociocultural components that impinge on and contribute to identity formation. As a minority literature – both produced by a minority population and comprising but a small portion of Mexican literary production – it nevertheless has the capacity to challenge hegemonic discourse, to incorporate difference, promote cultural pluralism and broaden the notion of *mexicanidad*. (Lockhart 2013b, 11)

In other words, any literary expression by Jewish-Mexican authors can – and must – be treated in relation to the official discourse, to formative works of Mexican majority literature and to the concept of national collective identity (intensely discussed again on the occasion of the 500th anniversary of the discovery of America). The "notion of *mexicanidad*" (Lockhart) is then called into question, broadened, and diversified. Nevertheless, heterogeneous Jewish literatures in Mexico should not be viewed as infected by that "morbo por la identidad nacional" (Seligson), but as the product of communities with rich traditions and entangled experiences not only with other Jewish literature in Mexico and Latin America, but with national majority literature and global literature(s) as well.

---

4 On Latin American post-boom literature and the role of female writers, cf. Shaw 1999.

As mentioned above, Saúl Sosnowski characterizes Jewish life and identity in Latin America and Mexico as "life on the hyphen" (Sosnowski 1987, 23), the hyphen being the third element in the continuous and dynamic interplay between the other two (the national present and the diasporic absent element), separating and uniting, the marker and semantic qualifier of a condition or situation in between. Questions regarding labelling and the discussion as to which adjectives and which nouns in which order are "privileged in terms of defining identity" (Lockhart 2013b, 10) have been intense and ongoing. In this regard, Lockhart opts for the term "Jewish-Mexican", "without placing primacy on either side of the hyphen [. . .] not to be taken as a conscious effort to value Jewishness over *mexicanidad*" (Lockhart 2013b, 10). In this article, I will go a step further and use the adjectives in a more performative way, changing their order from time to time to emphasize the aforementioned dynamics and to give readers the experience of there being no fixed attribution or labelling.

2 Ashkenazic Migration to Mexico: Facts and Figures

Ashkenazic migration to Mexico forms part of a larger Jewish migration to Latin America that occurred from the nineteenth until the mid-twentieth century and involved quite heterogeneous Jewish communities with different languages and traditions: Sephardic (Ladino-speaking), Arab-speaking (from Lebanon and Syria), and Ashkenazic, Yiddish-speaking Jews from Eastern Europe, particularly Russia, Ukraine, Lithuania and Poland: The latter group started migrating between the end of the nineteenth and the beginning of the twentieth century amid an increasing number of pogroms in their countries of origin as well as immigration policies that were (relatively) propitious for white Europeans, especially in Argentina (cf. Dolle 2020b, 306 and Cánovas 2011, 26). Their migration was supported by the Jewish Colonisation Association (JCA), founded by the German Jew Baron Maurice de Hirsch in 1891. The JCA had considered Mexico to be the country of destination for their settlement project, but due to "the negative reports that were given by the experts that [. . .] the potential settlers would not be able to compete with the cheap local labor work" (Hamui 2007, 140; cf. Sefamí and Lehmann 2018, 8), the settlement project was realized in Argentina instead (as well as in Brazil and Canada). In the 1890s, large-scale migration to Argentina began (cf. Avni et al. 2007, 427–429; Dolle 2020b, 306). For a while, there was even a discussion as to whether this settlement was the new Zion, as Theodor Herzl proposed in *The Jewish State* in 1896 (cf. Feierstein 2010, 7–8).

According to Avni et al. (cf. 2007, 430), the number of Jewish citizens in Argentina in 1919 was 125,000 (compared to 6,000 in 1895). As for Mexico, the situation is different: In the 1920s, Ashkenazic migration to Mexico (and to all of Latin America) increased because of ever tighter migration controls and restrictions in the US in the context of the Quota Act of 1921 and the Johnson Act of 1924. Migrants therefore had to turn to Latin America as their second option (cf. Cánovas 2011, 31–45, esp.

34–38; Waldman 2001, 431). In this decade alone, the Jewish population in Mexico increased to ca. 21,000 due to the immigration of about 9,000 Ashkenazic and 6,000 Sephardic Jews, with communities in Mexico City and then later – starting in the 1930s – Guadalajara and Monterrey as well (cf. Hamui 2007, 140; 143).[5]

During the Nazi regime, which was responsible for the death of more than six million Jews, half a million Jews were able to migrate, of which 92,351 went to Latin America and probably less than 2,000 to Mexico (1,850 according to Hamui 2007, 141; 1,631 according to Cánovas 2011, 28–29). Mexico received about 15,000 refugees from the Second Spanish Republic but was more restrictive and reluctant to accept Jewish refugees during the Cárdenas administration of 1934–1940 (cf. Senkman 1994, 67–68; Cánovas 2011, 37). Curiously, this restrictive attitude was not perceived as such by the Jews themselves, at least not by those who were admitted to the country and who held on to the myth of Mexico as a country of open doors.[6]

Immigration to Mexico was not followed, though, by direct re-emigration to the State of Israel after its founding in 1948, as the numbers show: In the first five years after 1948, with open door policies established by the Law of Return of 1950 (cf. Ran 2009, 25), only ca. 40 per year of the total 65,000 immigrants to Israel came from Mexico (cf. Della Pergola 2011, 319).[7]

Throughout the twentieth century and continuing to present times, Mexico, with a percentage of 0.4 % of the total population, has the third largest Jewish community in Latin America, following Argentina (4.7%) and Brazil (0.5%) (cf. DellaPergola 2011, 314–317). Sefamí and Lehmann (2018, 9, n. 2) refer to the Jewish Virtual Library (retrieved in 2018), which estimates that 40,000 Jews live in Mexico in 2017, which would constitute even less than 0.4%, i.e., only 0.00325% of the total population of nearly 130 million. In contrast, the Mexican Census of 2010 estimated that around 67,000 citizens were of Jewish faith.[8] Until quite recently, Ashkenazic communities

---

[5] For further research on this topic, cf. Martínez Assad 2008.

[6] Cf. Gleizer 2011, especially 145–146; Bokser 2011, 287–291, who points out the dynamics of the position vis-à-vis Jewish migrants from the Cárdenas regime onwards, and Pérez-Rosales 1996. Cf. also the documentary film *Visa al paraíso* (2010) and the corresponding book *De viva voz. Vida y obra de Gilberto Bosques* (2015), made by the Jewish-Mexican filmmaker Lilian Liberman on Bosques, Mexican consul in France between 1939 and 1942, who gave visas to more than 40,000 refugees from the Nazi regime and organized their travel to Mexico. This film on a very remarkable person and his humanitarian policy makes clear the extent to which the perspective is dependent on those who survived and still can speak.

[7] Hamui states that since 1948, "nearly 4,000 Mexican Jews have made *aliyah*" (Hamui 2007, 145; cf. DellaPergola 2011, 319–325).

[8] Cf. INEG – Panorama de las religiones en México, pdf http://internet.contenidos.inegi.org.mx/contenidos/productos/prod_serv/contenidos/espanol/bvinegi/productos/censos/poblacion/2010/panora_religion/religiones_2010.pdf (10 January 2020).

formed the majority of Jewish communities in Mexico; however, this seems to have changed as of the year 2000, as Hamui points out (cf. Hamui 2007, 144).[9]

By 1912, the first public religious association was created, followed by reviews and newspapers in Yiddish (cf. Sefamí and Lehmann 2018, 10). The first work of Ashkenazic literature in Mexico is a work of poetry, *Drai vegn*, written in Yiddish by the migrants Jacobo Glantz (the father of Margo Glantz), Itzjok Berliner and Moishe Glikovsky, and published in 1927.[10] In 1931, the "Unión de literatos y artistas judíos" was founded. In 1936, Berliner published his poems *Shtot fun Palatzn* (cf. Waldman 2001, 432). Gilda Waldman considers literary production in Yiddish among the first generation of Ashkenazic immigrants to be "absolutamente marginal" (Waldman 2001, 440), whereas the second generation of writers, born on Mexican territory and writing in Spanish, took on a much more visible role (cf. Waldman 2001, 447). Nevertheless, this literature still is a minority literature, as Lockhart (cf. 2013b, 11) emphasizes, while some of its representatives are seen as representatives of Mexican literature in general.

3 The Current State of Research

While several reliable and extensive works on the formation of Ashkenazic communities and cultural activities in Mexico were completed during the twentieth century (cf. Cimet Singer 1992; 1997; Gojman de Backal 1993; 2011; Gurvich Peretzman 2009), apart from Gilda Waldman's crucial article (2001) on the literature of Jewish immigration to Mexico, there are no historical or survey articles explicitly dedicated only to Ashkenazic Mexican literature.[11] Waldman (cf. 2001, 429) and Sefchovich (cf. 2008, 40)

---

9 As far as equality among different religious, non-Catholic groups is concerned, 1992 is a milestone for the acceptance of diversity, as Hamui points out: "The reforms of 1992 in the Constitution, related to the legal recognition of the religious institutions and their public activities, attempted to normalize the common practices. This kind of legality recognizes the legitimacy of group consolidation through the religious identification. Religious associations became another channel of collective expression. The religious and ideological diversity in the society increased in correlation with a greater democratization of political and cultural life. Gradually the participation of the Jews in these areas is becoming wider and less questioned every day, and the presence of Jews in senior official posts is becoming more frequent." (2007, 144)
10 Cf. Sefamí and Lehmann 2018, 10; Cánovas 2011, 61–62; Lockhart 2013b, 15–16. A selection of passages from this foundational text was translated into Spanish by Becky Rubinstein and published with the title *Tres caminos* in 1997.
11 For Sephardic female literature (and readers), as a literature beyond national boundaries: cf. Díaz-Mas and Ortega 2016. As far as Latin American Jewish studies in general are concerned, I agree with Ranaan Rein, who in 2004 stated that "studies have impressively advanced and the body of works devoted to the subject has grown enormously" (Rein 2004, 1). In this vein, I'd like to mention briefly the works of DiAntonio 1993; Agosín 1999c; 2002; 2005; Bokser de Liwerant and Gojman de

state that Mexican literature from the twentieth century spent relatively little time dealing with the lives of immigrants. This literature instead deals with Mexico (from colonial times onward) as a country marred (only) by the violent encounters between indigenous groups and Spanish Catholic (white) intruders, resulting in *mestizaje* – a topic intensely discussed during the revision of Spanish master narratives on the discovery of America and the conquest of Mexico that took place on the occasion of the five-hundredth anniversary of Columbus's "discovery" of the "Indies" in 1992 – without (the need for) mention of the cultural, ethnic, or religious integration of other groups (cf. Waldman 2001, 429).

This has to do with the fact, as various scholars and writers agree, that Mexico has never been, nor has it considered itself to be, a traditional country of immigration (cf. Martínez Assad 2008). On the contrary, it has displayed a quite skeptical attitude towards strangers, as the first encounter between indigenous people and white (Spanish) foreigners resulted in the violent conquest of Mexican territory and the rape of indigenous women by the Spaniards in the sixteenth century, a traumatic heritage that has become a supposed collective characteristic of the mestizo people, according to Octavio Paz in his essay *El laberinto de la soledad* (1950). Ashkenazic Mexican writer Sara Sefchovich (2008) also points to this attitude as being one of the reasons for the long-standing and continuous non-integration of immigrants in Mexico.[12]

Sefchovich views the Jewish position in the Mexican majority community quite negatively. In her article "Historia de una desconfianza", she supports the provocative hypothesis that immigrants have not been welcome in Mexico (unlike Argentina or the USA, cf. Sefchovich 2008, 40) from colonial times to the present and that consequently, there is a lack of cultural integration and no *mestizaje* as a symbiosis of cultures in that respect. At the same time, she holds that often even the immigrants have not been willing to integrate themselves (cf. Sefchovich 2008, 36–37), resulting in a multi-cultural parallel existence: "El desencuentro de miradas el agua y aceite de los extranjeros y los mexicanos terminó llevando a una situación que hasta hoy existe: aquéllos han hecho sus comunidades y con poquísimas excepciones, no se han mezclado con éstos." (Sefchovich 2008, 49) With respect to present times, she believes that Mexico, with its multiple cultures, is not a product of the integration of foreigners but rather the result of global pressure, a "resultado de corrientes culturales

---

Backal 1999; Huberman and Meter 2006. In anthologies of Latin American Jewish literature in English or German translation, a broader public interested in global literature is addressed, e.g. Burghardt and Schmidt 1998; Agosín 1999a; Sadow 1999.

12 As far as exiled Republicans from Spain are concerned, the situation is different. Unlike Yiddish-speaking Jews, they did not have a linguistic problem and their cultural background was much more similar to the Mexican one due to a common (colonial) past and basically the same religion, i.e., Catholicism. Therefore, they did not have to face the Mexican prejudices against Jews (cf. Senkman 1994, 67).

universales muy poderosas" (Sefchovich 2008, 50). Furthermore, she addresses the crucial topic of the official Mexican ideology of *mestizaje*, which in theory means ethnic miscegenation but in practice is characterized by a deeply rooted racism with a hierarchy in which people with white skin and blonde hair are ranked the highest (cf. Sefchovich 2008, 47) – this being one of the reasons for interest in "blanqueamento" (skin whitening).

Nevertheless, as Waldman states, recent literature on the topic of Jewish immigration is "relativamente vasta" (2001, 429) in poetry and prose, referring to Gloria Gervitz's poem *Yizkor* (1987), Margo Glantz's *Genealogías* (1981), Sabina Berman's *La bobe* (1992), and José Woldenberg's novel *Las ausencias presentes* (1992). (Survey) articles, books, book chapters, or special issues of reviews are either dedicated to Jewish Mexican literature in general (cf. Cánovas 2011, Ch. I.2; Lockhart 2013a; Sefamí and Lehmann 2018) or explicitly to Jewish Mexican female writers. The focus on the latter is due to their outstanding, if not overwhelming, presence in the last five decades. There are monographs such as Cortina (2000) dedicated to (Ashkenazic) writers Glantz, Levi Calderón, Krauze and Sefchovich;[13] Loyola's PhD thesis on "Género, etnicidad y Nación en la narrative [sic] judío-mexicana de Angelina Muñiz-Huberman, Rosa Nissán y Sara Levi Calderón" (2004); and Guadalupe Pérez-Anzaldo's monograph (2009) on *Memorias pluridimensionales en la narrative* [sic] *mexicana*, namely Berman, Nissán, Glantz and Levi Calderón. Nonetheless, writers such as Berman and Glantz are no longer labelled as "Jewish" or marginal, but have gained a status in the "center" of Mexican literature, as e.g. Lockhart points out (cf. 2013b, 12). Gloria Gervitz figures, without any further labelling attributes, in a volume on contemporary Mexican poetry (cf. Vergara 2015). Balutet's monograph *Poética de la hibridez en la literatura mexicana posmodernista* (2016) is on the literary representation of marginalized groups – women, homosexuals, Jews – in Mexican literature and is based on three works published between 1978 and 1982: Laura Esquivel's *Como agua para chocolate*, Luis Zapata's *El vampiro de la colonia Roma*, and Margo Glantz's *Las genealogías*. With his theoretical approach based on the key concept of hybridity, Balutet goes beyond ethnic ascriptions and compartmentalization, instead focusing on more current literary questions and concepts.

---

[13] In her book *Invenciones multitudinarias: escritoras judíomexicanas contemporáneas* (2000), Cortina focusses on Glantz, *Las genealogías* (1981); Ethel Krauze, *Entre la cruz y la estrella* (1990); Sara Levi Calderón, *Dos mujeres* (1990); and Sara Sefchovich, *Demasiado amor* (1990), which was awarded the prestigious Premio Agustín Yáñez (cf. Cortina 2000, 124). Cortina points out that these texts on cultural identity differ from the traditional (and negative) way in which Jewish people were represented in Mexican literature (cf. Cortina 2000, 23; Palomares Salas 2017), mentioning Justo Sierra's *La hija del judío*, V. Riva Palacio's *El libro rojo*, Josefina Estrada's *Malagato* and J. E. Pacheco's *Morirás lejos* (whereas Van Delden [2014, 569–570], highlights this latter novel as a reflection on the atrocities and evil persistent throughout all times).

In addition to monographs, there are also quite a few articles on female Jewish Mexican writers, including Magdalena Maíz-Peña's "Mapping the Jewish female voice in contemporary Mexican narrative" (1999); Caufield (2015) on the Ashkenazim Berman, Glantz and Seligson and the Sephardi Muñiz-Huberman; and Dabbah, who provides a list of 32 female and 15 male Jewish Mexican writers of the twentieth and twenty first centuries (cf. Dabbah 2016, 149) and deals with 11 female writers, including the Ashkenazi Becky Rubinstein and the Sephardim Anhalt, Nissán, Moscona and Montiel in addition to the aforementioned writers.

Critical Approaches to Jewish-Mexican Literature, edited by Darrell Lockhart (2013a), contains a thorough treatment of the topic (Lockhart 2013b), covering Sephardic, Ashkenazic, and Shami literature. With exhaustive articles dedicated to the works of Margo Glantz (cf. Sosnowski 2013), Muñiz-Huberman (2 articles), Seligson (cf. Senkman 2013), Berman (3 articles; cf. Baer Barr 2013), Nissán (3 articles), Gervitz (cf. Sefamí 2013), Sefchovich (cf. Cypess 2013), Krauze (cf. Weingarten-Ruderman 2013), Moscona, Levi Calderón (cf. Lefter 2013), Mexican-born US-American Ilan Stavans (cf. Muñiz-Huberman 2013), Sefamí, Woldenberg (cf. Oropesa 2013) and, more generally, to the works of lesser-known male authors (Lockhart 2013c), it establishes or confirms a contemporary canon of Jewish-Mexican authors.

A special issue of *iMex. México interdisciplinario*, edited by Jacobo Sefamí and Matthias Lehmann (2018), is dedicated to the "Experiencia judía en México" in past and present. In the section on literature, it deals with the contemporary writers of Ashkenazic descent Margo Glantz (cf. Poot Herrera 2018) and Esther Seligson (cf. Senkman 2018) as well as Sephardic writer Myriam Moscona (cf. Lockhart 2018).

Another writer of Ashkenazic origin who has received academic attention is Sara Levi Calderón (cf. Loyola 2004; Pérez-Anzaldo 2009). This is due to her autobiographical novel *Dos mujeres* (1990), which provoked a scandal and was highly successful in Mexico, as it describes for the first time the coming out of a lesbian Jewish-Mexican woman – a topic taken up in another autobiographical novel or autofiction of hers from 2015: *Vida y peripecias de una buena hija de familia* (cf. Marquet 2016).

What one can also see is that there are not many male Ashkenazic Mexican writers, nor are they often the subject of academic research. Rodrigo Cánovas[14] deals with Salomón Laiter and José Woldenberg, both of whom were (or, in the latter case, are still) active figures in Mexican cultural life (Laiter as film director, painter, etc. and Woldenberg as political writer and journalist). In his overview articles, Lockhart refers to this point and gives a brief characterization of those authors whose works are out of stock (even very difficult to acquire on the antiquarian book market) and therefore overlooked by critics. In addition to Laiter, Lockhart mentions Sergio Lan

---

14 Cánovas, dealing with 14 authors and 25 texts, groups them according to four topics: Sefarad, Holocaust, memory, and "Casa Patriarcal" (cf. 2011, 62). He also provides an outlook on the new generations, which are marked by collages and fragmented narrations (cf. 2011, 96–99).

Mischne, Manuel Levinsky, and José Gordon (cf. 2013b, 19–20) and deals with Gerardo Kleinburg and Víctor Weinstock (2013c).

The present handbook article, however, cannot deal in depth with the Ashkenazic Mexican authors mentioned above, nor can it enter into competition with the exhaustive articles gathered in Lockhart (2013a). The focus of this article is on the specificity of Ashkenazic Mexican literature written by second and third generation immigrants. It draws on Goldberg's classification of Jewish Latin American literature as model of memory and recuperation of the absent (cf. Goldberg 2011, 745–746) while at the same time trying to avoid the risk of othering and compartmentalization.[15]

In the following, I will first outline the works of Mexican Ashkenazic literature written in Spanish in the 1970s and 1980s that gave literary visibility to that part of Mexican society for the first time (4.1). Secondly, particular attention will be paid to autobiographical explorations of hybridity and hyphenated identity, which reach an unsurpassed peak in 1990 (4.2). Thirdly, I will focus on female empowerment and the challenging of patriarchal hierarchies (4.3). Finally, I will deal with works that focus on migration to Mexico and (post-traumatic) memory in addition to the dynamics between remembering and oblivion (4.4).

4 Mexican Ashkenazic Literature in Spanish

4.1 Becoming Visible

In Argentina (cf. 549 in this volume), Ashkenazic journalist Alberto Gerchunoff published his volume of short stories *Los gauchos judíos* in Spanish as early as 1910, contributing to a discourse on Argentinian national identity that was still under construction.[16] In contrast, the literary visibility of Jewish minorities in Mexico was something that emerged much later and took a different form. This is due to the fact that the situation in Mexico was quite different from the one in Argentina. As mentioned above, strong cultural nationalism was one of the by-products of the Mexican Revolution of the 1910s, propagating an idealized mestizo identity supported

---

15 To give an example of best practice for the awareness of diversity: In the electronic catalogue of one of the most important libraries on Latin America, the Ibero-American Institute (Prussian Cultural Heritage Foundation) in Berlin, the explanatory notes on Myriam Moscona say "Mexican writer with Bulgarian Sephardic origins", but no similar information is provided for Margo Glantz, Rosa Nissán, Sabina Berman or Esther Seligson. https://lhiai.gbv.de/DB=1/SET=8/TTL=11/SHW?FRST=15 (11 April 2019).
16 Gerchunoff was born in the Russian Empire in 1883 and came with his parents to Argentina in 1889 in the first immigration movement. Cf. Feierstein 2010; Aizenberg 2015; Dolle 2020b.

by the PRI, which governed without interruption from the 1920s until 2000 in a one-party system (cf. Fuentes 1997; Foster 2009, xviii, n. 1).

The literary field was largely dominated by white men who were part of a patriarchal system. There were female writers, but only very few.[17] From the 1970s onwards, female narrative started to break through, with the movement growing stronger, louder and more successful with every decade. This new writing focused on challenging homogenizing national discourse and narrow-mindedness and featured commentaries on global topics, claiming ethnic but also gender plurality in addition to the right to sexual self-determination and a space for homosexuality, a topic that was formerly considered taboo and not treated openly in literature (cf. Balutet 2016, 19–24).

In a similar vein, Jewish topics become visible in Mexican literature in Spanish in the 1970s: The Sephardi Angelina Muñiz-Huberman's historical novel *Morada interior* (1972), on the life of a (Sephardic) nun in colonial New Spain, is the first work in Jewish-Mexican literature written in Spanish, and her *Tierra adentro* (1977), another historical novel on a Sephardic boy in Golden Age Spain, is often named as the second (cf. Lockhart 2013b, 16; Schuvaks 1996; cf. 527–539 in this volume).

However, from the 1970s onwards, we see an ever growing presence of Ashkenazic topics written by Ashkenazic authors born in Mexico, who are much more familiar with the Spanish language than their parents or grandparents: The first example to name here is Esther Seligson's first and prize-winning novel *Otros son los sueños* (1973), followed by Salomón Laiter's novel *David* (1976) and, very prominently, writer and playwright Sabina Berman, who successfully writes plays on Mexican identity, conquest and Sephardic heritage in Mexico (cf. Cypess 2010).

Writing in Spanish as a descendent of Ashkenazic immigrants to Mexico, i.e., in the second or third generation, firstly meant that Spanish had been appropriated as a second language (in the majority of cases not as the mother tongue). Yiddish was often spoken at home and Hebrew was taught at the Jewish schools.[18] Spanish was and remains the official language of Mexico and is widely spoken in non-Jewish contexts.

Secondly, writing in Spanish as a descendent of Ashkenazic immigrants to Mexico meant becoming acquainted with the hybridity of a diasporic existence on

---

17 The volume of short stories by Mexican female writers with the suggestive title *Atrapadas en la casa* (2001), compiled by the Ashkenazim Ethel Krauze and Beatriz Espejo, critically examines traditional gender roles.
18 Regarding the discussion in the field of education as to which language to teach in the Ashkenazic schools, Hebrew (propagated by the Zionists) or Yiddish, cf. Zadoff 2001, 139, and Cimet Singer (1992; 1997). Apart from the question of language, the schools in Ashkenazic communities became a battlefield with regards to Zionist ideology in 1940–1950. When the community was small, a *convivencia* was possible, but as the number of members increased and the financial standing of the community grew, ideological and ethnic divergencies emerged (cf. Zadoff 2001, 143).

the "hyphen" vis-à-vis the hegemonic notion of *mexicanidad*. Third, it meant coping with the (transgenerational) traumatic memories not only of the loss of property and former social standing in Europe, but also of relatives murdered in the Holocaust, of pogroms, persecutions, flight and migration experienced by the surviving parents and grandparents, in addition to awareness of the fact that their ancestors'/(grand) parents' place of origin had been destroyed forever by the turmoil of World War II and the Shoah. Lastly, it meant that Yiddish, the language they considered to be their mother tongue, was about to die out. At the same time, the younger, Mexican-born offspring had to accept the strangeness of their own (grand)parents vis-à-vis their surroundings and find a position for themselves in what Bhabha so convincingly has called "un-homeliness".[19]

From the 1970s until her death in 2010, Esther Seligson was a prolific and renowned writer. Born in Mexico City in 1941 to Ashkenazic parents who had migrated to Mexico from Russia and Poland (cf. Seligson 2010, 28), she was active in various genres, writing essays (on French literature and philosophy, Cioran, and other Latin American Jewish writers, e.g. Alejandra Pizarnik and Clarice Lispector; cf. Seligson 1988) and journalistic works, working as a translator and editor of (Jewish) reviews, and authoring several short stories (sometimes so short that they can be considered *microrrelatos*), often in a fantastic vein,[20] as well as theatrical pieces, novels and poetry (cf. Castro Ricaldo 2017; Gutiérrez de Velasco and Domenella 2017b). Over the course of her life, she refused to be labelled and compartmentalized as a "Jewish" writer (cf. Dabbah 2016, 160).[21] Seligson's multifaceted work takes up Jewish traditions, among them the Kabbalah and Talmud, but goes far beyond that, dealing also with Hinduism, Tibetan religion, New Age philosophy and cultural syncretism (cf. Senkman 2018, 105–106; Lindstrom 2018, 96).

Moreover, Seligson was very mobile in a global world. Her travels to Asia, India and Israel led to her having somewhat of a nomadic existence, representing what Flusser called the freedom of the migrant – the nomadic existence without roots as *conditio sine qua non* for a creative, innovative work (cf. Flusser 2013, 17–18), an approach that Esther Seligson makes very clear in her autobiography from 2010, *Todo aquí es polvo*. Her work *Otros son los sueños* (1973), on a woman experiencing a life

---

19 The linguistic gap between the first generation of Yiddish-speaking immigrants and the later generations familiar with Spanish is a topic addressed by several writers, including Woldenberg, Seligson in her short story "Herencia", Berman and Gervitz. Ilan Stavans opted to write his autobiographical work *On Borrowed Words: A Memoir of Language* (2001) in English, his fourth language (cf. Stavans 2002, 88), and, perhaps for the same reason, is quite enthusiastic about the hybrid form of Spanglish (cf. Dolle 2020a).
20 Her fantastic stories on the sphinx, on (gender) difference and alienness, refer to Brazilian Jewish writer Moacyr Scliar, whose famous novel *O centauro no jardim* (1980) can be (and has been) read as an allegory of Jewish existence as the eternal experience of being different.
21 For her biography, cf. Gutiérrez de Velasco/Domenella 2017b, 18–19. Seligson became editor of the renowned Mexican journal *Cuadernos del viento* in the 1960s.

crisis, pondering her Jewish heritage during a train ride (and therefore, with allusions to the French New Novel, especially Michel Butor's novel *La modification* [1957]), was awarded the prestigious national Xavier Villaurrutia prize.

Whereas the focus of Seligson's novel is on her family history and her own Jewish cultural heritage, Salomón Laiter's novel *David*, completed in 1973 and published in 1976 (3,000 copies) by the influential Mexican publishing house Joaquín Mortiz,[22] deals with the difficult process faced by Ashkenazic immigrants from Central and Eastern Europe as they adapted to their new country in the 1940s and 1950s. It also focuses on the horrors and the trauma of the Holocaust and the fate of the survivors or those who were able to flee from the Nazi regime (cf. Van Delden 2014, 570). Salomón Laiter (born to Ashkenazic parents in 1937 in Mexico D.F. and deceased in 2001) was active as a writer and painter and became known above all as a film director and screenwriter in the 1960s and 1970s. *Las puertas del paraíso* (1971), which he directed and co-wrote with Elena Garro, won the prestigious Ariel Award of the Mexican film academy in 1972.

As far as I know, Laiter is the first Jewish Mexican author who writes about the Holocaust and Ashkenazic migration to Mexico in Spanish, building on an issue already taken up by renowned Mexican authors such as Carlos Fuentes and José Emilio Pacheco in *Cambio de piel* (1967) and *Morirás lejos* (1967) respectively (cf. Van Delden 2014, 570). *David*, however, goes beyond that period. It touches on the atrocities of World War II, the Nazi regime and the Cold War in addition to the atomic bomb tests conducted at Bikini Atoll, the McCarthy era and its obsessive persecution of dissenters, and the Vietnam War, all of which is seen as the persistence of evil. Rodrigo Cánovas views the form of the text as grotesque "viñetas" representing deformed bodies, places, and souls.[23] As the literary form "vignette" already suggests, the novel consists of short descriptions uttered by an extra-heterodiegetic narrative voice, is action-centered, and contains place names and years. Relatively little weight is given to the characters' thoughts and meditations. Thus, it is similar to filmic writing.[24] The plot's point of departure is the arrival of a Jewish boy, the eponymous David, in Mexico D.F. together with his parents. It traces how they adapted to their

---

22 The novel was published in the series *Nueva narrativa hispánica*, which was dedicated not only to authors from Mexico, but also to authors from other Spanish American countries. The series does not focus on ethnic heterogeneity, but rather on the innovative nature of the works. On Laiter's novel, cf. Cánovas 2011, 71–74; Van Delden 2014, 570; Lockhart 2013b, 19.

23 Cf. 2011, 71–73. "[. . .] sobre la vida de los inmigrantes en Ciudad de México y en los barrios de Brooklyn y Manhattan, exponiendo las miserias de una comunidad judía apartada de sí misma, pasiva, que no respeta los deberos religiosos básicos del cuidado de los débiles y los enfermos, y que apenas se sostiene en un tronco familiar ya de por sí debilitado por la muerte y la dispersión geográfica" (Cánovas 2011, 71).

24 At the same time, they remind the reader of Gerchunoff's foundational text *Los gauchos judíos*, which was based on literary "vignettes" or sketches that had been published earlier (cf. Aizenberg 2015, 19).

new country during World War II as well as David's time in New York, where he goes to receive medical attention.

In addition to the migrants' fate in Mexico, the novel looks at utopian discourse in general, or rather the Jewish and human longing for a promised land – and its failures in reality. By 1976, when the novel was published, Latin American leftist utopian dreams had turned into nightmares, as cruel right-wing dictatorships (e.g., Pinochet in Chile, Varela in Argentina) had taken a stronghold.

Conveying a strong anti-American position, the text severely criticizes US-American utopian discourse and the country's claim to be a (promised) land of freedom, referring to it rather as a dystopia, a "sueño americano al revés" (Cánovas 2011, 73). The allegorical dimension is woven into the text and already obvious in the title, with the US playing the role of Goliath (cf. Cánovas 2011, 73–74). Through the extra-heterodiegetic narrative, the US is revealed to be deeply characterized by poverty, racism and social inequality (cf. Lockhart 2013b, 19–20). In contrast to this, from the protagonists' perspective, Mexico becomes the land where dreams can – at least in a modest way – be realized. The novel underscores the role of Mexico as a place of immigration and refuge during World War II ("[Óscar, i.e. el padre de David] Se nacionalizó mexicano de inmediato y se prometió a sí mismo respetar la realidad política del país que le brindaba asilo" (Laiter 1976, 12), sketching the situation faced by the immigrants arriving from Europe who were forced to flee the Spanish Civil War, Nazi persecution and other atrocities ("En México le había gustado la gente y esta sensación le producía tranquilidad y reposo entre refugiados de todas partes de Europa", Laiter 1976, 13). It depicts their struggle for a new and better life, resulting in a modest degree of social ascent and economic progress (cf. the first trip by the own car, Laiter 1976, 134), and touches on Ashkenazic social life in Mexico D.F.

As mentioned above, the text shows individuals, communities, and a whole Western world deeply marked and deformed by the persistence of (global) wars, violence, and evil. This is highlighted by the central episode of the novel, David's "accident". It turns out to have been caused on purpose by his playmate Juan, to whom the protagonist ascribes an "instinto asesino" (Laiter 1976, 29), as he pushes him when he tries to step over a beam on a construction site (cf. Laiter 1976, 28). The narrator does not provide any more clues concerning the circumstances or the ethnicity of the playmate, nor regarding his motives. It therefore proves futile to focus on anti-Semitic motives only, and may be more adequate to interpret the episode as representative of the persistence of evil between human beings in general.[25]

Lockhart, in his lemma on the author in *Jewish Writers of Latin America: A Dictionary* (2013d) harshly criticizes the fragmented form of the novel as unconvincing

---

[25] Voluntary damage to a non-Jewish playmate is at the core of another, more recent novel by the Brazilian Ashkenazic writer Michel Laub (*Diário da queda*, 2011), who makes reference to the complex dynamics of anti-Semitic attitudes resulting in Jewish individuals defending themselves and having to endure emotional damage.

and overlooks, in my opinion, the author's filmic writing style, whereas Cánovas relates it to the narrated fragmented lives: "párrafos discontinuos que hacen aparecer y desaparecer estos cuerpos migrantes, marcados por la Era Nazi y luego envueltos por el estalinismo, y [. . .] el macartismo y finalmente consumidos y sacrificados en la ciudad del pecado, New York" (Cánovas 2011, 72). I would go further and regard the form not as artistically "unsuccessful", but as a narration of (transgenerational) trauma with some typical characteristics such as fragmented narration, psychical deformation, and recurring motifs including the countdown of the atomic bomb tests, carried out by the US-American army between 1946 and 1958, at Bikini Atoll that structure the story (cf. Laiter 1976, 7, 153, 156 passim; regarding trauma, cf. Kühner 2008, 38–39; Dolle 2020c, 106).

The novel is narrated in chronological jumps by an extra-heterodiegetic voice, focusing on the eponymous protagonist David, growing up in Mexico City, and on his parents, a German father and a Lithuanian mother, both Ashkenazic Jews, who fled the Nazi regime and emigrated to Mexico (cf. 1976, 11–14). The retrospective focus on the inner worlds of the boy and his parents reveal the city as an exotic (and positive) refuge full of secrets for exiled persons fleeing Spain and the Nazis: "México era un jardín secreto, de misterios, de alimentos prohibidos" (Laiter 1976, 8).

This refers to the millennial Jewish search for a "homeland", a promised land in which to have a safe harbor, while also containing a critical comment on the foundation of Israel that takes into account the perspective of the Palestinians as well ("un pueblo triunfaba, otro perdía", 1976, 138). The role and the image of the US as a possible place to end this search is rejected. This is visible not only in the case of the father, who rejected an immigration permit to the United States and chose to settle down in Mexico instead (cf. Laiter 1976, 13),[26] but also in the dystopian characterization of the US as far from being a place to realize any "American dream". The image of poor, filthy and racist New York – with a Mexican doctor warning David of racist "gringos" (Laiter 1976, 58) and Brooklyn depicted as a nightmarish ghetto and limbo[27] – is intriguing. The real "new world" cannot be the US, and the dream to settle down in a promised land can possibly be realized in Mexico instead: "Sí, allá, la gente era mejor. [. . .] se podía vivir y respirar" (cf. Laiter 1976, 93–94). This comment might refer in a positive way to the *mestizaje* discourse. And even if the Ashkenazic community in Mexico is not as peaceful as it could be – its heterogeneity is stressed during a discussion about how to appropriately bury a friend who was a political activist and Zionist, murdered

---

[26] Family memory is presented in short paragraphs in an elliptical style, with one family member surviving Dachau, another one fleeing before World War II, an allusion to social Jewish life in Puebla and Mexico D.F., a mention of Nazi atrocities (cf. Laiter 1976, 22–24), and references to historical events such as the beginning of the Korean War (cf. Laiter 1976, 155, when the protagonist is 11 years old).
[27] "Brooklyn a la caída de la tarde. [. . .] Vidrios rotos. La miseria era general. Los ancianos esperaban, muertos en vida, su pensión alimenticia [. . .]. Los adultos reían del mito del esplendor económico". (Laiter 1976, 69–70).

in a robbery referred to as an "crimen idiota" (Laiter 1976, 76) – it is much less morally depraved than the Ashkenazic community in North America.

In 1978, Esther Seligson published 3,000 copies of her volume of four short stories *Luz de dos* with the publishing house Joaquín Mortiz in the series "del volador", for which she was awarded the Magda Donato prize. The volume does not cover specifically Ashkenazic topics, but it does involve Sephardic history. Two of the volume's stories figure in English translation in Kalechofsky's aforementioned anthology *Echad* – "A Wind of Dry Leaves" and "Luz de Dos" (Seligson in: Kalechofsky 1980, 157–170) – in which Seligson is the only author from Mexico. The eponymous short story "Luz de dos" is about relationships between lovers, contrasting the medieval historical lovers Inês de Castro and Peter I of Portugal (thus bearing a connection to Spanish and Portuguese literature) with a twentieth century tourist couple visiting historical places in Cuenca and Coimbra, including the graves of the aforementioned lovers. By this means, parallels are drawn between historical and contemporary human/Jewish existence – not only in terms of emotional relations in crisis, but also in terms of the Jewishness of Inês and the fate of Sephardic Jews in the Middle Ages: "Exodus her only patrimony and assurance", comments the narrative voice (Seligson in: Kalechofsky 1980, 164). With respect to "Luz de dos", Caufield stresses its dimension of:

> cultural diversity [that] points to an interconnectedness that, although rooted in México, participates in a global world extending beyond Mexican borders not only in space, but also in time. [. . .] [this] short story by Esther Seligson serves to demonstrate the way in which drawing on different cultural elements, including Jewish, creates a rich polysemic story that is not stereotypically Mexican, yet belongs to the Mexican national literature. (Caufield 2015, 16)

Another story from the volume, "Viento de hojas secas", i.e. "A Wind of Dry Leaves" in its English version in *Echad*, covers at first glance only the emotional challenges of adolescence. It is a story about the recurring nightmare of a boy who dreams about girls' bodies that eventually lose their flesh and turn into skeletons.[28] Such a story could be seen not only in the same vein as fantastic literature (and thus refer to literature of the Southern Cone),[29] but also as a (post-traumatic) reference to the atrocities of the Holocaust. At the very least, this could be an interpretation suggested by the framing of the story in *Echad*.[30]

---

28 "[. . .] the girls' dresses began to unravel in long white threads and their flesh began to disappear, as though someone were peeling their skin down from head to foot. [. . .] One of the woman [sic] was coming toward him rattling her skeleton loudly under her rags. Seized by panic, Tomás stared at the page in his hand. At that instant the wind blew through his now empty skull. His fingers were losing their flesh". (Seligson in: Kalechofsky 1980, 158) The nightmare finds it drastic outcome when the boy encounters a pubescent girl and, scared by her sexual advances, pushes her over a precipice (cf. Seligson in: Kalechofsky 1980, 170).
29 For a recent interpretation, cf. Castro Ricalde 2017.
30 The Spanish volume *Luz de dos* was republished in 2002 with the title *Toda la luz* (for a critical appraisal, cf. Castro Ricalde 2017).

La morada en el tiempo (1981) is Seligson's most famous (and enigmatic) text, "uno de los textos hispanoamericanos más polisémicos", according to Senkman (2013, 69). Still today, it has drawn the most critical attention as a paradigmatic work explicitly detailing the Jewish condition. It is a work that oscillates between genres, challenging traditional classification and alternately characterized as philosophical essay, poetic prose, novel or even (in my opinion less convincingly) autobiography.[31] *La morada en el tiempo* (that was successful enough to achieve a second edition in Spanish in 1992) is a "historia extensa" with synchronic and diachronic dimensions (cf. Goldberg 2011, 754–755) dealing with the millennia-old history of Jewish exile and persecution from Biblical times through the Holocaust.[32] One might also ponder if the reference in its title to *La morada interior*, Muñiz-Huberman's groundbreaking novel on Sephardic heritage in Mexico, is accidental.

Through a hetero- and extradiegetic narrative voice, it offers a transtemporal view of Jewish migration, exodus, persecution, and murder[33] as well as of the search for a "Promised Land": "Doce hombres, uno por cada tribu, avanzan rumbo a la tierra de promisión" (Seligson 1981, 23). In five numbered chapters, it mainly consists of recurring but slightly varying scenes[34] of Biblical conversations between Rebecca, Rachel, Leah, Esau and his brother Jacob, as well as an unidentifiable dreamer ("alguien

---

31 Cf. Lindstrom 2018, 93–94; Cánovas 2011, 69–71; Glantz 1995, 127, n. 2. Boixò and Ordiz Vázquez 2019 place it, in my opinion mistakenly, in a category with Margo Glantz's autobiographical text *Las genealogías*, despite its completely different tone. *La morada en el tiempo* touches on prophecies and religious speech, prayers, litanies, and prayer formulas; in its tone, it refers to dialogicity and polyphony in a Bakhtinian sense and bears resemblance to the French New Novel of the 1970s, particularly Robert Pinget's *Fable*; with respect to the latter novel, cf. Dolle 1999, 107–121.

32 It is considered by some scholars as a rewrite of the prophet Jeremiah's vision in present times, as "historia del pueblo judío en sus manifestaciones místicas" (Muñiz-Huberman in Cánovas 2011, 70, n. 41), as well as "[e]xperiencia contemporánea de sentirse huérfana de Dios" (Cánovas 2011, 71). Senkman (cf. 2013, 71, n.5) stresses the fact that Seligson herself refused to be labelled as and reduced to be a Jewish writer and reads the text as universal, situated in "un tiempo mítico que rehusa el espacio nacional y no desea aquerenciarse en una sola comarca" (Senkman 2013, 71). Lindstrom recently pointed out its anti-authoritarian quality, with a kind of utopia and freedom becoming visible in the last chapter (cf. Lindstrom 2018, 102–103) which might be understood as a reference to the 1981 Mexican state's failure to realize the utopia of the Revolution).

33 Various references are made to the persecution and execution of Jews, e.g. the Sephardic Jews Luis de Carvajal and Hernán de Alonso under the rule of the Spanish Empire in Mexico in the sixteenth century (end of ch. II), and thus to important foundational figures for Jewish identity in Mexico, to the burning of Gonsalvo Molina on Plaza Saint Etienne by the Inquisition (Seligson 1981, 66); to Kristallnacht in Nazi Germany, children murdered with Zyklon B (Seligson 1981, 92) and the concentration and extermination camps of the Holocaust (Seligson 1981, 147–148). In its diachronic dimension, the text takes into account the Jewish fate of exile and persecution in past and present.

34 These frequent variations of a basic situation – "Como la Amante al Amado hablaré" (Seligson 1981, 115; 136), "como la Amada al Amante hablaré" (pass.) or "como el Amado a la Amante hablaré" (Seligson 1981, 173) – recall the Song of Songs and stress the elegiac tone of the text.

sueña"), all in conflict with the authoritarian voice of God: "[. . .] en ambos [Rebeca and Jacob] bullía el desafío a la autoridad (i.e., God, V.D.), un loco sueño de evasión y libertad. Poseer el reino de lo inasible" (Seligson 1981, 17). Migration consists of flight, exodus and the timeless question of what to leave behind forever and what to take with you during the process of dreaming ("soñar"), walking ("caminar") and arriving ("llegar"):[35]

> Camina Jacob. Lleva por único patrimonio la piedra donde descansó su cabeza la noche anterior. Se dirije hacia una tierra que desconoce, siempre lejana, prometida en un sueño, visión de lo inasible [. . .]. Hijo del hijo de un arameo errante, la imagen concreta de esa tierra de promisión va a fundirse en su sangre con el vasto rumor del infinito. (Seligson 1981, 57)

The frequent use of personal pronouns such as "el/ella" (Seligson 1981, 105–106) instead of names stresses the paradigmatic, never-ending nature of migration as a Jew and, I would say, as a human being: "todo ser será un ser en exilio" (Seligson 1981, 109). In a similar way, the arrival at a new place takes on a paradigmatic character, as we see in the dialogue between the sedentary "Hijo de la tierra" (Seligson 1981, 130) and the newly arrived "son of captivity" ("el hijo de la cautividad", Seligson 1981, 129), who discuss and quarrel about the rights of the first arrival, with the former defending his older rights against the latter, who blames God for his destiny. This is symbolic of the permanent process of taking and losing roots (of rootedness and rootlessness):

> Una y otra vez seremos vomitados de entre las naciones y las tierras donde creeremos encontrar refugio. ¿Que compensará de haber perdido tantas veces la patria? Sefarad yace postrada como antaño Sión – [. . .] y no hay consuelo posible. (Seligson 1981, 130)

Even the slightest hope of reaching the promised land, or at least of an improvement of conditions, is destroyed, alluding to the Holocaust and the passivity and refusal of other nations to give shelter to Jewish refugees:

> [. . .] menos precaria y provisional que la que se había abandonado, de prisa y no por propia voluntad, expulsión al fin y al cabo, sin liberación y sin Moisés, exilio nuevamente. Y los trenes fueron furgones de muerte y muerte los barcos que nadie quiso dejar llegar a puerto.
> (Seligson 1981, 134)[36]

---

35 The imagination of a place of desire, the real trip and the reactions to the experiences made in the new place are paradigmatic for both past and present migration and often treated in works of fiction, as Olsson (2016) has pointed out for contemporary Mexican novels on (undocumented) migration to the United States.
36 This refers to the odyssey of the *St. Louis*, with 937 (mostly German) Jews who were not allowed to disembark in Cuba, the USA or Canada in May and June 1939, forcing them to return to Europe. They were finally allowed to disembark in Antwerp and the refugees were taken in by Belgium, France, the Netherlands and Great Britain in June 1939. According to recent research, 254 of them later died at the hands of the Nazi regime (https://de.wikipedia.org/wiki/Irrfahrt_der_St._Louis; 5 January 2019).

La morada en el tiempo ends with a slight glimmer of hope concerning Jewish destiny, but does not make any reference to a positive arrival or to taking root in a new territory.[37] Thus, it differs considerably from Margo Glantz's vision offered in *Las genealogías*, which was published in the same year. Glantz's text is the first of a prolific series of autobiographical texts written and published by female Ashkenazic authors until 1990. These autobiographies take stock of the authors' cultural and ethnic origin and reflect upon their relationship with the country that received their families as immigrants.

4.2 Taking Stock – Autobiographical Explorations

Las genealogías (1981) by the scholar Margo Glantz (born 1930 in Mexico City) is one of the first and most successful autobiographical Ashkenazic Mexican texts ever written.[38] Awarded the Magda Donato Prize in 1982, it has garnered widespread attention and become a canonical work, as various critics point out (cf. Waldman 2001; Cánovas 2011; Klahn 2012; Dolle 2004; 2012; 2020b; Poot Herrera 2018; Sefamí and Lehmann 2018). As the title suggests, the work is about the author's own Jewish-Mexican-Christian identity and cultural roots: "parezco judía y no lo parezco y por eso escribo –éstas– mis genealogías" (Glantz 2006, 19). Attention should be paid to the fact that this is the first time in Mexican literature that a Jewish I expresses her subjectivity in a text no longer presented as fictitious or hidden in third-person narrators in (historical) novels with autobiographical elements. Here, the I makes herself fully visible as a member of a marginal group.

In the form of interviews, the female I-narrator explores the past and the memories of her parents who migrated from Eastern Europe to Mexico in the 1920s (cf. Sosnowski 2013).[39] Particular attention is paid to the father, an outstanding intellectual, poet, and co-author of the aforementioned first Yiddish anthology of poetry, *Drai vegn*, which was published in Mexico in 1927. With its combination of various mediums – text, photos, documents – *Las genealogías* goes beyond traditional (male) autobiographies and can be viewed as (new) non-traditional female life-writing (cf.

---

37 Cf. Senkman 2013, 78–79.
38 *Las genealogías*, México, Martín Casillas, 1981; re-editions: México, SEP 1987; Alfaguara, 1997 and Valencia (Spain), Pre-Textos, 2006. English translation: *The Family Tree: An Illustrated Novel*, translated by Susan Bassnett. London: Serpent's Tail, 1991.
39 Saúl Sosnowski characterizes the narrator, having settled in Mexico, as "product of another place and of a minority culture and, as such, forced to negotiate her own territory in the lands of indigenous peoples who lost theirs to foreign conquerors. Food is one front [. . .]. Language is another" (Sosnowski 2013, 48–49).

Dolle 2012; Poot Herrera 2018). The text consistently foregrounds cultural hybridity (Goldberg 2011, 753, sees it as belonging to the "mestizaje" model), where no fixed compartmentalization is possible and identity is negotiated in a ludic manner, without essentialization. We see this not only in the fragmented oral style of the text, but also in the dynamic relationship between the text and the photos.[40]

Without focusing on a single historical truth and opting instead for a coexistence of controversial versions, the emphasis is placed on oral storytelling and a wandering memory. The process of adapting to a new country is highlighted not only in the text but also in the photos taken from the author's private family album. As I have demonstrated in another article, the photos of her parents dressed up for carnival or of her father "Mexicanizing" with a sombrero on his head, dressed up as a farmer, are strongly performative and ludic, subverting any essentializing concept of identity (cf. Dolle 2012, 171–172).

Following in the footsteps of Margo Glantz's 1981 work, Ethel Krauze, Sabina Berman, and Sara Levi Calderón all published their autobiographical texts in 1990. This represents an astonishing breakthrough of autobiographical Jewish Ashkenazic texts on identity. In intersectional works that speak out against the religious, ethnic, or national hegemonic discourses of patriarchal systems, these female writers make Jewish migration and *mexicanidad* visible beyond a male-centered mestizo discourse (cf. Cortina 2000, 124).

4.3 Female Empowerment: Writing to Oppose Patriarchal Hierarchies

For Mexican literature, the 1990s are characterized by the increasing visibility and commercial success of female writers such as Ángeles Mastretta, Carmen Boullosa and Laura Esquivel, who had their literary breakthrough at the beginning of that decade, in the "post-boom phase". During the same period, Mexican literature was also characterized by discussions of the 500th anniversary of the discovery and conquest of America in 1492. Stress was also placed on the importance of this event as the foundational narrative of the modern Mexican state, a frequent theme in Mexican literature and culture (cf. Dolle 2014 regarding this topic as treated in Mexican theatre).

Sara Sefchovich (born 1949 in Mexico City) is a sociologist, novelist and translator. She has published some highly successful novels, in which Jewishness, though, does not play a significant role. Her first novel *Demasiado amor* (1990), which was awarded the Agustín Yáñez Prize and brought to the screen in 2002, as well as her prize-winning second novel *Señora de los sueños* (1993) deal with a "model of empowered femininity" (cf. Castillo 1998, and Cypess 2013, 168) that seems to challenge

---

40 Cf. Dolle 2012, in particular 164–174 and Balutet 2016, in particular 352–355.

traditional Mexican male (*machista*) hierarchies. Easy to read, Sefchovich addresses a topic that has proven to be extremely successful economically speaking and draws from a pattern started by the most successful Hispanic American female writer of all time, the Chilean Isabel Allende (Cypess 2013, 170, refers to intertextual links to Allende and Esquivel).

Señora de los sueños deals with the imagination of a house wife whose nationality is not revealed but whom we may assume to be Mexican. For her, reading fiction serves as a means of escape from her restrictive, boring life and from her sense of discontent. In a hetero-extradiegetic manner, the narrator tells the story of a female protagonist who, after reading books on different historical periods, imagines herself in their respective cultures and times meeting crucial male protagonists (Fidel Castro in Cuba, Gandhi in India). After a spiritual encounter with Gandhi, she has an epiphany, becoming content with her life. Her personality seems to have been positively affected by these imaginary trips, so that she even is accepted by her daughter as a role model (cf. Cypess 2013, 182). In the sense of Lotman, however, the ending is quite conservative, as it does not really involve changes in structures and patriarchal hierarchies, but rather seems to accept the ruling system.

Jewish global history is also present in the protagonist's trips (cf. Cypess 2013, 176): The first episode of escape in the novel involves the protagonist as a Moorish woman in fifteenth-century Spain experiencing expulsion in 1492, the beginning of Sephardic existence in exile. She then moves on to a nineteenth-century Ashkenazic village in Russia and a kibbutz in Israel (cf. Cánovas 2011, 85) in the twentieth century where she is confronted with a kaleidoscope of minority (not only Jewish) ethnic experiences of difference, migration and exile, with the common denominator being transtemporal and transspatial experiences of gender difference and hierarchy.

The novel seems to be quite typical of the female literature of the 1990s, not only in Spanish-speaking countries. Focus is placed on female agency and its questioning of *machista* and patriarchal hegemonic structures, and women are given a narrative voice, as in the Mexican author Laura Esquivel's bestselling novel *Como agua para chocolate* (where cooking is a way to escape from real-life patriarchy) or the Mexican Ashkenazic poet Becky Rubinstein's volume *Hijas de la rueca* (1994), in which female agents – mostly seen as taking a secondary role to famous men by official male-written historiography – are foregrounded in their subjectivity.

As Cortina points out, Levi Calderón's 1991 autobiographical novel *Dos mujeres* (translated as *The two mujeres*), the novel *Amora* by Rosamaría Roffiel and the poem collection *Lunas* by Sabina Berman created a new category of literature in Mexico, drawing attention to homosexuality and lesbianism and to a new perspective on female sexuality, which up until then were absolutely taboo topics in conservative Mexico (cf. Cortina 2000, 91: "Levi Calderón rechaza la narrativa paterna y maternina sino que se inventa y construye una propia a partir de su identidad sexual"). From the 1970s on, feminism was not only a Mexican, but a global (Western) movement – and clearly directed against patriarchal, macho thinking. Levi Calderón, for instance, enters into dialogue with Hispanic American boom literature, rewriting and appropriating canonical male texts such as Cortázar's *Rayuela* in her reinterpretation of the famous and controversial seventh chapter, in which the narrative voice speaks disrespectfully of a female (passive) reader as "lector hembra" (cf. Cortina 2000, 112–113).

Considering the upswing of female empowerment and ideas of feminism in the 1980s and 1990s, it is not surprising that also colonial female agency in intercultural and hegemonic contexts comes into focus and is highlighted by many authors. Sabina Berman and Margo Glantz have written on the colonial period in New Spain and focused on situations of male dominance, submission, the role ascribed to women, intercultural and interreligious (violent) encounters and negotiations of difference. These include not only the encounters between indigenous peoples and Spanish intruders, mediated by an indigenous woman known as Malintzin/Malinche (cf. Glantz 1983; 1994), but also the Sephardic heritage of New Spain and the atrocities of the Inquisition. In Glantz's interpretation, Malinche was crucial for the Spanish victory over the Aztec rulers as female mediator and communicator.[41] Ashkenazic writer Sabina Berman (born 1955) deals with similar themes in her plays of the 1970 and 1980s, e.g., *Herejía* (renamed *En el nombre de Dios*) or *Aguila o sol*,[42] "expos(ing) the lie inherent in the concept that Mexican cultural identity is a single, monotone, hegemonic voice" (Cypess 2010, 6).

Sor Juana Inés de la Cruz is another historical figure who has been given a great deal of attention by Margo Glantz and other scholars. She is the most famous criollo poet of the second half of the seventeenth century. Sor Juana, probably an illegitimate child, a brilliant mind, and a nun who enjoyed certain liberties at court but was strongly controlled by ecclesiastic men, may often serve as an object of projection for contemporary minds dealing with the themes of ecclesiastic hierarchy, gender inequality and exclusion of the Other. Moreover, there are also quite a few voices who attribute her marginal position in colonial society to a clandestine Jewish faith (cf. Lockhart 2013b, 13–14). In other words, every Ashkenazic author dealing with her might deal (metonymically) with the fate and legacy of (female) Jews in the Spanish empire and use her as a surface of projection for contemporary topics.[43] Sor

---

41 Cf. Glantz 1983, an interpretation contrary to Octavio Paz's macho interpretation in *El laberinto de la soledad*, where he calls Malinche a "traitor" to the native Mexican people.
42 Cf. Dabbah 2016; Goldberg 2011, 754.
43 Therefore, it is very intriguing to see how Ashkenazic writers, as members of an ethnic group that has "recently" arrived, that does not have the same historical experience of belonging or claim to Mexican territory, position themselves vis-à-vis the native ethnic minorities (heterogeneous tribes, different languages) located there for thousands of years but conquered by Spanish Catholics and ruled by their descendants, the criollos, since colonial times. An examination of this topic has, as far as I know, not been made for Mexican, but for US-American literature. The US, with its "melting pot" ideology, favors a different concept of belonging, characterized by (religious) tolerance towards all (white) immigrants but neither towards the native (first) people nor towards the imported black

Juana's crucial role becomes evident, for example, in *Hijas de la rueca* (1994) by the forementioned Becky Rubinstein (born 1948 in Mexico City). In this book of poetry, a lyrical I addresses important mythological and historical women from the Old and the New World in a monologue, from Eve, Salome, and Penelope to Frida Kahlo, Virginia Woolf, Marilyn Monroe, the singer Madonna and Lady Diana, transcending historical, national and religious boundaries. Whereas Rubinstein generally dedicates a single poem to each of the above-mentioned women, she dedicates an entire chapter, comprising ten poems, to Sor Juana, each of them addressed to "Hermana Juana" (Rubinstein 1994, 57–66) and the "madre de los descastados" (Rubinstein 1994, 60). This latter attribute refers to the position ascribed to Sor Juana in Mexican scholarship as a representative of outlaws, marginalized outsiders, and those without "casta", with no social standing.[44] Rubinstein's poetry volume can furthermore be placed in a global context. Here, the role of women – mythological and historical – was stressed from the 1970s onwards, with criticism of (patriarchal) hierarchy and of the silencing of women informing global feminist movements and postcolonial studies (cf. Spivak's famous essay from 2008, "Can the subaltern speak?"). In this context, there are quite a few literary works dealing with women who were formerly only known in their supposedly "ancillary role" with respect to their male partners. These seem to have reached a certain climax in the 1980s and 1990s – not only in Mexico, but in Germany as well. They can be seen as postmodern reactions, as questionings of the *grands récits* featuring (and very often told by) male agents.[45]

Another Ashkenazic Mexican poet is Ethel Krauze (born 1954 in Mexico City). The *Diccionario de escritores mexicanos* mentions her without any reference to her Ashkenazic origin despite her autobiographical work from 1990, *La cruz y la estrella*.[46] Instead, the focus is on the feminist traits of her oeuvre and on her engagement with gender-related topics due to her groundbreaking novel *Infinita* (1992) on lesbian-

---

slaves and their descendants. Dean J. Franco's *Ethnic American Literature* (Charlottesville/London: University of Virginia Press 2006) deals with contemporary Chicano and Jewish literatures in the US, while Rachel Rubinstein's *Members of the Tribe: Native America in the Jewish Imagination* (Detroit: 2010) deals with the literary history of Jewish representations of American Indians, giving insight into the question of how Jews connect to them and what their self-concept is vis-à-vis an imagined community of the American nation.

44 For comments on another poetry volume of hers, *Cuéntame una de vaqueros*, cf. Dabbah 2016, 183–186. In *Hijas de la rueca*, Jewishness is mentioned explicitly only in the poem on "Santa Miroslava, la judía" (Rubinstein 1994, 48–49) and in the poem on "Shejiná" (Rubinstein 1994, 54), a Hebrew word from the rabbinic literature denoting the dwelling of the divine presence of God.

45 Cf. the bestseller *Hättest Du geredet, Desdemona. Ungehaltene Reden ungehaltener Frauen*, by Christine Brückner (1983).

46 This is in contrast to Enrique Krauze, a Mexican historian whose descent from Polish Jews who came to Mexico during World War II is pointed out in the same dictionary (cf. "Ethel Krauze" and "Enrique Krauze", *Diccionario de escritores mexicanos*).

ism.⁴⁷ Ethel Krauze has not only been a prolific poet to date (producing, for instance, four poetry volumes between 2015 and 2019) but has also gained widespread visibility through her work on the interpretation of poetry (*Cómo acercarse a la poesía*, 1992), which has become canonical in Mexico. Furthermore, it would be too narrow and limiting to reduce her work (as well as that of other writers with Ashkenazic origins) to Jewish topics alone. One poem ("AYOTZINAPA") from her poetry volume *Convocaciones, desolaciones e invocaciones* (2015) deals with the recent Mexican history of violence and unsolved crimes, referring to the 2014 massacre of Ayotzinapa, in which 43 male students were forcibly abducted and later murdered, probably by members of the local drug cartel (cf. Krauze 2015, 50–52). Her poetry volume *Un nombre con olor a almizcle y a gardenias* (2018), on the other hand, deals with the relationship between an anonymous group named "we" and an unnamed figure, referring to certain Jewish and Kabbalistic beliefs that the name of the Deity is not to be uttered.⁴⁸

4.4 Migration and Intercultural (Post-)Traumatic Memory

Case Study I: Sabina Berman's *La bobe* (1990): Entangled History and Transgenerational Traumatic Memory

When Sabina Berman published her autobiographical text in 1990, she had been positioned as a well-known and successful playwright for around two decades, having written plays on Mexico's colonial past, cultural encounters between indigenous people and Spaniards, Mexico's Sephardic heritage and the impact of the Inquisition (see above). In *La bobe*, she addresses her own Ashkenazic family history. Its foreign, non-Spanish title alone foregrounds linguistic alterity and cultural difference. It was published by a large and renowned publishing house, Editorial Planeta, in the series Colección Fábula, in 4,000 copies. The linguistic strangeness of the title is mitigated by the illustration on the front cover, which depicts an elderly woman with grey hair so that even the unexperienced reader who only reads Spanish will easily deduce that "bobe" might mean grandmother, a fact that is further underlined by an explanation on the bastard title. *La bobe* is, without any doubt, an identity-centered work (cf. Loyola 2004) that reflects upon the author's own cultural and ethnic foundations (Goldberg calls it "mestizaje amplio", 2011, 753). Moreover, it presents the plurality

---

47 In *La cruz y la estrella*, she takes stock of her cultural roots like the other female Ashkenazic Mexican writers mentioned above.
48 Krauze is thus another example of Mexican hybrid literary production (cf. Balutet 2016) that goes beyond narrow concepts of ethnicity or the idea that a certain literature and certain writers might be supposed to deal with specific subjects only. Eloy Urroz (of Ashkenazic origin) is among the authors of the Mexican manifesto *Crack* (1996), which refuses such a compartmentalization.

of "mexicanidad" as a heterogeneous society where immigrants belong. However, to a considerable degree, it is also about the family's transgenerational (traumatic) memory of expulsion, displacement, and flight from the Nazis. Furthermore, it sheds light on twentieth century Mexican history and on crucial events such as 1968 and the massacre of Tlatelolco, which is related to the decay of the grandfather, representing the entanglement of history and transcultural memory. Like Woldenberg, Berman incorporates episodes of violence from both Ashkenazic and Mexican history.

An extradiegetic and autodiegetic I-narrator, the adult granddaughter, reflects on her grandparents' and parents' history as refugees from Poland and as Ashkenazic immigrants to Mexico, on flight and arrival. The scene that serves both as point of departure and as ending, framing the narration, is the body of her grandmother found dead in the bathtub. Over the course of 126 pages with unnumbered and untitled chapters, the I-narrator recalls, in non-chronological fashion, episodes with her grandmother; the visits they paid to fellow immigrants; the complex and emotional family relationships, especially between mother(s) and daughter(s); accompanying her mother to the psychoanalyst; the psychic deformation suffered by her mother; her own process of growing up and of distancing herself from her grandmother, whom she perceived as having fallen out of time; and her own process of self-discovery.

The narration of the flight from the Nazis, which the grandmother described to the mother of the I-narrator when she was a child as a 'blessed trip' in order to avoid making her cry, is especially intriguing: "Hasta el día de hoy me parece una hazaña que mi abuela le haya relatado a su hija la escapada de los nazis como un viaje bendito." (Berman 1990, 27) When the grandmother is asked by the granddaughter to tell her what the war and her flight from Russia had really been like (cf. Berman 1990, 38–39), the grandmother bluntly defies the granddaughter's image of the Holocaust, which is based on narratives, films and magazines. Instead, she tells her a very special story: that of her and her daughter saying goodbye to three fat grazing cows from the train with a white handkerchief (cf. Berman 1990, 40). This is obviously no random episode but is deeply related to the Jewish history of exodus, exile and persecution, in particular to the parable of the fat cows in Egypt. Thus, the grandmother inserts her own history into paradigmatic collective history, presenting it as the Jewish fate to leave one place in order to go to another (better) one.[49]

One of the core passages, if not the climax of the 126 pages – both in terms of content and in terms of style – is formed by the four-page episode in which the I-narrator imagines the family's exodus, leading finally to Mexico (cf. Berman 1990, 27–30). Apart from the first sentence, the sentences are not separated by any paragraphs or periods. Instead, they are only structured by commas, suggesting a certain breath-

---

[49] "¿Por qué cuando huían de Polonia, a punto de ser invadida por los nazis, no le explicó aquello de que los judíos eran considerados una raza maldita, que debía ser borrada de la faz del planeta? Por qué le contó ese otro cuento absurdo: que Dios los sacaba de Polonia, como antes lo había hecho de Egipto, y los conducía como entonces a un país más pródigo?" (Berman 1990, 25–26)

lessness, speed of movement and density of memories. The elliptical accumulation of images and scenes evokes mobility: the exodus from Poland, fleeing by train on the Transsiberian Railway, via Japan, "rumbo a América" ("mi abuelo, mi abuela, sus hijos, caminando sobre la nieve [. . .], ellos durmiendo en establos, en bodegas, abordando trenes atiborrados de gente. . ., [. . .] por fin en Tokio" (Berman 1990, 28), permanently threatened by airplane attacks ("silban los remotos aeroplanos, crucecitas negras en lo azul marino, y de súbito estallidos", Berman 1990, 27), the grandfather handing over the keys to his own factory until the establishment of a new factory and his first steps as a salesman in Mexico.[50]

In *La bobe*, as in other Ashkenazic narrations of immigration to Mexico (starting with Laiter), the topic of the US as the generally preferred or desired place and promised land is addressed. This is a crucial topic, as it reveals the author's stance towards the country that received her family and towards the concept of "mexicanidad". In Berman, the US is the family's desired destination (as for many European Jews), imagined as the promised land – a fact that is rhetorically exposed, with all the components of an "American dream", in a triple, climatic accumulation: "ellos en el barco japonés rumbo a América, la tierra de la libertad, la tierra de la oportunidad, el reducto heroico de la democracia" (Berman 1990, 28). Yet this promised land does not give them permission to enter; only Mexico does, but Mexico – at that moment – is perceived as the "wrong place": "ellos desembarcando *en el lugar equivocado*, en Manzanillo, en la costa de México" (Berman 1990, 29, italics mine, V.D.). Nevertheless, even if Mexico is not viewed as the promised land (at all) at that moment, there is at least one aspect conferring positive features to the new destination for the I-narrator's family. Referring to a crucial event of nineteenth-century Mexican history, the grandfather makes possible a common ground for both ethnic groups, Mexican and Jewish:

> [. . .] [México], un país al que una sola referencia los ligaba: allí, el siglo pasado, el rubio archiduque Maximiliano, sobrino del emperador Franz Josef de Austrohungria, luego de un reinado bienintencionado, torpe, impopular, y finalmente breve; había sido fusilado por órdenes de un señor de raza indígena, un tal Benito Juárez, suceso admirable que les hermanaba secretamente la sangre de judíos vilipendiados con la de aquel indio que no solo había hecho caso omiso de la noción de razas superiores (las europeas) sino que había derramado la sangre de uno de sus ejemplares más aristocráticos. (Berman 1990, 29–30)

Beyond anecdotal episodes, in the context of the "Quinto Centenario" and the discussion of the relationship between European intruders and native inhabitants, Berman explicitly points out features of Mexican and Jewish history that form a common denominator, connecting the latter to the receiving society and thereby giving a new

---

[50] The grandfather lost his social position over the course of emigration. Formerly a rich and influential factory owner in Poland involved in important cultural activities and a large network, he became a marginal figure in Mexico (Berman 1990, 104–105). Deeply traumatized, he never really overcame the war: "Para él [. . .] nunca acabó la Guerra" (Berman 1990,106), as one of the female members of the family comments.

meaning to the concept of "mexicanidad", creating an intercultural memory and thus an imagined entangled community. Contrary to the immigrants' first impression in *La bobe*, Mexico becomes visible as a destination for immigration and as a shelter from persecution. Mexico City even appears to be the home of many Jewish inhabitants: "Colonia Hipódromo [. . .] caminar por ese camellón era caminar por la ilusión de una ciudad de abundante judería." (Berman 1990, 71)

Case Study II: Thinking about Form: José Woldenberg, *Las ausencias presentes* (1992)

Within the panorama of Ashkenazic literary expression from the 1970s onwards, José Woldenberg (born 1952 in Monterrey), a highly prolific journalist, political analyst and sociologist, adopts a special position with his first and only (autobiographical) novel *Las ausencias presentes*.[51] It was published in 1992, in 2,150 copies, by Cal y Arena, the publishing house of renowned Mexican writers such as Héctor Aguilar Camín, Enrique Florescano, and Angeles Mastretta.

1992 is no arbitrary date as far as the hegemonic Mexican literary discourse is concerned. The 1980s and 1990s in Mexico were characterized by the controversial transatlantic discussion of the status of the "Quinto Centenario", the commemoration of 500 years of discovery and conquest of America. The central question was whether this was an event worth celebrating (a tendency followed by Spanish official discourse) or rather an occasion for mourning because of the genocide perpetrated against the autochthonous population of America. There was also a certain boom of new historical novels linked to this event (cf. Menton 1993), which focus on and reinterpret crucial events of Mexican-European relations from colonial times to the present. Such novels reflect critically on the status and interpretation of sources and memory and on the notion of historical truth, giving a carnivalesque, grotesque form to previously undisputed foundational events and personalities. In this vein, Carlos Fuentes's metafictional novel *Cristóbal Nonato* (1987) and Fernando del Paso's *Noticias del imperio* (1987) on the last Habsburgian Kaiser in Mexico, Maximiliano, and his wife Carlota should also be mentioned. In the same period, quite a few plays deal with the encounter between Cortes, Malinche and Moctezuma and with the conquest of Mexico, also drawing historical parallels to the present (cf. Seydel 2014). In other words, foundational episodes of Mexican identity and of the becoming of the modern state are reinterpreted by Mexican authors.

José Woldenberg's autobiographical novel is to be situated in this tendency, explicitly directed towards crucial events of twentieth century Mexican history, seen from an outsider's viewpoint: it is the first work that explicitly reflects on the relationship

---

51 Cf. the lemma "José Woldenberg" in the aforementioned *Diccionario de Escritores Mexicanos*.

between the Mexican majority community and the marginal position of (Jewish) immigrants as well as on their adaptation process.⁵² *Las ausencias presentes* is a complex text with metafictional elements that is structured by means of an interview of the autodiegetic protagonist by a young female sociologist, who turns out to have a migratory background herself as the daughter of Spanish refugees from the Civil War (cf. Woldenberg 1992, 40–41). The text consists of three parts dealing with the memories of an elderly Jew who immigrated to Mexico in 1922 after surviving a pogrom perpetrated by Russians in his home town (cf. Woldenberg 1992, 12, 17–18). It stands out because of its multiple perspectives, its critical reflection on individual and official memory and its acute awareness of the process of writing and forming texts – that is to say, it possesses strong metatextual elements, taking oral history into account.

The plot deals with the protagonist's arrival, and his process of adapting to Mexico. Obviously, he regards the country very positively, as a kind of paradise of the senses, of tastes and flavors: "E imaginarse ahí (i.e., in the market, V.D.), sin gente, solo, ensimismado, como Adán en el paraíso" (Woldenberg 1992, 23). Furthermore, he proudly stresses the socio-cultural and linguistic expertise regarding codes which he has gained since his arrival, as can be seen, for instance, in the novel's opening paragraph. Here, the male "I" reflects in fluent Spanish upon the incumbent president of Mexico and his physical appearance:

> Ese día caminaba tranquilamente pensando en la corbata del presidente. Era una imagen desconcertante. No había sido fácil conocer –o pensar que conocía– al país, y ahora una de sus caras se me aparecía retocada, artificialmente dócil y apacible como si alguien con un simple artificio me quisiera dar gato por liebre. (Woldenberg 1992, 11)⁵³

His degree of Mexicanization and cultural expertise is not only exposed here, but in another episode on the Spanish conquest of Mexico, on one of the foundational fictions preserved in Mexican cultural memory and discussed in the context of the "Quinto Centenario" in 1992. When he considers one of the central elements of the historical narrative, Moctezuma's treasure being hidden from the Spaniards during the *Noche Triste*, to be a *bobe maintze*, a Yiddish term for an invented story such as a tale told by one's grandmother (cf. Woldenberg 1992, 32–33), the I-narrator reveals not only how well informed he is about Mexican history, but also his critical distance from its narratives.

---

52 Even if there is no reference thereto, Woldenberg's text can also be seen as a reaction to, or comment on, a project of oral history that gathered the testimonies of Jewish immigrants in Yiddish and published them in 1990 as *Testimonios judíos de historia oral en México* (cf. Cimet 2013, 30). Oropesa (cf. 2013, 242–244) highlights the oximoron of the novel's title, interpreting it as allusion to the "cristianismo exclusivo" as propagated and practiced by high Mexican culture.
53 Some pages later, the typical Mexican expression "platicar" (Woldenberg 1992, 13) is used instead of the more common Peninsular Spanish expression "charlar" (to talk).

There is, however, a discrepancy between the aforementioned competence regarding Mexican history, politics and culture on the one hand and language on the other, as the linguistic incompetence of the newly arrived immigrant, which he never really overcomes despite his concerns about speaking correctly, is mentioned several times (cf. Woldenberg 1992, 13), as well as his rootedness in Yiddish as the only language in which he is able to express his ideas "con fidelidad" (Woldenberg 1992, 56). Moreover, there is a discrepancy between form and content, considering the idiomatic Mexican Spanish of the text itself, which, however, is finally "solved" by the unique construction of the text. It is written, as it turns out at the end of the novel, not by the supposed autodiegetic narrator, but by the female interviewer and Spanish native speaker (cf. Woldenberg 1992, 40) who writes in the first person – "que ella como si fuera yo, un relato en primera persona del singular. . . el narrador podía hablar con una tercera persona imaginaria tanto de él como de su entrevistadora" (Woldenberg 1992, 103) – and circles back to the beginning of the novel, repeating its first sentence: "'Ese día [. . .]'" (Woldenberg 1992, 103).[54]

Whereas the marginality of the Jewish Other is, due to this construction of the text, not visible at a linguistic level (i.e., *discours* in terms of Genette), it becomes quite frequently evident at the *histoire*-level, especially when the I-Narrator emphasizes the perception of himself as Other, as completely different ("mi absoluta extranjería", Woldenberg 1992, 17), or when he focuses on the history of Mexico in the 1920s, after the Mexican Revolution, and connects it to Jewish immigration in the same decade. Here, he reveals his critical distance from hegemonic historical discourse via his reference to the Cristero War of the 1920s in which Catholic farmers fought against secular Mexican troops defending their right to practice their religion and hold their services, a right that was forbidden by President Calles in 1926.[55] It is described from the perspective of a newly arrived immigrant, himself also persecuted for religious reasons, who does not take part in the confrontation but observes and echoes the ideas and key words expressed by both parties:

> Durante los primeros años de mi estancia en México escuché que se les perseguía. Escuché que en su mayoría eran campesinos. Escuché que aquello sucedía en Guanajuato, Jalisco, Michoacán. Escuché que se habían cerrado las Iglesias. Escuché que los obispos condenaban la violencia. Escuché que el gobierno culpaba a los obispos. [. . .] Escuché las letanías: 'gesta por la fe', 'cruzada contra el fanatismo'. (Woldenberg 1992, 34)

---

54 Ilan Stavans, a US-American citizen of Mexican Ashkenazic origin, tackles this linguistic problem in a different, subversive way. His "memoir of language" *On Borrowed Words* (2001) is written in a recently learned language (English). He uses the distance he has to this foreign language to make the process of creation more fruitful and to reflect upon the relationship between one's mother tongue and one's identity (cf. 2002, 88 and Dolle 2020b; 2021). María Barbetta from Argentina deliberately writes in German, a foreign language, in order to avoid the implications and connotations of her mother tongue.
55 On the Cristero War, cf. Meyer 2013.

This passage, containing multiple instances of parallelism and anaphora (in the whole chapter, "Escuché", I heard, is repeated 42 times), condenses political key words used by the parties to motivate their fights. Through the rhetorical device of accumulation, every political and ideological idea and intention turns into a mere (empty) slogan, especially because there is no connection to an enunciating agent, but only the free-floating words received, without differentiation between opposing ideological stances, by the immigrant: "Escuché al coro de voces: tiranía, Dios, leyes, revolución, reacción, heroísmo, libertad, humillación, progreso." (Woldenberg 1992, 34) In such a condensed form, the keywords attributed to both parties have an alienating effect and make the reader contemplate critically the value of political propaganda in general.

Furthermore, the I-narrator expresses a certain understanding of and identification with the Catholic victims of the conflict due to his own biography as survivor of a pogrom, e.g.: "imaginé la sangre derramada" (Woldenberg 1992, 34), "casi compartí", "creí comprender", "y entendí" (Woldenberg 1992, 35). However, he lays out his own position in favor of a secular Mexican constitution, concerned that a Christian ideology might be too dangerous for Jews: "Escuché llamamientos levantíscos [sic] que me crisparon los nervios: '¡México Guadalupano, México de Cristo Rey, México Hispánico!'" (Woldenberg 1992, 35) Forming the climax of the passage, the final paragraph breaks up the chapter's anaphoric structure, culminating in the I-narrator's observation: "Me invadía un sentimiento de misericordia mezclado con algunos gramos de alivio. Por el momento, los judíos eran los otros." (Woldenberg 1992, 36)[56]

From the Jewish immigrant's point of view, Mexican history of the 1920s is characterized as a double bind, "(años) (t)erribles" (Woldenberg 1992, 36) on the one hand, full of political violence, murders and attacks on leading politicians such as Obregón, Villa, and Serrano (cf. Woldenberg 1992, 35–37), and a fruitful period – "(años) pacibles" (Woldenberg 1992, 36) – for the Jewish community, on the other. His community was able to put down roots: "Época de grandes asesinatos políticos y de echar raíces. [. . .] estábamos, con pie firme, edificando una comunidad" (Woldenberg 1992, 36). The novel offers an alternative view on the decade of the 1920s, emphasizing the entangled character of history (according to Randeria, cf. 2009), the building of new communities and thus, diversity and plurality in Mexico and Mexican history beyond a focus only directed towards national "mestizo" identity and post-revolutionary turmoil.

In a similar vein, the I-narrator points out a certain arbitrariness as far as nationality and date of birth are concerned ("tuve que ser polaco para quienes me exigían papeles. Porque en un mundo ordenado, es necesario tener un lugar de origen

---

56 Drawing on Graff Zivin's book title from 2008, it becomes clear here that the "signifier" wandered – that time – to another group persecuted for religious reasons.

reconocido y con capacidad de expedir pasaporte" [1992, 50]),[57] which can be understood as a critical comment on any official discourse of national identity as an essence and therefore also on "mexicanidad". The misconception he experiences on the part of some Mexicans who see him as a "Russian" – he who fled from Russian persecution and pogroms (cf. Woldenberg 1992, 16–17) – underlines the absurdity and arbitrariness of national ascription and classification and how misleading essentializing conceptions of the "mestizo" might be in comparison.

But contrary to national categorization, which is dependent on circumstances, the I-narrator speaks of an unalienable, indelible Jewish belonging, i.e., the other part of the hyphen is – for him – that which is not arbitrary, but unequivocal: "[. . .] no había confusión: propios y extraños (in Eastern Europe, V.D.) sabían que éramos judíos. No había vuelta de hoja. Se es lo que se es." (Woldenberg 1992, 50)[58]

At the same time, Woldenberg's novel is characterized by its attempt to translate cultural differences between autochthonous Mexicans and newly arrived Jewish immigrants, as when the I-narrator tries to explain Jewish rites and habits (probably perceived as strange, weird or different, he assumes) to his interviewer of Spanish descent and – in extension – to his Mexican, Catholic readership, concluding that the situation of the Jewish community in Mexico has improved in comparison to Eastern Europe:

> En un camión rumbo a Laredo, va un hombre corpulento que al amanecer se envuelve en un manto blanco y en el brazo y la cabeza se enrede unas tiras de cuero. ¿Qué piensa y se imagina el resto del pasaje? Lo mínimo: que se trata de un loco. [. . .] me pregunto ¿qué somos los judíos a los ojos de los otros? En la vieja casa (i.e. Eastern Europe, V.D.), cuyos recuerdos salados no logran diluir la ternura propia de la melancolía, éramos conspiradores, asesinos de Cristo, criminales en los actos rituales, usureros, parásitos. En nuestro nuevo hogar, solamente somos otros.
> (Woldenberg 1992, 53)

The novel, however, is not only characterized by this attempt of cultural translation. It is also characterized by an explicit metatextual dimension in line with theoretical reflections about the significance of oral memory and its written articulation. According to the I-narrator, the text is an "archivo de la palabra – una historia a través de testimonios de emigrantes a México" (Woldenberg 1992, 14). But how these testimonies are generated by the questions of the interviewer, is critically reflected by the I-narrator: He wonders if the answers elicited by the questions of

---

57 In a similar way, Glantz exposes this national arbitrariness, in the Heideggerian sense of "Geworfensein", for the newcomers in *Las genealogías* (cf. Dolle 2012, 169–170 and Dolle 2020b, 311–312).
58 Seligson treats the indelibility of Jewishness in her autobiography in a similar way (cf. 2010, 122). For Woldenberg's I-narrator, however, Europe does not evoke any nostalgia or homesickness, as his home was destroyed in a pogrom and no longer exists: "Entonces comparaba el pasado y el presente, y si bien éste no parecía la tierra prometida, estaba seguro que aquello no había sido el paraíso perdido" (Woldenberg 1992, 18). And Mexico, instead of the US, is the "nuevo y definitivo hogar" (Woldenberg 1992, 71).

the interviewer, which, according to him, are directed towards the spectacular or extraordinary (cf. Woldenberg 1992, 23) really go to the core of the emigrant's life or if they systematically fail to do so (cf. Woldenberg 1992, 15), presenting instead only a "historia convencional de un emigrante judío en México" (Woldenberg 1992, 23).[59] These doubts – which pertain, *pars pro toto*, to all immigrants' memories or to all oral histories put into scripture – remain and incite us, the readers, to reflect upon the official discourse of Mexican history of the last 500 years, on the quality of its sources and its texts as constructions.

Case Study III: Gloria Gervitz: Between Memory and Oblivion

There are several renowned poets among the Ashkenazic Mexican writers. These include Gloria Gervitz, Ethel Krauze and Becky Rubinstein. For more than 40 years, Gloria Gervitz has been explicitly rewriting her only work and lifelong oeuvre *Migraciones*.[60] This work is a dynamic text, a collection of different poetry books of hers: *Shajarit* (1979), extended and published in 1986 with the title *Fragmentos de ventana*, *Yiskor* (1987) and *Leteo*, put together under the title *Migraciones* in 1991 and extended by four more parts by 2003 (Pythia, Equinoccio, Treno, and Septiembre).[61] This structure of seven books has been quite consistent since then. However, since the 2016 edition, the titles of the respective parts have been removed, as well as all capitalizations and all punctuation marks apart from question marks. The poems have undergone permutations, variations, and – often only slight stylistic – changes since the work's first publication in 1991 or, in Derrida's words, it is a signifier that is never fixed, revolving around a void, and permanently being re-elaborated. According to Karageorgou-Bastea (2019, 96), *Migraciones* is "un libro que ha crecido desde sus entrañas [. . .] es otra migración". It deals with female corporeality and desire but also with the poetics of memory in relation to Jewish immigration to Mexico (cf. Sefamí 2013; Vergara 2015, 164; Karageorgou-Bastea 2019 and Dolle in press) and with attempts at transgenerational dialogue between daughters and absent/dead mothers.

Gervitz, a former professor and translator of poetry and fiction from French, Russian, and Portuguese, was born in 1943 in Mexico City as the daughter of an Ashkenazic father whose mother was an immigrant from Ukraine, and a Catholic mother stemming from Puebla. Even if she is thus, strictly speaking, not Jewish in a traditional sense, her work revolves around Jewish topics and deals with the cultural

---

59 I would like to draw attention to the wording in this paragraph: The text always uses the term "emigrant", not immigrant, and thus stresses the place of origin and the fact of being new and alien in the receiving country. These nuances should not be overlooked (as is the case, e.g., in the Spanish translation of Stavans's *On Borrowed Words*, cf. Dolle 2021, 341).
60 The latest editions of *Migraciones* were published in 2016, 2017 and 2020.
61 For the history of *Migraciones* until 2016, cf. Karageorgou-Bastea 2019, 95, n. 1.

and emotional legacy of her Jewish and Cristian ancestors. Without any qualifying ethnic attributes, Gloria Gervitz forms part of the contemporary Mexican canon of poetry, as is highlighted by Gloria Vergara in her article "La memoria y el olvido en la poesía de Gloria Gervitz", published in *Historia crítica de la poesía Mexicana* (cf. 2015, 163).

In the version from 2020 used here, *Migraciones. Poema 1976–2020* has 269 pages containing untitled poems of various lengths written mostly in Spanish but with parts in Hebrew, Yiddish, Arabic and English, and a glossary that explains typical Yiddish, Hebrew and Mexican expressions, drinks and meals, but also Portuguese "saudades" (Gervitz 2020, 271–277). In the first 70 pages, it describes the lyrical female I's intention to access her past (i.e., to enter into contact with her own late mother and grandmother) and to measure the emotional dimensions of migration and its impact on the following generations.[62] It does so taking a crucial scene in family history, the arrival of a Jewish woman from Kiev in the Port of Veracruz, as a point of departure for its "divagación" – as Sefamí (2013, 158) calls it – along with several variations of that scene. In contrast to Margo Glantz's *Genealogías,* where real photos (i.e. those printed in the text) play an important role (see above), Gervitz only describes them in brief ekphrases (cf. e.g. Gervitz 2020, 48–49; Vergara 2015, 170; Dolle in print). Nevertheless, unlike in the work of Glantz, this medium does not lead to any act of remembering or approach to the person represented in the photo:

> la fotografía no nos descubre nada (todavía es una mujer joven)
>
> Yo nunca la conocí
>
> ¿en qué momento aquellos sueños comenzaron a perseguirme?
> (Gervitz 2020, 55)

In a monologue formed as dialogue directed towards the absent mother/grandmother – who never respond ("¿me oyes?" [Gervitz 2020, 26, 30] or repeatedly "¿me escuchas?" [Gervitz 2020, 29]) and thus whose answers are imagined – the female lyrical I tries to access the hidden, submerged family history centered around three generations of women: her grandmother, her mother and herself. It is dedicated, thus, to a central topic for the Jewish community, as Florinda Goldberg (2011) among others (cf. Cánovas 2011) pointed out: the memory of the absent. *Migraciones*, especially the variations of the arrival scene, are in this vein, and have, furthermore, a fantasmatic dimension, beyond memory, trying to figure out what the cultural and individual heritage consists of:

---

[62] In this chapter, I sketch briefly some ideas on the emotional dimensions of migration in *Migraciones* that are discussed more in detail in my article "'*El calor como colmillo de jabalí*': los momentos de llegada del inmigrante entre experiencia histórica y dimensión poética en *Migraciones* de Gloria Gervitz" (in print).

>   aquella muchacha sola en el muelle
>   esta imagen para siempre
>   ¿qué vida fue ésta?
>   y mi voz confundiéndose con la tuya
>   los pájaros golpeándose contra la luz
> el verano desbordándose
> y ella escribiendo cartas en un idish que ya nadie habla
>   ¿esa mujer soy yo?
>   (Gervitz 2020, 57)

But this approach by imagination with the photos as a starting point, is also marked by the tension between the will to remember and the will to forget and/or to be forgotten, as it is demonstrated in the imagined dialogue between the daughter's (nearly obsessive) attempts to remember and the refusal of the person who has gone to be remembered:

> déjame ir
> suéltame
> no regreses
> no quiero quedar atrapada en tu sueño sin poder despertar
>   ¿hacia dónde ir?
>   (Gervitz 2020, 33)

Even if a concrete direction and orientation towards the future ("¿hacia dónde ir?") do not become clear, oblivion might be an aliviation and an option to get rid of the obsessive weight of the past, as is underlined by the lyrical I's comment "ella no quiere que yo la recuerde" (Gervitz 2020, 56).

Migraciones is a collection of poems that stands out not only on account of its reflection on the dynamics between memory and oblivion in an individual history but also because of its religious, cultural, and linguistic hybridity. This latter quality is made evident by its frequent references to Christian prayers to the Virgin Mary and to Jewish prayers (cf. Vergara 2015, 165; Dolle in print) recited in the course of the day and the year. It is also visible in the litany-like repetitive tone woven throughout the text. The lyrical I inserts herself into an Ashkenazic as well as a Mexican Christian tradition, according to the author's aforementioned biography: There are supplications and the invocation of a (her) mother, e.g., "oh madre ten piedad de mí/ oh madre misericordiosa/ ten piedad de mí" (Gervitz 2020, 33) or "Yo digo Kadish por ti y por mi [. . .]/Madre de Dios ruega por nosotras" (Gervitz 2020, 31). Here, the boundaries between personal invocation and religious Catholic prayer to the Virgin Mary are blurred – and a hybridization and appropriation of Jewish and Catholic religious practices takes place, as we can see in the female form that is used in the Ave María: "Madre de Dios ruega por nosotras".

Furthermore, the lyrical I inscribes herself into the Hispanic American literary tradition of the twentieth century: This ranges from allusions to Latin America's most paradigmatic poets, Alejandra Pizarnik (cf. Sefamí 2013, 160–161) and Pablo Neruda, and to references to Mexican culture and literature such as Carlos Fuentes's novel on the Mexican revolution, *La muerte de Artemio Cruz*, and contemporary Mexican poet, Ululame González (cf. Vergara 2015, 167–171). There might also be allusions to one of the most canonical novels of twentieth century Mexican literature, Juan Rulfo`s *Pedro Páramo*:

> busco en la tierra mojada un lugar para morir
> ¿cómo encontrarte?
>
> (Gervitz 2020, 62)

and

> nunca sabré no sé si estás oyéndome
> ¿qué recuerdan los muertos?
> afuera enmudece la lluvia
>
> (bendíceme madre)
>
> (Gervitz 2020, 66)

I see this passage as an intertextual reference to *Pedro Páramo* in which a son's (failed) search for his father and his conversation with others who are buried (and dead) in wet soil is rewritten with female protagonists – the daughter's attempt to enter into contact with her (dead) mother. These references to Mexican and Hispanic American literature in general make visible Gervitz's appropriation of surrounding cultural traditions and literatures in Spanish but still reveal a diasporic, migratory, i.e., not only Mexico-centric context. This approach becomes directly visible in her use of multilingualism in *Migraciones*.[63]

Quite often, the lyrical voice evokes Jewish immigrants' adaptation process to Mexico in the course of time (two generations) and makes clear that there is still a discrepancy between the spoken language at present (Spanish) and the former languages of parents and grandparents that are no longer in use: "cartas en un idish que ya nadie habla" (Gervitz 2020, 57). But despite this reference to missing communication between generations due to the loss of linguistic competence and practice, the poetry volume does indeed contain passages in foreign languages, thus showing its cosmopolitanism and what we could call "world literature" according to Damrosch, who conceives it "not as an infinite, ungraspable canon of works but rather a mode of circulation and of reading [. . .]" (Damrosch 2003, 5).

Apart from Spanish as main language English,[64] Arabic (Sufi), Hebrew and Yiddish are used as embedded languages (cf. Helmich 2016, 20) – the latter two

---

[63] On the different functions of multilingualism in Romance poetry, cf. Helmich 2016, 156–169, 486–487, who stresses the linguistic cosmopolitanism as one of them.
[64] The English-language parts in the volume stem from anglophone poets, as is listed in the glossary (cf. Gervitz 2020, 279), such as US-American Charles Olson, Lorine Niedecker, British William Blake and Irish W.B. Yeats.

mostly in Hebrew letters and therefore not decipherable for those without knowledge of Hebrew. But very often, the Yiddish lines in Hebrew letters are immediately followed by a transcription into Latin letters and then by a translation into Spanish ("*es iz bashert*/ así tenía que ser/ así estaba escrito", Gervitz 2020, 234), thus representing an attempt to keep the language alive, at least as one that is practiced in literature. The volume does not expose the reader to a total experience of foreignness and lack of communication and understanding, as it provides – directly or, at the latest, in the glossary – a translation into Spanish. In general, with its quotes from different languages and prestigious poets it creates a poetic universe far beyond national (linguistic) frontiers and limitations, referring, at the same time, to the diasporic condition of Ashkenazic Mexican literature and highlighting the complex cultural and linguistic background of the author. For Stavans, a US-American citizen with Mexican-Ashkenazic origins, the state of "translationality" and linguistic hybridization without an original text is the chief characteristic and foundational feature of his own (nomadic) existence and may, beyond this, be paradigmatic of the twenty first century lives of Jews and migrants but also of a global literature marked by the intertwinement of various languages and cultures (cf. Stavans 2001, 88; Dolle 2021, 342–343).

It thus becomes obvious that the hegemonic Mexican mestizo ideal, with Spanish supposedly being the only official language and the miscegenation of indigenous and Catholic Spanish people and religions the (only) official cultural model, is put into question. *Migraciones* reveals the hybridity of cultural origins and literary practices on Mexican soil and characterizes itself as part of "world literature", situated in a net of Latin American, Yiddish, Arabic and English-language literatures.

5 Conclusion

Mexican Ashkenazic literature in Spanish became visible in the 1970s due to a stronger heterogenization of Mexican literature and a crisis in hegemonic discourse. Like Sephardic literature in Spanish that appeared in the same decade, the first steps were fictional texts, plays, short stories and novels written in the third-person singular (Berman, Seligson, Laiter) on topics involving colonial encounters and the persecution of the religious Other, female self-discovery, Ashkenazic immigration to Mexico, and traumatic experiences of the Holocaust and the flight from the Nazis. From 1981 to 1991, we see a decade in which Ashkenazic cultural roots, gender differences, and the hybrid Jewish existence are assessed, with the emergence of an extraordinary number of works of life-writing in the first-person singular drawing on collective (Seligson) and individual experiences (M. Glantz, Krauze, Levi Calderón, Berman). With this, it becomes obvious that Mexico in the twentieth and twenty first century is not only a country of mestizos but also a country of immigrants with transgenerational memories of (traumatic) departures, journeys, arrivals, and adaptation to new surroundings, including their feelings of being different or being in the "wrong place" (Mexico instead of the desired and promised land, the USA) and the stories of how the latter were overcome. Personal voices expressing cultural, ethnic and gender differences from mainstream Mexico come to the fore in these autobiographical texts. This trend is continued in the 1990s with works of fiction and poetry that question patriarchal, macho systems and articulate female agency (Sefchovich, Rubinstein, Krauze). Woldenberg's novel from 1992 focusses on entangled history and parallel lives, featuring the violent period in the aftermath of the Mexican Revolution and Ashkenazic immigration to Mexico, a destination experienced as a safe harbor and even a "paradise of senses", in the 1920s. At the same time, Woldenberg's *Las ausencias presentes* is the single work among the corpus of Mexican Ashkenazic literature that most strongly and critically reflects on the problematics of content and (linguistic) form, on how oral history and memories are conveyed in the literary text and if an access to an underlying truth or authenticity is possible in such a construction. Gloria Gervitz with her "obra única" *Migraciones* underlines another option in the attempt to access the past: One of the key scenes is the dialogue between the lyrical I who tries to bring into focus the blurred, vague memories of her own past and her dead mother who wants to be forgotten. So, once memory/memories (of migration) and cultural roots have been written down and explored extensively, forgetting might be an option that enables the author to look ahead, get rid of the weight of the past, and accept and reassert the present corporeal moment, as read the last lines of the volume:

> estoy aquí
> en este instante
> que es todos los instantes
> estoy viva

(Gervitz 2020, 269)

Bibliography

Works Cited

Agosín, Marjorie, ed. *The House of Memory. Stories by Jewish Women Writers of Latin America*. New York: Feminist Press at the City University of New York, 1999a.
Agosín, Marjorie (1999b). "Introduction." In: *The House of Memory*. 1999a. 1–29.
Agosín, Marjorie, ed. *Passion, Memory and Identity: Twentieth-Century Latin American Jewish Women Writers*. Albuquerque: University of New Mexico Press, 1999c.
Agosín, Marjorie. *Invisible Dreamer: Memory, Judaism, and Human Rights*. Santa Fe, New Mexico: Sherman Asher, 2002.
Agosín, Marjorie. *Memory, Oblivion and Jewish Culture in Latin America*. Austin: University of Texas Press, 2005.
Aizenberg, Edna. *Parricide on the Pampa? A New Study and Translation of Alberto Gerchunoff's Los gauchos judíos*. Madrid/Frankfurt a.M.: Iberoamericana/Vervuert, 2015 [2000].

Assmann, Aleida. *Der lange Schatten der Vergangenheit. Erinnerungskultur und Geschichtspolitik.* München: C.H. Beck, 2006.
Assmann, Jan. "Kollektives Gedächtnis und kulturelle Identität." *Kultur und Gedächtnis.* Eds. Jan Assmann and Tonio Hölscher. Frankfurt a. M.: Suhrkamp, 1988. 9–19.
Avni, Haim, Ignacio Klich, and Efraim Zadoff. "Argentina." *Encyclopaedia Judaica.* Vol. 2. Eds. Michael Berenbaum and Fred Skolnik. Detroit: Macmillan, [2]2007. 426–450.
Bachtin, Michail M. *Die Ästhetik des Wortes.* Frankfurt a. M.: Suhrkamp, 2010 [1979].
Balutet, Nicolás. *Poética de la hibridez en la literatura mexicana posmodernista: (Laura Esquivel, Margo Glantz, Luis Zapata).* Madrid: Editorial Pliegos, 2014.
Berman, Sabina. *La bobe.* México D.F.: Editorial Planeta Mexicana, 1990.
Bokser de Liwerant, Judit, and Alicia Gojman de Backal. *Encuentro y alteridad. La vida y la cultura judía en América Latina.* México D.F.: Universidad Nacional Autónoma de México, 1999.
Bokser de Liwerant, Judit. "Dinámicas de inclusión y exclusión. Aproximaciones a la construcción identitaria judía en México." *La memoria archivada. Los judíos en la configuración del México plural.* Coord. Alicia Gojman de Backal. Mexicó D.F.: Universidad Nacional Autónoma de México, 2011. 281–298.
Borsò, Vittoria, Yasmin Temelli, and Karolin Viseneber, eds. *México: migraciones culturales, topografías transatlánticas. Acercamiento a las culturas desde el movimiento.* Frankfurt a.M: Vervuert, 2012.
Burghardt, Tobias, and Delf Schmidt, eds. *Jüdische Literatur Lateinamerikas/Letras judías latinoamericanas = Rowohlt Literaturmagazin* 42 (1998).
Cánovas, Rodrigo. *Literatura de inmigrantes árabes y judíos en Chile y México.* Madrid: Iberoamericana, 2011.
Cánovas, Rodrigo. "Voces judaicas en México y en Chile. Nuevos acogimientos, antiguas huerfanías." *Múltiples identidades. Literatura judeo-latinoamericana de los siglos XX y XXI.* Ed. Verena Dolle. Madrid: Iberoamericana, 2012. 227–242.
Castro, Alan. *Yiddish South of the Border: An Anthology of Latin American Yiddish Writing.* Albuquerque: University of New Mexico Press, 2003.
Castro Ricalde, Maricruz. "*Luz de dos* de Esther Seligson: el modo fantástico y los procedimientos narrativos." *Esther Seligson. Fugacidad y permanencia: "Soy un reflejo de sol en las aguas. . .".* Eds. Luzelena Gutiérrez de Velasco and Ana Rosa Domenella. México D.F.: Universidad Autónoma Metropolitana (Col. Desbordar el canón), 2017. 101–114.
Caufield, Catherine L. "Diversity in the Public Sphere: Works of Fiction by Jewish-Mexican Women Writers." *Women in Judaism: A Multidisciplinary Journal* 12.2 (2015): 1–21.
Cimet Singer, Adina. *The Ashkenazi Jewish Community in Mexico, PHD thesis.* New York: Columbia University, 1992.
Cimet, Adina. *Ashkenazi Jews in Mexico: Ideologies in the Structuring of a Community.* Albany: State University of New York Press, 1997.
Cimet, Adina. "Anatomy of a Legacy: Immigrant Jewish Writers in Mexico." In Lockhart 2013a. 27–41.
Cortina, Guadalupe. *Invenciones multitudinarias. Escritoras judíomexicanas contemporáneas.* Newark: Juan de la Cuesta, 2000.
Cypess, Sandra M. "Mexican and Jewish Identity in *Herejía*, Sabina Berman's Play on Luis de Carbajal and the Inquisition." *Sephardic Horizons* 1.1 (2010): 1–9.
Cypess, Sandra M. "Love Preserves: Ethnicity and Desire in the Narratives of Sara Sefchovich." In Lockhart 2013a. 168–183.
Dabbah Mustri, Herlinda. "Identidad escindida. Autoras judeomexicanas." *Tejidos culturales: las mujeres judías en México.* Coords. Natalia Gurvich, Liz Hamui, and Linda Hanono. México D.F.: Universidad Iberoamericana, 2016. 149–192.

Damrosch, David. "Goethe Coins a Phrase." *What is World Literature?* Princeton: Princeton University Press, 2003. 1–36.
DellaPergola, Sergio. "¿Cuántos somos hoy? Investigación y narrativa sobre población judía en América Latina." *Pertenencia y alteridad. Judíos en/de América Latina: cuarenta años de cambios*. In: Avni Haim, Judith Bokser Liwerant, Sergio DellaPergola, Margalit Bejerano and Leonardo Senkman 2011. 305–340.
DiAntonio, Robert E. *Tradition and Innovation: Reflections on Latin American Jewish Writing*. Albany: State University of New York Press, 1993.
Díaz-Mas, Paloma, and Elisa Martin, Ortega, eds. *Mujeres sefardíes lectoras y escritoras, siglos XIX–XXI*. Madrid: Iberoamericana, 2016.
Diccionario de escritores mexicanos. https://www.iifilologicas.unam.mx/dem/. 7 March 2022.
Dolle, Verena. *Tonschrift: die Romane Robert Pingets in der Spannung zwischen Stimme und Schrift*. Tübingen: Gunter Narr Verlag, 1999.
Dolle, Verena. "La construcción del sí mismo: memoria cultural e identidad en *Las Genealogías* de Margo Glantz." *Literatura – Historia – Política. Festschrift Karl Kohut*. Eds. Günther Maihold and Sonja Steckbauer. Frankfurt a. M.: Vervuert, 2004. 151–162.
Dolle, Verena. "Autorretratos. Las relaciones entre imagen y texto en *Las genealogías* de Margo Glantz." *Múltiples identidades. Literatura judeo-latinoamericana de los siglos XX y XXI*. Ed. Verena Dolle. Madrid: Iberoamericana, 2012. 151–179.
Dolle, Verena. "La Conquista, globalizada, y la metáfora de la frontera en el teatro mexicano contemporáneo." *La representación de la Conquista en el teatro latinoamericano de los siglos XX y XXI*. Ed. Verena Dolle. Hildesheim: Georg Olms Verlag, 2014. 35–57.
Dolle, Verena. "A Case Study in Latin American Literature: Ilan Stavans' *On Borrowed Words*." *Disseminating Jewish Literature – Knowledge, Research, Curricula*. Eds. Susanne Zepp, Claudia Olk, Natasha Gordinsky, Ruth Fine, Kader Konuk, and Galili Shahar. Berlin: De Gruyter, 2020a. 197–204.
Dolle, Verena. "Intercultural Memory and Violence in Jewish Literature." *The Cambridge Handbook of Intercultural Communication*. Eds. Guido Rings and Sebastian Rasinger. Cambridge: Cambridge University Press, 2020b. 302–318.
Dolle, Verena. "Trauma, Conquista y colonia." *Trauma y memoria cultural. Hispanoamérica y España*. Eds. Roland Spiller, Kirsten Mahlke, and Janett Reinstädler. Berlin: De Gruyter, 2020c. 105–124.
Dolle, Verena. "Nachwort: Leben, Sprechen und Schreiben in Übersetzung." Ilan Stavans, *Geborgte Worte*. Herausgegeben und aus dem Englischen und Spanischen übersetzt von Verena Dolle. Leipzig: Hentrich & Hentrich, 2021. 336–347.
Dolle, Verena. "'El calor como colmillo de jabalí': los momentos de llegada del inmigrante entre experiencia histórica y dimensión poética en *Migraciones* de Gloria Gervitz" (in print). Joint issue of *Modern Jewish Studies* and *Cadernos de Língua e Literatura Hebraica*.
Feierstein, Liliana Ruth. "Vorwort." Alberto Gerchunoff, *Jüdische Gauchos*. Ed. Liliana Ruth Feierstein. Berlin: Hentrich & Hentrich, 2010. 7–24.
Flusser, Vilém. *Von der Freiheit des Migranten*. Hamburg: CEP Europäische Verlagsanstalt, 2013.
Foster, David William. "Introduction: Latin American Jewish Cultural Production." *Latin American Jewish Cultural Production*. Ed. David William Foster. Nashville: Vanderbilt University Press, 2009. ix–xviii.
Frakes, Jerold C. "Literature, Jewish." *Encyclopedia Judaica*. Vol. 14. Eds. Michael Berenbaum and Fred Skolnik. Detroit: Macmillan Reference, ^{2}2007. 84–116.
Fuentes, Carlos. *Por un progreso incluyente*. México D.F.: Instituto de Investigaciones Sociales, 1997.
Gerchunoff, Alberto. *Los gauchos judíos*. Buenos Aires: Biblioteca Nacional, Ediciones Colihue, 2007 [1910].

Gerchunoff, Alberto. *The Jewish Gauchos*. Translated by Edna Aizenberg. Edna Aizenberg. *Parricide on the Pampa? A New Study and Translation of Alberto Gerchunoff's* Los gauchos judíos. Madrid/Frankfurt a. M.: Iberoamericana/Vervuert, 2015 [2000]. 35–162.
Gervitz, Gloria. *Migraciones*. México D.F.: Fondo de Cultura Económica, 1991.
Gervitz, Gloria. *Migraciones: poema 1976–2016*. Barcelona: Ediciones Paso de Barca, 2016.
Gervitz, Gloria. *Migraciones*. México D.F.: Editorial Mangos de Hacha/Secretaría de Cultura, 2017.
Gervitz, Gloria. *Migraciones: poema 1976–2020*. Madrid: Libros de la Resistencia, 2020.
Glantz, Margo. *La lengua en la mano*. México D.F.: Editorial Premià, 1983.
Glantz, Margo. *Las genealogías*. México D.F.: SEP (Lecturas Mexicanas), 1987.
Glantz, Margo. *Las genealogías*. Valencia: Editorial Pre-Textos, 2006 [1981].
Glantz, Margo. "Las hijas de la Malinche." *Literatura mexicana hoy. Del 68 al ocaso de la revolución*. Ed. Karl Kohut. Frankfurt/Madrid: Vervuert/Iberoamericana, 1995. 121–129.
Gleizer, Daniela. "México y el refugio judío: el mito de las puertas abiertas." *La memoria archivada: los judíos en la configuración del México plural*. Coord. Alicia Gojman de Backal. México D.F.: Universidad Nacional Autónoma de México, 2011. 141–152.
Gojman de Backal, Alicia, coord. *Generaciones judías en México: la Kehilá Ashkenazi, 1922–1992*. México D.F.: Comunidad Ashkenazí de México, 1993, 7 Vols.
Gojman de Backal, Alicia. *La memoria archivada. Los judíos en la configuración del México Plural*. México D.F.: Universidad Nacional Autónoma de México, 2011.
Goldberg, Florinda F. "Escritores judíos latinoamericanos: residencia en la frontera." *Pertenencia y alteridad. Judíos en/de América Latina: cuarenta años de cambios*. Eds. Haim Avni, Judith Bokser Liwerant, Sergio DellaPergola, Margalit Bejerano, and Leonardo Senkman. Madrid/Frankfurt a. M./México D.F.: Iberoamericana/Vervuert/Bonilla Artigas Editores, 2011. 743–760.
González Boixò, José Carlos and Francisco Javier Ordiz. "La narrativa en México." *Historia de la literatura hispanoamericana. T. III. Siglo XX*. Coord. Trinidad Barrera. Madrid: Cátedra, ²2019 [2008]. 183–214.
Gurvich Peretzman, Natalia. "Ni muy asimilados ni tan aculturados. La juventud judía ashkenazi, su adaptación y organizaciones, 1935–1945." *Sobre el judaísmo mexicano: diversas expresiones de activismo comunitario*. Coords. Shulamit Goldsmit Brindis and Natalia Gurvich Peretzman. México D.F.: Universidad Iberoamericana, 2009. 19–60.
Gutiérrez de Velasco, Luzelena, and Ana Rosa Domenella, eds. *Esther Seligson. Fugacidad y permanencia:"Soy un reflejo de sol en las aguas. . .".* México D.F.: Universidad Autónoma Metropolitana (Col. Desbordar el canón), 2017a.
Gutiérrez de Velasco, Luzelena, and Ana Rosa Domenella (2017b). "Introducción." In Gutiérrez de Velasco and Ana Rosa Domenella 2017a. 13–27.
Hamui, Liz. "Mexico." *Encyclopaedia Judaica*. Vol. 14. 137–146. https://jwa.org/encyclopedia/article/mexico.%20 (17 October 2019).
Helmich, Werner. *Ästhetik der Mehrsprachigkeit: Zum Sprachwechsel in der neueren romanischen und deutschen Literatur*. Heidelberg: Universitätsverlag Winter, 2016.
Huberman, Ariana, and Alejandro Meter, eds. *Memoria y representación: configuraciones culturales y literarias en el imaginario judío latinoamericano*. Rosario: Viterbo, 2006.
Igler, Susanne. "Identidades fragmentadas, fragmentos de identidad: procesos de negociaciones culturales de escritoras judeo-mexicanas." *Negociando identidades, traspasando fronteras: tendencias en la literatura y el cine mexicanos en torno al nuevo milenio*. Eds. Susanne Igler and Thomas Stauder. Madrid/Frankfurt a.M.: Iberoamericana/Vervuert, 2008. 99–110.
Kalechofsky, Robert, and Roberta Kalechofsky, eds. *Echad: an Anthology of Latin American Jewish Writings*. Marblehead: Micah Publications, 1980.

Kalechofsky, Roberta. "Introduction." *Echad. An Anthology of Latin American Jewish Writings*. Eds. Robert and Roberta Kalechofsky. Marblehead: Micah Publications, 1980. vi–ix.

Klahn, Norma. "Genealogías transterradas. Los nuevos territorios de la literatura y la nación: los casos de Glantz y Jacobs in México" In: Vittoria Borsó, Yasmin Temelli and Karolin Viseneber 2012. 225–242.

Kraus, Arnoldo. "Los múltiples rostros de la comunidad judía en México." In: Gojman de Backal 2011. 62–69.

Krauze, Ethel. *Entre la cruz y la estrella*. México D.F.: Corunda, 1990.

Krauze, Ethel. *Convocaciones, desolaciones e invocaciones*. México D.F.: Universidad Nacional Autónoma de México, 2015.

Krauze, Ethel. *Un nombre con olor a almizcle y a gardenias*. Madrid: Ediciones Torremozas, 2018.

Kühner, Angela. *Trauma und kollektives Gedächtnis*. Gießen: Psychosozial-Verlag, 2008.

Laiter, Salomón. *David*. México D.F.: Editorial Joaquín Mortiz, 1976.

Lefter, Alexandru V. "Keeping the identity question open: Jewish, Mexican, Lesbian Subjectivity in Sara Levi Calderón's *Dos mujeres*." In Lockhart 2013a. 203–218.

Levi Calderón, Sara. *Dos mujeres*. México D.F.: Editorial Diana, 1990 (English version: *The two mujeres*. San Francisco: Aunt Lute Books, 1991).

Levi Calderón, Sara. *Vida y peripecias de una buena hija de familia*. México: D.F.: Voces En Tinta, 2015.

Lindstrom, Naomi. "La comunicación profética en *La morada en el tiempo* de Esther Seligson." *Estudios Interdisciplinarios de América Latina y el Caribe* 29.1 (2018): 93–107.

Lockhart, Darrell. "Growing Up Jewish in México. Sabina Berman's *La bobe* and Rosa Nissan's *Novia que te vea*." *The Other Mirror. Women's Narrative in México, 1980–1995*. Ed. Kristine Ibsen. Westport: Greenwood Press, 1997. 159–173.

Lockhart, Darrell, ed. *Critical Approaches to Jewish-Mexican Literature (Chasqui. Revista de literatura latinoamericana*. Special Issue Series No. 4). Tempe, Arizona: 2013a.

Lockhart, Darrell. "Introduction. On the Socioliterary Dimensions of Jewish-Mexican Literature." (2013b). In Lockhart 2013a: 9–26.

Lockhart, Darrell. "Jewish (Men)ority Literature in Mexico." (2013c). In Lockhart 2013a: 254–264.

Lockhart, Darrell. *Jewish Writers of Latin America: A Dictionary*. New York: Routledge, 2013d [1997].

Lomnitz-Adler, Claudio, coord. *1968–2018: historia colectiva de medio siglo*. México D.F.: Universidad Nacional Autónoma de México, 2018.

Loyola, Beatriz. "Género, etnicidad y nación en la narrative (sic) judío-mexicana de Angelina Muñiz-Huberman, Rosa Nissán y Sara Levi Calderón" (2004). *University Libraries Digitized Theses 189x–20xx*. 180.

Maíz-Peña, Magdalena. "Mapping the Jewish Female Voice in Contemporary Mexican Narrative." In Agosín 1999c. 17–34.

Marquet, Antonio. "Los tres frentes de Sara Levi Calderón en *Vida y peripecias de una buena hija de familia*." *Tema y variaciones de literatura* 46 (2016): 147–163.

Martínez Assad, Carlos, coord. *De extranjeros a inmigrantes en México*. México D.F.: Universidad Nacional Autónoma de México, 2008.

Menton, Seymour. *Latin America's New Historical Novel*. Austin: University of Texas Press, 1993.

Menton, Seymour. *Historia verdadera del realismo mágico*. México D.F.: Fondo de Cultura Económica, 1998.

Meyer, Jean A. *La Cristiada: the Mexican People's War for Religious Liberty*. Garden City Park, NY: Square One Publishers, 2013.

Muñiz-Huberman, Angelina. *Tierra adentro*. México D.F.: Editorial Joaquín Mortiz, 1977.

Muñiz-Huberman, Angelina. "Ilán Stavans: la memoria en juego." In Lockhart 2013a. 219–230.

Olsson, Fredrik. *"Me voy pal Norte": la configuración del sujeto indocumentado en ocho novelas hispanoamericanas actuales (1992–2009)*. Madrid/Sevilla: Consejo Superior de Investigaciones Científicas/Diputación de Sevilla, 2016.

Oropesa, Salvador A. "El oxímoron judío y la inteligencia peregrina: *Las ausencias presentes* de José Woldenberg." In Lockhart 2013a. 241–253.

Palomares Salas, Claudio. "Sefardismo y ficción fundacional: *La hija del judío* de Justo Sierra O'Reilly." *Bulletin of Hispanic Studies* 94 (2017): 215–228.

Parra Lazcano, Lourdes. "Esther Seligson, más allá de las raíces." *Mexican Transnational Cinema and Literature*. Eds. Maricruz Castro Ricalde, Mauricio Díaz Calderón, and James Ramey. Oxford/Bern/Berlin: Peter Lang, 2017. 85–100.

Pérez-Anzaldo, Guadalupe. *Memorias pluridimensionales en la narrativa mexicana: las mujeres judeomexicanas cuentan sus historias*. México D.F.: Ediciones Eón/University of Texas at El Paso, 2009.

Pérez-Rosales, Laura. "Anticardenism and Antisemitism in Mexico, 1934–1940." *The Jewish Diaspora in Latin America: New Studies on History and Literature*. Eds. David Sheinin and Lois Baer Barr Sheinin. New York: Garland Publishing, 1996. 183–198.

Pettersson, Anders. "General Preface to the Series *Literary History: A Global Perspective*." *Literary History: Towards a Global Perspective*. Vol. 1. Eds. Anders Petersson, Gunilla Lindberg-Wada, Margareta Petersson, and Stefan Helgesson. Berlin: De Gruyter, 2006. ix–xii.

Poot Herrera, Sara. "Margo Glantz: razón y corazón a un tiempo." *iMex Revista. México Interdiscipliario/Interdiscplinary Mexico* 14.1 (2018): 88–99.

Ran, Amalia. "'Israel': An Abstract Concept or Concrete Reality in Recent Judeo-Argentinean Narrative?" *Latin American Jewish Cultural Production*. Ed. David Wiliam Foster. Nashville: Vanderbilt, 2009. 24–40.

Randeria, Shalini. "Entangled Histories of Uneven Modernities: Civil Society, Case Councils, and Legal Pluralism in Postcolonial India." *Comparative and Transnational History: Central European Approaches and New Perspectives*. Eds. Heinz-Gerhard Haupt and Jürgen Kocka. New York: Berghahn Books, 2009. 77–104.

Rein, Ranaan. "Introduction. New Approaches to Latin American Jewish studies." *Jewish History* 18 (2004): 1–5.

Rubinstein F., Becky. *Hijas de la rueca*. México D.F.: Nautilium, 1994.

Rubinstein F., Becky. *Tres caminos. El germen de la literatura judía en México*. México D.F.: Tucán de Virginia, 1997.

Sadow, Stephen A., ed. *King David's Harp. Autobiographical Essays by Jewish Latin American Writers*. Albuquerque: University of New Mexico Press, 1999.

Schmidt-Welle, Friedhelm. "Von der Identität zur Diversität. Mexikanische Essayistik im 20. Jh." *Mexiko heute: Politik, Wirtschaft, Kultur*. 3. vollständig neu bearbeitete Auflage. Eds. Walther L. Bernecker, Marianne Braig, Karl Hölz, and Klaus Zimmermann. Frankfurt a.M: Vervuert, 2004. 759–786.

Schuvaks, Daniela. "Esther Seligson and Angelina Muñiz-Huberman: Jewish Mexican Memory and the Exile to the Darkest Tunnels of the Past." *The Jewish Diaspora in Latin America: New Studies on History and Literature*. Eds. David Sheinin and Lois Baer Barr Sheinin. New York: Garland Publishing, 1996. 75–88.

Sefamí, Jacobo. "Sueño de evasión y libertad, entre la errancia y la utopía: *La morada en el tiempo*, de Esther Seligson." *Literatura Mexicana* 20.1 (2009): 119–141.

Sefamí, Jacobo. "La herida y el milagro en las *Migraciones* de Gloria Gervitz." In Lockhart 2013a. 155–167 (reprint of an article first published in 2005 in *Confluencias* 20.2 and in Borsò et al. 2012).

Sefamí, Jacobo, and Matthias Lehmann. "Editorial – La experiencia judía en México." *iMex Revista Mexicó Interdiscipliario/Interdiscplinary Mexico* 14.1 (2018): 8–13.
Sefchovich, Sara: *La señora de los sueños*. México D.F.: Aguilar, 2001 [1993].
Sefchovich, Sara. "Historia de una desconfianza." *De extranjeros a inmigrantes en Mexico*. In Martínez Assad 2008. 36–52.
Seligson, Esther. *Otros son los sueños*. México D.F.: Editorial Novaro, 1973.
Seligson, Esther. *Luz de dos*. México D.F.: Editorial Joaquín Mortiz, 1978 (published by Ediciones Sin Nombre in 2002 with the title *Toda la luz*).
Seligson, Esther. *La fugacidad como método de escritura*. México D.F.: Plaza y Valdés, 1988.
Seligson, Esther. *La morada en el tiempo*. México D.F.: Hoja Casa Editorial, 1992.
Seligson, Esther. *Hebras*. México D.F.: Ediciones Sin nombre, 1996.
Seligson, Esther. *Todo aquí es polvo*. México D.F.: Bruguera, 2010.
Senkman, Leonardo. "Parias und Privilegierte: Die jüdischen und spanischen Flüchtlinge in Mexiko und Argentinien 1939–1945. Eine vergleichende Studie." *Alternative Lateinamerika: das deutsche Exil in Zeiten des Nationalsozialismus* (BIA 51). Eds. Karl Kohut and Patrik von zur Mühlen. Frankfurt: Vervuert, 1994. 54–78.
Senkman, Leonardo. "Otra lectura de *La morada en el tiempo* de Esther Seligson." In Lockhart 2013a. 69–86.
Senkman, Leonardo. "Figuraciones y fulguraciones mexicanas en textos de Esther Seligson." *iMex Revista. Mexicó Interdiscipliario/Interdiscplinary Mexico* 14.1 (2018): 100–109.
Seydel, Ute. "Resignificaciones de la figura de la Malinche a partir del multiculturalismo y neocolonialismo." *La representación de la Conquista en el teatro latinoamericano de los siglos XX y XXI*. Ed. Verena Dolle. Hildesheim: Olms, 2014. 15–34.
Shaw, Donald L. *Nueva narrativa hispanoamericana: boom, posboom, posmodernismo*. Madrid: Cátedra, [6]1999 [1981].
Sosnowski, Saúl. *La orilla inminente. Escritores judíos argentinos*. Buenos Aires: Legasa, 1987.
Sosnowski, Saúl. "Margo Glantz: Inscribing Histories." In Lockhart 2013a. 42–51.
Stavans, Ilan. *On Borrowed Words. A Memoir of Language*. New York: Penguin, 2002 [2001].
Stavans, Ilan. *Palabras prestadas. Autobiografía*. Traducción de Lety Barrera. México D.F.: Fondo de Cultura Económica, 2013.
Van Delden, Maarten. "The Holocaust in Mexican Literature." *European Review* 22.4 (2014): 566–574.
Vergara, Gloria. "La memoria y el olvido en la poesía de Gloria Gervitz." *Historia crítica de la poesía mexicana*. T. II. Coord. Rogelio Guedea. México D.F.: Fondo de Cultura Económica, 2015. 163–172.
Waldman, Gilda. "La literatura de la inmigración judáica a México: dos momentos." *Judaica Latinoamericana* 4 (2001): 429–449.
Weingarten-Ruderman, Laura. "Ethel Krauze: Transcending Borders." In Lockhart 2013a. 184–191.
Woldenberg, José. *Las ausencias presentes*. México D.F.: Cal y Arena, 1992.
Zadoff, Efraim. "La disputa en torno al idioma nacional en los colegios judíos askenazíes de México a partir de la década de 1930." *Judaica latinoamericana* 4 (2001): 135–155.

Further Reading

Avni, Haim, Judith Bokser Liwerant, Sergio DellaPergola, Margalit Bejerano, and Leonardo Senkman, eds. *Pertenencia y alteridad. Judíos en/de América Latina: cuarenta años de cambios*. Madrid/Frankfurt a. M./México D.F.: Iberoamericana/Vervuert/Bonilla Artigas Editores, 2011.

Foote, Nicola, and Michael Goebel, eds. *Immigration and National Identities in Latin America.* Gainesville, FL: University Press of Florida, 2014.
Graff Zivin, Erin. *The Wandering Signifier: Rhetoric of Jewishness in the Latin American Imaginary.* USA, New York: Duke University Press, 2008.

Jacobo Sefamí
17 Sephardic Writing in Mexico

Abstract: This chapter provides a concise survey of the diversity of Sephardic literatures in Mexico. The term "Sephardic Jews" is used in the broadest sense possible, including first those who emigrated from Spain to many different regions of the world following the 1492 expulsion as well as subsequent generations who speak Judeo-Spanish and maintain traditions and customs from Spain. The term includes also those who converted to Catholicism but adhered to Judaism, also known as *anusim* or crypto-Jews. Thirdly, it refers to those with origins in a much larger geographical area including North Africa and the Middle East, as this also relates to (Sephardic) liturgy. In Latin America, the Sephardic identity has generally been defined in this broad manner associated with religious practices. This chapter offers representative close readings of four writers: Angelina Muñiz represents the crypto-Jewish experience through her weaving together of the life of Teresa de Jesús and contemporary events. Rosa Nissán portrays the autobiographical journey of a Sephardic woman who challenges a patriarchal society. Myriam Moscona confronts the death of her ancestors from Bulgaria and of the Judeo-Spanish language in a moving novel and experiments with poetry in Ladino. Lastly, Alejandro Tarrab memorializes a family history as ruins of a recollected past.

Key Terms: Sephardic Literatures, Mexico, Angelina Muñiz, Rosa Nissán, Myriam Moscona, Alejandro Tarrab

1 Crypto-Jewish Writing in Colonial Times

Conversos arrived in Mexico among the Spanish conquistadors and colonizers. Their presence is documented through the trials of the Office of the Inquisition. For example, it is known that Hernando Alonso, a member of Cortés's army, was one of the first conversos to be burned at the stake for his Judaizing practices (in 1528).[1] In that history of persecution, contradictions are also visible. When granting, in the capitulations of 1579, Luis de Carvajal the right to conquer and colonize the province of Nuevo León and to bring one hundred men, sixty of them married, King Felipe II instructed officers in Seville not to ask any of them for information (i.e., to verify that they were 'Old Christians').[2] To this day, Jewish presence in the north of Mexico is

---

[1] The Inquisitors in Spain delegated their power to local authorities. The Office established its own quarters in New Spain in 1571.
[2] "To our officers residing in Seville, in the *Casa de Contratación*, I order you to allow captain Luis de Carvajal to return to New Spain, taking with him a hundred men, sixty of whom married farmers with

noticeable, for example, in the city of Monterrey, where the culinary culture of the "cabrito" (lamb) prevails instead of pork. In addition, one scholar has been able to identify certain streets in the center of Mexico City where crypto-Jews lived: Donceles,

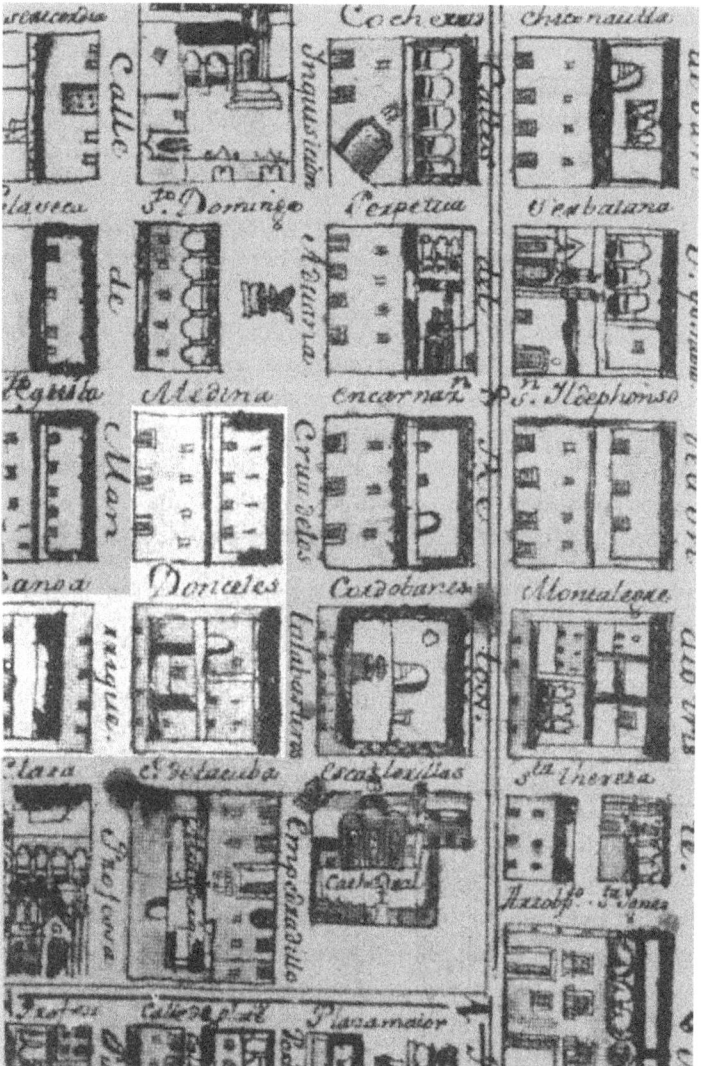

Figure 1: Mexico City in the colonial period, highlighting the area of settlement of crypto-Jews. (Hordes 2005, 47).[3]

---

their wives and sons and daughters, and the remaining soldiers and officers... without asking any of them information of any kind..." (qtd. in Temkin 2008, 86).

3 See the word "Inquisición" written vertically in the middle of the top row of squares and the Plaza Santo Domingo next to it (horizontal).

Tacuba, Manrique (currently Calle de la Palma); the interesting thing is that they were located just two blocks from the Office of the Inquisition, in the current Plaza de Santo Domingo (see Figure 1, and note the area illuminated in the map above).

There were periods of tolerance in which the inquisitors and the rulers "ignored" the practices of the small Jewish community that was so close to them. Persecution also had to do with power and finance. In this regard, the persecution of the Carvajal family is well-documented. It was when conflicts of a political and economic nature arose between the community and the Viceroy Marqués de Coruña in 1589 that the trials, the torture (with the aim of forcing prisoners to reveal other members of the community) and the autos-da-fé began. In addition to the well-known autobiography of Luis de Carvajal the Younger (the nephew of the one who had founded Nuevo León), who called himself Joseph Lumbroso, other trials have also come to light, including that of his sister, Leonor de Carvajal (1595), the records of which were acquired by the Bancroft Library of UC Berkeley. As the records reveal, over the course of more than six months, Leonor was forced to read the poems or sing the songs that were part of the Jewish cultural environment of her family in front of the court.[4] These texts incriminated her. To say, for example, that it is an obligation for the Jews to respect the Sabbath (Shabbat) as a day of rest was enough to justify her condemnation:

> En todas vuestras moradas
> Fuego no ençendáis
> En el sábado que holgáis
> Porque serán condenadas
> Las almas si tal obráis (qtd. in Hamilton 2000, 84)
>
> [In all of your homes
> Do not light a flame
> On the Sabbath of rest
> Because your soul will
> Be condemned for this act.][5]

Thus, the earliest Sephardic writing in Mexico can be found in the records of the trials of the Inquisition. More research on the respective archives[6] is badly needed in order to bring to light not only the literature embedded in these trials, but also the testimonies of the tortured crypto-Jews. Certainly, the story of Luis de Carvajal the Younger and of the whole Carvajal family[7] has had an impact on contemporary writing and film. The testament and autobiography of Carvajal should be considered a seminal work for all of Latin American Jewish literature. Arturo Ripstein's film *El Santo Oficio* (1974) and Sabina

---

4 Cf. Hamilton 2000.
5 Unless otherwise noted, all the translations from Spanish are my own.
6 There are more than 1,800 documents in the *Archivo de la Inquisición*, which forms part of the *Archivo General de la Nación* in Mexico City.
7 Cf. Toro 1944.

Berman's play *Herejía*⁸ (1983) both refer to the story. The portrayal of the auto-da-fé of Mariana de Carvajal (1601) in Diego Rivera's mural "Sueño de una tarde dominical en la Alameda Central" is also important.⁹ The Alameda (now a popular park in downtown Mexico City) was the site where crypto-Jews were burned at the stake.

2 Jewish Acceptance and Immigration

In 1865, during the French Intervention in Mexico, the freedom of religion was proclaimed by Emperor Maximilian, thanks to the previous triumph of Benito Juárez in the War of Reform and the Constitution of 1857, which separated church and state. Although wealthy Jews – especially from France, England and Germany – arrived in Mexico towards the end of the nineteenth century, the largest migration occurred shortly thereafter. First, Sephardim arrived from the different countries that made up the Ottoman Empire, pushed by internal wars and then by the First World War. They were then followed by Ashkenazim from Eastern Europe, particularly Russia, Ukraine, Lithuania and Poland, who were fleeing pogroms and famine.

In the last decade of the nineteenth century and the first two decades of the twentieth century, Jews settled mostly in the downtown area of Mexico City, in the proximity of *La Merced* (a popular and large food market). In 1912, they founded "Monte Sinai", the first public Jewish association in Mexico. At first, they did not differentiate members by their geographic origin, but a decade later, four separate communities were constituted (which are active to this day): 1) Eastern Europeans; 2) Sephardim from Turkey and Greece; 3) Syrians from Damascus; 4) Syrians from Aleppo. A few years after the foundation of "Monte Sinai," Jewish newspapers and magazines began to appear. The first Mexican Jewish literature of the twentieth century was written in Yiddish by Jacobo Glantz, Yitjok Berliner and Moishe Glikovsky.¹⁰ In 1936, Diego Rivera (who declared himself a descendant of conversos) illustrated the edition of Berliner's poems entitled *Shtot Fun Palatzn* (The City of Palaces), which was dedicated to certain slums of Mexico City (including Tepito). Glantz described his sense of belonging to the new Mexican environment, embodying the idea of a 'Neo-Sepharad', a second opportunity for Jews to flourish in a Spanish-speaking country. Previously, the same strategy had also worked for other Ashkenazic writers in Latin America, most notably Alberto Gerchunoff in his foundational novel *The Jewish Gauchos* (1910). Glantz also wrote a long poem titled *Kristobal Kolon* (written in 1934–1938 and published in 1949), in which he portrays Columbus as a converso and some of the other first explorers as Sephardim

---

8 A revised version of the play received the new title *En el nombre de Dios*.
9 Diego Rivera: "Sueño de una tarde dominical en la Alameda Central." https://mexicana.cultura.gob.mx/es/repositorio/detalle?id=_suri:ESPECIAL:TransObject:5bce55047a8a0222ef15d47a (9 March 2022).
10 Cf. Rubinstein 1997.

escaping oppression in search of liberty, just as Ashkenazic Jews were escaping the pogroms of Eastern Europe and finding a home (Jerusalem) in the New World.

The migration to Mexico of a handful of Ashkenazic Jewish writers who were refugees from the Spanish Civil War is also interesting. These include Máximo José Kahn, Max Aub, and the sisters Margarita and Carmen Eva Nelken, the latter of whom used the pseudonym Magda Donato. Kahn was born in Germany and nationalized as a Spanish citizen in 1931. He went to Salonica, Greece, as Spain's cultural consul during the Republic and later moved to France, Mexico (1941), and ultimately Argentina, where he resided until his death. Among other publications, he co-edited an anthology of Judah ha-Levi's writings and authored *Efraín de Atenas* (1950), a novel/chronicle about three generations of a Sephardic family in the context of the Shoah.

3 Contemporary Sephardic Writing

In the 1970s and 1980s, a new generation of Jewish writers emerged, many of them women. The historical novels of Angelina Muñiz (b. 1936), *Morada interior* (1972) and *Tierra adentro* (1977), address the conflicts of crypto-Jews in the hostile environment of sixteenth-century Spain. While the first novel reinvents a historical diary, revealing the intimate inner life of Saint Teresa of Jesus, the second centers on a trip to the Promised Land by a teenager.

Esther Seligson (1941–2010) published sinuous, suggestive, erotic books, recreations of intimate realms and poetic reveries. Her broad philosophical interests led her to explore Greek mythology, Hinduism, Taoism, the I Ching, Sufism and Kabbalah equally. *La morada en el tiempo* (1981) attempts a feminine rewriting of the Torah in which the constants of Jewish persecution are imagined by an "I" that absorbs all previous time and observes the (repeated and endless) history of the diaspora. She wrote this book in Spain, which likely influenced her inclusion of Sephardic themes.

The same generation of Jewish Mexican writers also includes Margo Glantz (b. 1930). Although her oeuvre is very large and covers a broad array of themes, *Las genealogías* (1982) is particularly relevant from a Jewish perspective. This novel reveals a critical, skeptical, playful, irreverent, ironic and scathing attitude, presenting Jewishness as a "motley", a hybrid mixture of traditions. While the first part of the book portrays the Yiddish cultural environment of Eastern Europe, centered on the figure of the author's father (the poet Jacobo Glantz), the second part depicts the Mexican intellectual sphere, centered on the Eastern European dishes of the Carmel, a restaurant in the Zona Rosa.

In *Novia que te vea* (1992) and *Hisho que te nazca* (1996), Rosa Nissán (b. 1939) represents the contemporary Sephardic world in Mexico through the story of a girl (later, a woman) from a Turkish family, incorporating Judeo-Spanish. Jacobo Sefamí (b. 1957) in *Los dolientes* (2004) and *Por tierras extrañas* (2019), Eloy Urroz (b. 1967) in *Un siglo tras de mí* (2004) and Ivonne Saed (b. 1961) in *Triple crónica de un nombre* all deal with Jews of Syrian origin (from Damascus and Aleppo) in their novels. Whether a family saga in Urroz, a portrayal of the dilemmas of three women from different generations in Saed, or a disquisition on mourning rituals in which the orality of Mexican slang is permeated by the Arabic and Hebrew lexicons in Sefamí, these works offer unusual perspectives given the preponderance of Ashkenazic representations.

Although there are also allusions to her Sephardic heritage in her early poetry, Myriam Moscona (b. 1955) produces the best representations of those origins in her later works *Tela de sevoya* (2012) and *Ansina* (2015) (see below). In the genre of the essay, Esther Cohen stands out with her brilliant analyzes of the Kabbalah and Ilan Stavans, who has served as an editor of countless works, has also reflected on Jewish identity on multiple occasions. Other Mexican Sephardic writers include: the prose writers Alberto Buzali Daniel (b. 1949), Vicky Nizri (b. 1954), Victoria Dana, and Teresa Zaga Cohen (b. 1984); the poets Jenny Asse (b. 1963), Alejandro Tarrab (b. 1972), and Salomón Mochón Esses (b. 1985); and the essayist Esther Charabati. Kabbalah is particularly relevant in Muñiz's essays and stories, Cohen's essays and Asse's poetry; family histories or historical recreations can be found in *Vida propia* (Nizri) and *A donde tú vayas, iré* (Dana); Jewish identity in Charabati's essays; the erasure of identity in *Litane* (Tarrab); and an antipoetic playfulness with vague references to Judaism in *Escardillo* (Mochón Esses).[11]

This short inventory is insufficient to establish a detailed guide, but it is a point of departure. I also should note that almost all – perhaps even all – of the Jewish authors mentioned above would refuse to be classified exclusively as Jews or as Sephardim. Their literature is, rather, a good example of the destabilizing, eccentric and irreverent character that they seek as a minority within the canonical literature of Mexico.

As mentioned earlier, since I am not able to provide an exhaustive analysis of the vast production of Sephardic writing in Mexico, I would like to concentrate in the following on four writers and their respective perspectives on Sephardic themes.

4 Crypto-Judaism, Kabbalah, and Exile in Angelina Muñiz

Starting with her first novel *Morada interior* (1972), Angelina Muñiz[12] has created a vast literary work that encompasses various literary genres (the short story, the novel, poetry, autobiography, the essay) and does so from multiple and diverse perspec-

---

[11] To this list, I would add Issac Dabbah Askenazi's work on the history of the Aleppine community in Mexico (1982) as well as the books (with abundant photographs) that trace the history of the overall Jewish presence in Mexico (Bokser de Liwerant), of Aleppine Jews (Hamui de Halabe), and of Damascene Jews (Smeke Darwich et al.).

[12] She published her first books under the name Angelina Muñiz. Later books were published under the name Angelina Muñiz-Huberman.

tives.¹³ All of her writings have focused on the experience of exile, combining the exile of refugees from the Spanish Republic as a consequence of the Civil War with the millennia-old Jewish diaspora, including the expulsion from Spain in 1492 and the (false) conversion to Catholicism.

Muñiz was born in Hyères, in the Provence region of France, to Spanish parents in 1936, after the Civil War had started. The family would move briefly to Cuba in 1939, and later to Mexico in 1942. Muñiz grew up believing that the return to Spain was imminent. A family secret was revealed to her when she was six or seven years old:

> One afternoon, on the balcony of my first home in Mexico, in Tamaulipas 185, my mother confessed to me that her origin was Jewish. That is, my maternal family had preserved this tradition for ever and ever. Her Judaism was already very diluted and she combined it with very diluted forms of Christianity. My grandmother Sebastiana knew a few words of Castilianized Hebrew. She had passed on to my mother, so that she would in turn pass it on to her children, a sign that would identify them as Jews. Such a sign is called *shaddai* and consists of joining the little and ring fingers and the middle and index fingers, with a separation in the middle. Later, I also learned that my mother's last name, Sacristán, apparently so Christian, was nothing but the translation of the Hebrew *Shamash* [caretaker in the synagogue]. Based on this discovery, reinforced by my mother's readings of the Bible, I took on the task of studying Judaism. When, many years later, I studied the works of Américo Castro at the university, the panorama of my origins became clearer. (Muñiz, *De cuerpo entero* 1991, 20)

Shaddai is one of the names of God. The word is alluded to in the *Sefer haZohar* (the Book of Splendor), and the three patriarchs of Judaism- Abraham, Isaac, and Jacob- are seen in its configuration.¹⁴ The word begins with the consonant *shin* [שׁ], which also refers to the Jewish heritage through another word that begins with the same letter: *Shemah*. This word, in turn, represents the main prayer of the liturgy: *Shemah Yisrael Adonai Elohenu Adonai Echad* (Hear O Israel, the Lord is our God, the Lord is one). The *shin* is also written on the parchment in the mezuzah, which contains the *Shemah* prayer to bless and protect the house. Thus, in the gesture made with the fingers of the hand, which alludes to the letter *shin*, there is an encrypted message to

---

13 Muñiz is a prolific writer. Among her many books, I should mention: *Tierra adentro* (1977), *El mercader de Tudela* (1998), *La burladora de Toledo* (2008), *En el jardín de la Cábala* (2008), *El sefardí romántico* (2014). She has received numerous awards including the Premio Nacional de Lingüística y Literatura (2018).
14 The *Sefer haZohar* reads, in the fragment related to Creation: "The letter Shin (שׁ) then entered and . . . defended the value of the initial of the divine word Shaddai, which is a Shin; it is convenient, she said, that the initial of the holy name Shaddai be used to carry out the Creation of the world. God replied: Indeed, you are worthy, good and honest. But the counterfeiters will use you to affirm their lies, associating you with the letters Kof and Resh to form the word Sheker (lie) . . . even if you are honest, oh letter Shin!, since the three patriarchs will meet in you, it is not convenient that I use you to carry out the Creation of the world, since you will often be associated with the two letters Kof and Resh that belong to the side of evil" (Zohar 1994, 27–28).

indicate belonging to a people, employed in order to preserve their identity. The fact that this is passed from generation to generation within the crypto-Jewish communities further emphasizes the idea of a secret language, almost as if it were a silent whisper testifying to its own prohibition (consider the sound "*sh*" or the *shin* in the word *sheket*, which means "silence" in Hebrew).

Morada interior (1972), Muñiz's first work of fiction, is presented as the "secret diary" of Teresa Sánchez de Cepeda y Ahumada (better known as Teresa de Ávila or as the mystic Santa Teresa de Jesús, 1515–1582), the granddaughter of Juan Sánchez, a declared converso from Toledo who moved to Ávila and changed his last name to Ahumada after being subjected to the persecution of inquisitors. Muñiz uses Teresa's *Las moradas del castillo interior* (The Interior Castle, written in 1577) and *Vida de Santa Teresa de Jesús* (her autobiography, ca. 1567) as paratexts.

The book can be analyzed within the context of the "new Latin American historical novel", representing, according to some scholars, its first instance in Mexican literature. The author takes the liberty to include vastly different time periods, mentioning (then) current events such as the moon landing and including anachronistic perspectives on the Spanish Civil War and the Shoah, which both serve as major references for the protagonist. Muñiz herself explains: "the central figure, Saint Teresa, became a contemporary self, without roots, without faith, in search of identity, in exile and in separation, at the center of a silent eroticism" (*De cuerpo entero*, 34).

From the beginning, the central idea of the novel is to explore the conflicts between celestial and earthly love, Christian and Jewish faiths, Spanish and Mexican identities, the public and the private spheres. That is, it captures the dilemma of the double self, the secrecy that accompanies crypto-Jews throughout their lives. Although there are no direct references to her Jewish background in the historical writings of Santa Teresa, Muñiz employs the idea of the "secret diary", in which the protagonist is able to freely express her innermost thoughts and feelings. The Inquisition is regarded as a transhistorical institution that persecutes and tortures people: "In the Nazi concentration camps, 1939–1945. In Spain, 1939–197... In Greece, 196... In Brazil, 196... In Biafra, 196... In My Lai, 1968 [...]" (*Morada interior*, 31).

Muñiz also includes Sephardic songs that have been passed down orally (in anticipation of her anthology *La lengua florida*). The novel abounds in the protagonist's references to her carnal love for her cousin. She describes the sexual act in an explicit way: "Am I not to let him make me get on the horse and wrap his hand around my waist and tire me like he tires the horse and then lay me down on the sweet grass and spread his black velvet cloak and lay me on it and one by one take off my clothes and, naked and white, run through my body until I become his in a fury of joy and pleasure?" (*Morada interior*, 53). There are also various passages in which she declares her desires for other men, including priests and confessors. At the same time, on the spiritual side, and almost concurrently with the carnal love, there are references to the "four stages of prayer" included in the book *Vida de Santa Teresa de Jesús*, which establish a guide to uniting with God. These culminate in a reflection on that unity: "You give everything, immense You, who make the union possible in the sweetest and most pleasant way. How to explain that joy that makes you forget joy? How to understand what is not understandable? How could words describe the ineffable, the ecstasy, the total immersion in that abyss that is Your love?" (*Morada interior*, 58). The culmination of both carnal and spiritual love is found on the next page, where the interlocutor "you" is, simultaneously, God, cousin, and an Israeli soldier (a reference to the desire to make *aliyah*, to be in Jerusalem at the Wailing Wall, in order to fulfill the spirit and erase the idea of exile that permeates the character). The notion of Jewish mysticism is lacking in this early book by Muñiz. She will later publish a book about Kabbalah.

Angelina Muñiz and Esther Cohen are the two main writers to convey and disseminate Kabbalistic studies in Mexico. Muñiz published *Las raíces y las ramas. Fuentes y derivaciones de la Cábala hispanohebrea* [The Roots and the Branches. Sources and Derivations of the Hispano-Hebrew Kabbalah] (1993) and Esther Cohen wrote *La palabra inconclusa (siete ensayos sobre cábala)* [The Inconclusive Word (Seven Essays on Kabbalah)] (1991) in addition to editing a compilation of studies on Kabbalah and deconstruction in the journal *Acta Poética* (1990, UNAM).

Muñiz's work on Kabbalah has two parts. In the first one, she deals with the "Roots", concentrating on the Spanish-Hebrew Kabbalists; in the second, she focuses on the "Derivations" of the Kabbalah in Christian thought and literature, i.e., in authors such as Ramón Llull, Marsilio Ficino, Pico della Mirandola, Juan Luis Vives and Miguel de Cervantes. That is, her book emphasizes the notion of Spain or the Iberian Peninsula (as well as the French Provence) as the place from which the great heritage of Jewish mysticism emanates. Although it is conceived as a work of dissemination (rather than original research), Muñiz articulates the structure of the study as if it were tracing the roots of her own origin, as if she were trying to draw the many faces of her past. This is what she affirms in the prologue: "It may happen that, because we cannot find the book that solves the doubts and concerns that afflict us, we decide to invent it" (*Las raíces y las ramas* 1993, 9). While *Las raíces y las ramas* serves to trace a theoretical genealogy, Muñiz's anthology *La lengua florida* (1989) forms the link to the literary praxis of the Sephardic heritage, drawing from a great Jewish Spanish "family" beginning in the medieval Golden Age (with literature written mostly in Arabic or Hebrew). It also encompasses the oral tradition, in which the fervor for a culture is demonstrated. And it adds appendices on the conversos and their experiences in New Spain, as if to mark the route to the new lands.

5 Against Sephardic Patriarchal Conventions: Rosa Nissán

The contemporary Sephardic world in Mexico is portrayed in Rosa Nissán's *Novia que te vea* (1992) and in its sequel *Hisho que te nazca* (1996)[15] through the story of a girl (and later, woman) who is the daughter of a Turkish mother and a Persian father. From the beginning of the first novel, the excitement lies in the establishment of a different way of perceiving Mexican-ness, i.e., through the inclusion of the Jewish variant. The novel also points out the differences between the diverse groups of Jews. Above all, the distinction between Iberian Jews and Arab Jews is highlighted. In Mexico, Jews from Syria separated, due to the antagonism between their places of origin, into two communities: the "Shami", from Damascus, and the "Halabi", from Aleppo. The mother of the protagonist says in reference to them: "Son atrasados y pesgados . . . a tu tía nunca la dejaron salir sola, traían maestro a la casa . . . ¡Uf!, ni amigas le desharon tener" ["They are backward and annoying . . . your aunt was never allowed to go out alone, they brought a teacher to the house . . . Ugh! They did not even allow her to have friends"] (Nissán 1992, 27).[16] There is also criticism of the father's family, who migrated from Iran to Israel/Palestine and then to Mexico. The mother continues: "Estos de Persia son el mismo shishit. ¿Cuál es la diferencia?, tu abuelo tiene a tu papa de esclavo . . . Yo, en Estambul iba a las mejores escuelas, mos daban las clases en francés. La familia de mi mamá sí es de categoría" ["The ones from Persia are the same *shishit*. What is the difference? Your grandfather treats your father like a slave . . . In Istanbul, I went to the best schools, they gave us classes in French. My mother's family is classy"] (Nissán 1992, 27).

Although the distinction between Sephardim and Mizrahim does not exist in Mexico in the same manner as in Israel,[17] Nissán's books insist on portraying Syrians as backwards, more religious, and misogynistic. The marriage between the aunt of the protagonist and a man from the Aleppo community serves to illustrate the differences: Syrians are more devout and remain faithful to their customs. Disputes run throughout the two novels, with recriminations voiced from both sides. Uncle "Halabi" says that "en el knis [sinagoga] donde él va, la oración se termina más tarde, porque es más

---

[15] The two novels were translated by Dick Gerdes and published together as *Like a Bride. Like a Mother* (University of New Mexico Press, 2013). Nissán has also published other books including *Las tierras prometidas* (1997), and *Los viajes de mi cuerpo* (1999).
[16] I also quote the original Spanish so that people who know the language can appreciate the inclusion of Judeo-Spanish in the novels. "Pesgados" means irritating or annoying in Judeo-Spanish.
[17] The Guatemalan American Sephardic writer Victor Perera emphasizes in his book *The Cross and the Pear Tree* the Sephardic identity as distinct from that of conversos or Jews from North Africa and the Middle East. He claims that his great-grandfather signed his will with the Hebrew letters *samech* and *tet* (ST), the initials of *Sephardi Tahor* ("true Sephardi"), implying his distance from both Eastern European Jews and converts (Perera 1995, 117).

completa. Lo dice recalcando que su judaísmo es superior al nuestro, porque según él no llevamos la religión como debe ser, y en shabat subimos en coche . . . dice que cómo es posible que haya micrófono en nuestro templo, que es utilizar electricidad y eso es pecado, y que los rabinos turcos son religiosos a su conveniencia" ["in the knis [synagogue] where he goes, the prayer ends later, because it is more complete. He says this emphasizing that his Judaism is superior to ours, because according to him we do not treat religion as we should, and on Shabbat we drive the car . . . he asks how it is possible that there is a microphone in our temple, which is to use electricity and that is a sin, and that the Turkish rabbis are religious at their convenience"] (Nissán 1992, 36–37). Nevertheless, the novel makes it clear that with the various groups living in the same city, intermarriages start to appear. The culmination of *Novia que te vea* is precisely the marriage of the protagonist to Lalo, a man with a Turkish father and a Syrian mother. But, curiously, instead of resolving the conflict, the differences accelerate it and, eventually, lead in *Hisho que te nazca* not only to divorce, but also to the separation of the protagonist from the Jewish community and her integration and assimilation into non-Jewish society.

The distinction between Sephardic Jews and Syrian Jews was reformulated in the adaptation of the novel to the cinema, in the film *Like a Bride*, which was produced and directed by Guita Schyfter with a screenplay by Schyfter herself, Rosa Nissán and Hugo Hiriart. Here, the dramatic tension is raised by means of the dialogue between two friends, one Sephardic and the other Ashkenazic. Two scenes in particular clearly allude to the differences between the two communities. In one of them, at the request of the protagonist to study painting, the Sephardic mother and her friends complain that the Ashkenazic friend (Rifke Groman) "puts ideas into her head". The Ashkenazim are the ones who transgress the tradition: "las idishicas son todas atavanadas" ["the Yiddish girls are all crazy"], says one of the women. Rifke's mother, on the other hand, claims in the following scene that "los sefaraditas son atrasados, *schlepers*, son ignorantes" ["the Sephardic Jews are backward, *schlepers* [stupid], they are ignorant"]. However, the father defends them by continuing the phrase ironically – "ignorant like Maimonides and Baruch Spinoza" – to which the mother reacts by reducing Sephardic wisdom to a moment in the past, unrelated to the circumstances of the present: "that was a long time ago".

Nissán challenges the prevailing patriarchal system not only among Syrian Jews but also among Sephardim. In *Hisho que te nazca*, the protagonist's mother defends her son-in-law against her daughter, who has acquired a better economic position through the marriage but is thinking of leaving her husband anyway. The mother emphasizes the risks that her daughter would face if she attempted to assimilate into non-Jewish society: "¿*Atavanada* estás? ¡Cómo vas a *deshar* este modo de marido! Tienes casa, coche, dos *jismichías*, un hombre, todo el mundo te respeta, vives como una reina. Anda, boba no seas, tú hazme caso, *arrecóyete* otra vez, te vas a meter en *velás*. *Velás* con *parás*. Él va a tomar una *jovencica* soltera y hasta dote le van a dar; otra va a gozar de lo bueno que ganó contigo, porque cuando tú lo *tomates*, rico no era" ["Are you crazy? How are you going to leave your husband! You have a house, a car, two maids, a man, everyone respects you, you live like a queen. Come on, don't be silly, you pay attention to me, get yourself together or you're going to get into trouble. You will get problems with money. He is going to take a young single woman and her parents will even give him a dowry. Another woman is going to enjoy the good things that he gained with you, because when you married him, he was not wealthy"] (Nissán 1996, 141).[18]

The paradox in Nisan's books is that although her protagonist rebels against the conditions of the patriarchal tradition of Sephardic Judaism, it is precisely this world that gives meaning and appeal to her literature. Thanks to their portrayal of Sephardic customs and forms of daily life, Nissán's novels are an important contribution to the understanding of a more diverse and multicultural Mexico. In fact, Nissán is the first Mexican writer to introduce Judeo-Spanish into her texts. Moreover, she does this in a singular manner. While the mother and older family members in her novels use Ladino, the protagonist and her generation of Sephardic Jews employ standard Mexican Spanish. Nissán is also keen on orality and recreates the idioms, for example, of lower-class people such as domestic workers. The dialogues between the older (Judeo-Spanish) and younger characters (Mexico City Spanish) acquire, in this regard, a sense of novelty and originality.

6 Dialogues with the Dead: Myriam Moscona

The daughter of Sephardic Bulgarian parents who immigrated to Mexico before her birth, Myriam Moscona[19] carries with her, as an inheritance revealed through her writings, the sensation of displacement, of transcending latitudes, of looking longingly towards the future and at the same time going back and remembering the past.

---

18 Nissán is not the only woman to deal with the conflicting attitudes towards Sephardic (and, more generally, Jewish) patriarchal culture. The Argentine writer Liliana Mizrahi has expressed the dilemma as follows: "Being a Jewish and Sephardic writer is a complex experience ... My need to be a transgressive woman is getting stronger every day, every morning, when the men pray: 'Thank you, my God, for not having made me a woman' ... The Sephardi, the ancestor that inhabits me is also part of my Judaism that forces me to perpetuate myself in a static model. I fight to save myself as a Jew from the Jew that torments me. The one who believes that to be you have to repeat. The crystallized Jew. The one that says: I am the echo of an echo of an echo ... This internal struggle between the ancestral Jew and the transgressor makes explicit not only the struggle between two ways of relating to the Jewish tradition, but also between two aspects of Judaism." (Mizrahi 1990, 19–21).
19 Moscona is a well-known poet who has published numerous books including *Las visitantes*, *El que nada*, *Negro marfil*, and *La muerte de la lengua inglesa*. She has received several awards and prizes including the National (Mexican) Poetry Prize of Aguascalientes (1989), a Guggenheim Fellowship (2006), and the prestigious Xavier Villaurrutia Prize (2012).

It is the realm of the past to which she constantly returns, be it in the "Elegy" on the death of her mother or in the "Carta de naturalización" ["Letter of naturalization"], a poem written in the voice of the *apátrida* (stateless) in search of the roots that are lost in history. These roots are the rituals and liturgies, the ghosts that re-emerge in *Las visitantes* and later in the eroticism and the sacredness of *El árbol de los nombres* and *Vísperas*, although always with a skeptical, mocking tone that emerges from a powerful and critical female voice.

Moscona also felt the need to look back at the language of her grandmothers the Judeo-Spanish that is interspersed in her modern Spanish. She does this as if the language were the personification of a remote past returning from its ashes, the death that confirms agony but at the same time exhales a "feeling of promise and expulsion that remained like a breath thrown in the glass", a breath of life. *Tela de sevoya* (*Onioncloth*) (2012) is everything at once:

1) a book that, viewed as the entirety of its individual sections, manages with great complexity to represent the individual, family and collective voices of the Sephardic diaspora;
2) an autobiographical novel that recounts the adventures of a girl who lost her father at eight years of age ("Focal Length");
3) a travel diary of an adult woman who returns to her roots in Bulgaria and other Sephardic countries ("From the Travel Diary");
4) an informative manual on the exile of the Jews expelled from Spain and their dispersion throughout the world ("Paperweight");
5) a series of personal stories that gathers diverse voices of the diaspora ("The Fourth Wall");
6) a collection of poems about evanescence ("Kantikas Songs", which will later be integrated into *Ansina*); and
7) a ghostly account of the dreams and inner obsessions of a woman who talks to the dead ("Windmill").

The novel revolves around two fundamental circumstances: a) the female protagonist loses her father at the age of eight; b) she spends her childhood and puberty (from eight to fourteen) sharing a room with her grandmother. Gradually, she loses the rest of her family as well (her grandmothers and her mother) along with the language that they spoke. Later, she travels to Sofia and Plovdiv (Bulgaria) and to other sites of the Sephardic diaspora such as Thessaloniki (Greece), Istanbul and Izmir (Turkey), as well as Jerusalem and Madrid – all in search of traces of her past and heritage. Judeo-Spanish appears insistently (as in "Paperweight"), as if it were a mirror of the dispossession and the disappearance of the author's ancestors. But, at the same time, it works like a time machine, a return to the remote past, to the expulsion from Sepharad: "Konservamos kozas espanyolas ke vozotros ya tenesh olvidadas i pedridas. Podemos darvosh pedasikos del pasado en el presente" ["We preserved Spanish things that you have already forgotten and lost. We can return fragments of the past to you in the present"] (Moscona, *Onioncloth* 2012, 95).[20]

The conflictual relationship between the narrator/child and her grandmother is the most shocking, terrifying, and disturbing part of the book. Moscona breaks with the nostalgic cliché of the conventional grandmother and depicts an ugly, unpleasant, malicious, moody woman who represents traditional values:

> We sleep in the same room. When she takes off her clothes, I'm amazed by the long baggy underwear that covers half her body. Later she loosens the upper part and when she unfastens the armature of her brassiere, her gigantic breasts spill out, reaching almost to her waist. They seem to me like skin-covered watermelons with no flesh. She doesn't have the slightest modesty, yet she criticizes me for showing my legs with those miniskirts she detests [. . .] my flabby, sour faced abuela, [I know] her unpleasant smells and the stained underwear she takes off in front of me without the least concern. [. . .]// She is a hefty woman. She had surgery on one of her eyes and the patch is off-kilter; the gap is visible. I am afraid of her threats; she always tells me that her misfortunes are going to transfer to me. The opening where her eye should be is so very deep.
> (*Onioncloth*, 71, 112)

Thus, a dispute between the past and the present, between Ladino and Spanish, is presented, emphasizing changes in the role of women in society. The protagonist and her grandmother end up cursing each other. In a key scene, "an old woman lying in her bed turns her face to the left, lets out a sonorous bit of stomach gas, tells her granddaughter that she does not forgive her (*para una preta kriatura komo sos, no ai pedron/for an evil little girl like you there is no forgiveness*) and dies" (*Onioncloth*, 12). The protagonist will carry that burden with her, that responsibility of being a "last creature" of the Sephardic link, and the book will constitute a restitution, a way to compensate for the loss of her ancestors, her language, her culture. Since the grandmother is the main interlocutor in the story, it is through her that the past, childhood and language are recovered. This occurs by means of the *byervos i las dichas* (words and sayings) that emerge in the memory of the narrator and, somehow, compensate for the loss with their simple evocations.

The dialogue between one language and the other, between the world of the past and the world of the present, sometimes becomes humorous and, simultaneously, chilling. See, for example, this dialogue between the narrator and her grandmother: "– What time is it, abuela? / —*Ocho kere vente. Twenty to eight.*/ —Don't talk like that. What time is it, abuela? / —*Ocho kere kinze. Quarter to eight.*/ —You don't know how to tell time. What time is it, abuela? / —*Nunka ni no, hanum. Las ocho son. La ora de dormir. We can agree to disagree, hanum. Eight it is. Time to go to sleep.* / —I'm not tired. / —*A echar, hanum. A pishar i a echar. Time to lie down, hanum. To go to pee, and then to lie down.* / —No, I want to watch TV./ —*Deja esos maymunes. Leave those talking monkeys.*/ —No, why? Just so you know: my other grandmother lets me watch cartoons. / —*Le dire a tu*

---

[20] I use the English translation of the novel by Jen Hofer and John Pluecker (2017).

madre. I'll tell your mother./ —So, tell her./ —*Le dire a tu padre. I'll tell your father.*/ —My dad already died. / —*Yo avlo kon el kada noche. Kada noche me dize ke esta arraviado kon ti. I talk with him every night. Every night he tells me he's angry at you.*/ —Liar, he's not mad at me./ —*No se dize menteroza. We don't call people liars.*/ —You're crazy! / —*Me vas i a mi matar. A todos matatesh tu. You are going to kill me too. You killed everyone.*/ —I didn't kill anyone./ —*Lo matatesh a tu padre por muncho azerlo araviar.* You killed your father by making him angry so often" (*Onioncloth*, 8).

Later, Moscona and Sefamí co-edited *Por mi boka* (2013), an anthology of writings in Judeo-Spanish. We wanted to trace, in broad strokes, the trajectory of the Judeo-Spanish language from its beginnings in the diaspora, after the expulsion from Spain, to the most recent work from the twentyfirst century. Rather than representing each of the variants of the language that emerged in different regions and throughout history, we limited ourselves to a small selection that offered a perspective of early religious literature and then concentrated on contemporary works. Our intention was not to compile a comprehensive anthology, but rather to present some texts that illustrate styles compatible with contemporary writing.

With *Ansina* (2015), Myriam Moscona manages to give freshness to the Judeo-Spanish language (although this is paradoxical). She displays a critical attitude that demystifies the tragedy of the diasporic journey – just as she had done by transgressing the cliché of the grandmother in *Tela de Sevoya* – in addition to questioning the very genre of poetry. She is thus the first antipoet of Ladino, the first to incorporate a playful, avant-garde use of language, the first to refer to issues unrelated to the experience of exile, and the first to use humor.

Ansina contains thirty poems, each divided into five sections of irregular length. Although it is supposed to be a book entirely written in Judeo-Spanish, Spanish does not completely disappear. It is present in the "Exordium", in the "Spelling Clarifications", in all the epigraphs (except one), and as a counterpoint – that is, in minimal phrases embedded in a dialogue – in thirteen of the thirty poems. That is to say, Moscona avoids the "purity" of a single language and prefers dialogism and hybridity. As a Mexican and as a Sephardi, Moscona has learned to combine her worlds, to mix languages, even to reinvent them (words such as "empolvaduras", "morideros", or "eskrivideros" are not commonly used in Ladino and it could be said that they are linguistic inventions of the author).

"Eskrivir de amor o sensya" [To Write of Love or Science] could serve to explicate the poetics of the entire book. Rather than being limited to an oral tradition that collects romances, sayings or songs as a vehicle to rediscover family heritage, Ladino should also be used for worldly, scientific and other matters:

la lingua sirve   [language serves
para el rakonto   to count
de estreyas   stars
para studiar   to study

insektos	insects
para apanyar	to trap
ladrones	thieves
i kriyar ijos	and to create children
i pajaros	and birds
...	...
(para limpiarse	(to clean
los dientes	teeth
la lingua	language
se guadra mui	is kept way
detrás).	back)]

(Moscona, *Ansina* 2015, 54–55)

It is for this reason that the book deals equally with family memory ("Empolvaduras"/ Dusty Matters), with the dead who are grieving ("De Morideros"/Deadlands), with science ("De Sensya"/On Science), with the (Kabbalistic) Creation of the universe ("De Kreaziones i Undimientos"/Of Creations and Sinking) and with writing itself ("De Eskrivideros"/Of Writinglands).

With its critical attitude, *Ansina* mocks itself; it inherits the Dadaist nihilism, calling into question the very concept of art or poetry. At the same time, it maintains a certain musicality in the back and forth of prose and verse and in its use of simple colloquial language (often with notes in Spanish). In "Papel de kuatro" [Paper in Four], the desire to write, the effort to preserve the old, and the idea of resistance to the imminent death of the Ladino language are called into question. Instead, the poem uses humor to mock the solemnity with which the lyrical genre is usually associated: "Eskrivo una kantika kada diya (I write a poem each day)/*es mentira* (*it's a lie*)/ la dovlo en kuatro (I fold it in four)/i esos papeles (and those papers)/kon eskritura antikua (with old writing)/a la perra sirven (are for the dog)/para pishar en eyos (to pee on):/*es verdad* (*it's true*) (*Ansina*, 64).

Ansina is a book that is fully embedded in the contemporaneity of Mexican poetry, in a line that continues the erudite antipoetry of Gerardo Deniz. Simultaneously, it manages to revive the musicality of the Ladino language inherited from the fifteenth century and to place it in a dialogue with humor, uneasiness, the interweaving of languages, and the nihilism of our time.

7 Sephardic Ruins and Burial: Alejandro Tarrab

He who seeks to approach his own buried past must conduct himself like a man digging. Above all, he must not be afraid to return again and again to the same matter; to scatter it as one scatters earth, to turn it over as one turns over soil.

Walter Benjamin

In *Litane* (2006), Alejandro Tarrab[21] explores a poetics of dispossession that is carefully constructed, incorporating citations from various authors. It is a reflection on loss and perhaps on the crisis of an identity that has endured annihilation and to which one returns, drawn by an inheritance at once buried and alive. *Litane*'s initial epigraph (from Paul Celan) underscores this sense of abandonment. It is a prayer of desolation, an expression of horror at the scene of a crime, a supplication and a complaint in the form of an inverted psalm: "It was blood, it was/what you shed, Lord. // It shined. // It cast your image into our eyes, Lord./Eyes and mouth stand so open and void, Lord./We have drunk, Lord./The blood and the image that was in the blood, Lord. // Pray, Lord./We are near" (trans. John Felstiner). Such a litany (indeed, *litane* means litany) cries out as a collective plea formed from the ashes of pain.

And it is just this notion of a sensorial poetry in dialogue with a vast tradition that obtains in the first section of *Litane*, which, above all, investigates a family's past. It is through the residue, the ruins, the sensations evoked in the mind of the author that an understanding of ancestry can be pieced together. In "the family (remembrance XV–VIII–XXV)" an old photograph is reproduced from a bar mitzvah that took place on 15 August 1925.

Figure 2: "The Family (remembrance XV-VIII-XXV)", included in *Litane*.

---

21 In addition to *Litane*, Tarrab has published *Degenerativa* (2010), *Maremágnum* (2013), *Ensayos malogrados: resabios sobre la muerte voluntaria* (2016), and *Caída del búfalo sin nombre: ensayos sobre el suicidio* (2017).

The child at the center of the photo is most likely accompanied by his mother (to his right) and his father (possibly to his left). Among the predominantly male crowd, four men seated in the front row with ample beards stand out; most likely they are the rabbis who officiated the ritual. One can conclude from a later poem that this is the bar mitzvah of Jacobo Tarrab Bazbaz, which took place in Damascus, Syria, only a few months before he left for Mexico. *Litane* pays special attention to this ancestor (the author's grandfather) in poems that trace his migratory voyage and in verses that reflect upon his death and burial. Instead of the nostalgia one might derive from a family photo, the poem points to an origin known to be lost, as if this were an image of a hidden, irrecoverable episode that elicits only pain and a sense of isolation:

> the family congregates
> extends its slender black thread
> out to an expanse it doesn't know
> *the blood and the image that was in the blood, Lord.*
>
> it makes sense to draw back delicately
> from the remembrance-tree
> *the tallit with its five knots in each one of eight filaments*
>
> (Tarrab, *Litane* 2006, 35)[22]

If the poem in which the photo of the bar mitzvah appears asked "essential questions" culled from a wound or a suture, knowing full well that answers are impossible, here the genealogical tree plants an atomization, a dilution, a loss of that point of departure. The quote from Celan, echoing the book's epigraph, sets the scene in a most desolate place, with the blood of God consumed by the horror of tragedy. It is this return to tradition (the tallit that recalls the five books of the Torah and the eight days preceding circumcision as per the covenant between Abraham and God) that cuts off the past and dissolves the possibility of going back; the "remembrance-tree" that grows, perhaps in rhizomes, threads that don't bind, family sketches that will disintegrate with time. "Notes on the margins," *Litane*'s final section, closes with an aphorism that frames the volume's *ars poetica*: "Maintain each work as a precious amputated being/ as the persistent prosthesis/with which to see the sky" (*Litane*, 173).

In the same way, it is interesting to note that Jacob Tarrab Maslatón (1843–1923), who shares the name of the author's grandfather and was perhaps in turn his grandfather or great-grandfather, was one of the most important rabbis in Damascus during the final period of the Ottoman Empire until its collapse. The photo thus indicates a privileged heritage, since the author's ancestors represent a tradition carried out by the family for centuries. Jacob Tarrab Bazbaz himself served as Head of Mount Sinai School in Mexico City for thirty years, thus linked to the Talmud (the commentaries

---

[22] I quote from the English translation of the book by Clare Sullivan (2017).

and oral discussions about the Torah that were taught in the school) and at the same time to its perpetuation through teaching (the literal meaning of *Talmud*).

In *Litane*, at least three poetic manifestations of Jacobo Tarrab stand out: his duty to put on the tefillin (in connection with the bar mitzvah of the previous poem), his migration from Damascus to Mexico, and the ritual of his burial. In "gradual canticle (jacobo tarrab bazbaz hangs upon the perpetual wind)", the ritual of connecting with the Divinity through the symbolism of two small boxes that bear the name of God offers a positive, sacred precept:

> take this tefillah and circle your left arm seven times
>   near your soul
> place this other on your forehead root of understanding
> both come from a pure animal
> here are the letters of emanation of creation of formation
>   of realization
>   yud hei vav hei   (*Litane*, 45)

To bear the name of God near one's heart and mind guarantees a certain spiritual peace. But the text also reveals the other side: a prelude to death, a prayer of lamentation, of an anguish that gnaws at the speaker:

> and you will raise your eyes to the plains
> and you will walk through fire as I do now
>
> *adonai*
> *i enter the razor sharp edge of the waters*
> *wounded to the depths*
> *like the darkest fish*
> *i break away*   (*Litane*, 47)

The poem "saga" recreates a migratory voyage. My research has confirmed that it reproduces fragments of an interview from an oral history archive that was collected toward the end of the 1980s. The interviews documented the stories of Jews of various origins who had immigrated to Mexico. During his interview, Jacobo Tarrab was asked about experiences ranging from his childhood in Damascus to his travels, his time in Mexico, and his work in the community. In the poem (also written in prose without punctuation), the voices of the interviewer and of Jacobo Tarrab himself alternate without any typographical distinction: "where did you sail for when you left damascus? to beirut to beirut he went with your uncle what was your uncle's name? isaac isaac and his last name? . . ." (*Litane*, 71). In this way, the poem creates echoes, as if to stress the words, to confirm names and places, recalling a voyage that would prove irreversible. But the author weaves himself into the poem as well, skillfully inserting another, more poetic narrative that transforms the journey into a spiritual experience touched by the everyday: "we turned out the light and a candlestick created splendor on all the walls tiny stars more terrible than in the sky because we could reach them they made us vulnerable *i can say* we touched them with the same contraction as when you brush by it for the first time with a stretching out" (*Litane*, 71). The text ends with dispersal, death and oblivion. The question "remember?" is repeated twice and is answered with "not much" and "they already died," in reference to the descendants of Jacobo Tarrab's travel companions on the boat.

In "onen", the ancestor is buried, and with him that marvelous origin. In the Jewish tradition, *onen* refers to someone who is mourning a loved one before performing the *keriah*, the tear in his garment that sets him apart in his pain. (After that, the person is considered *avel*, a mourner.) But *onen* distinguishes an individual still subject to the shock of death, an experience that culminates right before the burial ceremony:

> at the burial
> [they are submerged like egyptians
> without their tiny felt boat]
> one of his hands fell
> long and transparent
> as the utterance from those skies
> as the other side
> order you depart
> pitiless
>
> (*Litane*, 49)

Almost like a copy or a mirror, there is another poem in the last section of the (first edition of the) book that is also called "onen", complementing the previous one. This time written in prose, it again shows how the body sinks into its shroud to enter into a dialogue with the I, the *onen*, who proclaims in alarm "i could sense his hand as it came loose from the sheet." He concludes with a gesture that is typical in Jewish cemeteries and that reaffirms the possibility of further life for the soul: "i placed a stone's eternity upon your tomb" (*Litane*, 189).

It should be noted that the family heritage of the poetic voice does not only contain hidden Jewish origins but also a Catholicism that has been buried as well. In "second errors in reasoning," a religious void is emphasized through a logical sequence that leads to *nothing*, pronounced in a place where one practices communion: "i take communion *christ* in silence/i take communion *christ* without having confessed my sins because i am a jew// i say *jew* like saying *atheist* like saying *nothing* in confession/on the playground of this school// 'cause it's a shame to kneel down in the confines of the sacraments without religion/'cause it's a shame to scatter like a plague for the sick/i pronounce *nothing* in prayer as an antidote/*sick* i pronounce *plague* in this eucharist [emphasis from the original]" (*Litane*, 121). More than cultural hybridity or religious syncretism, what stands out is precisely the annulment of dogma, even though *Litane* is permeated by a kind of spiritual melancholy, an anguish born of the crisis endured by the subject.

That break with Jewish family origins is emblematic of a personal genealogical inquiry, but in a larger arena this fracture is amplified, as if in expansive waves, to the author's own Mexican identity or to the territory of the word, of language and of writing.

8 Conclusion

This essay has examined the production of Sephardic writing in Mexico. It began with a historical overview before focusing on contemporary writing, as most Sephardic writing in Mexico started to appear in the late twentieth century. As there is an abundance of books, I was unable to give a detailed account of each of them. The second part of the chapter presented works by four authors in more detail, providing insight into the kinds of approaches to Sephardic culture respectively exemplified.

I would summarize Sephardic writing in Mexico through the following topics:
1) Historical accounts of crypto-Jews as provided by Luis de Carvajal the Younger or appearing in Inquisition trials; contemporary revisions of those stories told by Ashkenazic and non-Jewish authors;
2) The experience of conversos in Spain and in the diaspora as it appears in various books by Angelina Muñiz;
3) The dissemination of Kabbalah studies by Angelina Muñiz; scholarship on contemporary issues regarding otherness by Esther Cohen; Kabbalistic notions in Muñiz's fiction and in Jenny Asse's poetry;
4) Incorporation of Judeo-Spanish in combination with Spanish, as seen in Rosa Nissán's novels and Myriam Moscona's fiction and poetry;
5) Incorporation of Arabic and Hebrew idioms representing the orality of Syrian Jews in Jacobo Sefamí's *Los dolientes*;
6) Feminist approaches to patriarchal structure in Nissán's works;
7) Portrayals of the customs of mourning rituals as they apply to the Syrian community;
8) Migration stories in Vicki Nizri and Victoria Dana;
9) Travel narratives that center on the return to places of origin in Moscona's *Tela de sevoya* and Sefamí's *Por tierras extrañas*;
10) Confrontations with the death of ancestors in Moscona and Tarrab; consciousness of a moribund Judeo-Spanish language;
11) Antipoetry that questions the clichés associated with diasporic stories of sadness and nostalgia.

I encourage readers to continue studying any of the books mentioned. As can be seen in the above, Sephardic writing in Mexico is rich and stimulating. It offers different perspectives on diaspora, language, memory, and migration, pointing to various nuances vis-à-vis Mexican literature and culture.

Bibliography

Works Cited

Bokser de Liwerant, Judit, coord. *Imágenes de un encuentro: la presencia judía en México durante la primera mitad del siglo XX*. Mexico City: UNAM, Tribuna Israelita, Comité Central Israelita de México, Multibanco Mercantil Probursa, 1992.

Dabbah Askenazi, Isaac. *Esperanza y realidad. Raíces de la comunidad judía de Alepo de México. Fundación de la Sociedad de Beneficiencia "Sedaka y Marpe."* Mexico City: Libros de México, 1982.

Hamilton, Michelle. "La poesía de Leonor de Carvajal y la tradición de los Criptojudíos en Nueva España." *Sefarad* 60.1 (2000): 75–94.

Hamui de Halabe, Liz, coord. *Los judíos de Alepo en México*. Mexico: Maguen David, 1989.

Hordes, Stanley M. *To the End of the Earth. A History of the Crypto-Jews of New Mexico*. New York: Columbia University Press, 2005.

Mizrahi, Liliana. *Las mujeres y la culpa. Herederas de una moral inquisidora*. Buenos Aires: Grupo Editor Latinoamericano, 1990.

Moscona, Myriam. *Tela de sevoya*. Mexico City: Lumen, 2012.

Moscona, Myriam. *Ansina*. Mexico City: Vaso Roto Ediciones, 2015.

Moscona, Myriam. *Tela de sevoya. Onioncloth*. Trs. Jen Hofer and John Pluecker. Los Angeles: Les Figues Press, 2017.

Moscona, Myriam, and Jacobo Sefamí, eds . *Por mi boka. Textos de la diaspora sefardí en ladino*. Mexico City: Lumen, 2013.

Muñiz, Angelina. *Morada interior*. Mexico City: Joaquín Mortiz, 1972.

Muñiz, Angelina, ed. *La lengua florida. Antología de literatura sefaradí*. Mexico City: Fondo de Cultura Económica, 1989.

Muñiz, Angelina. *De cuerpo entero*. Mexico City: Universidad Nacional Autónoma de México, 1991.

Muñiz, Angelina. *Las raíces y las ramas. Fuentes y derivaciones de la Cábala hispanohebrea*. Mexico City: Fondo de Cultura Económica, 1993.

Muñiz, Angelina. *El canto del peregrino. Hacia una poética del exilio*. Sant Cugat del Vallès: Associació d'Idees Gexel, 1999.

Nissán, Rosa. *Novia que te vea*. Mexico City: Editorial Planeta, 1992.

Nissán, Rosa. *Hisho que te nazca*. Mexico City: Plaza y Janés, 1996.

Perera, Victor. *The Cross and the Pear Tree. A Sephardic Journey*. Berkeley: University of California Press, 1995.

Rubinstein, Becky. *Tres caminos. El germen de la literatura judía en México*. Mexico City: Ediciones el Tucán de Virginia, 1997.

Smeke Darwich, Jacobo, Sofia Mercado Atri, Gina Sacal de Abut, and Alberto Rayek Balas, eds. *Historia de una Alianza*. Mexico: Alianza Monte Sinai, 1999.

Tarrab, Alejandro. *Litane*. Tr. Clare Sullivan. Cardboard House Press, 2017.

Temkin, Samuel. "Luis de Carvajal and his People." *Association for Jewish Studies Review* 32. 1 (2008): 79–100.

Toro, Alfonso. *La familia Carvajal; estudio histórico sobre los judíos y la Inquisición de la Nueva España en el siglo XVI, basado en documentos originales y en su mayor parte inéditos, que se conservan en el Archivo General de la Nación de la Ciudad de Mexico*. Mexico City: Editorial Patria, 1944, 2 Vols.

Zohar. *Libro del Esplendor*. Traducción: Esther Cohen y Ana Castaño. Selección, prólogo y notas: Esther Cohen. Mexico City: Conaculta, 1994.

Further Reading

Gardner, Nathanial. *Though their Eyes: Marginality in the Works of Elena Poniatowska, Silvia Molina, and Rosa Nissán*. Bern: Peter Lang, 2007.

Medina, Manuel. "Imagining a Space In-Between: Writing the Gap Between Jewish and Mexican Identities in Rosa Nissán's Narrative." *Studies in the Literary Imagination* 33 (2000): 93–102.

Stavans, Ilan. "On Separate Ground." *Passion, Memory and Identity. Twentieth-Century Latin American-Jewish Women Writers*. Ed. Marjorie Agosín. Albuquerque: University of New Mexico Press, 1999. 1–16.

Saúl Sosnowski
18 Jewish Literatures from the Río de la Plata Region (Twentieth Century)

Abstract: After considering the rubric 'Latin American-Jewish literature,' this article traces the regional historical-cultural context, and considers literature produced by Jewish writers on both sides of the Río de la Plata: Buenos Aires and Montevideo. Without limiting writers to any single category, as most navigate across all these motifs, the analysis arranges and reviews texts written by the 'founders' (Gerchunoff, Tiempo, Grünberg, Eichelbaum), and those who address Israel-Diaspora relations (Rozitchner, Aguinis, Feierstein); the underside of official history (Bortnik, Rivera, Verbitsky, Viñas); issues of identity, integration, acculturation, assimilation and political militancy (Chejfec, Costantini, Dujovne Ortiz, Goloboff, Cozarinsky, Kohan, Orgambide, Rozenmacher); humor (Blaisten, Shua, Steimberg, Szichman) and poetry by Futoransky, Gelman, Kamenszain, Pizarnik, Szpumberg and Toker). On the Uruguayan side, the emphasis is on Porzecanski, and on Rosencof's militancy.

Key Terms: Latin American-Jewish literature, Río de la Plata Region, Integration, Political militancy, Minority discourse

> It is not your responsibility to finish the work of perfecting the list, but you are not free to desist from it either.
> Variation on a saying by Rabbi Tarfon, *Pirkei Avot*, 2:21

1 A Liminal Note

"This is a complex subject. To what extent do Jewish writers who write in Spanish, in a language other than Yiddish or Hebrew, make Jewish literature?" With this opening salvo, Juan Gelman (1930–2014) opened his talk on "Lo judío y la literatura en castellano" (Gelman 1992, 83) at a meeting of Latin American Jewish writers held in Buenos Aires in 1992. I shall address this, and related issues in the coming pages.

The sheer volume of works under the allocated rubric, make a comprehensive analysis impossible. A mere catalog, and certainly a discussion of all who merit closer attention, would exceed the allocated space. Guides and dictionaries included in the bibliography provide a more complete listing. I do not disregard the importance of many who are not included here, whether Jewish motifs are the driving force of their work, or whether such motifs are less obvious or absent from their texts. Perhaps without exception, all who are included here stride with varying degrees of (dis)comfort a line that pulls together being Jewish with being Argentine/Uruguayan. To provide a working document (always a work in progress), I emphasize a select number of authors, and in some cases of texts that, in my opinion, will serve to anchor future studies, including analyses of writers, poets and playwrights who, while also Jewish, do not ostensibly include the multiplicity of their being on a written page. The sequence, while at first chronological, follows a thematic route to weave together a composite view of Río de la Plata Jewish writing.

To focus on the Río de la Plata region instead of on "Argentina and Uruguay," underscores various significant issues when approaching literary/cultural production. Opting for the more commonly used 'national literatures' label, instead of the current one, would have sidelined or ignored the diversity found within formal borders. Diversity, a ceaseless and ongoing process, has resulted from the mix of the surviving original inhabitants with successive migrations, mostly from Europe, Africa and, now increasingly, from Asia. National boundaries, particularly when resulting from postwar arrangements and treaties, do not accurately define nor fully account for cultural markers. In this region, the literature produced in the capitals that face the river have a lot more in common than the literature that flows out of Buenos Aires with that of, for instance, Argentina's northern provinces or the far reaches of Patagonia. A parceling out according to cultural zones, moreover, calls into question canonical systematizations that respond to academic comfort rather than to the realities on the ground.

A second element to be considered is, of course, *What is Jewish Literature?* as Hana Wirth-Nesher titled her edited volume and discussed in her introduction. In a different context, Albert Memmi wrote that "To be a Jewish writer means by necessity to express the Jewish condition, to present it to others or, even to a certain degree, to make others accept it" (Memmi 1966, 157). For our purpose, we'll consider authors who self-define as such, regardless of any rabbinical dictum. To underscore such an approach, I quote Alicia Dujovne Ortiz (1940), author of, among others, the quasi biographical novel *El árbol de la gitana* (1997), who wrote in a personal message: "Yes, I consider myself a Latin American-Jewish writer, with a line in between, as you say, because I touch Jewish themes and I have a sense of humor that is not far from being Jewish, but my mother was goy and for me it is important to be loyal to both branches. The term 'Jewish-Latin American' seems to me an adequate definition; we are Jews in a particular way that I identify myself with. Moacyr Scliar is neither Bashevis Singer nor Philip Roth, but all three are Jewish, each in his own way. I declare myself 'judeolatinoamericana,' in some cases, when I know they'll understand what I mean." As she now, once again, lives in France, she added: "In France I would rarely say it because they have no idea what it means. Not even French Jews understand it; they think it is too exotic. I wonder: is the combination itself 'exotic'?" And she added: "Whether the combination, or either or both of the two terms, we are led to conclude that I'm seen as an 'other,' an 'outsider,' one who does not fit a common ethnic/national canon: a definition, as it were, of what for many a Jew is in the world."

Several aspects of Dujovne Ortiz's comments echo throughout other authors as they also challenge, disregard or totally ignore the Orthodox definition of who is

Jewish. Not less significant is that beyond self-defining as Jewish, though born out of a mixed marriage, and with due respect for both sides, she concluded her comment with 'what is a Jew.' The Jew as 'other,' as 'outsider,' emerged when thinking of her status in France, where she sees herself at least as a double minority. This issue lies at the core of a minority's national status, as Albert Memmi eloquently argued in 1957 for Algerian-French Jewry.

The context in which the authors and texts to be commented upon developed, would have required a more extended analysis of key historical and political events. These include, among others, immigration policies throughout the nineteenth and twentieth century, and particularly during the 1930s and 1940s; demographic and organizational considerations to explore the various immigrant communities, including the diversity within Ashkenazi and Sephardic constituencies; anti-Semitic ordnances and attacks ranging in Argentina form early on in the twentieth century through the 1990s; the impact of the creation of the State of Israel; Perón and the ongoing sequels of Peronism; life under authoritarian regimes and during democratic governments in both Argentina and Uruguay; the dictatorships of the 1970s and early 1980s and the role played by Jewish writers and other intellectuals during that time and in the reconstruction of civic democratic culture. The writers to be addressed now were certainly affected, whether in country, in exile or both; several of them also left their imprint on major issues and events on both sides of the Río de la Plata. While it is senseless to consider a ratio of population size – about 10 to 1 in the Jewish communities of Buenos Aires and Montevideo – to cultural production and aesthetic value, it is necessary to keep it in mind when considering the volume of Jewish literatures produced on the Argentine side of the river when compared with the significant but smaller number of Uruguayan works.

2 Founding Letters

It is widely acknowledged that any consideration of Latin American-Jewish literature, not just of a regional enclave, begins with Alberto Gerchunoff (1883–1950) and his defining *Los gauchos judíos* (1910).[1] Written as an immigrant's contribution to the centennial celebrations of Argentine independence, it served as Gerchunoff's literary application for citizenship and promptly became a point of reference for the

---

[1] A revised edition appeared in 1936: *Los gauchos judíos: nueva edición corregida y aumentada*. Buenos Aires: Gleizer, 1936. The additions were "El médico milagroso" and "El candelabro de plata." Edna Aizenberg translated the first edition and in her introduction pointed to changes in the two editions (11–29). Argentina's Biblioteca Nacional edition includes an introduction by Perla Sneh (9–33). Senkman dedicated several chapters to him in his *La identidad judía en la literatura argentina* (1983).

developing mass of texts adjudicated under the "Argentine/Latin American-Jewish literature" rubric.

From the elegiac to the dramatic, and from hopeful to collapsing dreams, *Los gauchos judíos* speaks of the safety net provided for Jews from the Pale by a planned agricultural project. It also addresses, albeit at times indirectly, the core issues of identity, acculturation and survival in alien settings. Gerchunoff has been the subject of probing and controversial analyses by scholars such as Leonardo Senkman and Edna Aizenberg. In her recent biography, Mónica Szurmuk offers a comprehensive view of Gerchunoff's life and work. Without diminishing his patriarchal standing within the corpus at hand, when considering his acculturation and integration it is necessary to point out that, as Senkman underscored, that he remained conspicuously silent during early attacks on Jews, while both Jewish and non-Jewish colleagues spoke out against nationalist outbursts. Also, that while legitimizing the incorporation of Jewish-Argentine writers into the national fabric, his ideological path was at times set by his association with the newspaper *La Nación*.

Even a cursory look at some of the topics Gerchunoff embraced, for instance, in *El cristianismo pre-cristiano* and *La jofaina maravillosa: agenda cervantina* (1924), reflect his choice of the Hispanic legacy as an entry point into the then dominant ideology. Throughout his life he embraced Cervantes as Gerchunoff claimed for himself a Spanish-language lineage that had been wrested from him in 1492. He did so again in his *Retorno a Don Quijote* (1951); saw Argentina in almost messianic terms in pages gathered for the posthumous *Argentina, país de advenimiento* (1952), and spoke with a more nostalgic and even morose voice in *Entre Ríos, mi país* (1950). At some point in the 1930s, perhaps uncomfortable with the various tendencies at play in his country's literary circles, Gerchunoff threw himself fully into journalism. The rise of European Fascism (he was more circumspect of the home-grown variety) and Nazism, and later the establishment of the State of Israel became his major concerns. He did emphasize, however, that Israel was a haven for Jews in distress and not for someone defined by Argentine citizenship who spoke the language of the Argentines.

Gerchunoff discovered – as many others do to this day – that to self-identify does not suffice; what also matters is how one is seen and named by others. At first enthusiastically, and through the 1930s and early 1940s under a more sobering gaze, he served as a model of successful Jewish integration into the cultural, and even the political, establishment. He was, unquestionably, though born elsewhere, an Argentine from the province of Entre Ríos, and for many, an Argentine-Jew.

Los gauchos judíos provided directed vignettes that aimed not just at becoming part of a new nation but also at cultural *mestizaje* – an issue that has been debated in Latin America and the Caribbean since the nineteenth century and appears reflected in the various names used for the region ("Indoamérica" being one of them). At the same time, as changes in the national economic structure were reducing the need for the skills associated with the gaucho, the "gaucho" was becoming a national myth and thus a useful image for Gerchunoff's goals.

The Jewish agricultural settlements in the Argentine provinces floundered, and with them the flawed dream that lay at their foundation. Meantime, Buenos Aires had quickly developed into a major Jewish cultural center. As integration into the national Spanish-speaking culture was taking place, Yiddish literature, press and theater were also flourishing. Yiddish theater was performed in Argentina as early as 1901; three Yiddish newspapers already existed in 1898; by 1914 there were 40 Jewish periodicals. The 1917-founded *Kolonist Kooperator* was directed at the Jewish colonists while *Di Presse* and *Di Yiddishe Zeitung*, founded a year later, at urban Jews concentrated mainly in the capital, along with the Spanish-language *Vida nuestra*, launched almost at the same time. Sociedad Hebraica Argentina, with Gerchunoff as an icon, was established in 1922, and in 1929, cognizant of local intellectual resources and expertise, YIVO opened a branch in Buenos Aires. The renaissance of the Hebrew language as a secular expression of Jewish culture was also transferred to Argentina: in 1921 *Habbimah Haivrith*, the first Argentine Hebrew periodical, began publication, and in 1938 *Darom* (significantly named 'South') appeared. It is noteworthy that Jewish publications in Spanish have existed since 1911; the Sephardic magazine *La luz*, for instance, has been published continuously since 1935 (it continues online). *Davar*, sponsored by the Sociedad Hebraica Argentina, achieved national and, indeed, international, prominence as a journal of Argentine and general, not solely Jewish, literature and culture.

Jews were making a literary mark on the national scene. In addition to Alberto Gerchunoff, at least two additional authors from that generation must be remembered: Samuel Eichelbaum (1894–1967) and César Tiempo (née Israel Zeitlin, 1906–1980). Eichelbaum's plays were to solidify a multiple sense of belonging and national acceptance. Whereas the 1926 play *El judío Aarón* spoke openly of Jewish roots, it was *Un guapo del 900* (1940), which was often staged and made into a film by director Leopoldo Torre Nilsson, that, by capturing one of Buenos Aires' idiosyncratic types, signaled the playwright's seamless entry and acceptance into mainstream Argentine culture.

A noted poet and prominent screen writer who blended Jewish motifs into the Buenos Aires landscape, the Ukranian-born César Tiempo followed a different path vis-à-vis Gerchunoff. Firmly ensconced in Buenos Aires ("porteño") culture, he showed others what an urban Jew feels, celebrates and is, and he did so both through poetry and on the stage. Several of César Tiempo's books are anchored in the Sabbath: *Libro para la pausa del Sábado* (1930) earned him the Municipal Prize in Poetry; three years later he published *Sabatión Argentino: antiguas y nuevas donas para la pausa del sábado* with a foreword by Rafael Cansinos Assens – whom Borges claimed as his own entry point into Judaism – and Enrique Méndez Calzada. In 1938 he published *Sábadomingo* and in 1955 *Sábado Pleno*. Ideologically, he also differed from Gerchunoff, feeling closer to the progressive and working-class politics of writers identified with "Boedo" – a counterpart to the more avant-garde group "Florida," named for the then elegant downtown street. With Fascism on the rise in Europe as well as locally, he publicly called out anti-Semitism during the "Infamous Decade" – a period that extended from 1930 into the 1940s that began with a coup against a democratically elected government and had successive authoritarian presidents. In 1935 he denounced in an open letter the anti-Semitic novels published by Hugo Wast, penname of Gustavo Martínez Zuviría, then director of the National Library. A prolific script writer for both theater and film, César Tiempo also collaborated with a number of newspapers and magazines. During Perón's government (1946–1955) he served for several years (1952–1955) as director of the literary supplement of the newspaper *La Prensa*, an expropriated daily that had previously (and again after Perón's overthrow) reflected the ideology of the Argentine oligarchy. During the Peronist return to power, he directed the Teatro Nacional Cervantes (1973–1975). In the context of this presentation, it is worth mentioning that he was an early supporter and co-founder of the Argentine-Uruguayan "Sociedad Amigos del Libro Rioplatense," a publishing venture that brought to light authors from both sides of the Río de la Plata.

To the Sabbath-based poetry aimed at those outside the Jewish community, it is important to add at least two plays, *El Teatro soy yo* (1933) and *Pan criollo* (1938), that addressed integration into the country. By 1942 César Tiempo had earned the National Award for Theater and three years later the Municipal Award for best movie script. A major figure across genres and in politics, César Tiempo is also remembered for an early publication under the name Clara Beter: *Versos de una. . .*, one of the earliest denunciations of the white slave trade. What is particularly noteworthy is that its publication in 1926 coincided with the release of *Don Segundo Sombra*, by Ricardo Güiraldes (1866–1927), and of *El juguete rabioso* by Roberto Arlt (1900–1942). A triad, as it were, of the rural pastoral scene and of the vanishing gaucho's values, in Güiraldes' case, and of the transformative decay that was already falling upon the seamier side of the city in Arlt's opening salvo. The Güiraldes-Arlt-Tiempo sequence, noted also by David Viñas (1927–2011) provides not just a glimpse (anticipatory in Arlt's novels) of the changes that were about to fall upon Argentina with the 1930 coup, but also a nuanced look at the immigrants' integration into the national scene. Still, the 1919 pogrom known as "The Tragic Week" had been a sobering reminder that, in spite of Gerchunoff's desire to see Argentina as the new Zion, 'the promised land' was, as it continues to be everywhere in the Diaspora, a work in progress.

"Identity" has remained a major motif in Latin American-Jewish literature, as much if not more than among other hyphenated cultural communities. Integration-acculturation-assimilation have been sustained concerns. Among the elders in the Argentine landscape, Carlos M. Grünberg (1903–1968) captured it in "Un diferente y su diferencia" (Toker 1999, 291–294): the title of a speech he delivered at the SADE (The Argentine Writers Association) on November 23, 1965, as part of the presentation of his book *Junto a un Río de Babel* (1965), which includes a poem on Gerchunoff (Grünberg 1965, 258) – a book that Jorge Luis Borges (1899–1986), who had written a glowing presentation of his earlier *Mester de judería* (1940), considered ideologically controversial and therefore refused to endorse it. A well-known lawyer, philologist and respected poet who contributed to the avant-garde magazine *Martín Fierro*, Grünberg translated the Passover *Haggadah* (*Narración de la Pascua*, 1946), directed the magazine *Heredad* (1946–1947), and was a vocal advocate for the nascent State of Israel. Florinda Goldberg pointed out that Grünberg, along with Lázaro Liacho (née Liachovitsky, 1896–1969) and, as we have seen, also César Tiempo, addressed in their poetry what it meant to be perceived as Jews within Argentina's national culture (Goldberg 1993, 77–79).

3 On Israel

The establishment of the State of Israel, along with local developments, called into question Gerchunoff's earlier assertion of Argentina as Zion – a recurrent motif for his and subsequent generations increasingly anchored in an Argentine identity, whether hyphenated or not. In this regard, it should also be noted that, *generally*, Israel's existence, though an influential force at the community level, has not been a major motif in Latin American-Jewish writing. This is not due to neglect, ignorance or denial; it was a tacit acknowledgement of living and producing within national cultural boundaries on issues integral to the country's history and dramatic transformation. The 1967 Six-Day War, however, brought forth a series of debates within Argentine intellectual and leftists circles that led León Rozitchner (1924–2011) to publish *Ser judío* (1967). In it he forcefully engaged Jewish leftists who reneged of one of their defining components to assert nationality. He spoke of that segment of Argentine Jewry that may have thought that non-Jews would act along similar lines and perceive Jews just as "regular Argentines" and not primarily as an anomaly in the national body politic and in what others described as the "true Argentine" social fabric. Against the echoes of anti-minority sentiments (and anti-immigration rhetoric dating back to at least the 1902 restrictive 'Laws of residence'), and especially when they are internalized by Leftist Jews, Rozitchner insisted on citizenship as a birthright. He spoke of the need of every Jew to reject and refute any argument that attempts to preempt him/her from the territory that, by virtue of nationality, is inherent to their being.

Rozitchner's both dated and timely text underscores that over half a century after a hoped for total integration into the country, there was still a sense of unease in sectors of the Jewish community, and that this was due to both local issues as well as to events that took place elsewhere. Just a few years earlier, the capture of the final solution's architect Adolf Eichmann (1960) in a Buenos Aires suburb, led to a resurgence of antisemitism – a dormant and never extinct component in Argentina's social fabric. While periodic anti-Semitic outbursts have not been uncommon, oftentimes linked to events in the Middle East, charges of the so-called 'dual loyalty' were not regularly raised, nor did such a specter prevent writers from addressing life in Israel.

Marcos Aguinis (1935), for instance, whose work is steeped, though not exclusively, in Jewish motifs, addressed the Palestinian issue in one of his earlier novels, *Refugiados: crónica de un palestino* (1969, though written several years before the 1967 war). From a drastically different and critical point of view, and without this being his sole dominant interest, Ricardo Feierstein (1942) incorporated his experience in Israel and the Yom Kippur War (1973) in his novel *El caramelo descompuesto* (1979), which became part of the trilogy *Sinfonía inocente* (1984).

4 Uncovering Layers

Of greater significance than Israeli politics and communal establishment concerns, is the roster of authors who tackled Argentine history, particularly of 'founding fathers' and patriots during the country's seminal stages, in order to unveil images and provide versions that allow for a rewriting of past events or, at the very least, for reinterpreting the role played by both venerated and berated figures. Many of David Viñas' novels, plays, and essays are structured along those lines. Among them novels such as *Los dueños de la tierra* (1958), *Hombres de a caballo* (1967), *Jauría* (1974) and *Cuerpo a cuerpo* (1979); plays that include *Lisandro* (1971) and *Dorrego* (1974), and the various studies in the constantly revised and updated *Literatura argentina y realidad política*.

Andrés Rivera (née Marcos Ribak, 1928–2016), a one-time textile worker, and a long-time militant journalist, is another prime example of a similar sustained effort with novels such as *La revolución es un sueño eterno* (1992), which earned him the National Prize for Literature, *La sierva* (1992), *El Farmer* (1996) and *El manco Paz* (2003). *Kadish* (2011), Rivera's last novel, reveals through his well-known character Arturo Reedson, not just numerous autobiographical references, which he had advanced in his 1982 *Nada que perder*, but an insight into what cuts across many other Latin American-Jewish authors. A dialectic cross section, as it were, of the composite elements of one who is cognizant of rightful nationality and, at the same time, of being Jewish as a mark of difference. Echoing, as we shall see, Rozenmacher's self-definition, Arturo, son of Mauricio or Moisés (Moishe, Moishele) Reedson, recognizes himself as "judío y bolchevique y porteño" (Rivera 2011, 17). Through lieutenant Barahona, later a coronel active during the dictatorship who is killed by an ERP operative, we also learn of the military's attitude to Jews. Barahona's Jewish wife, initially a suspect in his death, says: "for the military, to be Jewish (male or female), is synonymous with subversive, with Bolshevik" (Rivera 2011, 34). This is one of several instances in which Rivera intersperses historical events ranging from early twentieth-century repressive actions though Perón's government and his overthrow, and down to the last military dictatorship and the return to electoral democracy. These, in turn, are woven around his work as a textile worker and union activist beginning in 1945;

years later around being with Piri Lugones ("granddaughter of a poet and a torturer's daughter" [Rivera 2011, 53]), disappearances, and his own militancy at the gates of repression. At almost 82, a line attributed to Lenin, "Revolutionaries must die at 50" (Rivera 2011, 57) triggers selective memories of his father, of Marx and Engels, of a worker who survived Petliura's pogrom, of a few Jews (Einstein, Trotsky, Mailer, also Borges, who once congratulated himself for having had a Jewish grandmother), and of a quote from a book about the Plan Cóndor on the DAIA's statement that the Argentine dictatorships as such weren't anti-Semitic.

In a twelfth-floor apartment in the Belgrano neighborhood, in a Buenos Aires that is still "una fiesta," Arturo Reedson plows memories, chastises himself and others for things done and undone, quotes Paul Auster, Stalin and Neruda, Antony Beevor and Paul Krugman. A *lejaim* toast with Graham Greene's recommended JB whisky, finally stitches together his father's running a workplace where tailors feverishly sewed coats for those who resisted Hitler, with a lifelong struggle in his own country. *Kadish* is 'kadish' for his father, for unfulfilled dreams, perhaps, but more assuredly after his own hard hitting texts, for himself.

5 Committing Identities

Acknowledged and/or imposed by others, plural, constructed and shifting identities are markers that enable us to sift through a selection of authors and texts. In this case, they serve as a critical tool to avoid listing dozens of authors and hundreds of texts and focus, instead, as we have been doing, on cases that problematize that very category of being both Jewish and an Argentine/Uruguayan national (or vice versa). In the process, it is worth noting, as Latin American-Jewish writing became an accepted and increasingly popular category, a greater number of authors capitalized on such a recognition by peppering texts with folkloric references. Often, these are light weight samples of "Jewish in dishes," as it were, or "also Jewish," particularly when for many who exercised that prerogative, weight was entirely thrown on the other side of birth and belonging. In saying so, I certainly do not seek to forge a litmus test, nor to cast an entry requirement, but to point to an ongoing feature in literary production.[2] As I have analyzed elsewhere,[3] major defining elements of Latin American-Jewish literature (of authors, I hasten to add, who address such issues, and not just in passing) continue to be identity, the Holocaust, remembrance of traditional

---

[2] These issues were broached, for instance, by Ana E. Weinstein & Myriam E. Gover de Nasatsky in preparing the bibliography *Escritores judeo-argentinos. Bibliografía 1900–1987*, and in the more limited compilation published by David William Foster and Naomi Lindstrom in *Revista Interamericana de Bibliografía*.
[3] Some listed in the bibliography under Sosnowski.

and religious practices, migration and the associated aspects of integration and assimilation, and the socio-historical and political events of the authors' respective countries. In addition, and with or without Jewish references attached to them, we also find a concern for human rights and justice; a revolutionary zeal; an emphasis on the struggle for freedom from oppression; a need to unearth unethical patterns that affect the nation and the body politic and, at a more direct personal level, a drive to participate in national politics and even in armed struggle. All of these components are being directed, in one way or another, to affirm and exercise citizenship.

Examples of such commitment may be found, among others, in plays by Aída Bortnik (1938–2013), one of the founding members of "Teatro abierto" – an act of resistance by several playwrights against the dictatorship – and the script-writer of the 1986 Oscar-winning film, *The Official Story*. She also wrote the script for the Argentine film *Pobre mariposa*, set in the 1940s against World War II background and nascent Peronism. Years later, the unveiling of Argentine civilian and governmental complicity with Nazis, appears in several works by Patricia Suárez (1969), who is known for her award-winning fiction, poetry, and drama. *La Germania* (2006), for instance, brings together seven plays that have in common, not just Nazism, but its ongoing legacy and corollaries. Suárez's plays not just denounce, but propose to confront and challenge dehumanization and oppression, to seek justice in the face of silence, and to learn from a tattooed number on a forearm. This drive also appears, among others, in her trilogy on the Jewish white slave trade *Las polacas* (2001–2002) and in her 2017 play *Shylock*.

Social commitment is found with particular emphasis within the narrative realist tradition that Bernardo Verbitsky (1907–1979) exemplifies. While also associated with tango, film, and columns in a popular newspaper, his name is immediately linked to *Villa Miseria también es América* (1957) a descriptive and apt name he bestowed on Argentina's shantytowns. He wrote about being Argentine and Jewish before this classic novel in *Es difícil empezar a vivir* (1941), *En esos años* (1947), *Café de los Angelitos y otros cuentos porteños* (1949), but it is fully explored in the 1972 novel, *Etiquetas a los hombres*. In it the writer Cherniacoff is followed through his journeys to Rome, Israel and the Soviet Union. Each stop, including his return to Buenos Aires, generated feelings and memories that clash with his Third World ideology and underscore the desire to fight injustice as it clashes with his limited means to pursue it. The novel's last words are uttered by Daniel, Cherniacoff's future son-in-law, who had planned to move to Israel before being jailed for denouncing the murderers of a Leftist student. As his imprisonment ends he says: "I plan to go, but I'm still here, and there or here, anguish is healed through action, and there or here, I can only fight for the same things, and for being myself" (Verbitsky 1972, 638).

When in January 1978, the Jewish umbrella organization DAIA honored Verbitsky for the 1977 "Ricardo Rojas Prize" he had received, he said: "Many years had to pass for me to notice that with *Es difícil empezar a vivir*, a protagonist who was entirely Argentine and Jewish to the core entered the Argentine novel. Previously, only incidentally, some Jewish characters appeared in our novels. (...) I could have eluded the Jewish condition of the protagonist, but deliberately, out of loyalty to myself, in any case, I marked it clearly, without it affecting his condition as an Argentine... The same thing happens in the most recent one, *Etiquetas a los hombres*, a novel in which out of Buenos Aires a vast Jewish problem unfolds..." (Senkman 1983, 372–373).

It is noteworthy, as Verbitsky argued in "Ante mi obra," that *Villa Miseria*... and *Etiquetas*... – which he began to conceive after Eichmann's capture and trial – are "fundamentally identical" in their aim: to denounce crimes against humanity; to condemn the labeling of minorities, their being reduced to objects thus anticipating their erasure. His entire oeuvre confirms what moves him. In his remarks he added: "It simply happens that I care about the Jewish condition, but what fundamentally matters to me is the human condition, questioned wherever an injustice is committed..." (Verbitsky 1973, 89–90).

Bernardo Kordon (1915–2002) was a prolific short story writer, also known for essays based on his frequent travels to Mao's China, as well as for novels and film scripts – including the memorable "Alias Gardelito" (1961). He mined neighborhoods, and in "Andate paraguayo" (1972) a Villa Miseria, for therein he found the characters that define a fractured city. Whether set in Argentina, Brazil or Chile, the poor and downtrodden, wanderers, and outlaws populate chronicles that are easily recognizable within a realist tradition. *Kid Ñandubay* (1971) is one of the few Jewish characters that appear in his work. It tells the story of the Polish-born boxer Jacobo Berstein, bent on defending his Jewishness against neighborhood bullies at a time (1939–1940) whose significance could not be lost on his readers.

Every aspect, clash and contradiction we have been pointing out in other authors was embodied by Germán Rozenmacher (1936–1971). He also did so in masterful short stories and plays. As he described himself in an autobiographical note, he was an oddity. At one point he described himself as "feo, judío, rante y sentimental;" at another, as a Jew who was neither a Zionist nor and anti-Zionist, but a Peronist (Rozenmacher 2013, 33). To denounce Peronism's ban by the Argentine government, Rozenmacher participated with three other major playwrights – Roberto Cossa (1934), Ricardo Talesnik (1935) and Carlos Somigliana (1932–1987) – in *El avión negro* (1970), a reference to Perón's popularly anticipated return from exile aboard a black airplane. At another level, as we recall Gerchunoff's earlier claim to a Hispanic literary ancestry, it's worth noting that Rozenmacher staged a version of the Spanish classic *El lazarillo de Tormes* – an anonymous picaresque anti-clerical novel published in 1554 – and that in 1970 he authored the play *Simón Brumelstein, caballero de Indias*, staged posthumously in 1982 and published in 1987. While it is tempting to draw a line between Rozenmacher and Samuel Eichelbaum, the previous generation's leading Jewish-Argentine playwright, I share Mizraje's view that it is more appropriate to link him to Samuel Glusberg (Enrique Espinoza, 1898–1987), founder of Babel, the legendary publishing house and magazine, and author of, among others, *La levita gris: cuentos judíos de ambiente porteño* (1924). Glusberg, she rightly argued, was the first to write

Jewish-*porteño* stories; Rozenmacher wrote *porteño* stories with a Jewish atmosphere (Mizraje 2006, 19).

Rozenmacher's best known play, *Requiem for a Friday Evening*, which opened at the IFT Theater in 1964, weaves David's desire to be free from following the cantorial Jewish tradition inherited and embraced by Sholem, his father, with his love for María and his ambition to become a writer. Rozenmacher's unquestioned familiarity with Yiddish and Hebrew, with Jewish traditions and history – he grew up in a traditional Orthodox home and pursued Jewish studies – allowed him to instruct pointed nuances in the décor and in the characters' expressions. Sholem's brother, Max Abramson, the king of Yiddish operetta, opens the play. Brothers from a family of artists, they represent divergent paths: Max lives off the popular and slowly dying Yiddish stage in Buenos Aires; Sholem, an observant 62-year old Jew, follows his ancestors' legacy. Max's introduction informs the audience that this is a play about a family of artists, and also a "father and son story", a story that is "so terrible and so small, so sweet and so cruel" (Rozenmacher 2013, 273).

Born in Argentina, David entertains other options and as the drama unfolds, he seeks his father's approval for a choice that runs counter to Sholem's beliefs and expectations. The son's refusal and the decision to leave home and the embedded traditions, may be seen as the triumph of integration into the Argentine national fabric to the detriment of ancestral lore – a reading that would explain its then frequent broadcast on the official TV channel. Still, it is the father who emerges as the force that ultimately protects the son from the cold that awaits him. The play is dedicated to his wife, Chana and, significantly, to his parents for, as he states: without their love this play would not have been written.

The weight expressed in *Requiem* resurfaced in the *Simón Brumelstein* play underscoring that, though firmly anchored in national politics, Rozenmacher held on to the pull and confluence of both forces. This is all the more so as Simón threads a thin line between the imaginary and the fall into insanity. Echoing *Requiem*'s David he sees himself as an artist and not as a failed jewelry salesman. The powerful imagery of the Sabbath's sanctity and the protective mantle of the family are thrown into the mix as Simón wishes to be just a human being without any other descriptor. More than the father – whom he calls a "*Luftmensch*" – this time it is the Bobe who becomes the shield as she chastises Guadalupe's presence, his behavior and self-denial. What from a spectator's viewpoint may be seen as ironic in someone struggling to abandon what has been inherited and learned, is the frequent use of Yiddish and Hebrew references, of the phylacteries that the Bobe thrusts upon him, of the script's care not to mention God's name as when it is pronounced in an actual prayer, and of a reenactment of Abraham's binding of Isaac.

A number of these motifs – all about wounded or broken souls – also appear in several of Rozenmacher's short stories, notably among them: "El gato dorado" and "Tristezas de la pieza de hotel," published in the 1962 collection *Cabecita negra*, and "Blues en la noche" (*Los ojos del tigre*, 1967). His familiarity with Judaism, evident throughout his work, is further attested in the approximately 90 entries he prepared on Hebrew, Yiddish, and Spanish literatures for *Diccionario de la literatura universal* (Muchnik Editores, 1966). Having underscored the Jewish motifs in his work, I should note that a comprehensive analysis of his work would also have highlighted "Cabecita negra," "Cochecito," "Los ojos del tigre" and "Esta hueya la bailan los radicales," where, at their core, his politics and Peronist sympathies were transparent.

6 A Rooted Mantle

I believe it is safe to ascertain that, regardless of their use on the page or on stage, very few of the authors under study possessed such a thorough understanding of Jewish sources. For most, some words or allusions sufficed to provide a tone, an echo of things past. For instance, a protective gesture similar to the one cast in the closing moments of *Requiem for a Friday Evening*, was adopted years later by Pedro Orgambide in his 1976 novel *Aventuras de Edmund Ziller en tierras del Nuevo Mundo*. Having written mostly on non-Jewish issues (though in a personal letter, without elaborating on their tenor, he listed Jewish characters that appeared in his fiction) it is the experience of exile that provoked the conjunction of Judaism and Diaspora. Until then, his Jews were immigrants from previous generations.

In a comment about "*Eli, Eli, Lamma Sabajtani*", a poem written by Humberto Costantini (1924–1987) long before the 1976 coup forced both of them to exile in Mexico, Orgambide evoked the character of the "Wandering Jew" and the burden of life in the diaspora as it affected him and David Viñas, both born out of mixed marriages, and Costantini, an Argentine Sephardi of Italian origin. Immigration motivated by exile also affected, of course, other communities, as Orgambide recalled works by Nicolás Casullo (1944–2008) and Mempo Giardinelli (1947). It is noteworthy that both Orgambide and Costantini, well known for stories that portray an array of *porteño* characters, popular streets and tango sung in "Argentine," come together as survivors to evoke the patriarchal voice of their Jewishness. Costantini's poem, in a Spanish dotted with Hebrew and Italian, addresses the "Adonai of Turin" as the uncle who was civilized there by his grandparents, and suggests that He better stay there, in the peace of an earlier time, and leave him in America to invent it all, once again, from the beginning. No one, but a porteño-Jewish-Italian-Sephardi poet, could have closed with "Te Saluda, y a veces te recuerda/con pavota nostalgia:/tu sobrino" (Orgambide 1983b).

Jewish references in Costantini were not isolated. In "Don Iudá" (1958), for instance, the "Wandering Jew" is being persecuted in Lucena in 1108; centuries, or years, later once again in Spain and elsewhere; "Una vieja historia de caminantes" is set around Jerusalem at the time of Jesus. Costantini left unfinished a novel, "Rapsodia de Raquel Liberman," the story of a prostitute who denounced the white slave trade of the Zwi Migdal – a story that has since been researched by, among others, Nora Glickman (1945) in *The Jewish White Slave Trade and the Untold Story of Raquel Liberman* (2015), author also of the play "Una tal Raquel." Still, his best known stories, *Una vieja historia de caminantes* (1967) and *Háblenme de Funes* (1970), offer an array of characters that are at home in the *picaresca porteña*. His award winning novel *De dioses, hombrecitos y policías* (1979) and *La larga noche de Francisco Sanctis* (1984) center on the violence that led to the 1976 coup and to the dictatorial period. Before that, in 1973, he had authored *Libro de Trelew* about the 1972 execution of Peronist political prisoners.

There seems to be a seamless transition of scenarios in terms of location, time, and the oppressor-oppressed identification when denouncing persecution and injustice. What applies to Costantini can be said upon examining a series of works by Pedro Orgambide. An author who wrote biographies of Horacio Quiroga (1878–1937) and Ezequiel Martínez Estrada (1895–1964), the 1972 "Juan Moreira Supershow," a musical on Eva Perón (1986), and who was at home with every aspect of Buenos Aires life, also concentrated on the underside, on the less glamorous and sinister side of Argentina, when chronicling watershed historical events and when drawing immigrant stories of rejection and adaptation, whether in the early *Hotel familias* (1972) or later on in *El arrabal del mundo* (1983), *Hacer la América* (1984) and *Pura memoria* (1985).

[Gerardo] Mario Goloboff (1939) has sustained his poetry and fiction through the intersection of history, politics, and references to Jewish origins and traditions. His very first book of poetry, *Entre la diáspora y octubre* (1966), bridges revolutionary expectations with a diasporic presence. A decade later it unfolded in *Caballos por el fondo de los ojos* (1976), a novel in which integration into Argentina is sealed with the killing of one of the early immigrants' descendants who had joined a revolutionary movement. His blood becomes the ultimate proof of national belonging. Throughout his works, exile – which Goloboff experienced in France for over two decades – lurks as a threat and, at times, as a sustaining force. In a subsequent trilogy, he placed events in Algarrobos, a town that retrieves memories of Carlos Casares, one of the Jewish colonies where he was born. In *Criador de palomas* (1984), a direct reference to the murders that took place during the dictatorship, in *La luna que cae*, (1989) and in *El soñador de Smith* (1990) he follows the search undertaken by El Pibe. In 1995 he published the well documented story of an anarchist commune: *Comuna Verdad*. The title names the commune, but it can also be sounded "como una verdad:" as a possible, or as one version of truth. Goloboff is both cognizant of, and at ease with, working on the remnants of Jewish traditions set in local history and political debacles. As a literary scholar he has also analyzed the motifs that structure his fiction and poetry, and reflected on its impact in "De una lengua impura," in "Lo judío en mi obra," and in "Diálogo íntimo de dos obras: Mi Algarrobos natal ante la Ferrara de Giorgio Bassani."

Edgardo Cozarinsky (1939), like Goloboff, also a product of the Jews who settled in the agricultural colonies, has directed several films, written about films and literature

(*Borges en/y/sobre/cine* [1981]), and is the author of several novels that in recent years broached Jewish characters and motifs: *La novia de Odessa* (2001); *El rufián moldavo* (2004); *Maniobras nocturnas* (2007); *Lejos de dónde* (2009). Buenos Aires and Paris – a frequent duet for Argentine writers and intellectuals – lead to exile, and all that it provokes, uncovers and rewrites, is the core of his first novel, *Vudú urbano*, published in 1985 with prologues by Susan Sontag and Guillermo Cabrera Infante. Immigrants; wars and survivors; real, adopted and assumed identities, are some of his frequent motifs. In 2016 Cozarinsky published *Dark* and *Niño enterrado*. Memory and nostalgia in a narrative that sometimes stops short at a turn that is left for the reader to engage. *Niño enterrado* offers fragments to reconstruct his own past through a father, son of a Jewish gaucho from Entre Ríos (Gerchunoff's *Entre Ríos, mi país*), who joins the Argentine navy – an unusual move for a Jew. In tracing his father's absence he asks: what did being Jewish mean for him? And the reader then wonders: and for the son? Far from any conventional religious practice, are some of the paragraphs he dedicates to his parents a literary semblance of "kadish?" Or are they perhaps another way to pursue the travels that defined him for decades and that, inevitably, must also face coming home?

7 Humor and beyond

Humor – particularly of the kind that mutes laughter and poke holes in any given version of reality – has been a steadfast ingredient in several writers as a strategy to confront challenges and threats, as well as to show life's quirky side. Alicia Steimberg (1933–2012) was one of them, notably in this context, in *Músicos y relojeros* (1971), *Su espíritu inocente* (1981), and in the award winning *Cuando digo Magdalena* (1992). In these, and in subsequent works, certain obsessions remain constant: in addition to recreating family origins and experiences of the newly arrived, she plays, oftentimes satirically, with religion, sex, madness, and death. The narrators, uncomfortable in their own skin, are descendants of immigrants who have not quite managed to accept that birthplace grants both citizenship and place in a social class. Sex and Catholic imagery, which contrasts with their inherited sobriety, share the world of fantasy and sensual gratification, forcing Steimberg's characters to act against the dictates of the petty bourgeois family. They do so through humorous situations as they provide fragmentary family histories that underline the desire to be what they are not. In time they will realize that the majority they strive to join is not less fragmentary that the chronicles they aim to overcome.

When thinking of witty humor, the kind that may turn melancholy into playful wisdom, Isidoro Blaisten (1933–2004) immediately comes to mind. It is his signature in stories – some of which include Jewish characters – that appear in *La salvación* (1972), in *El mago* (1974), in the best-selling *Dublin al sur* (1980), as well as in the

Anticonferencias he delivered at the Sociedad Hebraica Argentina, and in *Cuando éramos felices* (1992), the most autobiographical, and because of that, the most painful of his recollections.

In Mario Szichman (1945–2018), introspection and a demurred smile cede to open laughter even as he unveils the hypocrisy that defines the society his characters wish to inhabit. In a personal note he wrote on *Los judíos del Mar Dulce* (1971) – a continuation of his earlier *Crónica falsa* (1969), which he would reissue in 1972 as *La verdadera crónica falsa* – and aware of the twist he imprinted on his own ghosts, he acknowledged traces from Scholem Aleichem and Philip Roth. Through the saga of the Pechof characters he developed in several novels, Szichman affixed satire as a defining feature of Argentine-Jewish letters. He did so, moreover, by taking on Evita Perón in *A las 20:25 la señora entró en la inmortalidad* (1981) – a direct reference to Evita's time of death on July 26, 1952 that was broadcast as a daily reminder until Perón's overthrow on September 16, 1955. Years later, Szichman would continue to deconstruct the national heroes of Venezuela, where he lived for many years before moving to the U.S. A full repertoire of Jewish-linked motifs can be found in tracking the Pechof family: the immigrants' arrival and the lingering memories of a *shtetl* or a bustling city; pogroms and the Shoa; the attempts to adapt to a new language and culture as well as to challenging habits, and the ultimate proof of successful integration: the ability to frame it all by blending Jewish humor with *picardía criolla* to create a unique picaresque saga.

The path to citizenship is usually a combination of an extended period of in-country residence and a paper trail subject to governmental willingness and regulations. Spilling Jewish blood in recalled European events, and particularly under Nazi rule, pointed to the lack of recognition of the Jew as a human being. The death of Jews in the literature under review has another meaning. I alluded to it in Goloboff's *Caballos por el fondo de los ojos*; it is also grounded in a historical event in Szichman's first novel when Natalio Pechof is executed in the José León Suárez garbage dump on June 10, 1956. The assassination of a group of innocent people carried out by military personnel during the so-called "Revolución libertadora" that overthrew Perón, is the subject of Rodolfo Walsh's 1957 investigative chronicle *Operación masacre* (1957), and serves explicitly as *Crónica falsa*'s historical setting.

Natalio's ideological transitions and actions point to his missteps and to those of an immigrant Polish-Jewish family, as uncovered by his son Berele/Bernardo. It is through him that defeat seals their fate. This is further anticipated in *Los judíos del Mar Dulce* with an epigraph from Albert Memmi: "I was a mestizo of colonization who understood everyone, because I was not totally anyone's." To uncover a family history is, in this case, to also unveil decades of national history and politics. Through a mordant satire that is radically anti-establishment, Szichman's signature is the unraveling of that chronicle in this novel, and perhaps even more so, in *A las 20:25*... Myths and histories are generated to fill gaps and meet needs. "Hacer la América" at one point ceases to mean economic wealth and becomes grafting Pechof upon the nation's pillars. As the Pechof antics reflect, there isn't a sole nor an acceptable version of Jewish immigration. Contrary to earlier literary iterations, there aren't model immigrants nor a privileged chronicle of integration or assimilation into the national core. Threads are loosened; it all becomes part of a segmented "petit histoire."

David Viñas framed *Los judíos del Mar Dulce* against both Gerchunoff's *Los gauchos judíos* and Rozenmacher's *Requiem*... pointing to "insolence" as Szichman's narrative anchor. What he finds in Szichman's avoidance of self-pity, his demystifying tender myths and memories – a *chutzpah* Viñas doesn't name as such – is what he himself carried out throughout his career in novels, plays, and critical essays. Viñas, who consistently aimed at unearthing what lies under the nation's official history, under its authoritarian, militaristic and repressive veins, lends his weight to this then young author by saying: "may we with Szichman be talking about a Jewish literature of the Third World?" In the context of this reading such a comment propelled the novel unto a broader category. By the time the Pechof saga hit the bookstores, Latin American-Jewish literature was no longer confined to a ghettoized or specialized readership; it had become mainstream literature. Currently, moreover, as has been the case for a while, most Jewish-Argentine authors are "just Argentine."

Ana María Shua (1951), a prolific author at home in several genres, including micro-fictions and children's literature, sees herself "With All That I Am." As she herself said, in whatever order those terms are listed, she is woman, Latin American, Jewish, Writer (2004, 51). Devoid of drama and the introspection that were, and in some cases continue to be, almost a trademark of Argentine-Jewish letters, Shua opts for humor that is at once wholesome and occasionally biting. In the quoted essay she recalls a childhood in which being Jewish was an important matter for both her Sephardic and Ashkenazi grandparents. For her, it had to do with learning what Jewish is, and what a woman writer is, almost haphazardly; with believing in a sense of equality among all when reminders pointed in different direction. *Los amores de Laurita* (1984) a bestselling novel with a Jewish protagonist; the 1994 novel *El libro de los recuerdos* about an Argentine-Jewish family, are two targeted instances. Familiarity and recognition of her multiple roots are also evident in the humorous Jewish cookbook (*Risas y emociones de la cocina judía* [2003]), in the collection of *Sabiduría popular judía*, and in her popularizing for a Spanish-speaking public the wisdom of Chelm's wizards (*El pueblo de los tontos: humor tradicional judío*).

8 Chiseling Words

In search of a hidden form, some writers plow through letters and silences to seek meaning or just a voice in poetry. Some felt at home in any language and in more than one genre; for others only one landing was granted: a sole identity, as it were, in poetry. For Alejandra Pizarnik (1936–1972), forever in search of language as an aesthetic project, that which is "Jewish is the unrecognized, the relegated and declared alien, that of which in her poetry, deliberately, she did not want to speak." So states Florinda Goldberg in one of her readings. And still, as Goldberg also indicates, it explicitly appears, for instance, in the poem "La muerte y la muchacha (Schubert)" and in the prose text "Los muertos y la lluvia." Senkman perceived in her peculiar mode of wandering an unmistakable Jewish voice (Goldberg 1987, 60; Senkman 1983, 337). More than in explicit motifs, references or allusions, in Pizarnik's poetry there is a perception of otherness, of being an outlander, of being estranged from everything but the inevitable drive to pour into poetry what some entries in her diaries would somehow also manage to hold. At some point she wrote: "I believe that being Jewish is a perfectly grave fact. . . my Jewish traits are ambiguous. On the one hand, a special intelligence of things. On the other, a ghetto spirit. And, first and foremost, a deep disorder, as if I had done nothing but travel." Perhaps it was the not always hidden nostalgia of the samovar that also lay under an endless search for place, for an elusive or non-existent meaning to life, as much as for the inevitability of writing, and then for silence.

In reflecting on his own poetic reworking of Judah ha-Levi's Medieval Spanish-Jewish poetry, as well as of Kabbalistic texts, Juan Gelman's words undergird what stayed unspoken in others: "Language is much more than a worldview. It has an unconscious, a centuries-old reservoir. In language's unconsciousness, everything Jewish that fits in the Spanish language is housed." And later on, as he was addressing a Conference of Latin American-Jewish writers, he added: ". . .I believe that in the work of all of us there is indeed a Jewish dimension. I also believe that it is written with the body, but I find it impossible, in my case, to define the Jewishness that constitutes my subjectivity and that, undoubtedly, nurtures [encourages me in] what I write" (Gelman 1992, 84). Gelman, who among other honors, was the recipient of Argentina's National Prize for Poetry (1987) and of the 2007 Cervantes Prize, was already considered among the leading poets of his generation for earlier books such as *Gotán* (1962), *Los poemas de Sydney West* (1970), *Cólera Buey* (1971), and *Hechos y relaciones* (1980). He was also known as a journalist, and for his political work in the Montoneros movement. Forced into exile in 1975, after several years in Europe, he settled in Mexico City.

In an interview with Leonardo Senkman (Senkman 1992, 106–113), which took place in the context of the cited conference, Gelman traced his childhood in a Russian- and Yiddish-speaking home, and how in 1983 he began to write in Sephardic. His fascination with Ibn Gabirol and Judah ha-Levi – this time marked by the overwhelming impact of his own exile experience – led to *Com/Posiciones*. It is the interior, and not just the bodily personal impact of exile, that traverses this and several subsequent collections of poetry. Medieval Spanish-Jewish poets and Kabbalistic mystics echo throughout *Dibaxu* (1994), poems he wrote from 1983 to 1985, while in exile, and which follow the also exilic *Citas y comentarios* of 1978–

1979. In *Dibaxu*'s "Scholion" he comments: ". . .I know that the Sephardic syntax gave me back a lost candor, and its diminutives, a tenderness of other times that is alive and, therefore, full of consolation. Perhaps this book is just a reflection on language from its most calcined place, poetry" (Gelman 1994, 7). For this non-Sephardic Argentine Jew, exile from the beloved homeland finds another home, as it were, in retrieving the language of the Jews expelled from Spain in 1492. There is in exile a sense of being physically out-of-country, and through poetry out-of-oneself: an ecstatic experience that finds itself in the poet's longing for the country he was forced to leave.

In a 1992 interview in *Nueva Sión*, Gelman said that he never had a conflict with the Jewishness in him, which may also explain, he added, why he never had a conflict with the Argentine in him (15).[4] For him, Jewish culture, built for centuries without any support from a formal state structure; a culture that expresses itself in a myriad of languages, is diverse, universal, pluralistic, and, as it was built (and continues to build) from the bottom up, democratic. In reading Gelman's adoption and adaptation of Sephardic sources and language, particularly as it emerged from his own exile, it is worth remembering Gerchunoff's aim to retrieve Spanish literature (not necessarily Jewish-Spanish Medieval sources) to find roots in Argentina and to legitimize his use of the Spanish language.

Political militancy, when chosen, is a citizen right that has been, and is, pursued by immigrants throughout the world. Many – including innocent bystanders – paid with their lives, with prison, torture and/or exile, when confronting state-sponsored terrorism, as was the case during the last Argentine dictatorship (1976–1983), and also during the immediately prior rule of Isabel Perón. Argentine Jews, whose participation in the country's civil political life dates over a century, were also part of the opposition to military rule. Their participation covered a wide range of activities and included involvement in the armed struggle. The high percentage of Jews among the disappeared attests to their total integration into the national fabric; in the way many prisoners were treated, also to the anti-Semitic vein of the armed forces and paramilitary groups.

Rhetoric akin to that heard in earlier pogroms, and certainly by other perpetrators, were not uncommon. During this period, a significant number of writers being considered here, were forced into exile; several, including the already mentioned Viñas and Gelman, lost family members. Poet Alberto Szpunberg (1940), a militant fighter (co-founder of the Brigada Masetti) who had taught literature and worked as a journalist, was one of those who had to leave Argentina in 1977. He settled in Masnou, near Barcelona, where he continued to publish poetry, which earned him several major international awards, until his return to Buenos Aires.

---

4 H[oracio] L[utzky], "Juan Gelman: una cultura democrática," *Nueva Sión* [Buenos Aires], August 22, 1992, p. 15.

Szpunberg is fluent in Yiddish and very familiar with Jewish culture and traditions, from which his poetry continues to draw, as it also speaks of what cuts across his country and also Israel. A major example of his tying together the strands that define him appears in "Charlas con Ana" (1984): to be Jewish and Argentine; to draw from Hasidic tales; to conjugate poetry and politics; Che Guevara and Roque Dalton; to seek the source of poetry and face the challenge to go on living. The desire to change the world, anchored in Jewish sources, in Argentine and Latin American history, in the life of the militant, in ancestral memory and in the streets of Buenos Aires, which also appeared in a number of earlier collections of poetry, achieves its most powerful expression in the 77 poems of *La Academia de Piatock* (2010), meticulously explored by Mijal Gai.

In Luisa Futoransky (1939), who journeyed from music to law to art and literature, Jewishness, rooted from childhood in the Yiddish language, appears explicitly throughout her work. It is found in immigrant voices in her novels, in the search for place, in classic references asserting the identity that weave her poems. It is a sustained search whether undertaken in Buenos Aires, China, in other countries where she also resided, or in France, where she has been living since 1981, as well as from her frequent visits to Israel. Futoransky's Jewishness, as she wrote to me in a personal statement, is that of a non-observant, emancipated Jew, and still it is very explicit in her poetry, having overcome the more naïve, Chagall-like aura of her earlier publications. In her novels, fictions of self, that dimension shows up in a halo, as it were, that is wrapped around her characters. A composite of her poetry could weave threads where exile is absence; the land, almost every land but particularly Israel, a cauldron of memories; love, when not a pastime, lasts when granted, only to be lost and rekindled time and again; humor, a means to survive pain and the injustice of misery. In tune with the street and with history, with the ceaseless legacy of violence, with the political decisions that mar humanity, and with the encounters that still make it all worthwhile, Futoransky never averts her eyes from the points that cross her itinerary. "I do not descend from any parsimonious civil servant/but of simple people/angry and unhappy" – she writes in *Prender de gajo* (2006). And once again in "Jerusalem: A Glass of Vertigo": "The roses of Jerusalem are complicated./The pilgrims despair./The way of the roses of truth/is absolute/And it hurts/me so much" (*La sanguina* [1987]). A sort of loving and enthralled Jewish stubbornness, of survival in spite of it all, of language as the safety valve that names it all.

Tamara Kamenszain (1947–2021), an award-winning poet and essayist who is widely recognized for her theoretical approaches to the act of writing, for creative and probing analyses of some of Latin America's leading poets, as well as of poets of her own generation, titled her participation in the 1986 congress on the Jewish component in Latin American literature "All Writing is Female and Jewish." She explained it by recalling the Biblical and Talmudic stories she heard from her grandfather, notably the story of Bruria, Rabbi Meir's wife, who transgressed the restrictive patriarchal order on learning driven by her own desire to achieve knowledge. Familiarity with canonical texts, as well as with Yiddish and Hebrew, allowed Kamenszain her own reworking of stories that found their way in her first book, *De este lado del Mediterráneo* (1973) and later in *Los no* (1977) and in *La casa grande* (1986). The very term 'Hebrew' denotes crossing to the other side. It is almost an incitement, though not necessarily to transgress, to seek out what lies elsewhere, be that other genres beyond poetry – as Kamenszain continues to practice in essays and theoretical explorations – or outside the ghetto of her language (Kamenszain 2006, 157–169). *El ghetto* (2003), a collection of poetry in her father's memory, adds: "In your last name I install my ghetto." In it, brilliantly analyzed by Adriana Kanzepolsky, Kamenszain elicits some of the queries on language, identity, death and memory, belonging, sense of (and freedom from) place that she made explicit in her introspective look at how poetry and essay are somehow affected by the journeys that ultimately conduct her to an in-between space, to knowing what is Argentine and Jewish. With a twist so often found in exegetical analyses, one could be led to read in the language's interstices, that to know what it is to be Argentine it is necessary to come to it, and at it, from the outside, from exile, through a language that, like no other, is intimately associated with that experience.

Throughout this reading I pointed out the presence, significance, and/or use of Yiddish in a number of writers. In the entire registry of poets born in Argentina, including many who could not be included here, only one can bear "Buenos Aires Yiddish" associated to his name: Eliahu Toker (1934–2010). The intimacy he had with Yiddish language and culture comes through in his poetry, which he wrote in Spanish, in the work on writers such as Carlos M. Grünberg and César Tiempo, and in the translations of some of the major Yiddish-language poets. One home with two languages, in close vicinity with Hebrew, may describe the ease with which he did *not* need to cross borders. This is evident as we read his anthology of twentieth century Yiddish poetry, *El resplandor de la palabra judía* (1981), or the briefer selection in *El ídish es también Latinoamérica* (2003?). It is unequivocally one home when we pause at the dedication of *Papá, mamá y otras ciudades* (1988): "For Jacob, my father, from whom I received the language of the tribe and whom I still embrace to wrestle with him, as the patriarch with the angel, that he may bless me."

Toker's work as a translator underscored a sense of mission for a living language; a mission that also embraced what his home country, and within it, the Jewish community, were living through. The questions that weave together "Saga judía" (1990) end with a balance that defined Toker's life, his poetic drive and intellectual commitment: "How many years can you live between two countries?/Of course there is a lot to do here, as an Argentinean./And there is the language, the street, people, friends,/ [but] there is a living Israel that calls me/and a Jerusalem with which I have had an appointment for centuries." A saga that is part of the ongoing dialogue Gelman's opening question continues to pose for us all. Or does it?

9 Always In

Sergio Chejfec (1956) throws a number of the issues that we have been addressing into a different landing or, at least, places them into a reflective mode that almost skips a generation. While nostalgia and evoked Jewish motifs appear in both *Lenta biografía* (1990) and in *Los planetas* (1999), it is the "obsessively cerebral way" he recognizes in his writing that carves out a separate niche in this constellation. In a number of essays he questions a closed-off Latin American Jewish writing preferring an open field in which such works would find their own meaning. The referential world that defines so much of that category is for him a launch pad to write about writing; to push out set boundaries and dissolve borders; to find in being displaced (having left Argentina, he lived in Venezuela and is now in New York) the shifting motifs of nostalgia, tradition and adaptation that shape a new identity (Chejfec 2005, 119–133; Chejfec 2006, 113). In Chejfec's works, both fiction and essay, there is a desire to break down limits and to explore other venues to say that which seeks a presence, a definition. In a number of his literary ventures I find that in a labyrinthine way they mask, though not always too subtly, an affirmation of Jewish-Argentine-Latin American identity, in the anywhere place that had traditionally defined (at least until 1948) a Jewish geography. It is a geography that is not so much grounded in a land, as in the craft of language. Having said that, isn't the endless inquiry into the meaning and design of every letter another way of retrieving a world that has not been lost?

In Molloy and Siskind's edited volume, *Poéticas de la distancia. Adentro y afuera de la literatura argentina* – in which two thirds of the essays are by Jewish writers – Martín Kohan (1967) writes in his self-presentation: "I never lived or plan to live anywhere but in Buenos Aires. I learned two foreign languages: Latin and Hebrew. The first one I couldn't use because it's dead; the second because I don't travel to Israel and because my grandparents speak Yiddish, not Hebrew. The lack of use made me forget those two languages almost completely. I would like, in compensation, to perfect my Rioplatense Spanish, at least in writing" (Kohan 2006,130, my translation). Almost a century after Gerchunoff's defining first book, the terms of the Argentine-Jewish equation have been radically transformed. It is no longer a matter of setting foot on Argentine soil and strive to become integrated and accepted by the population and the dominant culture; now, leaving the city in which he is rooted acquires a different meaning and generates a different reaction: "...the choice is not Argentina but Judaism. Suddenly, as in the miracle of revelations, I discover myself a Jew. A Jew without God, according to the formula adopted by Peter Gay to refer to Freud, and without a State, because Israel does not enter into the definition (without God and without a State: in Judaism, though only in Judaism, I function as an anarchist). A completely diffuse Judaism and, at the same time, if not by my will, terribly concrete (that is, inscribed on my body). From Judaism one cannot emigrate, among other things because emigration in good measure constitutes it, it has to do with its tradition, makes its tradition" (Kohan 2006, 136–137, my translation).

Kohan's has written about his heroes: about the writer Esteban Echeverría (1805–1851), the military genius and liberator José de San Martín (1778–1850), also the subject of his doctoral dissertation, and about the wandering-non emigrating Jewish theorist and critic Walter Benjamin (1892–1940). Known for major books about each one of them and for the incisive analysis in *El país de la guerra* (2014), he has also authored some of the most powerful novels about the dictatorship: *Dos veces junio* (2002) and *Ciencias morales* (2007), among others.

10 Upon Arrival

As easy as it was to use the 1910 publication of *Los gauchos judíos* as a point of departure to canvas Argentine-Jewish literature, it is increasingly difficult to establish one or more points of arrival. The reason is rather felicitous: Argentine-Jewish prose fiction writers, poets and playwrights cover a myriad of issues, approaches, ideologies, degrees of inclusion and exclusion of ready-made Jewish motifs... In adopting the universe as a literary patrimony, they follow Borges' admonition in "El escritor argentino y la tradición." This in itself may signal the transformation of a port into a home.

11 Uruguay's Landscape

The Jewish population on the other side of the river, in the República Oriental del Uruguay, currently stands at no more than 20,000. Most Jews landed there from Eastern Europe, with a significant number also from Sephardic communities in the Middle East. Having arrived during the early decades of the twentieth century, they promptly established community institutions, including a strong network of Jewish schools. The first community publications were in Yiddish, beginning in 1920; *Nuestra vida*, a Sephardic bulletin, began in 1934. That same year a publication sponsored by the "Sociedad de Actores Israelitas en Argentina y Uruguay" was launched, stressing the close connections between professional actors on both sides of the river. Another publication dedicated to Jewish theater began two years later. What makes the proliferation of publications, mostly bulletins from various ideological quarters, impressive is that at that time the Jewish community was barely over half a percentage point of the total 2.1 million population of the country. In 1949 *Páginas artísticas y literarias* was launched in Yiddish, and in 1983 Egon Friedler (1932) – one of Uruguay's leading performing art critics and chronicler of the Jewish community – and Mauricio Zielenic started the monthly *Identidad*. In *El Uruguay judío. Demografía e identidad* (2006), looking at the religious, ethnic and national dimensions of the community, Rafael Porzecanski has traced its transformations and social mobility, development into the professional sectors, adscription to Jewish education and cultural values, and ideological affiliations within the country as well as attitudes towards Israel.

Writers who are widely recognized in, and by, the Uruguayan-Jewish community, and some whose books have achieved recognition among a wider public, include Roberto Cyjon (1951), an engineer by training, who has authored several novels – among them *Flaco, yo me saco el pasaporte* (2003) and *Marcados para siempre* (2006) – and the 2013 collection of short stories *La verdad siempre esquiva*. Economist Mauricio Bergstein (1961) is known particularly for his travel books, including the award winning *Páginas de arena* (2000) and *La fiesta de los dioses* (2011). Julia Galemire (1923), of Sephardic origin, is well-known both as a poet and as a major cultural promoter, having founded in 1994 the group "La Tertulia." Her books include *Fabular de la niebla* (1997) and *Memoria silenciosa* (2013). In 2015 Galemire received the "Morosoli Prize" for lifetime achievement.

Alicia Migdal (1947) is an established writer, critic and academic whose columns appeared in a number of Uruguay's leading publications. Her books include the prose poems of *Mascarones* (1981) and the 1986 book of poems *Historias de cuerpos*. She has also published fiction: *La casa de enfrente* (1988); *Historia quieta* (1993), which earned her the "Bartolomé Hidalgo Prize" and was translated into French, and *Muchachas de verano en días de marzo* (1999). *En un idioma extranjero* (2008) includes her three previous nouvelles and a new text; it earned Migal the "Premio Nacional de Narrativa."

12 Militant Heterodoxy

Teresa Porzecanski (1945), born in Montevideo to Ashkenazi and Sephardic parents, is well known both for her fiction and for her anthropological scholarly work; for a focus on the Jewish community in both disciplines, and also for her work on other minority identities, including oral histories of Charrúas, Guaraníes and Afro-Uruguayans. Translated into several languages, she is the recipient of numerous awards, including several from Uruguay's Ministry of Culture and from the City of Montevideo, of the "Premio de la Crítica Bartolomé Hidalgo" (1994), "Premio a la Cultura Uruguaya 'Morosoli de Plata' in Literature" (2004), as well as Fulbright and Guggenheim grants. In her heterodoxy, she comfortably brings together various belief systems, including Kabbalistic references, Messianic characters and African practices, as she also sensually brings to life ancestral figures and the far from epic folk that populate her literary system. In many of her novels and short stories a muted landscape brings forth the power of women who recreate a home and tales of struggle and survival, whether in a Syrian town, or in the Uruguay of the 1930s and under the 1970s dictatorship. Her explorations of the self and the eroticism of the female body, are also cast in an imaginary dimension where fractured, or at the very least, uncommon characters address their reality.

A seamless navigation across borderless 'reality' and 'fantasy' is one of her signatures. It may be a reality silenced by oppression, whether patriarchal or political, or one whose meaning awaits an alternate interpretation. Often, we come across the unsettling but still invigorating atmosphere where reason fails and imagination takes over. *Una novela erótica* (1986), *Mesías en Montevideo* (1989), and particularly *Perfumes de Cartago* (1994), which tells the story of the five women of the Mualdeb family as they arrive to settle in Montevideo, weave together Porzecanski's distinct tapestry. These threads, built on common or distant origins and ancestors, also appear in more recent works, as new questions and desires arise.

In titling a text that addressed the theme of Israel for Latin American Jewish writers, "Separación, travesía, incorporación," Porzecanski conveyed three instances that articulate her own fiction. Though aiming at a different issue, she also made explicit how her different practices as a writer and as an anthropologist come together: "Latin American Jewish literature tries to pick up on its diasporic path something that was forbidden, that without exile would not have existed: the descent into the human diversity, knowledge of oneself, which is the knowledge of the other" (253). It is through such a journey, she adds, that one may achieve the ability to be totally free. A freedom that we find sometimes in the title of a book, such as *Irse y andar* (2011), in tracing the character known as Shoshani (?–1968), in addressing her country's history and myths of singularity, and even in having anticipated its fracture.

In 1989, Mauricio Rosencof (Florida, Uruguay, 1933) and Eleuterio Fernández Huidobro (Montevideo, 1942–2016), two of the nine Tupamaro leaders held as 'hostages' by the military dictatorship, published *Memorias del calabozo* – a three-volume conversation recounting their lengthy imprisonment and torture (1973–1985). It received the Premio Bartolomé Hidalgo in the "Testimonio" category; an advance of that experience was published in 1987 in "Literatura del calabozo." Long before his incarceration, Rosencof was known for the chronicles published in the influential *Marcha*, some of which were later included in *Las crónicas del Tuleque* (1986), for *La rebelión de los cañeros* (1969), for children's books, and for his work as a playwright. After the seven surviving hostages were freed, several were elected or appointed to Uruguay's highest offices; Rosencof served as Montevideo's Director of Culture (2005–2010). Since his liberation, he published a string of books and plays that confirmed the degree to which crafting them in his mind contributed to defeating the avowed goal of the military to drive the hostages insane.

In comments about several Argentine authors, I pointed out how the experience of exile led some to retrieve and incorporate Jewish origins into their literature. In Rosencof's case it was his torture and incarceration, mostly in solitary confinement, that would lead to *Las cartas que no llegaron* (2000) and *Diez minutos* (2013), among his sustained production in fiction, poetry, theater, and even a script he wrote with Carlos Maggi (1922–2015) to stage the opera *Il Duce* (2013). Literature is memory, survival, and legacy. In isolation, imagination is a recourse to fight off insanity. These are some of the terms that emerge from Rosencof's own retelling of his experience and from various passages in both novels that blend him into his parent's European past, to atrocities, to the deathly silence that marked the letters' absence. And also, less than three decades later, to the torture and enforced silence he suffered, to the brief meeting with the father who can't recognize that handcuffed figure across the table as his son.

The "Letter" from prison that Moishe [Mauricio's Jewish name] writes to his father includes childhood memories, his father's experience in World War I, an understanding of things he had heard and dismissed. Being confined, he feels connected to his family, to the losses during the Shoa, to a past from which he had always felt alienated. Past and present: ". . . Jews play the violin and not the piano because they live light of luggage, if you run away from a pogrom you don't carry a piano, you get in the car, and between the cage of chickens and the trunk of bedding, you draw the violin and you play *Eli Eli* or the *Hatikva*, that I played and that I don't even remember, Dad; and don't you dare send me the violin here; you don't, but Mom has these things, she asks me if I watch TV; cobwebs, Viejo [Old Man], the rest is silence. But I still sometimes stand in the center of my two square meters and fit the violin under my chin (. . .) I mark the beat, Viejo. . . but what comes out is a tango, what-can-you-do!" (Rosencof 2000, 60). The letter leads from a reference to a pogrom, to World War II, to the Uruguayan military; from a liturgical piece and the Israeli anthem to a tango: the course of arrival and integration. Writing letters he couldn't write in his cell, he recalls and indicts his parents' exile from their place to an old-age home after his arrest: Uruguay had become a daily pogrom, a country to flee from. His father's flawed Spanish and his own ignorance of Yiddish, and still a bridge between them. The image of lost relatives, a name that assures continuity, a taste of food forever present: lines that trace lineage and political commitment; an anchor in a past that leads to fighting for social justice no matter the cost and wherever a country of one's own finally is.

13 Pending

In the quote that precedes this essay, I suggested that this is an opening or, more appropriately, a continuation of readings of Latin American-Jewish authors to be enriched and expanded by other researchers. Had space been unlimited (time certainly isn't) I would have expanded not just these readings but also included prose fiction writers and poets such as Cecilia Absatz (1943), Alberto Adellach (1933–1996), Marcos Aguinis (1935), Marcos Ricardo Barnatán (1946), Alicia Borinsky (1946), Antonio Elio Brailovsky (1946), Marcelo Cohen (1951), Mario Diament (1942), Osvaldo Dragún (1929–1999), Ricardo Feierstein (1942), Jacobo Fijman (1898–1970), Manuela Fingueret (1945–2013), Daniel Guebel (1956), Nora Glickman (1944), Daniel Gutman (1954), Ricardo Halac (1935), Ariana Harwicz (1977), Liliana Heker (1943), Gisela Heffes (1971), José Isaacson (1922), Noé Jitrik (1928), Fernando Klein (1970), Santiago

Kovadloff (1942), Denise León (1974), Lázaro Liacho (1906–1969), Liliana Lukin (1951), Leo Masliah (1954), María Gabriela Mizraje (1965), Sandra Pien (1960), Silvia Plager (1942), José Rabinovich (1903–1978), Diana Raznovich (1943), Mercedes Roffé (1954), Reina Roffé (1951), Daniel Samoilovich (1949), Mario Satz (1944), Ricardo Talesnik (1935), Susana Thénon (1933–1991), Paulina Vinderman (1944), Elina Wechsler (1952), Héctor Yánover (1929–2003), Saúl Yurkievich (1931–2005). A task to be continued...

Bibliography

Works Cited

Aguinis, Marcos. *Refugiados: crónica de un palestino*. Buenos Aires: Planeta, 1976.
Aizenberg, Edna. *Parricide on the Pampa? A New Study and Translation of Alberto Gerchunoff's 'Los gauchos judíos'*. Madrid: Iberoamericana, 2000.
Aizenberg, Edna. *Books and Bombs in Buenos Aires. Borges, Gerchunoff, and Argentine-Jewish Writing*. Hanover: University Press of New England, 2002.
Aizenberg, Edna. "The 'Other' Gerchunoff and the Visual Representation of the Shoah." *The New Jewish Argentina. Facets of Jewish Experiences in the Southern Cone*. Eds. Adriana Brodsky and Raanan Rein. Leiden: Brill, 2013.131–145.
Barylko, Jaime et al, eds. *Pluralismo e identidad: lo judío en la literatura latinoamericana*. Buenos Aires: Milá, 1986.
Blaisten, Isidoro. *La salvación*. Buenos Aires: CEDAL, 1972.
Blaisten, Isidoro. *El mago*. Buenos Aires: Ediciones del Sol, 1974.
Blaisten, Isidoro. *Dublin al sur*. Buenos Aires: El Cid, 1980.
Blaisten, Isidoro. *Anticonferencias*. Buenos Aires: Emecé, 1983.
Blaisten, Isidoro. *Cuando éramos felices*. Buenos Aires: Emecé, 1992.
Bortnik, Aída. *Teatro Abierto*. Buenos Aires: Corregidor, 1991–1992.
Chejfec, Sergio. *Lenta biografía*. Buenos Aires: Puntosur, 1990.
Chejfec, Sergio. *Los planetas*. Buenos Aires: Alfaguara, 1999.
Chejfec, Sergio. "Marcas en el laberinto. Literatura judía y territorios." *El punto vacilante. Literatura, ideas y mundo privado*. Buenos Aires: Norma, 2005. 119–133.
Chejfec, Sergio. "La pesadilla." *Poéticas de la distancia. Adentro y afuera de la literatura argentina*. Eds. Sylvia Molloy and Mariano Siskind. Buenos Aires: Norma, 2006. 103–114.
Costantini, Humberto. *Una vieja historia de caminantes*. Buenos Aires: CEDAL, 1967.
Costantini, Humberto. *Háblenme de Funes*. Buenos Aires: Sudamericana, 1970.
Costantini, Humberto. *Libro de Trelew*. Buenos Aires: Granica, 1973.
Costantini, Humberto. *De dioses, hombrecitos y policías*. La Habana: Casa de las Américas, 1979.
Costantini, Humberto. *La larga noche de Francisco Sanctis*. Buenos Aires: Bruguera, 1984.
Cozarinsky, Edgardo. *Borges en/y/sobre/cine*. Madrid: Fundamentos, 1981.
Cozarinsky, Edgardo. *Vudú urbano*. Barcelona: Anagrama, 1985.
Cozarinsky, Edgardo. *La novia de Odessa*. Buenos Aires: Emecé, 2001.
Cozarinsky, Edgardo. *El rufián moldavo*. Buenos Aires: Emecé, 2004.
Cozarinsky, Edgardo. *Maniobras nocturnas*. Buenos Aires: Emecé, 2007.
Cozarinsky, Edgardo. *Lejos de dónde*. Barcelona: TusQuets, 2009.
Cozarinsky, Edgardo. *Dark*. Barcelona: TusQuets, 2016.

Cozarinsky, Edgardo. *Niño enterrado*. Buenos Aires: Entropía, 2016.
Dujovne Ortiz, Alicia. *El árbol de la gitana*. Buenos Aires: Aguilar, 1997.
Eichelbaum, Samuel. *El judío Aarón*. Buenos Aires: Talía, 1926.
Eichelbaum, Samuel. *Un guapo del 900*. Buenos Aires: CEDAL, 1968.
Feierstein, Ricardo. *Sinfonía inocente (El caramelo descompuesto, Entre la izquierda y la pared, Escala uno en cincuenta)*. Buenos Aires: Pardés, 1984.
Feierstein, Ricardo, and Stephen A. Sadow, eds. *Recreando la cultura judeoargentina /2, literatura y artes plásticas*. Buenos Aires: Milá, 2004.
Foster, David William, and Naomi Lindstrom. "Jewish Argentine Authors: A Registry." *Revista Interamericana de Bibliografía*, Part 1 in XLI, 3 (1991): 478–503; Part 2 in XLI, 4 (1991): 655–682.
Futoransky, Luisa. *La sanguina*. Barcelona: Ediciones Taifa, 1987.
Futoransky, Luisa. *Prender de gajo*. Madrid: Ediciones Calambur, 2006.
Gai, Mijal. "El lenguaje poético de Alberto Szpunberg en *La Academia de Piatock*." Academia.edu
Gelman, Juan. *Com/posiciones*. Barcelona: Llibres del Mall, 1986.
Gelman, Juan. "Lo *judío* y la literatura en castellano." *Hispamérica*, XXI, 62 (1992): 83–90.
H[oracio] L[utzky]", Juan Gelman: una cultura democrática," *Nueva Sión* [Buenos Aires], August 22, 1992, p. 15
Gelman, Juan. *Dibaxu*. Buenos Aires: Seix Barral, 1994.
Gerchunoff, Alberto. *Los gauchos judíos* [1910]. *El hombre que habló en la Sorbona* [1926]. Estudio preliminar de Perla Sneh. Buenos Aires: Biblioteca Nacional, Colihue, 2007.
Gerchunoff, Alberto. *La jofaina maravillosa: Agenda cervantina*. Buenos Aires: Babel, 1922.
Gerchunoff, Alberto. *El cristianismo precristiano*. Buenos Aires: Asociación Hebraica, 1924.
Gerchunoff, Alberto. *Entre Ríos, mi país*. Buenos Aires: Futuro, 1950.
Gerchunoff, Alberto. *Retorno a Don Quijote*. Buenos Aires: Sudamericana, 1951.
Gerchunoff, Alberto. *Argentina, país de advenimiento*. Buenos Aires: Losada, 1952.
Glickman, Nora. "Una tal Raquel." *Cuatro obras de Nora Glickman*. Buenos Aires: Nueva Generación, 2000. 19–60.
Glickman, Nora. *The Jewish White Slave Trade and the Untold Story of Raquel Liberman*. London: Routledge, 2015.
Glusberg, Samuel. *La levita gris: cuentos judíos de ambiente porteño*. Buenos Aires: Babel, 1924.
Goldberg, Florinda F. "Alejandra Pizarnik: Palabra y sombra." *Noah*, I, 1 (1987): 58–62.
Goldberg, Florinda F. "The Complex Roses of Jerusalem: The Theme of Israel in Argentinian Jewish Poetry." *Tradition and Innovation. Reflection on Latin American Jewish Writing*. Eds. Robert DiAntonio and Nora Glickman. Albany: SUNY Press, 1993. 73–86.
Goldberg, Florinda F. *Alejandra Pizarnik: "Este espacio que somos."* Gaithersburg: Ediciones Hispamérica, 1994.
Goloboff, Mario. *Entre la diáspora y octubre*. Buenos Aires: Stilcograf, 1966.
Goloboff, Mario. *Caballos por el fondo de los ojos*. Barcelona: Planeta, 1976.
Goloboff, Mario. *Criador de palomas*. Buenos Aires: Bruguera, 1984.
Goloboff, Mario. "De una lengua impura." *Pluralismo e identidad. Lo judío en la literatura latinoamericana*. Eds. Jaime Barylko et al. Buenos Aires: Milá, 1986. 123–127.
Goloboff, Mario. *La luna que cae*. Barcelona: Muchnik, 1989.
Goloboff, Mario. "Diálogo íntimo de dos obras: Mi Algarrobos natal ante la Ferrara de Giorgio Bassani." *Hispamérica*, XX, 60 (1991): 85–92.
Goloboff, Mario. *Comuna verdad*. Madrid: Muchnik, 1995.
Goloboff, Mario. "Lo judío en mi obra." *Recreando la Cultura juedeoargentina*. Eds. Ricardo Feierstein and Stephen A. Sadow. Buenos Aires: Milá, 2002. 309–310.
Grünberg, Carlos M. *Mester de judería*. Intr. Jorge Luis Borges. Buenos Aires: Argirópolis, 1940.

Grünberg, Carlos M. *Haggadah Buenos Aires*. Buenos Aires: Editorial Fundación para el Fomento de la Cultura Hebrea, 5706/1946.
Grünberg, Carlos M. *Junto a un río de Babel*. Buenos Aires, Acervo Cultural/Editores, 1965. Xilografías de Víctor Marchese.
Kamenszain, Tamara. *De este lado del Mediterráneo*. Buenos Aires: Noé, 1973.
Kamenszain, Tamara. *Los no*. Buenos Aires: Sudamericana, 1977.
Kamenszain, Tamara. *La casa grande*. Buenos Aires: Sudamericana, 1986.
Kamenszain, Tamara. "Toda escritura es femenina y judía." *Pluralismo e identidad: lo judío en la literatura latinoamericana*. Eds. Jaime Barylko et al. Buenos Aires: Milá, 1986. 129–132.
Kamenszain, Tamara. "El ghetto de mi lengua." *Poéticas de la distancia. Adentro y afuera de la literatura argentina*. Eds. Sylvia Molloy and Mariano Siskind. Buenos Aires: Norma, 2006. 157–169.
Kamenszain, Tamara. *El ghetto*. México: Literal, 2012.
Kanzepolsky, Adriana. "'Aquí llegamos, aquí no veníamos', acerca de *El ghetto* de Tamara Kamenszain." *Hispamérica*, XXXIX, 115 (2010): 104–112.
Kohan, Martín. *Dos veces junio*. Buenos Aires: Sudamericana, 2002.
Kohan, Martín. "La emigración en ciernes." *Poéticas de la distancia. Adentro y afuera de la literatura argentina*. Eds. Sylvia Molloy and Mariano Siskind. Buenos Aires: Norma, 2006. 129–140.
Kohan, Martín. *Ciencias morales*. Barcelona: Anagrama, 2007.
Kohan, Martín. *El país de la Guerra*. Buenos Aires: Eterna Cadencia, 2014.
Kordon, Bernardo. *A punto de reventar seguido de Kid Ñandubay*. Buenos Aires: Losada, 1971.
Lockhart, Darrell B. *Jewish Writers of Latin America. A Dictionary*. New York: Garland, 1997.
Memmi, Albert. *La liberation du Juif*. Paris: Gallimard, 1966.
Migdal, Alicia. *Mascarones*. Montevideo: Arca, 1981.
Migdal, Alicia. *Historias de cuerpos*. Montevideo: Arca, 1986.
Migdal, Alicia. *La casa de enfrente*. Montevideo: Arca, 1988
Migdal, Alicia. *Historia quieta*. Montevideo: Trilce, 1993.
Migdal, Alicia. *Muchachas de verano en días de marzo*. Montevideo: Cal y Canto, 1999.
Migdal, Alicia. *En un idioma extranjero*. Montevideo: Rebeca Linke Editoras, 2008.
Mizraje, María Gabriela. "Una retórica del cruce: lazos de sangre en los textos identitarios de Germán Rozenmacher." *Sambatión. Estudios judíos desde Latinoamérica*, I, 1 (2006): 17–42.
Mizraje, María Gabriela. "Germán Rozenmacher y un judío afán: la argentinidad como consigna." *Hispamérica*, XLVI, 137 (2017): 3–14.
Molloy, Sylvia, and Mariano Siskind, eds. *Poéticas de la distancia. Adentro y afuera de la literatura argentina*. Buenos Aires: Norma, 2006.
Muchnik, Mario.. *El ídish es también Latinoamérica*. Buenos Aires: Ediciones Instituto Movilizador de Fondos Cooperativos (2003?).
Orgambide, Pedro. *Hotel familias*. Buenos Aires: Ediciones de la Flor, 1972.
Orgambide, Pedro. *Aventuras de Edmund Ziller en tierras del Nuevo Mundo*. México: Grijalbo, 1977.
Orgambide, Pedro. *El arrabal del mundo*. Buenos Aires: Bruguera, 1983a.
Orgambide, Pedro. "Notas sobre un poema de Humberto Costantini." *Hispamérica*, XII, 36 (1983b): 45–52.
Orgambide, Pedro. *Hacer la América*. Buenos Aires: Bruguera, 1984.
Orgambide, Pedro. *Pura memoria*. Buenos Aires: Bruguera, 1985.
Pizarnik, Alejandra. *Textos de sombra y últimos poemas*. Buenos Aires: Sudamericana, 1985.
Porzecanski, Teresa. *Una novela erótica*. Montevideo: Margen, 1986 [Montevideo: Planeta, 2000].
Porzecanski, Teresa. *Mesías en Montevideo*. Montevideo: Signos, 1989.
Porzecanski, Teresa. *Perfumes de Cartago*. Montevideo: Trilce, 1994.

Porzecanski, Teresa. "Separación, travesía, incorporación." *Pluralismo e identidad: lo judío en la literatura latinoamericana*. Eds. Jaime Barylko et al. Buenos Aires: Milá, 1986. 251–255.

Porzecanski, Rafael. *El Uruguay judío. Demografía e identidad*. Montevideo: Trilce, 2006.

Porzecanski, Teresa. *Irse y andar*. Montevideo: Ediciones B, 2011.

Ramos-Izquierdo, Eduardo and Federica Rocco. "Escribir hoy desde París: Laura Alcoba, Alicia Dujovne Ortiz y Luisa Futoransky." *Hispamérica*, XLVI, 137 (2017): 49–62.

Rivera, Andrés. *Nada que perder*. Buenos Aires: CEDAL, 1982.

Rivera, Andrés. *La revolución es un sueño eterno*. Buenos Aires: Alfaguara, 1992a.

Rivera, Andrés. *La sierva*. Buenos Aires: Alfaguara, 1992b.

Rivera, Andrés. *El Farmer*. Buenos Aires: Alfaguara, 1996.

Rivera, Andrés. *El manco Paz*. Buenos Aires: Alfaguara, 2003.

Rivera, Andrés. *Kadish*. Buenos Aires: Seix Barral, 2011.

Rosencof, Mauricio. *Las cartas que no llegaron*. Montevideo: Santillana, 2000.

Rosencof, Mauricio. *Diez minutos*. Montevideo: Santillana, 2013.

Rosencof, Mauricio and Carlos Maggi. *Il Duce. Texto para una ópera*. Montevideo: Alfaguara, 2013.

Rozenmacher, Germán. *Obras completas*. Ed. Matías H. Raia. Buenos Aires: Biblioteca Nacional, 2013.

Rozitchner, León. *Ser judío*. Buenos Aires: Ediciones de la Flor, 1967.

Senkman, Leonardo. *La identidad judía en la literatura argentina*. Buenos Aires: Pardés, 1983.

Senkman, Leonardo. "Juan Gelman (Entrevista)". *Noaj*, 7–8 (1992): 106–113.

Shua, Ana María. *Los amores de Laurita*. Buenos Aires: Sudamericana, 1984.

Shua, Ana María. *El libro de los recuerdos*, Buenos Aires: Sudamericana, 1994.

Shua, Ana María. *El pueblo de los tontos: humor tradicional judío*. Buenos Aires: Alfaguara, 1995.

Shua, Ana María. *Sabiduría popular judía*. Rosario: Ameghino, 1998.

Shua, Ana María. *Risas y emociones de la cocina judía*. Buenos Aires: Shalom, 2003.

Shua, Ana María. "Con todo lo que soy. Mujer, argentina, judía y escritora." *Recreando la cultura judeoargentina 2: Literatura y artes plásticas*. Eds. Stephen A. Sadow and Ricardo Feierstein. Buenos Aires: Milá, 2004.

Steimberg, Alicia. *Músicos y relojeros*. Buenos Aires: CEDAL, 1971.

Steimberg, Alicia. *Su espíritu inocente*. Buenos Aires: Pomaire, 1981.

Steimberg, Alicia. *Cuando digo Magdalena*. Buenos Aires: Planeta, 1992.

Sosnowski, Saúl. *La orilla inminente: Escritores judíos-argentinos*. Buenos Aires: Legasa, 1987.

Suárez, Patricia. *La Germania*. Buenos Aires: Losada, 2006.

Szichman, Mario. *Crónica falsa*. Buenos Aires: Jorge Álvarez, 1969.

Szichman, Mario. *Los judíos del Mar Dulce*. Buenos Aires-Caracas: Galerna-Síntesis 2000, 1971.

Szichman, Mario. *La verdadera crónica falsa*. Buenos Aires: CEDAL, 1972.

Szichman, Mario. *A las 20:25 la señora entró en la inmortalidad*. Hanover: Ediciones del Norte, 1981.

Szpunberg, Alberto. "Charlas con Ana.". *Hispamérica*, XIII, 38 (1984): 47–56.

Szpunberg, Alberto. *La Academia de Piatock*. Córdoba: Alción, 2010.

Szurmuk, Mónica. *La vocación desmesurada. Una biografía de Alberto Gerchunoff*. Buenos Aires: Sudamericana, 2018.

Tiempo, César. *Versos de una. . . [Clara Beter]*. Buenos Aires: Claridad, 1926.

Tiempo, César. *Libro para la pausa del Sábado*. Buenos Aires: Gleizer, 1930.

Tiempo, César. *Sabatión Argentino: antiguas y nuevas donas para la pausa del sábado*. Buenos Aires-Montevideo: Sociedad Amigos del Libro Rioplatense, 1933.

Tiempo, César. *El teatro soy yo*. Buenos Aires: Anaconda, 1933.

Tiempo, César. *Sábadomingo*. Buenos Aires: Porter, 1938.

Tiempo, César. *Pan criollo*. Buenos Aires: Porter, 1938.

Tiempo, César. *Sábado Pleno*. Buenos Aires: Gleizer, 1955.

Toker, Eliahu. *El resplandor de la palabra judía. Antología de la poesía idish del siglo XX.* Buenos Aires: Pardés, 1981.
Toker, Eliahu. *Papá, mamá y otras ciudades.* Buenos Aires: Contexto, 1988.
Toker, Eliahu. *Un diferente su diferencia. Vida y obra de Carlos M. Grünberg.* Madrid: Taller de Mario Muchnik, 1999.
Verbitsky, Bernardo. *Es difícil empezar a vivir.* Buenos Aires: Losada, 1941.
Verbitsky, Bernardo. *En esos años.* Buenos Aires: Futuro, 1947.
Verbitsky, Bernardo. *Café de los Angelitos y otros cuentos porteños.* Buenos Aires: Siglo Veinte, 1949.
Verbitsky, Bernardo. *Villa Miseria también es América.* Buenos Aires: Kraft, 1957.
Verbitsky, Bernardo. *Etiquetas a los hombres.* Barcelona: Planeta, 1972.
Verbitsky, Bernardo. "Ante mi obra." *Hispamérica*, II, 6 (1973): 83–90.
Viñas, David. *Los dueños de la tierra.* Buenos Aires: Losada, 1958.
Viñas, David. *Hombres de a caballo.* La Habana: Casa de las Américas, 1967.
Viñas, David. *Lisandro.* Buenos Aires: Merlín, 1971.
Viñas, David. *Jauría.* Buenos Aires: Granica, 1974.
Viñas, David. *Dorrego: Teatro.* Buenos Aires: Galerna, 1974.
Viñas, David. *Cuerpo a cuerpo.* México: Siglo XXI, 1979.
Viñas, David. *Literatura argentina y política I, II.* Buenos Aires: Sudamericana, 1995–1996.
Weinstein, Ana E. ,and Myriam E. Gover de Nasatsky. *Escritores judeo-argentinos. Bibliografía 1900–1987.* Buenos Aires: Milá, 1994, 2 Vols.
Wirth-Nesher, Hana, ed. *What is Jewish Literature?* Philadelphia-Jerusalem: The Jewish Publication Society, 1994.

Further Reading

Aizenberg, Edna. Books and Bombs in Buenos Aires. Borges, Gerchunoff, and Argentine-Jewish Writing. Waltham: Brandeis University Press, 2002.
Goldemberg, Isaac, comp. *El gran libro de América judía.* San Juan: Editorial de la Universidad de Puerto Rico, 1998.
Lockhart, Darrell B., ed., Jewish Writers in Latin America: A Dictionary. New York: Routledge, 2016.
Ran, Amalia. Made of Shores. Judeo-Argentinean Fiction Revisited. Bethlehem: Lehigh University Press, 2011.
Senkman, Leonardo. La identidad judía en la literatura argentina. Buenos Aires: Pardés, 1983.

V Contemporary Contexts

Leonardo Senkman

19 Historiography and Literary Essays on Latin American Jews in the New Millennium

Abstract: Since the beginning of the new millennium, the historiography of Latin American Jews has been enriched by pioneering works and innovative lines of research. A novel analytical lens has been adopted for examining the ethnicity, nationality and citizenship of immigrant communities that have negotiated their particular identities vis-à-vis the national identities of the Latin American countries of which they are citizens by birth or by naturalization. The objective of this essay is to review the impact of this epistemological shift, beginning in the year 2000, within both historiographical research and cultural studies on the past and present of Jews in Latin America.

The theory of the novel analytical approach examined here was expressed in brief in 2006 in the first joint article by Jeffrey Lesser and Raanan Rein: *Challenging Particularity: Jews as a Lens on Latin American Ethnicity* (Lesser and Rein 2006). Both historians express an interest in shifting from the dominant paradigm of ethnicity in the study of communities of immigrant origin in Latin America and in returning to the "nation" as a prominent analytical paradigm.

Key Terms: Jewish Latin America, Argentine, Immigration, Twenty-first Century

1 The Brill Series: Jewish Latin America – Issues and Methods

The explicit goal of Lesser and Rein is to propose a change to students of the ethnicity of minorities whose ancestors' religions were characterized as non-Catholic. In challenging the traditional historiography that primarily characterized Jews as members of the Jewish Diaspora, both authors propose the use of the term "Jewish-Latin Americans" rather than "Latin American Jewry." Their theoretical aim is to highlight that the scholarly history of Jews in Latin America should be a subject of Latin American studies.

The first comprehensive analytical study by Raanan Rein that made use of this new paradigm appeared in his *Argentine Jews or Jewish Argentines? Essays on Ethnicity, Identity, and Diaspora* (2010), followed one year later by its Spanish translation (Rein 2011). Argentina, a multiethnic and culturally diverse society, presented a multifaceted case study to which the author could apply his paradigm, which differentiates between the terms Argentinian Jews and Jewish Argentinians. In Rein's analysis, Jews are not a monolithic collective but rather fragmented residents and citizens according to place of origin, social class, political ideology, and ethno-linguistic formation. His main objective is to challenge essentialist conceptions of Jewry along with an overemphasis on Jewish particularity, as well as to review the frequent historical discourse of Jewish victimhood.

However, the topics and issues selected in Rein's book do not differentiate between the public sphere of citizenship among Jewish Argentinians and their ethnicity within the Argentinian Jewish community. Out of ten chapters, two explore attitudes among Argentinian Jewish citizens toward social and political conflicts that affect them in relation to the organized Argentinian Jewish community. One chapter, *Nationalism, Education and Identity: Argentinian Jews and Catholic Religious Instruction*, deals with the first Peronist government, while another, *Argentinian Jews and the Accusation of Dual Loyalty*, deals with post-Peronist governments until 1966.

In order to study the individual reactions of Argentinian Jewish citizens to the mandatory imposition of Catholic teaching during the years 1946–1954, it would have been necessary to conduct a comparative analysis which included the reactions of other non-Catholic religious communities. Such an analysis would have needed to tackle personal sources such as memoirs, life stories, autobiographical literary texts, and petitions of relatives of students in order to analyze active and passive reactions. The chapter lacks interviews on the accusation of dual loyalty during the Israel-Argentina diplomatic conflict over the kidnapping of Eichmann and the anti-Semitic wave of nationalist organizations such as Tacuara and GRN. Rein only documents this issue using sources from the official diplomatic archives of Israel and the USA and from international Jewish organizations such as AJC in addition to the Israeli and Argentinian press and the weekly *Mundo Israelita*. Undoubtedly, the best chapters of the book are those which are based on diplomatic sources regarding Israel-Argentina relations and those which are based on sources from the Israeli press (Rein 2010, Ch. 6, 7, 10).

Directly following the impact of Raanan Rein's book, Brill Publishing House decided to appoint him as the editor of a new series, *Jewish Latin America: Issues and Methods*. Since its inception in 2011, eleven books have been published for readers of English. Their broad range of themes and methodologies contributes to the development of a more subtle approach to the study of Jewish identity in Latin America. However, most of the books are devoted to studying the Argentinian case, with the exception of one study of Mexico (Gleizer 2013).

The first volume is an anthology of Latin American Jewish experiences, focusing on identity as represented in culture, literature and society from a variety of disciplinary perspectives (Ran and Cahan 2011). The more innovative articles in this volume deal with literature and culture. They include the work of literary critics including Saúl Sosnowski (*Jewish and lo Latinoamericano in the Arts: Borges and the Kabbalah: Pre-Texts to a Text*); Edna Aizenberg (*Jewishness as Literary Representation: Should We Bury the Jewish Gaucho? A New Gerchunoff for the Twenty-First Century*); Sergio Waisman (*The Jewish Latin American Writer and Tradition: The Case of Sergio Chejfec*); Nelson Vieira (*Beyond Identity: Clarice Lispector and the Ethical Transcendence of

Being for the Other); and Tzvi Tal (*Jewish Puberty in Contemporary Latin American Cinema: Constructing Judeo-Latinidad*)

Diverse facets of Jewish Argentina are thoroughly covered in the series through a variety of subjects and authors on history, culture and memory, about both individual Jews and Argentina's Jewish community (Brodsky and Rein 2012; Wassner 2013; Levine and Zaretsky 2015; Gurwitz 2017; Kahan 2018).

Two pioneering scholarly studies on Jewish Latin America are also welcome additions: *Mazal Tov, Amigos! Jews and Popular Music in the Americas*, edited by Amalia Ran and Moshe Morad (2016) and *Splendor, Decline, and Rediscovery of Yiddish in Latin America*, edited by Malena Chinski and Alan Astro (2018). Also deserving of praise is a comparative collection of studies on sports: *Muscling in on New Worlds: Jews, Sport, and the Making of the Americas*, edited by Raanan Rein and David Sheinin (2014).

The ninth volume is a collection of articles that were presented at an international workshop held at Tel Aviv University (Rein et al. 2017). Among various discussions of issues and methods, the volume offers new comparative approaches to ethnic collectivities, including a study of the role of Jews and Palestinian Arabs in the formation of the middle class in Chile, of the representation of individuals from diverse ethnic groups in contemporary Chilean media, and of the voices of women, non-affiliated Jews, and intellectuals (Stern 2017). The stated goal of the volume is to show the extent to which ethnic community institutions are not at center stage; instead, the editors chose topics pertaining to social conflicts and national tensions faced by non-affiliated Jews in order to challenge images of homogeneity in those communities.

The most interesting articles in this volume are those which investigate arguments regarding the role of nationalism, ethnicity and cultural legacy in assessing claims of inclusion/exclusion into citizenship among Arab-Argentinians who, rather than being unaffiliated, were involved with both the institutions of the populist movement and with ethnic Syrian-Lebanese associations. Paradoxically, the volume includes an article called *For an Arab, There Can Be Nothing Better Than Another Arab: Nation, Ethnicity and Citizenship in Peronist Argentina*, by Ariel Noyjovich and Raanan Rein, which shows that Peronist authorities granted full recognition of cultural and ethnic differences to both Arab-Argentinian and Jewish-Argentinian citizens through their collective representative communal institutions (*colectividades*). This perspective could be complemented by an examination of how Peronist policies on inclusion/exclusion into citizenship (in the legal or political sense, or in the sense of identity) were the outcome of a bargaining process and why populist regimes accepted the collective identity of ethno-national communities in granting legitimacy to their inclusion in political citizenship (Dumbrava 2012).

In a particularly interesting chapter, Valeria Navarro-Rosenblatt discusses the importance of non-affiliated Jewish voices in Chile during the half-century between 1940 and 1990. However, the chosen case study proves exactly the opposite of what the author intends. Using oral history, the author attempts to uncover the stories of leftist Jews who do not appear in the official community narrative. She makes her point by briefly examining the Centro Cultural Sholem Aleijem, which was important in the 1950s but whose membership was not mentioned in official central Jewish community records. The reason for the exclusion of these communist-affiliated Jews was obviously not ethnic but ideological.

Navarro-Rosenblatt also looks at a Socialist Party activist, Hanne G., to understand why official Jewish organizations refused to assist her after Pinochet's coup. Joel Horowitz points out very accurately in his book review that both examples adduced by Navarro-Rosenblatt are important but in fact challenge her assumption that "those who belong to no (central) Jewish organizations represent unaffiliated Jews" (2017, 142). The reviewer's explanation is that Centro Cultural members were obviously affiliated Jews, and both Hanne G. and her husband were involved with a leftist Jewish organization not recognized by the official community for ideological reasons.

Only several chapters in Volume Nine grapple with the issue of ethnicity and its complexities for the analysis of multiple identities. In *Factory, Workshop, and Homework: A Spatial Dimension of Labor Flexibility Among Jewish Migrants in the Early Stages of Industrialization in Buenos Aires*, Nadia Zysman refrains from asking any theoretical questions linked to the complex concepts of ethnicity, social class, cultural differences and multiple identities. To describe this lacuna in Horowitz's own words:

> Were Jewish communists in Argentina in the textile or the furniture industry in the first decades of the twentieth century thinking of themselves primarily as Jews, communists, or Argentinians, or some combination? Did other identities have an impact? Did many of them belong to 'Jewish' labor or general political organizations? (2017, 143)

In a similar way, Mariusz Kałczewiak, in his chapter *Becoming Polacos: Landsmanshaftn and the Making of a Polish-Jewish Sub-ethnicity in Argentina*, refrains from asking how Polish Jewish immigrants in Argentina confronted the cancellation of their Polish citizenship after the German Nazi invasion of 1939, which rendered them Jews without a homeland. Nor does the author raise the question of how the closing of the Polish Embassy affected Polish Jews. Did they replace their abolished Polish nationality with the Jewish-Polish sub-identity represented by the Polisher Jewish Farband as a central Ashkenazic communal institution? To raise this issue in a different way: it might have been worthwhile to dedicate more attention to crucial questions of identity, otherness and ethnicity.

Another interesting volume in the series is *Argentinian Jews in the Age of Revolt. Between the New World and the Third World* (Gurwitz 2017). This historical study by Beatrice D. Gurwitz examines the discourse of Jewish activists during a period of radical challenges faced by Argentinian youth in the years of transition between civil and military rule (1955, 1963, 1966); massive social turmoil and protest; escalating violence prior to and during the return of populism; and the impact of the last military dictatorship (1976–1983). It is to the author's credit that she traces ongoing efforts among Argentinian Jews affiliated with the organized institutions of Buenos Aires Jewry to rethink Argentinian nationality, membership in the Jewish community and the shifting meaning of Jewishness itself within the local context between the overthrow of Juan Perón and the restoration of democracy in 1983. This is achieved through an examination of the shifting ideas of nation, ethnicity and belonging among a broad spectrum of Jewish activists during the years of waves of anti-Semitism, mounting labor unrest, and the questioning of Argentina's liberal myths caused by recurring political instability.

A second achievement is the author's desire to understand such conflicting political issues within the context of the ideological impact of the rise of the New Left and the flocking of many young Jews to Third World movements, which entailed the disavowal of their Jewishness and of their Zionism at the height of revolutionary ferment during the 1960s and the Peronist years.

Finally, the third achievement is the volume's assessment of the radical framing of Jewish ethnicity, Socialist Zionism and national belonging against the backdrop of "national liberation" in Argentina and across the Third World's ideological development.

However, the author refrains from examining the personal impact of these processes on young Jews who were not affiliated with Jewish institutions and pays little attention to the political, cultural and social participation of Jews in the open public sphere beginning in 1958. Although the volume's analytical lens aims to examine how Argentinian Jews reassessed notions of Argentinian nationhood and the shifting meaning of Jewishness itself, such an objective would have required a chapter completely devoted to scrutinizing how the majority of unaffiliated Argentinian Jews faced ideological and political challenges.

The second and fourth chapters could have offered more detailed information on the participation of Jewish intellectuals and politicians in the public sphere during the first major national democratization process that began during the presidency of Arturo Frondizi (1958–1962). For example, there is no mention of the fact that, for the first time in Argentinian history, two provincial Jewish governors were elected on the initiative of President Frondizi. One case occurred when the National Territory of Formosa gained the constitutional status of a province and its constitution was the first in Argentina to allow non-Catholic citizens to assume the rank of governor. Luis Gutnisky, a member of Frondizi's party Unión Cívica Radical Intransigente (UCRI), was the first deputy elected at the convention that drafted the Provincial Constitution of Formosa in 1957, and one year later he was elected governor. The second such case was that of Angel Edelman, who was born in a JCA colony in Entre Rios, supported Arturo Frondizi's presidential candidacy from the creation of the Intransigent Radical Civic Union party, and was one of the drafters of the Constitutional Convention of Neuquén in 1957. One year later, Edelman was the first elected governor of the newly established Province of Neuquén, with Alfredo Asmar, a UCRI activist of Lebanese origin, as his lieutenant governor.

At the national level, the first time a Jew was appointed minister was due to president Frondizi's public policy of the national integration of citizens irrespective of their religion. The lawyer and politician David Blejer, born to Jewish settlers in the JCA San Antonio Colony (Colón, Entre Ríos Province), was appointed by Frondizi first as

Undersecretary of the Interior and then as Minister of Labor. After serious hardships with labor unions, he was obliged to resign in 1961 and appointed as Argentinian Ambassador to Mexico.

In addition, it is necessary to remember that the "developmentalist" movement (*desarrollismo*),[1] which made the political triumph of Frondizi possible, was represented by several talented native Jewish intellectuals. The case of Ismael Viñas is not mentioned in Gurwitz's volume, even though an article about him does appear in the bibliography; nor does the volume mention the journalist and politician Marcos Merchensky, another *desarrollista,* who collaborated with Rogelio Frigerio on the ideological publication QUE and was the author of an important developmentalist essay. Merchensky became vice president of the committee of the Integration and Development Movement (MID) in Buenos Aires Province and completed his political career as a national deputy in the broad FREJULI block led by the Peronists in 1973 (see Amato 1983).

If Merchensky was the only elected Jewish deputy on this historical Peronist list, other Jews in the Cámpora-Perón government also deserve to be remembered, such as José Ber Gelbard, who was nominated as Minister of the Economy by President Peron. He is mentioned only once in the book, as the victim of an anti-Semitic political campaign waged by the right-wing Peronist minister Lopez Rega.

Unfortunately, another aspect neglected by Gurwitz's book is the participation of José Ber Gelbard and other Jewish businessmen in the General Economic Confederation (CGE), which was founded with the aim of boosting a project of economic development and the defense of the domestic market. This program was formulated by a group of national entrepreneurs in the CGE when its constitution was written in 1952. In addition to Gelbard, who owned the synthetic rubber company FATE, other leading Jewish CGE figures were Julio Broner, owner of one of the most important automobile parts companies, and Israel Dujovne, an entrepreneur in the urban construction industry (see Broner and Larriqueta 1969).

The political importance of the CGE was on full display when President Perón decided to draft his Social Pact between employers and workers (June 1973), an agreement in which both CGE president Broner and economic minister Geldbard played crucial roles (Jáuregui 2005; Leyba 2003; Fiszbein and Rougier 2006, 54–60; Senkman 2006).

The importance of the newspaper *La Opinión*, founded by Jacobo Timerman together with Abrasha Rotenberg in May 1971, could have been more strongly accentuated. *La Opinión* attracted a nucleus of talented Jewish intellectuals and journalists.

---

1 *Developmentalism* is a cross-disciplinary school of thought that gave way to an ideology of development policy as a key strategy for economic growth. Many Jews in Argentina and Brazil were adherents of political leaders who were engaged in economic development at the center of their political endeavors and institutions in Argentina and Brazil in the 1960s. This was a means to participate in the political sphere.

The writer and playwright Mario Diament became editor-in-chief after working in the international section, while Horacio Verbitsky was political editor and Juan Gelman was cultural editor (Rotenberg 1999; Mochkofsky 2004).

The chapter entitled *The Challenge of the New Left: 1967–1973* unfortunately omits a discussion of the young Jews who fought against the dictatorship of General Juan C. Onganía. Although the chapter deals with political militancy during the 1960s and 1970s, it leaves out the names of three significant Jewish militants: Carlos Goldenberg, Daniel Hopen and Eduardo Sigal. Daniel and his sister Isabel took part in the armed struggle in the Ejército de Liberación Nacional (ELN). Eduardo Sigal was affiliated with the Communist Youth Federation starting in 1965 and was forced to change college for the third time after being involved in physical clashes together with his communist comrades who were attacked by anti-Semitic nationalists of the Tacuara organization. A similar anti-communist attack would be repeated at Mariano Moreno National College in the Once neighborhood to which Sigal had relocated and eventually turned politically to the Peronist left.

The political and ideological trajectory of Marcos Osatinsky is highly significant. Both Marcos and his wife Sara Solarz were born in Tucumán Province, as was another Jewish communist, Sergio Paz Berlin. All three militants were involved in the failed FAL guerrilla takeover of Garin in 1970. Many Jews had become active members of the urban guerrilla FAL; Osatinsky and a group of Jewish communist militant comrades became leaders in FAL and were also well-known revolutionary Peronist activists.

Alejo Levenson studied chemistry at the Faculty of Exact Sciences of the University of Buenos Aires (UBA), where he joined the communist youth organization FJC. His parents, Gregorio Levenson and Elsa Rabinovich, had been active communist militants, and his brother Bernardo would later become a militant in the ranks of the FAR as well. Marcelo Kurlat studied chemistry and, together with his wife, was an important student leader of the FJC at UBA (González Canosa 2012, 89–120; 2016).

Finally, the name Daniel Hopen could have been added to this chapter dealing with the participation of Jews in the struggle against the dictatorship of General Onganía. A sociology graduate and lecturer at the UBA, Hopen was one of the founders of the Workers' Revolutionary Party (PRT) in 1965; a member of the Leninist group starting in 1973; and one of the leaders of the People's Revolutionary Army (ERP) guerrilla faction that broke with the Trotskyite party led by Roberto Santucho (Tillet 2010; Tarcus 2007).

2 Jewish Latin America Series (University of New Mexico)

Since 1997, Ilan Stavans has been the editor of the Jewish Latin America series at the University of New Mexico Press. The selected volumes are obviously marked indelibly by Stavans' literary tastes, his heterogeneous research and his multicultural interests. He is recognized for his explorations of Jewish culture in the Hispanic world. In 1994, he published the anthology *Tropical Synagogues: Stories by Jewish-Latin American Writers* and, in 2005, *The Schocken Book of Modern Sephardic Literature*, for which he received the National Jewish Book Award. Some of his essays on Jewish topics are included in *The Inveterate Dreamer: Essays and Conversations on Jewish Literature* (2001). In addition, he had published a collection of essays that brings together three cultures: Jewish, American, and Mexican (*A Critic's Journey*, 2009).

As a sociolinguist, Stavans is known as a world authority on Spanglish, the hybrid form of communication that emerges at the crossroads where Spanish and English speakers interact. He has edited a dictionary of Spanglish called *Spanglish: The Making of a New American Language* (2003). According to Stavans's transcultural and transnational outlook, Spanglish is today's manifestation of *mestizaje*, the hybridization of the racial, social and cultural traits of Anglos and Latinos, similar to what occurred during the colonization of the Americas in the sixteenth century. Stavans also establishes differences across generational and geographical lines, stating that recent immigrants are prone to use a type of Spanglish that differs from that of second or third-generation Latinos. He addresses Spanglish by making comparisons with Black English and with Yiddish, as well as with Yinglish (the type of Yiddish used by Jewish immigrants to the United States and their children).

Given this transnationalist, translinguistic and transcultural background, it is not surprising that the most interesting titles published by Stavans in his series are literary texts by Latin American Jewish authors that have been translated into English. The first book is the classic *Los Gauchos Judíos*, by Alberto Gerchunoff (1998), in the same translation produced by Prudencio de Pereda for the first English edition in 1959. The two volumes that follow are paradigmatic of the new Argentinian Jewish narrative.

In *Mestizo* (1988, ²1994; English edition: 2001), Ricardo Feierstein fictionalizes the conflict between the ethnicity and citizenship of a Jew who, for many years, yearns to be Argentinian – a *mestizo* who transcends cultures and belongings – without renouncing his diasporic origin.[2] Gerardo Mario Goloboff's trilogy, *The Algarrobos Quartet*, is a lyric elegiac Kaddish memorializing the once dreamed-of country (homeland), now evoked by an orphan child from an abandoned neighborhood of the Mauricio Colony; a melancholic remembrance of a pioneering Jewish agricultural settler in the pampas of his childhood: a utopian land that Argentinian military terrorism erased.[3]

---

[2] See also Feierstein's reflections on the *mestizaje* of Jews in his essay, *Contraexilio y mestizaje. Ser judío en la Argentina* (1996).
[3] The *Algarrobos Quartet* is a series of four short, enigmatic novels, all located in Algarrobos, in the vicinity of Colonia Mauricio, in the rural district of Carlos Casares in Buenos Aires Province. The *Algarrobo* saga comprises: *Criador de palomas* (Breeder of Pigeons, 1984); *La luna que cae* (Moon that

Another successful literary selection in the series was authored by Moacyr Scliar (1999), the most well-known Brazilian Jewish writer. This anthology is comprised of six lesser-known collections of Scliar's fiction, yet all these powerful stories – humorous, bleak, or haunting – together provide a compelling perspective on the Jewish Diaspora in Brazil. In *The Carnival of the Animals*, Scliar uses political allegory to convey what was normally censored during the height of repression under Brazil's military regime. *The Ballad of the False Messiah* develops the theme of why Jewish redemption is always postponed in a vain wait for the Messiah. In *The Tremulous Earth*, the author explores the role of cruelty and violence in the tenuous lives of his characters. Scliar expands his use of fantasy and magical realism in *The Dwarf in the Television Set*, which deals with topics that range from Jewish prophets to marital revenge. *The Enigmatic Eye* has been described as a masterpiece evoking the enigmas of art and life, and in *Van Gogh's Ear*, Scliar uses dark and subtle humor in a collection of biblical parables. A final autobiographical piece, in which Scliar discusses his membership in the Jewish, medical, gaucho, and Brazilian "tribes," ties the collections together.

Other Latin American writers whose works were translated for the series are the Venezuelan Alicia Freilich, author of the novel *Cláper* (1998), and the Mexican Sephardic writer Rosa Nissán, author of *Like a Bride and Like a Mother* (2013). The latter title is one single volume that brings together the translations of Nissán's two well-known novels *Novia que te Vea* (1992) and *Hisho que te Nazca* (1999).

In 1999, two thematically novel anthologies comprised of autobiographical texts appeared in the series. Marjorie Agosín edited one of them, *Passion, Memory and Identity: Twentieth-Century Latin American Jewish Women Writers*. A varied group of academics, literary critics and essayists from the US and Latin America explore issues of gender, memory and hybrid conditions in the experience of Latin American Jewish women while also exploring their own relationships with their respective countries. The volume includes Ilan Stavans and Magdalena Maiz-Peña on Mexico, David William Foster on Argentina, Regina Igel and Nelson Vieira on Brazil, Elizabeth Ross Horan on Chile and Uruguay, Joan Friedman on Venezuela, and Ruth Behar, Ester Shapiro Rok, and Rosa Lowinger on Cuba.

The anthology *King David's Harp: Autobiographical Essays by Jewish Latin American Writers*, edited by Stephen A. Sadow (1999), comprises fifteen essays. Jewish Latin American authors write about their lives, their literary work, their formative experiences, and the Jewish communities in Latin America and the United States. This volume includes writers from Argentina, Brazil, Chile, Cuba, Mexico, Guatemala, Peru, and Venezuela – some half of whom, significantly, live outside their country of origin, as in the case of José Kozer and Ilan Stavans. Many, including Ariel Dorfman

---

falls, 1989); *El sonador de Smith* (The dreamer of Smith, 1990) and *Comuna Verdad* (1995). Regarding the first novel, see Aizenberg (1988).

and Alcina Lubitch Domecq, have changed countries, languages, and political systems; others, like Ricardo Feierstein and Margo Glantz, remain in their country of birth. Most are multilingual; the editor, in his introduction, writes that these complex individuals move back and forth among different worlds, giving the impression of being in perpetual motion.

Another anthology, *Pomegranate Seeds: Latin American Jewish Tales*, by anthologist Nadia Grosser Nagarajan (2005), is an almost unknown collection of both texts written in Spanish and Yiddish by Latin American by different authors and testimonies or autobiographical stories. One merit of the book is that it presents, for the first time, a collection of the oral tradition of Latin American Jews in English. These 34 short tales span the 500 years of Jewish presence in Latin America and the Caribbean. The folktales and oral narratives were often based on actual events, recorded not only from the Ashkenazic perspective but from the Sephardic and Mizrahi ones as well. In addition to gathering stories from 11 Latin American countries, the anthologist found material in the United States and Israel as well. As she says herself, all of the stories come from a common cluster, like dispersed pomegranate seeds, yet each is a separate kernel.

Finally, Stavans's series is enriched by the writers and poets selected by Alan Castro, with his own excellent introduction, for the book titled *Yiddish South of the Border: An Anthology of Latin American Yiddish Writing* (2003). With this collection, Castro has compiled the first anthology of Latin American Yiddish writings translated into English. The volume includes works of fiction, poetry, and nonfiction from Argentina, Brazil, Chile, Mexico, Uruguay, and Cuba, with one brief memoir by a Russian rabbi who arrived in San Antonio, Texas, in 1910. *Yiddish South of the Border* features a fascinating assortment of peddlers and moneylenders. The central figure in "Jésus", by Pinkhes Berniker, is a rabbi in Cuba who makes a fortune selling Catholic icons because his beard reminds the peasants of Jesus. Other stories involve a peddler selling goods in installments and Jewish involvement in moneylending and prostitution as well as testimonies of settlers in the agricultural colonies of the Argentinian provinces. It should be emphasized that this pioneering English translation was updated 15 years later in a volume published in 2018 by Brill and jointly edited by Malena Chinski and Alan Castro under the title *Splendor, Decline, and Rediscovery of Yiddish in Latin America* (Chinski and Castro 2018).

By contrast, two books in the Jewish Latin America series, pertaining to the realm of history and social science, are themselves reprints of former English editions: *The Martyr Luis de Carvajal, A Secret Jew in Sixteenth-Century Mexico*, by Martin Cohen, with an introduction by Ilan Stavans (2001);[4] and *Secrecy and Deceit: The Religion of*

---

4 The first edition of Martin Cohen, *The Martyr. The Story of a Secret Jew and the Mexican Inquisition in the Sixteenth Century*, was published in 1973, six years after the seminal work *Los judíos en México y América Central* was published in Spanish by Seymour Liebman, another prominent American historian (Liebman 1967).

the Crypto-Jews, by David Gitlitz (2002). The latter was a reprint of a work already published in English in 1996 which historically documents the religious customs of crypto-Jewish culture in Spain, Portugal and their American colonies, principally Mexico, Peru, and Brazil (Gitlitz 1996).

Given the evident value of these reprints of books in English, it is perplexing that other Latin American researchers on the Inquisition and crypto-Jewish issues who are completely unknown to English readers have not been translated in the Jewish Latin America series. Among the researchers whose works undoubtedly deserve to be known by English readers are the Mexican historians Eva Uchmany and Alicia Gojman de Backal as well as the pioneering Brazilian historian Anita Novinsky. All of them, basing their research on primary archival sources, provide comprehensive accounts of crypto-Jewish beliefs, superstitions, birth customs, education, marriage and sex, holidays, dietary laws, conversions and burial practices.[5]

In *Oy, My Buenos Aires Jewish Immigrants and the Creation of Argentine National Identity* (2013), Mollie Lewis Nouwen explores how Yiddish-speaking Ashkenazic immigrants helped create a new urban strain of the Argentinian national identity through a very interesting interplay of nationality and ethnicity. Her focus lies on the daily lives of ordinary Jews in Buenos Aires, many of them working-class or middle-class professionals. Although her express goal is to explore the diversity of the experiences of non-affiliated Jews in the articulation and overlapping of their multiple identities, Lewis Nouwen is more convincing when she examines press and police records to trace criminality or advertisements to study popular culture, gender and gastronomy. She succeeds in bringing in sources that reveal scenes from the lives of the mothers, daughters and wives of immigrant Jews. Less convincing is her effort to discuss how these Jews contribute to the development of Porteño citizen identity.

While criminality and illegal games are a legitimate aspect of public life when it comes to satisfactorily exploring the involuntary interaction between Jews and gentiles, other aspects remain much less examined with regards to identifying crucial questions on the overlapping of diverse identities. One such aspect is the phenomenon of immigrants who were affiliated ideologically with labor groups or Argentinian political parties and who took active membership in the political and sociocultural institutions of well-known Jews. Lewis Nouwen attempts to explain how Jewish immigrants like Enrique Dickmann, who arrived in Buenos Aires after a short rural experience in a JCA agricultural colony in Entre Ríos, had to familiarize themselves with markers of urban Argentinian national identity. Abandoning his former gaucho dress and creole habits, Dickmann ate Argentinian foods and wore the same clothing as other Porteños. Reading Dickmann's memoir, the author overestimates the role of

---

5 Regarding Mexico, see the pioneering work of Eva A. Uchmany, including *La vida entre el judaísmo y el cristianismo en la Nueva España. 1580–1606* (1992), and Alicia Gojman Goldberg (1984). Regarding Brazil, see Anita Novinsky's books (Novinsky 1972, 2006).

the markers of everyday Porteño existence – eating local food and wearing the same clothing as others – in helping Dickmann set about becoming Argentinian. Instead of examining in depth the extent to which Dickmann's political militancy and ideology as a member of the Socialist Party were the major factors in his embrace of ideas about nationality and citizenship, the author prefers to become immersed in the everyday Porteño urban markers. Without undervaluing the relevance of those markers for acquiring an identity as a citizen, it is crucial to note that Dickmann's ideas on national identity were forged by the political and patriotic socialist actions that took center stage in his life. Focusing on markers of national identity, however, Lewis Nouwen turns – after referring to the ombú tree as a symbolic icon in the national imagination of immigrants – to diverse icons of urban *criollismo* and to the realm of social life as new national urban markers allowing immigrants to adjust to the Porteño microcosmos of *Argentinidad*.

Lewis Nouwen offers an excellent examination of the new cultural habits that Jews adapted from creole Porteños in the 1920s and 1930s, such as dancing the tango and drinking *mate* while reading the Yiddish press of Buenos Aires. However, her account refrains from mentioning any stereotyped image of the Jew in the popular theatre of *sainetes* in Buenos Aires. She ignores a short play, *Hermanos Nuestros* by F. Defilippis Novoa, that premiered on November 5, 1923, and was described as a "*comedia dramática en dos actos*." The playwright focuses the drama's plot on the purity of race (and religion) in conflict with assimilation. Jews are not ridiculed, yet the play presents devout Jews as creating their own problems by not wanting to change and become completely assimilated Argentinians.

In 1932, in another successful *sainete* called *La Policía no se Equivoca Nunca*, by Florecio B. Chiarello, the main character, *El judío Jacobo*, is described as an "*estafador de estafadores*" and a "*seductor de mujeres*". Jacobo's only 'crime' is that he asked a Christian woman to marry him. The subtle message of the *sainete*: intermarriage between the "creolized" sons and daughters of immigrants and creoles is acceptable. However, when intermarriage is between an immigrant Jew and a creole woman, it is assumed that this is for immoral reasons and the man is subject to arrest. The old myth that Jewish men are corrupters of Christian women was still alive on the Buenos Aires stage in 1932 (Castro 1995).

Undoubtedly, as Lewis Nouwen writes, social life was indeed particularly important for middle-class Jews in Buenos Aires, who used social events to have fun, display their status, make business contacts, and look for possible marriage partners for their children. However, upper-class Jews also participated in this socialization process. Poor and working-class Jews, however, did not have the same breadth of social life because they did not have the money to attend the many fundraisers, dances, and banquets that constituted the middle-class social season.

It is true that social life was the essential marker of status for the urban Jewish middle class. However, it is not possible to establish a sharp class divide during the 1920s and 1930s between workers and artisans on the one hand and merchants, professionals and businessmen on the other. Very often, all attended the parties and picnics organized by the "*landsmanshaftn*" (immigrant associations) without differentiation between rich and poor, middle class and upper class; instead of class, it was their common regional origin in villages in Eastern Europe or the Ottoman Empire that created a social bond.

Middle-class Jews were a minority among Ashkenazic Jewish immigrants in Buenos Aires, yet they were typically the leaders of the institutions, publications, and events that were specifically created by and for Jews. Jewish immigrants, like other groups living in Buenos Aires in the early twentieth century, socialized with family, friends, and coworkers in a variety of ways. However, socialization at picnics, theatres and bars was part and parcel of a mixed network of social, ideological, educational and religious institutions.

3 Research on Latin American Jewry Through the Lens of Transnationalism

Since the start of the new millennium, issues and methods based on the sociohistorical and political study of transnationalism have increasingly influenced important historiographic and socio-cultural works on Jews in Latin America and their communities. Seminal works by Judit Bokser Liwerant introduced "Diaspora" and "transnationalism" as key conceptual categories for understanding the old and new dynamic lives of Latin American Jews as well as changes occurring today (Bokser Liwerant 2002, 2006).

By analyzing how migration and the relocation of Jewish life develops along a sustained dynamic of incorporation, integration and continuity, some of Liwerant's works contributed to the discussion of basic conceptual and methodological dilemmas of the old Jewish historiography that the social sciences still face today. Significant works in the social science research of contemporary Jewry tend to leave out the transnational dimension of Jewish life in a global era, focusing on national cases and, therefore, underscoring exceptionalism. On the other hand, the approach of the transnational Jewish experience contributes to overcoming a methodological nationalism that equates social processes with national or state borders. In addition, it contributes to overcoming the limitations of methodological individualism and its focus on the migrants and their networks, which – while certainly significant – cannot serve as the exclusive unit of analysis. Liwerant's pioneering work on the transnationalism of Latin American Jews also serves as a methodological warning by pointing out some limitations both of the approaches solely dedicated to ethnic studies and, on the opposite extreme, of the approach of transnational studies of migrants in a global, post-national world which focus on unconnected individuals and their links and networks of social relations as the principal units of analysis (Bokser Liwerant 2009).

The first theoretical works by Liwerant highlight the singularity of the Jewish case in general, and Latin American Jewry in particular, reassessing mainly its trajectory of being grounded in the collective Diaspora dimension, in the institutional underpinnings of the historical worldwide transnationalism of the Jewish people. In addition, she reminds us that the individual and communal levels interact through dense and stable Jewish associational and institutional channels that enhance informal ethnic links (Bokser Liwerant 2007, 2008).

In Diaspora studies, the Jewish case has been attenuated, losing its centrality, whereas transnational studies tend to lose sight of the persistence of boundaries and the diasporic density present in contemporary migratory movements. The singularity of the Jewish case, and of Latin American Jewry in particular, refers mainly to its trajectory of being grounded in the collective dimension of peoplehood. A transnational analytical perspective in new works published since the beginning of the current millennium provides a conceptual tool with relevant implications for better understanding Jews as both citizens of a given nation-state as well as members of a transnational Diaspora (Senkman 2008, 2013, 2014).

The first anthology devoted completely to Latin American Jewry, *Pertenencia y Alteridad, Judíos en/de América Latina: Cuarenta Años de Cambio* (2011), provides a comprehensive analysis of important changes in the composition, institutional organizations, collective identity, and cultural production of Jewish communities in Latin America since 1967.

A theoretical and methodological article written by Judit Bokser Liwerant, *Los judíos de América Latina. Los signos de las tendencias: juegos y contrajuegos* (2011, 115–164), follows a collective introduction written by the editors of the volume and expresses the shifting paradigms for analyzing 40 years of transformations.

Luis Roniger's essay *Globalización, Transnacionalización y las Comunidades judías: el impacto del Chavismo en Venezuela* (2011, 271–304) shares the same analytical outlook. A similar perspective is provided in several sociocultural works also contained in the anthology by Sergio Della Pergola, Ezequie Erdei and Rene Daniel Decolon the gravitation toward globalization and transnationalism; in addition, the essays by Marta F. Topel, Perla Sneh, and Florinda Goldberg provide insights for better understanding phenomena in the realm of Jewish orthodoxy and literature through the transnational lens.

Two years later, the seventh volume of *Judaica Latinoamericana* (2013), edited by the AMILAT Israeli research association, published innovative articles conceived through a transnational lens.[6]

Finally, in the eighth volume of *Judaica Latinoamericana* (2017), devoted to studying a range of facets of Latin American Jewish life, almost all articles deal with issues

---

6 See *Judaica Latinoamericana* 7, esp. the following essays in the section *New trends in research*: Bokser Liwerant and Senkman (2013), Della Pergola (2013), Roniger (2013) and Schenkolewski-Kroll (2013).

examined through a transnational lens. Contributors write about the transnational identity of communist Argentinian Jews; transnationalism in the cultural expressions of Jewish Italian immigrants to Uruguay; and a transnational approach to exploring anthropological facets of religious identities among Argentinian and Mexican Jews, among other articles.[7] A section explicitly titled *Transnational Diasporas* comprises various historical and sociological essays on networks of Jews in Miami, Mexico and Israel.[8]

Another section dealing with the findings and theoretical assumptions of a study on Latin American Jewish educators presents a variety of essays.[9] This voluminous final issue of *Judaica Latinoamericana* then concludes with two innovative literary essays, also written from a transnational point of view.[10]

In summary, the transnational approach to studying the Jewish experience has been adopted by researchers with very different historiographic, sociological and literary conceptions, both in Israel and in Latin America.[11]

4 Literary Criticism, Transnationalism, Multiculturalism and Multilingualism

Transnational approaches to Jews in Latin America are not restricted to history, sociology or international relations. Cultural studies and literary theories are influenced by the transnational lens as well. Two books written by Erin Graff Zivin, in 2008 and 2014, provide fascinating examples of ethical discussions on aesthetics of transnational social imaginary. The books were published by university publishing houses that include general studies on Latin American literature, history and criticism.

The first book, *The Wandering Signifier: Rhetoric of Jewishness in the Latin American Imaginary* (Graff Zivin 2008a),[12] deals with the ethics of representation within literary texts and the process of interpretation of Jewish belonging, both understood as aesthetic devices. Jewishness becomes the sign of alterity and of a transnational social imaginary by signifying "the other words" within a context such as Latin American multiethnic diversity. But instead of analyzing the plight of the Jews through Latin American literature, Graff Zivin's examination of the rhetoric of

---

[7] See *Judaica Latinoamericana* 8: Senkman (2017), Marsiglia (2017), Bargman (2017) and Levy (2017).
[8] See Roniger (2017), Bejarano (2017), Aizencang Kne (2017) and Kershenovich Schuster, (2017).
[9] Bokser Liwerant, Della Pergola and Siman (2017), Goldstein (2017), Dorfsman (2017) and Schenkolewski-Kroll (2017).
[10] Goldberg (2017) and Igel (2017).
[11] See, for example, Rein (2014), Yalonetzky (2019).
[12] One chapter has been published in a collection of essays devoted to rethinking Jewish-Latin Americans (Graff Zivin 2008b).

Jewishness contributes to better understanding the territorial spaces and zones that cross national, ethnic and religious boundaries.

Graff Zivin's provocative theory of the wandering signifier evokes in the reader the legendary figure of the wandering Jew by re-signifying her literary device with the mobility of the Jew himself, who wanders from one place to another. Ultimately, Graff Zivin suggests that the core of the wandering signifier is an absent one: a non-place that ultimately may be filled with diversified fields of meaning to capture the various significations of a literary work.

In short, according to her literary theory, the rhetoric of Jewishness can be implanted in any imaginary surroundings, including Latin American spaces, which appear not as surprising, out-of-place territories, but as legitimate scenarios for the negotiation of identities and of acceptance and marginalization.[13]

Graff Zivin's second book, *Figurative Inquisitions: Conversion, Torture, and Truth in the Luso-Hispanic Atlantic* (Graff Zivin 2014a), deals with the resurgence of figures in the theatrical and film narratives of the fourteenth and twentieth centuries in Latin America. The figures analyzed are Luis de Carvajal and Antonio José da Silva. Separated by two hundred years, both men belonged to families of crypto-Jews and faced the trials of the court of the Holy Office. Graff Zivin is interested in studying the tensions and anxieties of the converted Marrano and his passage from one space of Jewish existence to another as a simulated Catholic. Using the idea of the "spectre" according to the thought of Jacques Derrida, she proposes an interpretation of the historical figure of the convert as a *spectrology* within a theory of allegory (see Graff Zivin 2017). Her ultimate intention is a transhistorical and transdisciplinary – rather than historical – look at literary, theatrical and filmic texts (from Mexico, Brazil and Portugal). The literary theorist analyzes the phenomenon of torture and its impact on individual subjectivity. According to Graff Zivin, the aesthetic discourse of Inquisitorial interrogation and the final confession of the Marrano is "a way of understanding what truth is, and how the truth emerges and can be produced through torture and to conversion."

Through this fascinating lens, Graff Zivin proposes a transatlantic dialogue on transnational imaginaries, specifically the "Marrano imaginary", as it is called in the first chapter. However, the author states that the book "seeks to identify links between classical torture, Inquisitional interrogation, and contemporary forms of political violence on both sides of the Atlantic."

To make things even more complex, the author delves into the logic of the Inquisition in her discussion on the aesthetic representations of inquisitional interrogation and confessions in different temporal and spatial scenarios. Thus, the ultimate purpose of the book is to discuss if the emergence of truth, is linked to the aestheti-

---

13 See reviews of Erin Graff Zivin (2008a) in *Estudios Interdisciplinarios de América Latina y el Caribe* 21.2 (2010), in *Comparative Literature Studies* 48.2 (2011), and in *Revista de Estudios Hispánicos* 46.1 (2012); very significantly, one sole review has been published by a Jewish journal – see *Shofar* 28.2 (2010).

cization of torture by inquisitional logic in those centuries and today. Marrano thinking and the Marrano imaginary are completely opposed to the inquisitional logic, which, for Graff Zivin, is the definitive metaphor for all violence in modernity. If the logic of the Inquisition comprises the ideas of identity as an omnipresent essence, of sovereignty, and of politics as a friend-enemy opposition, Marrano thinking, on the contrary, also includes contemporary notions such as subalternity, deconstruction, infra-politics and post-hegemony.[14]

A second fascinating example of a transatlantic dialogue on transnational imaginaries is Monique Rodrigues Balbuena's book *Homeless Tongues* (2016).[15] The focus of this talented Brazilian literary critic lies on contemporary Ladino poetry that shares the common linguistic context of a threatened Jewish language. Poems written by three different Jewish multilingual poets – the Argentinian Juan Gelman, the Israeli Margalit Matitiahu and the Algerian Sadia Lévy – have been positioned amid different languages – Spanish, Hebrew, and French – which provide different expressions of Sephardic cultural legacy. All poets are multicultural and multilingual Jews. Juan Gelman, the only Latin American poet of the group, turned to Ladino to express his "homeless tongues" as an Argentinian exiled after the loss of his homeland during the last terrorist military dictatorship. At the same time, when Gelman was engaged abroad in resisting the cruel dictatorship, the Jewish poet transformed his European exile into a transnational diaspora from whence he could express nostalgia for his national homeland through elegies in Ladino. Writing in Ladino as a second language, in opposition to his de-territorialized national writing, Gelman needed to turn to the languages of the Jews expatriated from Spain to write *Dibaxu* (1994). The exiled Argentinian poet consciously turned to a language that was not his own to write 29 untitled, numbered poems in Ladino, translated by the author into Spanish and presented side by side on opposite pages.

In her chapter titled *Juan Gelman's Journey to Ladino*, Monique Balbuena lucidly suggests first examining Gelman's own exploration of a language that resulted from years of political exile. Thus, the first station in Gelman's journey to Ladino was his book *Citas y Comentarios* (1978–1979; Gelman 1986), in which he delved into the history of the Spanish language, soon followed by *Com/posiciones* (1988–1989; Gelman 1998). Only after addressing the questions raised by these two previous books does Balbuena analyze Gelman's *Dibaxu* (1994).

By focusing on Gelman's choice to turn to Ladino, Balbuena proves that multilingual and multicultural Jewish poetic works written in the current era of transnationalism need political and historical contextualization. As she accurately affirms,

---
[14] See Graff Zivin's explanation (Graff Zivin 2014b); see some reviews of Graff Zivin's book in *Revista de Estudios Hispánicos* 52.1 (2018); *Arizona Journal of Hispanic Cultural Studies* 20 (2016).
[15] As in the case of Graff Zivin's books, Balbuena's research has not been published in the Jewish Latin America series, perhaps because her analysis challenges the usual canons both of Jewish literature and of Jewish languages.

> His own personal exile pushes Gelman to uncover the foundations of his language and of his self, peeling away layers in his downward search. His diction – 'substratum' and 'roots' – reinforces this downward orientation as a representation of the past, as he burrows down through both geographical distance and historical time. (Balbuena 2016, 113)

5 Some Conclusions

The review of historiographic publishing and literary studies on the past and present of Latin American Jews provides a rich and varied bibliography from the beginning of the new millennium through three important series of Jewish studies publishing houses in the US and Israel. The promoters and directors of these series have university links (Tel Aviv University, Hebrew University of Jerusalem, University of New Mexico); the works reviewed, along with frequent international academic symposia and conferences, reveal the importance of contemporary Jewish studies in the field of Latin American Studies. In that context, it is worth noting the institutional stimulus to promote research and publications by LAJSA, AMILAT and the former Liwerant Center, which have sponsored and promoted numerous published books over the past twenty years.

Last but not least, the transnational approach to studying the Jewish experience has frequently been adopted by researchers with very different historiographical, sociological and theoretical literary conceptions, whether in the US, in Israel or in Latin America.

Bibliography

Works Cited

Aizenberg, Edna. "The Writing of the Disaster: Gerardo Mario Goloboff's *Criador de palomas*." *Inti: Revista de literatura hispánica* 28 (1988): 27–73.

Aizencang Kne, Perla. "El doble momento diaspórico: Diáspora judía, diáspora Israelí y vida transnacional en el caso de migrantes israelíes que residen en México." *Judaica Latinoamericana* 8. Ed. AMILAT. Jerusalem: Magnes Press, 2017. 373–400.

Amato, Alberto. *Cuando Fuimos Gobierno – Conversaciones con Arturo Frondizi y Rogelio Frigerio*. Buenos Aires: Paidos, 1983.

Bargman, Daniel. "Topografías judaicas y redes transnacionales: una aproximación antropológica a las identidades y religiosidades judías en Buenos Aires." *Judaica Latinoamericana* 8. Ed. AMILAT. Jerusalem: Magnes Press, 2017. 215–240.

Bejarano, Margalit. "Transnational Sephardi Zionism in a historical perspective: Salomon Garazi and the Cuban Chapter of FESELA in Miami." *Judaica Latinoamericana* 8. Ed. AMILAT. Jerusalem: Magnes Press, 2017. 351–372.

Bokser Liwerant, Judit. "Globalization and Collective Identities." *Social Compass* 49.2 (2002): 253–271.

Bokser Liwerant, Judit. "Globalización, diversidad y pluralismo." *Multiculturalismo: Perspectivas y Desafíos*. Coord. Daniel Gutiérrez Martínez. México: UNAM, 2006. 79–102.

Bokser Liwerant, Judit. "Jewish Life in Latin America: A Challenging Experience." *Journal of the Rabbinical Assembly*, New York: 2007.

Bokser Liwerant, Judit. "Latin American Jewish Identities: Past And Present Challenges. The Mexican Case In A Comparative Perspective." *Identities in an Era of Globalization and Multiculturalism*. Eds. Judit Bokser Liwerant, Eliezer Ben-Rafael, Yossi Gorny and Raanan Rein. Leiden/Boston: Brill, 2008. 81–105.

Bokser Liwerant, Judit. "Latin American Jews: A Transnational Diaspora." *Transnationalism. Diasporas and the Advent of a New (Dis)order*. Eds. Eliezer Ben-Rafael, Yitzhak Sternberg, Judit Bokser Liwerant and Yossi Gorny. Leiden/Boston: Brill, 2009. 351–374.

Bokser Liwerant, Judit. "Los judíos de América Latina. Los signos de las tendencias: juegos y contrajuegos." *Pertenencia y alteridad: Judíos en de América Latina: cuarenta años de cambio*. Eds. Haim Avni, Judit Bokser, Margalit Bejarano and Sergio Della Pergola. Frankfurt (Main)/Madrid: Vervuert Verlagsgesellschaft, 2011.115–164.

Bokser Liwerant, Judit and Leonardo Senkman. "Diasporas and Transnationalism: New Inquiries Regarding Latin American Jews Today." *Judaica Latinoamericana 7*. Ed. AMILAT. Jerusalem: Magnes Press, 2013. 11–72.

Bokser Liwerant, Judit, Sergio Della Pergola and Yael Siman. "Los educadores judíos latino-americanos: múltiples identidades e identificación con Israel" *Judaica Latinoamericana 8*. Ed. AMILAT. Jerusalem: Magnes Press, 2017. 431–492.

Brodsky, Adriana, and Raanan Rein, eds. *The New Jewish Argentina. Facets of Jewish Experiences in the Southern Cone*. Leiden/Boston: Brill, 2012.

Broner, Julio, and Daniel Larriqueta. *The Argentine Industrial Revolution*. Buenos Aires: Sudamericana, 1969.

Castro, Donald S. *But We Are a Separate Race! The Image of the Jew in the Argentine Popular Theatre, 1890–1935 (A Question of the Other)*. Paper presented at the 1995 meeting of the LASA, September 28–30, 1995.

Chinski, Malena, and Alan Castro. *Splendor, Decline, and Rediscovery of Yiddish in Latin America*. Leiden/Boston: Brill, 2018.

Della Pergola, Sergio. "National Uniqueness and Transnational Parallelism: Reflections on the Comparative Study of Jewish Communities in Latin America." *Judaica Latinoamericana 7*. Ed. AMILAT. Jerusalem: Magnes Press, 2013. 73–100.

Dorfsman, Marcelo I. "New perspectives for the training of transnational educators." *Judaica Latinoamericana 8*. Ed. AMILAT. Jerusalem: Magnes Press, 2017. 513–530.

Dumbrava, Costica. *Nationality, Citizenship and Ethno-Cultural Membership*. Florence: European University Institute, 2012.

Feierstein, Ricardo. *Mestizo*. Buenos Aires: Editorial Milá, 1988.

Feierstein, Ricardo. *Mestizo*. Buenos Aires: Editorial Planeta, 1994.

Feierstein, Ricardo. *Contraexilio y mestizaje. Ser judío en la Argentina*. Buenos Aires: Editorial Milá, 1996.

Feierstein, Ricardo. *Mestizo. A novel*. Tr. Stephen A. Sadow, Prol. Ilan Stavans. University of New Mexico Press, 2001.

Fiszbein, Martín, and Marcelo Rougier. *La frustración de un proyecto económico: el gobierno peronista de 1973–1976*. Buenos Aires: Manantial, 2006.

Gelman, Juan. "Citas y Comentarios." *Interrupciones 1*. Buenos Aires: Libros de Tierra Firme, 1986. 189–307.

Gelman, Juan. *Dibaxu*. Buenos Aires: Seix Barral, 1994.

Gelman, Juan. "Com/posiciones." *Interrupciones 2*. Buenos Aires: Seix Barral, 1998. 149–212.

Gerchunoff, Alberto. *The Jewish Gauchos of the Pampas*. Tr. Prudencio de Pereda, Intro. Ilan Stavans. University of New Mexico Press, 1998.
Gitlitz, David M. *Secrecy and Deceit: The Religion of the Crypto-Jews*. Philadelphia: Jewish Publication Society, 1996.
Gleizer, Daniela. *Unwelcome Exiles. Mexico and the Jewish Refugees from Nazism, 1933–1945*. Leiden/Boston: Brill, 2013.
Gojman Goldberg, Alicia. *Los conversos en la Nueva España*. México: Enep-Acatlan, UNAM, 1984.
Goldberg, Florinda F. "El viajero del siglo de Andres Neuman." *Judaica Latinoamericana* 8. Ed. AMILAT. Jerusalem: Magnes Press, 2017. 637–660.
Goldstein, Yosi J. "Educación y educadores judíos latinoamericanos. La construcción de una diáspora transnacional de conocimiento en un mundo globalizado." *Judaica Latinoamericana* 8. Ed. AMILAT. Jerusalem: Magnes Press, 2017. 493–512.
González Canosa, Mora. *Las Fuerzas Armadas Revolucionarias. Orígenes y desarrollo de una particular conjunción entre marxismo, peronismo y lucha armada (1960–1973)*. Unpublished dissertation. Universidad Nacional de La Plata, 2012.
González Canosa, Mora. "Aportes al estudio de la radicalización política en la Argentina de los años sesenta y setenta: el caso de las Fuerzas Armadas Revolucionarias." *Pacarina del Sur* 7.26 (2016).
Graff Zivin, Erin. *The Wandering Signifier: Rhetoric of Jewishness in the Latin American Imaginary*. Duke University Press, 2008a.
Graff Zivin, Erin. "The Scene of the Transaction: 'Jewishness', Money and Prostitution in the Brazilian Imaginary." *Rethinking Jewish-Latin Americans*. Eds. Raanan Rein and Jeffrey Lesser. Albuquerque: University of New Mexico Press, 2008b. 106–131.
Graff Zivin, Erin. *Figurative Inquisitions: Conversion, Torture, and Truth in the Luso-Hispanic Atlantic*. Evanston: Northwestern University Press, 2014a.
Graff Zivin, Erin. "Beyond Inquisitional Logic, or, Toward an An-archaeological Latin Americanism." *CR: The New Centennial Review* 14.1 (2014b): 195–211.
Graff Zivin, Erin, ed. *The Marrano specter, Derrida and Hispanism*. New York: Fordham University Press, 2017.
Gurwitz, Beatrice D. *Argentinian Jews in the Age of Revolt. Between the New World and the Third World*. Leiden/Boston: Brill, 2017.
Tarcus, Horacio. *Diccionario biográfico de la izquierda argentina. De los anarquistas a la "nueva izquierda" (1870–1976)*. Buenos Aires: Emecé, 2007.
Horowitz, Joel. "Book review: Raanan Rein, Stefan Rinke, and Nadia Zysman, eds. The New Ethnic Studies in Latin America." *Estudios Interdisciplinarios América Latina y el Caribe-E.I.A.L.* 28.2 (2017): 142–143.
Igel, Regina. "The wandering Jew in Brazilian literature." *Judaica Latinoamericana* 8. Ed. AMILAT. Jerusalem: Magnes Press, 2017. 571–598.
Jáuregui, Aníbal. "¿Industria sustitutiva o sustitución de industriales? Los empresarios argentinos y el peronismo (1945–1955)." *Revista de Sociología e Política* 25 (2005).
Kahan, Emmanuel Nicolás. *Memories that Lie a Little: Jewish Experiences during the Argentine Dictatorship*. Leiden/Boston: Brill, 2018.
Kershenovich Schuster, Paulette. "Perspectivas transculturales de mujeres judeo-mexicanas que viven en Israel." *Judaica Latinoamericana* 8. Ed. AMILAT. Jerusalem: Magnes Press, 2017. 401–430.
Lesser, Jeffrey, and Raanan Rein. "Challenging Particularity: Jews as a Lens on Latin American Ethnicity." *Latin American and Caribbean Ethnic Studies* 1.2 (2006): 249–263.
Levine, Annette, and Natasha Zaretsky, eds. *Landscapes of Memory and Impunity. The Aftermath of the AMIA Bombing in Jewish Argentina*. Leiden/Boston: Brill, 2015.

Levy, Leonel. "Una Mirada transnacional al fenómeno religioso al comienzo del siglo XXI. Estudio sobre una nueva comunidad en México DF." *Judaica Latinoamericana* 8. Ed. AMILAT. Jerusalem: Magnes Press, 2017. 241–266.

Lewis Nouwen, Mollie. *My Buenos Aires Jewish Immigrants and the Creation of Argentine National Identity*. Albuquerque: University of New Mexico Press, 2013.

Leyba, Carlos. *Economía y política en el tercer gobierno de Perón*. Buenos Aires: Biblos, 2003.

Liebman, Seymour B. *The Enlightened: The Writings of Luis de Carvajal, el Mozo*. Tr. and ed. Seymour B. Liebman. Coral Gables: Univ. of Miami Press, 1967.

Marsiglia, Edith. "Expresiones culturales transnacionales fruto de la diáspora judeo-italiana en Argentina y Uruguay durante el fascismo (1938–1976)." *Judaica Latinoamericana* 8. Ed. AMILAT. Jerusalem: Magnes Press, 2017. 161–184.

Mochkofsky, Graciela. *Timerman, el periodista que quiso ser parte del poder*. Buenos Aires: Sudamericana, ³2004.

Novinsky, Anita. *Cristãos-novos na Bahia: 1624–1654*. Perspectiva, Universidade de São Paulo, 1972.

Novinsky, Anita. *O Santo Ofício da Inquisição no Maranhão. A Inquisição de 1731*. São Luís: Universidade Estadual de Maranhão, 2006.

Rein, Raanan. *Argentine Jews or Jewish Argentines? Essays on Ethnicity, Identity, and Diaspora*. Leiden/Boston: Brill, 2010.

Rein, Raanan. *¿Judíos argentinos o argentinos judíos? Ensayos sobre identidad, etnicidad y diáspora*. Buenos Aires: Lumiere, 2011.

Rein, Raanan. "A Trans-National Struggle with National and Ethnic Goals: Jewish-Argentines and Solidarity with the Republicans during the Spanish Civil War." *Journal of Iberian and Latin American Research* 20.2 (2014): 171–182.

Rein, Raanan, Stefan Rinke and Nadia Zysman. *The New Ethnic Studies in Latin America*. Leiden/Boston: Brill, 2017.

Rodriguez Balbuena, Monique. *Homeless Tongues*. Stanford University Press, 2016.

Roniger, Luis. "Globalización, Transnacionalización y las Comunidades judías: el impacto del Chavismo en Venezuela." *Pertenencia y alteridad: Judíos en de América Latina: cuarenta años de cambio*. Eds. Haim Avni, Judit Bokser, Margalit Bejarano and Sergio DellaPergola. Frankfurt (Main)/Madrid: Vervuert Verlagsgesellschaft, 2011. 271–304.

Roniger, Luis. "Iberoamerica and Iberoamerican Jews in the Perspective of Regional and Transnational Studies." *Judaica Latinoamericana* 7. Ed. AMILAT. Jerusalem: Magnes Press, 2013. 101–118.

Roniger, Luis. "New and old transnationalism: Inter-state alliances and transnational networks in Latin America." *Judaica Latinoamericana* 8. Ed. AMILAT. Jerusalem: Magnes Press, 2017. 323–350.

Rotenberg, Abrasha. *Historia confidencial. La Opinión y otros olvidos*. Buenos Aires: Sudamericana, 1999.

Schenkolewski-Kroll, Silvia. "Changes in the Transnational Relationship of the World Zionist Organization and Latin America Jewry, Informal Education, 1968–2006." *Judaica Latinoamericana* 7. Ed. AMILAT. Jerusalem: Magnes Press, 2013. 465–486.

Schenkolewski-Kroll, Silvia. "Transnationalism and non-formal Jewish education in Buenos Aires's Hebraica and Macabi." *Judaica Latinoamericana* 8. Ed. AMILAT. Jerusalem: Magnes Press, 2017. 531–546.

Scliar, Moacyr. *The Collected Stories of Moacyr Scliar*. Tr. Eloah F. Giacomelli. Intro. Ilan Stavans. The University of New Mexico, 1999.

Senkman, Leonardo. "Populismo y empresarios judíos: actuación pública de Horacio Láfer y José B. Gelbard durante Varga y Perón." *Araucaria* 8.15 (2006): 46–76.

Senkman, Leonardo. "Klal Yisrael at the Frontiers: The Transnational Jewish Experience in Argentina." *Identities in an Era of Globalization and Multiculturalism*. Eds. Judit Bokser Liwerant, Eliezer Ben-Rafael, Yossi Gorny and Raanan Rein. Leiden/Boston: Brill, 2008. 125–152.

Senkman, Leonardo. "The Latin American Diasporas: New Collective Identities and Citizenship Practices." *Shifting Frontiers of Citizenship: The Latin American Experience*. Eds. Mario Sznajder, Luis Roniger and Carlos A. Forment. Leiden/Boston: Brill, 2013. 385–410.
Senkman, Leonardo. "Anti-Zionist discourse of the Left in Latin America. An Assessment." *Reconsidering Israel-Diaspora Relations*. Eds. Eliezer Ben-Rafael, Judit Bokser Liwerant and Yosef Gorny. Leiden/Boston: Brill, 2014. 309–333.
Senkman, Leonardo. "Identidad transnacional de judeocomunistas argentinos en los albores del ICUF." *Judaica Latinoamericana* 8. Ed. AMILAT. Jerusalem: Magnes Press, 2017. 131–160.
Stern, Claudia. "Otherness in Convergence: Arabs, Jews, and the Formation of the Chilean Middle Classes, 1930–1960." *The New Ethnic Studies in Latin America*. Eds. Rein, Raanan, Stefan Rinke and Nadia Zysman. 99–127.
Tillet, Agustín. "La Cultura como campo de batalla: El PRT-ERP." *VI Jornadas de Sociología de la Universidad Nacional de La Plata* (December 2010).
Uchmany, Eva A. *La vida entre el judaísmo y el cristianismo en la Nueva España. 1580–1606*. México: FCE y Archivo General de la Nación, 1992.
Wassner, Dalia. *Harbinger of Modernity: Marcos Aguinis and the Democratization of Argentina*. Leiden/Boston: Brill, 2013.
Yalonetzky, Romina. "Just like Us, but Jewish: Jewishness, Ethnicity, Class Affinity and Transnationality in Lima." *Ethnicities* 19.6 (2019): 1001–1120.

Further Reading

Elkin, Judith Laikin. *The Jews of Latin America*. New York: Holmes & Meier, 1998.
Mate, Reyes, Forster, Ricardo. *El judaísmo en Iberoamérica. Enciclopedia Iberoamericana de Religiones 6*. Madrid: Editorial Trotta, 2007.
Ran, Amalia, and Jean Cahan, eds. *Returning to Babel. Jewish Latin American Experiences, Representations and Identity*. Leiden/Boston: Brill, 2011.

Dieter Ingenschay

20 Contemporary Jewish Narrative in Twenty-first Century Latin America

Abstract: This chapter highlights the diversity of contemporary Jewish narrative in Latin America in the last 20 years. As this period has been particularly eventful in both political and cultural terms, a set of methodological considerations will be presented first. This will be followed by a brief section devoted to cultural theory. The main part of the chapter will then examine, on the basis of carefully chosen examples, key genres such as the historical novel, fiction focused on language, transgenerational novels, autofiction, and novels that reflect on the sacred and the profane.

Key Terms: Jewish-Latin American Literatures, Diasporas, Twenty-first Century

1 Jewish-Latin American Literatures in the Twenty-first Century

To this day, there has been no comprehensive study covering the entire sociopolitical and/or cultural development of Jewish topics in Latin America during the last two decades. Nevertheless, several scholars have contributed to the discourses on Jewish culture and literature in South America at the beginning of the twenty-first century. With *Pertenencia y alteridad*, Judit Bokser Liwerant et al. have published a more than 800-page collective volume with very substantial studies on 'forty years of change', as the subtitle indicates, with respect to cultural and political matters. These include questions of education, identity (politics), migration, language and Latin American-Israeli relations. In this volume, Arie M. Kacowicz's description of the changes and developments occurring until 2007 is particularly pertinent to the present study on account of its timeliness and its prospective reflections (Kacowicz 2011). Some of the contributors to *Pertenencia y alteridad* treat literary subjects; Saúl Sosnowski, a pioneer of Jewish-Latin American literatures, takes stock of four decades under the programmatic title "Sin desierto y sin tierra prometida" (Sosnowski 2011). Moreover, there have been other recent publications that deal with the field of literature (and cover early twenty-first century publications), such as Rodrigo Cánovas's book *Literatura de inmigrantes árabes y judíos en Chile y México* (Cánovas 2011), which deals with the literary production of Jewish (and Arab) writers from the two countries mentioned in the title. Another contribution worth mentioning is the volume *Múltiples identidades*, edited by Verena Dolle, which offers a survey of personal (autobiographical) and fictional Jewish-Latin American writing from the entirety of the twentieth century (Dolle 2012, 14).

Of course, the new millennium does not constitute a fixed threshold, neither in sociopolitical terms nor in terms of cultural/literary production; many authors of "Jewish-Latin American literature" – a term whose implications we shall discuss later – have written both before *and* after this temporal divider. Although this chapter will focus on literary works published since 2000, earlier works may be mentioned where necessary and helpful. If South American literatures of the 1980s and 1990s were characterized by a post-boom literary aesthetic and then by the post-dictatorship era, Jewish authors (and others as well) were struck by a new wave of anti-Semitism culminating in the attack on the AMIA in Buenos Aires on 18 July, 1994, which some critics later called a Jewish 9/11. Therefore, the period we are dealing with begins with a feeling of helplessness, of a lack of understanding of these events, which, however, soon culminated in a renaissance for many Jewish-Latin American authors. Subsequently, the first fifteen years of the new century may be characterized by three main (and somewhat contradictory) tendencies represented by three groups of authors: Firstly, one notices a growing integration of Jewish writers into the cultural industries of their respective countries, which leads to a neglect or complete displacement of traditional religious topics in favor of other questions. (This is only partly due to the effects of globalization, e.g. of the Latin American/Spanish book market, and probably has more to do with long-term assimilation processes[1]). There is an increasing number of novelists, poets and playwrights of Jewish belonging in whose writings Jewish religious life does not play any role at all.[2] These authors will only be mentioned in passing in the following observations. – Among a second group of authors, the aspect of a "Jewish identity" appears when cultures of remembrance are at stake, whether personal or family memories or remembrances of Jewish traditions, of pogroms, of the Shoah and the traumatic experiences involved. This is much more than a side effect of the worldwide boom of 'cultures of memory'. The uniqueness of Jewish experience (before, but above all) during the twentieth century explains the prevalence and continuance of memorial writing, which Yosef Hayim Yerushalmi thoroughly analyzed as a 'memory technique' dating back to the Middle Ages in his study *Zakhor. Jewish History and Jewish Memory* (cf. Yerushalmi 1996). – In the third group, we find a clear tendency to focus more intensely on Jewish history and on the Jewish lifeworld and to process them literarily. This group is comprised

---

1 An additional factor is the decline of the Jewish Latin American population: "La depresión demográfica ocurrió en la mayoría de los países sudamericanos. Entre 1980 y 2002 el número de judíos descendió en un 18%. Las causas principales fueron la disminución de la tasa de natalidad; la gran cantidad de matrimonios mixtos y la asimilación; y la migración negativa." (Kacowicz 2011, 262)

2 In fact, this is not exclusively a phenomenon of the twenty-first century. The novelist Ana María Shua previously observed this tendency in important Argentine authors: "Grandes escritores e intelectuales como Liliana Heker o Noé Jitrik se negaron y se niegan todavía a ser considerados 'escritores judíos'" (Shua 2012, 31).

of authors tired of or disappointed by the anonymity of multiculturalism[3] or exposed to special personal experiences.[4] (This, incidentally, implies a new consolidation of Jewish belonging that goes hand in hand with the consolidation of the State of Israel.)

Not all novelists can be easily assigned to one of these three groups. Well-known authors such as the Mexican Margo Glantz or the Argentines Edgardo Cozarinsky and the recently deceased Mario Szichman refer to their Jewishness only in some of their writings. The young Argentine author Ariel Magnus even asserts that he defines himself as a son of the ESMA (the center of torture during the military dictatorship) rather than as a grandson of an Auschwitz survivor (cf. Magnus 2012, 134). The novelist Alicia Steimberg explains: "El tema judío, si es que mi judaísmo es un tema literario, sólo aparece manifiestamente en dos de mis libros" (Steimberg 2012, 28). Her colleague Silvia Plager, who after several novels that only indirectly deal with Jewish topics published a novel about a woman who decides to study the Torah and become a rabbi (*La Rabina*, 2005), stated in an interview that she is "Jewish of course", which means that Jewish tradition had been a subtle but constitutive part of her former novels too.

Only a few years ago, Ana María Shua asked herself one of the cardinal questions: "Pero entonces, ¿qué nos convierte en escritores judíos? ¿Los temas judíos, la madre judía, el apellido judío? Cualquiera de las tres posibilidades, supongo" (Shua 2012, 30). As this answer hardly appears robust enough for the twenty-first century, let us turn to a further reflection on what Jewish-Latin American literatures are and how to define them today. In his dictionary *Jewish Writers of Latin America*, Darrell Lockhart explains:

> By writers whose works directly reflect a Jewish identity I mean to say that their writing in large parts deals with the so-called Jewish concerns, which include but are not limited to the problems of identity, assimilation, traditions, immigrations, the Sephardic heritage of Latin America, Yiddishkeit, Judaism/Jewishness, self-hatred, anti-Semitism, the Holocaust, Zionism and Israel.
> (Lockhart 2013, viii)

---

[3] Again, I refer to Ana María Shua: "Hoy la tendencia se invirtió y el movimiento multiculturalista impulsa a los escritores judíos a buscar sus raíces. Muchos autores están escribiendo sobre temas judíos sin que esa elección los haga sentirse menos argentinos. Es imposible mencionarlos todos" (Shua 2012, 32).

[4] The case of the Argentine novelist and scriptwriter Marcelo Birmajer (best known for *El abrazo partido*) is a good example. Birmajer had always been considered particularly 'Israel friendly' (cf. Birmajer 2002). When he lost his brother, who lived in Jerusalem as a rabbi, in an attack by militant Palestinians, his admiration became a veritable declaration of love: "Israel es, para mí, garantía de que puedo defender mi vida y mi libertad, y la vida y la libertad de los míos, y de los inocentes en general. Israel es un milagro que ninguna explicación racional, geopolítica o filosófica puede abarcar. Es un milagro que tampoco puede explicar la religión. Es tan parecido a un sueño, que incluso sus fundadores buscaron modos de subvalorarlo, para podérselo creer. [. . .] Israel es la única entidad a la que puedo relacionar con la palabra *amor*, como si se amara a una persona, una mujer o un hijo. Israel es el triunfo del bien, de la verdad y de la voluntad. Israel es una declaración de protesta y de amor, al mismo tiempo, respecto de Dios. Israel es el fruto varias veces milenario de un pueblo de dura cerviz. Israel es insolencia, desparpajo, libertad." Birmajer, "Que significa Israel para mí" (2011).

Among the many possible answers to the question of how to define Jewish literature, this chapter (like this Handbook as a whole) opts for a broad, post-essentialist definition based on the above statement and taking into account certain intrinsic features such as the importance of narration or 'storytelling' in Jewish history or the difference between an internal (Jewish) and external (non-Jewish) perspective. Hence, Jewish-Latin American literature of the twenty-first century is understood as an open corpus of literary works that contribute to the discussion, continuation and (re)shaping of the (self-)consciousness of the group of people who 'identify' as Jewish-Latin Americans. That is to say: not every author of Jewish origin writes Jewish-Latin American literature, and it is possible to imagine cases of non-Jewish authors who participate in the process described. This definition means that there are authors of Jewish descent who do not produce, for instance, Jewish-Argentine, but simply Argentine literature. Moreover, there are many novelists (including outstanding authors) who have written both Latin American and 'Jewish-Latin American' novels.[5]

2 Beyond the Hyphen: Jewish-Latin American Cultural Theory Today

The larger context of these observations on Jewish-Latin American literatures is provided by Saúl Sosnowski's so-called "hyphen theory". In his study *La orilla inminente. Escritores judíos argentinos* (1987a), Sosnowski reflects on the 'extraordinary and unexpected' terms that delineate 'literatures with a hyphen', such as Jewish-Latin American or Jewish-Argentine, Jewish-Chilean, etc. Sosnowski postulates that this is not a matter of simply combining two attributes in an additive way, but that the new term contains a self-referential element that proclaims the union of difference (cf. Sosnowski 1987a, 23). From the combination of two attributions, something different arises, and emphasis is placed on the intersections (hybridizations and resistances) that make up an identity in crisis, in the process of change and transformation (according to Cánovas 2011, 135). In his 'apology of the hyphen', Sosnowski notes: "When Judaism cannot be affirmed solely on the basis of a national territory, [. . .] Jewish identity in literature must per force acquire an aura of ethnicity as a defining feature. But it can also acquire [. . .] an internal code of ethics that rises above history's latest atrocities. Ethnicity and heterodoxy are

---

[5] This definition corresponds largely, though not completely, to the latest definition by Sosnowski (2011, 711): "Al referirme a 'literatura judía-latinoamericana' pienso en autores nacidos en la región que son judíos en una acepción más generosa que la estrictamente ortodoxa. Su identidad es nacional/latinoamericana y simultáneamente judía por herencia [. . .] no me limito a un criterio contendentista para incorporar o excluir del acotado 'canon judío-latinoamericano'."

the signs of Judaism's incorporation into Latin American literature" (Sosnowski 1987b, 305). In a more recent publication, he questions – in terms similar to those of many critics who doubt the universal validity of the notion of identity – the unambiguousness of identity concepts: "Somos plurales, transnacionales, pluriculturales, multilingües, casi ineludiblemente urbanos. [. . .] La identidad dejó de ser cifrada en singular. Hablamos y vivimos poseídos de identidades múltiples y fluctuantes." (Sosnowski 2011, 718)

The critical literature on the theories and histories of Jewish-Latin American literary production after Sosnowski is abundant. In this context, Sander Gilman reformulates a key concept of Latin American Studies – the opposition between center and periphery – in such a way that the center is no longer defined in opposition to the periphery, but as a border area, "a zone of diffuse contours in which different sociocultural entities communicate, mix, adapt and confront each other" (Gilman 1999, 20). That is to say, his definition postulates a dynamics between sameness and otherness – in Gilman's own words: "My sense of the frontier is one in which all voices can be articulated" (Gilman 1999, 21). Following Sosnowski's hyphen theory, Sander Gilman's reflections on the frontier and Leonardo Senkman's observations on Jewish identity, Florinda Goldberg has formulated the thesis that Jewish authors in Latin America since the 1980s have been able to reflect on Jewish belonging mainly as a borderline experience (Goldberg 2012). From the perspective of Jewish cultures, she explains, Latin America has become a "middle ground" (a term formerly applied to the Mexican-US borderlands that Goldberg borrows from Gilman).

Edward Friedman has emphasized the intrinsically political character of Jewish-Latin American literatures, enumerating the ways in which these literatures stand out by providing 'fruitful examples': they express an aesthetic of the margins, of what used to be called the periphery, in relation to the omissions of history or the problematic position of the latecomer (Friedman 1996).

A key concept that Latin American Studies has borrowed from Jewish cultural history is that of the diaspora. After José Saldívar reflected on a "Global North" and a "Global South" (Saldívar 2012), Robin Cohen added the "Global Diasporas" (Cohen 2008), using the most 'classical' concept to describe the cohesion of the Jewish communities throughout the world (outside of Israel). At first glance, Cohen's reflections are easily compatible with many of the definitions of Jewish Studies. However, a closer look reveals that his search for a definition goes beyond Jewish historical experience when he defines diaspora as "a special case of ethnics: They are imagined, transnational communities which unite segments of people that live in territorially separated locations" (Cohen 2008, 13). Following this definition to the letter, Alfonso de Toro has proposed to redefine the notion of diaspora as a hybrid and performative concept which may also include the Hispanic minorities of the USA or Germans with a Turkish background (de Toro 2013). With this proposal, de Toro moves beyond the theory of Robin Cohen, according to which the 'global' diasporas are a consequence of Western imperialism.[6] At the same time, de Toro refers to Stuart Hall's concept of "new ethnicity". However, in the case of the Jewish-Latin American diasporas, we are not confronted with 'new' ethnicities, but with established minority groups that have settled and resettled almost everywhere on the American continent. The transposition of the concept of diaspora to non-Jewish contexts (which began with the incorporation of Cubans outside the island into a 'Cuban diaspora') may be attractive, but the categorial and historical specificity of the diasporic experiences of Jews in Latin America is lost in the process of this generalization. The life of a Latin American Jew is hardly comparable, for example, with that of a Cuban in Miami or of a German with a Turkish family history at the beginning of the twenty-first century. In Jewish contexts, the concept of diaspora today is a variation – as Hopkins Rodríguez aptly describes it (Hopkins Rodríguez 2012) – of the notion of identity when it has lost its former territorial reference point and is attached instead to an 'imagined community'.

The particular quality of Jewish-Latin American literatures emerges – and here all of the critics mentioned would agree – from their internal diversity, their multifaceted character. This includes Brazil as a Portuguese-speaking country, as Nelson H. Vieira already stated twenty years ago: "Brazilian-Jewish literary expression signals the gaps, fissures, and fractures within cultural alterity." (Vieira 1995, 214). The issues and the general challenges of a supposed 'Jewish identity' are not limited to the binary model of the two parts that precede or follow the hyphen in the term "Jewish-Latin American", nor to the question of which of these parts has priority, but to a much more complex configuration. That is one of the reasons why this chapter discusses Jewish *identities*, intentionally using the plural form. Others have proposed different terms such as *hinge identity* ("Identidade em dobradiça", Igel 1987), giving even more importance to the 'hyphen', while others still have reservations regarding concepts of identity altogether. Arie Kacowicz, for instance, has emphasized that the main danger faced by Latin American Jews does not emerge from the discussion of identity but rather from a complex general sociopolitical context.[7]

Yet, Goldberg warns: "Refutar la identidad no equivale a eliminarla" (Goldberg 2012, 218). This is why this chapter refers to the concept of identity in a plural form, as a composite, nonlinear concept. These plural "Jewish identities" do not refer to homogenous, but to extremely diverse and dispersed groups throughout the entire continent, which include people of Sephardic and Ashkenazic descent, of different languages (whether native or adopted), of different religious rites (from orthodoxy to atheism), and of completely different social environments. This fact makes the Jewish-Latin

---

[6] Another example related to de Toro's argumentation is Paul Gilroy's notion of the "Black diasporas". For a more detailed discussion, cf. Ingenschay 2018.
[7] "Los mayores peligros e incertidumbres que deben enfrentar los judíos de las comunidades de Latinoamérica no surgen de su identidad judía sino del contexto general social y político que afecta a la población latinoamericana en su totalidad y que incluye el contexto internacional." (Kacowicz 2011, 269)

American literatures of the twentieth and twenty-first centuries an exemplary reflection of social dynamics and forms of coexistence.

3 A Multilayered Map: Methodological Remarks on Jewish-Latin American Narratives Today

In spite of the heuristic advantages of the hyphen theory, this survey of the Jewish-Latin American literary production of the twenty-first century does not make divisions according to the criterion of national origins, an approach that would produce very long parts on Argentine, Chilean and Brazilian literary production and rather short remarks on some other countries. However, as the respective origins of the authors under consideration and the circumstances of their writing are of uncontested relevance, their nationalities will be indicated in the first part of the bibliography below. By leaving out the 'national' side of the hyphenated attributions, the present chapter makes evident that the 'national' aspect is of less importance than the unifying property of literatures perceived as (diasporic) *Jewish* (rather than 'national').

Renouncing a nationally organized structure leaves us with the question of how to classify the complex field of current Jewish literary production in Latin America. According to the definition proposed above, the following section outlines thematic and generic constellations which convey 'Jewishness' in the sense of the modified statement of Darrel Lockhart – that is, constellations of genres such as historical novels, fiction with a focus on language, transgenerational novels, personal memoires and autobiographically inspired works as well as (un)religious novels. There are undoubtedly overlaps between these constellations, and more than one attribute will be applicable to a given literary work. However, a majority will fit particularly well into one of these categories, allowing for a systematization of current trends.

3.1 Historical Novels

Just as everywhere else, historical landmarks are highly significant for Latin American Jewish novels. Again and again, cardinal events that have influenced the Jewish community (from the Edict of Expulsion from the Iberian Peninsula in 1492 to the Nazi regime and the founding of the State of Israel in 1948) are continuously referenced both in fiction and in everyday life. Given the almost proverbial importance of history in Jewish cultures (see also the above-mentioned book by Yerushalmi [1996]) and the uninterrupted importance of material and spiritual history from Abrahamic times until today, the strong presence of historical subjects in twenty-first century Jewish-Latin American literature is hardly surprising. It is even less so if we consider the importance of historical novels in Latin America, including the so-called New Historical Novel (*nueva novela histórica*), a particularly witty and ingenious subgenre.[8] Isaac Goldemberg's *El nombre del padre* (Goldemberg 2001) can be considered such an innovative 'New Historical Novel' as it provides, among other curious elements departing from 'material' history, a speculative vision of an early pre-Columbian encounter between Jewish immigrants and Native Americans leading to nothing less than a paradisiacal state.[9] (This utopia is developed along the same lines as Antonio Brailovsky's novel *Identidad* [1980], which narrates a mythical Jewish Empire in the sixteenth century Mexican jungle.) Eduardo Hopkins Rodríguez explains that Goldemberg's vision juxtaposes the idea of migration as a traumatic experience with the idea of migration as an enrichment of 'identity' (Hopkins 2012, 181), while the concept of 'identity' is not pure and united but rather hybrid, a result of "interacción, integración, contaminación, fusión, sincretismo" (Hopkins 2012, 182).

A less 'postmodern' but nevertheless 'New Historical Novel' is Angelina Muñiz Huberman's *El sefardí romántico. La azarosa vida de Mateo Alemán II* (2005). In earlier works, Muñiz Huberman (who famously introduced the Talmud to Mexican writing) was inspired by Martin Buber, whereas this 'New Historical Novel', an audacious mixture of genres, refers in its title to the Jewish converso Mateo Alemán, author of the picaresque novel *Guzmán de Alfarache* (1599/1604) and an ancestor of Mateo Alemán II, the protagonist of Muñiz-Huberman's narrative. The protagonist, a new *pícaro*, crosses time and space, traveling through Europe from the Spanish Civil War to Holland, fascist Italy and Berlin shortly before Hitler's appointment as chancellor of the Reich. After enjoying the bars of Berlin together with Walter Benjamin, Mateo Alemán II ends up in Mexico with many of the exiled Spanish Republicans. The novel thus combines, according to Alicia Rico (2015), references to the expulsion of the Jews from Spain in 1492 with the exile from Francoist Spain. Among the characters encountered by the *pícaro* are important historical figures who were forced into exile, such as Stefan Zweig, María Zambrano, and Margarita Nelken. When a Mexican asks Mateo for his nationality, his answer sounds like a comment on Sosnowski's above-cited remark about *identidades múltiples y fluctuantes*: "judío, español republicano, jienense, sefardí, mexicano en prospecto, europeo, americano, universal" (Muñiz Huberman 2005, 190).

---

[8] The *nueva novela histórica* has been defined by several scholars (Seymour Menton, Fernando Aínsa, Karl Kohut and others). A common aspect is certainly the irreverent handling of historical facts and the loss of history's mandatory truth.

[9] "[...] lo que voy a referir... sucedió en épocas de la colonia... cuando los españoles quemaban a indios y a judíos por igual por el simple hecho de negarse a abandonar sus prácticas religiosas. [...] Pero un día, los indios y los judíos de Río Negro se sublevaron... los españoles los masacraron. [...] El hecho es que los sobrevivientes de la matanza, tanto judíos como indios, decidieron huir, juntos, hacia la selva, donde estaban seguros de que nadie los iba a encontrar. Así lo hicieron y fundaron en plena selva el pueblo ese del que hablaba: Paradés. Y en eso lo convirtieron, en un paraíso. [...] Y ahí indios y judíos crearon una sociedad perfecta." (Goldemberg 2001, 63–65)

A somewhat peculiar combination of Jewish and Latin American history of the twentieth century can be found in Ariel Bibliowicz's latest novel, *Migas de pan* (Bibliowicz 2013). Whereas in earlier narratives Bibliowicz offered a humorous view of Jewish-Latin American reality, this text – situated in Colombia in the 1980s – combines descriptions of the practice of kidnapping, a particularly violent form of crime that was rampant across Latin America at the time, with flashbacks to stories of escape from the Shoah and Stalinist persecution. Josué, the father of the protagonist, was a victim of Stalin's pogroms, and his wife Leah was a survivor of Auschwitz. Their son Samuel, living in the US as a medical doctor, returns to his parents' elegant home in Bogotá to lead a committee in charge of negotiating the liberation of his kidnapped father. Samuel spends most of his time on the second floor of the family home, where his father has installed a true 'cabinet of wonders', a sort of private museum of curiosities. A plan of the house and its architecture is added at the end of the novel. While Samuel keeps waiting for new calls from the kidnappers, his memories turn back to his father. He is described as a quite peculiar man who nevertheless has infused his son with a profound humanistic knowledge (including a restructuring of chronometry that takes into account the greatest crimes against mankind from the Holocaust to the gulags, from colonialism to cruel dictatorships, from Cambodia to the Chinese Cultural Revolution) (Bibliowicz 2013, 143–144). This universal humanistic dimension of the father's mental universe is enriched with elements of the Cabbala, with the theory and practice of remembering and the loss of memory, and above all with trauma. Trauma in fact represents the primary subject of the narration, as the past serves as a backdrop for the interpretation of the present experience of the kidnapping – because, as the text points out, "Lo vivido no se borraba con facilidad" (Bibliowicz 2013, 111). The father processed his traumatic experience of the Shoah and the Stalinist pogroms in his "Theater of Memory" (*Teatro de la memoria*), a part of the house in which he reenacted the past in the concrete political dimensions of Columbia in the grip of the terrorism of the 1980s.

While Bibliowicz's *Migas de pan* closes the historical gap between the 1920s and 1930s – years of Stalinist and Nazi persecution – and the violence of the 1980s and thereby may qualify as transhistorical, Cynthia Rimsky's *Poste restante* (2000) and *Los perplejos* (2009) can be classified as 'post-memory' narratives (in the sense of Marianne Hirsch [2008]). The rise of a post-memory discourse in Jewish history is explained by Cánovas: "la memoria judaica no está adscrita necesariamente a un pueblo, sino a una memoria actual de un mundo globalizado donde se han perdido los referentes utópicos" (Cánovas 124). Whereas *Poste restante* is at the same time a conspicuous 'post-identitarian' novel (which denies the usual identification with the ancestors of memory narratives), *Los perplejos* refers to one of the major works of Jewish philosophical history, Maimonides's *Guide for the Perplexed* (*Guía de los perplejos*), written in Judeo-Arabic in twelfth century Spain. Rimsky's novel presents two first-person narrators: Maimonides himself and a young student who is writing her doctoral thesis on the critical philosopher in the present. Thus, there is a permanent shift between the two narrators and between the Spain of al-Andalus and contemporary times, even if some of the problems of the past return in very similar ways. This is not only true when it comes to the levels of understanding, the sense of speech and writing, and the relation between words and reality (which may be literal, moral, allegorical or anagogical) but also with regard to the relation of (wo)man to spiritual questions, to Job's experience, to Jehovah. By taking the medieval philosopher as a point of reference who was severely attacked both by his orthodox contemporaries and by later generations, Rimsky does not only reinstate a Jewish tradition in Latin America but offers at the same time an illustrative example of the possibilities of re-actualizing Jewish self-consciousness in the globalized context of Latin American academia. In a similar way, Esther Seligson undertakes in her novel *La morada en el tiempo* (1981) to 're-write the Torah from the perspective of a contemporary Jeremias', as she herself has put it. As we have seen, historical references in contemporary Latin American novels include aspects of medieval philosophy as well as Spanish history from the twelfth to the sixteenth century, pre-Columbian cultures, persecutions in the twentieth century and reflections on Jewishness in the context of global historical processes.

3.2 Fiction Focused on Language

The majority of Latin American Jewish literature of the twenty-first century is written in Spanish (and sometimes also in Brazilian Portuguese or American English), i.e., in languages that have been acquired or 'borrowed' by immigrants (provided they do not belong to the Sephardic or Ladino-speaking minorities). Hebrew has maintained its position as a spiritual, ritual language, but Yiddish has almost completely lost the importance it carried a century ago. However, Yiddish is very much present as a subject of literary production. Language, obviously always crucial for the medium of literature, thus features even more prominently in the novels presented here. In general, language is largely considered a cardinal marker of identity, and the languages of Jewish immigrants to (Latin) America exist in a complex field of tensions between selfhood and integration, identity and acculturation, etc. For this very reason, Ilan Stavans titled his early autobiography *On borrowed words. A memoir of language* (2001), leaving it open whether the 'borrowed words' are to be understood as his primary means of communication before or after his arrival in the Americas. "I have made the conscious decision to find my voice in a language and habitat not my own. The Wandering Jew" (Stavans 2001, 7). Stavans, who as a specialist in identity shifts is interested in phenomena such as Spanglish, is not the only one to write memoirs of language. Gedalia Rimetka, the patriarch of a family clan and the protagonist of Ana María Shua's novel *El Libro de los recuerdos* (Shua 1994), decides from one day to the next that only Spanish shall be spoken in the huge mansion of the prosperous Ashkenazic family who immigrated years ago from Eastern Europe to

Argentina. In a chapter entitled "El idioma", the grandmother comments on the shift from Yiddish to Spanish without actually referring to the Yiddish language. In Ricardo Feierstein's novel *Mestizo* (Feierstein 1988), the protagonist suffers from memory loss after a traffic accident and has to reappropriate Yiddish as his own language.

In the novel *Lenta biografía* by Sergio Chejfec (Chejfec 2007), Yiddish plays an even more central role than in Feierstein's *Mestizo*. Chejfec's novel presents the story of a textual subject – Katja Carillo Zeiter refers to him as the "son-narrator" – who fails in his attempt to write his autobiography because it is so closely intertwined with the life story of his father. The father, for his part, affirms that he could write his autobiography, but only in Yiddish, an almost mythical language that the son does not understand but which has fascinated him since the days when he listened to his father reading almost silently *Di Presse*, the Argentine paper in Yiddish. In her careful analysis of the stylistic details of the novel, Carillo Zeiter has stated: "para el hijo-narrador el idisch marca más bien una tierra incógnita y un pasado oculto que despierta su curiosidad" (Carillo 2012, 201). The memories of the past include the feeling of helplessness, of the vulnerability of the European Jews who were denied their agency in view of the Nazi terror, and Carillo adds that "la sensación de ser víctimas [. . .] se convierte en un *leitmotiv*" (2012, 201). The core of the story is the silence of the father regarding what he and his family lived and suffered in Europe during the Holocaust and the son's futile attempts to learn more about these experiences. This silence obviously indicates the impossibility of overcoming the experienced trauma.

With the decline of speakers of Yiddish in Latin America, the language has also been less present as a topic of literature in the past 20 years than it used to be in the preceding decades. However, if actual memories of Yiddish have become infrequent, the consciousness of the language problem still exists and has developed additional facets. The tension between Yiddish and Spanish has been superseded by the presence not only of English and Hebrew[10] but also – on a smaller scale – of different Sephardic variants (Ladino, formerly spoken by Southeast European Jews, and Hakitía, spoken in Northern Africa).[11] – Fragmented memories of the Ladino language appear in Rosa Nissán's novel *Novia que te vea* (1992 – the movie version by Guita Schyfter is considered to be the first Mexican film on Jewish-Mexican communities) and – within the period under consideration here – in Vicky Nizri's *Vida propia* (Nizri 2000; for

---

10 Stavans is not the only author to opt for English as his language of literary creation; authors like Ruth Behar (from Cuba) could also be mentioned. Samuel Pecar, an Argentine author who emigrated to Israel, went on writing in Spanish – see the novels *El Segundo genesis de Janán Saridor* (1994) and *La última profecía* (2011).
11 In 1996, the Knesset founded the "Autoridad Nasional del Ladino i su Kultura" as an organization for all Israeli speakers of Judeo-Spanish variants, thus establishing the term "Ladino" as a general designation for these groups of speakers. For information about the Ladino language in Latin America, see Monique R. Balbuena 2012. Florinda Goldberg reveals another aspect of the new boom of Ladino when she reports that Juan Gelman decided to learn Ladino and wrote poetry in this language; see Goldberg 2011, 752.

further details, cf. Cánovas 2011, 89–91) and Myriam Moscona's *Tela de Sevoya*. The female protagonist of *Vida propia*, Esther, daughter of immigrants from Serbocroatia, arrives in Southern Chile as a very young child together with her family and suffers under the chauvinism of her culture: "Los hijos son de Dios, las hijas de los hombres, es varón y no hembra quien inaugura la historia humana y Dios es Él y no Ella" (Nizri 2000, 108). Women, in this view, are reduced to giving birth and have no agency beyond that. As Esther is forced to marry an older man she does not love, there is no room for hope whatsoever in this text.[12] The Ladino language appears in biblical quotes in the epigraph of each chapter[13] and in a handful of proverbs – frequently enough to form a counterbalance to the rude reality of Esther's family life. Nevertheless, the prohibition to speak to non-Jews appears in Ladino as well: "prohibido todo modo de avladero kon cristianos" (Nizri 2000, 57).

The Ladino language fulfills a very different function in *Tela de Sevoya* (Moscona 2012), a novel by Myriam Moscona (*1955), who stems from a Bulgarian-Sephardic family. The widely ramified plot unfolds a mixture of dreams, reflections, anecdotes and essays focused on the subject of (fantastical) travel. One chapter ("La cuarta pared"), in which the narrator ("la tía Ema") finds herself in a garden with old tombstones, is written entirely in Ladino (and printed in italics). In another chapter ("Del diario de viaje"), we find quotes from a variety of people, among them Julia Kristeva, Juan Gelman and Albert Cohen. Thus, the travel motive is not only realized via the trips to Sofia, Istanbul, Smyrna and other cities but also in relation to other people who seem to belong to a global canon. In this novel, the Ladino language evokes things past in a manner similar to the Yiddish language in the aforementioned novels by Shua and Chejfec. – As we have seen, questions of language as a literary medium and as part of a plot characterize Latin American Jewish literatures. The tension between the traditional languages that have been 'brought along' and the 'borrowed' new ones as well as the problems of language loss and language acquisition play an important role and raise, in their very own ways, complex questions of identity and Jewishness.

3.3 Transgenerational Novels

Tradition may be broadly defined as the transfer of cultural and personal knowledge across generations. Research on memory has described the cardinal role of the family in these transmission processes. The literature discussed in the following shows that especially under the conditions of diaspora, the passing on of tradition is what

---

[12] There are other Jewish-Latin American women writers who wrote about repression and sexual abuse, among them Teresa Porzecanski, *Felicidades fugaces* (2002).
[13] "E serésh como el uerto ke no tener agua, e será el forte ídolo fetcho estopa." Isaías 30, 31 (as quoted by Cánovas 2011, 90).

guarantees its survival. Thus, grandparents, uncles and aunts have a special role in many Jewish-Latin American narratives, as seen already in the examples above. An important model for this category is Mario Szichman's fictional Pechof family in several of his novels since the 1970s. In fact, the novels of this series, spanning several generations, overlap very often with historical or (auto-) biographical texts, but it makes sense to emphasize their function in the context of contemporary Jewish-Latin American narrative.

Ariel Magnus (*1975) is the author of two novels of this type: *La abuela* (Magnus 2006), the story of his grandmother, and *El que mueve las piezas* (Magnus 2017), inspired by episodes from the life of his grandfather. *La abuela* is a typical *novela testimonio*, a testimony novel in the sense of the well-known Latin American genre, based on interviews with a person who has had a particular historical experience. In this case, the grandson interviews his grandmother, born in the German city of Wuppertal, where she went to the train station one day in the 1930s to buy a train ticket to Theresienstadt to visit her blind mother. Separated from her mother and sister, both of whom are killed, she survives Auschwitz, arrives in Latin America after an unimaginable journey, and settles in Brazil. In the dialogues that the novel represents, the grandson stays in the background and leaves the main voice to his grandmother, who is without doubt a traumatized character but who tries to add a touch of humor to her memories. Magnus also had some other files and records at hand, including several statements his actual grandmother had made during interviews conducted by a Jewish-Brazilian committee. The text's framing is 'factual' as well – the visit of the grandmother to Germany, for instance, where the author Magnus used to live. The novel-testimony operates with fictional surnames but is accompanied by a whole series of authentic photos of the life of the grandmother (for further details, see Ingenschay 2015b).

Magnus's novel about his grandfather's life, in contrast, is much less biographical (Magnus 2017). It gives an excellent account of the circumstances of a German Jew who immigrated to Argentina in the 1930s (and combines the story of the grandfather's literary ambitions with intertextual references to Italo Calvino and others, but above all to Stefan Zweig's *Schachnovelle*, first published in Buenos Aires in 1942).

Grandfathers (and the remembrance of the pogroms and the Shoah) play an important role in some other recent Jewish-Latin American transgenerational novels. In his fifth novel, Michel Laub (*1973) presents his readers with a diary consisting of nine chapters, *Diário da Queda* (Laub 2011), in which titles like "Algumas coisas que sei sobre o meu avô", "Algumas coisas que sei sobre o meu pai", etc., alternate with other, more metaliterary chapters simply called "Notas", which contain reflections on his writing. Whereas Magnus, in his novel *La abuela*, succeeds in making his grandmother talk about Auschwitz (with difficulties and consciousness of the trauma), silence prevails in Laub's novel. The protagonist's grandfather, a survivor of Auschwitz, remains quiet, is unable to speak about the loss of his entire family, and is thus cut off from his own past, living on in a world of shadows. The narrator only learns the details of the horrors that his grandfather survived through his father, who serves as a mediator between the generations preceding and succeeding him.[14]

The title of Tatiana Levy Salem's *A chave de casa* (2007) refers to the fact that Portuguese Jews used to take the keys of their houses with them when anti-Jewish riots forced them to leave their homes in the fifteenth century – a historical experience shared by the ancestors of Levy Salem (*1979). With clear autobiographical references, the narrator discovers one day that her grandfather's brother kept the key to his family's home. This discovery prompts her to travel back to Turkey, as the family had initially fled from Portugal to the Ottoman Empire, where her grandfather was born.

Among the range of Jewish-Argentine novels with a transgenerational topic, *El libro de los recuerdos* by María Shua (*1951) stands out (Shua 1994). The novel presents the saga of the Rimetka family, which is fictional but inspired by Shua's own family history (a family of Moroccan and Lebanese origin, as revealed in her own comment on the book, Shua 2012). The novel combines the history of European Jewish immigrants embarking in Odessa with falsified passports with a socio-historical reflection on twentieth century Argentina.

El salmo de Kaplan is a novel written by the author and journalist Marco Schwartz (*1956), published in 2005 and adapted to the screen in 2015 (Schwartz 2005). Again, it is a family novel, told from the personal perspective of Jacobo ('Yakuv') Kaplan, who immigrated to Colombia in the 1920s from Eastern Europe. The old man is an active member of the Jewish community of Santa Maria, a fictional city with unmistakable resemblances to Colombia's multicultural center Barranquilla. The story exposes the gradual loss of traditions as a consequence of assimilation among the Jewish community of Colombia in an increasingly globalized world, with intermarriages[15] and children emigrating to Europe or the US. Together with a beautiful study of customs, the plot unfolds in a manner similar to a detective story: Kaplan, already elderly and ill, suspects that the German leader of a neo-Nazi organization lives near his city. So, inspired by the kidnapping of Eichmann in Argentina, he tries to capture this man with the help of a strange ex-policeman. *El salmo de Kaplan* combines the exotic aesthetics of the boom novel with the theme of contemporary Jewish-Latin American identities (see Ingenschay 2015a).

In her novel *Judite no país do futuro* (2008), Adriana Armony (*1969) recounts the life of the protagonist Judite, born in Tsfat (Palestine) in late Ottoman times (1917). Set in 2004, the protagonist looks back on her long and difficult personal history, on her jobs as a housemaid and later as a teacher of Hebrew in Brazil. Her biggest frustration consists in the loss of Jewish traditions. Regina Igel has discussed the novel's allusion

---

14 For more details on the novels by Laub and Salem Levy, see de Oliveira 2013.
15 Apparently, this is a recurrent subject in contemporary Jewish-Latin American novels, e.g. in Ana Vásquez-Bronfman's *Las jaulas invisibles* (2002), where the loss of Jewish traditions and the history of intermarriage are treated in a humorous way.

to Stefan Zweig's book *Brasilien, Land der Zukunft* (1941) and to his suicide. Igel explains Judite's disillusion with reference to the changes brought about in the course of the last century: "Ao final, expressa desilusão ao ver que os laços que sustentaram seu grupo familiar durante a juventude e grande parcela de sua vida adulta se diluíam diante dos seus olhos. [. . .] As tendências assimilatórias se aprofundavam com o passar dos anos e a narradora penetra por diálogos intergeneracionais, expondo um abismo diferencial entre a geração do princípio do século 21 e suas experiências e sensibilidade, formada entre as tribulações do século 20" (Igel 2012, 139).

Jorge Scherman's novel *Por el ojo de la cerradura* (Scherman 1999) is a typical family saga spanning three generations of the fictional Gleiser family, who leave Moldavia after Vieira Gleiser, one of the main characters, has been searching for her brother, a Trotskyist persecuted by Stalin's henchmen, in the streets of Moscow. While the family at the center of the narrative leads a normal life in Chile, most of the European members of the family are killed in concentration camps.

The collapse of the family as a haven of rest and a shelter of values is the central proposition of Andrea Jeftanovic's novel *Escenario de guerra* (2000), told from a girl's point of view, where the decomposition of the family implies the concealment of Jewishness.

A very special contribution to the transgenerational discourse can be found in Ricardo Feierstein's complex narrative *La logia del umbral* (Feierstein 2001). Whereas in his earlier novel *Mestizo* (1988) the protagonist was an Argentine Jew who lost his memory after an accident and has to work through his roots – including the Yiddish language – to regain it,[16] *La logia del umbral* spans five generations. Starting with the first Jewish settlers in Argentina, the famous 'Jewish Gauchos' in Moisesville (Province of Santa Fe), where the government has allotted them a patch of land, the novel contains references to Alberto Gerchunoff's famous book *Los gauchos judíos* (1910). As a manifest sign of their successful integration and their gratitude towards their new homeland, the present day Schvel family decides to bring a wooden box with a shovelful of soil from Santa Fe to the Plaza de Mayo in the very center of Buenos Aires.[17] When the youngest offspring of the family passes by the AMIA building in Tucumán Street, he becomes an eyewitness of the terrorist attack of July 18, 1994. This event destroys his father's dream: Mariano Moisés Schvel, representative of the fourth generation of the family, is the one to enter the city, in the first chapter of the novel, on horseback, with the firm intention to (re)assure himself of his 'hyphenated identity' as a Jewish-Argentine. Mariano's reflections on identity and assimilation are

---

[16] For a detailed interpretation of *Mestizo* on the basis of Deleuze/Guattari's theory of *littérature mineure*, see Edna Aizenberg 1993.
[17] A map of the horsemen's itinerary from Moisesville to D.F. is included in the book (Feierstein 2001, 241). Feierstein's novel is packed with intertextual allusions to Latin American literary history, in particular to Julio Cortázar.

reminiscent of Gerchunoff's dream of integration;[18] printed in italics, they open and close the whole narrative like parentheses. His ideas are elevated to the more universal level of early twenty-first century societies when Edith, one of his relatives, argues for another new global order: "no debe ser solo para judíos. Si bregamos por la integración, ello debe darse desde organizaciones pluralistas. [. . .] Todas las minorías. [. . .] Negros, homosexuales, indígenas, gitanos, armenios, desplazados por la política económica, organismos de derechos humanos. [. . .] – Hay consenso" (Feierstein 2001, 226). If the central part of the book consists, among other things, in a retrospect of the history of discrimination against Jews in Argentina and relativizes the narrative of integration, the AMIA attack of July 1994 makes evident the difference between the majority and minorities and specifies the position of Argentinian Jews in the context of multicultural societies. Feierstein's transgenerational novel is thus undoubtedly one of the most important commentaries on contemporary Latin American societies.

The above examples illustrate how, especially in the context of multicultural societies, family traditions play a cardinal role. If the family saga, narrating the lives of several generations, is already one of the most popular forms of Latin American literature, this applies in a special way to the Latin American Jewish novel: The awareness of belonging to a diaspora makes the transmission of cultural knowledge from generation to generation even more essential.

3.4 Personal Memories and (Auto)biographically Inspired Works

The underlying feature of many of the novels to be discussed in the present section may be described as the personal, individual side of larger historical developments witnessed by the respective authors. In this sense, they are testimonials. In addition to the generally growing tendency towards (auto)biographical texts, memories and descriptions of personal *vitae* have determined the character of Jewish-Latin American writing for the last several decades, from Salomón Laiter's *David* (Laiter 1976) to Marjorie Agosín's *Sagrada memoria. Reminiscencias de una niña judía en Chile* (Agosín 1996) and Milan Platovsky's *Sobre vivir. Memorias* (Platovsky 1997).[19] An additional, rather unique autobiographical text is Rudi ("Rodolfo") Haymann's *El tren partió a las 20.30. Memorias de un migrante: desde Berlín hasta Chile* (2005) insofar as the author – born in Berlin – emigrated to Palestine in 1938, while his parents and sister went into exile in Chile. As a young man, Haymann actively took part in the Second World War as a Palestinian soldier in the service of Great Britain, later joining his family in

---

18 The novel contains details, backed by a photo collage, of the discrimination of Jews in Argentina over the decades. Gerchunoff's dream of total integration collapses, in Feierstein's view, with the attack on the AMIA building. Hopkins, however, believes that the Shoah already made Gerchunoff's dream impossible (Hopkins Rodríguez 2012).
19 For more details on these novels, as well as on Haymann's text, see Cánovas 2011, 129.

Latin America after the war. With the help of the Chilean writer Carlos Cerda (who had been exiled to the German Democratic Republic during the Pinochet era and received his PhD from Humboldt University), he wrote his memoirs many decades later, still bearing hatred towards German and Italian fascists.

Whereas authors like Ricardo Feierstein or Sergio Chejfec employ the subtle registers of a literary idiom that oscillates between the speakable and the unspeakable, Vilma Faingezicht (*1946), writer and Director of the Historical Museum of the Jewish community of Costa Rica, introduces the naive voice of a child to comment on the life and customs of Polish immigrants after the Second World War and the experience of cultural alterity amidst the Christian community of this Central American country. The narrator of *En tierras ajenas* (Faingezicht 2012), rather a collection of stories than a novel, is a girl of about ten years of age who suffers under the missionary ambitions of Christian children and finally concludes in a tone of resignation, "¡Éramos diferentes!" (Faingezicht 2012, 50). The children identify themselves as Poles, and on Christmas Day they become aware that "a los 'polacos', el Niño no les trae juguetes" (Faingezicht 2012, 50).

Roberto Brodsky's novel *Bosque quemado* (Brodsky 2007) has structural parallels to Chejfec's *Lenta Biografía* insofar as both novels address the life stories of fathers and sons. Brodsky (*1957) constantly shifts between the respective biographies of father and son, for example, when narrating Pinochet's coup d'état in 1973 from the point of view of Moisés Brodsky, a successful doctor and staunch communist who has to flee from Chile, leaving his son behind (who – traumatized – will later try to retrace his father's itinerary after he dies from Alzheimer's in the late 1980s). Here, Rodrigo Cánovas identifies the figure of the Wandering Jew with the "hijo de las diásporas latinoamericanas del último tercio del siglo XX" (Cánovas 2011, 122).

Critics may encounter a particular kind of autofiction (combined with metafiction) in Jacques Fux's novel *Antiterapias* (Fux 2012). In this experimental, postmodern short text, Fux (*1977), who studied mathematics, astrophysics and literary studies, introduces as a sort of *alter ego* a contemporary young man, originating from a small conservative Jewish community, in search of his place in contemporary Brazilian society (and persecuted by a bad ghost [*dibouk*] driving him towards sexual pleasure). Among the manifold stories that are told, two main subjects come to the fore: literary intertexts (from Proust to Pessoa) and historical memories that go back to the perpetrators of the Holocaust, to Himmler, Martin Bormann, and the Nazis who today 'guarantee' the protagonist's personal 'identity'.[20] Some years later, Fux published *Meshugá: um romance sobre a loucura* (Fux 2016), in which he classifies some prominent people (Woody Allen, Sarah Kofman, Bobby Fischer) under what he calls a special kind of Jewish lunacy.

---

[20] Jacques Fux is one of the main paradigms in Joanna Moszczynska's PhD thesis *A memória da Destruição na escrita judaico-brasileira depois de 1985: Por uma literatura pós-Holocausto emergente no Brasil* which will be published in 2022 by Peter Lang.

Let me conclude this section with several non-fictional biographies. The first deals with the activities of the criminal organization Zwi Migdal, which lured a great number of young women from Poland and other Central European countries to South America, where they were forced to work as prostitutes. This dark chapter of Jewish-Latin American history has inspired many fictional works, both novels and films, from Sholem Aleichem's *Der Mentsch fun Buenos Aires* (1909) to Edgardo Cozarinsky's melancholic novel *El rufián moldavo* (2004). It appears again in Myrtha Schalom's biography *La Polaca* (Schalom 2003), an impressive compilation of her investigations into the life of one of these women, Raquel Liberman, whose case was brought to trial in the 1930s. – The second text worth mentioning in this context is the biography of Abraham Spiegel written by Jacqueline Goldberg (a writer from Venezuela who previously published many novels which do not treat Jewish subjects at all). In *Abraham Spiegel, un luchador* (Goldberg 2015), she retraces the extraordinary life of this man who survived four concentration camps, was a member of the *Livui Sheirut* group who tried to liberate the road from Tel Aviv to Jerusalem, co-founded the *Jayot Hanéguev* (Animals of the Desert), was a member of the Kibbutz Nitzanim, and took part in the Korean War as an American soldier. In the context of the Latin American novel, the works dealt with here are particularly suited to transferring the individual aspects of a life – childhood and youth, displacement and migration, fear and trauma – into the discourse of the novel and thus reflecting on the relationship between the individual and the larger Jewish community.

3.5 (Un)religious Novels

A large part of the corpus of Latin American Jewish novels is characterized by complex expressions of Jewish tradition, some of which – contrasting with the non-Jewish world in which they are set – critically explore or question religious beliefs including even the principles of the Torah and the Talmud. Jacobo Sefamí delves into contemporary Jewish life in his novel *Los dolientes* (Sefamí 2004; for more details, see Cánovas 2011, 91–92). If cultural anthropologists have noticed a restructuring of the Syrian-Sephardic communities of Mexico City according to their origins (*shamis* from Damascus, *halebis* from Aleppo, and *shajatos*, which rather describes an attitude), Sefamí's novel attests to the vivid power of Jewish tradition. The story opens with the death of the father of the protagonist Simón Galante, on the eve of Shabbat, Friday, 13 September 1996 (29 Elul 5756), and follows the family's traditional mourning procedure over the course of the next ten days (with each day corresponding to one chapter of the book). We witness tradition between grief and humor, with sacred and profane voices.

Silvia Plager, who had seldom treated Jewish topics in her previous novels, published *La Rabina* in 2005. The novel tells the story of Esther Fainberg, a young Argentine-born woman who came to the US and married a wealthy lawyer. When she decides to embrace her Jewish identity, her family supports her – but only up to a certain point. In an act of rebellion, she travels to Israel for half a year, where she falls in love with a Uruguayan doctor. However, she stands firm in her convictions and sticks to her plan to study the Torah and to become a rabbi. The novel references several female archetypes (such as the traditional orthodox homemaker or daughter), but above all the archetype of introspection and of a passionate religious search often presented in metaphors of light and darkness. Florinda Goldberg also describes how the novel deals with Israel as an expression of Jewishness and as a setting for the plot (Goldberg 2014).

One narrative that is highly critical of Jewish traditions is Eduardo Halfon's *Monasterio* (Halfon 2014), a novel including several autobiographical allusions. Written from the point of view of one of the sons, Halfon (*1971) tells the story of the trip of a (very secular) family – parents and two sons – from Guatemala to Jerusalem, where the daughter/sister has previously moved to study the Torah in a *yeshiva* for women, a decision which seemed strange to the rest of the family. She fell in love with a North American Haredi man, both wanted to marry, and the family – though quite skeptical about this union – decided to travel to Israel to prepare the wedding. At the airport, the narrator meets a young German flight attendant, a former lover whom he had met in a bar in Guatemala, and the encounter with her seems to become more important to him than his sister's marriage to a man who lives in a world completely different from his own. Most of the family's ancestors were Jews from the Arab world (which brings about some conflicts in everyday life in Jerusalem). The narrator's grandfather, however, was Polish, and the grandson has traveled to Warsaw in search of his roots, which reappear as flashes of ghetto life in the grandson's memory. The story explores not only the cultural, but also the conceptual differences and the differing practice of daily routines among members of the same family, despite the shared memories of the Shoah and similar experiences of the diaspora. At the end of the story, the son conveys his hopeless message to the girl he has found again: everyone believes in his own lies, and in the end, no one will be saved.

María Paz Oliver has highlighted the role of travel in this book (Paz Oliver 2016), while Alexandra Ortiz Wallner has measured the dimensions of a "gran laberinto de identidades vinculado a los orígenes (judío, árabe, polaco, guatemalteco) del autor y de su recurrente narrador-protagonista", postulating that "la narración es solo posible en tanto narrativa oblicua" (Ortiz Wallner 2014).

The issue of matrilineality in Judaism is at the center of Gerardo Kleinburg's novel *No honrarás a tu padre* (Kleinburg 2004; for details about this novel, see Cánovas 2011, 94–95). The Ashkenazic Mexican protagonist Pedro Roth is shown a photo of a baby on a Shabbat eve in 1964. It shows his son Alejandro just born to a gentile mother. Pedro stands up and leaves the room without commenting on the event. Seventeen years later, he gets a phone call from his son, again on Shabbat, and once more, he feels unable to speak to the young man who is (according to common opinion) his son. In response to this repeated act of failed communication, Alejandro begins a relationship with his teacher while listening to Tannhäuser under Karajan's direction.

Even more irreverent are some parodic narratives such as Alejandro Jodorowsky's *Donde mejor canta un pájaro* (Jodorowsky 2005), a family saga that starts with the story of Teresa Groisman, who is angry with God because her son lost his life in an inundation of the Dnieper river due to 37 copies of the Talmud in the chest where the boy had been placed. Her reaction contradicts Job's message: "¡Eres un monstruo! ¡Creaste un pueblo elegido solo para torturarlo! ¡Llevas siglos riéndote a costa de nosotros!" (Jodorowsky 2005, 14 [as quoted by Cánovas 2011, 125]).

The biblical intertext is treated in the manner of a pastiche in Rafael Bán Jacobsen's *Uma leve simetria* (2009), an alternate version of the David and Jonathan story which constructs a homosexual relationship between the protagonists, with Hebrew letters marking the chapters and further biblical intertexts (such as the Psalms). (For more details on Jacobsen's narrative, see Igel 2012, 145.) To summarize these observations: The Latin American Jewish novel of the twenty-first century prototypically reflects current forms of Jewishness in the diaspora, while at the same time making creative use of a 'disrespectful' postmodernism, playfully critiquing religion, tradition, and God – and sometimes bordering on outright blasphemy.

4 Summary

This survey, although focusing on exemplary texts rather than providing an exhaustive account, nevertheless allows us to conclude with some thoughts on the developments within Jewish-Latin American literatures in the twenty-first century. The presence of Jewish topics and of the traces of Jewish culture and consciousness is unbroken and remains strong in spite of the declining number of people who define themselves as Latin American Jews. Cultures of memory continue to occupy an important place, above all in transgenerational literature and family sagas in general. The question of language has not disappeared but is hardly ever presented as a problem; instead, it is part of the aesthetics of remembrance. The Shoah and other persecutions still serve as a clear point of reference, but autobiographical and testimonial forms have become considerably less frequent. Religious Jewish life does serve as a subject, but fiction (and non-fiction) criticizing orthodox beliefs and practices is just as common. Among the noticeable changes is an increased role of 'multicultural' processes; stylistically 'postmodern' writing and experimental forms prevail. As for content, 'Jewishness' has extended not only to 'national' framings – a process which started with Gerchunoff – but also to 'continental' references (to Native Americans, to borderland cultures) and to global movements. Ultimately, these reflections confirm some statements made several years ago in the introduction to the complex volume *Pertenencia y alteridad*: First, that the Jewish experience in Latin American countries is diverse and plural and thus difficult to conceptualize (Avni et al. 2011, 13); second, that a sort of global Jewishness is at play which is necessarily dual and sometimes contradictory:

entre la búsqueda judía de legitimidad, de igualdad y de diversidad, entre la sociabilidad de vidas individuales de ciudadanos judíos dentro de las sociedades nacionales latinoamericanas y el gregarismos en sus propias instituciones colectivas, entre la identidad sociocultural de los judíos en total sincronía con el *ethos* nacional de cada país latinoamericano, y una identidad y creatividad específicas cuyo centro simbólico e intelectual se encuentra en otra parte, en tanto son también parte de una nación, de una *pueblitud* (*peoplehood*) judía global. (Avni et al. 2011, 17)

This tension has proved to be positive. It safeguards a literary production which may be hard to conceptualize but which is prolific and exciting and which by way of its thematic and stylistic diversity, the internationality of its references and their diasporic character has become exemplary of modern writing per se.

Bibliography

Works Cited

The country of residence ('nationality') of the authors is added in parentheses.

Agosín, Marjorie. *Sagrada memoria. Reminiscencias de una niña judía en Chile*. Santiago: Cuarto propio, 1994. (Chile)
Aizenberg, Edna. "Jewish Identity, Pluralism, and Survival: Feierstein's *Mestizo* as Minority Discourse." *Reflections on Latin American Jewish Writing. Tradition and Innovation*. Eds. Robert DiAntonio and Nora Glickman. Albany: New York State University Press, 1993. 197–118.
Armony, Adriana. *Judite no país do futuro*. Rio de Janeiro: Record, 2005 [reed. 2008]. (Brazil)
Avni, Haim, Judit Bokser Liwerant, Sergio Della Pergola, Margalit Bejarano and Leonardo Senkman, eds. *Pertenencia y alteridad. Judíos en/de América Latina: cuarenta años de cambios*. Madrid: Iberoamericana, 2011.
Balbuena, Monique R. "Ladino in Latin America. An old language in a New World." *Contemporary Sephardic Identity in the Americas. An Interdisciplinary Approach*. Eds. Margalit Bejarano and Edna Aizenberg. Syracuse Univ. Press, 2012. 161–183.
Bibliowicz, Azriel. *Migas de pan*. Bogotá: Alfaguara, 2013. (Colombia)
Birmajer, Marcelo. *Ser judío en el siglo XXI*. Buenos Aires: Milá, 2002.
Birmajer, Marcelo. "Que significa Israel para mí." *La Ilustración liberal* 47 (2011) https://www.clublibertaddigital.com/ilustracion-liberal/47/que-significa-israel-para-mi-marcelo-birmajer.html (4 March 2022).
Brailovsky, Antonio E. *Identidad*. Buenos Aires: Sudamericana, 1980. (Argentina)
Brodsky, Roberto. *Bosque quemado*. Santiago: Mondadori, 2007. (Chile)
Cánovas, Rodrigo. *Literatura de inmigrantes árabes y judíos en Chile y México*. Madrid: Iberoamericana, 2011.
Carillo Zeiter, Katja. "Acercándose al pasado: *Lenta biografía* de Sergio Chejfec." *Múltiples identidades*. Ed. Verena Dolle. Frankfurt(Main)/Madrid: Vervuert Verlagsgesellschaft, 2012. 199–212.
Cohen, Robin. *Global Diasporas: An Introduction*. New York/London: Routledge, 1999 [reed. 2008].
Cozarinsky, Edgardo. *El rufián moldavo*. Buenos Aires: La Bestia Equilatera, 2004. (Argentina)
Chejfec, Sergio. *Lenta biografía*. Buenos Aires: Alfaguara, 2007. (Argentina)

Dolle, Verena, ed. *Múltiples identidades. Literatura judeo-latinoamericana de los siglos XX y XXI*. Frankfurt(Main)/Madrid: Vervuert Verlagsgesellschaft, 2012.
Faingezicht, Vilma. *En tierras ajenas*. San José: El Atabal, 2012. (Costa Rica)
Feierstein, Ricardo. *Mestizo*. Buenos Aires: Milà, 1988. (Argentina)
Feierstein, Ricardo. *La logia del umbral*. Buenos Aires: Galerna, 2001.
Friedman, Edward. "Theory in the margin. Latin American Literature and the Jewish subject." *The Jewish Diaspora in Latin America. New Studies on History and Literature*. Eds. David Sheinin and Lois Baer Barr. New York/London: Garland Publishers, 1996. 21–31.
Fux, Jacques. *Antiterapias*. Belo Horizonte: Scriptum, ²2014. (Brazil)
Fux, Jacques. *Meshugá. Um romance sobre a loucura*. Rio de Janeiro: José Olimpio, 2016.
Gilman, Sander L. "Introduction." *Jewries at the Frontier. Accomodation, Identity, Conflict*. Eds. Sander L. Gilman and Milton Shain. Univ. of Illinois Press, 1999. 1–25.
Goldberg, Florinda F. "Escritores judíos latinoamericanos: Residencia en la frontera." *Pertenencia y alteridad: Judíos en de América Latina: cuarenta años de cambio*. Eds. Haim Avni, Judit Bokser, Margalit Bejarano and Sergio Della Pergola. Frankfurt (Main)/Madrid: Vervuert Verlagsgesellschaft, 2011. 743–760.
Goldberg, Florinda F. "¿Tiempo en disolución? Sobre fronteras identitarias y escritura judía en América Latina." *Múltiples identidades*. Ed. Verena Dolle. Frankfurt(Main)/Madrid: Vervuert Verlagsgesellschaft, 2012. 213–226.
Goldberg, Florinda F. "Gender, Religion, and the Search for a Modern Jewish Identity in *La rabina* by Silvia Plager." *Reconsidering Israel–Diaspora Relations*. Eds. Eliezer Ben-Rafael, Judit Bokser Liwerant and Yosef Gorny. Leiden: Brill Academic Pub, 2014. 223–233.
Goldberg, Jacqueline. *Abraham Spiegel. Un luchador*. Caracas: Equinoccio, 2015. (Venezuela)
Goldemberg, Isaac. *El nombre del padre*. Lima: Santillana, 2001. (Peru)
Halfon, Eduardo. *Monasterio*. Barcelona: Libros del Asteroide, 2014. (Guatemala)
Haymann, Rodolfo. *El tren partió a las 20.20. Memorias de un migrante. Desde Berlín hasta Chile. 1938–1948*. Santiago: La Fuente, 2005. (Chile)
Hirsch, Marianne. "The Generation of Postmemory." *Poetics Today* 29.1 (2008): 103–128.
Hopkins Rodríguez, Eduardo. "La construcción de identidad en *El nombre del padre* de Isaac Goldemberg." *Múltiples identidades*. Ed. Verena Dolle. Frankfurt (Main)/Madrid: Vervuert Verlagsgesellschaft, 2012. 181–198.
Igel, Regina. *Imigrantes judeos – escritores brasileiros. O componente judaico na literatura brasileira*. São Paulo: Perspectiva, 1997.
Igel, Regina. "Os novos escritores brasileiro-judeos: geração dos anos 70." *Múltiples identidades*. Ed. Verena Dolle. Frankfurt (Main)/Madrid: Vervuert Verlagsgesellschaft, 2012. 135–150.
Ingenschay, Dieter. "In der Spannung zwischen jüdischer Identität und lateinamerikanischer Lebenswirklichkeit bringt Marco Schwartz Komik und Ernst zusammen." Nachwort zu Marco Schwartz, *Kaplans Psalm*. Berlin: Hentrich & Hentrich, 2015a. 186–193.
Ingenschay, Dieter. "Die Erfahrung des Lagers in zwei argentinischen Gegenwartstexten: Ariel Magnus' *La abuela* und Susana Romano Sued, *Procedimiento*." *Poetik des Überlebens. Kulturproduktion im Konzentrationslager*. Ed. Anne-Berenike Rothstein. Berlin: De Gruyter, 2015b. 68–83.
Ingenschay, Dieter. "Las literaturas 'judeo-latinoamericanas' frente a nuevos desafíos glocales." *Aspectos actuales del hispanismo mundial. Literatura – Cultura – Lengua*. Vol. 2. Ed. Christoph Strosetzki, in cooperation with La Asociación Internacional de Hispanistas. Berlin: De Gruyter, 2018. 21–34.
Jacobsen, Rafael Bán. *Uma leve simetria*. Porto Alegre: Não, 2009. (Brazil)
Jeftanovic, Andrea. *Escenario de guerra*. Santiago: Alfaguara, 2000. (Chile)
Jodorowski, Alejandro. *Donde mejor canta un pájaro*. Santiago: Mondadori, 2005. (Chile)

Kacowicz, Arie M. "Israel, Las comunidades judías y América Latina en un escenario internacional cambiante." *Pertenencia y alteridad: Judíos en de América Latina: cuarenta años de cambio*. Eds. Haim Avni, Judit Bokser, Margalit Bejarano and Sergio Della Pergola. Frankfurt (Main)/Madrid: Vervuert Verlagsgesellschaft, 2011. 251–270.
Kleinburg, Gerardo. *No honrarás a tu padre*. México: Sudamericana, 2004. (Mexico)
Laub, Michel. *Diário da Queda*. São Paulo: Companhia das Letras, 2011. (Brazil)
Levy Salem, Tatiana. *A chave de casa*. Rio de Janeiro: Record, 2007. (Brazil)
Lockhart, Darrell. *Jewish Writers of Latin America. A Dictionary*. New York: Routledge, 1997 [repr. 2013].
Magnus, Ariel. *La abuela*. Buenos Aires: Planeta, 2006. [German version: *Zwei lange Unterhosen der Marke Hering. Die erstaunliche Geschichte meiner Großmutter*. Tr. Silke Kleemann. Köln: Kiepenheuer & Witsch, 2012.] (Argentina)
Magnus, Ariel. *El que mueve las piezas. Una novela bélica*. Buenos Aires: Tusquets, 2017.
Moscona, Myriam. *Tela de Sevoya*. México: Lumen, 2012. (Mexico)
Moszczynska, Joanna. *A memória da Destruição na escrita judaico-brasileira depois de 1985: Por uma literatura pós-Holocausto emergente no Brasil*. Berlin/Bern: Peter Lang, 2022.
Muñiz-Huberman, Angelina. *El sefardí romántico. La azarosa vida de Mateo Alemán II*. México: Debolsillo, 2005. (Mexico)
Nissán, Rosa. *Novia que te vea*. México: Planeta, 1992. (Mexico)
Nizri, Vicky. *Vida propia*. México: El Pirul, 2000. (Mexico)
Oliveira, Jessica Sabrina de. A chave de casa, *de Tatiana Salem Levy, e* Diário da Queda, *de Michel Laub: Notas da inscripção do judaísmo na literature brasileira contemporânea*. Dissertação Recife 2013. https://repositorio.ufpe.br/handle/123456789/11464 (4 March 2022).
Ortiz Wallner, Alexandra. "Autorretrato en Jerusalén." *Iowa literaria* 2014.1 https://www.academia.edu/7039378/_Autorretrato_en_Jerusal%C3%A9n_sobre_Monasterio_de_Eduardo_Halfon (4 March 2022).
Paz Oliver, María. "Los paseos de la memoria: representaciones de la caminata urbana en Cynthia Rimsky, Sergio Chejfec y Eduardo Halfon." *Iberoromania* 83 (2016): 16–34.
Plager, Silvia. *La rabina*. Buenos Aires: Planeta, 2005. (Argentina)
Porzecanski, Teresa. *Felicidades fugaces*. Montevideo: Planeta, 2002. (Uruguay)
Rico, Alicia. "Reflexiones y representaciones del exilio: de *Canto del peregrino* (1999) a *El sefardí romántico* (2005)." *Anales de Literatura Hispanoamericana* 44 (2015): 47–57.
Rimsky, Cynthia. *Poste restante*. Santiago: Sudmericana, 2000. (Chile)
Rimsky, Cynthia. *Los perplejos*. Santiago: Sangría, 2009.
Saldívar, José D. *Trans-Americanity: Subaltern Modernities, Global Coloniality, and the Cultures of Greater Mexico*. Durham/London: Duke University Press, 2012.
Salem Levy, Tatiana. *A chave de casa*. Rio de Janeiro: Record, 2007. (Brazil)
Schalom, Myrtha. *La polaca*. Buenos Aires: Norma, 2003. (Argentine)
Scherman, Jorge. *Por el ojo de la cerradura*. Santiago: Cuarto Propio, 1999. (Chile)
Schwartz, Marco. *El salmo de Kaplan*. Bogotá: Norma, 2005. (Colombia)
Sefamí, Jacobo. *Los dolientes*. México: Plaza & Janés, 2004. (Mexico)
Seligson, Esther. *La morada en el tiempo*. México: Artífice, 1981. (Mexico)
Shua, Ana-María. *El libro de los recuerdos*. Buenos Aires: Sudamericana, 1994. (Argentina)
Shua, Ana María. "'¿Vos, escritora judía?', dijo mi bobe." *Múltiples identidades*. Ed. Verena Dolle. Frankfurt (Main)/Madrid: Vervuert Verlagsgesellschaft, 2012. 29–42.
Sosnowski, Saúl. *La orilla inminente. Escritores judíos argentinos*. Buenos Aires: Legasa, 1987a.
Sosnowski, Saúl. "Latin-American Jewish Writers: Protecting the Hyphen." *The Jewish Presence in Latin America*. Eds. Judith Laikin Elkin and Gilbert W. Merkx. Boston: Allen & Unwin, 1987b. 297–357.

Sosnowski, Saúl. "Sin desierto y sin tierra prometida: cuarenta años de literatura judía-latinoamericana." *Pertenencia y alteridad: Judíos en de América Latina: cuarenta años de cambio*. Eds. Haim Avni, Judit Bokser, Margalit Bejarano and Sergio Della Pergola. Frankfurt (Main)/Madrid: Vervuert Verlagsgesellschaft, 2011. 709–718.
Stavans, Ilan. *On Borrowed Words. A memoir of Language*. New York: Viking Press, 2001.
Stavans, Ilan. "Jewish Literature and Latin America." *Judaism: A Quarterly Journal of Jewish Life and Thought* 52 (2003): 246–260.
Steimberg, Alicia. "Recuerdos y reflexiones sobre la constitución de mi condición de escritora judía latinoamericana." *Múltiples identidades*. Ed. Verena Dolle. Frankfurt (Main)/Madrid: Vervuert Verlagsgesellschaft, 2012. 23–28.
Toro, Alfonso de. "Performativ-hybride Diasporas." *Alteritäten: Literatur, Kultur, Sprache*. Eds. Grit Melhorn, Hans-Christian Trepte, Alina Jurasz and Danuta Rytel-Schwarz. Hildesheim: Olms, 2013. 78–99.
Vásquez-Bronfman, Ana. *Las jaulas invisibles*. Santiago: Lom, 2002. (Chile)
Vieira, Nelson H. *Jewish Voices in Brazilian Literature. A Prophetic Discourse of Alterity*. University of Florida Press, 1995.
Yerushalmi, Yosef Hayim. *Zakhor. Jewish History and Jewish Memory*. Seattle: University of Washington Press, 1996.

Further Reading

Wassner, Dalia. "Harbingers of Modernity: Jews in the Hispanic World; A Conversation with Ilan Stavans." *Journal of Modern Jewish Studies* 12.2 (2013): 313–327.
Zivin, Erin Graff. *The Wandering Signifier: Rhetoric of Jewishness in the Latin American Imaginary*. Durham, NC: Duke University Press, 2008.

Florinda F. Goldberg
21 Writing Cuban Belonging through Jewish Eyes

Abstract: The emergence of a Cuban political diaspora in the 1960s reinforced the notion of an association between Cuban and Jewish identities – both in the social imaginary and in theoretical approaches such as those of José Martí in the nineteenth century. A number of authors, both on the island itself and in the American diaspora, have found in the "Jewish wandering signifier" a means of exploring the hybridity of Cuban and Cuban-American identities in our times. The present article elaborates on this issue as it is reflected in the novels of Achy Obejas, Oscar Hijuelos, and Leonardo Padura.

Key Terms: Cuban cultural history, Jewish belonging, political diaspora of the 1960s, contemporary novels

1 Introduction

José Martí, the writer, politician and essayist known as the "Apostle of Cuban Independence", famously sympathized with Jewish history. One prominent quote reflecting this attitude is the following: "We are somehow Hebrew in matters of fortune, and we are always waiting for a Messiah that never comes. Every day I am in danger of giving my life for my country and for my duty [...] and my sling is David's sling."[1] The scope of these elective affinities was enlarged with the emergence of a Cuban political diaspora in the 1960s. As Ruth Behar has remarked:

> [...] it is well known that Cubans as a whole like to think of themselves as the 'Jews of the Caribbean.' On the island, Cubans see Cuba and Israel as similarly fierce and independent nations [...] [which strive] to build paradise on earth. Cuban exiles and immigrants, in contrast, see themselves as diasporic in the classical Jewish sense. (Behar 2007, 41)

This homologization, often present in the works of Jewish Cuban writers, becomes particularly relevant when it appears in the works of non-Jewish Cuban authors, for whom Jewish history seems to enable a better perception and a particular resolution of the issue of Cuban identities. This hypothesis is examined below in three case studies of novels by authors born in Cuba or of Cuban heritage: *Days of Awe* (2001) by Achy Obejas; *A Simple Habana Melody* (2002) by Óscar Hijuelos; and *Heretics* (*Herejes*,

---

[1] "Somos un tanto hebreos en punto a fortuna, y esperamos siempre a un Mesías que nunca llega" (Martí 1963–1973, Vol. 9, 288); "[...] estoy todos los días en peligro de dar mi vida por mi país y por mi deber [...] y mi honda es la de David" (Martí 1963–1973, Vol. 20, 161) (my translations).

2013) by Leonardo Padura. Achy Obejas belongs to the Cuban post-revolution American diaspora; Óscar Hijuelos was born in the U.S. into a family who had emigrated in the 1940s for non-political reasons; and Leonardo Padura was born and remained in Havana. Though produced in different contexts, representing the various contemporary "Cubanities", the novels all represent the multifaceted existential reality of Cuban identities that followed the Cuban Revolution and the exile of a large number of Cubans in its aftermath.[2] This condition has been defined by Gustavo Pérez Firmat as a "life in the hyphen" (Pérez Firmat 1996). The three novels represent different dynamics in the construction of hyphenated belongings by means of integrating fragments of Jewish history, which we shall summarize after the particular analyses of the texts.[3]

One important theoretical notion for this context is found in Erin Graff Zivin's reflections on the semantics of Jewish cultural history: "By reading 'Jewishness' as a *wandering signifier*, a mobile sign that travels between literary texts and sociohistorical contexts, I simultaneously pursue two avenues of inquiry: literary representations of 'Jewishness' and anxiety surrounding difference in modern Latin American culture" (Graff Zivin 2008, 2). According to Graff Zivin, "the 'figurative Jew', that is, the idea of Jewishness that pervades Western culture [...] representing 'other others'" (Graff Zivin 2008, 3) "exhibits the particular ability to signify contradiction [...] [T]he 'Jew' often comes to stand for [the] others in literature [...] as a marker of a more generic form of alterity and marginality" (Graff Zivin 2008, 17).

In the following, we shall examine how this "wandering signifier" affects plots and characters in the different contexts of the three novels under consideration.

2 *Days of Awe* (2001) by Achy Obejas: "The great Cuban-Jewish novel"

Achy Obejas (Havana 1956) belongs to what Rubén Rumbaut called "the one and a half generation". With this concept, Rumbaut referred to people born in Cuba and taken to the US at a very early age, who "form a distinctive cohort in that in many ways they are marginal to both the old and the new worlds, and are fully part of neither of them" (Rumbaut 1991, 61). Gustavo Pérez Firmat indicates that this generation undergoes "two crisis-producing and identity-defining transitions: (1) adolescence [...] and (2) acculturation and the task of managing the transition from one sociocultural environment to another" (Pérez Firmat 1996, 4).

---

2 This multiplicity also affects Cubans who continue to live on the island as "the exile of those who stay behind, watching as everyone departs" (Behar 1995a, 14).
3 The scope of this chapter does not allow for a discussion of whether writers of Latin American origin who live in the United States and write in English (generally known as Latino or Hispanic) are or are not part of Latin American literature. My contention is that they are; see Goldberg (2021).

The author of the novel, Achy Obejas, is a translator and a journalist, a writer and a poet. Obejas is active in civil movements both for alternative sexualities and for contact between the island and the American Cuban diaspora. Her first two books focus on these issues. The short stories of *We Came All the Way from Cuba So You Could Dress Like This?* (1994) represent cultural and intergenerational conflicts. Her novel *Mambo Memoir* (1996) stresses the significations of the mambo for Cuban identitie(s), both as a Cuban rhythm developed in the US and as a dance consisting in one step forward and two steps backwards. Obejas grew up in a neighborhood with many Jewish immigrants. Since her childhood, she enjoyed visiting the synagogue during festivities, and up to this day she takes part in Passover dinners (even boasting of knowing by heart the four ritual questions). She finds much in common between Cubans and Jews:

> I honestly believe there is tremendous cultural affinity, if not overlap, between Cubans and Jews. I have a whole list in *Days of Awe*, kind of tongue-in-cheek, which ends with both groups thinking they're god's chosen people. But some things are real: the emphasis on education, the intense importance of family, all the weird tensions and ambivalences around assimilation and what it means, the stubbornness too – although that plays more to stereotypes. We share some of those too: being passionate, and loud, and the whole connection with commerce. Cubans are called the Jews of the Caribbean, and that springs from a prejudice toward both groups. I think what's most important for me is that we're both dynamically spiritual people – and by that I don't necessarily mean religious. What I'm talking about is having a sense of the divine in everyday life, not just awe but also a sense of accessibility and intimacy: among Cubans we call that speaking to god as "tú" instead of "usted".
> (Obejas in Sheppard-Brick 2002)

When the author learned that "Obejas" is a surname of Spanish converso or crypto-Jewish origin (an episode included in the novel), she decided to read about Sephardic and Judeo-Cuban history and embarked on the project of writing "the great Cuban-Jewish novel" (Obejas in an interview with Tatiana de la Tierra, quoted in Wolfenzon 2010, 116.)

Obejas has affirmed on several occasions that the plot of her novel is fictional, but it clearly includes many autofictional components, mainly in the figure of the protagonist and narrator Alejandra San José (Ale). Ale's syncretic belonging is established in the foundational episode that opens the novel. She is born on January 1, 1959 (the day Fidel Castro's revolutionary forces arrived in Havana) and declared to be "the first new life of this new day" (Obejas: *Days of Awe* 2001, 2). Suffering from a supposed incompatibility between her parents' blood factors, she is treated with transfusions (mainly of her father's blood) and other varied resources. A priest prays for her life; her mother lights candles for the Virgen de la Caridad del Cobre but also performs *Santería* rituals;[4] her father holds her in his arms while mumbling the words of a Hebrew prayer: *"Ner Adonai nishmat adam"* (*Days of Awe*, 4).[5]

---

4 "Our Lady of Charity" or "Our Lady of El Cobre" is the Virgin Mary's title as Patroness of Cuba. *Santería* is a syncretic religion developed in Cuba which combines African and Catholic beliefs.
5 "God's candle is the soul of man" (Proverbs 20:27) – a Jewish prayer against the danger of death.

Ale is two years old when the family flees Cuba led by her father's employer, a survivor of the Holocaust who, upon their arrival in Miami, shouts in Yiddish to the people on the beach, *"Mir sint pleitim!"* (We are refugees!) (*Days of Awe*, 30). Thus, their exile carries the signs of both the Cuban and the Jewish historical experience.

The author incorporates many of her own experiences in her account of Ale's life: a childhood among Jewish neighbors, romantic relations with Jewish boys and girls, and her profession as a translator, which positions her between two languages and two cultures that complement each other.

What triggers Ale's search for a new sense of belonging is when somebody tells her that her grandmother's name, Sima, is not Spanish but Hebrew and suggests that she ask her father about it: "Maybe you'll get an interesting family story out of it" (*Days of Awe*, 113). The father reacts in anger and reluctantly tells her that Sima was a convert – which confirms Ale's suspicion that there is more to be clarified.

The process of solving this mystery is linked with Ale's wish to recover her Cuban roots – both against the will of her parents. Her two trips to the island follow the paradigm of the journey of discovery and self-discovery. Ale gets to know the country and its people as they really are (and not through the eyes of the exiled). She also meets Moisés Menach, an open Cuban Jew and a life-long friend of her father. Moses plays the role of 'guide for the perplexed', and he will gradually and wisely help Ale unveil the family secret and establish its meaning for her own life.

In brief, the "mystery" is as follows: Ale's father Enrique San José was born into a Jewish family whose ancestors had fled Seville and arrived in Cuba. Secretiveness had become such an integral part of their Jewish practices that it remained also for the following generations, even when it became possible to live openly as Jews. Enrique was raised as a Jew by his uncle Ytzak (as it is spelled in the text), who felt deeply Jewish *and* Cuban. But Enrique suffered two traumatic experiences in his youth – a Nazi demonstration in Havana and the episode of the *St. Louis*[6] – that made him return defensively to a crypto-Jewish attitude. Enrique prays every day and (surreptitiously) celebrates the Jewish holidays, but he is careful that nobody except his wife should know about this, hiding it above all from his daughter.[7] Only on his deathbed will he ask her to help him with *tefillin* and prayers. Socolovsky indicates that the way Ale experiences this scene – "each prayer sung sending powerful vibrations down his

---

[6] The *St. Louis* set sail from Hamburg in May 1939 with 937 Jewish passengers who had purchased Cuban visas, but the Havana authorities only validated 23 of them. The ship returned to Europe, and it is estimated between 300 and 600 of its passengers perished in the Holocaust. See Bejarano (1991; 2014); Gordon Thomas and Max Morgan, *Voyage of the Damned* (1974); and Stuart Rosenberg's film based on this book (1976).

[7] Socolovsky correctly remarks that the different approaches of father and daughter to translation reiterate their respective approaches to Jewishness: "For Enrique, words gain meaning only through the act of translation, just as his sense of identity comes through negotiating the trace – the absence and voids – in his history", while "his daughter yearns for unity through translation" (Socolovsky 2004, 230, 231).

spine, into me" (*Days of Awe*, 280) – turns it into a reflection of the transfusions and prayers following her birth (Socolovsky 2004, 244–245).

Enrique instructs his family not to perform any religious funeral rites ("no shive, no mass", *Days of Awe*, 287) and entrusts Ale with the task of throwing his ashes into the sea in Havana, an assertion of his Cubanity. However, when her mother arranges a mass 'to save appearances', Ale decides to perform the other half of the funeral rites: "sit on boxes, say kaddish for eleven months, pray every day" (*Days of Awe*, 299). Ale chooses for the ritual of the ashes the eve of Yom Kippur, pronouncing by way of a *kaddish* her father's favorite poem by Judah ha-Levi: "Judah ha-Levi may or may not have made it to his Zion, but here, through me, my father is at rest in his" (*Days of Awe*, 357).

Ale tries to explore and resolve her discordant belongings: believer or atheist, Jewish or Christian, Cuban or American, monosexual or bisexual, which she experiences as parallel components of her self that reflect each other.[8] The symbol she chooses for this process is the Days of Awe, the ten-day period between Rosh Hashanah and Yom Kippur that is devoted to self-examination and inner reconciliation. The Days of Awe function in the novel on different levels. As the factual date of her trip to Cuba to fulfill her father's last wish, they become a *mise en abyme* that metaphorizes Ale's journey in search of herself/her-selves. For Enrique, "his life is *only* made of Days of Awe" (Wolfenzon 2010, 107; emphasis in the original); but while he conceives of the final destiny of his ashes as a symbolic fusion with Cuba, Alejandra understands that unifying her own dualities is impracticable because history cannot be reverted. She cannot simply be Jewish after 500 years of exile, and she cannot not be Jewish being her father's daughter. She cannot establish herself in Cuba because her parents left the island forty years ago, but neither can she simply be American. When, at the end of the novel, somebody urges her, "You have to choose", her answer is "I don't have to [. . .]. I can wonder. I can live with both possibilities" (*Days of Awe*, 336). In an interview, Obejas affirmed:

> But the more I studied and researched for *Days of Awe*, the more immersed I became in Jewish history and lore, the more complicated I saw any claim to identity. What I've said before is that *I don't have Jewish damage*; that is, I wasn't raised with any of the negative effects. *I have Cuban damage, which is probably close enough.* (Sheppard-Brick 2009, 2; my emphasis)

According to Goldman, her Jewish experience helps Ale to understand that "displacement and diaspora take the place of more conventional structures of subject-formation and, in doing so, palimpsestically mask an absence that they can never fully eradicate" (Goldman 2004, 63). Through the metaphor of the palimpsest, her contradictory belongings – religious, national and sexual – are made to interconnect by way of a

---

8 I do not elaborate here on the issue of Ale's bisexuality. Goldman emphasizes "the chiasmus of Judaism and sexuality that is enacted in Ale's relationships: she experiences her ethnicity through episodes that are introduced as moments of sexual self-discovery and, conversely, narrates her most intensely sexual encounter during her exploration of her family heritage in Cuba" (Goldman 2004, 65).

dynamics of presence/absence, affirmation/negation, search and acceptance. Obejas summed it up in a brief essay in 1999, in which we can perceive the thoughts that were guiding the composition of her novel at the time:

> My responsibility [...] is: to believe, fervently, reverentially, that everything is worth thinking, every life worth exploring, every condition worth discussing. No idea is too dangerous, even one as crazy as thinking that being a Jew could save me. In many ways – in all the gifts faith and community has brought me – it already has, just like lesbian love, just like that particular brand of Cuban craziness.
>
> (Obejas 1999, 48)

3 *A Simple Habana Melody* (2002) by Óscar Hijuelos: The Convergence of Cubanity and the Holocaust

Óscar Hijuelos (New York, 1951–2013) was born to Cuban parents who emigrated in the 1940s, and therefore his experience is not one of political exile. Nevertheless, his narrative themes include the hybridization of Cuban and American cultures, as in his novel *The Mambo Kings Play Songs of Love*, which won the Pulitzer Prize in 1989. Like Obejas, he also took for granted some Jewish converso presence in his genealogy:

> The name Hijuelos is a hard one to track down. And there's a whole side of my family that looks very Semitic. I was intrigued by the idea I could have some Sephardic blood, even if it's centuries old. A converso somewhere, generations back. My cousin got me thinking about identity and how one is defined by a name, by an appearance. As Carlos Fuentes once said, there's not a Spaniard walking around without these roots.
>
> (Hijuelos in Freedman 2013, 47)

The author's interest in Jewishness arose from his fortuitous acquaintance with Holocaust survivors and his perception of the universal significance of the Holocaust:

> Hijuelos also drew subtly on the several survivors he had known during his formative years – one the baker at a summer camp where Hijuelos was a counselor, another a female colleague in an ad agency where he wrote copy. [...] Hijuelos told me, "People in the thirteenth century said God died with the coming of the plague. But for me, like other people, God died in the Holocaust."
>
> (Freedman 2013)

A Simple Habana Melody was inspired by the singular biography of the Cuban musician Moisés Simons (1890–1945), a composer of light operas and popular music, particularly renowned for his rumba "El manisero" ("The peanut vendor"), the most famous piece of that Cuban song-dance. In spite of his name and surname, Simons belonged to a traditional Catholic family. His bad luck had it that he was in Paris on an artistic tour when the city was occupied by the Nazis, whom he could not convince that he was not Jewish. Though he was not deported, probably because of his popularity, his royalties were confiscated and he suffered frequent threats.

After two years, in 1942, he was finally allowed to go to Spain and from there he returned to Cuba.[9] In the "Author's note" at the end of the novel, Hijuelos explains the genesis of his novel:

> While this is a work of fiction, certain events depicted in its narrative were based on the life of Cuban [. . .] Moisés Simons (1890–1945) [. . .] composer of [. . .] *El manisero* [. . .]. [I]t was Simons's life as a Cuban exile in Paris of the 1930s and his eventual persecution by the Germans during the Second World War that became the basis for *this novel's convergence with the Holocaust*. That the creator of one of the most life-embracing and joyful of rumbas could have found himself in such an evil circumstance seemed *too powerful an irony to resist* when it came to the portrayal of my own protagonist, Israel Levis, whose dreams are the dreams of those who wish the world well.
> (Hijuelos: *A Simple Habana Melody* 2002, 343, my emphasis)

Like his historical model, the novel's hero bears an ambiguous name, Israel Levis,[10] and is a celebrated composer of popular music as well as a renowned classical pianist. Belonging to a very Catholic family of Spanish origin, Levis has benign fantasies about his plausible remote Jewish roots, and his name does not seem problematic to him:

> [. . .] it never bothered Levis in later years when strangers mistook him [. . .] for an Irishman or, more commonly, a *marrano* – a Jew – or a *polaco*. [. . .] [W]hat Spaniard did not have a descendant somewhere with Jewish or Arab blood? [. . .] Of course, it had never occurred to Israel Levis that he would one day get into trouble because of the apparent Jewishness of his name. [. . .] The family name, Levis, originated with some distant Catalan ancestor, who may or may not have had some Jewish blood. [. . .] Judaism had never been a matter of discussion [. . .]. [T]here had been a monsignor named Sebastiano Levis [. . .]. All that the young Levis knew was that he had been given his first name, Israel, after a great-uncle who had been a doctor in Spain [. . .].
> (*A Simple Habana Melody*, 49–50)

Jeremy Cass notes "a tripartite symbolic transformation in Israel Levis" over the course of the novel.[11] Samuel Freedman finds in it:

> three depictions of Levis: in the prewar years as the gifted musician, grown literally and metaphorically fat on his talents; during the Nazi occupation as the naïf too gradually awaking to the danger around him, and after the war as a shattered specimen.
> (Freedman 2003, 47)

At the height of his fame in Cuba in the 1920s, Levis – with his big body, his elegant clothes and his refined manners – enjoys a successful image as an artist and as an imposing male, enhanced by stories about his gastronomic pantagruelism and his sexual feats. However, below this public image – the way he is seen – *in his own eyes* he endures secret ambiguities and is deeply shy to the point that he never declares his love to the woman he adores and is above all ashamed of his repressed homosexual desires.

---

9 See the various entries on "Moisés Simons" in the bibliography.
10 According to Freedman (2003, 47), this surname is an intentional homage to Primo Levi.
11 "Hijuelos crafts what I view as a tripartite symbolic transformation in Israel Levis, in which we witness the evolution of his physical stature and presence, his sexual energy, and his creative viability." (Cass 2012, 8)

The golden period of his life ends suddenly with the dictatorship of Gerardo Machado (1925–1933). Levis is indifferent to politics, but some misunderstandings bring about violent acts of repression against his family, and he prudently leaves Cuba for what he considers a short-term exile. His professional success in Europe as conductor and composer lead him to postpone his return, and so he finds himself in Paris at the time of the German invasion.

As it happened with Moisés Simons, the Nazis consider him Jewish and forbid his performances: "what a pompous and deluded fool he had been, to assume that he, a Cuban Catholic with a name like Israel Levis, was immune to the terrors descending upon the Jews of Europe" (*A Simple Habana Melody*, 37). Nevertheless, the hardest blow to his sense of self comes when he understands that *in the eyes of the Nazis*, being Cuban – the argument he has considered to be his best defense – is not much better than being Jewish; both are, in their eyes, "inferior races".

In spite of this and to his surprise, it turns out that Germans like Cuban music and are familiar with his famous rumba, to the point that a general serving in the Buchenwald concentration camp takes him along to perform his music there. Once in the camp, this "protection" does not confer any privileges upon him; like any other Jewish internee, he has a number engraved on his forearm and suffers all the same miseries – particularly, considering his previous habits, hunger.

From time to time, the general takes him to play at the officers' canteen. The description of one such "concert" forms the central episode of the novel, the climax of Levis's erasure as a man and as an artist. First, he is introduced not even as a Cuban and certainly not as a Jew, but as "Monsieur Sebastiano of Paris [...] so as not to offend and repulse the Germans with the Jewishness of 'Israel Levis'" (*A Simple Habana Melody*, 304).[12] To disguise his identity as an internee, he is provided with 'civil' clothes – obviously stolen from Jews – which are never his size, always too big or too small. Moreover, there is the obvious contrast between a "normal" concert – the usual elegance of the venue and the people, the silence and respect of the public towards the performer – and the factual context of his playing at the canteen: the noise of people eating and talking, waiters coming and going, the scarce attention paid to music and musician, his miserable appearance in his inadequate clothes. All of these factors contribute to the annihilation of his identity: he is neither a Cuban nor a Jew; he is neither admired nor even listened to; his false name and his ridiculous clothing are metonymies of this annihilation, and the artist is reduced to a non-existent and sad clown. The only positive aspect of the performances is that the cook allows Levis to gather leftovers ... which certainly contributes to the fact that, in the end, he survives the camp.

---

12 "Playing for the first time in his life under another name – 'Monsieur Sebastiano of Paris' – Levis becomes entirely separated from 'Levis' as both signifier and signified." (Socolovsky 2005, 140). Moreover, the fake name becomes ironical when we remember Levis's uncle the bishop, "Monseñor Sebastiano".

Levis's identity and fate are therefore always overdetermined by the gaze of others: during his golden age in Cuba, during his plight in Europe, and also after his return to Cuba, where he lives as a shadow of himself, both physically and morally, and above all emptied of any creative capacity. Even his family and friends find it hard to recognize him; their astonished gaze confirms his shattered self. As in the past, when he found it difficult to cope with his personal ambiguities, now he is unable to overcome his European experience and be a Cuban again: "Israel Levis [. . .] essentially becomes a Jew" (Freedman 2003, 47). Ironically, his mother confirms this probability (which is terrible in her view): "My son, the idea has come to me that perhaps your father was a Jew. And that is why God has been acting so cruelly to us" (*A Simple Habana Melody*, 81). Paradoxically, he will recover his legendary stature only after his death, in the homage paid to him throughout Cuba.

Some critical reactions to Hijuelos's novel considered that the inclusion of the Holocaust was inappropriate. In his study on the novel, Socolovsky summarized some of them:

> In giving us a Catholic Cuban composer and putting him through a concentration camp, Hijuelos seems to be collapsing worlds and confusing the reader's expectations of what a 'Cuban-American' voice should or can produce. Reviewers of the book are uncomfortable with the Holocaust element of the text: the *New York Times* book review, for example, finds that the episode of Levis being mistaken for a Jew "is not used by Mr. Hijuelos to make a larger point about history or persecution, but simply becomes another instance in the composer's story in which he succumbs to his fatalistic tendencies and fails to seize control of his life" (Kakutani 44), while *Publisher's Weekly* feels "a faintly contrived air about Levis's experience of the Holocaust" (Zaleski 46).
> (Socolovsky 2005, 120)

On the other hand, Socolovsky considers that it is precisely the "Holocaust element" that contributes to the *Cuban* relevance of the novel:

> Hijuelos draws upon the Holocaust in order to present the uneasy clash and combination of aesthetics and politics that have for a long time determined, on an extra-textual level, the way in which *Cuban-American writers* have been assessed. Furthermore, his novel is precisely 'Cuban' in that it imagines the island as a provisional space even for its early twentieth century Cuban citizens-artists, and creates Cuba as an ideal only in memory, rather than in actuality [. . .] *even the most vivid and loving descriptions of Havana in the novel are, structurally, post-Holocaust recollections that are contaminated by exile and the horrors of inarticulate experiences* [. . .] Death and the Holocaust mediate the aesthetics with which he speaks about and remembers Cuba and in this way *it comes to define the center of Cuba*.   (Socolovsky 2005, 120, 129; my emphases)

American literary historian Sander Gilman, writing from a Jewish multicultural perspective, arrives at a similar conclusion:

> The novel, a Cuban-American novel of Havana, becomes a novel of the Cuban as Holocaust survivor [. . .]. The Cuban history that marks him, such as the political despotism of the Cuban dictatorship of Gerardo Machado, is paralleled to the rise of the Nazis [. . .]. The elision between the Cuban, seen through the eyes of the Cuban-American writer, and the Jew in the Shoah is as complete [. . .]. The Jew truly does not exist, except in the fantasy of the persecutors. Israel Levis

takes on the mantle of the Jew in this American multicultural novel. His actual difference as a fat man, as a bisexual man, and as creative genius is in the end defined by his difference as a Jew.

(Gilman 2006, 176)

4 *Herejes* (2013) by Leonardo Padura: "The eyes of young E. A."

While Obejas and Hijuelos write from the perspective of diasporic situations and strive to configure a hyphenated belonging through the mediation of the figure of the Jew, Leonardo Padura (Havana, 1955) lives and writes in Cuba.[13] His writing exhibits his involvement in configuring intra-Cuban identity, particularly with regards to his own generation, the Cubans born in the 1950s, who were raised with the principles of the Revolution and felt sincerely loyal to them until they gradually became aware of their limited application in Cuban reality.[14] In *Herejes* [Heretics] (2013), Padura turns to Jewish history as a means of finding an answer to the question of how to be a Cuban in present-day Cuba.

What attracted Padura to Jewish historical experience was mainly the demand for submission to a rigid regime as a condition of belonging to the community, which may turn the exercise of personal freedom into dissidence – heresy – and result in anathema and total exclusion. *Heretics* succeeds in correlating Jewish and Cuban historical experience by means of a complex plot, in which the Jewish sections become a prism that allows for better understanding of contemporary Cuban issues – with heresies included in both.

The following summary does not do justice to the richness of the plot. In the 1930s, the Kaminsky family in Cracow intends to flee from a menacing Europe. Ten-year-old Daniel is sent to Cuba to the care of his paternal uncle Joseph, who is already established in Havana. After some time, father, mother and their little daughter embark

---

13 "And I, in a rational manner, decided to remain in Cuba. I have been in the United States, in France, in Spain. I said: 'No, I stay here because I am a Cuban writer and I want to write about Cuba. I want to make my career here in spite of the difficulties'". / "Y yo, racionalmente, decidí permanecer en Cuba. Estuve en Estados Unidos, en Francia, en España, en Italia. Dije: 'No, yo me quedo aquí porque soy un escritor cubano y quiero escribir sobre Cuba, y quiero hacer mi carrera aquí a pesar de estas dificultades'" (Padura in Granovsky 2013, n.p.; my translation).
14 See, in note 16, Padura's portrait of Conde's (and his own) generation in the novel, and his lecture "La libertad como herejía" (Padura 2013b). However, throughout his work, Padura has been careful to ascribe the failure of the revolutionary project to endemic local evils such as corruption, inefficiency and indifference rather than to the project itself. His latest and monumental novel *Como polvo en el viento* (Like Dust in the Wind) (2020) elaborates on this issue and on the permanent Cuban choice between remaining or leaving the island.

on the infamous *St. Louis*.¹⁵ They trust that if necessary, they will be able to 'buy' an immigration permit with a small painting by Rembrandt, "Head of Christ", which for mysterious reasons came into the possession of the Kaminsky family in the seventeenth century. However, something goes wrong and the three are forced to return to Europe, where their final destiny will be Auschwitz. Uncle Joseph, being deeply religious, manages to cope with the tragedy, but a desperate Daniel reacts by rejecting Judaism and its cruel God, in later years even converting to Christianity.

Twenty years later, Daniel finds the painting at the house of a high government official by pure chance and has no doubts that he is the one who received the bribe from the Kaminsky family but did not provide them with their visas. Daniel is determined to kill him, but somebody else does it before him, and again the painting disappears. Some time afterwards, Daniel leaves for Miami, where he will return to Judaism, more out of interest than out of conviction.

Almost half a century after that, his son Elías Kaminsky, himself a painter, accidentally finds the Rembrandt included in the catalogue of a London auction. Elías travels to Cuba and hires the services of Mario Conde in order to discover the painting's mysterious itinerary. Mario Conde, a hard-boiled detective of the kind familiar from other works of fiction, is the hero of seven previous novels by Padura, in which he functions as the author's partial alter ego. Though disappointed by his personal life and no less by his environment, like many other Cubans he does not rebel and strives to find his own place in the country's everyday reality.¹⁶

Conde succeeds in solving some of the mysteries, but neither he nor Elías will ever know the original history of the painting, which is the reader's privilege alone. The second part of the novel takes place in Amsterdam in the seventeenth century, where a young Jew, Elías Ambrosius de Montalbo, strives to become a painter in spite of the categorical Jewish prohibition of representative art. By means of a trick, Elías succeeds in becoming an apprentice at Rembrandt's studio and is even used by him as a model for a portrait of Christ.¹⁷ When his heresy is uncovered, Elías decides to flee the city before the anathema which will expel him from the Jewish people is pronounced, and the Master gives him his portrait as a farewell present. It is only in the last section of the novel that the discovery of a letter signed "E. A." reveals that Elías arrived in Poland, at the time convulsed by wars and pogroms, that he decided to

---
15 See note 7.
16 "At the age of 54, Conde knew he was a paradigmatic member of what years before he and his friends considered to be the hidden generation, those [. . .] that [. . .] had evolved (involved in fact) to be the most disenchanted or fucked generation inside the new country on its way". / "A sus 54 años cumplidos, Conde se sabía un paradigmático integrante de lo que años atrás él y sus amigos calificaban como la generación escondida, los [. . .] que [. . .] habían evolucionado (involucionado en realidad) para convertirse en la generación más desencantada o jodida dentro del nuevo país que se iba configurando" (Padura: *Herejes* 2013, 24).
17 Rembrandt painted several studies of the "Head of Christ"; as he lived in the Jewish neighborhood, it is very likely that his models were Sephardic youngsters.

join Shabbetai Zvi's messianic movement in Palestine,[18] and that before leaving he gave the painting to a rabbi, who in his turn used it to pay for the services of a doctor Kaminsky, an ancestor of Daniel and his family.

In the third section of the novel, the story turns to a new plot. Conde is hired to elucidate the disappearance and murder of young Judith Torres. His investigation leads him to discover a novel Cuban variety of heresy: the "urban tribes", groups of youngsters from well-to-do families who have chosen to live outside the expectations of their society. They do not work or study, pursue only immediate pleasure and often commit acts of self-harm because they do not believe in the national project and decide to stay out of it.[19] As his friends Yoyi and Candito explain to Conde:[20]

> What happens with all those kids is that they do not want to be as you, Conde [...] They try to be different, but above all, they want to be what they decide to be and not *as they are told to be*, as it happens all the time in this country, *where people are always being ordered what to do*.
> (Padura: *Herejes* 2013, 353, my emphases)[21]

A chance conjunction of characters from both plots connects Judith's murder with the story of Rembrandt's painting, bringing together Jewish and Cuban heresies. Jewish history appears in the novel through three chronotopes that represent different constellations of acceptance/submission versus revolt/heresy. In seventeenth century Amsterdam, the rigidness of the Jewish community turns Elías Ambrosius's choice to become a painter into a heresy (with the added heresy of having served as the model for a portrait of Christ). The decision he makes once in Poland is a paradox between submission and heresy; anxious to return to the Jewish community but feeling himself an alien among Polish Jews, he travels to Palestine to join the Messianic-heretic movement of Shabbetai Zvi.

In liberal Cuba in the middle of the twentieth century, personal choice is possible without committing heresy. Uncle Joseph remains an orthodox Jew even when he marries a Christian *mulata*. Daniel is free to forsake Judaism in protest of the Jewish God who demands complete submission – "[. . .] without God's oppression and tyranny, what else is to be Jewish?" – but fails to save his family (*Herejes*, 65).[22]

---

18 Rabbi Shabbetai Zvi (Turkey, 1626–1676) proclaimed himself as the Messiah and called for the return of Jews to Palestine. Threatened with death by the Sultan, he converted to Islam, forsaking the great mass of his followers. His are considered the greatest heresy and collective treason in Jewish history.
19 On the "urban tribes", see Padura (2013b) and Yulzarí (2016).
20 I did not have access to the English translation of the novel; all quotes are my own translations; the original texts that appear in footnotes are quoted from Padura 2013.
21 "Lo que pasa con todos esos muchachos es que no quieren parecerse a la gente como tú, Conde [...] Tratan de ser distintos, pero, sobre todo, quieren ser como ellos decidieron ser y no como *les dicen que tienen que ser*, como hace rato pasa en este país, *donde siempre se está mandando a la gente*".
22 "[. . .] sin la opresión de ese Dios y sin su tiranía, ¿qué cosa era ser judío?"

At the beginning of the twenty-first century, Daniel's son Elías feels that his comfortable identity as an American non-observant Jew is unsatisfactory and insufficient: "[I am] a Jew of the periphery" (*Herejes*, 96); "sometimes I feel I belong nowhere, or belong to different places, I am like a puzzle that always can be taken apart" (*Herejes*, 112).[23]

Elías Ambrosius's Amsterdam and Conde's Cuba are both repressive environments: "As it has always been and will always be in human history, somebody decides what freedom is and how much of it is due to the individuals that some power represses or takes care of. Also in countries of freedom" (*Herejes*, 322).[24] There is only one way out of such oppressions: heresy. In a lecture, Padura indicated that his novel intends to represent:

> [. . .] the dose of heresy that, in different societies, historical moments and individual lives conceals the aim of exercising freely individual choices, that is, the natural wish to exert the freedom that [. . .] only human beings can conceive and search for in a conscious way.[25]

In Padura's own words, his aim was "to raise" the specific Cuban experience to "the level of the permanent and the global", linking Elías, a seventeenth century Sephardic Jew who pursues freedom in the Old World, with Daniel, a twentieth century Ashkenazic Jew who finds freedom in a remote island in the Caribbean.[26]

Heresies in the novel – whether religious or ideological, Jewish or Cuban – are motivated sometimes by an outside cause, sometimes by a personal goal. Those that emerge only as an aftereffect appear less valuable, as when Daniel Kaminsky reacts to his family's tragedy with a straightforward revolt (*Herejes*, 128).[27] Judy Torres and her

---

23 "[Soy] un judío de la periferia"; "a veces siento que no pertenezco a ningún sitio, o pertenezco a varios, soy como un rompecabezas que siempre se puede desarmar."
24 "Como siempre habría sido y sería en la historia humana, alguien decidía qué era la libertad y cuánto de ella les correspondía a los individuos a los que ese poder reprimía o cuidaba. Incluso en tierras de libertad."
25 "[. . .] la dosis de herejía que, en distintas sociedades, momentos históricos y vidas individuales podía revestir la pretensión de poner en práctica un libre ejercicio del albedrío individual, o sea, el natural deseo de ejercitar la libertad que [. . .] solo los seres humanos tenemos la posibilidad y la capacidad de buscar conscientemente" (Padura 2013b, 5).
26 " Si quería asomarme por encima de lo coyuntural y contingente, de lo doméstico y singular, debía levantar la mirada hacia *un horizonte más abierto* que la específica encrucijada cubana, y entregarle a mi pretensión una capacidad de funcionar en lo permanente y global [. . .]" (Padura 2013b, 6, my emphasis). "[Traté] de penetrar [. . .] en la personalidad de un judío, o de dos judíos: el sefardí que, sintiéndose un hombre libre para tomar sus decisiones, le serviría de modelo a Rembrandt para sus [. . .] 'cabezas de Cristo' y el del asquenazí que, poco antes del inicio de la Segunda Guerra Mundial, siendo todavía un niño, llega a Cuba y encuentra en la para él remota isla del Caribe, el mundo de libertad que ningún judío europeo de esos tiempos podía imaginar [. . .]" (Padura 2013b, 13).
27 "[. . .] in that moment he was only able to feel in the depths of his soul the mechanisms of an obscure primitive origin, those of the unredeemed Jew revolting against submission, the nomad of the desert". / "[. . .] en aquel momento solo era capaz de sentir cómo en su alma profunda se movían los mecanismos de un tapiado origen primitivo, los del judío irredento que se rebelaba ante la sumisión, el nómada del desierto [. . .]."

"generation of heretics with a cause" (*Herejes*, 442)[28] react in a merely negative and passive way that is devoid of any project – a useless heresy. On the other hand, Elías Ambrosius de Montalbo's heresies are goal-oriented and guided by his free choices: he first intends to establish himself as an artist and then strives to maintain his sense of belonging to the Jewish people (*Herejes*, 143).[29]

Nevertheless, the model heretic in the novel is, to the reader's surprise, Uncle Joseph, the deeply orthodox Jew: only towards the middle of the story do we learn that it was he who murdered the man who betrayed the Kaminsky family. More than vengeance – which of course was also a motive – his intention was to prevent Daniel from becoming a murderer, even at the price of his own self-condemnation for breaking a basic commandment:

> He did it so [Daniel] [...] would not do it [...] He ran the risk of being shot [...] but above all he killed him to save Daniel [...] he knew very well [...] that he was losing his God's forgiveness [...] that there was no salvation for his soul [...] but he died satisfied for having fulfilled the word he gave his brother one day [...] to take care of his son [...] as if he were his own son. (*Herejes*, 187)[30]

Through the stories of the Jewish heretics Elías Ambrosius and Joseph Kaminsky, Conde learns a new way of considering Cubanity, including the almost apocalyptic lives of the urban tribes. At the end of the novel, after reading the fragment of E.A.'s letter, Conde is capable of a different vision, pessimistic but stronger, while looking out on Havana from the roof of his house:

> *Behind the eyes of Mario Conde, in his mind, were the open eyes of young Jewish E.A.*, apprentice to a painter, dead three and a half centuries ago, probably following, as so many men in so many places and throughout the centuries, the trail of other self-acclaimed messiahs and saviors, capable of promising everything, only to finally reveal himself as a liar, sick with the thirst of power, and with an overwhelming passion to dominate other people and their minds. That story was too familiar and close for Conde. And he thought that maybe Judith Torres, in her search for liberty, has been closer than many to a disheartening truth: there is nothing to believe in, no messiah to follow. The only thing is to join the tribe you have freely chosen. Because if it were possible that even God has died, if he did exist at all, and if it happened that so many messiahs turn into manipulators in the end, the only thing left to you, the only thing that really belongs to you, is *your freedom of choice*. To send a picture or donate it to a museum. To belong or to stop belonging. To believe or not to believe. Even to live or to die. (*Herejes*, 513, my emphases)[31]

---

[28] "generación de herejes con causa".
[29] Rembrandt is also depicted in the novel as a heretic in the realm of art, "endowed with the spirit of perennial nonconformism, indefatigable pursuer of human and artistic freedom" / "premiado con el espíritu de la inconformidad perenne, perseguidor incansable de la libertad humana y artística."
[30] "Lo hizo para que [Daniel] [...] no lo hiciera [...] Corrió el riesgo de que lo fusilaran [...] pero sobre todo lo mató para salvar a Daniel [...] sabía muy bien [...] que estaba perdiendo el perdón de su Dios [...] que su alma no tenía salvación [...] pero murió satisfecho de haber cumplido con la palabra que un día le había dado a su hermano [...] cuidar de su hijo [...] como si fuera su propio hijo."
[31] "*Detrás de los ojos de Mario Conde*, en su mente, estaban abiertos *los ojos del joven judío E. A.*, aprendiz de pintor, muerto hacía tres siglos y medio, posiblemente siguiendo, como tantos hombres

5 Conclusions

The authors of these three novels are part of a fascinating body of Latin American Jewish and non-Jewish writers who have found in the "wandering signifier" a productive means to elaborate their take on a post-essentialist belonging. A number of them live in countries that are outside Latin America, and their multiple belongings are the explicit challenge that has attracted them to the complex models of Jewish identities throughout history. In addition, the particular history of Cuba in contemporary times – the split between homeland and diaspora together with their mutual attraction and tension – is undoubtedly a privileged background for such a literary elaboration.

Involuntarily turned into an exile by her parents' decision, Achy Obejas's protagonist Alejandra searches for a better understanding and a way of resolving her multiple belongings. Her father's experiences as a secret Jew – historical exile, fear of difference, and nevertheless the maintenance of a secret identity – lead her to understand the dangers of negation and concealment, but above all the possibility of positively embracing the components of her double self.

Exile enters the life of Oscar Hijuelos's protagonist Israel Levis as a temporary solution to an unexpected plight, and in his first years in Europe, he even enjoys his otherness as a successful Cuban artist. Nazism reveals to him – as it did to so many well-established European Jews – the dangers of being *other*. However, not only is he wrongly considered Jewish and treated as such; he discovers that any difference, including being Cuban, is assimilated to a similar devaluation and potential doom. Back in Cuba, his shattered self is not able to recover, as was the case with many Holocaust survivors, and his recovered Cubanity remains forever linked to the indelible number carved on his arm.[32]

Leonardo Padura's Mario Conde struggles with both his disappointment in the principles he once believed in and his reluctance to be a "heretic" of the Cuban revolutionary project. The story of Elías Ambrosius teaches him that free choice and heresy are the duty of the self-responsible individual and that, whatever these are in

---

en tantos sitios y a lo largo de los siglos, la estela de otro autoproclamado mesías y salvador, capaz de prometerlo todo para terminar revelándose como un farsante enfermo con la sed de poder, con la avasallante pasión del dominio de otros hombres y sus mentes. *Aquella historia a Conde le resultaba demasiado familiar y cercana.* Y pensó que tal vez, en sus búsquedas libertarias, en algún momento Judy Torres había estado más próxima que mucha gente a una desoladora verdad: ya no hay nada en que creer, ni mesías que seguir. Sólo vale la pena militar en la tribu que tú has elegido libremente. Porque si cabe la posibilidad de que, de haber existido, incluso Dios haya muerto, y la certeza de que *tantos mesías hayan terminado convirtiéndose en manipuladores*, lo único que te queda, lo único que en realidad te pertenece, es tu libertad de elección. Para vender un cuadro o donarlo a un museo. Para pertenecer o dejar de pertenecer. Para creer o no creer. Incluso, para vivir o para morirte."

32 Which is, in fact, an artistic license, as only Auschwitz prisoners had numbers carved on their forearms – but it serves a clear symbolic purpose in the novel.

the eyes of the powers that be, the free individual can continue feeling him/herself to be part of his or her community.

Seeing and being seen are decisive in all three novels: Alejandra San José has to learn to see herself as a unified, palimpsestic self in which one layer is Jewish. Israel Levis is transformed into a Jew by a hostile and destructive gaze. Mario Conde ends up seeing himself as a would-be heretic Jew. The three novels considered in this chapter apply the "wandering signifier" of the 'figurative Jew' to the construction of complex Cuban belongings, each of them choosing different components of Jewishness and different fictional dynamics.

Bibliography

Works Cited

Behar, Ruth. *Bridges to Cuba – Puentes a Cuba*. Ann Arbor: University of Michigan Press, 1995a.
Behar, Ruth. "Juban América." *Poetics Today* 16.1 (1995b): 151–170.
Behar, Ruth. *An Island Called Home: Returning to Jewish Cuba*. New Brunswick: Rutgers University Press, 2007.
Bejarano, Margalit. "The Jewish Community of Cuba between Continuity and Extinction." *Jewish Political Studies Review*. 3.1 & 2 (1991): 114–140.
Bejarano, Margalit. *The Jewish Community of Cuba: Memory and History*. Jerusalem: Magnes Press, 2014.
Cass, Jeremy L. "Imagining Cuba in Hijuelos's *A Simple Habana Melody*." *Label Me Latina/o* 2.1 (2012): 1–17.
Freedman, Samuel G. "Oscar Hijuelos' Yiddishe Neshama." *Tablet* (News). 15 October 2013.
Freedman, Samuel G. "With Truth on His Side." *The Jerusalem Report*. 10 March 2003. 46–47.
Gilman, Sander L. *Multiculturalism and the Jews*. New York: Routledge, 2006.
Goldberg, Florinda F. "Aurora Levins Morales: 'A Child of Many Diasporas'." *Judaica Latinoamericana IX*. Ed. AMILAT. Jerusalem: Magnes, 2021.
Goldman, Dara E. "Next Year in the Diaspora: The Uneasy Articulation of Transcultural Positionality in Achy Obejas's *Days of Awe*". *Arizona Journal of Hispanic Cultural Studies*. Vol. 8 (2004): 59–74.
Graff Zivin, Erin. *The Wandering Signifier. Rhetoric of Jewishness in the Latin American Imaginary*. Durham: Duke University Press, 2008.
Granovsky, Martín. "El hombre que no amaba a los fanáticos" (The man who did not like fanatics). Interview with Leonardo Padura. *Página12*. 12 May 2013.
Guerra, Mirna. "In Memoriam: Moisés Simons." *Worldwide Cuban Music*. 27 June 2016.
Hijuelos, Oscar. *A Simple Habana Melody*. New York: Harper Collins, 2002.
Kakutani, Michicko. "Book of the Times: Examining a Life Defined by Loves and Pleasures Lost." *New York Times*. 31 May 2002. Section E, Column 1, 44.
Martí, José. *Obras Completas*. La Habana: Editorial Nacional de Cuba, 1963–1973.
"Moisés Simons". *EnCaribe*. http://www.encaribe.org/es/article/moises-simons/423 (2 February 2019).
"Moisés Simons", *EcuRed*. https://www.ecured.cu/Mois%C3%A9s_Simons. (2 February, 2019).
Obejas, Achy. "Writing and Responsibility." *Discourse: Journal for Theoretical Studies in Media and Culture* 21.3 (1999): 42–48.
Obejas, Achy. *Days of Awe*. New York: Ballantine, 2001.

Padura, Leonardo. *Herejes*. Barcelona: Tusquets, 2013a; Barcelona: Tusquets, col. Maxi, 2014.
Padura, Leonardo: "La libertad como herejía (para qué se escribe una novela)." *La libertad como herejía. Apostillas a "Herejes"*. Ed. Leonardo Padura. Barcelona: Tusquets, 2013b.
Padura, Leonardo. *Heretics*. New York: Farrar, Straus & Giroux, 2017.
Pérez Firmat, Gustavo. *Life on the Hyphen. The Cuban-American Way*. Austin: University of Texas Press, 1996.
Rumbaut, Rubén. "The Agony of Exile: A Study of the Migration and Adaptation of Indochinese Refugee Adults and Children." *Refugee Children: Theory, Research, and Services*. Eds. Frederick L. Ahearn, Jr. and Jean L. Athey. Baltimore: Johns Hopkins University Press, 1991. 53–91.
Sheppard-Brick, Laura. "*Days of Awe* by Achy Obejas – Interview with Achy Obejas." *The Jewish Reader*, July 2002. http://www.yiddishbookcenter.org/node/327. (2 February 2019).
Socolovsky, Maya. "Deconstructing a Secret History: Trace, Translation, and Crypto-Judaism in Achy Obejas's *Days of Awe*". *Contemporary Literature* 44.2 (2004): 225–249.
Socolovsky, Maya. "From Rumba to Funeral March: Remembering Cuba in Oscar Hijuelos's *A Simple Habana Melody (From When the World Was Good)*". *South Atlantic Review*. 70.1 (2005): 117–147.
Wolfenzon, Carolina. "*Days of Awe* and the Jewish Experience of a Cuban Exile: The Case of Achy Obejas." *Hispanic Caribbean Literature of Migration: Narratives of Displacement*. Ed. Vanessa Pérez Rosario. New York: Palgrave Macmillan, 2010. 105–118.
Yulzarí, Emilia: "Ser hereje en una realidad que está hereje. Aproximaciones a *Herejes*, de Leonardo Padura." *Otro Lunes*. July 2016.
Zaleski, Jeff. "A Simple Habana Melody." *Publisher's Weekly*. 20 May 2002. 249:20. 46.

Further Reading

Bettinger-López, Caroline. "'Hebrew with a Cuban Accent': Jewbans in the Diaspora." *Cuba: Idea of a Nation Displaced*, Ed. Andrea O'Reilly Herrera. Albany, NY: State University of New York Press, 2007. 107–122.
Corrales Capestany, Maritza. "De libertades y exilios. José Martí y los hebreos cubanos." *Judaica Latinoamericana VI*. Ed. AMILAT. Jerusalem: Magnes, 2009. 193–214.
Davis, Rocío G. "Vulnerable Observation in An Island Called Home: Ruth Behar's Story of the Jews of Cuba." *Prooftexts: A Journal of Jewish Literary History* 31.3 (2011): 263–286.
Perelmuter, Rosa. "From Havana to the Hub: Cuban-Jewish Responses to Exile." *Yiddish/Modern Jewish Studies* 12.4 (2001): 108–114.
Sefamí, Jacobo. "The Family, the World: The Poetry of José Kozer." *Tradition and Innovation: Reflections on Latin American Jewish Writing*, Ed. DiAntonio, Robert and Nora Glickman, Albany, NY: State University of New York Press, 1993. 201–210.

Index

'Arūḍ modificado 67
A Chave da Casa 460, 616
A Columna 391
A donde tú vayas, iré 528
A Guerra no Bom Fim 468
A Hora da Estrela 462
A Maçã no Escuro 461
A memória da Destruição na escrita judaico-brasileira depois de 1985: Por uma literatura pós-Holocausto emergente no Brasil 619
A Paixão Segundo G. H. 461
A prece 465
A Simple Habana Melody 627, 632–635
A Tomb for Boris Davidovich 440
A Vida Secreta dos Relógios e Outras Histórias 453
ABC Islands 178, 268, 270, 300–301, 303–306, 308, 309, 310–312, 368–369
Abd al-Raḥmān III, 45, 59
Abenatar Melo, David 254, 273
Aboab of Venice, Imanuel 170, 264
Abraham (Patriarch) 467, 529, 540, 558, 609
Abraham, Ben 452
Abrahamic 433, 435, 609
Abraham Spiegel, un luchador 620
Abravanel, Jonas 277
Abū Bakr Yaḥyà b. Aḥmad ibn Baqī al-Qurṭubī/al-Ṭulayṭulī, see Ibn Baqī
Abulafia, Todros 43
Academias 161, 272, 276
Academias de las musas 272
Acapulco 175
Adafina 90
Adriatic 168
Afia, Aron 256
Africa(n) 171, 174, 299, 303–304, 308, 359, 361, 363, 548, 570, 629
Aggadah 324, 328
Agosín, Marjorie 589, 618
Agrarian Fraternity 381
Agraz, Juan 100, 110
Água viva 461
Agudat Israel 389
Aguilar, Grace 439
Aguinis, Marcos 12, 554, 572
Aitta Tettauen 419

Aizenberg, Edna 549–550, 582
Aizim, Lúcia 450
Ajzenberg, Bernardo 450
Al-Andalus 4–5, 18–19, 21, 39–45, 55–61, 67, 70–71, 75–76, 612, 187
Al-Andalus (journal) 63–64
Al-Hidāya ilā farāʾiḍ al-qulūb 49
Al-Muʿtamid of Seville 59, 76
Alameda Central 526
Alami, Salomón 31
Alarcón, García Álvarez de 95
Alarcón, Pedro Antonio de 419
Alberro, Solange 175, 176, 361, 362, 366, 367
Albo, R. Yosef 31
Alcalá, Ángel 35, 83, 87, 91, 97, 108, 114, 115, 124, 127, 191
Alcalá de Henares 32, 92, 161
Alcobaça 88
Aleichem, Sholem 562, 620
Alemán, Mateo 6, 185, 194–196, 203–209, 212, 610
Aleppo 321, 385, 400, 476, 526, 528, 532, 620
Alessandri, Arturo 396
Alfonso II of Aragon 20
Alfonso V of Aragon (Alfonso the Magnanimous) 22, 102, 104, 107
Afonso V of Avís 118
Alfonso VI of Castile 21
Alfonso VII of Castile 21
Alfonso X of Castile (Alfonso el Sabio) 21, 55, 60, 74, 130, 159
Alfonso XI of Castile 21, 27, 85–86, 89
Alfonso el Inocente 116
Algarrobos 560, 588
Alhambra Edict of 1492 433, 436
Aliyah 387, 389, 392–393, 399, 410, 531
Aljamas 22, 25–27, 30–31, 103
Aljamiado 159
Aljubarrota 88, 130
Allaigre, Claude 197, 198, 201
Allen, Woody 619
Allende, Isabel 479, 498
Allende, Salvador 396–397
Alliance israélite universelle ("the Alliance") 331, 332, 336, 337, 344, 407
Alma Pastora das Coisas 450

Almeida Bernal, Isaac 269, 277
Almohads 21, 60
Almoravids 21, 60
Alonso, Dámaso 62
Alonso, Hernando 175, 523
Altares, Moses 257, 263
Alter ego 129, 421, 619, 637
Altona 171–172
Álvarez de Ayllón, Per 125
Álvarez de León, Garci 93
Álvarez de Toledo, García (Duke of Alba) 116
Álvarez de Villasandino, Alfonso 89, 96–97
Álvarez Gato, Juan 101, 112–115, 120,124
Amador de los Ríos, José 94, 419
Amâncio, Moacir Aparecido 451–452
Ambato 402
American Dream 442, 503
American Jewish Committee (AJC) 582
American War of Independence 311
Americas 157, 170, 177, 298, 313, 355, 357, 361–362, 364, 367, 435, 438, 583, 588, 612
AMIA attack of July 1994 384, 604, 617–618
AMIA (Asociación Mutual Israelita Argentina) 384, 388, 398, 617
AMILAT (Asociación israelí de investigadores del judaísmo latinoamericano) 594, 598
Amsterdam 6, 8, 161, 166, 171–174, 178, 251, 254, 256–262, 264–265, 268–270, 272, 274–288, 290, 297–298, 300, 303–310, 313, 320, 334, 356, 361, 368, 437, 637–638, 639
Anacephaleosis 111
Anarchist 386, 560, 568
Anatolia 320, 322, 330–333, 339, 342, 344
Ancona 168
Andalusia 27, 35, 39–51, 74, 76, 123, 194, 202, 251, 274
Anilevich, Mordejai 399
annus mirabilis 436
Ansina 528, 535, 537–538
Anti-authoritarianism 478, 494
Anti-Judaism/Anti-Jewish 27, 83–85, 94, 95, 97, 100, 106–107, 112, 117, 127, 129, 161, 165, 185, 266, 378, 380, 383, 387–388, 419, 458, 477, 605, 616
– Anti-Semitism, see anti-Judaism
Antilles 251
Antiterapias 454, 619

Antwerp 165–166, 168–169, 171, 173, 258, 275, 277, 495
Anu(s)sim 84, 158, 320, 322, 523
Apartamiento 118
Aphrodite 233–235
Arab(ic) 5,10, 18–19, 23, 39, 44, 46, 49, 55–78, 159, 187, 202, 221, 236–247, 307, 333, 343, 395, 419,427, 433, 435–436, 467, 481, 510, 512–513, 531–532, 543, 583, 603, 611, 621, 633
Arab-Argentinian 583
Aragon 20, 22–24, 29, 31, 35, 75, 83, 88, 99, 102–104, 119–121, 128, 162, 436
Aramaic 40, 157
Arbell, Mordechai 305–306
Archivo de Protocolos Notariales of Saragossa 127
Argentina 10, 354, 375–377, 379, 380–393, 395, 398, 401, 403, 404, 408, 411, 423, 424, 447, 481, 482, 484, 487, 491, 506, 527, 548–554, 556–558, 560, 562, 564, 565, 567–569, 581–586, 588–590, 613, 615, 616–618
Argentina, país de advenimiento 550
Argentine Federation of Maccabean Community Centers (Federación Argentina de Centros Comunitarios Macabeos, FACCMA) 390
Argentine Jews or Jewish Argentines? Essays on Ethnicity, Identity, and Diaspora 581
Argentine Patriotic League 383
Argentinian Jews in the Age of Revolt. Between the New World and the Third World 584
Arias Dávila, Diego 112, 120
Arias Dávila, Pedro 112, 114, 120
Aristophanes 235
Aristotle 225–229, 238, 240
Arlt, Roberto 552
Armenian 321, 327
Armony, Adriana 616
Arte mayor 120
Aruba 308
Asentistas 177
Ashkenazi(m/c) 10–11, 172, 262, 301, 306, 335, 341, 384–385, 387–388, 395–398, 400, 403–404, 406–407, 418–419, 424, 434, 442–443, 475–493, 496–514, 526–528, 533, 543, 549, 563, 570, 584, 590–591, 593, 608, 612, 621, 639
Asire Hatikvah 285

Asmar, Alfredo 585
Assa, Abraham 324, 326, 327
Asse, Jenny 528, 543
Assimilation/ assimilated 6, 12, 95, 159,
    162–163, 179, 306, 308, 312–314, 321,
    369, 394–395, 412, 425, 449, 454, 456,
    465, 477, 533, 547, 552, 562–563, 592,
    604–605, 616–617, 629, 641
Association of Israelite Societies of Peru
    (Asociación de Sociedades Israelitas de
    Perú) 405
Asturias 107–108
Aterritorality 434–439
Atheism 608
Athias, Yomtob/Atias, Yom Tov 168, 255–256
Atlantic 161, 166, 169, 301, 307, 376, 378, 464,
    596
Attias, David 329, 330
Aub, Max 527
Auerbach, Erich 4, 233, 239
Auschwitz 458, 605, 611, 615, 637, 641
Austria 333, 398, 408, 436, 456
Authoritarianism 112, 549, 563
autobiographical 272, 274, 427, 434, 434–435,
    438, 475–476, 486–487, 489, 494,
    496–498, 500–501, 504, 514, 523, 535,
    554, 557, 562, 582, 589, 590, 603, 616,
    618, 621–622
(Auto)biography 175, 208, 260, 340, 343,
    434, 439–440, 442, 458, 472, 489,
    494, 507–508, 511, 525, 528, 530, 550,
    612–613
Auto-da-fé/Auto de fe/autodafé 175, 190,
    269, 277, 284, 285, 367, 368, 438, 440,
    525, 526
Auto de la Pasión 121
Autoridad Nasional del Ladino i su Kultura 613
Aviso para Cuerdos 122
Avni, Haim 377
Ayotzinapa 501
Ayuso, Arbós 82
Azancot, Leopoldo 418

B'nai B'rith 403–404, 410–411
Ba'alei ha-batim 323, 324
Baena, Juan Alfonso de 90–91, 94, 97–100
Baer, Yitzhak 63
Bagdad 19, 56
Baḥya ibn Paqūda of Saragossa 49–50, 266

Bakhtin, Mikhail 244, 467, 494
Balaam 42
Balak 42
Balfour Declaration 387, 392, 395
Balkans 157, 168, 252, 320, 322, 330–333, 336,
    339, 342, 344, 376, 379, 419, 437
Baptism 27–29, 33, 160, 215, 222
Baqqasha 50
Barba, Juan 121
Barbados 178, 306, 308–309
Barbetta, María 506
Barcelona 19–20, 23–24, 27, 65, 377, 565
Barechu 92
Barnatán, Marcos Ricardo 418, 572
Baroque 173, 186, 260, 268, 270, 271, 274, 275,
    280, 282, 286, 289, 290
Barranquilla 312, 406, 616
Barrientos, Lope de 32, 123
Barrios, Miguel de (Daniel Levi) 173, 178, 251,
    254, 258, 261, 265, 267, 270, 274–276,
    279, 284–286, 290, 434, 439
Barros Basto, Arthur Carlos de 378
Bartolomé Pons, Esther 420
Basque (Country, language) 20, 166–167, 187
Batavian Republic 311
– Battle of Aljubarrota, see Aljubarrota
    Battle of Montiel, see Montiel
Bautista Pérez, Manuel 177
Bayonne 8, 166–167, 251, 257, 297
Beatriz of Portugal 83
Behar, Ruth 589, 613, 627
Beinart, Haim 17, 23–26, 45, 84, 92, 93, 95–97,
    100, 105, 111, 114, 116, 118, 122, 123, 127,
    129, 131, 160, 355, 356
Beira 161
Belgium 251, 394, 495
Belle du Seignior 439
Belles-lettres 319, 320, 328, 330, 333,
    36–344
Belmonte 379
Belmonte, Manuel de 282
Belmonte, Moses 277
Belonging 2, 4, 8, 10–13, 163–164, 199,
    201–202, 212, 222, 224, 242, 251, 297,
    313, 362–364, 365, 368, 402, 418, 425,
    427–429, 447, 450, 453, 455, 462–463,
    477, 497, 499, 508, 526, 530, 551, 555, 560,
    567, 585, 588, 595, 605, 607, 618, 628,
    633, 636, 640, 641–642

Bendahan Cohen, Esther 10, 417–418, 426–429
Benjamin, Walter 569, 610
Benveniste, Immanuel 258
Beracha Ve-Shalom 310
Bergstein, Mauricio 570
Berlin 63, 333, 453, 487, 610, 618
Berliner, Itzjok 483, 526
Berman, Sabina 11, 475, 485–489, 497–499, 501–504, 513, 525–526
Bernáldez, André 28, 125
Berniker, Pinkhes 590
– *Berurim*, see *neemanim*
Bet din 26
Bet Israel 171
Bible/biblical 7–9, 18, 21, 33–34, 39–48, 51, 55, 63, 68–69, 72, 75–76, 78, 91, 122, 165, 176, 222, 227, 237, 245, 251, 253–257, 259, 261–263, 266–268, 272–274, 280–281, 286–287, 289–290, 301, 307, 322–326, 344, 433, 435, 437–439, 451, 453, 462, 467–468, 494, 529, 566, 589, 614, 622
– *Biblia en lengua española traduzida palabra por palabra de la verdad hebraica por muy excelentes letrados*, see Ferrara Bible
Bibliowicz, Ariel 611
Bidache 166
Bienveniste, Abraham 91
Bildungsroman 453, 455
Bikini Atoll 490, 492
Bilingual(ism) 58, 76, 161, 164, 252, 256
Birmajer, Marcelo 605
Birobidjan 392
Black English 588
Blaisten, Isidoro 12, 561
Blanche of Navarre 103
Blank, Paulo 453
Blasphemy 33, 41, 96, 126, 282, 622
Blejer, David 585
Bobe maintze 505
Bodian, Miriam 307
Bodrum 342
Boer, Harm den 310
Bogotá 354, 406–407, 611
Bokser Liwerant, Judit 401, 402, 478, 479, 483, 528, 593–595, 598, 604
Bolivia 354, 380, 402, 403
Bolívar, Simón 303, 369
Bolshevik 383, 406, 554
Bom Retiro 453, 459

Bom Retiro: o Bairro da Infância 459
Bonaire 308
Book of Beliefs 31
Book of Daniel 343
Book of Principles (Séfer ha-Iccarim) 31
– *Book of Splendor (Sefer haZohar)*
Book of Taḥkemoni 43
Boom latinoamericano 479–480, 497, 499, 604, 616
Bordeaux 166–167, 174, 251, 257
Borges, Jorge Luis 420–421, 428, 440, 454, 551, 552–553, 555, 561, 569, 582
Bormann, Martin 619
Borovaya, Olga 322, 330, 335, 337–339
Bortnik, Aída 12, 547, 556
Bosque quemado 619
Boullosa, Carmen 479, 497
Bourdieu, Pierre 199
Bourgeoisie 119, 163, 302, 331, 469
Bozales 299
Braganza 222, 378
Brailovsky, Antonio 610
Brandão, Ambrósio Fernandes 447–448
Brann, Ross 41
Brasilien, Land der Zukunft 617
Brazil(ian) 3, 10–11, 164, 174, 176–178, 298, 300, 302–303, 305, 375–376, 379–382, 391–395, 401, 408, 411, 447–472, 477, 481–482, 489, 491, 530, 557, 586, 589–591, 596–597, 608–609, 612, 615–616, 619
Brazilian Association A Hebraica (Associaçao Brasileira A Hebraica) 394
Brazilian Committee of Aid to the Victims of the War 391
Brazilian Communist Party (PCB) 392
Brazilian Society in support of Judaic Colonization in the Soviet Union (Sociedade Brasileira Pro-Colonizacao Judaica nao Union Sovietica, BRAZCOR) 392
Bridgetown 308
British 8, 266, 298–299, 301–304, 307, 311–312, 392
British Library 127
Brody, Haim 63
Brodsky, Moisés 619
Brodsky, Roberto 619
Brooklyn 490, 492
Brussels 166, 275, 281, 284
Brut 288

Buber, Martin 610
Bubonic plague 22
Buchenwald 634
Buenos Aires 12, 382–391, 394, 397, 417–418, 421, 423–424, 464, 547–561, 565–568, 584–593, 604, 615, 617, 620
Bulgaria 12, 342, 344, 440, 487, 523, 534, 535, 614
Bundist/bundism 380, 386, 389, 392, 398, 411
Burgos 34, 110, 123–124
Burgos, Cantera 81
Burgos, Diego de 120, 124
Burial Society (Sociedad de Entierros) 384–385, 388
Bursa 323
Buzali Daniel, Alberto 528

Caballos por el fondo de los ojos 560
Cabbala 611
Cabra 59, 76
Cabra, Maestre Pedro de la 127
Cabral, Pedro Álvares de 176
Cabrera Infante, Guillermo 561
Cáceres, Francisco de 256
Cahal 23, 25
Calderón de la Barca 281, 285
Caleoni, Gioanne 257
Cali 406
Caliph 'Abd al-Rahman III 45, 59
Calles, Plutarco Elías 506
Caloña 21
Calvino, Italo 440, 615
Cambio de piel 490
Cambodia 611
Cambridge 238
Canada 384, 405, 481, 495
Canary Islands 96, 437
Cáncer, Gerónimo 279
Cancioneiro 5, 81–82, 85, 89, 129, 131
Cancioneiro da Ajuda 89
Cancioneiro geral 5, 81, 89, 128–131
Cancionero (Songbook) 5, 81–85, 88–92, 97–98, 101–102, 105–106, 109, 113–122, 124, 126, 127, 130–131, 241
Cancionero de Baena 81, 89–100, 104, 131
Cancionero de Egerton 119, 127
Cancionero de Estúñiga 102–103, 105, 109
Cancionero de Gallardo 119
Cancionero de Herberay 103

Cancionero de Juan Fernández de Híjar 119
Cancionero de Martínez de Burgos 110
Cancionero de obras de burla 122, 125–126
Cancionero de Oñate-Castañeda 120
Cancionero de Otte Brahe 110
Cancionero de Palacio 81, 90, 98–101, 103, 105, 121, 124, 131
Cancionero de Pedro Manuel de Urrea 121
Cancionero de Pero Marcuello 121
Cancionero de Ramón de Llavia 121
Cancionero de Rennert 125
Cancionero de Roma 109
Cancionero de Salvá 103
Cancionero de San Román 104–105
Cancionero de Venecia 109
Cancionero de Vindel 107
Cancionero del Conde de Haro 109–110
Cancionero general 5, 81, 122, 124–127, 131
Cancionero llamado guirlanda esmaltada de galanes 125
Cancioneros enriqueños 104, 110, 131
Canetti, Elias 10, 433, 434, 440, 443
Cañizares, Ginés de 124
Cánovas, Rodrigo 486, 490, 603, 611, 619
Cansinos Assens, Rafael 10, 417–418, 420–423, 427–429, 551
Cantigas de escárnio e maldizer 91, 129
Capriles Goldish, Josette 312–313
Caput Castellae 110
Cape Verde Islands 175
Cárcel de amor 120
Cardinal Cisnero 124
Cardoso, Isaac (Fernando) 266
Caribbean 8–9, 176, 178, 297–300, 303–313, 369, 375–376, 437, 550, 590, 629, 639
Carmona 117
Caro Baroja, Julio 159, 355
Caro, Yosef 257
Carolingian(s) 119
Carpentier, Alejo 479
Carreiras Cortadas 450
Carrillo, Alonso (Archbishop of Toledo) 116–117
Carillo Zeiter, Katja 613
Carta-privilegio que Juan II dio a un fijodalgo 105
Cartagena, Alonso de 34, 109, 111
Cartagena de Indias 175, 177, 354, 360, 363, 365
Cartagena, Pedro de 124
Carvajal, Juan de 127

Carvajal, Leonor de 525
Carvajal, Luis de 175, 494, 523, 590, 596
Carvajal, Luis de, the Younger (Joseph Lumbroso) 175, 434, 438–439, 525, 543
Carvajal, Mariana de 526
Casa da Índia 165
Casa Universal de los Sefardís 419
Castelar, Emilio 419
Castes 160, 299–302, 313, 359
Castiglione, Baldassare 224, 225
Castile/Castilian 4–5, 17, 20–36, 55, 60, 74, 76–78, 81, 83, 84–104, 109–111, 114–122, 125, 128, 130–131, 157, 159, 161–162, 173, 272, 290, 323, 334, 359–360, 419, 436, 529
Castilian Civil War 21–22, 35, 83, 87–88, 106, 118
Castilian Jews 5, 17, 21, 26, 27, 29, 35, 81, 84, 86–88, 93–96, 98–102, 111, 115–116, 120, 122, 128, 130–131, 173
Castilian poetry 81, 83, 85, 87–88, 90, 93, 97–103, 114, 116, 118, 119–120, 131, 272, 290
Castillo, Diego del 110
Castillo, Enríquez del 112
Castro, Alan 590
Castro, Américo 81, 119, 160, 188, 437, 443, 529
Castro, Estevão de 170
Castro, Fidel 498, 629
Castillo, Hernando del 81, 124–126, 129
Castillo, Pedro del 102
Castro, Rodrigo de 171
Castro Sarmento, Jacob de 258
Castro Tartas, David de 258, 269
Cass, Jeremy 633
Casullo, Nicolás 559
Catalan 58, 60–61, 102, 119, 186, 633
Catalonia 19–20, 22–23, 35
Catherine of Lancaster 29–30
Catholic Monarchs (Reyes Católicos) 5, 28, 35, 81, 11, 117–124, 128, 131, 159, 222, 436
Catholic/Catholicism 5, 8, 10, 28, 35, 84, 87, 95, 98, 111, 117–125, 128, 131, 158–166, 171, 173, 175, 203, 224, 231–232, 246, 251, 259, 265–266, 268, 273, 275, 282, 285, 289, 297, 303, 312, 355, 357, 376, 379, 382, 395, 397, 399, 401, 411, 418, 436–437, 441, 443, 449, 483–484, 506–509, 511, 513, 523, 529, 542, 561, 581–582, 585, 590, 596, 629, 632–635
Católica Impugnación 123
Centenera, Antonio de 119
Center of Research and Diffusion of the Sephardic Culture (Centro de Investigación y Difusión de la Cultura Sefaradí, CIDICSEF) 385
Central America 409–410, 619
Central Council of Education *Vaad Hajinuj Hamerkazí* (Consejo Central de Educación) 390
Central Jewish Committee of Mexico (Comité Central Judío de México) 400
Centro Cultural Sholem Aleijem 584
Centro Sefarad-Israel 418, 426
Cerdaña 19
Cerda, Carlos 619
Cervantes, Miguel de 2, 126, 194–196, 199–200, 438, 531, 550
Céu Subterrâneo 467
Chamorro, Violetta 411
Chanzas del ingenio y dislates de la musa 283–284
Charabati, Esther 528
Charlemagne 19, 247
Charles II of Navarre 20
Charles II of Spain 162, 284
Charles III of Navarre 20
Charles V 165, 195, 222, 283, 284
Charles the Bald 19
Chávez, Hugo 404
Chejfec, Sergio 12, 568, 613, 614, 619
Cherubim 47
Chiarello, Florecio B. 592
Chile/an 375, 380–382, 395–397, 404, 427, 479, 491, 498, 557, 583, 589–590, 606, 609, 614, 617–619
China 175, 230, 231, 557, 566
Chinese Cultural Revolution 611
Chinski, Malena 583, 590
Chirino, Hernán Alfonso 102
Chuetas 161
Christian(ity) 2–4, 6, 8, 9, 17, 19, 21–35, 43, 49, 56, 59, 82, 84, 91–98, 101–102, 105, 107, 109–110, 112, 114, 116, 118, 121–124, 128, 130, 157–178, 190–199, 203, 209–215, 221–226, 230–232, 235–240, 244–247, 251, 253, 255–261, 266–281, 289, 297,

300, 302, 306–308, 313, 320–321, 327, 332, 335, 353–368, 376, 378, 425, 433–438, 441, 475, 496, 511, 523, 529–531, 592, 619, 631, 637–638
Christian Spain 23, 25, 157
Citas y Comentarios 564, 597
Citizenship 205, 206, 321, 376, 377, 420, 549, 550, 553, 556, 561, 562, 581–584, 588, 592
Ciudad Real 160
Ciudad Rodrigo (Extremadura) 161
Clergy 160, 171, 257, 449
Cochabamba 403
Cochim 174
Coelho, Jorge d'Albuquerque 176
Coexistence 2, 75, 81, 87–88, 91, 159, 302, 433, 497, 609
CL Salmos de David 273
Cohen, Albert 10, 433, 439, 614
Cohen de Lara, David 171, 264, 286
Cohen, Dov 334, 335
Cohen, Esther 528, 531, 543
Cohen Nassy, David de Isaac 310–311
Cohen Plan 394
Cohen, Reina 343
Cohen, Robert 301, 304, 311
Cohen, Robin 607
Colocci-Brancuti 89
Colonial(ism) 8–9, 167, 174–177, 297, 332–333, 353–368, 419, 447–448, 484, 488, 499–501, 504, 513, 523–524, 611
Colores Siguientes 451
Colombia 303, 313, 354–355, 369, 406–407, 611, 616
Columbus 111, 222, 224, 353–354, 437, 484, 526
Comedia 280–288
Comedia de Amán y Mardoqueo 286
Com/Posiciones 564, 597
Commercial Center of Charity (Centro Comercial de Beneficiencia, Chile) 395
Committee for the Protection of the Israelite Immigrant of Santiago 396
Committees in Support of Hebrew Palestine (Comités Pro-Palestina Hebrea) 380, 399, 405, 408
Communist/communism 380, 386, 388–389, 392–393, 398, 406–407, 411, 440, 472, 584, 587, 595, 619

Community 17–30, 45, 76–77, 84, 131, 161, 164–179, 192, 195, 199, 204, 207–208, 210, 215, 236, 246, 251, 253, 255, 257–258, 260, 262, 264, 269–270, 275–276, 279, 282–283, 285, 288, 297, 299–308, 310, 312, 321, 330–331, 336, 341, 365, 368–369, 375, 377–380, 383–411, 420–421, 424–425, 428, 435, 437, 443, 447–449, 468–471, 476–477, 482, 484, 488, 492–493, 500, 504–505, 507–508, 510, 525, 528, 532–533, 541, 543, 552–553, 567, 569–570, 582–584, 608–609, 616, 619–620, 632, 636, 638, 642
Communities 4–5, 8–9, 20, 22–23, 24–26, 36, 51, 56, 59, 62, 75–76, 87, 91–92, 158–175, 178, 187, 193, 201–202, 208, 211, 213, 230, 232, 245, 251, 255–271, 276–278, 280, 288–289, 297–309, 312–313, 320–323, 331, 333, 336, 339–345, 353, 356, 361, 364, 368–369, 375–380, 382, 384–386, 388, 390–391, 393, 396, 398, 401, 403, 405–407, 410–411, 418–419, 424–425, 428, 434–435, 439, 466, 476–477, 481–483, 488, 491, 507, 526, 530, 532–533, 549, 552, 559, 569, 581–583, 589, 593–594, 607, 613, 620
Cómo acercarse a la poesía 501
Como agua para chocolate 485, 498
Como polvo en el viento 636
Compagnie des Îles d'Amérique 299
Compendio de Dinim 263
Comuna Verdad 560, 588, 589
Concepción 396
Conciliador 266, 275
Confederation of Israelite Organizations of Venezuela (Confederación de Organizaciones Israelitas de Venezuela) 404
Confesos antiguos 125
– *Confesos de los viejos*, see *confesos antiguos*
Confusión de confusiones 271
Conjeturas sagradas sobre los Profetas Primeros 257
Consolação às tribulações de Israel 254, 260, 272
Consolatoria de Castilla 121
Constantinople 18, 111, 165, 167, 439
Constitution 164, 328, 376–378, 394, 419, 437, 483, 507, 526, 585–586

Contemporary period 12–13, 185–186, 417–429, 434, 448, 451, 469, 486, 493, 495, 499, 500, 510, 512, 525–532, 537, 534, 581–642
Contos do Imigrante 447, 449, 464
Contra la verdad no hay fuerza 285–286
Conversion(s) 4–6, 17–18, 27, 29–31, 35, 84, 91–95, 98, 118, 120, 122–124, 128, 130, 158, 160, 162–163, 167–168, 198–199, 203–204, 213, 223, 232, 256, 376, 425–426, 436–437, 439, 529, 591, 596
Conversos 5–10, 26–36, 81–131, 157–163, 166, 168–170, 175–178, 185–216, 251–289, 297, 305, 307, 310, 320, 353–368, 418–426, 434–437, 441–443, 523, 526, 530–532, 543, 610, 629, 632
Convivencia 81–82, 426–427, 433, 435, 437
Convocaciones, desolaciones e invocaciones 501
Copenhagen 174
Coplas 113, 115, 278, 324, 328, 329, 343
Coplas de la Gala 104
Coplas de la Pasión con la Resurrección 121
Coplas de Mingo Revulgo 114–115
Coplas de Vita Christi 115, 119
Coplas del Provincial 115–116, 119
Coplas del tabefe 123
Coplas por a.b.c 127
Cordoba 18–19, 21, 45, 56, 59, 61, 69, 91, 101, 117, 126, 285
Cordoba, Jacob de 258
– Cordova, see Cordoba
Coro (Venezuela) 303, 312
Coro de las musas 275, 284
Corpus de poesìa mozárabe 65
Corriente, Federico 57–58, 67
Cortázar, Julio 479, 499, 617
Cortes Generales 118
Cortés, Hernán 175, 504, 523
Cosimo de' Medici 168
Cosmopolitanism 187, 245–247, 289, 475, 478, 512
Cossa, Roberto 557
Costantini, Humberto 12, 559–560
Costa Rica 312, 409–410, 619
Costa, Isaac da 257, 300
Costa, Uriel da 264
Cota, Alonso 114
Cota, Rodrigo 115, 124

Council of Constance 31
Council of Toledo 17
Council of Vienne 21
Counter-Reformation 223, 232, 260
Coup d'état 87, 619
Court Jews 23–24
Cousas de folgar e gentilezas 129
Cozarinsky, Edgardo 12, 560, 561, 605, 620
Crack manifesto 479, 501
Cracow 636
Credo glosado contra los judíos 127
Creole (*Criollos*) 299, 499, 591–592
Creole languages 308–309
Criador de palomas 560, 588, 589
Crianza y virtuosa dotrina 122
Cristero War 506
Cristóbal Nonato 504
Critical Approaches to Jewish-Mexican Literature 486
Cromwell, Oliver 174, 300
Crónica de Juan II 29
Crónica de los Reyes Católicos 28
Crónica del Halconero 106
Crown 17, 21–23, 50, 52, 83, 87–88, 93, 101, 111, 117, 125, 161–162, 164, 166, 300
Crypto-Catholics 172
Crypto-Jews 84, 103, 109–111, 116, 122–123, 126, 130–131, 158, 160–162, 166–167, 175, 177, 190, 194, 210, 215, 297, 301, 310, 362–367, 378–379, 433–443, 523–530, 543, 591, 596, 629–630
Cuaderna vía 87, 92
Cuba(n) 13, 313, 354–355, 378–379, 495, 498, 529, 589–590, 608, 613, 627–642
Cuban Revolution 628, 641
Cuenca (Ecuador) 402
Cuenca (Spain) 32, 88, 493
Cueva, Beltran de la (Duke of Alburquerque) 116, 118
Cultural syncretism 489
Curaçao 178, 268, 270, 300–301, 303–306, 309, 310–312, 368–369, 403
Curationum Medicinalium Centuriae Septem 169
Curationum Medicinalium Centuriae Septem 169
Curiel, Moises (Jerónimo Nunes da Costa) 283
Curitiba 391, 466
Cuzary 266

Cyjon, Roberto 570
Cytrynowicz, Roney 453

da Silva, Antônio José 447, 448, 596
Damascus 43, 385, 400, 476, 526, 528, 532, 540, 541, 620
Damiani, Bruno 197, 198, 201
Dana, Victoria 528, 543
Danielillo 257, 267
Danish 165, 172, 302, 312
Danon, Abraham 334, 342
Dante, Alighieri 122, 232
Danza de la Muerte 122
Danzig 173
Dār al-tirāz 64
Dark 561
– Dark Ages, see Middle Ages
Daras 268
Darom 551
Davar 390, 462, 551
David 488, 490–493, 618
David the Psalmist 110
Davidson, William 266
Davihuelo 95
Dayán 26
Days of Awe 627–631
De dioses, hombrecitos y policías 560
De magia y prodigios 476
De Musica Libri Septem 123–124
Declaração das 613 encomendanças de nossa Sancta Ley 263
Defensorium unitates cristianos 34
Delegation of Argentine Israelite Associations (Delegación de Asociaciones Israelitas Argentinas, DAIA) 385, 387–388, 398, 555–556
Delicado, Francisco 6, 185, 194–203
Demasiado amor 485, 497
Der andere Prozess 440
Der Avangard 386
Der Mentsch fun Buenos Aires 620
Der Unhoib 392
Derrida, Jacques 192, 509, 596
Derush 260
Deuteronomy 324
Developmentalism/Desarrollismo 586
Di Presse and Di Yiddishe Zeitung 551, 613
Dialect(s) 58–59, 61, 75, 157, 271, 278, 333, 554
Dialoghi d'amore 7, 221–227, 245–246, 256

Diálogo de Mercurio y Carón 257
Diálogo dos montes 283
Diálogo entre el Amor y un viejo 114
Dialogue (literary form) 91, 94, 96, 99, 211, 223–228, 254–256, 260, 267, 271, 280, 283, 289, 435, 437, 448, 466, 495, 509–511, 514, 533–538, 615
Dialogues of the Great Things of Brazil 448
Diamant Fishenfeld, Janette 454
Diament, Mario 572, 587
Diário da Queda 457, 491, 615
Diario de un testigo de la Guerra de Africa 418
Diaspora/ic 1, 6–9, 12, 23, 26, 51, 157–158, 161, 164–174, 188, 197, 201, 205, 214, 245, 247, 251–262, 266–289, 298, 307, 312–313, 319–320, 329–330, 334, 340, 344, 361–364, 403, 426, 428, 433–436, 442–444, 451, 456, 463, 477, 481, 488, 512–513, 527, 529, 535, 537, 543, 547, 552, 559–560, 571, 581, 588–589, 594–595, 597, 603, 607–609, 614, 618, 621–22, 627–631, 636, 641
Dias, André 129
Dias, Damião 170
Dias, Estevão 267
Días penitenciales 247
Díaz de Toledo, Fernán/Fernando 32–33, 109
Dibaxu 442, 564, 565, 597
Diccionario de escritores mexicanos 500, 504
Dickmann, Enrique 591, 592
Die Blendung 440
Diglossia 58, 164, 168
Dines, Alberto 453
Discursos académicos 271
Disillusion (*desengaño*) 160
Disraeli, Benjamin 439
Dissertations sur le Messie 278
Diversity 1, 3–4, 6, 9, 11–13, 17, 159, 297, 418, 458, 476, 478–479, 483, 487, 493, 507, 523, 548–549, 571, 591, 595, 603, 608, 623
Dīwān 46, 69
Do Objeto Útil 451–52
Docendo Docemur 311
Dogma(tic) 95–96, 160, 214, 230–231, 233, 236, 260, 542
Dolle, Verena 11, 603
Domínguez Ortiz, Antonio 84, 98, 118, 160, 354, 355
Dom Pedro, Count of Barcelós 89

Donde mejor canta un pájaro 622
Don Dinís of Portugal 129
Don Quijote 2, 91, 126, 194–196, 199, 438
– *Don Quixote*, see *Don Quijote*
Doña Mencía de Cisneros 89
Donin, Nicholas 31
Dordrecht 258
Dos mujeres 485–486, 498
Dostoevsky, Fyodor 339, 467
Drai vegn 483, 496
Dublin 174
Duc de Richelie 166
Dumas, Alexandre 337
Dunash ben Labrat 44–46
Dueñas, Juan de 105–106, 110
Duero 20
Dutch 8, 165–166, 173–174, 177–178, 258, 269, 279–280, 282, 288, 297–311, 368, 433, 437, 457
Duties of the hearts 266
Dutton, Brian 85, 127
Early modern period. 1–3, 6–10, 82–83, 125, 157–161, 170, 179, 221–225, 237–238, 246, 251–254, 258, 260, 262, 273, 278, 358, 443
Ebrei levantini 170
Ebreo, Leone (Judah ben Isaac Abrabanel) 7, 221–229, 236, 246, 256
Ecclesiastical 21, 27, 160, 163, 200
Echeverría, Esteban 569
Écija 27, 84
Ecuador 303, 354, 380, 402
Edelman, Angel 585
Edict of Expulsion (1492)/ Alhambra Decree 377, 433, 437, 609
Edict of Expulsion (1290) 300
Edirne 323, 334, 336, 340, 342
Efraín de Atenas 527
Egypt(ian) 42–43, 64, 237, 330, 404, 436, 502, 542
Eichelbaum, Samuel 12, 547, 551, 557
Eichmann, Adolf 383, 553, 557, 582, 616
Eighteenth century 1–2, 9, 96, 117, 167, 170, 187, 251–252, 257–261, 267, 271, 279, 281, 284, 288, 298, 301, 304, 306–307, 310–311, 313, 319–345, 418, 439
El árbol de los nombres 535
El abrazo partido 605
El avión negro 557
El Buscón 194–196, 216

El caramelo descompuesto 554
El cristianismo pre-cristiano 550
El ghetto 567
El judío Aarón 551
El Jugeton 336
El laberinto de la soledad 479, 484, 499
El lazarillo de Tormes 557
El libro de los recuerdos 563, 612, 616
El Lunar 335, 340
El Macabeo 170, 273
El Manadero 335
"El manisero" ("The peanut vendor") 632–633
El Nasyonal 335
El nombre del padre 610
El otro, el mismo 420
El Paso 400
El perseguido dichoso 287
El que mueve las piezas 615
El Ropero (Antón de Montoro) 100–101, 114, 117–121, 124, 126–127, 131
El rufián moldavo 561, 620
El salmo de Kaplan 616
El Salvador 410
El Santo Oficio 436, 525
El sefardí romántico. La azarosa vida de Mateo Alemán II 610
El Segundo genesis de Janán Saridor 613
El Sidiello 77–78
El soñador de Smith 560, 588, 589
El Telegrafo 335
El Tiempo 335
El tren partió a las 20.30. Memorias de un migrante: desde Berlín hasta Chile 618
Eleventh Century 49, 55, 60, 74, 225, 231, 239, 242, 247
Eli Nazareno 177
Eliezer ben rabbi Isaac Papo 327
Elogios a la felice memoria 269
Emancipation 3, 6, 172, 179, 245, 252, 312, 332, 468
Emden 172
Emigrants 174, 178, 403
En tierras ajenas 619
En un vergel deleitoso 95
Encina, Juan del 121, 125
Encyclopaedia Judaica 221, 480
England 36, 40, 165, 173–174, 247, 257–258, 297–298, 300–301, 369, 436, 526

Enlightenment 3, 187, 225, 237, 246, 311, 319, 320, 333, 343, 433, 444
Enrique II of Castile 21, 27, 83, 85–87
Enrique III of Castile 29, 97
Enrique IV of Castile 102, 104–109, 113, 115–120
– Enrique of Trastámara, see Enrique II of Castile
Enríquez Gómez, Antonio 167, 272–273, 279, 281–282
Enríquez, Juana 103
Enseña a pecadores 264
Enslavement 18, 20, 175–178, 237, 297–304, 308–309, 312, 359, 500, 552, 556, 560
Entangled history 475, 479–480, 501–504, 507, 514
Entre Ríos 550, 561, 585, 591
Entre Ríos, mi país 550
Entremeses 279, 282, 287
Epigraphs 308, 537
Epitalamio burlesco 114
Ercole II 168
Erlich, Sara Riwka 454
Esau 33, 286, 494
Escavias, Pedro de 120
Escobar, Ferrando Filipo / Fernando Felipe 104, 110, 119
Escardillo 528
Escenario de guerra 617
ESMA 605
España, Franco y los Judíos 377
España, Juan de 93–94
Españoles sin patria 420
Espejo de la vanidad del mundo 264
Espejo fiel de vidas 273, 310
Espina, Alonso de 28, 97
Esquivel, Laura 479, 485, 497–498
Essai historique sur la colonie de Surinam 311
Estado Novo (Brazil) 394, 449
Estella 20
Estrella Lusitano 273
Ethnicity 158, 307, 447, 478, 479, 491, 501, 581–585, 591, 606, 608, 631
Etiquetas a los hombres 556
Ets Haim 172, 270, 279
Etz Chaim 305
Euripides 235
Europe(an) 1, 3–4, 6, 7, 19, 21, 31, 36, 43, 56–58, 61–64, 76, 88, 111, 131, 157–158, 165, 167, 169, 172–174, 177–178, 186–188, 221–222, 224–226, 245–246, 252, 258, 268, 270, 275–276, 280, 281, 284, 297, 298–300, 302–304, 306–308, 310, 312–313, 319–321, 330–334, 336–337, 341, 356, 359–364, 367–368, 376–379, 385–388, 393, 399, 402–403, 405–406, 408, 419, 433, 435–437, 444, 447, 449, 456, 460, 465–466, 489, 491, 495, 503–504, 508, 527, 532, 548, 550, 552, 562, 564, 572, 610, 613, 616–617, 620, 630, 634–637, 641
– Central Europe 62, 75, 306, 321, 379, 404
– Eastern Europe 306, 331, 369, 379, 385, 391–392, 395, 400, 404–405, 407, 449, 455, 462, 465, 468, 477, 481, 490, 496, 508, 526–527, 569, 593, 612, 616
– Northern Europe/North Europe/ North European 157, 170–171, 178, 281
– Southern Europe 246
– Western Europe 40, 83, 246, 256, 320, 331, 364, 379, 384, 395, 399, 404
Evangelized 354, 359
Evian conference 398, 409, 411
Exame das tradições fariseas 264
Excelencias de los hebreos 266
Exclusion 6, 25, 30, 99, 158–159, 303, 342, 499, 569, 583–584, 636
Exegesis 267, 322, 324
Exile 19, 22, 48, 72, 105, 122, 128, 157–158, 162, 169, 172, 187–188, 195, 197–198, 201, 206, 208, 214, 237, 272, 279, 320, 326, 424–425, 427–428, 440, 451–452, 455–456, 460, 462, 466, 469, 484, 492, 494, 498, 502, 528–531, 535, 537, 549, 557, 559–561, 564–567, 571–572, 597–598, 610, 618–619, 627–635, 641
Exodus 42, 47, 51, 208, 269, 287, 324, 397, 493–495, 502–503
Expulsion 5, 10, 28, 35, 81, 128, 159, 162, 165, 167, 169, 188, 190, 193, 195, 198–199, 206, 255, 300, 302, 319, 320–322, 326, 328, 353, 375–377, 423, 433–436, 440, 495, 498, 502, 523, 529, 535, 537, 609–610
Expulsion of Jews from Spain 1492 10, 35, 128, 159, 162, 165, 167, 188, 190, 193, 198, 319, 320, 353, 376, 377, 423, 433–436, 440, 498, 523, 529, 609, 610
Extremadura 160–161, 424
Eyck, Jan Van 109
Ezekiel prophecies 100, 308

Ezrá 24
Ezrah Society 384

Faingezicht, Vilma 619
Fall of Tenochtitlán 175
Family Lexicon 440
Farrar, Abraham 263
Farsa de Ávila 112
Farsi 241, 244
Faṣaḥa 44
Fascist(s) 394, 440, 610, 619
Fausto, Boris 454
Federation of Argentine Israelite Communities *Vaad Hakehilot* (Federación de Comunidades Israelitas Argentinas) 390
Federation of Cultural Jewish Entities of Argentina (ICUF) 389
Federation of Jewish Communities of Colombia (Federación de Comunidades Judías de Colombia) 407
Federation of Jewish Communities of Spain 424
Feierstein, Ricardo 12, 481, 487, 547, 554, 572, 588, 590, 613, 617–619
Feiner, Shmuel 333, 342
Feitoria 165
Felicidades fugaces 614
Feminism 11–12, 189, 199, 224, 478, 498–500, 543
Ferdinand/Fernando I of Aragon 31
Ferdinand/Fernando II of Aragon (Ferdinand the Catholic) 111, 120
Ferdinand I of Castile and León 20
Ferdinand/Fernando III of Castile 159
Fernandes Carvajal, António 165
Fernandes Villareal, Manuel 257
Fernández, Lucas 121
Fernández de Velasco, Pedro 109
Fernández Huidobro, Eleuterio 571
Fernández Samuel, Alfonso 96–97
Ferrara 168, 255–257, 259, 262–262, 272–274, 289
Ferrara Bible 255, 259, 261–262, 272–274, 289–290
Ferrer, Vincent 29–31, 84, 94, 102
Ferruz, Pero 92–92
Feuchtwanger, Lion 423
Ficino, Marsilio 225, 228, 531
Fictional/autofictional/metafictional/non-fictional 194, 199, 237, 254, 260, 320, 339–340, 456, 467, 603, 475, 504–505, 513, 588, 615–617, 620, 629, 642
Fifteenth century 5, 21, 27, 29–31, 84–101, 117–118, 122–131, 159–161, 224, 321, 358, 376, 425, 427, 435, 498, 538, 616
Figurative Inquisitions: Conversion, Torture, and Truth in the Luso-Hispanic Atlantic 595
Fine, Ruth 160, 187, 189–191, 199, 273
Finta 305
– First World War, see World War I
Fischer, Bobby 619
Fischer, Susann 308–309
Five Scrolls 326, 328
Flemish 165, 275
Flor de Apolo 275, 284
Flos Sanctorum Vida de los Santos 273
Fons vitae (Yanbu' al-Hayat) 225, 435
Fonseca, Rodrigo da 170
Fontaine, Jean de la 329
Formosa 585
Founding of the State of Israel in 1948 380, 482, 609
Fortalitium fidei 97
Fortuna variabilis 92
Foucault, Michel 221, 226, 231, 236, 243, 460
France 6, 19, 22, 36, 40, 43, 64, 161, 166, 167, 172–173, 187, 247, 251, 257, 281, 284, 288, 297–298, 302, 310, 312, 331–332, 337, 344, 394, 439–434, 482, 495, 526–527, 529, 532, 548–549, 560, 566, 636
Franco, Antonio 124
Franco, Francisco 377, 421
François I 103
Francoist Spain 610
Frankel, Rachel 308
Fray Alonso de Oropesa 109
Fray Diego de Valencia de Don Juan 93, 95–96
Fray Hernando de Talavera 119, 123
Fray Íñigo de Mendoza 115, 119–120, 124
Fray Luis de León 111, 437, 441
Freedman, Samuel 633
Freemasons 303
French 8, 10, 20, 36, 40, 58, 61, 103, 166–167, 173–174, 202, 222, 224, 236, 252, 278–279, 281–282, 285, 288, 297–298, 302, 311–312, 321, 331, 333, 336–338–339, 342, 360, 419, 433, 435, 479, 489–490, 494, 509, 526, 532, 548–549, 570, 597
French Revolution 167, 252

Fresco, David 335, 340
Freud, Sigmund 240, 568
Friedler, Egon 569
Friedman, Edward 607
Frings, Theodor 64
Frondizi, Arturo 585, 586
Fuente de la Gracia 109
Fuentes, Carlos 479, 490, 504, 512, 632
Fuero of Escalona 21
Fuero of Nájera 21
Furtado 107
Futoransky, Luisa 12, 566
Fux, Jacques 454, 619

Gabay 305
Gabbay, Rosa 343
Gai, Mijal 566
Galanté, Abraham 342
Galemire, Julia 570
Galicia(n) 20, 35, 85, 88–89, 122, 131, 161, 186, 333, 386
Galician-Portuguese 85, 89, 91, 96, 100
Gaon, Moshe David 334
Garcia de Resende 81, 89, 128, 129–131
García Gómez, Emilio 64–67
Garden of Eden 46
Gartenberg, Alfredo 454
Gaucho 550, 552, 561, 589, 591
Gavilán, Moses 282, 288
Gazal 239, 241, 244
Gazeta de Amsterdam 334
Geiger, Abraham 63
Gelbard, José Ber 586
Gelman, Juan 12, 442, 547, 564, 565, 567, 587, 597, 598, 613, 614
Genesis 222, 279, 324, 325, 461
Genoa 204–206, 222
Gerchunoff, Alberto 12, 487, 490, 526, 547, 549–553, 557, 561, 563, 565, 568, 582, 588, 617, 618, 622
German 36, 57–58, 63, 65, 165, 241, 247, 306, 333, 341, 398, 405–408, 435–436, 440–441, 456, 468, 481, 484, 492, 494, 506, 584, 607–608, 615–616, 619, 621, 633–634
Germany 64, 173, 257, 276, 284, 369, 376, 383, 394, 398, 402, 404, 408, 457, 468, 494, 500, 526–527, 615
Gernert, Folke 197–202

Gervitz, Gloria 11, 475, 485–486, 489, 509–514
Ghetto 168, 256, 282, 456, 492, 564, 567, 621
Ghetto Novissimo 170
Ghivelder, Zevi 454
Giardinelli, Mempo 559
Gibraltar 19, 419–420
Gilman, Sander 607, 635
Gilroy, Paul 608
Ginzburg, Natalia 440
Girona 19, 24
Gitlitz, David M. 98, 362, 365, 443, 491
Glantz, Jacobo 483, 526–527
Glantz, Margo 11, 475, 483, 485–487, 494, 496–497, 499, 508, 510, 590, 605, 527
Glickman, Nora 560, 572
Glikovsky, Moishe 483, 526
Globalización, Transnacionalización y las Comunidades judías: el impacto del Chavismo en Venezuela 594
Globalization 479, 594, 604
Glorious Revolution 276
Glückstadt 171
Glusberg, Samuel 557
Goa 174, 362
Goldberg, Florinda 13, 477, 487, 501, 510, 553, 564, 594, 607, 608, 613, 621
Goldberg, Jaqueline 620
Goldemberg, Isaac 610
Golden Age of medieval Iberian Hebrew verse 4–5, 19, 39–40, 43–44, 47–48, 51, 55, 72
Goldman, Silvio 450
Goloboff, Mario 12, 560, 562, 588
Gómez Manrique 88, 110, 112, 118–120
Gómez Silveira, Abraham 267, 270, 277–278, 290
González Boixò, J.C. 475
González de Mendoza, Pedro (Archbishop of Toledo) 97, 119
González, Fernán 20
Gracia Dei, Pedro de 120–122
Gracioso 279, 287–288
Graetz, Heinrich 341
Graff Zivin, Erin 595–597, 628
Gran Colombia 303
Gran viraje 84
Granada 19, 35, 45, 69, 71, 76, 86, 111, 119–121, 159, 222
Grão-Pará 176

Great Britain 284, 377, 495, 618
Great Complicity (*gran complicidad*) 177, 362, 365, 367
Greece 344, 433, 443, 456, 526, 527, 530, 535
Greek 18, 56, 157, 167, 225, 233–235, 244, 329, 439, 527
Greek Mythology 225, 527, 232–235
Gringuinho 465
Grosser Nagarajan, Nadia 590
Grossmann, Judith 455
Grotius, Hugo 172
Grünberg, Carlos M. 12, 552, 553, 567
Grunebaum, Gustave 64
Grynberg, Halina 455
Guadalajara (Mexico) 363, 482
Guadalajara (Spain) 77–78
Guatemala 354, 399, 410, 589, 621
Guayaquil 402
Guide for the perplexed (*Guía de los perplejos*) 225, 256, 436, 611, 630
Guinsburg, Jacó 447, 449, 455
Gulags 611
Guianas 297–298
Guillén de Ávila, Diego 122
Guillén de Segovia, Pero 104, 117, 120, 122, 124
Guinsburg, Jacó 447, 449, 455
Güiraldes, Ricardo 552
Gurwitz, Beatrice D. 583, 584, 586
Gutnisky, Luis 585
Guzmán de Alfarache 6, 194, 196, 203, 610
Guzmán, Enrique de 110
Guzmán, Gaspar de (Count-Duke of Olivares) 367
Guzmán, Leonor de 21, 85

Ha-Kohen, Elijah 327
Ha-Magid 342
Habbimah Haivrith 501
Ḥabīb 74, 77
Habsburg crown 164, 504
Hafez 241, 244
Haham 258, 264, 305, 310
Haiti 312, 437
Hajsharot 387
Haketía 253
Hakitía 613
Halabi 476, 532
Halajá 24, 40, 257, 323–324, 328
Halakha/Halakkah, see *Halajá*

Halebis 620
Halfon, Eduardo 621
Hall, Stuart 608
Halorki, Joshua 91, 100
Hamagid 340
Hamas 404
Hamburg 8, 171, 174, 251, 257, 264, 273, 277–278, 280, 286, 297, 320, 361, 630
Hanoar Hatzioni 405, 408, 410
Hanukkah 328, 421
Hanseatic 165, 171, 275
Haphtarot 262
Haredi 621
Hashomer Hatzair 394, 399
Hasid, David Yosef 339
Haskalah (Jewish Enlightenment) 319, 320, 333, 334, 340–343, 433
Havana 628, 631, 635–636, 640
Haymann, Rudi 618
Hazará betshubá 393
"Head of Christ" 637
Hebraica (Paraguayan magazine) 408
Hebraica-Macabi 399
Hebraica veritas 199, 255
Hebraeo Mastix 100
Hebrei hispani 168
Hebrew 2, 4, 5, 8, 10, 18–19, 28, 39–100, 127, 157–160, 166, 168, 170, 172–173, 187, 190, 198–200, 223–224, 242–243, 251–275, 285, 289, 301–311, 319, 322–330, 334–343, 380, 386–387, 396–399, 405–410, 419, 433–443, 451, 453, 462, 480, 488, 500, 510, 512–513, 528–532, 543, 547, 551, 558–559, 567–568, 597–598, 612–613, 616, 622, 627, 629–630
– Hebrew Andalusi verse 39–51
– Hebrew Battalion 387
– Hebrew Bible 39, 42, 55, 68, 72, 75, 78, 433, 438, 462
– Hebrew Federation 407
– Hebrew Immigrant Aid Society (HIAS) 398
– Hebrew Nation 301, 303
– Hebrew poetry 4–5, 39–51, 55–78, 90, 127, 271, 273–275, 328, 434–435, 451
– Hebrew Vestry Act 306
Hebron 301, 305
Heger, Klaus 65
Heine, Heinrich 436, 441
Heker, Liliana 604

Henry II 166
Herberay des Essarts, Nicolas 103
Herejes/Heretics 627, 636–639
Herejía 499, 526
Herem 25–437
Heresy/heresies 28, 34, 165, 176, 355, 365, 456, 636–641
Heritage 8, 13, 51, 121, 159, 176, 179, 236–238, 308, 313, 320, 359, 363, 376, 427, 439, 455, 460, 477, 484, 487–488, 490, 494, 499, 501, 510, 528–529, 531, 535, 537, 540, 542, 605, 627, 631
Hermanos Nuestros 591
Hernández Coronel, Francisco 124
Herrera de Toro, Juan 115
Hervás (Cáceres) 424–426
Herzl, Theodor 391, 481
Heschel, Abraham Joshua 442
Hijas de la rueca 498, 500
Hijuelos, Oscar 13, 627–628, 632, 633, 635–636
Himmler, Heinrich 619
Hinduism 174, 489, 527
hinge identity 608
Hirsch, Baron Maurice de 379, 381, 481
Hisho que te nazca 527, 532–533, 589
Hispanic America 9, 176, 353–369, 475, 490, 498, 499, 511, 512
Hispaniola 313, 354–355, 437
Hispano-Moroccan War 418
Historia crítica de la poesía Mexicana 510
Historical Academy Madrid 63
Historical Museum of the Jewish community of Costa Rica 619
Historical novel 13, 423, 464, 488, 496, 504, 527, 530, 603, 609–610
Historiography 2–4, 10–11, 129, 158–159, 163, 187–188, 196, 260, 263, 320, 334, 340–341, 345, 443, 498, 581, 593
Hitchcock, Richard 66
Hitler, Adolf 555, 610
Hoenerbach, Wilhelm 64
– Holland, see Netherlands
Holocaust 344, 375, 380, 393, 423, 489, 490, 493–495, 502, 513, 555, 611, 613, 619, 630, 632, 635
– Holy Brotherhood, see Santa Hermandad
Holy Land 19, 237, 264, 305
Holy Office 28, 125, 162, 356, 596
Holy Roman Empire 36

Homeless Tongues 597
Hopen, Daniel 587
Hopkins Rodríguez, Eduardo 608, 610
Honduras 411
Hooghe, Romein de 269
Horowitz, Joel 584
Huesca 22
Hugo, Victor 339
Huli, Jacob R. 324, 325
Humas o cinco libros de la Ley divina 262
Humboldt University 619
Hurtado de Mendoza, Juan 115
Hybridity 6, 119, 158, 179, 190, 198, 213, 229, 242, 244, 437, 450, 468–469, 475, 485–489, 497, 501, 511, 513, 527, 537, 542, 588–589, 606–607, 610, 627, 632
Hyphen(ated) 475, 477, 481, 487, 489, 508, 552–553, 606–609, 617, 628, 636
"hyphen theory" 606–607, 609

I. L. Peretz Cultural Association (Asociación Cultural I. L. Peretz) 400
Iberian 4–10, 12, 17, 25, 35, 40, 41, 43, 48, 81–85, 87–88, 90–92, 97–98, 102, 105, 117–122, 124–125, 128–131, 157–158, 164–178, 213, 222, 233, 242, 245, 251, 253–255, 258–260, 265, 267–269, 271–289, 297–298, 306–308, 313, 319, 356, 358, 360–361, 364, 375, 379–380, 426, 440–441, 532
Iberian Jewish 5–7, 17, 92, 157, 167–168, 170, 174, 178–179
Iberian Peninsula 2, 4–7, 9–10, 17–22, 27, 29, 36, 43, 51, 56, 59–61, 81–84, 90, 95, 102–106, 117, 123, 128, 157–169, 179, 188, 221–222, 242, 245–246, 251, 280, 307, 320, 358, 361–362, 366, 411, 433, 435, 438, 531, 609
Ibero-Romance 5, 55, 60–61, 67, 157
Ibn Adret, Shlomo 24
Ibn al-Jaṭīb, Lisān al-dīn 86
Ibn Baqī 69–73, 76
Ibn Caprel al-Kātib, Yosef 76–78
Ibn Ezra, Abraham 40, 42–43, 111, 261
Ibn Ezra, Moshé/Moses 19, 39, 42, 45–48, 71–72, 78, 435
Ibn Ferruziel, Yosef 77
Ibn Gabirol, Shlomo (Avicebron) 19, 39, 41, 43, 45, 47–50, 225, 435, 441, 564

Ibn Ghiath, Isaac 50
Ibn Quzmān 61
Ibn Shaprut, Ḥasdai 18, 45
Ibn Verga, Shlomo 84, 261
Ibn Zarzar, Abraham 87
Ideas posibles 271
Identidad 610
Identities 2, 7, 84, 99, 119, 161, 172–173, 478, 530, 555, 561, 570, 581, 584, 591, 595–596, 608, 616, 627–628, 641
Identity 1–2, 6, 101, 120–121, 157, 160, 163, 173, 175, 191–192, 199, 206, 209, 211, 224, 251–252, 258–259, 265, 267, 272, 287, 307, 312–313, 332, 338, 364, 390, 393–394, 417–419, 421–422, 424, 426–428, 435–436, 443, 448–449, 460–464, 468–469, 475–481, 485, 487–488, 494, 496–497, 499, 501, 504, 506–508, 528, 530, 532, 539, 543, 547, 550, 552, 553, 555, 563, 566–568, 581–584, 589, 591–592, 594–595, 597, 603–608, 610, 612, 614, 617, 619–620, 628, 630–636, 639, 641
Ideology/ Ideological 111, 160, 188, 194–195, 213, 222–223, 247, 326, 329, 331, 358, 377, 384, 386–387, 398, 389–394, 397–398, 411, 476, 485, 483, 488, 499, 507, 550, 552, 556, 562, 569–570, 581, 584–587, 592, 593, 639
Igel, Regina 448, 449, 589, 616–617
Imagens no meu Espelho 454
Imberti 257
Immigrants 161, 171–172, 175, 279–281, 312, 320, 353, 359, 362, 375–376, 379, 381–382, 385–386, 392, 394–396, 399–409, 411, 424–425, 441, 448–449, 453, 455–457, 459–460, 468–472, 475, 479–484, 487–491, 496, 499, 502, 504–505, 508–509, 512–513, 552, 559–565, 584, 588, 591–595, 610, 612, 614, 616, 619, 627, 629
Imperio de Dios en la armonía del mundo 275
Imposta da naçao 305
Inclusion 159, 197, 200, 205, 212, 426, 527, 532, 569, 583, 635
India 165, 174, 176–178, 230–231, 437, 298, 368, 437, 489, 498
Indies 175, 306, 312, 359, 439, 484
Infantes de Aragón 99, 102, 105
Infinita 500

Inquisition 9, 28, 35, 81, 96, 98, 112, 121–127, 159–168, 173–177, 198, 200, 204, 256, 264, 272, 278, 282, 302, 310, 353–368, 376–379, 418–419, 425, 436–439, 447–448, 453, 494, 499, 501, 523, 525, 530, 543, 591, 596–597
Instution of the *inhabilidad* 160
Instrucción del Relator 109
Integration 2–3, 12, 30, 81, 87, 95, 98–99, 160, 162, 166, 179, 199, 205, 216, 311, 332–333, 360, 393, 405, 407, 424, 469, 472, 484, 533, 547, 550–553, 556, 558, 560, 562–563, 565, 572, 585–586, 593, 604, 612, 617–618
Intertextual/ intertextuality 60, 68, 72–73, 75, 78, 254, 468, 512, 615, 617
Invasion 118, 177, 211, 330, 584, 634
Iolovitch, Marcos 455
Iran 241, 404, 433, 532
Iraq 45, 433, 414
Isaac (Patriarch) 467, 529, 558
Isabel I of Castile (Isabel the Catholic) 35, 108, 111, 114–129, 222, 436–437
Isabella of Aragon and Castile, Queen of Portugal 125, 128–129
Ishmaelites 33
Isidro, Gabay 269
Islam(ic) 3, 7, 45–46, 55–56, 58–61, 68, 95, 167, 222, 230, 237–245, 331–333, 342, 433, 435, 439, 638
Islamic Spain 55–56, 58
Islas inútiles 297
Isolation 157, 308, 540, 571
Israel(i/te) 12, 25, 30, 33–34, 42, 48–51, 78, 93, 178, 237, 255, 264, 287, 336, 344, 375, 380–411, 418–420, 426–427, 434–435, 440–443, 457, 459, 462–463, 447, 482, 489, 492, 498, 529, 531–532, 547, 549–556, 566.572, 582, 590, 594–598, 603, 605, 607, 609, 613, 621, 627
Israel Garzón, Jacobo 418–421, 424
Israel, Jonathan 158
Israelite Alliance of Paraguay (Alianza Israelita de Paraguay) 407
Israelite Center of Bogotá (Centro Israelita de Bogotá) 406
Israelite Central Committee of Uruguay (Comité Central Israelita del Uruguay) 398
Israelite Circle (Círculo Israelita, Chile) 396–397

Israelite Circle of La Paz (Círculo Israelita de La Paz) 403
Israelite Commercial and Industrial Center (Centro Comercial e Industrial Israelita, Brazil) 398
Israelite Congregation of the Argentine Republic (Congregación Israelita de la República Argentina, CIRA) 384, 389–390
Israelite Philanthropic Association (Asociación Filantrópica Argentina) 385
Israelite-Sephardic Community Association (Asociación Comunidad Israelita-Sefaradí) 385
Israelite Society of Venezuela 404
Israelite Worker Union (Unión Obrera Israelita) 384
Israelite Youth Association (Chile) 396
Istanbul 169, 321–324, 326–328, 330, 334–336, 339–340, 342–343, 532, 535, 614
Italian 19, 61, 83, 90, 103, 109, 121, 165–172, 200, 204–208, 221, 223–224, 267, 271, 276, 281–282, 321, 329, 419, 430, 435, 440, 443, 559, 595, 619
Italy 6, 40, 43, 62, 64, 89, 102, 105, 131, 161, 165, 170, 187, 195–196, 206, 221, 223, 238, 247, 251, 256–257, 260, 271, 278, 281, 320, 333, 433, 437, 439–440, 443, 467, 610
Izmir 321, 323, 324, 327, 329, 334–336, 535

Jabad (Chabad) 389, 393, 401
Jacob (Patriarch) 286, 467, 494, 529
Jacob Ben Meir Tam 40, 43
Jacob, Paulo 456
Jacobsen, Rafael Bán 622
Jaén 117
Jaffe, Noemi 456
Jahacob e Essau 286
Jamaica 178, 301–302, 304, 308, 310, 312, 354
James I of Aragon 22
James II of Aragon 22
– *Jarcha*, see *khardja*
Jayot Hanéguev (Animals of the Desert) 620
Jeremiah 72, 494
– Jerónimo de Santa Fe, see Yehoshua ha-Lorqui
Jerusalem 18–19, 23, 30, 41, 63, 69–70, 73, 111, 173, 189, 257, 305, 324, 338, 342, 419, 433, 436, 440, 527, 531, 535, 559, 565, 567, 598, 605, 620–621
Jessurun, Rehuel (Paulo de Pina) 283

Jesús 590
Jesus Christ 28, 30, 32–34, 126, 205, 230–231, 236, 239, 273, 278, 281, 439, 542, 559, 590, 637–638
Jew's Tribute 301
Jewish authors 5, 31, 311, 475, 528, 554, 572, 588, 604, 635
Jewish calendar 43
Jewish Colonisation Association (JCA) 379, 381, 384, 389, 391, 394–395, 481, 585, 591
Jewish Community Foundation (Oficina de Relaciones Humanas de la Fundación de la Comunidad Judía, Colombia) 407
Jewish identity 175, 265, 272, 390, 393–394, 417, 421–422, 424, 428, 460, 477, 494, 528, 582, 604–608, 620
Jewish identities 608, 627, 641
Jewish Latin America: Issues and Methods 582
Jewish-Latin 417, 548, 581, 588, 595, 603–609, 611, 614–616, 618, 620, 622
Jewish-Latin American literatures 603, 605–608, 622
Jewish Literature: A Very Short Introduction 444
Jewish National Fund (KKL) 391
Jewish New Year 274
Jewish World Congress 377
Jewish Writers of Latin America: A Dictionary 491, 605
Jewishness 55, 75, 77–78, 158, 163, 172, 437–438, 464, 477, 481, 493, 497, 500, 508, 527, 557, 559, 564–566, 585, 595–596, 605, 609, 612, 614, 621–622, 628, 630, 632–634, 642
Jewry 8, 40, 45, 62, 164, 171–172, 178, 221, 298, 321–322, 328, 330, 341–343, 549, 553, 581–582, 584, 593–594
Jiménez de Enciso 283
Jitrik, Noé 604
Joana of Portugal 108
João II 129, 162
João III 163
João Rodrigues de Castelo Branco (Amatus Lusitanus) 169
Joden Quartier 300, 304
Joden Savanne 301, 304, 308, 310
Jodorowsky, Alejandro 622
Johnson Act of 1924 481
Joly, Monique 202, 207

Jones, Alan 66–67
Joset, Jacques 197–202
Journal Israelit 335
Juan I of Castile 27, 83–84, 88
Juan I of Navarra 103
Juan II of Castile 91, 94, 97–99, 102–103, 109
Juan Carlos I 377
Juana of Castile 118
Juárez, Benito 503, 526
Judah Al-Ḥarizi 43
– Judah ben Isaac Abrabanel, see Leone Ebreo
Judah Ha-Levi 5, 19, 39, 42, 45, 47–48, 55, 62–64, 69–78, 266, 434–435, 441, 524, 564, 631
Judaica Latinoamericana 594, 595
Judaism 7–8, 19, 28, 30–33, 49, 62–63, 84, 122, 158, 160, 162–164, 168–169, 171–173, 177–179, 198, 225, 230, 236–238, 245–246, 251–267, 272–279, 289, 307, 310, 312–313, 320, 323, 325, 342, 356, 361, 364–368, 376–380, 383, 386–388, 393, 396, 398, 400–403, 410, 417, 420–421, 424–429, 433–439, 447, 450, 456, 458, 463, 467, 476–477, 523, 528–529, 533–534, 551, 558–559, 568, 605, 606–607, 621, 631, 633, 637–638
Judaizantes/Judaizers/*judaizar*/*judaizado*/ judaize 28, 107, 111, 118, 158, 170, 176–177, 199, 215, 265, 360, 362, 365, 425, 437, 447, 523
Judeo-Arabic 333, 611
– Judeo-converts, see conversos
Juderías 84, 88, 91, 93, 100, 422, 435, 503
Judezmo 157, 253, 437
Judite no país do futuro 616
Juego de naipes 103
Junto a un Río de Babel 552

K 457
Kabbalah/Kabbalistic 173, 265, 270, 275, 322, 324, 434, 441, 468, 489, 501, 527–528, 531, 538, 543, 564, 570, 582
Kacowicz, Arie M. , 608
Kaddish 588, 631
Kadima United Zionist Organization (Organización Sionista Unida Kadima) 400
Kafka 444, 450, 457
Kahn, Máximo José 527
Kałczewiak, Mariusz 584

Kalechofsky, Roberta 476, 493
Kamenszain, Tamara 12, 566, 567
Kandiyoti, Dalia 422, 428
Kaplan, Yosef 8, 158, 169, 255, 297, 362, 364
Kashrut 105
Kayserling, Meyer 158, 254
Kehilá Israelite Circle (Kehilá Círculo Israelita, Chile) 397
Keren Hayesod 388
Keter Malkhut 50
Ketuvim 324–326
Khabbāz 57
kharadjāt/ *khardja* 5, 55, 57–78, 242
Khazars 435
Kibbutz Bror Jail 393
Kibbutz Nitzanim 620
Kibbutzim 387, 393
Kid Ñandubay 557
King David's Harp: Autobiographical Essays by Jewish Latin American Writers 589
King Solomon 245, 436
Kingston 308
Kiš, Danilo 10, 443, 440
Kitab al-Ḥujjah wal-Dalil fi Nuṣr al-Din al-Dhalil (Sefer ha-Kuzari) 435
Kleinburg, Gerardo 487, 621
Knight, Franklin 299
Kofman, Sara 619
Kohan, Martín 12, 568, 569
Kolelim 393
Kolonist Kooperator 551
Kordon, Bernardo 557
Korean War 492, 620
Krausz, Luis Sérgio 456
Krauze, Ethel 485–486, 497, 500–501, 509, 513–514
Kristeva, Julia 614
Kristobal Kolon 526–527
Kucinsk, Meir 457
Kucinski, Bernardo 457

La abuela 615
La Academia de Piatock 566
La bobe 485, 501–504
La Buena Esperansa 335
La Celestina 114, 160, 257, 434, 437, 441
La certeza del camino 264
La Corónica 67
La cruz y la estrella 485, 500–501

La Dame aux camélias 232, 337
La Epoka 335
La Germania 556
La Guerta de Oro 329, 330, 332, 343
La jofaina maravillosa: agenda cervantina 550
La larga noche de Francisco Sanctis 560
La lengua florida 530–531
La lozana andaluza 6, 194–197
La logia del umbral 617
La luna que cae 560, 588, 589
La luz 551
La Machabea 273
La mayor hazaña de Carlos VI 283
La morada en el tiempo 494–496, 527, 612
La Opinión 586
La orilla inminente. Escritores judíos argentinos 606
La palabra inconclusa (siete ensayos sobre cábala) 531
La Paz 403
La Plata region 176, 547–448
La Polaca 620
La Policía no se Equivoca Nunca 592
La Prensa 552
La rabina 605, 620
La Reconquista 24, 61, 436
La última profecía 613
La vara de Juda 260
La venganza de Tamar 287
La vida es sueño 281
Laberinto de fortuna 101
Ladino (Judeo-Spanish) 8–10, 12, 122, 157, 221, 223, 253, 257, 261, 273, 308, 319–345, 419, 433, 437, 440, 442, 476, 523, 527, 532, 534–538, 543, 597, 612–614
Laiter, Salomón 486, 488, 490, 513, 618
LAJSA (Latin American Jewish Studies Association) 598
Landau, Trudi 457
Landsmanshaft 593
Largman, Esther Regina 457
Las ausencias presentes 485, 504–509
Las genealogías 585, 494, 496–497, 508, 527
Las jaulas invisibles 616
Las khardjas de la serie árabe en su marco 65
Las luminarias de Janucá 421–423, 428
Las moradas del castillo interior 530
Las muchachas modernas 343

Las raíces y las ramas. Fuentes y derivaciones de la Cábala hispanohebrea 531
Las Trescientas 101
Las visitantes 534–535
Latin 18, 33, 56, 58–59, 61, 65, 47, 91, 101, 159, 173, 176–177, 224, 226, 234, 238, 243–244, 252, 261, 266, 271–272, 326, 329, 334, 376, 513, 568
Latin America(n) 1, 3, 8–10, 12–13, 303, 309, 336, 344, 353, 369, 375–377, 379–380, 385, 389, 399, 401, 403–404, 408, 411, 417, 425, 476–477, 479–484, 487, 489, 491, 511, 513, 523, 525–526, 530, 547–555, 563–564, 566, 568, 571–572, 581–583, 587–598, 603–622, 628, 641
Latin American Department of the Jewish Agency 380
Latin American Jewish novel(s) 609, 620, 622
Latin American literature(s) 417, 476, 479, 487, 566, 595, 603–609, 618, 622, 628
Latin American Rabbinical Seminary (Seminario Rabínico Latinoamericano) 389
Latin American Sephardic Federation (Federación Sefaradí Latino-Americana, FESELA) 385
Latin American Zionist Congress 387, 408
Latin Israelite Congregation 384
Laub, Michel 457, 459, 491, 615–616
Laudário 129
Law of Moses 276, 285
Law of Return of 1950 482
Laws of Valladolid of 1412 30–31
Lazarillo de Tormes 2, 203, 434, 437, 441, 557
Lazarus, Emma 436, 441, 443
Leão, Manuel de 270, 276
Lebanon/Lebanese 401, 404, 583, 585, 616
Lehmann, Matthias B. 326–330, 476, 481–486
Leiden 257
Lenin 555, 587
Lenta Biografía 568, 613, 619
Leo of Rozmital 110
León 20, 23, 83
León, Diego de 104
León, Fray Luis de 111, 437, 441
León, Pedro de 110–11
Leon Templo, Jacob Judah 266
Leonor of Navarre 103
Lerner, Jaime 459
Lesser, Jeffrey 449, 581

Levant(ine) 168–170, 210, 330, 433, 435
Levantine and Spanish *schole* 170
Levenson, Alejo 587
Levi Calderón, Sara 485–486, 497–499, 513
– Levi, Daniel, see Miguel de Barrios
Levi Mortera, Saul 263, 267–268
Levi, Primo 10, 433, 435, 440, 443, 633
Levi, Shlomo 91
Lévi-Provençal, Évariste 64
Levin, Eliezer 459
Leviticus 324
Levy, Tatiana Salem 460, 616
Lewis Nouwen, Mollie 591, 592
Li, Andrés de 121
Liacho, Lázaro 553
Liberal(ism) 207–208, 236, 303, 306, 313, 326, 376, 378, 382, 389, 393, 395, 397, 399, 403, 406, 478, 585, 638
Liberman, Raquel 559, 620
Libro de la tesubá 264
Libro de las Aphtaroth 262
Libro de los pensamientos variables 120
Libro de Trelew 560
Libro del Alborayque 85
Libro del mantenimiento del alma 257, 263
Like a Bride (film) 533
Like a Bride and Like a Mother 532, 589
Lima 175, 177, 354, 363, 405
– *Limpieza de sangre*, see *statutes of purity of blood*
Lingua Franca 309, 319, 334, 433
Lisbon 128, 162, 165, 176, 178, 221–222, 269, 310, 378–379, 460
Lispector, Clarice 448, 450, 460–462, 489
Lispector, Elisa 462
Litane 528, 539–543
Litany 511, 539
Literary canon 3, 6, 12, 46, 59, 185, 187, 197, 212, 215, 223–224, 243, 244–245, 259, 289, 325, 337, 342, 422, 435–436, 486, 496, 499, 501, 510, 528, 548, 567, 597, 606, 614
Literatura de inmigrantes árabes y judíos en Chile y México 603
Lithuania 391, 481, 492, 526
Liturgical literature 4–5, 39–51, 62, 102, 168, 252–253, 256, 258–262, 322, 435, 442, 572
Livornine edict 170

Livorno 170, 174, 178, 251, 257, 271, 276, 281–282, 286, 320, 329–330, 343, 361
Livro de cantigas 89
Livui Sheirut group 620
Lloret Florenciano, Asunción 308–309
Llull, Ramon 94, 531
Lockhart, Darrell 480–481, 483, 485, 486, 487, 491, 605, 609
Lodeña, Pedro de 360
Loker, Zvi 302, 309
London 8, 158, 165, 174, 178, 251, 259, 270, 273, 297, 300, 303, 309, 313, 320, 459, 637
Lope, Mosén 107
Lopes, Rodrigo 165
Lopes da Costa, James 172
López de Haro, Diego, 122
López de Mendoza, Íñigo (Marquis of Santillana 89, 97, 100, 110, 115, 120
López Laguna, Daniel Israel 258, 273, 310
López Rega, José 586
Los amores de Laurita 563
Los conversos 424, 426
Los dolientes 527, 620
Los encantos de la culpa 285
Los gauchos judíos 487, 490, 526, 549, 550, 563, 569, 588, 617
Los israelitas españoles y el idioma castellano 419
Los judíos de América Latina. Los signos de las tendencias: juegos y contrajuegos 594
Los judíos del Mar Dulce 562, 563
Los perplejos 611
Love 7, 55, 70–78, 82, 90, 92, 95, 98–103, 105, 107, 110, 114, 121, 124, 125, 221–247, 337, 338, 530, 531
Lovers of Zion 386
Lucena 59–60, 76, 559
Lucena, Juan de 114
Lumbroso, Joseph 438, 525
Lumen ad revelationem gentium 109
Luna, Álvaro de 99–102, 106–107, 109
Lunas 498
Luz de dos 493

Ma'amad 305
Macabi youth organization 377
Macedonia 344, 395
Macedonian Center (Centro Macedónico) 395
Machado, Gerardo 634–635

Machismo 480, 498–499, 514
Macías (troubadour) 88–89
Madeira 379
Madrid 63, 65, 95, 112, 161, 171, 195, 264, 268, 377, 418–422, 424, 426–428, 435
Magdalene 278
Maggi, Carlos 571
Maghreb 167, 170
Magic Realism 479, 589
Magnus, Ariel 605, 615
Maguén David Community (Comunidad Maguén David) 400
Mahamad 171–172, 253, 283
Mahveret 18–19
Mahzor (*Orden de Ros Hasanah y Kipur*)
Maimónides (Moshé ben Maimón) 19, 223–225, 258, 264, 322, 435, 442, 435, 533, 611
Majlis 46–47
Makom-haMakon 452
Malaga 377
Maldonado de Silva, Francisco 177
Malinche 499, 504
Mallorca 22–23, 35, 161
Malsines 26
Malvinas War 384
Mambo Memoir 629
Mameloschn: Memória em Carne Viva 455
Mancha region/ La Mancha 161, 438
Manhattan 490
Mañozca, Juan de 368
Manrique, Jorge 118
Mantua 103
Manuel I of Portugal (Manuel o Venturoso) 128–129, 162
Manuel de Lando, Ferrán 91
Manuscript literature 66, 69, 99, 109, 258–260, 267, 272, 277–279
María de Portugal 86
Marmolejo, Juan 100, 110
Marrakesh Dialogues 254
Marrano/Marranismo 91, 130–131, 158, 163, 168, 176, 178, 190, 194, 204–206, 255, 265, 275, 289, 362, 364, 378, 433, 436, 596–597, 633
Marrano-Portuguese Committee 378
Martí, José 627
Martín Fierro 553
Martínez de Burgos, Fernán 110
Martínez de Burgos, Juan 110

Martínez de Medina, Diego 99
Martínez de Medina, Gonzalo 99
Martínez Estrada, Ezequiel 560
Martínez, Ferránd 27, 29, 84
Maskilim 332–334, 340–342
Masnou 565
Masse und Macht 440
Mastretta, Ángeles 497, 504
Matatia Aboab, Isaac de 287
Mateus Ventura, Maria d.G.A. 363
Mattancherry 174
Mauricio Colony (Colonia Mauricio) 588
Maury, Laurence 257
Maximiliano of Mexico 503–504, 526
Mayores 23
McCarthy era 490
Me'am Lo'ez 9, 319, 324–327, 333, 343, 344
Medellín 406
Medianos 23
Medieval 1, 4–7, 17–26, 39–40, 43, 46, 48, 51, 61, 64, 75, 81–84, 91–92, 100–105, 129, 157, 159, 178, 221–222, 225, 230, 234, 237–238, 246–247, 278, 427, 434–435, 441, 443, 493, 531, 564–565, 612
Medina Sidonia family 35
Mediterranean 39, 157, 164–169, 320, 332, 419, 437
Memmi, Albert 548, 549, 562
Memorial de los misterios de Christo 93
Memorias del calabozo 571
Memory 11–12, 49, 76, 120, 131, 159–160, 163, 179, 189, 191, 193, 196, 199, 201, 203, 206, 208, 210, 216, 269, 272, 277, 423, 443, 451, 453, 455, 458, 463, 465, 467, 475, 486, 487, 492, 497, 501–502, 504–505, 508–509, 510, 511, 514, 536, 538, 543, 561, 566, 567, 571, 583, 589, 604, 611, 613, 614, 617, 621, 622, 635
Mena, Juan de 101–102, 110, 124, 126–127
Menahem ben Saruq 18, 46
Menasseh ben Israel 173–174, 258, 266–268, 275
Mendes de Solla, Samuel 269, 310
Mendes, Diogo and Francisco 165
Méndez Calzada, Enrique 551
Mendoza family 120
Menéndez Pidal, Ramón 64, 83, 237
Menéndez y Pelayo, Marcelino 63, 82, 116
Menina e moça 256

Menocal, María Rosa 48, 237, 238, 242, 246
Mensch: a Arte de Criar um Homem 453
Menudos 23
Merchant(s) 98, 127, 161–162, 164–169, 171, 175, 177, 252, 258–259, 261, 264–266, 270–271, 276, 287, 289, 298–300, 302, 304, 308, 320, 329–330, 360–361, 363, 382, 409, 435, 592
Merchant of Venice 165
Merchensky, Marcos 586
Meshugá – um Romance sobre a Loucura 454, 619
Messiah 30, 42, 111, 321, 439, 627, 638, 640
Messianic 30, 55, 77–78, 111, 160, 171, 174, 270, 285, 321, 434, 439, 550, 570, 638
Mestizo/mestizaje 306, 478, 479, 484, 485, 492, 497, 501, 550, 588, 613, 617
Mesummad 84
Mexía, Hernán 113
Mexican Revolution 479, 487, 494, 506–507, 512, 514
Mexicanidad 475, 478, 480–481, 489, 497, 502, 504, 508
Mexico(an) 3, 9, 11–12, 175, 354, 362–368, 375, 380, 384, 398–402, 438, 441–442, 475–514, 523–543, 559, 582, 586–598, 605–607, 610, 613, 621
Mexico City 175, 354, 363, 438, 478, 482, 489, 492, 496, 497, 500, 504, 509, 524–526, 534, 540, 564, 620
Mezuzah 434, 529
Miami 404, 595, 608, 630, 637
Micas, João (Joseph Nasi) 169
Mikve Israel 306, 310, 368–369
Middle Ages 1–3, 20, 39–40, 50, 76, 88, 114, 162, 221, 225–226, 231, 233, 239, 247, 255, 327, 338, 419, 493, 604
Middle East 405, 435, 440, 523, 532, 553, 569
Midrash(im/ic) 47, 283, 322, 324, 328
Migas de pan 611
Migdal, Alicia 570
Migraciones 509–514
Migrant Sites 428
Migration(s) 6, 9–11, 157, 162, 179, 198, 206, 252, 312–313, 353, 357–358, 369, 392, 405, 428, 475, 481, 487, 489–490, 494–498, 501, 510, 514, 526–527, 541, 543, 548, 556, 593, 603, 610, 620
Milan 103, 278

Millás Vallicrosa, José María 63
Millet 321
Mimesis: The Representation of Reality in Western Literature 4, 233
Minority/ minorities 1, 17, 22–23, 27, 29–30, 35–36, 57, 86, 91, 98, 111, 129, 159–160, 166, 199, 201, 210, 213–214, 272, 299, 302, 359, 362, 387, 392, 398, 436, 447, 449, 458, 464, 466, 472, 480, 483, 487, 496, 498–499, 528, 547, 549, 553, 557, 570, 581, 593, 607–608, 612, 618, 623
Miranda de Ebro 88
Mise en abyme 631
Mishna 322, 324
Mitrani, Barukh 334, 342
Mizrahi 389, 433, 440, 441, 532, 590
Moab(ites) 42
Mochón Esses, Salomon 528
Moctezuma 504–505
Modern period/Modernity 4, 8–10, 39, 44, 48, 51, 62, 71, 75, 84, 111, 113, 159–160, 172, 187, 214, 222, 226, 231, 237–238, 240, 243, 254, 263–264, 272, 297, 328, 330, 332–334, 337, 339–340, 344, 353, 355, 357–358, 368, 378, 401, 418–420, 439, 443–444, 476, 479, 477, 504, 535, 597, 623, 628
Moisesville 617
Moldavia 617
Molière 339
Molotov-Ribbentrop Pact 398
Monarchy 21, 26, 86–88, 91, 95–96, 101, 106, 111–112, 118, 123, 162, 170, 276
Monasterio 621
Monastir 395
Monotheism 233, 235, 236, 245
Monroe, James T. 67
Monsieur Chouchani 441
Montaigne, Michel de 166, 224
Montalto, Eliyahu 267, 277
Monterrey 482, 504, 524
Montevideo 12, 397–399, 408, 441, 547, 549, 570, 571
Montiel 83, 87, 486
Montilla 251
– Montoro, Antón de, see El Ropero
Morada interior 488, 494, 527–528, 530–531
Moral Epistle (Iggeret musar) 31
Morales, Abraham 282

Morgan, Max 630
Morirás lejos 485, 590
Morisco 35, 159, 188, 202–203, 213
Morocco/ Moroccan 10, 158, 174, 253, 369, 377–378, 384–385, 418–419, 424, 426–427, 429, 616
Moscovich, Cíntia 463–464
Moscow 389, 617
Moscona, Myriam 12, 442, 486–487, 523, 528, 534–537, 543, 614
Moses 42, 51, 276, 279, 285, 287
Moshe ben Abraham Zarzar 87, 97
– Moshé ben Maimón, see Maimónides
Moszczynska, Joanna 619
Mount Sinai 51, 283
Mount Sinai Charity Society 400
Moyal, Esther 343
Mozarabic 5, 55, 59–61, 74, 193–194
Mr. Mani 440
Mu'allaqāt 56
Mugnon, David 257, 265
Muhammad V, King of Granada 86
Mukadamim 24
Multicultural/multiculturalism 55, 58, 443, 479, 534, 588, 595, 597, 616, 618, 622, 635–636
Multilingualism 10–11, 58–59, 61, 187, 252, 433, 512, 590, 595, 597
Múltiples identidades 603
Mundo Israelita 582
Muñiz Huberman, Angelina 10, 433, 435, 441, 476, 485–486, 488, 494, 523, 527–531, 610
Muñoz Molina, Antonio 423
Muqaddam Qabrī 59, 76
Murcia 124
Musar 9, 322–328, 343
Muslim 2–4, 18, 35, 39, 47, 49, 56, 59, 76, 86, 110, 158, 175, 194, 203, 237–238, 240, 242–243, 246–247, 321, 326–327, 331–332, 376, 427, 435–436, 460
Mussafia, Benjamin 171
Muwashaḥ 5, 55, 44, 47–48, 57, 59–60, 65–68, 73, 76–77, 242
Muwaššaḥāt, see Muwashaḥ
My heart is in the East 435, 436
Mysticism/mystic/Mystery 160, 228, 232, 239–244, 247, 265, 421, 434, 441, 452, 467, 530, 531, 564, 630

Naar, Isaac 267
Nação 6, 8, 161, 163, 168, 173, 176–177, 267, 297–298, 305, 362–365, 469
Nahon, Gérard 311
Nájera 21, 88
Nantes 166, 173
Naples 103, 170, 221–222
Napoleon 237, 330
Narrative 3, 11, 13, 42, 86, 92, 102, 158, 164, 192, 195–196, 204, 207, 210, 224, 233, 238, 240, 264–265, 269, 328, 363, 427–428, 433, 437–438, 455, 463, 465, 475, 485, 486, 488, 490–499, 505, 541, 556, 561, 563, 583, 588, 603, 610, 615, 617–618, 621–622, 632–633
Natal 391
Navarre 20, 23–24, 29, 83, 103
Navarro-Rosenblatt, Valeria 583, 584
Navigation Act of 1651 299
Nazi(sm) 377, 379, 383, 395–397, 401–402, 406–408, 411, 458, 463, 465, 482, 490–492, 495, 530, 562, 584, 611, 613, 616, 630, 633
Neapolitan court 102–103
Neemanim 24
Nehama, Judah 334, 340, 341
Nekrycz, Chaim 452
Nelken, Carmen Eva (Magda Donato) 527
Nelken, Margarita 527, 610
Neo-Platonism/Neo-Platonic 225, 226, 228, 229, 237, 241
Netanyahu, Benzion 31, 35, 84, 98, 106, 108, 109, 122, 179, 355
Netherlands (Holland) 161, 166–167, 173–174, 251–252, 258, 273, 276, 279, 288, 298, 311–312, 394, 437, 434, 495, 610
Neuquén 585
New Age philosophy 489
New Amsterdam 178, 298
New Castile 161
New Christians 2, 4, 8–9, 27–34, 84, 95, 98, 101, 109, 114, 116, 118, 121, 123–124, 157–158, 161–178, 190–196, 203, 209–215, 251, 257–259, 267, 269, 281, 289, 297, 300, 307, 313, 353–368, 434, 438, 441, 447
"New ethnicity" 608
New Granada 354, 366, 368
New Historical Novel (*nueva novela histórica*) 504, 610

New Jews 6–8, 169–171, 179, 266, 272, 297, 364, 437
New Millennium 581–598, 604
New Spain 175, 363, 438, 488, 499, 523, 531
New Testament 34, 257, 335
New World 6, 9, 157, 174, 177, 251, 268, 309, 320, 355, 359–363, 366, 368, 376, 438, 492, 500, 527
New York 178, 251, 380, 444, 464, 491, 492, 568, 632
New York Times 635
Nicaragua 354, 355, 411
Nicene Council (325 CE) 230
Nichthauser, Joseph 464
Nicomachean Ethics 225, 228
Nidjei Isroel 400
Nieto, David 258–259, 267
Nieto, Miguel 424
Nineteenth century 1, 3, 8–9, 11, 39, 62, 158, 170, 186–187, 230, 233, 241, 244, 256, 302, 306, 308, 309, 311–312, 319–345, 353, 369, 376, 378–379, 382, 399, 404, 411, 418–419, 435, 437, 439, 441, 442, 447, 481, 498, 503, 526, 549–550, 627
Niño enterrado 561
Nissan, Rosa 12, 485–487, 523, 527, 532–534, 543, 589, 613
Nizri, Vicky 528, 543, 613
No Exílio 462
Noche Triste 505
Nomologia o discursos legales 170, 264
Non-Jews/non-Jewish 167, 252, 255–259, 330, 407, 443, 458, 465–466, 468, 472, 476–477, 488, 491, 533, 543, 550, 553, 559, 606, 608, 614, 620, 627, 641
Non-Catholic 159, 303, 377, 382, 436, 483, 581–582, 585
Normandy 166
North Africa 18–19, 21, 27, 157, 202, 252–253, 333, 376, 378–379, 405, 419, 433, 437, 440, 476, 523, 532, 613
North America 8, 174, 299, 362, 493
North Sea 164, 171
Nostalgia 237, 428, 472, 508, 540, 543, 561, 564, 568, 597
Noticias del imperio 504
Novela testimonio 615
Novia judía 418
Novia que te vea 527, 532–533, 589, 613

No honrarás a tu padre 621
Novoa, F. Defilippis 592
Nubes no ofenden al sol 284
Nuestra Tribuna 407
Nuestra vida 569
Nuevo León 175, 438, 523, 525
Núñez Bernal, Abraham 269, 277
Núñez Coronel, Antonio 124
Núñez Coronel, Luis 124

Obejas, Achy 13, 627–629, 631–632, 636
O Centauro no Jardim 468
O Ciclo das Águas 468
O homem que voltou ao frio 463
O profeta 465
O Reino das Cebolas 463
O Saco Plástico 451
Occitan 64, 233, 240
Octavas reales 92
Odessa 616
Old Catalan 58
Old Christians 2, 27, 32, 34–35, 84, 95–96, 98, 102, 105, 107, 112, 114, 116, 118, 122, 162, 175, 203, 211, 213–214, 272, 359, 366–367, 437, 523
Old Portuguese 58
Old Spanish 58
Old Testament 34, 50, 267, 273
Oligarchy 172, 406, 552
Olim 380
Oliveira, Solomon de 264, 286
On borrowed words. A memoir of language 489, 506, 509, 612
Once Jews: Stories of Caribbean Sephardim 312
Onganía, Juan C. 587
Opinions of the ancient philosophers on the Soul 256
– *Orden de Ros Hasanah y Kipur*, see mahzor
Ordenações Manuelinas 128
– Ordinance of Alcalá, see *Siete Partidas*
Ordiz Vázquez, J. 475, 494
Orgambide, Pedro 12, 547, 559, 560
Organism of Direct Aid to the Jewish Victims of the War in Europe 388
Organización Sionista Femenina Argentina (OSFA) 387
Orient/oriental 56, 57, 62–64, 67, 237, 238, 341, 387
Orobio de Castro, Isaac 267, 269, 275, 277

Oropesa, Antonio de 28
Orthodox Christians 196, 232, 321, 327
Orthodox(y) 7, 162, 166, 196, 232, 260, 321, 327, 389, 393, 401, 403, 411, 424, 548, 558, 594, 608, 612, 621–622, 638, 640
Ortiz Cota, María 114
Ortiz Wallner, Alexandra 621
Oruro 403
Os Deuses de Raquel 468
Osatinsky, Marcos 587
Ostrabanda 306
Otherness 112, 358–360, 378, 402, 499, 506, 543, 564, 584, 607, 641
Otros son los sueños 488–489
Ottoman Empire 167–170, 174, 252–253, 297, 319–324, 327, 329–340, 342, 344, 356, 362, 369, 379, 385, 395, 420, 433–434, 439, 526, 540, 593, 616
Ottoman Jews 321, 333, 335, 338, 340–341, 343
Ovid 234
Oxford 63, 66, 67, 77, 238
Oy, My Buenos Aires Jewish Immigrants and the Creation of Argentine National Identity 591

Pacheco, José Emilio 485, 490
Pacheco, Juan (Marquis of Villena) 112
Pachuca 175–176, 363
Pacifism 478
Padura, Leonardo 13, 627–628, 636–639, 641
Páginas artísticas y literarias 569
Palatnik, Rosa 464
Palestine/Palestinian 283, 336, 380, 397, 399–400, 405, 408–409, 532, 616, 618, 638
Palma, Alonso 114
Pamplona 20
Panama 303, 306, 312, 354–355, 403, 410
Panegírico a la Reina doña Isabel 122
Papal States 168
Papiamento 308–309
Papo, Laura 343
Paraguay 354, 407, 408, 464, 557
Paramaribo 306, 308, 311
Parashiot 262
Paravicino, Hortensio 269
– *Pardes soshanim*, see *Asire Hatikvah*
Pardo, David 263
Pardo, Yoshiahu 305
Paris 167, 238, 334, 341, 402, 441, 461, 632–634

Parnas 305, 310
Paso, Fernando del 504
Passion, Memory and Identity: Twentieth-Century Latin American Jewish Women Writers 589
Passover 28, 70, 468, 553, 629
Pastorellos 22
Paul 230, 231, 236, 239
Paul et Virginie (Pablo y Virginia) 337, 338
Paytan 45, 49
Paz, Octavio 479, 484, 499
Paz Oliver, María 621
Pecar, Samuel 613
Pecho 25
Pedrarias affair 112, 120
Pedro I of Castile 21, 83, 86–88, 108
Pedro IV of Aragon 22, 83
Pedro Páramo 479, 512
Pele Yo'ets 327
Penso de la Vega, Joseph 261, 270–271, 285–286, 290
Pentateuch 262, 266, 289, 324, 326, 328
Pequeño cancionero del marqués de la Romana 114
Pereira, Abraham 264–265
Perelis, Ronnie 310, 364–365
Pérez Firmat, Gustavo 628
Pérez de Guzmán, Fernán 110, 120
Pérez Galdós, Benito 419
Perfumes de Cartago 571
Pernambuco 176–178, 251, 298, 303
Pernidji, Maurício Eskenazi 464
Perón, Eva (Evita) 560, 562
Perón, Isabel 565
Perón, Juan Domingo 383, 549, 552, 554, 557, 562, 585, 586
Peronism/Peronist 549, 552, 556–560, 582–587
Perpignan 22
Persecution(s) 6, 22, 160–161, 175, 179, 189, 191, 212, 214, 256, 269, 272–273, 277, 280, 361, 366–368, 377, 379, 424, 460, 489–491, 494, 502, 504, 508, 513, 523, 525, 527, 530, 560, 611–612, 622, 633, 635
Persian 56, 61, 243–244, 532
Pertenencia y alteridad. Judíos en/de América Latina: cuarenta años de cambios 594, 603, 622
Perto do Coração Selvagem 460

Peru 9, 167, 177, 354, 362–368, 380, 404–406, 479, 589, 591
Petrarcha 124, 230
Petronila of Aragon 20
Peyrehorade 166
Phaedra 234, 235
Philip II of Spain/Felipe II 175, 252, 256, 523
Philip IV/ Felipe IV 162, 367
Philippines 175
Phillipson Colony 381
Philosephardism /philosephardi 419–421
Pícaro/picaresque 2, 160, 206–212, 278, 437, 557, 560, 562, 610
Pina, Jacob (Manuel) de 275, 277, 279, 286
Pinkás 25
Pinochet, Augusto 419, 619
Pinto Delgado, João (Moses) 167, 251, 257, 273, 277, 434
Pires, Diogo 129, 272
Pisa 168, 170, 257, 271, 282
Piyyut(im) 5, 39–40, 44, 48–51, 328
Pizarnik, Alejandra 12, 489, 564, 511, 547
Plager, Silvia 605, 620
Plato/Platonism 225–229, 232–237
Platovsky, Milan 618
Plaza de Mayo 617
Pleito del Perro de Alba 127
Plotinus 225, 226
Poalei Zion (Workers of Zion) 386–387, 389, 400
Poema de la reina Ester 273
Poeta, Juan 108, 119
Poetae minores 76
Poética de la hibridez en la literatura mexicana posmodernista 485
Pogrom(s) 27, 92, 162, 246, 383, 449, 481, 489, 505, 507–508, 526–527, 552, 555, 562, 565, 572, 604, 611, 615, 637
Poland 386, 392, 407, 409, 449, 452, 455, 457, 464, 466, 468, 481, 489, 502–503, 526, 620, 637–638
Polish 378, 407, 409, 442, 444, 453, 457, 464, 500, 557, 562, 584, 621, 638
Pomegranate Seeds: Latin American Jewish Tales 590
Ponce de León family 35
Ponentino 169–170
Pope Benedict XIII 30–31
Pope Gregory IX 31
Pope Paul IV 168
Pope Sixtus IV 28
Popular literature 67, 75, 97, 129, 157, 242, 278, 319–320, 332, 335, 337–338, 344, 555, 563
Populism/Populist 583, 584
Por el ojo de la cerradura 617
Por los modernos 343
Por mi boka 537
Por Que Sou Gorda, Mamãe? 463
Por tierras extrañas 527, 543
Port Royal 301
Porto 176, 378–379
Porto Alegre 391, 457–458, 463, 468
Porto Cabello 303
Portugal 6, 8–9, 81–89, 108, 121, 125, 128, 129, 130, 157–165, 172, 175, 178, 222–224, 251, 256, 260, 263, 269, 272, 276, 281, 297–298, 300, 305, 310, 358, 360–363, 367, 375–379, 411, 433, 436, 448, 453, 460, 493, 591, 596, 616
Portuguese India 174, 176
Portuguese Jewish 8, 158, 161, 252, 268–269, 279–280, 283, 297, 301, 307, 309
Portuguese Nation 158, 165–166, 171, 173, 177, 265, 363
Portuguese New Christians 161, 164, 167–168, 171, 177
Porzecanski, Rafael 569
Porzecanski, Teresa 547, 569–571, 614
Postcolonialism 500
Poste restante 611
Postmodern(ism) 440, 466–467, 500, 610, 619, 622
Potosí 177, 403
Prague 389
Premio Bartolomé Hidalgo 570–571
Prince Carlos of Viana 103
Prince Juan de Trastámara 125
Prince Miguel of Portugal 125
Princess Isabel 122
Privilege(s) 21–22, 26–27, 162,168, 175, 222, 298, 231, 243, 301–303, 477, 634, 637
Proops, Solomon 258
Propostas 264
Prospopeia 176, 448
Protestant 165, 171, 178, 213, 246, 302, 303, 308, 313
Protocols of the Elders of Zion 394
Provence 40, 237, 529, 531

Proverbios en rimo del sabio Salamón, Rey de Israel 110
Proverbios morales 86–87, 119
Provisiones of March 31, 1492 122
Psalms/Psalmists 46, 72, 110, 255, 259, 265, 273–274, 289, 310, 420, 539, 622
Publisher's Weekly 635
Puebla 175, 492
Puerto Rico 313, 354–355
Pulgar, Fernando Del 28, 114, 118, 198
Pulido y Fernández, Ángel 419–421
Punishment 17, 25–26, 31, 264
Purim 282, 286, 287, 328
Pyrenees 19–20, 119, 237

Qaṣīda 44–45, 56–58, 76
Qiṭ'a 44
Quaestio 260, 267
Quatro Irmaos Colony 381, 470
Queen María Cristina 419
Querido, Selomoh 258
Quevedo, Francisco de 173, 194–196, 216, 279
Quinto Centenario 503–505
Quiroga, Horacio 560
Quito 402
Quota Act of 1921 481
Qur'ān 58, 68, 78, 97, 240–244

– Rabbenu Tam, see Jacob Ben Meir Tam
Rabbi Angel Kreiman 397
Rabbi David Nieto of London 258–259, 267
Rabbi Isaac Aboab de Fonseca 177, 269, 286
Rabbi Isaac Athias 257, 263
Rabbi Isaías Raffalovich 391
Rabbi Jacob Abendana 266, 269
Rabbi Jacob ibn Núñez 108
Rabbi Moses de Toledo 257
Rabbi Moses Raphael de Aguilar 266, 269, 286
Rabbi Samuel David Luzzatto 62
Rabbi Saul Levi Mortera 263, 267–268, 277, 283–284
Rabbi Simuel 108
Rabbi Sion Levy 403
Radical Worker Center (Centro Obrero Radical, Mexico) 400
Radio Sefarad 424
Ragusa 169
Rahmeijer, Bento Guilhelmo 278
Ramiro of Aragon 20

Ramon Berenguer IV 20
Ramón Ferreira, Juan 424
Rawet, Samuel 447–449, 464–466
Recife 177, 368, 391, 454, 467
Reconquista 24, 61, 196, 436
Red de juderías de España 424
Redondo, Augustin 189
Reformed church 172, 302
Refranes 278
Refugees 161, 164, 167, 178, 257, 303, 376–380, 385, 394, 396, 398, 401–403, 405, 407–409, 466, 482, 495, 502, 505, 527, 529, 630
Refugee Economic Corporation (REC) 409
Refugiados: crónica de un palestino 554
Regimiento de príncipes 119
Reibscheid, Samuel 466
Rein, Ranaan 377, 378, 424, 483, 581–583, 595
Relación de los zelos de San Joseph de hombre 96
Relator 32–33
Rembrandt van Rijn 637, 639–640
Remembrance 71, 209, 457, 539, 540, 555, 588, 604, 615, 622
Renaissance 90, 114, 121, 129, 186–187, 223, 226–227, 231, 235–236, 255, 261, 267, 434, 441, 443
Representative Committee of the Israelite Collectivity of Chile (Comité Representativo de la Colectividad Israelita de Chile) 396
Repression 159–160, 172, 383, 392, 447, 555, 589, 614, 634
Republican Period 9, 353, 369
Requiem for a Friday Evening 557, 559
Réquiem para um solitário 465
Resende, García de 81, 89, 128–131
Reshit Hokhma 265
Reshuyot 49, 51
Resistance 159, 164, 201, 216, 228, 288, 449, 538, 556
Resurrección de los muertos 264
Retallat 102
Retorno a Don Quijote 550
Révah, I. S. 161, 163, 166, 172, 355
Revue des Études Juives 341
Reyes, Alfonso 479
– *Reyes Católicos*, see Catholic Monarchs
Rhodes 323
Ribera, Suero de 104

Ricardo, Mordechay 303
Rico, Alicia 610
Rimsky, Cynthia 611–612
Rio de Janeiro 391, 450, 453–454, 455, 460
Rio de la Plata 12, 176, 547–548, 552
Rio Grande do Sul 381, 455, 459, 468, 470–472
Ripstein, Arturo 525–526
Ritual 99, 159–161, 177, 234, 540–541, 612, 629
Rivera, Andrés 12, 554, 555
Rivera, Diego 526
Rivkin, Ellis 128, 355
Rodela 30
Rodriga, Daniel 169
Rodrigues Balbuena, Monique 597
Rojas, Fernando de 437
Rolnik, Malka Lorber 466
Román, Diego 121
Romance Kharjas in Andalusian Arabic muwashshaḥ poetry. A palaeographical analysis 66
Romanso 337, 338
Romantic 158, 221, 230–238, 241–242, 244, 337, 426–427, 436, 529, 610, 630
Romanticism 230, 237, 238, 436
Rome 163, 168, 169, 177, 195, 202, 206, 556
Romero, Elena 327, 339
Roncaglia, Aurelio 64
Rosanes, Shlomo Abraham 341
Rosenbaum, Paulo 467
Rosenberg, Stuart 630
Rosencof, Mauricio 571
Rosenzweig, Franz 63
Rosh Hashanah 274, 631
Rosh Kallah 44–45
Roth, Cecil 158, 443
Rotterdam 174, 281
Rouen 166–167, 257
Roussillon 19
Rovere, Vittoria della 282
Royal African Company 304
Royal Library of Denmark 110
Rozenmacher, Germán 12, 547, 554, 557, 558, 563
Rozitchner, León 12, 547, 553
Rubinstein, Becky 483, 486, 498, 500, 509, 514
Rulfo, Juan 479, 512
Rumbaut, Rubén 628
Rumbos peligrosos 271

Russia/Russian 321, 333, 381, 383, 386, 444, 449, 455, 467, 481, 489, 498, 502, 505, 508, 509, 526, 564, 590

Saar Hasamaim 174
Sabbatai Zvi 171, 264, 275, 278, 285, 321, 341, 439, 638
Sabbatanism 439
Sabbath 25, 28, 161, 269, 300, 302, 525, 551–552, 558/ Shabbat 435, 465, 533, 620–621, 525
Sadow, Stephen A. 484, 589
Saed, Ivonne 527–528
Sáenz de Mañozca, Juan 368
Safed 305, 325
Sagrada memoria. Reminiscencias de una niña judía en Chile 618
Sainete 592
Saint-Domingue 312
Salamanca 34, 161
Salazar, António de Oliveira 378
Saldívar, José 607
Salom Gallego, Joseph 264
Salonica (Thessaloniki) 167, 169, 218, 257, 264, 321–329, 334–336, 339–341, 343–344, 527, 535
Salvador de Bahia 176, 391
Samuel ben Negrela 19
Samuel ha-Levi Abulafia 87
Samuel ha-Nagid 39, 45, 48, 434, 435
San Antonio (Texas) 590
San Antonio Colony 585
Sanbenitos 160
Sánchez, Francisco 166
Sánchez Cota, Rodrigo 114
Sánchez de Arévalo, Rodrigo 91
Sánchez, Juan (Juan Ahumada) 530
Sancho IV of Castile 21
Sancho the Great 20
San Martín, José de 569
San Pedro, Diego de 120
Sandinista 411
Sanskrit 56
Sansón nazareno 273
Santa Cruz 403
Santa Fe 617
Santa Hermandad 35
Santa María, Pablo de 29, 34, 91, 98, 104
Santa Teresa de Jesús (Teresa de Ávila) 437, 441, 523, 530

Santería 629
Santes Pagnino 261
Santiago de Chile 177, 395–396
Santiago de Compostela 20, 277
Santo Domingo 354
Sao Paulo 391, 393–394, 450, 452–457, 459, 464, 466–467, 470
Sappho 233, 234
Saragossa 19–20, 24, 49, 67, 127, 206, 207
Saraiva, Antônio José 163, 268
Sarajevo 329, 330, 343
Sardinian 74
Sarmiento, Pedro 27, 98, 106, 109
Savary, Jacques 329
Schachnik, Isaac 467
Schachnovelle 615
Schalom, Myrtha 620
Scherman, Jorge 617
Scholastic, Scholasticism 225, 226, 260, 267, 328
Schnaiderman, Boris 467
Schvel, Mariano Moisés 617
Schwarcz, Luis 467
Schwartz, Marco 616
Schwartz, Samuel 378
Schyfter, Guita 533, 613
Scliar, Moacyr 468–469, 489, 548, 589
Scrutinium Scripturarum 91
Second Spanish Republic 482, 527, 529, 610
– Second World War, see World War II
Secrecy and Deceit: The Religion of the Crypto-Jews 443, 590
Secretum 225, 227
Secular(ism/ization) 4–5, 7–9, 18, 39–51, 55, 63, 90, 161, 210, 239, 241, 251–252, 261, 270, 276, 284, 290, 306, 308, 311, 313, 329, 331, 334, 344, 378, 382, 393, 397, 401, 403, 418–419, 425, 469, 506–507, 551, 621, 633
Sefamí, Jacobo 11, 482–483, 486, 510, 527–528, 537, 543, 620
Sefardica 385
Sefchovich, Sara 479, 483–486, 497–498, 514
Segura, Diego de 127
Segura, Pedro de 127
Seligson, Esther 476, 478–479, 486–487, 489, 493–494, 508, 513, 527, 612
Sem Tob de Carrión (Šem Ṭov ben Ishaq ibn Arduṭiel) 86–87

Sendero de vidas 264
Senegal 174
Seneor, Abraham 108, 124
Senkman, Leonardo 12, 13, 383, 387, 389, 482, 484, 486, 489, 502, 504, 549, 550, 557, 564, 586, 594, 595, 607
Señora de los sueños 497–498
Sentencia Arbitral de Medina del Campo 112
Sentencia-Estatuto 27, 98, 106, 109
Sephardic/Sefarad/Sepharad/Sefardim/ Sephardim 4–12, 31, 39–51, 129, 157–159, 167–179, 198–199, 251–290, 297–313, 319–345, 361, 364, 369, 377–379, 385, 387, 391, 395–409, 418–428, 433–444, 476–477, 481–483, 486–488, 493–495, 498–501, 513, 523–543, 549, 551, 559, 564–565, 569–570, 590, 597, 605, 608, 612, 614, 620, 629, 632, 637, 639
Sephardic communities 174, 257, 259–260, 264, 267, 276–277, 303, 305–307, 309, 312, 323, 344, 378, 391, 569, 620
Sephardic congregation of Amsterdam 172, 174, 258, 269–270, 276, 283–284, 286
Sephardic Federation of Spain (Federación Sefaradí de España) 377
Serbia 344, 440
Serbocroatia 614
Serenissima 169
Sermons 8, 29–30, 84, 94, 102, 161, 173, 254, 258, 260, 263, 268–270, 277, 283, 289, 310, 322, 324
Settlement(s) 4, 17–18, 21, 164–166, 174, 179, 251, 297–301, 304, 359, 375, 378–382, 388, 393, 385, 400, 481, 524, 551
Seventeenth Century 159–174, 185, 186, 188, 191, 195, 199, 215, 224, 254–281, 297, 298, 303, 303, 307, 310, 320–322, 341, 355–358, 368, 499, 637–639
Seville 10, 27, 59, 76, 84, 159, 166, 175, 363, 377, 417–418, 523, 630
Sfarad 433
Sha'ar Hashamayim 258
Sha're Mizrah (Las Puertas de Oriente) 334, 335
– Shabbetai Sevi or Shabbetai Zvi, see Sabbatai Zvi
Shacharit 92
Shaddai 529
Shajatos 620
Shakespeare 165, 339

Shalom Yahuda, Abraham 419–422
Shami 476, 486, 532, 620
Shavuot 283
Shem Tob ben Shem Tob 31
Shem'a Yisrael 92, 529
Sheerit Israel 178
Shevet Musar 327
Shevet Yehudah 84, 261
Shmuel ha-Nagid 434, 435
Shoah 379, 411, 443, 452, 463–465, 489, 455, 527, 530, 604, 611, 615, 618, 621, 622
Shtot fun Palatzn 483, 526
Shúa, Ana María 12, 563, 604, 605, 612, 614, 616
Siete edades del mundo 92, 110
Siete Partidas 24
Sigal, Eduardo 587
Silva Miranda, Samuel da 269
Silveira, Fernam da 130
Silveira, Miguel de 170, 273
Simons, Moisés 632–634
Sinagoga del Tránsito 87, 425
Sinfonía inocente 554
"Sin desierto y sin tierra prometida" 603
Šir 'ezor 57
Six-Day War 383, 399, 424, 553
Sixteenth Century 70, 83, 89, 122, 125–128, 153, 159–175, 185, 186, 188, 191, 195, 200, 215, 224, 251–259, 265, 267, 271, 272, 280, 281, 301, 322, 326, 327, 339–343, 354, 438, 484, 494, 527, 588, 610, 612
Smyrna 169, 439, 460, 614
Soares, Mario 378
Sobre a ubrigação dos sábios 269
Sobre vivir. Memoria 618
Socialist 336, 386, 392, 400, 406, 584–585, 592
Sociedad Amigable 278
Sociedad Amigos del Libro Rioplatense. 552
Sociedad Hebraica Argentina 390, 551, 562
Society of Israelite Ladies (Sociedad de Socorros de Damas Israelitas) 384–385
Socolovsky, Maya 630, 635
Sofia 614
Sola-Solé, José María 65–66
– Solomon Ha-Levi, see Santa María, Pablo de
Somigliana, Carlos 557
Song of Songs 76, 78, 325
– Songbook, see *cancionero*

Sontag, Susan 561
Sor Juana Inés de la Cruz 441, 499–500
Sosnowski, Saúl 12, 477, 481, 496, 582, 603, 606–607
South America(n) 175–178, 309, 603–604, 620
Southern Cone 384, 493
Soviet Union (USSR) 388–389, 392, 398, 556
Spain 5–6, 9–10, 17–35, 39–40, 55–58, 63–64, 75, 109, 157–178, 187, 192–215, 222–224, 238, 242, 247, 251, 253–256, 260–261, 264, 269, 273, 280–281, 284, 287–288, 297–298, 300, 304, 310, 313, 319–322, 326, 353, 357–359, 362–363, 367, 375–379, 384, 398, 411, 417–443, 484, 488, 492, 496, 498–499, 523, 527, 529–531, 535, 537, 543, 559, 565, 591, 597, 610–612, 633, 636
Spalato 169
Spanglish: The Making of a New American Language 588
Spanglish 489, 588, 612
Spanish American War 418
Spanish Civil War 420, 441, 491, 505, 527, 530, 610
Spanish Empire 178, 188, 303, 313, 494, 49
Spanish Golden Age 119, 131, 185–215, 254, 281, 426, 488
Spanish Main 301, 302, 304
Spanish Republicans 610
Spectrality/spectre/spectral 6, 185, 191–198, 203, 215, 216, 596
Spiegel, Abraham 620
Spinoza, Baruch de 172, 173, 224, 264, 437, 533, 557
Splendor, Decline, and Rediscovery of Yiddish in Latin America 583, 590
Sranan Tongo 309
St. Augustin 34
St. Jean-de-Luz 173
St. Louis (ship) 495, 630, 637
St. Thomas 302–303, 312
Stalin(s)/Stalinist 555, 611, 617
Statutes of purity of blood 2, 9, 27, 106, 160, 357–360, 193, 436
Stavans, Ilan 10, 486, 489, 506, 513, 528, 587–590, 612–613
Steimberg, Alicia 12, 561, 605
Stern, Samuel Miklos 63–64
Stigma 128, 159–160, 163, 198–199, 469
Stoics 225, 226

Studemund-Halévy, Michael 255, 308
Suárez, Patricia 556
Sucre 403
Sufism 49, 527
Sugar 165, 176, 178, 297–304, 309, 312
Sulhan Arukh 257, 325
Sultan Bayezid II 320
Suma de la Política 91
Suriname 178, 258, 300–302, 304, 306–311
Surowitz-Israel, Hilit 305
Symposium 225, 234, 235
Synagogue 49, 92, 105, 166, 172, 177, 255, 262, 269, 283, 285, 289, 305–306, 325, 344–345, 368, 376–378, 391, 393, 398, 420–421, 533, 629
Synod of Zamora 21
Syrian-(s) 385, 401, 403, 476, 526, 528, 532–533, 543, 570, 583, 620
Szichman, Mario 12, 562, 563, 605, 615
Szpunberg, Alberto 565, 566
Szurmuk, Mónica 550
Szwarc, Samuel 470

Tacanot 25
Tacuara 582, 587
Tahlīth al-waḥdāniyyab (*La trinidad de la unidad*) 95
Taifa 20–21
Talesnik, Ricardo 557
Tallante, Mosén Juan 124
Talmud 24, 26, 30–31, 40, 94, 171–173, 269, 276, 283, 323, 325–326, 389, 401, 435, 441, 489, 540–541, 566, 610, 620, 622
Talmud Torah 172, 269, 276, 283, 323
Taoism 527
Tarrab, Alejandro 12, 523, 528, 538–543
Tarrab Maslatón, Jacob 540
Teitelbaum, Célia Igel 470
Tefillin 541, 630
Tefillah 541
Teixeira, Bento 176, 447
Tel Aviv 441, 444, 464, 583, 598, 620
Tela de Sevoya 442, 528, 535, 537, 614
Temple of Jerusalem 23, 173
Temuco 395–396
Tenochtitlán 175
Teresa of Ávila (Teresa de Jesús) 12, 240, 437, 441, 523, 527, 530
Tertulias 161, 278

Tesoro de preceptos 257, 263
Tesouro dos Dinim 263, 265
Tetouan 418, 427–428
The Algarrobos Quartet 588
The Ballad of the False Messiah 469, 589
The Carnival of the Animals 469, 589
The Dwarf in the Television Set 589
The Encyclopedia of the Dead 440
The Enigmatic Eye 477, 589
The Hague 174, 279
The Jewish State 481
The Knesset 613
The Mambo Kings Play Songs of Love 632
The Schocken Book of Modern Sephardic Literature 588, 443
The Spaniard from Oran 284
The Structure of Spanish History 443, 588
The Tremulous Earth 385
The Trumpet 257
The Voices of Marrakesh: A Record for a Visit 433
The Wandering Signifier: Rhetoric of Jewishness in the Latin American Imaginary 595
"Theater of Memory" (*Teatro de la memoria*) 611
Theresienstadt 615
Thesoro de la Pasión 121
– Thessaloniki, see Salonica
Thomas, Gordon 630
Tiberias 305
Tibetan religion 489
Tiempo, César 423, 551–553, 567
Tierra adentro 476, 488, 527, 529
Tikkun olam 453
Timoneda, Joan de 124
Tirso de Molina 287
Tlatelolco 478–479, 502
Tmeim 386
Tnuat Aliá 383
Todo aquí es polvo 489–490
Ṭodros Abū l-ʿĀfiya 74–75
Toker, Eliahu 12, 567
Tokheḥa 50
Toledo 17, 23–24, 28, 32–34, 69, 87, 92, 98, 100, 105–109, 111, 114, 116–119, 121, 124, 178, 187, 257, 425, 435, 530
Topel, Marta 393, 594
Torah 21, 45–46, 51, 97, 105, 262, 268–269, 276, 283, 323–325, 527, 540–541, 605, 612, 620–621

Toro, Alfonso de 607
Torquemada, Juan de 33–34
Torquemada, Tomás de 33
Torre, Alfonso de la 102, 256
Torre, Fernando de la 103
Torre Nilsson, Leopoldo 551
Torres, Juan de 100–101
Tortosa 18–19, 30–31, 95,100
Tosefta 322
Toulouse 166
Tractatus contra medianitas eismaelitas advesarios et detractores fidelium qui de populo iraelitico originem traxerum 33
Tractatus Theologico-Politicus 437
Tradition(s) 1–5, 7–10, 12, 17–18, 24, 39, 40, 43, 48, 56, 59–62, 64, 69–70, 73, 75–77, 89, 91, 102, 104, 122, 129, 159, 161, 172–173, 177, 179, 196, 212, 221–222, 225, 230, 233–234, 237–241, 246, 263, 274, 278, 283, 286, 297, 305, 307–308, 320, 325, 327–328, 341, 364, 369, 378–379, 392, 397, 399, 403, 422, 433–435, 437, 439–440, 443–444, 449–452, 455, 462, 468, 475, 476–477, 480–481, 489, 511–512, 523, 527, 529, 531, 533–534, 537, 539–540, 542, 556–558, 560, 566, 568, 590, 604–605, 612, 614, 616, 618, 620–621, 622
Traduzindo Hannah 470
Tragic Week 383, 552
Transgenerational 489, 492, 501–502, 509, 513, 603, 609, 614–618, 622
Transgenerational novel(s) 603, 609, 614–615, 618
Transhistorical 530, 596, 611
Trauma/traumatic 6, 179, 188, 191, 455, 457–458, 463, 475, 478, 487, 489, 490, 492–493, 501–502, 513, 604, 610–611, 613, 615, 620, 630
Trás-os-Montes 161, 378
Trastámara 21, 22, 38, 83, 85–86, 88–89, 95, 99, 101, 103, 111, 125
Tratado de la oración y meditación y conocimiento propio del Dio 257
Tratado de penitencia 264
Tratado del temor divino 265
Treaty of Tordesillas 297
Tribunal of the inquisition 163–164, 175–177, 353–357, 362, 365–367

Trinity 95, 198
Triple crónica de un nombre 527–528
Triunfo da união 270
Triunfo del gobierno popular 270, 276
Triunfo del Marqués de Santillana 120
Trobes en lahors de la Verge Maria 119
Troki, Isaac 267
Trotsky 555, 587, 617
Troubadours 62, 64, 88, 90, 92, 96, 101, 103, 105, 114, 230, 233, 240
Tsfat 616
Tshuvá 393
Tucumán Province 587
Tudela 19, 20, 69, 75
Tulip Period (1718–1730) 321
Tunis 321
Turkey 340, 342, 344, 385, 433, 437, 443, 526, 535, 616, 638
Turkish 61, 285, 331–337, 341–343, 419, 437, 527, 532, 533, 607, 608
Tuscany 168, 170, 329
Twelfth Century 40, 70, 74, 242, 611, 612
Twentieth Century 1, 3, 9–11, 63, 76, 83, 230, 237, 242, 311–312, 335–336, 339, 341, 369, 375–411, 417–429, 433–443, 447–472, 475–514, 523–543, 547–573, 584, 593, 596, 603–604, 609, 611–612, 616, 635, 638–639
Twenty-first Century 3, 12–13, 185, 187–188, 398, 407, 418, 429, 442, 447, 475, 582–583, 603–612, 618, 622, 639
Tzdaká 384
Tzur Israel / Zur Israel 177, 368

Ucko, Enrique 312
Ukraine 450, 460, 462, 467, 481, 509, 526
Uma leve simetria 622
Un guapo del 900 551
Un nombre con olor a almizcle y a gardenias 501
UN Resolution 3379 402
(Un)religious novels 609, 620
Un siglo tras de mí 527–528
Unión Cívica Radical Intransigente (Intransigent Radical Civic Union) 585
Unión de literatos y artistas judíos (Mexico) 483
United Nations (UN) 399, 409
United Nations Special Committee on Palestine (UNSCOP) 399, 410

United States (US, U.S., USA) 298, 303, 306, 309, 312, 336, 344, 377, 380, 384, 388, 389, 398–403, 405, 410, 411, 418, 435, 437, 441, 476, 481, 484, 486, 491–492, 495, 499–500, 503, 506, 508, 512–514, 562, 582, 588–590, 598, 607, 611, 616, 620, 628–629, 636
Universidad Nacional Autónoma de México (UNAM) 478
University of Pisa 170
Urgel 19
Urioste, Carmen de 420–421
Urroz, Eloy 501, 527–528
Uruguay 354, 375, 380–382, 388, 392, 397–399, 401, 408, 441, 547–549, 552, 555, 569–572, 589, 590, 595, 621
Usque, Abraham 168, 255–256, 261
Usque, Samuel 254, 260, 263, 272, 290
Usque, Solomon 282
Uziel, Jacobo 273
Uziel, Rafael 334, 335

Vaad Hajinuj 388
Vaez, Abraham 257
Valdés, Alfonso de 257
Valencia(n) 19, 22, 27, 35, 102, 119, 124, 127, 377, 496
Valencia, Nicolás de 96
Valera, Diego de 102, 105, 111
Valle Saldaña, David del 278, 288
Valley of Dry Bones 308
Valparaíso 396
Van Gogh's Ear 477, 589
Varela, Jorge Rafael 491
Vargas, Getulio 394, 470
Vargas Llosa, Mario 479
Variações Goldman 450
Vásquez-Bronfman, Ana 616
Vaticana 89
Vega, Lope de 280
Venezuela 303, 312, 354, 355, 369, 382, 404, 411, 562, 568, 589, 620
Venice 169, 170, 172, 199, 222, 251, 256, 257, 259, 264, 265, 271, 282, 325, 356
Vera, Hernando de 123
Veracruz 363, 510
Verbitsky, Bernardo 12, 556, 557
Vergara, Gloria 510
Veritas hebraica 199, 255

Viceroy Marqués de Coruña 525
Vida de Santa Teresa de Jesús 530
Vida nuestra 551
Vida propia 528, 613–614
Vida y peripecias de una buena hija de familia 486
Vidal de Elvas 129
Vidas, Eliahu de 265
Vieira, António 268–269
Vieira, Nelson H. 582, 589, 608
Vienna 276, 321, 327, 330, 336
Vietnam War 490
Villegas, Alonso de 273
Villena, Enrique de 123
Viña del Mar 396
Viñas, David 12, 552, 554, 559, 563, 565
Viñas, Ismael 586
Virgin Islands 298
Virgin Mary 28, 33, 121, 281, 511, 629
Visigoths 17, 111
Visión deleitable de todas las ciencias 102–103, 256, 266
Vísperas 535
Voloch, Adão 470
Voltaire 282, 288
Voyage of the Damned 630
Vudú urbano 561

Wailing Wall 531
Waldman, Gilda 483, 485
Walsh, Rodolfo 562
"Wandering signifier" 596, 628, 641–642
War of Reform (Mexico) 526
Warsaw 453, 621
Waššāḥūn 57, 73, 76
We Came All the Way from Cuba So You Could Dress Like This? 629
West India Company (WIC) 173, 177, 298–299
Western Sephardic Diaspora 7, 157, 168, 173, 251–252, 254–262, 267–268, 270–271, 276–279, 283–284, 286, 289, 329, 334, 361
Western Sephardic Literature 6–8, 251–290, 295–313, 319–345, 433–444, 523–543
Western Sephardim 7, 158, 167, 251–254, 259–260, 263, 268–269, 272, 276, 288, 290, 313
Westernization/Westernizer 319, 330–336
– Wild Coast, see Guianas
Willemstad 306

Wirth-Nesher, Hana 447, 548
Wissenschaft des Judentums 39, 62, 340–341
Woldenberg, José 485–486, 489, 502, 504–509, 514
Wolodarsky, Solly 10, 417–418, 423–424, 426–427, 429
Workers Center Morris Vinchevsky 392
Works of the Little Devil of Pierced Hand 448
World War I 331–332, 382, 421, 572
World War II 337–378, 380, 448, 453, 460, 489–492, 500, 556, 572, 618
World Zionist Organization (WZO) 380, 386–387, 399
Wrobel, Ronaldo 470
Wuppertal 615
Wurman, Samy 471

Yachia, Guedellah 256
Yanbu' al-Hayat 435
Yaron Ben-Naeh 320–323, 327, 337, 340
Yehoshua ha-Lorqui 30
Yehoshua, A. B. 440, 443
– Yehuda ha-Lewi/Yehudá ha-Levy, see Judah ha-Levi
Yerushalmi, Yosef Hayim 356, 358, 443, 604
Yeshivah 264, 305/ Yeshiva 305, 323, 621
Yeshivot 276, 322, 393, 401
Yiddish 286, 383, 385, 388–392, 400–401, 439, 442, 444, 455, 457, 464, 470, 476, 477, 480, 481, 483, 484, 488, 489, 496, 505, 506, 510, 512, 513, 526, 527, 533, 547, 551, 558, 559, 564, 566, 567–569, 572, 583, 588, 590–592, 605, 612–614, 617, 630

Yiddish South of the Border: An Anthology of Latin American Yiddish Writing 590
Yinglish 588
Yoatzim 24
Yom Kippur 274, 435, 631
Yom Kippur War 383, 554
Yosef Da'at (El Progreso) 340
Young Men's Hebrew Association (Mexico) 400

Zacatecas 363
Zaga Cohen, Teresa 528
Zakhor 443, 451, 604
Zakhor. Jewish History and Jewish Memory 604–605
Zambrano, María 610
Zamora 21, 119
Zapata, Luis 485
– Zaragoza, see Saragossa
Zeitschrift für Romanische Philologie 65
Zielenic, Mauricio 577
Zion(ism/t) 62, 336, 380, 383, 385–411, 436, 477, 481, 488, 492, 552–553, 557–558, 605, 631
Zionist Federation of Chile (Federación Sionista de Chile) 395–396
Zionist Israelite Center of Costa Rica (Centro Israelita Sionista de Costa Rica) 410
Zionist Youth Federation of Uruguay 399
Zohar 265, 441
Zweig, Stefan 453–454, 610, 615, 617
Zwi Midgal 560, 620
Zysman, Nadia 584

www.ingramcontent.com/pod-product-compliance
Lightning Source LLC
Chambersburg PA
CBHW081942230426
43669CB00019B/2900